THE ROUGH GUIDE TO
SPAIN

T0372569

ROUGH
GUIDES

This eighteenth edition updated by
**Libby Davies, Sally Davies, Mary-Ann Gallagher,
Agnish Ray and Daniel Stables**

Contents

THE GARDENS OF THE GENERALIFE AND THE ALHAMBRA, GRANADA

Introduction to
Spain

First-time visitors be warned: Spain is addictive. You might book a city break, villa holiday or hiking trip, but soon you'll find yourself distracted by something quite different – swept up in the excitement of a fiesta, hooked on the local cuisine, or stunned by Barcelona's otherworldly architecture. Even in the best-known destinations – from Madrid to the *costas*, from the high Pyrenees to the Moorish cities of the south – there are genuinely surprising attractions at every turn, whether that be cool restaurants in the Basque country, the wild landscapes of the central plains, or cutting-edge galleries in the industrial north. Soon, you'll notice that there is not just one Spain but many – and indeed, Spaniards themselves often speak of Las Españas (the Spains).

This diversity is partly down to an almost obsessive regionalism, stemming from the creation in the late 1970s of seventeen *comunidades autonomías* (autonomous regions) with their own governments, budgets and cultural ministries, and even police forces. You might think you are on holiday in Spain but your hosts are more likely to be adamant that you're actually visiting Catalunya, and will point to a whole range of differences in language, culture and artistic traditions, not to mention social attitudes and politics. Indeed, the old days of a unified nation, governed with a firm hand from Madrid, seem to have gone forever, as the separate kingdoms that made up the original Spanish state reassert themselves in an essentially federal structure.

Does any of this matter for visitors? As a rule – not really, since few tourists have the time or inclination to immerse themselves in contemporary Spanish political discourse. Far more important is to look beyond the clichés of paella, matadors, sangría and siesta if you're to get the best out of a visit to this amazingly diverse country.

Even in the most over-touristed resorts of the Costa del Sol, you'll be able to find an authentic bar or restaurant where the locals eat, and a village not far away where an age-old bullfighting tradition owes nothing to tourism. The large cities of the north, from Barcelona to Bilbao, have reinvented themselves as essential cultural destinations (and they don't all close down for hours for a kip every afternoon). And now that the world looks to Spain for culinary inspiration – the country has some of the most acclaimed chefs and innovative restaurants in the world – it's clear that things have changed. Spain, despite some lingering economic uncertainty, sees itself very differently from a generation ago. So should you – prepare to be surprised.

Where to go

Spain's cities are among the most vibrant in Europe. Exuberant **Barcelona**, for many, has the edge, thanks to Gaudí's extraordinary *modernista* architecture, the lively promenade of the Ramblas, five kilometres of sandy beach and one of the world's best football teams. The capital, **Madrid**, may not be as pretty, but nor is it quite so over-run with tourists. Its many devotees have seen the city immortalized in the movies of Pedro Almodóvar, and it is shot through with a contemporary style that informs everything from its major-league art museums to its carefree bars and summer *terrazas*. Then there's **Seville**, home of flamenco and all the clichés of southern Spain; **Valencia**, the vibrant capital of the Levante, with a thriving arts scene and nightlife; and **Bilbao**, a not-to-miss stop on Spain's cultural circuit, due to Frank Gehry's astonishing Museo Guggenheim.

Not only are Spain's modern cities and towns lively and exciting, they are monumental – literally so. The country's history is evident everywhere, adding an architectural backdrop that varies from one region to another, dependent on their occupation by Romans, Visigoths or Moors, or on their role in the medieval Christian Reconquest or in the later Golden Age of imperial Renaissance Spain. Touring **Castilla y León**, for example, you can't avoid the stereotypical Spanish image of vast cathedrals

FACT FILE
- Spain's land **area** is around half a million square kilometres – about twice the size of the UK or Oregon. The **population** is almost 48 million – some eighty percent of whom declare themselves nominally Catholic, though religious observance is patchy.
- Politically, Spain is a **parliamentary monarchy**; democracy was restored in 1977, after the death of General Franco, the dictator who seized power in the Civil War of 1936–39.
- Spaniards read fewer **newspapers** than almost any other Europeans – tellingly, the best-selling daily is *Marca*, devoted purely to football.
- **Spanish** (Castilian) is the main official language, but sizeable numbers of Spaniards also speak variants of **Catalan** (in Catalunya, parts of Valencia and Alicante provinces, and on the Balearic Islands), **Galician** and **Basque**, all of which are also officially recognized languages.
- A minority of Spaniards attend **bullfights**; it doesn't rain much on the **plains**; and they only dance **flamenco** in the southern region of Andalucía.
- The highest **mountain** on the Spanish peninsula is Mulhacén (3483m), and the longest **river** is the Rio Tajo (716km).
- Spain has fifty sites on **UNESCO's World Heritage** list – nearly twice as many as the US.
- Between them, **Real Madrid** and **Barcelona** have won the Spanish league title 63 times and the European Cup (Champions League) twenty times and counting.

and hundreds of *reconquista* castles, while the gorgeous medieval university city of Salamanca captivates all who visit. In northerly, mountainous **Asturias** and the **Pyrenees**, tiny, almost organically evolved, Romanesque churches dot the hillsides and villages, while in **Galicia** all roads lead to the ancient, and heartbreakingly beautiful cathedral city of Santiago de Compostela. **Andalucía** has the great mosques and Moorish palaces of Granada, Seville and Córdoba; **Castilla-La Mancha** boasts the superbly preserved medieval capital of Toledo; while the harsh landscape of **Extremadura** cradles ornate *conquistador* towns built with riches from the New World.

The Spanish **landscape**, too, holds just as much fascination and variety as the country's urban centres. The evergreen estuaries of Galicia could hardly be more different from the high, arid plains of Castile, or the gulch-like desert landscapes of Almería. In particular, Spain has some of the finest **mountains** in Europe, with superb walking – from short hikes to week-long treks – in a dozen or more protected ranges or *sierras* – especially the Picos de Europa and the Pyrenees. There are still brown bears and lynx in the wild, not to mention boar, storks and eagles, while a near-five-thousand-kilometre coastline means great opportunities for fishing, whale-watching and dolphin-spotting.

Agriculture, meanwhile, makes its mark in the patterned hillsides of the wine- and olive-growing regions, the baking wheat plantations and cattle ranches of the central plains, the *meseta*, and the rice fields of the eastern provinces of Valencia

and Murcia, known as the Levante. These areas, although short on historic monuments and attractions, produce some of Spain's most famous exports, and with the country now at the heart of the contemporary European foodie movement, there's an entire holiday to be constructed out of simply exploring Spain's rich **regional cuisine** – touring the Rioja and other celebrated wine regions, snacking your way around Extremadura and Andalucía in search of the world's best *jamón serrano* (cured mountain ham), or tucking into a paella in its spiritual home of Valencia.

And finally, there are the **beaches** – one of Spain's greatest attractions, and where modern tourism to the country began in the 1960s. Here, too, there's a lot more variety than the stereotypical images might suggest. Long tracts of coastline – along the **Costa del Sol** in Andalucía in particular – have certainly been massively

> ## SPANISH TIME
>
> Spanish time is notionally one hour ahead of the UK – but conceptually Spain might as well be on a different planet. Nowhere else in Europe keeps such late hours. Spaniards may not take a traditional midday **siesta** as much as they used to, but their diurnal rhythms remain committedly nocturnal. They'll saunter out around 8pm or 9pm in the evening for a **paseo**, to greet friends and maybe have a drink and tapas, and if they're eating out, they'll normally start at 10pm or 11pm, often later in Madrid, where it's not unusual for someone to phone around midnight to see if you're going out for the evening.
>
> Like everything else, practices differ somewhat by region. Madrid – its inhabitants nicknamed **los gatos** or "the cats" for their nocturnal lifestyle – is famed for staying up the latest, with Andalucía a close second. In the north, particularly in Catalunya, they keep more northern European hours. And, of course, **summer nights** never seem to really end.

and depressingly over-developed, but delightful pockets remain, even along the biggest, concrete-clad *costas*. Moreover, there are superb windsurfing waters around Tarifa and some decidedly low-key resorts along the **Costa de la Luz**. On the **Costa Brava**, in the northeast in Catalunya, the string of idyllic coves between Palamos and Begur is often overlooked, while the cooler Atlantic coastline boasts the **surfing beaches** of Cantabria and Asturias, and the unspoiled coves of Galicia's estuaries. Offshore, the **Balearic Islands** – Ibiza, Formentera, Mallorca and Menorca – also have some superb sands, with party-fuelled Ibiza in particular offering one of the most hedonistic backdrops to beachlife in the whole Mediterranean.

Hedonism, actually, brings us full circle, back to one of the reasons why Spain is pretty much irresistible and infectious. Wherever you are in the country, you can't help but notice the Spaniards' wild – often overbearing – enthusiasm for **having a good time**. Festivals are a case in point – these aren't staid celebrations; they are raucous reaffirmations of life itself, complete with fireworks, fancy dress, giants, devils, bonfires, parties, processions and sheer Spanish glee. But even outside *fiesta* time there's always something vibrant and noisy happening – from a local market to a late-night bar, a weekend football match to a beachside dance club. Meals are convivial affairs – for most Spaniards the rushed sandwich or chain-restaurant takeaway just won't do – and

ON THE TAPAS TRAIL

Everyone thinks they know tapas – the little nibbles served up in bars – yet nothing can prepare you for the variety available on their home soil. If all you've ever encountered is deep-fried squid and spicy potatoes, then a treat awaits. That's not even to say that those dishes aren't authentic – but the truth is that your first beachfront plate of Andalucían **calamares** or **patatas bravas** in back-street Barcelona will really make you sit up and take notice. The proper way to eat tapas is to wander from one bar to another to sample a particular speciality, since the best bars tend to be known for just one or two dishes and the locals wouldn't dream of ordering anything else. So you might duck into one place for **jamón serrano** (cured ham), another for **pulpo gallego** (pot-cooked octopus), a third for **pimientos de Padrón** (small green peppers – about one in ten being fiery-hot), and then maybe on to a smoky old bar that serves just **fino** (dry sherry) from the barrel along with slices of **mojama** (dried, pressed roe). And that's not counting the creative, new-wave bars where sculpted **montaditos** (canapés), yucca chips, samosas, sushi-fusion titbits or artisan-produced cheese and meat are all vying for your attention. Once you've nibbled your way around town, it's time to tackle the serious business of dinner.

long lunches and late dinners are the norm throughout the country. And with family at the heart of Spanish society, there's a genuine welcome for, and interest in, you and yours, whether at a resort hotel or a rustic guesthouse. "*A pasarlo bien*!" (Have a good time!), as the Spanish say.

When to go

If Spain is a country of many regions, it's also a country of many **climates** (see page 51). The high central plains (which include Madrid) suffer from fierce extremes – stiflingly hot in summer, bitterly cold and swept by freezing winds in winter. The Atlantic coast, in contrast, has a tendency to be damp and misty, with a relatively brief, humid summer. The Mediterranean south is warm virtually all year round, and in parts of Andalucía it's positively subtropical – it's often pleasant enough to take lunch outside, even in the winter months. On a general holiday or city break, in most regions spring, the early part of summer and autumn are the best times to visit. Temperatures will be fairly mild, sites and attractions open, and tourist numbers relatively low – worth considering, especially if your destination is one of the beach resorts or main cultural attractions. Spain is one of the most-visited countries on the planet – it plays host to about sixty million tourists a year, rather more than the entire population – and all main tourist destinations are packed in high summer. Even the Pyrenean mountains aren't immune, swapping winter ski crowds for summer hikers and bikers. August is Spain's own holiday month – when the *costas* are at their most crowded, though inland cities (including Madrid) are, by contrast, pretty sleepy, since everyone who can leaves for their annual break.

Author picks

Our hard-travelling authors have visited every corner of Spain – from the *rías* of Galicia to the white towns of Andalucía – to bring you some unique travel experiences. These are some of their own, personal favourites.

Fiestas and ferias Get boozy at Sanlúcar de Barrameda's sherry festival (see page 280), play with fire at Valencia's Las Fallas (see page 746), or celebrate at Seville's Feria de Abril (see page 247).

Seafood heaven Fill up on aromatic Valencian paella (see page 754) or feast on L'Escala anchovies (see page 674). Adventurous eaters can try *percebes*, prestigious little crustaceans from Galicia (see page 513), or *ortiguillas*, deep-fried sea anemones from the Cádiz area (see page 273).

Classic journeys The legendary Camino de Santiago route (see page 523) is a life must-do. For train thrills the Catalan Cremallera (see page 699) is a blast.

Delightful towns Not famous, no fanfares, but thoroughly lovely – Beget in Catalunya (see page 692), El Burgo de Osma in Castilla y León (see page 376) and Andalucía's Zahara de la Sierra (see page 245).

Amazing views The jagged remains of Las Médulas are eerily captivating (see page 412), while the views from the walls of Ávila (see page 141) and Barcelona from the cross-harbour cable car (see page 630) are unforgettable.

Hip and hot nightlife Join the gin craze in Barcelona (see page 646), let your hair down at *Ibiza Rocks* in Ibiza (see page 799), or hit *Coco's* fashionable dancefloors in Madrid (see page 109).

Fine sands In a land of long sandy stretches and limpid, turquoise waters the competition for best beach is tough. Top of the table are: Conil in Andalucía (see page 273), Águilas in Murcia (see page 783) and Ibiza's Cala D'Hort (see page 798).

Stunning architecture Gaudí's Parc Güell (see page 632), Chillida in San Sebastián (see page 426) and the vertical garden in Madrid's CaixaForum (see page 87) are all eye-popping masterpieces.

> Our author recommendations don't end here. We've flagged up our favourite places – a perfectly sited hotel, an atmospheric café, a special restaurant – throughout the Guide, highlighted with the ★ symbol.

MILESTONE OF THE WAY OF ST JAMES

SEVILLE'S APRIL FAIR

25

things not to miss

It's not possible to see everything that Spain has to offer in one trip – and we don't suggest you try. What follows, in no particular order, is a selection of the country's highlights, including spectacular architecture, outstanding natural wonders, flamboyant local festivals and a few culinary treats. Each entry has a page reference to take you straight into the Guide, where you can find out more. Coloured numbers refer to chapters in the Guide section.

1 FLAMENCO IN SEVILLE

See page 265

The stamp of heels and heart-rending lament of a *cante jondo* encapsulate the soul of the Spanish south.

2 SHERRY TASTING IN JEREZ

See page 283

There are few greater pleasures than a chilled glass of fino or manzanilla, and there's no better place to sample them than in the sherry heartland of Jerez.

3 BURGOS CATHEDRAL

See page 391

What is perhaps Spain's finest Gothic cathedral dominates the lively small city of Burgos.

4 IBIZA AND FORMENTERA'S HIDDEN COVES

See page 791

The islands' little-developed beaches range from gem-like coves to sweeps of white sand.

5 CLUBBING IN IBIZA

See page 795

Forget sleep, and experience everything else to excess, on Ibiza – the ultimate party island.

6 SEGOVIA

See page 148

At eight hundred metres long the extraordinary Roman aqueduct of Segovia is one of Spain's most breathtaking ancient monuments.

7 TEATRE-MUSEU DALÍ, FIGUERES

See page 689

The Dalí museum in Figueres is as surreal as its creator – who lies in a mausoleum within.

8 TOLEDO

See page 118

The capital of medieval Spain, Toledo has changed little since its depiction in El Greco's paintings.

9 LA MEZQUITA, CÓRDOBA

See page 293

Nothing can prepare you for the breathtaking Grand Mosque of Córdoba – one of the world's most beautiful buildings.

10 PARADORES

See page 36

Converted castles, monasteries and special monuments provide many of Spain's most atmospheric hotels.

11 BODEGAS YSIOS
See page 451
Raise a glass to the Rioja
region's amazing designer
temple of wine.

12 LAS ALPUJARRAS
See page 326
Drive over lemons and
walk old mule paths in
this picturesque region of
mountain villages nestled
in the southern folds of the
Sierra Nevada.

13 SEMANA SANTA
See page 214
Easter week sees processions
of masked penitents, with
the biggest events in Seville
and Málaga.

14 FUNDACIÓ JOAN MIRÓ
See page 628
Admire the instantly
recognizable colours and
forms of Joan Miró's life's work
in this Barcelona museum.

15 SANTIAGO DE COMPOSTELA
See page 510
The pilgrim route left a
swathe of Gothic and
Renaissance churches, not
least the great Catedral.

11

12

13

14

15

16 PARQUE NACIONAL COTO DE DOÑANA
See page 286
Look for Doñana's myriad birds and other wildlife – including the rare Iberian lynx on an African-style safari.

17 PICOS DE EUROPA
See page 482
Take a hike along the stunning Cares Gorge, the most popular walk in glorious Picos de Europa National Park.

18 MUSEO DEL PRADO, MADRID
See page 78
Spain's greatest art museum is an obligatory visit on any trip to the capital.

19 ROMAN RUINS OF MÉRIDA
See page 199
Wander at will around the ancient Roman ruins of Mérida, the most extensive such remains in the country.

20 MUSEO GUGGENHEIM, BILBAO
See page 441
Frank Gehry's flagship creation of undulating titanium has become one of the iconic buildings of our age.

17

18

19

20

21

22

23

21 SEVILLE
See page 247

The quintessential Andalucian city with sun-drenched plazas, winding alleyways, Moorish monuments and more bars than seems remotely feasible.

22 LAS FALLAS
See page 746

In March, Valencia erupts in festivities as giant models are burnt and fireworks crackle across town to celebrate San José.

23 THE ALHAMBRA, GRANADA
See page 309

The legendary Moorish palace complex is a monument to sensuality and contemplative decoration.

24 SAGRADA FAMÍLIA, BARCELONA
See page 622

One of Spain's truly essential sights – Antoni Gaudí's unfinished masterpiece, the church of the "Sacred Family".

25 A NIGHT ON THE TILES, MADRID
See page 106

Delight in the capital's most traditional of rituals – a night of bar-hopping and clubbing rounded off by a dawn reviver of *chocolate con churros*.

Itineraries

Spain is a vast and varied country, and you can't cover all of it in a single trip. Our Grand Tour concentrates on Spain's major cities and outstanding sights, while our other suggested routes focus on two captivating regions, one in the south, one in the north. Each itinerary will take a packed two weeks to cover; if you only have one week to spare you can cover part of one route and get a flavour of the whole country or a feel for one of its fascinating regions.

GRAND TOUR OF SPAIN

Two weeks in Spain and no idea where to start? Our "Grand Tour" puts you on the right track.

❶ **Madrid** The vibrant capital is at the heart of all that makes modern Spain tick, from world-class art collections to a buzzing café society and a wild nightlife. See page 60

❷ **Toledo** With time for just one side trip from Madrid, head to Toledo. This old rock-bound city is the home of El Greco and is packed with magnificent buildings. See page 118

❸ **Seville** You could spend weeks exploring Andalucía (see page 210) – but for a taster, Seville combines gorgeous buildings with a vibrant flamenco and tapas scene. See page 247

❹ **Valencia** The rapidly changing city of Valencia – cultural hub of the east, not to mention the spiritual birthplace of paella. See page 739

❺ **Barcelona** The cool Catalan capital, with its Art Nouveau architecture, designer shops, and stylish bars and clubs. See page 600

❻ **Figueres** The two-hour journey from Barcelona towards the French border is made with only one destination in mind – the extraordinary Teatre-Museu Dalí. See page 689

❼ **Logroño** This handsome city sits at the heart of the Rioja region, and while it may be small there's nothing modest about its superb tapas and wine bars. From here, you could detour along the northern coast (see page 23). See page 383

❽ **Valladolid** Relive Spain's Golden Age in the capital of Castilla y León, whose majestic Plaza Mayor has no equal. See page 366

❾ **Salamanca** The most beautiful city in Spain has buildings fashioned from a honey-coloured stone that glows as the sun sets. See page 346

THE BEST OF ANDALUCÍA

❶ **Málaga** This transport hub is the obvious place to start, but it's also worth lingering for a day to enjoy this vibrant coastal city. See page 213

❷ **Ronda** Sited astride a towering gorge is the queen of Andalucía's white towns. See page 240

Create your own itinerary with Rough Guides. Whether you're after adventure or a family-friendly holiday, we have a trip for you, with all the activities you enjoy doing and the sights you want to see. All our trips are devised by local experts who get the most out of the destination. Visit **www.roughguides.com/trips** to chat with one of our travel agents.

❸ Seville The essence of all things *andaluz*, with a stunning cathedral, Moorish Alcázar and atmospheric old quarter. See page 247

❹ Córdoba A must-see destination, boasting one of the world's greatest Moorish buildings, the Mezquita, at its heart. See page 293

❺ Baeza and Úbeda These twin Renaissance architectural jewels are filled with a wealth of golden monuments. See pages 304 and 305

❻ Cazorla Natural Park A stunning array of wildlife inhabits the rugged mountains, gorges and forested valleys of Cazorla. See page 307

❼ Granada Overlooked by the seductive Alhambra, this historic city is one of Spain's most compelling attractions. See page 308

❽ Almuñécar The Costa Tropical's main resort has great beaches and plenty of places to eat, drink and dance the night away. See page 228

NORTHERN SPAIN, ALONG THE ATLANTIC COAST

❶ Bilbao Revitalized by the success of its Guggenheim Museum, the energetic city of Bilbao is set amid the spectacular green hills of the Basque Country. See page 439

❷ San Sebastián This elegant seaside resort boasts one of Europe's best city beaches; its superb cuisine is at its most affordable in the *pintxos* bars of the old quarter. See page 422

❸ Pamplona An intriguing destination, which comes alive during the bull-running of July's San Fermín festival. See page 452

❹ Santillana del Mar Often hailed as Spain's prettiest village, Santillana is an exquisite medieval ensemble with some gorgeous hotels. See page 477

❺ Picos de Europa These peaks are interspersed with lush meadows and ancient settlements, and offer superb hiking. See page 482

❻ Llanes Delightful seaside towns dot the Asturian coast, but bustling little Llanes, close to superb beaches and soaring mountains, is perhaps the finest of all. See page 494

❼ Oviedo Visigothic churches pepper the hills here – though you'll have to tear yourself away from cider-houses to see them. See page 502

❽ The Rías of Galicia Galicia's fjord-like estuaries cradle dramatic scenery, with the wild Rías Altas in the north and the gentler Rías Baixas to the south. See pages 525 and 536

❾ Santiago de Compostela For over a thousand years, this magnificent cathedral city has welcomed footsore pilgrims; its historic core remains irresistible. See page 510

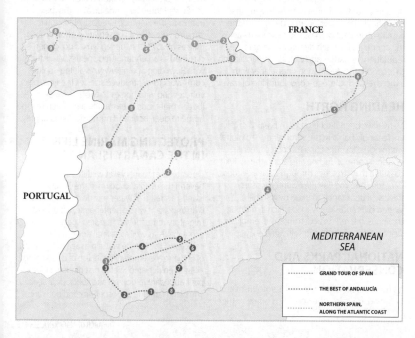

FRANCE

PORTUGAL

MEDITERRANEAN SEA

.... GRAND TOUR OF SPAIN

.... THE BEST OF ANDALUCÍA

.... NORTHERN SPAIN, ALONG THE ATLANTIC COAST

Sustainable travel

For decades, it was famed for beach breaks and all-inclusives – but look past the fiestas and you'll discover the greener, wilder, eco-conscious side of Spain.

After receiving a record 85 million tourists in 2023, and with 90 million expected in 2024 at the time of writing, Spain is on its way to becoming the world's most highly visited country – but the environmental concerns accompanying the surge are hard to shake off. The high visitor numbers generate an alarming carbon footprint and the over-urbanization of Spain's coastlines has damaged biodiversity, while holidaymakers have also been linked to excessive water usage contributing to droughts. But the approach to holidaying in Spain has been changing. In order to curb the damaging impact of mass tourism, efforts across the country have been discarding its dated reputation for parties and excess, instead aiming to reconcile the destination's popularity with a more responsible, eco-conscious kind of travel.

HEADING NORTH

Many have been ditching beach breaks (increasingly harsh in the summer due to global warming) in favour of Spain's cooler, greener northern corridor. Journeying along the 2500km coastline that stretches through Galicia, Asturias, Cantabria and the Basque Country, visitors traverse a geography marked by lush hills, jagged cliffs and sinewy roads. Rich in farming traditions, the region's gastronomy exemplifies seasonality, proximity and self-sufficiency.

NATIONAL PARKS AND CONSERVATION

It's no wonder ecotourism and agrotourism are booming in Spain – the country is home to the

world's largest number of UNESCO Biosphere Reserves, while 28 percent of Spanish land (among the highest rates in Europe) is protected for its natural significance. Spain's sixteen stunning national parks range from the Picos de Europa mountains in the north of the mainland to the Doñana wetlands in the south. Its diverse landscape encompasses the snowy peaks of the Pyrenees and the arid deserts of Almería. Rare animal species are found in such areas, from the lynx (around five hundred are said to roam the Sierra Morena in Andalucía) to the ibex (native to the Sierra de Gredos). Although it remains vulnerable, conservation efforts mean that, as of 2024, the Iberian lynx is no longer classified as an endangered species. Volunteers with Rewilding Spain (www.rewilding-spain. com) work to reintroduce species like lynx, black vultures and wild horses to the 2.1-million-acre Iberian highlands in eastern Spain, which is also home to deer, boar and numerous birds of prey.

PROTECTING MARINE LIFE IN THE CANARY ISLANDS

Opportunities to marvel at wildlife extend beyond the mainland: down in the Canary Islands, a stretch of water southwest of Tenerife is an important whale heritage site, acting as a migratory route for two hundred specimens of pilot whales, as well as several dolphins and other cetaceans. The Mar de las Calmas sea to the south of El Hierro – exemplary for its use of clean energy – has been declared Spain's first marine national park, abundant in tropical and subtropical species. The Islands' unique atmospheric conditions are

THE ARCH OF MACARENA, SEVILLE

MONASTERY OF SAN XULIÁN DE SAMOS IN GALICIA

ideal for observing other natural phenomena too – like stargazing in La Palma.

GREEN SPACES IN CITIES

Spain's urban destinations have also been upping their eco-conscious game. Valencia was named European Green Capital in 2024 for its reduced energy consumption, water purification and wetlands protection. Visitors soak up the city while enjoying its extensive pedestrianized spaces; its wealth of greenery includes the Turia Garden, stretching for 9km along the river, while the new Central Park project is adding 230,000 square kilometres of green space to the city centre.

APPS FOR ENVIRONMENTAL AWARENESS

Further south, the Andalucían capital of Seville aims to be carbon neutral by 2030 and is excelling in smart tourism, with a range of new apps available for visitors to encourage accessibility, mobility, safety and environmental awareness. The city is a cyclist's paradise too, boasting 180km of bike lanes, while the Isla de la Cartuja district is taking steps towards becoming a fully renewable and electric zone.

SUSTAINABILITY IN THE BALEARIC ISLANDS

Visitors to the Balearic Islands have been paying a Sustainable Tourism Tax since 2016 that has funded eco-conscious projects like new cycling and walking routes in Mallorca and Ibiza. There are also efforts to preserve Formentera's marine

seagrass (*Posidonia oceanica*), which oxygenates the underwater ecosystem – home to over four hundred plant and a thousand animal species – but has been damaged by excessive yachting. A new app now lets yachts know where they can and can't moor – and there's even an intimate, zero-emissions music festival on the island for just 350 people that supports the Save Posidonia project.

ECO-CONSCIOUS ACCOMMODATION

Hotels across Spain are eliminating plastic, making organic choices in their design and looking to alternative energy resources – but for a truly ecological experience, live and volunteer in one of Spain's numerous *ecoaldeas* (eco-villages), where self-sustaining communities cohabit consciously and responsibly with nature.

EATING PULPO A LA GALLEGA WITH POTATOES IN GALICIA

Basics

Getting there

Madrid and Barcelona are the two main Spanish airports, though the summer holiday trade to the costas and the Balearics, and extensive coverage by European budget airlines, has opened up regional airports right across Spain. Taking the train to Spain is a greener option and has much to recommend it – and now you can do the whole journey from London to Barcelona or Madrid in a day. Driving is more of an adventure, but there are several routes that can save you time, like the direct ferry services from Portsmouth and Plymouth to Santander and Portsmouth to Bilbao.

Flights from the UK and Ireland

Flight time to Spain is two to three hours, depending on the route, and usually the cheapest flights are with the no-frills **budget airlines** such as easyJet (http:// easyjet.com), Jet2 (http://jet2.com), Ryanair (http:// ryanair.com) and Vueling (http://vueling.com), who between them fly from over twenty regional UK airports direct to **destinations all over Spain** – not just Madrid and Barcelona, but also to smaller regional Spanish airports like Málaga, Alicante, Santander, Valencia and those in the Balearics. Note that London flights tend to depart from Stansted or Luton, while it's always worth double-checking the exact Spanish airport used – some "Barcelona" flights, for example, are actually to Girona (1hr to the north) or Reus (1hr 15min to the south). **Fares** for flights on all routes can be very cheap, particularly if you fly without checked baggage. However, book last minute in the summer and you can expect to pay considerably more, particularly on more popular routes.

For flights **to the costas and Balearics**, it's also worth checking holiday and charter companies such as First Choice (http://firstchoice.co.uk), Thomas Cook (http://thomascook.com) and TUI (http://tui.co.uk). You might not get the rock-bottom deals of the budget airlines, as schedules and prices are geared towards the summer holiday season, but flights depart from convenient regional airports around the UK.

The widest range of **scheduled flights** is with Iberia (http://iberia.com) and British Airways (http:// britishairways.com), with direct services from London Gatwick or Heathrow to half a dozen Spanish cities (most frequently to Madrid and Barcelona, but also Valencia, Bilbao, Málaga and Alicante) and connections on to most other airports in Spain. You'll also be able to arrange add-on sections to London from regional English airports such as Manchester or Newcastle or from Scotland.

From Ireland, you can fly with Iberia from Dublin to Madrid, or with Aer Lingus (http://aerlingus.com) from Dublin or Cork to several Spanish airports (including Barcelona, Bilbao, Málaga and Alicante). Ryanair also connects Dublin with most of the same destinations. Prices rise sharply for last-minute bookings or to popular summer destinations.

Flights from the US and Canada

The widest choice of scheduled flights **from the United States** to Spain is with Iberia (http://iberia. com), which flies direct, nonstop from New York, Los Angeles, Miami and Chicago to Madrid. Journey time (typically overnight) is between seven and eleven hours, depending on the route. The advantage of flying with Iberia is that it offers connecting flights to almost anywhere in Spain, which can be very good value if booked with your transatlantic flight.

Other airlines offering Spain routes (some on a code-share basis with Iberia or other airlines) include American Airlines (http://aa.com), Delta (http://delta. com) and United (http://united.com). Level (http:// flylevel.com) is the first "budget" airline to offer trans-Atlantic flights. They offer direct flights from Los Angeles or San Francisco to Barcelona. Flights can be found for as low as €350 return, though double that is more realistic. You can also fly to Spain with airlines such as Air France, KLM, Lufthansa, TAP or British Airways, for example, which tend to fly via

A BETTER KIND OF TRAVEL

At Rough Guides we are passionately committed to travel. We believe it helps us understand the world we live in and the people we share it with – and of course tourism is vital to many developing economies. But the scale of modern tourism has also damaged some places irreparably, and climate change is accelerated by most forms of transport, especially flying. We encourage all our authors to consider the carbon footprint of the journeys they make in the course of researching our guides.

their respective European hubs – in which case, you can add three to four hours to your total travel time, depending on the connection.

From Canada, Air Canada (http://aircanada.com) flies nonstop from Toronto to Madrid and Barcelona. It also sells connecting and/or code-sharing flights from Toronto and Montréal to Madrid, Barcelona, Valencia, Malaga and Bilbao. Alternatively, you can fly with one of the major European airlines via their respective hubs.

Flights from Australia, New Zealand and South Africa

There are no direct flights to Spain **from Australia or New Zealand**, but many airlines offer through-tickets with their partners via their European or Asian hubs. Flights via Asia are generally the cheaper option, but fares don't vary as much between airlines as you might think, and in the end you'll be basing your choice on things like flight timings, routes and possible stop-offs on the way. If you're seeing Spain as part of a wider European trip, you might want to aim first for the UK, since there's a wide choice of cheap flights to Spain from there and it's generally cheaper to fly from Australasia to London than it is to Spain. Or consider a Round-the-World fare, with most basic options able to offer Madrid or Barcelona as standard stopovers.

From **South Africa**, Iberia (http://iberia.com) offers direct flights between Johannesburg and Madrid. One of the more convenient non-direct routes is offered by Ethiopian Airlines (www.ethiopianairlines. com) who fly the Johannesburg to Madrid route with a transit in Addis Ababa. Otherwise many other European airlines fly from their respective hubs to Johannesburg and all can offer connections onto Spain.

Package holidays, tours and city breaks

The basic, mass-market **package holidays** to the traditional resorts on the Costa del Sol, Costa Brava, Costa Blanca and others are not to everyone's taste, but bargains can be found online or at any UK high-street travel agent, from as little as £250 for a seven-night flight-and-hotel package. There are often really good deals for families, either in hotels or in self-catering apartments, though, of course, if you are tied to school holidays you will pay significantly more.

A huge number of **specialist tour operators** offer a wider range of activity holidays or tours, from hiking in the Pyrenees to touring the artistic highlights of Andalucía. We've given a flavour of what's available in the listed reviews at the end of this section, but the options are almost endless. Prices vary wildly depending on the quality of accommodation offered and whether the tours are fully inclusive or not. Many hiking or bicycle tours, for example, can either be guided or done on a more independent (and cheaper) self-guided basis, which makes for an exciting trip. Spanish-based tour operators offer some of the more interesting, off-the-beaten-track options, but for these you'll usually have to arrange your own flights to Spain, while many foreign-based operators also tend to quote for their holidays exclusive of airfares.

Some operators and websites specialize in **city breaks**, with destinations including Barcelona, Madrid, Seville and Granada. UK prices start at around £200 for three-day (two-night) breaks, including return flights, airport transfer and B&B in a centrally located one-, two- or three-star hotel. Adding extra nights or upgrading your hotel is possible, too, usually at a fairly reasonable cost. The bigger US operators, such as American Express and Delta Vacations, can also easily organize short city breaks to Spain on a flight-and-hotel basis, while from Australia World Journeys (https://worldjourneys.com.au) can arrange two- or three-night packages in most Spanish cities.

Other deals worth considering are fly-drive offers, where you'll get a **flight, accommodation and car rental** arranged through your tour operator. Some companies specialize in villas and apartments, or off-the-beaten-track farmhouses and the like, while on other holiday packages you can tour the country's historic paradores, with car rental included in the price.

CYCLING TOURS

Bravobike Spain http://bravobike.com. Offers a variety of cycle tours from one day in Madrid, Segovia or Toledo, for example, to themed week-long tours in *conquistador* country or along the Camino de Santiago. Tour lengths vary widely, from a half-day trip round Madrid, up to an eight-day guided wine tour of Rioja.
Iberocycle Spain http://iberocycle.com. An English-run, Spain-based company specializing in supported or self-guided cycling tours of northern Spain in particular (Cantabria, Asturias, Basque Country, Catalunya).

FOOD AND DRINK TOUR

A Taste of Spain Spain http://atasteofspain.com. Organizes gourmet culinary tours of Catalunya, the Basque region/La Rioja, Andalucía and central Spain, with tastings, meals and cookery lessons. Trips vary from a day's excursion to taste Iberico ham, up to a week-long gastronomic whizz through the Basque country, Catalunya and Madrid.

HISTORY, ART AND CULTURE TOUR

Madrid and Beyond Spain http://madridandbeyond.com. Classy customized holidays and special experiences, from private gallery tours to fashion-expert-led shopping trips in Barcelona and Madrid. Variable prices.

HORSERIDING TOUR

Fantasia Adventure Holidays Spain http://fantasiaadventureholidays.com. British-run company offering riding breaks on the Costa de la Luz, from five to fifteen days.

Trains

Travelling **by train from the UK to Spain** is a viable – and fun – option, with total journey times from London of under twelve hours to Barcelona, and fifteen hours to Madrid. You can now do the journey in one (admittedly very long) day, if you take the early **Eurostar** (http://eurostar.com) from London St Pancras International to Paris and change there for the double-decker TGV Duplex, which arrives in Barcelona (via Figueres and Girona) in the mid-evening. From Barcelona, you can catch a high-speed AVE train, which will get you to Madrid (via Zaragoza) at around midnight. You'll have to book well in advance on all services to get the lowest prices. If you don't mind the journey to Spain taking a whole lot longer, there are also minor routes that cross the central Pyrenees (via Canfranc or Puigcerdà), though you may have to spend the night at either of the border towns if you want to see the mountains in daylight.

The best first stop for information about train travel to Spain is the excellent http://seat61.com, which provides full route, ticket, timetable and contact information. You can book the whole journey online with **Rail Europe** (http://raileurope.com), or contact a specialist rail agent like Ffestiniog Travel (http://ffestiniogtravel.com) or the Spanish Rail Service (http://renfe.com). For the French trains try http://oui.sncf, which can book Eurostar and TGV tickets and advise about **rail passes** (principally InterRail and Eurail), which have to be bought before leaving home (see page 30).

Buses

You can reach most major towns and cities in Spain by bus from the UK with **National Express** services (http://nationalexpress.com). The main routes are from London (though inexpensive add-on fares are available from any British city) to Madrid (27hr), with connections on to other Spanish destinations, but it's a long time to spend cooped up in a bus. Standard return fares are often significantly pricier than advance deals and special offers – it's always cheapest to book online. Eurolines also has a **Eurolines Pass**, which allows unlimited travel on Eurolines routes between forty-odd cities, but only between Madrid, Barcelona and Alicante within Spain, so it's not much use for a Spanish tour.

Driving to Spain

Driving to Spain from the UK is an interesting way to get there, but with fuel, road toll and overnight costs it doesn't compare in terms of price with flying or taking the train. It's about 1600km from London to Barcelona, for example, which, with stops, takes almost two full days to drive; it's another 600km on to Madrid.

Many people use the conventional **cross-Channel ferry links**, principally Dover–Calais, though services to Brittany or Normandy might be more convenient depending on where you live (and they cut out the trek around Paris). However, the quickest way of crossing the Channel is to use the **Eurotunnel** (http://eurotunnel.com), which operates drive-on, drive-off shuttle trains between Folkestone and Calais/Coquelles. The 24-hour service runs every twenty minutes throughout the day; though you can just turn up, booking is advised, especially at weekends and in summer holidays, or if you want the best deals.

The best way to cut driving time is to use one of the direct **UK–Spain ferry crossings**, especially if you're heading for the Basque region, Galicia, Castilla y León or even Madrid. Brittany Ferries (http://brittany-ferries.co.uk) operates car and passenger ferry services from **Portsmouth to Santander** (2 weekly; 24hr) and **Bilbao** (3 weekly; 24–32hr) and **Plymouth to Santander** (2 weekly; 20hr). Fares start at around £320 one-way for a car and two passengers, but it costs significantly more in summer, particularly August – it's cheaper for foot-passengers, though everyone has to book some form of seating or cabin accommodation.

Any ferry company or travel agent can supply up-to-date schedules and ticket information, or you can consult the encyclopedic http://directferries.com, which has details about, and links to, every European ferry service.

Getting around

Most of Spain is well covered by public transport. The rail network reaches all the provincial capitals and the main towns along the inter-city lines, and there's an expanding high-speed network that has

slashed journey times on major cross-country routes from Madrid. Inter-city bus services are often more frequent and cheaper than the regular trains, and will usually take you closer to your destination, as some train stations are a few kilometres from the town or village they serve. Driving a car, meanwhile, will give you the freedom to head away from the major tourist routes and take in some of the spectacular scenery at your own pace.

One important point to remember is that all public transport, and the bus service especially, is drastically reduced on **Sundays and public holidays** – don't even consider travelling to out-of-the-way places on these days. The words to look out for on timetables are *diario* (daily), *laborables* (workdays, including Sat), and *domingos y festivos* (Sun and public hols).

By train

Spanish trains, operated by **RENFE** (http://renfe.com), tend to be efficient and comfortable, and nearly always run on time. There's a confusing array of services, though the website has a useful English-language version on which you can check timetables and buy tickets with a credit card (printing them out at home before you travel).

Cercanías are local commuter trains in and around the major cities, while **media distancia** (regional) and **larga distancia** (long-distance) trains go under a bewildering number of names, including Avant, Alaris, Intercity (IC), Regional and Talgo services. The difference is speed, service and number of stops, and you'll always pay more on the quickest routes (sometimes quite a lot more).

The premier services are the high-speed trains, such as the **Euromed** from Barcelona to Alicante, or the fast-expanding **AVE** (Alta Velocidad Española)

network from Madrid to Seville, Málaga, Valencia, Segovia/Valladolid, Zaragoza, Barcelona, Alicante and Huesca; and from Barcelona to Seville and Málaga; and from Valencia to Seville. The AVE trains have cut travelling times dramatically, with Madrid to Seville, for example, taking two and a half hours compared with six to nine hours on the slower trains. The AVE network also runs across the border from Madrid and Barcelona to Marseille, and from Barcelona to Paris, Lyon and Toulouse, and is set to expand right across the peninsula over the next decade, northwest to Castilla y León and Galicia, the Basque Country and Asturias, and west to Lisbon in Portugal.

Tickets, fares and rail passes

Although you can just turn up at the station for short hops, **advance booking** is essential (and seat reservations obligatory) for long-distance journeys. Advance tickets can be bought at stations between sixty days and five minutes before departure, but don't leave it to the last minute, as there are usually long queues (and often separate windows for the different types of train). Automatic **ticket machines** at main stations take some of the hassle out of queuing and waiting a long period of time.

The best deals are always available **online** on the RENFE website, which has a range of different promotional fares offering discounts of up to sixty percent on the full fares. Otherwise, **return fares** (*ida y vuelta*) are discounted by ten to twenty percent, depending on the service – you can buy a single, and so long as you show it when you buy the return, you'll still get the discount. There's also a whole range of other **discounted fares** of between 25 and 40 percent for those over 60 or under 26, travellers with disabilities, children aged 4 to 11 years, and those travelling in groups.

Actual fares vary wildly, but as an example, you'll pay around €20 on the regional service from Madrid to Salamanca (2hr 50min trip), while on the Madrid to

---

ALL ABOARD

As well as the main Spanish rail system, there are also several private and regional train lines offering a different view of some spectacular parts of the country, mainly in the north.

The best is probably the **narrow-gauge railway** (see page 468), which runs right across the wild northwest, from Santander in Cantabria, through Asturias to Ferrol in Galicia. Catalunya has its own local commuter line, the **FGC** (see page 638), which operates the mountain rack-railway to **Montserrat**, as well as the **Cremallera**, the "zipper" (see page 699), another rack-and-pinion line that slinks up a Pyrenean valley to the sanctuary and ski station of Núria.

In the Sierra Guadarrama, just north of Madrid, the narrow-gauge line from **Cercedilla** to the ski station at Puerto de Navacerrada and then on to Cotos is a great way to see the mountainous landscape (see page 138).

THE SPANISH DRIVING EXPERIENCE

If it's your first time out on a Spanish road, especially in one of the bigger cities, you could be forgiven for thinking you've stumbled upon the local chapter of *Mad Max* devotees, out for a burn-up. In fact, those wild-eyed, dangerously speeding, non-signalling, bumper-hogging, mobile-talking, horn-sounding road warriors are normal Spanish citizens on their way to work. **Traffic lights** and **pedestrian crossings** in particular present a difficult conceptual challenge – if you are going to stop at either, make sure you give plenty of warning to avoid another vehicle running into the back of you, and keep an eye out for cars crossing your path who have jumped the lights. **Signposting** is universally poor (yes, *that* was the turn you wanted), even on main roads and highways, while joining and exiting **autopistas/autovías** can be particularly dangerous, as it's almost a point of honour not to let anyone in or out, and slip roads are often very short. Many of the worst **accidents** are on the N roads, which have only a single carriageway in each direction, so take particular care on these. Major roads are generally in good **condition**, though some minor and mountain roads can be rather hairy and are little more than dirt tracks in the more remote regions, awash with sheep, goats and cattle. That said, things are getting more orderly and drivers are a bit more careful because of the increased use of radar and speed controls. The police are also setting up more **drink-driving** controls than before, though you have to remember that this is a country where it's considered a good idea to have bars in motorway service stations.

Barcelona route you could pay from as little as €50 on the high-speed AVE service (around 3hr).

The major pan-European **rail passes** (InterRail and Eurail) are only worth considering if you're visiting the country as part of a wider European tour. Both schemes also have single-country Spain rail passes available, which might be better value depending on your Spanish itinerary. The **InterRail Spain Pass** (http://interrail.eu) is only available to European residents and allows three, four, six or eight days' train travel within one month, with under-26 years, second- and first-class versions available. For anyone else, **Eurail** (http://raileurope.com) has various Spain passes available, typically offering three days' travel in two months, again in various classes. You can check current prices on the websites, but bear in mind that it often works out cheaper to buy individual tickets in Spain as you need them, and it's certainly more convenient to be free to choose long-distance buses on some routes. All passes have to be bought before you leave home, and you'll still be liable for supplements and seat reservations on long-distance and high-speed trains.

By bus

Buses will probably meet most of your transport needs, especially if you're venturing away from the larger towns and cities. Many smaller villages and rural areas are only accessible by bus, almost always originating in the capital of their province. Services are pretty reliable, whether it's the two-buses-a-day local run, or the regular services between major cities (the latter often

far more conveniently scheduled than the equivalent train services). **Fares** are very reasonable, too: Madrid to León (3hr 30min), for example, costs around €35, Madrid to Santander (6hr) around €40. On inter-city runs, you'll usually be assigned a seat when you buy your ticket. Some destinations are served by more than one **bus company**, but main bus stations have posted timetables for all services (and, sometimes, someone who can speak English). Or you can check timetables on the company websites, which, while not always up to date, do at least give an idea of available services. Major companies like Alsa (http://www.alsa.com) and Avanzabus (http://www.avanzabus.com) have nation-wide services, and have full or partly English-language versions of their websites.

There are only a few cities in Spain (Madrid, Barcelona and Valencia, for example) where you'll need to use the **local bus** network, and all the relevant details are given in the Guide. You'll also sometimes need to take a local bus out to a campsite or distant museum or monastery; fares are very cheap, rarely more than a euro or two.

By car

Spain has an extensive system of highways, both free and with tolls. The **autopistas** are the most comfortable and best-kept roads. The second-grade roads, **autovías** (prefixed E), often follow similar routes, but their speed limits are lower. Many *autopistas* and some *autovías* are toll roads, and relatively expensive but worth paying for the lighter traffic encountered. You can usually pay with

DISTANCE CHART (KM)

	Alicante	Barcelona	Bilbao	Burgos	Córdoba	Granada	Jaén	León	Madrid	Málaga
Alicante	–	552	814	645	513	372	417	762	420	480
Barcelona	552	–	609	629	893	889	840	818	630	1022
Bilbao	814	609	–	160	795	820	730	350	400	930
Burgos	645	629	160	–	640	664	581	178	245	776
Córdoba	513	893	795	640	–	238	110	736	404	168
Granada	372	889	820	664	238	–	98	761	424	125
Jaén	417	840	730	581	110	98	–	677	342	211
León	762	818	350	178	736	761	677	–	349	871
Madrid	420	630	400	245	404	424	342	349	–	543
Málaga	480	1022	930	776	168	125	211	871	543	–
Murcia	82	602	785	634	482	297	342	749	408	414
Pamplona	723	490	152	210	841	869	791	404	456	993
Salamanca	630	835	398	248	604	634	543	208	219	674
San Sebastián	769	525	249	300	924	949	854	489	534	1065
Santander	837	715	103	186	820	856	762	280	428	967
Santiago de Compostela	1033	1165	596	526	1009	1032	949	364	607	1124
Seville	606	1055	861	711	149	261	300	674	537	231
Toledo	439	710	472	317	391	413	326	412	78	527
Valencia	183	365	651	590	536	510	454	702	361	649

a credit card, although it's wise to have enough cash just in case. Toll roads are usually designated by an "AP" or "R" or the words *peaje/Telpeaje/Via T*.

The Spanish **drive on the right**, and **speed limits** are enforced throughout the country. On most *autopistas* it is 120km/h, on the *autovía* 90km/h, and in towns and villages 50km/h. Police have the power to fine drivers on the spot for speeding or any other transgressions, and if you don't have any cash, they will escort you to the nearest cash machine and issue you with a receipt there and then. You can pay by credit card at most petrol stations for **fuel** (*gasolina*), the main companies being Cepsa and Repsol.

A UK or EU **driver's licence** is sufficient to drive in Spain. US, Canadian, Australian and New Zealand licences should also be enough, though you may want to get an International Driver's Licence as well, just to be on the safe side. If you are bringing your own car, you will need your vehicle registration and insurance papers – and check with your insurers that you are covered to drive the car abroad. It's also compulsory to carry two hazard triangles and reflective jackets in case of accident or breakdown. Rear seat belts are also compulsory, as are child seats for infants. An official first-aid kit and a set of spare bulbs is also recommended.

Parking can be a big pain in the neck, especially in big cities and old-town areas. Metered parking zones usually have stays limited to a couple of hours, though parking between 8pm and 8am, on Saturday afternoons and all Sundays tends to be free. Green or blue bays signify pay-parking areas in most cities, but it's always worth double-checking that you're allowed to park where you've just left your car, as any illegally parked vehicle will be promptly towed. Some cities (like Granada) have also introduced old-town **congestion charges**, which you might unwittingly trigger as a casual visitor. It's nearly always best to pay extra for a hotel with parking or use a pay car park, for which you'll need to budget anything from €15 to €25 a day.

Car rental

Car rental is cheapest arranged in advance through one of the large multinational agencies (Avis, Budget, EasyCar, Europcar, Hertz, Holiday Autos, National or Thrifty, for example). There are hundreds of pick-up offices in Spain, including regional airports and major train stations. Rates start from around €250 a week for a two-door Renault Clio or similar, more for larger vehicles and in peak holiday periods. Local Spanish companies (such as Pepecar; http://pepecar.com) can sometimes offer better value for money and you can also get some very good low-season rates.

You'll need to be 21 or over (and have been driving for at least a year) to rent a car in Spain. You will also need

Murcia	Pamplona	Salamanca	San Sebastián	Santander	Santiago de Compostela	Seville	Toledo	Valencia
82	723	630	769	837	1033	606	439	183
602	490	835	525	715	1165	1055	710	365
785	152	398	249	103	596	861	472	651
634	210	248	300	186	526	711	317	590
482	841	604	924	820	1009	149	391	536
297	869	634	949	856	1032	261	413	510
342	791	543	854	762	949	300	326	454
749	404	208	489	280	364	674	412	702
408	456	219	534	428	607	537	78	361
414	993	674	1065	967	1124	231	527	649
–	772	604	812	817	1015	531	420	233
772	–	453	97	264	742	924	529	524
604	453	–	554	370	437	467	273	573
812	97	554	–	350	836	2022	631	612
817	264	370	350	–	499	896	508	769
1015	742	437	836	499	–	901	672	970
531	924	467	2022	896	901	–	507	684
420	529	273	631	508	672	507	–	378
233	524	573	612	769	970	684	378	–

a credit card to cover the initial deposit, and have both your driving license photo card and paper license. It's essential to check that you have adequate **insurance cover** for your rental car, and that all visible damage on a car you're picking up is duly marked on the rental sheet. It's definitely worth considering paying the extra charge to reduce the "excess" payment levied for any damage, but these waiver charges (by the day) soon add up. However, you can avoid all **excess charges** in the event of damage by taking out an annual insurance policy with http://insurance4carhire.com, which also covers windscreen and tyre damage.

By bike

Bike rental is not common, save in resort areas or in tourist-oriented cities such as Barcelona and Madrid, where you can expect to pay €20 a day, or around €30 for a half-day bike tour. Barcelona, Seville and some other cities also have bike-transit schemes, where you join (by paying a deposit) and then pick up bikes (free or low-cost) to ride around the city from one depot to another. However, dedicated cycle paths are rare (again, Barcelona is an exception), and cycling around most major Spanish cities can be a hair-raising, if not downright dangerous, business.

Outside towns and cities, cycling is a great way to see parts of the country that might otherwise pass you by, though bear in mind that Spain is one of the most mountainous countries in Europe and there are often searing high-summer temperatures with which to contend. You also need to be extremely careful on the road (single file only, at all times), since Spanish drivers don't generally expect to see cyclists and don't take much care when they do. Off-road biking is a far better idea, and increasing numbers of mountain bikers are taking to the trails in national parks or following long-distance routes like the Camino de Santiago.

Ferries and planes

Anyone heading from the Spanish mainland to the Balearic Islands will probably do so by **ferry** or **catamaran** express ferry (from Alicante, Barcelona, Dénia or Valencia) – all the details are in the relevant city and island chapters. However, there's also an extensive network of internal Spanish **flights**, including to and between the Balearics, with Iberia (http://iberia.com) and other smaller operators such as Vueling (http://vueling.com). These can be worth it if you're in a hurry and need to cross the entire peninsula, or if you can snap up a bargain web fare, but otherwise tourists rarely use flights to get around Spain. The main exception has always been Europe's busiest air route, that between Madrid and Barcelona, though this is now facing stiff competition from the

SPAIN'S BEST DRIVES

There are some fantastic driving routes in this land of big scenery, big horizons and big surprises – here's our choice of Spain's best drives.

Alt Empordà Track the coastline in northern Costa Brava as you take in Greek and Roman ruins at Empúries and Salvador Dalí's former home outside the picturesque town of Cadaqués. See page 662.

Cañón de Río Sil Gaze upon Galicia's most arresting landscape along this dramatic canyon that is also home to one of the country's foremost wine-producing regions. See page 553.

The Cincó Villas Lose yourself in small-town Aragón on the 80km drive linking the historic "five towns", from Tauste to Sos del Rey Católico. See page 570.

El Escorial to Ávila The most scenic route out of Madrid province, an hour's drive from Felipe II's colossal monastery and over the hills to the historic walled city of Ávila. See page 134.

Gipuzkoa Head inland from San Sebastián and immerse yourself in Basque culture at Tolosa's lively carnival and historic Oñati, with its distinctive *casas torres*. See page 431. Or, for a more coastal Basque view, drive the wiggly and spectacular coastal route (N364 and BI3438) between San Sebastián and Bilbao, stopping for a swim at any one of the hidden coves. See page 431.

Huelva province Take the A416 north from Minas de Río Tinto towards Aracena in Huelva and you'll see some stunning effects of the wealth of minerals in the region. The road leads to a mirador overlooking the El Cerro Colorado mine and travels low over the point at which two alternately coloured reservoirs – the Embalse de Gossán and the Embalse del Agua – meet.

Inland from Benidorm It's the juxtaposition between hedonistic sun-and-sand and quiet, rural inland Valencia that marks this leisurely 55km excursion, from Calpe to Alcoy. See page 767.

Puerto de las Palomas to Zahara de la Sierra One of the most dramatic descents in Andalucía starts from the "Pass of the Doves" and corkscrews dizzily downwards to the ancient Moorish village of Zahara, with spectacular views across the sierras. See page 244.

Sierra de la Demanda Mountain monasteries, verdant valleys and bare upland vistas on the two-hour drive (LR113) from La Rioja to the Castilla y León heartland. See page 389.

Through the Valle de Jerte Track the Río Jerte for 70km (N110 out of Plasencia towards Barco de Ávila) on one of the most picturesque drives in Spain – carpeted in cherry blossom every spring. See page 183.

Valldemossa to Lluc The Ma10 tracks the dramatic coastline of northern Mallorca, a roller coaster of a ride through hilltop villages via the island's highest peaks. See page 813.

Vielha to Esterri d'Aneau Snowy peaks, thickly forested slopes and, above all, utter mountain stillness – this 42km drive over the Bonaigua Pass (2072m) is pure Pyrenees. See page 712.

---

high-speed AVE train, which is comparable in overall centre-to-centre journey time, and often cheaper.

Accommodation

There's a great variety of accommodation in Spain, ranging from humble family-run *pensiones* to five-star luxury hotels, often in dramatic historic buildings. The mainstay of the coastal resort is the typical beachfront holiday hotel, though renting an apartment or a villa gives you more freedom, while farm stays, village B&Bs, rural guesthouses and mountain inns are all increasingly popular options.

Compared with other European countries, accommodation in Spain is still pretty good value. In almost any town, you'll be able to get a no-frills double room in a *pensión* or small hotel for around €65, sometimes even less, especially outside the main resorts. As a rule, you can expect to pay from €120 for something with a bit of boutique styling, and from €180–300 for five-star hotels, historic paradores and luxury beach-front resorts. However, the trend is bucked by Madrid and Barcelona, in particular, and some fashionable coastal and resort areas, where rooms are often appreciably more expensive in all categories.

Advance reservations are essential in major cities and resort areas at peak holiday, festival or convention times. Local festivals and annual events also tend to fill all available accommodation weeks in advance. That said, as a general rule, if you haven't booked, all you have to do is head for the cathedral or main square of any town, which is invariably surrounded by an old quarter full of *pensiones* and hotels. You don't always pay more for a central location; indeed, the newer three- and four-star properties tend to be located more on the outskirts. **Families** will find that most places have rooms with three or even four beds at not a great deal more than the double-room price; however, **single travellers** often get a comparatively bad deal, and can end up paying sixty to eighty percent of the price of a double room.

Accommodation prices are **seasonal**, but minimum and maximum rates should be displayed at reception. In high season on the *costas*, many hotels only take bookings for a minimum of a week, while some

ACCOMMODATION PRICE CODES

Accommodation throughout the Guide is organized into price codes. Unless otherwise stated, this represents the price for the **cheapest available double or twin room in high season** (ie usually Christmas/New Year, Easter, and June–September, though local variations apply – summer prices might be high-season on the Costa del Sol but will be low-season in scorching inland Andalucía, for example). Consequently, at many times of the year, or during special promotions, you'll often find a room for a lower price than that suggested. For **youth hostels** and anywhere else with **dorm beds**, we give codes for dorms (and doubles if available). Note that **eight percent tax** (IVA) is added to all accommodation bills, which might not be specifically stated until it is time to pay, so always ask if you're uncertain. Hotel prices don't usually include **breakfast**, which is almost always an optional extra; often it's much cheaper to find a nearby bar to eat in.

$\bar{\textbf{€}}$ = under €65
$\bar{\textbf{€€}}$ = €65–100
$\bar{\textbf{€€€}}$ = €100–150
$\bar{\textbf{€€€€}}$ = over €150

---

also require at least a half-board stay. However, it's worth noting that high season isn't always summer, in ski resorts for example, while inland cities such as Madrid tend to have cheaper prices in August, when everyone heads for the coast. Easter, though, tends to be very busy in many cities.

Where possible, **website** bookings nearly always offer the best deals, especially with the larger **hotel groups** that have made big inroads into Spain – it's always worth checking *NH Hotels* (http://nh-hotels.com), *Accor* (http://all.accor.com) and *Meliá* (http://melia.com) for current deals.

Unless otherwise stated all our listed accommodation includes free wi-fi.

Private rooms and B&Bs

The cheapest beds are usually in **private rooms**, in someone's house or above a bar or restaurant. The signs to look for are *habitaciones* (rooms) or *camas* (beds), or they might be touted at resort bus and train stations in summer as you arrive. The rooms should be clean, but might well be very simple and timeworn; you'll probably share a communal bathroom.

The number of private **"bed-and-breakfast"** establishments (advertised as such) is on the increase, and while some are simply the traditional room in someone's house, others – especially in the major cities – are very stylish and pricey home from homes and make a delightful stay.

Pensiones, hostales and hotels

Guesthouses and hotels in Spain go under various anachronistic names – *pensión, fonda, residencia,* *hostal*, etc – though only **hotels and pensiones** are recognized as official categories. These are all star-rated (hotels, one- to five-star; *pensiones*, one- or two-star), but the rating is not necessarily a guide to cost or ambience. Some smaller, boutique-style *pensiones* and hotels have services and facilities that belie their star rating; some four- and five-star hotels have disappointingly small rooms and an impersonal feel.

At the budget end of the scale are **pensiones** (marked P), **fondas** (F) – which traditionally had a restaurant or dining room attached – and **casas de huéspedes** (CH), literally an old-fashioned "guesthouse". In all such places you can expect straightforward rooms, often with shared bathroom facilities (there's usually a washbasin in the room), while occasionally things like heating, furniture (other than bed, chair and desk) and even external windows might be too much to hope for. On the other hand, some old-fashioned *pensiones* are lovingly cared for and very good value, while others have gone for a contemporary, boutique style.

Next step up, and far more common, are **hostales** (Hs) and **hostal-residencias** (HsR), which are not hostels, in any sense, but budget hotels, generally offering good, if functional, rooms, usually with private bathrooms and – in the better places – probably heating and air conditioning. Many also have cheaper rooms available without private bathrooms. Some *hostales* really are excellent, with good service and up-to-date furnishings and facilities.

Fully fledged **hotels** (H), meanwhile, have a star-rating dependent on things like room size and staffing levels rather than any intrinsic attraction. There's often not much difference in price between a one-star hotel and a decent *hostal*, for example, and the *hostal* might be nicer. At three and four stars, hotel prices start to increase and you can expect soundproofing, an elevator, an English-language channel on the TV and a buffet breakfast spread. At five stars, you're in the luxury class, with pools, gyms, Jacuzzis, and prices to match, and some hotels differentiate themselves again as five-star "deluxe" or "gran classe" (GL).

You can pick up lists of local accommodation from any Spanish tourist office, and there are countless websites to look at, too, including the excellent **Rusticae** (http://rusticae.es), which highlights scores of stylish rural and urban hotels across the country.

Paradores

Spain has over ninety superior hotels in a class of their own, called **paradores** (http://parador.es), which are often spectacular lodgings converted from castles, monasteries and other Spanish monuments (although some are purpose-built). They can be really special places to stay, sited in the most beautiful parts of the country, or in some of the most historic cities, and prices are very good when compared with the five-star hotels with which they compete. Overnight rates depend on location and popularity, and start at around €120 a night, though €180 is more typical. That said, a whole host of special offers and web deals (through the official website) offer discounted rates for the over-55s, the under-30s, or for multi-night stays.

A popular approach is to take a fly-drive holiday based around the paradores. There is no end of routes you could choose, but good options include the area around Madrid and through the Sierra de Gredos; along the Cantabrian coast, past the Picos de Europa; or along the French–Spanish border and through the foothills of the Pyrenees. Another popular route takes you through Galicia, and on to *Hostal dos Reis Católicos*, one of the most sumptuous paradores of all in Santiago de Compostela. Three-night **packages**, where you stay in a different parador every night yet only pay for two nights, start at around €200 per person (based on two sharing, car rental not included). All the details are on the website, or contact the official parador **agents**, Keytours International in the UK (http://keytoursinternational.co.uk) or Petrabax in the US (http://petrabax.com).

Villas, apartments and rural tourism

Most UK and European tour operators can find you a self-catering **villa** or **apartment**, usually on one of the *costas* or in the Balearics. They are rented by the week, and range from simple town-centre apartments to luxury coastal villas with private pools. Prices, of course, vary wildly, but the best deals are often packages, including flights and car rental, with endless **agencies** including TUI Villa Holidays (www.tui.co.uk).

Casas rurales (rural houses), or *casas de pagès* in Catalunya, are where many Spanish holiday-makers stay. It's a wide-ranging concept, from boutique cave dwellings to restored manor houses, many with pools and gardens. You can rent by the room, or by the property, either on a B&B basis or self-catering, depending on the accommodation. Many places also offer outdoor activities such as horseriding, walking, fishing and cycling. They are generally excellent value for money, starting at around €50 per person, even cheaper if you're in a group or staying for longer than a night or two. While some are fairly basic and clearly just a sideline to the owners' real work, others are run more along the lines of intimate boutique hotels. In many cases they are the choice place to stay.

ASETUR (http://ecoturismorural.com), the association for rural tourism in Spain, has an excellent website where you can search thousands of properties by region, while many Spanish tourist-office websites also carry information on *casas rurales*. Holiday companies in your own country may also have Spanish rural properties available, or contact Spain-based **agencies** like Ruralia (Cantabria and Asturias; http://ruralia.com), Rustic Blue (Andalucía; http://rusticblue.com), Agroturisme (Catalunya; http://agroturisme.cat), or Casas de Gredos (Ávila and Gredos area; http://casasgredos.com). Vrbo (http://vrbo.com) is a country-wide option.

Youth hostels

There are around 250 youth hostels (*albergues juveniles*) in Spain under the umbrella of the **Red Española de Albergues Juveniles** (REAJ; http://reaj.com), the Spanish youth hostel association that is affiliated to the parent organization, Hostelling International (HI; http://hihostels.com). There are full details of each hostel on the REAJ website (English-language version available), and we've included some of the best in the Guide.

However, many HI hostels are only open in the spring and summer, or tend to be inconveniently located in some cities; they may also be block-booked by school/youth groups. You'll need an HI membership card, though you can buy one at most hostels on your first night. And at €25–40 a night in high season (less for under-26s, and out of season) for a bunk bed with shared facilities, they're no cheaper than a basic double room in a *hostal* or *pensión*. That said, hostels are good places to meet other travellers, and there are some really gorgeously located ones, especially in Andalucía and in the hiking regions of northern Spain.

PICK OF THE PARADORES

Nearly all of Spain's **paradores** (http://parador.es) have a quirky history, a story to tell or a magnificent location – here's our choice of the best, from former palaces to pilgrims' hospitals.

Hostal dos Reis Católicos, Santiago de Compostela Apparently the oldest hotel in the world, the *Hostal dos Reis Católicos* is impressively set in a fifteenth-century hospital at the end of the Camino de Santiago. See page 522.

Parador Castillo de Santa Catalina, Jaén Occupying a stunning, crag-bound thirteenth-century Moorish fortress, this is one of the most spectacular locations in Spain. See page 304.

Parador Condes de Alba y Aliste, Zamora Occupying a grand palace in the middle of a quiet town, Zamora's parador is gentility defined. See page 364.

Parador Cristobal Colón, Andalucía An impeccable four-star hotel set high above the Costa de la Luz's Mazagón beach – a

pristine stretch with sandstone cliffs and lapping Atlantic waters.

Parador de Jarandilla de la Vera, Jarandilla Majestic former imperial palace, set in the verdant Vera valley.

Parador de Lerma, Lerma A remarkable ducal palace facing a broad plaza of elegant beauty. See page 398.

Parador Marqués de Villena, Alarcón There are just fourteen rooms in this atmospheric Arabic castle perched on the rocky promontory above the Río Júcar. See page 174.

Parador de Tortosa, Tortosa Tortosa's highest point, the splendid Castillo de la Suda, looms majestically over the lush Ebre valley.

Some cities and resort areas also have a wide range of **independent backpacker hostels**. Prices are similar, they tend to be far less institutional, and open all year round, and you won't need a membership card. Also, many are brand-new, often with private rooms as well as dorms, and with excellent facilities (en-suite rooms, cafés, bike rental, tours, etc).

Mountain refuges, monasteries and pilgrim accommodation

In mountain areas and some of the national parks, climbers and trekkers can stay in **refugios**, simple dormitory huts, generally equipped only with bunks and a very basic kitchen. They are run by local mountaineering organizations, mostly on a first-come-first-served basis, which means they fill up quickly in high summer, though you can book in advance at some (or bring a tent and camp outside). Overnight prices start around €20 per person (or €35–40 with a meal included).

It is sometimes possible to stay at Spanish **monasterios** or **conventos**, which may let empty cells for a small charge. There are some particularly wonderful monastic locations in Galicia, Castilla y León, Catalunya and Mallorca. If you're following the Camino de Santiago, you can take full advantage of monastic accommodation specifically reserved for **pilgrims** along the route (see page 518).

Camping

There are literally hundreds of authorized campsites in Spain, mostly on the coast and in holiday areas. They work out at about €7 or €8 per person plus the

same again for a tent, and a similar amount for each car or caravan. The best-located sites, or the ones with top-range facilities (restaurant, swimming pool, bar, supermarket), are significantly more expensive. If you plan to camp extensively, buy the annual *Guía de Campings*, which you can find in large bookshops, or visit http://vayacamping.net. The price quoted in our campsite reviews in this book refers to the cost for two people, a pitch and a car.

In most cases, **camping outside campsites** is legal – but there are certain restrictions. You're not allowed to camp "in urban areas, areas prohibited for military or touristic reasons, or within 1km of an official campsite". What this means in practice is that you can't camp on the beach, while in national parks camping is only allowed in officially designated areas. Aside from these restrictions, however, and with a little sensitivity, you can set up a tent for a short period almost anywhere in the countryside. Whenever possible, ask locally first.

Food and drink

Spanish cuisine has come a long way in recent years, and Spanish chefs are currently at the forefront of contemporary European cooking. You know a power shift has taken place when *Restaurant* magazine's annual "World 50 Best Restaurants" list regularly cites three or four Spanish eateries in the top ten, and when there are more gourmet places in the Basque Country worth making a special trip for than in Paris. There's some

TEN UNUSUAL PLACES TO STAY

Take ancient buildings, magnificent locations, historic charm, designer flair and sheer Spanish style – and the result is enough **unusual places to rest** your head for a whole lifetime's worth of holidays.

La Casona de Calderón, Andalucía Immerse yourself in Osuna's history in this seventeenth-century *pensión*, complete with museum which has, among other rare findings, a display of the towns cow bells.

Castilla Termal Monasterio de Valbuena, Castilla y León Classy hotel rooms and a spa within a sprawling monastery that is hidden high in the Riojan hills.

Hotel Castell d'Empordà, Catalunya Eight-hundred-year-old hilltop castle that Salvador Dalí once tried to buy. See page 673.

Hotel España, Barcelona Boutique hotel, yes, but also a peerless *modernista* artwork. See page 640.

Hotel El Mudayyan, Aragón Venture into the medieval tunnels (as far as you dare) under this lovely Moroccan-style boutique hotel. See page 577.

Hotel Real Colegiata de San Isidoro, León Stay in an old royal college and church, part of which dates back to 1063 and doubles up as a museum.

Hotel Toruño, Andalucía Spot flamingos, herons, avocets and more without leaving your bed. See page 287.

Jallambau Rural, Galicia Enjoy expansive views over Ría de Muros from this spectacularly perched, stone B&B. See page 536.

Hostal Posada de San José, Castilla-La Mancha Precariously situated in a mansion perched on the edge of the gorge next to Cuenca's famous "hanging houses". See page 171.

Refugio Marnes, Valencia Sleep like a sultan in this sumptuous Bedouin tent in the middle of the Valencian countryside. See page 765.

Santuari de Lluc, Mallorca Enjoy complete peace and quiet, by spending the night at this monastery that has been a tranquil retreat since the thirteenth century. See page 814.

---

fantastic food to be had in every region, and not just the fancy new-wave stuff either – the tapas, gazpacho, *tortilla* and paella that you may know from home are simply in a different league when made with the correct ingredients in their natural surroundings.

Of course, not every restaurant is a gourmet experience and not every dish is a classic of its kind. Tourist resorts – after all, where many people go – can be disappointing, especially those aimed at a foreign clientele, and a week on one of the *costas* can just as easily convince you that the Spanish national diet is egg and chips, *sangría*, pizza and Guinness. However, you'll always find a good restaurant where the locals eat, and few places in Europe are still as good value, especially if you have the *menú del día*, the bargain fixed-price lunch that's a fixture across the country.

Breakfast, snacks and sandwiches

The traditional Spanish **breakfast** (*desayuno*) is *chocolate con churros* – long, extruded tubular doughnuts served with thick drinking chocolate or coffee. Some places specialize in these but most bars and cafés also serve cakes and pastries (*bollos* or *pasteles*), croissants and toast (*tostadas*), or crusty sandwiches (*bocadillos*) with a choice of fillings (try one with omelette, *tortilla*). A "sandwich", incidentally, is usually a less appetizing ham or cheese sandwich in white processed bread. Other good places for snacks are **cake shops** (*pastelerías* or *confiterías*) or the local bakery (*panadería*), where they might also have savoury pasties and turnovers.

Bars, tapas and raciones

One of Spain's glories is the phenomenon of **tapas** – the little portions of food that traditionally used to be served up free with a drink in a bar. (The origins are disputed but the word is from *tapar*, "to cover", suggesting a cover for drinks' glasses, perhaps to keep the flies off in the baking sun.) A *menú de tapeo* (tapas menu) is found in many restaurants or bars and can include just about anything – a handful of olives, a slice or two of cured ham, a little dish of meatballs or chorizo, spicy fried potatoes or battered squid. They will often be laid out on the counter, so you can see what's available, or there might be a blackboard menu. Most bars have a speciality; indeed, Spaniards will commonly move from bar to bar, having just the one dish that they consider each bar does well. Conversely, if you're in a bar with just some pre-fried potatoes and day-old Russian salad on display, and a prominent microwave, go somewhere else to eat.

Aside from a few olives or crisps sometimes handed out with a drink, you often pay for tapas these days (the provinces of Granada and Jaén, León and parts of Galicia are honourable exceptions). **Raciones** or a **media racion** are simply bigger plates of tapas: a *ración*, or two or three half *raciones* are enough for a meal – you're sometimes asked if you want a *tapa* or a *ración* of whatever it is you've chosen.

There are big regional variations in tapas. They are often called **pinchos** (or *pintxos*) in the Basque provinces, where typically tapas come served on a slice of baguette, held together with a cocktail stick. When you've finished eating, the sticks are counted up to work out your bill. This kind of tapas can be as simple as a cheese cube on bread or a far more elaborately sculpted concoction; they are also known as **montaditos** (basically, *canapés*). Famously good places across Spain for tapas-tasting include Madrid, León, Logroño, San Sebastián, Granada, Seville and Cádiz.

Most cafés and bars have some kind of tapas available, while you'll also find a decent display in **tascas**, **bodegas** and **tabernas** (kinds of taverns) and **cervecerías** (beer-houses). It's always cheapest to stand at the bar to eat; you'll pay more to sit at tables and more again to sit outside on a terrace.

Restaurants

The simplest kind of restaurant is the **comedor** (dining room), often a room at the back of a bar or the dining room of a *hostal* or *pensión*. Traditionally, they are family-run places aimed at lunching workers, usually offering a straightforward set meal at budget prices. The highway equivalent are known as **ventas** or **mesones** (inns), and are dotted along the main roads between towns and cities. These have been serving Spanish wayfarers for centuries – some of them quite literally – and the best places are immediately picked out by the line of cars and trucks outside. Proper restaurants, **restaurantes**, come in a myriad of guises, from rustic village restaurants to stylish Michelin-starred eateries; **asadores** specialize in grilled meats, **marisquerías** in fish and seafood.

Almost every restaurant serves a weekday, fixed-price lunchtime meal, the **menú del día**, generally three courses including wine for €15–18, occasionally even cheaper, depending on where you are in Spain. This is obviously a terrific deal; the *menú del día* is only sporadically available at night, and sometimes prices are slightly higher (and the menu slightly fancier) at weekends. The very cheapest places are unlikely to have a written menu, and the waiter will tell you what the day's dishes are. In smarter restaurants in bigger cities and resorts, there will still be a *menú del día*, though it might be a shadow of the usual a la carte menu, and drinks may be excluded. Even so, it's a way of eating at a restaurant that might normally cost you three or four times as much. Top city restaurants often also feature an upmarket *menú* called a **menú de degustación** (tasting menu), which again can be excellent value, allowing you to try out some of the country's finest cooking for anything from €75 to €150 a head.

Otherwise, in bars and so-called *cafeterías*, meals often come in the form of a **plato combinado** – literally a combined dish – which will be a one-plate meal of something like steak, egg and chips, or

---

IT'S FOOD, JIM, BUT NOT AS WE KNOW IT

King of molecular gastronomy, and godfather of Spanish contemporary cuisine, **Ferran Adrià**, started it all, with his liquid-nitrogen-frozen herbs, seafood-reduction Rice Krispies and exploding olive-oil droplets. Although his multi-Michelin-starred *El Bulli* restaurant on the Costa Brava has now closed and turned into a cookery foundation and "centre for creativity" (see page 678), the influences of Spain's best-known chef have shaken the restaurant scene, as his former employees, acolytes and disciples have gone on to make the country one of the most exciting places to eat in the world.

The style city of Barcelona, not surprisingly, is at the forefront of this innovative form of cooking, with **Carles Abellán**'s *Tapas24* (see page 644) typical of the breed, while the **Roca brothers**' celebrated *Celler de Can Roca* in Girona (see page 687) keeps Catalunya firmly in the vanguard of new-wave cuisine. However, it's in the Basque Country that many of the hottest chefs are currently in action: **Andoni Aduriz** at *Mugaritz*, Errenteria, San Sebastián (see page 430), father-and-daughter team **Juan Mari and Elena Arzak** at *Arzak*, San Sebastián (see page 430), and **Martín Berasategui** at *Restaurante Martín Berasategui*, Lasarte-Oria, San Sebastián (see page 430), are all cooking sensational food in restaurants that regularly feature in lists of the world's best. Maybe it's a northern thing, but there's less fuss in the south of the country about the so-called *cocina de autor*; in Madrid, perhaps only **Sergi Arola** cuts the new-wave mustard with his surprisingly affordable venture *Vi-Cool* (see page 102).

SPANISH CUISINE

There really is no such thing as traditional "Spanish" cuisine, since every region claims a quite separate culinary heritage. That said, you'll find similar dishes cropping up right across the country, whatever their origin, while typical Mediterranean staples are ubiquitous – olive oil, tomatoes, peppers, garlic, onions, lemons and oranges.

It's usual to start your meal with a **salad** or a plate of cold cuts, while **soups** might be fish or seafood or, in the north especially, hearty broths such as the Galician cabbage-and-potato *caldo gallego*. Boiled potatoes with greens, or a thick minestrone of vegetables, are also fairly standard starters, while depending on the season you might be offered grilled asparagus or artichokes, or stewed beans with chunks of sausage.

Anywhere near the coast, you really should make the most of what's on offer, whether it's the fried fish of Málaga, Basque shellfish or the seafood specialities in Galicia, notably octopus (*pulpo*). Fish stews (*zarzuelas*) can be memorable, while seafood rice dishes range from *arroz negro* ("black rice", cooked with squid ink) to the better-known **paella**. This comes originally from Valencia (still the best place for an authentic one), though a proper paella from there doesn't include fish or seafood at all but things like chicken, rabbit, beans and snails.

Meat is most often grilled and served with a few fried potatoes. Regional specialities include *cordero* (lamb) from Segovia, Navarra and the Basque Country, as well as *cochinillo* (suckling pig) or *lechal* (suckling lamb) in central Spain. **Cured ham**, or *jamón serrano*, is superb, produced at its best from acorn-fed Iberian pigs in Extremadura and Andalucía, though it can be extremely expensive. Every region has a local **sausage** in its locker – the best known is the spicy chorizo, made from pork, though others include *morcilla* (blood sausage; best in Burgos, León and Asturias), and *butifarra*, a white Catalan sausage made from pork and tripe. **Stews** are typified by the mighty *fabada*, a fill-your-boots Asturian bean-and-meat concoction.

Cheeses to look out for include Cabrales, a tangy blue cheese made in the Picos de Europa; Manchego, a sharp, nutty cheese made from sheep's milk in La Mancha; Mahon, a cow's-milk cheese from Menorca, often with paprika rubbed into its rind; Idiazábal, a smoked cheese from the Basque Country; and Zamorano, made from sheep's milk in Castilla y León.

In most restaurants, **dessert** is nearly always fresh fruit or *flan*, the Spanish crème caramel, with the regions often having their own versions such as *crema catalana* in Catalunya and the Andalucian *tocino de cielo*. There are also many varieties of *postre* – rice pudding or assorted blancmange mixtures – and a range of commercial ice-cream dishes.

If you want to know more about the food in the region where you're travelling, turn to the special **features**:

Andalucía See page 215	**Castilla y León and La Rioja** See page 351
Aragón See page 568	**Catalunya** See page 664
Around Madrid See page 130	**Extremadura** See page 182
Asturias See page 495	**Galicia** See page 513
Balearics See page 791	**Madrid** See page 103
Basque Country See page 429	**Valencia and Murcia** See page 739
Castilla-La Mancha See page 168	

calamares and salad, often with bread and a drink included. This will generally cost in the region of €8–15.

If you want a menu in a restaurant, ask for **la carta**; *menú* refers only to the fixed-price meal. In all but the most rock-bottom establishments it is customary to leave a small **tip**, though five percent of the bill is considered sufficient and service is normally included in a *menú del día*. IVA, the eight percent **tax**, is also

charged, but it should say on the menu if this is included in the price or not.

Spaniards generally eat very late, with **lunch** served from around 1pm (you'll be the first person there at this time) until 4pm, and **dinner** from 8.30pm or 9pm to midnight. Obviously, rural areas are slightly earlier to dine, but making a dinner reservation for 10.30pm or even later is considered perfectly normal in many cities in Spain. Most restaurants **close one day a**

week, usually Sunday or Monday. The opening hours given in this book provide a rough idea, but bear in mind that many restaurants in Spain will close early or not open at all during quiet periods.

Increasingly, more upmarket restaurants are using **WhatsApp** as a means of making and confirming bookings.

Vegetarians

Vegetarians generally have a fairly hard time of it in Spain, though there's an increasing number of veggie restaurants in the bigger cities, including some really good ones in Madrid (see page 102) and Barcelona (see page 645). In more rural areas, there's usually something to eat, but you may get weary of fried eggs and omelettes. However, many tapas favourites, especially in the south, are veggie (like fried aubergine, or spinach and chickpeas in Seville), while superb fresh fruit and veg, and excellent cheese, is always available in the markets and shops.

In restaurants, you're faced with the extra problem that pieces of meat – especially ham, which the Spanish don't regard as real meat – and tuna are often added to vegetable dishes and salads. You'll also find chunks of chorizo and sausage turning up in otherwise veg-friendly soups or bean stews. The phrases to get to know are Soy vegetariano/a. Como sólo verduras. Hay algo sin carne? ("I'm a vegetarian. I only eat vegetables. Is there anything without meat?"); you may have to add y sin marisco ("and without seafood") and y sin jamón ("and without ham") to be really safe.

Some salads and vegetable dishes are strictly **vegan**, but they're few and far between. Fruit and nuts are widely available, nuts being sold by street vendors everywhere.

Coffee, tea and soft drinks

Café (coffee) is invariably an espresso (café solo); for a large cup of weaker, black coffee, ask for an americano. A café cortado is a café solo with a drop of milk; a café con leche is made with lots of hot milk. Spaniards almost only drink this kind of coffee at breakfast time and you'll get strange looks if you order it at any other time of the day unless you're in a tourist hotspot. Coffee is also frequently mixed with brandy, cognac or whisky, all such concoctions being called carajillo. Iced coffee is café con hielo. **Chocolate** (hot chocolate) is a popular breakfast drink, or for after a long night on the town. It's usually thick and rich. For a thinner, cocoa-style drink, ask for a brand name, like Cola Cao.

Spaniards usually drink **té** (tea) black, so if you want milk it's safest to ask for it afterwards, since ordering té con leche might well get you a glass of warm milk with a tea bag floating on top. Herbal teas (infusions) are widely available, like manzanilla (camomile), poleo (mint tea) and hierba luisa (lemon verbena).

Local soft drinks include **granizado** (crushed ice) or **horchata** (a milky drink made from tiger nuts or almonds), available from summer street stalls, and from milk bars (horchaterías, also known as granjas in Catalunya) and ice-cream parlours (heladerías). Although you can drink the **water** almost everywhere, it tastes revolting in some cities and coastal areas – inexpensive agua mineral comes either sparkling (con gas) or still (sin gas).

Wine

One of the great pleasures of eating out in Spain is the chance to sample some of the country's excellent **wines**. Over fifty percent of the European Union's vineyards lie in Spain and vino is the invariable accompaniment to every meal. At lunchtime, a glass or small pitcher of the house wine – often served straight from the barrel – is usually included in the menú del día; otherwise, restaurant wine starts at around €8–15 a bottle, although the sky's the limit for the really good stuff. And there's plenty of that, since in recent years Spanish wine has enjoyed an amazing renaissance, led largely by the international success of famous wine-producing regions like La Rioja and Ribera del Duero. Other regions – not perhaps so well-known abroad – are also well worth investigating, like Galicia or the Priorat in Catalunya, and every wine-producing area is set up for bodega (winery) visits, tastings and tours. In Andalucía, meanwhile, the classic wine is **sherry** – vino de jerez – while champagne in Spain means the Catalan sparkling wine, **cava**.

The festival and tourist drink is, famously, **sangría**, a wine and fruit punch that's often deceptively strong; a variation in Catalunya is sangría de cava. Tinto de verano is a similar red-wine-and-soda or -lemonade

SPAIN'S TOP 6 BODEGA VISITS

Bodegas Codorníu, Penedès Spain's first producers of cava, located in outstanding Catalan Art Nouveau premises. See page 716.

Bodegas Marqués de Riscal, La Rioja Alavesa Terrific wine, and an extraordinary Frank Gehry-designed building to boot. See page 451.

Bodegas Ysios, La Rioja Alavesa Located in a stunning building by Santiago Calatrava. See page 451.

Condes de Albarei, Galicia Cooperative *bodega* turning out excellent Albariño wines. See page 539.

González Byass, Jerez One of the biggest sherry producers, makers of the Tío Pepe brand. See page 283.

Costers del Siurana, Priorat Investigate the Priorat region wines in deepest Catalunya. See page 726.

combination; variations on this include *tinto de verano con naranja* (red wine with orangeade) or *con limón* (lemonade).

Beer

Beer (*cerveza*) is nearly always lager, though some Spanish breweries also now make stout-style brews, wheat beers and other types. It comes in 300ml bottles (*botellines*) or, for about the same price, on tap – a *caña* of draught beer is a small glass, a *caña doble* larger, and asking for *un tubo* (a tubular glass) gets you about half a pint. Mahou, Cruz Campo, San Miguel, Damm, Estrella de Galicia and Alhambra are all decent beers. A **shandy** is a *clara*, either with fizzy lemon (*con limón*) or lemonade (*con casera* or *con blanca*).

Spirits and shots

In mid-afternoon – or, let's face it, sometimes even at breakfast – Spaniards like to take a *copa* of liqueur with their coffee, such as *anís* (which is similar to Pernod) or *coñac*, the local **brandy**, which has a distinct vanilla flavour. Most brandies are produced by the great sherry houses in Jerez (like Lepanto, Carlos I and Cardinal Mendoza), but two good ones that aren't are the Armagnac-like Mascaró and Torres, both from Catalunya. Instead of brandy, at the end of a meal many places serve **chupitos** – little shot glasses of flavoured schnapps or local firewater, such as Patxarán in Navarra and the Basque Country, Ratafía in Catalunya or Orujo in Galicia. One much-loved Galego custom is the *queimada*, when a large bowl of *aguardiente* (a herb-flavoured fiery liqueur) with fruit, sugar and coffee grains is wheeled out and set alight, and then drunk hot.

You should order **spirits** by brand name, since there are generally less expensive Spanish equivalents for standard imports, or you could simply specify *nacional*. Larios gin from Málaga, for instance, is about half the price of Gordon's. Measures are staggeringly generous – bar staff generally pour from the bottle until you suggest they stop. Long drinks include the universal Gin-Tónic and the Cuba Libre (rum and Coke), and there are often Spanish Caribbean rums (*ron*) such as Cacique from Venezuela or Havana Club from Cuba.

The media

The ubiquitous Spanish newspaper kiosk is your first stop for regional and national newspapers and magazines, though hotels and bars nearly always have a few kicking around for customers. The bigger cities, tourist towns and resorts will also have foreign newspapers available (some of which are actually published in Spain), generally on the day of issue or perhaps a day late. Television is all-pervasive in bars, cafés and restaurants, and you're going to find yourself watching more bullfighting, basketball and Venezuelan soap operas than perhaps you'd bargained for. Most hotel rooms have a TV, too, though only in the fancier places will you get any English-language programming, and then probably only the BBC News, CNN or Eurosport satellite channels.

Newspapers

Of the Spanish **national newspapers** the best are the Madrid-based centre-left *El País* (http://elpais.com) and the centre-right *El Mundo* (http://elmundo.es), both of which have good arts and foreign news coverage, including comprehensive regional "what's on" listings and supplements every weekend. The **regional press** is generally run by local magnates and is predominantly right of centre, though often supporting local autonomy movements. Nationalist press includes *Avui* in Catalunya, printed in Catalan, and the Basque papers *El Correo*, *Deia* and *Gara*, the last of which is very strongly nationalist. All that said, the paper with the highest circulation is *Marca* (http://marca.com), the country's top **sports daily**, which is mainly football-dominated; there's also *As* (http://as.com), *El Mundo Deportivo* (http://mundodeportivo.com) and *Sport* (http://sport.es). The main cities are also awash with **free newspapers**, which are dished out at bus and metro stops.

Magazines

There's a bewildering variety of **magazines** specializing in celebrity gossip (known collectively as *la prensa rosa*), ranging from the more traditional *Hola* to the sensationalist *QMD! (Qué Me Dices)*. *El Jueves* ("The Thursday" – strapline: "The magazine that comes out on Wednesdays") is a weekly comic-strip-style satirical magazine, while the online daily *El Confidencial* (http://elconfidencial.com) gives the inside track on serious economic and political stories. There are also various **English-language magazines** and papers produced by and for the expatriate communities in the main cities and on the *costas*, such as *Madrid Metropolitan* (http://madridmetropolitan.com), *Barcelona Metropolitan* (http://barcelona-metropolitan.com), and – for southern Spain – *Sur in English* (http://surinenglish.com) and *The Olive Press* (http://theolivepress.es).

Radio

There are hundreds of local radio channels, broadcasting in Spanish and regional languages, alongside a handful of national ones. The state-run Radio Nacional de España, or **RNE** (http://rtve.es/radio), covers five stations: Radio Nacional, a general news and information channel; Radio Clásica, broadcasting mainly classical music and related programmes; the popular music channel Radio 3; Radio 4, in Catalan; and the rolling news and sports channel Radio 5. Radio Exterior is RNE's international shortwave service. Other **popular channels** include Cadena Ser and Onda Cero (news, talk, sports and culture); the Catholic Church-run COPE; Los 40 Principales (for the latest hits, Spanish and otherwise); and Cadena 100 (music and cultural programming). Radio Marca (dedicated sports radio) is also very popular.

Television

RTV (http://rtve.es/television) provides the main, state-run channels, namely La 1 (ie, "Uno"), a general entertainment and news channel, and its sister La 2 ("Dos"). Private national stations are Antena 3, Cuatro (Four), Telecinco (Five) and La Sexta (Sixth). There are also plenty of **regional channels**, the most important being Catalunya's TV3 and Canal 33, both broadcast in Catalan, and the Basque Country's ETB channels (in Basque), though there are also stations in Galicia (TVG) and Andalucía (Canal Sur) with local programming. The main satellite channel is Canal+.

Festivals

It's hard to beat the experience of arriving in some small Spanish village, expecting no more than a bed for the night, to discover the streets decked with flags and streamers, a band playing in the plaza and the entire population out celebrating the local fiesta. Everywhere in Spain, from the tiniest hamlet to the great cities, devotes at least a couple of days a year to partying, and participating in such an event propels you right into the heart of Spanish culture.

Local saints' days aside, Spain has some really major events worth planning your whole trip around such as the great Easter processions of Semana Santa (Holy Week). There are also fiestas celebrating deliverance from the Moors, safe return from the sea, or the bringing in of the grapes – any excuse will do. One thing they all tend to have in common is a curious blend of religious ceremony and pagan ritual – sombre processions of statuary followed by exuberant merrymaking – in which fire plays a prominent part.

The **annual festival calendar in this section** concentrates on the country's most notable fiestas. For more regional and local fiestas turn to the **feature boxes** found in the Guide.

Outsiders are always welcome at fiestas, the only problem being that it can be hard to find a hotel, unless you book well in advance. The other thing to note is that while not every fiesta is a national **public holiday** (see page 56), or vice versa, you may well get stuck if you arrive in town in the middle of an annual event, since pretty much everything will be closed.

JANUARY

5: Cabalgata de Reyes When the "Three Kings" *(reyes)* arrive to bring the children their presents for Epiphany. Most cities stage a spectacular cavalcade as the Three Kings are driven through the streets throwing sweets to the crowds.

16–17: Sant Antoni Bonfires and saint's day processions, especially on the Balearic Islands.

TOP 5 FIESTAS

Feria de Abril Seville. See page 214
Fiesta de San Fermín Pamplona. See page 454
Las Fallas Valencia. See page 746
La Tomatina Buñol. See page 755
Semana Santa Andalucía. See page 214

FEBRUARY

Week preceding Ash Wednesday and Lent: Carnaval An excuse for wild partying and masques, most riotous in Cádiz (Andalucía), Sitges, Catalunya and Águilas (Valencia).

MARCH

12–19: Las Fallas Valencia has the biggest of the bonfire festivals held for San José, climaxing on the Nit de Foc (Night of Fire) when enormous caricatures are burnt, and firecrackers let off in the streets. See page 746.

EASTER

March/April: Semana Santa Holy Week is celebrated across Spain, most theatrically in Seville, Málaga, Murcia and Valladolid, where *pasos* – huge floats of religious scenes – are carried down the streets, accompanied by hooded penitents atoning for the year's misdeeds. Maundy Thursday and Good Friday see the biggest, most solemn processions.

APRIL

22–24: Fiestas de Moros y Cristianos Mock battle between Moors and Christians in Alcoy, Valencia. See page 768.

23: Sant Jordi A day of celebration across Catalunya, especially Barcelona (see page 604) for the region's patron saint – Sant Jordi, St George. Being the birth date of Cervantes, it's also celebrated as National Book Day throughout Spain.

Last week: Feria de Abril Spectacular week-long fair in Seville, with a major bullfighting festival.

MAY

Early May: Horse Fair Jerez (Andalucía). Horsey high jinks – show-jumping, parades and the famous "dancing Andalusian horses" – turn Jerez into equine heaven.

15: San Isidro Madrid's patron saint's day sees a two-week fiesta either side of the actual date.

Seventh Sunday after Easter: Pentecostés Pentecost is celebrated by the Romería del Rocío – the great pilgrimage-fair – at El Rocío, near Huelva (Andalucía). See page 214.

Thursday after Trinity Sunday: Corpus Christi Religious processions accompanied by floats and penitents, notably in Toledo, Granada and Valencia, plus the spectacular costumed events of Berga's Festa de la Patum, Catalunya (see page 697).

Last week: Feria de la Manzanilla The big annual sherry festival celebrates the famous tipple of Sanlúcar de Barrameda (Andalucía).

JUNE

Second or third week: Sónar Europe's biggest electronic music and multimedia bleep-fest, held over three days in Barcelona. See page 604.

23–24: San Juan Midsummer's eve is celebrated with bonfires and fireworks all over Spain, marking a hedonistic welcome to the summer –particularly in San Juan de Alicante and in Barcelona.

JULY

7–14: San Fermín The famed "Running of the Bulls" at Pamplona. See page 454.

25: Santiago Spain's patron saint, St James, is honoured at Santiago de Compostela, with fireworks and bonfires.

Last three weeks: Pirineos Sur World music festival on a floating stage at Lanuza, near Sallent de Gállego, in the Pyrenees.

AUGUST

10–11: Misteri d'Elx Elche, Valencia (see page 741), hosts mock battles between Christians and Moors, ending with a centuries-old mystery play.

Last week: Los Santos Niños *Gigantones* (giant puppets) are paraded in Alcalá de Henares, near Madrid.

Last Wednesday: La Tomatina Buñol, near Valencia, hosts the country's craziest fiesta, a one-hour tomato fight. See page 755.

SEPTEMBER

First week: Vendimia The grape harvest is celebrated wildly in Valdepeñas (Castilla-La Mancha), Jerez (Andalucía) and many other wine towns.

21: San Mateo The annual Rioja wine harvest bash coincides with the local saint's day in Logroño (La Rioja).

Third Week: Festa de Santa Tecla Human castles (*castells*) and processions of gegants (giant puppets) in Tarragona.

24: La Mercè Barcelona's biggest annual party (either side of the saint's day, 24th) sees a week's worth of giants' parades, fireworks and human-castle-building.

OCTOBER

1: San Miguel Villages across the country celebrate their patron saint's day.

12: La Virgen del Pilar Honouring the patron saint of Aragón is an excuse for bullfights, dancing and celebrations in Zaragoza and elsewhere.

DECEMBER

24: Nochebuena Christmas Eve is particularly exuberant, with parties and carousing early in the evening before it all suddenly stops in time for family dinner or Mass.

31: Nochevieja New Year is celebrated by eating a grape for every stroke of the clock in Plaza del Sol in Madrid, Pza. de Catalunya in Barcelona, and the main squares and bars throughout the country.

Culture and etiquette

Spain is a fantastically welcoming, vibrant country, characterized by its love of life. With a population of almost 48 million it's a diverse place, too, with regional identities as characteristic as their local

landscapes, and the Basques, Galicians and Catalans all add their own languages and cultures to the mix. No matter where you decide to visit though, many of the clichés of Spanish life, such as the siesta, busy bars and restaurants open late into the night, and towns celebrating lively festivals, still pretty much ring true.

Social life and etiquette

One of the most important aspects of Spanish life is the **family**; no celebration would be complete without an extended gathering, although this is more common away from the busy cities where modern life takes its toll. Even so, the elderly are respected, and it's not uncommon to have older relatives being cared for in the family home. Likewise, children are absolutely adored, and included in everything. There is no better country in Europe in which to holiday as a family.

Food plays an important part in Spanish family life, with lunch (*la comida*) the biggest meal of the day, often lasting from 2 to 4pm. It's common for shops and whole villages to come to a standstill for the "siesta" (which today really means just lunch rather than actually sleeping) especially in more out-of-the-way places. Evening meals, which often start as late as 10pm, are usually preceded by a leisurely stroll, or **paseo**, when you may take in an aperitif in a bar or two.

Friends are more likely to meet in restaurants for meals, but if you are **invited to someone's house** for dinner, you should take a small gift for any children, along with chocolates, a bottle of wine, or some flowers (though avoid dahlias, chrysanthemums and flowers in odd numbers as these would only be given at funerals). Also bear in mind that **drinking** too much isn't common; although there seems to be a bar on every corner, this is more for coffee and socializing than heavy boozing.

The Spanish are among the biggest **smokers** in Europe, with an estimated twenty percent of the population smoking regularly. Attitudes are changing, however, and the law now bans smoking in all public places, including shops, public transport, bars and restaurants.

Tipping is common in Spain, although not always expected, but locals are small tippers and twenty cents on a bar table or five percent in a restaurant is usually enough. It is also common practice to tip taxi drivers, hotel porters and the like in small change.

If you are planning to indulge in any topless **sunbathing**, consider local feelings first, and try to stick to beaches where people are already doing it. You also need to make sure you are properly covered if you enter a **church**; shorts and sleeveless tops should be avoided.

Greetings

If you're **meeting someone** for the first time, you should shake their hand. If you become friends, you may well move on to hugging (men) or kisses on each cheek (women), starting with the left. Men are also more likely to kiss women hello and goodbye, than to shake their hand. To say **hello**, use *Buenos días* before lunch and *Buenos tardes* after that. Bear in mind that in Spain the sense of time is somewhat elastic, so unless you're meeting for business (when being late is very bad form) don't be offended if you are left waiting for a good ten or twenty minutes.

Sports and outdoor activities

Spain is nothing if not enthusiastic about sport, with football and basketball all but national obsessions, and bullfighting – whether or not you agree that it's a "sport" – one of its cultural highlights. There are also plenty of opportunities to get out and enjoy the country's stunning outdoors, whether it's ambling around a golf course, skiing in the southern slopes, chasing surf off the Basque Country coast or canyoning in the Pyrenees.

Basketball

In Spain, **basketball** (*baloncesto*) comes second only to football in national interest, and the 2014 World Championships were held here, the second time the country has hosted the world's biggest basketball tournament. In 2019 Spain became the basketball world champions. Domestically, there are eighteen professional teams competing in the national league, **ACB** (http://acb.com), whose season runs from September to June; while other big competitions include the Copa del Rey and the Europe-wide Euroleague. The two biggest teams are, not entirely coincidentally, owned by the two most successful football teams, Barcelona and Real Madrid, and have won the ACB (until 1983 known as the Liga Nacional) dozens of times between them. There's more basketball information on the Federacion Española de Baloncesto website (http://feb.es). Games are broadcast on TV, and match tickets cost from around €25.

Bullfighting

The **bullfight** is a classic image of Spain, and an integral part of many fiestas. In the south, especially, any village that can afford it will put on a *corrida* for an afternoon, while in big cities such as Madrid or Seville, the main festival times are accompanied by a season of prestige fights. However, with the exception of Pamplona, bullfighting is far more popular in Madrid and all points south than it is in the north or on the islands. Indeed, many northern cities don't have bullrings, while the regional governments of both Catalunya and the Balearics have gone so far as to **ban bullfighting** (although Catalunya's ban was overturned by the Constitutional Court in 2016). Spain's main opposition to bullfighting is organized by **ADDA** (Asociación Defensa Derechos Animal; http://addaong.org), whose website has information (in English) about international campaigns and current actions.

Los Toros, as Spaniards refer to bullfighting, is certainly big business, with the top performers, the matadors, on a par with the country's biggest pop and sports stars. To aficionados (a word that implies more knowledge and appreciation than mere "fan"), the bulls are a ritual part of Spanish culture – with the emphasis on the way man and bull "perform" together – in which the *arte* is at issue rather than the cruelty. If pressed on the issue of the slaughter of an animal, supporters generally fail to understand. Fighting bulls are, they will tell you, bred for the industry; they live a reasonable life before they are killed, and, if the bullfight went, so too, would the bulls.

If you decide to attend a *corrida*, try to see a big, prestigious event, where star performers are likely to despatch the bulls with "art" and a successful, "clean" kill. There are few sights worse than a matador making a prolonged and messy kill, while the audience whistles and chucks cushions. The most skilful events are those featuring mounted matadors, or *rejoneadores*; this is the oldest form of *corrida*, developed in Andalucía in the seventeenth century.

The **bullfight season** runs from March to October, and **tickets** for *corridas* start from around €8 – though you can pay much more (up to €200) for the prime seats and more prominent fights. The cheapest seats are *gradas*, the highest rows at the back, from where you can see everything that happens without too much of the detail; the front rows are known as the *barreras*. Seats are also divided into *sol* (sun), *sombra* (shade) and *sol y sombra* (shaded after a while), though these distinctions have become less crucial as more and more bullfights start later in the day, at 6pm or 7pm, rather than the traditional 5pm. The *sombra* seats are more expensive, not so much for the spectators' personal comfort as the fact that most of the action takes place in the shade.

The corrida

The **corrida** begins with a procession, to the accompaniment of a *pasodoble* by the band. Leading the procession are two *alguaciles*, or "constables", on horseback and in traditional costume, followed by the three matadors, who will each fight two bulls, and their *cuadrillas*, their personal "team", each comprising two mounted *picadores* and three *banderilleros*.

Once the ring is empty, the first bull appears, to be "tested" by the matador or his *banderilleros* using pink and gold capes. These preliminaries conducted (and they can be short, if the bull is ferocious), the **suerte de picar** ensues, in which the *picadores* ride out and take up position at opposite sides of the ring, while the bull is distracted by other *toreros*. Once they are in place, the bull is made to charge one of the horses; the *picador* drives his short-pointed lance into the bull's neck, while it tries to toss his padded, blindfolded horse, thus tiring the bull's powerful neck and back muscles. This is repeated up to three times, until the horn sounds for the *picadores* to leave. For many, this is the least acceptable stage of the *corrida*, and it is clearly not a pleasant experience for the horses, who have their ears stuffed with oil-soaked rags to shut out the noise, and their vocal cords cut out to render them mute.

The next stage, the **suerte de banderillas**, involves the placing of three sets of *banderillas* (coloured sticks with barbed ends) into the bull's shoulders. Each of the three *banderilleros* delivers these in turn, attracting the bull's attention with the movement of his own body rather than a cape, and placing the *banderillas* while both he and the bull are running towards each other.

Once the *banderillas* have been placed, the **suerte de matar** begins, and the matador enters the ring alone, having exchanged his pink-and-gold cape for the red one. He (or she) salutes the president and then dedicates the bull either to an individual, to whom he gives his hat, or to the audience by placing his hat in the centre of the ring. It is in this part of the *corrida* that judgements are made and the performance is focused, as the matador displays his skills on the (by now exhausted) bull. He uses the movements of the cape to attract the bull, while his body remains still. If he does well, the band will start to play, while the crowd *olé* each pass. This stage lasts around ten minutes and ends with the kill. The matador attempts to get the bull into a position where he can drive a sword between its shoulders and through to the heart for a *coup de grâce*. In practice, they rarely succeed in this, instead taking a second sword, crossed at the end, to cut the bull's spinal cord; this causes instant death.

If the audience is impressed by the matador's performance, they will wave their handkerchiefs and shout for an award to be made by the president. He can award one or both ears, and a tail – the better the display, the more pieces he gets – while if the matador has excelled himself, he will be carried out of the ring by the crowd, through the *puerta grande*, the main door, which is normally kept locked.

Popular **matadors** include the veteran Enrique Ponce, Julián "El Juli" López, Granada's David "El Fandi" Fandila, César Jiménez and Manuel Jesús Cid Sala "El Cid". But the *torero* who sets most male aficionados' hearts aflutter (and many female ones, too) is the moody, quixotic and media-shy José Tomás Román Martín; fighting under the name José Tomás, his fans claim that his courageous, high-risk style – he has been seriously gored on numerous occasions – has taken the art back to its roots.

Football

Until its poor performance in the 2014 World Cup, Spain had one of the greatest national teams of all time. Spain became World Cup winners in 2010 and won back-to-back European championships in 2008 and 2012, returning to pre-eminence in 2024 with another victory in the Euros. Meanwhile, Barcelona – mercurial *tiki-taka* (pass-and-move) masters – and big spenders Real Madrid are regular finalists of the European Champions League. Certainly, if you want the excitement of a genuinely Spanish sporting event, watching a Sunday-evening game in **La Liga** (http://laliga.com) is unsurpassed.

For many years, in fact, the country's two dominant teams have been **Real Madrid** and **FC Barcelona**, each boasting one of the world's two best footballers in, respectively, Cristiano Ronaldo and Lionel Messi. Their monopoly was broken by **Atlético Madrid**, who surprised everyone by winning the league title in 2014, but other challengers struggle to keep up. These usually include **Valencia**, the Andalucian powerhouse of **Sevilla** and the emerging forces of **Villarreal**, who have experienced a rags-to-riches success story under president and ceramics tycoon Fernando Roig, and **Real Sociedad** from San Sebastián. Also powerful are **Athletic Bilbao**, who only draw on players from Euskal Herria (the Basque Country in Spain and France, and in Navarra) and those who come through the club's youth ranks.

The league **season** runs from late August until May, and most games kick off at 5pm or 7pm on Sundays, though live TV usually demands that one key game

kicks off at 10pm on Saturday and 9pm on Sunday. With the exception of local derbies, major European games, and the so-called *clásicos* between Real Madrid and Barcelona, **tickets** are not too hard to get. They start at around €35 for La Liga games, with the cheapest in the *fondo* (behind the goals); *tribuna* (pitchside stand) seats are much pricier, while to see an average Real Madrid (see page 94) or Barcelona (see page 633) game could easily cost you up to €120.

Golf

When Cantabria boy Severiano "Seve" Ballesteros died in 2011, aged just 54, the whole nation mourned. He and his fellow golfers, like José María Olazábal, Sergio García and Miguel Ángel Jiménez, have raised the country's golf profile immeasurably in recent years, and with around three hundred **golf courses**. Spain is one of the best European destinations for the amateur golfer too. Temperatures, especially favourable in the south, mean that you can play more or less year-round on the Costa del Sol, while a number of courses have been built away from the traditional centres, for example along the Costa de la Luz and the Atlantic coast, which, while not as nice in winter, tend to be a little cheaper. There are increasing concerns, however, about the amount of water used by courses in a country that is experiencing a severe water crisis.

Plenty of tour operators can arrange golf-holiday packages, while for more information visit the very useful **Golf Spain** website (http://golfspain.com), which details all the country's golf courses and golf schools, plus green fees and golf-and-resort packages.

Hiking and mountain sports

Spain is one of the most mountainous countries in Europe, and as such is hugely popular with walkers. Aside from the classic long-distance routes, there are fantastic day-hikes, climbs and circuits possible almost everywhere, though you'll need to be properly equipped with a map, compass or GPS, hiking boots and mountain gear.

In Andalucía, the **Sierra Nevada** mountain range and national park offers spectacular walking among the highest peaks in Europe after the Alps. It can be pretty hard going, but there are less challenging hikes in the foothills, particularly the lush valleys of Las Alpujarras. For the best trekking in central Spain, head for the **Sierra de Gredos**, two hours' drive from Madrid, where there are lots of excellent one- and two-day hikes in the shadow of the highest peak, Almanzor (2592m). To the north, in the Pyrenees, the largest concentration of peaks lies in the eastern half of the range, particularly in Catalunya's **Parc Nacional d'Aigüestortes i Estany de Sant Maurici**, where there are walks of all levels, from afternoon rambles to multi-day expeditions. Further challenges abound to the west, where the **Aragonese Pyrenees** are home to the two highest peaks in the range, Aneto (3404m) and Posets (3375m), while in Aragón's **Parque Nacional de Ordesa** there are both rewarding day-hikes and more intensive climbs. If asked to choose just one corner of Spain, though, many would plump for the rugged **Picos de Europa** in Cantabria and Asturias, which, although only 40km or so across, offers a surprising diversity, from easy day-treks to full-blown expeditions.

Rafting and canyoning

There's **rafting** (see page 705) in various rivers across Spain, though the fast-flowing Noguera Pallaresa in the eastern Pyrenees is the most popular choice for expeditions. The season runs roughly from March to October, during which time you can fling yourself down the rapids in an inflatable raft from around €50 for a two-hour trip, and more like €180 for an all-day trip with lunch.

The Parque Natural Sierra de Guara (http://guara. org) and the Parque Nacional de Ordesa (http:// ordesa.net) provide some of the best locations in Europe for **canyoning** (*barranquismo*) – hiking, climbing, scrambling and abseiling in caves, gorges and rivers. Operators in most of the local villages (including Alquézar and Torla) offer equipment and guides, with prices starting from around €90 for a full day's expedition. The park websites have more information on routes and local organizations.

Skiing and snowboarding

Spain offers a decent range of slopes, and often at lower prices than its more mountainous European neighbours. It is also home to the southernmost skiing in Europe, in the form of the Sol y Nieve resort in the **Sierra Nevada** (Andalucía), which has the longest season in Spain, running from November to April and sometimes even May, allowing you to ski in the morning and head to the beach in the afternoon – really, the only thing the resort's got going for it. Much more challenging skiing is to be had in the north of the country in the Pyrenees. The **Aragonese Pyrenees** are home to a range of resorts catering for beginners to advanced skiers, while the resorts in the **Catalan Pyrenees**, to the east, encompass Andorra; the biggest resort here is Soldeu/El Tarter. Other options include the more intimate **Alto Campoo**, near Santander, and, for a day's excursion, easy-to-intermediate skiing just outside Madrid at **Valdesqui** and **Navacerrada**.

There are ski deals to Spain from tour operators in your home country, though it often works out cheaper if you go through a local Spanish travel agent or even arrange your trip directly with local providers. Many local hotels offer ski deals, and we've covered some options in the Guide. Equipment rental will set you back around €30–40 a day as a general rule, and weekly lift-passes from around €150, although the longer you rent or ski for, the cheaper it will be.

Watersports

Spain offers a vast range of watersports, especially along the Mediterranean coast where most resorts offer **pedalo**, **kayak**, **paddleboard and canoe rental** (from €15/hour), sailing/kitesurfing tuition, and **boat rental** (€50/hour) and **waterskiing** (from €40/15min).

Surfing is best on the Atlantic coast, backed up by the fact that the area plays regular host to a number of prestigious competitions such as the Ferrolterra Pantín Classic and the Goanna Pro Breaks such as the legendary Mundaka (Costa Vasca), considered by many as the best left-hander in Europe (but one that's notoriously fickle), along with a superb run of beaches with waves for all abilities, make the region's

SPAIN'S CLASSIC HIKES

The country's **major footpaths** are known as GR (Grande Recorrido) or PR (Pequeño Recorrido), some of which make up part of the trans-European walking routes that extend across the entire continent. GR paths are the longest, and are marked by red-and-white stripes, while the smaller PR routes (yellow-and-white) can usually be done in a day. The best-known routes are the GR11, which crosses the Pyrenees from coast to coast and takes at least forty days, via Andorra; the GR65 and its variants, the Camino de Santiago; and the GR7, which starts from Tarifa in Andalucía, heads through the Sierra Nevada and up the Catalan coast before reaching the Pyrenees.

Baixa Garrotxa A 28-kilometre loop through the spectacular Garrotxa volcanic region of northeastern Catalunya. See page 693.

Camino de Santiago The legendary, month-long pilgrimage route runs from the Pyrenees to Santiago de Compostela, by way of Romanesque architecture in Navarra (see page 458), mighty Gothic cathedrals in Castilla y León (see page 398), fine wines in La Rioja and beautiful green Galicia scenery (see page 523).

Cañón de Añisclo Much less visited and wilder than its neighbour Ordesa, this spectacular river gorge is overlooked by wedding-cake palisades. See page 594.

Carros de Foc The trans-park circuit takes in the most scenic corners of the Parc Nacional d'Aigüestortes i Estany de Sant Maurici, a challenging route linking nine overnight refuges. See page 708.

Circo de las Cinco Lagunas A scintillating one-day walk in the Sierra de Gredos, with sparkling mountain lakes and the possibility of seeing half-tame Gredos ibex. See page 147.

Circo de Soaso The best sampling of Aragón's Parque Nacional de Ordesa – upstream along the valley to a superb waterfall, and back via a spectacular corniche route called the Faja de Pelay. See page 593.

Desfiladero de Cares The classic Picos de Europa hike – through the Cares Gorge – is a dramatic 12km route along a path hewn out of the cliff face. See page 482.

Pedraforca One of the most revered peaks in Catalunya is a relatively easy one to bag, with a variety of routes up. See page 700.

reputation. The surfing season runs roughly from September to April, meaning that a full wetsuit is a basic requirement in the cold Atlantic waters. If you prefer to surf in warmer waters, note that the Atlantic Andalucian coastline has a few decent spots. For more information, get hold of the superb *Stormrider Surf Guide: Europe*, which gives full details of all the best spots in Spain (and elsewhere in Europe).

Tarifa on the Costa de la Luz is *the* spot in Spain – indeed, in the whole of Europe – for **windsurfing and kitesurfing**, with strong winds almost guaranteed, and huge stretches of sandy beach to enjoy. You'll also find schools dotted around the rest of the coast, with another good spot being the rather colder option of the Atlantic coast in Galicia. Prices are around €45 for an hour's board and sail rental, while lessons start at €60 for two hours including board rental.

Travelling with children

Spain is a fabulous country to travel with children of any age; they will be well received everywhere, and babies and toddlers, in particular, will be the centre of attention. You will probably have to change your usual routine, since young children stay up late in Spain, especially in the summer. It's very common for them to be running around pavement cafés and public squares after 10pm or 11pm, and yours will no doubt enjoy joining in. It's expected that families dine out with their children, too, so it's not unusual to see up to four generations of the same family eating tapas in a bar, for example.

Holidays

Many holiday hotels and self-contained club-style resorts offer things like kids' clubs, babysitting, sports and entertainment. The only caveat is that, of course, you're unlikely to see much of Spain on these family-oriented holidays. The two best cities to take children, hands down, are Madrid and Barcelona, which have loads of child-friendly attractions. Otherwise, Spain has various theme parks and leisure activities specifically aimed at kids, while the long Spanish coastline has a bunch of popular **water parks**.

Museums, galleries and sights throughout Spain either offer **discounts** or **free entry** for children (it's often free for under-4s or even under-7s), and it's the same on trains, sightseeing tours, boat trips and most other usual tourist attractions.

Accommodation

If you're travelling independently, finding **accommodation** shouldn't be a problem, as *hostales* and *pensiones* generally offer rooms with three or four beds. Bear in mind that much budget accommodation in towns and cities is located on the upper storeys of buildings, often without lifts. It's also worth noting that some older-style *pensiones* don't have heating systems – and it can get very cold in winter. If you want a cot provided or **babysitting** services, you'll usually have to stay in a more expensive hotel – and even then, never assume that babysitting services can be provided, so always check in advance. **Self-catering accommodation** offers the most flexibility; even in major cities, it's easy to rent an apartment by the night or week and enjoy living like a local with your family.

Products, clothes and services

Baby food, disposable nappies, formula milk and other standard items are widely available in pharmacies and supermarkets, though not necessarily with the same brands that you will be used to at home. Organic baby food, for example, is hard to come by away from the big-city supermarkets, and most Spanish non-organic baby foods contain small amounts of sugar or salt. Fresh milk, too, is not always available; UHT is more commonly drunk by small children. If you require anything specific for your baby or child, it's best to bring it with you or check with the manufacturer about equivalent brands. Remember, too, the airline restrictions on carrying liquids in hand luggage if you're planning to bring industrial quantities of Calpol to see you through the holiday.

For **babies' and children's clothing**, Prénatal (http://prenatal.es) and Chicco (http://chicco.es) are Spain's market leaders, with shops in most towns and cities. Or you can always try the local El Corte Inglés department store.

Families might eat out a lot, but things like **highchairs and special children's menus** are rare, except in the resorts on the *costas* and islands. Most bars and cafés, though, will be happy to heat milk bottles for you. **Baby-changing areas** are also relatively rare, except in department stores and shopping centres, and even where they do exist they are not always up to scratch.

Attitudes

Most establishments are **baby-friendly** in the sense that you'll be made very welcome if you turn up with a child in tow – a refreshing change from parts of northern Europe. Many museum cloakrooms, for example, will be happy to look after your pushchair as you carry your child around the building, while restaurants will make a fuss of your little one. Discreet **breast-feeding** in public is acceptable. **Noise** is the other factor that often stuns visiting parents. Spain is a loud country, with fiesta fireworks, jackhammers, buzzing mopeds and clamouring evening crowds all adding to the mix. Babies sleep through most things, but you might want to pick and choose accommodation with the location of bars, clubs, markets, and the like, firmly in mind.

Travel essentials

Accessible travel

The classic tourist images of Spain – the medieval old towns, winding lanes, the castles and monasteries – don't exactly fill you with confidence if you use a wheelchair. However, Spain is changing and facilities are improving rapidly, especially in the more go-ahead, contemporary cities. There are accessible rooms and hotels in all major Spanish cities and resorts and, by law, all new public buildings (including revamped museums and galleries) are required to be fully accessible. Public transport is the main problem, since most local buses and trains are virtually impossible for wheelchairs, though again there are pockets of excellence in Spain. The AVE high-speed train service, for example, is fully accessible, as is every city and sightseeing bus in Barcelona (and large parts of its metro and tram network, too). In many towns and cities, acoustic traffic-light signals and dropped kerbs are common.

Some organizations at home may be able to advise you further about travel to Spain, like the very useful UK-based **Tourism For All** (http://tourismforall.org.uk). **Access Travel** (www.travelwithaccess.com) offers Barcelona city breaks and holidays to five other Spanish resorts and, at the very least, local tourist offices in Spain should also be able to recommend a suitable hotel or taxi company.

Addresses

Addresses are written as: C/Picasso 2, 4° izda. – which means Picasso Street (*calle*) no. 2, fourth floor, left- (*izquierda*) hand flat or office; dcha. (*derecha*) is right; cto. (*centro*) centre. Where no house number is known, s/n (*sin número*) is commonly used in Spain. Avenida is often abbreviated to Avda. (Avgda. in Barcelona, Catalunya and the Balearics) in addresses.

Other confusions in Spanish addresses result from the different spellings, and sometimes words, used in Catalan, Basque and Galician – all of which are replacing their Castilian counterparts; for example, *carrer* (not *calle*) and *plaça* (not plaza) in Catalan.

Climate

Overall, spring, early summer and autumn are ideal times for a Spanish trip – though the weather varies enormously from region to region. Note that the chart below shows **average temperatures** – and while Seville, the hottest city in Spain, can soar high into the 90s at midday in summer, it is a fairly comfortable 23–27°C (75–80°F) through much of the morning and late afternoon. Equally, bear in mind that temperatures in the north or west, in Extremadura or León for example, can approach freezing at night in winter, while mountainous regions can get extremely cold much of the year.

Complaints

By law, all establishments (including hotels) must keep a *libro de reclamaciones* (**complaints book**). If you have any problems, you can usually produce an immediate resolution by asking for the book, since most establishments prefer to keep them empty, thus attracting no unwelcome attention from officialdom. If you do make an entry, English is acceptable but write clearly and simply; add your home address, too, as you are entitled to be informed of any action, including – but don't count on it – compensation. Or take your complaint to any local *turismo*, which should attempt to resolve the matter while you wait.

Costs

There are few places in Europe where you'll get a better deal on the cost of simple meals and drinks. Public transport remains very good value, as does car rental, certainly out of season.

It's difficult to come up with **a daily budget** for the country, as your €2 glass of wine and €40 *pensión* room in rural Andalucía might be €7 and €70, respectively, in Madrid or Barcelona. However, as a very rough guide, if you always stay in youth hostels or the cheapest hotels, use public transport and stick to local restaurants, you could get by on between €70 and €100 a day. Stay somewhere a bit more stylish

AVERAGE TEMPERATURES						
	Jan	Mar	May	Jul	Sept	Nov
ALICANTE, COSTA BLANCA						
°C/°F	16/61	20/68	26/78	32/90	30/86	21/70
BARCELONA, CATALUNYA						
°C/°F	13/56	16/61	21/70	28/83	25/77	16/61
MADRID, CASTILE						
°C/°F	9/49	15/59	21/70	31/88	25/77	13/56
MÁLAGA, COSTA DEL SOL						
°C/°F	17/63	19/67	23/74	29/84	29/84	20/68
MALLORCA, BALEARICS						
°C/°F	14/58	17/63	22/72	29/84	27/80	18/65
PONTEVEDRA, GALICIA						
°C/°F	14/58	16/61	20/68	25/77	24/75	16/61
SANTANDER, CANTABRIA						
°C/°F	12/54	15/59	17/63	22/72	21/70	15/59
SEVILLE, ANDALUCÍA						
°C/°F	15/59	21/70	26/78	35/95	32/90	20/68

EMERGENCY NUMBERS

112 All emergency services
061 Ambulance
080 Fire service
062 Guardia Civil
091 Policía Nacional

or comfortable, eat in fancier restaurants, and go out on the town, and you'll need more like €150–200 a day, though, of course, if you're holidaying in Spain's paradores or five-star hotels, this figure won't even cover your room.

Visiting museums, galleries, churches and monasteries soon adds up. Check to see if there are tourist cards available that give discounts on entry. Accordingly, it pays to take along any **student/youth or senior citizen cards** you may be entitled to, as most attractions offer discounts (and make sure you carry your passport or ID card). Some museums and attractions are **free** on a certain day of the week or month (though note that this is sometimes limited to EU citizens only; you'll need to show your passport). Any **entrance fees** noted in the Guide are for the full adult price; children (as well as seniors) usually get a discount, and children under 4 years old are often free in many places.

Crime and personal safety

The police in Spain come in various guises. The **Guardia Civil**, in green uniforms, is a national police force, formerly a military organization, and has responsibility for national crime, as well as roads, borders and guarding public buildings. There's also the blue-uniformed **Policía Nacional**, mainly seen in cities, who deal with crime, drugs, crowd control,

identity and immigrant matters, and the like. Locally, most policing is carried out by the **Policía Municipal**, who wear blue-and-white uniforms, and these tend to be the most approachable if you're reporting a crime, for example. In certain of the autonomous regions, there are also regional police forces, which are gradually taking over duties from the Guardia Civil and Policía Nacional. The **Mossos d'Esquadra** in Catalunya (blue uniforms with red-and-white trim) and the Basque **Ertzaintza** (blue and red, with red berets) have the highest profile, though you're most likely to encounter them on traffic and highways duty.

If you do get robbed, go straight to the police, where you'll need to make an official statement known as a **denuncia**, not least because your insurance company will require a police report. Expect it to be a time-consuming and laborious business – you can do it online (details on http://policia.es), but you'll still have to go into the station to sign it. If you have your passport stolen, you need to contact your embassy or consulate.

Avoiding trouble

Pickpocketing and **bag-snatching** is, unfortunately, a fact of life in major Spanish cities and tourist resorts, though no more so than anywhere else in Europe. You need to be on guard in crowded places and on public transport, but there's no need to be paranoid. Drivers shouldn't leave anything in view in a **parked car**. **On the road**, be cautious about accepting help from anyone other than a uniformed police officer – some roadside thieves pose as "good Samaritans" to persons experiencing car and tyre problems, some of which, such as slashed tyres, may have been inflicted at rest stops or service stations in advance. The thieves typically attempt to divert your attention by pointing out a problem and then steal items from the vehicle while you are looking elsewhere.

STAYING SAFE IN SPANISH CITIES

Certain Spanish cities – Madrid, Barcelona and Seville particularly – have a bad reputation as far as petty crime is concerned. While it's easy to get spooked by lurid tales of local thievery (hoteliers often go to great pains to warn guests of the dangers), taking the usual sensible **precautions** should help make your stay safe.

Know where your belongings are at all times (don't leave **bags** unattended, even if you're looking at rooms upstairs in a *hostal*). Carry handbags slung across your neck, not over your shoulder; don't put wallets in your back pocket; leave passport and tickets in the hotel safe; and keep a photocopy of your passport, plus notes of your credit card helplines and so on.

On the street, beware of people standing unusually close at street kiosks or attractions, or of those trying to distract you for any reason (pointing out "bird faeces" – in reality, planted shaving cream – on your jacket, shoving a card or paper to read right under your nose). Next thing you know, your wallet has gone.

Incidentally, if you are stopped by a proper police officer for a **driving offence**, being foreign just won't wash as an excuse. They'll fine you on the spot, cash or card.

Sexual harassment

Spain's macho image has faded dramatically, and these days there are relatively few parts of the country where **women travelling alone** are likely to feel intimidated or attract unwanted attention. There is little of the pestering that you used to have to contend with, and the outdoor culture of terrazas (terrace bars) and the tendency of Spaniards to move around in large, mixed crowds, help to make you feel less exposed. *Déjame en paz* ("leave me in peace") is a fairly standard rebuff, and if you are in any doubt, take a taxi back to your accommodation, always the safest way to travel late at night.

The major **resorts** of the *costas* have their own artificial holiday culture, where problems are more likely to be caused by other alcohol-fuelled holiday-makers. You are actually more vulnerable in isolated, **rural regions**, where you can walk for hours without coming across an inhabited farm or house, though it's rare that this poses a threat – help and hospitality are much more the norm. Many single women happily tramp the long-distance pilgrim footpath, for example, though you are always best advised to stay in rooms and *pensiones* rather than camping wild.

Electricity

Plugs in Spain are of the two-prong, standard European type. The current in Spain is 220v – bring an adaptor (and transformer) to use UK and US laptops, mobile phone chargers, and other electronic devices.

Entry requirements

EU citizens (and those of Norway, Iceland, Liechtenstein and Switzerland) need only a valid national identity card or passport to enter Spain. Other Europeans, including UK nationals, and citizens of the **United States**, **Canada**, **Australia** and **New Zealand**, require a passport but no visa, and can stay as a tourist for up to ninety days. UK nationals must hold a passport valid for at least six months beyond their return date. Other nationalities (including South Africans) will need to get a visa from a Spanish embassy or consulate before departure. Visa requirements do change, and it's always advisable to check the current situation before leaving home for travelling. At the time of writing, plans were afoot to introduce an ETIAS visa (https://travel-europe.europa.

eu/etias_en), effective from mid-2025, for visitors to the EU, including those from the UK.

Most non-EU citizens who want to stay in Spain for longer than three months, rather than just visit as a tourist, need to register at a provincial **Oficina de Extranjeros** (Foreigners' Office), where they'll be issued with a residence certificate; you'll find a list of offices (eventually) on the Ministry of Interior website (www.interior.gob.es). You don't need the certificate if you're an EU citizen living and working legally in Spain, or if you're legally self-employed or a student (on an exchange programme or otherwise). US citizens can apply for one ninety-day extension, showing proof of funds, but this must be done from outside Spain. Other nationalities wishing to extend their stay will need to get a special visa from a Spanish embassy or consulate before departure.

Health

The **European Health Insurance Card (EHIC)** gives EU citizens access to Spanish state public-health services under reciprocal agreements. While this will provide free or reduced-cost medical care in the event of minor injuries and emergencies, it won't cover every eventuality – and it only applies to EU citizens in possession of the card – so travel insurance is essential. British nationals may now apply for the **UK Global Health Insurance Card (GHIC)** before travelling to Spain but EHIC cards issued before Brexit are still valid until they expire.

In Spain the worst that's likely to happen to you is that you might fall victim to an upset stomach. To be safe, wash fruit and avoid tapas dishes that look as if they were prepared last week. Water at public fountains is fine, unless there's a sign saying "*agua no potable*", in which case don't drink it.

For minor complaints, go to a **farmacia** – pharmacists are highly trained, willing to give advice (often in English) and able to dispense many drugs that would be available only on prescription in other countries. They keep usual shop hours (Mon–Fri 9am–1.30pm & 5–8pm), but some open late and at weekends, while a rota system (displayed in the window of every pharmacy) keeps at least one open 24 hours in every town.

If you have special medical or dietary requirements, it is advisable to carry a letter from your doctor, translated into Spanish, indicating the nature of your condition and necessary treatments. With luck, you'll get the address of an English-speaking **doctor** from the nearest *farmacia*, police station or tourist office – it's obviously more likely in resorts and big cities. Treatment at **hospitals** for EU citizens in possession

ROUGH GUIDES TRAVEL INSURANCE

Looking for travel insurance? Rough Guides partners with top providers worldwide to offer you the best coverage. Policies are available to residents of anywhere in the world, with a range of options whether you are looking for single-trip, multi-country or long-stay insurance. There's coverage for a wide range of adventure sports, 24-hour emergency assistance, high levels of medical and evacuation cover and a stream of travel safety information. Even better, roughguides.com users can take advantage of these policies online 24/7, from anywhere in the world – even if you're already travelling. To make the most of your travels and ensure a smoother experience, it's always good to be prepared for when things don't go according to plan. For more information go to http://roughguides.com/bookings/insurance.

of the EHIC card is free; otherwise, you'll be charged at private-hospital rates, which can be very expensive.

Like the rest of the world, Spain was hit hard by the Covid-19 pandemic, but at the time of writing, there were no longer any vaccination or testing requirements in place for entering the country. Check www.gov.uk/foreign-travel-advice/spain for the latest guidelines and updates regarding all travel to Spain.

In **emergencies**, dial 112 for an ambulance.

Insurance

You should take out a comprehensive **insurance policy** before travelling to Spain, to cover against loss, theft, illness or injury. A typical policy will provide cover for loss of baggage and tickets, as well as cancellation or curtailment of your journey. When securing baggage cover, make sure that the per-article limit will cover your most valuable possession. Most policies exclude so-called **dangerous sports** unless an extra premium is paid: in Spain, this can mean that most watersports are excluded (plus rafting, canyoning, etc), though not things like bike tours or hiking.

If you need to make a claim, you should keep receipts for medicines and medical treatment, and in the event you have anything stolen, you must obtain an official statement from the police.

Internet

Wi-fi (pronounced "wee-fee" in Spain) is widespread in cafés, bars, hotels and other public "hotspots" – Barcelona city council, for example, operates Spain's largest free public network. Otherwise, you can get online at computer shops and phone offices (*locutorios*), where you'll pay as little as €1 an hour, though it can cost two or three times as much. Since most accommodation in Spain has free wi-fi too, reviews in the Guide only highlight places where there is no wi-fi or you have to pay for it.

Laundry

You'll find a few coin-operated self-service laundries (*lavanderías automáticas*) in the major cities, but you normally have to leave your clothes for a service wash and dry at a *lavandería*. A dry cleaner is a *tintorería*. Note that by law you're not allowed to leave laundry hanging out of windows over a street, and many *pensiones* and *hostales* expressly forbid washing clothes in the sink.

LGBTQ+ travellers

There are plenty of LGBTQ+-friendly hotels, clubs and bars, as well as resorts such as Torremolinos (Costa del Sol), Maspalomas (Gran Canaria), Playa de las Américas (Tenerife) and Sitges (Costa Brava) that cater specifically for a LGBTQ+ clientele. Madrid hosts the largest Gay Pride in Europe; the rest of the year the scene is centred around the city's Chueca district. In Barcelona, the place to go is the Eixample district. There are several LGBTQ+ internet sites relating to Spain, including www.gaybarcelona.com, www.visitlgbtq.com, www.gaytravel4u.com/gay-madrid-guide/, and www.benamics.com in the Balearics.

Mail

Post offices (*Correos*; http://correos.es) are normally open weekdays from 8am to 2pm and again from 5pm to 7.30pm, though branches in bigger places may have longer hours, may not close at midday and may open on Saturday mornings. There's an office-finder on the website, which also gives exact opening hours and contact details for each post office in Spain. As you can also pay bills and buy phonecards in post offices, queues can be long – it's often easier to buy **stamps** at tobacconists (look for the brown-and-yellow *estanco* sign).

Outbound mail is reasonably reliable, with letters or cards taking around three days to a week to the UK and the rest of Europe, a week to ten days to North America, New Zealand and Australia, although it can be more erratic in the summer. There's also a whole host of express-mail services (ask for *urgente* or *exprés*).

Maps

You'll find a good selection of **road maps** in most Spanish bookshops and service stations. Most widely available are the regional Michelin maps (1:400,000), covering the country in a series of nine maps, though there are also whole-country maps and atlas-format versions available. Other good country and regional maps are those published by Distrimapas Telstar (http://distrimapas-telstar.es), which also produces reliable indexed **street plans** of the main cities. Any good book or travel shop in your own country should provide a decent range of maps, or buy online from specialist stores such as http://stanfords.co.uk or http://randmcnally.com.

You can buy **hiking/trekking maps** from specialist map/travel shops in Spain, including La Tienda Verde in Madrid and Llibrería Quera (http://espaiquera.com/llibreria) or Altaïr (http://altair.es) in Barcelona. These and other bookshops stock the full range of **topographical maps** issued by two government agencies – the Instituto Geográfico Nacional and the Servicio Geográfico del Ejército – available at scales of 1:200,000, 1:100,000, 1:50,000 and occasionally 1:25,000. The various SGE series are considered to be more up to date, although neither agency is hugely reliable. A Catalunya-based company, Editorial Alpina (http://editorialalpina.com), produces useful 1:40,000 or 1:25,000 map/booklet sets for most of the Spanish **mountain and foothill areas** of interest, and these are also on sale in many bookshops.

Money

Spain's currency is the **euro** (€), with notes issued in denominations of 5, 10, 20, 50, 100, 200 and 500 euros, and coins in denominations of 1, 2, 5, 10, 20 and 50 cents, and 1 and 2 euros. Up-to-the-minute currency **exchange rates** are posted on http://oanda.com.

By far the easiest way to get money is to use your bank **debit card** to withdraw cash from an **ATM**, found in villages, towns and cities all over Spain, as well as on arrival at the airports and major train stations. You can usually withdraw up to €300 a day, and instructions are offered in English once you insert your card. Make sure you have a personal identification number (PIN) that's designed to work overseas, and take a note of your bank's emergency contact number in case the machine swallows your card. Some European debit cards can also be used directly in shops to pay for purchases; you'll need to check first with your bank.

All major **credit cards** are accepted in hotels, restaurants and shops, and for tours, tickets and transport, though don't count on being able to use them in every small *pensión* or village café. If you use a foreign credit card in some shops, you may also be asked for photo ID, so be prepared to show a driving licence or passport. Make sure you make a note of the number for reporting lost or stolen cards to your credit card company.

Spanish **bancos** (banks) and **cajas de ahorros** (savings banks) have branches in all but the smallest villages. **Banking hours** are usually Monday to Friday 8.30am to 2pm, with some city branches open Saturday 8.30am to 1pm (except June–Sept when all banks close on Sat), although times can vary from bank to bank. Outside these times, it's usually possible to change cash at larger hotels (generally with bad rates and high commission) or with travel agents – useful for small amounts in a hurry.

In tourist areas, you'll also find specialist **casas de cambio**, with more convenient hours (though rates vary), while some major tourist offices, larger train stations and most branches of El Corte Inglés department store have exchange facilities open throughout business hours.

Opening hours

Almost everything in Spain – shops, museums, churches, tourist offices – closes for at least two hours in the middle part of the day (commonly called a siesta but today few Spaniards actually sleep at this time). There's a lot of variation (and the siesta tends to be longer in the south), but you'll get far less aggravated if you accept that the early afternoon is best spent having lunch or at the beach.

Basic **working hours** are Monday to Friday 9.30am to 2pm and 5pm to 8pm. Many **shops** open slightly later on a Saturday (at 10am) and close for the day at 2pm, though you'll still find plenty of places open in cities, and there are regional variations. Department and chain stores and shopping malls tend to open a straight Monday to Saturday 10am to 9pm or 10pm.

Museums and galleries, with very few exceptions, also have a break between 1pm or 2pm and 4pm. On Sundays, most open mornings only, and on Mondays many close all day (museums are also usually closed Jan 1 & 6, May 1, Dec 24, 25 & 31). Opening hours vary from year to year, though often not by more than half an hour or so. Some are also seasonal, and usually in Spain, "summer" means from Easter until September, and "winter" from October until Easter.

The most important **cathedrals, churches and monasteries** operate in the same way as museums,

SPANISH NATIONAL PUBLIC HOLIDAYS

Jan 1 *Año Nuevo,* New Year's Day

Jan 6 *Epifanía,* Epiphany

March/April *Viernes Santo,* Good Friday

May 1 *Fiesta del Trabajo,* May Day

Aug 15 *La Asunción,* Assumption ofthe Virgin

Oct 12 *Día de la Hispanidad,* National Day

Nov 1 *Todos los Santos,* All Saints

Dec 6 *Día de la Constitución,* Constitution Day

Dec 8 *Inmaculada Concepción*

Dec 25 *Navidad,* Christmas Day

with regular visiting hours and admission charges. Other churches, though, are kept locked, generally opening only for worship in the early morning and/or the evening (between around 6pm and 9pm).

Public holidays

Alongside the Spanish **national public holidays** (see page 56) there are scores of regional holidays and local fiestas (often marking the local saint's day), any of which will mean that everything except hotels, bars and restaurants locks its doors.

In addition, **August** is traditionally Spain's own holiday month, when the big cities are semi-deserted, with many shops and restaurants closed. In contrast, it can prove nearly impossible to find a room in the more popular coastal and mountain resorts at these times; similarly, seats on planes, trains and buses in August should if possible be booked in advance.

Shopping

The great city **markets** of Spain are attractions in their own right – bustling, colourful and hugely photogenic – but even so they are emphatically not "just for tourists". Local people still do their daily shop in places like La Boquería in Barcelona, Valencia's Mercado Central or Madrid's Mercado de San Miguel, while a visit to any town's local market is a sure way to get a handle on regional produce and specialities. Independent **food shops** thrive too, from traditional bakeries to classy delis serving the finest cured meats, while the bigger cities support whole enclaves of foodie shops – in Barcelona's La Ribera neighbourhood, for example, you can flit from alley to alley to buy hand-crafted chocolates, artisan-made cheeses, home-roast coffee, organic olive oil and the like. They make great souvenirs.

Leatherwork, such as belts, bags, purses and even saddles, are best sourced in Andalucía. The town of Ubrique (Cádiz) has been a centre of leather production since medieval times, and you can browse and buy from the workshops that line the main street.

Ceramics are widely available, but are especially good in Andalucía (Córdoba and around Seville) and in Catalunya (at La Bisbal, northwest of Palafrugell).

In Andalucía you'll also be able to pick up the most authentic **flamenco** accessories such as dresses, fans, shawls and lace.

Smoking laws

Since 2006, smoking in public places in Spain has been regulated by law, and tougher restrictions introduced in 2011 mean that it's now forbidden to smoke in all public buildings and transport facilities, plus bars, restaurants, clubs and cafés. Compared to other countries with smoking restrictions in force, you'll find there's still an awful lot of puffing going on, though the ban is generally observed.

Taxes

Local sales tax, **IVA** (pronounced "eeba"), is ten percent in hotels and restaurants, and twenty-one percent in shops. It's usually included in the price though not always, so some hotel or restaurant bills can come as a bit of a surprise – though quoted prices should always make it clear whether or not tax is included. **Non-EU residents** are able to claim back the sales tax on purchases that come to over €90. To do this, make sure that the shop you're buying from fills out the correct paperwork, and present this to customs before you check in at the airport for your return flight.

Telephones

Spanish **telephone numbers** have nine digits; mobile numbers begin with a 6 or 7, freephone numbers begin 900, while other 90-plus- and 80-plus-digit numbers are nationwide standard-rate or special-rate services. To **call Spain from abroad**, dial your country's international access code + 34 (Spain's country code) + the nine-digit Spanish number.

Public telephones have instructions in English, and accept coins, credit cards and phonecards. **Phonecards** (*tarjetas*) with discounted rates for calls are available in tobacconists, newsagents and post offices, issued in various denominations either by Telefónica (the dominant operator) or one of its rivals. Credit cards are not recommended for local and national calls, since most have a minimum charge that is far more than a normal call is likely to cost. It's also best to avoid making calls from the phone in your hotel room, as even local calls will be slapped with a heavy surcharge.

You can make international calls from any public payphone, but it's cheaper to go to one of the ubiquitous phone centres, or **locutorios**, which specialize in discounted overseas connections. **Calling home from Spain**, you dial 00 (Spain's international access code) + your country code (44 for the UK) + city/area code minus initial zero + number. For **reverse-charge calls**, dial the international operator (1008 Europe, 1005 rest of the world).

Most European **mobile phones** will work in Spain, though it's worth checking with your provider whether you need to get international access switched on. Since June 2017, EU mobile phone companies are no longer allowed to charge extra roaming fees for using a mobile (including text and data services) in another EU nation.

Time

Spain is one hour ahead of the UK, six hours ahead of Eastern Standard Time, nine hours ahead of Pacific Standard Time, eight hours behind Australia, ten hours behind New Zealand, and the same time as South Africa. In Spain, the clocks go forward in the last week in March and back again in the last week in October. It's worth noting, if you're planning to cross the border, that Portugal is an hour behind Spain throughout the year.

Toilets

Public toilets are generally reasonably clean but don't always have any paper. They can very occasionally still be squat-style. They are most commonly referred to and labelled *Los Servicios*, though signs may point you to *baños*, *aseos* or *lavabos*. *Damas* (Ladies) and *Caballeros* (Gentlemen) are the usual distinguishing signs for sex, though you may also see the potentially confusing *Señoras* (Women) and *Señores* (Men).

Tourist information

The Spanish national tourist office, **Turespaña** (http://spain.info), is an excellent source of information when planning your trip. The website is full of ideas, information and searchable databases, and there are links to similar websites of Turespaña offices in your own country.

There are **oficinas de turismo** (tourist offices) in virtually every Spanish town, usually open Monday to Friday 9am to 2pm and 4pm to 7pm, Saturday and Sunday 9am to 2pm, but hours vary considerably from place to place. In major cities and coastal resorts the offices tend to remain open all day Saturday and on Sunday morning between April and September.

The information and help available in *oficinas de turismo* also varies: some are very good, and some do little more than hand out a map and ask where you're from. Not all staff speak English, especially in the more rural and out-of-the-way destinations. There's also often more than one information office, especially in bigger towns and cities, where responsibility for local tourism is split between municipal and provincial offices. As a rough rule, the municipal offices are better for specific city information, the provincial offices are best for advice about where to go in the region.

Madrid

PLAZA MAYOR

1 | Madrid

Madrid became Spain's capital simply by virtue of its geographical position at the heart of Iberia. When Felipe II moved the seat of government here in 1561, his aim was to create a symbol of the unification and centralization of the country, and a capital from which he could receive the fastest post and communication from every corner of the nation. The site itself had few natural advantages – it is 300km from the sea on a 650m-high plateau, freezing in winter, boiling in summer – and it was only the determination of successive rulers to promote a strong central capital that ensured Madrid's survival and development.

Today, Madrid is a vast, predominantly modern city, with a population of some six million and growing. The journey in – through a stream of soulless suburbs and high-rise apartment blocks – isn't pretty, but the streets at the heart of the city are a pleasant surprise, with pockets of medieval buildings and narrow, atmospheric alleys, dotted with the oddest of shops and bars, and interspersed with eighteenth-century Bourbon squares. Compared with the historic cities of Spain – Toledo, Salamanca, Seville, Granada – there may be few sights of great architectural interest, but the monarchs did acquire outstanding picture collections, which formed the basis of the **Prado** museum. This, together with the **Reina Sofía** and the **Thyssen-Bornemisza** museums, state-of-the-art homes to fabulous arrays of modern Spanish painting (including Picasso's *Guernica*) and European and American masters, has made Madrid a top port of call on the European art tour.

Aside from these heavyweight cultural attractions, there is a host of smaller museums and palaces which can be almost as rewarding. Sports fans will inevitably be drawn to the Santiago Bernabéu, home to Real Madrid, one of the most glamorous and successful clubs in world football, while a scattering of parks and gardens provide a welcome respite from the hustle and bustle of the city centre.

However, monuments and sights are not really what Madrid is about and as you get to grips with the place, you soon realize that it's the lifestyle of the inhabitants – the **madrileños** – that is the capital's key attraction: hanging out in traditional cafés or summer *terrazas*, packing the lanes of the Sunday Rastro flea market or playing hard and very late in a thousand **bars**, clubs, discos and *tascas*. Whatever Barcelona, Valencia or San Sebastián might claim, the Madrid scene, immortalized in the movies of Pedro Almodóvar, remains the most vibrant and fun in the country.

Over the last twenty years, Madrid has undergone a series of urban rehabilitation programmes focused on the city's older *barrios* (districts). Improvements have been made to the transport network, with extensions to the metro, the construction of new ring roads, and the excavation of a honeycomb of new road tunnels designed to bring relief to Madrid's congested streets. Several of the city centre shopping streets have been pedestrianized, new cycle lanes have been built, while an ambitious regeneration scheme along the Manzanares has turned the river into a focal point for leisure and recreation. Now that the economic crisis is in the past and unemployment has dropped, the city is only on the up, and remains one of the most vibrant and welcoming destinations for any visitor.

A brief history

Madrid's history dates back to the ninth century when **Muslims** established a defensive outpost on the escarpment above the River Manzanares which later became known as "Mayrit" – the place of many springs.

MATCH BETWEEN ATLÉTICO MADRID AND REAL MADRID

Highlights

❶ **Palacio Real** Marvel at the over-the-top opulence in this grandiose former residence of the Spanish monarchs. See page 72

❷ **El Rastro** Take a Sunday stroll from Plaza Mayor through Madrid's shambolic flea market. See page 74

❸ **The Prado** The Goya, Velázquez and Bosch collections alone are worth a trip to one of the world's greatest museums. See page 78

❹ **Guernica** Behold this icon of twentieth-century art at the Reina Sofía. See page 84

❺ **Museo Arqueológico Nacional** The archeological museum houses a stunning array of ancient treasures, including the iconic Iberian bust known as the Dama de Elche. See page 93

❻ **Real Madrid** Watch the fifteen-times European champions' dazzling roster of big-name players parade their footballing skills at the Santiago Bernabéu stadium. See page 94

❼ **Tapas** Sample the mouthwatering range of tasty specialities as you hop from bar to bar in the Huertas, La Latina, Chueca or Malasaña districts. See page 101

❽ **A night on the tiles** Start late at a bar, then go on to a club and try to make it into the early hours before collapsing over *chocolate con churros*. See page 109

HIGHLIGHTS ARE MARKED ON THE MAP ON PAGE 62

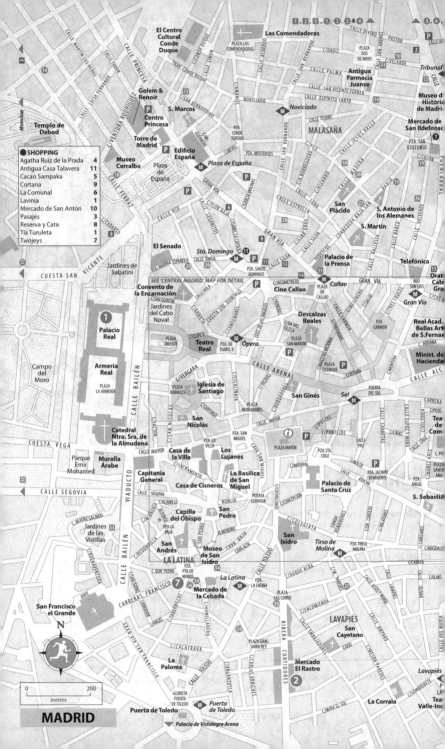

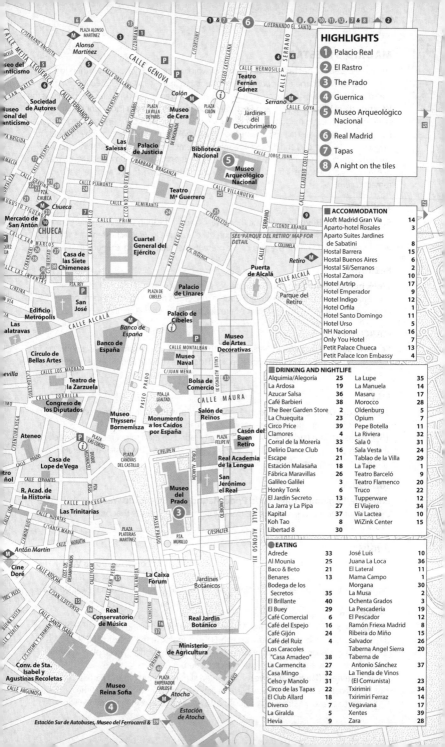

HIGHLIGHTS

1 Palacio Real
2 El Rastro
3 The Prado
4 Guernica
5 Museo Arqueológico Nacional
6 Real Madrid
7 Tapas
8 A night on the tiles

ACCOMMODATION

Aloft Madrid Gran Via	14
Aparto-hotel Rosales	3
Aparto Suites Jardines de Sabatini	8
Hostal Barrera	15
Hostal Buenos Aires	6
Hostal Sil/Serranos	2
Hostal Zamora	10
Hotel Artrip	17
Hotel Emperador	9
Hotel Indigo	12
Hotel Orfila	1
Hotel Santo Domingo	11
Hotel Urso	5
NH Nacional	16
Only You Hotel	7
Petit Palace Chueca	13
Petit Palace Icon Embassy	4

DRINKING AND NIGHTLIFE

Alquimia/Alegoría	25	La Lupe	35
La Ardosa	19	La Manuela	14
Azucar Salsa	36	Masaru	17
Café Barbieri	38	Morocco	28
The Beer Garden Store	2	Oldenburg	5
La Chuequita	23	Opium	7
Circo Price	39	Pepe Botella	11
Clamores	4	La Riviera	32
Corral de la Morería	33	Sala 0	31
Delirio Dance Club	16	Sala Vesta	24
Escape	21	Tablao de la Villa	29
Estación Malasaña	18	La Tape	1
Fábrica Maravillas	26	Teatro Barceló	12
Galileo Galilei	3	Teatro Flamenco	20
Honky Tonk	6	Truco	22
El Jardín Secreto	13	Tupperware	12
La Jarra y La Pipa	27	El Viajero	34
Kapital	37	Vía Lactea	10
Koh Tao	8	WiZink Center	15
Libertad 8	30		

EATING

Adrede	33	José Luís	10
Al Mounia	25	Juana La Loca	36
Baco & Beto	21	El Lateral	11
Benares	13	Mama Campo	1
Bodega de los Secretos	35	Morgana	30
El Brillante	40	La Musa	2
El Buey	29	Ochenta Grados	3
Café Comercial	6	La Pescadería	19
Café del Espejo	16	El Pescador	12
Café Gijón	24	Ramón Frieza Madrid	8
Café del Ruiz	4	Ribeira do Miño	15
Los Caracoles "Casa Amadeo"	38	Salvador	26
La Carmencita	27	Taberna Angel Sierra	20
Casa Mingo	32	Taberna de Antonio Sánchez	37
Celso y Manolo	31	La Tienda de Vinos (El Comunista)	23
Circo de las Tapas	22	Txirimiri	34
El Club Allard	18	Txirimiri Ferraz	14
Diverxo	7	Vegaviana	17
La Giralda	5	Xentes	39
Hevia	9	Zara	28

1

MADRID'S FIESTAS

There are dozens of **fiestas** in Madrid, some of which involve the whole city, others just an individual *barrio*. The more important dates celebrated in the capital are listed below.

Also well worth checking out are cultural festivals organized by the city council, in particular the **Veranos de la Villa** (July–Aug) and **Festival de Otoño a Primavera** (Nov–June). Many events are free and, in the summer, often open-air, taking place in the city's parks and squares. Annual festivals for gastronomy (Jan–Feb), flamenco (June), books (end May), photography (mid-July to August), jazz (November) and dance (November–December) are also firmly established on the cultural agenda. Full programmes are published in the monthly what's-on magazine *esMadrid*, free from any of the tourist offices (see page 98) and from the city's tourist website (http://esmadrid.com).

JANUARY

5: Cabalgata de Reyes To celebrate the arrival of the gift-bearing Three Kings there is a hugely popular, gigantic evening procession through the city centre in which children are showered with sweets. It's held on the evening before presents are traditionally exchanged in Spain.

FEBRUARY

Week before Lent: Carnaval An excuse for a lot of partying and fancy-dress parades, especially in the LGBTQ+ zone around Chueca. The end is marked by the bizarre parade, El Entierro de la Sardina (The Burial of the Sardine), on the Paseo de la Florida.

MARCH/APRIL

Semana Santa (Holy Week) Celebrated with a series of solemn processions around Madrid, although for a more impressive backdrop head for Toledo (routes and times of processions are available from tourist offices).

MAY

2: Fiesta del Dos de Mayo Held throughout Madrid, with music, theatre productions and flamenco shows, though a bit low-key in recent years.
15: Fiestas de San Isidro Festivities to honour Madrid's patron saint are spread a week either side of this date, and are among the country's biggest festivals. The fiestas also herald the start of the bullfighting season.

JUNE/JULY

End June/beginning July: World Pride Madrid (LGTBQ+ Pride Week) Week-long party throughout Chueca, culminating in a massive carnival-style parade that brings the city centre to a standstill.

AUGUST

6–15: Castizo (Traditional fiestas of San Cayetano, San Lorenzo and La Virgen de la Paloma) in La Latina and Lavapiés *barrios*. Much of the activity – processions, dancing and live music – takes place around C/Toledo, the Pza. de la Paja and the Jardines de las Vistillas.

DECEMBER

25: Navidad During Christmas, Pza. Mayor is filled with stalls selling festive decorations and displaying a large model of a Nativity scene. El Corte Inglés, at the bottom of C/Preciados, has an all-singing, all-dancing clockwork Christmas scene (Cortylandia), which plays at certain times of the day to the delight of assembled children.
31: Nochevieja (New Year's Eve) is celebrated at bars, restaurants and parties all over the city. Puerta del Sol is the customary place to gather, waiting for the strokes of the clock – it is traditional to swallow a grape on each stroke to bring good luck in the coming year.

1

It remained a relatively insignificant backwater until 1561 when Felipe II designated the city his **imperial capital** by virtue of its position at the heart of the recently unified Spain. The cramped street plan in the city centre provides a clue as to what the city would have been like at this time and the narrow alleys around the Pza. Mayor are still among Madrid's liveliest and most atmospheric. With the **Bourbons** replacing the Habsburgs at the start of the eighteenth century, a touch of French style, including the sumptuous Palacio Real, was introduced into the capital by Felipe V.

It was the "King-Mayor" **Carlos III**, however, who tried to convert the city into a home worthy of the monarchy after he ascended to the throne in 1759, ordering the streets to be cleaned, sewers and lighting to be installed and work to begin on the Prado museum complex.

Upheaval and political polarization

The early **nineteenth century** brought invasion and turmoil to Spain as Napoleon established his brother Joseph (or José to Spaniards) on the throne. Madrid, however, continued to flourish, gaining some very attractive buildings and squares, including the Pza. de Oriente and Pza. de Santa Ana. With the onset of the **twentieth century**, the capital became the hotbed of the political and intellectual discussions that divided the country; *tertulias* (political/philosophical discussion circles) sprang up in cafés across the city (some of them are still going) as the country entered the turbulent years of the end of the monarchy and the foundation of the Second Republic.

The Civil War

Madrid was a Republican stronghold during the **Civil War**, with fierce battles raging around the capital as Franco's troops laid siege to the city, eventually taking control in 1939. The Civil War, of course, caused untold damage, and led to forty years of isolation. The city's great spread to **suburbia** began during the Franco era and it has continued unabated ever since, with unbridled property speculation taking its toll on the green spaces that surround the capital. Franco also extended the city northwards along the spinal route of the Paseo de la Castellana, to accommodate his ministers and minions during development extravaganzas of the 1950s and 1960s.

The post-Franco era

The Spanish capital has changed immeasurably, however, in the five decades since Franco's death, initially guided by a poet-mayor, the late **Tierno Galván**. His efforts

---

ORIENTATION

Madrid's layout is fairly straightforward. At the city's heart is the large oval-shaped plaza **Puerta del Sol** (often referred to as just "Sol"). Around it lie the oldest parts of Madrid, neatly bordered to the west by the **River Manzanares**, to the east by the park of **El Retiro** and to the north by the city's great thoroughfare, the **Gran Vía**.

Madrid's main sights occupy a compact area between the **Palacio Real** and the gardens of **El Retiro**. The great trio of museums – the **Prado**, **Thyssen-Bornemisza** and **Reina Sofía** – lie in a "golden triangle" just west of El Retiro and close to Paseo del Prado. Over towards the river are the oldest parts of the city, centred on the splendid, arcaded **Pza. Mayor**, an area known as **Madrid de los Austrias** after the Habsburg monarchs who built it.

To get a feel for the city you should experience the contrasting character and life of the various neighbourhoods (*barrios*). The most central and rewarding of these are the areas around **Pza. de Santa Ana and C/Huertas**, east of Sol; **La Latina and Lavapiés**, south of Pza. Mayor, where the Sunday market, El Rastro, takes place; and **Malasaña and Chueca**, north of Gran Vía. By happy circumstance, these *barrios* have some of Madrid's finest concentrations of tapas bars and restaurants.

1

– the creation of parks and renovation of public spaces and public life – left an enduring legacy, and were a vital ingredient of the *movida madrileña* "the happening Madrid" with which the city broke through in the 1980s. From the early 1990s until 2015, the centre-right Partido Popular (PP) was in control, bringing with it a more restrictive attitude towards bar and club licensing. Mayor Alberto Ruiz Gallardón oversaw significant urban renewal schemes, but also rampant property speculation and a subsequent collapse that bequeathed the city a massive debt crisis. Support for the PP plummeted in the 2015 elections and the left-of-centre Ahora Madrid group, led by mayor Manuela Carmena, began to pick up the pieces. They slashed debt and simultaneously increased public spending, which aroused suspicion regarding their spending practices, a controversy which would ultimately dominate Ahora Madrid's time in office and see the pendulum swing back to PP in 2019. New mayor José Luis Martínez-Almeida has scrapped Madrid's low-emission zone and been accused of corruption in the handing out of contracts during Spain's Covid-19 pandemic.

In recent years there has been a tendency in Madrid towards homogenization with the rest of Europe, as franchised fast-food joints and coffee bars have sprung up all over the city centre. Nevertheless, in making the transition from provincial backwater to major European capital, Madrid has still managed to preserve its own stylish and quirky identity.

Madrid de los Austrias

Madrid de los Austrias (Habsburg Madrid) was a mix of formal planning – at its most impressive in the expansive and theatrical Pza. Mayor – and areas of shanty-town development, thrown up as the new capital gained an urban population. The central area of old Madrid still reflects both characteristics, with its twisting grid of streets, alleyways and steps, and its Flemish-inspired architecture of red brick and grey stone, slate-tiled towers and Renaissance doorways.

Puerta del Sol

Ⓜ Sol

The obvious starting point for exploring Madrid de los Austrias (and most other areas of the centre) is the **Puerta del Sol**. This square marks the epicentre of the city – and, indeed, of Spain. It is from this point that all distances are measured, and here that six of Spain's *Rutas Nacionales* officially begin. On the pavement outside the clock-tower building on the south side of the square, an inconspicuous stone slab shows **Kilometre Zero**.

The square, which conceals a subterreanean transport hub, is a popular meeting place, especially by the statue of a bear pawing a *madroño* (strawberry tree) – the city's emblem – at the start of C/Alcalá and the equestrian bronze of King Carlos III. Statues apart, there's little of note in the square apart from the **Casa de Correos**, built in 1766, originally the city's post office and now home to the main offices of the Madrid regional government. At New Year, the square is packed with people waiting for the clock that crowns the Neoclassical facade to chime midnight. Sol's main business, however, is shopping, with giant branches of the **department stores** El Corte Inglés and the French chain FNAC in C/Preciados, at the top end of the square.

Plaza Mayor

Ⓜ Sol

Follow C/Mayor (the "Main Street" of the medieval city) west from the Puerta del Sol and you could easily walk right past Madrid's most important landmark: **Pza. Mayor**.

1

Set back from the street and entered by stepped passageways, it appears all the more grand in its continuous sweep of arcaded buildings. It was planned by Felipe II – the monarch who made Madrid the capital – as the public meeting place of the city, and was finished thirty years later in 1619 during the reign of Felipe III, who sits astride the stallion in the central statue. The architect was Juan Gómez de Mora, responsible for many of the civic and royal buildings in this quarter.

The square, with its hundreds of balconies, was designed as a theatre for public events, and it has served this function throughout its history. It was the scene of the Inquisition's *autos-de-fé* (trials of faith) and the executions that followed; kings were crowned here; festivals and demonstrations passed through; plays by Lope de Vega and others received their first performances; bulls were fought; and gossip was spread.

Nowadays, Pza. Mayor is primarily a tourist haunt, full of expensive outdoor cafés and restaurants (best stick to a drink), buskers and caricaturists. However, an air of grandeur clings to the plaza, which still performs public functions. In the summer months and during the major *madrileño* fiestas, it becomes an outdoor **theatre** and **music stage**; and in the winter, just before Christmas, it becomes a **bazaar** for festive decorations and religious regalia. Every Sunday, too, stamp and coin sellers set up their stalls.

Casa Panadería
Royalty would watch the more important of the historic public events from their apartments in the central **Casa Panadería**, a palace named after the bakery that it replaced. It was rebuilt after a fire in 1692 and subsequently decorated with frescoes. However, the present delightful, and highly kitsch, array of allegorical figures that adorn the facade was only added in 1992. Today, the palace houses municipal offices and a tourist office (open daily).

Mercado de San Miguel
Set back from the road, near the entrance to the Pza. Mayor, is the splendid decorative ironwork of the **Mercado de San Miguel**. Built in 1916, it was formerly one of the old-style food markets scattered throughout the city, but it has been refurbished and

---

MADRID'S FREEBIES

Free entrance can be gained to many of Madrid's premier attractions. Sites classed as Patrimonio Nacional, such as the Palacio Real, the Convento de la Encarnación, El Pardo and the Monasterio de las Descalzas, are free to EU citizens at various times during the week (bring your passport). Museums run by Madrid City Council, including the Museo de San Isidro, La Ermita de San Antonio, the Templo de Debod and the Museo de Historia de Madrid, do not charge admission. Most museums are free for children, and give substantial discounts to retirees and students (bring ID in all cases). In addition, many museums and sights that normally charge entry set aside certain times when entrance is free, and nearly all are free on World Heritage Day (April 18), International Museum Day (May 18), the Día de Hispanidad (Oct 12) and Día de la Constitución (Dec 6). The following are free at these times:

Museo de América Sun 10am–3pm.

Museo Reina Sofía Mon, Wed–Sat 7–9pm, Sun 1.30pm–7pm.

Museo Arqueológico Nacional Sat 2–8pm, Sun 9.30am–3pm.

Museo de Artes Decorativas Thurs 5–8pm (Sept–June), Sat 2–3pm, Sun 10am–3pm.

Museo Cerralbo Thurs 5–8pm, Sat 2–3pm, Sun 10am–3pm.

Museo Lázaro Galdiano Mon, Wed–Sat 3.30–

4.30pm, Sun 2–3pm.

Museo del Prado Mon–Sat 6–8pm, Sun 5–7pm.

Museo del Romanticismo Sat 2–6.30pm (May–Oct till 8.30pm), Sun 10am–3pm.

Museo Sorolla Sat 2–8pm, Sun 10am–3pm.

Museo Thyssen-Bornemisza Mon noon–4pm.

Museo del Traje Sat 2.30–7pm, Sun 10am–3pm.

Palacio Real Oct–March: Mon–Thurs 4–6pm, April–Sept: 6–8pm.

Real Academia de Bellas Artes Wed 10am–3pm.

1

A WALKING TOUR OF MADRID DE LOS AUSTRIAS

To get a feel for what the old city might have been like when it was first designated the Spanish capital in the sixteenth century take a stroll around the area known as **Madrid de los Austrias**.

Start off at **Pza. de la Villa**, probably the oldest square in the city and home to some of its most ancient buildings, including the fifteenth-century Torre de los Lujanes. Then take the narrow, elbow-shaped C/Codo out of the northeastern corner of the plaza, passing the Convento de los Carboneras where the nuns still sell traditional cakes and biscuits, continuing downhill to the tranquil backstreet C/San Justo. If you bear left past the splendid **Baroque Basílica de San Miguel** you will emerge on to bustling C/Segovia, one of the ancient entrances into the old city. From here wander down Cava Baja with its succession of traditional *tascas*, former coaching inns and stylish tapas bars. You will end up in **Pza. Humilladeros**, which buzzes with people sitting at the terrace bar in the middle of the square and is flanked by the graceful lines of the Iglesia de San Andrés and the mansion that is now home to the Museo de San Isidro. Walk past the splendid domed church and turn right into **Pza. de la Paja**, one of the old market squares that once littered the medieval city. Wealthy families would have lived in the mansions that line the square, each with a small garden similar to the peaceful Jardín de Anglona situated at the bottom of the plaza.

Take a right along C/Príncipe de Anglona and shady C/Nuncio to rejoin C/Segovia and bear left up **C/Cuchilleros**, named after the knife-makers who once plied their trade on the street. Here you will pass the renowned restaurant **Botín**, a *madrileño* institution that lays claim to be the oldest eating establishment in the world, followed by a string of cellar bars offering flamenco and traditional tapas. Don't miss the beautiful wrought-ironwork of the **Mercado de San Miguel** before finishing up with a circuit of the arcaded splendour of the **Pza. Mayor**.

converted into a stylish, though pricey, tourist-oriented emporium complete with oyster bar, a sherry corner and smoked cod stall.

The alley taverns

In the alleys just below the square, such as C/Cuchilleros and C/Cava de San Miguel, are some of the city's oldest *mesones*, or **taverns**. Have a drink in these in the early evening and you may be serenaded by passing *tunas* – musicians and singers dressed in traditional costume of knickerbockers and waistcoats who wander around town playing and passing the hat. These men-only troupes are attached to various faculties of the university and are usually students earning a bit of extra cash to make ends meet.

Plaza de la Villa and around

West along C/Mayor, towards the Palacio Real, is **Pza. de la Villa**, an example of three centuries of Spanish architectural development. Its oldest surviving building is the eye-catching fifteenth-century **Torre de los Lujanes**, a fine Mudéjar (Moors working under Christian rule) tower, where Francis I of France is said to have been imprisoned in 1525 after his capture at the Battle of Pavia in Italy. Opposite is the former town hall, the **ayuntamiento** (**Casa de la Villa**), begun in the seventeenth century, but remodelled in Baroque style. Finally, fronting the square is the **Casa de Cisneros**, which was built by a nephew of Cardinal Cisneros in the sixteenth-century Plateresque ("Silversmith") style.

Basílica de San Miguel

C/San Justo 4 • Free • Ⓜ La Latina

Just around the corner from Pza. de la Villa is the flamboyant **Basílica de San Miguel**. Designed by Italian architects at the end of the seventeenth century, the Basílica, with its convex facade, is one of the few examples of a full-blown Baroque church in Madrid and has been entrusted to the Opus Dei organization since 1959.

Ópera and the Palacio Real

1

Dominated by the imposing **Palacio Real** and the elegant Pza. de Oriente, **Ópera** is one of the most pleasant and relaxed *barrios* in the city. The area contains the lavishly decorated **Teatro Real**, the tranquil gardens of the **Campo del Moro** and the **city cathedral**, while the two unobtrusive monastery complexes of **La Encarnación** and **Las Descalzas Reales** conceal an astounding array of treasures.

San Ginés

C/Arenal 13 • Free • Ⓜ Sol/Ópera

Situated midway between Sol and Ópera along C/Arenal is the ancient church of **San Ginés**. Of Mozarabic origin (built by Christians under Moorish rule), it was completely reconstructed in the seventeenth century. There is a splendid El Greco canvas of the moneychangers being chased from the temple in the **Capilla del Cristo** (on show Mon 12.30pm). Alongside, in somewhat uneasy juxtaposition, stands a cult temple of modern times, the *Joy Madrid* nightclub, and, behind it, the **Chocolatería San Ginés**, a Madrid institution, which at one time catered for the early-rising worker but now churns out *chocolate con churros* at any time of day or night. (see page 110).

Descalzas Reales

Pza. de las Descalzas Reales 3 • Guided tours (some in English) • Charge, joint ticket with Convento de la Encarnación available • http://patrimonionacional.es • Ⓜ Sol/Callao

A couple of blocks north of San Ginés is one of the hidden treasures of Madrid, the **Monasterio de las Descalzas Reales**. It was founded in 1557 by Juana de Austria, daughter of the Emperor Carlos V, sister of Felipe II, and, at the age of 19, already the widow of Prince Don Juan of Portugal. In her wake came a succession of titled ladies (*Descalzas Reales* means "Barefoot Royals"), who brought fame and, above all, fortune to the convent, which is unbelievably rich, though beautiful and tranquil, too. It is still in use, with shoeless nuns tending patches of vegetable garden.

Whistle-stop **guided tours** conduct visitors through the cloisters and up an incredibly elaborate stairway to a series of chambers packed with art and treasures of every kind. The **former dormitories** are perhaps the most outstanding feature, decorated with a series of Flemish tapestries based on designs by Rubens and a striking portrait of St Francis by Zurbarán. These were the sleeping quarters for all the nuns, including St Teresa of Ávila for a time, although the empress María of Germany preferred a little more privacy and endowed the convent with her own luxurious private chambers. The other highlight of the tour is the **Joyería** (Treasury), piled high with jewels and relics of uncertain provenance. The nuns kept no records of their gifts, so no one is quite sure what many of the things are – there is a bizarre cross-sectional model of Christ – nor which bones came from which saint. Whatever the case, it's an exceptional hoard.

Convento de la Encarnación

Pza. de la Encarnación • Guided tours (usually in Spanish only) • Charge, joint ticket with the Monasterio de las Descalzas available • http://patrimonionacional.es • Ⓜ Ópera

Just to the north of Pza. de Oriente is the **Convento de la Encarnación**. This was founded a few years after Juana's convent, by Margarita, wife of Felipe III, though it was substantially rebuilt towards the end of the eighteenth century. It houses an extensive but somewhat disappointing collection of seventeenth-century Spanish art, and a wonderfully bizarre library-like reliquary, reputed to be one of the most important in the Catholic world. The most famous relic housed here is a small glass bulb said to contain the blood of the fourth-century doctor martyr, St Pantaleon,

1

whose blood supposedly liquefies on his feast day, July 27. The tour ends with a visit to the Baroque-style church, which features a beautifully frescoed ceiling.

Teatro Real

Pza. de Isabel II • Charge • https://teatroreal.es • Ⓜ Ópera

◼ ACCOMMODATION				● EATING			
Hostal Gala	3	Numa Script	12	Almendro 13	34	Casa Mortero	8
Hostal Gonzalo	19	Petit Palace Ópera	9	Ana La Santa	22	Casa Paco	27
Hostal Ivor	8	Petit Palace Posada del Peine	14	Artemisa	16	CEBO	14
Hostal La Macarena	16	Petit Palace Puerta del Sol	10	La Barraca	1	Cervecería Cervantes	23
Hotel Mayerling	21	Posada del Leon de Oro	22	La Bola	2	Chocolatería San Ginés	9
Hotel Meninas	6	Radisson Blu Madrid Prado	23	El Botín	24	Círculo de Bellas Artes	5
Hotel Palacio de		Room Mate Alicia	18	Las Bravas	15	Dos Cielos Madrid	3
San Martín	6	Room Mate Laura	7	Café de Oriente	6	Honest Greens	4
Hotel San Lorenzo	1	Room Mate Mario	5	Casa del Abuelo	18	Lhardy	11
Hotel Urban	11	Villa Real	13	Casa del Abuelo II	19	Mercado de San Miguel	20
Hotel Vincci The Mint	2	The Westin Palace, Madrid	15	Casa González	25	La Musa Latina	31
ME Madrid Reina Victoria	17			Casa Labra	7	Museo del Jamón	10
NH Palacio Tepa	20			Casa Lucio	36	Palacio de Anglona	29

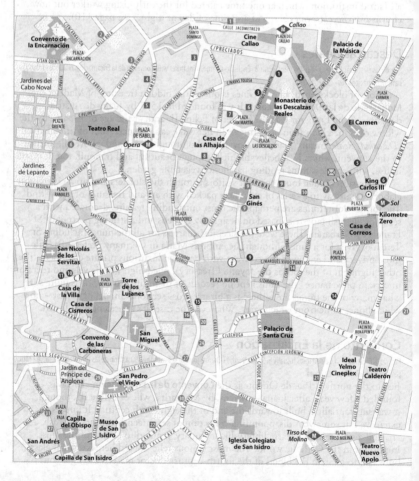

West of Sol, C/Arenal leads to the **Teatro Real**, or **Ópera**, which gives this area its name. Built in the mid-nineteenth century, it almost sank a few decades later as a result of subsidence caused by underground canals and was forced to close in 1925; it finally reopened in 1997 after an epic ten-year refurbishment that ended up costing a mind-boggling €150 million. The interior is suitably lavish and merits a visit in its own right, and it makes a truly magnificent setting for opera, ballet and classical concerts (see

La Platería	32	**■ DRINKING AND NIGHTLIFE**			**● SHOPPING**	
Posada de la Villa	30	Alhambra	11	La Fidula	25	El Arco Artesania	15
Prada a Tope	17	Café Berlín	1	Gin Club/Mercado de la Reina	5	Area Real Madrid	5
Qoritika	12	Café Central	23	The Glass Bar	10	Casa de Diego	6
La Sanabresa	33	Café Jazz Populart	24	Joy Madrid	9	Casa Mira	8
Taberna del Chato	21	Las Carboneras	19	Museo Chicote	4	Casa Yustas	9
Taberna La Dolores	28	Cardamomo	14	La Quimera	20	La Central	1
La Tapería del Prado	35	Cervecería Alemana	22	Ricks	3	Desnivel	16
El Tempranillo	37	Cervecería Santa Ana	21	Salmon Guru	17	El Flamenco Vive	7
Vi-cool	26	Club 33	28	El Sol	12	FNAC	2
Yerbabuena	13	Coco	7	El Son	12	Geppetto	10
		La Coquette	8	Tablao Flamenco 1911	6	Imaginarium	4
		Del Diego	2	Torero	18	José Ramírez	14
		De Mercado	27	La Venencia	13	La Librería	11
		Dos Gardenias	26	Viva Madrid	15	Mariano Madrueño	3
						Mercado de San Miguel	12
						Seseña	13

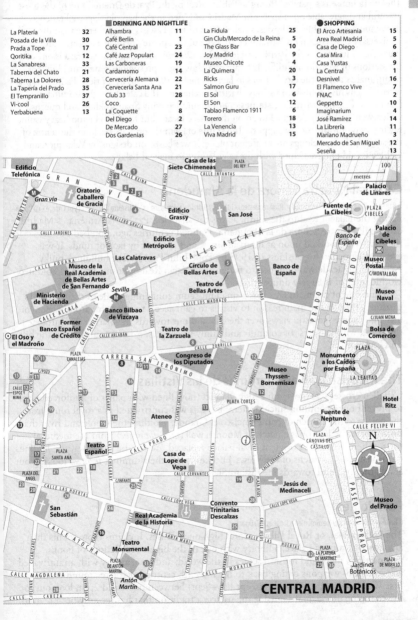

CENTRAL MADRID

1

page 112). You can take a general tour or tours focusing on the artistic or technical elements of productions.

Plaza de Oriente

Ⓜ Ópera

The opera house is separated from the Palacio Real by the **Pza. de Oriente**, one of the most graceful and agreeable open spaces in Madrid and used in the bad old days by Franco as the venue for his public addresses; small groups of neo-Fascists still gather here on the anniversary of his death on November 20. One of the square's main attractions – and the focus of its life – is the Parisian-style *Café de Oriente*, whose summer *terraza* is one of the stations of Madrid nightlife. The café (which is also a prestigious restaurant) looks as traditional as any in the city but was in fact opened in the 1980s by a priest, Padre Lezama, who ploughs his profits into various charitable schemes. The café apart, the dominant features of Pza. de Oriente are **statues**: 44 of them, depicting Spanish kings and queens, which were originally designed to go on the palace facade but found to be too heavy (some say too ugly) for the roof to support. The **statue of Felipe IV** on horseback, in the centre of the square, clearly belongs on a different plane; it was based on designs by Velázquez, and Galileo is said to have helped with the calculations to make it balance.

Catedral Nuestra Señora de la Almudena

C/Bailén 8–10 • **Catedral** Free (small donation requested) • http://catedraldelaalmudena.es • **Museum** Charge • **Crypt** Charge • Ⓜ Ópera

Facing the Palacio Real to the south, across the shadeless Pza. de la Armería, is Madrid's cathedral, **Nuestra Señora de la Almudena**. Planned centuries ago, bombed out in the Civil War, worked upon at intervals since, and plagued by lack of funds, it was eventually opened for business in 1993 by Pope John Paul II. The building's bulky Neoclassical facade was designed to match the Palacio Real opposite, while its cold neo-Gothic interior is largely uninspiring.

To one side of the main facade is a small **museum** containing some of the Catedral's treasures, though the main reason to visit is to gain access to the dome from where you can enjoy some fantastic views over the city and out towards the Sierra. The entrance to the **crypt**, with its forest of columns and dimly lit chapels, is to be found down the hill on C/Mayor.

The Moorish wall and Jardines de las Vistillas

C/Bailén crosses C/Segovia on a high **viaduct** (now lined with panes of reinforced glass to prevent once-common suicide attempts); this was constructed as a royal route from the palace to the church of San Francisco el Grande, avoiding the rabble and river that flowed below. Close by is a patch of **Moorish wall** (*muralla árabe*) from the medieval fortress here, which the original royal palace replaced. Across the aqueduct, the **Jardines de las Vistillas** ("Gardens of the Views") beckon, with their summer *terrazas* looking out across the river and towards the distant Sierra.

Palacio Real

C/Bailén • Charge • http://patrimonionacional.es • Ⓜ Ópera

The **Palacio Real**, or Royal Palace, scores high on statistics. It claims more rooms than any other European palace; a library with one of the biggest collections of books, manuscripts, maps and musical scores in the world; and an armoury with an unrivalled assortment of weapons dating back to the fifteenth century. If you're around on the first Wednesday of the month (except July–Sept) between noon and 2pm, look out for the **changing of the guard** outside the palace, a tradition that has recently been revived.

Guided tours in various languages are available, but a more relaxing option is to hire an audio-guide and make your own way through the luxurious royal apartments, the Royal Armoury Museum and the Royal Pharmacy. This will give you more time to appreciate the extraordinary opulence: acres of Flemish and Spanish tapestries, endless Rococo decoration, bejewelled clocks and pompous portraits of the monarchs.

The palace also houses an impressive exhibition space, the **Galería de Pinturas**, which displays work by Velázquez, Caravaggio and Goya, among others, and also hosts temporary **exhibitions**.

The palace

The Habsburgs' original palace burnt down on Christmas Eve, 1734. Its replacement, the current building, was based on drawings made by Bernini for the Louvre. It was constructed in the mid-eighteenth century and was the principal royal residence from then until Alfonso XIII went into exile in 1931; both Joseph Bonaparte and the Duke of Wellington also lived here briefly. The present royal family inhabits a considerably more modest residence on the western outskirts of the city, using the Palacio Real on state occasions only.

The **Salón del Trono** (Throne Room) is the highlight for most visitors, containing as it does the thrones installed for former monarchs Juan Carlos and Sofía as well as the splendid ceiling by Tiepolo, a giant fresco representing the glory of Spain – a remarkable achievement for an artist by then in his seventies. Look out, too, for the marvellous **Sala de Porcelana** (Porcelain Room) and the incredible oriental-style **Salón de Gasparini**.

The outbuildings and annexes

The palace outbuildings and annexes include the **Armería Real**, a huge room full of guns, swords and armour, with such curiosities as the suit of armour worn by Carlos V in his equestrian portrait by Titian in the Prado. Especially fascinating are the complete sets of armour, with all the original spare parts and gadgets for making adjustments. There is also an eighteenth-century **Farmacia**, a curious mixture of alchemist's den and laboratory, whose walls are lined with jars labelled for various remedies. The **Biblioteca Real** (Royal Library) can now only be visited by prior arrangement for research purposes.

The gardens
Occasionally closed for state visits

Immediately north of the palace are the **Jardines de Sabatini**, which provide a shady retreat and venue for summer concerts, while to the rear is the larger, and far more beautiful, **Campo del Moro** (access only from the far west side, off the Paseo de la Virgen del Puerto), a leafy English-style garden with shady paths, monumental fountains and a splendid view of the western facade of the palace.

South of Plaza Mayor

The areas south of Pza. Mayor have traditionally been tough, working-class districts, with tenement buildings thrown up to accommodate the expansion of the population in the eighteenth and nineteenth centuries. In many places, these old houses survive, huddled together in narrow streets, but the character of **La Latina** and **Lavapiés** has changed as their inhabitants, and the districts themselves, have become younger, more fashionable and more cosmopolitan. The streets in and around Cava Baja and Cava Alta in La Latina, for example, include some of the city's most popular bars and restaurants. These are attractive *barrios* to explore, particularly for bar-hopping or during the Sunday-morning flea market, El Rastro (see page 74), which takes place along and around the Ribera de Curtidores (ⓂLa Latina/Tirso de Molina).

EL RASTRO

Madrid's flea market, **El Rastro**, is as much a part of the city's weekend ritual as a Mass or a *paseo*. This gargantuan, thriving shambles of a street market sprawls south from Metro La Latina to the Ronda de Toledo, especially along Ribera de Curtidores. Through it, crowds flood between 10am and 3pm every Sunday and on public holidays, too. On offer is just about anything you might – or more likely might not – need, from secondhand clothes and military-surplus items to flamenco fans and antiques.

Some of the goods are so far gone that you can't imagine any of them ever selling. Others may be quite valuable, but on the whole it's the stuff of markets around the world you'll find here: pseudo-designer clothes, bags and T-shirts. Don't expect to find fabulous bargains, or the hidden Old Masters of popular myth: the serious antique trade has mostly moved off the streets and into the surrounding shops, while the real junk is now found only on the fringes. Nonetheless, the atmosphere of El Rastro is always enjoyable, and the bars around these streets are as good as any in the city. One warning, though: keep a close eye on your bags, pockets, cameras (best left at the hotel) and jewellery. The Rastro rings up a fair percentage of Madrid's tourist thefts.

Around La Latina

La Latina is a short walk south from Pza. de la Villa and, if you're exploring Madrid de los Austrias, it's a natural continuation, as some of the squares, streets and churches here date back to the early Habsburg period. One of the most attractive pockets is around **Pza. de la Paja**, a delightful square behind the large church of **San Andrés**, and once home to one of the city's medieval markets. In summer, there are a couple of *terrazas* here, tucked well away from the traffic.

Iglesia de San Andrés, Capilla del Obispo and Capilla de San Isidro

Pza. de San Andrés & Pza. de la Paja • **Iglesia de San Andrés** Free • **Capilla del Obispo** Charge, guided visits only • http://museocatedral.archimadrid.es/capilla-del-obispo • Ⓜ La Latina

The **Iglesia de San Andrés** and the **Capilla de San Isidro** can be reached from Pza. de San Andrés. Inside is a beautifully sculpted dome depicting angels laden with fruit and a red-marble backdrop fronted by black columns and sculptures of saints. The chapel of San Isidro was built in the mid-seventeenth century to hold the remains of Madrid's patron saint (since moved to the Iglesia de San Isidro). The adjoining Gothic **Capilla del Obispo** (entrance on Pza. de la Paja), with its impressive polychromed altarpiece and alabaster tombs, reopened in 2010 following a forty-year restoration saga.

Museo de San Isidro: Los Orígenes de Madrid

Pza. San Andrés 2 • Free • www.madrid.es/museosanisidro • Ⓜ La Latina

Alongside the church of San Andrés is one of the city's newer museums, the **Museo de San Isidro**, housed in a sixteenth-century mansion owned by the counts of Paredes and supposedly once the home of Madrid's patron saint. The museum traces the city's origins through to its establishment as the Spanish capital. The **archeological collection**, which consists of relics from the earliest settlements along the River Manzanares and nearby Roman villas, is in the basement. The rest of the museum is given over to exhibits on the later history of the city and also to **San Isidro** and his miraculous activities, including the well from which he is said to have rescued his own son.

San Francisco el Grande

Pza. de San Francisco 11 • Charge, with guided tour • 913 653 800 • Ⓜ La Latina

A couple of minutes' walk southwest of the Museo de San Isidro down the hill is one of Madrid's grandest, richest and most elaborate churches, **San Francisco el Grande**. Built towards the end of the eighteenth century as part of Carlos III's renovations of the city, it has a dome even larger than that of St Paul's in London. The interior, which you can only visit with a guided tour, contains splendid paintings by, among others, Goya and Zurbarán, and some magnificent frescoes by Bayeu.

Iglesia Colegiata de San Isidro
C/Toledo 37 • Ⓜ La Latina

The vast **Iglesia Colegiata de San Isidro** was originally the centre of the Jesuit Order in Spain. After Carlos III fell out with the Order in 1767, he redesigned the interior and dedicated it to the city's patron, whose remains are entombed within. The church acted as the city's cathedral prior to the completion of the Almudena by the Palacio Real, but relics and altarpiece aside, its chief attribute is its size. Next door is the **Instituto Real**, a school that has been in existence considerably longer than the church and counts among its former pupils such literary notables as Calderón de la Barca, Lope de Vega, Quevedo and Pío Baroja.

Puerta de Toledo
Ⓜ Puerta de Toledo

If you proceed south to the end of Ribera de Curtidores, whose antique shops (some, these days, extremely upmarket) stay open all week, you'll see a large arch, the **Puerta de Toledo**, at one end of the Ronda de Toledo. The only surviving relation to the Puerta de Alcalá in the Pza. de la Independencia, this gate was originally designed to be built as a triumphal arch to honour the conquering Napoleon. However, it was not constructed until after his defeat in the Peninsular War, so instead became a symbol of the city's freedom. Adjacent to the arch is the Mercado Puerta de Toledo, once the site of the city's fish market, and now a teaching centre for one of the local universities.

Lavapiés

A good point at which to start exploring the multicultural *barrio* of **Lavapiés** is the Pza. Tirso de Molina (Ⓜ Tirso de Molina). From here, you can follow C/Mesón de Paredes, stopping for a drink at one of the city's most traditional bars, the *Taberna Antonio Sánchez* at no. 13, past rows of wholesale clothes shops to **La Corrala**, on the corner of C/Sombrerete. This is one of many traditional *corrales* – tenement blocks – in the quarter, built with balconied apartments opening onto a central patio. Plays, especially farces and *zarzuelas* (a kind of operetta), used to be performed regularly in Spanish *corrales*, and the open space here usually hosts a few performances in the summer. It has been sympathetically renovated and declared a national monument.

From Metro Lavapiés, you can take **C/Argumosa** towards the Museo Reina Sofía. Don't miss out on the opportunity to sample some of the excellent local bars on this pleasant tree-lined street while you're here.

Cine Doré
C/Santa Isabel 3 • 913 691 125 • Ⓜ Antón Martín

To the north of the quarter is the **Cine Doré**, the oldest cinema in Madrid, dating from 1922, which has a late modernist/Art Nouveau facade. It has been converted to house the Filmoteca Nacional, an art-film centre (see page 112) with bargain prices that often shows English-language films and has a pleasant and inexpensive **café/restaurant**.

East of Sol: Plaza de Santa Ana to Plaza de Cibeles

The **Pza. de Santa Ana/Huertas** area lies at the heart of a triangle, bordered to the east by the Paseo del Prado, to the north by C/Alcalá and along the south by C/Atocha,

1

with the Puerta del Sol at the western tip. The city reached this district after expanding beyond the Palacio Real and the Pza. Mayor, so the buildings date predominantly from the nineteenth century. Many of them have literary associations: there are streets named after Cervantes and Lope de Vega (where one lived and the other died), and the *barrio* is host to the Atheneum club, Círculo de Bellas Artes (Fine Arts Institute), Teatro Español and the Congreso de los Diputados (parliament). Just to the north, there is also an important museum, the **Real Academia de Bellas Artes de San Fernando**.

For most visitors, though, the major attraction is that this district holds some of the best and most beautiful **bars** and **tascas** in the city. They are concentrated particularly around Pza. de Santa Ana and the streets that run into Huertas.

Plaza de Santa Ana and around

Ⓜ Sol/Sevilla

The bars around **Pza. de Santa Ana** really are sights in themselves. On the square itself, the dark wood-panelled *Cervecería Alemana* was a firm favourite of Hemingway's and has hardly changed since the turn of the twentieth century. Flanking one side of the plaza is the elegant facade of the emblematic *ME Madrid Reina Victoria* hotel, once a favourite of bullfighters and now the designer showpiece for the Sol-Meliá chain, while at the other end are the polished lines of the nineteenth-century Neoclassical pile, the Teatro Español.

Viva Madrid, on the northeast corner at C/Manuel Fernández y González 7, should be another port of call, if only to admire the fabulous tile work, original zinc bar and a ceiling supported by wooden caryatids.

Huertas

The area around pedestrianized **C/Huertas** itself is workaday enough – sleepy by day but buzzing by night – and, again, packed with bars. North of here, and parallel, are two streets named in honour of the greatest figures of Spain's seventeenth-century literary golden age, Cervantes and Lope de Vega. Bitter rivals in life, both are probably spinning in their graves now, since Cervantes is interred in the **Convento de las Trinitarias** on the street named after Lope de Vega, while the latter's house, the **Casa de Lope de Vega**, finds itself on C/Cervantes. In 2015, forensic scientists found a casket in the convent crypt containing human remains and labelled with Cervantes' initials. The remains were reburied in the Iglesia de San Ildefonso which lies within the convent.

Casa de Lope de Vega

C/Cervantes 11 • Free • http://casamuseolopedevega.org • Ⓜ Antón Martín

The charming little **Casa de Lope de Vega** provides a fascinating reconstruction of life in seventeenth-century Madrid; behind the innocuous wooden door you will be taken on a tour of the Spanish Golden Age dramatist's former home, which includes a chapel containing some of his relics and a delightful little patio garden.

El Congreso

C/San Jerónimo s/n • Free; passport essential • http://congreso.es • Ⓜ Sevilla

El Congreso de Los Diputados is an unprepossessing nineteenth-century building where the Congress (the lower house) meets. Sessions can be visited by appointment only, though anyone can turn up for the tour on Saturday mornings. You're shown, among other things, the bullet holes left by Colonel Tejero and his Guardia Civil associates in the abortive coup attempt of 1981.

Círculo de Bellas Artes

C/Alcalá 42 • Charge • http://circulobellasartes.com • Ⓜ Sevilla

Cut across to C/Alcalá from Pza. de las Cortes and you'll emerge close to the **Círculo de Bellas Artes**, a strange-looking 1920s building crowned by a statue of Pallas Athene. This is one of Madrid's foremost arts centres, and includes a theatre, music hall, cinema, exhibition galleries and a very pleasant bar – all marble and leather decor, with a nude statue reclining in the middle of the floor. It attracts the capital's arts and media crowd but is not in the slightest exclusive, and there's an adjoining terraza and a great rooftop bar, too. The Círculo is theoretically a members-only club, but it issues €5 day-membership on the door, for which you get access to the roof terrace and exhibitions.

Plaza de la Cibeles and Real Academia de Bellas Artes

Close to the Círculo and past an imposing array of grandiose buildings on C/Alcalá lies one of Spain's leading art galleries, the **Real Academia de Bellas Artes**, one for art buffs who have some appetite left after the Prado, Thyssen-Bornemisza and Reina Sofía. Half a kilometre to the east is **Pza. de la Cibeles**. Awash in a sea of traffic in the centre of the square are a **fountain** and statue of the goddess Cibeles, which survived the bombardments of the Civil War by being swaddled from helmet to hoof in sandbags. It was designed, as were the two other fountains gushing magnificently along the Paseo del Prado, by Ventura Rodríguez. The fountain is the scene of celebrations for victorious Real Madrid fans (Atlético supporters bathe in the fountain of Neptune just down the road).

Palacio de Cibeles, CentroCentro and Casa de América

Casa de América Charge • http://casamerica.es/visitas • Ⓜ Banco de España

The monumental wedding-cake building on the eastern side of Pza. de Cibeles was until quite recently Madrid's main post office. Constructed from 1904 to 1917, **Palacio de Cibeles** is vastly more imposing than the parliament and runs the Palacio Real pretty close. The city council took a shine to it and it now provides a home for the burgeoning **municipal offices**. It is also home to a smart exhibition space **CentroCentro**, with a viewing gallery (charge), a café, an expensive restaurant and an overpriced terrace bar. Adjacent, a palatial eighteenth-century mansion built by the Marqués de Linares is home to the **Casa de América**, a cultural organization promoting Latin American art and hosting temporary exhibitions which runs guided tours at weekends.

Real Academia de Bellas Artes de San Fernando

C/Alcalá 13 • Charge, free Wed • http://realacademiabellasartessanfernando.com • Ⓜ Sevilla

The **Real Academia** has traditionally been viewed as one of the most important art galleries in Spain. Admittedly, you have to plough through a fair number of dull academic canvases, but there are some hidden gems. These include a group of small panels by **Goya**, in particular *The Burial of the Sardine* and two revealing self-portraits, and a curious *Family of El Greco*, which may be by the great man or his son. Two other rooms are devoted to foreign artists, in particular Rubens. Upstairs, there is a series of sketches by Picasso, and a brutally graphic set of sculptures depicting the *Massacre of the Innocents* by José Ginés. It is also home to the national chalcography (copper or brass engraving) collection (closed Aug), which includes a number of Goya etchings used for his *Capricho* series on show at the Prado.

The Paseo del Arte

Madrid's three world-class art museums, the Prado, Thyssen-Bornemisza and Reina Sofía, are all along or close to the Paseo del Prado within a kilometre of each other in what is commonly known as the **Paseo del Arte**. The most famous of the three galleries is the **Prado**, which houses an unequalled display of Spanish art, an outstanding Flemish collection and an impressive assemblage of Italian work. The

1

Thyssen-Bornemisza provides an unprecedented excursion through Western art from the fourteenth to the late twentieth centuries. The final member of the trio, the **Reina Sofía**, is home to the Spanish collection of contemporary art, including the Miró and Picasso legacies and the jewel in the crown – *Guernica*.

Museo del Prado

C/Ruiz de Alarcón 23 • Charge; free for under-18s, students under 25 and travellers with disabilities • http://museodelprado.es • Ⓜ Banco de España/Atocha

The **Museo del Prado** is Madrid's premier attraction – well over two million visitors enter its doors each year – and one of the oldest and greatest collections of art in the world. Built as a natural science museum in 1775, the Prado opened to the public in 1819, and houses the finest works collected by Spanish royalty – for the most part, avid, discerning and wealthy buyers – as well as Spanish paintings gathered from other sources over the past two centuries. The €152 million Rafael Moneo-designed **extension**, which includes a stylish glass-fronted building incorporating the eighteenth-century cloisters of the San Jerónimo church, houses the restaurant and café areas, a shop, an auditorium, temporary exhibition spaces, restoration and conservation workshops and a sculpture gallery.

The museum's highlights are its early Flemish collection – including almost all of **Bosch**'s best work – and, of course, its incomparable display of Spanish art, in particular that of **Velázquez** (including *Las Meninas*), **Goya** (including the *Maja*s and the *Black Paintings*) and **El Greco**. There's also a huge section of Italian painters (**Titian**, notably) collected by Carlos V and Felipe II, both great patrons of the Renaissance, and an excellent collection of seventeenth-century Flemish and Dutch pictures gathered by Felipe IV, including **Rubens**' *Three Graces*. The museum also hosts an increasing number of critically acclaimed temporary displays. Even in a full day you couldn't hope to do justice to everything here, and it's perhaps best to make a couple of more focused visits, returning when entry is free at the end of the day.

INFORMATION AND TOURS   **MUSEO DEL PRADO**

Tickets are purchased at the Puerta de Goya opposite the *Hotel Ritz* on C/Felipe IV, and the **entrances** are round the back at the Puerta de los Jerónimos, which leads into the new extension, or at the side at the Puerta de Goya Alta. If you want to avoid the lengthy queues for tickets, a better option is to buy them in advance via the museum website (http://museodelprado.es). The Puerta de Murillo entrance, opposite the botanical gardens, is for school and university groups only.

Tours What follows is, by necessity, only a brief guide to the museum contents. If you want more background on the key paintings pick up an audio-guide (charge; children's version also available), a visitor's guide covering 50 key masterpieces, or the comprehensive 480-page Prado guide in the bookshop. A lunchtime or early-evening visit is often a good plan if you want to avoid the worst of the crowds and tour groups.

Exploring the museum

To follow the **route** proposed by the museum, bear right after the Puerta de los Jerónimos entrance and head into the central hallway – the Sala de las Musas. From here you are guided through the early Flemish, Italian and Spanish collections on the ground floor before being directed upstairs. A tour of the sixteenth- and seventeenth-century Italian and French collections in the northern wing gives way to the Flemish

---

PASEO DEL ARTE COMBINED ENTRY TICKET

If you plan to visit all three art museums on the Paseo del Prado during your stay, it's worth buying the under-advertised **Paseo del Arte ticket**, which is valid for a year and allows one visit to each museum at a substantial saving, although it does not include the temporary exhibitions. It's available at any of the three museums and gives you a significant saving on full-price tickets.

1

and Dutch galleries on the second floor where work from Rubens and Rembrandt is to the fore. Back on the first floor, visitors are ushered through the Spanish Golden Age collections with their heavyweight contributions from El Greco, Velázquez and Murillo before enjoying the delights of Goya which stretch up to the second floor once again. From there you return to the ground floor for Goya's *Black Paintings* before concluding the visit with a tour of the grandiose historical epics that make up the remainder of the nineteenth-century Spanish collection.

Spanish painting

The Prado's collections of Spanish painting begin on the ground floor (rooms 50–52C) with the striking cycles of twelfth-century **Romanesque frescoes** reconstructed from a pair of churches from the Mozarabic (Muslim rule) era in Soria and Segovia. **Early panel paintings** – exclusively religious fourteenth- and fifteenth-century works – include a huge *retablo* (altarpiece) by Nicolás Francés; the anonymous *Virgin of the Catholic Monarchs*; Bermejo's *Santo Domingo de Silos*; and Pedro Berruguete's *Auto-da-Fé*.

The Golden Age: Velázquez and El Greco

Upstairs, the collections from Spain's Golden Age – the late sixteenth and seventeenth centuries under Habsburg rule – are prefigured by a fabulous array of paintings by **El Greco** (1540–1614), the Cretan-born artist who worked in Toledo from the 1570s. You

---

PRADO HIGHLIGHTS

The Prado is much too big for a single visit to do the collection justice; however, if you are pressed for time here is a list of some of the **works you should not miss**.

The Garden of Earthly Delights by Bosch. A surrealistic masterpiece years ahead of its time.

The Triumph of Death by Pieter Brueghel. A disturbing and macabre depiction of hell by the Flemish master.

The Annunciation by Fra Angelico. A groundbreaking early Renaissance work.

Self-portrait by Dürer. Insightful self-portrait by the German genius.

The Descent from the Cross by Van der Weyden. An emotive and colourful depiction of the Deposition.

The Romanesque frescoes. Stunning frescoes from the Romanesque churches in Segovia and Soria.

David and Goliath by Caravaggio. The Italian's theatrical use of chiaroscuro at its best.

The Adoration of the Shepherds by El Greco. One of a series of revolutionary Mannerist works by the Greek-born painter.

Las Meninas by Velázquez. One of the most technically adroit and fascinating paintings in Western art.

Artemisa by Rembrandt. The Dutchman used his wife Saskia as a model for this portrayal of the heroic queen.

Sir Endymion Porter by Van Dyck. A superlative work by the Dutch court painter famous for his portraits of Charles I.

The Three Graces by Rubens. One of the great classically inspired works by the Flemish genius.

Charles V at Mühlberg by Titian. A magnificent equestrian portrait of the Holy Roman Emperor.

The Lavatorio by Tintoretto. Epic masterpiece depicting Christ washing the feet of the disciples, that once belonged to Charles I.

La Maja Desnuda and **La Maja Vestida** by Goya. A pair of supremely seductive portraits of a woman reclining on a bed of pillows, one clothed, one naked.

Dos and Tres de Mayo by Goya. Timeless and iconic images on the horror of war.

Goya's Black Paintings. A series of penetrating and haunting images from the latter part of Goya's career.

1

really need to have taken in the works in Toledo to appreciate fully his extraordinary genius, but the portraits and religious works here (rooms 8B–10B), ranging from the Italianate *Trinity* to the visionary late *Adoration of the Shepherds*, are a good introduction.

In rooms 9A and 10–15A, you confront the greatest painter of Habsburg Spain, **Diego Velázquez** (1599–1660). Born in Portugal, Velázquez became court painter to Felipe IV, whose family is represented in many of the works: "I have found my Titian," Felipe is said to have remarked on his appointment. Velázquez's masterpiece, *Las Meninas*, is displayed in the octagonal central gallery (room 12) alongside studies for the painting. Manet remarked of it, "After this, I don't know why the rest of us paint," and the French poet Théophile Gautier asked "But where is the picture?" when he saw it, because it seemed to him a continuation of the room. *Vulcan's Forge*, *Las Hilanderas*, showing the royal tapestry factory at work, *Christ Crucified* and *Los Borrachos* (*The Drunkards*) are further magnificent paintings. In fact, almost all of the fifty or so works on display (around half of the artist's surviving output) warrant close attention. Don't overlook the two small panels of the *Villa Medici*, painted in Rome in 1650, in virtually Impressionist style. There are several Velázquez canvases, including *The Surrender at Breda*, in the stunning collection of royal portraits and works depicting Spanish military victories.

In the adjacent rooms are examples of just about every significant Spanish painter of the seventeenth century, including many of the best works of **Francisco Zurbarán** (1598–1664), **Bartolomé Esteban Murillo** (1618–82), **Alonso Cano** (1601–67), **Juan de Valdés Leal** (1622–60) and **Juan Carreño** (1614–85). Note, in particular, Carreño's portrait of the last Habsburg monarch, Carlos II, rendered with terrible realism. There's also a fine selection of paintings by **José Ribera** (1591–1625), who worked mainly in Naples, and was influenced there by Caravaggio. His masterpieces are considered to be *The Martyrdom of St Philip* and the dark, realist portrait of *St Andrew*; look out, too, for the bizarre *Bearded Lady*.

Goya

The final suite of Spanish rooms (32 and 34–38), which continue up onto the second floor (85–94) and then down on to the ground floor (64–67), provides an awesome and fabulously complete overview of the output of **Francisco de Goya** (1746–1828), the largest and most valuable collection of his works in the world, with some 140 paintings and 500 drawings and engravings. Goya was the greatest painter of Bourbon Spain, a chronicler of Spain in his time, and an artist whom many see as the inspiration and forerunner of Impressionism and modern art. He was an enormously versatile artist: contrast the voluptuous *Maja Vestida* and *Maja Desnuda* (*The Clothed Belle* and *The Naked Belle*) with the horrors depicted in the *Dos de Mayo* and *Tres de Mayo* (moving, on-the-spot portrayals of the rebellion against Napoleon in the streets of Madrid and the subsequent reprisals). Then there is the series of pastoral cartoons – designs for tapestries – and the extraordinary Black Paintings (room 67), a series of disconcerting murals painted on the walls of his home by the deaf and embittered painter in his old age. The many portraits of his patron, Carlos IV, are remarkable for their lack of any attempt at flattery, while those of Queen María Luisa, whom he despised, are downright ugly.

The nineteenth century

The Prado's collection of melodramatic nineteenth-century Spanish art can be found in the ground-floor rooms 60–66 and 75. Theatrical works by Eduardo Rosales and Antonio Gisbert are combined with some fine luminous canvases by Spanish Impressionist Joaquin Sorolla.

Italian painting

The Prado's Italian galleries begin on the ground floor (49 and 56B) and are distinguished principally by **Fra Angelico**'s *Annunciation* (c.1445) and by a trio of panels by **Botticelli** (1445–1510). The latter illustrate a deeply unpleasant story from the *Decameron* about a woman hunted by hounds; the fourth panel (in a private collection in the US) gives a happier conclusion. Here too are major works by **Raphael** (1483–1520), including the fabulous *Portrait of a Cardinal*.

With the sixteenth-century Renaissance, the collection really comes into its own. The Prado is said to have the most complete collection of Titians and painters from the Venetian School of any single museum. On the first floor there are epic masterpieces from the Venetians **Tintoretto** (1518–94), such as the beautifully composed *Lavatorio*, bought by Felipe IV when Charles I of England was beheaded and his art collection was auctioned off, and **Veronese** (1528–88), as well as **Caravaggio** (1573–1610), whose brutal *David with the Head of Goliath* is another highlight. The most important works, however, are by **Titian** (1487–1576) in rooms 24–27 and 41–44. These include portraits of the Spanish emperors *Carlos V* and *Felipe II* (Carlos' suit of armour is preserved in the Palacio Real), and a famous, much-reproduced piece of erotica, *Venus, Cupid and the Organist* (two versions are displayed here), a painting originally owned by a bishop.

Flemish, Dutch and German painting

The biggest name in the **early Flemish collection** (room 56A) is **Hieronymus Bosch** (1450–1516), known in Spain as "El Bosco". The Prado has several of his greatest triptychs: the early-period *Hay Wain*, the middle-period *Garden of Earthly Delights* and the late *Adoration of the Magi* – all familiar from countless reproductions but infinitely more chilling in the original. Bosch's hallucinatory genius for the macabre is at its most extreme in these triptychs, but is reflected here in many more of his works, including three versions of *The Temptations of St Anthony* (though only the smallest of these is definitely an original). Don't miss, either, the amazing table-top of *The Seven Deadly Sins*.

Bosch's visions find an echo in the works of **Pieter Brueghel the Elder** (1525–69), whose *Triumph of Death* must be one of the most frightening canvases ever painted. Another elusive painter, **Joachim Patinir**, is represented by four of his finest works. From an earlier generation, **Rogier van der Weyden**'s *Descent from the Cross* is outstanding; its monumental forms make a fascinating contrast with his miniature-like *Pietà*. There are also important works by Memling, Bouts, Gerard David and Massys.

The collection of **later Flemish and Dutch art** is on the first floor (rooms 16B and 28–29), and there are enough works here to make an excellent comparison between the flamboyant Counter-Reformation propaganda of Flanders and the more austere bourgeois tastes of Holland. **Rubens** (1577–1640) is extensively represented, with the beautifully restored *Three Graces*, *The Judgement of Paris* and a series of eighteen mythological subjects designed for Felipe IV's hunting lodge in El Pardo (though Rubens supervised rather than executed these). There is, too, a fine collection of canvases by his contemporaries, including **Van Dyck**'s dramatic and deeply moving *Piedad*, and his magnificent portrait of himself and Sir Endymion Porter. **Jan Brueghel**'s representations of the five senses and **David Teniers**' scenes of peasant lowlife also merit a closer look. For political reasons, Spanish monarchs collected few works painted from seventeenth-century Protestant Holland; an early **Rembrandt**, *Judith at the Banquet of Holofernes*, in which the artist's pregnant wife served as the model, is, however, an important exception.

The **German room** (55B) on the ground floor is dominated by **Dürer** (1471–1528) and **Lucas Cranach the Elder** (1472–1553). Dürer's magnificent *Adam and Eve* was saved from destruction at the hands of the prudish Carlos III only by the intervention of his court painter, Mengs, whose own paintings are on the first and second floors in rooms 20 and 89. The most interesting of Cranach's works is a pair of paintings depicting Carlos V hunting with Ferdinand I of Austria.

French and British painting

Most of the **French** work held by the Prado is from the seventeenth and eighteenth centuries (rooms 2, 3, 19, 21 and 39 on the first floor). Among the outstanding painters represented is **Nicolas Poussin** (1594–1665), with his Baroque work shown to best effect

1

in *Triumph of David*, *Landscape with St Jerome* and *Mount Parnassus*. The romantic landscapes and sunsets of **Claude Lorraine** (1600–82) are well represented, and look out for **Hyacinthe Rigaud**'s (1659–1743) portrayal of the imperious *Louis XIV*.

British painting is thin on the ground – a product of the hostile relations between the Spanish and English from the sixteenth to nineteenth centuries. There is, however, a small sample of eighteenth-century portraiture from **Joshua Reynolds** (1723–92) and **Thomas Gainsborough** (1727–88) in room 20 on the first floor.

The Tesoro del Dauphin

The museum's basement houses the **Tesoro del Dauphin** (Treasure of the Dauphin), a display of part of the collection of jewels that belonged to the Grand Dauphin Louis, son of Louis XIV and father of Felipe V, Spain's first Bourbon king. The collection includes goblets, cups, trays, glasses and other pieces richly decorated with rubies, emeralds, diamonds, lapis lazuli and other precious stones.

Museo Thyssen-Bornemisza

Paseo del Prado 8 • Charge; combined admission with Paseo del Arte ticket (see page 78); free for under-18s and on Mon for Mastercard holders only • http://museothyssen.org • Ⓜ Banco de España

The **Museo Thyssen-Bornemisza** occupies the old Palacio de Villahermosa, diagonally opposite the Prado, at the end of Pza. de las Cortes. This prestigious site played a large part in Spain's acquisition – for a knock-down $350 million in June 1993 – of what many argue was the world's greatest private art trove after that of the British royals: some seven hundred paintings accumulated by father-and-son German-Hungarian industrial magnates. The son, Baron Hans Heinrich Thyssen, died in April 2002 aged 81. Another trump card was the late baron's fifth wife, Carmen Cervera (aka "Tita" Cervera), a former Miss Spain, who steered the works to Spain against the efforts of Britain's Prince Charles, the Swiss and German governments, the Getty foundation and other suitors.

The museum had no expense spared on its design – again in the hands of the ubiquitous Rafael Moneo, responsible for the remodelling of Estación de Atocha and the extension at the Prado – with stucco walls (Carmen insisted on salmon pink) and marble floors. A terribly kitsch portrait of Carmen with a lapdog hangs in the great hall of the museum, alongside those of her husband and King Juan Carlos and Queen Sofía. Pass beyond, however, and you are into seriously premier-league art: **medieval to eighteenth-century** on the second floor, **seventeenth-century Dutch** and **Rococo and Neoclassicism to Fauves and Expressionists** on the first floor, and **Surrealists**, **Pop Art** and the **avant-garde** on ground level. Highlights are legion in a collection that displays an almost stamp-collecting mentality in its examples of nearly every major artist and movement: how the Thyssens got hold of classic works by everyone from Duccio and Holbein, through El Greco and Caravaggio, to Schiele and Rothko, takes your breath away.

Carmen has a substantial collection of her own (over six hundred works), which has been housed in the **extension**, built on the site of an adjoining mansion and cleverly integrated into the original format of the museum. It is particularly strong on nineteenth-century landscape, North American, Impressionist and Post-Impressionist work. The ground floor is home to a large temporary exhibition space, which has staged a number of interesting and highly successful shows.

There's a handy cafeteria and restaurant on the ground floor of the extension, overlooking a pleasant outdoor terrace; there's also a shop, where you can buy a wide variety of art books, guides to the museum, postcards and other souvenirs. Advance tickets for the museum, a good idea in high season, are available via the website.

The second floor: European old masters and Carmen's collection

Take a lift to the second floor and you will find yourself at the chronological start of the museum's collections: European painting (and some sculpture) from the fourteenth to the eighteenth century. The core of these collections was accumulated in the 1920s and 1930s by the late baron's father, Heinrich, who was a friend of the art critics Bernard Berenson and Max Friedländer. He was clearly well advised. The early paintings include incredibly good (and rare) devotional panels by the Sienese painter **Duccio di Buoninsegna**, and the Flemish artists **Jan van Eyck** and **Rogier van der Weyden**. You then move into a fabulous array of Renaissance portraits (room 5), which include three of the very greatest of the period: **Ghirlandaio**'s *Portrait of Giovanna Tornabuoni*, **Hans Holbein**'s *Portrait of Henry VIII* (the only one of many variants in existence that is definitely genuine) and **Raphael**'s *Portrait of a Young Man. A Spanish Infanta* by **Juan de Flandes** may represent the first of Henry VIII's wives, Catherine of Aragón, while the *Young Knight* by **Carpaccio** is one of the earliest-known full-length portraits of the king. Beyond these is a collection of **Dürer**s and **Cranach**s to rival that in the Prado, and as you progress through this extraordinary panoply, display cases along the corridor contain scarcely less spectacular works of sculpture, ceramics and gold- and silverwork.

Next in line, in room 11, are **Titian** and **Tintoretto**, and three paintings by **El Greco**, one early, two late, which make an interesting comparison with each other and with those in the Prado. **Caravaggio**'s monumental *St Catherine of Alexandria* (room 12) is the centrepiece of an important display of works by followers of this innovator of chiaroscuro. As you reach the eighteenth century, there is a room containing three flawless **Canaletto** views of Venice (room 17). Tagged onto this floor are the first galleries (lettered A–H) that make up the initial section of Carmen's collection. **Luca Giordano**'s monumental *Judgement of Solomon* and a **Van Dyck** *Crucifixion* (room A) are two of the early highlights. Gallery C traces the development of landscapes from early Flemish works through to the nineteenth century. Beyond are some interesting works by North American and European artists that complement the baron's collection and some soothing Impressionist offerings by **Degas**, **Renoir**, **Pissarro**, **Monet** and **Sisley**. Constable's *Lock*, however, is no longer in the collection, Carmen having, controversially, sold it for £22.4 million in 2012 because she had "no liquidity", a decision that prompted the resignation of museum trustee Sir Norman Rosenthal.

The first floor: Americans, Impressionists and Expressionists

The route now takes you downstairs through the remainder of Carmen's collection (rooms I–P), beginning with further Impressionist work, taking in some delightful canvases by **Gauguin** and the Post-Impressionists and ending with some striking Expressionist pieces by **Kandinsky** and **Robert Delaunay**.

From room P, walk along the corridor to rejoin the baron's collection. After a comprehensive round of seventeenth-century Dutch painting of various genres, Rococo and Neoclassicism, you reach some **English portraiture** by Gainsborough, Reynolds and Zoffany (room 28) and **American painting** in rooms 29 and 30. The collection, one of the best outside the US, concentrates on landscapes and includes James Goodwyn Clonney's wonderful *Fishing Party on Long Island Sound*, and works by James Whistler, Winslow Homer and John Singer Sargent.

As with Carmen's collection, **Impressionism** and **Post-Impressionism** are another strong point, with a selection of paintings by Vincent van Gogh, including one of his last and most gorgeous works, *Les Vessenots* (room 32). **Expressionism**, meanwhile, is represented by some stunning works by Ernst Ludwig Kirchner, Franz Marc, Wassily Kandinsky and Max Beckmann.

The ground floor: avant-garde

Works on the ground floor run from the beginning of the twentieth century through to around 1970. The good baron didn't, apparently, like contemporary art: "If they can throw colours, I can be free to duck," he explained, following the gallery's opening.

The most interesting work in his "experimental avant-garde" sections is from the **Cubists**. There is an inspired, side-by-side hanging of parallel studies by Picasso

1

(*Man with a Clarinet*) and Braque (*Woman with a Mandolin*). Later choices include a scattering of Joan Miró, Jackson Pollock, Dalí, Rauschenberg and Lichtenstein. In the **Synthesis of Modernity** section, there are some superbly vivid canvases by Max Ernst and Marc Chagall, a brilliant portrait of George Dyer by Francis Bacon, and a fascinating **Lucian Freud**, *Portrait of Baron Thyssen*, posed in front of the Watteau *Pierrot* hanging upstairs (both in room 47).

Museo Reina Sofía

C/Santa Isabel 52 • Charge, free last two hours of opening and Sunday afternoons; free for under-18s and over–65s; or Paseo del Arte ticket (see page 78) • http://museoreinasofia.es • ⓜ Atocha

It is fortunate that the **Museo Reina Sofía**, facing Estación de Atocha at the end of Paseo del Prado, keeps slightly different opening hours and days to its neighbours. For this leading exhibition space and permanent gallery of modern Spanish art – its centrepiece is Picasso's greatest picture, *Guernica* – is another essential stop on the Madrid art circuit, and one that really shouldn't be seen after a Prado-Thyssen overdose.

The museum, a vast former hospital, is a kind of Madrid response to the Pompidou Centre in Paris, with transparent lifts shuttling visitors up the outside of the Sabatini building to the permanent collection. Like the other two great art museums, it also underwent a major **extension** programme – the French architect Jean Nouvel added a massive state-of-the-art metal-and-glass wing behind the main block in 2005. If the queues at the main entrance are too long, try the alternative one in the new extension on the Ronda de Atocha. You can also buy tickets in advance via the website.

The Santini building

It is for **Picasso's Guernica** that most visitors come to the Reina Sofía, and rightly so. Superbly displayed, this icon of twentieth-century Spanish art and politics carries a shock that defies all familiarity. Picasso painted it in response to the bombing of the Basque town of Gernika by the German Luftwaffe, acting in concert with Franco, in the Spanish Civil War. In the fascinating preliminary studies, displayed around the room, you can see how he developed its symbols – the dying horse, the woman mourning her dead, the bull, the sun, the flower, the light bulb – and then return to the painting to marvel at how he made it all work.

The painting was first exhibited in Paris in 1937, as part of a Spanish Republican Pavilion in the Expo there, and was then loaned to the Museum of Modern Art in New York, until, as Picasso put it, Spain had rid itself of Fascist rule. The artist never lived to see that time, but in 1981, following the restoration of democracy, the painting was, amid much controversy, moved to Madrid to hang (as Picasso had stipulated) in the Prado. Its transfer to the Reina Sofía in 1992 again prompted much soul-searching and protest, though for anyone who saw it in the old Prado annexe, it looks truly liberated in its present setting. Many Basques believe the painting's rightful home is with them, but studies have revealed cracks and fissures that make the painting too fragile to move once again.

Guernica hangs midway around Collection 1 on the second floor. It is displayed adjacent to rooms dedicated to the Spanish Pavilion in the 1937 Expo. There are strong sections on **Cubism** and the **Paris School**, in the first of which Picasso is again well represented, alongside work by French artist Georges Braque and Spaniard Juan Gris.

Dalí and **Miró** make heavyweight contributions to the nearby halls. Miró, who once claimed that he wanted "to assassinate painting", is represented with a series of characteristically striking and enigmatic canvases. The development of Dalí's work and his variety of techniques are clearly displayed here, with works ranging from the classic *Muchacha en la Ventana* to famous surrealist works such as *El Gran Masturbador* and *El Enigma de Hitler*. There is an impressive collection of Spanish sculpture to be found in the final rooms.

The fourth floor, which houses Collection 2, covers themes from the postwar years up to the late 1960s and includes Spanish and international examples of **abstract** and **avant-garde** movements. Outstanding pieces from **Francis Bacon** (*Reclining Figure*), **Henry Moore** and **Graham Sutherland** give a British context, while challenging work from **Antoni Tapiès**, **Antonio Saura** and **Eduardo Chillida** provide the Spanish perspective. If the avant-garde work all gets too much, you'll find some more accessible offerings from the Spanish realists here too.

The Area Nouvel

The extension, or the **Nouvel wing** as it is known, consists of three buildings built around an open courtyard topped by a striking delta-shaped, metallic, crimson-coloured roof. It is home to Collection 3 which deals with themes from the final years of the Francoist dictatorship through to the present day. The new wing also houses an auditorium, a library, a café-restaurant and a bookshop that sells a wide range of glossy coffee-table volumes, as well as more academic tomes and the informative museum guidebook, which examines eighty key works in detail.

Parque del Retiro and around

When you get tired of sightseeing, Madrid's many parks are great places to escape for a few hours. The most central and most popular of them is **El Retiro**, a delightful mix of formal gardens and wider open spaces. Nearby, in addition to the Prado, Thyssen-Bornemisza and Reina Sofía galleries, are a number of the city's **smaller museums**, plus the startlingly peaceful **Jardines Botánicos**.

Parque del Retiro

Free • Ⓜ Retiro

Originally the grounds of a royal retreat (*retiro*) and designed in the French style, the **Parque del Retiro** has been public property for more than a hundred years. In its 330 acres you can jog, row in the lake (you can rent boats by the Monumento a Alfonso XII), picnic (though officially not on the grass), have your fortune told and – above all – promenade. The busiest day is Sunday, when half of Madrid, replete with spouses, in-laws and kids, turns out for the *paseo*. Dressed for show, the families stroll around, nodding at neighbours and building up an appetite for a long Sunday lunch.

Strolling aside, there's almost always something going on in the park, including a good programme of **concerts** and **fairs** organized by the city council. Concerts tend to be held in the Quiosco de Música in the north of the park. The most popular of the fairs is the Feria del Libro (Book Fair), held in early June, when every publisher and half the country's bookshops set up stalls and offer a 25 percent discount on their wares. At weekends, there are **puppet shows** by the Puerta de Alcalá entrance, and on Sundays you can often watch groups of South American musicians performing by the lake.

A number of **stalls and cafés** along the Paseo Salón del Estanque sell drinks, *bocadillos* and *pipas* (sunflower seeds), and there are *terrazas*, too, for *horchata* and *granizados*. The park has a safe reputation, at least by day; in the late evening, it's best not to wander alone.

Palacio de Velázquez, Palacio de Cristal, Casa de Vacas and the Bosque del Recuerdo

Palacio de Velázquez & Palacio de Cristal Free • 915 746 614 • **Casa de Vacas** Free; closed Aug

Temporary art exhibitions are frequently housed in the beautifully tiled **Palacio de Velázquez**, the splendid glass and wrought-iron **Palacio de Cristal** and the more modest **Casa de Vacas**, all of which are inside the park. Look out, too, for **El Ángel Caído** (Fallen Angel), the world's only public statue to Lucifer, in the south of the park. There is

1

also the **Bosque del Recuerdo**, 192 olive trees and cypresses planted in the Paseo de la Chopera in memory of those who died in the train bombings at the nearby Atocha station on March 11, 2004.

Puerta de Alcalá

Ⓜ Retiro/Banco de España

The Parque del Retiro's northwest corner gives access to the Pza. de la Independencia, in the centre of which is one of the two remaining gates from the old city walls. Built in the late eighteenth century, the **Puerta de Alcalá** was the biggest in Europe at that time and, like the bear and *madroño* tree, has become one of the city's monumental emblems.

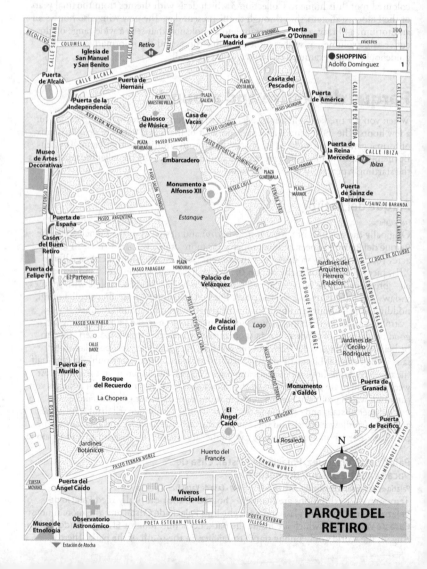

PARQUE DEL RETIRO

Museo de Artes Decorativas

C/Montalbán 12 • Charge, free Thurs evenings, Sat afternoons, Sun and Jul & Aug • http://culturaydeporte.gob.es/mnartesdecorativas • Ⓜ Banco de España/Retiro

Just south of Puerta de Alcalá is the **Museo de Artes Decorativas**, housed in a graceful-looking mansion close to the Retiro. The eclectic collection of furniture, glass, carpets, toys, clocks, jewellery and fans is interesting enough but the highlight is undoubtedly the beautifully tiled Valencian kitchen on the fourth floor with its superb painted *azulejos*.

Museo Naval

Paseo del Prado 5 • Free (bring ID), though a voluntary donation is requested • http://armada.mde.es/museonaval • Ⓜ Banco de España

A couple of blocks west of the Museo de Artes Décoratives in a corner of the Naval Ministry is the **Museo Naval**, strong, as you might expect, on maritime paintings, models, charts and navigational aids from or relating to the Spanish voyages of discovery. Exhibits include the first map to show the New World, drawn in 1500, a cannon from the Spanish Armada and part of Cortés' flag used in the conquest of Mexico.

San Jerónimo el Real

C/Ruiz de Alarcón 19 • Free • Ⓜ Banco de España/Estación del Arte

Just behind the Prado is **San Jerónimo el Real**, Madrid's society church, where in 1975 Juan Carlos (like his predecessors) was crowned. Despite significant remodelling and the addition of two Gothic towers, the old form of the church is still clearly visible; but the seventeenth-century cloisters have fallen victim to the Prado extension.

Real Academía Española de la Lengua

C/Felipe IV 4 • Ⓜ Banco de España/Estación del Arte

Opposite the church is the **Real Academia Española de la Lengua** (Royal Language Academy; not open to the public), whose job it is to make sure that the Spanish language is not corrupted by foreign or otherwise unsuitable words. The results are entrusted to their official dictionary – a work that bears virtually no relation to the Spanish you'll hear spoken on the streets.

Real Jardín Botánico

Pza. de Murillo 2 • Charge, under-18s free • www.rjb.csic.es • Ⓜ Estación del Arte

Immediately south of the Prado is the delightful, shaded **Real Jardín Botánico**. Opened in 1781 by Carlos III (known as *El Alcalde* – "The Mayor" – for his urban-improvement programmes), the garden once contained over 30,000 plants. The numbers are down these days, though the worldwide collection of flora is fascinating for any amateur botanist; don't miss the hothouse with its tropical plants and amazing cacti or the bonsai collection of former prime minister Felipe González. Temporary exhibitions take place in the Palacio Villanueva within the grounds.

La CaixaForum

Paseo del Prado 36 • Charge; prices differ depending on exhibit • http://obrasociallacaixa.org • Ⓜ Estación del Arte

Opposite the botanical gardens is **La CaixaForum**, an innovative and stylish exhibition space opened in 2008 by the powerful Catalan bank, which complements the existing attractions on the Paseo del Arte. The centre, which hosts a variety of high-quality temporary art shows, concerts and workshops, is flanked by an eye-catching vertical

1

garden designed by French botanist Patrick Blanc in which some 15,000 plants form an organic carpet extending across the wall. Inside, there's a decent art bookshop and a neat top-floor restaurant that serves a fine lunchtime set menu.

Estación de Atocha

Ⓜ Estación del Arte

On the far side of the botanical gardens from La CaixaForum is the sloping Cuesta de Moyano, lined with **bookstalls**; although it's at its busiest on Sundays, many of the stalls are open every day. Across the way, the **Estación de Atocha** is worth a look even if you're not travelling out of Madrid. It's actually two stations, old and new, the latter now sadly infamous as the scene of the horrific train bombings that killed 191 people and injured close to 2000 in March 2004. The original station, a glorious 1880s glasshouse, was revamped in the early 1990s with a spectacular tropical-garden centrepiece. It's a wonderful sight from the walkways above, and train buffs and architects will want to take a look at the high-speed AVE trains and the station beyond.

Museo Nacional de Antropología/Etnología

C/Alfonso XII 68 • Charge, under-18s & over-65s free, free Sat afternoons & Sun • http://culturaydeporte.gob.es/mnantropologia • Ⓜ Estación del Arte

Also in this area is the **Museo Nacional de Antropología/Etnología**, designed to give an overview of different cultures of the world, in particular those intertwined with Spanish history. The most unusual exhibits are to be found in a side room on the ground floor – a macabre collection of deformed skulls, a Guanche (the original inhabitants of the Canary Islands) mummy and the skeleton of a circus giant (2.35m tall).

Real Fábrica de Tapices

C/Fuentarrabia 2 • Charge • Tours on the hour must be booked in advance • http://realfabricadetapices.com • Ⓜ Estación del Arte / Menéndez Pelayo

The **Real Fábrica de Tapices** still turns out handmade tapestries, many of them based on the Goya cartoons in the Prado. They are fabulously expensive, but the entrance fee is a bargain, with the tour tracing the fascinating manufacturing process, barely changed in the three hundred years of the factory's existence.

The Gran Vía, Chueca and Malasaña

The **Gran Vía**, Madrid's great thoroughfare, runs from Pza. de Cibeles to Pza. de España, effectively dividing the old city to the south from the newer parts northwards. Permanently crowded with shoppers and sightseers, it's the commercial heart of the city, and – if you spare the time to look up – quite a monument in its own right, with its early twentieth-century, palace-like banks, offices and theatres. Look out for the **Edificio Metrópolis** (1905–11) on the corner of C/Alcalá, complete with cylindrical facade, white stone sculptures, zinc-tiled roof and gold garlands, and the towering **Telefónica** building, which was the chief observation post for the Republican artillery during the Civil War, when the Nationalist front line stretched across the Casa de Campo to the west.

North of the Telefónica building, C/Fuencarral heads north to the Glorieta de Bilbao. To either side of this street are two of Madrid's most characterful *barrios*: **Chueca**, to the east, and **Malasaña**, to the west. Their chief appeal lies in an amazing concentration of bars, restaurants and, especially, nightlife. However, there are a few reasons – cafés included – to wander around here by day.

Chueca

Once rather down at heel, Chueca is now one of the city's most vibrant *barrios* and the focal point of Madrid's **LGBTQ+ scene**. At the centre is the lively **Pza. de Chueca** (ⓂChueca), which is fronted by one of the best old-style *vermút* bars in the city, *Taberna de Ángel Sierra*. The whole area has become gentrified, with the rise of a host of stylish bars, cafés and restaurants and the opening of the refurbished Mercado de San Antón.

Paseo de Recoletos

From Pza. de Chueca east to **Paseo de Recoletos** (the beginning of the long Paseo de la Castellana) are some of the city's most enticing streets. Offbeat restaurants, small private art galleries and odd corner shops are in abundance, and the **C/Almirante** has some of the city's most fashionable clothes shops, too. To the north, on Paseo de Recoletos, are a couple of the city's most lavish **traditional cafés**, the *Café Gijón* at no. 21 and *Café del Espejo* at no. 31 (see page 106).

Sociedad General de Autores

C/Fernando VI 4 • Ⓜ Alonso Martínez

On the edge of the Santa Bárbara *barrio*, is the **Sociedad de Autores** (Society of Authors), housed in the only significant *modernista* building in Madrid designed by José Grasés Riera, who was part of the Gaudí school. It features an eye-catching facade that resembles a melted candle.

Museo Nacional del Romanticismo

C/San Mateo 13 • Charge, free on Sat afternoons, Sun • http://museoromanticismo.mcu.es • Ⓜ Tribunal

Reopened in 2009 after a nine-year, seven-million-euro restoration, the **Museo Nacional del Romanticismo** shows the lifestyle and outlook of the late Romantic era through an evocative re-creation of a typical bourgeois residence in the turbulent reign of Isabel II (1833–68), and this it does brilliantly. Overflowing with a marvellously eclectic and often kitsch hoard of memorabilia, the mansion is decorated with some beautiful period furniture and ceiling frescoes. There's also a relaxing garden café serving a selection of teas, coffees and cakes.

Museo de Historia de Madrid

C/Fuencarral 78 • Free • Ⓜ Tribunal

Just around the corner from the Museo del Romanticismo, the **Museo de Historia de Madrid** reopened in late 2014 after a lengthy restoration programme. The building itself features a flamboyant Churrigueresque (Spanish Baroque) facade by Pedro de Ribera. Inside, the holdings include a large chronological collection of paintings, photos, cartoons, maps, sculptures and porcelain, all relating to the history of the city since it was designated capital in 1561. One of the highlights is a fascinating 1830s scale model of the city.

Malasaña

The heart, in all senses, of **Malasaña** is the **Pza. Dos de Mayo**, named after the insurrection against Napoleonic forces on May 2, 1808; the rebellion and its aftermath are depicted in Goya's famous paintings at the Prado. The surrounding district bears the name of one of the martyrs of the uprising, 15-year-old Manuela Malasaña, who is also commemorated with a street (as are several other heroes of the time). On the night of May 1, Madrid honours its heroes, though the plaza is no longer the site of the traditional festivities.

More recently, the quarter was the focus of the *movida madrileña*, the "happening scene" of the late 1970s and early 1980s. As the country relaxed after the death of Franco and the city developed into a thoroughly modern capital under the leadership

1

of the late mayor, Tierno Galván, Malasaña became a focal point for the young. Bars appeared behind every doorway, drugs were sold openly in the streets and there was an extraordinary atmosphere of new-found freedom. Times have changed and a good deal of renovation has been going on in recent years, but the *barrio* retains a somewhat alternative – nowadays rather grungy – feel, with bar customers spilling onto the streets and an ever-lively scene in the Pza. Dos de Mayo *terrazas*.

The streets have an interest of their own and are home to some fine traditional bars, while on C/Manuela Malasaña you can take your pick from some of the trendiest cafés in town. There are also some wonderful old shop signs and architectural details, best of all the **Antigua Farmacia Juanse** on the corner of C/San Andrés and C/San Vicente Ferrer, with its irresistible 1920s *azulejo* scenes depicting cures for diarrhoea, headaches and suchlike.

San Antonio de los Alemanes
Calle de la Puebla 22 • Charge • Ⓜ Callao

One of the few specific sights in this quarter, and a real gem it is too, is **San Antonio de los Alemanes**, a delightful, elliptical church with dizzying floor-to-ceiling frescoes by Neapolitan artist Luca Giordano depicting the life of St Anthony.

Plaza de España, Moncloa and beyond

Pza. de España provides a breathing space from the densely packed streets to the east. Beyond the square lies a mixture of leafy suburbia, university campus and parkland, including the green swathes of Parque del Oeste and Casa de Campo. Sights include some fascinating minor museums and, further out, the royal palace of *El Pardo*. The airy *terrazas* along Paseo del Pintor Rosales provide ample opportunity for refreshment.

Plaza de España
Ⓜ Pza. de España

The **Pza. de España** at the west end of Gran Vía was home, until the flurry of corporate building in the north of Madrid, to two of the city's tallest buildings: the **Torre de Madrid** and the **Edificio de España**; the latter is now the 600-room **Hotel Riu Plaza España**. These rather stylish 1950s buildings preside over an elaborate monument to Cervantes in the middle of the square, which in turn overlooks the bewildered-looking bronze figures of Don Quixote and Sancho Panza.

After the recent renovations, the plaza is now a pleasant green space filled with gardens, fountains and olive trees. To the north **C/Martín de los Heros** is a lively place, day and night, with a couple of the city's best cinemas, and behind them the **Centro Princesa**, with shops, clubs, bars and a 24-hour branch of the ubiquitous VIPS – just the place to buy a box of chocolates or a bite to eat before heading on to a small-hours club.

Conde Duque
Ⓜ Ventura Rodríguez

Up the steps opposite the Centro Princesa is **C/Conde Duque**, an atmospheric street that contains an intriguing selection of cafés, restaurants and shops, and one that is dominated by the massive former barracks of the royal guard, constructed in the early eighteenth century by Pedro de Ribera. The barracks have been turned into a dynamic cultural centre, **El Centro Cultural de Conde Duque**, housing the city's contemporary art collection (C/Conde Duque 11; http://condeduquemadrid.es). Just to the east of this is the **Pza. de las Comendadoras** – named after the convent that occupies one side of the square – which is a tranquil space bordered by a variety of interesting craft shops, bars and cafés.

Museo Cerralbo

C/Ventura Rodríguez 17 • Charge, free Thurs evenings, Sat afternoons, Sun • http://culturaydeporte.gob.es/mcerralbo • Ⓜ Pza. de España

A block to the west of Pza. de España, a beautiful mansion houses the refurbished **Museo Cerralbo**, endowed with the collections of the reactionary politician, poet, traveller and archeologist, the seventeenth Marqués de Cerralbo. The rooms, stuffed with paintings, furniture, armour and artefacts, provide a fascinating insight into the lifestyle of the nineteenth-century aristocracy. The highlight is the exquisite mirrored ballroom complete with frescoes and marble decor.

Parque del Oeste

Pza. de España • Ⓜ Argüelles/Ventura Rodríguez

The **Parque del Oeste** stretches northwest from the Pza. de España, following the rail tracks of Príncipe Pío up to the suburbs of Moncloa and Ciudad Universitaria. In summer, there are numerous *terrazas* in the park, while, year-round, a **teleférico** shuttles its passengers high over the river from Paseo del Pintor Rosales to the middle of the Casa de Campo, where there's a bar-restaurant with pleasant views back towards the city. Just below the starting point of the *teleférico* (see website for opening times as they differ throughout the year; charge, http://teleferico.emtmadrid.es) is the beautiful **Rosaleda**, a vast rose garden at its best in May and June.

Templo de Debod

C/Ferraz 1 • Free • http://madrid.es/templodebod • Ⓜ Pza. de España

On the south side of the park, five minutes' walk from Pza. de España, is the **Templo de Debod**, a fourth-century BC Egyptian temple given to Spain in recognition of the work done by Spanish engineers on the Aswan High Dam (which inundated its original site). Reconstructed here stone by stone, it seems comically incongruous, and even more so with the multimedia exhibition on the culture of Ancient Egypt housed inside.

La Ermita de San Antonio de la Florida

Glorieta de la Florida 5 • Free; guided tours by prior reservation only • http://madrid.es/ermita • Ⓜ Príncipe Pío

Almost alongside the famous roast chicken and cider restaurant *Casa Mingo* is **La Ermita de San Antonio de la Florida**. This little church on a Greek-cross plan was built by an Italian, Felipe Fontana, between 1792 and 1798, and decorated by **Goya**, whose frescoes are the reason to visit. In the dome is a depiction of a miracle performed by St Anthony of Padua. Around it, heavenly bodies of angels and cherubs hold back curtains to reveal the main scene: the saint resurrecting a dead man to give evidence in favour of a prisoner (the saint's father) falsely accused of murder. Beyond this central group, Goya created a gallery of highly realist characters – their models were court and society figures – while for a lesser fresco of the angels adoring the Trinity in the apse, he took prostitutes as his models. The *ermita* also houses the artist's mausoleum, although his head was stolen by phrenologists for examination in the nineteenth century.

Moncloa

The wealthy suburb of **Moncloa** contains the Spanish prime ministerial residence and merits a visit even if you are not using the bus terminal for El Pardo and El Escorial. The metro will bring you out next to the mammoth building housing the Air Ministry and the giant Arco de la Victoria, built by Franco in 1956 to commemorate the Nationalist victory in the Civil War. Beyond this lie the leafy expanses of the Parque del Oeste and the campuses of the **Ciudad Universitaria**. During termtime, the area becomes one giant student party on weekend evenings, with huddles of picnickers and singing groups under the trees.

1

Museo de América

Avda. de los Reyes Católicos 6 • Charge, free on Sun & Thurs after 2pm • http://culturaydeporte.gob.es/museodeamerica • Ⓜ Moncloa

Near the Arco de la Victoria is the **Museo de América**, which contains a fine collection of artefacts, ceramics and silverware from Spain's former colonies in Latin America, displayed thematically. The highlight is the fabulous Quimbayas treasure – a breathtaking collection of gold objects and figures from the Quimbaya culture of Colombia.

Faro de Moncloa

Avenida de los Reyes Católicos 6 • Charge • Ⓜ Moncloa; take the Pza. de Moncloa exit

Next to the Museo de América is the **Faro de Moncloa**, a futuristic 110m-high viewing tower, which offers fantastic views over the city, Casa de Campo and out towards the mountains.

Museo del Traje

Avda. de Juan de Herrera 2 • Charge; free for under-18s, Sat afternoons and all day Sun • http://culturaydeporte.gob.es/mtraje • Ⓜ Moncloa

Across the busy road from the Museo de América down towards the university is the **Museo del Traje**, a fascinating excursion through the history of clothes and costume. Exhibits include clothes from a royal tomb dating back to the thirteenth century, some stunning eighteenth-century ball gowns and a selection of Spanish regional costumes, as well as shoes, jewellery and underwear. Modern Spanish and international designers are also featured, with a Paco Rabanne miniskirt and stylish dresses from Pedro del Hierro. The upmarket restaurant in the grounds has a cool garden terrace for summer use.

Casa de Campo

Ⓜ Batán/Lago, bus (#33) from Príncipe Pío or *teleférico* (see page 91)

If you want to jog, play tennis, swim (pool open daily June–Sept 11am–8.30pm; €6), picnic, go to the fairground or see pandas, then the **Casa de Campo** is the place. This enormous expanse of heath and scrub is in parts surprisingly wild for a spot so easily accessible from the city; other sections have been tamed for more conventional pastimes.

Picnic tables and café-bars are dotted throughout the park and there's a **jogging track** with exercise posts, a municipal open-air **swimming pool** close to Ⓜ Lago, tennis courts and rowing boats for rent on the **lake** (again near Ⓜ Lago). Sightseeing attractions include a large and well-organized **zoo** and a popular amusement park, the **Parque de Atracciones** (see page 113), complete with the obligatory selection of heart-stopping, stomach-churning gravity rides. Be aware that some of the **access roads** through the park are frequented by prostitutes, though there are few problems during daylight hours.

El Pardo

Nine kilometres northwest of Madrid in the former royal hunting ground of **El Pardo** is where Franco had his principal residence. A garrison still remains in the town – where most of the Generalísimo's staff were based – but the stigma of the place has lessened over the years, and it is now a popular weekend excursion for *madrileños*, who come here for long lunches in the terraza restaurants, or to play tennis or swim at one of the nearby sports clubs.

Palacio del Pardo

C/Manuel Alonso • Charge • http://patrimonionacional.es • Buses (#601) from Moncloa

Rebuilt by the Bourbons on the site of a hunting lodge of Carlos V, the **Palacio del Pardo** is the tourist focus of the area. The interior is pleasant enough, with its chapel and theatre, a portrait of Isabel la Católica by her court painter Juan de Flandes and an excellent collection of tapestries, many after the Goya cartoons in the Prado. Guides detail the uses Franco made of the *palacio*, but pass over some of his stranger habits

– he kept by his bed, for instance, the mummified hand of St Teresa of Ávila. The country-house retreat in the grounds known as the **Casa del Príncipe** was, like the *casitas* (pavilions) at El Escorial, designed by Prado architect Juan de Villanueva, and is highly ornate (visit by appointment only; charge; 913 761 500).

Salamanca and the Paseo de la Castellana

Salamanca, the area north of the Parque del Retiro, is a smart address for apartments and, even more so, for shops. The *barrio* is the haunt of *pijos* – universally denigrated rich kids and their well-heeled parents – and the grid of streets between C/Goya and C/José Ortega y Gasset contains most of the city's designer emporiums. Most of the buildings are modern and undistinguished, though there are some elegant nineteenth-century mansions and apartment blocks. A scattering of museums, galleries and exhibition spaces might tempt you up here, too – in particular the **Sorolla** and the **Lázaro Galdiano** museums, two little gems that are often ignored by visitors.

Plaza de Colón and around

If you tackle the area from south to north, the first point of interest is **Pza. de Colón** (ⓜColón), endowed at street level with a statue of Columbus (Cristóbal Colón) and some huge stone blocks arranged as a megalithic monument to the discovery of the Americas. Below the plaza and underneath the cascading waterfall facing the city's longest, widest and busiest avenue, the Paseo de la Castellana, is the **Teatro Fernán Gómez** arts centre.

Museo Arqueológico Nacional

C/Serrano 13 • Charge • http://man.es • ⓜ Colón/Serrano

Adjacent to Pza. de Colón is the **Museo Arqueológico Nacional**, revitalized after a lengthy refurbishment. The collections have been given a new lease of life with their arrangement around a naturally lit central atrium, while the labelling and video explanations (in English and Spanish) put the exhibits into context. As befitting a national collection, the museum holds some very impressive pieces, among them the celebrated Celtiberian busts known as *La Dama de Elche* and *La Dama de Baza*, and a wonderfully rich hoard of Visigothic treasures found at Toledo. The museum also contains outstanding Roman, Egyptian, Greek and Islamic finds.

Museo de Arte Público

Paseo de la Castellana 41 • Free • ⓜ Rubén Darío

North from the Museo de la Biblioteca Nacional, up the Paseo de la Castellana, the **Museo de Arte Público** is an innovative attempt at using the space underneath the Juan Bravo flyover. However, its haphazard and rather stark collection of sculptures, including the six-tonne suspended block titled *The Meeting* by Eduardo Chillida and Joan Miró's primitive bird-woman figure *Mère Ubu*, appears to be more appreciated by the city's skateboard community.

Museo Sorolla

C/Martínez Campos 37 • Charge, free under-18s, Sat afternoons, Sun • http://culturaydeporte.gob.es/msorolla • ⓜ Gregorio Marañon/Iglesia

Not far north of here, across the Paseo de la Castellana, is a little gem of a gallery, the **Museo Sorolla**, which has a large collection of work by the painter **Joaquín Sorolla** (1863–1923), tastefully displayed in his beautifully preserved old home. The most striking of his paintings, which include beach scenes, portraits and landscapes, are impressionistic plays on light and texture. His old studio is much as he left it, and the house itself, with its cool and shady Andalucian-style courtyard and gardens, is worth the visit alone and makes a wonderful escape from the traffic-choked streets.

1

Museo Lázaro Galdiano

C/Serrano 122 • Charge, free last hour of opening • www.museolazarogaldiano.es • ⓂGregorio Marañón/Rubén Darío

The **Museo Lázaro Galdiano** is just northeast of the Museo Sorolla at the intersection of C/Serrano and C/María Molina. This formerly private collection was given to the state by José Galdiano in 1948 and spreads over the four floors and 37 rooms of his former home. It is a vast jumble of artworks, with some very dodgy attributions, but includes some really exquisite and valuable pieces. Among painters represented are El Greco, Bosch, Gerard David, Dürer and Rembrandt, as well as a host of Spanish artists, including Berruguete, Murillo, Zurbarán, Velázquez and Goya. Other exhibits include a collection of clocks and watches, many of them once owned by Carlos V.

Museo de Ciencias Naturales

C/José Gutiérrez Abascal 2 • Charge • http://mncn.csic.es • ⓂGregorio Marañón

Set back from the busy road, halfway along the Paseo de la Castellana, is the **Museo de Ciencias Naturales** (Natural History Museum), whose displays are split between two buildings. One is now home to a renovated exhibition space focusing on biodiversity and Mediterranean fauna, with a collection of stuffed animals, skeletons and audiovisual displays on the evolution of life on earth, the other is home to some rather dull fossil and geological exhibits.

To the Bernabéu

North along the Paseo de la Castellana, you reach the **Zona Azca** (ⓂNuevos Ministerios/ Santiago Bernabéu), a business quarter, once home to the city's tallest skyscraper, the 157-metre Torre Picasso designed by Minori Yamasaki (also the architect of New York's infamous Twin Towers), although now dwarfed by the four new towers erected beyond Pza. Castilla. It is only a short hop across the Castellana to Real Madrid's magnificent **Santiago Bernabéu** stadium, easily the most famous sight in this part of town.

Estadio Santiago Bernabéu

C/Concha Espina 1 • Charge • http://realmadrid.com • ⓂSantiago Bernabéu

The **Santiago Bernabéu** stadium provides a suitably imposing home for one of the most famous clubs in world football, Real Madrid – particularly after a significant

---

FÚTBOL IN MADRID

The "Galactico" era of the likes of David Beckham, Zinedine Zidane, Ronaldo and Luís Figo may be over, but **Real Madrid** remains one of the most glamorous teams in club football with an ample quota of superstars including the world's two most expensive players in Gareth Bale and Cristiano Ronaldo. The fifteen-time winners of the European Cup and 36-time Spanish champions play at the **Bernabéu**, venue of the 1982 World Cup final and a ground that ranks as one of the world's most fabled sporting arenas.

Tickets to games – which have become more difficult to get hold of in recent years – cost from €40 up to €750 for big matches and usually go on sale a couple of weeks before a game; Real runs a telephone and online booking service (http://realmadrid.com). They can be purchased by credit card on the ticket line or online for all but the biggest matches. If you don't get lucky, you can still catch a glimpse of the hallowed turf by taking the stadium tour.

The capital is also home to another of the country's biggest teams, 2014 league champions **Atlético Madrid** (http://clubatleticodemadrid.com; tickets from around €35, on sale via the website), who moved to their **Wanda Metropolitano** stadium on the eastern edge of the city (ⓂLas Musas/Estadio Olímpico) at the start of the 2017–18 season. The more modest Leganés (http://cdleganes.com), Getafe (http://getafecf.com) and Rayo Vallecano (http:// rayovallecano.es) are based in working-class suburbs of the city.

1

renovation was completed in 2024. Even if you can't get to see a match, you can take the **stadium tour** which, though exorbitantly priced, is understandably popular. It starts with a panoramic view of the massive 85,000-capacity stadium and takes in a visit to the dressing rooms and a walk through the tunnel onto the pitch. Also included is the **trophy exhibition**, complete with endless cabinets of gleaming silverware, with pride of place given to the team's twelve European Cups and video footage of their greatest triumphs. The tour ends with the obligatory visit to the overpriced club shop – where you soon come to realize why Real is one of the richest football clubs in the world. As part of the new renovations (which also increased seating capacity by more than three thousand), the stadium will feature a food area with six restaurants; this was yet to open at the time of writing, but should be operational by the time you read this.

Plaza Castilla
Ⓜ Pza. Castilla

The Paseo de la Castellana ends with a flourish at **Pza. Castilla** with four giant skyscrapers constructed on Real Madrid's former training ground, the result of a controversial deal that allowed the club to solve many of its financial problems. The two tallest towers, one of which is designed by Norman Foster, soar some 250m into the sky.

ARRIVAL AND DEPARTURE   MADRID

Whatever your point of **arrival** in Madrid, it's an easy business getting into the centre of the Spanish capital. The airport is connected by a speedy metro link, shuttle buses and taxis, while the city's main train and bus stations are all linked to the metro system only a short ride from the centre.

BY PLANE

Aeropuerto Adolfo Suárez Madrid-Barajas (http://www.aena.es), renamed in honour of the late Spanish prime minister who oversaw the transition to democracy after the death of Franco, is 16km east of the city. It has four terminals, including the state-of-the-art T4 building designed by Richard Rogers and Carlos Lamela, which has helped double the capacity to some seventy million passengers a year. All Iberia's domestic and international flights, as well as airlines that belong to the Oneworld group, such as British Airways and American Airlines, use T4 (a 10min shuttle-bus ride from the other terminals); other international flights and budget airlines, including Aer Lingus, easyJet and Ryanair, go from T1, while Air France, KLM, Alitalia and Lufthansa use T2.

Metro link From the airport, the metro link (Line 8) takes you from T4 and T2 to the city's Nuevos Ministerios station in just 20min. From there, it's a 15min metro ride to most city-centre locations.

Airport buses The route by road to central Madrid is more variable, depending on rush-hour traffic, and can take anything from 20min to 1hr. The bright-yellow airport express buses run round the clock from each terminal to Cibeles and Atocha, with a journey time of around 40min.

Taxis are always available and charge a fixed tariff (including an airport supplement) to the centre.

Train A cercanías train line takes you from T4 to Chamartín in the north of the city in around 12min or to Atocha in the

south in 25min.

Car rental Half a dozen or so car rental companies have stands at the airport terminals and can generally supply clients with maps and directions.

Airport facilities Other airport facilities include 24hr currency exchange, ATMs, a post office, left-luggage lockers, a RENFE office for booking train tickets, pharmacies, tourist offices and hotel reservations desks.

BY TRAIN

Two main stations, Estación de Chamartín and Estación de Atocha, serve destinations in Spain and further afield.

Estación de Chamartín Serves trains from France or northern and western Spain (including the high-speed links to Segovia and Valladolid); a modern terminal isolated in the north of the city, connected by metro with the centre and by regular commuter trains (cercanías) with Estación de Atocha.

Destinations A Coruña (5–10 daily; 5hr 30min–11hr 30min); Ávila (20–25 daily; 1hr 25min–2hr); Bilbao (2–4 daily; 5hr–6hr 40min); Burgos (6–12 daily; 2hr 15min–4hr 35min); Ferrol (1–3; 6hr 50min–12hr 10min); Gijón (5–7 daily; 4hr 30min–7hr 10min); León (10–12 daily; 2hr 45min–5hr 10min); Lisbon (daily; 10hr 40min); Oviedo (5–7 daily; 4hr–6hr 40min); Pamplona (6–8 daily; 3hr 5min–4hr 10min); Pontevedra (2–5 daily; 6hr 20min–11hr 20min); Salamanca (7–12 daily; 1hr 35min–3hr); San Sebastián (7–9 daily; 4hr 50min–8hr); Santander (6–8 daily; 4hr 5min–6hr 50min); Santiago (4–6 daily; 5hr–11hr); Segovia (AVE 12–14 daily; 25min; 7 daily; 1hr 50min–2hr 10min); Sigüenza (4–5 daily; 1hr 30min–1hr 55min); Soria (2–3 daily; 3hr); Valladolid (AVE 20 daily; 55min–1hr 10min; 7 daily; 1hr 50min–2hr 50min); Vigo (4–8 daily; 5hr 55min–12hr 5min); Vitoria (AVE 2 daily; 3hr

1

35min; 3 daily; 5hr 40min); Zamora (3–6 daily; 1hr 25min–1hr 35min). Plus most other destinations in the northeast and northwest.

Estación de Atocha Centrally located at the end of the southern end of Paseo del Prado, it has two interconnected terminals: one for local services, the other for all points in southern and eastern Spain, including the high-speed AVE trains to Barcelona, Seville, Toledo, Málaga, Valencia and Zaragoza.

Destinations Albacete (11–15 daily; 1hr 25min–2hr 55min); Alcalá de Henares (every 5–20min; 35min); Algeciras (3 daily; 5hr 15min–6hr 5min); Alicante (8–11 daily; 2hr 10min–3hr 35min); Almería (2 daily; 6hr 15min–6hr 30min); Aranjuez (every 15–30min; 45min); Badajoz (4–6 daily; 5hr 40min–6hr 40min); Barcelona (25–35 daily; 2hr 45min–3hr 10min); Cáceres (3–5 daily; 3hr 55min–4hr 20min); Cádiz (7–13 daily; 3hr 55min–5hr 30min); Cartagena (3–5 daily; 4hr 50min–6hr 15min); Ciudad Real (16–25 daily; 50min–1hr); Córdoba (25–30 daily; 1hr 40min–2hr); Cuenca (AVE 6–11 daily; 55min; Regional 4 daily; 3hr); El Escorial (every 20–30min; 1hr 5min); Granada (4 daily; 3hr 55min; final section by bus); Guadalajara (AVE 9 daily; 25min; regional every 15–30min; 55min); Huelva (4–8 daily; 3hr 40min–5hr 45min); Huesca (2–4 daily; 2hr 15min–3hr 35min); Jaén (4–8 daily; 4hr 15min); Jerez (8–12 daily; 3hr 20min–4hr 45min); Lleida (10 daily; 2hr); Málaga (13–15 daily; 2hr 20min–2hr 50min); Marseilles (daily; 7hr); Mérida (4–6 daily; 4hr 50min–6hr); Seville (18–24 daily; 2hr 20min–3hr); Toledo (11–15 daily; 33min); Valencia (10–15 daily; 1hr 40min–3hr 30min); Zaragoza (14–20 daily; 1hr 15min–1hr 45min). Plus most destinations in the south and west.

Príncipe Pío If you're coming from local towns around Madrid, you may arrive at Príncipe Pío (aka Estación del Norte), fairly close to the centre below the Palacio Real, which is also connected to the metro network.

Information and reservations http://renfe.com. Tickets can be bought at the individual stations, at Aeropuerto de Barajas arrivals in T1 and T4 and at registered travel agents. Bear in mind that you'll need to book in advance for most long-distance trains, especially at weekends or holiday time.

BY BUS

Bus terminals are scattered throughout the city. The largest – used by all of the international bus services – is the Estación Sur de Autobuses at C/Méndez Álvaro 83 on the corner of C/Retama, 1.5km south of the Atocha station (914 684 200; ⓜ Méndez Álvaro). There are other bus stations at the *intercambiadoras* in Avda. de América (ⓜ Avda. de América), Conde de Casal (ⓜ Conde de Casal), Moncloa (an underground terminal just above ⓜ Moncloa), Príncipe Pío (ⓜ Príncipe Pío) and Pza. Elíptica (ⓜ Pza. Elíptica). Leading bus companies that operate from Madrid include Alsa

(http://alsa.es), Arriva (http://arriva.es) Avanzabus (www.avanzabus.com), Samar (http://samar.es), and Socibus (www.socibusventas.es).

Estación Sur de Autobuses destinations Albacete (10–20 daily; 2hr 45min–3hr 35min); Alicante (6 daily; 4hr 50min–5hr); Almería (6 daily; 6hr 15min–6hr 45min); Aranjuez (Mon–Fri every 30min, Sat & Sun hourly; 40min); Arenas de San Pedro (1–5 daily; 2hr 15min); Ávila (5–10 daily; 1hr 20min–1hr 45min); Badajoz (7–8 daily; 4hr 40min–5hr 45min); Cáceres (8 daily; 3hr 55min–4hr 55min); Ciudad Real (1–3 daily; 2hr 30min); Córdoba (6 daily; 4hr 45min); Cuenca (8 daily; 2hr 5min–2hr 30min); Gijón (11 daily; 5hr 30min–6hr 30min); Granada (15 daily; 4hr 30min–5hr 30min); Jaén (15 daily; 4hr 30min–5hr); León (19 daily; 3hr 30min–4hr 30min); Lisbon (3 daily; 7hr); Málaga (5–8 daily; 5hr 50min–6hr); Marbella (6 daily; 7hr); Mérida (8 daily; 4–5hr); Oviedo (15–25 daily; 5hr–6hr 15min); Palencia (12 daily; 3hr 15min–3hr 30min); Pontevedra (5 daily; 8hr 15min); Salamanca (20–25 daily; 2hr 30min); Santiago (4 daily; 8hr 30min–9hr 30min); Seville (8 daily; 6hr 30min); Trujillo (10 daily; 3hr 10min–4hr); Valencia (8–12 daily; 4hr 15min); Valladolid (15 daily; 2hr 30min); Vigo (5–7 daily, 7hr 10min–8hr 50min); Zamora (4–6 daily; 3hr–3hr 15min); and international services to France.

Intercambiador de Avda. de América destinations Alcalá (every 15–20min; 40min); Barcelona (10–15 daily; 7hr 20min–8hr 40min); Bilbao (10–15 daily; 4hr 15min–4hr 45min); Guadalajara (every 30min; 40–55min); Logroño (9 daily; 4hr–4hr 15min); Pamplona (12 daily; 5hr 15min–6hr 5min); San Sebastián (10 daily; 5hr 15min–5hr 45min); Santander (12 daily; 5hr 15min–5hr 45min); Soria (9–10 daily; 2hr 30min); Vitoria (11 daily; 4hr 10min–4hr 45min); Zaragoza (18 daily; 3hr 30min–4hr 15min).

Intercambiador de Moncloa destinations El Escorial (approx every 15–30min; 55min–1hr). Onward connections to El Valle de los Caídos.

Intercambiador de Pza. Elíptica destination Toledo (every 30min; 1hr–1hr 30min).

Intercambiador de Príncipe Pío destination Segovia (every 30min; 1hr 45min).

Intercambiador Conde de Casal destination Chinchón (daily every 30min–1hr; 45–55min).

BY CAR

All the main roads into Madrid bring you right into the city centre, although eccentric signposting and even more eccentric driving can be very unnerving. The two main ring roads – the M40 and the M30 – and the Paseo de la Castellana are all notorious bottlenecks, although virtually the whole city centre can be close to gridlock during the peak rush-hour periods (Mon–Fri 7.30–9.30am & 6–8.30pm). Be prepared for a long trawl around the streets to find parking, and even then in most central areas you'll have to buy a ticket at one of the roadside meters. Another option is to put your car in one of the many signposted parkings. Your own transport is really only of use for out-of-town excursions, so it's advisable to find a hotel with or near a car park and keep your car there during your stay in the city. If you are staying more than a couple of weeks, you can get long-term parking rates at some neighbourhood garages.

Free maps of the whole central area of Madrid are available from any of the *turismos* (see page 98).

GETTING AROUND

THE METRO

The clean and highly efficient metro (http://metromadrid. es) is by far the quickest way of getting around Madrid, serving most places you're likely to want to get to. Multi-trip tickets are available which are good value and can be used on buses, too. The metro operates a paperless ticketing system so you will have to purchase a *tarjeta multi* transport card and then load up the card with the trips you want to take. Alternatively, buy a tourist travel pass (see page 97). The network has undergone massive expansion in recent years and some of the outlying commuter districts are now connected by light railways, which link with the existing stations (separate tickets are needed for some of these). Lines are numbered and colour-coded, and the direction of travel is indicated by the name of the terminus station. You can pick up a free colour map of the system (*plano del metro*) at any station.

BUSES

The comprehensive urban bus network (www.emtmadrid. es) is another good way to get around and see the sights: in the text, where there's no metro stop, we've indicated which bus to take. There are information booths in the Pza. de Cibeles and Puerta del Sol, which dispense a huge route map (*plano de los transportes de Madrid*), and – along with other outlets – sell bus passes. Fares are the same as for the metro, but note that you can only buy single tickets on the buses themselves (try to have the right money). Buses run from 6am to midnight. In addition, there are *búho* (owl) night buses that operate on twenty routes around the central area and out to the suburbs.

TAXIS

One of the best things about getting round Madrid is that there are thousands of taxis – white cars with a diagonal red stripe on the side – which are reasonably cheap; €15 will get you to most places within the centre and, although it's common to round up the fare, you're not expected to tip. Supplements are charged for the airport, train and bus stations, the IFEMA congress centre, going outside the city limits and for night trips (10pm–6am). In any area in the centre, day and night, you should be able to wave down a taxi (available ones have a green light on top of the cab) in a short time, although it is more difficult at weekends when half the population is out on the town. To phone for a taxi, call 915 478 600 (also for wheelchair-friendly cabs), 914 051 213, 913 712 131 or 914 473 232. If you want to make a complaint take the driver's number and ask for the *hoja de reclamaciones* (a claim form). If you leave something in a taxi, ring 914 804 613.

LOCAL TRAINS

The local train network, or *cercanías*, is the most efficient way of connecting between the main train stations and provides the best route out to many of the suburbs and to nearby towns such as Alcalá de Henares. Most trains are air-conditioned, fares are cheap and there are good connections with the metro. Trains generally run every 15 to 30min from 6am to midnight. For more information, go to the RENFE website at http://renfe.com and click on the *cercanías* section for Madrid.

BICYCLES

Madrid is not a particularly bike-friendly city, but things are improving. A new network of cycle paths is being constructed in some of the central areas and a municipal bike hire scheme known as BiciMad (www.bicimad.com) has also been introduced though it is still in its infancy. You can pick up and return a bike at one of the stations dotted all over the city centre, though you will have to pay a returnable credit card deposit.

THE TOURIST TRAVEL PASS

If you're using public transport extensively, it could be worth getting a **tourist pass** (*abono túristico*), covering the metro, train and bus. These are non-transferable, and you'll need to show your passport or identity card at the time of purchase. **Zone A** cards cover central Madrid, and **Zone T** cards cover the whole region including buses to Toledo and Guadalajara but not those to the airport. They are available for a duration of one to seven days and can be purchased at all metro stations, the airport and tourist offices. If you're staying longer, passes (*abonos*) covering the metro, train and bus, and available for each calendar month, are worthwhile.

1

CITY TOURS

The *turismo* in Pza. Mayor (see page 98) can supply details of a variety of guided English-language walking tours around the city (http://esmadrid.com/visitas-guidas-por-madrid). For a bus tour of all the major city sights, wait at the pick-up points outside the Prado, Pza. de España, Pza. de Colón and Pza. de Cibeles. Tickets (http://madrid.city-tour.com) allow you to jump on and off throughout the day at various places throughout the city.

INFORMATION

There are **Turismo** at the following locations, which are open all year round:

Barajas International Airport in T1 (913 058 656), T2 and T4 (913 338 248).

Estación de Atocha (915 284 630).

Estación de Chamartín (913 159 976).

Pza. Mayor 27 (915 787 810; ⓜ Sol/Ópera).

Pza. de Colón In the underground passageway, accessed at the corner of C/Goya (ⓜ Colón).

CentroCentro, Palacio de Cibeles (ⓜ Banco de España).

Turismo booths Next to the Reina Sofía, in Pza. de Cibeles and in Pza. de Cibeles off Gran Vía (daily 9.30am–8.30pm).

Website and phone numbers The Madrid tourist board is at http://esmadrid.com, while the regional authority has one covering the whole of the province (http://turismomadrid.es). There's tourist information available in English on 902 100 007, a premium number that links all the regional tourist offices mentioned above, and on 914 881 636.

ACCOMMODATION   SEE MAPS PAGES 62 AND 70

Business hotels apart, most of Madrid's **accommodation** is pretty central. With increasing competition, many *hostales* and hotels have been busy upgrading their facilities and a new breed of stylish, design-conscious, medium-priced hotels have emerged. Many of the expensive hotels do special weekend offers, and prices drop substantially in August when temperatures soar towards 40ºC (air-conditioning is usual and a welcome extra). You'll notice that buildings in the more popular hotel/*hostal* areas often house two or three separate establishments, each on **separate floors**; these are generally independent of each other. One thing to bear in mind is **noise**; bars, clubs, traffic and roadworks all contribute to making Madrid a high-decibel city, so avoid rooms on the lower floors, or choose a place away from the nightlife if you want a bit of peace and quiet. Madrid has just one **campsite**, located on the outskirts, but there are an increasing number of backpackers' **hostels** right in the centre.

If you want to be at the heart of the old town, the areas around **Puerta del Sol**, **Pza. de Santa Ana** and **Pza. Mayor** are the ones to go for; if you're into nightlife, **Malasaña** or **Chueca** may also appeal; for a quieter location and a bit of class, you should opt for the **Paseo del Prado**, **Recoletos** or **Salamanca** areas; if you have children the areas around the parks are good options.

SOL, ÓPERA AND MADRID DE LOS AUSTRIAS

This really is the heart of Madrid, and prices are a bit higher than other central areas, though you can still find bargains in the streets around the Pza. Mayor.

Hostal Ivor C/Arenal 26, 4º, www.hostalivor.com; ⓜ Ópera/Sol. Great budget option just a few minutes from Sol. Rooms range from singles to family (sleeps four), and are bare-bones – white walls, pine beds, tiled floors – but perfectly comfortable. Some rooms have small balconies. €

Hotel Mayerling C/Conde de Romanones 6, http://mayerlinghotel.com; ⓜ Tirso de Molina. A stylish mid-range hotel with 22 rooms, housed in a former textile warehouse close to C/Atocha. Clean lines and black-and-white decor predominate in the simple, neat rooms. Continental breakfast is included in the price and there's free internet as well as a sun terrace. €€

★ **Hotel Meninas** C/Campomanes 7, http://hotel meninas.es; ⓜ Ópera. A stylish, 37-room hotel owned by the same group as the nearby *Ópera*, and similarly good value, with a prime location in a quiet street by Pza. Ópera. As well as doubles, they offer triple rooms, suites and family rooms. Very helpful staff, excellent attic rooms and flat-screen TVs. Breakfast included for web reservations. €€

Hotel Palacio de San Martín C/Pza. de San Martín 5, http://intelier.com; ⓜ Ópera/Sol. Situated in a historic building in an attractive square alongside the Monasterio de las Descalzas Reales. This hotel has 94 bright spacious rooms with period decor, a small gym and sauna, plus a restaurant with a terrace in the plaza. €

Pension Foster C/La Estrella 5, 2ºizda, http://pension foster.com; ⓜ Santo Domingo/Callao. A creatively-decorated *hostal* just off lively Gran Vía. Rooms are a little on the small side but are cosy, comfy and have en suite bathrooms. Great location. €

Petit Palace Arenal C/Arenal 16, http://petitpalace arenal.com; ⓜ Sol/Ópera. A member of the Petit Palace chain, with sleek, modern rooms, all with a/c, and some family-friendly rooms and some for groups with bunk beds too. Two other members of this chain, the *Posada del Peine* (www.petitpalaceposadadelpeine.com) and the *Puerta del Sol* (www.petitpalacepuertadelsol.com), are close at C/Postas 17 and C/Arenal 4. €€

★ **Posada del Leon de Oro** C/Cava Baja 12, http://

posadadelleondeoro.com; ⓜLa Latina. This former inn has been converted into a chic, designer hotel with seventeen large, individually decorated rooms complete with walk-in showers. Three-night minimum stay at some times of the year. €€

★ **Room Mate Mario** C/Campomanes 4º, http://room-matehotels.com/mario; ⓜÓpera. Hip, designer hotel with a perfect spot on a pleasant street close to the Teatro Real. Compact, ultra-cool rooms, neat bathrooms and friendly staff. Buffet breakfast is included. There is another member of the chain, the *Laura*, at nearby Travesía de Trujillos 3 (917 011 670). €€

AROUND PLAZA DE SANTA ANA AND HUERTAS

Pza. de Santa Ana and the Huertas area are the focal point of Madrid nightlife, with bars and cafés open until very late at night. The following are all within a few blocks of the square, with the metro stations Antón Martín, Sevilla and Sol close by. Go for rooms on the higher floors if you want to avoid the worst of the noise.

Hostal Barrera C/Atocha 96, 2º, http://hostalbarrera.com; ⓜAntón Martín. A friendly, good-value fourteen-room *hostal* only a short distance from Atocha station and run by an English-speaking owner. Smart a/c rooms are a cut above the rest in this category and the bathrooms are modern. €

★ **Hotel Urban** Carrera San Jeronimo 34, http://hotelurban.com; ⓜSevilla/Sol. Ultra-cool, fashion-conscious, five-star hotel offering a glut of designer rooms, a rooftop pool, summer terrace and *pijo* cocktail bar. It even has its own small museum, consisting of items from owner Jordi Clos' collection of Egyptian and Chinese art. Look out for special deals online. €€€€

ME Madrid Reina Victoria Pza. Santa Ana 14, http://melia.com; ⓜSol. Once a favourite haunt of bullfighters, this giant white wedding-cake of a hotel is now part of Meliá's exclusive ME chain. Features include minimalist decor, designer furnishings, high-tech fittings, a super-cool penthouse bar and a chic restaurant serving fusion-style food. Special offers can bring the price down. €€€

★ **NH Palacio Tepa** C/San Sebastian 2, http://nh-hoteles.com; ⓜAntón Martín. This luxurious five-star, 85-room hotel is right in the heart of Huertas, close to Pza. Santa Ana and a stone's throw from the big museums. It has a range of large, plush rooms including some two-storey suites and wooden-beamed attics. There's also a restaurant and bar onsite. €€€

★ **Room Mate Alicia** C/Prado 2, http://room-mate hotels.com/alicia; ⓜSol/Sevilla. Perched on the corner of the plaza, the 34-room *Alicia* is in a great location – if a little noisy. Seriously cool decor, stylish rooms, including some suites with a sun terrace, and great value if you manage to get one of the web offers. €€

AROUND PASEO DEL PRADO AND ATOCHA

This is a quieter area, though still very central, and it is close to the main art museums, the Parque del Retiro and Estación de Atocha. Some of the city's most expensive hotels are here – as well as a few more modest options.

★ **Hostal Gonzalo** C/Cervantes 34, 3º, http://hostal gonzalo.com; ⓜAntón Martín. This has to be one of the most welcoming *hostales* in the city. It has fifteen simple, bright, en-suite rooms – all of which have a/c – and a charming owner. €

Hotel Artrip C/Valencia 11, http://artriphotel.com; ⓜLavapiés. This self-styled "Art Hotel" is conveniently located close to the Reina Sofia and other art galleries in the area. Its seventeen sleek, design-conscious rooms, which include family options, combine the modern with the traditional. Buffet breakfast included in website booking. €€

NH Nacional Paseo del Prado 48, http://nh-hoteles.com; ⓜEstación del Arte. A large, well-run hotel, part of the NH chain, attractively situated opposite the Jardines Botánicos at near Estación de Atocha. Special offers can reduce the price substantially. €€€

Numa Script Pza. de los Cortes 4, 7º dcha., http://numastays.com; ⓜBanco de España. Boutique accommodation in this neat B&B in the heart of the art-museum quarter. The rooms have an appropriately cool, arty decor, and there's a communal kitchen where you can self-cater if you wish. €

★ **Radisson Blu Madrid Prado** C/Moratín 52, http://radissonblu.com/pradohotel-madrid; ⓜEstación del Arte. Designer hotel located along the Paseo del Prado featuring sleek rooms in black, brown and white, photos of the Madrid skyline adorning the walls, black-slate bathrooms and coffee machines. There is a small gym, a spa area and indoor pool, a whisky bar and a restaurant too. €€€

Villa Real Pza. de las Cortes 10, http://hotelvillareal.com; ⓜSevilla. Aristocratic hotel with its own art collection owned by Catalan entrepreneur Jordi Clos. Each of the 96 luxurious double rooms has a spacious sitting area and many have balconies over the plaza. The rooftop restaurant, *Bar East 47*, whose walls are decorated with Andy Warhol originals, affords splendid views over the Congresos de Diputados and down towards the Paseo del Prado. €€€

The Westin Palace, Madrid Pza. de los Cortes 7, http://marriott.com/hotels/travel/madwi-the-westin-palace-madrid; ⓜEstación del Arte/Banco de España. A colossal, sumptuous hotel with every imaginable facility, a spectacular, glass-covered central patio and luxurious rooms – plus none of the snootiness of the *Ritz* across the road. It was commissioned by King Alfonso XII in 1912 and still retains its historic grandeur. Look out for website offers. €€€€

PLAZA DE ESPAÑA, GRAN VÍA AND BEYOND

The huge old buildings along the Gran Vía – which stretches

1

all the way from Pza. España to C/Alcalá – hide a vast array of hotels and *hostales* at every price, often with a delightfully decayed elegance, though they also suffer from traffic noise.

Aloft Madrid Gran Via C/Jacometrezo 4, 7º, http:// marriott.com; Ⓜ Callao. Comfortable smart hotel with spacious rooms. Funky, yet stylish communal spaces and great views from the rooftop bar and pool area. €€

Aparto-hotel Rosales C/Marqués de Urquijo 23, http:// apartohotel-rosales.com; Ⓜ Argüelles. Large, comfortable apartments with separate bedroom, living area and kitchenette. Close to the Parque del Oeste and in one of the quieter areas of town, so a good option if you're travelling with children. €€

Aparto Suites Jardines de Sabatini Cuesta San Vicente 16, http://jardinesdesabatini.com; Ⓜ Pza. España/Príncipe Pío. Convenient location in between Pza. España and Príncipe Pío station, this upmarket apartment complex with a rooftop terrace overlooking the royal palace offers studios and suites with small kitchen areas that sleep up to three people. €€

Hostal Buenos Aires Gran Vía 61, 2º, 915 420 102, http:// hostalbuenosaires-madrid.com; Ⓜ Pza. de España. Twenty-five pleasantly decorated rooms with a/c, satellite TV and modern bathrooms, plus double-glazing to keep out much of the noise. €

★ **Hostal Gala** C/Costanilla de los Ángeles 15, http:// hostalgala.com; Ⓜ Callao. An upmarket, very tasteful *hostal* close to the shopping areas around Gran Vía. The slickly decorated rooms have a/c and power showers. Some have small balconies and there are family rooms available too. €€

Hotel Emperador Gran Vía 53, http://emperadorhotel. com; Ⓜ Santo Domingo/Pza. de España. The main reason to come here is for the stunning rooftop swimming pool with its magnificent views. Otherwise, this 232-room hotel is rather impersonal, though the rooms are large and well-appointed. €€€

★ **Hotel Indigo** C/Silva 6, http://indigomadrid.com; Ⓜ Santo Domingo. Boutique-style hotel close to Gran Vía with a rooftop infinity pool and terrace bar. The design-conscious rooms have large beds, flat-screen TVs, coffee machines and modern bathrooms with walk-in showers. €€€

★ **Hotel Santo Domingo** C/San Bernardo 1, http:// hotelsantodomingo.es; Ⓜ Santo Domingo. What with the jungle paintings adorning the car park, the private art collection and the rooftop swimming pool with views over the city, this hotel is full of nice surprises. Rooms have tasteful individual decor, carpeted floors, large beds and walk-in shower rooms. €€€

Hotel Vincci The Mint Gran Vía 10, www.vinccithemint. com; Ⓜ Gran Vía. Housed in a historic lemon-yellow villa at the smarter end of Gran Vía, this hotel has smart, contemporary rooms with lovely marble bathrooms, a rooftop with a fun food-and-drink truck, and a decent bar-restaurant. €€€

NORTH OF GRAN VÍA AND CHUECA

North of Gran Vía, there are further wedges of *hostales* and hotels on and around C/Fuencarral and C/Hortaleza, near Ⓜ Gran Vía. Chueca, to the east of C/Fuencarral, is another nightlife centre and the city's *zona gay*, home to numerous bars, clubs and restaurants.

Hostal Zamora Pza. Vázquez de Mella 1, 4º izqda, http:// hostalzamora.com; Ⓜ Gran Vía. There are seventeen well-kept, simple rooms in this pleasant *hostal* overlooking the plaza. All have modern bathrooms, TV and a/c. There are good-value family rooms, too. Closed Aug. €

Hotel San Lorenzo C/Clavel 8, www.hotel-sanlorenzo. com; Ⓜ Gran Vía. A former *hostal* that has been upgraded to a neat and tidy three-star hotel offering clean and comfortable rooms with a/c and bathrooms; quadruples available too. Breakfast available. €

★ **Only You Hotel** C/Barquillo 21, http://onlyyouhotels. com; Ⓜ Chueca. This boutique-style hotel, housed in a refurbished nineteenth-century building, is in a great location between Chueca and Recoletos. There are seventy very swish, individually decorated rooms, including seven elegant suites, as well as a gastro and cocktail bar and a small gym. €€€€

Petit Palace Chueca C/Hortaleza 3, 3º, http:// petitpalacechueca.com; Ⓜ Gran Vía. Upgraded from an old *hostal* a few years back, this is now one of the self-styled Petit Palace chain. Its 58 sleek rooms come complete with all manner of mod cons. Family rooms available. €€

MALASAÑA AND SANTA BÁRBARA

Malasaña, west of C/Fuencarral and centred around Pza. Dos de Mayo, is a former working-class district, and now one of the main nightlife areas of Madrid.

Hostal Sil/Serranos C/Fuencarral 95, 2º & 3º, http:// silserranos.com; Ⓜ Tribunal. Two well-managed *hostales*, run by a friendly owner, at the quieter end of C/Fuencarral, offer functional rooms with a/c, modern bathrooms and TV. Triple and quadruples available. €€

★ **Hotel Urso** C/Mejía Lequerica 8, http://hotelurso.com; Ⓜ Alonso Martínez. A new, upmarket hotel with spacious, well-equipped, comfortable rooms. There is a small spa area and a pleasant bar and bamboo-fringed indoor terrace. €€€

PASEO DE RECOLETOS AND SALAMANCA

This is Madrid at its most chic: the Bond Street/Rue de Rivoli region of smart shops and equally well-heeled apartment blocks. It's a safe, pleasant area, just north of the Parque del Retiro, though a fair walk from the main sights.

★ **Hotel Orfila** C/Orfila 6, http://hotelorfila.com; Ⓜ Colón/Alonso Martínez. Exclusive boutique hotel housed in a beautiful nineteenth-century mansion on a quiet street north of Alonso Martínez. Twelve of the exquisite rooms are suites, and there's an elegant terrace for tea and drinks, as well as an upmarket restaurant run by Michelin-star chef Mario Sandoval. Of course, none of this comes cheap. €€€€ **Petit Palace Icon Embassy** C/Serrano 46, www. petitpalace.com; Ⓜ Colón/Goya. A four-star member of the sleek Petit Palace Hotels chain, close to Pza. Colón and in the middle of the upmarket Salamanca shopping district. The *Embassy* has 75 rooms, including ten family rooms for up to four people. €€€

EATING
SEE MAPS PAGES 62 AND 70

Madrid's range of **eating** establishments is wide, and includes tapas bars, cafés, *marisquerías* (seafood bars) and *restaurantes*. At almost any of our recommendations you could happily eat your fill – money permitting – though at bars, *madrileños* usually eat just a tapa or share a *ración* of the house speciality, then move on to repeat the procedure down the road. While cafés do serve food, they are much more places to drink coffee, have a *copa* or *caña*, or read the papers. Some also act as a meeting place for the semi-formal *tertulia* – a kind of discussion/drinking group, popular among Madrid intellectuals of the past and revived in the 1980s.

SOL, PLAZA MAYOR AND ÓPERA
The central area is the most varied in Madrid in terms of price and food. Indeed, there can be few places in the world that rival the streets around Puerta del Sol for sheer number of places to eat and drink. Around the smarter Ópera district, you need to be more selective, while on Pza. Mayor itself, stick to drinks. Unless indicated otherwise, all these places are easily reached from Metro Sol.

CAFÉS
Café de Oriente Pza. de Oriente 2, http://grupolezama.es; Ⓜ Ópera. Sophisticated Parisian-style affair with a popular *terraza* looking out towards the Palacio Real. €

TAPAS BARS
Las Bravas C/Alvarez Gato 3, http://lasbravas.com. As the name suggests, *patatas bravas* (spicy potatoes) are the tapa to try at this bar, which has patented its own version of the sauce; the *tortilla* is pretty good, too. On the outside of the bar are novelty mirrors, a hangover from the days when this was a barber's and the subject of a story by Valle Inclán. Standing room only and bright lights mean it is not to everyone's liking, though. Other branches nearby at C/Espoz y Mina 13 and Pasaje Mathéu 5. €€
★ **Casa del Abuelo** C/Victoria 12, http://lacasadelabuelo. es. This tiny, highly atmospheric *madrileño* institution serves cloyingly sweet red house wine, beer and a classic array of tapas. Try the cooked prawns *al ajillo* (in garlic) or *a la plancha* (fried). €€
Casa del Abuelo II C/Núñez de Arce 5, http://lacasa delabuelo.es. There's a *comedor* at the back of this down-to-earth bar, where you can order a selection of traditional *raciones* – the *croquetas* are especially good – and a jug of house wine. €€
Casa Labra C/Tetuán 12, http://casalabra.es. A very popular, long-standing bar-restaurant, where the Spanish

Socialist Party was founded back in 1879. Order a drink and a *ración* of *bacalao* (cod fried in batter) or some of the best *croquetas* in town at the counter to the right of the door. There's a fairly expensive restaurant at the back with classic *madrileño* food on offer. €€€
Lhardy C/San Jerónimo 8, http://lhardy.com. Dating back over 175 years, *Lhardy* is one of Madrid's most famous and expensive restaurants. Once the haunt of royalty, it's a beautiful place but greatly overpriced. Downstairs, however, there's a wonderful bar/shop, where you can snack on *canapés*, *fino* (dry sherry) and consommé, without breaking the bank. €€€€
★ **Mercado de San Miguel** Pza. de San Miguel, http://mercadodesanmiguel.es. Transformed from a traditional neighbourhood market into a hip location for an *aperitivo* and a spot of tapas, this beautiful wrought-iron *mercado* is worth exploring at almost any time of day. There's something for everyone, from vermouth and champagne to salt cod, oysters and sushi. €€
Museo del Jamón C/Gran Vía 72. The largest branch of this ubiquitous Madrid chain, from whose ceilings are suspended hundreds of *jamones* (hams). The best – and they are not cheap – are the *jabugos* from the Sierra Morena, though a ham croissant certainly won't break the bank. €€€

RESTAURANTS
El Botín C/Cuchilleros 17, http://botin.es; Ⓜ Sol/Tirso de Molina. Established in 1725, the picturesque *El Botín* is cited in the *Guinness Book of Records* as Europe's oldest restaurant. Favoured by Hemingway, inevitably it's become a tourist haunt but not such a bad one, with quality Castilian roasts – especially suckling pig (*cochinillo*) from Segovia and roast lamb (*cordero asado*). €€
★ **El Buey** Pza. de la Marina Española 1, http:// restauranteelbuey.com; Ⓜ Santo Domingo. A meat-eaters' paradise specializing in steak – which you fry up yourself on a sizzling hotplate. Very good side dishes, too, including a superb leek and seafood pie, and excellent home-made desserts. €€
Casa Paco Pza. Puerta Cerrada 11, http://casapaco1933. es; Ⓜ La Latina/Sol. This classic, traditional *comedor*, with no-nonsense service, dishes out some of the best-prepared meat dishes in town. Specializes in sirloin steak (*solomillo*) and another delicious cut known as *cebón de buey*. €€

PLAZA DE SANTA ANA AND HUERTAS
You should spend at least an evening eating and drinking

1

MADRID'S VEGETARIAN RESTAURANTS

Madrid has a growing number of good-value **vegetarian restaurants**, scattered about the centre. These include:

Artemisa C/Ventura de la Vega 4, http://restaurantes vegetarianosartemisa.com; ⓜ Sevilla; C/Tres Cruces 4; ⓜ Gran Vía; see map page 70. There are two branches of this long-standing popular vegetarian (you may have to wait for a table), which is good for veggie pizzas and wok dishes and has an imaginative range of salads and soups too. Reasonable prices, particularly for the lunchtime set menu. €€

Casa Mortero C/Zorrilla 9, http://casamortero.com; ⓜ Sevilla; see map page 70. With a darkly hip interior – think polished concrete and soft hanging lights – this stylish place puts a modern spin on classic Spanish dishes. This is a chance to try regional specialities like *remojon andaluz* – an Andalusian salad of orange, cod, and olives – while the hearty one-pot dishes, like duck and asparagus stew, are superb. €€

Honest Greens C/Fuencarral 95, www.honestgreens. com; ⓜ San Bernardo/Bilbao; see map page 62. Part of a small but international chain, with a few other outlets in Madrid, this bustling, energetic spot specializes in salads and plant-based pastas, and health bowls, although meat options are also available. €€

★ **Mama Campo** Pza. Olavide, www.mamacampo. es; ⓜ Quevedo/Iglesia; see map page 62. You'll find organic food for vegetarians and non-vegetarians alike in this cool and airy restaurant/bar perched on the edge of a popular tree-lined plaza. There are two spaces, one for meals, the other (*La Cantina*) for tapas and snacks. Always something interesting on offer in the seasonal menu. €€

Vegaviana C/Pelayo 35, 913 080 381; ⓜ Chueca; see map page 62. There's a wide range of vegetarian options with an international twist at this small eatery in the heart of Chueca, plus a free-range chicken option for non-veggies, too. Very good value, with big portions, meaning you'll struggle to break the €20 mark. €

★ **Yerbabuena** C/Bordadores 3, 915 99 48 05; ⓜ Ópera; see map page 70. A cut above most of its competitors, this friendly vegetarian has an extensive and well-presented range of dishes. Spinach crêpes, aubergine burgers, fennel soup and mushroom pie are among the mains. The set lunch is good value, as is the evening set menu. €€

at the historic, tiled bars in this central area. Restaurants are good, too, and frequented as much by locals as tourists.

TAPAS BARS

★ **Ana La Santa** Pza. Santa Ana 14, http://encompania delobos.com; ⓜ Sol/Antón Martín. A stylish bar-restaurant housed in smart surroundings in the lobby of the *ME Victoria* hotel at one end of Pza. Santa Ana. On offer is a mixture of classic *raciones* with a modern touch: mussels with lime and coriander, roast asparagus with rosemary, and fried baby squid, for example. €€€

★ **Casa González** C/Leon 12, http://casagonzalez.es. As you'd expect, this great little bar on the busy C/Leon has an extensive range of wines and cheese on offer, but it also serves up other great tapas including a fantastic *salmorejo* (cold tomato soup), a range of speciality sausages from around Spain and some imaginative *tostas* covered in a variety of tasty pâtés. €€

Cervecería Cervantes Pza. de Jesús 7, 914 296 093; ⓜ Antón Martín. Prawns are the speciality here – the *tosta de gambas* is delicious – but there's a wide range of other tapas, and the beer is good, too. An excellent place for an *aperitivo*. €€

Taberna del Chato C/Cruz 8, http://tabernadelchato. com; ⓜ Sol/Antón Martín. Reasonable prices, friendly service and some very good tapas are on offer in this increasingly popular bar. There is a selection of starters featuring tiny dishes of chicken curry, *morcilla*, *paté de perdiz* (partridge pâté), tuna tartare and so on, while there are more substantial dishes on offer too. €€

★ **Taberna La Dolores** Pza. de Jesús 4, 914 292 243; ⓜ Antón Martín. Splendid *canapés* at this popular and friendly tiled bar at the bottom of Huertas. The beer is good, and the food specialities include Roquefort and anchovy, and smoked-salmon *canapés*. Get here early if you want a space at the bar. €€

RESTAURANTS

Prada a Tope C/Príncipe 11, http://pradaatopemadrid. com; ⓜ Sevilla. There's quality produce from El Bierzo in León at this branch of the restaurant chain; the *pimientos asados*, *morcilla* and *tortilla* are extremely tasty. €€

La Sanabresa C/Amor de Diós 12, 914 290 338; ⓜ Antón Martín. A real local with an endless stream of customers who come for its good-quality and reasonably priced dishes. Don't miss the grilled aubergines. €

Vi-cool C/Huertas 12, 914 294 913, http://vi-cool.com; ⓜ Antón Martín. This place was originally established by Catalan celebrity chef Sergi Arola as a more affordable outlet for his renowned food. The low-key, minimalist interior provides the setting for some simple, but very classy and creative offerings including fried langoustines in a curry and mint sauce, as well as gourmet hamburgers and pizzas. €€€

LA LATINA AND LAVAPIÉS

South from Sol and Huertas are the quarters of La Latina and Lavapiés, whose patchwork of tiny streets retains an appealing neighbourhood feel, and are home to a great selection of bars and restaurants.

TAPAS BARS

★**Almendro 13** C/Almendro 13, http://almendro13.com; ⓜLa Latina. Always packed at weekends, this fashionable wood-panelled bar serves great *fino* from chilled black bottles. Tuck into the house specials of *huevos rotos* (fried eggs on a bed of crisps) and *roscas rellenas* (rings of bread stuffed with various meats). €€

Los Caracoles "Casa Amadeo" Pza. Cascorro 18, www.caracolesdeamadeo.com; ⓜLa Latina. A favourite since the 1940s, and as the name suggests the *caracoles* (snails) are the thing to eat. The place to come after a trek around the Rastro – although it will be heaving and keep an eye on the bill. €€€

★**Juana La Loca** Pza. Puerta de Moros 4, https://juanalaloca.es/en/; ⓜLa Latina. Fashionable hangout serving inventive tapas – a local favourite for spectacular *tortilla* with caramelized onion, grilled artichokes with parmesan and smoked salmon with curry sauce – and a great selection of very tasty, but fairly pricey, *canapés*. €€

La Musa Latina C/Costanilla San Andrés 12, http://grupolamusa.com; ⓜLa Latina. Another style-conscious restaurant on the La Latina scene. Serves a great set menu and a decent selection of modern tapas. It has a cool brick-walled bar downstairs with DJ sessions in the evenings. €€

Taberna de Antonio Sánchez C/Mesón de Paredes 13, http://tabernaantoniosanchez.com; ⓜTirso de Molina. Said to be the oldest *taberna* in Madrid, this Lavapiés bar has an appropriately dark, wooden interior complete with stuffed bulls' heads (one of which killed Antonio Sánchez, the son of the founder). *Rabo de toro* (oxtail), *tortilla*, *callos* (tripe) and *caracoles* (snails) are among the classic *madrileño* tapas on offer. €€

★**El Tempranillo** Cava Baja 38; ⓜLa Latina. A stylish little bar serving tasty tapas and a vast range of Spanish wines by the glass – a great place to discover a new favourite. €€

★**Txirimiri** C/Humilladero 6, http://txirimiri.es; ⓜLa Latina. Fantastic range of tapas and *pintxos* in this friendly and very popular bar just beside the Mercado de la Cebada. Mouthwatering combinations include *tortilla* with caramelized onion, langoustine *croquetas*, mushroom risotto and the house speciality, the Unai hamburger *pintxo* (a tempura burger with porcini sauce). €€

RESTAURANTS

Casa Lucio C/Cava Baja 35, http://casalucio.es; ⓜLa Latina. A Madrid institution famous for its Castilian specialities such as *cocido*, *callos* (tripe) and roasts, cooked to perfection. Booking is essential. If you can't stretch to a full meal, try some of the specialities in the front bar. €€€

Palacio de Anglona C/Segovia 13, http://palaciodeanglona.com; ⓜLa Latina/Ópera. This good-value restaurant housed in the cellars of an old La Latina mansion boasts minimalist black and white decor. Mains include black spaghetti with prawns, mini hamburgers and marinated langoustines. Cocktails are served in the lounge bar. €€

★**Posada de la Villa** C/Cava Baja 9, http://posadadelavilla.es; ⓜLa Latina. The most attractive-looking restaurant in La Latina, spread over three floors of a seventeenth-century mansion. Cooking is typically *madrileña*, including superb roast lamb. €€€

★**Xentes** C/Humilladero 13, http://xentes.es; ⓜLa Latina /Puerta de Toledo. Deservedly popular restaurant with a Galician accent and wide-ranging menu, including excellent *arroz caldoso* (rice dishes) accompanied by a range of seafood. There is also a very tasty selection of steaks. There's a good value taster menu alongside the à la carte offerings. €€

GRAN VÍA, PLAZA DE ESPAÑA AND BEYOND

On the Gran Vía, burger bars and fast-food joints fill most of the gaps between shops and cinemas. However, there are a few good restaurants in and around the great avenue.

MADRID CUISINE

Thanks to its status as Spanish capital, Madrid has long provided a home to **almost every regional style of Spanish cooking** from Castilian roasts, Galician seafood and Andalucian fried fish, to Asturian stews, Valencian paellas and Basque *nueva cocina*.

The city also has its own range of home-spun dishes with the famous *cocido madrileño*, a three-course stew of various cuts of meat, chorizo, chickpea and vegetables, topping the list. Other traditional favourites include *callos* (tripe in a spicy tomato sauce), *oreja* (pig's ears), *caracoles* (snails) and a range of offal-based dishes.

But Madrid is becoming increasingly cosmopolitan and dozens of **foreign cuisines** have appeared on the scene in recent years. There are some good Peruvian, Argentinian, Middle Eastern and Italian places and a growing number of Asian-influenced restaurants with some inventive fusion-style cuisine.

1

CAFÉS

Círculo de Bellas Artes C/Alcalá 42, http://circulo bellasartes.com; ⓂBanco de España. A stylish bar, where you can loll on sofas and have drinks at "normal" prices. Outside, in summer, there's a comfortable terraza. €€

TAPAS BARS

★ **Circo de las Tapas** C/Baja de San Pablo 21, https:// circodelastapas.com; ⓂSanto Domingo/Callao. You'll find a fabulous array of tapas and toasted sandwiches in this popular bar north of Gran Vía. The mussel casserole and grilled sirloin sandwich are both superb, but all the dishes are excellent. The service is friendly and the prices are reasonable too. €€

Txirimiri Ferraz C/Ferraz 38, http://txirimiri.es; ⓂArgüelles/ Ventura Rodríguez. Branch of an excellent small chain of tapas bars specializing in Basque-style *pintxos* and *raciones*. Apart from the house speciality Unai hamburger, the marvellous hot *pintxos* include steak, caramelized onion and pepper, cod in tempura and pâté with fig marmalade. If you want something more substantial the risottos are a good bet. €€€

RESTAURANTS

★ **La Barraca** C/Reina 29, http://labarraca.es; ⓂGran Vía/Banco de España. Step off the dingy street into this little slice of Valencia for some of the best paellas in town. Service is attentive but not overfussy, the starters are excellent and there's a refreshing lemon sorbet for dessert. €€€

La Bola C/Bola 5, http://labola.es; ⓂSanto Domingo. Established in 1870, this is one of the places to go for *cocido madrileño* (soup followed by chickpeas and other vegetables and then a selection of meats), only served at lunchtime. Don't plan on doing anything energetic afterwards, as it is incredibly filling. Service can be a little surly. No cards. €€

★ **Casa Mingo** Paseo de la Florida 34, www.casamingo. es; ⓂPríncipe Pío. Noisy, crowded and fun, *Casa Mingo* is a reasonably priced Asturian chicken and cider house just up the road from the Príncipe Pío. Tables are like gold dust, so loiter with your bottle of *sidra* in hand. €€

CHUECA AND SANTA BÁRBARA

Chueca – and Santa Bárbara to its north – have a combination of some superb traditional old bars and stylish new restaurants, as well as a vast amount of nightlife.

CAFÉS

Café Comercial Glorieta de Bilbao 7, http://cafecomercial madrid.com; ⓂBilbao. Reopened and spruced up after threatened closure (though they've kept the marble tables), the *Comercial* has retained much of its appeal as a traditional *madrileño* meeting point. Best for breakfasts and afternoon coffee and cakes, though it now also has a restaurant. €

TAPAS BARS

★ **Baco & Beto** C/Pelayo 24, http://baco-beto.com; ⓂChueca. Creative, mouthwatering tapas in this small bar in the heart of Chueca. The constantly changing menu features a selection of fresh ingredients and innovative raciones. €€

★ **Celso y Manolo** C/Libertad 1, 915 318 079, http:// celsoymanolo.es; ⓂChueca. Named in honour of the original owners of the old *taberna* that used to occupy the site, this bar now offers a wide-ranging menu with delicious raciones such as *croquetas de bacalao* (cod croquettes), great rice dishes and a fantastic selection of tomato salads. €€

★ **Taberna Angel Sierra** C/Gravina 11, Pza. Chueca, http://tabernadeangelsierra.es; ⓂChueca. One of the classic bars of Madrid, with a traditional zinc counter, constantly washed down. Everyone drinks *vermút*, which is on tap and delicious, and free tapas of the most exquisite *boquerones en vinagre* are despatched; *raciones*, however, are a bit pricey. €€€

RESTAURANTS

Benares C/Zurbano 5, http://benaresmadrid.com; ⓂColón. Michelin-star chef Atul Kochhar heads up this posh and correspondingly pricey Indian in Madrid. There are two taster menus available at different prices, while slightly cheaper a la carte options are also on offer. €€€€

La Carmencita C/Libertad 16, http://tabernalacarmencita. es; ⓂChueca. A traditional *taberna* with roots dating back to 1854 and which remains faithful to its origins by serving up an authentic range of classic dishes with carefully sourced ingredients including traditional stews, *pollo en pepitoria*

SUMMER IN MADRID

Although things have changed as Madrid has come into line with the rest of Europe, the Spanish capital still experiences a **partial shut-down in the summer**; from the end of July, you'll suddenly find that many of the bars, restaurants and offices are closed, and their inhabitants gone to the coast and countryside. Only in September does the city open fully for business again.

Luckily for visitors, and those *madrileños* who choose to remain, the main sights and museums stay open, and the summer nightlife takes on a momentum of its own in outdoor terrace bars, or *terrazas*. In addition, the city council organizes a major programme of entertainment, Los Veranos de la Villa, and overall it's not a bad time to be in town, so long as you can cope with the soaring temperatures and you're not trying to get anything done.

TOP CHEFS IN MADRID

Aside from the burgeoning international cuisine scene in Madrid, further good news for gastronomes is that several of the **country's top chefs** have established flagship restaurants in the capital.

El Club Allard C/Ferraz 2, http://elcluballard.com; Ⓜ Argüelles; see map page 62. Dominican María Marte took over the Michelin-starred *El Club Allard* in 2013 after working her way up from office cleaner to leading the kitchen. She has kept up its good reputation since with her supremely creative set menus combining a range of flavours and textures. €€€€

Diverxo C/Padre Damian 23, http://diverxo.com; Ⓜ Tetuán; see map page 62. Now located in the *NH Madrid Eurobuilding* hotel, Madrid's only restaurant in possession of three Michelin stars is run by chef David Muñoz and has a deserved reputation for stunning presentation, mouthwatering food and unpretentious service. As you would expect, prices are sky-high, but worth it for those who can afford it. €€€€

Dos Cielos Madrid Cuesta Santo Domingo 5, 915 416 700; Ⓜ Ópera/Santo Domingo; see map page 70. Run under the auspices of Michelin-starred brothers Sergio and Javier Torres and head chef Damián González, Dos

Cielos is housed in the elegant surroundings of the Gran Meliá Palacio de los Duques. Prices are more accessible than many of the other top restaurants; there is a taster menu with a selection of delicious bite-size samples of fish, meat and vegetable dishes. €€€€

Ramón Freixa Madrid C/Claudio Coello 67, http://ramonfreixamadrid.com; Ⓜ Serrano; see map page 62. Catalan chef Ramon Freixa's flagship two-Michelin-star restaurant is situated in the luxury surroundings of the *Selenza* hotel. Creative and impeccably presented dishes from an ever-changing menu feature superb meat and fish options and new twists on Spanish classics. A la carte dishes and taster menus are both available. Only space for 35 diners, so book well in advance. €€€€

CEBO Hotel Urban Cra de San Jerónimo 34, www.cebomadrid.com; Ⓜ Sevilla; see map page 62. Javier Sanz and Juan Sahuquillo run this Michelin-starred restaurant, which has two stunning menus: one classic, and one more contemporary and experimental. €€€€

(chicken in an almond sauce) and stuffed peppers. Also open for breakfast and weekend brunches, and serves up an excellent range of *vermút* for a pre-lunch *aperitivo*. €€€

★ **Morgana** C/Libertad 5, https://restaurantemorgana.es; Ⓜ Chueca. Superbly done Asian-influenced Galician food is the order of the day at this laid-back contemporary restaurant. Try the curry laksa mussels and the grilled octopus with kimchi. €€€

Salvador C/Barbieri 12, http://casasalvadormadrid.com; Ⓜ Chueca. A blast from the past, with bullfighting decor and specialities such as *rabo de toro* (bull's tail), *gallina en pepitoria*, fried *merluza* (hake) and *arroz con leche* (rice pudding), all of which are excellent. Set menus are decent value. €€€

La Tienda de Vinos (El Comunista) C/Augusto Figueroa 35, 915 217 012; Ⓜ Chueca. A long-established, down-to-earth, no frills *comedor*; its unofficial (but always used) name dates back to its time as a student haunt under Franco. Home-cooking at its best: the garlic soup is recommended as are the *lentejas* (lentils) and the *croquetas*. €€

Zara C/Barbieri 8, http://restaurantezara.com; Ⓜ Chueca/Gran Vía. There's excellent food at very good prices at this Cuban restaurant that has just relocated round the corner from its original home: *ropa vieja* (strips of beef), fried yucca, minced beef with fried bananas and other specialities; the *daiquiris* are very good, too. Prices are moderate. €€

MALASAÑA AND CHAMBERÍ

Malasaña is another characterful area, with a big nightlife

scene and dozens of bars. Farther north, in Chamberí, the area around Pza. de Olavide – a real neighbourhood square – offers some good-value places, well off the tourist trail.

CAFÉS

Café del Ruiz C/Ruiz 11, 914 461 232; Ⓜ Tribunal/Bilbao. A traditional café, serving coffee, cakes and cocktails. A top spot for a late drink or a pep-up coffee, and they often offer sets by local jazz, swing and folk artists on the small stage. €

TAPAS BAR

★ **La Musa** C/Manuel Malasaña 18, http://grupolamusa.com; Ⓜ Bilbao. It's easy to see why *La Musa* – a café, bar and restaurant combined – has become such a firm favourite on the Malasaña scene. A variety of imaginative – and very tasty – tapas, generous helpings, a strong wine list and chic decor are all part of the recipe for success. €€

RESTAURANTS

La Giralda C/ de Claudio Coello 12, http://restaurantes lagiralda.com; Ⓜ Bilbao. An *andaluz* fish and seafood restaurant of very high quality: perfectly cooked *chipirones*, *calamares* and all the standards, plus wonderful *mero* (grouper). €€€

★ **Ochenta Grados** C/Manuela Malasaña 10, http://ochentagrados.com; Ⓜ Bilbao. The idea behind *Ochenta Grados* is to serve traditional main-course dishes in miniature and it works wonderfully. Forget the idea of

1

a starter and a main; just order a selection of dishes to share from the inventive menu, maybe steak tartare with mustard, parmesan ice cream or prawn risotto. €€

★ **Ribeira do Miño** C/Santa Brigida 1, http://marisqueria ribeiradomino.com; ⓂTribunal. A fabulous-value *marisquería*, serving a superb seafood platter for two. Go for the slightly more expensive Galician white wine Albariño to accompany it. Fast, efficient and friendly service. €€

PASEO DEL PRADO, PASEO DE RECOLETOS AND EL RETIRO

This is a fancier area with few bars of note but some extremely good, if expensive, restaurants, well worth considering, even if you're not staying at the *Ritz*.

CAFÉS

★ **Café del Espejo** Paseo de Recoletos 31, http://restauranteelespejo.com; ⓂColón. This opened in 1991 but you wouldn't guess it – mirrors, gilt and a wonderful glass pavilion, plus a leafy outside terraza. €

Café Gijón Paseo de Recoletos 21, http://cafegijon.com; ⓂBanco de España. A famous literary café – and a centre of the intellectual/arty *movida* in the 1980s – decked out in Cuban mahogany and mirrors. Has a summer terraza. €

TAPAS BARS

El Brillante Glorieta de Emperador Carlos V 8, http://barel brillante.es; ⓂAtocha. Down-to-earth, brightly lit bar next to the Reina Sofía that's open all day. Claims to serve the best *calamares bocadillo* (filled baguette) in Madrid. Perfect for a quick snack between museum visits, but not the place for a meal. €

La Platería C/Moratín 49, 914 291 722; ⓂAntón Martin/Estación del Arte. Just across the square from *La Tapería* (see below), this touristy but conveniently placed bar has an enormously popular summer terraza and a good selection of reasonably priced tapas. €€

La Tapería del Prado Pza. Platerías de Martínez 1, http://latapeia.es; ⓂAntón Martin/Estación del Arte. A modern and slightly pricey bar opposite the Prado serving up an inventive range of tapas and *raciones* from an all-day kitchen. €€€

RESTAURANTS

Adrede C/Alfonso XI 13, http://restauranteadrede.com; ⓂRetiro/Banco de España. An atmospheric brick-walled restaurant with a varied menu of meat, seafood and veggie dishes. The sardines with garlic and parsley, duck gyozas and truffle-fried artichokes are all superb. €€€

Al Mounia C/Recoletos 5, http://restaurantealmounia.es; ⓂColón/Banco de España. High-quality Moroccan cooking in the most established Arabic restaurant in town, offering a romantic setting with attentive service. There is a taster menu and a more affordable lunchtime option. €€€

★ **Bodega de los Secretos** C/San Blas 4, http://bodega delossecretos.com; ⓂAtocha. Located in an atmospheric brick-lined wine cellar (access is difficult) just behind the Caixa Forum exhibition space, this restaurant offers a range of stylishly presented Spanish dishes with a modern twist and, as you'd expect, has an excellent wine list. €€€

Qorotika C/Marqués de Cubas 16, 689 36 21 28; ⓂBanco España. Lovely Peruvian food is served up in a homely environment at this laid-back restaurant, with ceviche, seafood rice, and tres leches cake to finish. €€

SALAMANCA

Salamanca is Madrid's equivalent of Bond Street or Fifth Avenue, full of designer shops and expensive-looking natives. The recommendations below are correspondingly pricey but high quality.

TAPAS BARS

Hevia C/Serrano 118, http://heviamadrid.com; ⓂNúñez de Balboa. Plush venue and wealthy clientele who come for expensive but excellent tapas and *canapés*. The smoked fish, *salmorejo* (cold tomato soup) and squid are superb. €€€

José Luís C/Serrano 89, http://joseluis.es; ⓂSerrano. A classy tapas place with dainty and delicious sandwiches laid out along the bar. You take what you fancy and cough up at the end, in the safe knowledge that the owner will have notched up another few hundred euros to expand his chain of bars in the Americas. €€

El Lateral Paseo de la Castellana 89, http://lateral.com; ⓂSantiago Bernabéu/Nuevos Ministerios. A swish place serving a good variety of classic dishes such as *croquetas* and *pimientos rellenos* (stuffed peppers) with a modern twist. Other branches at Castellana 42, C/Velazquez 57 and C/Fuencarral 43. €€€

RESTAURANTS

La Pescadería C/Hermosilla 46, https://lapescaderia dehermosilla.es; ⓂVelázquez. The speciality at this roomy restaurant is seafood, with delicately presented octopus carpaccio, black paella with squid ink, juiy prawns with mango and avocado, and more. Good wine list, too. €€€

El Pescador C/José Ortega y Gasset 75, http://marisqueriaelpescador.net; ⓂLista. One of the city's best seafood restaurants, run by Gallegos and with specials flown in from the Atlantic each morning. The clientele can be a bit intimidating, but you'll rarely experience better seafood cooking. If the restaurant is too much you can always sample some of the dishes in the bar. €€€

DRINKING AND NIGHTLIFE

SEE MAPS PAGES 62 AND 70

Madrid **nightlife** is a pretty serious phenomenon. This is one of the few cities in Europe where you can get caught in traffic jams in the early hours of the morning when the clubbers are either going home or moving on to the dance-past-dawn discos. As with everything *madrileño*, there is a bewildering variety of nightlife venues. Most common are the **discobares**, whose unifying feature is background (occasionally live) pop, rock, dance or salsa music. These get going from around 11pm and stay open routinely until 2am, as will the few quieter **cocktail bars** and **pubs**.

For *discotecas*, entry charges are quite common, but tend to cover you for a drink or two. Free passes can often be picked up from public relations personnel who hang around in the streets outside, in tourist offices or bars. Be aware that many *discotecas* are fairly ephemeral institutions and frequently only last a season before opening up somewhere else under a different name, so it's a good idea to consult listing magazines *La Guía del Ocio, Metrópoli, esMadrid* or the website https://tickets.nightlifemadrid.com for the very latest information.

BARS

Madrid's bar scene caters to every conceivable taste in terms of drinks, music and atmosphere, though in recent years, the notoriously late opening hours have been somewhat curtailed by the local authorities, with most bars closing at 2am or 3am depending on their licence.

SOL, PLAZA DE SANTA ANA AND HUERTAS

Alhambra C/Victoria 5, 915 210 718; Ⓜ Sol. A friendly tapas bar by day, *Alhambra* transforms itself into a fun *discobar* by night with the crowds spilling over into the *El Buscón* bar next door.

Cervecería Alemana Pza. Santa Ana 6, http://cerveceria alemana.com; Ⓜ Sol. Refurbished once again but it remains a stylish old beer house, once frequented by Hemingway. Order a *caña* and go easy on the tapas, as the bill can mount up fast.

Cervecería Santa Ana Pza. Santa Ana 10, http://cerveceriasantaana.com; Ⓜ Sol. Old-styled wood-panelled bar which has actually only been around since the mid-1980s. Cheaper than the *Alemana*, with tables outside, friendly service and a good selection of tapas.

Dos Gardenias C/Santa María 13; 627 003 571; Ⓜ Antón Martín. Intimate and relaxed little bar in the Huertas area where you can chill out in their comfy chairs, sip on a mojito and escape from the hubbub of the city outside.

La Fidula C/Huertas 57, http://lafidula.es; Ⓜ Antón Martín. Head here to sip a beer, cocktail or *fino* to the accompaniment of live music – usually singer-songwriters – performed on the tiny stage. Cover charge on some nights.

The Glass Bar C/San Jeronimo 34, http://hotelurban.com; Ⓜ Sevilla. Housed in the ultra-chic five-star *Hotel Urban*, this glamorous, glass-fronted cocktail bar has become a compulsory stop for the well-heeled crowd. In summer, there's a terrace bar on the sixth floor.

Salmon Guru C/Echegaray 21, http://facebook.com/

SalmonGuru; Ⓜ Sevilla/Antón Martín. There are excellent cocktails in this fun gastrobar run by star bartender Diego Cabrera. Mirrors, neon lights and comic-book-hero speech bubbles adorn the walls, while behind the bar the cocktail menu includes classics like Tom Collins and Long Island Ice Tea as well as non-alcoholic "mocktails".

★ **La Venencia** C/Echegaray 7, 914 29 73 13; Ⓜ Sol. For a real taste of old Madrid, this is a must: a dilapidated wood-panelled bar, serving just sherry – try the extra-dry *fino* or the crisp *manzanilla* – cured tuna (*mojama*) and delicious olives. The decoration has remained unchanged for decades, with ancient barrels and yellowing posters, while the bill is chalked up old-style on the wooden bar.

Viva Madrid C/Manuel Fernández y González 7, http://restaurantevivamadrid.com; Ⓜ Antón Martín. A fabulous tiled bar-restaurant – both outside and in – offering a wide selection of food and tapas, but best for a drink.

GRAN VÍA

★ **Del Diego** C/Reina 12, http://deldiego.com; Ⓜ Gran Vía. An elegant New York-style cocktail bar set up by a former *Museo Chicote* waiter and now better than the original place. There's a friendly, unhurried atmosphere, and it's open until the early hours. The house special is the vodka-based Del Diego, but the mojitos and margaritas are great, too.

Estación Malasaña C/Pez 16, www.estacionmalasana.es; Ⓜ Noviciado. Original and fun, this long, narrow comedy club and lounge bar is designed to look like the interior of a luxurious old train carriage, while landscapes are projected onto the "windows" to create the sensation of movement. There is an extensive cocktail menu in the evenings and regular live comedy too.

Gin Club/Mercado de la Reina C/Reina 16, http://grupomercadodelareina.es; Ⓜ Gran Vía. Multipurpose tapas bar, restaurant and *bar de copas*. At the back, with its mirror ceilings and black leather chairs, is the chill-out cocktail bar, the *Gin Club*, which offers over 20 different brands. You can also get a decent mojito here if you prefer something different.

El Jardín Secreto C/Conde Duque 2, https://eljardin secretomadrid.es; Ⓜ Pza. de España. Cosy, fairy-tale-style bar and eatery on the corner of a tiny square close to Pza. de España, serving reasonably priced drinks and cocktails. Service is friendly and the atmosphere unhurried.

Museo Chicote Gran Vía 12, http://grupomercado delareina.es; Ⓜ Gran Vía. Opened back in 1931, *Chicote* was once a haunt of Buñuel and Hemingway. It's lost some of its charm but is still a very fashionable place, with evening music sessions.

LA LATINA AND LAVAPIÉS

★ **Café Barbieri** C/Ave María 45, https://cafe barbieri1902.com; Ⓜ Lavapiés. A relaxed bar-café in the heart of Lavapiés, with unobtrusive music, old-style decor, newspapers and a wide selection of coffees.

De Mercado Cost.ª de San Andrés, 20 , 914 912 406; ⓜ Antón Martín. Classic Madrid café-bar on the southwest corner of Plaza de la Paja, with good-value cocktails, beer and wine alongside some hearty home cooked food options like big plates of roasted chicken legs.

El Viajero Pza. de la Cebada, http://elviajeromadrid.com; ⓜ La Latina. You'll find a bar, disco, restaurant and summer terraza on different floors of this fashionable La Latina nightspot. Great views of San Francisco el Grande from the terraza at the top. Reasonably priced *raciones*, while there are steaks and burgers if you want something more substantial.

CHUECA, MALASAÑA AND SANTA BÁRBARA

★ **La Ardosa** C/Colón 13, http://laardosa.es; ⓜ Tribunal. One of the city's classic *tabernas*, offering limited but very tasty tapas including great *croquetas*, *salmorejo* (cold tomato soup) and an excellent home-made *tortilla*. Prides itself on its draught beer and Guinness and serves a great pre-lunch *vermút* (vermouth) too.

La Manuela C/San Vicente Ferrer 29 (just off Pza. Dos de Mayo), 915 313 598; ⓜ Tribunal. An irresistible old

neighbourhood *bodega*, with a traditional bar counter, marble columns and *vermút* on tap. An ideal place to start the evening. Packed out at weekends.

Masaru C/Santo Tomé 7, www.masarumadrid.com; ⓜ Colón/Alonso Martínez. A stylish Japanese cocktail bar, with dim lighting, a Zen-industrial aesthetic and a great range of Japanese whiskies, sakes and cocktails.

Pepe Botella C/San Andrés 12 (on Pza. Dos de Mayo), 915 224 309; http://facebook.com/cafepepebotella; ⓜ Tribunal. An old-style elegance still clings to this little bar, with its friendly staff, marble-topped tables and low-volume music.

Tupperware C/Corredera Alta de San Pablo 26, 914 485 016; ⓜ Tribunal. You'll find a refreshingly cosmopolitan musical diet at this legendary Malasaña nightspot which is often packed to the rafters.

Vía Lactea C/Velarde 18, 914 467 581; ⓜ Tribunal. Call in here to see where the *movida* began. *Vía Lactea* was a key meeting place for Spain's designers, directors, pop stars and painters in the 1980s, and it retains its original decor from the time, billiard tables included. There's a stage downstairs. It attracts a young, studenty clientele and is packed at weekends.

SALAMANCA

Alquimia/Alegoría C/Villanueva 2 (entrance on C/Cid),

TERRAZAS

Since the banning of smoking inside bars and restaurants, **terrazas** (terraces) have become more popular than ever in Madrid and many places now have at least a few tables set up on the city pavements year-round.

In summer many more bars migrate on to the streets. Beyond **Pza. de Colón** and up to the **Bernabéu** more fashionable *terrazas* with music, a posey clientele and higher prices often appear in the summer. Be aware, however, that many of the *terrazas* run by clubs vary their sites year by year as they fall foul of the increasingly strict licensing and noise regulations.

Atenas Parque de Atenas (just off C/Segovia), http:// terrazaatenas.com; ⓜ Ópera. Lively summer terraza set in the park down by the river in the shadow of the Catedral and not far from the bars and clubs of La Latina.

Paseo del Pintor Rosales ⓜ Argüelles. There is a clutch of *terrazas* catering for all tastes and popular with families along this avenue on the edge of the Parque del Oeste.

Paseo de Recoletos and Paseo de la Castellana On the nearer reaches of Paseo de Recoletos is the refined garden terraza at the *Casa de América* (no. 2) and those of the old-style cafés *Gijón* (no. 21) and *Espejo* (no. 31), popular meeting points for *madrileños* of all kinds.

Pza. de Comendadoras ⓜ Ventura Rodríguez. One of the city's few traffic-free squares, this has a couple of very popular *terrazas* – attached to the *Café Moderno* and to the Mexican restaurant next door.

Pza. de Oriente ⓜ Ópera. The *Café de Oriente terraza* is a station of Madrid nightlife and enjoys a marvellous

location next to the opera house, gazing across the plaza to the Palacio Real.

Pza. de la Paja ⓜ La Latina. One of the most pleasant *terrazas* in the heart of old Madrid can be found in this former market square in La Latina.

Pza. San Andrés ⓜ La Latina. Just the other side of the church of San Andrés a host of bars spills out onto this atmospheric plaza. The place is buzzing in the summer, and makes a great meeting place before a bar crawl around the area.

Pza. de Santa Ana ⓜ Sol. Several of the *cervecerías* here have outside seating, and there's a *chiringuito* (a makeshift bar) in the middle of the square throughout the summer.

Terraza de Las Vistillas C/Bailén (on the south side of the viaduct); ⓜ Ópera. This popular terraza is good for a relaxing drink while enjoying the *vistillas* ("little vistas") over towards the Almudena Catedral and the Guadarrama mountains to the northwest.

CRAFT BEER

The fashion for craft beers has reached Madrid and there are a number of excellent establishments, some of which brew their own beer on site, springing up over the city. These include:

The Beer Garden Store C/Juan de Asturia 23 , www.thebeergardenstore.com; ⓂIglesia; see map page 62. With a decor not unlike a traditional British pub, there's a top-drawer range of self-brewed beers here, from IPAs and sour ales to pilsners and stouts.

Fábrica Maravillas C/Valverde 29, www.fmaravillas.com; ⓂGran Vía; see map page 62. Opened in 2012 in this rejuvenated street running perpendicular to Gran Vía, *Fábrica* has helped promote the trend for craft beers in Madrid. A tasty selection of ales on offer, including the fruity Malasaña, stout and an excellent IPA.

Oldenburg C/Hartzenbusch 12, 914 482 341; ⓂBilbao;

see map page 62. This bar has been around for 25 years and was one of the first to break the stranglehold of the mass-produced local brews like Mahou. Has featured in the *Guinness Book of Records* for having the highest concentration of different beers per metre squared of any bar in the world.

La Tape C/San Bernardo 88, http://latape.com; ⓂSan Bernardo; see map page 62. Seven craft beers on tap, most of which are changed on a regular basis. They also have a great selection of bottled beers and some excellent food too. Downstairs is the bar and takeaway section, upstairs the restaurant.

915 772 785; ⓂRetiro. A restaurant-bar-club modelled on an English gentleman's club, with over-the-top Baroque decor. It's a popular backdrop for media presentations and photo shoots.

La Jarra y La Pipa C/Alcalá 147, www.facebook.com/lajarraylapipa; ⓂGoya. There's a great selection of beers on tap at this friendly, pub-like *cervezería*, as well as *bocadillos*, *tostas*, and other light snacks.

DISCOTECAS

Discotecas – or clubs – aren't always that different from *discobares*, though they tend to be bigger and flashier, with a lot of attention to the lighting, sound system and decor. They start late and stay open until around 4am, some till 6am and a couple till noon. In summer, some of the trendier clubs suspend operations and set up outdoor *terrazas* (see page 108).

SOL, ÓPERA AND PZA. DE SANTA ANA

Coco C/Alcalá 20, http://mondodisko.es; ⓂSevilla. Uber-modern decor in this slick club that is one of the most fashionable stations of the night on the Madrid scene. House, funk and hip-hop in the *Mondo Disko* sessions on Thursday and Saturday nights from midnight till the early morning hours.

Joy Madrid C/Arenal 11, http://joy-eslava.com; ⓂSol/Ópera. *Joy Madrid* may not be at the cutting edge of the club scene, but judging by the queues, it remains one of the city's most popular and successful clubs. If you can't get in, console yourself with the *Chocolatería San Ginés* on the street behind (see page 110).

Torero C/Cruz 26; ⓂSol/Sevilla. A very popular and enjoyable two-storey disco right in the heart of the Santa Ana area. The first floor focuses on sounds from the 1980s and 1990s, the second has a more contemporary menu. Packed at weekends.

PASEO DEL PRADO/ATOCHA

Azucar Salsa C/Atocha 107, http://azucarsalsadisco.com; ⓂAtocha/Antón Martín. Fun salsa disco, which also runs dance classes, with frequent Cuban and Bachata nights and amateur dance competitions where the virtuosos get a chance to strut their stuff.

Kapital C/Atocha 125; https://madridlux.com; ⓂAtocha. A seven-storey macro-disco, complete with three dancefloors, lasers, go-go dancers, a cocktail bar and a top-floor terrace. House, funk and R&B.

GRAN VÍA AND PLAZA. DE ESPAÑA

Morocco C/Marqués de Leganés 7, http://salamorocco madrid.com; ⓂSanto Domingo. Fun, unpretentious disco with a slightly older clientele and a varied diet of Spanish pop.

Sala 0 Pza. de Callao 4; www.sala0madrid.com; ⓂCallao. Previously known as *Sala Bash* and a mainstay of the club scene, this venue in the elegant Palacio de la Prensa is a popular performance space for touring bands and DJs.

CHUECA/SANTA BÁRBARA

Teatro Barceló C/Barceló 11, http://teatrobarcelo.com; ⓂTribunal. Formerly known as *Pachá*, this club, housed in a fantastic Art Deco building, remains a popular station of the Madrid night scene, with its varied offering of resident DJ sessions, concerts and party nights.

SALAMANCA AND THE NORTH

Koh Tao C/Alberto Alcocer 32, https://madridlux.com; ⓂColombia/Cuzco. Despite the exclusive location, this is a light-hearted club determined to keep the clientele happy with its party atmosphere, actors and go-gos. There is a popular summer terraza too.

Opium C/José Abascal 56, http://opiummadrid.com; ⓂGregorio Marañon. There's electronic/house music from

1

CHOCOLATE BEFORE BED

If you stay up through a Madrid night, then you must try one of the city's great institutions – the **Chocolatería San Ginés** (http://chocolateriasangines.com; daily 24hrs; see map page 70) on Pasadizo de San Ginés, off C/Arenal between the Puerta del Sol and Teatro Real. Established in 1894, this serves *chocolate con churros* to perfection – just the thing after a night's excess. There's an almost mythical *madrileño* custom of winding up at San Ginés after the clubs close (not that they do any longer), before heading home for a shower and then off to work.

resident DJs in this reopened club which is popular with *pijos* – fashion-conscious rich kids – and the trendsetting glamour crowd.

MUSIC, FILM AND THEATRE SEE MAPS PAGES 62 AND 70

Most nights in Madrid, you can take in performances of **flamenco**, **salsa**, **rock**, **jazz**, **classical music** and **opera**. Often, it's the smaller, offbeat clubs that are the more enjoyable, though there are plenty of large auditoria for big-name concerts. In summer, events are supplemented by the council's **Veranos de la Villa** cultural programme, and in autumn the **Festival de Otoño a Primavera**. These also encompass **theatre** and **film**, both of which have healthy year-round scenes.

FLAMENCO

Flamenco underwent something of a revival in Madrid back in the 1990s, in large part owing to the "new flamenco" artists, like Ketama, Pata Negra and Radio Tarifa, who were unafraid to mix it with a bit of blues, jazz, even rock. Since then a new generation of younger but more traditional artists such as Niña Pastori and Estrella Morente have become more popular. Madrid has its own flamenco festival (Suma Flamenca) in June, when you stand a chance of catching some of the bigger names such as Tomatito, José Mercé or Eva Yerbabuena. The club listings below span the range from purist flamenco to crossover experiments, and most artists – even major stars – appear in them. A *sala rociera* is where the public dances *sevillanas*, while a *tablao* is where professional artists sing and/or dance. Although the following may open earlier, be aware that in many cases performances won't really get going until around midnight.

Tablao de la Villa C/Torija 7, https://tablaodelavilla. com; ⓜ Santo Domingo. One of the oldest flamenco clubs in Madrid (though under a recent name change), with a dinner-dance spectacular. It's expensive, but the music is authentic. Reservations are essential (sessions at 8pm & 10.30pm) and you can either opt for the show and a drink or have a meal too.

Las Carboneras C/ Conde de Miranda, http://tablaolas carboneras.com; ⓜ Sol. It's geared up for the tourist market but this *tablao* has gained a decent reputation and is a good option if you want to get a taste of flamenco.

Cardamomo C/Echegaray 15, http://cardamomo.com; ⓜ Sevilla/Sol. This flamenco bar has evolved into a well-

respected fully blown *tablao* in recent years.

La Quimera C/de Cuchilleros 7, https://tablaolaquimera. com; ⓜ Tirso de Molina. A small but very popular flamenco *tablao* that gets its share of big names. The best nights are Thurs and Fri.

Corral de la Morería C/Morería 17, 913 658 446, http://corraldelamoreria.com; ⓜ La Latina. A renowned and atmospheric, if expensive, venue for some serious flamenco acts but, again, expensive at about €40 for show plus a drink and double that if you want to dine in the restaurant.

Tablao Flamenco 1911 Pl. de Santa Ana 15, http://flamencocandela.com; ⓜ Antón Martín. A lovely, ornate venue decked out in mock-Moorish style and with an Andalusian food menu to match the authentic flamenco music and dance on stage.

Teatro Flamenco C/del Pez 10, http://teatroflamenco madrid.com; ⓜ Noviciado. There's a little slice of Andalucía in this *sala rociera* where it's easy to imagine you've been transported to Seville as you watch the professionals strut their stuff. Drinks are expensive, but it's the most professional show in town.

POP, ROCK AND BLUES

Although not as popular as Barcelona, Madrid is on the international rock-tour circuit and you can catch big (and small) American and British acts in front of enthusiastic audiences. Large arenas such as the WiZink Center and Las Ventas bullring are used for some of the biggest acts, while in the smaller clubs, you have a chance of seeing a very wide range of local bands.

CLUBS AND BARS

La Coquette C/Hileras 14; ⓜ Ópera. A small, crowded basement jazz and blues bar, where people sit around in the near-dark watching blues bands perform on a tiny stage.

Honky Tonk C/Covarrubias 24, http://clubhonky.com; ⓜ Alonso Martínez. This late-opening bar just north of Alonso Martínez has nightly blues and rock sets.

★ **Libertad 8** C/Libertad 8, http://libertad8cafe.es; ⓜ Chueca. *Libertad 8* made its name during the *movida*,

LGBTQ+ MADRID

Much of Madrid's nightlife has a big LGBTQ+ input and **gay men** especially will feel at home in most of the listings in our "Discotecas" section. However, Pza. Chueca and the surrounding streets, especially C/Pelayo, harbour at least a dozen exclusively LGBTQ+ bars and clubs, as well as a café that's traditionally LGBTQ+ – the *Café Figueroa* at C/Augusto Figueroa 17. The **lesbian scene** is more disparate.

The main LGBTQ+ organization in Madrid is **Coordinadora Gay de Madrid**, C/Puebla 9 (http://cogam.org; ⓂGran Vía), which can give information on health, leisure and LGBTQ+ rights. Feminist and lesbian groups are based at the **Federacion Estatal de Lesbianas, Gais, Transexuales y Bisexuales** at C/Infantas 40, 4º izqda (http://felgtbi.org; ⓂBanco de España/Chueca). The website http://shangay.com has listings and information about upcoming events.

BARS AND DISCOTECAS

La Chuequita C/Gravina 10; ⓂChueca. Comfortable café, with an Art Deco frontage and kitsch, colourful decor. The perfect place for a quiet drink, and popular with a mixed crowd.

Club 33 C/Cabeza 33, http://club33madrid.es; ⓂTirso de Molina/Antón Martín. Formerly women-only, now a mixed club in Lavapiés with a friendly vibe.

Delirio Dance Club C/Pelayo 59, http://deliriochueca. com; ⓂChueca. Fun atmosphere with drag queens, shows and lightweight pop sounds from Britney Spears to Madonna.

Escape C/Gravina 13; ⓂChueca. Originally a lesbian club, but now popular with the LGBTQ+ crowd too. A fun and friendly atmosphere.

La Lupe C/Torrecilla del Leal 12; ⓂAntón Martín. A mixed LGBTQ+ and alternative bar. Good music, cheap drinks and occasional cabaret.

Ricks C/Clavel 8; ⓂGran Vía. A varied-clientele *discobar* that gets packed at weekends when every available space is used for dancing. Open and light, with a friendly atmosphere – but drinks are pricey.

Truco C/Gravina 10; ⓂChueca. A long-established women's bar with a popular summer terraza that spills out onto Chueca's main plaza.

but this friendly little bar in Chueca still acts as a venue for up-and-coming singer-songwriters and even has its own record label.

El Sol C/Jardines 3, http://salaelsol.com; ⓂSol/Gran Vía. Over thirty years on the scene, this down-to-earth club hosts around twenty live concerts a month, but continues afterwards (usually from about 1am) as a disco, playing house, soul and acid jazz. Cover charge includes a drink.

Sala Vesta C/Barquillo 29, http://salavesta.com; ⓂChueca. On the site of the legendary club Bogui Jazz, Sala Vesta is holding the flag proudly with great club nights and a live music programme including jazz, folk, rock and soul.

MAJOR EVENT VENUES

Circo Price Ronda de Atocha 35, http://teatrocircoprice. es; ⓂAtocha/Lavapiés. Big enough to hold some major shows and concerts, but small enough to retain a sense of intimacy, the Circo Price hosts a popular Christmas circus, an annual magic season and many of the concerts in the Veranos de la Villa season.

La Riviera Paseo Bajo Virgen del Puerto s/n, Puente de Segovia, http://salariviera.com; ⓂPuerta del Ángel. A fun disco (weekends only) and concert venue right next to the river, which has hosted its fair share of major artists including Paul Weller and the Black Eyed Peas.

WiZink Center Avda. Felipe II s/n, http://wizinkcenter.es; ⓂGoya. This, the city's sports arena, replaces the one that burned down in 2001 and has been renamed on several occasions. It's used for big shows of the Harry Styles, Bruno Mars, Rihanna variety.

LATIN MUSIC

Madrid attracts big-name Latin artists, who tend to play at the venues below. The local scene is a good deal more low-key, but there's enjoyable salsa, nonetheless, in a handful of clubs.

TICKETS

Tickets for most big rock concerts are sold by Fnac, C/Preciados 28, http://fnac.es (ⓂCallao), El Corte Inglés, C/Preciados 1–4 http://elcorteingles.es (ⓂSol) and http:// ticketea.com. For theatre and concert tickets try Entradas.com, http://entradas. com and Ticketmaster http://ticketmaster. es. The website http://atrapalo.com also sells discount tickets for the theatre and musicals.

1

Galileo Galilei C/Galileo 100, http://salagalileogalilei. com; ⓜIslas Filipinas. A bar, concert venue and disco all rolled into one. Latin music is regularly on offer, but you'll need to check the website to find out which night, as it also hosts cabaret, flamenco and singer-songwriters.

El Son C/Victoria 6; www.facebook.com/DISCOTECAELSON; ⓜSol. You'll find live salsa music, dance classes and disco at this small Latin club, which has picked up where its predecessor *Massai* left off. There's no space to stand and watch, though, so make sure you bring your dancing shoes.

JAZZ

Madrid doesn't rank up there with London, Paris or New York on the jazz front, but the clubs are friendly, unpretentious places. Look out for the annual jazz festival, which is staged at a variety of venues in November.

★ **Café Berlín** C/Jacometrezo 4, http://berlincafe.es; ⓜCallao/Santo Domingo. Jazz and blues sessions often take place in this good-looking Art Nouveau café just off the Gran Vía. It also stages soul, flamenco and tango concerts.

Café Central Pza. del Ángel 10, www.cafecentralmadrid. com; ⓜSol. A small and relaxed jazz club that gets the odd big name, plus strong local talent. The Art Deco café is worth a visit in its own right.

Café Jazz Populart C/Huertas 22, http://cafepopulart. com; ⓜAntón Martín. Nightly sets from jazz and blues bands.

Clamores C/Alburquerque 14, http://salaclamores.com; ⓜBilbao. A large, low-key and enjoyable jazz bar with accomplished (if not very famous) artists, not too exorbitant drinks and a nice range of snacks.

CLASSICAL MUSIC AND OPERA

The Teatro Real is the city's prestigious opera house and the Auditorio Nacional de Música is home to the Orquesta Nacional de España. Equally enjoyable are the salons and small auditoria for chamber orchestras and groups.

Auditorio Nacional de Música C/Príncipe de Vergara 146, www.auditorionacional.mcu.es; ⓜCruz del Rayo. Home of the Spanish National Orchestra and host to most international visiting orchestras.

Teatro Real Pza. Isabel II, https://teatroreal.es; ⓜÓpera. Madrid's opulent opera house, and a fantastic setting for

some prestigious productions. Tickets range from €12 (with very restricted views) to close to €500, and you'll need to book well in advance for the best seats.

Teatro Zarzuela C/Jovellanos 4, http://teatrodelazarzuela. mcu.es; ⓜSevilla. The main venue for Spanish operetta. Also hosts classical music and dance.

FILM

Cines – cinemas – can be found all over the central area, and there's a handful of grand old picture houses strung out along the length of the Gran Vía. These offer major releases dubbed into Spanish, though a number of cinemas have regular original language screenings, with subtitles; these are listed in a separate *versión original/subtitulada* (*v.o.*) section in the newspapers. Most cinemas have a *día del espectador* (usually Mon or Wed) when tickets are heavily discounted. Be warned that on Sunday night half of Madrid goes to the movies, and queues can be long.

Filmoteca/Cine Doré C/Santa Isabel 3; ⓜAntón Martín. A beautiful old cinema, now home to an art-film centre, with imaginative programmes of classic and contemporary films, all shown in *v.o.* at a low admission price. In summer, there are open-air screenings on a little terraza – they're very popular, so buy tickets in advance.

Golem, **Renoir** and **Princesa** C/Martín de los Heros 12 & 14 and C/Princesa 3, http://golem.es, http://cinesrenoir. com; ⓜPza. de España. These three multiscreen cinemas, within 200m of each other, show regular *v.o.* films.

Ideal Yelmo Cineplex C/Doctor Cortezo 6, http:// yelmocines.es; ⓜSol/Tirso de Molina. A centrally located, nine-screen complex that shows a good selection of *v.o.* films.

THEATRE AND CABARET

Madrid is enjoying a renaissance in theatre; you can catch anything from Lope de Vega to contemporary and experimental productions, and there's also a new wave of cabaret and comedy acts. Look out, too, for the annual Festival de Otoño a Primavera which runs from September to May.

Teatro de Bellas Artes C/Marqués de Riera 2, http:// teatrobellasartes.es; ⓜBanco de España. The *teatro* stages a wide range of productions from Shakespeare to Hansel and Gretel.

MADRID LISTINGS

Listings information is in plentiful supply in Madrid. The newspapers *El País* (http://elpais. es) and *El Mundo* (http://elmundo.es) have excellent daily listings, and on Fridays both publish supplements devoted to events, bars and restaurants in the capital. El Pais's supplement, *La Guía del Ocio* (https://guiadelocio.es/madrid), is also available for the rest of the week at any kiosk. The *ayuntamiento* publishes a monthly pamphlet *esMadrid* (in English and Spanish), which is free from any of the tourist offices and lists forthcoming events in the city (also see http://esmadrid.com).

1

Teatro Español C/Príncipe 25, http://teatroespanol.es; ⓂSol/Sevilla. A classic Spanish theatre on the site of one of the city's old *corrales*.
Teatro Fernán Gómez Pza. de Colón, http://teatrofernan gomez.es; ⓂColón. A range of dramas, dance and musical productions as well as exhibitions are on at this arts centre named after the late Spanish actor.
Teatro María Guerrero C/Tamayo y Baus 4, http://dramatico.mcu.es; ⓂColón. This is the headquarters of the Centro Dramático Nacional, which stages high-quality Spanish and international productions in a beautiful neo-Mudéjar interior.

Teatro Nuevo Apolo Pza. Tirso de Molina 1, http://summmusic.com; ⓂTirso de Molina. Madrid's principal venue for major musicals, dance spectacles and ballet.
Teatro Valle-Inclán C/Pza. de Lavapiés, http://dramatico.mcu.es; ⓂLavapiés. The state-of-the-art Valle-Inclán provides a second home for the Centro Dramático Nacional.
Teatros del Canal C/Cea Bermúdez 1, www.teatroscanal.com; ⓂRíos Rosas. Two large theatres in this complex host music, dance and drama. One of the spaces is used for the regional theatre festival in the spring and for acclaimed touring productions.

CHILDREN

Many of the big sights may lack child-specific services or activities, but there's plenty to keep kids occupied for a short stay. There are various **parks** (El Retiro being a particular favourite), a host of well-attended public **swimming pools** and an increasing number of **child-oriented attractions**. Children are welcome in nearly all cafés and restaurants.

IN THE CITY
Museo de Cera (Wax Museum) Paseo de Recoletos 41, http://museoceramadrid.com; ⓂColón. Expensive, tacky and the figures bear little resemblance to the originals, but it's nevertheless popular with children. There's also a train of horrors and a film history of Spain.
Museo del Ferrocarril Paseo de las Delicias 61, http://museodelferrocarril.org; ⓂDelicias. An impressive collection of engines, carriages and wagons that once graced the railway lines of Spain. Of more interest to the younger ones is the fascinating collection of model railways and the mini railway. There's an atmospheric little cafeteria housed in one of the more elegant carriages. The station was used as a backdrop in the film classic *Doctor Zhivago*.
Parque de Atracciones Casa de Campo, http://parquedeatracciones.es; ⓂBatán/bus #33 & #65. A theme park packed full of rides, whose attractions include the 100km/hr Abismo roller coaster, the swirling Tarantula ride, the 63m vertical drop La Lanzadera and the whitewater-rafting ride Los Rápidos. Discounts for children between 1m and 1.40m tall (reductions for advance purchases via the website); children under 1m tall go free.
Planetario Parque Tierno Galván, http://planetmad.es; ⓂMéndez Álvaro. Exhibition halls, audiovisual displays and projections on a variety of astronomical themes (all in Spanish).

Zoo–Aquarium Casa de Campo, http://zoomadrid.com; ⓂCasa de Campo/Batán, bus #33 from Príncipe Pío. Over 2000 different species, including big cats, gorillas, koalas, venomous snakes and the star attraction baby panda Chulina, plus an impressive aquarium with sharks, a children's zoo, a parrot show and a dolphinarium.

SWIMMING POOLS AND AQUAPARKS
Outdoor swimming pools are open between mid-May and mid-September. The Piscina Canal Isabel II, Avda. de Filipinas 54 (ⓂRíos Rosas), is a large and well-maintained pool, and the best central option. Alternatively, try the open-air *piscina* in the Casa de Campo (ⓂLago). There are also two aquaparks around the city, the closest being Aquópolis de San Fernando (http://san-fernando.aquopolis.es), 16km out on the N-II Barcelona road (buses #281, #282 and #284 from the *intercambiador* at Avda. de América; trains from Atocha to San Fernando de Henares, then bus #L1).

OUT OF THE CITY
Faunia Avda. de las Comunidades 28, http://faunia.es; ⓂValdebernardo, bus #71 from Pza. Manuel Becerra (ⓂManuel Becerra). An innovative nature park re-creating a series of ecosystems that provide a home to 720 different animal species. Highlights are the Arctic dome with its penguins, the komodo dragons and the storms in the indoor tropical rainforest. An entertaining and educational experience for children of all ages.
Palacio de Hielo C/Silvano 77, www.palaciodehielo.com; ⓂCanillas. There's an 1800-square-metre ice rink, a 24-lane bowling alley and an indoor play park in this massive leisure/shopping complex on the eastern side of the city.

SHOPPING   SEE MAPS PAGES 62, 70 AND 86

Shopping districts in Madrid are distinctly defined. The biggest range of stores is along the Gran Vía and the streets running north out of Puerta del Sol, which is where the **department stores** – such as El Corte Inglés – have their main branches. For **fashion** (*moda*), the smartest addresses are calles Serrano, Goya, Ortega y Gasset and Velázquez in the Salamanca *barrio*, while more alternative designers are in Malasaña and Chueca (C/Almirante, especially). For street fashion, there's plenty on offer around C/Fuencarral and the nearby area known as triBall. The **antiques** trade is centred

1

towards the Rastro, on and around C/Ribera de Curtidores, while for **general quirkiness**, it's hard to beat the shops just off Pza. Mayor, where luminous saints rub shoulders with surgical supports. If you want international shops or chain stores, head for La Vaguada, a large shopping centre next to ⓜ Barrio de Pilar. There is a smaller, more upmarket mall at ABC Serrano, with entrances at C/Serrano 61 and Paseo de la Castellana 34 (ⓜ Rubén Darío).

Most areas of the city have their own **mercados del barrio** – indoor markets, devoted mainly to food. A whole host of these have been refurbished and geared up to the tourist market including **Mercado de San Miguel** (just west of Pza. Mayor), **Mercado de San Antón** in Chueca (ⓜ Chueca), and **Mercado de San Ildefonso and Mercado Barceló**, both in Malasaña (ⓜ Tribunal). There are more traditional markets in the Pza. de los Mostenses (ⓜ Pza. de España) and C/Santa Isabel (ⓜ Antón Martín). The city's biggest market is, of course, **El Rastro** – the flea market – which takes place on Sundays in La Latina, south of Pza. Cascorro (see page 74). Other specialized markets include the secondhand bookstalls on Cuesta del Moyano, near Estación de Atocha, and the stamp and coin markets in Pza. Mayor on Sundays.

CRAFTS AND MISCELLANEOUS

★ **Antigua Casa Talavera** C/Isabel la Católica 2, http://antiguacasatalavera.com; ⓜ Santo Domingo. Packed to the rafters with a massive selection of traditional Spanish ceramics, this old-fashioned family business is a great place to pick up a souvenir.

★ **El Arco Artesania** Pza. Mayor 9, www.facebook.com/elarcoartesania; ⓜ Sol. This shop may be at the heart of tourist Madrid, but the goods are a far cry from the swords, lace and castanets that fill most stores in the area. Handmade crafts and objets d'art include ceramics, leather, wood, jewellery and textiles.

Area Real Madrid C/Carmen 3, 915 217 950; ⓜ Sol. Club store just off Sol where you can pick up replica shirts and all manner of – expensive – souvenirs related to the club's history. There is another branch in the shopping centre at Real's Bernabéu stadium at C/Padre Damián gate 55 (ⓜ Santiago Bernabéu).

★ **Casa de Diego** Puerta del Sol 12, http://casadediego.info; ⓜ Sol. An old-fashioned shop with helpful staff selling a fantastic array of Spanish fans (*abanicos*) ranging from cheap offerings to beautifully handcrafted works of art.

Casa Yustas Pza. Mayor 30, http://casayustas.com; ⓜ Sol. Madrid's oldest hat shop, established back in 1894. Pick from traditional designs for men's and women's hats (*sombreros*), caps (*gorras*) and berets (*boinas*). There's also a large range of souvenir-style goods including Lladró porcelain figurines.

El Flamenco Vive C/Condé de Lemos 7, http://elflamencovive.com; ⓜ Ópera. A fascinating little piece of Andalucía in Madrid, specializing in all things flamenco, from guitars and

CDs to polka-dot dresses and books.

José Ramírez C/Paz 8, http://guitarrasramirez.com; ⓜ Sol. The Ramírez family have been making hand-crafted guitars since 1882 and, even if you are not a budding flamenco artist, this beautiful shop still merits a visit to appreciate these works of art.

Seseña C/Cruz 23; http://sesena.com; ⓜ Sol. A tailor specializing in traditional *madrileño* capes for royalty and celebrities. Clients have included Luis Buñuel, Gary Cooper and Hillary Clinton.

BOOKS AND MAPS

★ **La Central** C/Postigo de San Martín 8, www.lacentral.com; ⓜ Callao. Stunning bookshop occupying four floors of a beautifully decorated building just off Pza. Callao. A comprehensive collection of Spanish, Latin American and English classics.

Desnivel Pza. Matute 6, http://libreriadesnivel.com; ⓜ Antón Martín. This centrally located bookshop stocks a good range of guides and maps covering mountaineering and hiking in all parts of Spain.

FNAC C/Preciados 28, http://fnac.es; ⓜ Callao. The book department of this huge store is a good place to sit and peruse books and magazines in all languages. Also sells CDs, computer equipment and electronic goods.

La Librería C/Mayor 80, http://edicioneslalibreria.com; ⓜ Sol. A tiny place full of books only about Madrid. Most are in Spanish, but many would serve as coffee-table souvenirs. It's also a good place to pick up old prints and photos of the city.

Pasajes C/Genova 3, http://pasajeslibros.com; ⓜ Alonso Martínez/Colón. Specializes in English and foreign-language books. Also has a useful notice board service for apartment-sharing and Spanish classes.

CLOTHES

Adolfo Domínguez C/Serrano 5, http://adolfodominguez.com; ⓜ Retiro. Domínguez has a massive five-storey flagship store for his classic modern Spanish designs – a wide range of colours and lines for both men and women.

Agatha Ruiz de la Prada C/Serrano 27, http://agatharuizdelaprada.com; ⓜ Colón/Goya. Outlet for the brightly coloured clothes and accessories of this *movida* designer. There's a children's line, stationery and household goods, too.

Cortana C/Jorge Juan 12, http://cortana.es; ⓜ Chueca. Spanish clothes for women, with beachy, boho designs in neutral colours.

Twojeys C/Fuencarral 71, http://kling.es; ⓜ Gran Vía. There's fun, young clothing for men at reasonable prices in this popular store on a buzzing street in Chueca.

FOOD AND DRINK

★ **Cacao Sampaka** C/Orellana 4, http://cacaosampaka.com; ⓜ Alonso Martínez/Colón. Every conceivable colour, shape and flavour of chocolate is available in this chocoholics' paradise. The only surprise is that the restaurant has so¡me non-chocolate snacks on the menu.

Casa Mira C/San Jerónimo 30, http://casamira.es; Ⓜ Sol. An old, established *pastelería*, which was set up 150 years ago and sells delicious *turrón, mazapán, frutas glaseadas* and the like.

Lavinia C/José y Gasset 16, http://lavinia.es; Ⓜ Núñez de Balboa. Massive wine shop in the upmarket *barrio* of Salamanca, with a great selection from Spain and the rest of the world.

★ **Mariano Madrueño** C/Postigo San Martín 3, http:// marianomadrueno.es; Ⓜ Callao. Traditional wine sellers established back in 1895 and the place to get *Pacharán* (aniseed liqueur with sloe berries).

★ **Mercado de San Antón** C/Augusto Figueroa 24, http://mercadosananton.com; Ⓜ Chueca. Like the Mercado de San Miguel near Pza. Mayor, this local market has been transformed into a trendy meeting place on the Chueca scene, with gourmet food stands, a wine bar, a café, a sushi stall and a stylish terrace restaurant.

★ **Reserva y Cata** C/Conde de Xiquena 13, www. reservaycata.com; Ⓜ Colón/Chueca. Well-informed staff at this friendly specialist shop will help you select from some of the best new wines in the Iberian Peninsula. There is a wide selection of Spanish liqueurs too.

★ **La Comunal** C/Mejia Lequerica 1, 915 321 876; Ⓜ Alonso Martínez. Outlet for olive growers' cooperative boasting around ninety different varieties of olive oil.

CHILDREN

Geppetto C/Mayor 78, http://geppettoitalia.com; Ⓜ Sol. Handmade wooden toys and trinkets from Italy which make perfect gifts for small children.

Imaginarium C/Carmen 15, http://imaginarium.es; Ⓜ Sol. Toys, games and activities with an educational twist for children of all ages.

Tía Turuleta, Pl de la Habana, http://tiaturuleta.com, Ⓜ Barrio del Pilar. Sustainably made teddies, dolls, and other traditional toys.

DIRECTORY

Bicycles To rent a bike or for tours outside the city, get in touch with Bravo Bike at Juan Mendizábal 19 bajo izda (http://bravobike.com; Ⓜ Ventura Rodríguez) or Bike Spain at Pza. de la Villa 1 (http://bikespain.com; Ⓜ Ópera).

Access for travellers with disabilities Madrid is slowly getting geared up for visitors with disabilities (*minusválidos*). The local authority has produced a practical guide known as Accessible Madrid at www.esmadrid.com/ en/accessible-madrid. The Organización Nacional de Ciegos de España (ONCE; National Organization for the Blind, C/ Prim 3, www.once.es) provides more specialist advice, as does the Federación de Asociaciones de Minusválidos Físicos de la Comunidad de Madrid (FAMMA; C/Galileo 69, http:// famma.org); http://discapnet.es is also a useful source of information (Spanish only). Wheelchair-friendly taxis can be ordered from Eurotaxi (630 026 478 or 687 924 027) and Radio Taxi (915 478 200 or 915 478 600).

Embassies Australia, Torre Espacio, Paseo de la Castellana 259D (913 536 600, http://spain.embassy. gov.au; Ⓜ Begoña); Britain, Torre Espacio, Paseo de la Castellana 259D (917 146 300 or 902 109 356, http://gov. uk/government/world/spain; Ⓜ Begoña); Canada, Torre Espacio, Paseo de la Castellana 259D (913 828 400, http:// canadainternational.gc.ca; Ⓜ Begoña); Ireland, Paseo de la Castellana 46, 4º (914 364 093, http://dfa.ie/irish-embassy/ Spain; Ⓜ Rubén Darío); New Zealand, C/Pinar 7, 3º (915 230 226, www.mfat.govt.nz; Ⓜ Gregorio Marañon); South Africa, C/Claudio Coello 91 (914 363 780, www.gov.za; Ⓜ Rubén Darío); USA, C/Serrano 75 (915 872 200, http://

es.usembassy.gov; Ⓜ Rubén Darío).

Health First-aid stations are scattered throughout the city and open 24hr, including Carrera San Jerónimo 32, close to Puerta del Sol (913 690 491; Ⓜ Sol). Central hospitals include El Clínico San Carlos, C/Profesor Martín Lagos s/n (913 303 000; Ⓜ Islas Filipinas); Hospital Gregorio Marañon, C/Dr Esquerdo 46 (915 868 000; Ⓜ O'Donnell); Ciudad Sanitaria La Paz, Paseo de la Castellana 261 (917 277 000; Ⓜ Begoña). Many doctors speak English but there is a private English-speaking clinic, the Anglo-American Medical Unit, C/Conde de Aranda 1 (914 351 823; Mon–Fri 9am–8pm, Sat 10am–1pm; Ⓜ Retiro). The Clinica Dental Pza. Prosperidad at Pza. Prosperidad 3, 2ºB (914 158 197, http://clinicadentalplazaprosperidad.com; Ⓜ Prosperidad), has some English-speaking dentists, as does the Clinica Dental Cisne at C/Magallanes 18 (914 463 221, http:// cisnedental.com; Ⓜ Quevedo).

Left luggage Facilities (*consignas*) at Barajas Airport in terminals 1 & 4; the Estación Sur bus station and lockers at Atocha and Chamartín.

Pharmacies Open 24hr: C/Mayor 13 (913 664 616; Ⓜ Sol); C/Toledo 46 (913 653 458; Ⓜ La Latina); C/Atocha 46 (913 692 000; Ⓜ Antón Martín); C/Goya 12 (915 754 924; Ⓜ Serrano).

Police stations (*comisarías*) at C/Leganitos 19 (915 487 945; Ⓜ Pza. de España/Santo Domingo), C/Huertas 76 (913 221 027; Ⓜ Antón Martín) and C/Luna 29 (915 211 236; Ⓜ Callao). To report a crime go to the nearest police station or ring 901 102 112/915 488 537.

Around Madrid

TOLEDO

Around Madrid

The lack of historic monuments in Madrid is more than compensated for by the region around the capital. Within a radius of 100km – and within an hour's travel by bus and train – are some of Spain's greatest cities. Not least of these is Toledo, which preceded Madrid as the country's capital. Immortalized by El Greco, who lived and worked there for most of his later career, the city is a living museum to the many cultures – Visigothic, Moorish, Jewish and Christian – which have shaped the destiny of Spain. If you have time for just one trip from Madrid, make it this.

That said, **Segovia**, with its extraordinary Roman aqueduct and irresistible Disney-prototype castle, puts up strong competition, while Felipe II's vast palace-cum-mausoleum of **El Escorial** is a monument to out-monument all others. And there are smaller places, too, less known to foreign tourists: **Aranjuez**, an oasis in the parched Castilian plain, famed for its asparagus, strawberries and lavish Baroque palace and gardens; the beautiful walled city of **Ávila**, birthplace of St Teresa; and Cervantes' hometown, **Alcalá de Henares**, with its sixteenth-century university. For walkers, too, trails amid the sierras of **Gredos and Guadarrama** provide enticing escapes from the midsummer heat.

All of the towns in this chapter can be visited as easy day-trips from Madrid, but they also offer interesting jumping-off points into Castile and beyond.

Toledo

TOLEDO remains one of Spain's great cities. Redolent of past glories, it is packed with memorable sights – hence the whole city's status as a National Monument and UNESCO Patrimony of Mankind – and enjoys an incomparable setting. Be aware, however, that the extraordinary number of day-trippers can take the edge off what was once the most extravagant of Spanish experiences.

Set in a landscape of abrasive desolation, Toledo sits on a rocky mound where every available inch has been built upon: churches, synagogues, mosques and houses are heaped upon one another in a haphazard, cobblestoned spiral.

To see the city at its best, it is advisable to avoid peak holiday periods and weekends and stay at least a night: a day-trip will leave you hard-pressed to see everything. More importantly, in the evening with the crowds gone and the city lit up by floodlights – resembling one of **El Greco**'s moonlit paintings – Toledo is a different place entirely.

There are two main entrances to the old city of Toledo: via the mechanical staircase that scales the hill from the Puerta de Bisagra opposite the tourist office and leaves you close to the Convento de Santo Domingo Antiguo, or up C/ Real del Arrabal to the Pza. Zocodover. Once there, the street **layout** can appear confusing, but the old core is so small that it should never take too long to get back on track; part of the city's charm is that it's a place to wander in and absorb. Don't leave without seeing at least the El Grecos (many of which have been redisplayed since the four hundredth anniversary of the painter's death in 2014), the Catedral, the synagogues and Alcázar, but give it all time and you may just stumble upon things not listed in this or any other guidebook. Enter any inviting doorway and you'll find an array of stunning patios, rooms and ceilings, often of Mudéjar workmanship.

THE AQUEDUCT IN SEGOVIA

Highlights

① A tour of El Greco's Toledo Explore the churches and museums of this historic city in search of evocative masterpieces by the Greek painter. See pages 118 and 127

② Toledo's Catedral An astonishing construction featuring a heady mixture of opulent decorations and styles befitting a former capital. See page 124

③ Savour strawberries and cream at Aranjuez Indulge in the town's famous sweet treat at the street cafés by the royal palace. See page 131

④ El Escorial Marvel at Felipe II's massive monastery complex perched spectacularly in the foothills of the Sierra de Guadarrama. See page 134

⑤ Hiking in the sierra Head for the hills of Guadarrama or Gredos for a break from the city heat. See pages 138 and 146

⑥ A walk along the walls at Ávila Superb views of the town and the austere Castilian landscape. See page 144

⑦ The aqueduct at Segovia A marvel of Roman engineering situated at the entrance to the historic mountain city. See page 148

⑧ The fountains at La Granja A beautiful display at the royal retreat near Segovia. See page 155

HIGHLIGHTS ARE MARKED ON THE MAP ON PAGE 120

Brief history

Toledo was known to the Romans, who captured it in 192 BC, as Toletum, a small but well-defended town. Taken by the Visigoths, who made it their capital, it was already an important cultural and trading centre by the time the **Moors** arrived in 712. The period that followed, with Moors, Jews and Mozárabes (Christians subject to Moorish rule) living together in relative equality, was one of rapid growth and prosperity and Toledo became the most important northern outpost of the Muslim emirates. Though there are few physical remains of this period, apart from the enchanting miniature mosque of **Cristo de la Luz**, the long domination has left a clear mark on the atmosphere and shape of the city.

When the Christian king Alfonso VI "reconquered" the town in 1085, with the assistance of El Cid, Moorish influence scarcely weakened. Although Toledo became the capital of Castile and the base for campaigns against the Moors in the south, the city itself

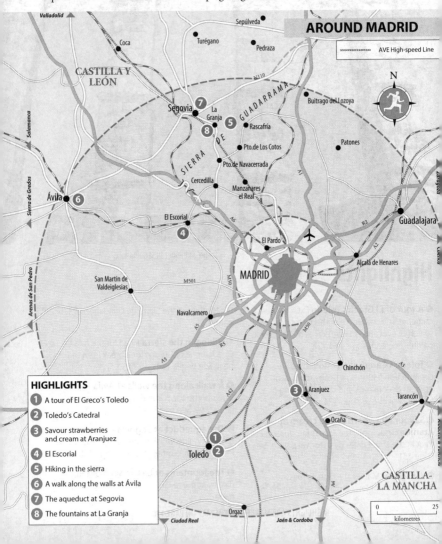

AROUND MADRID

〰〰〰〰〰 AVE High-speed Line

N

CASTILLA Y
LEÓN

Valladolid

Coca

Sepúlveda

Turégano

Pedraza

N110

SEGOVIA ⑦
La
Granja ⑤
⑧

SIERRA DE GUADARRAMA

Buitrago del Lozoya

Rascafría

Pto. de Los Cotos

Patones

Pto. de Navacerrada

Cercedilla

A1

Manzanares
el Real

Ávila ⑥

El Escorial ④

A6

El Pardo

Guadalajara

R2

A2

Alcalá de Henares

San Martín de
Valdeiglesias

M501

MADRID

M50

Navalcarnero

A5

R5

M50

Chinchón

A3

A5

A42

Aranjuez ③

Tarancón

Ocaña

HIGHLIGHTS

① A tour of El Greco's Toledo

② Toledo's Catedral

③ Savour strawberries
and cream at Aranjuez

④ El Escorial

⑤ Hiking in the sierra

⑥ A walk along the walls at Ávila

⑦ The aqueduct at Segovia

⑧ The fountains at La Granja

Toledo ①②

Orgaz

CASTILLA-
LA MANCHA

0 ____ 25
kilometres

Ciudad Real   Jaén & Córdoba

FIESTAS

FEBRUARY–APRIL

First Sunday in February: Santa Agueda Women's Festival Married women take over city administration and parade and celebrate in traditional costume.
Semana Santa (Holy Week): Formal processions in Toledo and a Passion play on Saturday in the Pza. Mayor at Chinchón.
Mid-April: Fiesta del Anís y del Vino, Chinchón Ample tastings of these two local products.

2

MAY–AUGUST

Thursday after Trinity, possibly in June: Corpus Christi Solemn, costumed religious procession in Toledo when the Catedral's magnificent sixteenth-century *custodia* is paraded around.
June 24–29: San Juan y San Pedro Lively procession with floats and music in Segovia.
August 15: Virgen de la Asunción Chinchón's celebrations include an *encierro*, with bulls running through the street;
August 15: Virgen del Sagrario Amazing fireworks display in Toledo.
August 17–25: Entertaining fiestas in La Granja (near Segovia) Parades, bullfighting, fireworks and the fountains in full flow, and in Orgaz (near Toledo) which honours its patron saint with further celebrations.
Last week in August: Spectacular parades of giant puppets, and theatre, music and dance in Alcalá de Henares.

SEPTEMBER & OCTOBER

First weekend in September: Motín de Aranjuez Re-enactment of the Mutiny of Aranjuez in Aranjuez.
September 27: La Virgen de la Fuencisla The image of Segovia's patron saint is carried from the sanctuary in the Eresma valley to the Catedral.
October 25: San Frutos Fiestas, Segovia Concerts, celebrations and parades in honour of the city's patron saint.

was a haven of cultural tolerance. Not only was there a school of translators revealing the scientific and philosophical achievements of the East, but Arab craftsmen and techniques remained responsible for many of the finest buildings of the period: look, for example, at the churches of **San Román** or **Santiago del Arrabal** or at any of the old **city gates**.

At the same time Jewish culture remained powerful. There were, at one time, at least seven **synagogues** – of which two, **Santa María la Blanca** and **El Tránsito**, survive – and Jews occupied many positions of power. The most famous was Samuel Levi, treasurer and right-hand man of Pedro the Cruel until the king lived up to his name by torturing Levi to his death and stealing his fortune. From this period, too, dates the most important purely Christian monument, Toledo's awesome **Catedral**.

This golden age ended abruptly in the sixteenth century with the transfer of the capital to Madrid, following hard on the heels of the Inquisition's mass expulsion of Muslims and Jews; some of the latter responded by taking refuge in Catholicism, becoming known as *conversos*. The city played little part in subsequent Spanish history until the Civil War with the siege of the Alcázar (see page 121) and it remains, despite the droves of tourists, essentially the medieval city so often painted by El Greco.

The Alcázar and the Museo del Ejército

C/Unión s/n • Charge, free Sun • http://ejercito.defensa.gob.es

2

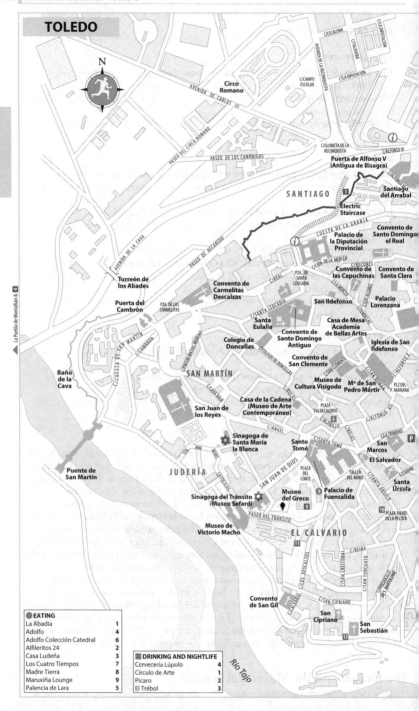

TOLEDO

N

Circo Romano

AVENIDA DE CARLOS III

C/ESCALONA
C/LA DIPUTACIÓN
AVENIDA DE LA RECONQUISTA
C/TLA DIPUTACIÓN
C/CAMPO ESCOLAR

PASEO DEL CIRCO ROMANO

PASEO DE LOS CANÓNIGOS

C/GLORIETA DE LA RECONQUISTA
C/ALFONSO VI

Puerta de Alfonso V
(Antigua de Bisagra)

SANTIAGO

Electric Staircase

Santiago del Arrabal

CUESTA DE LA GRANJA

AVENIDA DE LA CAVA

PASEO DE RECAREDO

Palacio de la Diputación Provincial

Convento de Santo Domingo el Real

C/BUZONES
C/GERARDO LOBO
C/SION DE LA MERCED

Convento de las Capuchinas

Convento de Santa Clara

Torreón de los Abades

PZA. DE LAS CARMELITAS

Convento de Carmelitas Descalzas

C/REAL
PZA. DE SANTA LEOCADIA

C/ALFILERITOS
C/SAN MIGUEL

San Ildefonso

Palacio Lorenzana

Puerta del Cambrón

Santa Eulalia

C/SANTA LEOCADIA

Convento de Santo Domingo Antiguo

Casa de Mesa Academia de Bellas Artes

Iglesia de San Ildefonso

Colegio de Doncellas

C/COLEGIO DE DONCELLAS

C/SAN CLEMENTE

Baño de la Cava

CUESTA DE SAN MARTÍN

C/CAMBRÓN

SAN MARTÍN

Convento de San Clemente

Museo de Cultura Visigodo

Mº de San Pedro Mártir

PLZ DEL P. MARIANA

C/CAVA BAJA

C/BULAS

Casa de la Cadena (Museo de Arte Contemporáneo)

PLAZA VALDECALEROS

C/ALFONSO XII

San Juan de los Reyes

C/ÁNGEL

Santo Tomé

C/ALJIBILLO

C/BULAS

Sinagoga de Santa María la Blanca

C/SANTO TOMÉ

San Marcos

C/LA TRINIDAD

P

STA. ANA
C/REYES

JUDERÍA

C/TOLEDO OHIO
SAN JUAN DE DIOS

PLAZA DEL CONTE

TALLER DEL MORO

El Salvador

Santa Úrsula

Sinagoga del Tránsito /Museo Sefardí

Museo del Greco

Palacio de Fuensalida

C/SANTA ÚRSULA
C/CIUDAD

PASEO DEL TRÁNSITO

PLAZA JUEGO DE LA PELOTA

Museo de Victorio Macho

EL CALVARIO

C/REINA

C/SAN CRISTÓBAL
C/LOS DESCALZOS
C/SAN JUAN TORCUATO

C/CALVARIO
C/SAN CIPRIANO

Convento de San Gil

San Cipriano

San Sebastián

C/SAN BARTOLOMÉ

Río Tajo

La Puebla de Montalbán &

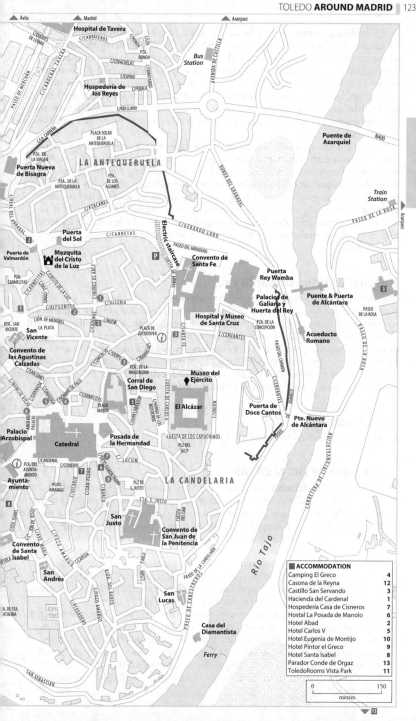

2

ACCOMMODATION

Camping El Greco	4
Casona de la Reyna	12
Castillo San Servando	3
Hacienda del Cardenal	1
Hospedería Casa de Cisneros	7
Hostal La Posada de Manolo	6
Hotel Abad	2
Hotel Carlos V	5
Hotel Eugenia de Montijo	10
Hotel Pintor el Greco	9
Hotel Santa Isabel	8
Parador Conde de Orgaz	13
ToledoRooms Vista Park	11

0   150
metres

If one building dominates Toledo, it's the bluff, imposing fortress of the **Alcázar**. Originally the site of a Roman palace, Emperor Carlos V ordered the construction of the current fortress in the sixteenth century, though it has been burned and bombarded so often that little remains of the original building. The monument enjoyed iconic status during the Franco era after the Nationalist forces inside, under siege by the Republican town, were eventually relieved by an army heading for Madrid which took severe retribution on the local inhabitants. After the war, Franco's regime completely rebuilt the fortress as a monument to the glorification of its defenders.

Following a tortuous relocation and refurbishment programme lasting the best part of a decade, the Alcázar is now home to an impressive state-of-the-art **Museo del Ejército** (army museum). Encompassing a new building constructed over the archeological remains of the original fortress, the museum offers two fascinating routes which navigate visitors through its extensive collections – one historic and one thematic. Spain's military history, the organization of its armed forces and the art of war are all dealt with in exhaustive detail, while exhibits include everything from medieval swords and suits of armour to toy soldiers and Civil War memorabilia.

Hospital y Museo de Santa Cruz

C/Cervantes 3 • Charge, free Tues–Sat after 6pm • http://cultura.castillalamancha.es

Just north of the Alcázar, off Pza. de Zocodover, is the **Hospital y Museo de Santa Cruz**, a superlative Renaissance building with a fine Plateresque facade, housing some of the greatest El Grecos in Toledo, including *The Immaculate Conception* and *The Holy Family* as well as outstanding works by Luca Giordano and Ribera. The **museum** also contains an impressive collection of exhibits dating from prehistory through to the twentieth century, including archeological finds, ceramic and sculpture. Don't miss the patio with its ornate staircase – the entrance is beside the ticket office.

The Catedral

C/Cardenal Cisneros • Charge • http://catedralprimada.es

THE SIEGE OF THE ALCÁZAR

At the outset of the **Spanish Civil War**, on July 20, 1936, Colonel José Moscardó – a leading Nationalist rebel – and the cadets of the military academy under his command were **driven into the Alcázar**. They barricaded themselves in with a large group that included six hundred women and children, and up to a hundred left-wing hostages (who were never seen again).

After many phone calls from Madrid to persuade them to surrender, a Toledo attorney phoned Moscardó with an ultimatum: within ten minutes the Republicans would shoot his son, captured that morning. Moscardó declared that he would never surrender and told his son, "If it be true, commend your soul to God, shout Viva España, and die like a hero." (His son was actually shot with others a month later in reprisal for an air raid.) Inside, though not short of ammunition, the defenders had so little food they had to eat their horses.

The number of Republican attackers varied from 1000 to 5000. Two of the three mines they planted under the towers exploded but nothing could disturb the solid rock foundations, while spraying petrol all over the walls and setting fire to it had no effect. Finally, General Franco decided to relieve Moscardó and diverted an army that was heading for Madrid. On September 27, General José Varela commanded the successful attack on the town, which was followed by the usual bloodbath. The day after Franco entered Toledo to consolidate his victory, he was declared head of state.

In a country overflowing with massive religious institutions, the metropolitan **Catedral** has to be something special – and it is. A robust Gothic construction that took over 250 years (1227–1493) to complete, it has a richness of internal decoration in almost every conceivable style, with masterpieces of the Gothic, Renaissance and Baroque periods. The exterior is best appreciated from outside the city, where the hundred-metre spire and the weighty buttressing can be seen to greatest advantage. From the street it's less impressive, so hemmed in by surrounding houses that you can't really sense the scale or grandeur of the whole.

2

The coro

Inside the Catedral, the central nave is divided from four aisles by a series of clustered pillars supporting the vaults, 88 in all, the aisles continuing around behind the main altar to form an apse. There is magnificent **stained glass** throughout, mostly dating from the fifteenth and sixteenth centuries, particularly beautiful in two rose windows above the north and south doors. Beside the south door (Puerto de los Leones) is a huge, ancient **fresco of St Christopher**.

At the physical heart of the church, blocking the nave, is the **coro**, itself a panoply of sculpture. The wooden stalls are in two tiers. The lower level, carved in 1489–95 by Rodrigo Alemán, depicts the conquest of Granada, with each seat showing a different village being taken by the Christians. The portraits of Old Testament characters on the stalls above were executed in the following century, on the north side by Philippe Vigarni and on the south by Alonso Berruguete, whose superior technique is evident. He also carved the large **Transfiguration** here from a single block of alabaster. The *reja* (grille) that encloses the *coro* is said to be plated with gold, but it was covered in iron to disguise its value from Napoleon's troops and has since proved impossible to renovate.

The Capilla Mayor and Transparente

The **Capilla Mayor** stands directly opposite the *coro*. Its gargantuan altarpiece, stretching clear to the roof, is one of the triumphs of Gothic art, overflowing with intricate detail and fanciful embellishments. It contains a synopsis of the entire New Testament, culminating in a Calvary at the summit.

Directly behind the main altar is an extraordinary piece of fantasy – the Baroque **Transparente**. Wonderfully extravagant, with marble cherubs sitting on fluffy marble clouds, it's especially magnificent when the sun reaches through the hole punched in the roof for just that purpose. A red cardinal's hat hangs from the vaulting just in front. Spanish primates are buried where they choose, with the epitaph they choose and with their hat hanging above them, where it stays until it rots. One of them chose to be buried here, and there are other pieces of headgear dotted around the Catedral.

The Capillas

There are well over twenty **chapels** embedded into the walls of the Catedral, all of which are of some interest. Many of them house fine tombs, particularly the **Capilla de Santiago**, the octagonal **Capilla de San Ildefonso** and the gilded **Capilla de Reyes Nuevos**.

In the **Capilla Mozárabe**, Mass is still celebrated daily according to the ancient Visigothic rites. When the Church tried to ban the old ritual in 1086 the people of Toledo were outraged. The dispute was put to a combat, which the Mozárabe champion won, but the Church demanded further proof: trial by fire. The Roman prayer book was blown to safety, while the Mozárabe version remained, unburnt, in the flames. Both sides claimed victory, and in the end the two rituals were allowed to coexist. If you want to attend Mass, be there at 9am and look out for the priest – you may well be the only member of the congregation.

2

The Tesoro, Sacristía and Sala Capitular

The **Tesoro** (Treasury) houses the riches of the Catedral, most notably a solid silver *custodia* (repository for Eucharist wafers) commissioned by Cardinal Cisneros in 1515; it's three metres high and weighs over two hundred kilos.

An even more impressive accumulation of wealth is displayed in the **Sacristía** (Sacristy) with its magnificent ceiling fresco, *The Clothing of Saint Ildephonsus* by Luca Giordano, while the paintings include a *Disrobing of Christ* and portraits of the Apostles by El Greco, Velázquez's portrait of *Cardinal Borja* and Goya's *Christ Taken by the Soldiers*. The adjoining rooms house works of art that were previously locked away or poorly displayed. Among them are paintings by Caravaggio, Gerard David and Morales, and El Greco's most important piece of sculpture, a polychromed wooden group of *Saint Ildephonsus and the Virgin*.

The **Sala Capitular** (Chapter House) has a magnificent sixteenth-century *artesonado* (wooden sculptured) ceiling and portraits of all Spain's archbishops to the present day.

Santo Tomé and the Burial of the Count of Orgaz

Pza. del Conde 4 • Charge • http://santotome.org

A little way to the west of the Catedral is one of Toledo's outstanding attractions: El Greco's masterpiece, **The Burial of the Count of Orgaz**. It's housed, alone, in a small annexe to the church of **Santo Tomé** and depicts the count's funeral, at which SS Stephen and Augustine appeared in order to lower him into the tomb. It combines El Greco's genius for the mystic, exemplified in the upper half of the picture where the count's soul is being received into heaven, with his great powers as a portrait painter and master of colour. The identity of the sombre-faced figures watching the burial has been a source of endless speculation. On two identities, however, there is universal agreement; El Greco painted himself seventh from the left, looking out at the viewer, and his son in the foreground. Less certain are the identities of the rest of the mourners, but the odds are on for Felipe II's presence among the heavenly onlookers, even though he was still alive when it was painted. A search for the count's bones came to an end in early 2001 when they were unearthed from a tomb located, appropriately enough, directly below the painting.

Museo del Greco

Paseo del Tránsito • Charge, free Sat after 2pm & Sun • www.cultura.gob.es/mgreco/inicio.html

From Santo Tomé, the C/Alamillo leads down to the old **Judería** (Jewish quarter) and the **Museo del Greco**, which is devoted to the life and work of the Greek-born artist so closely associated with the city. This refurbished exhibition space houses his famous *View and Map of Toledo*, a full series of the *Twelve Apostles*, completed later than the set in the Catedral and subtly different in style, and a fascinating selection of other work by the painter and his disciples. Several of the rooms also re-create the atmosphere of the artist's original living quarters in the city, though this is not the actual house in which he lived. The exhibits are well explained in both Spanish and English, and short videos explain the artist's life and the techniques he used.

Sinagoga del Tránsito

C/Samuel Levi • Charge, free Sat after 2pm & Sun • http://culturaydeporte.gob.es/msefardi

Almost next door to the Museo del Greco is the **Sinagoga del Tránsito**. Built along Moorish lines by Samuel Levi in 1366, it became a church run by the military order of Calatrava after the expulsion of the Jews. The interior is a simple galleried hall, brilliantly decorated with polychromed stuccowork and superb filigree windows. Hebrew inscriptions praising God, King Pedro and Samuel Levi adorn the walls. It houses a small **Museo Sefardí** and the Museo Sefardí (Sephardic Museum) tracing the distinct traditions and development of Jewish culture in Spain.

Museo de Victorio Macho
Pza. de Victorio 2 Macho • Charge • http://realfundaciontoledo.es

Opposite the Sinagoga del Tránsito, splendidly situated on a spur overlooking the Río Tajo and in a delightfully tranquil garden, is the **Museo de Victorio Macho**, which contains the sculptures, paintings and sketches of the Spanish artist Victorio Macho (1887–1966). The auditorium on the ground floor shows a documentary (available in English) about the city and its history.

Sinagoga de Santa María la Blanca
C/Reyes Católicos 4 • Charge • 925 227 257

The only other surviving synagogue apart from the Sinagoga del Tránsito, **Santa María la Blanca** is a short way further down C/Reyes Católicos. Like El Tránsito, which it predates by over a century, it has been both church and synagogue, though, as it was built by Mudéjar craftsmen, it actually looks more like a mosque. Four rows of octagonal pillars each support seven horseshoe arches, all of them with elaborate and individual designs moulded in plaster, while a fine sixteenth-century *retablo* has been preserved from the building's time as a church. The whole effect is quite stunning, accentuated by a deep-red floor tiled with decorative *azulejos*.

Monasterio de San Juan de los Reyes
C/San Juan de los Reyes 2 • Charge, free under-10s • http://sanjuandelosreyes.org

Down C/Reyes Católicos from Santa María la Blanca you come to the superb church of **San Juan de los Reyes**, its exterior bizarrely festooned with the chains worn by Christian prisoners from Granada released on the reconquest of their city. It was originally a Franciscan convent founded by the "Catholic Kings", Fernando and Isabel, to celebrate their victory at the Battle of Toro. Designed in the decorative

EL GRECO AND TOLEDO

Even if you've never seen **Toledo** – and even if you've no idea what to expect – there's an uncanny familiarity about your first view of it, with the Alcázar and the Catedral spire towering above the tawny mass of the town. This is due to **El Greco**, whose constant depiction of the city (as background, even, for the Crucifixion) seems to have stuck, albeit unwittingly, somewhere in everyone's consciousness.

Domenikos Theotokopoulos, "the Greek", was born in Crete in 1541 and worked in Venice and Rome before going to Spain. He had originally hoped to get work on the decoration of El Escorial, but after being rejected by Felipe II, he arrived in Toledo in about 1577. His first major commission was to produce the altarpiece for the church of Santo Domingo el Antiguo and many others followed, including his most famous work: *The Burial of the Count of Orgaz*. El Greco remained in the city until his death in 1614 which came while he was working on a commission for the Hospital de Tavera. He was buried in Santo Domingo el Antiguo.

Many of El Greco's extraordinary paintings – some of the most individual, most intensely spiritual visions of all Spanish art – remain scattered throughout the city. Years ahead of his time, his work went on to influence artists for centuries to come, including Manet, Cezanne and Picasso.

Hortension Félix Paravicino, a Spanish preacher and poet who was a subject of one of El Greco's paintings, commented "Crete gave him life and the painter's craft, Toledo a better homeland, where through death he began to achieve eternal life."

Gothic Hispano-Flemish style sometimes referred to as Isabelline (after the queen), its double-storeyed cloister is quite outstanding: the upper storey has an elaborate Mudéjar ceiling, and the crests of Castile and Aragón – seven arrows and a yoke – are carved everywhere in assertion of the new unity brought by the royal marriage.

Convento de Santo Domingo el Antiguo

Pza. Santo Dominguo el Antiguo • Charge • 925 222 930

2

A little way to the north of San Juan de los Reyes and close to the mechanical staircase leading out of the old city is the **Convento de Santo Domingo el Antiguo**. The church's chief claim to fame is that it contains El Greco's remains, which can be glimpsed through a peephole in the floor. The nuns display their art treasures in the old choir, but more interesting is the high altarpiece of the church, El Greco's first major commission in Toledo. Unfortunately, most of the canvases have gone to museums and are here replaced by copies, leaving only two *St John*s and a *Resurrection*.

Iglesia de San Ildefonso (Iglesia de los Jesuitas)

Pza. Juan de Mariana 1 • Charge • 925 251 507

A short distance to the south of the Convento de Santo Domingo el Antiguo stretching along C/San Román and facing on to the Pza. Juan de Mariana is the imposing Baroque facade of the **Iglesia de San Ildefonso**, more commonly known as the **Iglesia de los Jesuitas**. The church, modelled on the Jesuit headquarters, the Gesú in Rome, was completed in 1765, over 150 years after work began and only two years before the brotherhood was expelled from Spain by Carlos III. Although the interior is pleasing enough, the main reason to visit is to make your way up the tower for some magnificent views of the city.

The Puerta del Sol and Mezquita del Cristo de la Luz

Cuesta de los Carmelitos Descalzos 10 • Charge • 925 254 191

If you leave the old city by the Cuesta de Armas, which runs out of the Pza. de Zocodover and down the hill, you will come across the battlements of the **Puerta del Sol**, a great fourteenth-century Mudéjar gateway. Tucked behind the gateway on the Cuesta de los Carmelitas Descalzos is the tiny mosque of **Mezquita del Cristo de la Luz**. Although this is one of the oldest Moorish monuments in Spain (it was built by Musa Ibn Ali in the tenth century on the foundations of a Visigothic church), only the nave, with its nine different cupolas, is the original Arab construction. The apse was added when the building was converted into a church, and is claimed to be the first product of the Mudéjar style. According to legend, as King Alfonso rode into the town in triumph, his horse stopped and knelt before the mosque. Excavations revealed a figure of Christ, still illuminated by a lamp, which had burned throughout three and a half centuries of Muslim rule – hence the name Cristo de la Luz. The outstandingly elegant mosque, set in a small park and open on all sides to the elements, is so small that it seems more like a miniature summer pavilion, but it has an elegant simplicity of design that few of the town's great monuments can match.

Santiago del Arrabal and the Puerta Bisagra

Pza. Santiago del Arrabal 4

Below the Puerta del Sol on the way out of the old city is the intriguing brickwork exterior of the Mudéjar church of **Santiago del Arrabal**, while at the foot of the hill and marooned in a constant swirl of traffic is Toledo's main gate, the sixteenth-century **Puerta Nueva de Bisagra**. Its patterned-tile roofs bear the coat of arms of Carlos V.

Alongside is the gateway that it replaced, the ninth-century Moorish portal through which Alfonso VI and El Cid led their triumphant armies in 1085.

Hospital de Tavera

C/Duque de Lerma 2 • Charge • 925 220 451

Beyond the city walls along the Paseo de Merchán is the **Hospital de Tavera**. This Renaissance palace with beautiful twin patios houses the private collection of the Duke of Lerma. The gloomy interior is a reconstruction of a sixteenth-century mansion and is dotted with fine paintings, including a *Day of Judgement* by Bassano; the portrait of Carlos V by Titian is a copy of the original in the Prado. The hospital's archives are kept here, too: thousands of densely handwritten pages chronicling the illnesses treated. The museum contains several works by El Greco, and Ribera's celebrated portrait of a freak "bearded woman" breast-feeding a baby. Also here is the death mask of Cardinal Tavera, the hospital's founder, and in the church of the hospital is his ornate marble tomb – the last work of Alonso de Berruguete.

ARRIVAL AND DEPARTURE · TOLEDO

By train A high-speed train service departs from Atocha station in Madrid (15–18 daily; 30min; it's essential to book in advance at the station or via the website http://renfe.com). Toledo's magnificent neo-Mudéjar train station is some way out on the Paseo de la Rosa, a 20min walk – take the left-hand fork off the dual carriageway and cross the Puente de Alcántara – or a bus ride (#5 or #6 or the tourist shuttle) to the heart of town.
Destinations Albacete (5–8 daily; 2hr 25min–3hr 37min); Cuenca (3–6 daily; 1hr 50min–3hr).

By bus Every 30min from the Pza. Elíptica terminal in Madrid (1hr). The bus station is on Avda. de Castilla la Mancha in the modern, lower part of the city; bus #5 runs to Pza. Zocodover, though if you take shortcuts through the *barrio* at the bottom of the hill just inside the walls, it's a mere 10min walk to the Puerta Nueva de Bisagra.
Destinations Ciudad Real, for the south (2–4 daily; 1hr 30min–2hr 30min); Cuenca (Mon–Fri 1–2 daily; 2hr); Guadamur (3–5 daily; 20min); Orgaz (5–8 daily; 40min); Talavera de la Reina, for Extremadura (6–13 daily; 1hr 15min).

By car The best places to park are in the streets beyond the Circo Romano in the new town or in the underground car park close to the mechanical staircase that leads up into the old city.

GETTING AROUND

On foot Walking is the only way to see the city itself, but be aware that resident cars have a tendency to roar along even the tiniest alleyways in the centre. Information on an array of walking tours is available at the *turismo* (see page 129). You can also check out http://toledofreetour.com and http://toledo3culturas.com.

INFORMATION

Regional tourist office Opposite Puerta Nueva de Bisagra outside the city walls (http://turismocastillalamancha.com).
Local tourist offices In the train station (925 239 121); at the top of the mechanical staircase leading into the city from the Puerta de Bisagra (Cuesta de la Granja s/n; Mon–Fri 10am–6pm – until 7pm in July & Aug – Sat 10am–7pm & Sun 10am–3pm; 925 248 232); the kiosk in Pza. Zocodover (Sept–June: Mon–Sat 9am–6pm, Sun 10am–3pm; July & Aug: Mon–Sat 9am–5pm & Sun 10am–3pm) and in the plaza next to the Catedral (Mon–Sat 9am–4pm, Sun 10am–3pm; 925 254 030, http://toledo-turismo.com).
Tickets You can save on the entry fees to a number of the sights such as the synagogue of Santa María la Blanca, San Juan de los Reyes, Santo Tomé and the Iglesia de los Jesuitas if you invest in the tourist wristband. Alternatively, depending on how much you want to visit, check out the range of discount tourist cards available from the high-speed train station and many of the larger hotels.

ACCOMMODATION · SEE MAP PAGE 122

Booking a room in advance is important in Toledo, especially at weekends, or during the summer. The tourist offices have lists of all the **accommodation** available in town. Be aware that prices in many places almost double at Easter, bank holidays and at Corpus Christi, but that outside these times and midweek, hotels often offer substantially reduced rates.
Casona de la Reyna C/San Sebastián 26, http://casonadelareyna.com. Situated in the quiet San Cipriano area of the old town close to the Judería, this functional mid-range hotel has 25 spacious, classically decorated rooms with a/c

2

and private parking for an extra charge. €€

Castillo San Servando Across the Puente de Alcántara and just off Paseo de la Rosa on Cuesta de San Servando, http://hihostels.com. Toledo's youth hostel is across the river from the Alcázar and in a wing of the fourteenth-century Mudéjar-style Castillo San Servando, a 15min walk (signposted) from the train station. It has a fine view of the city, a pool and communal areas. Booking is advised and a YH card required; accommodation is in two- or four-room dormitories. €

★ **Hacienda del Cardenal** Paseo de Recaredo 24, http://haciendadelcardenal.com. A splendid old mansion with 27 very comfortable, classically decorated rooms, a well-regarded but pricey restaurant, a chill-out bar and delightful patio gardens, located outside the city wall, near Puerta Nueva de Bisagra. Discounts available on the website. €€

Hospedería Casa de Cisneros C/Cardenal Cisneros, http://hospederiacasadecisneros.com. A boutique-style *hostal* in a refurbished sixteenth-century townhouse with ten small, en-suite, wooden-beamed a/c rooms situated opposite the Puerta de Leones entrance of the Catedral. €€

★ **Hostal La Posada de Manolo** C/Sixto Ramón Parro 8, http://laposadademanolo.com. An atmospheric *hostal* in a carefully refurbished period house close to the Catedral, with small, simple, brick-lined, beamed rooms, all with a/c. €

Hotel Abad C/Real del Arrabal 1, http://hotelabad.com. A smart hotel situated in a former ironworks close to the Mezquita de la Luz. The 22 tastefully decorated rooms have brick-lined walls and warm colours, and those in the loft are particularly nice. There are family apartments available too. €€

Hotel Carlos V Pza. Horno de la Magdalena 4, http://carlosv.com. The rooms in this well-established hotel, tucked away in a little side street close to the Alcázar, have been given a makeover and offer a choice between the more traditional standard option and the slightly slicker,

clean-lined premium ones. The big attraction is the terrace bar with its great views over the city. €€€

Hotel Eugenia de Montijo Pza. del Juego de la Pelota 7, http://marriott.com. Plush 40-room boutique-style hotel in the heart of the old town close to the Catedral with its own spa and a top-notch restaurant. €€

★ **Hotel Pintor el Greco** C/Alamillos de Tránsito 13, http://hotelpintorelgreco.com. A well-equipped and nicely furnished four-star hotel in a refurbished seventeenth-century bakery situated in the old Jewish quarter. It has 56 comfortable rooms, many with fine views across the Tajo, and private parking. €€

Hotel Santa Isabel C/Santa Isabel 24, http://hotelsanta isabeltoledo.es. A mid-range hotel occupying a converted nobleman's house right in the centre of town. It has neat, unfussy rooms (some with views), wood-panelled floors and safe parking. Special offers available on website. €

Parador Conde de Orgaz Cerro del Emperador s/n, http://paradores.com. Superb views of the city from the terrace of Toledo's top hotel, but the drawback is that it's a fair walk from the centre. Light and airy rooms and a splendid outdoor pool that's tempting if the heat gets too much in summer. €€€

ToledoRooms Vista Park Paseo del Transíto 5, http://toledorooms.com. Very good value, centrally located *budget hotel* handy for the main sights. As the name suggests, rooms overlook a lovely green park. €

CAMPING

Camping El Greco Carretera de Toledo–Puebla de Montalbán, http://campingelgreco.es. There are great views of the city from this riverside campsite – and a bar to enjoy them from – plus a swimming pool to cool off in after a hard day's sightseeing. A 30min walk from the Puerta de Bisagra: cross the Puente de la Cava towards Puebla de Montalbán, then follow the signs. €

CUISINE AROUND MADRID

The **food** to be found in most of the areas **around Madrid** owes much to **Castilian tradition**, with roast meats such as *cochinillo* (suckling pig) and *cordero* (roast lamb) providing the signature dishes in many restaurants. Cooked to perfection so the meat is deliciously tender and falling off the bone (in some restaurants they even cut the *cochinillo* with plates), meals are served with almost no side dishes, bar the odd chip or potato.

But one of the chief pleasures of eating in the areas around the Spanish capital is that **local specialities** still remain. In Toledo, for example, many of the more traditional restaurants offer *carcamusa* – a meat in a spicy tomato sauce, and game such as partridge (*perdiz*), pheasant (*faisán*) and quail (*cordoniz*). In Segovia Castilian roasts are to the fore, while in nearby La Granja the rather healthier *judiones* (large white beans) are on offer. Like La Granja, Ávila is also renowned for its beans, this time haricot beans with sausage (*judias del barco*), as well as its delicious, and massive, T-bone steaks (*chuletón de Ávila*), and for the most sickly sweet of desserts, the *yemas de Santa Teresa* (candied egg yolks). If all that proves too much, head for the oasis of Aranjuez where vegetables (in particular asparagus) and fresh strawberries are the local speciality.

EATING
SEE MAP PAGE 122

Toledo is a major tourist centre and inevitably many of its **cafés**, **bars** and **restaurants** are geared to passing trade. However, the city is also popular with Spanish visitors, so decent, authentic places do exist – and there's a bit of nightlife, too.

★ **La Abadía** Pza. San Nicolás 3, http://abadiatoledo.com. There's a three-course set lunchtime menu in this popular restaurant which also serves some decent specialities such as partridge and venison. €€

Adolfo C/Hombre de Palo 7, http://grupoadolfo.com. One of the most prestigious restaurants in town, tucked behind a marzipan café, in an old Jewish townhouse (ask to see the painted ceiling in the eleventh-century cellar downstairs). They serve imaginative, high-quality but pricey food, using local ingredients such as partridge. €€€€

Adolfo Colección Catedral C/Nuncio Viejo 1, http://grupoadolfo.com. If you can't afford to eat at the *Adolfo* restaurant (above), have a glass of wine and some designer tapas or the lunchtime menu at this elegant little bar run by the same people. €€

★ **Alfileritos 24** C/Alfileritos 24, http://alfileritos24.com. A cool, relaxed, brick-lined bar-restaurant serving an imaginative and tasty assortment of tapas in the bar and more sophisticated options in the restaurant. In the evening a la carte options include aubergine with tiger prawns and cheese or venison steak with mushrooms. The taster menu with its array of starters, meat and fish dishes will set you

back a fair amount but certainly won't leave you hungry. €€€

Casa Ludeña Pza. Magdalena 13. One of many places around this square, but this down-to-earth bar-restaurant is the most authentic. It offers some of the best *carcamusa* in town (see page 130) and is great value. €€

★ **Los Cuatro Tiempos** C/Sixto Ramón Parro 5 (close to the Catedral), http://restauranteloscuatrotiempos.com. An excellent restaurant with local specialities such as *cochinillo*, *perdiz* and *cordero* given a modern twist. €€€

Madre Tierra Bajada Triperla 2, https://restaurante madretierra.com. A plant-based restaurant is a rare thing in Toledo, even nowadays, which makes this fantastic place stand out even more. Fish-free sushi, seitan moussaka and vegan cakes are among the delicious offerings on the menu, served artfully in a stylish environment. €€€

Maruxiña Lounge Travesía Descalzos 1, http://maruxina lounge.com. Slick, modern, minimalist decor provides the backdrop, while the food is a nice combination of the old and new with creative takes on classic dishes such as partridge, venison and pork as well as fusion-style options including red-curry vegetables and Thai salad. There's a lounge bar and terrace too. €€€

Palencia de Lara C/Nuncio Viejo 6, www.asador palenciadelara.es. Two branches of a popular Toledano group of restaurants (there's another one next to the Catedral in the Pza. del Ayuntamiento which closes on Tuesdays) serve up good, classic Castilian food. €€€

DRINKING AND NIGHTLIFE
SEE MAP PAGE 122

By Spanish standards, Toledo's **nightlife** is rather tame. You'll find most late-night bars running along C/Sillería and its extension C/Alfileritos, west of Pza. de Zocodover. In the old core, there are several bars close to Pza. de Zocodover, while in the new town the area around Pza. de Cuba is packed with bars and clubs. Out of the tourist season, between September and March, classical concerts are held in the Catedral and other churches; details can be obtained from the *turismo*.

Cervecería Lúpolo C/Aljibillo 4, www.facebook.com/ lupulocraftbeer. You'll find a good variety of craft beers – including the locally brewed Domus brand – decent music and a friendly atmosphere at this bar in the historic centre.

Círculo de Arte Pza. de San Vicente, http://circuloarte toledo.org. A converted chapel now used as a venue for live music, exhibitions, poetry reading and the like. Also makes a classy location for a coffee or drink.

Pícaro C/Cadenas 6, http://picarotoledo.com. This popular discobar-café has regular concerts and DJ sessions. It's spread over three levels and is not far from Pza. de Zocodover.

El Trébol C/Santa Fé 1, http://cerveceriatrebol.com. Very popular bar between Pza. Zocodover and the Museo de Santa Cruz serving up decent breakfasts, great tapas and the house speciality *bombas* (potatoes stuffed with meat and fried). A tasty range of *bocadillos* and some good *tortillas* too.

Aranjuez

A short train journey from Madrid is **ARANJUEZ**, a little oasis at the confluence of the Tajo and Jarama rivers on the southern edge of the province of Madrid, where the eighteenth-century Bourbon rulers set up a spring and autumn retreat. The beauty of Aranjuez is its greenery – it's easy to forget just how dry and dusty most of central Spain is until you come upon this town, with its lavish palaces and luxuriant gardens, which inspired the composer Joaquín Rodrigo to write the famous *Concierto de Aranjuez*. Famed for its summer strawberries (served with cream – *fresas con nata* – at roadside stalls) and asparagus, Aranjuez functions principally as a weekend escape from Madrid and most people come out for the day, or stop en route to or from Toledo.

Palacio Real

Plaza de Parejas Palace Charge, free Wed & Thurs 5–8pm (3–6pm Oct–March) for EU citizens • **Gardens** Free • http://patrimonionacional.es

The showpiece eighteenth-century **Palacio Real** and its **gardens** were an attempt by the Spanish Bourbon monarchs to create a Versailles in Spain; Aranjuez clearly isn't in the same league, but it's a very pleasant place to while away a few hours. The palace, placed by the river, is more remarkable for the ornamental fantasies inside than for any virtues of architecture. There seem to be hundreds of rooms, all exotically furnished, most amazingly so the **Porcelain Room**, which is entirely covered in decorative ware from the factory that used to stand in Madrid's Retiro park. Most of the palace dates from the reign of the "nymphomaniac" Queen Isabel II, and many of the sexual scandals and intrigues that led to her removal from the throne in 1868 were played out here.

Outside, on a small island, are the decorative fountains and neatly tended gardens of the **Jardín de la Isla**. The **Jardín del Príncipe**, on the other side of the main road, is crisscrossed with shaded walks along the river and plenty of spots for a siesta.

Real Casa del Labrador

Poligono, Plaza Jardines Histórico Art, 1 • Charge • http://patrimonionacional.es

At the far end of the **Jardín del Príncipe** is the **Casa del Labrador**, an opulent house containing more silk, marble, crystal and gold than would seem possible in so small a place, as well as a huge collection of fancy clocks. The guided tour (limited numbers on each one) goes into great detail about the weight and value of every item.

Museo de Faluas Reales

Jardín Del Príncipe • Free, included with entrance to the Palacio Real • http://patrimonionacional.es

In the gardens, by the river, is the small **Casa de los Marinos** or **Museo de Faluas Reales**, which houses the brightly coloured launches in which royalty would take to the river. You can do the modern equivalent and take a boat trip through the royal parks from the jetty by the bridge next to the palace (charge; www.elcuriosity.com).

ARRIVAL AND DEPARTURE | ARANJUEZ

By train An old wooden steam train (http://trendelafresa.es), the *Tren de la Fresa*, also runs between Madrid and Aranjuez; it leaves the Museo del Ferrocarril at Paseo de las Delicias 61 in Madrid at 10am and returns from Aranjuez at 7pm. The price includes a guided bus tour in Aranjuez, entry to the main monuments and *fresas* on the train. The less romantic, but highly efficient, standard trains leave every fifteen to thirty minutes from Atocha, with the last train returning from Aranjuez at about 11.30pm.

By bus Buses run every half-hour during the week and every hour at weekends from Estación Sur (40min).

INFORMATION AND GETTING AROUND

Turismo Casa de Infantes, facing the Pza. de San Antonio (daily 10am–6pm; 918 910 427, http://aranjuez.es or http://aranjuez.com).

Getting around A bus service occasionally connects the various sights and if you have children the *chiquitren*, a motorized mini-train that departs from the Palacio Real, is a good option, but everything is within easy walking distance, and the town's a very pleasant place to stroll around.

ACCOMMODATION

It's essential to reserve a room in advance, as **accommodation** is not plentiful.

★ **Hotel El Cocherón 1919** C/Montesinos 22, http://elcocheron1919.com. This boutique-style hotel, close to the Palacio and gardens, has eighteen individually decorated rooms, a large and tranquil central patio area and a small bar/cafeteria. **€€**

Hotel Jardin de Aranjuez C/Príncipe 26, http://hotel jardindearanjuez.com. A comfortable hotel, with a good range of rooms, close to the royal palace and across the road

from the Jardín del Príncipe. Family rooms are available. €€
NH Collection Palacio de Aranjuez C/San Antonio 22, http://nh-hoteles.com. Refurbished NH hotel that is part of its more upmarket "Collection" range, complete with 86 spacious, well-equipped rooms. The hotel has all the usual business facilities, a bar and restaurant, and is conveniently located next to the palace. €€

EATING AND DRINKING

The splendid nineteenth-century **Mercado de Abastos** on C/Stuart is a good place to buy your own food for a picnic (including, in season, the famous locally grown strawberries and asparagus).
La Alegria de la Huerta Carretera de Madrid 4, http://lalegriadearanjuez.es. This place, near to the bridge across the Tajo on the main road in from Madrid, offers a speciality *arroz con bogavante* (lobster), pheasant and *cochinillo*. Lunchtime menu has dishes such as rabbit and steak followed by the obligatory strawberries and cream. €€
Casa José C/Abastos 32, http://casajose.es. Renowned restaurant serving high-quality *nueva cocina* featuring local produce. Offers an excellent seasonal taster menu and a chef's choice menu that brings local produce, fruit and

CAMPING

Samay Camping Aranjuez On a far bend of the Río Tajo, http://campingaranjuez.com. This large campsite with 162 pitches is equipped with a swimming pool, a supermarket and a children's club, and rents out bicycles and canoes. €

vegetables to the fore. €€€
★ **Casa Pablete** C/Stuart 108, http://casapablete.com. A traditional bar good for tapas and *raciones* with excellent *montados de calamares* and *solomillo*. €
Casa Pablo C/Almíbar 42, http://casapablo.net. Castilian food at a reasonable price is served in traditional surroundings in this long-standing Aranjuez favourite, whose walls are covered with pictures of local dignitaries and bullfighters. €€
El Rana Verde Pza. Santiago Rusiñol s/n, http://elrana verde.com. Probably the best-known restaurant in the area, but mainly because of its pleasant riverside location. It dates back to the late nineteenth century and serves up a range of decent, if unspectacular, menus for good value. €€

Chinchón

CHINCHÓN, 45km southeast of Madrid, is an enchanting little place, with a fifteenth-century castle and a picture-postcard **Pza. Mayor**, encircled by whitewashed buildings festooned with wooden balconies. Providing the backdrop to the Pza. Mayor is the Neoclassical **Iglesia de la Asunción**, which houses Goya's depiction of the Assumption. The town is best known for being the home of *anís* – a mainstay of breakfast drinkers across Spain. Your best bet for a sample of the spirit is one of the local bars or the Alcoholera de Chinchón, a shop on the Pza. Mayor. The **Museo Etnológico** (charge), at C/Morata 5, off the Pza. Mayor, has some of the traditional *anís*-making machines on display.

ARRIVAL AND INFORMATION
CHINCHÓN

By bus From Aranjuez #430 from Avda. de las Infantas (Mon–Fri hourly, Sat & Sun 8 daily; 55min); from Madrid #337 every 30min from the bus station at Avda. Mediterraneo 49 (Ⓜ Conde Casal); 45–55min.

Turismo Pza. Mayor (summer: Mon–Fri 10am–3pm & 5–8pm, Sat & Sun 10am–3pm, winter daily 10am–7pm; 918 935 323, http://ciudad-chinchon.com).

ACCOMMODATION

Hostal Chinchón C/Grande 16, http://hostalchinchon. com. Near the Pza. Mayor, modest but pleasant with ten decent-sized, nicely decorated a/c doubles and triples. There is a terrace pool and restaurant/bar. €
★ **Parador de Chinchón** C/Los Huertos 1, http://

paradores.com. Situated in a sixteenth-century former Augustinian monastery close to the Pza. Mayor, this historic parador has an outdoor pool, tranquil patio gardens, large rooms and a very good restaurant. Look out for offers on the website. €€€

EATING AND DRINKING

★ **Casa de Pregonero** Pza. Mayor 4, http://lacasadel pregonero.com. Adds modern touches to traditional dishes and has some mouthwatering starters such as scallops with strawberry, lime and truffle dressing and a creamy rice dish

with mushrooms. There is a set menu, but reckon on at least €40 a head if you go a la carte. €€€
Mesón La Balconada Pza. Mayor, 918 941 303. Quality restaurant in one of the balconied buildings overlooking

the plaza, serving top-quality Castilian specialities such as *cochinillo* and *cordero* as well as some quality fish dishes. An extensive wine list too. €€€

Mesón Cuevas del Vino C/Benito Hortelano 13, http://cuevasdelvino.com. Situated in an old olive oil mill, with its own *bodega*, this restaurant first opened its doors back in 1964, with luminaries such as Orson Welles and Yul Brynner passing through its doors in the early years. There is a taster menu, which includes *cordero* or *cochinillo*, available. €€€

Mesón El Duende C/Grande 36, 918 940 807. One of the more reasonably priced restaurants in town in a little courtyard not far from the Pza. Mayor, serving traditional Castilian food with a set lunch. €€

La Villa Pza. Mayor 45, http://restaurante-lavilla.es. With a history dating back over 70 years, this restaurant was originally set up as a bar by two workers in one of the town's *anís* distilleries. Nowadays they serve up some excellent creative tapas as well as the Chinchón standards of *cordero* and *cochinillo*. €€€

San Lorenzo del Escorial and El Valle de los Caídos

Northwest of Madrid, in the foothills of the Sierra de Guadarrama, is one of Spain's best known and most visited sights – Felipe II's colossal monastery-palace complex of **El Escorial**. The vast granite building, which contains a royal palace, a monastery, a mausoleum, four thousand rooms, fifteen cloisters and one of the finest libraries of the Renaissance, embodies all that was important to one of the most powerful rulers in European history. The town around the monastery, **San Lorenzo del Escorial**, is an easy day-trip from Madrid; for onward travel, rail and road routes continue to Ávila and Segovia.

Tours from Madrid to El Escorial often take in the forbidding Francoist monument **El Valle de los Caídos** where the dictator and many Civil War dead are buried.

El Escorial

Av Juan de Borbón y Battemberg, San Lorenzo del Escorial • Charge (entry covers monastery, Palacio de los Borbones, outlying lodges and gardens); free Wed & Thurs 5–8pm (3–6pm Oct–March) for EU citizens • http://patrimonionacional.es

The monastery of **El Escorial** was the largest Spanish building of the Renaissance: rectangular, overbearing and austere, from the outside it resembles a prison more than a palace. Built between 1563 and 1584 to commemorate the victory over the French at the battle of San Quentin on August 10, 1557 (San Lorenzo's Day), it was originally the creation of Juan Bautista de Toledo, though his one-time assistant, **Juan de Herrera**, took over and is normally given credit for the design. **Felipe II** planned the complex as both monastery and mausoleum, where he would live the life of a monk and "rule the world with two inches of paper". Later monarchs had less ascetic lifestyles, enlarging and richly decorating the palace quarters, but Felipe's simple rooms remain the most fascinating.

Visits to the **Real Monasterio del Escorial** have become more relaxed in recent years, and you can use your ticket (purchased in the **visitors' entrance**) to enter, in whatever sequence you like, the basilica, sacristy, chapterhouses, library and royal apartments. To escape the worst of the crowds, avoid Wednesday and Thursday afternoons in the high season and try visiting just before lunch or late in the day.

The Biblioteca and Patio de los Reyes

A good starting point is the west gateway, the traditional **main entrance**, facing the mountains. Above it is a gargantuan statue of San Lorenzo holding the gridiron on which he was martyred. Within is the splendid **Biblioteca** (Library), adorned with shelves designed by Herrera to harmonize with the architecture, and frescoes by Tibaldi and his assistants that show the seven Liberal Arts. Its collections include the tenth-century *Codex Albeldensis*, St Teresa's personal diary, some gorgeously executed Arabic manuscripts and a Florentine planetarium of 1572 demonstrating the movement of the planets according to the Ptolemaic and Copernican systems. Beyond is the **Patio de**

los Reyes, named after the six statues of the kings of Israel on the facade of the basilica straight ahead.

Basílica

In the **Basílica**, notice the flat vault of the *coro* above your head as you enter, which is apparently entirely without support, and the white marble Christ carved by Benvenuto Cellini and carried here from Barcelona on workmen's shoulders. The east end is decorated by Italian artists: the sculptures are by the father-and-son team of Leone and Pompeo Leoni, who also carved the two facing groups of Carlos V with his family and Felipe II with three of his wives; Mary Tudor is excluded. The reliquaries near the altar are said to hold the entire bodies of ten saints, plus 144 heads and 306 arms and legs.

2

Sacristía, Salas Capitulares and the Panteón Real

The **Sacristía** and **Salas Capitulares** (Chapter Houses) contain many of the monastery's religious treasures, including paintings by Titian, Velázquez and José Ribera. Beside the sacristy a staircase leads down to the **Panteón Real**, the final resting place of all Spanish monarchs since Carlos V, with the exception of Felipe V and Fernando VI. The deceased monarchs lie in exquisite gilded marble tombs: kings (and Isabel II) on one side, their spouses on the other.

Just above the entry is the Pudridero Real, a separate room in which the bodies (which are covered in lime) rot for twenty years or so before the cleaned-up skeletons are moved to the final resting place. The royal children are laid in the **Panteón de los Infantes**; the tomb of Don Juan, Felipe II's bastard half-brother, is grander than any of the kings', while the wedding-cake babies' tomb with room for sixty infants is more than half full.

Museos Nuevos, Salones Reales and Claustro Grande

What remains of the Escorial's art collection – works by Bosch, Gerard David, Dürer, Titian, Zurbarán and many others, which escaped transfer to the Prado – is kept in the elegant suite of rooms known as the **Museos Nuevos** (New Museums). Don't miss the **Sala de las Batallas**, a magnificent gallery lined with an epic series of paintings depicting the most notable imperial battles. The surprisingly modest **Salones Reales** (Royal Apartments) contain the austere **quarters of Felipe II**, with the chair that supported his gouty leg and the deathbed from which he was able to contemplate the high altar of the basilica. However, Felipe's successors occupied the more lavish **Palacio de los Borbones**, which takes up the northeastern corner of the complex.

Claustro Grande and Patio de los Evangelistas

You can wander at will in some of the Escorial's courtyards; most notable is the **Claustro Grande**, with frescoes of the *Life of the Virgin* by Tibaldi, and the secluded gardens of the **Patio de los Evangelistas** which lie within, while on the southern flank lies a series of parterre gardens known as the Jardín de los Frailes.

Outlying lodges

Charge

The **Casita del Príncipe** (aka Casita de Abajo) and the **Casita del Infante** (aka Casita de Arriba) are two eighteenth-century royal lodges located within the grounds of El Escorial, both full of decorative riches, and built by Juan de Villanueva, Spain's most accomplished Neoclassical architect – so worth seeing in themselves as well as for their formal gardens.

The Casita del Infante, which served as the former monarch Juan Carlos' student digs, is a short way up into the hills and affords a good view of the Escorial complex. The Casita del Príncipe, in the Jardines del Príncipe below the monastery, is larger and more worthwhile, with an important collection of Giordano paintings and four pictures made from rice paste.

2

Silla de Felipe

Around 3km out of town is the **Silla de Felipe** – "Felipe's Seat" – a chair carved into a rocky outcrop with a great view out towards the palace. His majesty is supposed to have sat here to watch the construction going on. You can reach it on foot by following the path through the arches beyond the main entrance to the monastery by the Biblioteca; keep to the left as you go down the hill and then cross the main road and follow the signs. If you have a car, take the M505 Ávila road and turn off at the sign after about 3km.

El Valle de los Caídos

Carretera de Guadarrama • Charge, free Wed & Thurs 4–7pm (3–6pm Oct–March) for EU citizens • http://patrimonionacional.es

Nine kilometres north of El Escorial nestled among the mountains is **El Valle de los Caídos** (The Valley of the Fallen). This is an equally megalomaniac yet far more chilling monument: an underground basilica hewn out by political prisoners under Franco's orders, allegedly as a memorial to the Civil War dead of both sides, though in reality as a shrine to the *generalísimo* and his regime.

It remains a controversial place to this day. In 2007, the socialist government of José Luis Rodríguez Zapatero tried to depoliticize the site and passed a law to prevent its use

---

COMING TO TERMS WITH THE PAST

El Valle de los Caídos is probably the most controversial and emotive physical expression of the **Francoist dictatorship** that still remains in present-day Spain. Partly built by Popular Front prisoners in the 1940s and 50s, this pharaonic memorial to the fascist triumph in the **Civil War** towers over a valley that conceals tens of thousands of corpses moved there under Franco's orders. After the burial of the founder of the Falange Party, **José Antonio Primo de Rivera**, and Franco himself, the mausoleum became a place of homage for neo-fascists who continued to commemorate the dictator's death every November 20 by parading their fascist paraphernalia at the site. But the future of the monument has finally been exposed to official scrutiny following the decision of the former socialist government to set up a committee to decide how to turn the site into a monument to reconciliation.

The removal of Franco's remains is one option, but the destruction of the giant cross appears to have been dismissed, as has the possibility of evicting the **Benedictine monks** who inhabit the site. The most likely outcome is the establishment of a museum or interpretation centre which will put the monument in its context and use it as a reminder of the horrors that resulted from the Civil War. But the debate has shown how raw feelings remain in Spain and how problematic the country has found the experience of coming to terms with its traumatic past.

It was not until 2007, over thirty years after the death of the dictator, that the then socialist government introduced what became known as **the "historical memory" law**, which recognized victims of the Franco regime, prohibited political events at the Valle de los Caídos and provided some state help for the identification and eventual exhumation of the victims of Francoist repression whose corpses still lie in over two thousand mass graves scattered across Spain. Even that step was resisted by opponents who preferred to turn a blind eye to the deep wounds left by the Civil War and its aftermath. But grassroots campaigns to dig up the mass graves, often led by relatives of the victims, forced the government to break its silence and confront the issue.

The conservative **Partido Popular** government, which came to power in 2011, has been reluctant to follow up the initiative of their predecessors and have cut funding for the exhumations but the pressure is on to try to force Spain to come to terms with matters that have been swept under the carpet for so many years. As Catalan photographer Francesc Torres, a leading light in the movement to shed light on Spain's unexamined past, has said: "History is resilient. You can cover it, but it's not going away."

by Falangist supporters keen to glorify the Franco era, while it also set up a commission to decide how to turn it into a monument symbolizing reconciliation rather than Nationalist victory and oppression (see page 136).

To get to the monument itself you have to travel some 6km along a road which winds its way up from the main entrance gate. Above is a vast 150-metre-high cross, reputedly the largest in the world, and visible for miles along the A6 motorway towards Segovia.

The **basilica complex** denies its claims of memorial "to the Civil War dead of both sides" almost at a glance. The debased and grandiose fascist-style architectural forms employed, the grim martial statuary, the constant inscriptions "Fallen for God and for Spain" and the proximity to El Escorial intimate the complex's true function: the glorification of General Franco and his regime. The dictator himself lies buried behind the high altar, while the only other named tomb, marked simply "José Antonio", is that of his guru, the Falangist leader José Antonio Primo de Rivera, who was shot dead by Republicans at the beginning of the war. The "other side" is present only in the fact that the complex was built by the Republican army's survivors – political prisoners on quarrying duty.

ARRIVAL SAN LORENZO DEL ESCORIAL AND EL VALLE DE LOS CAÍDOS

By train There are trains every 15–30min from Madrid (5.45am–11.30pm; 1hr) from Atocha, calling at Chamartín. If you arrive by train, get straight on the local bus that shuttles you up to the centre of town – they leave promptly and it's a long uphill walk.

Destinations Ávila (15 daily; 1hr); Madrid (30 daily; 1hr). If you want to go on to Segovia you will have to backtrack down the train line to Villalba and then take one of the trains from Madrid.

By bus Buses (#661 & #664 from the *intercambiador* at

Moncloa) run every 15min on weekdays and hourly at weekends and take around an hour to arrive. Stay on the bus and it will take you right up to the monastery. To get to El Valle de los Caídos from El Escorial, take local bus #C660A that runs from the bus station at C/Juan de Toledo 3, just north of the visitors' entrance to the monastery (departs 3.15pm, returns 5.30pm).

Destinations Guadarrama (every 30min–1hr; 15min); Madrid (every 15–30min; 1hr); Valle de los Caídos (daily; 15min).

INFORMATION

Turismo C/Grimaldi 4 (http://sanlorenzoturismo.org), on the small street to the north of the visitors' entrance to the

monastery, running into C/Floridablanca.

ACCOMMODATION

Most **hotels** are close to the monastery. In summer the town is a favourite retreat from the heat of Madrid, so it's wise to book in advance.

HOTELS AND HOSTALES

Hotel Florida C/Floridablanca 12–14, http://hflorida. com. A well-appointed traditional mid-range place, with a restaurant and café serving a buffet breakfast for an extra charge. There are fifty rooms with a/c and for an extra price you can get a superior room with views of the monastery. €€

Los Lanceros C/Calvario 47–49, http://loslanceros.com. A five-minute walk from the monastery complex, this three-star hotel has 36 functional rooms, a terrace restaurant and friendly service. €€

Posada Don Jaime C/San Antón 24, http://posadadon jaime.es. You'll find three cosy doubles, a superior double

with a terrace and four suites in this homely hotel in an old mansion house in the centre of the town. There is parking for a small number of cars and a compact garden where breakfast can be served in summer. €€

San Lorenzo Suites C/Timoteo Padrós 16, http:// botanicohotel.com. Lovely old townhouse converted into a modern apart-hotel, with suites bearing a contemporary style while retaining original features like brick walls and wooden beams. All rooms have kitchenettes. €€

CAMPING

Caravaning El Escorial Carretera de Guadarrama a El Escorial km 3.5, http://campingelescorial.com. A very well-equipped campsite with several swimming pools and three tennis courts situated 6km out on the road back towards Guadarrama. A little noisy during summer weekends. €

EATING AND ENTERTAINMENT

Scattered about town are plenty of small **bars**, which offer snacks and tapas. For evening **entertainment**,

the eighteenth-century Real Coliseo de Carlos III at C/ Floridablanca 20 offers flamenco, jazz and classical concerts and theatrical productions year-round. Details of shows can be picked up from the *turismo*, or check out website http://sanlorenzoturismo.org.

Algóra C/Juan de Toledo 19, http://algorarestaurante.com. Located back down in the town by the railway station, this well-regarded restaurant serves up an array of traditional staples and seasonal dishes, including an excellent selection of starters and salads. €€

El Charolés C/Floridablanca 24, http://charolesrestaurante.com. Renowned for its fish and stews, this old-school restaurant with attentive service is at the top end of the scale. It does a set menu on weekdays with an excellent, but stomach-bursting, *cocido* on Mon, Wed & Fri in winter

(book ahead); otherwise, a la carte options are good and plentiful. €€€

La Cueva C/San Antón 4, http://mesonlacueva.com. An atmospheric wooden-beamed *mesón* that is a good bet for both tapas and a larger meal. Menu offerings include mains of steak or hake. There is *cocido* on Thursdays at good value. €€

★ **Montia** C/Juan de Austria 7, http://montia.es. The best restaurant in town by a long shot – with a price list to match – is this Michelin-starred modern masterpiece from Daniel Ochoa, who forages and farms many of the ingredients which make it to your plate. Among his "wild cuisine" ingredients are tripe and sea urchins, presented beautifully and served in a cosy, almost Scandi-like interior. €€€€

The Sierra de Guadarrama

The routes from Madrid and El Escorial to Segovia strike through the heart of the **Sierra de Guadarrama** (http://parquenacionalsierraguadarrama.es), and it is a beautiful journey. The road is occasionally marred by suburban development, especially around **Puerto de Navacerrada**, Madrid's main ski station, but from the train it's almost entirely unspoiled. There are plenty of opportunities for walking, but make sure you buy the appropriate maps in Madrid.

If you want to base yourself in the mountains for a while you'd do best to head for **Cercedilla**. Alternatively, over to the east, there is **Manzanares el Real**, with its odd medieval castle and reservoir-side setting.

In the shadow of the mountains to the north lies the Valle de Lozoya. At the western end are the village of **Rascafría** and the nearby Benedictine monastery of El Paular, and to the east the old fortified town of **Buitrago**, with its medieval core and small Picasso museum.

Cercedilla

CERCEDILLA is an alpine-looking village perched at the foot of the valley leading up to the Puerto de la Fuenfría and it makes an excellent base for summer walking. It is much frequented by *madrileños* at weekends, as it has the advantage of being accessible.

The village is the starting point for a very pleasant five-hour round-trip **walk** along the pine-fringed Calzada Romana (old Roman road) up to the Puerto de la Fuenfría (1796m), with its striking views down into Segovia province. Follow the signs up to Las Dehesas where there is an a *turismo* (see page 138) which provides maps and advice on walks in the area, then head past the meadows and follow the clearly indicated path up to the Puerto.

ARRIVAL AND INFORMATION CERCEDILLA

By bus #684 every half-hour (50min–1hr 10min) from the *intercambiador* in Moncloa.
By train Madrid–Segovia line, over 20 daily 6am–11pm from Atocha calling at Chamartín, 3–4 daily going on to Segovia; 40–50min; Cotos (5 daily; 40min); Puerto de Navacerrada (5 daily; 25min).

Turismo Pza. Mayor 3 (Wed–Sat 11am–3pm & 4–7pm, Sun 9am–3pm; July–Sept Tues–Fri 10am–3pm, Sat 10am–2pm & 4–7pm, Sun 10am–3pm; 918 523 704); Las Dehesas (daily 9am–4.30pm; July & Aug 9am–8pm; 918 522 213, http://cercedilla.es).

ACCOMMODATION AND EATING

Los Frutales Carretera de las Dehesas 41, http://los-frutales.com. This hotel-restaurant with six charming rooms

has a delightful bucolic setting (breakfast included in price). The restaurant serves good *croquetas*, *trucha* (trout) and

meat dishes, and has a cool terrace in summer. €€€
Hostal Longinos – El Aribel C/Emilio Serrano 71, http://
hostalaribel.com. In a convenient location close to the
railway station, but otherwise nothing special, this alpine-
style *hostal* has 23 en-suite rooms and a café-bar. €

Luces del Poniente C/Lina de Ávila 4, http://
lucesdelponiente.com. A tranquil rural hotel with thirteen
spacious, individually decorated rooms, a covered pool and
spa area and a relaxing garden terrace. Breakfast included.
€€

Puerto de Navacerrada and Cotos

From Cercedilla, you can embark on a wonderful little train ride to the **Puerto de Navacerrada**, the most important pass in the mountains and the heart of the ski area, or a little farther on to **Cotos** where a number of well-maintained walks around the **Parque Natural de Peñalara** begin. The train runs hourly over weekends and holidays, and passes through the *parque natural*, an extension of the upper Manzanares basin: watch out for roe deer and wild boar. In winter it is possible to ski in both Navacerrada and Cotos, but be prepared for long queues and traffic jams at weekends.

Hiking in the high peaks

Navacerrada is also the starting point for a number of impressive walks along the **high peaks**, while Cotos is the gateway to the highest peak in the Sierra, Peñalara (2430m). It can be reached in about four hours, but is a reasonably tough ascent and should not be attempted in winter. Less challenging but very enjoyable is the easy, well-indicated hike to the glacial lake, the Laguna Grande.

INFORMATION **COTOS**

Information There is a small information booth just above the small café close to the Cotos train station that will give advice on all routes (918 520 857).

Monasterio del Paular and Rascafría

Off Hwy M-604, 35 miles (56km) north of Madrid • Guided tours in Spanish only • Free • http://monasteriopaular.com • Bus #194 links with Madrid (intercambiador Pza. Castilla) 2–3 times a day; 2hr 5min

Some 10km below Cotos in the beautiful Valle de Lozoya just outside the pleasant mountain village of **Rascafría** stands the **Monasterio de Santa María de El Paular**, originally a Carthusian monastery founded at the end of the fourteenth century, and now home to a handful of Benedictine monks who provide guided tours of the silent cloisters and the main church.

ACCOMMODATION **RASCAFRÍA**

Los Espinares Avda. de Cascajales 52, www.losespinares.
net. A lovely, tranquil hotel on the edge of Rascafría, with
cosy rooms with brick or wood-panelled walls and wrought-
iron beds. Also has a health suite with sauna and jacuzzi. €€

Hostal Rural El Valle Avda. del Valle 39, http://hotel
ruralelvalle.com. A good-value, cosy option close to the
village. Thirty rooms, including some triples and quadruples
which have their own cooking facilities. €€

Manzanares el Real

Some 50km north of Madrid, on the shores of the Santillana *embalse* (reservoir), lies **MANZANARES EL REAL**, a town which in former times was disputed between the capital and Segovia. Nowadays it's geared to Madrid weekenders, whose villas dot the landscape for miles around. The town's one attraction is the castle (charge), which despite its eccentric appearance is a perfectly genuine fifteenth-century construction, built around an earlier chapel. It was soon modified into a palace by the architect Juan Guas, who built an elegant gallery on the south side and false machicolations on the other, and studded the tower with stones resembling cannonballs. The interior has been heavily restored, but it makes for an interesting visit. Alongside is a reconstructed Renaissance garden with a kitchen garden, orchard and vineyard and a maze.

ARRIVAL AND INFORMATION
MANZANARES EL REAL

By bus #724 from the *intercambiador* in Pza. de Castilla (⊕ Plaza de Castilla) hourly; 45min.

Turismo (Tues–Fri 9.30am–2.30pm, Sat, Sun & hols 9am–3pm; http://manzanareselreal.org). For information about the region as a whole consult the website http://sierranorte.com.

ACCOMMODATION

La Fresneda Carretera M608, km19.5, http://camping lafresneda.com. An upgraded campsite on the road towards Soto del Real with a pool bar area, small playground and shady pitches. €

El Ortigal C/Montañero 19, 918 530 120. Campsite at the foot of La Pedriza, with great views and its own pool, situated on the northern side of the town. €

EATING AND DRINKING

Restaurante Parra C/Panaderos 15, http://restaurante parra.es. Better value than many of the Sierra restaurants, this one serves up similar fare, with Castilian meat dishes and paellas topping the bill. A decent wine list too. There is a lunchtime menu for great value, but if you go a la carte expect to pay significantly more. €€

La Pedriza

Access limited to 350 cars a day at weekends • Free • http://parquenacionalsierraguadarrama.es • Bus #724 from the *intercambiador* in Pza. de Castilla in Madrid

Rising behind Manzanares el Real is the ruggedly beautiful **La Pedriza**, a spur of the Sierra de Guadarrama that has been declared a regional park. There are some enjoyable walks by the river and around the granite dome El Yelmo, as well as some much-revered technical climbs, notably the ascent to the jagged Peña del Diezmo. The park is also home to a very large colony of **griffon vultures**.

Buitrago de Lozoya

East of La Pedriza, beyond the road to Burgos, lies the attractive little town of **BUITRAGO DE LOZOYA**, a fortified settlement with defensive walls that date from the twelfth century, a ruined castle, a fine Mudéjar church, Santa María del Castillo and, more surprisingly, a small **Picasso museum** (free). The collection, based on work donated by the artist to his friend and local barber Eugenio Arias, features an interesting selection of sixty minor pieces dating from between 1948 and 1972.

ARRIVAL AND INFORMATION
BUITRAGO DE LOZOYA

By bus Hourly buses (#191) from the *intercambiador* in Pza. de Castilla; 1hr 20min.

Turismo C/Tahona 19 (http://buitrago.org).

Patones de Arriba

On the southern edge of the so-called Sierra Pobre is the picturesque mountain village of **PATONES DE ARRIBA**, abandoned in the 1930s but since restored and now a fashionable weekend destination for many *madrileños*. The black slate architecture of the village is undeniably beautiful, the views are good, and you can be assured of a fine meal, but there is little else to detain the casual visitor. You will need to leave vehicles in the car park in nearby Patones de Abajo and walk the 2.5km up the signposted path.

ARRIVAL AND INFORMATION
PATONES DE ARRIBA

By bus Two or three buses (#197) daily from the *intercambiador* in the Pza. de Castilla in Patones Abajo.

Turismo http://patones.net.

ACCOMMODATION

★ **El Mirador de las Jaras** Travesía del Ayuntamiento 5 y 7, http://elmiradordelasjaras.com. Luxury boutique hotel with seven individually decorated rooms (some with small balconies) housed in one of the beautiful slate cottages in this tranquil village. The owner Paco Bello is also the chef at the excellent *El Poleo* restaurant which is contained within the hotel. €€€

EATING AND DRINKING

El Poleo Travesía del Arroyo 3, www.elmiradordelasjaras. com. Attached to the hotel *El Tiempo Perdido* and owned by Cordobés chef Paco Bello, this restaurant takes a creative angle on the local cuisine with dishes such as roast lamb with honey and couscous. You can eat outside on the picturesque patio in summer. €€€

El Rey de Patones C/Azas 13, http://reydepatones. com. Serving up an appetizing mixture of local produce and seasonal specials, this was the first restaurant to be established in the abandoned village and it has the pick of the views over the black slate houses. Ask for one of the tables on the terrace in summer. €€€

Ávila

Two things distinguish **ÁVILA**: its eleventh-century **walls**, two perfectly preserved kilometres of which surround the old town, and the mystic writer **Santa Teresa**, who was born here and whose shrines are a major focus of religious pilgrimage. Set on a high plain, with the peaks of the Sierra de Gredos as a backdrop, the town is quite a sight, especially if you approach with the evening sun highlighting the golden tone of the walls and the details of the 88 towers. The walls make orientation straightforward, with the **Catedral** and most other sights contained within. Just outside the southeast corner is the city's main square, **Pza. Santa Teresa**, and the most imposing of the old gates, the **Puerta del Alcázar**.

Convento de Santa Teresa

Pza. de la Santa 2 • **Chapel & Reliquary** Free • **Museum** Charge • http://museosantateresa.com

The obvious place to start a tour of Teresa's Ávila is the **Convento de Santa Teresa**, built over the saint's birthplace just inside the south gate of the old town and entered off the Paseo del Rastro. Most of the convent remains *de clausura*, but you can see the very spot where she was born, now a fabulously ornate chapel in the Baroque church, which is decorated with scenes of the saint demonstrating her powers of levitation to various august bodies. A small **reliquary**, beside the gift shop, contains memorials of Teresa's life, including not only her rosary beads, but also one of the fingers she used to count them with. In the crypt of the monastery is a **museum** dedicated to the saint's life and work. Packed full of memorabilia, accounts of her miraculous deeds and numerous translations of her work, it provides a truly hagiographic vision of Teresa's life.

Palacio de los Superunda

Pza. Corral de Las Campanas 3 • Charge • 920 354 000

This Renaissance mansion, with its marvellous two-storeyed interior patio, now houses a collection of work by Italian artist Guido Caprotti, who lived in the city from 1916 until the Civil War. His work gives an evocative insight into the people and customs of the city in the early twentieth century.

Monasterio de la Encarnación

Paseo de la Encarnación s/n • Charge • 920 211 212

Heading through the old town, and leaving northwards by the Puerta del Carmen, you can follow a lane, C/Encarnación, to the **Monasterio de la Encarnación**. The entrance

ÁVILA

Río Adaja

Puente Románico

0 — 100 meters

Segovia (N110) | Train Station | Madrid (C505)

Parque de San Antonio

Bus Station

Monasterio de Santa Ana
Convento de las Gordillas
Jardín del Recreo
San Andrés
Basílica de San Vicente
Convento de San José
Ermita de Ntra. Sra. de las Vacas
Museo de Ávila
Santo Tomé el Viejo
Santa María de la Antigua
Palacio de los Serrano
San Pedro
Convento de la Concepción
Puerta de S. Vicente
Palacio de los Aguila
Puerta de Carnicerías
Catedral
Puerta del Alcázar
Convento de Ntra. Sra. de Gracia
Palacio de los Verdugo
Palacio de los Valderrábanos
Santiago
Puerta del Mariscal
Capilla de Mosén Rubí
Ayuntamiento
Palacio de los Dávila
Puerta del Rastro
San Martín
Parador
Torreón de los Guzmanes
Parque del Rastro
San Nicolás
Puerta del Carmen
Palacio de los Polentinos
Convento de Santa Teresa
Palacio de los Superunda
San Esteban
Palacio de los Núñez-Vela
Puerta de Sta. Teresa
Ermita de Santa María de la Cabeza
Puerta del Puente
Ermita de San Segundo

Monasterio de la Encarnación
Monasterio de Santo Tomás & Museo Oriental
Toledo (N403)
Cáceres
Los Cuatro Postes & Salamanca (N 501)

DRINKING AND NIGHTLIFE
La Bodeguita de San Segundo	1

ACCOMMODATION
Las Cancelas	7
Hostal Bellas	6
Hostal Don Diego	2
Hostal Le Vintage	3
Hotel Las Leyendas	8
Palacio de Valderrábanos	5
Palacio de los Velada	4
Parador de Ávila	1

EATING
El Almacén	2
Bar El Rincón	3
Bococo	7
Las Cancelas	8
Doña Cayetana	6
El Molino de la Losa	1
La Posada de la Fruta	5
Soul Kitchen	4

to the museum is in the patio – ring the bell and wait if it appears to be unattended and you will eventually be ushered in. Teresa lived here for much of the time between 1535 and 1574, the last three years as the prioress. Each room is labelled with a miraculous act she performed or vision that she witnessed, while everything she might have touched or looked at is also on display. A small museum section also provides a reasonable introduction to the saint's life, with maps showing the convents, papal bulls and a selection of her sayings – the pithiest, perhaps, "Life is a night in a bad hotel".

Convento de San José

Pza. de las Madres 4 • Charge • 920 222 127

A third Teresan sight lies five minutes east of the Catedral outside the city walls. This is the **Convento de San José**, the first monastery that the saint founded, in 1562. Its museum contains relics and memorabilia, including the coffin in which Teresa once slept and a signed handkerchief stained with her blood. The tomb of her brother Lorenzo is in the larger of the two churches, which was the work of one of the El Escorial architects, Francisco de Mora.

Los Cuatro Postes

You might want to make your way up to **Los Cuatro Postes**, a little four-posted shrine, 1.5km along the Salamanca road west of town and a fine vantage point from which to admire the walls of the town. It was here, aged 7, that the infant Teresa, running away with her brother to seek Christian martyrdom fighting the Moors, was recaptured by her uncle.

The Catedral

Pza. de la Catedral • Charge, under-12s free • http://catedralavila.es

Ávila's **Catedral** was started in the twelfth century but has never been finished, as evidenced by the missing tower above the main entrance. The earliest Romanesque parts were as much fortress as church, and the apse actually forms an integral part of the city walls.

Inside, the succeeding changes of style are immediately apparent; the **Romanesque** parts are made of a strange red-and-white mottled stone, then there's an abrupt break and the rest of the main structure is pure white stone with **Gothic** forms. Although the proportions are exactly the same, this newer half of the Catedral seems infinitely more spacious. The *coro*, whose elaborate carved back you see as you come in, and two chapels in the left aisle, are **Renaissance** additions. Here you can admire the elaborate marble tomb of a fifteenth-century bishop known as El Tostado (the "toasted" or "swarthy"), while the thirteenth-century *sacristía* with its star-shaped cupola and gold inlay decor, and the treasury-museum with its monstrous silver *custodia* and ancient religious images are also worth a visit.

Basílica de San Vicente

Pza. de San Vicente 1 • Charge • 920 255 230

The **Basílica de San Vicente** marks the site where San Vicente was martyred, and his tomb narrates the gruesome story of torture and execution by the Romans. Legend has it that following the martyrdom a rich Jew, who had been poking fun at the martyrs, was enveloped and suffocated by a great serpent that miraculously emerged from the rocks. On the verge of asphyxiation he repented and converted to Christianity, later building the church on the very same site, and he, too, is said to be buried here. In the crypt you can see part of the rocky crag where San Vicente and his sisters were executed and from which the serpent later supposedly appeared. Like the Catedral, the building is a mixture of architectural styles. The warm pink glow of the sandstone of the church is a characteristic feature of Ávila, also notable in the **church of San Pedro** (charge) on Pza. de Santa Teresa.

Capilla de Mosén Rubí

Pza. de Mosén Rubí 9 • Free

One of the most eye-catching of the city's monuments, the polygonal **Capilla de Mosén Rubí** was started in the fifteenth century, but owing to a lengthy legal dispute and a lack of funds it was not completed until the following century. The delay explains the chapel's two distinct architectural styles – Gothic and Renaissance – which are evident in the interior design. The magnificent marble tombs of the benefactors take pride of place in the centre of the chapel.

City walls

Charge, tickets available from the green kiosk by the Puerta del Alcázar and the tourist office at Puerta de Carnicerías

The **city walls**, a mixture of red limestone, granite and brick, were built under Alfonso VI, following his capture of the city from the Moors in 1090; they took his Muslim prisoners nine years to construct. At closer quarters, they prove a bit of a facade, as the old city within is sparsely populated, most of modern life having moved into the new developments outside the fortifications. It's possible to walk along two sections of the walls, from Puerta de Carnicerías to Puerta del Carmen and from Puerta del Alcázar to Puerta del Rastro, the former being the best as it has some memorable views of the town.

Museo de Ávila

Pza. del Navaillos 3 • Charge • http://museoscastillayleon.jcyl.es

Just outside the city walls, through the Puerta de Carnicerías, is the small **Museo de Ávila (Museo Provincial)**, housed in the sixteenth-century Palacio de los Deanes where the Catedral's deans once lived. Today, its eclectic exhibits include collections of archeological remains, ceramics, agricultural implements and traditional costumes, as well as some fine Romanesque statues and a wonderful fifteenth-century triptych depicting the *Life of Christ*. The ticket also allows you entry to the museum storeroom in the church of Santo Tomé El Viejo just opposite.

SANTA TERESA DE ÁVILA

Santa Teresa (1515–82) was born to a noble family in Ávila and from childhood began to experience visions and religious raptures. Her religious career began at the Carmelite convent of La Encarnación, where she was a nun for 27 years. From this base, she went on to reform the movement and found convents throughout Spain. She was an ascetic, but her appeal lay in the mystic sensuality of her experience of Christ, as revealed in her autobiography, for centuries a bestseller in Spain. As joint patron saint of Spain (together with Santiago), she remains a central pillar in Spanish Catholicism and schoolgirls are brought into Ávila by the busload to experience first-hand the life of the woman they are supposed to emulate. She died in Alba de Torres just outside Salamanca, and the Carmelite convent, which contains the remains of her body and a dubious reconstruction of the cell in which she passed away, is another major target of pilgrimage. On a more bizarre note, one of Santa Teresa's mummified hands has been returned to Ávila after spending the Franco years by the bedside of the dictator.

Monasterio de Santo Tomás

Pza. de Granada 1 • Charge • http://monasteriosantotomas.com

The **Monasterio de Santo Tomás** is a fifteen-minute walk southeast of the old city. Established by the Reyes Católicos Fernando and Isabel in the later fifteenth century, the monastery is set around three cloisters and contains a fine, carved Gothic choir in the main church. Within are the tombs of Don Juan, the only son of the Reyes Católicos, and the notorious Torquemada, Isabel's confessor and later head of the Inquisition. Alongside is the **Museo Oriental**, which contains memorabilia brought back from the Far East by Dominican missionaries and a small natural history collection full of stuffed animals.

ARRIVAL AND DEPARTURE

ÁVILA

By train From Madrid (Chamartín station) there are up to twenty trains a day to Ávila (1hr 25min–2hr 10min). The train station is a 15min walk to the east of the old town, and a local bus connects it with Pza. Victoria, a little west of the Catedral. On foot, follow the broad Paseo de la Estación to its end, by the large church of Santa Ana, and head straight on to reach Pza. Santa Teresa.
Destinations El Escorial (6 daily; 1hr); Madrid (20 daily; 1hr 25min–2hr 10min); Medina del Campo (12 daily; 40–50min); Salamanca (10 daily; 1hr 10min–1hr 30min).
By bus Buses are less frequent (Estación del Sur; 8–11

daily; 1hr 25min–1hr 45min) and use a terminal on the Avda. de Madrid, a little closer in: walking from here, cross the small park opposite, then up C/Duque de Alba, or take a local bus to Pza. Victoria.
Destinations Arenas de San Pedro (daily Mon–Fri; 1hr 30min); Madrid (8–11 daily; 1hr 25min–1hr 45min); Salamanca (5–8 daily; 1hr 10min–1hr 30min); Segovia (4 daily; 55min).
By car Follow signs for the walls (*murallas*) or the parador and you should be able to park just outside the old town.

INFORMATION

Visitors' centre Avda. de Madrid 39, just beyond the Basílica de San Vicente (www.avilaturismo.com). Here you can buy the Ávila tourist pass (under-12s free) which will provide entry to most of the leading sights for a period of 48 hours. They also offer a selection of themed walking tours of

the city (charge; see website for details).
Turismo Casa de las Carnicerías, C/San Segundo 17 (July to mid-Sept Mon–Sat 9.30am–2pm & 5–8pm, Sun 9.30am–5pm; mid-Sept to June Mon–Sat 9.30am–2pm & 4–7pm, Sun 9.30am–5pm; 920 211 387, www.avilaturismo.com).

ACCOMMODATION

SEE MAP PAGE 142

There are numerous cheap **hostales** around the train station and along Avda. José Antonio, but you should be able to find something nearer the walled centre of town.
★ **Las Cancelas** C/Cruz Vieja 6, http://lascancelas.com. This converted fifteenth-century building has fourteen functional a/c rooms, some with good views of the Catedral and walls. There's a decent bar and a very pleasant patio restaurant serving regional specialities, too. €€
Hostal Bellas C/Caballeros 19, http://hostalbellas.es. Eager-to-please owners run this centrally located *hostal*. There are sixteen simple en-suite rooms, including one for families, and discounts out of season. €
Hostal Don Diego C/Marqués de Canales y Chozas 5, 920 255 475. A friendly, family-run and good-value *hostal* just opposite the parador with its own parking and restaurant. All twelve simple but neatly decorated rooms have bath or shower. €
Hostal Le Vintage C/Comuneros de Castilla 3, 920 251 475. Rebranded and refurbished, this centrally located *hostal* has a smart, modern feel with a selection of neatly decorated en-suite rooms, including some triples. €
★ **Hotel Las Leyendas** C/Francisco Gallego 3, http://

lasleyendas.es. This sixteenth-century mansion has nineteen tastefully refurbished rooms, with exposed brick and stonework on some of the walls, wooden beams and minimalist decor. Some rooms have views of the Sierra. Its restaurant, *La Bruja*, serves up a refreshing mix of modern tapas and Castilian classics. €€
Palacio de Valderrábanos Pza. de la Catedral 9, http://hotelpalaciovalderrabanos.com. A refurbishment has spruced up the rooms and given this former bishop's palace next to the Catedral a much more modern feel. Good cut-price deals available through the website. €€
★ **Palacio de los Velada** Pza. de la Catedral 10, http://hotelpalaciodelosvelada.com. A beautifully converted sixteenth-century palace with a stunning cloistered bar. The large, airy, classically decorated rooms – many with views over the patio – are all very competitively priced if you book via the website. €€
Parador de Ávila C/Marqués de Canales y Chozas 2, http://paradores.com. A converted fifteenth-century mansion close to the city walls. While not the most exciting parador in Spain, it is pleasant enough and has all the usual comforts. €€€

EATING

SEE MAP PAGE 142

Ávila has a decent if unexceptional array of **bars** and **restaurants**, some of them sited just outside the walls. Local specialities include the Castilian *cordero asado* (roast lamb), *judías del barco con chorizo* (haricot beans with sausage), *mollejas* (cow's stomach) and *yemas de Santa Teresa* (candied egg yolk) – the last of these sold in confectioners all over town.

★ **El Almacén** Carretera Salamanca 6, http://restaurante elalmacen.com. One of the best restaurants in the province, situated in a former storehouse across the river, close to Los Cuatro Postes, with great views of the city walls. It serves quality meat and fish dishes with a creative touch and excellent desserts, and boasts a lengthy wine list. €€€

Bar El Rincón Pza. Zurraquín 6. To the north of Pza. de la Victoria, this down-to-earth bar attached to a *hostal* serves up a generous three-course menu for great prices. Excellent *calamares* and seafood dishes on offer too. €

★ **Bococo** C/Estrada 11, http://bococo.es. Deservedly popular eatery just outside the city walls, serving up an excellent array of traditional dishes with a modern touch; goat's cheese with caramelized apple, hake in martini sauce and partridge with mushrooms are some of the delicious offerings. €€€

Las Cancelas C/Cruz Vieja 6, http://lascancelas.com. Next to the Catedral and in the hotel of the same name, this friendly restaurant with a great interior patio is popular with locals and serves up some excellent *cordero asado* (roast lamb) and *chuletón de Ávila* (succulent locally bred steak). €€€

Doña Cayetana Pza. de Pedro Dávila 6, 920 256 139. Popular, and very good value, two-storey restaurant with a nice interior patio in this plaza by the Puerta del Rastro, specializing in Castilian meat dishes and fish, with a reasonably priced set lunch. €€

★ **El Molino de la Losa** C/Bajada de la Losa 12, http://elmolinodelalosa.com. A beautiful location in a converted fifteenth-century mill out by Los Cuatro Postes, this restaurant has a deserved reputation for quality cuisine. The taster menu with salmon and shoulder of pork and wine is superb. €€€

La Posada de la Fruta Pza. de Pedro Dávila 8, http://posadadelafruta.com. With its attractive, sunny, covered courtyard, this is a nice place for a drink, and it also serves some tasty regional cuisine, with a selection of set menu options. €€€

Soul Kitchen C/Caballeros 13, http://soulkitchen.es. A favourite on the Ávila scene, with its sleek minimalist lines, stripped wood tables and creative menu, which includes gourmet hamburgers, octopus and avocado salad, and cod confit. There is an excellent set lunch and a decent wine list too. €€

DRINKING AND NIGHTLIFE

SEE MAP PAGE 142

For nightlife, head outside the city walls to C/Capitán Peña where the strip of four *bares de copas* next to each other keeps the walking to a minimum.

La Bodeguita de San Segundo C/San Segundo 19. Buried into the wall by the Puerta de Carnicerías, this wine bar has a wide selection from Rioja, Ribera de Duero, Rueda, Penedes, Somantano and Galicia, and serves up a decent range of accompanying, but rather pricey, tapas too.

The Sierra de Gredos

The **Sierra de Gredos** continues the line of the Sierra de Guadarrama, enclosing Madrid to the north and west. A major mountain range, with peaks in excess of 2500m, Gredos offers the best trekking in central Spain and is worth the trip for keen walkers, including some high-level routes across the passes, as well as more casual walks around the villages.

By bus, the easiest access to this spectacular region is from Madrid to Arenas de San Pedro, from where you can explore the range, and then move on west into the valley of La Vera in Extremadura. If you have your own transport, you could head into the range south from Ávila along the N502. Stop at any one of the villages on the north side of the range, along the Tormes valley, such as Hoyos del Espino or Navarredonda, and explore the spectacular circular walks from there.

Arenas de San Pedro and around

ARENAS DE SAN PEDRO is a sizeable town with a somewhat prettified fifteenth-century castle, the Castillo de la Triste Condesa, a Gothic church and the half-built eighteenth-century palace, the Palacio del Infante Don Luis de Borbón.

Grutas del Águila
Carr. de las Cuevas del Águila Daily • Charge, free for under-5s • http://grutasdelaguila.es

Some 9km away, close to the village of Ramacastañas, are the caves known as the **Grutas (or Cuevas) del Águila**, which are lined with an impressive array of bizarre limestone formations stained with orange, yellow and brown from the trace elements in the rocks.

Walks to the Gredos watershed
The main reason to stop at Arenas is to make your way up to the villages of **EL HORNILLO** and **El ARENAL**, 6km and 9km to the north respectively, the trailheads for **walks up to the Gredos watershed**. There are no buses but it's a pleasant walk up from Arenas to El Arenal on a track running between the road and the river – start out past the sports centre and swimming pool in Arenas.

Valle del Tormes
On the north side of Gredos is the beautiful **Valle del Tormes**, which enjoys spectacular views across to the highest peaks in the range. The village of **HOYOS DEL ESPINO**, 20km west along the AV941, makes a good base, as there are several places to stay, a few decent bars, and shops where you can stock up on supplies. A few kilometres to the east is **Navarredonda**, another good base from which to explore the area, while the nearby picturesque village of San Martín del Pimpollar is the base of the excellent **Gredos Guides** (http://gredosguides.es), a small business run by local expert

---

WALKS IN GREDOS
The **two classic walks** in the Gredos mountains are best approached from the so-called Plataforma, at the end of a twelve-kilometre stretch of paved road running from the village of Hoyos del Espino (see page 147), where you can purchase detailed maps of the area. You could also reach this point by walking up from El Hornillo or El Arenal on the southern side of the range, although it makes for a tougher challenge. A functional pamphlet of the area can be obtained from the tourist office at C/Triste Condesa 1, in Arenas de San Pedro (http://arenasdesanpedro.es).

CIRCO DE LAGUNA GRANDE
The **Circo de Laguna Grande** is the centrepiece of the Gredos range, with its highest peak, Almanzor (2593m), surrounded by pinnacles sculpted into utterly improbable shapes. The path begins at the car park at the end of the road coming from Hoyos and climbs towards the high Pozas meadow. From there you can reach the large glacial lake at the end of the valley, a spectacular two-hour walk that winds its way down the slopes on a well-defined path. The route is best done in late spring, summer or early autumn, as snow makes it a treacherous walk in winter.

CIRCO DE LAS CINCO LAGUNAS
For a tougher and much longer route – the **Circo de las Cinco Lagunas** – you can continue on from the Laguna Grande, where there is a *refugio* and camping area, to the Cinco Lagunas (allow 8hr from the Plataforma). Take the signposted path to the right just before the lake, which follows an old hunting route used by Alfonso XIII, up to the Portilla del Rey pass. From there you will be able to look down on the lakes – which are reached along a sharp, scree-laden descent. The drop is amply rewarded by virtual solitude, even in midsummer, and sightings of *Capra pyrenaica victoriae*, the graceful (and almost tame) Gredos mountain goat. There are also species of salamander and toad found only in the area. It is another four to five hours on to the village of Navalperal de Tormes, which is 14km west of Hoyos del Espino.

and fluent English-speaker Juanfran Redondo who organizes a fantastic range of personally tailored ecological and adventure activities throughout the local area, from birdwatching and hiking to mushroom hunting and snow-shoe walking.

ARRIVAL AND DEPARTURE

By bus Buses run from the Estación Sur in Madrid to Arenas de San Pedro (4–6 daily; 2hr 15mins) and to Hoyos del Espino (1 bus daily; 4hr). There are daily buses from Ávila

SIERRA DE GREDOS

that call at Hoyos on their way to Barco de Ávila and a twice-daily service to Arenas.

ACCOMMODATION

The *casas rurales* that are scattered throughout the villages often make a good base, especially if you are travelling in a group (information line http://casasgredos.com).

ARENAS AND GUISANDO

Hostal El Fogón de Gredos C/Linarejo 6, http://fogondegredos.com. If you want a mountain location, then this is your best bet. Situated a couple of kilometres outside Guisando on the flanks of the mountains, this two-star *hostal* has eleven simple, comfortable rooms and a decent restaurant. Breakfast included. €

Posada de la Triste Condesa C/Dr Juan Torres 9, http://posadatristecondesa.com. Rustic accommodation with five cosy, comfortable, tastefully designed double rooms around a delightful plant-strewn interior patio. Breakfast included. €

VALLE DEL TORMES

Camping Navagredos Navarredonda, http://navagredos.com. Large, pine-forested campsite with three hundred pitches on the fringes of the Sierra and close to the Río Tormes. Wooden bungalows on offer. €

★ **Hotel Milano Real** Hoyos del Espino, http://elmilanoreal.com. Luxury hotel on the outskirts of the

village with a high-quality restaurant serving some excellent regional and Spanish specialities and a seasonal menu. Eight suites (each decorated according to an international theme from Arabic to Japanese, Colonial to Manhattan, five comfortable doubles and a delightful garden area. €€€

★ **Hotel Rural las 4 Calles** C/Mayor 57, San Martín del Pimpollar, http://gredosguides.es. A very friendly local hotel in a picturesque village, with five en-suite rooms and a cosy little seating area. The owner, Juanfran, can organize a range of outdoor activities for visitors, from birdwatching to hikes and mountain biking. Price includes breakfast, and there are special deals if you stay for two nights or more. €

Parador de Gredos Navarredonda, km10 on the AV941, http://paradores.com. Spain's first-ever parador, which has undergone a major refurbishment programme and enjoys some great views across the mountains from the terraces. The rustic rooms are large and comfortable while the restaurant serves up some high-quality local produce. €€

Youth hostel Navarredonda, http://reaj.com. Well-situated youth hostel not far from the parador on the outskirts of the village, with a large summer pool, good communal areas and some great views of the mountains. Two- and four-bed rooms. YH card needed. €

Segovia

After Toledo, **SEGOVIA** is the standout trip from Madrid. A relatively small city, strategically sited on a rocky ridge, it is deeply and haughtily Castilian, with a panoply of squares and mansions from its days of Golden Age grandeur, when it was a royal resort and a base for the Cortes (parliament). It was in Segovia that Isabel la Católica was proclaimed queen of Castile in 1474.

For a city of its size, there is an extraordinary array of architectural monuments. Most celebrated are the breathtaking **Roman aqueduct**, the Gothic **Catedral** and the fairy-tale **Alcázar**, but the less obvious attractions – the cluster of ancient churches and the many mansions found in the lanes of the old town, all in a warm, honey-coloured stone – are what really make it worth a visit. If you have time, take a walk out of the city alongside the river and out to the fascinating church of **Vera Cruz**.

The aqueduct

The most photographed sight in Segovia is the magnificent **aqueduct**. Over 800m of granite, supported by 166 arches and 120 pillars and at its highest point towering some

30m above the Pza. de Azoguejo, it stands up without a drop of mortar or cement. No one knows exactly when it was built, but it was probably around the end of the first century AD under either the emperor Domitian or Trajan. It no longer carries water from the Río Acebeda to the city, and in recent years traffic vibration and pollution have been threatening to undermine the entire structure, but the completion of a meticulous restoration programme should ensure that it remains standing for some time to come. If you climb the stairs beside the aqueduct you can get a view looking down over it from a surviving fragment of the city walls.

2

Museo Zuloaga

Pza. de Colmenares s/n • Charge • http://museoscastillayleon.jcyl.es

Some 200m up the hill to the right of the aqueduct and nestled against the walls is the **Museo Zuloaga**, a museum dedicated to the ceramicist Daniel Zuloaga and housed in the Romanesque Iglesia San Juan de los Caballeros, where the noble families of the city used to meet. Its limited opening hours mean that Wednesdays are the only time you can see the striking display of the artist's work, including some marvellous painted tiles and a scene of the Apostles with Christ that was designed to surround the family fireplace and which were modelled on those at the Monasterio de Santo Domingo de Silos in Burgos.

Casa de los Picos and the Alhóndiga

Passing under the aqueduct and up the hill along C/Cervantes and C/Juan Bravo, you will be directed towards the old city past the curious fifteenth-century **Casa de los Picos** (House of Spikes), with its waffle-like facade made up of pyramid-shaped stones to your right, and the former corn exchange, the **Alhóndiga**, down a few steps on your left.

Plaza de San Martín

A short distance northwest of Casa de los Picos is the **Plaza de San Martín**, one of the city's grandest squares, whose ensemble of buildings includes the fourteenth-century **Torreón de Lozoya** and the twelfth-century **church of San Martín**, which demonstrates all the local stylistic peculiarities. It has the characteristic covered portico, a fine arched tower and a typically Romanesque aspect; like most of Segovia's churches, it can be visited only when it's open for business, during early morning or evening services. In the middle of the plaza is a **statue of Juan Bravo**, a local folk hero who led the *comuneros* rebellion against Carlos V in protest against tax increases, the undermining of local power and the influence of foreign advisers.

La Trinidad and Plaza San Esteban

Charge, free Sat & Sun

North of Pza. de San Martín, the church of **La Trinidad** preserves the purest Romanesque style in Segovia: each span of its double-arched apse has intricately carved capitals, every one of them unique. Nearby – and making a good loop to or from the Alcázar – is the **Plaza San Esteban**, worth seeing for its superb, five-storeyed, twelfth-century church tower.

The Catedral

Pza. Mayor • Charge • http://catedralsegovia.es

C/Juan Bravo eventually leads on to the bar-filled **Pza. Mayor**. Dominating one corner of the plaza are the exuberant lines of the **Catedral**. Construction began in 1525, on

2

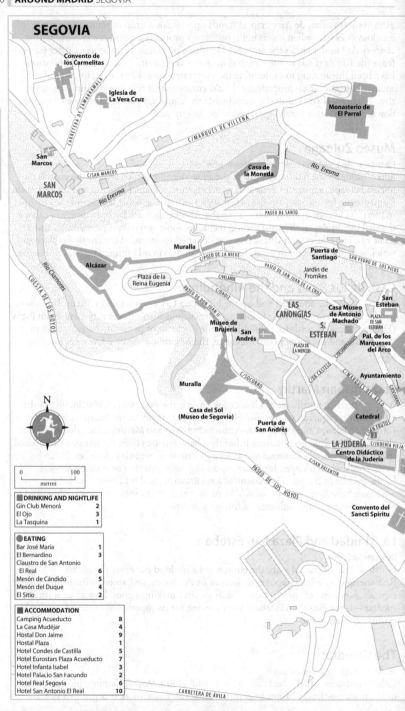

SEGOVIA

Convento de
los Carmelitas

Iglesia de
La Vera Cruz

CARRETERA DE ZAMARRAMALA

C/MARQUES DE VILLENA

Monasterio de
El Parral

San
Marcos

C/SAN MARCOS

Casa de
la Moneda

Río Eresma

SAN
MARCOS

Río Eresma

PASEO DE SANTO

Río Clamores

Muralla

C/POZO DE LA NIEVE

Puerta de
Santiago

SAN PEDRO DE LOS PICOS

Alcázar

Plaza de la
Reina Eugenia

PASEO DE SAN JUAN DE LA CRUZ

Jardín de
Fromkes

CUESTA DE LOS HOYOS

C/VELARDE

C/DAOIZ

PASEO DE DON JUAN II

Museo de
Brujería

San
Andrés

LAS
CANONGIAS

Casa Museo
de Antonio
Machado

S.
ESTEBAN

San
Esteban

PLAZA
DE SAN
ESTEBAN

C/DESAMPARADOS

Pal. de los
Marqueses
del Arco

PLAZA DE
LA MERCED

C/SOCORRO

C/DR CASTELÓ

C/MARQUES DEL ARCO

Ayuntamiento

C/ESCUDERO

Muralla

Casa del Sol
(Museo de Segovia)

Puerta de
San Andrés

Catedral

C/SAN FRUTOS

LA JUDERÍA

C/JUDERÍA VIEJA

Centro Didáctico
de la Judería

C/SAN VALENTIN

PASEO DE LOS HOYOS

Convento del
Sancti Spiritu

N

0   100
metres

CARRETERA DE ÁVILA

DRINKING AND NIGHTLIFE

Gin Club Menorá	2
El Ojo	3
La Tasquina	1

EATING

Bar José María	1
El Bernardino	3
Claustro de San Antonio El Real	6
Mesón de Cándido	5
Mesón del Duque	4
El Sitio	2

ACCOMMODATION

Camping Acueducto	8
La Casa Mudéjar	4
Hostal Don Jaime	9
Hostal Plaza	1
Hotel Condes de Castilla	5
Hotel Eurostars Plaza Acueducto	7
Hotel Infanta Isabel	3
Hotel Palacio San Facundo	2
Hotel Real Segovia	6
Hotel San Antonio El Real	10

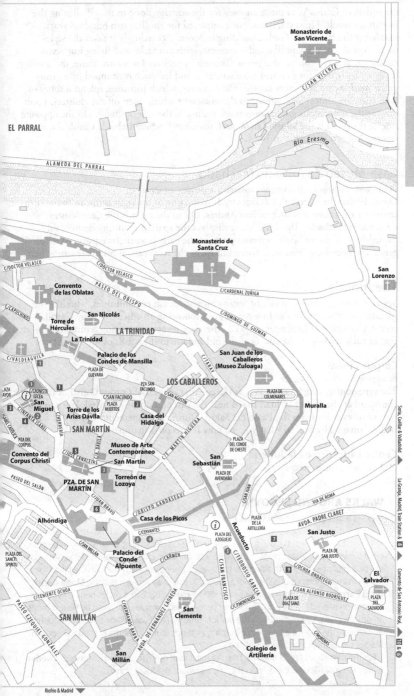

2

the orders of Carlos V, to make amends for the damage done to the city during the *comuneros* revolt. However, it was not completed for another two hundred years, making it the last major Gothic building in Spain. Accordingly it takes the style to its logical – or perhaps illogical – extreme, with pinnacles and flying buttresses tacked on at every conceivable point. Though impressive for its size alone, the interior is surprisingly bare for so florid a construction and its space is cramped by a great green marble *coro* at its very centre. The treasures, which include a splendid series of tapestries, are almost all confined to the **museums** which open off the cloisters. Look out for the marvellous golden *artesonado* ceiling in the *sala capitular*. On the opposite side of the plaza is the **Iglesia San Miguel**, the church where Isabel la Católica was crowned queen of Castile in 1474.

Casa-Museo de Antonio Machado

C/Desamparados 5 • Charge, free Wed • http://turismodesegovia.com/es/antonio-machado

Down beside the Catedral, C/Daoiz leads past a line of souvenir shops to the twelfth-century Romanesque church of San Andrés. Off to the right is the **Casa-Museo de Antonio Machado**. This little house displays the spartan accommodation and furnishings of one of Spain's greatest poets of the early twentieth century; Machado is generally more associated with Soria, but spent the last years of his life teaching here.

The Judería

Segovia was once home to one of Spain's biggest Jewish communities, who like the Muslims were forced to live in separate areas following an edict issued by Castilian regent Catherine of Lancaster in 1412. There are several interesting remnants from that period tucked away in the streets of the old **Judería** to the south of the Pza. Mayor.

Corpus Christi

Plaza del Corpus 7 • Charge • 921 463 429

The **synagogue**, which now serves as the convent church of **Corpus Christi**, is in a little courtyard at the end of C/Juan Bravo near the east end of the Catedral. You can see part of its exterior from the Paseo del Salón. During the nineteenth century it was badly damaged by fire, so what you see now is a reconstruction.

Centro Didáctico de la Judería

C/La Judería Vieja 12 • Charge, free Wed

WALKS AROUND SEGOVIA

Segovia is an excellent city for **walks**. Drop down onto the path that winds its way down into the valley from the Alcázar on the north side of the city wall and you'll reach the Río Eresma. Head west and you'll pass close to Vera Cruz and the Convento de los Carmelitas, with some great views of the Alcázar, before turning back towards the city; head east and you can follow the beautiful tree-lined path alongside the river and wend your way back up the hill to the old town in a round trip of a little over an hour. On your way you can visit the **Monasterio de El Parral** (entry by donation); or better still, follow the track that circles behind Vera Cruz to the monastery. El Parral is a sizeable and partly ruined complex occupied by Hieronymites, an order found only in Spain. Ring the bell for admission and you will be shown the cloister and church; the latter is a late Gothic building with rich sculpture at the east end. Gregorian Masses can be heard on Sundays at noon.

For the best view of all of Segovia, take the main road north for 2km or so towards **Cuéllar**. A panorama of the whole city, including the aqueduct, gradually unfolds.

Close by Corpus Christi is the **Centro Didáctico de la Judería**, which houses a limited exhibition about Jewish culture and is located in the former house of Abraham Senneor, a rabbi who lived in Segovia in the fifteenth century.

Puerta de San Andrés and the Museo de Segovia

C/Martínez Campos • Charge, free Sat & Sun • http://turismodesegovia.com/es/muralla

Just west of the Catedral is the **Puerta de San Andrés**, one of the old gates into the Judería which houses an information centre about the city walls and from which you can walk along the parapet. Back towards the Alcázar, and housed in the old Jewish slaughterhouse (Casa del Sol), is the **city museum**, which contains an absorbing and comprehensive range of exhibits detailing the history of Segovia from prehistoric times to the present day. There is an informative explanatory video on the construction of the aqueduct and some fascinating Visigoth and medieval exhibits. Across the other side of the valley you can see the old **Jewish cemetery**.

The Alcázar

Plaza Reina Victoria Eugenia • Charge • http://alcazardesegovia.com

Beyond the Pza. Mayor and the Judería, perched on the northwestern tip of the city walls, is the **Alcázar**. An extraordinary fantasy of a castle, with its narrow towers and flurry of turrets, it will seem eerily familiar to just about every visitor, having apparently served as the model for the Disneyland castle in Orlando. It is itself a bit of a sham; although it dates from the fourteenth and fifteenth centuries, it was almost completely destroyed by a fire in 1862 and rebuilt as a deliberately hyperbolic version of the original. Nevertheless the rooms contain some fascinating furnishings and artefacts and it is worth the entry fee alone for the beautiful *artesonado* ceilings and the magnificent panoramas from the tower.

Vera Cruz and the Convento de las Carmelitas

Tr. Zamarramala • Charge, free Tues • 921 432 475

The most striking of Segovia's ancient churches is undoubtedly **Vera Cruz**, a remarkable twelve-sided building outside town in the valley facing the Alcázar, which can be reached by taking the path down to Paseo San Juan de La Cruz. It is traditionally thought to have been built by the Knights Templar in the early thirteenth century on the pattern of the church of the Holy Sepulchre in Jerusalem, and once housed part of the True Cross (hence its name; the sliver of wood itself was moved to the nearby village church of La Magdalena at Zamarramala). Inside, the nave is circular with ghostly vestiges of beautiful murals still visible on the walls, and its heart is occupied by a strange two-storeyed chamber – again twelve-sided – in which the knights, as part of their initiation, stood vigil over the cross. Climb the tower for a highly photogenic vista of the city.

While you're over here you could take in the prodigiously walled **Convento de las Carmelitas** (free/voluntary donation), which is also referred to as the monastery of San Juan de la Cruz, and contains the gaudy mausoleum of its founder saint.

Casa de la Moneda

C/Moneda • Charge, free Wed • http://casamoneda.es

Located in a picturesque setting down by the River Eresma, a little further east of Vera Cruz, is the **Casa de la Moneda**, the former royal mint established by Felipe II in the late sixteenth century and designed by El Escorial architect Juan de Herrera. Inside is a museum tracing the history and the methods used in the production of royal coinage and an interpretation centre about the aqueduct. There is a refreshing riverside café too.

Convento de San Antonio Real

C/San Antonio el Real • Charge

If you follow the line of the aqueduct away from the old city you will come to the **Convento de San Antonio Real**, a little gem of a palace, and now also serving as a luxury hotel (see page 154). Originally founded by Enrique IV in 1455, it contains an intriguing collection of Mudéjar and Hispano-Flemish art, some outstanding *artesonado* ceilings and a wonderful fifteenth-century wooden calvary.

ARRIVAL AND DEPARTURE   SEGOVIA

By train The high-speed train from Chamartín station in Madrid (15–20 daily) takes just 27min, though the train station is quite a way out of town (take the #11 bus, which goes to the aqueduct every 15min). If you take a regional train it will take you a lot longer (3 daily; 2hr 5min), but it goes to the old station nearer to the centre (then take bus #8) and costs around €13.

Destinations Cercedilla (4–5 daily; 35–40mins); Madrid (20 daily; 28min–2hr).

By bus There are regular buses from Madrid (operated by La Sepulvedana, Intercambiador de Moncloa; ⓂMoncloa; every 30min; 1hr 15min; €7.89 single) that drop you at the bus station to the west of the aqueduct.

Destinations Ávila (2–4 daily; 1hr); La Granja (20 daily; 25min); Madrid (every 30min; 1hr 15min); Salamanca (2 daily; 2hr 45min); Valladolid (hourly; 1hr 50min–2hr 30min).

INFORMATION

Turismo Offices at: Pza. Mayor 10 (Mon–Sat 9.30am–2pm & 5–7/8pm, Sun 9.30am–5pm, 921 460 334, http://turismocastillayleon.com); the high-speed train station C/Campos de Castilla 1 (Mon–Fri 8.15am–3.15pm, Sat & Sun 10.30am–1.30pm & 4–6.30pm); and the bus station on Paseo Ezequiel González.

Local council visitors' reception office Pza. de Azoguejo, by the aqueduct (http://turismodesegovia.com). You can sign up for a variety of guided tours (charge). For a modest fee you can purchase a Segovia Tourist Card which will give you a range of discounts on entry fees and at restaurants and hotels.

ACCOMMODATION   SEE MAP PAGE 150

Most of the **accommodation** is to be found in the streets around the Pza. Mayor and Pza. de Azoguejo, but rooms can be hard to come by even out of season, so it's worth booking ahead. Be warned that in winter, at over 1000m, the nights can be very cold and sometimes snowy.

★ **La Casa Mudéjar** C/Isabel Católica 8, http://lacasamudejar.com. Characterful hotel located in a restored mansion sandwiched between the Pza. Mayor and the Judería. Well-appointed rooms with historic touches such as beautiful carved *artesonado* ceilings, a patio restaurant that serves some traditional *sefardí* dishes with fruit sauces and a small spa area (extra charge). €€

Hostal Don Jaime C/Ochoa Ondátegui 8, http://hostaldonjaime.com. A decent budget option, this old-style but comfortable sixteen-room *hostal* is close to the aqueduct. All doubles have their own bathroom. €

Hostal Plaza C/Cronista Lecea 11, http://hotelesmhsegovia.es. A smart *hostal*, centrally located just off the Pza. Mayor, with twenty small a/c doubles and four triples, all with simple but stylish decor. It also has its own bar/café and a garage. €

★ **Hotel Condes de Castilla** C/José Canalejas 5, http://hotelcondesdecastilla.com. Refurbished, reformed and rebranded, this hotel, housed in a beautiful old building overlooking the church of San Martín, now has thirteen imaginatively decorated rooms, each named after a Castilian noble. €€

Hotel Eurostars Plaza Acueducto Avda. Padre Claret 2–4, http://eurostarsplazaacueducto.com. Probably the best view of the aqueduct in the whole city is from the terrace bar in this well-appointed, modern four-star hotel. Many of the rooms also have great views over this masterpiece of Roman engineering. Child rooms and triples also available. €€€

Hotel Infanta Isabel Pza. Mayor 12, http://hotelinfantaisabel.com. A very comfortable hotel with 37 rooms (including four triples and eight superior-class doubles with views over the plaza) done out with nineteenth-century-style furnishings and ideally positioned right on the Pza. Mayor. €€

★ **Hotel Palacio San Facundo** Pza. San Facundo 4, http://palaciosanfacundo.com. An old Segovian mansion not far from the Pza. Mayor converted into a swish business-style hotel with slickly decorated rooms and a stylish, covered patio bar. Look out for offers on the website. €€

Hotel Real Segovia C/Juan Bravo 30, http://hotelrealsegovia.com. Another refurbished and rebranded hotel in the historic core, though it still retains some of the 1950s-style decor of its heyday. Rooms come complete with tea and coffee-making facilities, wooden floors and modern bathrooms. €€

★ **Hotel San Antonio El Real** San Antonio El Real s/n,

http://sanantonioelreal.es. Luxury hotel located inside a splendid old convent just up from the aqueduct. The 51 rooms are large, sumptuously decorated and with all the facilities you could want, while the garden cloister is the perfect place for a relaxing drink. €€

EATING

SEE MAP PAGE 150

Segovia takes its cooking seriously, with restaurants of Madrid quality – and prices to match. Culinary specialities include *cochinillo asado* (roast suckling pig) and *judiones*, large white beans from La Granja.

Bar José María C/Cronista Lecea 11, just off Pza. Mayor, http://restaurantejosemaria.com. Bar-annexe to one of Segovia's best restaurants, serving delicious and modestly priced tapas. If you want to splash out, try the main restaurant which serves up classic Segovian fare with a taster menu including *cochinillo* and wine. €€€

★ **El Bernardino** C/Cervantes 2, http://elbernardino.com. A friendly place serving the Castilian classics of *cochinillo* and *cordero*, but better value than some of the city's more famous restaurants. The *menú segoviano* with *cochinillo* is good value, as is the kids' menu. €€

Claustro de San Antonio El Real San Antonio El Real s/n, http://sanantonioelreal.es. Located in the interior of this luxury hotel in a converted monastery, this restaurant serves up an excellent and surprisingly reasonable set

CAMPING

Camping Acueducto Avda. Don Juan de Borbón 49, http://campingacueducto.com. The nearest campsite, 3km out on the road to La Granja; take a #6 "Nueva Segovia" bus from the Pza. Mayor. A quiet site with a swimming pool with great views of the sierra and plenty of shade. Closed mid-Oct to Easter. €

menu for lunch and dinner, with options such as mushroom risotto, *cochinillo* and tuna, and mandarin tiramisu for dessert. €€€

Mesón de Cándido Pza. Azoguejo 5, http://mesondecandido.es. This is the city's most celebrated restaurant: the place for *cochinillo* and other roasts cooked to perfection. €€€

Mesón del Duque C/Cervantes 12, http://restauranteduque.es. Rival to the nearby *Cándido*, and also specializing in Castilian roasts, though it claims to be the oldest restaurant in the city. Offers a range of different menus including the obligatory *cochinillo* and *cordero*. €€€

El Sitio C/Infanta Isabel 9, http://elsitiorestaurante.com. Popular bar with an upstairs restaurant close to the Pza. Mayor. A good range of tapas is on offer in the bar, while upstairs there are more substantial dishes, ranging from the locally grown *judiones de la Granja* (broad beans) to cuttlefish in garlic mayonnaise as well as the usual Castilian roasts and home-made desserts. €€

DRINKING AND NIGHTLIFE

SEE MAP PAGE 150

Pza. Mayor, with its cathedral backdrop, makes a great place for a drink and a snack, but the biggest clusters of **bars** can be found in the narrow streets that lead off the plaza and back down by the aqueduct along Avda. Fernández Ladreda.

Gin Club Menorá C/San Frutos 21, 921 460 468. A good range of beers, cocktails and gin and tonics are available in this relaxing two-floored bar close to the Catedral. Friendly service and atmosphere.

El Ojo Pza San Martín 6, http://restaurantenarizotas.es. Small *bar de copas* perched on the edge of this charming little plaza and serving well-poured draught beer accompanied by a soundtrack of jazz, rock and pop.

La Tasquina C/Valdeláguila 3, 921 463 914. Popular wine bar close to the Pza. Mayor serving some tasty tapas to accompany a wide selection of wines and cavas.

Around Segovia

Segovia has a major outlying attraction in the elegant Bourbon summer palace and gardens of **La Granja**, 10km southeast of the town on the CL601 Madrid road, and connected by regular bus services. True Bourbon aficionados, with time and transport, might also want to visit a second palace and hunting museum 12km west of La Granja at **Riofrío**.

La Granja

Pza. de España 17 • Charge • http://patrimonionacional.es

The **Palacio Real de la Granja de San Ildefonso** was built by the reluctant first Bourbon king of Spain, Felipe V, no doubt homesick for the luxuries of Versailles. Its glories are the mountain setting and the extravagant wooded grounds and

2

gardens, but it's also worth casting an eye over the **palace**. Though destroyed in parts and damaged throughout by a fire in 1918, much has been well restored and is home to a superlative collection of sixteenth-century tapestries, one of the most valuable in the world. Everything is furnished in plush French imperial style, but it's almost all of Spanish origin; the majority of the huge chandeliers, for example, were made in the **glass factory** in the village of San Ildefonso (charge; free Wed from April to Sept 3–6pm; http://fcnv.es). Here you can visit an exhibition on the history of the craft and still see the glass being blown and decorated in the traditional manner.

The highlight of the **gardens** is its series of **fountains**, which culminates in the fifteen-metre-high jet of La Fama. They're fantastic and really not to be missed, which means timing your visit for 5.30pm on Wednesdays and Saturdays or 1pm on Sundays when some are switched on (they may not be switched on during periods of water shortage, so it's best to check on 921 470 019 or on the website beforehand). Only on three saints' days in the year – normally May 30 (San Fernando), July 25 (Santiago) and August 25 (San Luís) – are all of the fountains set to work, with accompanying crowds to watch. The enormous monumental fountain known as the Baños de Diana usually operates on Saturday nights in summer and is illuminated together with the palace facade.

NORTH FROM SEGOVIA: A CASTLE TOUR

Of some five hundred **castles** that remain in reasonable state of repair in Spain, Segovia province has an especially rich selection. Drivers en route to Valladolid and the Río Duero (see page 375) can construct an enjoyable route to see the best of them; there are buses (from Segovia or Valladolid), but you may end up spending the night in places that really only warrant a quick stop.

Fifty kilometres northwest of Segovia, the fortress (charge; http://castillodecoca.com) at the small town of **Coca** is the prettiest imaginable, less a piece of military architecture than a country house masquerading as one. Built in about 1453, as the base of the powerful Fonseca family, it's constructed from pinkish bricks, encircled by a deep moat and fantastically decorated with octagonal turrets and elaborate castellation – an extraordinary design strongly influenced by Moorish architecture. There are five **buses** a day here from Segovia, though Coca itself is fairly unremarkable; drivers should push on to **Medina del Campo** in Castilla y León for lunch (see page 372), itself the site of another fabulous castle.

The castle at **Turégano** (charge), 28km north of Segovia, is essentially a fifteenth-century structure enclosing an early thirteenth-century church. However, it's east of here, off the main Segovia–Soria road (N110), that the most rewarding diversions are to be made. Eight kilometres east of Turégano, **Pedraza** in particular is almost perfectly preserved from the sixteenth century. The village is protected on three sides by a steep valley; the only entrance is the single original gateway (which used to be the town prison), from where the narrow lanes spiral up towards a large Pza. Mayor, still used for a bullfighting festival in the first week in September. The **Castillo de Pedraza** (charge; http://elcastillodepedraza.es) is where the 8-year-old dauphin of France and his younger brother were believed to be imprisoned in 1526, given up by their father François I who swapped his freedom for theirs after he was captured at the battle of Pavia. Within is a museum dedicated to the Basque artist Ignacio Zuloaga. **Sepúlveda**, a little further north (and off the highway between Madrid and Burgos), is less of a harmonious whole, but has an even more dramatic setting, strung out high on a narrow spit of land between the Castilla and Duratón river valleys. Its physical and architectural high point is the distinctive Romanesque church of **El Salvador**, perched high above its ruined castle. Ask at the tourist office (Pza. del Trigo 6 Sepúlveda; http://turismosepulveda. es) for details of routes down into the spectacular gorge that is home to one of the country's biggest colonies of griffon vultures.

Riofrío

Bosque de Riofrío • Charge • http://patrimonionacional.es

The palace at **Riofrío** was built by Isabel, the widow of Felipe V, in the fear that she would be banished from La Granja by her stepson Fernando VI. He died, however, leaving the throne for Isabel's own son, Carlos III, and Riofrío was not occupied until the nineteenth century, when Alfonso XII moved in to mourn the death of his young queen Mercedes. He, too, died pretty soon after, which is perhaps why the palace has a spartan and slightly tatty feel.

The complex, painted in dusty pink with green shutters, is surrounded not by manicured gardens but by a **deer park**, into which you can drive but not wander. Inside the palace, you have to join a guided tour, which winds through an endless sequence of rooms, none stunningly furnished. About half the tour is devoted to a **museum of hunting**; the most interesting items here are reconstructions of cave paintings, including the famous Altamira drawings.

ARRIVAL AND INFORMATION

By bus Buses depart to La Granja from the bus station in Segovia (20 daily, 10 daily at weekends; 25min).

By train There are three to six local trains a day from Segovia to Navas de Riofrío (10min). From there it is a 1km walk to Riofrío. Regional line trains from Chamartín station

AROUND SEGOVIA

in Madrid to Segovia also stop at Navas de Riofrío (2–5 daily; 1hr 45min–2hr).

Turismo La Granja Pza. de los Dolores 1 (Mon, Tues & Sun 10am–2pm, Wed–Sat 10am–2pm & 3.30–7.30pm; http://turismorealsitiodesanildefonso.com).

ACCOMMODATION

Hotel Roma C/Guardas 2, San Ildefonso de la Granja, http://hotelrestauranteroma.es. Friendly two-star hotel right outside the palace gates with sixteen slightly dated but comfortable rooms and a restaurant serving local specialities. €€

Parador de la Granja Casa de los Infantes, C/Fuentes 3,

San Ildefonso de la Granja, http://paradores.com. A plush parador with a rooftop pool and spa area housed in the eighteenth-century Casa de los Infantes built by Carlos III for two of his sons. Large, modern rooms and an excellent restaurant specializing in local dishes such as *judiones*, lamb and suckling pig. €€€

EATING AND DRINKING

Casa Zaca C/Embajadores 6, http://casazaca.com. Great place in La Granja to stop off for lunch, this former posthouse has been serving up quality home-style local cuisine, including the local speciality broad beans, since 1940 and remains a family business. Good value, too. €€

La Taberna del Pelón C/Carral 4, http://lataberna delpelon.com. Located close to the Palacio Real, this little

restaurant is a delight, with a great line in traditional dishes of the Castilian variety and beyond. The classics are all here – *croquetas*, meatballs, grilled octopus and the like – but to get the most out of your visit, try something different, like the bull's tail rosti or lamb sweetbreads with caramelized onion. €€€

Alcalá de Henares

ALCALÁ DE HENARES, a little over 30km east from Madrid, is one of Europe's most ancient university towns, and renowned as the birthplace of **Miguel de Cervantes**. In the sixteenth century the university was a rival to Salamanca's, but in 1836 the faculties moved to Madrid and the town went into decline. Almost all the artistic heritage was lost in the Civil War and nowadays it's virtually a suburb of Madrid. It is not somewhere you'd want to stay longer than it takes to see the sights.

Universidad Antigua

Pza. San Diego • Charge • http://visitasalcala.es

The **Universidad Antigua** stands at the heart of the old town. It was endowed by Cardinal Cisneros (also known as Cardinal Jiménez) at the beginning of the sixteenth century, and features a fabulous Plateresque facade; a Great Hall, the **Paraninfo**, with a gloriously decorated Mudéjar *artesonado* ceiling; and a series of beautiful patio areas. Next door, the **Capilla de San Ildefonso** has another superb ceiling, intricately stuccoed walls and the Italian marble tomb of Cardinal Cisneros, although his actual remains are buried in the Catedral in Pza. de los Santos Niños.

Museo Casa Natal de Cervantes

C/Mayor 48 • Free • http://museocasanataldecervantes.org

The **Museo Casa Natal de Cervantes** on the porticoed C/Mayor claims to have been the birthplace of Cervantes in 1547, though the house itself was actually constructed in 1956. It's authentic in style, furnished with genuine sixteenth-century objects, and contains a small museum with a few early editions of *Don Quixote* and other curiosities related to the author.

Corral de Comedias

Pza. de Cervantes 15 • Charge • http://corraldealcala.com

Just off the central Pza. Cervantes is the oldest surviving public theatre in Europe, the **Corral de Comedias**, which has been brought to life once more after a twenty-year restoration programme. Originally dating from 1601, the theatre was discovered beneath a crumbling old cinema by three drama students in 1980. Like Shakespeare's Globe, it was a hub of rowdy heckling and lively dramatics throughout the first half of the seventeenth century.

The Catedral

Pza. de los Santos Niños • Charge • http://visitacatedraldealcala.com

Elevated to the status of **Catedral** in 1991 when Alcalá separated from the diocese of Madrid, the Gothic church of San Justo and San Pastor was restored in the late twentieth century after being badly damaged in the Civil War. The remains of Cardinal Cisneros, regent of Spain on two separate occasions during the era of the Catholic Kings, lie within. The best views of the historic core of the city are from the tower.

Complutum

Camino del Juncal • Charge • http://complutum.com

The ruins of the forum of the Roman town of **Complutum**, on the outskirts of Alcalá, were rescued and re-excavated after being partially destroyed by construction work in the 1960s. The original complex dates from the first century AD, although it was replaced by another two centuries later. You can make out the remains of buildings, roads and other Roman urban infrastructure, including the market and the baths on the site.

Museo Arqueológico and the Casa de Hippolytus

Museo Arqueológico Free • Casa de Hippolytus Charge • www.turismoalcala.es/turismo/museo-arqueologico-regional

Situated next to the Monasterio de San Bernardo, the regional **Museo Arqueológico** houses an array of Roman finds. On the outskirts of town on Avenida de Madrid are the foundations of a Roman villa, the **Casa de Hippolytus**, which was originally a school for the children of wealthy Romans, complete with a temple, baths, and a garden containing exotic animals. The centrepiece is a magnificent mosaic signed by Hippolytus, depicting fishermen at sea and a vast array of aquatic life.

ARRIVAL AND INFORMATION

ALCALÁ DE HENARES

By train From Madrid's Chamartín or Atocha stations; daily every 15–30min from 5.30am–11.45pm from Madrid. For a more atmospheric trip you could catch the *Tren de Cervantes* (www.renfe.com/es/es/experiencias/trenes-tematicos/tren-de-cervantes; check website for timetables), complete with staff in period costume, and including a guided tour of the main sights.

By bus Daily every 15min, from the *intercambiador* at Avda. de América in Madrid.

Turismo Just off the central Pza. de Cervantes (daily: June to mid-Oct 10am–2pm & 5–8pm; mid-Oct to May 10am–2pm & 4–7pm; 918 892 694, http://turismoalcala.es); also at Pza. de los Santos Niños (same hours; 918 810 634). Organizes a range of guided tours (usually leaving at noon & 5pm; charge).

EATING AND DRINKING

Casino Pl. de Cervantes 9, www.casinoalcala.es. Not far from the railway station, this stylishly appointed spot – bare brick walls, marble bar – with a menu of beautifully presented, if slightly pricey, dishes. Highlights include grilled octopus and black rice. The set lunch menu is decent value, but still a little more expensive than many other places in town. €€€

★ **Hostería del Estudiante** C/Los Colegios 3, http://paradores.com. Run by the Parador chain and situated in part of the old university, this is probably the best restaurant in town, serving up local cuisine such as *migas* (breadcrumbs, garlic, chorizo and pepper) and roast meats. €€€

El Quinto Tapón C/Teniente Ruiz 3, 918 775 749. One of the most popular stops on Alcalá's tapas trail, and it is easy to see why: hip decor, generous helpings, decent beer and wine, friendly service and a good range of tapas on offer. €€

2

Castilla-La Mancha and Ex- tremadura

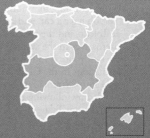

STATUE OF FRANCISCO PIZARRO

Castilla-La Mancha and Extremadura

The vast area covered by this chapter includes some of the most travelled, yet least visited, parts of Spain. Once south of Toledo, most tourists thunder nonstop across the plains of Castilla-La Mancha to Valencia and Andalucía, or follow the great rivers through Extremadura into Portugal. At first sight this is understandable. Castilla-La Mancha, in particular, is Spain at its least welcoming: a huge, bare plain – the name La Mancha comes from the Arab *manxa*, meaning steppe – burning hot in summer, chillingly exposed in winter. But this impression is not an entirely fair one – away from the main highways the villages are as friendly as any in the country, and in the northeast, where the mountains start, is the extraordinary cliff-hanging city of Cuenca and the historic cathedral town of Sigüenza. Castilla-La Mancha is also the agricultural and wine-growing heartland of Spain and the country through which Don Quixote cut his despairing swathe.

It is in **Extremadura**, though, that there is most to be missed by just passing through. This harsh environment was the cradle of the *conquistadores*, men who opened up a new world for the Spanish Empire. Remote before and forgotten since, Extremadura enjoyed a brief golden age when its heroes returned with their gold to live in splendour. **Trujillo**, the birthplace of Pizarro, and **Cáceres** were built with *conquistador* wealth, the streets crowded with an array of perfectly preserved and very ornate mansions of returning empire builders. Then there is **Mérida**, the most completely preserved Roman city in Spain, and the monasteries of **Guadalupe** and **Yuste**, the one fabulously wealthy, the other rich in imperial memories. Finally, for some wild scenery and superb fauna, northern Extremadura has the **Parque Natural de Monfragüe**, where even the most casual birdwatcher can look up to see eagles and vultures circling the cliffs.

Castilla-La Mancha

The region that was for so long called **New Castile** – and that until the 1980s held Madrid in its domain – is now officially known as **Castilla-La Mancha**. The main points of interest are widely spaced on an arc drawn from Madrid, with little between. If you are travelling east on **trains and buses** towards Aragón, the only worthwhile stops are Sigüenza (en route to Zaragoza) or Cuenca (en route to Teruel). To the south, Toledo has bus links within its own province, but if heading for Andalucía or Extremadura you'd do better returning to Madrid and starting out again; the Toledo rail line stops at the town.

If you have a **car**, and are **heading south**, the Toledo–Ciudad Real road, the Montes de Toledo and the wetland Parque Nacional de las Tablas de Daimiel all provide good alternatives to the sweltering A4 *autopista*. **Heading east**, through Cuenca to Teruel, the best route is to follow the Río Júcar out of the province, by way of the weird rock formations in the Ciudad Encantada and the source of the Río Tajo. The A5 **heading west** into Extremadura is one of the dullest and hottest roads in Spain and can be avoided by following the M501/CL501 through the Sierra de Gredos or by cutting onto it from Talavera de la Reina; this would bring you to the Monastery of Yuste by way of the lush valley of La Vera.

The following sections cover the main sights and routes of Castilla-La Mancha in a clockwise direction, from northeast to southwest of Madrid.

CHERRY BLOSSOMS, VALLE DEL JERTE

Highlights

❶ **Museo de Arte Abstracto, Cuenca** One of the famous hanging houses is the wonderful setting for this gem of a museum. See page 171

❷ **La Ciudad Encantada** Explore the weird and wonderful limestone formations near Cuenca. See page 172

❸ **Jamón** Treat yourself to a *ración* of the cured dried ham washed down with *pitarra* wine. See page 182

❹ **Cherry blossoms, Valle de Jerte** Take in the spectacular display in this picturesque valley when the trees burst into bloom for ten days in spring. See page 183

❺ **Vulture spotting, Parque Natural de Monfragüe** You don't have to be a dedicated ornithologist to be impressed by these prehistoric-looking creatures. See page 188

❻ **Trujillo** A visit to the birthplace of Pizarro is worthwhile for the view of the town from the Cáceres road alone. See page 189

❼ **Evening in Cáceres** Wander around the atmospheric historic core at night. See page 194

❽ **The Roman ruins in Mérida** Marvel at the stunning array of Roman buildings and artefacts. See page 199

HIGHLIGHTS ARE MARKED ON THE MAP ON PAGE 164

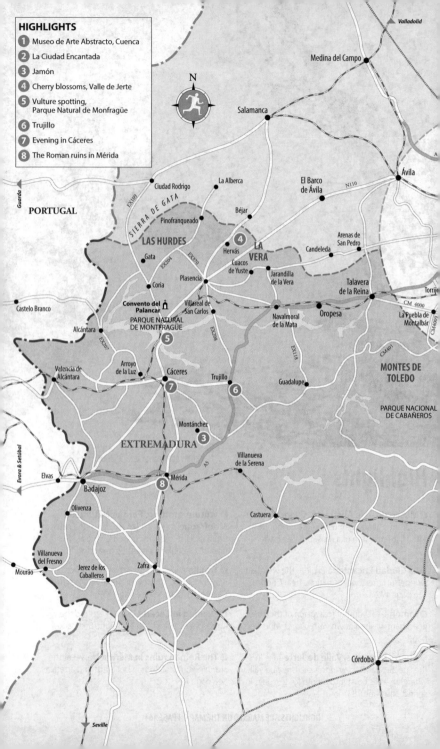

HIGHLIGHTS

1. Museo de Arte Abstracto, Cuenca
2. La Ciudad Encantada
3. Jamón
4. Cherry blossoms, Valle de Jerte
5. Vulture spotting, Parque Natural de Monfragüe
6. Trujillo
7. Evening in Cáceres
8. The Roman ruins in Mérida

N

Valladolid

Medina del Campo

Salamanca

Ávila

Guarda

PORTUGAL

Ciudad Rodrigo

La Alberca

El Barco de Ávila

N110

SIERRA DE GATA

EX109

Pinofranqueado

Béjar

LAS HURDES

Arenas de San Pedro

Gata

EX204

EX370

Hervás

LA VERA

Candeleda

Cuacos de Yuste

Coria

Plasencia

Jarandilla de la Vera

Talavera de la Reina

Torrije

Castelo Branco

Convento del Palancar

Villareal de San Carlos

Navalmoral de la Mata

Oropesa

CM 4000

La Puebla de Montalbá

CM4009

Alcántara

PARQUE NATURAL DE MONTFRAGÜE

EX208

CM401

MONTES DE TOLEDO

Valencia de Alcántara

EX207

Arroyo de la Luz

Cáceres

Trujillo

EX118

Guadalupe

PARQUE NACIONAL DE CABAÑEROS

Évora & Setúbal

Montánchez

EXTREMADURA

A5

Villanueva de la Serena

Elvas

Badajoz

Mérida

Castuera

Olivenza

Villanueva del Fresno

Jerez de los Caballeros

Zafra

Mourão

Córdoba

Seville

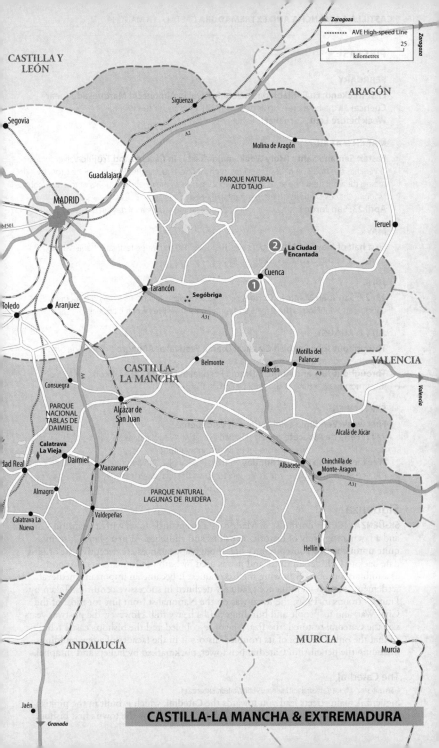

CASTILLA-LA MANCHA & EXTREMADURA

3

FIESTAS

FEBRUARY

First weekend: La Endiablada ancient festival in Almonacid Marquesado (near Cuenca) All the boys dress up as devils and parade through the streets.
Week before Lent: Carnaval Everywhere.

MARCH & APRIL

Easter: Semana Santa (Holy Week) major fiestas in Cáceres and Trujillo Valverde de la Vera has the tradition of Los Empalaos, men who re-enact Jesus's journey to the Cross by roping their outstretched arms to huge wooden bars as they walk the streets of town at night. Magnificent celebrations (floats, penitents) in Cuenca.
April 23: San Jorge Enthusiastic celebrations continue for several days in Cáceres.

MAY

First half of May: WOMAD At Cáceres. Renowned world music festival set against the wonderful backdrop of the historic core.

JUNE

23–27: San Juan Manic in Coria A bull is let loose for a few hours a day, with people dancing and drinking in the streets and running for their lives when it appears.

JULY & AUGUST

Throughout July: Spanish Classical Drama Festival at Almagro Golden Age drama takes the stage at this prestigious festival.
Throughout July and August: Drama Festival in Mérida Classical works performed in the atmospheric setting of the original Roman theatre.

SEPTEMBER

First week: Vendimia celebrations at Valdepeñas
7–17: Feria de Albacete Hugely popular festival with regular parades and bullfights, while a host of kiosks and attractions are set up in the showground.
Week leading up to third Sunday Festivals in Jarandilla and Madrigal de la Vera with bulls running in front of cows – which are served up on the final day's feast.

Sigüenza

SIGÜENZA, 120km northeast of Madrid, is a sleepy little town with a beautiful Catedral and a fascinating array of historic mansions and churches. At first glance it seems quite untouched by contemporary life, though appearances are deceptive. Its origins date back to Celtiberian times and it was used by both the Romans and Visigoths as a military outpost. Following the Reconquest it became an important medieval settlement, though its influence gradually declined in successive centuries. Taken by Franco's troops in 1936, the town was on the Nationalist front line for most of the Civil War, and its people and buildings paid a heavy toll. However, the postwar years saw the Catedral restored, the Pza. Mayor re-cobbled and the bishop's castle rebuilt, so that the only evidence of its troubled history is in the facades of a few buildings, including the pencil-thin Catedral bell tower, pockmarked by bullets and shrapnel.

The Catedral

C/Serrano Sanz • Charge (Cathedral and Museum) • http://catedralsiguenza.es

Sigüenza's main streets lead you towards the **Catedral**, which is built in the pinkish yellow stone that characterizes the town. Begun in 1150 by the town's first bishop,

Bernardo of Agen, it is essentially Gothic, with three rose windows, though it has been much altered over the years. Facing the main entrance is a huge marble *coro* with an altar to a thirteenth-century figure of the Virgin. To the right of the *coro* is the Catedral's principal treasure, the alabaster tomb of Martín Vázquez de Arce, known as El Doncel (the page boy); a favourite of Isabel la Católica, he was killed fighting the Moors in Granada. On the other side of the building is an extraordinary doorway: Plateresque at the bottom, Mudéjar in the middle and Gothic at the top – an amazing amalgam, built by a confused sixteenth-century architect. Take a look, too, at the sacristy, whose superb Renaissance ceiling has 304 heads carved by Covarrubias. In a chapel opening off this (with an unusual cupola, best seen in the mirror provided) is an El Greco *Annunciation*.

Museo Diocesano de Arte Sacro

Pza. Obispo Don Bernardo • Charge, free third Wed of the month

Housed in a refurbished sixteenth-century mansion close to the Catedral, the **Museo Diocesano de Arte Sacro** displays artworks from the Stone Age to the twentieth century, including Greek and Roman sculptures, textiles, manuscripts and a vast array of sacred

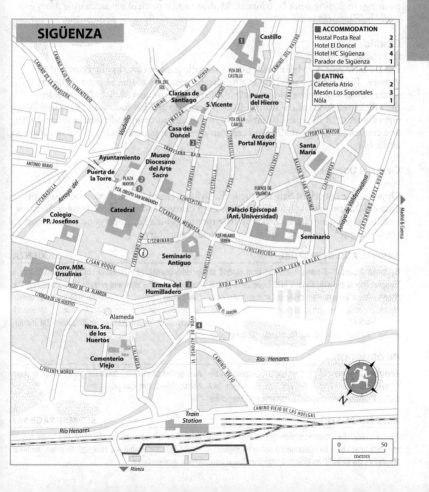

SIGÜENZA

ACCOMMODATION
Hostal Posta Real	2
Hotel El Doncel	3
Hotel HC Sigüenza	4
Parador de Sigüenza	1

EATING
Cafetería Atrio	2
Mesón Los Soportales	3
Nöla	1

3

CASTILLA-LA MANCHA CUISINE

La Mancha is renowned for its simple, down-to-earth **cuisine** based on local ingredients and traditional recipes made famous in Cervantes' classic *Don Quixote*. Dishes such as *gazpacho manchego* (a stew usually made from rabbit mixed with pieces of unleavened bread), *atascaburras* (puréed potato with salted cod and garlic) and *pisto manchego* (a selection of fried vegetables in a tomato sauce and often topped with a fried egg) are among the staples. The region is famed for its garlic and saffron, but perhaps the most celebrated of all foods from the region is **Manchego cheese** of which there is a bewildering array, though it can be divided into two main types: *semi-curado* (semi-cured) and *curado* (cured) – both must come from the local Manchegan breed of sheep, though the latter is stronger and more expensive. To accompany the cheese, there is nothing better than a glass of wine: the Valdepeñas vineyards, which have traditionally been known more for the quantity than the quality of their product, have improved significantly in recent years.

paintings including work by Morales, Madrazo and a particularly saccharine *Mary as a Child* by Zurbarán.

Castillo
Pza. del Castillo

From **Pza. Mayor**, C/Mayor leads up to the castle passing close by the **church of San Vicente**. The **Castillo** started life as a Roman fortress, was adapted by the Visigoths and further improved by the Moors as their Alcazaba. Reconquered in 1124, it became the official residence of the warlike Bishop Bernardo and his successors. The Civil War virtually reduced the castle to rubble, but it was almost completely rebuilt in the 1970s and converted into a parador. You can visit the central patio even if you are not staying at the hotel.

Casa del Doncel
Free

Opposite the church of San Vicente is the striking Gothic construction known as the **Casa del Doncel**, dating back to the thirteenth century and one of the most emblematic buildings in Sigüenza. The Mudéjar-style interior, which has undergone refurbishment, is worth a peek if you are here at the weekend (hours vary).

ARRIVAL AND DEPARTURE
SIGÜENZA

By train Around 4–7 trains a day run from Madrid to Sigüenza (1hr 30min–1hr 55min). RENFE operates a special "tren medieval" excursion which leaves Chamartín station in Madrid (most Sat late April to late June & mid-Sept to mid-Nov; departs Chamartín 10am, arrives Sigüenza 11.37am, returns 7.45pm arriving at Chamartín 9.24pm; price includes dramatized explanations of the region's history, a guided tour of the town and entry to the main sights). The train station is 5min from the centre of this compact town. Destinations Madrid (5–6 daily; 1hr 40min); Medinaceli (2 daily; 20min); Zaragoza (2 daily; 2hr 21min–2hr 36min).

INFORMATION

Turismo To the west of the Catedral at C/Serrano Sanz 9 (Mon–Thurs 10am–2pm & 6–7pm, Sun 10am-2pm, 949 347 007, http://turismocastillalamancha.es). The office runs guided tours of the town for groups of ten or more people (12-4.30pm; charge).

ACCOMMODATION
SEE MAP PAGE 167

The town makes for a relaxing stopover en route to Soria and the north or as a base for exploring the rest of the region. **Hostal Posta Real** C/San Vicente 1, http://postareal.com. Located in the centre of the old town, this *hostal* has 23 simple, but comfortable and quite stylish en-suite rooms as well as a cafeteria. €€

Hotel El Doncel Paseo de la Alameda 3, http://eldoncel.com. A stylishly refurbished seventeen-room hotel, with smart rooms mixing the traditional and the modern. The *Doncel* is also home to a very good restaurant serving some high-quality regional cuisine, including an extensive taster menu. €€

Hotel HC Sigüenza C/Alfonso VI 7, 949 391 974, http://hotelhcsiguenza.com. Next to the shady Alameda park with its summer terraza bars, this modern three-star hotel, with its individually decorated rooms, is a good mid-range option. €€

★ **Parador de Sigüenza** Pza. del Castillo s/n, http://parador.es. Located in the town's twelfth-century castle, this atmospheric parador enjoys a stunning hilltop location, with fine views from the rooms on the upper floors. High-quality local specialities and seasonal produce are served up in the imposing dining room. Midweek prices are considerably lower. €€

EATING SEE MAP PAGE 167

For **meals**, try the hotel restaurants at *El Doncel* and the *Parador de Sigüenza*, as well as the options below.

Cafetería Atrio Pza. Obispo Don Bernardo 6, http://atrio-siguenza.es. In the shadow of the Catedral, this relaxed bar serves excellent tapas, has a good home-made set lunch and has a great summer terraza. €€

Mesón Los Soportales Pza. Mayor 3, 949 347 349. A great location opposite the Catedral, this bar makes a good base for a drink and a spot of tapas. €

★ **Nöla** Plaza de San Vicente, http://nolarestaurante.com. This classy restaurant, which featured on the TV series *The Trip to Spain*, fits the bill with its creative seasonal menu, featuring mains such as free-range chicken with figs and Grand Marnier sauce and desserts that include foamed yoghurt with mango sorbet and passion fruit. The taster menus are great value. €€€

Cuenca and around

The mountainous, craggy countryside around **CUENCA** is as dramatic as any in Spain. Located 166km east of Madrid, the city, the capital of a sparsely populated province, is an extraordinary-looking place, enclosed on three sides by the deep gorges of the Huécar and Júcar rivers, with balconied houses hanging over the clifftop – the finest of them tastefully converted into a wonderful museum of abstract art. To get the most from a visit, try to come on a weekday, and stay overnight; with this much time, you can make the short trip to see the bizarre limestone formations of the Ciudad Encantada and visit the picturesque source of the Río Cuervo.

The Ciudad Antigua

At the centre of the rambling **Ciudad Antigua** is the Pza. Mayor, a fine space, entered through the arches of the Baroque *ayuntamiento* and ringed by cafés and ceramic shops. Follow the road out of the Pza. and up the hill and you get some fantastic views of the surrounding countryside.

The Catedral

Pza. Mayor • Charge (joint entry with Museo Tesoro available)

Occupying most of the east side of the Pza. Mayor is the **Catedral**, whose incongruous, unfinished facade betrays a misguided attempt to beautify a simple Gothic building after the tower collapsed. The interior is much more attractive, especially the carved Plateresque arch at the end of the north aisle and the chapel next to it, with distinctly un-Christian carvings round its entrance.

Alongside is a small **Tesoro Catedralicio**, which contains some beautiful gold and silver work, as well as wooden doors by Alonso Berruguete.

Museo Tesoro

C/Obispo Valero 3 • Charge • www.catedralcuenca.es

Next to the Catedral, further religious treasures are to be found in the adjacent **Museo Tesoro**, including two canvases by El Greco, a magnificent *Crucifixion* by Gerard David and a Byzantine diptych unique in Spain. The museum also houses a marvellous collection of tapestries and carpets.

Museo de Cuenca

C/Obispo Valero 12 • Charge

Right opposite the Museo Tesoro is the excellent **Museo de Cuenca**, which traces the city's history from prehistoric times and showcases a good Roman collection from local finds.

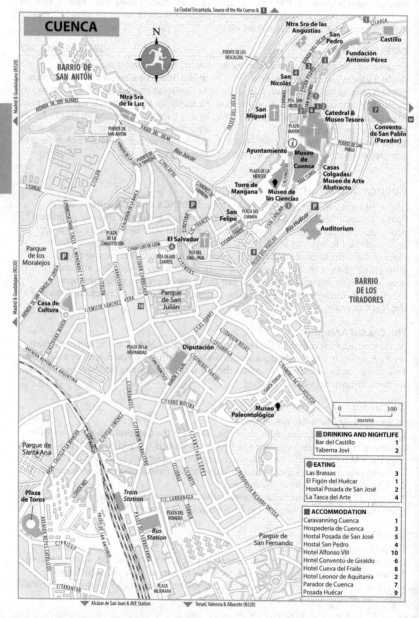

CUENCA

La Ciudad Encantada, Source of the Río Cuervo &

Madrid & Guadalajara (N320)

BARRIO DE SAN ANTÓN

Ntra Sra de la Luz

AVENIDA DE LOS ALFARES

PASEO DEL JÚCAR

PUENTE DE SAN ANTÓN

Río Júcar

PUENTE DE LA TRINIDAD

PLAZA DE LA MERCED

Torre de Mangana

El Salvador

PLAZA DE LA CONSTITUCIÓN

San Felipe

PLAZA DEL CARMEN

Parque de los Moralejos

Casa de Cultura

Parque de San Julián

PLAZA DE LA HISPANIDAD

Diputación

AVENIDA REPÚBLICA ARGENTINA

Parque de Santa Ana

Train Station

Plaza de Toros

Bus Station

PLAZA MEJORADA

Ntra Sra de las Angustias

San Pedro

Castillo

PUENTE DE LOS DESCALZOS

Fundación Antonio Pérez

San Nicolás

San Miguel

PLAZA MAYOR

Catedral & Museo Tesoro

Convento de San Pablo (Parador)

PUENTE DE SAN PABLO

Ayuntamiento

Museo de Cuenca

Casas Colgadas/ Museo de Arte Abstracto

Museo de las Ciencias

Río Huécar

Auditorium

BARRIO DE LOS TIRADORES

Museo Paleontológico

Parque de San Fernando

0   100
metres

DRINKING AND NIGHTLIFE
Bar del Castillo	1
Taberna Jovi	2

EATING
Las Brassas	3
El Figón del Huécar	1
Hostal Posada de San José	2
La Tasca del Arte	4

ACCOMMODATION
Caravanning Cuenca	1
Hospedería de Cuenca	3
Hostal Posada de San José	5
Hostal San Pedro	4
Hotel Alfonso VIII	10
Hotel Convento de Giraldo	6
Hotel Cueva del Fraile	8
Hotel Leonor de Aquitania	2
Parador de Cuenca	7
Posada Huécar	9

Madrid & Guadalajara (N320)

Alcázar de San Juan & AVE Station

Teruel, Valencia & Albacete (N320)

Museo de Arte Abstracto
Casas Colgadas • Free • http://march.es/arte/cuenca

The artistic highlight of Cuenca has to be the nearby **Museo de Arte Abstracto**, a gallery established in the 1960s by Fernando Zóbel, one of the leading artists in Spain's "abstract generation". It is now run by the prestigious Fundación Juan March, which displays works from a core collection of abstract painting and sculpture by, among many others, Eduardo Chillida, José Guerrero, Lucio Muñoz, Antonio Saura, Antonio Tàpies and Fernando Zóbel, and hosts some of the best exhibitions to be found in provincial Spain. The museum itself is a stunning conversion of one of the extraordinary Casas Colgadas ("Hanging Houses"), a pair of fifteenth-century houses, with cantilevered balconies, literally hanging from the cliff face.

For the best views of the houses cross the Puente de San Pablo **footbridge** that heads across the gorge to the parador.

Fundación Antonio Pérez
C/Julián Romero 20 • Charge • http://fundacionantonioperez.com

Housed in a former Carmelite convent which dates back to the seventeenth-century, the **Fundación Antonio Pérez** is home to a contemporary art museum that acts as a perfect complement to the **Museo de Arte Abstracto.** Within the labyrinthine building lies a significant and thought-provoking collection of paintings, sculptures, photographs, and other objets d'art amassed by the patron, including work by Spanish surrealist Antonio Saura.

Museo de las Ciencias
Pza. de la Merced 1 • Charge, free Wed • http://pagina.jccm.es/museociencias

Housed in an old convent and an adjoining modern extension, the **Museo de las Ciencias** is an ambitious and largely successful attempt to explain the origins of the universe and the history of the earth in the context of the local region. It contains a host of fascinating interactive exhibits, including a planetarium which has some shows in English, and makes a great visit if you are with children.

ARRIVAL AND DEPARTURE CUENCA AND AROUND

By train Cuenca is connected to the AVE high-speed train network and is now just a 50min trip from Madrid on the line to Valencia. The Fernando Zóbel AVE station is some 3km out of town and has regular bus connections to the city centre (line #1). The slower but considerably cheaper regional trains stop at the more central station at C/Mariano Catalina 10, which has a regular bus link (line #1 or #6) to the old town.
Destinations Madrid (AVE 10–11 daily, 55min; regional 4 daily, 3hr); Valencia (AVE 7 daily, 1hr; regional 4 daily, 3hr–4hr).

By bus The bus station is on the southern edge of the modern part of town close to the old train station at C/ Fermin Caballero 20.
Destinations Albacete (2–4 daily; 1hr 45min); Madrid (7–10 daily; 2hr–2hr 30min); Valencia (2 daily; 3hr–3hr 15min).
By car The old town of Cuenca – the Ciudad Antigua – stands on a high ridge, looped to the south by the Río Huécar and the modern town and its suburbs. If you're driving in, follow signs for the Catedral and try one of the car parks beyond that up at the top of the old town.

INFORMATION

Turismo Pza. Mayor 1 (Mon–Thurs & Sun 10am–2pm & 5–8pm, Fri & Sat 10am–8pm; 969 241 051, http://turismo.cuenca.es). There is also a visitor reception centre at C/Cruz

Roja 1 on the way into town on the Madrid road (Mon–Sat 10am–2pm & 5–7pm, Sun 10am–2pm; 969 241 050).

ACCOMMODATION SEE MAP PAGE 170

You'll find many **places to stay** in the new town, with a concentration of *hostales* along C/Ramón y Cajal, but the most atmospheric options are up in the old town.
Hospedería de Cuenca C/San Pedro 27, http://hospederia decuenca.com. Comfortable *hostal* in the old town just up

the hill from the Pza. Mayor. Fourteen individually decorated rooms with retro wooden furnishings and modern bathrooms scattered over the six floors of this old mansion. €€

★ **Hostal Posada de San José** C/Julián Romero 4, http://posadasanjose.com. A lovely old building with a

3

tranquil garden in the old town near the Catedral. It has a variety of rooms, ranging from small individual rooms with no bathrooms to large suites with seating areas and views over the gorge. There's a good-quality restaurant, too (see page 172), and the slightly more expensive rooms will get you a room with a view over the gorge. €€

Hostal San Pedro C/San Pedro 34, http://hostalsanpedro. es. This comfortable little *hostal* in a great position up in the old town close to the Catedral has eight small but neat rooms, some with views and seating areas, and all with smart bathrooms. €€

Hotel Alfonso VIII C/Parque de San Julián 3, http://hotel-alfonsoviii.com. A nicely located, functional and good-value three-star hotel in the new town, facing the park. They also offer two-room apartments, which make a good family option. €

Hotel Convento de Giraldo Ctra. C/San Pedro 12, http:// hotelconventodelgiraldo.com. An upmarket 34-room, four-star hotel housed in a refurbished seventeenth-century mansion in the heart of the old town. Simple but smart, comfortable rooms (some with four-poster beds and beamed ceilings), which combine the old and the new. €€

Hotel Cueva del Fraile Ctra. Cuenca-Buenache km7, http://hotelcuevadelfraile.com. A sixteenth-century former monastery 5km out from Cuenca. The rooms are pleasantly furnished in antique style and the extensive grounds include a pool. It also has its own restaurant serving local specialities. Family rooms available. €€

Hotel Leonor de Aquitania C/San Pedro 60, http://hotel leonordeaquitania.com. Slightly frayed at the edges but a great situation in an eighteenth-century nobleman's house in the old town; many of the rooms in this hotel have great views over the gorge. There is a small spa and fitness area and a restaurant too. €

Parador de Cuenca Convento de San Pablo, http:// parador.es. Expensive compared to much of the accommodation in Cuenca, but the parador does have a fine summer pool, superb views across the gorge to the Casas Colgadas and a very good restaurant. €€€

Posada Huécar C/Paseo del Huécar 3, http://posada huecar.com. A friendly and characterful inn on the banks of the Río Huécar with rustic furnishings in the old-style rooms, all of which have en-suite bathrooms. €

CAMPING

Caravanning Cuenca 6km north of the city on the CM2105 (no bus), http://campingcuenca.com. There's a riverside location for this extremely well-appointed campsite with a great pool, surrounded by shady pines. Log cabins for rent too. Closed mid-Oct to mid-March. €

EATING
SEE MAP PAGE 170

Many of the hotels in the old town have good restaurants attached to them, and there are a host of smaller eateries tucked into the streets by the Pza. Mayor.

Las Brassas C/Alfonso VIII 105, 969 235 520. This place is the real thing. *Jamónes* hanging from the ceiling, tables always crowded with locals, and a cheap and cheerful menu of succulent grilled meat – try the suckling lamb. €€

★ **El Figón del Huécar** C/Julián Romero 6, http:// figondelhuecar.es. There's inventive cuisine in this place up in the old town, with views over the gorge. Dishes range from lamb stuffed with raisins, pine nuts and pâté to gilthead bream baked with prawn and sesame seeds. A la carte is available, or you could go for the taster menu with venison or lamb. €€€

Hostal Posada de San José C/Julián Romero 4, http:// posadasanjose.com. Tapas, *raciones* and full meals available in the restaurant of this characterful *hostal* in the old town. Local cuisine and seasonal ingredients are on offer: they do a taster dish of local specialities and the home-made *croquetas* are excellent. €€

La Tasca del Arte C/Fray Luis de León 9, www.la-tasca-del-arte.es. Popular restaurant and flamenco venue, with a food menu of traditional tapas and *raciones* – the monkfish rice, courgette flowers, and Cantabrian anchovies are particularly good – and top-notch flamenco performances in the evenings. €€€

DRINKING AND NIGHTLIFE
SEE MAP PAGE 170

The Pza. Mayor and the surrounding streets are the places to head for evening *copas*, with their vibrant and diverse range of bars. The liveliest joints are on C/Severo Catalina and in the little alleyways overlooking the Río Júcar. Another popular area is on and around C/Parque del Huécar by the Júcar, while the road up by the ruined castle at the top of town has a string of terrace bars.

Bar del Castillo C/Larga 13, 664 657 803. One of the popular down-to-earth bars by the castle. This one also serves food and specializes in meat dishes and barbecued chicken; it's a good option if you have children. Great views over the gorge and back into town from the terrace.

Taberna Jovi C/Colmillo 10, http://tabernajovi.es. Cosy cocktail bar with dark-wood walls and your grandma's stained-glass lampshades. A homely place for a drink – the martinis are particularly good – and some generously portioned tapas.

La Ciudad Encantada

19km (12 miles) northeast of Cuenca • Charge • http://ciudadencantada.es

The classic excursion from Cuenca is to the **Ciudad Encantada**, a twenty-square-kilometre "park" of karst limestone outcrops, sculpted by natural erosion into a bizarre series of abstract, natural and animal-like forms. A few of the names – "fight between an elephant and a crocodile", for example – stretch the imagination a little, but the rocks are certainly amazing, and many of the creations really do look knocked into shape by human hands. The fantasy landscape was used as a backdrop for Arnold Schwarzenegger's first major film, *Conan the Barbarian*.

The most interesting area of sculptures is enclosed and the extensive car park and restaurants outside testify to its popularity with weekending *madrileños*. However, off season, or during the week, you can have the place almost to yourself. Just outside the entrance there are signs to the **Mirador de Uña**, providing excellent views over the valley. You will need your own transport to get to the park, which is around 20km northeast of Cuenca, on signed back roads towards Albarracín. If you get stuck, you might like to seek out the quiet and functional *hostal*, the *Ciudad Encantada* (http://hostalciudadencantada.es), opposite the entrance gate.

Serranía de Cuenca

To the north of the Ciudad Encantada is the **Parque Natural Serranía de Cuenca**, a wild mountain area crisscrossed by spectacular ravines, river gorges and rock formations and repopulated by wolves and bears. Within the park is the **Parque de El Hosquillo**, a nature reserve which can only be visited on a guided tour booked in advance (weekends mid-March to Dec and most days in Aug; charge; http://parqueelhosquillo.com). At the northern top of the park on the CM2106 past Tragacete is the **source of the Río Cuervo**, a moss-covered crag peppered with waterfalls, and further on is the spectacular gorge of the **Hoz de Beteta**.

The route east from the Ciudad Encantada towards Albarracín is a delight, edging through the verdant **Júcar Gorge** and across the scarcely populated mountains; you'll need your own transport. En route, still in Cuenca province, you might stop at **UÑA**, a village sited between a lagoon and a barrage. Just over the provincial border, in Teruel province, the road between Uña and Frías de Albarracín runs past a point known as García, close to the **source of the Río Tajo** where the great river begins its journey across Iberia to the Atlantic.

ACCOMMODATION	SERRANÍA DE CUENCA
Hotel Uña Serranía Encantada C/Egido 23, Uña, http://hotelluna.es. This lakeside hotel has twelve very decent	rooms (triples and quadruples available), as well as a panoramic restaurant and a pleasant garden bar. €

Segóbriga

Charge • http://en.www.turismocastillalamancha.es

Just south of the A3 motorway that runs between Madrid and Valencia, near the village of Saelices, **SEGÓBRIGA** makes a worthy detour for anyone interested in Roman ruins. References to the town date back to the second century BC and it developed into a prosperous settlement largely thanks to the presence of nearby gypsum mines. The town reached its peak about four centuries later, but declined under the Visigoths and was effectively abandoned during the Arab occupation. The best-preserved structures are the theatre and amphitheatre – which had a capacity for 5500 people – but there are also some interesting additions made by the Visigoths. An informative interpretation centre on the site recounts the history of what was a fairly important settlement.

Alarcón

Just off the old NIII road between Honrubia and Motilla del Palancar is the lively little town of **ALARCÓN**, occupying an imposing defensive site sculpted by the burrowing of the Río Júcar. Almost completely encircled and walled, the village is accessible by a spit of land just wide enough to take a road that passes through a succession of **fortified gateways**.

At the top of the village is an exquisite **castle**, eighth-century in origin and captured from the Moors in 1184 after a nine-month siege.

ACCOMMODATION AND EATING   ALARCÓN

The parador, with its atmospheric dining hall, is probably the best **place to eat**, and there is cheaper fare served at the bars on the main Pza. de Don Juan Manuel.

La Cabaña de Alarcón C/Alvaro de Lara 21, http://restaurantelacabanadealarcon.es. A friendly, good-value restaurant with a cool library-like interior and a terrace overlooking the valley, serving up a range of well-presented locally inspired dishes. €€

Hostal Don Juan C/Marqués de Villena 4, http://hostal

donjuan.es. An affordable option, this *hostal* has five good-sized neat doubles, some with seating areas. Book ahead in summer and at weekends. €

★ **Parador de Alarcón** Avda.Amigos de los Castillos 3, http://parador.es. The Arabic fortress has now been converted into one of the country's smallest and most atmospheric paradores, with just fourteen, brick-lined doubles. Book ahead in summer and at weekends. €€€

Albacete province

Travelling between Madrid or Cuenca and Alicante or Murcia, you'll pass through **Albacete province**, one of Spain's more forgettable corners. Hot, arid plains for the most part, the province shelters the lovely **Alcalá del Júcar** and the humdrum provincial capital, **Albacete**. Scenically, the only relief is in the hyperactive **Río Júcar**, which, in the north of the province, sinks almost without warning into the plain.

Alcalá del Júcar

If you are driving, it's certainly worth making a detour off the main roads east to take the scenic route along the banks of the Río Júcar, between Valdeganga and the stunning village of **ALCALÁ DEL JÚCAR**. Almost encircled by the river, the village is an amazing sight, with its houses built one on top of the other and burrowed into the white cliff face. Several of these **cuevas** (caves) have been converted into bars and restaurants and make a great place for a drink, with rooms carved up to 170m through the cliff and windows overlooking the river on each side of the loop. They're open daily in summer but otherwise only at weekends.

Alcalá also boasts a **castle** – adapted at intervals over the past 1500 years, though today just a shell – with great views and an unusual teardrop-shaped bullring (charge).

ACCOMMODATION   ALCALÁ DEL JÚCAR

La Finca de los Olivos Carretera de Tolosa, http://fincalosolivos.com. A four-star spa hotel and holiday cottage complex built on the banks of the river on the edge of the village. Hotel rooms are very sleek and some have terraces looking out towards the castle, plus there is a great pool and a good-value restaurant. Cottages, with one to three bedrooms, are also available. The complex runs a range of outdoor activities including rafting and kayaking. €€€

Hostal Pelayo Avda. Constitución 4, http://hotelpelayo.

net. This place has comfortable, modern rooms and its own restaurant and terrace next to the river. Pay a little extra and you can have a balcony and a hydro-massage bathtub. Breakfast included. €

Hostal Rambla Paseo de los Robles 2, http://hostal rambla.es. Another decent option in a shady spot by the river. Simple, pleasantly decorated, comfortable rooms, some with small balconies, and a restaurant. €€

EATING AND DRINKING

Casa El Moli Av. Los Robles 5, http://restaurantecasaelmoli. com. This down-to-earth restaurant by the river offers home cooking with local specialities. The set lunch is good value and there are some good à la carte options such as the *gazpacho manchego* or the *judias con perdíz*. €€

Las Cuevas del Diablo C/Tal y Cual 12, http://cuevas

deldiablo.com. A series of bars, a disco and even a small museum have been carved out of this seventy-metre tunnel that ends in a fantastic *mirador* across the valley. The "diablo" is eccentric owner Juan José Martínez, a self-confessed Don Juan character with a comedy Dalí-esque moustache. Entry fee includes a drink. €€

Albacete

ALBACETE was named **Al-Basit** – "the plain" – by the Moors, but save for a few old backstreets, it is basically a modern city. The **Catedral** is noteworthy for the presence of Ionic columns instead of normal pillars astride its nave. The **Pasaje Lodares** is also worth seeking out. A stunning iron-and-glass gallery constructed in 1925, it is adorned with neo-Baroque and modernist decoration and lined with shops.

Museo de Albacete

Parque de Abelardo Sánchez • Charge • http://cultura.castillalamancha.es/museos/nuestros-museos/museo-de-albacete

The **Museo de Albacete**, whose prize exhibits are five small Roman dolls, perfectly sculpted and jointed, and an array of local Roman mosaics, has a more than respectable archaeological and ethnographical collection. Local-born painter Benjamin Palencia donated 120 works that form the basis of the art collection.

Museo de la Cuchillería

Pza. de la Catedral • Charge • www.museocuchilleria.es

For Spaniards, Albacete is synonymous with high-quality knives and the **Museo de la Cuchillería**, housed in the intriguing green-tiled mock-Gothic Casa Hortelano by the Catedral, will tell you all you want to know about this speciality that, as with Toledo, can be traced back to the Moors.

ARRIVAL AND INFORMATION   ALBACETE

By train Albacete is connected to the high-speed train network on the route between Madrid and Valencia. The new train station is on C/Federico García Lorca on the northeastern edge of the city.
Destinations Alicante (8–10 daily; 50min–1hr 15min); Madrid (15–18 daily; 1hr 30min–2hr 30min); Valencia (4–6 daily; 1hr 40min–2hr 10min).
By bus The bus from Madrid takes around 3hr and drops you at the terminus by the high-speed train station on C/Federico García Lorca.
Destinations Alicante (9 daily; 2hr–2hr 20min); Cuenca (3–5 daily; 2hr 25min–3hr); Madrid (20 daily; 2hr 45min–3hr).
Turismo Pza. Altozano (summer: Mon–Sat 10am–2pm & 5–9pm, Sun 10am–2pm; winter: Mon–Sat 10am–2pm & 4–8pm, Sun 10am–2pm; 967 630 004, http://en.www.turismocastillalamancha.es).

ACCOMMODATION AND EATING

The city is full of **tapas bars** and **restaurants** serving high-quality local produce with several good options to be found in the streets around the Catedral.
L'Arruzz Albacete C/Purísima 1, http://larruzzalbacete.com. This centrally located restaurant offers creative dishes, friendly service and reasonable prices. The *pulpo* and the rice dishes are particularly good. €€
Hotel Los Llanos Avda. España 9, http://sercotelhoteles.com. This four-star hotel, part of the *Sercotel* chain, is centrally located and offers modern business-style comfort with large rooms. €€
Nuestro Bar C/Alcalde Conangla 102, http://nuestrobar.es. Renowned local bar serving great tapas and a vast range of regional cuisine, all at reasonable prices. €€

Ciudad Real and the heartland of La Mancha

There is a huge gap in the middle of the tourist map of Spain between Toledo and the borders of Andalucía, and from Extremadura almost to the east coast. This, the province of **Ciudad Real**, comprises the heartland of **La Mancha**. The tourist authorities try hard to push their Ruta de Don Quixote across the plains, highlighting the windmills and other Quixotic sights: the signposted central part of the route, which starts at Belmonte and finishes at Consuegra, can be done in a day, but much of it is fanciful and, unless you're enamoured with the book, it's only of passing interest.

Nonetheless, a few places merit a visit if you've got time to spare, most notably **Consuegra**, for its magnificent windmills; **Almagro**, for its arcaded square and medieval theatre; and **Calatrava**, for the castle ruins of its order of knights. It is also the heart of wine-producing country, and many of the *bodegas* in **Valdepeñas** offer free tastings. The **website** http://turismocastillalamancha.es gives more information about the area.

Consuegra

CONSUEGRA lies just to the west of the A4 *autovía*, roughly midway from Madrid to Andalucía, and has the most picturesque and typical of Manchegan settings, below a ridge of eleven restored (and highly photogenic) windmills. The first of these is occupied by the town's **turismo** while others house shops and workshops. They share their plateau with a ruined **castle** (charge; http://consuegra.es), which was once the headquarters of the Order of St John in the twelfth century and offers splendid views of the plain from its windswept ridge. The town below is also attractive, with a lively Pza. Mayor and many Mudéjar churches.

INFORMATION   CONSUEGRA

Turismo Occupies the first windmill and the office on Avda. Castilla la Mancha (http://consuegra.es). Good for information on the Ruta de Don Quixote.

ACCOMMODATION AND EATING

Hostal-Restaurante San Poul Avda. Alcázar de San Juan 50, http://sanpoul.es. Small, old-fashioned, but very welcoming *hostal* with a decent restaurant, situated on the eastern side of town below the windmills. €

NATIONAL PARKS AND RESERVES IN LA MANCHA

A respite from the arid monotony of the Castilian landscape, and a treat for birdwatchers, is provided by the oasis of **La Mancha Húmeda** ("Wet La Mancha"). This is an area of lagoons and marshes, both brackish and fresh, along the high-level basin of the Río Cigüela and Río Guadiana. Drainage for agriculture has severely reduced the amount of water in recent years, so that the lakes effectively dry up in the summer, but there is still a good variety of interesting plant and bird life. You're best off visiting from April to July when the water birds are breeding, or from September to midwinter when migrating birds pass through.

PARQUE NACIONAL DE LAS TABLAS DE DAIMIEL

Major parks between Ciudad Real and Albacete include the **Parque Nacional de las Tablas de Daimiel**, 11km north of Daimiel itself, which is renowned for its bird life (over two hundred species visit the park over the course of the year). There's an information centre (http://lastablasdedaimiel.com) alongside the marshes. The park is accessible only by car or taxi, and Daimiel has little accommodation on offer.

Hostal Las Brujas Paseo del Carmen, Daimiel, http://restaurantelasbrujas.es. Excellent-value place on the outskirts of town with simply furnished rooms, a popular restaurant and a summer terrace. €

Hotel Las Tablas C/Virgen de la Cruces 5, Daimiel, http://hotellastablas.com. Comfortable 30-room hotel in the centre of town from which you can organize guided trips of the park. Price includes breakfast. €€

PARQUE NATURAL DE LAS LAGUNAS DE RUIDERA

More traveller-friendly, but crowded in the summer months, is the **Parque Natural de las Lagunas de Ruidera**, northeast of Valdepeñas (frequent buses from Albacete). You'll find an information centre (926 528 116) on the roadside, as you enter Ruidera from Manzanares, and several nature trails inside the park, as well as swimming and boating opportunities. Accommodation includes:

Los Batanes Ctra. Las Lagunas km 8, Ruidera, http://losbatanes.com. Campsite with a large pool and grassy sunbathing area close to the Laguna Redondilla. €

Doña Ruidera Pedazo de lo Alto, Ruidera, http://hotelruidera.es. Good-value aparthotel with large rooms and a couple of two-bedroom apartments with views of the lake. €€

Hotel Albamanjon Laguna de San Pedro, Ossa de Montiel, http://albamanjon.net. Picturesque rural hotel/restaurant overlooking one of the lakes. The large rooms have terraces and seating areas. €€€

Hotel Entrelagos Ctra. Las Lagunas, http://entrelagos.com. Two-star hotel with simple en-suite rooms and its own little beach on the edge of one of the lakes. €

Vida de Antes C/Colón 2, http://lavidadeantes.com. A cosy little hotel with nine individually designed rooms laid out around an interior patio of a traditional Manchego house. €€

Ciudad Real

The city of **CIUDAD REAL**, capital of the province at the heart of this flat country, makes a good base for excursions and has connections by bus with most villages in the area. It has a few sights of its own, too, including a Mudéjar gateway, the **Puerta de Toledo**, which fronts the only surviving fragment of its medieval walls, at the northern edge of the city on the Toledo road. Further in, take a look at the fourteenth-century **church of San Pedro**, an airy, Gothic edifice, housing some exquisite chapels and an elaborate fifteenth-century alabaster *retablo*. The Pza. Mayor, with its impressive neo-Gothic town hall and clock with its mechanical figures of Cervantes, Don Quixote and Sancho Panza, is also worth a visit.

Museo Provincial

C/Prado 4 • Charge • http://ciudadreal.es

The **Museo Provincial** is made up of two buildings, the first a modern one opposite the Catedral, which exhibits local archeological finds, and the former Convento de la Merced, which houses a decent art collection including work by Dalí, Chillida, Tàpíes and Saura.

Museo de Don Quijote

Ronda de Alarcos 1 • Free • www.ciudadreal.es

In the entertaining **Museo de Don Quijote**, personalities from the story guide you round the exhibits, which include some smart audiovisuals that bring the tale to life.

ARRIVAL AND DEPARTURE   CIUDAD REAL

By train Ciudad Real's train station, with high-speed AVE connections to Madrid and south to Seville and Córdoba, lies out of town at the end of Avda. de Europa; bus #5 connects with the central Pza. de Pilar.
Destinations Almagro (6 daily; 15min); Cordoba (16–20 daily; 50min–1hr 5min); Madrid (18–25 daily; 55min–1hr);

Sevilla (12–14 daily; 1hr 45min–2hr).
By bus The bus station is on Ctra. de la Fuensanta.
Destinations Almagro (1–8 daily; 20min); Madrid (3 daily; 2hr 50min); Toledo (4 daily; 1hr 30min–2hr 5min); Valdepeñas (5 daily; 1hr 15min).

INFORMATION

Turismo The main tourist office is on the Pza. Mayor (Tues–Sat 10am–2pm & 5–7pm, Sun 10am–2pm; July & Aug Tues–Sun 10am–2pm; 926 200 641, http://ciudad- real.es/turismo). There is also an information booth at the train station.

ACCOMMODATION

Keep in mind that finding a **place to stay** is not always easy, so it's worth booking ahead.
Hotel NH Ciudad Real Avda. Alarcos 25, http://nh-hotels. com. Centrally located, ninety-room business-style hotel, which is part of the slickly run if slightly faceless NH chain. €
Hotel Santa Cecilia C/Tinte 3, http://santacecilia.com. A competitively priced four-star hotel in the centre of town. Rooms are cosy and it has its own pool. €

EATING AND DRINKING

Ciudad Real has an impressive range of **tapas bars**. The town's **nightlife** at the weekend generally starts off with tapas on C/Palma, carrying on to the bars along Avenida Torreón del Alcázar and around.
La Casuca C/Palma 10, 926 255 480. This popular bar- restaurant close to the centre of town offers homemade cooking at reasonable prices and a decent range of wines. €€
El Portalón Pza. Mayor 9, 926 216 588. Welcoming wood-panelled bar serving drinks, *bocadillos* and a decent selection of tapas. €

Almagro

Twenty kilometres southeast of Ciudad Real is **ALMAGRO**, an elegant little town, which for a period in the fifteenth and sixteenth centuries was quite a metropolis in southern

3

DON QUIXOTE

Not a novel in the modern sense, **Miguel de Cervantes'** *Don Quixote de La Mancha* (published in 1604) is a sequence of episodes following the adventures of a country gentleman in his fifties, whose mind has been addled by romantic tales of chivalry. In a noble gesture, he changes his name to Don Quixote de La Mancha, and sets out on horseback, in rusty armour, to right the wrongs of the world. At his side throughout is Sancho Panza, a shrewd, pot-bellied rustic given to quoting proverbs at every opportunity. During the course of the book, Quixote, an instantly sympathetic hero, charges at windmills and sheep (mistaking them for giants and armies), makes ill-judged attempts to help others and is mocked by all for his efforts. Broken-hearted but wiser, he returns home and, on his deathbed, pronounces: "Let everyone learn from my example … look at the world with common sense and learn to see what is really there."

Cervantes' life was almost as colourful as his hero's. The son of a poor doctor, he fought as a soldier in the sea battle of Lepanto, where he permanently maimed his left hand and was captured by pirates and put to work as a slave in Algiers. Ransomed and sent back to Spain, he spent the rest of his days writing novels and plays in relative poverty, dying ten years after the publication of *Don Quixote*, "old, a soldier, a gentleman and poor".

Spanish academics have spent as much time dissecting the work of Cervantes as their English counterparts have Shakespeare's. Most see *Don Quixote* as a satire on the popular romances of the day, with the central characters representing two forces in Spain: Quixote the dreaming, impractical nobility, and Sancho the wise and down-to-earth peasantry. There are also those who read in it an ironic tale of a visionary or martyr frustrated in a materialistic world, while others see it as an attack on the Church and establishment. Debates aside, this highly entertaining adventure story is certainly one of the most influential works to have emerged from Spain.

Castile, partly thanks to the influence of the Fuggers, bankers to the Habsburg king and Holy Roman Emperor Carlos I (Charles V).

Corral de las Comedias

Pza. Mayor 18 • Charge • http://corraldecomedias.com

Almagro's main claim to fame today is the **Corral de las Comedias**, a perfectly preserved seventeenth-century open-air, balconied theatre, unique in Spain. Plays from its seventeenth-century heyday – the Golden Age of Spanish theatre – are performed regularly in the tiny auditorium, and throughout July it hosts a fully fledged theatre festival (http://festivaldealmagro.com).

Museo Nacional del Teatro

C/Gran Maestre 2 • Charge, free Sat 4–6pm & Sun morning • http://museoteatro.mcu.es

A short walk north of the main square, the **Museo del Teatro** houses costumes, photos, posters, model theatres and other paraphernalia documenting the history of drama from Greek and Roman times to the present, but is probably only of passing interest to anyone other than theatre buffs.

Museo de Encaje

Callejón del Villar • Charge • http://almagro.es

As well as its theatre festival, Almagro is renowned for its lace and embroidery work, showcased in the **Museo de Encaje**, which also looks at the techniques, origins and history of the craft.

Plaza Mayor

The **Plaza Mayor** is magnificent: more of a wide street than a square, it is arcaded along its length, and lined with rows of green-framed windows – a north-European influence brought by the Fugger family, Carlos V's bankers, who settled here. Also resident in Almagro for a while were the Knights of Calatrava (see page 179), though their power was on the wane by the time the **Convento de la Asunción de Calatrava** was built in the early sixteenth century. Further traces of Almagro's former importance are dotted throughout the town in the grandeur of numerous **Renaissance mansions**.

Back in the Plaza Mayor, you can have an open-air snack or browse among the shops in the arcades, where **lacemakers** at work with bobbins and needles are the main attraction. On Wednesday mornings there's a lively **market** in C/Ejido de San Juan.

ARRIVAL AND INFORMATION   ALMAGRO

By train Almagro is connected to Madrid with one train a day (2hr 35min) and to Ciudad Real with five trains (15min); the train station is a short distance from the centre of town along the Paseo de la Estación.

By bus Buses, connecting the city to Ciudad Real, stop near the *Hotel Don Diego* on the Ronda de Calatrava.

Turismo C/Ejido de Calatrava s/n (Jan–March & Oct–Dec Tues–Fri 10am–2pm & 4–7pm, Sat 10am–2pm & 4–6pm, Sun 10am–2pm; April–June, Aug & Sept Tues–Fri 10am–2pm & 5–8pm, Sat 10am–2pm & 5–7pm, Sun 10am–2pm; July Tues–Fri 10am–2pm & 6–9pm, Sat 10am–2pm & 6–8pm, Sun 10am–2pm; 926 860 717, http://ciudad-almagro.com).

ACCOMMODATION

Almagro is a great **place to stay**, although accommodation can be fairly limited during the theatre festival and at holiday weekends, so make sure that you book ahead.

★ **Casa del Rector** C/Pedro Oviedo 8, http://lacasadelrector.com. This stylish hotel has some delightful and well-appointed rooms, each with their own individual decor, set in three distinct areas; for atmosphere go for the ones around a beautiful interior patio. The hotel also has a spa (charged extra by the hour). €€

Hostal Los Escudos C/Bolaños 55, http://hostalescudos.com. There are thirteen individually decorated, a/c rooms in this upmarket little *hostal* on one of the main roads into town. €

★ **Parador de Almagro** C/Gran Maestre, http://parador.es. Housed in a sixteenth-century Franciscan convent, this historic parador features some peaceful interior courtyards and a great swimming pool. Look out for offers on the parador website. €€

EATING AND DRINKING

Tapas **bars** cluster around the Pza. Mayor; and the *bodega* at the parador is worth a stop for a drink, too.

La Posada de Almagro C/Gran Maestre 5, 659 185 872. There are two beautiful interior patios in this *hostal* restaurant that specializes in local delicacies. Very good value with a range of set menus available. €€

★ **Restaurante La Parrilla de San Agustín** C/San Agustín 18, http://grupoelcorregidor.es. Lovely restaurant with a traditional interior and a menu to match. Highlights include Iberian pork loin, fillet of turbot, and a selection of dishes described in *Don Quixote*, including Manchego porridge and *asadillo* (roasted red peppers and tomatoes). €€

★ **La Tabernilla de Almagro** C/Bolaños 3, http://latabernilladealmagro.com. Popular bar on the edge of the old town with friendly service and a great range of well-presented tapas including *pisto manchego*, pulpo and aubergines in red wine. €€€

El Campo de Calatrava

The area known as **El Campo de Calatrava**, in between Almagro and Ciudad Real, was the domain of the **Knights of Calatrava**, a Cistercian order of soldier-monks created in the twelfth century and which was at the forefront of the reconquest of Spain from the Moors.

So influential were they in these parts that Alfonso X created Ciudad Real as a royal check on their power. Even today, dozens of villages for many kilometres around are suffixed with their name.

Calatrava La Vieja

Carrión de Calatrava • Charge • http://turismocastillalamancha.es

Founded by the Moors back in the eighth century, the fortified settlement now known as **Calatrava La Vieja** (Qal'at Rabah in Arabic) acted as the power base of the Caliphate of Córdoba in this strategically important region. It was recaptured by the Christians in the mid-twelfth century and subsequently became the first headquarters of the Knights of Calatrava. You can clearly see the medieval walled fortress with its towers and the remains of buildings such as the *mezquita* during a visit.

Calatrava La Nueva
Aldea del Rey • Charge

In the opening decades of the thirteenth century, the knights pushed their headquarters south to a commanding hilltop 25km south of Almagro, protecting an important pass –the Puerto de Calatrava – into Andalucía. Here, in 1216, they founded **Calatrava La Nueva**, a settlement that was part monastery and part castle, and whose main glory was a great Cistercian church. Here you get a good idea of what must have been an enormously rich and well-protected fortress. The church itself is now completely bare but preserves the outline of a striking rose window and has an amazing stone-vaulted entrance hall. On the hill opposite is a further castle ruin, known as **Salvatierra**, which the knights took over from the Moors.

Valdepeñas and beyond

The road from Ciudad Real through Almagro continues to **VALDEPEÑAS**, centre of the most prolific wine region in Spain, just off the main Madrid–Andalucía motorway. You pass many of the largest **bodegas** on the slip road into town coming from the north and Madrid; most of them offer free tastings. Another option is the high-tech **Museo del Vino** at C/Princesa 39, close to Pza. de España (charge; http://museodelvinovaldepenas. es). The town holds a popular wine **festival** at the beginning of September. There is also a **windmill**, on C/Francisco Mejía, which the tourist office says "could be the biggest in Europe", and opposite there's a museum dedicated to the abstract drawings of local artist Gregorio Prieto (free; http://gregorioprieto.org), though there are also works by Picasso, Miró, Matisse, Chagall, Henry Moore and Francis Bacon.

Gorge of Despeñaperros

Heading south beyond Valdepeñas, you can enter Andalucía through the **Gorge of Despeñaperros**, a narrow mountain gorge once notorious for bandits and still a dramatic natural gateway that signals a change in both climate and vegetation, or as Richard Ford put it (travelling south to north), "exchanges an Eden for a desert".

INFORMATION   **VALDEPEÑAS**

Turismo Pza. España (Tues 4–7pm, Wed–Sat 9.30am– 2pm & 4–6pm, Sun 11am–2pm; 902 310 011, http:// valdepenas.es).

ACCOMMODATION

Hotel Central C/Capitán Fillol 4, http://hotelcentralval. com. There are 25 straightforward en-suite rooms in this decent-value hotel that has its own parking in the centre of town. Serves continental breakfast. €

Hotel & Spa Veracruz Pza. Veracruz, http://hotel veracruzplaza.com. A modern well-equipped hotel with large rooms and its own spa. Offers trips to the local *bodegas* and wine-therapy beauty treatments. €€

The Montes de Toledo

The **Montes de Toledo** cut a swathe through the upper reaches of La Mancha, between Toledo, Ciudad Real and Guadalupe. If you're heading into Extremadura, and have time and transport, the deserted little roads across these hills (they rise to just over 1400m) provide an interesting and atmospheric alternative to the main routes. This is an amazingly remote region to find so close to the centre of Spain.

Toledo to Navalmoral de la Mata

The CM4000, west of Toledo, provides a direct approach into **Extremadura**, linking with the A5 from Madrid to Trujillo, and with roads north into the valley of **La**

Vera (see page 181). It follows the course of the Río Tajo virtually all the way to uninspiring **TALAVERA DE LA REINA**, known for its manufacture of ceramics and as the site of one of Wellington's victories in the Peninsular War.

Oropesa and around

OROPESA is best known for its **castle**, a warm, stone building on a Roman site, rebuilt from Moorish foundations in the fifteenth century by Don García Álvarez de Toledo. Below it, stretches of the old town walls survive, along with a few noble mansions and a pair of Renaissance churches. There are great views from the neatly manicured gardens across to the hulking silhouettes of the Gredos mountains on the horizon, beyond which an attractive minor road, from **Oropesa**, with its castle parador, runs to **El Puente del Arzobispo** and south of the river to the Roman site of **Los Vascos**.

ACCOMMODATION   OROPESA

Parador de Oropesa Pza. Palacio 1, Oropesa, Toledo, http://parador.es. Installed in part of the splendid village castle, this is the best place to stay in the area. It has a great terrace pool, large communal areas and a good restaurant serving a range of local specialities. €€

Navalmoral de la Mata

West from Oropesa, **NAVALMORAL DE LA MATA** has nothing to offer other than its road, rail and bus connections to more engrossing places, such as the **Monasterio de Yuste** across the rich tobacco-growing area to the north, **Plasencia** to the west, and **Trujillo** and **Guadalupe** to the south.

Extremadura

Once neglected and overlooked by many visitors, **Extremadura** has established itself on the tourist trail – and deservedly so. The grand old *conquistador* towns of **Trujillo** and **Cáceres** are excellent staging posts en route south from Madrid or Salamanca; **Mérida** has some exceptional Roman remains and an exemplary museum of local finds; and there is superb bird life in the **Parque Natural de Monfragüe**. Almost inaccessible by public transport, but well worth visiting, is the great **monastery of Guadalupe**, whose revered icon of the Virgin has attracted pilgrims for the past five hundred years. The lush hills and valley of **La Vera** are the first real patch of green you'll come to if you've driven along the A5 west from Madrid.

La Vera

Characterized by its lovely *gargantas* – streams – **La Vera** lies just south of the Sierra de Gredos, a range of hills tucked above the **Río Tiétar** valley. In spring and summer, the area attracts bands of weekenders from Madrid to the picturesque villages of **Candeleda** and **Jarandilla**. At the heart of the region is the **Monasterio de Yuste**, the retreat chosen by Carlos V to cast off the cares of empire.

Jarandilla and around

The main village in these parts is **JARANDILLA DE LA VERA**, which has good **walking** around it. A track into the hills leads to the village of **El Guijo de Santa Bárbara** (4.5km) and then ends, leaving the ascent of the rocky valley beyond to walkers. An hour's trek away up the Garganta de Jaranda is a pool known as El Trabuquete and a high meadow with shepherds' huts known as Pimesaíllo. On the other side of the valley – a serious trek needing a night's camping and good area maps – is the **Garganta de Infierno** (Stream of Hell) and natural swimming pools known as **Los Pilones**.

3

3

EXTREMEÑO CUISINE

Given that **Extremadura** remains a largely agricultural region, it is hardly surprising that its **cuisine** is renowned for high-quality local ingredients, whether it be the trout from the streams in the Gredos mountains, the *pimentón* (paprika) from the Vera, the goat's cheese from Cáceres or the succulent cherries from the Valle de Jerte. Signature dishes include the humble *migas* (breadcrumbs, paprika, ham, garlic and olive oil) and *patatas revolconas* (delicious paprika-flavoured potatoes), but to most Spaniards ham is the gastronomic product that they most associate with Extremadura.

Together with the Sierra Morena in Andalucía, the Extremaduran sierra is the only place in the country that supports the pure-bred Iberian pig, source of the best **jamón**. For its ham to be as flavoursome as possible, the pig, a subspecies of the European wild boar exclusive to the Iberian Peninsula, is allowed to roam wild and eat acorns for several months of the year. The undisputed kings of hams in this area, praised at length by Richard Ford in his *Handbook for Travellers*, are those that come from Montánchez, in the south of the region. The village is midway between Cáceres and Mérida, so if you're in the area try some *jamón* in a bar, washed down with local red wine – but be warned that the authentic product is extremely expensive, a few thinly cut slices often costing as much as an entire meal. The local wine, *pitarra*, is an ideal accompaniment.

Monasterio de Yuste

Carretera de Yuste • Charge • http://patrimonionacional.es

There is nothing especially dramatic about the **Monasterio de Yuste**, the retreat created by Carlos V after renouncing his empire: just a simple beauty and the rather stark accoutrements of the emperor's last years. The monastery, which is signposted from Cuacos de Yuste on the Jarandilla–Plasencia road, had existed here for over a century before Carlos' retirement and he had earmarked the site for some years, planning his modest additions – which included a pleasure garden – while still ruling his empire from Flanders. He retired here with a retinue that included an Italian clockmaker, Juanelo Turriano, whose inventions were the emperor's last passion.

The imperial apartments are draped throughout in black, and exhibits include the little sedan chair in which Carlos was brought here, and another designed to support the old man's gouty legs. If you believe the guide, the bed and even the sheets are the very ones in which the emperor died, though since the place was sacked during the Peninsular War and deserted for years after the suppression of the monasteries, this seems unlikely. A door by the emperor's bed opens out over the church and altar so that even in his final illness he never missed a service. Outside, there's a snack bar and picnic spots, and you'll find a track signposted through the woods to Garganta La Olla (see page 182).

Cuacos de Yuste

The Monasterio de Yuste is 2km into the wooded hills from **CUACOS DE YUSTE**, an attractive village with a couple of squares, including the tiny Pza. de Don Juan de Austria, named after the house (its upper storey reconstructed) where Carlos' illegitimate son Don Juan lived when visiting his father. The surrounding houses, their overhanging upper storeys supported on gnarled wooden pillars, are sixteenth-century originals, and from the beams underneath the overhang tobacco is hung out to dry after the harvest.

Garganta La Olla

Just beyond Jaraíz de la Vera, a left turning leads for around 5km to **GARGANTA LA OLLA**, a beautiful, ramshackle mountain village set among cherry orchards. There is a signposted short-cut track to the Monasterio de Yuste, and several other things to look out for: the **Casa de Putas** (a brothel for the soldiers of Carlos V's army, now a butcher's but still painted the traditional blue) and the **Casa de la Piedra** (House of Stone), a house whose balcony is secured by a three-pronged wooden support resting on a rock. The latter is hard to find; begin by taking the left-hand street up from the square and then ask.

ARRIVAL   LA VERA

By bus Buses run from Príncipe Pío to the Monasterio de   Yuste (daily; 4hr 15min) and to Jarandilla (daily; 3hr 55min).

ACCOMMODATION

JARANDILLA AND AROUND
Camping La Mata Just outside Madrigal de la Vera east of Jarandilla along the EX203, http://campinglamata.com. Pleasant, grassy campsite with a decent bar/restaurant close to a natural swimming pool on one of the *gargantas*. Tent pitches and bungalows available. €€
Don Juan de Austria Hotel Rural and Spa Avda. Soledad Vega Ortiz 101, http://hoteldonjuandeaustria.com. This good mid-range option in the village has comfortable, well-equipped and furnished rooms, some with views of the Sierra and the castle, and a small spa. €€
Jaranda Ctra. EX203, km 47, http://campingjaranda. es. Attractive campsite by the river with plenty of shady pitches, cabins for rent, a pool and a supermarket. Closed mid-Sept to mid-March. €
★ **Parador Carlos V** Avda. García Prieto 1, http:// parador.es. A magnificent parador in the fifteenth-century castle where the emperor stayed during the construction of Yuste. It has a splendid palm-fringed courtyard, period

furnishings and a very good restaurant serving Extremeño cuisine, and an open-air pool in summer. €€
Posada de la Gula C/Ancha 26, http://lagulajarandilla. com. A comfortable and good-value option in a terracotta-coloured building, with no-frills but large, modern and comfortable en-suite rooms. Buffet breakfast included. €€

CUACOS DE YUSTE
★ **Hotel Abadía de Yuste** Avda. Constitución, http:// abadiadeyuste.com. Relaxing, fifteen-room hotel close to the Monasterio de Yuste, with atmospheric decor, a swimming pool and two restaurants. €€

GARGANTA LA OLLA
Hotel Rural Carlos I Avda. Libertad, http:// hotelcarlosprimero.com. A good-value option in this village. Individually decorated rooms, a couple of larger suites with sitting areas and a bar-restaurant serving up local dishes. €

El Valle de Jerte

Immediately north of La Vera, the main Plasencia–Ávila road follows the valley of the **Río Jerte** (from the Greek *Xerte*, meaning "joyful") to the pass of Puerto de Tornavacas, the boundary with Ávila province. The villages here are more developed than those of La Vera but the valley itself is stunning and renowned for its orchards of cherry trees, which for a ten-day period in spring cover the slopes with white blossom. If you're anywhere in the area at this time try to visit as it's a beautiful spectacle.

If you have transport, you can follow a minor route across the sierra to the north of the valley from **Cabezuela del Valle** to **Hervás**, following the highest road in Extremadura, which rises to 1430m.

On the **southern side**, the main point of interest is the **Puerto del Piornal** pass, just behind the village of the same name. The best approach is via **Casas del Castañar** and **Cabrero**. Once at the pass you can continue over to Garganta La Olla in La Vera.

Plasencia

Set in the shadow of the Sierra de Gredos, and surrounded on three sides by the Río Jerte, **PLASENCIA** looks more impressive from afar than it actually is. Once you get up into the old city the walls are hard to find – for the most part they're propping up the backs of houses – and the Catedral is barely half-built, but it still merits a visit. Opposite the Catedral is the **Casa del Deán** (Dean's House), with an intriguing balcony like the prow of a ship. Continuing away from the Catedral along C/Blanca you come out at the **Pza. de San Nicolás**, where, according to local tradition, the church was built to prevent two local families from shooting arrows at each other from adjacent houses.

Plasencia has some lively bars, delightful cafés and a fine, arcaded **Pza. Mayor**, the scene of a farmers' **market** every Tuesday morning, held here since the twelfth century.

Parque de la Isla

At the entrance to the city on the main road in from Ávila is the very pleasant **Parque de la Isla** on the banks of the Río Jerte; head here for a relaxing walk or picnic. A little north of here are the remaining 55 arches of the sixteenth-century **aqueduct**, designed by Juan de Flandes, that used to bring in the city's water supply.

The Catedral

Pza. de la Catedral • **La Catedral Nueva** Free • **La Catedral Vieja** Charge, under-12s free • http://catedralesplasencia.com

Plasencia's **Catedral** is in fact two churches – old and new – built back to back. Work began on the second church, **La Nueva,** at the end of the fifteenth century, but after numerous technical hitches it was eventually abandoned in 1760 when the open end was simply bricked up. It does have some redeeming features, however, most notably the Renaissance choir stall intricately carved by Rodrigo Alemán and described with some justice by the National Tourist Board as "the most Rabelaisian in Christendom".

The older, Romanesque part of the Catedral, known as **La Vieja,** was built between the thirteenth and fourteenth centuries and now houses a refurbished **museum** and **cloisters**.

Museo Etnográfico Textil Provincial

Plazuela Marqués de la Puebla • Free • http://plasenciaturismo.es/museo-etnografico-textil

The **Museo Etnográfico Textil Provincial** contains some colourful costumes and local crafts reflecting local traditions. Many of the exhibits are still much in evidence in the more remote villages in the north of Plasencia province.

ARRIVAL AND DEPARTURE
PLASENCIA

By train The train station is some distance away from the centre – take a taxi (around €5) unless you fancy the hike. Destinations Badajoz (1–3 daily; 2hr 50min); Cáceres (2–4 daily; 1hr 10min); Madrid (3–4 daily; 2hr 50min); Mérida (2–3 daily; 1hr 55min–2hr 15min).

By bus The bus station is about 15min walk from the centre, along the Avda. del Valle to the west. Destinations Cáceres (4–5 daily; 1hr 20min); Jarandilla (2–4 daily; 2hr); Madrid (2 daily; 4hr); Salamanca (3 daily; 2hr).

By car Be warned that the town is difficult to navigate, with a warren of narrow one-way streets and poor signing.

INFORMATION

Turismo C/Santa Clara 4, just off the Pza. de la Catedral (http://plasencia.es). There is also a provincial office in the Pza. Torre Lucia next to the city walls (http://plasenciaturismo.es).

ACCOMMODATION

La Chopera 2.5km out on the Ávila road, http://camping lachopera.com. A large riverside campsite with decent facilities, bungalows for hire and a swimming pool. €

Hostal La Muralla C/Berrozana 6, http://hostallamuralla. es. A professionally run thirteen-room *hostal*. Most of the simple, neat rooms are en-suite and all have a/c. A good central location close to the Pza. Mayor. €

Hotel Exe Alfonso VIII C/Alfonso VIII 32, http://hotel exealfonsoviii.com. A smart four-star hotel with bright, classically decorated rooms, located on the main road near the post office. All the facilities you'd expect of a hotel of this category. €€

Parador de Plasencia Pza. de San Vicente Ferrer s/n, http://parador.es. Housed in a beautiful restored fifteenth-century Gothic convent with large rooms, a cloister, stone staircases and a huge dining room, this parador also has a convenient central location. €€€

EATING AND DRINKING

This is the land of the **pincho**, a little sample of food provided free with your beer or wine – among which is the local *pitarra* wine. Finding good restaurants is not as easy as finding bars in Plasencia (try the area between the Catedral and the Pza. Mayor). There are over fifty bars in the old town alone, mostly found on C/Patalón (go down C/Talavera from the main square and it's the second turning on the left).

RESTAURANTS

Casa Juan C/Arenillas 2, http://restaurantecasajuan.com. You get good-quality regional dishes with some refined touches in this critically acclaimed restaurant in the old part of town. A la carte mains such as *cochinillo* or duck offer a good variety beyond the set menu. €€

Los Monges C/Sor Valentina Mirón 22, just up from Puerta Berronzana, http://restaurantelosmonges.com. A good-quality family restaurant serving up some fine local produce with a creative twist. €€€

Restaurante Succo C/Vidrieras 7, http://restaurantesucco.

es. This restaurant close to the Pza. Mayor offers minimalist decor, friendly service and excellent creative food at decent prices. The beautifully presented dishes include langoustine and scallop salad and goat confit. €€€

BARS

Chiqui C/Alfonso VIII 22, 607 258 064. A busy bar that is a good bet for *pinchos*, hot and cold tapas and a glass of *pitarra* wine. The portions are generous, and the house specials – *croquetas* and *torreznos* (pork scratchings) – are delicious.

Valle del Ambroz

A little further to the west of the Valle de Jerte and almost as pleasing to the eye is the **Valle del Ambroz**. Dotted with picturesque villages set against a backdrop of some magnificent mountain scenery, the valley, which follows the Roman Vía de la Plata, heads up towards the picturesque town of **Hervás** and on towards Bejar in the region of Castilla y León.

Hervás

Pleasant little **HERVÁS**, perched on the flanks of the valley, makes a good base from which to explore the area. It also has attractions of its own, including a fascinating former Jewish quarter and a couple of small museums.

Museo de la Moto Clásica

Carretera de la Garganta • Charge, under-12s free • http://museomotoclasica.com

The overpriced **Museo de la Moto Clásica**, housed in a series of conical pavilions on the edge of town, contains an impressive though eccentrically displayed private collection of classic motorbikes, cars, bicycles and carriages, including giant Cadillacs, World War II sidecars and horse-drawn carts.

Museo Pérez Comendador-Leroux

C/Asensio Neila 5 • Charge, free Sun • http://mpcl.net

The **Museo Pérez Comendador-Leroux**, which is situated in a splendid eighteenth-century mansion, is home to works of local sculptor Enrique Pérez Comendador, his French artist wife Magdalena Leroux and some of their friends and associates.

ARRIVAL AND INFORMATION   HERVÁS

By bus Twice daily from Cáceres via Plasencia (1hr 50min), twice daily from Salamanca (1hr 40min) and three times daily from Madrid (3hr 20min).

By car From Plasencia take the N630 north towards Salamanca and then the EX205 to Hervás.

Turismo C/Braulio Navas 6 (http://turismodehervas.com).

ACCOMMODATION AND EATING

★ **Jardín del Convento** Pza. del Convento, http://eljardindelconvento.com. A beautiful and tranquil little hotel in a refurbished former nineteenth-century convent, with six rooms and a small cottage apartment with space for four people that's set in the delightful gardens. €€

★ **Restaurante Mesón Nardi** C/Braulio Navas 19, http://restaurantenardi.com. Imaginative and well-presented dishes based on local ingredients and specialities are served in this friendly place on a pedestrian street in the centre of town. €€

Las Hurdes

Las Hurdes, the abrupt rocky lands north of Plasencia, have always been a rich source of mysterious tales. According to legend, the region was unknown to the outside world until the time of Columbus, when two lovers fleeing from the court of the Duke of Alba chanced upon it. The people who welcomed them were supposedly unaware of the existence of other people or other lands. Shields and other remnants belonging to the Goth Rodrigo and his court of seven centuries earlier were discovered by the couple, giving rise to the saying that the *hurdanos* are descendants of kings.

Sixty years ago, the inhabitants of the remoter areas were still so unused to outsiders that they hid in their houses if anyone appeared. In 1932, **Luis Buñuel** filmed an unflatteringly grotesque documentary here, *Las Hurdes: Tierra Sin Pan* ("Land Without Bread"), in which it was hard to discern any royal descent in his subjects. Modernity has crept up on the villages these days, though they can still feel wild and very remote, and the soil is so barren that tiny terraces have been constructed on the riverbeds as the only way of getting the stubborn land to produce anything.

Las Hurdes villages

You could approach Las Hurdes from Plasencia, Salamanca or Ciudad Rodrigo – the region borders the Sierra de Francia (see page 360). If you're coming from Plasencia the village of **PINOFRANQUEADO** marks the start of the region. It has a campsite, *hostales* and a natural swimming pool. Fifteen kilometres farther along on the road at Vegas de Coria you can turn off to reach **NUÑOMORAL**, the village best connected to the outside world. A good base for excursions, it also has a bank alongside its **hostal** – not a common sight in these parts.

A few kilometres to the north of Nuñomoral, the tiny village of **LA HUETRE** merits a visit; take a left fork just before the village of Casares de las Hurdes. The typical slate-roofed houses are in decent condition and have an impressive setting, surrounded by steep rocky hills. Walkers might also head for the remote and disarmingly primitive settlement of **EL GASCO**, at the top of Valle de Malvellido, the next valley to the south, where there is a huge waterfall beneath the Meancera Gorge.

ARRIVAL AND INFORMATION   LAS HURDES

By bus Early-morning buses connect Nuñomoral to both Ciudad Rodrigo and Plasencia.
By car From Plasencia take the EX370 and then the EX204.
Turismo Avda. de Las Hurdes, Caminomorisco

(Wed–Sun 10am–2pm & 4.30–7.30pm; 927 435 329, http://todohurdes.com). The website http://mancomunidadhurdes.org also has plenty of useful information on the region.

ACCOMMODATION AND EATING

Hotel Hospedería Hurdes Reales C/Factoría, Las Mestas, http://hospederiasdeextremadura.es. There are large rooms, a decent restaurant, an outdoor pool and a small spa area in this modern hotel, set in beautiful surroundings in the village of Las Mestas in the northern

part of Las Hurdes. €€
Pensión El Hurdano C/La Fuente 1, Nuñomoral, 927 433 012. An excellent and inexpensive *hostal* which also serves very ample dinners. €

The Sierra de Gata

The **Sierra de Gata** creates a westerly border to Las Hurdes, in a series of wooded hills and odd outcrops of higher ground, in parts stunningly beautiful. To explore the whole region, you need your own transport and certainly a detailed local **map** – regular Spanish road maps tend to be pretty sketchy.

The Sierra de Gata is almost as isolated as Las Hurdes – in some of the villages the old people still speak *maniego*, a mix of Castilian Spanish and Portuguese. For a trip into the heart of the region, take the EX204 south from Las Hurdes to **Villanueva de la Sierra** and follow the EX205 west. A couple of kilometres past the Río Arrago, a very minor road veers north towards **Robledillo de Gata**, a village of old houses packed tightly together. A shorter, easier detour, south of the EX205, around 5km on, goes to the hilltop village of **Santibáñez el Alto**, whose oldest houses are built entirely of stone, without windows. At the top of town, look out for a tiny bullring, castle remains and the old cemetery – there's a wonderful view over the Borbollón reservoir from here. Another 3km along the EX205, a turn-off to the north takes you on a winding road up to the pretty village of **Gata**. Farther west on the EX205 is the largest village of the region, **Hoyos**, which has some impressive mansions. Lastly, farther along the EX205, another turning leads north to **San Martín de Trevejo**, one of the prettiest of the many lonely villages around.

ARRIVAL AND DEPARTURE   SIERRA DE GATA

By car Take the EX370 from Plasencia and then the EX204   northwards before bearing west onto the EX205.

ACCOMMODATION

Campsite el Merino Sierra de Gata https://camping elmerino.com. Located 7km from the village of Gata beneath hills of olive groves, this campsite has a large outdoor pool, a small bar and plenty of shade. €

Finca El Cabezo Villamiel, http://elcabezo.com. Characterful and cosy *casa rural* with six large, rustic rooms. Breakfast included in the price. €€

Hospedería Conventual Sierra de Gata Camino del Convento 39, San Martín de Trevejo, http://hospederiasde extremadura.es. Spa hotel housed in a former convent dating from the fifteenth century and in the foothills of the Sierra de Gata. Rooms are comfortable and spacious, plus the hotel has its own restaurant and an outdoor pool for use in the summer months. €€

Coria

South of the Sierra de Gata, **CORIA** makes an interesting stop. It looks nothing much from the main road, but it's actually a cool, quiet old town with lots of stately whitewashed houses. The fifteenth-century **convent** (charge) with its Gothic-Renaissance cloister is enclosed within third- and fourth-century **Roman walls**.

The Catedral
Pza. de la Catedral • **Catedral** Free • **Museum** Charge

The **Catedral** has beautifully carved west and north portals in the Plateresque style of Salamanca and, inside, the choir stalls and *retablo* are worth seeing. The building overlooks a striking medieval bridge across fields, the river having changed course three hundred years ago.

Museo Carcel Real
C/Monjas 2 • Free

The former town prison now houses the local archeological museum, **Museo Carcel Real**, with exhibits dating from the time the Celtiberians first settled in the area.

Convento del Palancar
Voluntary donation; ring the doorbell

A detour off the EX109, south of Coria, will take you to the **Convento del Palancar**, a monastery founded by San Pedro de Alcántara in the sixteenth century and said to be the smallest in the world at only seventy square metres. It's hard to imagine how a community of ten monks could have lived in these cubbyholes, though San Pedro himself set the example, sleeping upright in his cubicle. A small monastic community today occupies a more modern monastery alongside; ring the bell and a monk will come and show you around.

   To reach Palancar, turn left off the EX109 just after Torrejoncillo and follow the road towards **Pedroso de Acim**; a left turn just before the village leads to the monastery.

ARRIVAL AND INFORMATION   CORIA

By car South from the Sierra de Gata along the EX109 towards Cáceres or take the EX08 or EXA1 from Plasencia.

Turismo Inside the *ayuntamiento* on Avda. de Extremadura (http://coria.org).

3

ACCOMMODATION

Hotel Los Kekes Avda. Sierra de Gata 49, 682 656 818. A modest hotel which has twenty pleasant, air-conditioned doubles and an adjoining restaurant. €

Hotel San Cristóbal Carretera Ciudad Rodrígo, http://hotelsancristobal.net. Comfortable three-star hotel with 35 modern rooms and a decent bar and restaurant. €

Parque Natural de Monfragüe

South of Plasencia, a pair of dams, built in the 1960s, has turned the **ríos Tajo and Tiétar** into a sequence of vast reservoirs. It's an impressive sight and a tremendous area for wildlife: almost at random here you can look up to see storks, vultures and even eagles circling the skies. The best area for concerted wildlife viewing – and some very enjoyable walks – is the **PARQUE NATURAL DE MONFRAGÜE**, Extremadura's only protected area, which extends over 44,000 acres to either side of the Plasencia–Trujillo road. Transport of your own is an advantage.

Walking in the park

If you're **walking** in Monfragüe, it's best to stick to the colour-coded paths leading from the park's headquarters at **Villarreal de San Carlos**. Each of them is amply paint-blobbed and leads to rewarding birdwatching locations. Elsewhere, it is not easy to tell where you are permitted to wander – it's very easy to find yourself out of the park area in a private hunting reserve.

The Green Route

The **Green Route**, to the Cerro Gimio, is especially good – a two-and-a-half-hour stroll looping through woods and across streams, in a landscape unimaginable from Villarreal, to a dramatic clifftop viewing station.

The Red Route

The longer **Red Route** heads south of Villarreal, over a bridge across the Río Tajo, and past a fountain known as the Fuente del Francés after a young Frenchman who died there trying to save an eagle. Two kilometres farther is a great crag known as the Peñafalcón, which houses a large colony of griffon vultures, and the Castillo de Monfragüe, a castle ruin high up on a rock, with a chapel next to it; there is an observation post nearby. All these places are accessible from the EX208 and if you're coming in on the bus, you could ask to get off here. There are also two routes of 8km and 12km respectively that have been designed for **cars** and include a number of viewing points.

The dehesas

On the south side of the park, towards Trujillo, you pass through the **dehesas**, strange Africa-like plains which are among the oldest woodlands in Europe. The economy of the *dehesas* is based on grazing, and the casualties among the domestic animals provide the vultures of Monfragüe with their daily bread.

MONFRAGÜE'S WILDLIFE

There are **over two hundred species of animals in Monfragüe**, including reptiles, deer, wild boar and the ultra-rare Spanish lynx. Most important is the bird population, especially the black stork – this is the only breeding population in western Europe – and birds of prey such as the black vulture (not averse to eating tortoises), the griffon vulture (partial to carrion intestine), the Egyptian vulture (not above eating human excrement), the rare Spanish imperial eagle (identifiable by its very obvious white shoulder patches), the golden eagle and the eagle owl (the largest owl in Europe). Ornithologists should visit Monfragüe in May and June, botanists in March and April, and everybody should avoid July to September, when the heat is stifling.

ARRIVAL AND DEPARTURE

By train The nearest train station is Monfragüe, 18km from Villarreal de San Carlos and a stop for slow trains on the Madrid–Cáceres line.

By bus There is just one bus along the road, which runs between Plasencia and Torrejón El Rubio (Mon–Fri; departs from Plasencia bus station 8.30am) and stops in Villarreal de San Carlos.

By car The easiest approach to the park is along the EX208 from Plasencia to Trujillo, which runs past the park headquarters at Villarreal de San Carlos.

INFORMATION

Information centre At the park's headquarters at Villarreal de San Carlos (http://parquedemonfrague.com). Pick up a leaflet with a map detailing a range of colour-coded walks from the village and details about activities such as horseriding and walking in the park. There is also a seasonal shop, selling wildlife T-shirts and the like, and a useful guide to the park (in Spanish).

ACCOMMODATION AND EATING

VILLARREAL DE SAN CARLOS

Casa Rural El Cabrerin C/Villareal 3, http://elcabrerin.com. There are four straightforward a/c en-suite rooms in this little *casa rural* which can also be rented out as a whole for larger groups. €

Casa Rural Al Mofrag C/Villareal 19, http://casaruralalmofrag.com. Right in the centre of the park, close to the information centre, this *casa rural* has six simple, a/c, comfortable rooms and an outdoor pool open in summer. €€

Casa Rural Monfragüe C/Villareal, http://monfraguerural.com. Owned by the same people as the *Cabrerin*, this *casa rural* has six large, airy a/c rooms with an option in some of them to add an extra bed. €

TORREJÓN EL RUBIO

Hospedería Parque de Monfragüe Plasencia-trujillo 208, http://hospederiasdeextremadura.es. A classy hotel with a pool and a good restaurant offering a range of local specialities and barbecues on the terrace in summer. Clean lines and simple decor in the sixty rooms. €€

Hotel Carvajal Pza. de Pizarro 54, http://hotelcarvajal.es. Located just to the south of the park, this simple thirteen-room hotel-restaurant is friendly and good value for money. €

CAMPING

Camping Monfragüe 12km north of Villarreal on the Plasencia road, http://campingmonfrague.es. A well-equipped, year-round site near the turning to the Monfragüe train station that has a swimming pool and restaurant. It also has bikes for rent to get to Monfragüe. €

Trujillo

TRUJILLO is the most attractive town in Extremadura: a classic **conquistador** stage set of escutcheoned mansions, stork-topped towers and castle walls. A very small place, still only a little larger than its extent in *conquistador* times, much of it looks virtually untouched since the sixteenth century, and it is redolent above all of the exploits of the conquerors of the Americas; Francisco Pizarro, the conqueror of Peru, was born here, as were many of the tiny band who with such extraordinary cruelty aided him in defeating the Incas.

Plaza Mayor

At the centre of a dense web of streets is the **Plaza Mayor**, a grand square overlooked by a trio of palaces and churches, and ringed by half a dozen cafés and restaurants, around which life for most visitors revolves. In the centre is a huge bronze statue of Pizarro – by American sculptor Charles Rumsey – which was bought by the Spanish government in the late 1920s.

Palacio de la Conquista

Pza. Mayor 1

In the square's southwest corner is the **Palacio de la Conquista**, the grandest of Trujillo's mansions, with its roof adorned by statues representing the twelve months. Just one of many built by the Pizarro clan, it was originally inhabited by Pizarro's half-brother and son-in-law Hernando, who returned from the conquests to live here with his half-Inca bride Yupanqui (Pizarro's daughter).

Iglesia de San Martín
Pza. Mayor • Charge

Diagonally opposite the Palacio de la Conquista, and with a skyline of storks, is the bulky church of **San Martín**. Its tombs include, among others, that of the family of Francisco de Orellana, the first explorer of the Amazon.

Palacio de los Duques de San Carlos
C/de Mingo Ramos

The **Palacio de los Duques de San Carlos** is home to a group of nuns who moved out of their dilapidated convent up the hill and restored this palace in return for the lodgings. The chimneys on the roof boast aggressively of cultures conquered by Catholicism in the New World – they are shaped like the pyramids of Aztecs, Incas and others subjected to Spanish rule.

Palacio de Juan Pizarro de Orellana
Pza. Juan Tena • Free

Of the many other town mansions, or **solares**, the most interesting is the **Palacio de Orellana-Pizarro**, just west of the main square. Go in through the superb Renaissance arched doorway to admire the courtyard, an elegant patio decorated with the alternating coats of arms of the Pizarros – two bears with a pine tree – and the Orellanas.

North of Plaza Mayor

From the plaza, C/Ballesteros leads up to the walled upper town, past the domed **Torre del Alfiler** with its coats of arms and storks' nests, and through the fifteenth-century gateway known as the **Arco de Santiago**.

Iglesia de Santiago
Palacio Viejo O de la Cade • Free

Built up against the walls of the Arco de Santiago is the **Iglesia de Santiago**, which dates from the thirteenth century and was sometimes used as a venue for council meetings in the Middle Ages, while opposite it is the **Palacio de los Chaves**, which was where the Reyes Católicos, Fernando and Isabel, stayed when they were in town.

Iglesia de Santa María Mayor
C/Santa María 17 • Charge

The most interesting and important of the town's many churches, **Santa María Mayor** is located a short way up the hill beyond the gateway. The building is basically Gothic but contains a beautiful raised Renaissance *coro* noted for the technical mastery of its almost flat vaults. There is a fine Hispano-Flemish *reredos* (altarpiece) by Fernando Gallego, while tombs include those of the Pizarros – Francisco was baptized here – and Diego García de Paredes, a man known as the "Sansón Extremeño" (Extremaduran Samson). Among other exploits, this giant of a man, armed only with his gargantuan sword, is said to have defended a bridge against an entire French army and to have picked up the font, now underneath the *coro*, to carry holy water to his mother. You are allowed to clamber up the **tower**, which provides magnificent views of the town, the parched plains over towards Cáceres and the Sierra de Gredos.

Casa Museo Pizarro and Fundación Xavier de Salas
Calleja del Castillo • **Casa Museo Pizarro** Charge • **Fundación Xavier de Salas** Free

Located in the Pizarros' former residence, the **Casa Museo Pizarro** is a small, relatively dull affair, with little beyond period furniture and a few panels on the conquest of Peru.

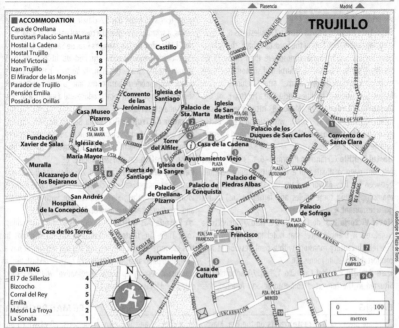

TRUJILLO

■ ACCOMMODATION

Casa de Orellana	5
Eurostars Palacio Santa Marta	2
Hostal La Cadena	4
Hostal Trujillo	10
Hotel Victoria	8
Izan Trujillo	7
El Mirador de las Monjas	3
Parador de Trujillo	1
Pensión Emilia	9
Posada dos Orillas	6

● EATING

El 7 de Sillerías	4
Bizcocho	3
Corral del Rey	5
Emilia	6
Mesón La Troya	2
La Sonata	1

For those who want to delve deeper, the **Fundación Xavier de Salas**, housed in an old Franciscan convent nearby, has more detailed exhibits on the Conquest.

Castillo

Pza. del Castillo • Charge

The **Castillo** is now virtually in open countryside; for the last hundred metres of the climb you see nothing but the occasional broken-down remnant of a wall clambered over by sheep and dogs. The fortress itself, Moorish in origin but much reinforced by later defenders, has been restored, and its main attraction is the panoramic view of the town and its environs from the battlements. As you look out over the town and on towards the distant horizon, the castle's superb defensive position is abundantly evident.

ARRIVAL AND DEPARTURE   TRUJILLO

By bus The town is well served by buses, with up to fourteen a day to and from Madrid (4–5hr) and nine from Cáceres (45min). Buses arrive in the lower town, a 5min walk from the Pza. Mayor.

By car If you're driving, follow the signs to the Pza. Mayor, and with luck you should be able to park beyond the square and farther along C/García de Paredes.

INFORMATION

Turismo Pza. Mayor (www.turismotrujillo.es). Sells discount tickets for combined visits to some of the main sites and provides guided tours (in Spanish) of the town at 11am and 4.30pm (charge).

ACCOMMODATION   SEE MAP PAGE 191

Trujillo could be visited easily enough as a day-trip from Cáceres, but it's definitely worth staying the night. **Places to stay** are in high demand – so book ahead if you can. The *turismo* can provide accommodation lists. The best rooms are in the old town close to the Pza. Mayor.

★ **Casa de Orellana** C/Palomas 5–7, http://casade orellana.com. There are just four doubles and a single in this delightful and exclusive little hotel that's located in a refurbished fifteenth-century mansion close to the Pza. Mayor. There is a patio garden with a swimming pool and the price includes breakfast. €€€

Eurostars Palacio Santa Marta C/Ballesteros 6, http://eurostarshotels.com. Part of the Eurostars chain, the *Palacio* nevertheless retains more atmosphere than many of its brethren, set in a beautiful, refurbished sixteenth-century mansion and tucked down a small street behind the Pza. Mayor. Slick, modern facilities, including a rooftop pool. €€

Hostal La Cadena Pza. Mayor 8, http://mesonhostal lacadena.es. A homely *hostal*, with simple, but nicely decorated a/c rooms overlooking all the action, and a decent café-restaurant. €

Hostal Trujillo C/Francisco Pizarro 4–6, 623 21 09 44. A pleasant *pensión* situated in a fifteenth-century building between the Pza. Mayor and the bus station. Twenty a/c rooms (including some triples and family rooms) and a good restaurant. €

Hotel Victoria Pza. de Campillo 22, http://hotelvictoria trujillo.es. A friendly three-star hotel in an elegant old nineteenth-century mansion, with a pool, restaurant and comfortable en-suite rooms. €€

Izan Trujillo Pza. del Campillo 1, http://izanhoteles.es. Situated in the converted Convento de San Antonio, this swish four-star hotel has 72 classically decorated double rooms, a swimming pool and a covered patio-bar area. €

★ **El Mirador de las Monjas** Pza. de Santiago 2, http://elmiradordelasmonjas.com. Situated up in the old part of town by the castle, this homely *hostería* has five comfy rooms with modern bathrooms and a good restaurant serving some excellent local produce and a varied, and very good quality, set lunch. €

Parador de Trujillo Pza. Santa Beatriz de Silva, http://parador.es. Top-end accommodation in a sixteenth-century former *convento* north of the Pza. Mayor. Two beautiful cloistered patio areas and large rooms. €€

Pensión Emilia Pza. Campillo 28, www.facebook.com/HostalRestauranteEmilia. A clean and comfortable *pensión* located down by the main road into town, with warm decor and a restaurant and bar downstairs. €

★ **Posada dos Orillas** C/Cambrones 6, http://dosorillas.com. There are thirteen individually designed rooms in this converted inn in the heart of the old quarter. It has a delightful patio area, where you can have breakfast, and a restaurant serving up some imaginative, well-presented salads and local specialities. €€

EATING

SEE MAP PAGE 191

There are plenty of **bar-restaurants** on the Pza. Mayor, and for budget eating, all the *pensiones* around Pza. Campillo have reasonably priced set menus on offer. At the weekend, **nightlife** revolves around the streets splaying out of Pza. Mayor and down in the newer parts of town.

El 7 de Sillerías Sillerías 7, http://el7desillerias.com. Friendly service, a café-bar area, a pleasant interior patio and a *menú del día* (Mon–Thurs lunch) that is a notch above many of the other restaurants in its class. Located close to the Pza. Mayor. €€

Bizcocho Pza. Mayor 11, http://restaurantebizcochoplaza.com. A reliable restaurant serving regional specialities and good meat dishes. It has two separate dining areas and a summer terrace looking out on to the plaza. €€

Corral del Rey Plazuela Corral del Rey 2, 689 19 09 35. Housed in a sixteenth-century mansion, this well-regarded restaurant specializes in roast meats, Extremeño stews, local cheeses and home-made desserts, all of which are delicious. €€

Emilia Pza. Campillo 28, http://facebook.com/Hostal RestauranteEmilia. A *pensión* located down towards the main road, which offers one of the most competitive set menus in town. €€

Mesón La Troya Pza. Mayor 10, http://mesonlatroya.es. Trujillo's best-known restaurant. Offers huge set menus at great prices, although it is a case of quantity over quality and they'll probably serve you a giant *tortilla* as a starter before you have even ordered. €€

La Sonata C/Ballesteros 10, 927 322 884. Tucked away in a street just north of the Pza. Mayor, this serves some well-presented Extremeño specialities. It does a good set lunch and more sophisticated à la carte options featuring mains such as duck and lamb. €€

Guadalupe

The small town of **GUADALUPE**, perched up in the sierra to the west of Trujillo, is dominated in every way by the great **Monasterio de Nuestra Señora de Guadalupe**, which for five centuries has brought fame and pilgrims to the area. It was established in 1340, on the spot where an ancient image of the Virgin, said to have been carved by St Luke, was discovered by a shepherd fifty or so years earlier. The delay was simply a question of waiting for the Reconquest to arrive in this remote sierra, with its lush countryside of forests and streams. In the fifteenth and sixteenth centuries, Guadalupe was among the most important pilgrimage centres in Spain: Columbus named the Caribbean island in honour of the Virgin here, and a local version was adopted as the patron saint of Mexico. Much of the monastic wealth, in fact, came from returning

conquistadores, whose successive endowments led to a fascinating mix of styles. The monastery was abandoned in the nineteenth-century Dissolution, but was later reoccupied by Franciscans, who continue to maintain it.

The town itself is a fitting complement to the monastery and countryside: a network of narrow cobbled streets and overhanging houses constructed around the Pza. Mayor, the whole overshadowed by the monastery's bluff ramparts. There's a timeless feel, only slightly diminished by modern development on the outskirts, and a brisk trade in plastic copies of religious treasures.

The church and monastery
Church Free • Monastery Charge • http://monasterioguadalupe.com

The **monastery church** opens onto the Pza. Mayor (aka Pza. de Santa María). Its gloomy Gothic interior is, like the rest of the monastery, packed with treasures from generations of wealthy patrons.

The entrance to the **monastery** proper is to the left of the church. The (compulsory) guided tour begins with a Mudéjar **cloister** – two brick storeys of horseshoe arches with a strange pavilion or tabernacle in the middle – and moves on to the **museums**, which has an apparently endless collection of rich vestments, early illuminated manuscripts and religious paraphernalia, along with some fine artworks including a triptych by Isenbrandt and a small Goya. The **Sacristía**, beyond, is the finest room in the monastery. Unaltered since it was built in the seventeenth century, it contains eight paintings by Zurbarán, which, uniquely, can be seen in their original context – the frames match the window frames and the pictures themselves are a planned part of the decoration of the room.

Climbing higher into the heart of the monastery, you pass through various rooms filled with jewels and relics before the final ascent to the Holy of Holies – the Camarín. From this tiny room high above the main altar you can look down over the church while a panel is spun away to reveal the highlight of the tour – the bejewelled and richly dressed **image of the Virgin**. The Virgin is one of the few black icons ever made – originally carved out of dark cedarwood, its colour has further deepened over the centuries under innumerable coats of varnish. The story goes that the image was originally carved by St Luke, made its way to Spain and was then hidden during the Arab occupation for over five hundred years. It was eventually rediscovered by a local cowherd on the banks of the Río Guadalupe at the beginning of the thirteenth century.

On the way out, drop in at the **Hospedería del Real Monasterio**, around to the right. The bar, in its Gothic cloister, with lovely gardens outside, is one of the world's more unusual places to enjoy a *Cuba libre*.

ARRIVAL AND DEPARTURE
GUADALUPE

By bus Buses leave from either side of Avda. de Barcelona, uphill from the *ayuntamiento*, 200m from the Pza. Mayor: Mirat operates services to Trujillo and Cáceres, Samar runs buses to Madrid (some change at Talavera de a Reina). Destinations Cáceres (2 daily; 2hr 30min); Madrid (1–2 daily; 3hr 45min); Trujillo (2 daily; 2hr–2hr 30min).

INFORMATION

Turismo Pza. Mayor (http://guadalupeturismo.com).

ACCOMMODATION

There are plenty of **places to stay** in Guadalupe and the only times you're likely to have difficulty finding a room are during Easter Week or around September 8, the Virgin's festival day.

★ **Hospedaría del Real Monasterio** Pza. Juan Carlos s/n, http://hospederiaguadalupe.es. Housed in a wing of the monastery and popular with Spanish pilgrims, this place is much better value than the parador, is very atmospheric and serves excellent food in the giant dining room, too. €€

Hostal Alba Taruta C/Alfonso Onceno 16, 670 44 91 76. Friendly, family-run *hostal* close to the main plaza with simple old-style rooms. The *comedor* downstairs serves an inexpensive range of *platos*. €

Parador de Guadalupe C/Marqués de la Romana 12, http://parador.es. A beautiful parador, housed in a fifteenth-century hospital and a former school, with a swimming pool and immaculate patio gardens. €€

CAMPING

Las Villuercas http://campinglasvilluercasguadalupe.es.

EATING

You can **eat** at most *hostales* and *pensiones*, with just about everywhere – including the restaurants on Pza. Mayor – serving good-value set menus.

Hospedaría del Real Monasterio Pza. Juan Carlos s/n, http://hospederiaguadalupe.es. A great setting for a meal, with a choice of the grand dining room or the outdoor courtyard. €€

Some 2km out of town towards Trujillo, close to the main road. A quiet campsite with a pool and bar-restaurant. €

★ **Posada del Rincón** Pza. Santa María de Guadalupe 11, www.posadadelrincon.com. Excellent regional cooking in this friendly restaurant close to the main square. Quality meat dishes and local specialities such as *morcillas de Guadalupe*. There are differently priced set menus on weekdays and weekends (cheaper during the week). €€

The Sierra de Guadalupe

A truly superb view of Guadalupe set in its sierra can also be enjoyed from the road (EX118) north to Navalmoral. Five kilometres out of town, the **Ermita del Humilladero** marks the spot where pilgrims traditionally caught their first glimpse of the monastery.

The surrounding **Sierra de Guadalupe** is a wild and beautiful region, with steep, rocky crags abutting the valley sides. If you have your own transport, you could strike northwest of the EX102 at Cañamero, up to the village of **Cabañas del Castillo**, nestling against a massive crag and ruined castle; the handful of houses are mostly empty, as only twelve inhabitants remain. Beyond here, you can reach the main **Navalmoral–Trujillo road** close to the **Puerto de Miravete**, a fabulous viewpoint, with vistas of Trujillo in the far distance. Another great driving route, again leaving the EX102 at Cañamero, is to follow the narrow road **through Berzocana** to Trujillo.

Cáceres

CÁCERES is in many ways remarkably like Trujillo. It features an almost perfectly preserved walled town, the Ciudad Monumental, packed with *solares* built on the proceeds of American exploration, while every available tower and spire is crowned by a clutch of storks' nests. As a provincial capital, however, Cáceres is a much larger and livelier place, especially in termtime, when the students of the University of Extremadura are in residence. With its Roman, Moorish and *conquistador* sights, and a number of great bars and restaurants, it is an absorbing and highly enjoyable city. It also provides a dramatic backdrop for an annual **WOMAD** (World of Music, Arts and Dance) festival, held over the second weekend in May and attracting up to seventy thousand spectators.

The walled **Old Town** stands at the heart of Cáceres, with a picturesque **Pza. Mayor** just outside its walls. These are basically Moorish in construction, though parts date back to the Romans – notably the **Arco del Cristo** – and they have been added to, refortified and built against throughout the centuries. The most intact section, with several original adobe Moorish towers, runs in a clockwise direction, facing the walls from the Pza. Mayor. Almost everything of interest is contained within – or a short walk from –this area; try to base yourself as close to it as possible.

The Old Town

Entering the Old Town – the **Parte Vieja**, as it's also known – from the Pza. Mayor, you pass through the low **Arco de la Estrella**, an entrance built by Manuel Churriguera in the eighteenth century. To your left is the **Torre de Bujaco** (charge), which dates from the twelfth century and is named after the Caliph Abú-Ya'qub who conquered the city in 1173. The tower houses an interactive exhibition about the history of the city. At the corner of the walls is one of the most imposing *conquistador solares*, the **Casa de Toledo-Moctezuma** with its domed tower. It was to this house that a follower of Cortés brought back one of the New World's more exotic prizes, a daughter of the Aztec

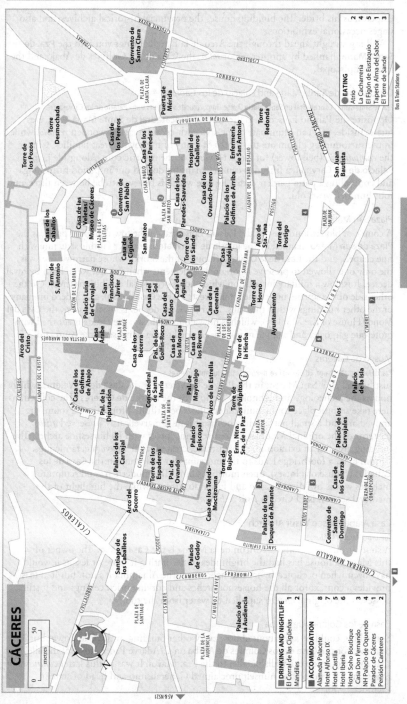

CÁCERES

0 ——— 50 metres

● EATING

Atrio	2
La Cacharrería	4
El Figón de Eustaquio	5
Tapería Alma del Sabor	1
El Torre de Sande	3

Bus & Train Stations ▶

■ **DRINKING AND NIGHTLIFE**

El Corral de las Cigüeñas	1
Mandiles	2

■ **ACCOMMODATION**

Alameda Palacete	8
Hotel Alfonso IX	7
Hotel Castilla	5
Hotel Iberia	6
Hotel Soho Boutique	3
Casa Don Fernando	4
NH Palacio de Oquendo	1
Parador de Cáceres	2
Pensión Carretero	2

Convento de Santa Clara
Torre Desmochada
Torre de los Pozos
Puerta de Mérida
Casa de los Pereros
C/PUERTA DE MÉRIDA
Torre Redonda
Casa Pablo Casa de los Sánchez Paredes
Hospital de Caballeros
Enfermería de San Antonio
San Juan Bautista
Casa de las Veletas / Museo de Cáceres
Convento de San Pablo
Casa de los Paredes-Saavedra
Casa de los Ovando-Perero
Palacio de los Golfines de Arriba
Casa de los Caballos
Erm. de S. Antonio
San Mateo
Casa de la Cigüeña
Torre de los Sande
Casa Mudéjar
Arco de Sta. Ana
Torre del Postigo
Palacio Luisa de Carvajal
San Francisco Javier
Casa del Sol
Casa del Águila
Casa de la Generala
Torre del Horno
Casa Árabe
Casa de los Becerra
Pal. de los Golfines-Roco
Casa del Mono
Casa de los Moraga
Casa de los Rivera
Ayuntamiento
Arco del Cristo
Casa de los Golfines de Abajo
Pal. de la Diputación
Concatedral de Santa María
Pal. de Mayoralgo
Arco de la Estrella
Torre de los Púlpitos
Torre de la Hierba
Palacio de la Isla
Palacio Episcopal
Erm. Ntra. Sra. de la Paz
Palacio de los Carvajales
Palacio de los Carvajal
Torre de los Espaderos
Pal. de Ovando
Casa de los Toledo-Moctezuma
Torre de Bujaco
Plaza Mayor
Casa de los Galarza
Convento de Santo Domingo
Arco del Socorro
Casa de los Duques de Abrante
Palacio de los Duques de Abrante
C/GENERAL MARGALLO
Santiago de los Caballeros
Palacio de Godoy
Palacio de la Audiencia

emperor, as his bride. The building houses the provincial historical archives, and also stages occasional exhibitions.

Walking straight ahead through the Arco de la Estrella brings you into the **Pza. de Santa María**, flanked by another major *solar*, the Casa de los Golfines de Abajo and the Palacio Episcopal.

Concatedral de Santa María and Palacio de los Carvajal

Pza. de Santa María • **Concatedral de Santa María** Charge • http://concatedralcaceres.com • **Palacio de los Carvajal** Free

Opposite the Palacio Episcopal is the Gothic **Concatedral de Santa María** – Cáceres' finest. Inside, you can illuminate a fine sixteenth-century carved wooden *retablo*, while in the surrounding gloom are the tombs of many of the town's great families. Climb the *campanario* (bell tower) for fantastic views of the historic core. Alongside is the **Palacio de los Carvajal**, a fifteenth-century mansion decked out in period furnishings and concealing a patio garden with a fig tree which is believed to be between three and four hundred years old.

3

Plaza San Mateo

A couple of blocks southwest of the Palacio Episcopal, at the town's highest point, is the **Plaza de San Mateo**, flanked by the **Iglesia de San Mateo**, another Gothic structure with fine chapels, and the **Casa de la Cigüeña** (House of the Stork), whose narrow tower was the only one allowed to preserve its original battlements when the rest were shorn by royal decree. It is now a military installation which holds occasional exhibitions (free). On the other side of the square, notice the **family crests** on the **Casa del Sol**, and indeed on many of the other buildings within the walls. Near the Casa del Sol is another *solar*, the **Casa del Mono** (House of the Monkey), which is now a public library; the facade is adorned with grotesque gargoyles and a stone monkey is chained to the staircase in the courtyard.

Museo de Cáceres

Pza. de las Veletas • Charge, EU citizens free, free Sun • http://turismo.caceres.es

Just behind Pza. San Mateo, in the Pza. de las Veletas, is the **Casa de las Veletas**, which houses the archeology and ethnology sections of the **Museo de Cáceres**. The collections here take second place to the building itself: its beautifully proportioned rooms are arrayed around a small patio, while below ground a marvellously preserved *aljibe* (cistern) of the original Moorish Alcázar remains intact with its horseshoe arches. The building also has an extraordinary balustrade, created from Talavera ceramic jugs.

From here, a footbridge leads to the museum's art collection in the **Casa de los Caballos** (House of Horses), open mornings only. The modern art and sculpture includes works by Miró, Picasso and Eduardo Arroyo, while the highlight of the medieval section is El Greco's *Jesús Salvador*.

Casa Árabe/Museo Yusuf Al Burch

Cuesta del Marqués 4 • Charge

A short stroll away along C/Rincón de la Monja is the **Casa Árabe**. The owner of this Moorish house has had the bright idea of decorating it more or less as it would have been when occupied by its original owner. The Alhambra it's not, but it at least provides a context for all the horseshoe arches and curving brick ceilings and it still possesses the original cistern supplied by water from the roof.

Casa de los Golfines de Arriba

Something could be said about almost every other building in the Old Town, but look out, too, for the **Casa de los Golfines de Arriba** on C/Adarve Padre Rosalío, the allcyway that runs alongside the walls parallel to the Pza. Mayor. It was in this latter *conquistador* mansion that Franco had himself proclaimed Generalísimo and head of state in October 1936.

Outside the walls

Outside the walls, it's worth wandering up to the sixteenth-century **church of Santiago de los Caballeros**, which fronts the plaza of the same name, opposite a more or less contemporary mansion, **Palacio de Godoy**, with its corner balcony. The church, open only for Masses, has a fine *retablo* by Alonso Berruguete. For a good **view** of the Old Town, exit the walls through the Arco del Cristo down to the main road and turn right onto C/Fuente Concejo, following the signs for about five minutes or so.

ARRIVAL AND DEPARTURE   CÁCERES

By train or bus Both the train and bus stations are around 3km out from the old town, at the far end of Avda. de Alemania. It's not a particularly enjoyable walk, so it's best to take bus #1, which runs down the *avenida* to Pza. de San Juan, a square adjoining the Pza. Mayor; an irregular shuttle bus from the train station (free if you show a rail ticket) also runs into town, to the Pza. de América, a major traffic junction west of the Old Town.

Train destinations Badajoz (4–6 daily; 1hr 45min); Madrid (4–5 daily; 3hr 45min–4hr 15min); Mérida (4–6 daily; 1hr). Bus destinations Alcántara (2–4 daily; 1hr 30min);

Badajoz (4 daily; 1hr 15min); Coria (2 daily; 1hr); Madrid (7 daily; 3hr 45min–4hr 50min); Mérida (3 daily; 1hr–1hr 30min); Plasencia (4 daily; 1hr 15min); Salamanca (8–9 daily; 3hr–3hr 45min); Seville (8 daily; 3hr 10min–3hr 45min); Trujillo (6 daily; 45min).

By car If you're driving, be warned that increasing pedestrianization is making access to some streets impossible by car; your best bet is to park on Avda. de España, on the main road in from Madrid, or outside the Old Town.

INFORMATION

Turismo C/Amargura 1 (Mon & Tues 8am–8.45pm, Sat 10am–1.45pm & 5–7.45pm; 927 255 597, http://turismo.

caceres.es). There is also tourist information on the local council website http://ayto-caceres.es.

ACCOMMODATION   SEE MAP PAGE 195

★ **Alameda Palacete** C/Margallo 45, http://alameda palacete.com. This delightful little hotel not far from the Pza. Mayor has eight fascinatingly decorated rooms, each with its own individual ambience. Breakfast included. €̄

Hotel Alfonso IX C/Moret 20, http://hotelalfonsoix.com. Well located on a pedestrianized street off C/Pintores, this 37-room hotel offers smart en-suite rooms with a/c and satellite TV. Apartments are also available through the website. €€€

Hotel Castilla C/Ríos Verdes 3, http://hotelcastillacaceres. com. Upgraded from a *hostal* to a hotel, the *Castilla* has neat, functional en-suite rooms and a good central location. €̄

Hotel Iberia C/Pintores 2, http://iberiahotel.com. A tastefully restored 37-room hotel, complete with period furnishings, located in a mansion in a corner of the Pza. Mayor. Breakfast included. €̄

★ **Hotel Soho Boutique Casa Don Fernando** Pza. Mayor 30, www.sohohoteles.com/en/hotel-soho-

boutique-casa-don-fernando-3-en. Perfectly situated on the main plaza, this slick, designer-style hotel has 38 stylishly furnished doubles, including some large attic rooms, and a decent café-bar. €̄

NH Palacio de Oquendo Pza. de San Juan 11, http://nh-hotels.com. Now part of the NH chain, this smart, well-appointed hotel is in a sixteenth-century palace, just outside the walls of the Old Town. Some of the pastel-coloured rooms have views over the plaza. €€

Parador de Cáceres C/Ancha 6, http://parador.es. The parador occupies an elegant and atmospheric *conquistador* mansion in the Ciudad Monumental. Prices vary considerably depending on the time of year. €€

Pensión Carretero Pza. Mayor 22, http://pension carretero.com. Basic, but great-value *pensión* with large doubles and spotless bathrooms – though some rooms can be noisy at the weekend. €̄

EATING   SEE MAP PAGE 195

There is a good range of **bars**, **restaurants** and **bodegas** in and around the Pza. Mayor, while the Old Town offers a bit more style at modest prices.

RESTAURANTS

★ **Atrio** Pza. de San Mateo 1, http://restauranteatrio. com. An exclusive Michelin-starred restaurant, located in the Old Town in a designer hotel of the same name, with

an extensive menu and sophisticated food. As you would expect the food is superlative, but so are the prices with the taster menus starting at over €100. €€€€

La Cacharrería C/Orellana 1, 927 030 723. One of the best places for tapas in the centre. The *salmorejo*, *croquetas* and *puntas de solomillo con torta* (small chunks of steak in sheep's cheese) are excellent, and most tapas are very cheap. You may have to wait for a table though, as they

3

don't take reservations. €

★ **El Figón de Eustaquio** Pza. de San Juan 12, http:// elfigondeeustaquio.com. This long-established and popular restaurant features an extensive list of regional dishes, cooked with care. €€

Tapería Alma del Sabor Pza. de las Veletas 4, http:// restaurantealmadelsabor.com. Located in an old square inside the walled town and next to the Museo de Cáceres,

this restaurant has some excellent regional tapas on offer and a wine list consisting solely of local varieties. €€

★ **El Torre de Sande** C/Los Condes 3, https://atriocaceres. com/en/the-bistro. Another top-class restaurant in the middle of the Old Town, from the people behind *Atrio*, with refined food and attentive service. There is a delightful summer terrace serving tapas and *raciones* too. €€€

DRINKING AND NIGHTLIFE

SEE MAP PAGE 195

In addition to the bars in and near Old Town, Cáceres has the best nightlife in the region – especially during termtime – with the night starting off in the bars along C/Pizarro, south of Pza. de San Juan, moving on to C/Dr Fleming and the discos in the nearby Pza. de Albatros. There are several late-night bars around Pza. Mayor and a string of interesting watering holes in and around C/Donoso Cortés, while live music can be heard in many places along the nearby C/General Ezponda.

★ **El Corral de las Cigüeñas** Cuesta de Aldana 6, http://

elcorralcc.com. A beautiful spot in the Old Town with tables in a large, palm-shaded courtyard. A great place to enjoy a breakfast snack, a lunchtime aperitivo or a night-time cocktail. Live music and other acts.

Mandiles C/Sergio Sanchéz 7, www.facebook.com/pequegin. This popular bar a few minutes' walk to the northwest of the Old Town is hard to miss with its pink exterior and dark wooden decor. A wide gin menu, and a good music selection at night with 1980s and 1990s classics at weekends.

Northwest of Cáceres

Northwest of Cáceres is the vast **Embalse de Alcántara**, one of a series of reservoirs harnessing the power of the Río Tajo in the last few kilometres before it enters Portugal. The scheme swallowed up large tracts of land and you can see the old road and railway to Plasencia disappearing into the depths of the reservoir (their replacements cross the many inlets on double-decker bridges), along with the tower of a castle.

The EX207 loops away to the south of the reservoir, through **Arroyo de la Luz** and **Brozas**, each with fine churches, before reaching **Alcántara**, with its superb Roman bridge across the Tajo. The Portuguese border – and the road to Costelo Branco and Coimbra – is just a dozen kilometres beyond.

Alcántara

The name **ALCÁNTARA** comes from the Arabic for "bridge" – in this case a beautiful six-arched **Puente Romano** spanning a gorge of the Río Tajo. Completed in AD 105, and held together without mortar, it was reputed to be the loftiest bridge ever built in the Roman Empire, although it's far from certain which bits, if any, remain genuinely Roman.

The bridge is quite a distance from the town itself, which is built high above the river; if you're on foot, don't follow the signs via the road – instead, head to the far side of the town and down the steep cobbled path.

Further Roman remains include a **triumphal arch** dedicated to Trajan and a tiny **classical temple**. The dominating landmark, however, is the restored **Convento San Benito**, erstwhile headquarters of the Knights of Alcántara, one of the great orders of the Reconquest. For all its enormous bulk, the convent and its church are only a fragment; the nave of the church was never built. Outside, the main feature is the double-arcaded Renaissance gallery at the back; it serves as the backdrop for a season of classical plays in August. There are frequent guided tours of the convent (free) with its cloister, Plateresque east end and elaborate wall tombs.

Alcántara also contains the scanty remains of a **castle**, numerous **mansions** and street after street of humble whitewashed houses. The place is marvellous for scenic walks, whether in the town, along the banks of the Tajo or – best of all – in the hills on the opposite bank.

ARRIVAL AND INFORMATION

By bus Buses, which run twice a day to and from Cáceres, stop at a little square ringed by cafés at the entrance to the historic part of the town.

Turismo Avda. de Mérida 21 (http://alcantara.es). Very helpful and can provide a town map.

ACCOMMODATION

Hospedería Conventual Carretera Poblado de Iberdrola s/n, http://hospederiasdeextremadura.es. A little way to the north of the town, this good-value thirty-room hotel is housed in a beautifully restored fifteenth-century convent. Large rooms, modern bathrooms, a pool and a good restaurant. €€

Mérida

Some 70km to the south of Cáceres on the N630 is the former capital of the Roman province of Lusitania, **MÉRIDA** (the name is a corruption of *Emerita Augusta*), which contains more **Roman remains** than any other city in Spain. Even for the most casually interested, the extent and variety of the remains here are compelling, with everything from engineering works to domestic villas, by way of cemeteries and places of worship, entertainment and culture. With a little imagination, and a trip to the wonderful modern museum, the Roman city is not difficult to evoke – which is just as well, for the modern city, in which the sites are scattered, is no great shakes.

Each July and August, the Roman theatre in the town hosts a **theatre festival** (http://festivaldemerida.es), including performances of classical Greek plays and Shakespeare's Roman tragedies.

The Roman sites

Built on the site of a Celtiberian settlement and founded by Emperor Augustus in 25 BC as a home for retired legionaries, Mérida became the tenth city of the Roman Empire and the final stop on the Vía de la Plata, the Roman road that began in Astorga in northern Castile. The old city stretched as far as the modern bullring and Roman circus, covering only marginally less than the triangular area occupied by the modern town.

The Puente Romano and Alcazaba

Pza. Roma 1a • Charge

The obvious point to begin your tour is the magnificent **Puente Romano**, the bridge across the islet-strewn Río Guadiana. It is sixty arches long (the seven in the middle are fifteenth-century replacements) and was still in use until the early 1990s, when the nearby **Puente de Lusitania** – itself a structure to admire – was constructed by Spanish architect Santiago Calatrava.

Defence of the old bridge was provided by a vast **Alcazaba**, built by the Moors to replace a Roman construction. The interior is a rather barren archeological site, although in the middle there's an *aljibe* to which you can descend by either of a pair of staircases.

Templo de Diana to the Arco Trajano

Museo de Arte Visigodo C/Santa Julia 1 • Charge, under 18s free • http://cultura.gob.es/mnromano/home.html

---

COMBINED TICKET IN MÉRIDA

The best way to see the Roman sites is to buy the excellent-value **combined ticket**, valid over a number of days. It covers the Teatro Romano and Anfiteatro, the Roman villas Casa del Anfiteatro and Casa del Mitreo, the Columbarios burial ground, the Circo Romano, the archeological site at Morerías, the Alcazaba and the Basílica de Santa Eulalia though not the Museo de Arte Romano, and is available at any of the sites.

3

MÉRIDA

EATING
Pepe Osorio	2
La Tahona, Casa de Comidas	1

ACCOMMODATION
Deluxe Hostel	1
La Flor de al-Andalus	2
Hostal Emeritae	5
Hostal Senero	4
Hotel Adealba	7
Hotel Ilunion Mérida Palace	6
Hotel Nova Roma	8
Parador Vía de la Plata	3

Cáceres (N630) & Madrid (A5)

Cáceres (N630) & Madrid (A5)

Acueducto de San Lázaro

Circo Romano

AVENIDA REINA SOFÍA

FERROCARRIL MADRID-BADAJOZ

C/CABO VERDE

Casa Romana del Anfiteatro

Termas

Anfiteatro

Museo Nac. de Arte Romano

Teatro Romano

Columbarios

Casa Romana del Mitreo

AVENIDA DE EXTREMADURA

Obelisco de Sta. Eulalia

Sta. Eulalia

Plaza de Toros

Pórtico del Foro Munic.

Templo de Diana

Train Station

Acueducto de Los Milagros

Restos del Foro Provincial

Arco de Trajano

Alcazaba y Conventual

Río Albarregas

Plaza de la Constitución

Morerías site

Museo de Arte Visigodo

Santa María la Mayor

Plaza de España

Puente Romano

Torre de Agua

Guadiana

Puente Romano

Río

Guadiana

Puente de Lusitania

AVENIDA J. FERNÁNDEZ LÓPEZ

Badajoz (A5) & Seville (N630)

N

0   250
metres

Bus Station

Northeast of the Alcazaba, past the airy sixteenth-century Pza. de España, the heart of the modern town, is the so-called **Templo de Diana**, adapted into a Renaissance mansion, and farther along are remains of the **Foro**, the heart of the Roman city. To the west of the plaza in C/Santa Julia, the Convento de Santa Clara houses the **Museo de Arte Visigodo**, which has a collection of about a hundred lapidary items. It will eventually be housed alongside the Museo Nacional de Arte Romano. Just behind here is the great **Arco Trajano**, once wrongly believed to be a triumphal arch; it was, in fact, a marble-clad granite monumental gate to the forum.

Morerías archeological site
Pza. Roma • Charge

Heading to the river from the Arco Trajano you'll also discover the **Morerías archeological site** along C/Morerías, where you can watch the digging and preservation of houses and factories from Roman through Visigoth to Moorish times – particularly of interest are the well-preserved Roman mosaics.

Teatro Romano, Anfiteatro and Casa Romana del Anfiteatro
Pza. Margarita Xirgu • **Teatro Romano and Anfiteatro** Charge

A ten-minute walk east of the Pza. de España will take you to Mérida's main archeological site containing the theatre and amphitheatre. The elaborate and beautiful **Teatro Romano** is one of the best preserved anywhere in the Roman Empire. Constructed around 15 BC, it was a present to the city from Agrippa, as indicated by the large inscription above the passageway to the left of the stage. The stage itself, a two-tier colonnaded affair, is in particularly good shape, and many of the seats have been entirely rebuilt to offer more comfort to the audiences of the annual July and August season of classical plays (http://festivaldemerida.es).

Adjoining the theatre is the **Anfiteatro**, a slightly later and very much plainer construction. As many as 15,000 people – almost half the current population of Mérida – could be seated to watch gladiatorial combats and fights with wild animals. The **Casa Romana del Anfiteatro** lies immediately below the museum, and offers an approach to it from the site. It has wonderful mosaics, including a vigorous depiction of grape-treading.

The Museo Nacional de Arte Romano
C/José Ramón Mélida • Charge, free Sat after 2pm & Sun am • www.cultura.gob.es/mnromano/home.html

The **Museo Nacional de Arte Romano**, constructed in 1986 above the Roman walls, is a wonderfully light, accessible building, using a free interpretation of classical forms to present the mosaics and sculpture as if emerging from the ruins. The exhibits, displayed on three levels of the basilica-like hall, include statues from the theatre, the Roman villa of **Mitreo** (see page 202) and the vanished forum, and a number of mosaics –the largest being hung on the walls so that they can be examined at each level. Individually, the finest exhibits are probably the three statues, displayed together, depicting Augustus, the first Roman emperor; his son Tiberius, the second emperor; and Drusus, Augustus' heir apparent until (it is alleged) he was murdered by Livia, Tiberius' mother.

The ruins outside the centre
Santa Eulalia Av. Extremadura 11 • Charge • **Casa del Mitreo and Columbarios burial ground** Calle Oviedo • Charge

The remaining monuments are on the other side of the train tracks. From the museum, it's a fifteen-minute walk if you cut down the streets towards Avenida de Extremadura and then head east out of the city to the **Circo Romano**, essentially an outline, where up to thirty thousand spectators could watch horse and chariot races. Across the road from here, a stretch of the **Acueducto de San Lázaro** leads off towards the Río Albarregas.

The more impressive aqueduct, however, is the **Acueducto de los Milagros**, of which a satisfying portion survives in the midst of vegetable gardens, west of the train station. Its tall arches of granite, with brick courses, brought water to the city in its earliest days from the reservoir at Proserpina, 5km away. The best view of the aqueduct is from a low and inconspicuous **Puente Romano** across the Río Albarregas; it was over this span that the Vía de la Plata entered the city.

Two further sights are the church of **Santa Eulalia**, by the train station, which has a porch made from fragments of a former temple of Mars, and a second Roman villa, the **Mitreo**, in the shadow of the Pza. de Toros, south of the museum and theatres. The villa has a magnificent but damaged mosaic depicting the cosmos. A short walk away is the **Columbarios burial ground**, which has two family sepulchres and an interesting series of exhibits on Roman death rites.

Proserpina and Cornalvo reservoirs

You can swim in the **Embalse de Proserpina**, a Roman-constructed reservoir 5km north of town (special bus #13 in the morning and afternoon from Paseo de Roma, June–Aug; charge), and a popular escape to cool off in summer; it's lined with holiday homes, has a campsite and a small beach area, but is best avoided at weekends. Alternatively, if you have transport, head to the **Embalse de Cornalvo**, 18km east of Mérida (turn left after the village of Trujillanos). There's a Roman dyke here, and a small national park has been created in the area with walking trails in the surrounding forest.

ARRIVAL AND DEPARTURE   MÉRIDA

By train The train station is pretty central, with the theatre site and Pza. de España no more than a 10min walk away.

Destinations Badajoz (6 daily; 40–55min); Cáceres (5 daily; 55min–1hr); Madrid (7 daily; 4hr 40min–5hr 40min); Plasencia (3 daily; 2hr–2hr 15min); Seville (daily; 3hr 40min).

By bus The bus station is on the other side of the river and is

a grittier 20min walk from the town centre, along Avda. de Libertad, which extends from the new single-arch bridge.

Destinations Badajoz (7–8 daily; 50min); Cáceres (3 daily; 1hr); Jerez de los Caballeros (1 daily; 1hr 55min); Madrid (7 daily; 4hr 15min); Salamanca (5 daily; 4hr 10min–5hr 5min); Seville (6 daily; 2hr 50min), Zafra (7–8 daily; 1hr 10min).

INFORMATION

Turismo Just outside the gates to the theatre and amphitheatre site (daily April–Sept 9am–9pm; Oct–March 9am–6.30pm; 924 330 722, http://turismomerida.org). There is another office (April–Sept Mon–Wed 9am–9pm,

Thurs–Sun 9.30am–2pm & 5.30–8.30pm, Oct–March Mon–Wed 9am–7.30pm, Thurs–Sun 9.30am–2pm & 5–7.30pm; 924 380 191) at C/Santa Eulalia 62.

ACCOMMODATION   SEE MAP PAGE 200

Deluxe Hostel C/Marquesa de Pinares 36, http://deluxe hostels.es. Well-positioned *hostal* with small, plain but comfortable, en-suite rooms. Some rooms have terraces, and there's an outdoor pool – welcome in the summer months. €

★ **La Flor de al-Andalus** Avda. Extremadura 6, http:// hostallaflordeal-andalus.com. A self-styled boutique *hostal* close to the train station and with eighteen rooms decorated in Andalucian style, each named after a flower and with a/c. Triples and quadruples available. €€

Hostal Emeritae C/Sagasta 40, http://hostalemeritae. com. A sophisticated *hostal* with nineteen cosy a/c doubles, two triples, one family room and a couple of suites. Pastel colours, stylish bathrooms and a neat little patio area. €

Hostal Senero C/Holguin 12, http://hostalsenero.com. A long-established, friendly *hostal* with neat a/c rooms situated around a quiet courtyard and close to the main plaza. €

Hotel Adealba C/Ramiro Leal 18, http://adealba.com. This design-conscious four-star hotel close to the Alcazaba has large rooms with wooden floors and clean lines and a spa. The high-season price is exorbitant, but look out for offers on the website, which can halve the price. €€

Hotel Ilunion Mérida Palace Pza. España 19, http:// ilunionmeridapalace.com. A 76-room, five-star hotel located in an elegant mansion on the Plaza España. Large, bright rooms with classically inspired decor, an outdoor pool and beautiful colonnaded entrance hall. €€€

Hotel Nova Roma C/Suárez Somonte 42, http://novaroma. com. A good location for this functional and well-established 55-room hotel. Rooms are neat, if a little old-fashioned, service is friendly and there is parking, though it costs extra. €

Parador Vía de la Plata Pza. Constitución 3, http:// parador.es. Well-run and friendly parador in an eighteenth-century Baroque convent, near the Arco de Trajano. Check the website for offers that will reduce the price. €€€

EATING

SEE MAP PAGE 200

There is a good selection of eateries in the area around the Roman sites and close to the train station.

Pepe Osorio C/Castelar 3, 677 099 994. Pleasant restaurant, offering good fish dishes and a varied *menú del día* as well as more sophisticated options such as partridge

salad or local speciality lamb with plums. €€

La Tahona, Casa de Comidas C/Alvarado 5, 924 338 774. Converted into a chic gastrobar, *La Tahona* offers carefully prepared and presented Extremeño-style dishes at reasonable prices. €€

Badajoz

The valley of the Río Guadiana, followed by road and rail, waters rich farmland between Mérida and **BADAJOZ**. The main reason for visiting this provincial capital, traditional gateway to Portugal and the scene of innumerable sieges, is still to get across the border. It's not somewhere you'd want to stay very long – crude modern development has largely overrun what must once have been an attractive old centre, and few of the monuments have survived – but food and lodging are cheap, and it does serve as a useful stopover. The city's troubled history, springing from its strategically important position on the Río Guadiana, is its main claim to fame. Founded by the Moors in 1009, Badajoz was taken by the Christian armies of Alfonso IX in 1230,

3

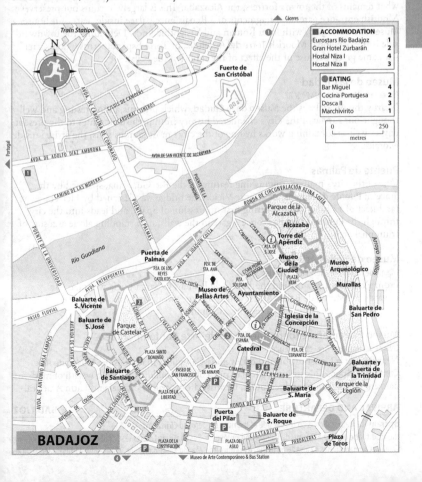

ACCOMMODATION
Eurostars Rio Badajoz	1
Gran Hotel Zurbarán	2
Hostal Niza I	4
Hostal Niza II	3

EATING
Bar Miguel	4
Cocina Portugesa	2
Dosca II	3
Marchivirito	1

BADAJOZ

SEE MAP PAGE 20?

> ## TO THE PORTUGUESE BORDER AND BEYOND
>
> The **Portuguese frontier** is 4km west of Badajoz. You can get to Elvas, the first sizeable town on the Portuguese side of the border, by local bus. From here there are up to seven long-distance buses to **Lisbon** each day.

used as a base by Felipe II against the Portuguese in 1580, stormed by British forces under the Duke of Wellington in 1812 and taken by Franco's Nationalist troops in 1936.

The Catedral and the museo
Pza. de España • **Catedral** Free • **Museo** Charge

At the heart of old Badajoz is the **Pza. de España** and the squat thirteenth-century **Catedral**, a fortress-like building, prettified a little during the Renaissance by the addition of a portal and the embellishment of the tower. The **museo** contains work by local-born artist Luís de Morales (1520–86).

Alcazaba
Museo Arqueológico • Free

Northeast of Pza. de España, C/San Juan leads to **Pza. Alta**, once an elegant arcaded concourse, whose facades are decorated with a dazzling Mudéjar-style design, and what remains of the town's fortress, the **Alcazaba**. This is largely in ruins but preserves Moorish entrance gates and fragments of a Renaissance palace inside. Part of it houses a **Museo Arqueológico**, with local Roman and Visigothic finds. Defending the townward side is the octagonal Moorish **Torre del Aprendiz**, or Torre Espantaperros ("dog-scarer") – a name given because of the effect of the sound of the bells).

Museo de la Ciudad
Pza. de Santa María • Free • 924 20 06 87

Nearby the Alcazaba is the **Museo de la Ciudad**, which presents an interesting and well-thought-out survey of the city's chequered history from prehistoric times to the present day, as well as containing works by one of the city's most famous sons, the artist Luís de Morales.

Puente de Palmas
One of the city's main distinguishing features is the Río Guadiana, spanned by the graceful **Puente de Palmas**, or Puente Viejo. The bridge was designed by Herrera (architect of El Escorial) as a fitting first impression of Spain, and leads into the city through the **Puerta de Palmas**, once a gate in the walls, now standing alone as a sort of triumphal arch.

Museo de Bellas Artes
C/Duque de San Germán • Free • http://muba.badajoz.es

From Pza. de España behind the Puerta de Palmas, C/Santa Lucía will take you towards the **Museo de Bellas Artes**, which includes works by Morales, three etchings by Goya and a couple of good panels by Zurbarán.

Museo Extremeño e Iberoamericano de Arte Contemporáneo
C/Virgen de Guadalupe • Free • http://meiac.es

Near Pza. de la Constitución and off Avenida Calzadillas Maestre is the **Museo de Arte Contemporáneo**. This striking, circular, rust-coloured building houses a wealth of modern paintings, installations and sculpture, by artists from Spain, Portugal and Latin America.

ARRIVAL AND DEPARTURE
BADAJOZ

By train The train station is on the far side of the river, up the road that crosses the Puente de Palmas and on Avda. Carolina Coronado. Buses #2 and #6 go to the city centre; it's around €6 in a taxi.

Destinations Cáceres (3–5 daily; 1hr 35min–1 hr 50min); Madrid (5–8 daily; 5hr 25min–8hr 45min); Mérida (4–6

daily; 35–45min).
By bus If you're arriving by bus, you'll have a 15min-plus walk to the centre, as the station is located on C/José Rebollo López towards the southern edge of the city. Your best bet is to hop on city bus #3 to Avda. de Europa.
Destinations Cáceres (4 daily; 1hr 15min–1hr 30min);

Córdoba (1–3 daily; 4hr 15min–4hr 30min); Madrid (7 daily; 4hr 40min–5hr 10min); Mérida (6 daily; 45min–1hr); Olivenza (9 daily; 25min); Seville (5–7 daily; 2hr 50min–3hr 10min); Zafra (5–8 daily; 1hr 10min).
By car For parking follow the signs to Pza. de Minayo where you'll find an attended underground car park.

INFORMATION

Turismo Paseo San Juan, just off Pza. de España (http://turismo.aytobadajoz.es). There is another office at Plaza San José 18.

ACCOMMODATION
SEE MAP PAGE 203

There's plenty of accommodation in Badajoz, much of it inexpensive, making it a good stopover on the way into Portugal.
Eurostars Río Badajoz Avda. Adolfo Díaz Ambrona 13, http://eurostarshotels.com. At the far end of Puente de la Universidad, this mid-range 101-room hotel, which is now part of the *Eurostars* chain, has a swimming pool, parking and a restaurant. €

Gran Hotel Zurbarán Gómez de Solís 1, http://granhotel zurbaranbadajoz.com. A sleek, business-style hotel, with swimming pool and bar-café. Look out for weekend deals that can bring the price down. €€
Hostal Niza I and II C/Arco Agüero 34 & 45, http://hostal-niza.es. There are very simple but clean rooms with en-suite bathrooms in these two well-located *hostales*. €

EATING
SEE MAP PAGE 203

The area around C/Muñoz Torrero, a couple of blocks below the Pza. de España, is the most promising for reasonably priced **food** and **tapas**.
Bar Miguel C/Rafael Lucenqui 4, 924 239 246. Popular, friendly and good-value bar with a range of excellent *raciones* and tapas. Fish dishes are particularly good, and there is a good selection of local wines too. €
Cocina Portuguesa C/Muñoz Torrero 7, http://cocina portuguesa.com. The best budget bet in Badajoz, with tasty, reasonably priced Portuguese cooking and a selection of good-value set menus. €€

Dosca II Avda. de Colón 3, just off Pza. Santo Domingo, http://dosca2.es. This place is very popular with locals, serving a wide range of satisfying, well-cooked specialities in the nautically themed restaurant. Does a generous weekday set lunch and a slightly pricier weekend version. €€
Marchivirito Nuestra Señora de Bótoa 37, http://marchivirito.com. High-quality restaurant out of town on the Cáceres road, with a great summer terrace, excellent starters and meat dishes and a very good wine list. The steak tartare is one of the star dishes. Prices are high, though. €€€

Southern Extremadura

The routes **south from Mérida** or **Badajoz** cross territory that is mostly harsh and unrewarding, fit only for sheep and the odd cork or olive tree, until you come upon the foothills of the Sierra Morena, on the borders of Andalucía. En route, **Olivenza**, a town that has spent more time in Portugal than Spain, is perhaps the most attractive stop, and offers a road approach to Évora, the most interesting city of southern Portugal.

LAND OF THE CONQUISTADORES

Extremadura is a tough country that bred tough people, if we are to believe the names of places like Valle de Matamoros (Valley of the Moorslayers), and one can easily understand the attraction that the New World and the promise of the lush Indies must have held for its inhabitants.

Francisco Pizarro, the conqueror of Peru, and **Francisco de Orellano**, the explorer of the Amazon, both came from Trujillo, while the ruthless **Hernán Cortés**, who led the destruction of the Aztec empire, hailed from Medellín in Badajoz. Jerez de los Caballeros also produced its crop of *conquistadores*. The two most celebrated are **Vasco Núñez de Balboa**, discoverer of the Pacific, and **Hernando de Soto** (also known as the Conqueror of Florida), who in exploring the Mississippi became one of the first Europeans to set foot in North America.

Olivenza

Twenty-five kilometres southwest of Badajoz, whitewashed **OLIVENZA** seems to have landed in the wrong country; long disputed between Spain and Portugal, it has been Spanish since 1801. Yet not only are the buildings and the town's character clearly Portuguese, the oldest inhabitants still cling to this language. There's a local saying here: "The women from Olivenza are not like the rest, for they are the daughters of Spain and the granddaughters of Portugal."

The walls, castle and the Museo Etnográfico

Museo Pza. Santa María • Charge • http://museodeolivenza.com

The town has long been strongly fortified, and traces of the **walls and gates** can still be seen, even though houses have been built up against them. They extend up to the **castle**, which has three surviving towers and holds the **Museo Etnográfico**, which displays an interesting and comprehensive range of exhibits detailing all aspects of life in the region, local archeological finds and a room containing part of a 150kg meteorite that fell in the area in 1924. It makes a great destination to visit.

Iglesias Santa María del Castillo and Santa María Magdalena

Free

Right beside the castle is the seventeenth-century church of **Santa María del Castillo** and, around the corner, **Santa María Magdalena**, built a century later. The latter is in the distinctive Portuguese Manueline style, with arcades of twisted columns; the former is a more sober Renaissance affair with three aisles of equal height and a notable work of art in the huge "Tree of Jesse" *retablo*. Just across the street from Santa María Magdalena is a former **palace**, now the public library, with a spectacular Manueline doorway.

INFORMATION   OLIVENZA

Turismo Pza. Santa María del Castillo (924 490 151).

ACCOMMODATION AND EATING

Hotel Los Amigos Avda. Nicaragua s/n, 924 490 386. Situated on the edge of town, this is a no-frills, straightforward, good-value place to stay and, as the name would suggest, service is friendly. Rooms are functional and all have a/c. The bar serves up some very good tapas. €

Jerez de los Caballeros

The road from Badajoz to **JEREZ DE LOS CABALLEROS** is typical of southern Extremadura, striking across a parched landscape whose hamlets – low huts and a whitewashed church strung out along the road – look as if they have been dumped from some low-budget Western set of a Mexican frontier town.

Churches

Free

Jerez de los Caballeros is a quiet, friendly place, through which many tourists pass but few stay. The towers dominate the walled old town: a passion for building spires gripped the eighteenth century, when three churches had new ones erected: the first is **San Miguel**, in the central Pza. de España, made of carved brick; the second is the unmistakeable red-, blue- and ochre-glazed tower of **San Bartolomé**, on the hill above it, with a striking tiled facade; and the third, rather dilapidated, belongs to **Santa Catalina**, outside the walls.

Museums

Museo de Arte Sacro Charge • https://jerezcaballeros.es/museo-del-arte-sacro • **Museo Casa Vasco Nuñez de Balboa** Free • http://casadebalboa.es

Jerez de los Caballeros has two museums of note. The **Museo de Arte Sacro** houses a modest but well-presented collection of religious art. The more ambitious Museo Casa

Vasco Nuñez de Balboa puts the life of the local-born conquistador, who became the first European to reach the Pacific Ocean from the New World, into context with exhibits on the Spanish conquests of America, the history of the Extremadura and the activities of the Knights Templar.

The Castle and the Iglesia de Santa María de Encarnación

Above the Pza. de España the streets climb up to the restored remains of a **castle** of the Knights Templar (this was once an embattled frontier town), mostly late thirteenth-century but with obvious Moorish influences. Adjoining the castle, and predating it by over a century (as do the town walls), is the **Iglesia de Santa María de Encarnación**. Built on a Visigothic site, it's more interesting seen from the battlements above than from the inside.

INFORMATION   JEREZ DE LOS CABALLEROS

Turismo Ayuntamiento, Pza. San Agustín 1 (Mon–Sat   http://jerezcaballeros.es/oficina-de-turismo).
10am–2pm & 4.30–6.30pm, Sun 10am–2pm, 924 730 372,

ACCOMMODATION

Posada de las Cigüeñas C/Santiago 7–9, http://   Some of the individually decorated rooms have balconies
laposadadelasciguenas.mydirectstay.com. A   seven-room   with great views over the town. €
posada with a pool, bar area, sun terrace and restaurant.

Zafra

If you plan to stick to the main routes or are heading south from Mérida, **ZAFRA** is rather less of a detour than Olivenza, though it's also more frequented by tourists. Two beautiful arcaded plazas, the Pza. Grande and the Pza. Chica, adjoin each other in the town centre. But the town is famed mainly for its **castle** – now converted into a parador – remarkable for the white marble Renaissance patio. The region is also renowned for its wines, and you can visit the **Bodega Medina**, C/Cestria 4 (http://bodegasmedina.es; by appointment).

Nuestra Señora de la Candelaria

C/Tetuán • Free; open just prior to and after Mass

The most attractive of several interesting churches is **Nuestra Señora de la Candelaria**, with nine panels by Zurbarán in the *retablo* and a chapel by Churriguera; the entrance is on C/José through a small gateway, around the side of the church.

INFORMATION   ZAFRA

Turismo Pza. de España 8 (Mon–Fri 10am–2pm &   turismozafra.com, http://rutadelaplata.com).
5.30–7.30pm, Sat & Sun 10am–2pm; 924 551 036, http://

ACCOMMODATION

★ **Casa Palacio Conde de la Corte** C/Pilar Redondo 2,   **Hotel Las Palmeras** Pza. Grande 14, http://hotellas
http://condedelacorte.com. A beautiful, luxurious boutique-   palmeras.net. Well-appointed, good-value *hotel* with
style hotel with bullfighting-themed rooms, a great   standard rooms, an elegant patio and bar-restaurant with
Andalucian patio area and a pool. Price includes breakfast. €€   a summer terraza. €
Hostal Carmen Avda. Estación 9, http://hostalcarmen.   **Parador de Zafra** Pza. Corazón de María 7, http://parador.
com. A very tidy *hostal* with facilities closer to that of a   es. Housed in a fifteenth-century castle, the rooms in this
hotel. Also boasts an excellent medium-priced restaurant   parador are suitably palatial. There's a splendid courtyard, a
with a varied set lunch. €   tranquil pool and an excellent restaurant too. €€

EATING

There are plenty of bars serving tapas and *raciones* in the   very popular restaurant (make a reservation first) in the
streets around Pza. de España.   centre of town, with a wide selection of high-quality local
★ **La Rebotica** C/Boticas 12, 924 554 289. A small and   dishes such as oxtail or steak with figs in brandy sauce. €€

Andalucía

ALHAMBRA, GRANADA

Andalucía

The popular image of Spain as a land of bullfights, flamenco, sherry and ruined castles derives from Andalucía, the southernmost territory and the most quintessentially Spanish part of the Iberian Peninsula. Above all, it's the great Moorish monuments that compete for your attention here. The Moors, a mixed race of Berbers and Arabs who crossed into Spain from Morocco and North Africa, occupied al-Andalus for over seven centuries. Their first forces landed at Tarifa in AD 710, and within four years they had conquered virtually the entire country; their last kingdom, Granada, fell to the Christian Reconquest in 1492. Between these dates, they developed the most sophisticated civilization of the Middle Ages, centred in turn on the three major cities of Córdoba, Seville and Granada.

Each one of Andalucía's major cities preserves extraordinarily brilliant and beautiful monuments, of which the most perfect is **Granada**'s Alhambra palace, arguably the most sensual building in all of Europe. **Seville**, not to be outdone, has a fabulously ornamented Alcázar and the grandest of all Gothic Catedrals. Today, Andalucía's capital and seat of the region's autonomous parliament is a vibrant contemporary metropolis that's impossible to resist. **Córdoba**'s exquisite Mezquita, the grandest and most beautiful mosque constructed by the Moors, is a landmark building in world architecture and is not to be missed.

These three cities have, of course, become major tourist destinations, but it's also worth leaving the tourist trail and visiting some of the smaller **inland towns** of Andalucía. Renaissance towns such as **Úbeda**, **Baeza** and **Osuna**, Moorish **Carmona** and the stark white hill towns around **Ronda** are all easily accessible by local buses. Travelling for some time here, you'll get a feel for the landscape of Andalucía: occasionally spectacularly beautiful but more often impressive on a huge, unyielding scale.

The region also takes in mountains – including the **Sierra Nevada**, Spain's highest range. You can often ski here in March, and then drive down to the coast to swim the same day. Perhaps more compelling, though, are the opportunities for walking in the lower slopes, **Las Alpujarras**. Alternatively, there's good trekking among the gentler (and much less known) hills of the **Sierra Morena**, north of Seville.

On the **coast**, it's easy to despair. Extending to either side of **Málaga** is the **Costa del Sol**, Europe's most heavily developed resort area, with its poor beaches hidden behind a remorseless density of concrete hotels and apartment complexes. However, the region offers two alternatives, much less developed and with some of the best beaches in all Spain. These are the villages **between Tarifa and Cádiz** on the Atlantic, and those **around Almería** on the southeast corner of the Mediterranean. The latter allow warm swimming in all but the winter months; those near Cádiz, more easily accessible, are fine from about June to September. Near Cádiz, too, is the **Parque Nacional Coto de Doñana**, Spain's largest and most important nature reserve, which is home to a spectacular range of flora and fauna.

The realities of life in contemporary Andalucía can be stark. **Unemployment** in the region is the highest in Spain – over forty percent in some areas – and has been a problem for some time, and a large proportion of the population still scrapes a living from seasonal agricultural work. The *andaluz* villages, bastions of anarchist and socialist groups before and during the Civil War, saw little economic aid or change during the Franco years, and although much government spending has been

PAMPANEIRA

Highlights

❶ Semana Santa Andalucía's major Holy Week festival is memorably celebrated in Seville, Málaga, Córdoba and Granada. See page 214

❷ Seville The region's pulsating capital city is a treasure house of churches, palaces and museums. See page 247

❸ Flamenco The passionate dance, song and music of the Spanish south. See page 265

❹ Sipping sherry in Jerez Andalucía's classic wine is made in Jerez and makes the perfect partner for tapas. See page 283

❺ Coto de Doñana Explore Spain's largest and most important wildlife sanctuary. See page 286

❻ Mezquita, Córdoba This 1200-year-old Moorish mosque is one of the most beautiful ever built. See page 293

❼ Alhambra Granada's Moorish palace is the pinnacle of Moorish architectural splendour in Spain. See page 309

❽ Las Alpujarras A wildly picturesque region dotted with traditional mountain villages. See page 326

HIGHLIGHTS ARE MARKED ON THE MAP ON PAGE 212

channelled into improving infrastructure such as hospitals and road and rail links throughout the region, the lack of employment opportunities away from the coastal tourist zones persists.

For all its poverty, however, Andalucía is also Spain at its most exuberant – those wild and extravagant clichés of the Spanish south really do exist and can be absorbed and enjoyed at one of the hundreds of thrilling annual **fiestas**, **ferias** and **romerías**.

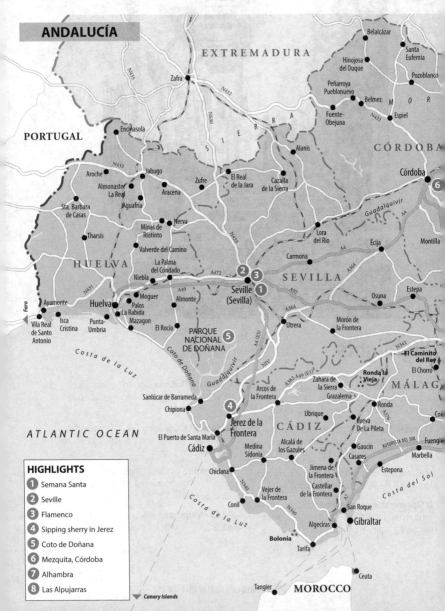

HIGHLIGHTS

1. Semana Santa
2. Seville
3. Flamenco
4. Sipping sherry in Jerez
5. Coto de Doñana
6. Mezquita, Córdoba
7. Alhambra
8. Las Alpujarras

Málaga

MÁLAGA is the second city of the south (after Seville), with a population of over half a million. Though the clusters of high-rises look pretty grim as you approach, the city does have some compelling attractions. The elegant central zone is now largely pedestrianized with the focal and marble-paved **Calle Marqués de Larios** – lined with fashionable stores – its most elegant thoroughfare. This leads into the **Pza. de la Constitución**, the city's

FIESTAS

FEBRUARY

1: San Cecilio Fiesta in Granada's traditionally gypsy quarter of Sacromonte.
Week before Lent: Carnaval An extravagant week-long event in all the Andalucian cities. Cádiz, above all, celebrates, with uproarious street parades, fancy dress and satirical music competitions.

MARCH/APRIL

Easter: Semana Santa (Holy Week) Memorable processions and penitents at Seville, Málaga, Granada and Córdoba, and in smaller towns such as Jerez, Arcos, Baeza and Úbeda. All culminate with dramatic candlelight processions at dawn on Good Friday.
Last week of April: Feria de Abril Week-long fair at Seville: the largest *feria* in Spain.

MAY

First week: Cruces de Mayo Celebrated in Córdoba and includes a "prettiest patio" competition in a town full of prize examples.
Early May (week after Feria de Abril): Feria del Caballo A somewhat aristocratic horse fair is held at Jerez de la Frontera.
Pentecost: Romería del Rocío Horse-drawn carriages and processions converge from all over the south on El Rocío (Huelva).
Last week: Feria de la Manzanilla Prolonged binge in Sanlúcar de Barrameda to celebrate the town's excellent *manzanilla* wine, with flamenco and sporting events on the river beach.

JUNE

13: San Antonio Fiesta at Trevélez with mock battles between Moors and Christians.
Third week The Algeciras Feria Real is another major event of the south.
End June/early July: International Festival of Music and Dance Major dance/flamenco groups and orchestras perform in Granada's Alhambra palace, Generalife and Carlos V palace.

JULY

Early July: International Guitar Festival Brings together top international acts from classical, flamenco and Latin American music in Córdoba.
End of month: Virgen del Mar Almería's major annual shindig, with parades, horseriding events, concerts and lots of drinking.

AUGUST

First week The first cycle of horse races along Sanlúcar de Barrameda's beach, with heavy official and unofficial betting; the second tournament takes place two weeks later.
5: Trevélez observes a midnight *romería* to Mulhacén.
13–21: Feria de Málaga One of Andalucía's most enjoyable fiestas for visitors, who are heartily welcomed by the ebullient *malagueños*.
15: Ascension of the Virgin Fair With *casetas* (dance tents) at Vejer and elsewhere.
Noche del Vino Riotous wine festival at Competa (Málaga).
23–25: Guadalquivir festival Bullfights and an important flamenco competition, at Sanlúcar de Barrameda.

SEPTEMBER & OCTOBER

First two weeks of September: Feria de Ronda Ronda's annual *feria*, with flamenco contests and Corrida Goyesca – bullfights in eighteenth-century dress.
First/second week of September: Vendimia Celebrating the vintage at Jerez.
Sept 27–Oct 1: Feria de San Miguel In Órgiva (Las Alpujarras), featuring traditional dancing and a huge paella cook-up.

ANDALUCÍA'S CUISINE

The most striking feature of Andalucía's cuisine is its **debt to the Moors**. In their long period of hegemony over the region the North Africans introduced oranges and lemons as well as spices such as cumin and saffron and refined techniques for growing olives and almonds. Their chilled soups such as *ajo blanco* (made with ground almonds) and gazpacho are still a welcome refresher in high summer temperatures. Of course, gazpacho is today made with tomatoes and green peppers, both brought back from the Americas by Columbus, who sailed from Andalucía.

The region is also the birthplace of **tapas**, the classic titbits that Spaniards love to tuck into as they drink. Between 6pm and 9pm most evenings city bars are humming with conversations of *tapeadores* (as aficionados are termed). One of Andalucía's favourite tapas is **jamón serrano**, mountain-cured ham from prime producing zones in the Sierra de Aracena and the Alpujarras. The most prized ham of all is *jamón ibérico* from black Iberian pigs, and in the curing village of Jabugo this is graded into five levels of quality with the very best accorded five *jotas* or "j's" (for Jabugo). The taste is delicious (for those who can afford it) and far superior to the standard white-pig *jamón* sold in supermarkets.

Andalucía is also known in Spain as the *zona de los fritos* (fried food zone) and **fried fish** is a regional speciality. *Chanquetes* (whitebait), sardines, *calamares* and *boquerones* (anchovies) are all *andaluz* favourites and the seafood *chiringuitos* (beach restaurants) of Málaga are famous for their **fritura malagueña** (assorted fried fish).

Inland, Andalucía is a mountainous region and the specialities here are **carnes de caza** (game). *Jabalí* (wild boar), *venado* (venison), *cabrito* (kid) and *perdiz* (partridge) all make memorable meals in the hands of a competent chef.

The wine par excellence of Andalucía – particularly to accompany tapas – is **fino** (dry sherry) from Jerez de la Frontera, although nearby Sanlúcar de Barrameda's *manzanilla* and *montilla* (produced in Córdoba) are similar and display their own prized characteristics.

main square, with its monumental fountain flanked by slender palms, and the terraces of numerous cafés and restaurants. The centre has a number of interesting things to see, not to mention the **birthplace of Picasso** and the **Museo Picasso Málaga**, which houses an important collection of works by Málaga's most famous son. Perched on the hill above the town are the formidable citadels of the **Alcazaba** and **Gibralfaro**, magnificent vestiges of the seven centuries that the Moors held sway here.

Málaga is looking fresh after a city-wide revamp has restored the historic core back to its nineteenth-century splendour. It boasts a sleek port, lined by contemporary waterfront promenades **El Palmeral** and **Muelle Uno**, which feature a spectacular pergola stretched along a marina lined with shops, bars and restaurants. Building on the success of the Picasso museum, Málaga has turned itself into an art-lover's hotspot, with several excellent art museums. The Soho district, between the port and **CAC Málaga**, is the art neighbourhood, decked with murals and home to some of the city's most innovative places to eat.

Málaga is also renowned for its **fish** and **seafood**, which can be sampled at tapas bars and restaurants throughout the city, as well as at the old fishing villages of **El Palo** and **Pedregalejo**, now absorbed into the suburbs, where there's a seafront *paseo* lined with some of the best **marisquerías** and **chiringuitos** (beachside fish restaurants) in the province.

The Catedral

C/Molina Lario 9 • Charge • http://malagacatedral.com

The city's most conspicuous edifice seen from the heights of the Gibralfaro is the peculiar, unfinished **Catedral**. Constructed between the sixteenth and eighteenth centuries, it still lacks a tower on the west front because a radical *malagueño* bishop donated the earmarked money to the American War of Independence against the British. Unfortunately – and despite its huge scale – it also lacks any real inspiration and is distinguished only by an intricately carved seventeenth-century *sillería* (choir stall) by noted sculptor Pedro de Mena. However, **Iglesia del Sagrario** (same ticket and hours), on the Catedral's northern flank, is worth a look, if only for its fine Gothic portal, dating from an earlier, uncompleted Isabelline church. Inside, a restored and magnificent gilded Plateresque **retablo**, which is brilliantly illuminated during services, is the work of Juan de Balmaseda. Equally worthwhile is the climb (two hundred steps) up to the Catedral's

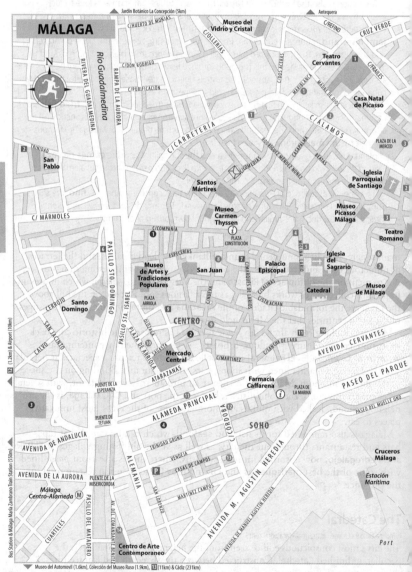

terracotta domed rooftops for a guided tour (English available – ask when you buy your tickets) round the perimeter from where you get sweeping views of the city centre.

Museo Picasso Málaga

C/San Agustín • Charge • http://museopicassomalaga.org

Just around the corner from the Catedral is the **Museo Picasso Málaga**, housed in the elegant sixteenth-century mansion of the counts of Buenavista. It was opened by the king and queen in 2003, 112 years after Picasso left Málaga at the age of 10 and to

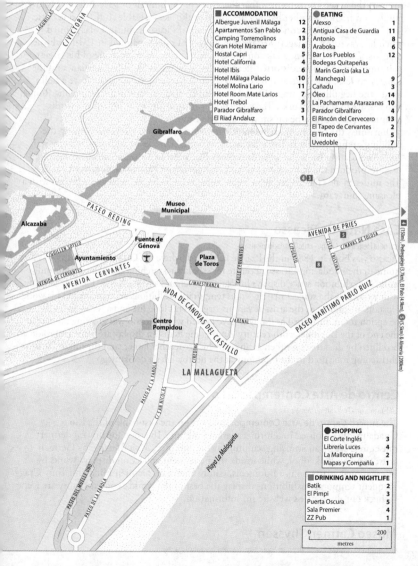

■ ACCOMMODATION	
Albergue Juvenil Málaga	12
Apartamentos San Pablo	2
Camping Torremolinos	13
Gran Hotel Miramar	8
Hostal Capri	5
Hotel California	4
Hotel Ibis	6
Hotel Málaga Palacio	10
Hotel Molina Lario	11
Hotel Room Mate Larios	7
Hotel Trebol	9
Parador Gibralfaro	3
El Riad Andaluz	1

● EATING	
Alexso	1
Antigua Casa de Guardia	11
Antonio	8
Araboka	6
Bar Los Pueblos	12
Bodegas Quitapeñas Marín García (aka La Manchega)	9
Cañadu	3
Óleo	14
La Pachamama Atarazanas	10
Parador Gibralfaro	4
El Rincón del Cervecero	13
El Tapeo de Cervantes	2
El Tintero	5
Uvedoble	7

● SHOPPING	
El Corte Inglés	3
Librería Luces	4
La Mallorquina	2
Mapas y Compañía	1

■ DRINKING AND NIGHTLIFE	
Batik	2
El Pimpi	3
Puerta Oscura	5
Sala Premier	4
ZZ Pub	1

where he returned only once for an unhappy, fleeting visit in his late teens. In later life, he toyed with the idea of "sending two lorries full of paintings" to set up a museum in Málaga but vowed never to set foot in Spain while the ruling General Franco – who described the artist's work as "degenerate" – was still alive. Picasso died in 1973 and was outlived by the dictator by two years.

The **permanent collection** consists of 120 paintings, sculptures and ceramics, displayed chronologically and donated or loaned by the foundation belonging to Bernard Ruiz-Picasso, the artist's grandson. The **temporary collection** comprises loaned works and special exhibitions (usually connected with Picasso). Though not on a par with the Picasso museums in Paris and Barcelona, the museum does allow you to see some of the lesser-known works that Picasso kept for himself or gave away to his lovers, family and friends – rather harshly described as the "less saleable stuff" by one critic.

Among the highlights on display are a portrait of Picasso's cousin Lola, painted when he was just a teenager; *Restaurante*, a piece of canvas painted in 1914 and stuck on glass; *Las Tres Gracias*, a take on the Grecian Three Graces and one of his largest paintings; *Siesta*, whose distorted sleeping figure is unmistakeably Picassian; and the *Cabeza de Toro*, where Picasso used a bike handlebars and saddle to recreate a bull's head. The beguiling yet tragic Dora Maar and Picasso's second wife, Jacqueline Roque, also feature in several works. The collection is rotated and thus not all the works mentioned above may be on show at any one time.

Don't miss the basement **archeological remains**, which were revealed during the building's refurbishment. These include substantial chunks of a Phoenician city wall and tower dating from the seventh century BC, parts of a Roman *salazones* factory, used to produce the famous *garum*, and vestiges of the **Palacio de Buenavista** cellar. The museum also has an excellent book store and gift shop as well as a *cafetería* with a pleasant courtyard.

Casa Natal de Picasso

Pza. de la Merced 15 • Charge • http://fundacionpicasso.es

Picasso was born in 1881 in the Pza. de la Merced, where the **Casa Natal de Picasso** is now home to the Fundación Picasso, a centre for scholars researching the painter's life and work. An exhibition space displays lithographs, etchings and washes by Picasso – mainly with women as the subject matter – plus temporary exhibitions centred around his work. Upstairs are photos of the artist at various stages in his long life and a reconstructed reception room, furnished as it might have looked when Picasso was growing up here at the end of the late nineteenth century. Among the items on display are some embroidered bed linen by the artist's mother, a canvas by his art-teacher father, and the infant Picasso's christening robe used in the ceremony at the nearby Iglesia de Santiago.

Centro de Arte Contemporaneo

C/Alemania s/n • Free • http://cacmalaga.eu

The superb **Centro de Arte Contemporaneo** sits on the east bank of the Río Guadalmedina, housed in a former market building. The tone for this modern art museum is set by an amusing sculpture at the entrance, *Man Moving,* by German artist Stephan Balkenhol, while inside the permanent collection displays works by international artists Louise Bourgeois, Cindy Sherman, Damien Hirst and Tony Cragg. Frequent temporary exhibitions display the best of the world's contemporary art scene – check out the centre's website for information.

Museo Carmen Thyssen

C/Compañia 10 • Charge, free Sunday from 5pm • http://carmenthyssenmalaga.org

Just off the west side of Pza. de la Constitución and housed in the refurbished sixteenth-century Palacio de Villalón is the **Museo Carmen Thyssen**, named after the spouse of the late baron whose collection forms the core of the Thyssen-Bornemisza museum in Madrid. Opened in 2011, the museum comprises 230 loaned works from Thyssen's personal collection of Spanish nineteenth-century art. Displayed on three floors (the fourth floor houses temporary exhibitions which have featured Monet, Hooper, Matisse, Miró and Van Gogh) and divided into sections titled "Romantic", "Naturalist Landscape", and "Fin-de-siècle", most of the works are perhaps more interesting for the glimpses they give of Spanish and *andaluz* life and times than for any intrinsic artistic merit or originality.

Centro Pompidou

Pasaje Dr. Carrillo Casaux • Charge, free Sunday from 4pm • http://centrepompidou-malaga.eu

Occupying the corner of Muelle Uno, Málaga's branch of the **Pompidou Centre**, known as **El Cubo** after its iconic multicoloured glass cube decorated by the French artist Daniel Buren, houses modern artworks on loan from its Parisian big sister. The main exhibition focuses on the human body, whole, in bits or in metamorphosis, and includes works by artists such as Bacon, Magritte, Giacometti and Léger. Highlights include portraits by Chagall, Kahlo and Picasso; Landau's *Barbed Hula*; Attia's rows of aluminium foil *Ghosts*; and sculptures by Brancusi, Miró and Schütte. Several temporary exhibitions take place every year; artists have included Miró, Starck and Buren as well as Dada cinema and modern French architects. Centro Pompidou also showcases the performing arts with concerts, dance performances and films throughout the year.

Museo de Málaga

Pza. de la Aduana • Charge • www.museosdeandalucia.es

Málaga waited almost twenty years for a museum to house its enormous archeological and fine art collections, previously kept in boxes in basements around the city. The **Museo de Málaga**, the largest museum in Andalucía and the fifth biggest in Spain, is housed in the old customs building adjacent to the Alcazaba. It's divided into two sections: archeology (on the third floor) where two thousand of the fifteen thousand pieces are on display; and fine art (on the second floor) with two hundred works of the total two thousand in store. The **archeology** is easily the most interesting section for non-locals and its exceptionally well curated spaces include several fine pieces, such as a Neolithic cheese-maker from the Cueva de la Pileta cave near Ronda; Roman marble figures; and a sixth-century BC bronze Corinthian mask excavated in the city centre. Roman mosaics and Moorish ceramics also form part of the display. Downstairs, the **fine art** section has a predominance of Málaga artists, mostly from the nineteenth century when the city's art school reached its heyday. Must-sees here include the sixteenth-century ceiling corbels, some fine Picasso sketches and Simonet's painting *And she had a heart!* (Anatomy of the heart), a romantic vision of an autopsy and one of the city's best-known artworks. Don't miss the magnificent main stairwell, the central courtyard with perhaps the tallest palms in Andalucía, and the roof whose six thousand aluminium tiles carry engravings of the Alcazaba, the Catedral and the museum itself.

Museo del Vidrio y Cristal

Pza. Santísimo Cristo de la Sangre 2 • Charge • http://museovidrioycristalmalaga.com

Housed in an eighteenth-century inn in the historic artisans' quarter, the **Museo del Vidrio y Cristal** contains one of the largest glass collections in Europe. The over three thousand pieces encompass the history of glass-making, from the Phoenicians to Lalique and Whitefriars in the mid-twentieth century via the Romans, Persians and Venetians. The museum also showcases stained-glass windows and antique furniture and paintings.

Museo del Automovil

Av. Sor Teresa del Prat 15, to the west of the city centre on bus #16 • Charge • http://museoautomovilmalaga.com

A must for car fans, **Museo del Automóvil** takes in the entire history of cars, from early models such as a 1912 Barron Acoryd to a 2010 hydrogen-powered prototype. Expect to see plenty of signature designs – the collection of Rolls-Royce and Italian cars is particularly large – as well as more unusual makes such as the Czech Tatra. Mannequins dressed in appropriate period costume accompany each car and there's also an impressive fashion display.

Colección del Museo Ruso

Av. Sor Teresa del Prat 15, to the west of the city centre on bus #16 • Charge, free Sunday from 4pm • http://coleccionmuseoruso.es

A restored tobacco factory (La Tabacalera, built in the 1930s and modelled on the Antigua Fábrica de Tabacos in Seville) houses the **Colección del Museo Ruso**, a collection from the Russian State Museum in St Petersburg, one of the largest in the world. The main exhibition changes annually in February – themes have included Russian icons, the four seasons and the Romanov dynasty – and the smaller exhibitions (two a year) focus on a particular artist such as Chagall, Filonov or Kandinsky or a Russian theme such as the Knave of Diamonds movement in the 1920s or Russian pop art. While many of the artists are relatively unknown in western Europe, their work offers an interesting insight into Russian culture and history. The museum also provides online access to the entire Russian State Museum collection and hosts Russian-themed concerts and conferences.

Jardín Botánico La Concepción

5km north of Málaga and signposted off the A45 *autovía* • Charge, free after 4.30pm in summer and after 2pm in winter • http:// laconcepcion.malaga.eu

A pleasant trip out of Málaga is to the **Jardín Botánico La Concepción**. A spectacular tropical garden, much of which was planted in the nineteenth century, this formerly private estate was founded in the 1850s by Amelia Loring, granddaughter of the British consul, and purchased in 1990 by the Málaga city council. Lack of public funds and mismanagement have led to the loss of some of the largest trees and several areas are anything but manicured. However, a walk round the garden (allow two hours) is still worthwhile.

Specimens on view include exotic blooms, thirty species of palm, and other trees of all shapes and continents, such as the Australian banyan with its serpentine aerial roots. The giant wisteria pergola, formally the Loring family's summer dining room, comes into full bloom from mid-March to the end of April, and is worth the visit alone.

A **taxi** costs about €20 one-way from the centre. The most convenient way to visit without your own transport, however, is to use the **Málagatour dedicated bus service** – see the Jardín's website for full timetable.

ARRIVAL AND DEPARTURE   MÁLAGA

BY AIR

From the airport (902 404 704), the electric local train (*Cercanías*) provides the easiest approach to Málaga (every 20min; 6.44am–00.54am). From the Arrivals hall or baggage carousels go to the exit and cross the forecourt to the train station "Aeropuerto". Buy a ticket from the machine for the C1 Cercanías line to the Centro-Alameda stop (12min). The train also makes a stop en route at the Málaga train station (María Zambrano), which is also convenient for the bus station next door. Alternatively, city bus Linea A leaves from outside the Terminal 3 Arrivals hall (roughly every 20 from 7am–midnight; then at 00.45am, 2am & 3.05am; €3), stopping at the train and bus stations en route to the centre and the Paseo del Parque near the port, from where you can also pick it up in the opposite direction when you're returning to the airport. A taxi (roughly 15min) into town from the rank outside the Arrivals hall will cost around €30 depending on traffic and time of day.

BY TRAIN

The city's impressive RENFE train station (María Zambrano) is southwest of the heart of town; buses #3 and #16 runs from here to the centre every 10min or so. For current timetables and ticket information, consult RENFE http://renfe.es.

Destinations Algeciras (1 daily, change at Bobadilla; 3hr 30min); Cádiz (3 daily, change at Dos Hermanas; 4hr 40min); Córdoba (6 daily; 1hr 5min; AVE 12 daily; 55min); Fuengirola (every 20min from airport; 35min); Madrid (AVE 16 daily; 2hr 40min); Ronda (1 daily; 1hr 50min); Seville (13 daily; 1hr 55min to 2hr 30min); Torremolinos (every 20min; 25min).

BY BUS

The bus station is just behind the RENFE station, from where all buses (run by several different companies) operate. In summer, it's best to arrive an hour or so early for the bus to Granada, since tickets can sell out. Bus timetables can be checked on http://estabus.malaga.eu.

Destinations Algeciras (7 daily; 2hr); Almería (3 daily; 3hr 15min); Almuñécar (8 daily; 1hr 15min); Antequera (14 daily; 1hr); Cádiz (4 daily; 4hr); Córdoba (4 daily; 2hr 30min); Fuengirola (2 daily; 45min); Gibraltar (stops at La Linea de la Concepcion border; 4 daily; 3hr); Granada (20 daily; 2hr); Jaén (4 daily; 3hr); Jerez de la Frontera (1 daily; 4hr 35min);

Madrid (8 daily; 6hr); Marbella (21 daily; 50min); Motril (8 daily; 2hr); Nerja (26 daily; 1hr); Ronda (3 daily; 2hr); Salobreña (7 daily; 1hr 45min); Seville (5 daily; 2hr 45min); Úbeda/Baeza (3 daily; 4hr).

BY CAR

Arriving in Málaga by car you face the serious problem of parking, and will have little choice but to use one of the many signed (and expensive) car parks around the centre or use a garage connected to your accommodation (you will still need to pay but many hotels offer discounts). Note that theft from cars is rampant in Málaga and you should never leave anything valuable in a street-parked vehicle, especially overnight.

BY FERRY

Málaga has a passenger ferry port, the Estación Marítima, which serves the Spanish enclave of Melilla in Morocco with Trasmediterranea (7hr; http://armastrasmediterranea. com). If you're heading for Fes and eastern Morocco, this is a useful connection – particularly for taking a car over – though most people use the quicker services at Algeciras and Tarifa to the west. A useful site for checking the latest ferry schedules is http://directferries.co.uk.

Destinations Melilla (1–2 daily in summer; see website for winter timetables; 6–8hr).

INFORMATION AND TOURS

Turismo Pza. de la Constitución 7 (952 308 911); can provide information on cultural events and accommodation, and sells a detailed city map.

Turismo municipal On Pza. de la Marina (daily 9am–6pm, April–Oct closes 7pm; 951 926 020), with other branches at the Alzacaba, bus station and airport arrivals.

Useful website http://guidetomalaga.com, with tourist information online and via an app.

Bus tours One way to get to grips quickly with the city is on an open-topped bus tour. This hop-on-hop-off service also includes entrance to the Museo Interactivo de la Musica (http://city-ss.es); buses leave the bus station every 30min (9.40am–6.30pm) with about a dozen stops around the centre (see website for route map), including the Catedral, Pza. de la Merced, the Alameda and the Gibralfaro.

ACCOMMODATION

SEE MAP PAGE 216

Málaga boasts dozens of hotels and *hostales* in all budget categories. The best places to start looking for cheaper **accommodation** are the Soho district just south of the Alameda Principal and the streets east and west of C/ Marques de Larios, which cuts between the Alameda and Pza. de la Constitución.

Albergue Juvenil Málaga Pza. de Pio XII, http://inturjoven.com. Modern youth hostel on the western outskirts of town, with double and single rooms, disabled facilities, its own sun terrace and restaurant. Tends to fill up in season, so book ahead. Buses #11, #25 and #31 heading west across the river from the Alameda will drop you nearby. €

Apartamentos San Pablo C/Trinidad 39, http://apartamentossanpablomalaga.com. Excellent apartments and studios (sleeping two to six people) in a building alongside the church of San Pablo on the west bank of the

Rio Guadalmedina. All come with well-equipped kitchen, plasma TV and lounge area. Just the place for a longer stay, with welcoming owners and (relatively) easy street parking nearby. Reductions for stays of over three days. €€

Camping Torremolinos Loma del Paraiso 2, http://campingtorremolinos.com. Torremolinos' campsite, 10km west of Málaga along the coast, has plenty of shade and good facilities although it's pricey in high season. It's 3km east of the centre of the resort on the main N340 Málaga–Cádiz highway, 500m from the sea and accessible by train from Málaga. €

★ **Gran Hotel Miramar** Paseo de Reding 22, http://granhotelmiramarmalaga.com. One of the few five-star options in town. Built in 1926 as a holiday residence, the huge white palace has been restored to its former glory, with all the luxury extras you'd expect – including butler service. Features include large rooms and suites, plus a pool,

4

spa and pleasant gardens on the seafront. There's also a private car park. €€€€

Hostal Capri Av. de Pries 8, www.hostalcaprimalaga.com. Near the bullring, this is one of the best budget places in the city, with cosy a/c en-suite doubles, friendly owners and the beach on the doorstep. €

Hotel California Paseo de Sancha 17, 500m east of the bullring, http://hotelcaliforniamalaga.com. Charming small hotel near the beach with flower-bedecked entrance. The well-appointed rooms come with a/c and safes, and the hotel has its own garage. Five-night minimum stay in August. Buses #11, #34 and #35 from the Alameda will drop you outside. €

Hotel Ibis Paseo Guimbarda 5, http://ibishotel.com. On the west bank of the Guadalmedina, this is part of the international chain, offering functional rooms at attractive prices with frequent further discounts online. Can arrange parking. €€

Hotel Málaga Palacio Cortina del Muelle 1, http://marriott.com. This central four-star hotel with harbour-view rooms pampers its guests with free minibar and bathrobes. Facilities include a rooftop pool and a restaurant with spectacular views and a gym. €€€€

Hotel Molina Lario C/Molina Lario 20, http://hotelmolinalario.com. This family-run four-star hotel is housed in a pair of handsome nineteenth-century buildings right in the city's historic core. Design-led rooms are cool and contemporary, though the best are in the high-ceilinged historical wings. The hotel's crowning glory, however, is its rooftop pool that's so close to the cathedral it feels like you could almost touch it. €€

Hotel Room Mate Larios C/Marqués de Larios 2, http://hotellariosmalaga.com. Modern, upmarket and central hotel inside the shell of an original Art Deco edifice; satellite TV, room safes, and a rooftop bar with panoramic views are among the features. €€€

Hotel Trebol C/Moreno Carbonero 3, http://hoteltrebol.com. Pleasant small hotel in the atmospheric market area with modern a/c rooms. Features include a TV and internet connections. Ask for a room facing the street as these get more light and air. €€

★ **Parador Gibralfaro** Monte de Gibralfaro, www.paradores.es. You won't get a better panoramic view of the coast than from this eagle's nest on top of the Gibralfaro hill. It's quite small as *paradores* go, which adds to its charm, plus there's a pretty good restaurant (see page 223) and it also squeezes in a pool and has its own garage. €€€€

El Riad Andaluz C/Hinestrosa 24, http://elriadandaluz.com. En-suite doubles, riad-style decor and an attractive interior patio are the main features of this friendly townhouse near Pza. de la Merced. They can help with parking. €€

EATING

SEE MAP PAGE 216

Málaga has no shortage of **places to eat and drink**, and, though it's hardly a gourmet paradise, the city has a justified reputation for seafood. Its greatest claim to fame is undoubtedly its **fried fish**, acknowledged as the best in Spain. You'll find many fish restaurants grouped around the Alameda, although for some of the very best you need to head out to the suburbs of Pedregalejo and El Palo, served by bus #11 (from Paseo del Parque). On the seafront *paseo* at **Pedregalejo**, almost all of the cafés and restaurants serve up terrific seafood. Farther on, after the *paseo* disappears, you find yourself amid fishing shacks and smaller, sometimes quite ramshackle, cafés in **El Palo**, an earthier sort of area for the most part, with a beach and huts, and – in summer or at weekends – an even better place to eat.

TAPAS BARS

Antigua Casa de Guardia C/Pastora at the junction with the Alameda, http://antiguacasadeguardia.com. This is one of Málaga's oldest bars, dating from the nineteenth century, and serving the traditional sweet Málaga wine (Falstaff's "sack"), made from muscatel grapes and dispensed from huge barrels. Try washing it down with shellfish sold from a stall at the rear of the bar. The new-season wine, *Pedriot*, is incredibly sweet; much more palatable is *Seco Añejo*, which has matured for a year. €€

Bodegas Quitapeñas Marín García (aka La Manchega) C/Marín García 4, http://quitapenas.es. Another fine old drinking den with its own off-site *bodega* (which can be visited). Good tapas selection and *jibias guisadas* (stewed cuttlefish) is a speciality. You can wash them down with Málaga's traditional Moscatel and Sierras de Málaga wines. €€

El Rincón del Cervecero C/Casas de Campo 5, http://elrincondelcervecero.com. Located in the heart of Soho, this ranks among the best craft beer venues in town. The beer list runs long and includes the in-house brew, which you can accompany with cold cuts and cheese. Regular tastings and beer-making classes. €€

★ **El Tapeo de Cervantes** C/Carcer 8, http://eltapeodecervantes.com. This Lilliputian but outstanding bar near the Teatro Cervantes merits at least one visit. Here you'll find a cosy ambience and some creative tapas priced competitively; be sure to sample their *atún rojo en con emulsión coliflor* (tuna in a cauliflower sauce). They also have an equally excellent restaurant, *El Mesón de Cervantes*, located just around the corner at C/Alamos 11. €€

Uvedoble C/Cister 15, http://uvedobletaberna.com. Modernistic bar offering "designer" tapas in a minimalist setting with a small but interesting tapas and *raciones* menu. Try their *alcachofas con chipirón* (artichokes with squid) or *ceviche de pez espada* (sword fish ceviche) and *tortilla de patatas trufada* (truffled potato omelette). €€

RESTAURANTS

Alexso C/Mariblanca 10, http://restaurantealexso.es. Small restaurant serving some of the most creative food in town, the best of which you can try in the two tasting menus. Sharing plates is another good way to sample the Risotto de Málaga *salchichón* (a Malaga sausage risotto), the *lubina con salsa de zanahoria* (sea bass with carrot sauce) or *cochinillo con chutney de manzana* (suckling pig with apple chutney). Finish with a "salmon sandwich with chips" for dessert. €€

Antonio C/Fernando Lesseps 7, http://mesonantonio. com. Popular small and central restaurant serving well-prepared *malagueño* dishes, with an outdoor terrace in an atmospheric cul-de-sac off the north end of C/Nueva. €€

Araboka C/Pedro de Toledo 4, http://arabokarestaurante. com. Wine bar and restaurant with a seasonal changing menu. Dishes may include calamari with *pisto* (Spanish version of ratatouille) and deer ragout. Excellent wine list and the maître d' offers good advice on suitable pairing. €€

Bar Los Pueblos C/Ataranzas 15, http://barlospueblos. wordpress.com. This popular and busy diner has one of the warmest welcomes in town. It serves up satisfying, inexpensive food all day – bean soups and *estofados* are its specialities; gazpacho is served in half-pint glasses. Good-value daily menu. €€

Cañadu Pza. de la Merced 21, http://canadu.es. Relaxed vegetarian restaurant serving a good selection of salads and pastas as well as Persian rice, burgers and moussaka accompanied by organic wines and beers. €€

Óleo C/Alemania, part of CAC Málaga, http://oleo restaurante.es. This Mediterranean kitchen and sushi bar

offers both modern and classic dishes with a twist. Try the black Iberian pork with olive oil and red onion chutney, Vietamese rolls or the tuna belly nigiri. If you don't want to eat, you can just sip a cocktail on the outdoor terrace next to the river. €€

La Pachamama Atarazanas C/Olózoga 10, http:// barlapachamama.com. Lovely Peruvian restaurant, with a lively atmosphere, floral wall art, and a tempting menu of hearty, flavoursome dishes – the ocean-fresh, zingy *ceviche* and lomo saltado (beef tenderloin) are very tasty. €€€

★ **Parador Gibralfaro** Monte Gibralfaro, http:// paradores.es. Superior dining on the terrace with spectacular views over the coast and town. The house specialities are *malagueño* fish and meat dishes, and the menu is excellent value, with reasonable wine prices too. There's also a vegetarian menu. Ring to book one of the best tables. €€

El Tintero Playa del Dedo, El Palo, http://eltinteromalaga. com. Right at the far eastern end of the seafront, just before the *Club Náutico* (bus #11; ask for "*Tintero*"), this is a huge beach restaurant where the waiters charge round with plates of fish and you shout for, or grab, anything you like. The bill is totalled according to the number of plates on your table at the end of the meal. The fish to go for are, above all, *mero* (cod) and *rosada* (dogfish and catfish), along with Andalucian regulars such as *boquerones*, *gambas* and *sepia* (cuttlefish). Haute cuisine it certainly isn't, but for sheer entertainment it's a must. €€

DRINKING AND NIGHTLIFE SEE MAP PAGE 216

Most of Málaga's **nightlife** is northeast of the Catedral along and around **calles Granada and Beatas** and the streets circling the nearby **Pza. de Uncibay**. In the summer months, there's also a scene nearer the sea at **Malagueta**, south of the bullring. At weekends and holidays, dozens of youth-oriented disco bars fill the crowded streets in these areas, and over the summer – though it's dead out of season – the scene spreads out along the seafront to the suburb of **Pedregalejo**. Here the streets just behind the beach host most of the action, and dozens of *discotecas* and smaller music bars lie along and off the main street, Juan Sebastián Elcano. Málaga's daily paper, *Sur*, is good for local entertainment **listings**; there's also an English edition (*Sur in English*) on Fridays, available from *turismos* and hotels.

Batik C/Alcazabilla 12, http://batikmalaga.com. This club and restaurant is located on the fourth four of the boutique *Alcazaba Premium Hostel*, and serves excellent food and drinks on the roof terrace, with views of the Alcazaba.

★ **El Pimpi** C/Granada 62, http://elpimpi.com. Cavernous

and hugely popular *bodega*-style bar serving up, among other concoctions, tasty *vino dulce* by the glass or bottle. There are tapas to go with the drinks and you can do a bit of celebrity-spotting on their wall of photos (which includes a young Antonio Banderas, whose flat is just next door). Don't miss a superb terrace (with Alcazaba view) out the back. A great place to kick-start or end the evening.

Puerta Oscura C/Molina Lario 5 near the Catedral, 952 221 900. Slightly incongruous classical-music-cum-*cafetería*-cum-cocktail-bar – sometimes with live performers – which also mounts art exhibitions; serves cocktails, ices and baguettes. T-shirts are definitely a no-no here.

Sala Premier C/Molina Lario 2, http://salapremier.com. Busy venue with Wild West memorabilia downstairs and a Hobbit-themed upstairs, packed with locals and tourists who come here to watch sport and play board games.

ZZ Pub C/Tejón y Rodríguez 6, http://zzpub.es. DJ plays all kinds of music from jazz and soul to pop and funk. Often hosts live gigs at weekends.

SHOPPING SEE MAP PAGE 216

El Corte Inglés Avda. de Andalucía 4, http://elcorteingles. es. A great department store with a basement supermarket and top-floor gourmet store that sell a terrific selection of

the nation's wines and spirits.

Librería Luces Alameda Principal 16, http://librerialuces. com. The town's most central general bookshop stocks a selection of titles in English.

La Mallorquina C/Sagasta 1 (near the market), http://facebook.com/lamallorquinaj. This is a good place to pick up *malagueño* cheeses, wines, almonds and dried fruit.

Mapas y Compañía C/Compañía 33, http://mapasycia.es. Málaga's best travel bookshop sells IGN walking maps, as well as 1:50,000 Mapas Cartografía Militar (military maps).

DIRECTORY

Currency exchange El Corte Inglés will change currency free of charge.

Consulates UK, Edificio Eurocom, C/Mauricio Moro Pareto 2, 952 352 300; US, Avda. Juan Gómez 8, Fuengirola, 952 474 891; Republic of Ireland, Avda. de los Boliches 15, Fuengirola, 952 475 108.

Football Since gaining promotion to La Liga's top flight in 2008 C.F. Málaga has endured a rollercoaster period. In the 2011–12 season the club qualified for the Champions League for the first time in its history and reached the quarter finals, although success didn't last – two successive relegations saw it start the 2023/24 season in the third tier for the first time ever. Games are at La Rosaleda stadium, Paseo de Martiricos s/n, at the northern end of the Río Guadalmedina. Tickets can be purchased from the stadium (http://malagacf.com).

Hospital Hospital Regional Universitario, Avda. Carlos Haya, 2km west of the city centre, 951 290 000.

Left luggage There are lockers and a *consigna* at the train station, and lockers at the bus station.

Pharmacy Farmacia Caffarena (24hr) on the Alameda at no. 2, near the junction with C/Marqués de Larios, 952 212 858, http://farmaciacaffarena.net.

Police The Policía Local are at Avda. La Rosaleda 19 (952 126 500); in emergencies, dial 092 (local police) or 091 (national).

Post office C/Santa Lucía.

Garganta del Chorro

Fifty kilometres northwest of Málaga lies the deep, rugged canyon of the Río Guadalhorce, known as the **Garganta del Chorro**. It's an amazing place – an immense five-kilometre-long cleft in a vast limestone massif, which has become Andalucía's major centre for rock climbers. The gorge's most stunning feature, however, is a concrete catwalk, **El Caminito del Rey**, which threads the length of the gorge, hanging precipitously halfway up its side. If you have no head for heights it's still possible to explore the rest of the gorge, and get a view of the *camino* by walking from **El Chorro**. A glimpse of both gorge and *camino* can also be had from any of the trains going north from Málaga – the line, slipping in and out of tunnels, follows the river for a considerable distance along the gorge, before plunging into a last long tunnel just before its head.

El Caminito del Rey

Charge • http://caminitodelrey.info

A WALK FROM EL CHORRO TO THE GORGE

Another good way to view Garganta del Chorro is to follow a 12km **walk** (vehicles should follow the same route) from the village of **El Chorro**. Take the road from the train station, signposted "Pantano de Guadalhorce", reached by crossing over the dam and turning right, then following the road north along the lake towards the hydroelectric plant. After 8km turn right at a junction to reach – after 2km – the bar-restaurant *El Mirador*, poised above a road tunnel and overlooking the various lakes and reservoirs of the Guadalhorce scheme. From the bar (where you should leave any transport) a dirt track on the right heads towards the gorge. Follow this and take the first track on the right after about 700m. This climbs for some 2km to where it splits into two small trails. The trail to the left leads after 300m to a magnificent **viewpoint** over the gorge from where you can see the Caminito del Rey clinging to the rock face. The right-hand track climbs swiftly to an obvious peak, the **Pico de Almochon**, with more spectacular views, this time over the lakes of the Embalse de Guadalhorce.

Built in the 1920s as part of a hydroelectric scheme, **El Caminito del Rey** was one of the wonders of Spain, but fell into a dangerous state of disrepair, which led to its closure to all but those with climbing gear in the late 1990s. In 2015, a new catwalk opened after a major feat of engineering (helicopters were used to position some of the structure) built it one metre above the line of the old one, and it's now one of the main tourist attractions in Málaga province. There is now a visitors' centre detailing the history of the site. To walk the 7.7km El Caminito trail (4.4km along the catwalk itself) you need to book in advance via the website, which also provides full details on how to get to the start point and return. Allow 3 to 4 hours for your visit.

ARRIVAL AND DEPARTURE GARGANTA DEL CHORRO

By train and bus El Chorro is served by one daily direct trains (55min; currently running at 9.06am), but no buses, from Málaga. There are five daily buses to El Chorro from nearby Álora, which is served by eight daily trains from Málaga.

By car To get there with your own transport, take the A357 heading west from Málaga towards Pizarra, turning here along the A343 to Álora. Continue beyond Álora for 15km and turn west at Valle de Abdalajís along the minor MA4401, a journey of around 65km in total.

ACCOMMODATION

Bar-Restaurante Garganta del Chorro http://lagarganta.com. Located near the station, this restaurant and accommodation complex has been refurbished since the new Caminito del Rey opened and provides pleasant rooms inside a converted mill overlooking a pool. €€€€
Camping Parque Ardales http://parqueardales.com. Located in a pine wood on the shores of the reservoir, this is a handy campsite for the Caminito del Rey. They also offer basic apartments, as well as tent pitches. They can also provide advice on rural accommodation. Open all year. €€

★ **Finca La Campana** http://fincalacampana.com. Signs from the station will direct you 2km to this complex, which consists of a rural farmhouse, bunkhouse, a cluster of attractive cottages (with fully equipped kitchen), and a pool. Run by Swiss climber Jean Hofer, the place also offers courses in rock climbing and caving, rents out mountain bikes, can arrange kayaks on the nearby reservoir, and does hiking excursions, as well as organizing tickets for the Caminito del Rey. For longer stays (two nights plus) transfers can be arranged from Álora or Málaga airport and camping is also possible. €

Antequera and around

ANTEQUERA, some 55km north of Málaga on the main rail line to Granada, is an attractive market town with some important monuments, a clutch of interesting churches and a fine old Pza. de Toros. The most famous of its sights, however, is a group of prehistoric dolmen caves on the northern edge of town that rank among the most important in Spain.

Nuestra Señora del Carmen

Pza. del Carmen • Charge

The finest of Antequera's collection of Baroque churches (the *turismo* can provide a full list) is **Nuestra Señora del Carmen** on Pza. del Carmen. The church's rather plain facade little prepares you for the eighteenth-century interior, now painstakingly restored to its former glory. The main altar's sensational 13m-high *retablo* – one of the finest in Andalucía – is a masterly late Baroque extravaganza of carved wood by Antonio Primo and Diego Márquez, its centrepiece a Virgin in a *camarín* (shrine) flanked by a bevy of polychromed saints and soaring angels.

The Dolmen caves

Avda. de Málaga 1 • Free

Antequera's most visited monuments are the group of prehistoric dolmen caves, a designated UNESCO World Heritage Site. They're on the town's northern edge, enclosed in a "dolmen park" with visitor centre, car park and a Centro de Interpretación. The grandest and most famous of these megalithic monuments is the **Cueva de Menga**, its roof formed by an immense 180-tonne monolith. Dating from around 2500 BC, a columned gallery leads to an oval burial chamber, probably the final resting place of an important chieftain. The nearby **Cueva de Viera**, dating from a century or two later, has cut stones but a smaller burial chamber. To reach the dolmens, take the Granada road out of town – an easy ten-minute walk – to the turning, rather insignificantly signposted, after about 1km on the left.

Two kilometres away is a third cave, **El Romeral**, which is different (and later) in structure, with a domed ceiling of flat stones; get instructions (and a map) of how to reach it from the visitor centre.

The Plaza de Toros

Paseo María Cristina s/n • Free

The **Plaza de Toros** in the newer part of town on the Alameda de Andalucía is also worth a look; it staged its first *corrida* in August 1848. Whatever your view on bullfighting, it's difficult not to pick up the atmosphere the old place generates, especially when you survey the amphitheatre from the matador's position in the centre of the burning sand.

INFORMATION
ANTEQUERA

Turismo Town maps and information on El Torcal are available from a very helpful tourist office on the central Pza. San Sebastián (Mon–Sat 9.30am–7pm, Sun 10am– 2pm; 952 702 505, http://turismo.antequera.es) alongside the church of the same name.

ACCOMMODATION AND EATING

A good base for visits to nearby El Torcal, Antequera has plenty of **accommodation** options and prices are reasonable. The Antequera *turismo* can provide information regarding some attractive *casas rurales* to rent near El Torcal.
★ **Hotel Arte de Cozina** C/Calzada 25, http://artede cozina.com. Comfortable and good-value a/c en-suite rooms with TV, plus a friendly welcome, make this a winner. It also has a very good restaurant. €
Hotel Los Dolmenes Cruce del Romeral, http:// hotellosdolmenes.com. Pleasant three-star hotel close to the dolmen caves, with spacious, comfortable rooms with terrace balcony and views. Ideal if you have a vehicle as their ample car park is free. Breakfast included. €
Mar de Gloria C/Infante Don Fernando 68, http://marde gloria.es. One of the best local restaurants, serving traditional local dishes in relaxed surroundings. Specialities include *porre antequerana*, a cold soup made of tomato and bread which is the local answer to gazpacho, only much thicker. €€
Parador de Antequera Paseo García del Olmo s/n, http:// parador.es. A modern parador, to the north of the Plaza de Toros, with well-appointed and well-equipped rooms, plus pleasant gardens, pool and stunning views. €€

Parque Natural El Torcal de Antequera

16km south of Antequera • http://torcaldeantequera.com

Approaching Antequera Málaga via Almogía and Villenueva de la Concepción, you reach **Parque Natural El Torcal**, whose haunting limestone sculptures make it one of the most geologically arresting of Spain's natural parks. A massive high plateau of glaciated limestone tempered by a lush growth of hawthorn, ivy and wild rose, it can be painlessly explored using the three walking routes that radiate from the centre of the park, outlined in a leaflet available from the **Centro de Visitantes**.

Trails

The best-designed and most exciting **trails** are the yellow and red routes, the former climaxing with suitable drama on a cliff edge with magnificent views over a valley. The latter gives fantastic vantage points of the looming limestone outcrops, eroded into vast, surreal sculptures. Because of the need to protect flora and fauna, the red route is in a restricted zone and can only be visited with a **guide** (ask at the *centro*). The **green** and **yellow routes** (waymarked) can be walked without a guide, the former taking about forty minutes if you don't dawdle, the latter about two hours. In early summer, on the popular green route you may find yourself competing with gangs of schoolkids, who arrive en masse on vaguely educational trips, excitedly trying to spot La Copa (the wine glass), El Lagarto (the lizard) and La Loba (the she-wolf), as well as other celebrated **rock sculptures**. Keep an eye on the skies while you're here, for griffon vultures are frequent visitors and, with their huge wingspans, make a spectacular sight as they glide overhead. The Centro de Visitantes also has its own **cafetería** with a *menú del día*.

ARRIVAL AND DEPARTURE

PARQUE NATURAL EL TORCAL

By bus Buses run from Málaga; ask the driver to drop you at the road for El Torcal from where it's a 4km uphill slog to the visitor centre.

By taxi turístico The most convenient way to visit the park without your own transport is the *taxi turístico*, which can be arranged through the *turismo* in Antequera; a taxi will drop off up to four passengers at the Centro de Visitantes and wait (roughly 1hr) until you have completed the green route before returning you to Antequera.

Nerja & Almuñécar

The eastern section of the Costa del Sol ribbons east of the city of Málaga as far as Almería, and is generally uninspiring. Inland there are plenty of attractive sierras to explore but, though far less developed than its twin coastal strip to the west of Málaga, there's little to tempt you to stop before you reach the twin resorts of **Nerja** and **Almuñécar** – which are its saving feature.

Nerja

Some 40km east out of Málaga, **NERJA** nestles in the foothills of the Almijara range. This was a village before it was a resort, so it has some intrinsic character, and villa development has been shaped around it.

The focus of the whitewashed old quarter is the **Bálcon de Europa**, a striking palm-fringed belvedere overlooking the sea. The beaches flanking this are also reasonably attractive, with a series of quieter coves within walking distance. There are plenty of other great **walks** around Nerja, too, well documented in the *turismo*'s own leaflets; at Smiffs Bookshop, C/Almirante Ferrandiz 10, you can buy individual leaflets detailing walks in the area by local resident and hiker Elma Thompson.

The Cuevas de Nerja

Carr. de Bajada a Playa de Maro 7pm • Charge • http://cuevadenerja.es

Nerja's chief tourist attraction, the **Cuevas de Nerja**, 3km east from the town, are a heavily commercialized series of caverns, impressive in size – and home to the world's longest-known **stalactite** at 63m – though otherwise not tremendously interesting. They also contain a number of prehistoric paintings, but these are not currently on public view.

ARRIVAL AND INFORMATION

NERJA

By bus The main bus station (actually a stand) is on C/San Miguel at the north end of town close to Pza. Cantarero; from here hourly buses leave for the *cuevas*. It's a 5min walk south from the bus station to the beach and centre.

Turismo C/Carmen 1 (http://nerja.org), next to the *ayuntamiento* and just west of the Balcón de Europa.

ACCOMMODATION

Note that Nerja's accommodation can be booked out solid in high season.

Hostal Marissal Paseo Balcón de Europa 3, http://hostalmarissal.com. This excellent *hostal* is in the town's prime location – actually on the belvedere. En-suite balcony rooms come with a/c, TV and strongbox, and many have sea views (try for rooms 102–105 or 204–205); it also rents apartments in the same location. Doubles €€, apartments €€€€

Hotel Mena Plaza Plaza de España 2, www.hotel menaplaza.es. Very comfortable, if rather uninspiring and business-like, rooms and suites at this central budget hotel. Apartments are also available and are slightly more homely, while there's a terrace pool to enjoy. €€

Hotel Paraiso del Mar C/Carabeo 22, http://hotel paraisodelmar.es. With similar views to the parador, this is a very pleasant hotel where all rooms come with Jacuzzi and many have sea-view balconies. There's also a pool, gardens and a sauna dug out of the cliff face. €€€

Parador Nacional C/Almuñécar 8, http://parador.es. Overlooking one of Nerja's most popular beaches, Playa de Burriana, to which you descend in a private lift, this is a modern parador with comfortable rooms and a pool situated in attractive gardens. €€€€

Almuñécar

The lively resort of **ALMUÑÉCAR** is marred by a number of towering holiday apartments, and the rocky grey-sand beaches are rather cramped, but the esplanade behind them, with palm-roofed bars (many serving free tapas with each drink) and restaurants, is fun, and the old quarter – clustered around a sixteenth-century castle – is attractive. The two main beaches, the **Playa San Cristóbal** and the **Playa Puerta del Mar**, are separated by the towering headland of the Peñon del Santo.

ARRIVAL AND INFORMATION   ALMUÑÉCAR

By bus The bus station, which has frequent connections to Málaga and Granada, is at the junction of avenidas Juan Carlos I and Fenicia, northeast of the centre.

Turismo In an imposing neo-Moorish mansion on Avda.

de Europa (daily 9.30am–1.30pm & 4.30–7pm; 958 631 125, http://turismoalmunecar.es), behind the Playa San Cristóbal beach at the west end of the town.

ACCOMMODATION

The pressure on **accommodation** in Almuñécar is not quite as acute as at Nerja. There are more than enough hotels to cope with the summer crush, while good-value *hostales* encircle the central Pza. de la Rosa in the old town. Note that some hotels require a minimum booking of two nights in high season.

Hostal San Sebastián C/Ingenio Real 16, http://hostal-sansebastian.com. Clean, friendly *hostal* in the north of town, offering colourful en-suite rooms with TV and ceiling fans. €

Hotel California Carretera de Málaga km 313, northwest of the town on the main road, http://hotelcaliforniaspain.com. Moorish-style, inviting hotel with balcony rooms and bar offering evening meals with plenty of veggie options.

Owners are keen paragliders and can also organize diving and skiing. €

★ **Hotel Casablanca** Pza. San Cristóbal 4 (aka Pza. Abderramán), http://hotelcasablancaalmunecar.com. The wonderful *Casablanca* is one of the most charming hotels on the coast. Fifty metres from the beach, and with a splendid neo-Moorish facade, the hotel boasts comfortable a/c terrace-balcony rooms with great sea views (on the front). The friendly family proprietors make this an all-round winner. Also has garage parking. €€

Hotel Toboso C/Larache 2, http://hoteltobosoalmunecar.com. Comfortable hotel a block south of the N340 offering a/c rooms with mountain or sea views plus garden and own parking. €€

EATING AND DRINKING

There are numerous **places to eat** along the seafront, many of them offering cheap, if unspectacular, fare. The town's more interesting possibilities are set further back in the *casco antiguo* or old quarter.

Bodega Francisco C/Real 15, north of Pza. Rosa, 958 630 168. Wonderful old bar with barrels stacked up to the ceiling and walls covered with ageing *corrida* posters and mounted boars' heads. The *fino* and *montilla* are both excellent, and the bar offers a wide range of tapas and cheap *platos combinados*. There's an adjoining dining area and impromptu flamenco sometimes adds to the fun. €€

Mesón Antonio C/Manila 9, http://facebook.com/meson antonio. One of several lively bars in the street and usually packed with locals, this *mesón* specializes in *carne a la brasa* (chargrilled meat) and octopus. €€

Mesón Gala Pza. Damasco 4, www.restaurantegala.es. Slightly higher-end option, popular with locals and one of several in an attractive square with a lively scene on summer nights. Specials include *bacalao con setas y langostinos* (cod with mushrooms and langoustines) and *berenjenas a la miel* (crispy fried aubergine with treacle). Tapas available at the bar and on part of the terrace. €€

The Costa del Sol resorts

West of Málaga – or more correctly, west of Málaga airport – the real **Costa del Sol** gets going, and if you've never seen this level of tourist development, it's quite a shock. These are certainly not the kind of resorts you could envisage anywhere else in Europe. The 1960s and 1970s hotel and apartment tower blocks were followed by a second wave of property development in the 1980s and 1990s, this time villa homes and leisure complexes, funded by massive international investment. It's estimated that 300,000 foreigners now live on and around the Costa del Sol, the majority of them British and other Northern Europeans, though marina developments such as Puerto Banús have also attracted Arab and Russian money.

Approached in the right kind of spirit, it is possible to have fun in resorts like **Torremolinos**, **Fuengirola** and, at a price, in **Marbella**. But if you've come to Spain to be in Spain keep going at least until you reach Estepona.

Marbella and around

Sheltered by the hills of the Sierra Blanca, **MARBELLA** stands in considerable contrast to most of what has come before. Since it attracted the attentions of the smart set in the 1960s the town has zealously polished its reputation as the Costa del Sol's most stylish resort. Glitz comes at a price, of course: many of the chic restaurants, bars and cafés cash in on the hype, and everything costs considerably more than elsewhere in the region. The resort has also attracted more than its fair share of Russian and Italian mafia over the years, plus several notorious British and Irish criminals, and there are periodic police raids and high-profile arrests. In addition, Marbella was the focus of one of Spain's largest municipal political corruption cases between 1991 and 2007. Nowadays, however, political life is relatively staid and Marbella features in the press mostly as a celebrity holiday spot. In an ironic twist of history, Arabs favour the area, particularly the west end of the resort where the late King Fahd of Saudi Arabia built a White House lookalike, complete with adjacent mosque.

South of Marbella's centre, there are three excellent **beaches** stretching east from Playa de la Bajadilla and Playa de Venus to Playa de la Fontanilla to the west, which gets progressively less crowded the farther west you go.

The old town

To be fair, Marbella has been spared the worst excesses of concrete architecture and also retains the greater part of its **old town** – set back a little from the sea and the new development. Centred on the attractive Pza. de los Naranjos and still partially walled, the old town is hidden from the main road and easy to miss. Slowly, this original quarter is being bought up and turned into clothes and jewellery boutiques

---

GETTING AROUND THE COSTA DEL SOL

One of the major selling points of the **Costa del Sol** is its ease of access. Hundreds of flights arrive here every week, and **Málaga airport** is positioned midway between **Málaga**, the main city on the coast, and **Torremolinos**, its most famous resort. You can easily reach either town by taking the electric train (*cercanía*) that runs every twenty minutes along the coast between Málaga and **Fuengirola**, 20km to the southwest. Frequent bus connections also link all the major coastal resorts, while a toll *autopista* (motorway) between Málaga and Sotogrande has taken the strain off the often overloaded coastal highways. Inland, Granada, Córdoba and Seville are all within easy reach of Málaga; so, too, are **Ronda** and the beautiful "White Towns" to the west, and a handful of relatively restrained coastal resorts, such as **Nerja**, to the east.

and restaurants, but the process isn't that far advanced. You can still sit in an ordinary bar in a small old square and look up beyond the whitewashed alleyways to the mountains of Ronda.

Puerto Banús

The seriously rich don't stay in Marbella itself. They secrete themselves away in villas in the surrounding hills or laze around on phenomenally large and luxurious yachts at the marina and casino complex of **Puerto Banús**, 6km west of town. As you'd expect, Puerto Banús has more than its complement of big-name designer boutiques, cocktail bars, beach clubs and restaurants, most of them very pricey.

ARRIVAL AND INFORMATION   MARBELLA

By bus From the bus station (952 764 401) in the north of the town, bus #2 will drop you close by the old town; otherwise, it's a 20min walk south along C/Trapiche.
Turismo Pza. de los Naranjos (mid-June to Sept Mon–Fri

8.30am–9.30pm, weekends 10am–9.30pm; Oct to mid-June Mon–Fri 8.30am–7.30pm, weekends 9am–2pm; 952 768 707). It can help with accommodation, and provides a street-indexed town map.

ACCOMMODATION

All Marbella's budget **accommodation** is in the old town and south of the Alameda. Pressure on rooms is tight in July and extremely so in August, when you'll need to book ahead.
Albergue Juvenil C/Trapiche 2, http://inturjoven.com. To the north of the old town, the *Albergue Juvenil* has economical beds in smart double and four-person en-suite rooms, and there's also a pool. €
Hostal Berlin C/San Ramón 21, http://hostalberlin.com. Sparkling and very friendly *hostal*; all rooms come with a bath, a/c and satellite TV. Bargain rates outside July and August. €€
★ **Hotel La Morada Mas Hermosa** C/Montenebros 16, http://lamoradamashermosa.com. Sited to the north of

Pza. de los Naranjos, this is an enchanting small hotel in a refurbished eighteenth-century townhouse, with elegant, individually styled a/c rooms (most with terraces). €€
The Townhouse C/Alderete 7, http://townhousemarbella. com. Attractive en-suite a/c rooms, most with balconies, set in a peaceful square in the heart of the old town. There's also a lovely rooftop terrace; breakfast is included. €€€€
La Villa Marbella C/Príncipe 10, www.lavillamarbella. com. Rooms and apartments located to the north of the old town in tranquil streets. Asian-style en-suite doubles with a/c, some with balcony and/or Jacuzzi, plus use of the pool and roof terrace. Breakfast included for direct bookings. Rooms €€€, apartments €€€€

EATING

Although there are several Michelin-starred restaurants (including double-starred chef Dani García at the restaurant of the *Hotel Puente Romano*), Marbella's best-value eating and drinking places aren't always the most obvious. Avoid the touristy and overpriced **restaurants** on the Pza. de los Naranjos, which turn the whole square into their dining terrace after dark –you're better off seeking out some of Marbella's excellent **tapas bars** and less brassy restaurants. Despite its high-roller reputation, it's possible to dine well in Marbella at normal *andaluz* prices.

TAPAS BARS

Bar Altamirano Pza. de Altamirano 4, http://bar altamirano.es. Great place for some of the freshest seafood tapas and *raciones* in town; has a terrace with tables spread across a small square. €€
El Estrecho C/San Lázaro 12, http://barelestrecho.com. Founded in 1954, this is an excellent and atmospheric little tapas bar with a wide range of choice. There's a small dining room off to the side if you want to make a meal of it, and

cool jazz sounds often float in the background. Try their *carne mechada* (slow-braised pork) or *pimento del piquillo* (peppers stuffed with tuna and spinach). €€
Sidrería La Paca C/Peral 16, http://tapaspaca.com. Asturias-themed tapas at reasonable prices, to eat inside at the bar or outside on the street terrace. Specials include generous salads, *tostas* (bread with toppings) and *sidra* (cider). €€

RESTAURANTS

★ **Gaspar** C/Notario Luís Oliver 19, west of Pza. de los Naranjos, http://tabernagaspar.es. A gem of a restaurant run by a friendly family from Rioja – which explains the comprehensive wine list. Besides their standard dishes – including *tortilla*, *cordero asado* (charcoal grilled lamb), and *pastel de berenjenas* (aubergine terrine) you can also order a few plates of *raciones* to share. If you have to wait for a table you can peruse the books in the restaurant's library, and impromptu flamenco sometimes happens when *cantantes* (singers) drop in for a meal. €€€

★ **Messina** Avda. Severo Ochoa 12, http://restaurante messina.com. This Michelin-starred restaurant consistently produces great food. Argentinean chef Mauricio Giovanni cooks Mediterranean dishes with a modern twist. Three tasting menus showcase his signature dishes *cigalas con foie y erizo* (crayfish with foie gras and sea urchin), Iberian pork curry and creamy parsnip with blue cheese, and Andalusian shrimp, or you can eat these dishes on their own from the à la carte menu. Extensive wine list. €€€€

Paellas y Más C/Hermanos Salom 3, http://restaurante paellasymas.com. There's not much they don't know about rice here, where paellas and *fideuas* (minimum order for two people) are the absolute stars of the show in both their traditional versions and with more unusual ingredients. Sharing plates and creative salads are also available. The spacious outdoor terrace makes for very pleasant dining. €€

Santiago Avda. Duque de Ahumada s/n, http://restaurantesantiago.com. For a splurge, head for *Santiago*, near the Puerto Deportivo, one of Marbella's swankiest and oldest restaurants, founded in the 1950s by Santiago Domínguez – who started out with a *chiringuito* on the beach opposite. Over fifty years later Santiago is still at the helm and is famous throughout Spain as one of the great restaurateurs. The menu showcases traditional *malagueño* cuisine (both fish and meat) with a creative touch. €€€€

DRINKING AND NIGHTLIFE

Marbella has one of the liveliest **nightlife** scenes on the *costa*, with action centred around Pza. Puente de Ronda, Pza. de Africa in the old town and Pza. de Olivos to the west of here. The once riotious Puerto Deportivo, the seafront yacht harbour, also has a scene, now mostly laidback *copas* bars with terraces filled with sofas and easy chairs.

Bar Guerola C/Padre Enrique Cantos 4, http://guerola marbella.wordpress.com. It's not all glitz and glamour in Marbella. For a taste of days gone by, head to this cosy and historic bar, dating back to 1960 and covered in black-and-

white photographs depicting times past. The wine list is varied and well-priced, and the tapas are generous.

Franks Corner C/Camino José Cela 12, http://franks cornermarbella.com. A classic on the Marbella live music scene, as well as one of the places to play pool and/or watch televised sport.

Gauguin Avda. Fontanilla 7, http://facebook.com/Gauguin Marbella. Popular lounge and Tiki-style cocktail bar with a long G&T menu and outdoor terrace (heated in winter). In-house DJs play music from the 1980s onwards.

Estepona and around

The coast continues to be upmarket (or "money-raddled", as Laurie Lee put it) until you reach **ESTEPONA**, about 30km west, which is about as Spanish as the resorts round here get. It lacks the enclosed hills that give Marbella character, but the hotel and apartment blocks that sprawl along the front are restrained in size, and there's space to breathe. The fine sand beach has been enlivened a little by a promenade studded with flowers and palms, and, away from the seafront, the old town is very pretty, with cobbled alleyways, two delightful plazas, plus over 24 murals (ask for a map at the *turismo*). At the beginning of July, the Fiesta y Feria week transforms the place, bringing out whole families in flamenco-style garb.

Plaza de Toros museum complex

Free

From May onward, Estepona's **bullfighting** season gets under way in a modern **bullring** reminiscent of a Henry Moore sculpture. This building has now taken on an additional role as the location for no fewer than three museums: the **Museo Etnográfico** (folk museum), the **Museo Paleontológico** (paleontology) and, perhaps the most interesting, the **Museo Taurino** (bullfighting), with fascinating exhibits and photos underlining the importance of *taurinismo* in Andalucian culture.

Selwo Adventure Park

Av. Parque Selwo • Charge • http://selwo.es

The **Selwo Adventure Park** is a landscaped zoo 6km to the east of town where the two-thousand-plus resident animals are allowed to roam in "semi-liberty" and there are re-creations of African Zulu and Masai villages. To reach the park, watch out for the signed exits indicated from the A7 and the AP7 Autopista del Sol, and there are regular buses from all the major Costa del Sol resorts.

Casares

Beyond Estepona, 8km along the coast, a minor road (the MA546) climbs a farther 13km into the hills to **CASARES**, one of the classic *andaluz* White Towns. In keeping with the genre, it clings tenaciously to a steep hillside below a castle, and has attracted its fair share of arty types and expats. But it remains comparatively little known; bus connections are just about feasible for a day-trip (Mon–Sat leaving 1pm, returning 4pm; 45min), or you may want to consider an overnight stay. Get further details from the *turismo*.

ARRIVAL AND INFORMATION   ESTEPONA AND AROUND

By bus The station is on Avda. de España, to the west of the centre behind the seafront.

Turismo The town's efficient and centrally located *turismo* is located inside the *ayuntamiento* at Pza. de las Flores s/n (Mon–Fri 9am–3.30pm, Sat 10am–2pm; 952 802 002); they will supply town maps and can help you find a room.

ACCOMMODATION AND EATING

Camping Parque Tropical 6km east of town on the A7, km162, http://campingparquetropical.com. Estepona's nearest campsite is set back a few hundred metres from the beach in a former tropical garden with plenty of shade plus a spectacular conservatory-pool and a restaurant. €

Casa de la Borrega C/Correo Viejo 9, north of Pza. de la Flores, http://casalaborrega.com. Functional, clean apartments sleeping two to four, in a restored sixteenth-century mansion with many original features such as a stunning central patio. Apartments are named after the Andalucian provinces. €€€€

★ **La Escollera** Puerto Pesquero, 952 806 354. Now into its eighth decade and sited at the foot of the lighthouse in the fishing harbour, adjoining the Puerto Deportivo, this is a vibrant, reasonably priced restaurant and tapas bar, with a wonderful sea-view terrace and excellent fish and *mariscos* dishes. At weekends you'll need to book ahead or arrive

early to get a table. €€€

Hostal La Malagueña C/Castillo s/n, close to Plaza de Las Flores, http://hlmestepona.com. Comfortable, welcoming and reliable *hostal*, offering a/c en-suite rooms with TV, plus a roof terrace solarium. Own car park. €

Hotel Mediterráneo Avda. de España 68, on the seafront to the east of C/Terraza, 952 800 895. Functional but good-value seafront hotel, where rooms have bath, a/c, TV and (most of them) sea views. Ask for a higher room on the front (these are quieter). €€

Restaurante El Gavilán del Mar C/Correo 1, actually on Pza. Arce, 952 802 856. A decent place for seafood (meat dishes are also on offer), specializing in paella, and with a terrace on this charming square. Try their *sardinas asadas* (grilled sardines) or a *zarzuela* (fish casserole) which is enough for two. €€

Gibraltar

GIBRALTAR's interest is essentially its novelty: the genuine appeal of the strange, looming physical presence of its rock, and the dubious one of its preservation as one of Britain's last remaining colonies. For most of its history it has existed in a limbo between two worlds without being fully part of either. It's a curious place to visit, but its recent "discovery" by British package tourists day-tripping from the Costa del Sol threatens both to destroy Gibraltar's highly individual hybrid society and at the same time to make it much more "British", after the fashion of the expat communities and huge resorts of the Costa.

The Town

The town has a necessarily simple layout, as it's shoehorned into the narrow stretch of land on the peninsula's western edge in the shadow of the towering Rock. **Main Street** (La Calle Real) runs for most of the town's length, a couple of blocks back from the port. On and around Main Street are most of the shops, together with many of the British-style pubs and hotels.

Trafalgar Cemetery
Prince Edward's Road • Free

To the south of the town centre, beyond the city walls, lies the evocative **Trafalgar Cemetery**, where some of those who perished at the Battle of Trafalgar are buried. A memorial to the battle stands in the cemetery grounds and a number of graves display a good line in imperial epitaphs.

The Gibraltar Museum
Bomb House Lane • Charge • http://gibmuseum.gi

BRITISH SOVEREIGNTY IN GIBRALTAR

Sovereignty of the Rock (a land area smaller than the city of Algeciras across the water) will doubtless eventually return to Spain, but at present a **stalemate** exists regarding the colony's future. For Britain, it's a question of divesting itself of the colony without incurring the wrath of Gibraltar's citizens who are implacably opposed to any further involvement with Spain. For Spain, there are unsettling parallels with the *presidios* (Spanish enclaves) on the Moroccan coast at Ceuta and Melilla – both at present part of Andalucía. Nonetheless, the British presence is in practice waning: they are running down the significance of the military base, and now only a token force of under a hundred British troops remains – most of these working in a top-secret high-tech bunker buried deep inside the Rock from where the Royal Navy monitors sea traffic through the Strait (accounting for a quarter of all the world's movement of shipping).

In 1967, just before Franco closed the border in the hope of forcing a quick agreement, the colony voted on the return to Spanish control of the Rock – rejecting it by 12,138 votes to 44. Most people would probably sympathize with that vote – against a Spain that was then still a dictatorship – but fifty years have gone by, Spanish democracy is now secure, and the arguments are becoming increasingly tenuous. May 1996 saw a change in the trend of internal politics, with the defeat of the colony's pugnaciously anti-Spanish Labour government (following two previous landslide victories) and the election of a new **Social Democratic administration** led by Peter Caruana. Caruana won further victories in 2000, 2004 and 2007 but was defeated in the 2011 election by a Labour-Liberal coalition, following which Labour leader Fabian Picardo became chief minister. Picardo won the last election held in 2015 and remains in power.

The ruling PP (Partido Popular) conservative **Spanish administration** formed a minority government after failing to win a majority in elections in 2015, but has repeated the claims over Gibraltar voiced by all its predecessors, and the political stalemate seems set to continue for as long as Britain uses the wishes of the Gibraltarians as a pretext for blocking any change in the colony's status – a policy that infuriates the Spanish government, whose former foreign minister, Abel Matutes, stated that the wishes of the residents "did not apply in the case of Hong Kong".

The UK's 2016 **Brexit referendum** on leaving or remaining in the EU also has had major implications for Gibraltar's future. Whereas in Britain the vote was narrowly in favour of leave, in Gibraltar (which was included in the poll) the vote to remain was an overwhelming 96 percent. At the time of writing, Spain had won an early concession from the EU guaranteeing it an important role in deciding Gibraltar's post-Brexit status, and Spain and the UK had reached an agreement in principle that Gibraltar would join the EU's Schengen Area, although this had still not come to pass at the time of writing.

In tune with their rejection of most things Spanish (although seven thousand of the Rock's citizenry, including Chief Minister Fabian Picardo, own second homes on the Spanish side of the frontier), Gibraltarians stubbornly cling to British status, and all their institutions are modelled on British lines. Contrary to popular belief, however, they are of neither mainly Spanish nor British blood, but an ethnic mix descended from Genoese, Portuguese, Spanish, Menorcan, Jewish, Maltese and British forebears. **English** is the official language, but more commonly spoken is what sounds to an outsider like perfect Andalucian Spanish. It is, in fact, *llanito*, an Andalucian dialect with the odd borrowed English and foreign word reflecting its diverse origins – only a Spaniard from the south can tell a Gibraltarian from an Andalucian.

4

The **Gibraltar Museum** is mainly concerned with gilding the imperial story, although the building also holds two well-preserved and beautiful fourteenth-century **Moorish baths** as well as a rather incongruous Egyptian mummy washed up in the bay.

Nelson's Anchorage

Rosia Road • Charge

At **Nelson's Anchorage** a monstrous **100-tonne Victorian gun** marks the site where Nelson's body was brought ashore – preserved in a barrel of rum – from HMS *Victory* after the Battle of Trafalgar in 1805.

The Top of the Rock

Main Street • Charge • http://naturereserve.gi/our-rock/top-of-the-rock

From near the southern end of Main Street you can hop on a **cable car**, which will carry you up to the summit – **The Top of the Rock** as it's logically known. Although the cable car's fare structure militates against it, after riding to the top it's possible to walk back down, a pleasant twenty- to thirty-minute stroll. From The Top of the Rock you can look over the Strait of Gibraltar to the Atlas Mountains of Morocco and down to the town, the elaborate water-catchment system cut into the side of the rock, and

4

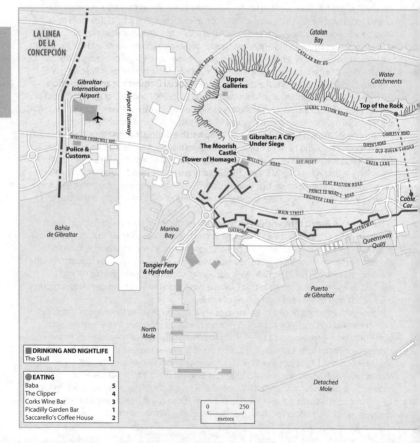

■ DRINKING AND NIGHTLIFE	
The Skull	1

● EATING	
Baba	5
The Clipper	4
Corks Wine Bar	3
Picadilly Garden Bar	1
Saccarello's Coffee House	2

ponder whether it's worth heading for one of the beaches such as Catalan Bay (see page 236). Or stay put for a glass of wine at the Mons Calpe Suite restaurant, whose floor-to-ceiling windows offer panoramic views.

Upper Rock Nature Reserve

Charge • http://naturereserve.gi/

The area at The Top of the Rock, designated the **Upper Rock Nature Reserve**, is home to six-hundred-plus plant and tree species, and also contains the Apes' Den (a fairly reliable viewing point to see the tailless monkeys), St Michael's Cave and other sights; the attractions in this zone are included in the Nature Reserve ticket, available from tourist offices or at each attraction. A grand tour of the Rock takes a half- to a full day.

From the cable-car stop at The Top of the Rock, it's an easy walk south along St Michael's Road through the Nature Reserve, to **St Michael's Cave**, an immense natural cavern that led ancient people to believe that the Rock was hollow and gave rise to its old name of Mons Calpe (Hollow Mountain). The cave was used during the last war as a bomb-proof military hospital and nowadays hosts occasional concerts. If you're adventurous, you can arrange at the tourist office for a guided visit to Lower St Michael's Cave, a series of chambers going deeper down and ending in an underground lake.

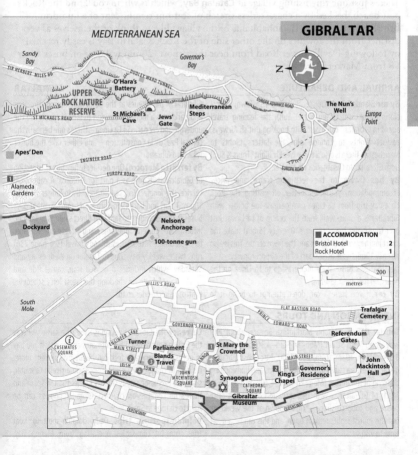

If you prefer to walk rather than take the cable car to the top, you could visit the **Tower of Homage**, reached via Willis' Road. Dating from the fourteenth century, this is the most visible surviving remnant of the old **Moorish Castle**. Near to the Tower of Homage on Willis' Road itself, and housed in a former ammunition store – with some eighteenth-century graffiti etched into its walls – is the **Gibraltar: A City Under Siege** exhibition, which uses tableaux to explain the various sieges the Rock has endured during its three hundred years as a British colony. Farther up the same road you'll find the **Upper Galleries** (aka the Great Siege Tunnels), which were blasted out of the rock during the Great Siege of 1779–82 in order to point guns down at the Spanish lines.

To **walk down** from The Top of the Rock, follow Signal Station Road and St Michael's Road to O'Hara's Road (passing O'Hara's Battery, a privately restored WWII gun emplacement) and the **Mediterranean Steps** – a very steep descent most of the way down the east side (not for those who suffer from vertigo), turning the southern corner of the Rock. You'll eventually pass through the **Jews' Gate** and into Engineer Road, from where the return to town is through the Alameda Gardens where there's a statue of Molly Bloom, Joyce's Gibraltar-born heroine in *Ulysses*.

Catalan Bay

There's just one tiny fishing village at **Catalan Bay**, which is where you'll find the Rock's best **beach**, backed by a characterless stretch of seafront reminiscent of a humdrum British holiday resort. The inhabitants of the village like to think of themselves as very distinct from the townies on the other side of the Rock. Catalan Bay is easily reached by following Devil's Tower Road from near the airport (20min walk) or on buses #4 or #8 from Market Place.

ARRIVAL AND DEPARTURE
GIBRALTAR

By air Blands Travel (Cloister Building, Irish Town; http://blandstravel.com; closed Sat & Sun), the leading travel agent in Gibraltar, can assist with booking British Airways, easyJet flights to London plus the latter's flights to Manchester. There is also a twice weekly flight (Thurs & Sun) from Gibraltar to Casablanca via Tangier.

By bus Owing to the relatively scarce and pricey accommodation, you're far better off visiting the Rock on a day-trip from La Línea or Algeciras. The border with Gibraltar is a 5min walk from the centre of La Línea. Just over the border buses (#5 or #10; every 15min) make the short journey to Main Street and the town centre. This is also an easy 10min walk across part of the airport runway.

Destinations Buses from Algeciras go to La Línea on the hour and half-hour (30min).

By car If you have a car, don't attempt to bring it to Gibraltar – the queues at the border are always atrocious and parking is a nightmare owing to lack of space. Use the underground car parks in La Línea – there's one beneath the central Pza. de la Constitución – and either take the bus or walk into Gibraltar.

By ferry (to Morocco) One decidedly functional attraction of Gibraltar is its role as a port for Morocco. A catamaran service, the *Tangier Med*, sails fortnightly to Tanger Med (Fri 10pm; 1.5hr) and back (Sun 5pm local time). On other days buses take passengers to Tarifa for direct sailings to Tangier. Information, current timetables and tickets are available to book online http://frs.es. Blands Travel (see page 236) runs twice-weekly day-trips to Tangier on Wednesday and Saturday, which includes a guided tour, camel ride and lunch. A useful site for checking the latest ferry schedules is http://directferries.co.uk.

INFORMATION AND TOURS

Tourist Office 13 John Mackintosh Square, about half way along Main Street (Mon–Fri 9am–4.30pm, Sat 9am–3.30pm, Sun 10am–1pm; 20045000, http://visitgibraltar.gi), and there's a sub-office in the customs and immigration building at the border (Mon–Fri 9am–4.30pm; 20050762). Much of Gibraltar – with the exception of the cut-price booze and tobacco shops – closes down at the weekend, but the tourist sights remain open, and this can be a quiet time to visit.

Currency The Gibraltar pound is used (the same value as the British pound, but different notes and coins); if you pay in euros, you generally fork out about five percent more. It's best to change your money once you arrive in Gibraltar, since the exchange rate is slightly higher than in Spain there's no commission charged. Gibraltar pounds can be hard to change in Spain.

Dolphin-spotting trips Daily dolphin-spotting boat trips, run by companies operating from Marina Bay, including Dolphin Safari (http://dolphinsafari.gi) and Dolphin Adventure (http://dolphin.gi). You should ring first to book places or ask the tourist office to do it for you. You can also book online with both companies, which will get you cheaper rates.

ACCOMMODATION SEE MAP PAGE 234

Shortage of space on the Rock means that **places to stay** are at a premium and there's little in the budget category. No **camping** is allowed on the peninsula, and if you're caught sleeping rough or inhabiting abandoned bunkers, you're likely to be arrested and fined.

Bristol Hotel Cathedral Square, http://bristolhotel.gi. Long-established three-star with refurbished rooms and a pool (there is a supplement for a sea view). $\overline{\underline{\underline{\in\in}}}$

Rock Hotel 3 Europa Rd, www.rockhotelgibraltar.com. Flagship hotel immediately below the Apes' Den, trading on its imperial connections – rooms are decorated in "colonial style" and come with ceiling fans and a trouser press; all have sea views and (some) balconies. $\overline{\underline{\underline{\in\in\in}}}$

EATING SEE MAP PAGE 234

Restaurants are far more plentiful than places to stay, and Main Street is crowded with touristy places. Things are still relatively expensive by Spanish standards; pub snacks or fish and chips are reliable stand-bys.

Baba 5 Governor's Parade, http://babagibraltar.com. This vibrant place boasts that they serve the best burgers in town, and it's hard to disagree. Alongside juicy cheeseburgers are more exotic offerings like a chilli burger and 'Xavi' burger with camembert cream; tacos, tapas and bao buns are also available. $\overline{\underline{\underline{\in\in}}}$

The Clipper 78 Irish Town, http://theclipper.gi. Spacious diner serving British-style pub grub – a house special is steak-and-ale pie – along with a variety of beers. $\overline{\underline{\underline{\in\in}}}$

Corks Wine Bar 79 Irish Town, http://corks.gi. This is a tranquil venue and offers breakfasts along with a variety of salads and pasta dishes as well as pub-style favourites such as steak-and-Guinness pie. $\overline{\underline{\underline{\in\in}}}$

Piccadilly Garden Bar 3 Rosia Rd, just beyond the Referendum Gates (aka South Port), www.facebook.com/piccadillygardenbar. A garden bar serving breakfasts (full British blowout or Spanish with *churros*) as well as meat and fish *raciones*. A Spanish kitchen ensures that the food is more authentic than most places – try the *sardines a la plancha*. Also has reasonable wine prices and later in the evening it transmutes into a drinks bar. $\overline{\underline{\underline{\in\in}}}$

Sacarello's Coffee House 57 Irish Town, http://sacarellos gibraltar.com. *Sacarello's* is a century-old local institution and a great place for tea and home-made cakes. It also does lunch dishes such as pies, quiche and lasagne. $\overline{\underline{\in}}$

DRINKING AND NIGHTLIFE SEE MAP PAGE 234

Gibraltarian **pubs** mimic traditional English styles (and prices), but are often rowdy, full of soldiers and visiting sailors.

The Skull 26 Cannon Ln, www.facebook.com/theskullgib. The décor is macabre (plastic skulls stacked all over the bar) but the vibes are fun at this English pub, with live sport and good Spanish food and pub grub.

Algeciras

ALGECIRAS occupies the far side of the bay from Gibraltar, spewing out smoke and pollution in the direction of the Rock. The last town of the Spanish Mediterranean, it must once have been an elegant resort; today, it's unabashedly a port and industrial centre, its suburbs extending on all sides. When Franco closed the border with Gibraltar at La Línea it was Algeciras that he decided to develop to absorb the Spanish workers formerly employed in the British naval dockyards, thus breaking the area's dependence on the Rock.

Most travellers are scathing about the city's ugliness, and unless you're waiting for a bus or train, or heading **for Morocco**, there's admittedly little reason to stop. However, once you start to explore, you'll discover that the **old town** has some very attractive corners that seem barely to have changed in fifty years, especially around Pza. Alta.

ARRIVAL AND INFORMATION ALGECIRAS

By train The train station (902 432 343) is at C/San Bernardo s/n, 1.2km behind the port. At Algeciras, the train line begins again, heading north to Ronda, Córdoba and Madrid. The route to Ronda – through spectacular mountain scenery – is one of the best rail journeys in Andalucía; there are four departures a day.

Destinations Córdoba: (5 daily; 3hr 15min); Granada (4 daily; 4hr 15min); Madrid (3 daily; AVE 5hr 30min); all Algeciras northbound trains go via Ronda (1hr 40min) and the Bobadilla junction.

By bus The main bus station (956 653 345) is in C/San Bernardo, behind the port, next to the *Hotel Octavio* and just short of the train station.

Destinations Cádiz (9 daily; 2hr); La Línea (for Gibraltar: every 30min; 30min); Jerez (8 daily; 1hr 30min); Madrid (8 daily; 8hr 45min); Seville (8 daily; 3hr 15min); Tarifa (every 30min; 45min).

By ferry Morocco is easily visited from Algeciras: in summer, there are crossings to Tangier and to the Spanish *presidio* of Ceuta, little more than a Spanish Gibraltar with a brisk business in duty-free goods, but a relatively painless way to enter Morocco. Tickets cost around €33 one-way to Tangier or Ceuta (depending on the company), and are sold at scores of travel agents along the waterfront and on most approach roads. Note that all ferries between Spain and Tangier (except for sailings from Tarifa) now dock at the new Tanger-Med port some 40km east of the town itself. The road connections

are good but it adds some 30–45min to the journey in either direction; a bus transfer between the city and port runs regularly. For up-to-date information on hydrofoils and fast-ferries, check with the *turismo* or with the ferry companies inside the harbour terminal: Trasmediterránea, Estación Marítima (http://armastrasmediterranea.com), or FRS (http://frs.es). FRS also do a daily all-inclusive day-trip to Tangier by fast-ferry, which includes a guided tour, lunch and time for shopping. They also offer a two-day excursion adding a night in a three-star hotel. Wait till Tangier – or if you're going via Ceuta, Tetouan – before buying any Moroccan currency; rates in the embarkation building kiosks are very poor. A useful site for checking the latest ferry schedules is http://directferries.co.uk. Destinations Ceuta (up to 25 daily; 35min); Tangier (up to 30 daily; 1hr–2hr 30min).

Turismo C/Juan de la Cierva s/n (Mon–Fri 9am–7.30pm, Sat & Sun 9.30am–3pm; 670 948 731, at the start of the pedestrianized avenue running east–west between the harbour and the train and bus stations. They can provide a town map, help with finding a room and have up-to-date ferry schedules.

White Towns southwest of Ronda

Andalucía is dotted with small, brilliantly whitewashed settlements – the **Pueblos Blancos** or "**White Towns**" – most often straggling up hillsides towards a castle or towered church. Places such as **Mijas**, up behind Fuengirola, are solidly on the tourist trail, but even here the natural beauty is undeniable. All of them look great from a distance, though many are rather less interesting on arrival. Arguably the best lie in a roughly triangular area between Málaga, Algeciras and Seville; at its centre, in a region of wild, mountainous beauty, is the spectacular town of **Ronda**.

Castellar de la Frontera

The first White Town on the route proper is **CASTELLAR DE LA FRONTERA**, 27km north of Algeciras, a bizarre village enclosed within the walls of a strikingly isolated thirteenth-century Moorish castle, whose population, in accord with some grandiose scheme, was moved downriver in 1971 to the "new" town of Nuevo Castellar, turning

---

TOWARDS RONDA FROM THE COAST

Of several possible approaches to Ronda from the coast, the stunningly scenic route up **from Algeciras**, via Gaucín, is the most rewarding – and worth going out of your way to experience. It's possible by either bus or train (a spectacularly picturesque option), or, if you've time and energy, can be walked in four or five days. En route, you're always within reach of a river and there's a series of hill towns, each one visible from the next, to provide targets for the day. Casares is almost on the route, but more easily reached from Estepona.

   From Málaga, most buses to Ronda follow the coastal highway to San Pedro before turning into the mountains via the modern A376 *autovía*, dramatic enough, but rather a bleak route, with no villages and only limited views of the sombre rock face of the Serranía; an alternative route, via Álora and Ardales, is far more attractive and is taken by a couple of daily buses. A single daily train from Málaga (two hours), is another scenic option.

the castle settlement into a ghost village. Although remote, much of the village inside the castle has been restored and now has a couple of bars and places to stay.

ACCOMMODATION   **CASTELLAR DE LA FRONTERA**

Hotel Castellar http://hotelcastellar.com. Of the two places to stay inside the castle walls, the B&B *Hotel Castellar* occupies part of the castle and has well-equipped rooms with fine views. The hotel also rents out a number of restored houses in the village, a decent restaurant, a spa and gym. €€

Jimena de la Frontera and around

JIMENA DE LA FRONTERA, 20km north of Castellar de la Frontera along the A405, is a far larger and more open hill town, rising to a grand Moorish castle with a triple-gateway entrance and round keep. In recent years it has become home to a considerable number of British expats who probably feel the need to be within working and shopping distance of Gibraltar.

Parque Natural de los Alcornocales

Jimena is also a gateway to the **Parque Natural de los Alcornocales**, a vast expanse of verdant hill country stretching south to the sea and north to El Bosque and covered with *alcornocales* (cork oaks). A haven for large numbers of birds and insects, the park is also a paradise for walkers. *Walking in Andalucía* by Guy Hunter-Watts (see page 859) describes half a dozen walks in the park, two starting in Jimena.

ACCOMMODATION AND EATING   **JIMENA DE LA FRONTERA**   **4**

Bar Ventorrillero Pza. de la Constitución 2, 956 640 997. Situated at the foot of C/Sevilla, the town's main artery, this is a friendly bar-restaurant with a good-value weekday lunchtime menu. €

Camping Los Alcornocales http://campinglos alcornocales.com. Jimena's campsite occupies a suberb location with great views on the north side of town (reached by following C/Sevilla to the end), and has its own restaurant. €

Casa Henrietta C/Sevilla 44, 956 648 130. Charming hotel with just thirteen rooms, all painted in pastel tones and adorned with cooling floor tiles. All have private bathrooms and a/c; the best have balconies overlooking the rolling hills and Moorish castle. A small restaurant serves up breakfasts, afternoon tea and light meals. €

Restaurante Bar Cuenca Avda. de los Deportes 31, on the way into town, http://facebook.com/restaurante cuenca1920. This is perhaps the town's best place to eat, serving tapas and meals in its main room and with a pretty terrace patio at the rear. €€

Gaucín

Beyond Jimena, it's 23km farther along the A405, passing through woods of cork oak and olive groves, to reach **GAUCÍN**. Almost a mountain village, Gaucín commands tremendous views (to Gibraltar and the Moroccan coast on a very clear day), and makes a great place to stop over.

ARRIVAL AND DEPARTURE   **GAUCÍN**

By bus and train You can reach Gaucín by bus or by train, but the train station (at El Colmenar on the fringes of the Cortés nature reserve) is 13km away. From here it's a bracing and mostly uphill hike to the village; a taxi can be arranged at *Mesón Flores* fronting the station (952 153 026). The *Flores* also does decent meals, and there are several other bars here. The train line between Gaucín and Ronda passes through a handful of tiny villages. En route, you can stop off at the station of Benaoján-Montejaque, from where it's an hour's trek to the prehistoric Cueva de la Pileta (see page 243). From Benaoján, Ronda is just three stops (30min) down the line.

ACCOMMODATION AND EATING

★ **Ahora Casa Rural** Bda. El Colmenar, 500m downhill from the train station, http://casaruralahora.com. This is a wonderful little oasis close to the train station, with en-suite cabin-style rooms surrounded by greenery. There's a communal room with *chimenea* (stove), library and games in addition to a wellbeing centre offering all kinds of alternative therapies plus a sauna and Jacuzzi. It also has its own restaurant, where you can book full or half board. €

Hostal Moncada Crt. De Campillos, Gaucín, www.hostal moncadagaucin.com. En-suite a/c rooms above a restaurant and next to the *gasolinera* (ask for a room at the back for a view and less noise) as you come into the village from

Jimena. It also offers some great facilities, including a pool, tennis court and coffee shop. €

Hotel Rural Fructuosa C/Luis de Arminan 67, Gaucín, http://lafructuosa.com. A more upmarket option in the village proper is the charming *Hotel Rural Fructuosa*, with its own – very good – mid-priced restaurant nearby. €€

Ronda

The full natural drama of **RONDA**, rising amid a ring of dark, angular mountains, is best appreciated as you enter the town. Built on an isolated ridge of the sierra, it's split in half by a gaping river gorge, **El Tajo**, which drops sheer for 130m on three sides. Still more spectacular, the gorge is spanned by a stupendous eighteenth-century arched bridge, the **Puente Nuevo**, while tall, whitewashed houses lean from its precipitous edges.

Much of the attraction of Ronda lies in this extraordinary view, or in walking down by the Río Guadalvín, following one of the donkey tracks through the rich green valley. Birdwatchers should look out for lesser kestrels nesting on the cliffs beneath the Alameda; lower down you can spot crag martins. The town has a number of **museums** and, surprisingly, has sacrificed little of its character to the flow of day-trippers from the Costa del Sol.

Ronda divides into three parts: on the south side of the bridge is the old Moorish town, **La Ciudad**, and farther south still, its **San Francisco** suburb. On the near north side of the gorge, and where you'll arrive by public transport, is the largely modern **Mercadillo** quarter.

La Ciudad

La Ciudad retains intact its Moorish plan and a great many of its houses, interspersed with a number of fine Renaissance mansions. It is so intricate a maze that you can do little else but wander at random. However, at some stage, make your way across the eighteenth-century **Puente Nuevo** bridge, peering down the walls of limestone rock into the yawning Tajo and the Río Guadalvín, far below.

Puente Nuevo
Charge • http://turismoderonda.es

The spectacular eighteenth-century **Puente Nuevo** bridge spanning the gorge between the Mercadillo and La Ciudad quarter was originally the town prison, and last saw use during the Civil War, when Ronda was the site of some of the south's most vicious massacres. Hemingway, in *For Whom the Bell Tolls*, recorded how prisoners were thrown alive into the gorge. The bridge itself is a remarkable construction and has its own **Centro de Información**, housed in the former prison above the central arch, with exhibits documenting its construction and history; entry is to the side of the parador in Pza. de España.

Casa del Rey Moro gardens
C/Santo Domingo 17 • Charge • http://casadelreymoro.org

The somewhat arbitrarily named **Casa del Rey Moro** (House of the Moorish King) is an early eighteenth-century mansion built on Moorish foundations. The gardens (but not the house itself) are open to the public, and from here a remarkable underground stairway, the Mina, descends to the river; these 365 steps (which can be slippery after rain), guaranteeing a water supply in times of siege, were cut by Christian slaves in the fourteenth century. There's a viewing balcony at the bottom where you can admire El

Tajo's towering walls of rock and its bird life, although the long climb back up will make you wonder whether it was worth it.

Palacio del Marqués de Salvatierra

C/Marqués de Salvatierra 26 • No access

The **Palacio del Marqués de Salvatierra** is a splendid Renaissance mansion with a fine portal depicting an oddly primitive, half-grotesque frieze of Adam and Eve together with the colonial images of four Peruvian Indians (or possibly Incas) supporting a pediment. Twin sets of Corinthian pillars flank the entrance, topped by an elegantly crafted wrought-iron balcony in the *rondeño* style. The house is still used by the family, and hence prohibits visits, but you can peep into the patio.

Baños Árabes

C/San Miguel • Charge • 656 950 937

At the foot of C/Santo Domingo are two old town bridges – the **Puente Viejo** of 1616 and the single-span Moorish **Puente de San Miguel**; nearby, on the southeast bank of the river, are the distinctive hump-shaped cupolas and glass skylights of the old **Baños Árabes**. Dating from the thirteenth century and recently restored, the complex is based on the Roman system of cold, tepid and hot baths and is wonderfully preserved; note the sophisticated barrel-vaulted ceiling and brickwork octagonal pillars supporting horseshoe arches.

Santa María La Mayor

Pza. Duquesa de Parcent • Charge

At the centre of La Ciudad, on Ronda's most picturesque square, the Pza. Duquesa de Parcent, stands the cathedral church of **Santa María La Mayor**, originally the Moorish town's Friday mosque. Externally, it's a graceful combination of Moorish, Gothic and Renaissance styles with the belfry built on top of the old minaret. Climb this to reach the rooftop walkway from where you get magnificent views of the town and countryside. The interior is decidedly less interesting, but you can see an arch covered with Arabic calligraphy, and just in front of the street door, a part of the old Arab *mihrab*, or prayer niche, has been exposed.

Palacio de Mondragón

Pza. de Mondragón s/n • Charge • http://museoderonda.es

Slightly west of Pza. Duquesa lies the fourteenth-century **Casa de Mondragón**, probably the real palace of the Moorish kings. Inside, three of the patios preserve original stuccowork and there's a magnificent carved ceiling, as well as a small museum covering local archeology and aspects of Moorish Ronda.

Museo Lara

C/Armiñán 29 • Charge • http://museolara.org

To the northeast of the Pza. Duquesa de Parcent, on C/Armiñán, which bisects La Ciudad, you'll find the **Museo Lara**, containing the collection of *rondeño* Juan Antonio Lara, a member of the family that owns and runs the local bus company of the same name. An avid collector since childhood, Señor Lara has filled the spacious museum with a fascinating collection of antique clocks, pistols and armaments, musical instruments and archeological finds, as well as early cameras and cinematographic equipment.

The southern end of La Ciudad

Near the southern end of La Ciudad, to the right, are the ruins of the **Alcázar**, once impregnable until razed by the French ("from sheer love of destruction", according to the nineteenth-century hispanist Richard Ford) in 1809. Beyond here, the principal gates of the town, the magnificent Moorish **Puerto de Almocabar**, through which passed the Christian conquerors (led personally by Fernando), and the triumphal **Puerta de Carlos V**, erected later during the reign of the Habsburg emperor, stand side by side at the entrance to the suburb of San Francisco.

Mercadillo and Plaza de Toros

Plaza de Toros • Pza. Teniente Arce • Charge • http://rmcr.org

The Mercadillo quarter, which grew up in the wake of the Reconquest, is of comparatively little interest, although it is now the town's commercial centre. There is only one genuine monument here, the eighteenth-century **Plaza de Toros** sited on Pza. Teniente Arce, close to the beautiful clifftop *paseo*, Paseo de Orson Welles, and offering spectacular views towards the Sierra de Ronda. Ronda played a leading part in the development of bullfighting and was the birthplace of the modern *corrida* (bullfight). The ring, built in 1781, is one of the earliest in Spain and the fight season here is one of the country's most important. At its September *feria*, the *corrida goyesca*, honouring Spain's great artist Goya, who made a number of paintings of the fights at Ronda, takes place in eighteenth-century costume. You can wander around the arena, and there's a **museum** inside stuffed with memorabilia such as famous bullfighters' *trajes de luces* (suits) and photos of the ubiquitous Ernest Hemingway and Orson Welles – both avid aficionados – visiting the ring.

ARRIVAL AND INFORMATION   RONDA

By bus Ronda's bus station – used by all bus companies – is on Pza. Redondo in the Mercadillo quarter, to the northeast of the bullring.

Destinations Arcos de la Frontera (3 daily; 2hr 5min); Cádiz (3 daily; 3hr 15min); Grazalema (2 daily; 45min); Jerez de la Frontera (3 daily; 2hr 30min); Málaga (10 daily; 1hr 45min); Marbella (6 daily; 1hr 15min); San Pedro de Alcantara (6 daily; 1hr 5min); Seville (8 daily; 2hr/2hr 30min); Ubrique (2 daily; 1hr 30min); Zahara de la Sierra (2 daily; 45min).

By train Ronda's train station lies a 5min walk east of the bus station on Avda. Andalucía, in the Mercadillo quarter to the northeast of the bullring. The station is a 10min walk or

an easy bus or taxi ride from the centre.

By car Arriving by car, your best bet for street parking is to park as far out as possible (near the train station is usually feasible where there's also a pay car park), or head straight for one of the central signposted pay car parks.

Turismo The tourist office lies opposite the south side of the bullring (952 187 119) and can help with accommodation, up-to-date opening times for Acinipo, and provide a map and information about visiting Ronda's *bodegas*.

Useful website http://turismoderonda.es is a good source of information.

ACCOMMODATION

Most of the **places to stay** are in the **Mercadillo** quarter, although there are a handful of upmarket hotels in the old Moorish quarter, **La Ciudad**, on the south side of El Tajo. Both zones are within easy walking distance of Pza. de España.

Alavera de los Baños C/San Miguel s/n, http://alaveradelosbanos.com. Enchanting small hotel with stylish rooms (some with terraces), garden, pool and views from rear rooms of grazing sheep on the hill across the river. It also has a couple of elegant suites. Breakfast included. €€€

Camping El Sur Carretera Ronda–Algeciras Km2.8, http://campingelsur.com. Ronda's campsite with pool, bar and restaurant, lies some 3km out of town along the Algeciras road (A369). €

Hotel Andalucía C/Martínez Astein 19, http://hotel-andalucia.net. Pleasant en-suite rooms in leafy

surroundings opposite the train station. €

Hotel Colón C/Pozo 1, on the Pza. de la Merced, http://hcolon.es. Charming small hotel with a/c en-suite facilities and – in rooms 301 & 302 – your own spacious roof terrace. Breakfast included. €

Parador de Ronda Pza. de España, www.parador.es. Ronda's imposing parador offers elegantly furnished rooms with spectacular views overlooking El Tajo, plus a pool, terrace bar and very good restaurant. €€€€

★ **Soho Boutique Palacio San Gabriel** C/José Holgado 19, La Ciudad, http://en.sohoteles.com. A lovely boutique hotel housed in a beautifully restored eighteenth-century mansion. It offers stylish a/c rooms, a library, an amusing five-seater cinema for guests and welcoming proprietors. €€

EATING AND DRINKING

Most of Ronda's bargain **restaurants** are grouped round   Pza. del Socorro and nearby Pza. Carmen Abela, though there are also some to be found near Pza. de España.

Casa Ortega Pza. del Socorro 17, http://restauranteortega.
es. Popular restaurant run by a local family whose specials
include *ensalada de tomate* (they grow their own variety –
marvel at the size of them piled on the counter) and home-
reared roast kid goat. €€

Churrería Alba C/Espinel 44, 952 871 009. Piping-hot
churros and excellent coffee. It has a street terrace and is on
a pedestrian thoroughfare. €

★ **Entrevinos** C/del Pozo 2, www.facebook.com/
entrevinosronda. Tiny venue with bar stools only but the
best place in town to try Ronda wines paired with tapas. The
wine list runs to nearly a hundred and there's a good choice
of tapas including *fideos negros* (black noodles) and mini-
burgers. Local craft beers also available. €

Las Maravillas Carrera Espinel 12, http://lasmaravillas
ronda.com. Friendly restaurant serving Mediterranean
tapas, generous salads and mains on the busy outside
terrace or inside in the dining area decorated with Ronda-
themed art and quotes or on the quieter patio. Try the
salmorejo con helado de mascarpone or the *carpaccio de
champiñón* (mushroom carpaccio). €€

Parador de Ronda Pza. de España, http://parador.es.
With a staggering clifftop location, the parador's upmarket
restaurant has an excellent choice of local and regional
dishes such as *rabo de toro* (bull's tail) and *solomillo de ciervo*
(venison loin). Set menu and a la carte both available. €€

★ **Restaurante Almocábar** Ruedo de Alameda 5, La
Ciudad, http://almocabarronda.es. Excellent restaurant
with a pleasant terrace serving creative variations on
regional dishes along with a range of salads such as the
ensalada almocábar, which includes figs, cheese, pears and
honey. House specials include *paté de perdiz* (partridge) and
cochinillo (suckling pig). €€

Toro Tapas C/Espinel 7, near the Pza. de Toros, http://
facebook.com/torotapasronda. Great hole-in-the-wall (and
one of Ronda's oldest tapas venues, having opened in 1946)
with a tempting menu recited verbally by the proprietor.
It's also a bar *taurino*, so the photos of past *torero* greats
plus Hemingway and Welles (all one-time customers) gaze
down from the walls. Try their *costillas* (pork ribs). It has a
small street terrace. €€

Tragatá C/Nueva 4, http://tragata.com/ronda. Catalan
super-chef Benito Gómez is best known for *Bardal*, his
covetable Ronda restaurant that scooped a Michelin star
within a year of opening, and a second two years later. If
your purse strings can't quite stretch to fine dining, try
sister restaurant *Tragatá* nearby. This low-key tapas bar
offers some of the same culinary wonders at a fraction of
the price. Try the squid sandwich on ink bread, fried pork ear
with spicy sauce, or duck *tataki* with rice. €€

Around Ronda

Ronda makes an excellent base for exploring the superb countryside of the Serranía de
Ronda to the south or for visiting the remarkable **Cueva de la Pileta**, with its prehistoric
cave paintings, and the Roman ruins of **Acinipo**.

Acinipo

Free

Some 12km northwest of Ronda are the ruins of a town and **Roman theatre** at a site
known as **Ronda la Vieja**, reached by turning right 6km down the main A374 road to
Arcos/Seville. At the site a friendly farmer, who is also the guardian, will present you
with a plan (in Spanish). Based on Neolithic foundations – note the recently discovered
prehistoric stone huts beside the entrance – it was as a Roman town in the first century AD
that Acinipo (the town's Roman name) reached its zenith. Immediately west of the theatre,
the site's most imposing ruin, the ground falls away in a startlingly steep escarpment
offering fine views all around, taking in the picturesque hill village of Olvera to the north.

Cueva de la Pileta

10km southwest of Ronda • Charge • http://cuevadelapileta.es

West from Ronda is the prehistoric **Cueva de la Pileta**, a fabulous series of caverns with
some remarkable paintings of animals (mainly bison), fish and what are apparently
magic symbols. These etchings and the occupation of the cave date from about 25,000
BC – hence predating the more famous caves at Altamira in northern Spain – to the
end of the Bronze Age. The tour lasts an hour on average, but can be longer, and is in

Spanish – though the guide does speak a little English. There are hundreds of bats in the cave, and no artificial lighting, so visitors carry lanterns; you may also want to take a jumper, as the caves can be extremely chilly. Be aware if you leave a car in the car park that thieves are active here.

ARRIVAL AND DEPARTURE   **CUEVA DE LA PILETA**

By train and bus To reach the caves from Ronda, take either an Algeciras-bound local train to Estación Benaoján-Montejaque (3 daily; 20min), or a bus, which drops you a little closer in Benaoján. There's a bar and restaurant at the train station if you want a bite to eat before the 6km walk (1hr) to the caves. Follow the farm track from the right bank of the river until you reach the farmhouse (30min). From here, a track goes straight uphill to the main road just before the signposted turning for the caves.

By car Follow the road to Benaoján and take the signed turn-off, from where it's about 4km.

White Towns northwest of Ronda

Ronda has good transport connections in most directions. Almost any route to the north or west is rewarding, taking you past a whole series of White Towns, many of them fortified since the days of the Reconquest from the Moors – hence the mass of "de la Frontera" suffixes.

Perhaps the best of all the routes, though a roundabout one, and tricky without your own transport, is to **Cádiz** via Grazalema, Ubrique and Medina Sidonia. This passes through the spectacular **Parque Natural Sierra de Grazalema** before skirting the nature reserve of **Cortes de la Frontera** (which you can drive through by following the road beyond Benaoján) and, towards Alcalá de los Gazules, running through the northern fringe of **Parque Natural de los Alcornocales**, which derives its name from the forests of cork oaks, one of its main attractions and the largest of its kind in Europe.

Grazalema

Twenty-three kilometres from Ronda, **GRAZALEMA** is a striking white village at the centre of the magnificent Parque Natural Sierra de Grazalema, a paradise for hikers and naturalists. The **Puerto de las Palomas** (Pass of the Doves – at 1350m the second-highest pass in Andalucía) rears up behind the village. Cross this (a superb half-day walk or short drive), and you descend to Zahara de la Sierra and the main road west (see page 245).

PUERTO DE LAS PALOMAS WALK

From the car park at the Puerto de las Palomas *mirador* there is a fine circular 5km (45min) **walk** offering spectacular views over the whole sierra. The walk has plenty of nooks to spot wild flowers and in the skies griffon vultures are frequent visitors. If you're very lucky you may even see the nimble Spanish ibex (*cabra montés*), the scimitar-horned wild goat, which is relatively common at this altitude. The hike begins from an opening in the fence at the left (northwest) side of the car park. The well-defined path heads uphill and circles the Cerro Coros peak (1327m) taking in stirring views of the village of Zahara de la Sierra and its lake (reservoir) and castle and, further away, the white splashes denoting the villages of Algodonales and Olvera, topped by its twin-towered church. After a couple of kilometres the path climbs and winds around the north side of the mountain before turning south along its eastern flank. Another ascent follows as fine views open up over the Sierra de Gaidovar and its river valley. The track then slowly descends to the Puerto de las Palomas where, beyond a gate, you enter the opposite side of the car park from where you started out.

INFORMATION

Turismo Located on Pza. Asomaderos, off the main square, Pza. de España (Tues–Sun 9am–3pm; 956 132 052). The tourist office can provide information about the park, accommodation in the village and activities such as horseriding, and it also sells good walking maps.

ACCOMMODATION AND EATING

The **bars and restaurants** on and around Pza. de España are generally reasonably priced, if not outstanding.

Cádiz El Chico Pza. de España 8, http://facebook.com/cadizelchico. Located on the main square, this is one of the town's better restaurants and specializes in the cuisine of the sierra – *cordero al horno de leña* (lamb in a wood-fired oven) is a signature dish. It also does good tapas in its bar. €€

Casa de las Piedras C/Las Piedras 6, http://casadelaspiedras.es. The only budget option, this friendly family-run *hostal* is located above the main square. It offers comfortable en-suite rooms and also rents out some apartments nearby. The *hostal's* restaurant, with a vine-covered patio for alfresco dining, serves local dishes with a creative edge. €

Hotel Villa de Grazalema Finca El Olivar s/n, http://villasdeandalucia.com. This three-star hotel lies in leafy surroundings on the village's northern edge (a 3min walk) and has comfortable rooms with terrace balconies and fine views. Facilities include a restaurant and bar, pool and free parking; they also rent out cottages sleeping up to four. €€

★ **La Mejorana** C/Santa Clara 6, http://lamejorana.net. One of the most attractive places to stay in the village, this welcoming *hostal* offers comfortably furnished rooms (many with views) in an elegant *casa señorial* complete with pool. Breakfast (extra) available. Minimum booking of two nights during high season. €€

Torreon C/Agua 44, www.facebook.com/restaurantstorreon.grazalema. Reliable, central traditional restaurant for dishes of the sierra including game and venison, *sopa de grazalema* (a hearty mountain soup), and fish dishes and salads. The wine list is fairly priced and you can eat in the cosy dining room upstairs or, in better weather, on a street terrace below. €€

Ubrique

From Grazalema, following the scenic A2302 towards Ubrique takes you through the southern sector of the natural park, a landscape of dramatic vistas and lofty peaks. The road snakes through the charming ancient villages of **Villaluenga del Rosario** and **Benaocaz**, and offers plenty of opportunities for hikes – perhaps down Benaocaz's six-kilometre-long paved Roman road – along the way. **UBRIQUE**, 20km southwest of Grazalema, is a natural mountain fortress and was a Republican stronghold in the Civil War. Today, it's a prosperous and bustling town, owing its wealth to the medieval guild craft of **leather working**. The highly skilled leather workers produce bags, purses and accessories for many of the big names (including Loewe, Louis Vuitton, Gucci) at unmarked workshops around the town. These high-value products are then whisked away to be sold in Madrid, Paris, Rome and London. Shops selling the output of numerous other workshops (footwear and bags, often at bargain prices) line the main street, Avda. Dr Solis Pascual.

ACCOMMODATION AND EATING

Hotel Ocurris Avda. Dr Solis Pascual 49, http://hotelocurris.com. This two-star hotel on the main street has pleasant enough en-suite rooms with a/c and TV plus its own tapas bar and restaurant. €€

El Laurel de Miguel C/San Juan Bautista 7, just behind the main street, http://ellaureldemiguel.com. Good tapas and *raciones* bar with a decent range of tapas and wines plus a street terrace. Try the *pluma ibérica* (pork loin) or *magret de pato* (duck breast). €€

Zahara de la Sierra

Heading directly to Jerez or Seville from Ronda, a scenic rural drive along the Grazalema park's eastern fringes, you pass below **ZAHARA DE LA SIERRA** (or *de los Membrillos* – "of the Quinces"), perhaps the most perfect example of these fortified hill towns. Set above a lake (in reality, the man-made *embalse*, or reservoir, which has dramatically changed the landscape to the north and east of town), Zahara is a landmark for many kilometres around, its red-tiled houses huddling round a church and castle perched on a stark outcrop

4

of rock. Once an important Moorish citadel, the town was captured by the Christians in 1483, opening the way for the conquest of Ronda – and ultimately Granada.

ACCOMMODATION   ZAHARA DE LA SIERRA

Hostal Marqués de Zahara C/San Juan 3, http:// marquesdezahara.com. A pleasant and central *hostal* with a/c en-suite balcony rooms, shady patio and a *cafetería*. €

Hotel Arco de la Villa Camino Nazarí s/n, http://tugasa. com. On the road leading up to the castle, this is a good-value modern hotel with its own restaurant and where all rooms enjoy spectacular views over the nearby *embalse*. €€

Hotel Los Tadeos Paseo de la Fuente s/n, http:// alojamientoruralcadiz.com. Smart, refurbished small hotel near the swimming pool on the eastern edge of the village. Terrace balcony a/c rooms have great views and come with wet room or Jacuzzi, plus there's an infinity pool, a decent restaurant and easy parking. €

Arcos de la Frontera

Of more substantial interest than Zahara de la Sierra, and another place to break the journey, is **ARCOS DE LA FRONTERA**, taken from the Moors in 1264, over two centuries before Zahara fell – an impressive feat, for it stands high above the Río Guadalete on a double crag and must have been a wretchedly impregnable fortress. This dramatic location, enhanced by low, white houses and fine sandstone churches, gives the town a similar feel and appearance to Ronda – only Arcos is poorer and, quite unjustifiably, far less visited. The streets of the town are if anything more interesting, with their mix of Moorish and Renaissance buildings. At its heart is the Pza. del Cabildo, easily reached by following the signs for the parador, which occupies one side of it. Flanking another two sides are the castle walls and the large Gothic-Mudéjar church of **Santa María de la Asunción**; the last side is left open, offering plunging **views** to the river valley. Below the town to the north lies **Lago de Arcos** (actually a reservoir) where locals go to cool off in summer.

INFORMATION   ARCOS DE LA FRONTERA

Turismo Located on the hill leading up from the new to the old town at Cuesta de Belén 5 (http://turismoarcos. es), the tourist office can provide a town map and has

details of daily guided morning tours of the old town (free, but excluding monument entry charges); there is also a nocturnal tour which includes a drink at a typical tapas bar.

ACCOMMODATION

The old town, formerly the exclusive preserve of a clutch of upmarket hotels, has added a number of **hostales** in recent years providing budget accommodation. Staying a little out of town, at the **Lago de Arcos**, where there are two hotels, is another possibility. There's a bus service to the lake.

IN TOWN

★ **La Casa Grande** C/Maldonado 10, http://lacasagrande. net. Perched along the same clifftop as the parador, this elegant hotel has beautiful rooms inside a restored *casa señorial* with a columned inner patio and a sensational view from the terrace of their bar across the river valley. They also offer more expensive suites for up to four people. €€

Hostal-Bar San Marcos C/Marqués de Torresoto 6, http://pensionsanmarcosdearcos.es. Excellent-value B&B *hostal* in the old town, offering pleasant rooms with bath. The friendly proprietors run a cosy and inexpensive bar-restaurant downstairs. €

★ **Parador de Arcos de la Frontera** Pza. del Cabildo, http://parador.es. Perched on a rock pedestal – with reassuringly reinforced foundations to prevent it from

sliding over the cliff – this is one of the smaller paradores, with spacious balcony rooms to enjoy the view. A former magistrate's mansion with parts dating from the sixteenth century, there's a delightful patio (open to the public for drinks and afternoon tea) and the "crow's nest" terrace has the best views in town. Also has a restaurant with a recommended *menú* at a good price. €€€

ON LAGO DE ARCOS

Hacienda El Santiscal 3km out of town on the lakeside, http://santiscal.com. Small country hotel in a beautiful converted *hacienda* with sumptuously decorated and furnished a/c rooms, restaurant and a pool in the grounds. Horseriding and other activities available. €€

Hotel Mesón de la Molinera Lago de Arcos, http:// mesondelamolinera.com. Tranquil location on the waterfront with stunning views towards Arcos on its hilltop. The hotel sports well-equipped balcony rooms with safe, its own bar and restaurant, and cheaper accommodation in chalet-style bungalows. Easy parking. €€

EATING AND DRINKING

There are plenty of places to **eat and drink** in Arcos in both the upper old town and the modern lower town.

Mesón Los Murales Close to the church of San Pedro, Pza. de Boticas 1, 685 809 661. One of the best low-priced options in the old town, with a pleasant terrace and traditional dishes of the sierra; there's an economical set menu of the day and a la carte options. €€

Taberna Jovenes Flamencos C/Dean Espinosa 11, near the Plaza del Cabildo, http://facebook.com/taberna. jovenesflamencos. Lively and popular flamenco-themed bar with a terrace, offering well-prepared *raciones* and *media-raciones*. Dishes include *pulpo a la gallega* (octopus) and *secreto ibérico* (iberian pork loin), and there are plenty of vegetarian options. Sometimes stages flamenco concerts. €€€

Seville (Sevilla)

"Seville," wrote Byron, "is a pleasant city, famous for oranges and women." And for its heat, he might perhaps have added, since **SEVILLE** is one of the hottest cities in mainland Europe. Its summers are intense and they start early, in May. Seville has three important monuments and an illustrious history, but what it's essentially famous for is its own living self – the greatest city of the Spanish south, of Carmen, Don Juan and Figaro, and the archetype of Andalucian promise. This reputation for gaiety and brilliance, for theatricality and intensity of life does seem deserved. It's expressed on a phenomenally grand scale at the city's two great festivals – **Semana Santa** (Holy Week at Easter) and the **Feria de Abril** (which starts two weeks after Easter Sunday and lasts a week). Either is worth considerable effort to get to. Seville is also Spain's second most important centre for **bullfighting**, after Madrid.

Despite its elegance and charm, and its wealth, based on food processing, shipbuilding, aircraft construction and a thriving tourist industry, Seville lies at the centre of a depressed agricultural area and has an unemployment rate of over thirty percent – one of the highest in Spain. The total refurbishment of the infrastructure boosted by the 1992 Expo – including impressive new roads, seven bridges, a high-speed rail link and a revamped airport – was intended to regenerate the city's (and the region's) economic fortunes, but has hardly turned out to be the catalyst for growth and prosperity promised at the time. Indeed, some of the colossal debts are still unpaid over two decades later.

Seville's **old city** – where you'll want to spend most of your time – is sited along the east bank of the Guadalquivir. At its heart, side by side, stand the three great monuments: the **Giralda tower**, the **Catedral** and the **Alcázar**, with the cramped alleyways of the **Barrio Santa Cruz**, the medieval Jewish quarter and now the heart of tourist life, extending east of them.

North of here is the main shopping and commercial district, its most obvious landmarks **Pza. Nueva**, **Pza. Duque de la Victoria** and the smart, pedestrianized **C/ Sierpes**, which runs roughly between them. From **La Campana**, the small square at the northern end of C/Sierpes, C/Alfonso XII runs down towards the river by way of the **Museo de Bellas Artes**, second in importance in Spain only to the Prado in Madrid. Across the river is the earthier, traditionally working-class district of **Triana**, flanked to the south by the **Los Remedios** *barrio*, the city's wealthier residential zone where the great April *feria* takes place.

The Catedral

Av. de la Constitución • Charge • http://catedraldesevilla.es

Seville's **Catedral** (properly titled Santa María de la Séde) was conceived in 1402 as an unrivalled monument to Christian glory – "a building on so magnificent a scale that posterity will believe we were mad". The canons, inspired by their vision of future repute, renounced all but a subsistence level of their incomes to further the building. The Catedral was completed in just over a century (1402–1506), an extraordinary

4

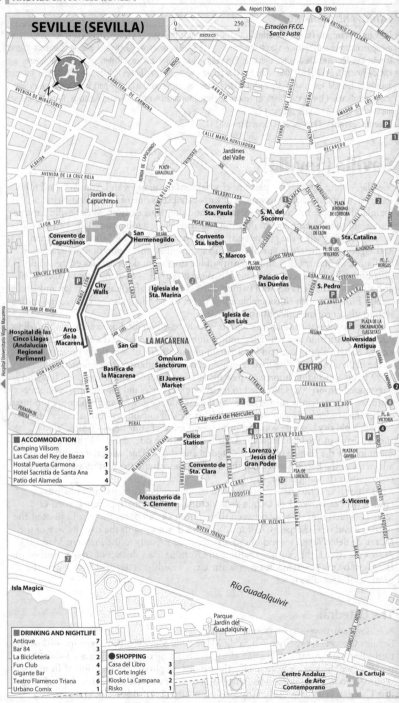

SEVILLE (SEVILLA)

Airport (10km)

(500m)

Estación FF.CC.
Santa Justa

0 — 250 metres

Jardines
del Valle

Convento
Sta. Paula

S. M. del
Socorro

PLAZA
JERONIMO
DE CÓRDOBA

Convento de
Capuchinos

San
Hermenegildo

Convento
Sta. Isabel

PLAZA PONCE
DE LEÓN

Sta. Catalina

S. Marcos

Jardin de
Capuchinos

City
Walls

Iglesia de
Sta. Marina

Palacio de
las Dueñas

S. Pedro

Iglesia de
San Luis

Hospital de las
Cinco Llagas
(Andalucian
Regional
Parliment)

Arco
de la
Macarena

San Gil

LA MACARENA

PLAZA DE LA
ENCARNACIÓN
(LAS SETAS)

Universidad
Antigua

Basílica de
la Macarena

Omnium
Sanctorum

CENTRO

El Jueves
Market

Alameda de Hércules

Police
Station

S. Lorenzo y
Jesús del
Gran Poder

PLAZA DE
GAVIDIA

Convento de
Sta. Clara

S. Vicente

Monasterio de
S. Clemente

Isla Magica

Río Guadalquivir

Parque
Jardín del
Guadalquivir

Centro Andaluz
de Arte
Contemporano

La Cartuja

ACCOMMODATION

Camping Villsom	5
Las Casas del Rey de Baeza	2
Hostal Puerta Carmona	1
Hotel Sacristía de Santa Ana	3
Patio del Alameda	4

DRINKING AND NIGHTLIFE

Antique	7
Bar 84	3
La Bicicletería	2
Fun Club	4
Gigante Bar	5
Teatro Flamenco Triana	6
Urbano Comix	1

SHOPPING

Casa del Libro	3
El Corte Inglés	4
Kiosko La Campana	2
Risko	1

Hospital Universitario Virgin Macarena

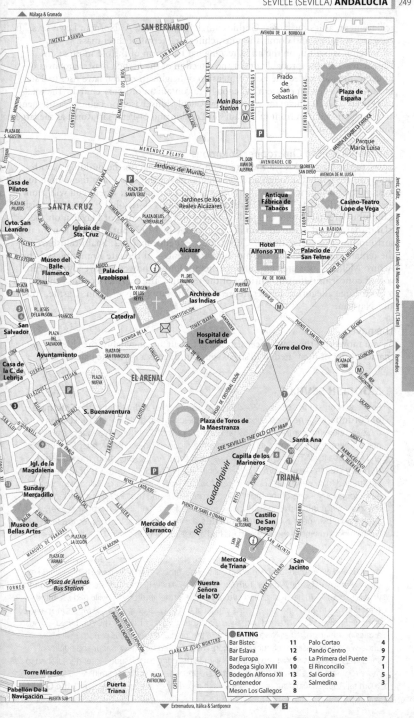

SAN BERNARDO

JIMÉNEZ ARANDA

SAN BERNARDO

DEMETRIO DE LOS RÍOS

CONTRERAS

AVENIDA DE MÁLAGA

AVENIDA DE CARLOS V

AVENIDA DE LA BORBOLLA

Prado
de
San
Sebastián

Plaza de
España

AVENIDA DE PORTUGAL

Main Bus
Station

AVDA DE CÁDIZ

Parque
María Luisa

PLAZA DE
S. AGUSTÍN

MENÉNDEZ PELAYO

Jardines de Murillo

AVENIDA DEL CID

PL. DON
JUAN DE
AUSTRIA

GLORIETA
SAN DIEGO

AVENIDA DE M. LUISA

Casa de
Pilatos

PLAZA DE
PILATOS

Jardines de los
Reales Alcázares

PLAZA DE
SANTA CRUZ

SANTA CRUZ

Antiqua
Fábrica de
Tabacos

Casino-Teatro
Lope de Vega

Cvto. San
Léandro

Iglesia de
Sta. Cruz

PLAZA DE LOS
VENERABLES

SAN FERNANDO

LA RÁBIDA

VÍRGENES

MATEOS GAGO

Alcázar

Hotel
Alfonso XIII

Palacio
de San Telme

Museo del
Baile
Flamenco

Palacio
Arzobispal

PL. DEL
TRIUNFO

AV. DE ROMA

PLAZA
ALFALFA

PL. VIRGEN
DE LOS
REYES

PUERTA
DE JEREZ

Archivo de
las Indias

SAMURJO

San
Salvador

PL. JESÚS
DE LA PASIÓN

FRANCOS

Catedral

CONSTITUCIÓN

TOMÁS IBARRA

PUENTE DE SAN TELMO

JUAN S. ELCANO

Casa de
la C. de
Lebrija

Ayuntamiento

PLAZA
DEL
SALVADOR

AVENIDA DE LA

PLAZA DE
SAN FRANCISCO

Hospital de
la Caridad

DOS DE MAYO

Torre del Oro

PLAZA DE
CUBA

ASUNCIÓN

SIERPES

TETUÁN

PLAZA
NUEVA

EL ARENAL

AV. REP
ARGENTINA

O'DONNELL

MENDEZ NUÑEZ

S. Buenaventura

CASTELAR

PASEO DE CRISTÓBAL COLÓN

SALADO

SAN PABLO

ZARAGOZA

Plaza de Toros de
la Maestranza

FARMACÉUTICO
E. M. HERRERA

ARDILLA

Santa Ana

SEE 'SEVILLE: THE OLD CITY MAP'

Igl. de la
Magdalena

Capilla de los
Marineros

TRIANA

Bodega Siglo XVIII

Sunday
Mercadillo

CANALEJAS

REYES CATÓLICOS

ALHIERA

Guadalquivir

PUENTE DE ISABEL II (TRIANA)

PL. DEL
ALTOZANO

Castillo
De San Jorge

PAGÉS DEL CORRO

Museo de
Bellas Artes

MARQUÉS DE PARADAS

PLAZA DE
LA LEGIÓN

Mercado del
Barranco

Río

SAN
JORGE

SAN JACINTO

Mercado
de Triana

San
Jacinto

PLAZA DE
ARMAS

C. DE ARJONA

Plaza de Armas
Bus Station

TORNEO

Nuestra
Señora
de la 'O'

PAGÉS DEL CORRO

Torre Mirador

AV. DEL CRISTO DE LA EXPIRACIÓN

CLARA DE JESÚS MONTERO

TEJARES

PLAZA
PATROCINIO

CASTILLA

Pabellón De la
Navegación

PUERTA SUR

Puerta
Triana

PUERTA TRIANA

Jerez, Cádiz ► Museo Arqueológico (1.6km) & Museo de Costumbres (1.5km) ► Remedios

4

● **EATING**

Bar Bistec	11	Palo Cortao	4
Bar Eslava	12	Pando Centro	9
Bar Europa	6	La Primera del Puente	7
Bodega Siglo XVIII	10	El Rinconcillo	1
Bodegón Alfonso XII	13	Sal Gorda	5
Contenedor	2	Salmedina	3
Meson Los Gallegos	8		

achievement, as it's the largest Gothic church in the world. As Norman Lewis says, "It expresses conquest and domination in architectural terms of sheer mass."

Though it is built upon the huge, rectangular base-plan of the old mosque, the Christian architects (probably under the direction of the French master architect of Rouen cathedral) added the extra dimension of height. Its central nave rises to 42m, and even the side chapels seem tall enough to contain an ordinary church. The total area covers 11,520 square metres, and new calculations, based on cubic measurement, have now pushed it in front of St Paul's in London and St Peter's in Rome as the largest church in the world.

The monument to Christopher Columbus

Entry to the Catedral is via the Puerta de San Cristóbal on the building's south side; you are guided through a reception area that brings you into the church to the west of the portal itself. Turn right once inside to head east, where you will soon be confronted by the **Tomb of Christopher Columbus** (Cristóbal Colón in Spanish). Columbus's remains were originally interred in the cathedral of Havana, on the island that he had discovered on his first voyage in 1492. But during the upheavals surrounding the declaration of Cuban independence in 1902, Spain transferred the remains to Seville, and the monumental tomb – in the late Romantic style by Arturo Mélida – was created to house them. Doubts, however, have always been voiced concerning the authenticity of the remains. The mariner's coffin is held aloft by four huge allegorical figures, representing the kingdoms of León, Castile, Aragón and Navarra.

The nave

As you move into the **nave**, sheer size and grandeur are, inevitably, the chief characteristics of the Catedral to strike you. But there is a rhythmic balance and

MOORISH SEVILLE

Seville was one of the earliest Moorish conquests (in 712) and, as part of the **Caliphate of Córdoba**, became the second city of al-Andalus. When the caliphate broke up in the early eleventh century it was by far the most powerful of the independent states (or *taifas*) to emerge, extending its power over the Algarve and eventually over Jaén, Murcia and Córdoba itself. This period, under a series of three Arabic rulers from the **Abbadid dynasty** (1023–91), was something of a golden age. The city's court was unrivalled in wealth and luxury and was sophisticated, too, developing a strong chivalric element and a flair for poetry – one of the most skilled exponents being the last ruler, al-Mu'tamid, the "poet-king". But with sophistication came decadence, and in 1091 Abbadid rule was overthrown by a new force, the **Almoravids**, a tribe of fanatical Berber Muslims from North Africa, to whom the Andalucians had appealed for help against the rising threat from the northern Christian kingdoms.

Despite initial military successes, the Almoravids failed to consolidate their gains in al-Andalus and attempted to rule through military governors from Marrakesh. In the middle of the twelfth century, they were in turn supplanted by a new Berber incursion, the **Almohads**, who by about 1170 had recaptured virtually all the former territories. Seville had accepted Almohad rule in 1147 and became the capital of this last real empire of the Moors in Spain. Almohad power was sustained until their disastrous defeat in 1212 by the combined Christian armies of the north, at Las Navas de Tolosa. In this brief and precarious period, Seville underwent a renaissance of public building, characterized by a new vigour and fluidity of style. The Almohads rebuilt the Alcázar, enlarged the principal mosque – later demolished to make room for the Christian Catedral – and erected a new and brilliant minaret, a tower over 100m tall, topped with four copper spheres that could be seen for miles around: **the Giralda**.

interplay between the parts, and an impressive overall simplicity and restraint in decoration. All successive ages have left monuments of their own wealth and style, but these have been limited to the two rows of side chapels. In the main body of the Catedral only the great box-like structure of the **coro** stands out, filling the central portion of the nave.

The Capilla Mayor

The *coro* extends and opens onto the **Capilla Mayor**, dominated by a vast **Gothic retablo** composed of 45 carved scenes from the Life of Christ. The lifetime's work of a single craftsman, Fleming Pieter Dancart, this is the supreme masterpiece of the Catedral – the largest and richest altarpiece in the world and one of the finest examples of Gothic woodcarving.

The Sacristía de los Cálices

Before proceeding around the edge of the nave in a clockwise direction it's best to backtrack to the church's southeast corner to take in the **Sacristía de los Cálices** where many of the Catedral's main art treasures are displayed, including a masterly image of *Santas Justa y Rufina* by Goya, depicting Seville's patron saints, who were executed by the Romans in 287. Should you be interested in studying the many canvases here or the abundance of major artworks placed in the various chapels, it's worth calling at the bookshop near the entrance to purchase a copy of the official *Guide to the Cathedral of Seville*.

The Sacristía Mayor

Alongside this room is the grandiose **Sacristía Mayor**, housing the treasury. Embellished in the Plateresque style, it was designed in 1528 by Diego de Riaño, one of the foremost exponents of this predominantly decorative architecture of the late Spanish Renaissance. Amid a confused collection of silver reliquaries and monstrances – dull and prodigious wealth – are displayed the **keys** presented to Fernando by the Jewish and Moorish communities on the surrender of the city; sculpted into the metal in stylized Arabic script are the words "May Allah render eternal the dominion of Islam in this city". Through a small antechamber here you enter the oval-shaped **Sala Capitular** (Chapter House), with paintings by Murillo and an outstanding **marble floor** with geometric design.

Puerta del Nacimiento

Continuing to the southwest corner and the **Puerta del Nacimiento** – the door through which pass all the *pasos* and penitents who take part in the Semana Santa processions – you then turn right (north) along the west wall, passing the Puerta Principal.

The Capilla de San Antonio

In the northwest corner, the **Capilla de San Antonio** has Murillo's *Vision of St Anthony* depicting the saint in ecstatic pose before an infant Christ. A magnificent work: try to spot where the restorers joined San Antonio back into place after he had been hacked out of the picture by thieves in the nineteenth century. He was eventually discovered in New York – where art dealers recognized the work they were being asked to buy – and returned to the Catedral. *The Baptism of Jesus* above this is another fine work by the same artist.

The Capilla Real

The nave's north side leads to the Puerta de la Concepción, through which you will exit – but before doing so, continue to the northeast corner to view the domed Renaissance **Capilla Real**, built on the site of the original royal burial chapel and containing the body of Fernando III (El Santo) in a suitably rich, silver shrine in front of the altar. The large tombs on either side of the chapel are those of Fernando's wife, Beatrice of Swabia, and his son, Alfonso the Wise. The chapel is reserved for services and private prayer and may only be viewed via the entrance in Pza. Virgen de los Reyes (Mon–Sat 8am–2pm & 4–7pm; free). You are now close to the entry to the Giralda tower.

The Patio de los Naranjos

To reach the Catedral's exit, move east along the nave's north side to reach the Puerta de la Concepción, passing through this to enter the **Patio de los Naranjos**. Along with the Giralda tower, this was the only feature to be spared from the original mosque. In Moorish times the mosque would have been entered via the Puerta del Pardon, now the visitor exit. Taking its modern name from the orange trees that now shade the patio, this was the former mosque's entrance courtyard. Although somewhat marred by Renaissance additions, the patio still incorporates a **Moorish fountain** where worshippers carried out ritual ablutions prior to worship. Interestingly, it incorporates a sixth-century font from an earlier Visigothic cathedral, which was in its turn levelled to make way for the mosque.

La Giralda

Same ticket as Catedral

The **entrance to the Giralda** lies to the left of the Capilla Real in the Catedral's northeast corner. Unquestionably the most beautiful building in Seville, the cathedral's square-sided tower was named after the sixteenth-century *giraldillo*, or weather vane, on its summit, and it dominates the city skyline. From the entrance you can ascend to the **bell chamber** for a remarkable **view** of the city – and, equally remarkable, a glimpse of the Gothic details of the Catedral's buttresses and statuary. But most impressive of all is the tower's inner construction, a series of 35 gently inclined ramps wide enough to allow two mounted guards to pass.

The minaret

The Giralda tower, before it was embellished with Christian additions, was the mosque's **minaret** and the artistic pinnacle of Almohad architecture. The Moorish structure took twelve years to build (1184–96) and derives its firm, simple beauty from the shadows formed by blocks of brick trelliswork (a style known as *sebka*), different on each side, and relieved by a succession of arched niches and windows. It was used by the Moors both for calling the faithful to prayer (the traditional function of a minaret) and as an observatory, and was so venerated that they wanted to destroy it before the Christian conquest of the city. This they were prevented from doing by the threat of Alfonso (later King Alfonso X) that "if they removed a single stone, they would all be put to the sword". Instead, it became the bell tower of the Christian Catedral. The original harmony has been somewhat spoiled by the Renaissance-era additions but it still remains one of the most important and beautiful monuments of the Islamic world.

Archivo de las Indias

Av. de la Constitución • Free • www.cultura.gob.es

If the Columbus tomb has inspired you, or you have a keen interest in the navigator's travels, visit the sixteenth-century **Archivo de las Indias**, between the Catedral and the Alcázar. Originally called La Casa Lonja, it served as the city's old stock exchange (*lonja*). Built in the severe and uncompromising style of El Escorial near Madrid, and designed by the same architect, Juan de Herrera, in the eighteenth century it was turned into a storehouse for the archive of the Spanish empire – a purpose it served for almost three hundred years. In 2006, this mountain of documentation (of vital importance to scholars) was moved to another building around the corner and the Archivo was renovated, enabling visitors to enjoy Herrera's masterpiece in all its splendour once again. The exterior is defined by four identical facades, while corner pyramids supporting weather vanes are the main decorative feature. Inside, the sumptuous marble floors, bookcases in Cuban wood, arcaded central patio, and grand staircase in pink and black marble are a visual feast. The upper floor houses temporary **exhibitions** of interesting documents from the archive; these frequently include items such as Columbus's log and a letter from a penurious Cervantes (pre-*Don Quixote*) petitioning the king for a position in the Americas – fortunately for world literature, he was turned down.

The Ayuntamiento

Pza. de San Francisco • Charge • http://sevilla.org

Another building worth a visit and sited slightly to the north of the Catedral is the sixteenth-century **Ayuntamiento**, which has a richly ornamented Plateresque facade by Diego de Riaño. The equally impressive interior – with Riaño's star-vaulted entrance hall and council chamber with gilded coffered ceiling – is open for guided visits.

The Alcázar

Casco Antiguo • Charge • http://alcazarsevilla.org

Rulers of Seville have occupied the site of the **Alcázar** from the time of the Romans. Here was built the great court of the **Abbadids**, which reached a peak of sophistication and exaggerated sensuality under the ruthless al-Mu'tadid – a ruler who enlarged the palace in order to house a harem of eight hundred women, and who decorated the terraces with flowers planted in the skulls of his decapitated enemies. Later, under the **Almohads**, the complex was turned into a citadel, forming the heart of the town's fortifications. Its extent was enormous, stretching to the Torre del Oro on the bank of the Guadalquivir.

4

Parts of the Almohad walls survive, but the present structure of the palace dates almost entirely from the Christian period. Seville was a favoured residence of the Spanish kings for some four centuries after the Reconquest – most particularly under **Pedro the Cruel** (Pedro I; 1350–69) who, with his mistress María de Padilla, lived in and ruled from the Alcázar. Pedro's rebuild of the palace forms the nucleus of the Alcázar as it is today and, despite numerous restorations necessitated by fires and earth tremors, it offers some of the best surviving examples of **Mudéjar architecture** – the style developed by Moors working under Christian rule. Later monarchs, however, have left all too many traces and additions. Isabel built a new wing in which to organize expeditions to the Americas and control the new territories; Carlos V married a Portuguese princess in the palace, adding huge apartments for the occasion; and under Felipe IV (c.1624) extensive renovations were carried out to the existing rooms. On a more mundane level, kitchens were installed to provide for General Franco, who stayed in the royal apartments whenever he visited Seville.

Entry to the Alcázar and the Patio de la Montería

The Alcázar is entered from the Pza. del Triunfo, adjacent to the Catedral. The gateway, flanked by original Almohad walls, opens onto a courtyard where Pedro I (who was known as "the Just" as well as "the Cruel", depending on one's fortunes) used to give judgement; to the left is his **Sala de Justicia** and beyond this the **Patio del Yeso**, the only surviving remnant of the Almohads' Alcázar. The main facade of the palace, the **Patio de la Montería** of the fourteenth-century Mudéjar, stands at the end of an inner court and, with its delicate, marble-columned windows, stalactite frieze and overhanging roof, is one of the finest things in the whole Alcázar.

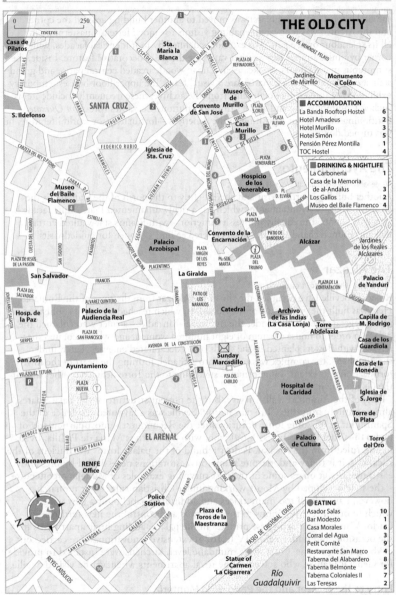

THE OLD CITY

ACCOMMODATION
La Banda Rooftop Hostel	6
Hotel Amadeus	2
Hotel Murillo	3
Hotel Simón	5
Pensión Pérez Montilla	1
TOC Hostel	4

DRINKING & NIGHTLIFE
La Carbonería	1
Casa de la Memoria de al-Andalus	3
Los Gallos	2
Museo del Baile Flamenco	4

EATING
Asador Salas	10
Bar Modesto	1
Casa Morales	6
Corral del Agua	3
Petit Comité	9
Restaurante San Marco	4
Taberna del Alabardero	8
Taberna Belmonte	5
Taberna Coloniales II	7
Las Teresas	2

The Salón del Almirante

As you will exit on the other side of the complex, it's probably better to look round the **Salón del Almirante** (or Casa de Contración de Indias), the sixteenth-century building on the right, before entering the main palace. Founded by Isabel in 1503, this gives you a standard against which to assess the Moorish forms. The only notable exception of overly heavy decor is the **Sala de Audiencias** (or Capilla de los Navigantes, Chapel of the Navigators) with its magnificent *artesonado* ceiling inlaid with golden rosettes;

within is a fine sixteenth-century *retablo* by Alejo Fernández depicting Columbus (in gold) and Carlos V (in a red cloak) sheltering beneath the Virgin. In the rear, to the left, are portrayed the kneeling figures of the Indians to whom the dubious blessings of Christianity had been brought by the Spanish conquest.

The royal apartments

Guided tours (charge) last 30min and take place every 30min

The **royal apartments**, known as the **Palacio Real Alto**, are open for visits when not in use, and a temporary desk located in front of the Salón del Almirante sells tickets for a guided tour. This takes in the **royal chapel**, with its fine early sixteenth-century *retablo* by Nicola Pisano; the so-called **bedroom of Pedro I**, with fine early Mudéjar plasterwork; and the equally splendid **Sala de Audiencias** – with more stunning plaster and tile decoration – which is still used by the royal family when receiving visitors in Seville.

Palacio de Pedro I

As you enter the main palace, the **Palacio de Pedro I**, the "domestic" nature of Moorish and Mudéjar architecture is immediately striking. This involves no loss of grandeur but simply a shift in scale: the apartments are remarkably small, shaped to human needs, and take their beauty from the exuberance of the decoration and the imaginative use of space and light. There is, too, a deliberate disorientation in the layout of the rooms – the palace seems infinitely larger and more open than it really is. From the entrance court a narrow passage leads straight into the central courtyard, the **Patio de las Doncellas** (Patio of the Maidens), its name recalling the Christians' tribute of one hundred virgins presented annually to the Moorish kings. The heart of the patio has been restored to its fourteenth-century original state after having been buried under a tiled pavement for four centuries. Archeologists have replanted the six orange trees that once grew in sunken gardens to either side of a central pool. The pool is now filled with goldfish – as it was in the time of Pedro I – a medieval way of eliminating mosquitoes in summer. The court's stuccowork, *azulejos* and doors are all of the finest Granada craftsmanship. Interestingly, it's also the only part of the palace where Renaissance restorations are successfully fused – the double columns and upper storey were built by Carlos V, whose *Plus Ultra* ("yet still farther") motto recurs in the decorations here and elsewhere.

Salons de Carlos V and Embajadores

Past the **Salón de Carlos V**, distinguished by a superb ceiling, are three rooms from the original fourteenth-century design built for María de Padilla (who was popularly thought to use magic in order to maintain her hold over Pedro – and perhaps over other gallants at court, too, who used to drink her bath water). These open onto the **Salón de Embajadores** (Salon of the Ambassadors), the most brilliant room of the Alcázar, with its stupendous *media naranja* (half-orange) wooden dome of red, green and gold cells, and horseshoe arcades inspired by the great palace of Medina Azahara outside Córdoba. Although restored, for the worse, by Carlos V – who added balconies and an incongruous frieze of royal portraits to commemorate his marriage here to Isabel of Portugal – the salon stands comparison with the great rooms of Granada's Alhambra. Adjoining are a long dining hall (*comedor*) and a small apartment installed in the late sixteenth century for Felipe II.

Patio de las Muñecas

The last great room of the palace – the **Patio de las Muñecas** (Patio of the Dolls), takes its curious name from two tiny faces decorating the inner side of one of the smaller arches. It's thought to be the site of the harem in the original palace, where Pedro is reputed to have murdered his brother Don Fadrique in 1358 and Abu Said of Granada was murdered for his jewels (one of which, an immense spinel that Pedro later gave to Edward, the "Black Prince", now figures in the British crown jewels). The upper storey of the court is a much later, nineteenth-century restoration. On the other sides of the patio are the **bedrooms** of Isabel and of her son Don Juan, and the arbitrarily named **Dormitorio del los Reyes Moros** (Bedroom of the Moorish Kings).

Palacio de Carlos V

To the left of the main palace loom the large and soulless apartments of the **Palacio de Carlos V** – something of an endurance test, with endless tapestries (eighteenth-century copies of the sixteenth-century originals now in Madrid) and pink, orange or yellow paintwork. Their classical style asserts a different and inferior mood.

The gardens

In the beautiful and rambling **Jardines de los Reales Alcázares** (gardens), you'll find the vaulted baths in which María de Padilla is supposed to have bathed (in reality, an auxiliary water supply for the palace), and the **Estanque de Mercurio** with a bronze figure of the messenger of the gods at its centre. This pool was specially constructed for Felipe V in 1733, who whiled away two solitary years at the Alcázar fishing and preparing himself for death through religious flagellation. Just to the left of the pool a path beyond the Puerta de Marchena leads to a pleasant **cafetería** with a terrace overlooking the gardens. South of here towards the centre of the gardens there's an entertaining **maze** of myrtle bushes and, nearby, the **pavilion** (*pabellón*) **of Carlos V**, the only survivor of several he built for relaxation.

4 Antigua Fábrica de Tabacos

Av. San Fernando • Free by appointment only • http://us.es

Immediately south of the Alcázar and fronting Avda. San Fernando lies the old tobacco factory and the setting for Bizet's *Carmen*. Now part of the university, the massive **Antigua Fábrica de Tabacos** was built in the 1750s and retains its position as the largest building in Spain after El Escorial. At its peak in the following century, it was also the country's largest single employer, with a workforce of some four thousand women, *cigarreras* – "a class in themselves", according to Richard Ford, who were forced to undergo "an ingeniously minute search on leaving their work, for they sometimes carry off the filthy weed in a manner her most Catholic majesty never dreamt of."

Parque María Luisa and Plaza de España

Ten minutes' walk to the south of the Alcázar, lies the **Parque de María Luisa** and the adjoining **Plaza de España**. These are wonderfully relaxing places to get away from the city bustle and are among the most pleasant – and impressive – public spaces in Spain.

The Parque de María Luisa used to form part of the vast grounds of the Palacio de San Telmo. The palace's nineteenth-century owner, the dowager duchess María Luisa, donated the park to the city in 1893 which then named it after her. Amid the ornamental pools and tree-shaded avenues lie various pavilions from the ill-fated Spanish Americas Fair. The Plaza de España was designed as the centrepiece of the fair, which was somewhat scuppered by the 1929 Wall Street crash. A vast semicircular complex, with its fountains, monumental stairways and mass of tile work, it would seem strange in most Spanish cities, but here it looks entirely natural, carrying on the tradition of civic display. At the fair, the plaza was used for the Spanish exhibit of industry and crafts, and around the crescent are *azulejo* scenes representing each of the provinces – an interesting record of the country at the tail end of a moneyed era. The buildings here fell into a terrible state in the latter part of the twentieth century, but have now been superbly restored and refurbished. The tiny strip of canal fronting the plaza has been refilled with water and *sevillanos* can be seen once again pottering about in the little rented boats.

Museo Arqueológico and Museo de Costumbres Populares

Pza. de América s/n • Charge • http://museosdeandalucia.es

Two opulent mansions at the southern end of the Parque de María Luisa – built for the 1929 Spanish Americas Fair – now house the city's archeological and folk museums.

The farthest south is the city's **Museo Arqueológico**, the most important archeology collection in Andalucía. The main exhibits include the **Carambolo Treasure**, a hoard of prehistoric gold jewellery found in the Seville suburb of Camas in 1958, and attributed to the land of Tartessus (the biblical Tarshish) which, although not yet identified, probably lay in the region between Seville and the mineral-rich hills of Huelva. The treasure is now displayed in its own section – with background information on the Tartessian culture – on the second floor. The remainder of the collection displays Roman mosaics and artefacts from nearby Itálica and a unique Phoenician statuette of Astarte-Tanit, the virgin goddess once worshipped throughout the Mediterranean.

Opposite is the fabulous-looking **Museo de Costumbres Populares** (Popular Arts Museum), with an equally fine patio. The museum has displays of costumes, implements, furniture, textiles, photos and posters from times past, with interesting displays relating to traditional arts and crafts and the April *feria*. The basement ceramic display – illustrating the regional developments of this craft inherited from the Moors – is a highlight. The first floor is currently closed for refurbishment.

Barrio Santa Cruz

The city's Jewish quarter until the Alhambra Decree of 1492, **Barrio Santa Cruz** is very much in character with Seville's romantic image. Its streets are narrow and tortuous in order to keep out the sun, the houses brilliantly whitewashed and festooned with flowering plants. Many of the windows are barricaded with *rejas* (iron grilles), behind which girls once kept chaste evening rendezvous with their *novios* who were forced to *comer hierro* ("eat iron") as passion mounted.

Casa de Pilatos

Pza. de Pilatos 1 • Charge • 954 225 298

Of the numerous mansions, by far the finest is the so-called **Casa de Pilatos**, built by the Marqués de Tarifa on his return from a pilgrimage to Jerusalem in 1519 and popularly thought to have been in imitation of the house of Pontius Pilate. In fact, it's an interesting and harmonious mixture of Mudéjar, Gothic and Renaissance styles, featuring brilliant *azulejos*, a tremendous sixteenth-century stairway and one of the most elegant domestic patios in the city.

Hospicio de los Venerables Sacerdotes

Pza. de los Venerables 8 • Charge • http://hospitalvenerables.es

Patios are a feature of almost all the houses in Santa Cruz: they are often surprisingly large and in summer they become the principal family living room. One of the most beautiful is within the Baroque **Hospicio de los Venerables Sacerdotes**, near the centre in a plaza of the same name – one of the few buildings in the *barrio* worth actively seeking out. The former hospice also displays some outstanding artworks including **sculptures** by Martínez Montañés and a painting of the *Last Supper* by Roelas, plus some wonderfully restored **frescoes** by Lucás Valdés and Valdés Leal in addition to a *Fray Pedro de Oña* by Zurbarán displaying the artist's special gift for portraying white draperies. The museum has recently added a **Centro Velázquez**, which – in addition to other works by the Spanish master – displays a fine *Santa Rufina* and a spectacular *Inmaculada Concepción*.

Museo del Baile Flamenco

C/Manuel Rojas Marcos 3 • Charge • http://museoflamenco.com

The **Museo del Baile Flamenco** is an innovative and entertaining museum dedicated to the history and evolution of this emblematic *andaluz* art form. Set up in collaboration with celebrated flamenco dancer Cristina Hoyos, the museum is interactive (and multilingual), employing the latest sound and image technology to familiarize visitors with the origins of flamenco and the range of dance styles or "*palos*", which can all be seen at the touch of a button. The museum also stages concerts of flamenco, which bring the art form to life at a very high standard.

Plaza de la Encarnación and Las Setas

Mirador and rooftop walkway Charge • **Museum** Charge • http://setasdesevilla.com

Almost at the geographical centre of the former walled city of Seville, the **Plaza de la Encarnación** was created in 1819 after Napoleon's invading forces demolished the convent of the same name that stood on the spot. Long criticized for its bleakness, at the start of the new millennium the city government decided to spectacularly raise its profile with a breathtaking piece of modern architecture.

Taking seven years to build, **Las Setas** or Metropol Parasol (as it is officially dubbed) is a 30m-high, 150m-long structure comprising a series of undulating wood-waffle flat-topped mushroom structures on giant concrete pillars. Claimed by its German architect, Jürgen Mayer, to be the world's largest timber construction, it incorporates a market, shopping mall, restaurant and a **basement museum** that imaginatively displays the ruins of Roman Sevilla – complete with mosaics – encountered during the preliminary excavations. The structure's high point (in all senses) is a spectacular undulating **walkway** across the roof to a sky deck with stunning views over the city. When unveiled in 2011 the structure attracted much criticism and its official name did not last more than a couple of days – *sevillano* residents took one look and tagged it Las Setas (the mushrooms), the name everyone uses today when debating how long it'll stay standing.

Río Guadalquivir and around

Down by the **Río Guadalquivir** are pedal-boats for idling away the afternoons, and at night, local couples come to sip beer on its banks. Very few people swim here, however, as the river's slow current means that it's closer to being a stagnant than a clean body of water. The main riverside landmark here is the twelve-sided **Torre del Oro**, built by the Almohads in 1220 as part of the Alcázar fortifications. It was connected to another small fort across the river by a chain that had to be broken by the Castilian fleet before their conquest of the city in 1248. The tower was later used as a repository for the gold brought back from the Americas – hence its name.

Hospital de la Caridad

Entry on C/Temprado 3 • Charge

The **Hospital de la Caridad** was founded in 1676 by Don Miguel de Mañara, the inspiration for Byron's *Don Juan*. According to one of Don Miguel's friends, "There was no folly which he did not commit, no youthful indulgence into which he did not plunge … (until) what occurred to him in the street of the coffin." What occurred was that Don Miguel, returning from a reckless orgy, had a vision in which he was confronted by a funeral procession carrying his own corpse. He repented his past life, joined the Brotherhood of Charity (whose task was to bury the bodies of vagrants and criminals), and later set up this hospital for the relief of the dying and destitute, for which purpose it is still used. Don Miguel commissioned a series of eleven paintings by Murillo for the chapel; seven remain (the French stole the others during the Napoleonic occupation), including a superlative image of *San Juan de Dios* for which Mañara himself posed as the model. Alongside hang two *Triumph of Death* pictures by Valdés Leal. One, depicting a decomposing bishop being eaten by worms (beneath the scales of justice labelled *Ni más, Ni menos* – No More, No Less), is so powerfully repulsive that Murillo declared that "you have to hold your nose to look at it". Their mood may reflect memories of the 1649 plague, which killed half of Seville's population.

Museo de Bellas Artes

Pza. del Museo 9 • Charge • 954 786 498

Near the Pza. de Armas bus station is one of Spain's most impressive art galleries, the **Museo de Bellas Artes**, housed in a beautiful former convent. The collection is frequently rotated, so not all the works mentioned here may be on show.

Room 1

Among the highlights is a wonderful late fifteenth-century sculpture in painted terracotta in Room 1, *Lamentation over the Dead Christ*, by the Andalucian **Pedro Millán**, the founding father of the Seville school of sculpture. A marriage of Gothic and expressive naturalism, this style was the starting point for the outstanding seventeenth-century period of religious iconography in Seville.

Rooms 2 to 4

A later example, in Room 2, is a magnificent *San Jerónimo* by the Italian **Pietro Torrigiano**, who spent the latter years of his life in the city. Room 3 has a *retablo* of the *Redemption* (c.1562), with fine woodcarving by Juan Giralte. Here also is displayed the grisly terracotta sculpture of the severed head of John the Baptist by Nuñez Delgado, not something you want to see too soon after lunch. Room 4 shows an impressive series by Francesco Pacheco, a protagonist in both the Naturalist and Mannerist schools before he tutored Velázquez, whose work also hangs here.

Room 5

Beyond a serene patio and cloister, Room 5 is located in the monastery's former church, where the recently restored paintings on the vault and dome by the eighteenth-century *sevillano*, Domingo Martínez, are spectacular. In addition to a monumental *Last Supper* by Alonso Vázquez, here also is the nucleus of the collection: **Zurbarán's** *Apotheosis of St Thomas Aquinas*, as well as a clutch of works by **Murillo** in the apse, crowned by the great *Immaculate Conception* – known as "*La Colosal*" to distinguish it from the other work here with the same name. Below this is displayed the same artist's *Virgin and Child*; popularly known as *La Servilleta* because it was said to have been painted on a dinner napkin, the work is one of Murillo's greatest.

Rooms 6 to 10

Upstairs, Room 6 (quadrated around the patio) displays works from the Baroque period, among which a stark *Crucifixion* by Zurbarán stands out. Room 10 contains more imposing canvases by Zurbarán, including *St Hugo visiting the Carthusian Monks at Supper* and another almost sculptural *Crucifixion* to compare with the one in Room 6. Here also are sculptures by **Martínez Montañés**, the sixteenth-century "Andalucian Lysippus", whose early *St Dominic in Penitence* and *San Bruno* from his mature period display mastery of technique.

Rooms 11 to 14

The collection ends with works from the Romantic and Modern eras. In Room 11 there's an austere late canvas by **Goya** of the octogenarian *Don José Duaso,* and in Room 12, Gonzalo Bilbao's *Las Cigarreras* is a vivid portrayal of the wretched life of women in the tobacco factory during the early years of the last century. Also here is a monumental canvas by nineteenth-century *sevillano* artist José Villegas Cordero, *La Muerte del Maestro*, depicting the death of a *torero*, which was purchased by the Junta de Andalucía in 1996.

Room 13 has an evocative image of *Sevilla en Fiestas* dated 1915 by Gustavo Bacarisas, and finally, in Room 14 there's *Juan Centeño y su cuadrilla* by Huelvan artist Daniel Vásquez Díaz, who worked in Paris and was a friend of Picasso. This stirring image of the *torero* and his team provides an appropriately *andaluz* conclusion to a memorable museum.

Triana

Over the Río Guadalquivir is the **Triana** *barrio*, scruffy, lively and well away from the tourist trails. This was once the heart of the city's *gitano* (gypsy) community and, more specifically, home of the great flamenco dynasties of Seville who were kicked out by developers early last century and are now scattered throughout the city. The *gitanos*, belonging to the Romani ethnic group, lived in extended families in tiny, immaculate communal houses called *corrales* around courtyards glutted with flowers. Today, only a handful remain intact. Triana is the starting point for the annual pilgrimage to El Rocío (end of May), when a myriad of painted wagons leave town, drawn by oxen. It houses, too, the city's oldest working **ceramics factory**, Santa Ana, where the tiles, many still in the traditional, geometric Arabic designs, are hand-painted in the adjoining shop.

La Cartuja
Charge • www.caac.es
At Triana's northern edge lies **La Cartuja**, a fourteenth-century former Carthusian monastery expensively restored as part of the Expo '92 World's Fair. Part of the complex is now given over to the **Centro Andaluz de Arte Contemporáneo** (same hours and ticket) which stages rotating exhibitions from a large and interesting collection of contemporary work by *andaluz* artists, including canvases by Antonio Rodríguez Luna, Joaquín Peinado, Guillermo Pérez Villalta, José Guerrero and Daniel Vásquez Díaz. Two other galleries stage temporary exhibitions by international artists and photographers (see website for details).

Isla Mágica
Pabellón de España • Charge • http://islamagica.es
The remnants of much of the **Expo '92 site** have been incorporated into the **Isla Mágica**, an amusement park based on the theme of sixteenth-century Spain, with water and roller-coaster rides, shows and period street animations (included in ticket price). The Aquapark has the usual water chutes and slides but requires a supplementary ticket (and you must enter the main park first).

Pabellón de la Navegación and Schindler Torre Mirador
Camino de los Descubrimientos 2 • Charge • 954 043 111
Another remnant of **Expo '92**, the **Pabellón de la Navegación** has been turned into an exhibition space dedicated to the history of Spanish navigation and discovery with lots of interactive gadgetry. The museum is divided into four sections: navigators, the history of navigation, shipboard life and the history of Seville, and the English translations are well done. Your entry ticket also allows you to ascend the 65m high **Schindler Torre Mirador** (taking its name from the Swiss company who built it), another Expo leftover, from where there are stunning views over the river and the old city.

Itálica and around
9km north of Seville • Charge • http://italicasevilla.org • Bus #M172 departs the Pza. de Armas station (every 30min, Sun every hour; stop 41; 20min); it makes its way into Santiponce before turning back on itself and heading out of town again, where you get off at the "Parada Monestario", 200m down from the gates to the Itálica site entrance. Buses return to Seville from this same stop
The Roman ruins and remarkable mosaics of **Itálica** and the exceptional Gothic **Monasterio San Isidoro del Campo** lie some 9km to the north of Seville, just outside

the village of **Santiponce**, where also lie the well-preserved remains of a Roman theatre.

Itálica was the birthplace of two emperors (Trajan and Hadrian) and one of the earliest Roman settlements in Spain, founded in 206 BC by Scipio Africanus as a home for his veterans. It rose to considerable military importance in the second and third centuries AD, was richly endowed during the reign of Hadrian (AD 117–138) and declined as an urban centre only under the Visigoths, who preferred Seville, then known as *Hispalis*. Eventually, the city was deserted by the Moors after the river changed its course, disrupting the surrounding terrain.

Throughout the Middle Ages, the ruins were used as a source of stone for Seville, but somehow the shell of its enormous **amphitheatre** – the third largest in the Roman world – has survived. Today, it's crumbling perilously, but you can clearly detect the rows of seats, the corridors and the dens for wild beasts. Beyond, within a rambling and unkempt grid of **streets** and **villas**, about twenty **mosaics** have been uncovered. Most are complete, including excellent coloured floors depicting birds, Neptune and the seasons, and several fine black-and-white geometric patterns. More recently, the site has been used as a filming location for *Game of Thrones*.

Monasterio San Isidoro del Campo
Free

A little over 1km to the south of Santiponce on the road back to Seville lies the former Cistercian **Monasterio San Isidoro del Campo**. Closed for many years, it has now been painstakingly and gloriously restored and shouldn't be missed.

Founded in the fourteenth-century by monarch Guzmán El Bueno of Tarifa, the monastery is a masterpiece of Gothic architecture, which, prior to its confiscation during the nineteenth-century Disentailment (government confiscation of property), was occupied by a number of religious orders. Among these were the *ermitaños jerónimos* (Hieronymites) who, in the fifteenth century, decorated the central cloister and the Patio de los Evangelistas with a remarkable series of **mural paintings** depicting images of the saints – including scenes from the life of San Jerónimo – as well as astonishingly beautiful floral and Mudéjar-influenced geometric designs. In the seventeenth century, the monastery employed the great *sevillano* sculptor Martínez Montañés to create the magnificent **retablo mayor** in the larger of the complex's twin churches.

ARRIVAL AND DEPARTURE
SEVILLE

BY PLANE
Seville's airport (flight information 954 449 000) lies 12km northeast of town along the A4 (NIV) *autovía* towards Córdoba. The airport bus (roughly hourly), takes 45min to the centre and terminates at the central Pza. de Armas bus station, stopping at the train station en route. A taxi can be taken from the airport taxi rank or booked in advance with Book Taxi Sevilla (typically for a twenty percent mark-up; http://booktaxisevilla.com).

BY TRAIN
Santa Justa train station is 5km out northeast of the city on Avda. Kansas City, the airport road. Bus #32 will take you from here to Pza. del Duque, from where all sights are within easy walking distance; alternatively, bus #C1 will take you to the Prado de San Sebastián bus station. For train timetables and information, consult RENFE 902 240 202, http://renfe.es. Alternatively, there's a RENFE office on C/

Zaragoza, where you can buy advanced tickets in person.
Destinations Algeciras (7 daily, change at Antequera or Bobadilla; 3hr 30min); Almería (4 daily; 5hr 40min); Barcelona (2 daily at 8.50am & 2.50pm; 5hr 30min); Cádiz (14 daily; 1hr 45min); Córdoba (AVE 19 daily, 45min; 5 *cercanías* daily, 1hr 20min); Granada (6 daily; 3hr 15min); Huelva (5 daily; 1hr 35min); Madrid (AVE 16 daily; 3hr 20min); Málaga (12 daily; 2hr 30min); Osuna (3 daily; 1hr).

BY BUS
Pza. de Armas Station On the square of the same name by the Puente del Cachorro on the river (954 908 040). Buses from this station are operated by Alsa (http://alsa.es) who cover long-distance national and international destinations; and Damas (http://damas-sa.es), who are the most prominent provider for longer routes within Andalucía. For the majority of coaches, you'll have an allocated seat.
Destinations Almería (3 daily; 3hr 30min); Aracena (2 daily;

1hr 20min); Ayamonte (6 daily; 2hr 45min); Córdoba (7 daily; 1hr 45min); El Rocío (2 daily; 1hr 30min); Faro (5 daily; 2hr 45min); Granada (8 daily; 3hr); Huelva (every 30min; 1hr 15min); Madrid (9 daily; 6hr); Málaga (8 daily; 2hr 45min); Matalascañas (7 daily; 2hr); Mérida (4 daily; 2hr 15min).

Prado de San Sebastián (954 417 111), the city's subsidiary bus station, is on Avda Carlos V, which runs along the north edge of the San Sebastián park. Both Alsa and Damas providers call here.

Destinations Albufeira (3 daily; 3hr 15min); Algeciras (4 daily; 3hr 50min); Cádiz (10 daily; 1hr 45min); Carmona (hourly; 45min); Écija (9 daily; 1hr 15min); Jerez de la Frontera (7 daily; 1hr 15min); Mérida (5 daily; 1hr 15min); Ronda (6 daily; 2hr 30min).

BY CAR

Driving in Seville is an ordeal, especially in the narrow streets of *barrios* such as Santa Cruz, which is supposed to be pedestrianized. As on-street parking spaces are almost impossible to find, your best bet for parking is to find a pay car park (they are signed all around the central zone), or to choose accommodation with a garage (for which you will be charged extra).

GETTING AROUND

By bus All inner-city bus journeys have a flat fare. Seville's bus & tram company, Tussam (http://tussam.es), also sells one-day or three-day *tarjetas turísticas* for unlimited journeys with a small card deposit. These are available from the Tussam offices at Prado San Sebastián, Plaza Ponce de León station, Avda. Andalucía 11 (one of the two local bus hubs with Puerta de Jerez), or at the Santa Justa train station. If you're staying for longer, it's worth buying a Tarjeta Multiviaje rechargeable card from a kiosk (also good for trams). A bus map detailing routes is available from the *turismo*.

By tram Confusingly called Centro-Metro, the city tram runs from Plaza Nueva to San Bernando bus station, stopping at Archivo de Indias, San Fernando and Prado de San Sebastian along the way. A single journey costs €1.40, and you buy tickets at the stops (you can also use the Tarjeta Multiviaje rechargeable card on board).

By metro Seville currently has just one, 18km-long metro line (three more are planned), connecting the suburbs beyond Triana with Montequinto to the east. It's efficient and well-air conditioned – convenient if you arrive at San Bernardo in the heat of the day and are staying close to or over the river.

By open-top bus tour Good if you're pressed for time, this hop-on-hop-off service is operated by City Sightseeing Sevilla (http://city-sightseeing.com); buses leave half-hourly from the riverside Torre del Oro, stopping at or near the main sites (half-price for kids). Information is provided by earphone commentary in sixteen languages.

By taxi The main central ranks are in Pza. Nueva, the Alameda de Hércules and the Pza. de Armas and Prado de San Sebastián bus stations. The basic charge for a short journey is around €5 but rates rise at night and at weekends. For a reliable taxi pick-up, try Radio Taxi (954 580 000).

By bike Seville is famous for its cyclists and the city is very accommodating to those who decide to discover it upon two wheels. There are Bici bike depots dotted throughout the city, where you can pick up some wheels for unlimited access for up to a week. Alternatively, lots of private companies do rentals by the hour.

INFORMATION

Turismo Pza. del Triunfo 1, close to the exit from the Alcázar (Mon–Fri 9am–7.30pm, Sat & Sun 9.30am–7.30pm; 954 210 005). This office tends to be overwhelmed in peak periods, but they have accommodation lists and can give you a copy of the very useful free listings magazine *El Giraldillo*.

Municipal tourist office Less chaotic, and therefore much more helpful, this office is inside the Castillo de San Jorge, across the Puente de Triana (aka Isabel II) on the west bank of the river (Mon–Fri 9.30am–1.30pm & 3.30–7.30pm, Sat & Sun 10am–1.30pm; 954 332 240, http://turismosevilla.org). There are information points dotted around the city, noticeable by their orange glow: the most helpful being at Santa Justa train station, Av. de la Constitución and inside the Mercado del Barranco.

ACCOMMODATION
SEE MAPS PAGES 248 AND 254

Seville has some of the finest **hotels** in Andalucía. The most attractive area to stay is undoubtedly the **Barrio Santa Cruz**, though this is reflected in the prices (especially in peak season). Slightly farther out, another promising area is to the north of the Pza. Nueva, and especially over towards the river and the Pza. de Armas bus station.

If you're arriving during any of the major **festivals**, particularly Semana Santa or the Feria de Abril (April fair), you're strongly advised to book ahead – be aware also that this is when hotel rates rise above the high season rates quoted below.

BARRIO SANTA CRUZ AND CATEDRAL AREA

La Banda Rooftop Hostel C/Dos de Mio 16, http://labandahostel.com. An artistic place that fosters community. There are shared "family" dinners up on the rooftop that overlooks the Catedral, where they also host live music & DJs. The four- to eight-bed dorms are clean and comfortable; and the kitchen's well equipped. 24hr reception. **€**

★**Las Casas del Rey de Baeza** Pza. Jesús de la Redención 2, http://hospes.com. Wonderful hotel with rooms arranged around an eighteenth-century *sevillano corral*. Stylishly furnished pastel-shaded rooms come with traditional exterior *esparto* blinds; the restaurant's just as special and there's a rooftop pool to cool off in – a surprisingly rare find in Seville. €€€€

Hostal Puerta Carmona Pza. de San Agustín 5, http://hostalpuertacarmona.com. Very pleasant *hostal* whose good-value modern en-suite rooms come with a/c and TV; they will advise on where to park nearby (solely in Spanish). €€

★**Hotel Amadeus** C/Farnesio 6, http://hotelamadeus sevilla.com. Welcoming hotel housed in an eighteenth-century *casa señorial* where there's a *sala de música*, a grand piano in the patio and you can loan a variety of musical instruments. Thoughtfully, the stylish rooms are also soundproofed and come with a/c, satellite TV, and their own laptops, which you're free to take and use anywhere in the hotel. It's topped off with a stunning roof terrace (with telescope and Jacuzzi) for breakfasting, which is available as late as 2pm. €€

Hotel Murillo C/Lope de Rueda 7, http://hotelmurillo.com. Traditional hotel in a restored mansion close to Pza. Santa Cruz with all facilities plus amusingly kitsch features, including suits of armour and paint-palette key rings. Also rents out fully equipped apartments nearby (see website). €

Hotel Simón C/García de Vinuesa 19, http://hotelsimon sevilla.com. Well-restored mansion in an excellent position across from the Catedral with parking nearby. All rooms are en suite and a/c, and this can be a bargain when booked online. €

Pensión Pérez Montilla Pza. Curtidores 13, http://pensionperezmontilla.com. Spotless *hostal* on a tranquil square with economically priced rooms. A few cheaper rooms come without bath; those with have a/c and (most) have TV. Ask for an exterior room as these have more light. €

★**TOC Hostel** C/Miguel Mañara 18–22, http://tochostels.com. So close to the Catedral that it almost sits in its shadow, *TOC* is a forward-looking place. They have the efficiency of a hotel coupled with the open atmosphere of a hostel. The brilliance is also in the detail: environmentally friendly automatic lighting and a fingerprint entry system. €

SANTA CATALINA, SAN PEDRO, ALAMEDA DE HÉRCULES

Hotel Sacristía de Santa Ana Alameda de Hércules 22, http://hotelsacristia.com. Beautiful hotel with delightful rooms – the external ones have Alameda views – inside a seventeenth-century *casa señorial* with many original features. Facilities include minibar, room safe and plasma TV. €€

Patio de Alameda Alameda de Hércules 31, http://patio delaalameda.com. Modern, pleasant and very friendly *hostal* overlooking the tree-lined Alameda. En-suite rooms are all exterior-facing with small balconies and come with a/c and a TV. €

CAMPING

Camping Villsom 10km out of town on the main Cádiz road, http://campingvillsom.com. A decent campsite with a pool and BBQ area. To reach it by public transport: take the C1 metro line from San Bernando to Dos Hermanos. The campsite is on the other side of the NIV highway from the Hospital San Augustín (around a 20min walk southwest). €

EATING
SEE MAPS PAGES 248 AND 254

Seville is packed with lively and enjoyable **tapas bars and restaurants**, and you'll be able to find something open at all hours. With few exceptions, anywhere around the major sights and the **Barrio Santa Cruz** will be expensive. The two most promising central areas are down **towards the bullring** and north of here towards the Pza. de Armas bus station. The **Pza. de Armas** area is slightly seedier but has the cheapest *comidas* this side of the river. Wander down C/ Marqués de Paradas, and up C/Canalejas and C/San Eloy, and find out what's available. Across the river in **Triana**, C/ Betis and C/Pureza are also good hunting grounds.

RESTAURANTS AND CAFÉS

BARRIO SANTA CRUZ AND AROUND THE CATEDRAL

Bar Modesto C/Cano y Cueto 5, http://modesto restaurantes.com. At the north end of Santa Cruz, *Modesto has* built a good reputation. It has a restaurant and a separate tapas bar opposite. House specials include brochetas: one of *solomillo ibérico* (pork sirloin), and another of monkfish. If one of their *menú gustacións* is out of budget, try their daily menu, which includes wine and, if you get there early, can be eaten on an attractive terrace. In both venues, the kitchen continues throughout the day. €€€

Corral del Agua Callejón del Agua 6, http://corraldelagua.es. You won't mind paying a little more for this *cocina andaluz* as the patio here is one of the most romantic spots in the city. For lunch, there's a daily menu; in the evening try the *lubina al Tío Pepe* (sea bass with sherry sauce). Perfectly located for a pre-flamenco meal. €€€

Restaurante San Marco C/Mesón del Moro 6, http://sanmarco.es. Good Italian food served inside a remarkable twelfth-century Moorish bathhouse which has attracted the likes of Tom Cruise and Madonna. €€€

TRIANA AND THE RÍO GUADALQUIVIR

Asador Salas C/Almansa 15, 954 217 796. The impeccable table linen and elegant scoured brick and tiled interior denote quality, and the food follows suit. The specialities of the house include grilled fish and meat dishes. There's a bar area serving tapas and two spacious dining rooms with efficient service. €€

Petit Comité C/Dos de Mayo 30, https://petitcomitesevilla. es. French-influenced menu in an elegant restaurant with wall-hung art and traditional floor tiles. Try the signature dish of anchovies marinated in dry sherry or the octopus with truffled parmentier potatoes. A great spot for dinner. €€€

La Primera del Puente C/Betis 66, http://laprimera delpuente.es. The riverside terrace of the restaurant over the road has one of the city's best vistas; soft-talk a waiter to get a frontline table. You can enjoy generous *raciones* or *media raciones* of fish, meat and seafood. Paella is a daily special and there's a reasonably priced wine list. €€

★ **Taberna del Alabardero** C/Zaragoza 20, http:// alabarderosevilla.es. Elegant nineteenth-century *casa-palacio sevillana* with attractive decor and an upmarket clientele. Pricey – and outstanding – cutting-edge restaurant upstairs where you can experience the excellent tasting menu. However, the bargain lunchtime menu in the bistro below comes from the same kitchen. They also offer a tapas menu in the bar. €€€

CENTRO, LA MACARENA, ALAMEDA AND SANTA JUSTA

Bodegón Alfonso XII Alfonso XII 9, 954 910 420 Cosy little restaurant beyond a lively tapas bar out front, with generous fish and meat dishes at a good price. The kitchen is non-stop and it also does breakfasts. €€

★ **Contenedor** C/San Luís 50, http://restaurante contenedor.com. Lively, colourful, slow-food restaurant whose founders are so proud of the veg they serve that they even decorate the tables with it. Always fresh, and local where possible, the ever-changing menu features dishes such as *pappardelle con setas y alchachofas* (pasta with mushrooms and artichokes) and *pato y arroz cruicante* (duck with crispy rice). Booking is recommended for the evenings, especially on Tuesday when there's live music. €€

Meson Los Gallegos C/Capataz Franco 1, http:// mesonlosgallegos.eatbu.com. Friendly and inexpensive restaurant in a tiny alley off C/Martín Villa, serving *Galician* specialities – try the excellent *pulpo gallego* (spicy boiled octopus) or fried fish plate. €€

Pando Centro C/San Eloy 47, http://pandorestaurantes. com. An ideal lunch stop as most *raciones* are available in tapas form. There's a wide range of rice dishes on offer, as well as meat and fish – try their *alcachofas con langostinos* (braised artichoke with langoustines). €€

TAPAS BARS

For casual eating and drinking and taking tapas – Seville's great speciality – there are bars all over town. The tapas venues all serve barrelled sherries from nearby Jerez and Sanlúcar (the locals drink the cold, dry *fino* with their tapas,

especially *camarones*, or shrimps); a *tinto de verano* is the local version of *sangria* – wine with lemonade, a great summer drink. Outside the centre, you'll find lively bars in the Pza. Alfalfa area, and across the river in Triana – particularly in and around C/Castilla and C/Betis. Over recent years, a zone that has emerged as a focus for artistic, student and LGBTQ+ bar-hoppers is the Alameda (de Hércules).

BARRIO SANTA CRUZ AND AROUND THE CATEDRAL

★ **Bar Europa** Junction of C/Alcaicería de Loza and C/ Siete Revueltas, www.facebook.com/BarEuropa1925. Approaching its centenary, this is a fine old watering hole with lots of cool tiled walls, plus excellent *manzanilla* and a variety of inventive tapas served on marble-topped tables. Their deliciously sweet and velvety *croquetas de jamón Ibérico* (jamón croquettes) are a must try. It has a large terrace and also does breakfasts. €€

★ **Casa Morales** C/García de Vinuesa 11, http://casa moralessevilla.es. Earthy, traditional bar (founded 1850) with wine barrels from bygone days now looming empty around the cosy dining area. House staples are *tablas* (tapas served on wooden boards) of regional meat and cheeses, including *morcilla* (blood pudding). The daily specials are written up on the huge barrels and may include things such as bonito fish with tomato or *revueltos* (scrambled egg with different ingredients). €€

Taberna Belmonte C/Mateos Gago 24, http://taberna belmonte.com. Named after bullfighting legend Juan Belmonte, the menu at this bar-restaurant is just as brave. If you sit on the romantic terrace out back, the waiter/ waitress will give you both a tapas and restaurant menu, from which the *alcachofas a la plancha* (grilled artichokes) and *champiñones rellenos de queso y jamón* (mushrooms stuffed with cheese and ham) are top picks. €€

Taberna Coloniales II C/Fernández y González 38, http:// tabernacoloniales.es. Offspring of the similarly named establishment in Pza. Cristo de Burgos, this is up to the same high standard. Tapas are served at the bar, but cornering a table (not always easy) will allow you to feast on a wide range including *solomillo al whisky* (pork loin in grog) and *papas a la brava* (potatoes in a spicy sauce); the *raciones* are meal-sized portions, so why bother with a restaurant? €€

Las Teresas C/Santa Teresa 2, http://lasteresas.es. Good beer and sherry are served in this atmospheric L-shaped bar, which has hanging cured hams and tiled walls lined with faded *corrida* photos. It's also worth stopping here for breakfast the morning after. Try the *pulpo a la gallega* (Galician octopus) and their *tortillitas de camarones* (shrimp fritters). €€

Sal Gorda C/Alcaicería de la Loza 23, 955 385 972. Gourmet tapas in hip corner bar. It's a popular place and there's not much space, so make sure you reserve. Try the sea bream with white garlic and *buñuelos de bacalao* (risotto with mushrooms and langoustines). €€

TRIANA AND THE RÍO GUADALQUIVIR

★ **Bar Bistec** C/Pelay y Correa 34, 954 274 759. Excellent, ancient and hearty Triana hostelry, with a sparkling Triana-tiled interior and outdoor tables in summer fronting the church of Santa Ana. Tasty dishes include *anchoas con salmorejo* (anchovies with a thick cold tomato soup) and *tortillitas de bacalao* (cod fritters). They also do *raciones* and sell good wine by the bottle, tempting you to make a meal of it. €€

Bodega Siglo XVIII C/Pelay y Correa 32, http://sigloxviii. com. The neighbour of *Bar Bistec* and another great Triana bar. House specialities include *cordero en salsa de frutos secos* (lamb in dried-fruit sauce). If you want to try a well-curated selection, opt for the six tapas tasting menu. €€€

CENTRO, LA MACARENA, ALMEDA AND SANTA JUSTA

Bar Eslava C/Eslava 3–5, http://espacioeslava.com. Very good and extremely popular bar – which often means you can't get through the door – with a mouthwatering range of tapas and some great veggie options. Try their *strudel de verduras* (pastry with veggie filling) or *pimiento relleno de* *merluza* (pepper stuffed with hake). €€

Palo Cortao C/Mercedes de Velilla 4, http://palo-cortao. com. Watch the culinary theatre unfold before you in the open kitchen at *Palo Cortao*. Head chef Angel leads the team in creating imaginative tapas like cuttlefish balls in red shrimp sauce, mackerel with mangetouts, and tuna tomato. Choose from over 30 sherries to wash down food. €€

★ **El Rinconcillo** C/Gerona 40, http://elrinconcillo. es. Seville's oldest bar (founded in 1670) does a fair tapas selection as well as providing a hang-out for the city's literati. Now with a more contemporary wing around the corner, it's renowned for *espinacas con garbanzos* (spinach with chickpeas), one of the city's most popular tapas; you could also try a tasty *bacalao en costra y crema de piquilllos* (encrusted cod with a chilli cream). Its dining rooms function as a very good mid-priced restaurant. €€

Salmedina C/Guardamino 1, 954 213 172. Classic tapas bar with a seafood focus in the vibrant Alfalfa *barrio* just off its main square. There's a spacious bar for winter dining but in summer everyone sits out on their terrace. House specials include razor clams and cuttlefish eggs as well as *bacalao a la Bilbaina* (cod in chilli sauce). €€

DRINKING AND NIGHTLIFE

SEE MAPS PAGES 248 AND 254

4

Seville is a wonderfully late-night city, and in summer and during fiestas, the streets around the central areas – particularly the Pza. de Alfalfa, Alameda de Hércules and Triana riverfront zones – are often packed out until the small hours. Throughout the summer, the Alcázar, the Prado de San Sebastián gardens and other squares host occasional **free concerts**. Information on these should be available from the *turismo*, the local press and the *El Giraldillo* listings magazine.

FLAMENCO

Flamenco music and dance is on offer at dozens of places in the city, some of them extremely tacky and expensive. Unless you've heard otherwise, avoid the fixed "shows", or *tablaos* (many of which are a travesty, even using recorded music) – the spontaneous nature of flamenco makes it almost impossible to timetable into the two-shows-a-night cabaret demanded by impresarios.

La Carbonería C/Levies 18, http://lacarbonerialevies. blogspot.com. An excellent bar that often has spontaneous flamenco almost every night of the week. It used to be the coal merchants' building (hence the name) and is a rambling and welcoming place. They also do tapas and *raciones*. Tricky to find, but well worth the effort.

Casa de la Memoria de al-Andalus C/Jiménez de Enciso 28, http://casadelamemoria.es. This cultural centre is dedicated to promoting the art of flamenco and features up-and-coming talent – many flamenco luminaries made their first appearances here. Space is limited and tickets must be booked in advance – in person or by phone or email. It's a great way to spend an evening.

Los Gallos Pza. Santa Cruz, http://tablaolosgallos.com. Professional *cantantes* do their best to create some *duende* (flamenco magic) and succeed when mesmerizing guitarists are granted solos and performers actually meet their cues. It's pricey, but the ticket includes a drink, which is brought to you at your seat; and with the longest running time of those listed, a real tableau of flamenco is able to form.

★ **Museo del Baile Flamenco** http://museoflamenco. com. Nightly concerts are staged in-a-round at the museum's atmospheric courtyard (see page 257). Visit their website for details and to reserve tickets, which is necessary in the summer months. Shows are on daily at 7pm.

Teatro Flamenco Triana C/Pureza 76, http://teatro flamencotriana.com. The only actual flamenco theatre in the city, this place is also a flamenco school run by the Cristina Heeren Foundation. Shows are performed by former students who have now turned professional and are on every day at 7.30pm. Tickets must be reserved in advance.

LIVE MUSIC, BARS & CLUBS

Earlier on in the evening, Seville's *discotecas* attract a very young crowd; the serious action starts after midnight and often lasts till well beyond dawn. For rock and pop music, the bars around Pza. Alfalfa and Alameda de Hércules have the best of the action.

Antique Avda. Matemáticos Rey Pastor y Castro s/n, http:// antiquetheatro.com. Popular with Seville's fancier dancers, this place comes with a transparent dancefloor, a summer terrace ("Rosso"), and sounds that range from Latin pop to heavier stuff.

Bar 84 Alameda de Hércules 84, 954 904 099. The terrace of this LGBTQ+-friendly bar is the perfect spot for a *tinto verano*, or four.

La Bicicleteria C/Feria 36, 676 412 010. The nucleus for Seville's alternative scene, this mysterious bar/club operates on a discretionary basis: who to let in, which laws to abide by and when to close. You'll have to knock on the door for entry (look for the bicycle frame above).

Fun Club Alameda de Hércules 86, http://funclubsevilla.

com. Popular weekends-only music and dance bar – favouring rock, reggae, hip-hop and salsa – with live bands.

Gigante Bar Plz. Alameda de Hercules 17, 955 294 529. Cosy, fun café-cum-bar on the Alameda. Perfect place for a post-dinner drink and dessert (try the piña colada and *tarta queso platano* – banana cheesecake).

Urbano Comix C/Matahacas 5, http://urbanocomix.es. Popular student bar – with hippy overtones – featuring zany urban decor. Sounds include grunge metal, rock, punk and R&B, often with live bands. Open 365 days per year.

SHOPPING

SEE MAP PAGE 248

Casa del Libro C/Velázquez 8, http://casadellibro.com. Central bookshop that stocks a range of books in English (and other languages) as well as maps.

El Corte Inglés Pza. Duque de la Victoria, http://lcorteingles.es. Seville's branch of Spain's major department store chain has designer fashions as well as an excellent supermarket, bookstore and, more recently, a travel agent. It also stocks the international press.

Kiosko La Campana La Campana s/n. The city's best news kiosk with a comprehensive range of international newspapers. It's located in front of the *pastelería La Campana* at the northern end of C/Sierpes.

Risko Avda. Kansas City 26, close to Santa Justa train station, http://risko.es. Stocks maps and a range of outdoor clothing and equipment.

Markets Entertaining Sunday *mercadillos* (roughly 8am–2pm depending on weather) take place on Pza. del Cabildo opposite the Catedral (stamps, coins, pins, ancient artefacts), and on Pza. del Museo in front of the Museo de las Bellas Artes (locally made art, tiles and woodcarvings). C/Feria's long-standing and vibrant El Jueves (Thursday market) with secondhand bric-a-brac and antiques, east of the Alameda de Hércules, is another good one.

DIRECTORY

Currency exchange Bureaux de change can be found on Avda. de la Constitución, Pza. Duque de la Victoria and Pza. Nueva.

Bullfights The season for *corridas* is mid-April to end of September, with the main *corridas* staged during the April *feria*. Details and tickets – which vary widely in price depending on seat and *toreros* – from the Pza. de Toros (902 223 506) on fight days from 4.30pm or in advance (with commission) from the Impresa Pagés ticket office at C/Adriano 37.

Football Seville has two major teams: Sevilla CF (who finished fourteenth in La Liga in 2024) plays at the Sánchez Pizjuán stadium (http://sevillafc.es); and Real Betis – promoted to the First Division of La Liga in 2011 and finishing seventh in 2024 – at the Manuel Ruiz de Lopera stadium (902 191 907, http://realbetisbalompie.es), in the southern suburbs. Match schedules are in the local or national press, and tickets are surprisingly easy to get hold of for many matches (check the stadium or *turismos*).

Hospital English-speaking doctors are available at Hospital Universitario Virgen Macarena, C/Dr Marañon s/n

(955 008 000), behind the Andalucía parliament building to the north of the centre. For emergencies, dial 061.

Left luggage There are coin-operated lockers (ask for the *consigna*) at the Santa Justa train station in a basement (to the right as you enter; 6am–12.30am). There are left luggage offices at the Prado de San Sebastián (daily 5.30am–midnight), and Pza. de Armas (9.30am–1.30pm & 3–6pm) bus stations; note that the latter one is not inside the bus station but around the right side of the building where there are taxis.

Lost property Oficina de Objetos Perdidos, C/Manuel V. Sagastizábal 3, next to the Prado de San Sebastián bus station (Mon–Fri 9.30am–1.30pm; 954 420 703).

Police Central local police stations are at C/Arenal 1 (954 275 509) and C/Credito 11 (954 289 555), off the north end of the Alameda de Hércules. Dial 092 or 112 (local police) or 091 (national) in an emergency.

Post office Avda. de la Constitución 32, by the Catedral; *Lista de Correos* (poste restante) Mon–Fri 8.30am–8.30pm, Sat 9.30am–1pm.

The Sierra Morena

The longest of Spain's mountain ranges, the **Sierra Morena** extends almost the whole way across Andalucía – from Rosal on the Portuguese frontier to the dramatic pass of Despeñaperros, north of Linares in the province of Jaén. Its hill towns marked the northern boundary of the old Moorish Caliphate of Córdoba, and in many ways the region still signals a break, with a shift from the climate and mentality of the south to the bleak plains and villages of Extremadura and Castilla-La Mancha. The range is not widely known – with its highest point a mere 1110m, it's not a dramatic sierra – and even Andalucians can have trouble placing it.

Aracena and around

Some 90km northwest of Seville, **ARACENA** is the highest town in the Sierra Morena, with sharp, clear air all the more noticeable after the heat of the city. A substantial but pretty place, it rambles partly up the side of a hill topped by the **Iglesia del Castillo**, a Gothic-Mudéjar church built by the Knights Templar around the remains of a Moorish castle. The town is flanked to the south and west by a small offshoot of the Sierra Morena – the **Sierra de Aracena** – a wonderfully verdant corner of Andalucía with wooded hills and villages with cobbled streets, which is perfect for hiking (see page 268).

Gruta de las Maravillas

C/Manuel Suirot, southwest of the Mueso del Jamón • Charge • http://aracena.es

Aracena's principal attraction is the **Gruta de las Maravillas**, the largest and arguably the most impressive cave in Spain. Supposedly discovered by a local boy in search of a lost pig, the cave is now illuminated and there are guided tours as soon as a couple of dozen or so people have assembled; to protect the cave there's now a strict limit of forty persons per visit. At weekends and holiday periods, try to visit before noon – coach parties with advance bookings tend to fill up the afternoon allocation. On Sunday, there's a constant procession, but usually plenty of time to gaze and wonder. The cave is astonishingly beautiful, and funny, too – the last chamber of the tour is known as the Sala de los Culos (Room of the Buttocks), its walls and ceiling an outrageous, naturally sculpted exhibition, tinged in a pinkish-orange light. Taking photos is prohibited, but if you're really keen to get a shot at the Gruta, there's a professional photographer capturing everyone as they walk in, and selling the prints.

4

SIERRA MORENA PRACTICALITIES

The Morena's **climate** is mild – sunny in spring, hot but fresh in summer – but it can be very cold in the mornings and evenings. A good **time to visit** is between March and June, when the flowers, perhaps the most varied in the country, are at their best. You may get caught in the odd thunderstorm, but it's usually bright and hot enough to swim in the reservoirs or splash about in the clear springs and streams, all of which are good to drink. If your way takes you along a river, you'll be entertained by armies of frogs and turtles plopping into the water as you approach, by lizards, dragonflies, bees, hares and foxes peering discreetly from their holes – and, usually, no humans for miles around.

GETTING AROUND

East–west **transport** in the sierra is very limited. Most of the bus services are radial and north–south, with Seville as the hub, and this leads to ridiculous situations where, for instance, to travel from Aracena to Cazalla de la Sierra, a distance of some 80km, you must take a bus to Seville, 70km away, and then another up to Cazalla – a full day's journey of nearly 150km.

Buses from Seville to the sierra leave from the Plaza de Armas station. If you just want to make a quick foray into the hills, **Aracena** is probably the best target (and the most regularly served town). If you're planning on some walking, it's also a good starting point: before you leave Seville, however, be sure to get yourself a decent **map** (see page 268) which, though it will probably be crammed with misleading information, should point you in the right direction to get lost somewhere interesting.

ARRIVAL AND DEPARTURE
ARACENA

By bus The station, Avda. de Sevilla s/n, lies on the southeast side of town close to the Parque Municipal and operates services to and from nearby pueblos and cities in the region. Buses leave for Seville twice daily. Check http://damas-sa.es for full schedule.

INFORMATION AND ACTIVITIES

Turismo At the Gruta (daily 10am–2pm & 4–6pm; 663 937 877, http://aracena.es).

Hiking You can get useful information (including maps and leaflets) on the surrounding Parque Natural Sierra de Aracena y Picos de Aroche from an information centre in the ancient *cabildo* (town hall), Pza. Alta 5. You should also ask at the Aracena *turismo* for the free *Senderos de la Sierra de Aracena y Picos de Aroche* map, which lists 23 waymarked routes, and they also sell a more detailed *Mapa Guía de la Sierra de Aracena y Picos de Aroche*. A good hiking guide, *Sierra de Aracena* by David and Ros Brawn, details 27 clearly described walks in the sierra ranging between four and fourteen kilometres. An accompanying map for the book is sold separately, and all walks have GPS waypoints identifying key locations en route.

ACCOMMODATION

Prices are for high season, which for Sierra de Aracena, begins mid-September (the cooler weather makes mountain trekking slightly more appealing than in summer, when most Andalucians head to the coast).

Camping El Madroñal 1km out of Fuenteheridos, along the HU8114 towards Castaño Robledo, http://camping elmadronal.com. Welcoming campsite with mature trees providing plenty of shade, and with decent facilities, including a large pool and restaurant. €€

Casa Manolo C/José Nogales 17, http://hotelessentia.es. There's a beachy feel about this laid-back hotel, with rattan lampshades, whitewashed walls and upcycled furniture. The on-site restaurant serves good seafood from the Huelva coast. €

Hospedería Reina de los Angeles Avda. Reina de los Angeles s/n, near the Gruta de las Maravillas, 959 128 367. A rather institutional-looking place that betrays its origins as a former student hostel. However, redecorated and refitted, its ninety en-suite and rather Spartan rooms are nevertheless clean, bright and good value. Easy street parking. €

Hotel Convento de Aracena C/Jesús María 19, http://hotelconventoaracena.es. The town's four-star luxury option is located inside a tastefully restored sixteenth-to-eighteenth-century former Dominican convent. Rooms overlook the cloisters and quadrangle, now planted with trees and aromatic herbs. Facilities include a spa and pool with a view over the mountains. A former convent herb garden now stands outside the hotel's top-notch restaurant, *Huerto*. €€€

Hotel Sierra de Aracena Gran Vía 21, http://hotelsierra dearacena.com. This traditional hotel has pleasant, decent-sized rooms, half of which have views of the castle. €

EATING AND DRINKING

Aracena is at the heart of a prestigious *jamón*-producing area, so try to sample some, as well as, when they're available, the delicious wild asparagus, and local snails, which are in the fields in spring and summer, respectively.

THE KING OF HAMS

Surrounding Aracena is a scattering of attractive but economically depressed villages, most of them dependent on the **jamón industry** and its curing factory at Jabugo. *Jamón serrano* (mountain ham) is a tapa or *bocadillo* standard throughout Spain, and some of the best, *jamón de bellota* (acorn-fed ham), comes from the Sierra de Aracena, where herds of sleek black pigs grazing beneath oak trees are a constant feature. In October, the acorns drop and the pigs, waiting patiently below, gorge themselves, become fat and are promptly whisked off to be slaughtered then cured in the dry mountain air. The meat of these black pigs is exceptionally fatty when eaten as pork but the same fat that marbles the meat adds to the tenderness during the curing process. This entails first of all covering the hams in coarse rock or sea salt to "sweat", after which they are removed to cool cellars to mature for up to two years. *Jamón serrano* from mass-produced white pigs is matured for only a few weeks, hence the incomparable difference in taste. At Jabugo the best of the best is then further graded from one to five *jotas* (the letter "J" for Jabugo) depending on its quality. A whole leg of *cinco jotas jamón* will set you back anything from €250 to €400. The *turismo* can provide details of where to sample and buy.

Setas (wild mushrooms) are another prized delicacy.

Casas Pozo La Nieve 40, http://restaurantecasas.es. One of the town's top three restaurants, this is sited near the Gruta de las Maravillas and is only open lunchtimes. All the pork-based dishes are excellent, as is the *jamón* and *salchichón* (salami) and there are some interesting hot and cold soups that incorporate the latter. Wine prices are reasonable, there's a good-value daily menu (including wine), and there's an outdoor terrace. €€

Puerta 20 Plaza Marqués de Aracena 20, www.facebook.com/puerta20restaurante. A large, friendly restaurant that certainly makes the most of Aracena's local produce. If you're in town Sept–Dec, be sure to order the *pataje de castañas y setas* (potatoes with chestnuts and mushrooms) and/or the *risotto de boletus con aciete de trufa* (risotto with mushrooms and truffle oil). Both come in *medio* or main-sized portions. €€

★ **Restaurante José Vicente** Avda. Andalucía 51, http://restaurantejosevicente.com. For a memorable splurge this is the place to come. Arguably the town's best restaurant, patrons gather to savour the five grades of Jabugo *jamón ibérico* (black-pig ham) under the approving gaze of owner/chef José Vicente Sousa. The daily menu, which often includes a mouthwatering *solomillo ibérico* (black-pig loin), is recommended. The *costillas de cerdo ibérico* (ribs) are also excellent and the *helado de castañas* (chestnut ice cream) makes a perfect end to a feast. €€€

La Serrana Pozo de la Nieve s/n, 959 127 613. The third of the triumvirate of Aracena's best restaurants, and located opposite *Casas*, this is another place where sierra cooking is at its best. All the pork dishes are recommended and there's a daily set menu during the week. €€€

Almonaster La Real

The **sierra villages** – Jabugo, Aguafría, Almonaster La Real – all make rewarding bases for walks, though all are equally ill-served by public transport (details from the Aracena *turismo*). The most interesting is **ALMONASTER LA REAL**, whose castle encloses a tiny ninth-century mosque, **La Mezquita** (free), with what is said to be the oldest *mihrab* in Spain. Tacked onto the mosque is the village bullring, which sees action once a year in August during the annual *feria*.

ACCOMMODATION AND EATING

ALMONASTER LA REAL

Luz Almonaster C/Urbanización la Real 19, 616 609 902. Lovely old red-brick townhouse, with spacious rooms decorated in a rustic yet luxurious *casa rural* style. Hearty breakfasts and sumptuous dinners showcase traditional Huelva cuisine. €€

Las Palmeras C/Carretera s/n, 647 885 451. A string of apartments on one side of the road, and a restaurant on the other, *Las Palmeras* is a promising place to arrive at. In their plant-bedecked terrace, they serve up sierra specialities including *parrillada de carne*. €€

The Costa de la Luz

Stumbling on the villages along the **Costa de la Luz**, between Algeciras and Cádiz, is like entering a new land after the parade of flashy high-rise resorts along the Costa del Sol. The journey west from Algeciras seems in itself a relief, the road climbing almost immediately into rolling green hills, offering fantastic views down to Gibraltar and across the Strait to the just-discernible white houses and tapering minarets of Moroccan villages. Beyond, the Rif mountains hover mysteriously in the background, and on a clear day, as you approach **Tarifa**, you can distinguish Tangier on the edge of its crescent-shaped bay. Beyond Tarifa lies a string of excellent golden-sand beaches washed by Atlantic breakers and backed by a clutch of low-key resorts such as **Conil**. Inland, the haunting Moorish hill town of **Vejer de la Frontera** beckons, while set back from the sea at Bolonia is the ancient Roman settlement of **Baelo Claudia**.

Tarifa

TARIFA, spreading out beyond its Moorish walls, was until the mid-1980s a quiet village, known in Spain, if at all, for its abnormally high suicide rate – a result, it is said, of the unremitting winds that blow across the town and its environs. Today, it's a prosperous, popular and, at times, very crowded resort, following its discovery as

Europe's prime **windsurfing** and **kitesurfing** spot. There are equipment-rental shops along the length of the main street, and regular competitions are held year-round. Development is moving ahead fast as a result of this new-found popularity, but for the time being it remains an attractive place for a stopover.

San Mateo
C/Sancho IV el Bravo 8 • Free

If windsurfing is not your motive for visiting Tarifa, there can still be an appeal in wandering the crumbling ramparts, gazing out to sea or down into the network of lanes that surround the fifteenth-century, Baroque-fronted church of **San Mateo**, which has a beautiful late Gothic interior.

Castillo de Guzmán
C/Guzmán el Bueno • Charge, free guided tour at noon

Worth a look is the **Castillo de Guzmán**, originally a tenth-century alcázar and the site of many a struggle for this strategic foothold into Spain. It's named after Guzmán el Bueno (the Good), Tarifa's infamous commander during the Moorish siege of 1292, who earned his tag for a superlative piece of tragic drama. Guzmán's 9-year-old son had been taken hostage by a Spanish traitor, and surrender of the garrison was demanded as the price of the boy's life. Choosing "honour without a son, to a son with dishonour", Guzmán threw down his own dagger for the execution. The story – a famous piece of heroic resistance in Spain – had echoes in the Civil War siege of the Alcázar at Toledo, when the Nationalist commander defied similar threats, an echo much exploited for propaganda purposes.

ARRIVAL AND INFORMATION

By bus Frequent services to Seville, Málaga, Cádiz and points in between. The station lies at the northern end of town near the *gasolinera* (petrol station) from where the main Algeciras–Cádiz road (C/Batalla del Salado) leads to the walled old town, a 5–10min walk. Along here there's a supermarket, fried-fish and *churro* stalls, and windsurfing-equipment shops.

By ferry Tarifa offers the tempting opportunity for a trip to Morocco – a day-trip by catamaran to Tangier is feasible. Information on schedules and fares is available from the *turismo*. A useful site for checking the latest ferry schedules is http://directferries.co.uk.

Turismo A welcoming *turismo*, on the central Paseo la Alameda (956 680 993), can help with maps and accommodation.

ACCOMMODATION

Tarifa has plenty of **places to stay**, though finding a bed in summer (or when there's a surfing tournament) can often be a struggle, with crowds of windsurfers cornering every available room. The town also sets a premium on its undoubted charms and room rates tend to be higher here than in other resorts along this coast. A little way out of town to the west, there are six **campsites** and the *turismo* can provide a list of these (or visit http://campingsandalucia. es). Be aware that high-season rates quoted below can fall by up to sixty percent outside July and August.

Casa Facundo C/Batalla del Salado 47, http://pension facundo.com. Reliable and friendly family *hostal* on the main road into town just outside the walls, offering rooms sharing bath and en-suite rooms with TV (same price for

---

WHALE- AND DOLPHIN-WATCHING TRIPS

Tarifa is home to **whale- and dolphin-watching** excursions in the Strait of Gibraltar, which leave daily from the harbour. The two-hour trip is fairly steep (reductions for under-14s), but includes another trip free of charge if there are no sightings. Places must be booked in advance from non-profit-making organization **FIRMM** (Foundation for Information and Research on Marine Mammals), C/Pedro Cortés 4, slightly west of the church of San Mateo (http://firmm. org). The latter also offers a more specialized tour in summer for spotting orca whales. A more commercial operation, **Turmares**, with an office on the beach road near the foot of the Paseo de la Alameda (http://turmares.com), also runs whale-spotting trips with a glass-bottomed boat.

both). They also own *Hostal Tarifa* (see below). €
Hospedaje Villanueva Av. Andalucía 11, www.
hospedajevillanuevatarifa.com. A minimalist, understated
hotel with a central location. Some rooms have balconies
but others are rather small, so ask to see a few before you
decide. €€€

★ **Hostal Africa** C/María Antonia Toledo 12, http://
hostalafrica.com. Charming, small *hostal* with clean and
simple rooms with and without bathrooms and offering
spectacular sea views from a communal terrace. En suite €€

Hostal La Calzada C/Justina Pertiñez 7, http://hostal
lacalzada.com. Popular and friendly *hostal* in the centre of
the old town, close by the church of San Mateo, offering a/c
en-suite rooms with TV. €€€
Hostal Tarifa C/Batalla del Salado 40, http://hostaltarifa.
com. This impressive three-star property is a hotel in all but
name. Pristine rooms come with all facilities, a/c, TV and
sparkling bathrooms and most have sit-out balconies. The
welcome is warm and they have their own garage. €€€

EATING AND DRINKING

Tarifa has a wide range of **places to eat**, divided between
the old town inside the walls and the new town beyond
then. This is another place to try Cádiz's tasty *urta* (sea
bream), available all over town. In summer, the council
erects *carpas* (**disco tents**) on the Playa de los Lances
beach.

★ **Bar El Francés** Paseo C/Sancho IV El Bravo 21, http://
facebook.com/pages/Bar-El-Francés. A highly popular
French tapas and *raciones* bar adding a subtly Gallic touch
to such staples as *calamares*, *rabo de toro* and *tortilla de
camarones* and *pulpo braseado* (octopus), besides adding a
few more exotic dishes such as *picaña* (Brazilian beefsteak).
It has a small street terrace. €€
Bar Morilla C/Sancho IV El Bravo 2, 956 681 757.
Central bar with an attractive terrace where *tarifeños*
gather to breakfast or munch early-evening tapas while
contemplating the ancient stones of nearby San Mateo.
Later, cloths are thrown over the tables as the restaurant

hits its stride. *Urta* is frequently on the menu, but the bar
also offers meat dishes as well as pasta and salads and
there's a good-value *menú del día*. €€
El Lola C/Guzmán el Bueno 52, www.ellolatarifa.com.
Lively tapas bar with a menu featuring all manners of *tataki*
(try the red tuna from Almadraba) along with Cádiz classics
like croquettes stuffed with ibérico ham and garlicky grilled
prawns. Come for the food, stay for the flamenco. €€
★ **Mandragora** C/Independencia 3, 956 681 291. One
of a number of restaurants and tapas bars in town offering
dishes from both sides of the straits. But this is a cut
above the rest and in addition to Moroccan couscous and
berenjenas bereber (aubergine), it does excellent *raciones*,
including *boquerones rellenos* (stuffed anchovies) and
tasty dishes like *rape con crema de erizos y setas* (monkfish
with wild mushrooms in a sea urchin sauce). Servings are
generous and a dish like lamb couscous is easily enough for
two. Also offers a range of vegetarian options. €€€

4

Tarifa Beach

Heading northwest from Tarifa, you find the most spectacular **beaches** of the whole of
the Costa de la Luz – wide stretches of yellow or silvery-white sand, washed by some
magical rollers. The same winds that have created such perfect conditions for windsurfing
can, however, sometimes be a problem for more casual enjoyment, sandblasting those
attempting to relax on towels or mats and whipping the water into breakers.

The beaches lie immediately west of town. They get better as you move past the tidal
flats and the mosquito-ridden estuary – until the dunes start and the first campervans
lurk among the bushes. At **TARIFA BEACH**, a little bay 9km from town, there are
restaurants, a windsurfing school, campsites and a string of pricey hotels, including the
exclusive *Hurricane*.

ACCOMMODATION   TARIFA BEACH

Tarifa's six campsites all lie to the west of the town and
are served by a bus service (July–Aug only; daily 7.50am–
11pm; roughly every 90min) from the bus station.
Camping Río Jara On the N340 road 4km northwest of
town, http://campingriojara.com. The nearest campsite to
the town fronts the beach and has plenty of shade; facilities
include supermarket and bar-restaurant and there's access
for disabled campers. €
Camping Torre de la Peña On the N340 7km northwest

of town, http://campingtp.com. Beachfront campsite with
plenty of shade; facilities include full-size pool, supermarket,
laundry and a restaurant. Also rents out timber bungalows. €
Hurricane Hotel Carretera Cádiz s/n, http://hotel
hurricane.com. Set in dense gardens 7km west of Tarifa at
the ocean's edge, this luxurious California-style B&B hotel
has tastefully decorated a/c rooms, fully equipped gym, two
pools, stables, windsurfing school and its own restaurant.
Rooms with sea view carry a supplement. €€€

Baelo Claudia Bolonia

Ensenada de Bolonia • Charge • Free guided tour all year Wed at noon

At the Roman town of **BOLONIA**, or *Baelo Claudia* as the Romans knew it, beyond a visitor centre and museum you can make out the remains of three temples and a theatre, as well as a forum, numerous houses, and a fascinating factory for making *garum* fish sauce, a Roman culinary passion. The ticket office provides you with a detailed site plan. Bolonia can be reached down a small side road that turns off the main Cádiz road 15km beyond Tarifa.

ARRIVAL AND DEPARTURE   BOLONIA

There's a bus service in July and August (3 daily) from Tarifa to the site. If you don't have your own transport you can take a taxi. Details on both from the Tarifa *turismo*.

ACCOMMODATION AND EATING

Bolonia has a fine **beach** with bars and eating places and a few **places to stay**. There are a couple of *chiringuitos* on the beach serving grilled fish – otherwise most of the places to eat are in the small village of Bolonia itself.

★ **Hostal La Hormiga Voladora** C/El Lentiscal 15, http://lahormigavoladora.com. This delightful retreat with en-suite garden rooms and apartments close to the beach is the best choice should you wish to stay. It's located at the eastern end of the village next to the *Panadería*

Beatriz. Breakfast is not provided but if you buy in your own vittles (from the bakery or nearby bar) you can dine on an enchanting patio shaded by a prodigious mulberry tree. €€

Las Rejas Close to the Hostal La Hormiga Voladora, http://lasrejasbolonia.es. *Las Rejas* is perhaps Bolonia's best restaurant. All the fish and *mariscos* are fresh – as is of course the tuna in season – and they can rustle up a decent paella if you're looking for a beach snack. There's a reasonably priced wine list and a terrace. €€

Vejer de la Frontera

While you're on the Costa de la Luz, be sure to take time to visit **VEJER DE LA FRONTERA**, a classically white, Moorish-looking hill town set in a cleft between great protective hills that rear high above the road from Tarifa to Cádiz. The drama of Vejer is in its isolation and elevated position, both easily appreciated from an approach road that winds upwards for a dizzying 4km. This eventually arrives at the Parque de los Remedios and a **car park**, which, given Vejer's tortuously narrow streets, one-way system and traffic congestion, you'd be strongly advised to make use of if you've arrived by car; this is also where the **bus** drops you. From here you'll need to ascend a further 300m along C/Los Remedios to reach La Plazuela, the effective centre of town.

Vejer has a remoteness and Moorish feel as explicit as anywhere in Spain. There's a castle and a church of curiously mixed styles (mainly Gothic and Mudéjar), but the main fascination lies in exploring the brilliant white and labyrinthine alleyways, wandering past iron-grilled windows, balconies and patios, and slipping into a succession of bars.

INFORMATION   VEJER DE LA FRONTERA

Turismo In the Parque de los Remedios, Avda. de los Remedios 2 (http://turismovejer.es); it can provide a useful town map.

ACCOMMODATION

Camping Vejer Ctra. N340, Km 39.5, http://campingvejer. es. Vejer's campsite lies below town on the main Málaga-to-Cádiz road. There's decent shade, and facilities include a pool, bar and supermarket. They also have cute bungalows sleeping from two to four people. €

★ **La Casa del Califa** Pza. de España 16, http://lacasadelcalifa.com. One of Vejer's most striking hotels is *La Casa del Califa*, occupying a refurbished, rambling house,

parts of which date back to Moorish times; the stylish rooms are decorated with Moroccan fittings and guests have use of two patios with fine views and a library. It also has a charming *casa rural* next door (*Las Palmeras del Califa*) with rooms and suites around a pool. €€€

Casa Rural Leonor C/Rosario 27, near the Castillo, 956 451 085. A charming *casa rural* in a converted Moorish dwelling with comfortable en-suite rooms, friendly proprietors, and

fabulous views towards Morocco from a roof terrace. €
★ **El Cobijo de Vejer** C/San Filmo 7, http://elcobijo.com. Excellent *hostal* inside a traditional house with delightful flower-filled patio and individual rooms on various levels. The higher-priced *Zahara* and *Xauen* (the latter has a fabulous terrace) with their own kitchens are the ones to go for. All rooms are a/c, and have fridges and satellite TV. A lavish breakfast (extra) is also available. €€

Hotel Convento de San Francisco La Plazuela, http://tugasa.com. Housed in a converted seventeenth-century convent on the smaller of the town's two main squares, this is a very pleasant hotel where the former monastic cells – with exposed stone walls – have been turned into attractive a/c rooms. Also has its own bar (the former refectory with fresco remnants) and restaurant. €€

EATING AND DRINKING

Bar Peneque Pza. de España 27, 956 450 209. Traditional and entertaining local bar built into a cave (though there's also a street terrace) with tables at the back for munching *raciones* should you not feel like joining in the domino games favoured by regulars. €€
El Jardín del Califa Pza. de España 16, http://califavejer.com. The mid-priced Michelin-recommended restaurant attached to the hotel of the same name has a Moroccan chef and serves up a variety of Moroccan and Middle Eastern-inspired dishes on a tree-shaded courtyard terrace. Specialities include tagines and spicy fish dishes. An

adjacent and stylish bar-*tetería* offers stunning views from its roof terrace. €€
Mercado de San Francisco C/San Francisco, behind La Plazuela. An innovative project has transformed Vejer's old marketplace and hall into a highly popular gastro-emporium where up to a dozen stalls sell or produce various offerings ranging from *almadraba* tuna sushi to *jamones* (cured ham), cheeses, *tortillas de camarones* (shrimp fritters), authentic pizzas and lots more. Prices are reasonable, a couple of stalls sell wines and beers, and there are tables outside where you can turn your purchases into a feast. €€

Conil

4

Some 10km northwest of Vejer, lies the increasingly popular resort of **CONIL**. Outside July and August, though, it's still a good place to relax, and in mid-season the only real drawback is trying to find a room. Conil Town, once a poor fishing village, now seems entirely modern as you look back from the beach, though when you're actually in the streets you find many older buildings, too. The majority of the tourists are Spanish, so there's an enjoyable atmosphere, and, if you are here in mid-season, a very lively nightlife.

The **beach**, Conil's *raison d'être*, is a wide bay of brilliant yellow sand stretching for many kilometres to either side of town and lapped by an amazingly, not to say disarmingly, gentle Atlantic – you have to walk a long way before it reaches waist height. The area immediately in front of town is the family beach; up to the northwest you can walk to some more sheltered coves, while across the river to the southeast is a topless and nudist area. If you walk along the coast in this direction, you'll see that the beach is virtually unbroken until it reaches the cape, the familiar-sounding **Cabo de Trafalgar**, off which Lord Nelson achieved victory and met his death on October 21, 1805. When the winds are blowing, this is one of the most sheltered beaches in the area. It can be reached by road, save for the last 400m across the sands to the rock.

ARRIVAL AND INFORMATION   CONIL

By bus Most buses use the Transportes Comes station (956 442 916) on C/Carretera; walk towards the sea and you'll find yourself in the centre of town.
Turismo Just south of the bus station at the junction of C/Carretera and C/Menéndez Pidal (daily: June–Sept

9am–2pm & 6–9pm; Oct–May 8.30am–2.30pm; 956 440 501, http://turismo.conil.org); it's worth picking up a copy of their useful free booklet *Conil en su Bolsillo*, which details all the town's tapas bars, restaurants and much more.

ACCOMMODATION AND EATING

Accommodation needs are served by numerous hotels and *hostales*, augmented in high season by a multitude of private rooms for rent; full details on all of these are available from the *turismo*. As with other resorts in this zone, room rates

fall sharply outside of July and August. Seafood is king here and Conil has lots of good **restaurants** along the seafront; try the *ortiguillas* – deep-fried sea anemones – which you see only in the Cádiz area.

Camping Fuente del Gallo Urbanización Fuente de Gallo s/n, http://campingfuentedelgallo.com. The nearest campsite to the town lies a stiff 3km walk (or easy taxi ride) north of the centre and is sited 400m inland from the superb Playa la Fontanilla. There are good facilities including a bar-restaurant and a pool. Tents €, bungalows €€

★ **Casa Alborada** C/G. Gabino Aranda 5, http://alborada conil.com. Delightful small boutique hotel with flamboyantly decorated and individually styled bedrooms and bathrooms – the bathroom of room 10 gets the star prize. It also has a stunning roof terrace/solarium with loungers and sofas offering spectacular views of the coast. €€

★ **La Fontanilla** Playa de la Fontanilla, http://lafontanilla.com. With a wonderful terrace overlooking the town's main beach, this is an outstanding fish and seafood restaurant where you can sample the very best of what the Cádiz sea coast has to offer. Next door, *Francisco la Fontanilla* is just as good. €€

Hostal La Posada C/Quevedo s/n, http://laposadadeconil.com. Dapper B&B *hostal* with clean and tidy en-suite a/c rooms with TV – many with sea views – plus a garden pool, and a good restaurant. High-season rate applies August only. €€

Hostal La Villa Pza. de España 6, 670 242 731. Economical en-suite rooms above a bar-restaurant on a central square. €

Hotel Flamenco Playa Fuente de Gallos, http://hipotels.com. Fronting the Fuente del Gallo beach, this elegant four-star one-hundred roomer is one of the resort's older luxury places (it's had a recent top-to-bottom refurb), and is set in a tranquil location. Well-appointed rooms have balcony terraces and sea views and there's a bar-restaurant, two garden pools and steps down to a fine strand. In July and August there's a minimum stay of two to four nights. €€€€

Cádiz

CÁDIZ is among the oldest settlements in Spain, founded about 1100 BC by the Phoenicians and one of the country's principal ports ever since. Its greatest period, however, and the era from which the central part of town takes most of its present appearance, was the eighteenth century. Then, with the silting up of the river to Seville, the port enjoyed a virtual monopoly on the Spanish–American trade in gold and silver, and on its proceeds were built the Catedral – itself golden-domed (in colour at least) and almost Oriental when seen from the sea – grand mansions, public buildings, dockyards, warehouses and the smaller churches.

Inner Cádiz, built on a peninsula-island, remains much as it must have looked in those days, with its grand, open squares, sailors' alleyways and high, turreted houses. Literally crumbling from the effect of the sea air on its soft limestone, it has a tremendous atmosphere – slightly seedy, definitely in decline, but still full of mystique.

Unlike most other ports of its size, Cádiz seems immediately relaxed, easy-going and not at all threatening, even at night. Perhaps this is due to its reassuring shape and compactness, the presence of the sea, and the striking **sea fortifications** and waterside **alamedas** making it impossible to get lost for more than a few blocks. But it probably owes this tone as much to the town's tradition of liberalism and tolerance – one maintained through the years of Franco's dictatorship even though this was one of the first towns to fall to his forces, and was the port through which the Nationalist armies launched their invasion. In particular, Cádiz has always accepted its substantial LGBTQ+ community, who are much in evidence at the city's brilliant **Carnaval** celebrations. In 2012 the city celebrated the bicentenary of the 1812 Constitution (Spain's first, called "La Pepa") and setting up of the Cortes (parliament), in opposition to the Napoleonic blockade. The major monument commemorating this event is a spectacularly beautiful **road bridge** – the longest in Spain – named "La Pepa", linking Puerto Real across the Bay of Cádiz with the old town. Crossing the bridge, which was designed by Javier Manterola, is a real adventure (the central span is 70m above the water) and enables an appreciation of the towering structure close up.

Cádiz has two main **beaches** – the excellent **Playa de la Victoria** (and its less commercial continuation the Playa de la Cortadura), to the left of the promontory approaching town (reached from the centre on bus #1 from Plaza de España), and the often overcrowded **Playa de la Caleta** on the peninsula's western tip.

Museo de Cádiz

Pza. de Mina • Charge • http://museosdeandalucia.es/web/museodecadiz

The **Museo de Cádiz**, the province's most important museum, overlooks the leafy Pza. de Mina and incorporates the **archeological museum** on the ground floor, which has many important finds and artefacts from the city's lengthy history, including two remarkable fifth-century BC Phoenician carved sarcophagi in white marble (one male,

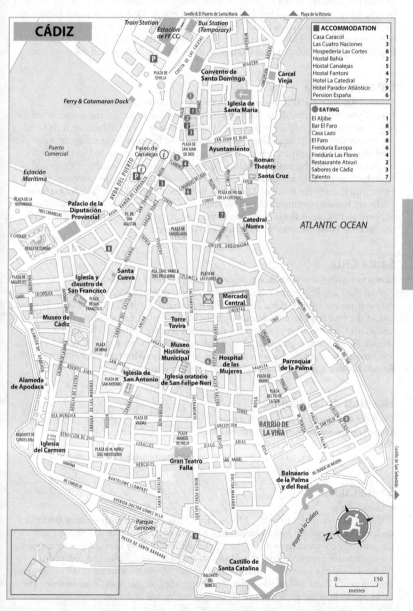

CÁDIZ

Train Station
Estación
de FF.CC.

Bus Station
(Temporary)

Seville & El Puerto de Santa María

Playa de la Victoria

PLAZA DE
SEVILLA

CUESTA DE LAS CALESAS

MIRADOR

HIGUERA

CONCEPCIÓN

ARENAL

Convento de
Santo Domingo

Cárcel
Vieja

Ferry & Catamaran Dock

Iglesia de
Santa María

ROSA

SOPRANIS

Puerto
Comercial

Paseo de
Canalejas

PLAZA DE
SAN JUAN
DE DIOS

SAN JUAN DE DIOS

FLAMENCO

Ayuntamiento

Roman
Theatre

Estación
Marítima

AVDA. DEL PUERTO

SAN FRANCISCO

ROSA

CONCEPCIÓN

Santa Cruz

PLAZA DE LA
HISPANIDAD

TRES CARABELAS

Palacio de la
Diputación
Provincial

AVDA. RAMÓN DE CARRANZA

VARGAS PONCE

COBOS

CHAMORRO DE CADIZ

COBOS

COMPAÑÍA

PLAZA DE PÍO XII
(DE LA CATEDRAL)

F. CATÓLICO

PLAZA DE ESPAÑA

PL. DE
SAN
AGUSTÍN

PLAZA DE
CANDELARIA

OBISPO URQUINAONA

COMPAÑÍA

SAN JUAN

Catedral
Nueva

ATLANTIC OCEAN

4

ZAPATA

TUDOURT

PLAZA DE
ARGÜELLES

LA CATÓLICA

ISABEL

BENDICIÓN DE DIOS

Santa
Cueva

PZA. GRAL. VARELA
(DEL PAULILERO)

COLUMELA

PLAZA DE
LAS FLORES

Iglesia y
claustro de
San Francisco

PLAZA
DE SAN
FRANCISCO

CÁNOVAS DEL CASTILLO

SACRAMENTO

Mercado
Central

LIBERTAD

Museo de
Cádiz

PLAZA
DE MINA

ANCHA

Torre
Tavira

CRUZ

CALLEJÓN
CARBÓN

CAMPO DEL SUR

ALAMEDA DE APODACA

COLUMELA DE LA ROSA

BUENOS AIRES

SAN JOSÉ

SAGASTA

Museo
Histórico
Municipal

Hospital
de las
Mujeres

HOSPITAL DE MUJERES

Parroquia
de la Palma

SAGASTA

Alameda
de Apodaca

ADOLFO DE CASTRO

ENRIQUE DE LAS MARINAS

PLAZA DE
SAN ANTONIO

Iglesia de
San Antonio

Iglesia oratorio
de San Felipe Neri

BENJUMEDA

SACRAMENTO

VALVERDE

TORRE

ROSA

PLAZA DE
VIUDAS

PLAZA
DEL TÍO DE
LA TIZA

PEÑUELA

CAMPO DEL SUR

VIRGEN DE LA PALMA

CALLEJÓN DE LA MANGA

VEA MURGUÍA

CERVANTES

PLAZA DE
VIUDAS

CONCEPCIÓN

BARRIO DE
LA VIÑA

M. FÉLIX

FEDUCHY

Castillo de San Sebastián

BALUARTE DE
CANDELARIA

Iglesia
del Carmen

GRAVINA

PLAZA DE M. NÚÑEZ
(DEL MENTIDERO)

CEBALLOS

PLAZA
MANUEL
DE FALLA

DIEGO

OBISPO

ARIAS

ROSA

SAN RAFAEL

Gran Teatro
Falla

HERCULES

SANTA ROSALÍA

AV. CARLOS III

BARTOLOMÉ LLOMPART

BENITO PÉREZ GALDÓS

DOCTOR MARAÑÓN

Balneario
de la Palma
y del Real

AVENIDA DOCTOR GÓMEZ ULLA

Parque
Genovés

PASEO DE SANTA BÁRBARA

Playa de la Caleta

AV. DUQUE DE NÁJERA

Castillo de
Santa Catalina

BALUARTE
DEL BONETE

0   150

metres

the other female), unique to the western Mediterranean. The upper floor houses the **Museo de Bellas Artes**. This contains a quite exceptional series of saints painted by Francisco Zurbarán, brought here from the Carthusian monastery at Jerez and one of only three such sets in the country (the others are at Seville and Guadalupe) preserved intact, or nearly so. With their sharply defined shadows and intense, introspective air, Zurbarán's saints are at once powerful and very Spanish – even the English figures such as Hugh of Lincoln, or the Carthusian John Houghton, martyred by Henry VIII when he refused to accept him as head of the English Church. Perhaps this is not surprising, for the artist spent much of his life travelling round the Carthusian monasteries of Spain and many of his saints are in fact portraits of the monks he met. Other important artists displayed here include Murillo, Ribera, Rubens and Alonso Cano.

Catedral Nueva

Pza. Catedral · **Catedral Nueva** Charge including museum, free Sun 11.30am–12.30pm · **Torre de Poniente** Charge

Even if you don't normally go for High Baroque, it's hard to resist the attraction of the huge and crumbling eighteenth-century **Catedral Nueva**, so titled because it replaced the former cathedral, Santa Cruz (see opposite). The building has undergone a ten-year (and astronomically expensive) restoration to preserve its interior and work will now begin on restoring the roof and "gilded" dome. The Catedral's interior is decorated entirely in stone, with no gold in sight, and in absolutely perfect proportions. In the crypt, you can see the tomb of Manuel de Falla, the great *gaditano* (as inhabitants of Cádiz are known) composer of such Andalucía-inspired works as *Nights in the Gardens of Spain* and *El Amor Brujo*. For a magnificent view over the city, you can also climb the **Torre de Poniente**, one of the Catedral's twin towers.

Santa Cruz

Catedral Pza. Fray Félix 6 · Free · **Roman theatre** C/Mesón 12 · Free, entry via the Centro de Interpretación

East of the Catedral on the edge of the Barrio del Populo, the city's oldest quarter dating from the Middle Ages, lies the "old" or original Cathedral, **Santa Cruz**. This was one of the buildings severely knocked about by the Earl of Essex during the English assault on Cádiz in 1596, causing the thirteenth-century church to be substantially rebuilt. A fine Gothic entry portal survived, and inside there's a magnificent seventeenth-century *retablo* with sculptures by Martínez Montañés. A first-century BC **Roman theatre** has been excavated behind, close to the sea.

Hospital de las Mujeres

C/Hospital de Mujeres 26 · Charge; ask the porter for admission

One of the most impressive Baroque buildings in the city, the chapel of the **Hospital de las Mujeres**, houses a brilliant **El Greco**, *St Francis in Ecstasy*. It's one of the Cretan artist's finest portrayals of the saint, although it's a rather sombre study using copious shades of grey.

Santa Cueva

C/Rosario s/n · Charge

A short walk southeast from the Museo de Cádiz is the eighteenth-century **Oratorio de Santa Cueva**, which houses three fine Goya frescoes. The church is divided into two dramatically contrasting parts. In the elliptical **upper oratory** beneath an elegant dome are three frescoes representing the *Miracle of the Loaves and Fishes*, the *Bridal Feast* (either side of the main altar) and the *Last Supper* (above the entrance), an unexpected depiction of Christ and the disciples dining sprawled on the floor, Roman style. The other works here are depictions of biblical scenes by minor artists.

In sharp contrast to the chapel above is the **subterranean chapel**, containing a sculpture of the Crucifixion whose manifest pathos adds a sombre note. An eighteenth-century work of the Genoa school, the image is said to have inspired visiting composer Joseph Haydn to write his *Seven Last Words* (of Christ) oratorio. A small museum has been added between the two chapels giving background information on the building's history and includes a display of Haydn's original score.

Plaza de las Flores and Mercado Central

Head west from the Catedral and it's a couple of blocks to the **Plaza de las Flores** (aka Pza. Topete), one of the city's most emblematic squares. Fronted by the striking early twentieth-century *Correos*, the square is a riot of colour most days due to the many flower sellers that have their stalls here. Adjoining the plaza to the west is the Pza. de la Libertad, the whole of which is taken up by the nineteenth-century **Mercado Central**, an elegant Neoclassical construction with a colonnade of Doric pillars enclosing the central area.. On weekday mornings it's a beehive of activity and not to be missed. In addition to the usual fish, meat, fruit and veg the new building has attracted a kaleidoscopic multitude of stalls selling everything from herbs and spices to exotic teas and world beers as well as sushi and even fish and chips.

ARRIVAL AND DEPARTURE | CÁDIZ

By train The station is on the periphery of the old town, close to Pza. de San Juan de Dios, busiest of the city's many squares. For current timetables and ticket information, consult RENFE 902 240 202, http://renfe.es.

Destinations Córdoba (10 daily; AVE 2hr 30min–3hr 30min normal); El Puerto de Santa María (19 daily; 30min); Granada (9 daily; change at Seville; 5hr 30min); Jerez (20 daily; 45min); Madrid (6 daily; 4hr 15min–5hr 30min); Seville (17 daily; 1hr 45min).

By bus A bus station is located on the east (or harbour) side of the train station on C/Astilleros. Either *turismo* will be able to provide the latest information.

Destinations Algeciras (8 daily; 1hr 45min); Arcos de la Frontera (9 daily; 1hr 30min); Conil (12 daily; 1hr 15min); El Puerto de Santa María (20 daily; 35min); Granada (4 daily; 5hr 30min); Jerez de la Frontera (21 daily; 35min); Málaga (4 daily; 4hr, 1hr 45 direct); Sanlúcar de Barrameda (5–12 daily; 1hr); Seville (8 daily; 1hr 45min); Tarifa (8 daily; 2hr); Vejer de la Frontera (10 daily; 1hr).

By car Coming by car, you'll soon discover sea-locked Cádiz's acute lack of parking space, and if you don't want to spend an age searching you'd be best off taking accommodation with a garage (all the hotels will assist with parking) or heading for a car park – two of the most central inside the city walls are by the train station and along Paseo de Canalejas near the port.

By ferry The only long-distance ferry services from Cádiz are to the Canary Islands. Trasmediterranea, Estación Marítima (https://armastrasmediterranea.com) currently operates a weekly sailing to Las Palmas and Tenerife. Local ferries sail across the bay to El Puerto de Santa María and the beach resort of Rota. The service to El Puerto is by catamaran (information/timetables in Spanish only: http://cmtbc.es). All three services including the boat to Rota sail from the same dock on the south side of the Puerto Comercial. A useful site for checking the latest ferry schedules is http://directferries.co.uk.

Destinations Las Palmas (1 weekly; 39hr); El Puerto de Santa María (catamaran: weekdays every 30min); Rota (weekdays 8 daily); Tenerife (2 weekly; 48hr).

INFORMATION

Turismo Avda. Ramón de Carranza (Mon–Fri 9am–7pm, Sat & Sun 10am–2pm; 956 203 191) near to Pza. San Juan de Dios; there's also a useful *turismo municipal* on the Paseo de Canalejas (July–Sept Mon–Fri 9am–7pm, Sat–Sun 9am–5pm; Oct–June Mon–Fri 8.30am–6.30pm, Sat & Sun 9am–5pm; 956 241 001).

ACCOMMODATION | SEE MAP PAGE 275

In tune with the city itself, much of Cádiz's budget **accommodation** has seen better days. Although things are slowly improving, the city has a shortage of good-quality accommodation in all categories. Radiating out from the Pza. San Juan de Dios is a dense network of alleyways crammed with *hostales* and *fondas* and a few less inviting options.

More salubrious places to stay are to be found a couple of blocks away, towards the Catedral or Pza. de la Candelaria.

★ **Casa Caracol** C/Suárez de Salazar 4, http://casacaracol cadiz.com. Friendly backpackers' place with dorm beds in a large house near Pza. San Juan de Dios; also has some double rooms sharing bathrooms and pricier en-suite

4

rooms in a new *hostal* nearby. Note that room prices rise significantly on Fri & Sat nights. Breakfast is included, guests have use of a communal kitchen, and the proprietors hire out cycles and surfboards. €

Las Cuatro Naciones C/Plocia 3, http://lascuatronaciones. com. A stone's throw from Pza. San Juan de Dios and close to the train and bus stations, this is a clean, unpretentious place with low-priced rooms sharing bathrooms. €

★ **Hospedería Las Cortes** C/San Francisco 9, http:// hotellascortes.com. Splendid B&B hotel in a stylishly restored *casa señorial*. Elegant rooms are well equipped and include a minibar. Facilities include sauna and gym, and there's a *cafetería* and restaurant. High-season price August only. €€€

Hostal Bahía C/Plocia 5, http://hostalbahiacadiz.com. Reasonable-value and conveniently located *hostal*, offering a/c rooms with baths. Request their more attractive balcony rooms. Pay car park nearby. €€

Hostal Canalejas C/Cristóbal Colón 5, http://hostal canalejas.com. Pleasant two-star *hostal* in completely restored townhouse. En-suite rooms come with a/c and TV, and there's a wi-fi zone plus car park nearby. Avoid the windowless interior rooms though. €€

Hostal Fantoni C/Flamenco 5, http://hostalfantoni. es. Good-value *hostal* in a renovated townhouse with lots of *azulejos* and cool marble, offering simple and en-suite rooms, the latter with a/c and TV. €

★ **Hotel La Catedral** Pza. de la Catedral 9, http://hotel lacatedral.com. Charming new small B&B hotel 50m from the Catedral's front door. Comfortable rooms are well equipped and many have balconies where you can feast your eyes on the Catedral's imposing facade. Add an infinity rooftop pool – where you seem to swim almost within touching distance of the Catedral's bell tower – and you have a perfect place to stay. Ring reception for the best available rate. €€€

Hotel Parador Atlántico Parque Genovés 9, http:// parador.es. Beyond an austere exterior – combining wood and rusting metal with stone and glass – lie 124 rooms and suites filled with five-star comforts, all with terrace balcony and sea view. Features include full-size rooftop pool, solarium, bars, restaurant and gardens. €€€€

Pension España Marqués de Cádiz 9, www.pension espana.es. Pleasant *hostal* inside a restored *casa palacio* offering reasonable en-suite rooms with fans (some sharing bath) ranged around a patio. €

EATING

SEE MAP PAGE 275

There are great **places to eat** all over town and you'll find good tapas bars and restaurants in the streets around Pza. San Juan de Dios, Pza. de las Flores and Pza. de la Libertad (containing the market). In sea-girthed Cádiz, of course, fish is king and nowhere more so than in the old fishermans' quarter, the Barrio de la Viña. Here in the streets surrounding a tiny square named Pza. Tío de la Tiza – particularly along C/Virgen de la Palma – *gaditanos* gather to stuff themselves at economical *marisquerías*.

El Aljibe C/Plocia 25, www.nosgustanuestrotrabajo.com. A very good restaurant serving up a range of traditional dishes. House specials include *frito gaditano* (fried fish) and *almejas a la marinera* (clams in garlic sauce); it also serves tasty tapas in its bar. *Menú de degustación* including wine, and main dishes. €€

★ **Bar El Faro** C/San Félix 15, http://elfarodecadiz.com/ la-barra.php. Tapas bar of the renowned restaurant (see below), and probably the best in town. A stand-up place where the *finos* are first-rate, the service is slick and the seafood tapas are mouth-wateringly delicious. House specials include *tortillitas de camarones* (shrimp fritters) and *tostaditas de pan con bacalao* (cod on toast). €€

Casa Lazo C/Barrie 17, north of the market, 956 229 499. Charming compact shop/bar with a tasty tapas and raciones selection. Try their *jamón*, *brochetas de pulpo* (octopus) or *croquetas caseras* (croquettes). Also does more substantial meat dishes and has a good wine cellar. €€

★ **El Faro** C/San Félix 15, http://elfarodecadiz.com. In the heart of the Barrio de la Viña, this is one of the best fish restaurants in Andalucía. House specialities include

---

A FEAST MADE IN HEAVEN

Takeaway **fried fish** was invented in Cádiz (despite English claims to the contrary), and there are numerous *freidurías* (fried-fish shops) around the town, as well as stands along the beach in season. Few eating experiences here can beat strolling the city streets while dipping into a *cartucho* (paper funnel) of *pescado frito*. In the bars, *tortilla de camarones* (shrimp fritter) is another superb local speciality. Worth seeking out are:

Freiduría Europa C/Hospital de Mujeres 21, 956 227 305; see map page 275. Excellent fried-fish shop, similar and near to *Freiduría Las Flores*. €€

★ **Freiduría Las Flores** Plaza de las Flores 4, 956 226 112; see map page 275. Outstanding fried fish is

cooked up here and if you buy a takeaway you can carry your *cartucho* to the terrace tables of the nearby bar, La Marina, in front of the post office. Order a glass (or bottle) of chilled white wine to wash it down with, and you've got a feast made in heaven. €€

pulpo (octopus), *merluza* (hake), *urta* (sea bream), and a delicious *arroz marinero* (Andalucian paella). There's a *menú de degustación* (excluding wine) which is good value, especially on weekdays. Their excellent tapas bar is also well worth a visit. €€

★ **Restaurante Atxuri** C/Plocia 7, http://atxuri.es. This is an outstanding and highly popular Basque fish restaurant where head chef Pedro Ladrón de Guevara has been satisfying diners for over forty years. His kitchen turns out delicious Basque- and *andaluz*-inspired fish dishes at reasonable prices. Also has an excellent tapas bar where they offer meal-sized *media raciones*. You'd best book for the restaurant. €€€

Sabores de Cádiz Pza. San Juan de Dios 6, 617 793 668. Traditional *gaditano* fish restaurant with an all-day kitchen offering good-quality fish dishes, which are served on a terrace facing the striking *ayuntamiento*. €€

Talento C/de la Palma 7, 685 572 213. In the old fishing quarter of the Barrio de la Viña, this is one of a number of good tapas bars along the focal C/La Palma. There are tables outside and a great atmosphere as this street becomes one big terrace at weekends. €€

El Puerto de Santa María

Just 10km across the bay, **EL PUERTO DE SANTA MARÍA** is the obvious choice for a day-trip from Cádiz, a traditional family resort for both *gaditanos* and *sevillanos* – many of whom have built villas and chalets along the fine **Playa Puntillo**. This strand is a little way out from town (10–15min walk or local bus ride), a pleasant place to while away an afternoon; there are friendly beach bars where for ridiculously little you can nurse a litre of *sangría* while munching a *ración* of local *mariscos*.

ARRIVAL AND INFORMATION   EL PUERTO DE SANTA MARÍA

By catamaran The catamaran from Cádiz (operated by Consorcio de Transportes http://cmtbc.es/catamaran.php) is quicker and cheaper than the bus; the 40min trip across the bay departs from the Muelle Reina Victoria jetty (near the train station) roughly half-hourly; the return timetable is similar. Check all return times when you board on the outward journey if you don't want to be stranded.

Turismo Housed in the splendid Baroque Palacio de Aranibar, Pza. del Castillo facing the Castillo de San Marcos (daily: May–Sept 9am–2pm & 6–8pm; Oct–April 10am–2pm & 5.30–7.30pm; 956 483 714, http://turismoelpuerto. com). Here you can pick up a detailed street map as well as a *Ruta del Tapeo* leaflet to help find the best tapas bars.

4

ACCOMMODATION

Camping Playa Las Dunas Paseo Marítimo Playa de la Puntilla, http://lasdunascamping.com. Large campsite near the beach with plenty of shade plus pool, restaurant and supermarket. Bus #2 from the Pza. de las Galeras Reales (ferry quay) will take you there. €

★ **Casa de Huespedes Santa María** C/Pedro Múñoz Seco 38, www.casadehuespedessantamaria.com. Very welcoming refurbished family *pensión*, for spotless rooms with bath, run by an ebullient *dueña andaluza* (female proprietor) and her son. Rooms come with a/c and fans. There's a guests' kitchen and if you want to practice your Spanish, here's the place to stay. €€

Hostal Loreto C/Ganado 17, http://pensionloreto.com. Pleasant *hostal* with a delightful patio. Rooms come with or without bath; en suites have ceiling fans, fridge and TV. €

Hotel Soho Boutique Puerto Avda. Bajamar s/n, http://

VISITING EL PUERTO'S SHERRY BODEGAS

El Puerto's principal attraction is a series of **sherry bodegas** – long, whitewashed warehouses flanking the streets and the banks of the river. Until the train was extended to Cádiz, all shipments of sherry from Jerez came through Santa María, and its port is still used to some extent. Many of the firms offer tours and tastings to visitors – the most worthwhile tours are offered by two of the town's major producers: Osborne, C/Los Moros 7 (visits: in English and Spanish daily; charge, tasting of 5 *finos* and a brandy; booking required; http://osborne.es/en/experiencia-bodega-osborne-cadiz-visita-catas); and Gutierrez Colosía, Avda. Bajamar 40 (in English/Spanish; no booking required; charge; http://gutierrezcolosia.com), who let you taste six *finos* and a brandy. The *turismo* can provide details of visits to smaller *bodegas*.

sohoteles.com. Good-value three-star riverfront hotel in a converted eighteenth-century *palacio* with a/c balcony rooms, restaurant, garage and rooftop pool. Not all rooms have fridges so request one at check-in if you want to be sure. €€

EATING

The best areas in town for **places to eat** are the Ribera del Marisco, a street upstream from the ferry dock that is lined with a variety of seafood restaurants and bars serving tapas and *raciones*, and the nearby Pza. de la Herrería.

Bar La Dorada Avda. de la Bajamar 26, http://ladorada restaurantes.com. Inexpensive meal-sized *raciones* are served up at this friendly bar with a terrace overlooking the river. The *pescado frito* is superb, and house specials include *choco a la plancha* (cuttlefish) and *tortillitas de camarones* (shrimp fritters). €€

Bar Vicente C/Abastos 7, near the market, http://facebook.com/BarVicenteElPuerto. This wonderful old bar first opened its doors well over a century ago and is now part of El Puerto folklore. Show an interest and the latest Vicente (in a long line) will tell you its story and show you an atmospheric photo of the bar in the early days (the wall tiles are the originals). Excellent tapas and *raciones* are also on offer and a house special is *atún encebollado* (tuna in onion sauce). €€

★ **Romerijo** Ribera del Marisco, http://romerijo.com. This enormous, economical and justifiably popular seafood bar dominates the strip here. You can get a takeaway of *mariscos* in a *cartucho* (paper funnel) from their shop and eat it at outdoor tables where buckets are provided for debris and waiters serve beer; the *cóctel de mariscos* (seafood cocktail) or any of the six types of *langostinos* (prawns) are delicious. The same firm's *freiduría* restaurant over the road is equally excellent. €€

Sanlúcar de Barrameda

Like its neighbour El Puerto, **SANLÚCAR DE BARRAMEDA**, 15km to the northwest, also has its sherry connections. Nine kilometres east of Chipiona and set at the mouth of the Guadalquivir, it's main depot for **manzanilla** sherry, a pale, dry variety much in evidence in the bars, which you can also sample during visits to the town's **bodegas**. Sanlúcar is also the setting for some exciting **horse races** along the resort's extensive beach in the first and third weeks of August (check with the *turismo* for exact dates), a great time to be here.

Barrio Alto

There's not a great deal to see in Sanlúcar, although the attractive old quarter in the upper town, or **Barrio Alto**, is worth taking time to explore. The town's port was the scene of a number of important maritime exploits: Magellan set out from here to circumnavigate the globe; Pizarro embarked to conquer Peru; and 4km upriver, from

---

A CRUISE INTO PARQUE NACIONAL COTO DE DOÑANA

One of the best things about Sanlúcar is its shell-encrusted **river beach** and warm waters, a couple of kilometres' walk from the town centre and usually quite deserted. This is flanked, on the opposite shore, by the beginnings of the **Parque Nacional Coto de Doñana** (see page 286), a restricted area whose vast marshy expanses signal the end of the coast road to the west. Visits to the park from Sanlúcar are possible with a boat cruise, which, while it doesn't allow for serious exploration, is nevertheless a wonderful introduction to this remarkable area. The trip lasts approximately three hours and allows two short, guided walks inside the park to spot wildlife. The **Real Fernando** – which has a *cafetería* on board – leaves daily from the Bajo de Guía quay (charge, under-12s half-price; booking essential, http://visitasdonana.com). Tickets should be collected at least 30min before sailing from the Fábrica de Hielo, Bajo de Guía s/n, the national park's **exhibition centre** opposite the *Real Fernando's* jetty. Also note that binoculars are pretty essential, and, while they can be hired on board, having your own is a distinct advantage.

the fishing harbour of Bonanza, Columbus sailed on his third voyage to the Americas. The few buildings of interest in the town are all located in the Barrio Alto, reached by following the Cuesta de Belén uphill from the lower town.

Bodega Antonio Barbadillo
C/Sevilla 25 • Charge • http://barbadillo.com

The town's major producer, **Bodega Antonio Barbadillo**, in the Barrio Alto near the castle, is one of the most interesting *bodegas* to visit, with a tasting and stop at their shop and museum thrown in at the end. A list of Sanlúcar's seven other *bodegas* offering visits is available from the *turismo* (see below).

Palacio de los Duques de Medina Sidonia
Pza. Condes de Niebla • Charge; book in advance • http://fcmedinasidonia.com

The most significant of the upper *barrio*'s buildings, this is the magnificent sixteenth- to eighteenth-century ducal palace of **Medina Sidonia**, and it's stuffed with paintings by Spanish masters, including Goya, Murillo and Zurbarán. Until her death in 2008 the duchess of Medina Sidonia (last in a family line going back to the Middle Ages) lived here and had been an inveterate opponent of the Franco regime (her nickname was La Duquesa Roja, "the Red Duchess"). The palace and family estate is now in the care of the foundation she created. The guided tour of the house and its beautiful gardens takes an hour. Part of the palace now houses a *hospedería* (hotel) and a very pleasant *cafetería*.

Nuestro Señora de la O
Pza. Condes de Niebla 3 • Free

Alongside the ducal palace is the thirteenth-century church (with later additions) of **Nuestro Señora de la O**, which was founded by the family of Guzmán El Bueno (see page 270). The impressive exterior has a fine Gothic-Mudéjar portal depicting, above an elegant arched doorway with archivolt molding, lions bearing the coats of arms of the Guzmáns. Inside there is a superb *artesonado* ceiling.

Castillo de Santiago
C/Eguilaz • Charge • http://castillodesantiago.com

The **Castillo de Santiago** was constructed by the second duke of Medina Sidonia in the fifteenth century. Fernando and Isabel once put up here when visiting the dukes, and it served as a barracks for the invading French army in the early nineteenth century and later as a prison. A ruin for most of the last century, it was extensively renovated over the last decade and opened to visitors. The audio-guided visits enable you to see the castle's barbicans as well as the Pza. de Armas and towers with stunning views over the town and the river towards the Parque Nacional Coto de Doñana.

INFORMATION   SANLÚCAR DE BARRAMEDA

Turismo Calzada de la Duquesa (July & Aug Mon–Sat 10am–2pm & 5–7pm, Sun 10am–2pm; March–June & Sept–Nov Mon–Fri 10am–2pm & 4–6pm, Sat & Sun 10am–2pm; Dec–Feb Mon–Sat 10am–2pm & 4–6pm, Sun 10am–2pm; 956 366 110, http://sanlucarturismo.com), near the start of the avenue leading to the river estuary. They can also inform about a number of free wi-fi zones in the centre of town.

ACCOMMODATION

There's a shortage of budget accommodation in Sanlúcar, and in August you'll be pushed to find anything at all. This is when a number of *casas particulares* open to mop up the overflow; enquire at the *turismo* for information about these.

Casa Miguel Pza. de San Roque, https://casamiguelsanlucar. com. Lovely collection of homely, modern apartments, set in a central position on this small plaza. €€€

★ **Hostal Gadir** C/Caballeros 19, 956 366 078. Wonderful and friendly, family-run *hostal* with sparkling a/c rooms, some with terraces others with jacuzzis. Rooms 3, 4, 5 & 10 (with Jacuzzi) and 11 have a superb view of the gardens of the Palacio de Orleáns y Borbón opposite. All rooms come with a/c and TV. A bargain even in high season, it's a steal at other times of the year. €

Hotel Barrameda C/Ancha 10, http://hotelbarrameda. com. A newish, central and welcome addition to the town's accommodation options offering light and airy a/c rooms with plasma TV, some with balconies. It also has a pleasant patio, solarium roof terrace and a *cafetería*. €€

★ **Posada de Palacio** C/Caballeros 11, http://posadade palacio.com. An elegant converted eighteenth-century *casa palacio* in the Barrio Alto with a delightful patio and tastefully furnished rooms with character. Rooftop terraces, bar and an intimate atmosphere make this rather special. €€€

EATING

For **tapas** you shouldn't miss *Casa Balbino*; for more elaborate fare, head to the Bajo de Guía – a river beach backed by a line of great seafood restaurants. You can take a taxi or walk there by continuing past the *turismo* to the end of the Calzada de la Duquesa and turning right (east) when you hit the river, about 1km from the town centre.

★ **Bar-Restaurante Casa Bigote** Bajo de Guía 10, http://restaurantecasabigote.com. Celebrated establishment and one of the "big two" on the waterfront which has edged in front of its neighbour, the *Mirador de Doñana*. You can eat outstanding tapas in their lively bar next door or more formally in the restaurant, where the fish and the house *arroz de marisco* (seafood paella) are outstanding. An upstairs dining room offers panoramic views across the river towards the Doñana national park. Reservation advised. €€

★ **Casa Balbino** Pza. del Cabildo 11, http://casabalbino. es. Behind an unassuming facade lies one of the best tapas

bars in Andalucía. Long-established, its walls are hung with faded photos and the obligatory bulls' heads, and the smoothly efficient bar staff will guide you through a daunting tapas menu. To kick off your session you could try their celebrated *tortilla de camarones* (shrimp fritters) or *caracolas* (whelks) or the renowned *langostinos de Sanlúcar* (large prawns). There is a (self-service) terrace on the square but serious *tapeadores* do it standing up. €€

Mirador Doñana Bajo de Guía s/n, http://miradordonana. com. The second of the Bajo de Guía's "big two", with a *mariscos* (shellfish and seafood) bar below and an upstairs restaurant with views towards Doñana. There's also a very pleasant outdoor terrace overlooking the river. House specials include *corvina a la plancha con tártara* (meagre with a tartar sauce) and the whole gamut of *sanluqueño* shellfish – *langostinos*, *gambas*, *cigales* (scampi) and *bogovante* (lobster). €€€

Jerez de la Frontera

JEREZ DE LA FRONTERA, 30km inland towards Seville, is the home and heartland of sherry (itself an English corruption of the town's Moorish name – *Xerez*) and also of Spanish brandy. An elegant and prosperous town, it's a tempting place to stop, arrayed as it is round the scores of *bodegas*, with plenty of sights to visit in between.

Life is lived at a fairly sedate pace for most of the year here, although things liven up considerably when Jerez launches into one or other of its two big **festivals** – the May Horse Fair (perhaps the most snooty of the Andalucian *ferias*), or the celebration of the vintage towards the end of September.

Centro Andaluz de Flamenco

Pza. de San Juan • Free • www.centroandaluzdeflamenco.es

Jerez is famous throughout Spain for a long and distinguished **flamenco** tradition, and if you're interested in finding out more about Andalucía's great folk art, then a visit to the **Centro Andaluz de Flamenco** in the atmospheric *gitano* quarter, the Barrio de Santiago, is a must. There's an audiovisual introduction to *El Arte Flamenco* (hourly on the half-hour), plus videos of past greats and information on flamenco venues in the town.

The Alcázar

Calle Alameda Vieja • Charge

The substantial **Alcázar** lies just to the south of the focal Pza. del Arenal. To reach the entrance, take a right off the southern end of Pza. del Arenal into Pza. Monti, at the end of which you turn left into C/María González. The entrance lies uphill on the left. Constructed in the twelfth century by the Almohads, though much altered since, the Alcázar has been extensively excavated and restored in recent years. The **gardens** have received particular attention: the plants and arrangements have been modelled as closely as possible – using historical research – on the original. The interior contains a well-preserved mosque complete with *mihrab* from the original structure, now sensitively restored to its original state after having been used as a church for many centuries. The eighteenth-century **Palacio de Villavicencio** constructed on the west side of the Alcázar's Patio de las Armas (parade ground) houses an entertaining **camera obscura** (same hours) offering views of the major landmarks of the town as well as the sherry vineyards and the sea beyond.

Catedral de San Salvador

Plaza Encarnación s/n • Charge, free Sun 10.30–11.30am

The eighteenth-century **Catedral de San Salvador** was rather harshly dismissed by Victorian British hispanist Richard Ford as "vile Churrigueresque" because of its mixture of Gothic and Renaissance styles, but an elegant facade – largely the work of Vincente Acero – is not without merit. Inside, over-obvious pointing gives the building an unfinished, breeze-block aspect, while, in the sacristy museum, there's a fine, little-known painting by Zurbarán – *The Sleeping Girl*. The most exciting time to be here is September, when on the broad steps of the Catedral, below the freestanding bell tower – actually part of an earlier, fifteenth-century Mudéjar castle – the wine harvest celebrations begin with the crushing of grapes.

Archeological Museum

Pza. del Mercado • Charge including useful English-language audio-guide (exhibit information is in Spanish only); free first Sun of each month

The city's excellent **Archeological Museum** lies five minutes north of the centre on the edge of the Barrio de Santiago. The itinerary opens with Jerez's impressive prehistoric past (look out for some four-thousand-year-old cylinder-shaped idols with starburst eyes from Cerro de las Vacas). Star exhibits in the Greek and Roman sections include a seventh-century BC Greek military helmet, Roman amphorae – many stamped with the maker's name – and in the Visigothic section

4

VISITING JEREZ DE LA FRONTERA'S BODEGAS

The **tours of the sherry and brandy processes** can be interesting – almost as much as the sampling that follows – and, provided you don't arrive in August when much of the industry closes down, there are a great many firms to choose from. The visits are conducted either in English (very much the second language of the sherry world) or a combination of English and Spanish and last for about an hour. Many of these *bodegas* were founded by British Catholic refugees, barred from careers at home by the sixteenth-century Supremacy Act, and even now they form a kind of Anglo-Andalucian tweed-wearing, polo-playing aristocracy (on display, most conspicuously, at the Horse Fair). The González cellars – the *soleras* – are perhaps the oldest in Jerez and, though it's no longer used, preserve an old circular chamber designed by Eiffel (of the tower fame). If you feel you need comparisons, you can pick up a list of locations and opening times of the other *bodegas* from the *turismo*.

TWO OF JEREZ'S MAJOR BODEGAS
Fundador C/San Ildefonso 3, https://bodegasfundador. site. Producers of one of Spain's best-selling brandies – including *Supremo*, winner of the world's best brandy in 2019 – they have also taken over production of the Harveys brand range of *finos*, one of which won the "best wine in the world" category at the 2016 International Wine Challenge.
González Byass (aka Tio Pepe) C/María González, http://bodegastiopepe.com. Makers of the famous Tio Pepe brand and also a major brandy producer. Wine tasting can be taken alone, or with accompanying tapas.

a fine sarcophagus carved with curious vegetable, animal and human symbols. The museum has added an expanded Moorish section with some fine ceramics – look out for an exquisite caliphal bottle vase – and interesting displays (with artefacts) relating to daily life in this period. Another section dealing with the Christian Middle Ages features an exquisite fifteenth-century alabaster relief carved in England, and depicting the Resurrection of Christ; this is one of a number of similar works found in the town and underlines the importance of trade – not only in wine – between Jerez and the British Isles in this period.

Real Escuela Andaluz del Arte Ecuestre

Avda. Duque de Abrantes s/n • Charge for performances and visits during training hours • http://realescuela.org

Evidence of Jerez's great enthusiasm for horses can be seen at the **Real Escuela Andaluz del Arte Ecuestre** (Royal Andalucian School of Equestrian Art), which offers the chance to watch them performing to music. Training, rehearsals (without music) and visits to the stables and museum take place on other weekdays.

ARRIVAL AND INFORMATION   JEREZ DE LA FRONTERA

By plane From Jerez airport (7km out of town on the NIV; 956 150 000), there are three daily buses to the centre between 6.30am and 7.15pm with a less frequent service from the bus station in the reverse direction. The airport also has a train station (on the opposite side of the airport car park) which connects with Jerez central station, a 10min journey. Trains currently run roughly hourly between 6.15am and 7.15pm, but it would be wise to confirm times with the airport's *turismo* or general information desk.

By train The train station, Estación de Ferrocarril, is at Pza. de Estación s/n (902 240 202), eight blocks (10min walk) east of the town's central square, Pza. del Arenal. To reach the centre, take #10 urban bus from outside the station.

Destinations Cádiz (12 daily; 40min); Córdoba (12 daily; 2hr 28min); Seville (13 daily; 1hr 15min).

By bus The bus station, Estación de Autobuses, is at Pza. Estación s/n (956 149 990), which is next to the train station. To reach the centre, take #10 urban bus from outside the station.

Destinations Algeciras (7 daily; 1hr 15min); Arcos de la Frontera (14 daily; 35min); Cádiz (3 daily direct, 6 daily via El Puerto; 45min); Córdoba (5 daily; 2hr 40min); El Puerto de Santa María (10 daily; 30min); Málaga (3 daily; 4hr); Ronda (2 daily; 2hr 30min); Sanlúcar de Barrameda (9 daily; 30min); Seville (12 daily; 1hr 30min); Vejer de la Frontera (3 daily via Cádiz; 1hr 30min).

By car Coming by car, you'll meet the familiar problem of finding a place to park; to avoid being clamped or towed, use the pay car parks signed in the centre or park farther out and walk in. There is a huge underground car park beneath the central Pza. del Arenal.

Turismo Pza. del Arenal, in the northwest corner of Jerez's main square (June–Sept Mon–Fri 9am–3pm & 5–7pm, Sat & Sun 9.30am–2.30pm; Oct–May Mon–Fri 9am–3pm & 4.30–6.30pm, Sat & Sun 9.30am–2.30pm; 956 341 711, http://turismojerez.com). Well stocked with information about the town and the area and can supply a detailed town map.

ACCOMMODATION

There's usually no problem finding **rooms** in Jerez except during April and May, when Semana Santa, the Festival de Jerez, the World Motorcycle Championship (held at the town's Formula 1 racing circuit) and the Feria del Caballo (May Horse Fair) come one after the other and fill the town to bursting point. During these events ("*temporada extra*") prices quoted can double or even treble.

Albergue Juvenil Avda. Blas Infante 30, www.inturjoven. com. Good-value seven-storey hostel with double a/c en-suite rooms and a pool; but out in the suburbs. Take bus #9 from outside the bus station. €

La Gitinilla C/Barranco 12, www.lagitanilla.com. Charming hotel inside a refurbished nineteenth-century town house. Rooms are cosy and traditional without feeling stuffy, and common areas include a comfy lounge and

shaded roof terrace (with loungers) for having breakfast or enjoying a fine view of the Catedral and surrounding town. Also has a couple of suites. €

Hotel Al Andalus C/Arcos 29, 956 323 400. Comfortable hotel with two pretty patios. Individually styled rooms come with bold colour schemes and the better ones – off the inner patio – are equipped with a/c and TV. €

Hotel Doña Blanca C/Bodegas 11, http://hoteldona blanca.com. One of the most central and intimate of the upper-range places, with well-equipped a/c balcony rooms with minibar and satellite TV, in a quiet street. Own garage. €€

★ **Hotel-Hostal San Andrés** C/Morenos 12, 956 340 983. Excellent and friendly hotel-*hostal* offering (in the *hostal*) both en-suite rooms, and those sharing bath; the hotel's rooms are all en suite with a/c and TV. There's also a charming patio below. €

Vivian's Guesthouse C/Higueras 17, http://vivians

EATING AND DRINKING

Jerez's expansive sherry trade ensures that the town's **restaurants** are kept busy, and a few of these are very good indeed. Befitting the capital of sherry production, Jerez also has a range of great bars where *fino* – the perfect partner for tapas – can be sampled on its own turf. In recent years there's been a revival of the **tabancos**, a combination of bar and wine store, serving food. Many old ones with character have been rediscovered and new ones have opened. The *turismo* can provide a list.

Almacén C/La Torre 6, just north of Pza. del Arenal, http://facebook.com/elalmacenvinosytapas. Atmospheric tapas bar installed in a former grocery store (*almacén*). Tapas and *raciones* include *patatas bravas* (potatoes with spicy sauce) as well as *tablas* (boards of cheese and cured meats to share) plus various vegetarian options. Make sure not to miss out on the *tarta de manzana templada con helado* (warm apple tart with ice cream) which can only be described as paradise on a plate. €€

★ **Bar Juanito** C/Pescadería Vieja 4, http://bar-juanito. com. In a small passage off the west side of Pza. del Arenal, this is one of the most celebrated tapas bars in town, with a menu as endless as the number of excellent *finos* on offer. Specials include *berza jerezano* (chickpea stew) and

guesthouse.es. The most central budget option, with clean and simple rooms (some en-suite) and dorms, with a shared kitchen and bright communal courtyard area. €

the *mariscos* of the coast. Their pleasant terrace restaurant serves a good-value *menú del día* (lunch only). €€

La Carboná C/San Francisco de Paula 2, http://lacarbona. com. Cavernous but wonderfully atmospheric mid-priced restaurant inside an old *bodega*, specializing in charcoal-grilled fish and meat and – in season – fresh tuna. Their *maridajes con vino de jerez* presents five courses, each accompanied by the appropriate Jerez wine. €€€

La Condesa Pza. Rafael Rivero, C/Tornería 24, www.hotel palaciogarvey.com. The Michelin-recommended restaurant of the *Hotel Palacio Garvey* is an excellent place for a meal, especially on their attractive terrace. A three-course menu is recommended and often features *solomillo en salsa oloroso* (pork loin in sherry sauce). House specials include a tasty *salmorejo de remolacha con mojama y feta* (beetroot gazpacho with tuna and feta cheese). €€

Tabanco Plateros C/Algarve 35, 956 104 458. Highly popular *tabanco* slightly northeast of the Pza. del Arenal. There's a good and extensive wine list (including the classics of Jerez) or excellent tapped beer to accompany a lengthy tapas menu. Standouts are *salchichón* (salami), *sardinas ahumadas* (smoked), *alcachofas con anchoas* (artichokes with anchovies). €€

Huelva province

The **province of Huelva** stretches between Seville and Portugal. With a scenic section of the Sierra Morena to the north and a chain of fine **beaches** to the west of the provincial capital, it has a lot to offer but suffers a mixed reputation. This is probably because it's laced with large areas of swamp – the *marismas* – and is notorious for mosquitoes. This distinctive habitat is, however, particularly suited to a great variety of wildlife, especially birds, and over 60,000 acres of the delta of the Río Guadalquivir (the largest roadless area in western Europe) have been fenced off to form the **Parque Nacional Coto de Doñana**. Here, amid sand dunes, pine woods, marshes and freshwater lagoons, live scores of flamingos, along with rare birds of prey, around 75 of the endangered **Iberian lynx**, mongooses and a startling variety of migratory birds.

CROSSING THE BORDER TO PORTUGAL

From Huelva you can head straight **along the coast to Portugal**. There are a number of good beaches and some low-key resorts noted for their excellent seafood, such as **Isla Cristina**, along the stretch of coastline between Huelva and the frontier town of **Ayamonte**. There is a good bus service along this route and a road suspension bridge across the Río Guadiana estuary and border, linking Ayamonte and **Vila Real de Santo Antonio** in Portugal. A fun alternative is catching the hourly ferry between these locations, over the river. A good first night's target in Portugal is **Tavira**, on the Algarve train line. Note that Portugal is an hour behind Spain throughout the year.

Parque Nacional de Doñana

The seasonal pattern of its delta waters, which flood in winter and then drop in the spring, leaving rich deposits of silt, raised sandbanks and islands, gives the **Parque Nacional de Doñana** its uniqueness. Conditions are perfect in winter for ducks and geese, but spring is more exciting; the exposed mud draws hundreds of flocks of breeding birds. In the marshes and amid the cork-oak forests behind, you've a good chance of seeing squacco herons, black-winged stilts, whiskered terns, pratincoles and sand grouse, as well as flamingos, egrets and vultures. There are, too, occasional sightings of the Spanish imperial eagle, now reduced to a score of breeding pairs. Conditions are not so good in late summer and early autumn, when the *marismas* dry out and support far less birdlife.

It is no Iberian Arcadia, however, and given the region's parlous economic state the park is under constant threat from development. Even at current levels the drain on the water supply is severe, and made worse by **pollution** of the Guadalquivir by farming pesticides, Seville's industry and Huelva's mines. The seemingly inevitable disaster finally occurred in 1998 when an upriver mining dam used for storing toxic waste burst, unleashing millions of litres of pollutants into the Guadiamar, which flows through the park. The noxious tide was stopped just 2km from the park's boundary, but catastrophic damage was done to surrounding farmland, with nesting birds decimated and fish poisoned. What is even more worrying is that the mining dams have not been removed (the mines are a major local employer) but merely repaired.

In June 2017, a large forest fire just 30km west of the park forced the evacuation of two thousand people. Though firefighters got the spread under control before it reached Doñana, one of the park's protected species, an Iberian lynx, died from stress. Some local people and environmental bodies are suspicious of arson by developers who they think have ulterior intentions for the area that's currently protected.

El Rocío

Set on the northwestern tip of the *marismas*, **EL ROCÍO** is a tiny village of white cottages and a church stockade where perhaps the most famous pilgrimage-fair of the south takes place annually at Pentecost. This, the **Romería del Rocío**, is an extraordinary spectacle, with whole village communities and local "brotherhoods" from Huelva, Seville and even Málaga converging in lavishly decorated ox carts and on horseback. Throughout the procession, which climaxes on the Saturday evening, there is dancing and partying, while by the time the carts arrive at El Rocío they've been joined by busloads of pilgrims, swelling numbers in recent years to over half a million. The fair

---

VISITING PARQUE NACIONAL COTO DE DOÑANA

Visiting Doñana involves (perhaps understandably) a certain amount of frustration. At present, it's open only to a **boat cruise** from Sanlúcar (see box, page 280) and to brief, organized **tours** by all-terrain thirty-seater buses – four hours at a time along one of five charted, 80km routes. Tours are run by the Doñana Reserva, based at Av. de la Canaliega, S/N 21750, El Rocío, Almonte, Huelva (http://donanareservas.com). Booking is essential, and should be done as far ahead as possible in high season. The tours are quite tourist-oriented and point out only spectacular species such as flamingos, imperial eagles, deer and wild boar (binoculars are pretty essential). If you're a serious ornithologist, enquire instead at the *centro* about organizing a private group tour.

There are excellent birdwatching **hides** at the El Acebuche, La Rocina and El Acebron reception centres, as well as a 1.5km footpath from El Acebuche, which creates a mini-trek through typical *cotos*, or terrains, to be found in the reserve. Although binoculars are on hire, they sometimes run out, and you're advised to bring your own. All three centres have exhibitions and displays covering the species to be seen in the park and the history of human activity within its boundaries.

commemorates the miracle of Nuestra Señora del Rocío (Our Lady of the Dew), a statue found in the thirteenth century – so it is said – on this spot and resistant to all attempts to move it elsewhere. The image, credited with all kinds of magic and fertility powers, is paraded before the faithful early on the Sunday morning.

In spring, as far as **birdwatching** goes, the town is probably the best base in the area. The adjacent *marismas* and pine woods are teeming with birds, and following tracks east and southeast of El Rocío, along the edge of the reserve itself, you'll see many species (up to a hundred if you're lucky).

ACCOMMODATION   EL ROCÍO

The village makes a nice **place to stay**, with wide, sandy streets, cowboy-hatted horseriding farmers and a frontier-like feeling, and prices for most of the year are reasonable. Though the daytime is bursting with tourists in newly purchased sombreros, tranquillity is restored by evening. That said, don't even think about getting a room during the *romería* as they not only cost over ten times normal prices, but are booked up years ahead. All the accommodation options listed below have their own decent restaurants.

Camping La Aldea http://campinglaaldea.com. El Rocío's campsite lies on the village's northern edge along the Almonte road (A483), and offers good facilities and a reasonable amount of shade. €

Hostal Cristina C/Real 58, www.pensioncristina.com.

One of El Rocío's oldest budget establishments, this is a welcoming place with en-suite a/c rooms (some with *marismas* views). €

Hotel La Malvasia C/Sanlúcar 38, http://hotellamalvasia.com. Recently refurbished to a very high standard, bird-themed rooms are host to traditional Andalucian tiling, balconies and sensational beds. Request room 13 (the *cigüeña blanca*/white stork) for a view of the *marismas*. €€

Hotel Toruño Pza. Acebuchal 22, 959 442 323. This is the pick of the more expensive places, offering B&B, the best restaurant, and comfortable rooms overlooking the *marismas*. There's a great view from room 225 but some of the ground-floor rooms (109, 111 & 115) also allow you to spot flamingos, herons, avocets and lots more while lying in bed. €€

The Columbus Trail

Other than to test out its title as Spain's Capital of Gastronomy of 2017, there's not much reason to linger at provincial capital **Huelva**. It is worth, however, crossing the Río Tinto estuary from here to visit a clutch of sites associated with the fifteenth-century **voyages of Christopher Columbus** (Cristóbal Colón in Spanish). It's a great place to visit.

La Rábida
8km from Huelva • Charge • http://monasteriodelarabida.com

La Rábida is a charming and tranquil fourteenth-century Franciscan monastery, whose fifteenth-century abbot was instrumental in securing funds from the monarchs Fernando and Isabel for Columbus's initial 1492 voyage. The guided tour (1hr 30min) includes the *Sala Capitular* (Chapter House), where the final plans for the voyage were made, and the monastery's fourteenth-century church where Columbus and his crew prayed before setting sail.

Muelle de las Carabelas
Paraje de La Rábida, s/n • Charge

On the Río Tinto estuary just behind La Rábida monastery, the **Muelle de las Carabelas** (Harbour of the Caravels) has impressive full-size replicas of the three caravels of Columbus's first voyage, while an adjoining museum features among its displays facsimiles of his geography books annotated in his surprisingly delicate hand.

San Jorge
C/Fray Juan Peréz 19, Palos de la Frontera • Free

The church of **San Jorge** in the village of **PALOS** is where, in August 1492, Columbus and his crew heard Mass before setting sail from the now silted-up harbour. The church's southern Mudéjar portal through which Columbus – flanked by his captains

4

– left the church, can be seen as well as the nearby La Fontanilla, a medieval well from which the ships took on water for the voyage.

Convento de Santa Clara

Pza. de Monjas 1, Moguer • Charge

At the whitewashed town of **MOGUER** is the fourteenth-century **Convento de Santa Clara**, in whose church Columbus spent a whole night in prayer as thanksgiving for his safe return. The tour also takes in some notable artworks and the ancient monastery's cloister and refectory.

GETTING AROUND   **THE COLUMBUS TRAIL**

By bus Frequent buses from Huelva's main bus station at   Moguer.
Avda. Dr Rubio s/n (902 114 492) link La Rábida, Palos and

ACCOMMODATION

Hotel La Pinta C/Rábida 79, Palos, 959 350 511. This pleasant two-star hotel is a good bet for a/c en-suite rooms and there's a decent restaurant, *El Paraíso*, a few doors away. €€

Pensión Platero C/Aceña 4 slightly east of Plaza del Cabildo, Moguer 13, 959 372 159. This central *hostal* has good-value en-suite rooms with a/c and windows which let in a ton of light. The friendly owner can advise on free parking nearby. €

Seville to Córdoba

4

The direct route from **Seville to Córdoba**, 135km along the valley of Guadalquivir, followed by the train and some of the buses, is a flat and rather unexciting journey. There's far more to see following the route just to the south of this, via **Carmona** and **Écija**, both interesting towns, and more still if you detour further south to take in **Osuna** as well. There are plenty of buses along these roads, making travel between the villages easy. Overnighting, too, is possible, with plenty of places to stay – although Carmona is an easy day-trip from Seville.

Carmona

Set on a low hill overlooking a fertile plain, **CARMONA** is a small, picturesque town made recognizable by the fifteenth-century tower of the Iglesia de San Pedro, built in imitation of the Giralda. The tower is the first thing you catch sight of and it sets the tone for the place – an appropriate one, since the town shares a similar history to Seville, less than 30km distant. It was an important Roman city (from which era it preserves a fascinating subterranean necropolis), and under the Moors was often governed by a brother of the Sevillan ruler. Later, Pedro the Cruel built a palace within its castle, which he used as a "provincial" royal residence.

To get your bearings, it's helpful to know that the town consists of the *casco antiguo* (old town) inside the walls entered through the impressive Puerta de Sevilla, and the more modern town to the west of this. The heart of the old quarter is the **Plaza de San Fernando** (often referred to as the "Plaza Mayor") which, though modest in size, is dominated by splendid Moorish-style buildings. Behind it, and just to the south, there's a bustling fruit and vegetable **market** most mornings in the porticoed Plaza del Mercado.

Iglesia de San Pedro

C/San Pedro s/n • Charge

The **Iglesia de San Pedro** is a good place to start exploring the town; its soaring tower, built in imitation of the Giralda and added a century later, dominates Carmona's main thoroughfare, C/San Pedro. Inside there's a splendid Baroque sacristy by Figueroa.

Puerta de Sevilla

Pza. Blas Infante s/n • Charge, free Mon • http://turismo.carmona.org/alcazar-puerta-de-sevilla/

From the Paseo del Estatuto, the modern town's main thoroughfare, looking east, you get a view of the magnificent Moorish **Puerta de Sevilla**, a grand, fortified Roman double gateway (with substantial Carthaginian and Moorish elements) to the old town. It now houses the *turismo*, which organizes guided tours of the gate's upper ramparts. The **old town** is circled by 4km of ancient walls, inside which narrow streets wind up past Mudéjar churches and Renaissance mansions.

Santa María la Mayor

Pza. de Ángel 1 • Charge

To the east of Pza. San Fernando, is **Santa María la Mayor**, a fine Gothic church built over the former Almohad Friday (main) mosque, whose elegant patio it retains, complete with orange trees and horseshoe arches. Like many of Carmona's churches, it is capped by a Mudéjar tower, possibly utilizing part of the old minaret.

Museo de la Ciudad

C/San Ildefonso 1 • Charge, free Tues

To the east of Pza. San Fernando, and housed in the graceful eighteenth-century Casa del Marqués de las Torres, is the **Museo de la Ciudad**, which documents the history of the town with mildly interesting displays of artefacts from the prehistoric, Iberian, Carthaginian, Roman, Moorish and Christian epochs. The museum has a *cafetería*, open to all.

Pedro's Alcázar

Parador bars, restaurants and public areas open to nonguests

Dominating the ridge of the town are the massive ruins of **Pedro's Alcázar**, an Almohad fortress transformed into a lavish residence by the fourteenth-century king. He employed the same Mudéjar craftsmen who worked on the Alcázar in Seville. The fortress was destroyed by an earthquake in 1504 and partly rebuilt by Fernando (after Isabel's death) but then fell into ruin. What remains has now been incorporated into a remarkably tasteful parador.

Puerta de Córdoba

Following C/Martín López and its continuations east from Pza. de San Fernando for 500m will bring you to an imposing Roman gateway, the **Puerta de Córdoba**, where the town comes to an abrupt and romantic halt. This was the start of the ancient Córdoba road (once the mighty Via Augusta heading north to Zaragoza, Gaul and finally Rome itself, now a dirt track) which dropped down from here to cross the vast plain below. Following the road for a few kilometres will lead you to a five-arched Roman bridge, just visible on the plain below.

Roman necropolis

Av. Jorge Bonsor 9 • Charge • 600 143 632

The extraordinary **Roman necropolis** lies on a low hill at the opposite end of Carmona; if you're walking out of town from San Pedro, take C/Enmedio, the middle street of three (parallel to the main Seville road) that leave the western end of Paseo del Estatuto and follow this for about 450m. Here, amid the cypress trees, more than nine hundred family tombs dating from the second century BC to the fourth century AD can be found. Enclosed in subterranean chambers hewn from the rock, the tombs are often frescoed and contain a series of niches in which many of the funeral urns remain intact. Some of the larger tombs have vestibules with stone benches for funeral banquets, and several retain carved family emblems (one is of an elephant, perhaps symbolic of long life). Most spectacular is the **Tumba de Servilia** – a huge colonnaded temple with vaulted side chambers. Opposite the site is a partly excavated **amphitheatre**.

4

ARRIVAL AND INFORMATION

By bus Buses from Seville stop on the central Paseo del Estatuto in sight of the landmark ancient gateway, the Puerta de Sevilla.

By car Your best bet is to use the reasonably priced car park beneath the Paseo de Estatuto, but if this is full the

CARMONA

somewhat unofficial-looking men in high-vis will usher you into a space on the road by the *puerta*.

Turismo The Puerta de Sevilla houses an efficient *turismo* (http://turismo.carmona.org), which is well stocked with information, and can provide a town map.

ACCOMMODATION

Carmona has a shortage of **places to stay**, especially in the budget category; particularly in spring and high summer, it's worth ringing ahead. The cheaper places lie outside the walls, while a clutch of more upmarket options all occupy scenic locations in the old town.

Convento Madre de Dios C/Aire s/n, 954 140 521. Great value and beautifully positioned budget hotel in a centuries-old working convent, with plain but comfortable rooms (complete with wall-hung crucifixes), a serene garden and generally peaceful atmosphere, and a staff of very friendly nuns. €

Hostal Comercio C/Torre del Oro 56, 954 140 018. Built into the Puerta de Sevilla gateway, this is a charming small and friendly family-run *hostal* with a history going back over

a century. It offers compact a/c en-suite rooms (without TV) around a pretty patio, some with views of the church. €

Hotel San Pedro C/San Pedro 3, http://hotelsanpedro.es. Near the church of San Pedro this is a central and pleasant budget option for a/c en-suite rooms with TVs. Below, there's a café that serves a decent breakfast. €

★ **Parador Nacional** Alcázar Rey Don Pedro, http://parador.es. Despite more recent competition at this end of the market, a superb location, patios and swimming pool ensure that this is still the nicest – and best value – of the luxury places in town. Pay a few euros extra for a room with a balcony. It's worth calling in for a drink at the bar, to enjoy the fabulous views from the terrace. €€€€

EATING AND DRINKING

There are plenty of places to eat both in the old and new towns, and you don't need to spend a fortune to eat well.

Bar Goya C/Prim 42, www.goyatapas.com. This lively tapas bar is housed in a fifteenth-century edifice off the west side of Pza. de San Fernando in the old town. There's also a pleasant terrace, and cheap house specials include *alboronía* (ratatouille) and *croquetas de merluza* (hake croquettes). €€

Bodega José María C/Domínguez de la Haza 1, 637 557 571. Tapas bar-restaurant offering a decent selection – try the *grilled artichokes with jamón*. Aside from a range of meat and fish dishes, the restaurant also offers a good-value menu of the day, and it's open for traditional Andalucian breakfast in the morning. €€

Mingalario Pza. Cristo del Rey 1, 954 143 893. In the old

town, facing the church of El Salvador, this is another fine old bar with excellent tapas. House specials include *gambas al ajillo*. €€

★ **Molino de la Romera** C/Pedro s/n, http://molinodelaromera.es. With a great terrace view across the *campiña* and housed in a sixteenth-century Moorish oil mill, this pleasant restaurant serves up regional dishes, has a good-value menu and also does *raciones* (try the pulpo in cream sauce). Its *dulces* are prepared by the nuns of the nearby Convento de Santa Clara. €€

Parador Nacional Alcázar Rey Don Pedro, http://parador.es. The restaurant of the parador is a model of baronial splendour which can be experienced on a *menú del día* that includes many local dishes; a la carte options are also available. They also offer vegetarian and diabetic menus. €€€

Écija

Lying midway between Seville and Córdoba in a basin of low sandy hills, **ÉCIJA** is known, with no hint of exaggeration, as *la sartenilla de Andalucía* ("the frying pan of Andalucía"). In mid-August, it's so hot that the only possible strategy is to slink from one tiny shaded plaza to another or, with a burst of energy, to make for the riverbank.

The heat is worth enduring, since this is one of the most distinctive and individual towns of the south, with eleven superb, decaying church towers, each glistening with brilliantly coloured tiles. It has a unique domestic architecture, too – a flamboyant style of twisted and florid forms, best displayed on C/Castellar, where the magnificent painted and curved frontage of the huge **Palacio de Peñaflor** (interior currently closed; enquire at the *turismo*) runs along the length of the street; the building has a fine patio and until recently housed Écija's public library. Other sights not to be missed are the beautiful polychromatic tower of the church of **Santa María**, overshadowing the main Pza. de España, and the **Palacio de**

Benamejí, a stunning eighteenth-century palace on C/Castillo, south of Pza. de España, that has a beautiful interior patio and has now been declared a national monument.

Museo Histórico Municipal

Palacio de Benamejí, C/Canovas de Castillo • Free • http://museo.ecija.es

The magnificent eighteenth-century Palacio de Benamejí, a short walk southwest of Pza. de España, is now home to the **Museo Histórico Municipal**, the town museum, which displays archeological finds from all periods. There is a particularly interesting section on Astigi's (the town's Roman name) role in the olive-oil trade – Spanish oil was prized in Imperial Rome. Don't miss the sensational **Amazona de Écija**, a beautifully sculpted first-century AD Roman statue depicting an Amazon resting against a pillar, accidentally discovered in the 2002 excavations to build a car park beneath the main square, Pza. de España. Two metres tall and still bearing traces of ochre paint, the statue has become the town's civic icon. The museum's upper floor displays a marvellous collection of **Roman mosaic pavements** which have been unearthed in excavations in and around the town.

Plaza Mayor

The town's focal **Plaza Mayor** (Pza. de España) was a building site for seven years during the construction of a controversial subterranean car park. Following this upheaval, the revamped square has been turned into a rather desolate, modernistic space jarring with the Baroque splendours surrounding it. A **Roman bath** discovered in the course of these works – just one of many archeological discoveries – can now be viewed under a canopy in the plaza's southeast corner.

4

INFORMATION ÉCIJA

Turismo Located at the Museo Histórico Municipal (June–Sept Tues–Fri 10am–2.30pm, Sat 10am–2.30pm & 8–10pm, Sun 10am–3pm; Oct–May Tues–Fri 10am– 1.30pm & 4.30–6.30pm, Sat 10am–2pm & 5.30–8pm, Sun 10am–3pm; 955 902 933, http://turismoecija.com).

ACCOMMODATION

Apartamentos Santiago Av. Miguel de Cervantes 35, http://hotelpirula.com. Good value, modern yet homely apartments, each one with a kitchenette so you can self-cater if you choose. €€

La Casa en el Centro C/Cinteria 15, www.lacasaenelcentro. com. The "house in the centre" certainly has an accurate name, but one which doesn't quite do justice to its gorgeous tiled courtyard and its unpretentious but lovely rooms, which pay homage to Moorish architecture with their floor tiles, turquoise wooden furniture and dark-wood shutters. €€

Hotel Platería C/Garcílópez 1, http://hotelplateria.net. Off the east side of the Pza. Mayor, this comfortable hotel has modern a/c rooms. Despite what the muted decor might lead you to believe, there's a lot of personality under the surface. The restaurant below serves up fun *pinchos* and *tostadas* including pork loin bites with Roquefort and mini hamburgers. They also offer laughter therapy for those inclined. €€

EATING

Ágora Tapas C/Barquette 38A, http://agoratapas.es. Food cooked with finesse in a light, spacious setting. They have a small, rotating menu which includes their deliciously sticky *milhojas de berenjena y queso de cabra* (aubergines with goat's cheese) and a three-course set menu for good value. €€

Café Central Pza. España 13, 744 650 484. Overlooking the Plaza España, this bar serves up the usual array of tapas and raciones but stands out for also offering a decent number of vegan options, including seitan stir-fries and plant-based burgers. €€

Cafetería Pasareli Pasaje Virgen del Rocío 2, www. facebook.com/Pasareli. Tucked away in a cul-de-sac off the east side of the Pza. de España, this bar-restaurant serves up a range of fish and meat dishes – including *pez espada a la maninera* (swordfish in seafood sauce) in season – and has a great-value budget menu. Also has a small terrace. €€

Osuna

OSUNA (like Carmona and Écija) is one of those small Andalucian towns that are great to explore in the early evening: slow in pace and quietly enjoyable, with elegant streets of tiled, whitewashed houses interspersed with fine **Renaissance mansions**. The best of these are off the main street, C/Carrera, which runs down from the central Pza. Mayor, and in particular on C/San Pedro, which intersects it; at no. 16, the **Cilla del Cabildo** has a superb geometric relief round a carving of the Giralda, and, farther along, the eighteenth-century **Palacio de El Marqués de la Gomera** – now a hotel and restaurant (see below) – is a stunning Baroque extravaganza. There's also a marvellous **casino** on Pza. Mayor, with 1920s Mudéjar-style decor and a grandly bizarre ceiling, which is open to all visitors and makes an ideal place for a cool drink. More recently featured as a filming location in the fifth season of popular series *Game of Thrones*, Osuna has seen a subsequent surge in tourism, dedicating a floor of its museum to the show.

The old university and Colegiata

Campo de Cipreses 1 • Charge

Two huge stone buildings stand on the hilltop: the **old university** (suppressed by reactionary Fernando VII in 1820) and the lavish sixteenth-century **Colegiata**, which contains the gloomy but impressive pantheon and chapel of the dukes of Osuna, descendants of the kings of León and once "the lords of Andalucía", as well as a museum displaying some fine artworks, including imposing canvases by Ribera. Opposite the entrance to the Colegiata is the Baroque convent of **La Encarnación** (same hours as Colegiata), which has a fine plinth of Sevillan *azulejos* round its cloister and gallery, and a patio where you can join the students for a café break.

INFORMATION   OSUNA

Turismo Housed in the town museum, Museo de Osuna, C/Sevilla 37, west of the main square (July–Aug Tues–Sat 10am–2pm & 5–8pm, Sun 10am–2pm; Sept–June Tues– Sat 10am–2pm & 5–8pm, Sun 10am–2pm; 954 815 732, http://osuna.es), the *turismo* has information on Osuna and can provide a map.

ACCOMMODATION

In Osuna **accommodation** is not plentiful, but outside of national holiday periods and the local *fería* (third or fourth week in May) there's usually no great problem finding a place to stay. All the same, it's worth ringing ahead.

Hostal Caballo Blanco C/Granada 1, 954 810 184. Welcoming and comfortable *hostal* with en-suite a/c rooms with TV in a remodelled old coaching inn. It has a large car park at the back. €

Hostal Five Gates C/de Carrera 79, 955 820 877. Friendly, modern *hostal* with communal kitchen and views over the plaza. Breakfast not included but the café opposite comes highly recommended. €

Hotel Esmeralda C/Tesorero 7, http://hotelesmeralda.es. Welcoming hotel with elegant a/c en-suite rooms. Stunning rooftop terrace with plunge pool and view towards the hilltop Colegiata. Free parking (reserve in advance). €

★ **Hotel Palacio Marqués de la Gomera** C/San Pedro 20, http://hotelpalaciodelmarques.es. The town's four-star option, set inside one of the most beautiful *casa palacios* in the country. A national monument in its own right, this eighteenth-century mansion has a strikingly attractive patio with a Baroque chapel just off it, and all rooms are tastefully and individually furnished. Room 7 was used by Franco Zeffirelli when he was here making a film about the life of María Callas and has a spectacular exterior balcony, while the irresistibly romantic room 10 is situated in the palace's tower. Rates increase by 15 percent Fridays and Saturdays. €€

EATING

Alfonso XII C/Alfonso XII 58, 664 053 079. Another of Osuna's lively and welcoming tapas bars, with a wide selection of dishes, mostly in the classic style. Try the tuna tartare and the *berenjenas fritos* (fried aubergines). Most dishes come in *tapa*, *medio* and *entera* sizes. €€

★ **Casa Curro** Pza. Salitre 5, www.facebook.com/ restaurantecasacurro. The town's best (and liveliest) tapas and *raciones* bar cooks up a tasty range of seafood and meat dishes, many with a creative slant. Choose from the specials chalked up on the numerous blackboards covering the walls. There's a superb restaurant in the back, and just around the corner, the owner's son has set up his own place – *Currito Chico* – that's definitely worth trying too. €€

Taberna Jicales C/Esparteros 11, http://tabernajicales. es. Excellent tapas bar with an outdoor terrace. There's a mouthwateringly long tapas *carta*, and house specials include *boquerones al limon* (anchovies with lemon) and *croquetas pollo bechamel* (chicken croquettes with béchamel sauce). Since the owner won the lottery, they're only open at lunchtime. €€

4

Córdoba

CÓRDOBA lies upstream from Seville beside a loop of the Guadalquivir, which was once navigable as far as here. It is today a minor provincial capital, prosperous in a modest sort of way. Once, however, it was the largest city of Roman Spain, and for three centuries it formed the heart of the western Islamic empire, the great medieval caliphate of the Moors.

It is from this era that the city's major monument dates: the **Mezquita**, the grandest and most beautiful mosque ever constructed by the Moors in Spain. It stands right in the centre of the city, surrounded by the old Jewish and Moorish quarters, and is a building of extraordinary mystical and aesthetic power. Make for it on arrival and keep returning as long as you stay; you'll find its beauty increases with each visit, as, of course, is proper, since the mosque was intended for daily attendance.

The Mezquita apart, Córdoba itself is a place of considerable charm. It has few grand squares or mansions, tending instead to introverted architecture, calling your attention to the tremendous and often wildly extravagant **patios**. These have long been acclaimed, and they are actively encouraged and maintained by the local council, which runs a "Festival of the Patios" in May. Away from the Mezquita, Córdoba's other remnants of Moorish – and indeed Christian – rule are not individually very striking. The river, though, with its great **Arab water wheels** and recently restored and pedestrianized **Roman bridge** (the Puente Romano), is an attractive area in which to wander.

Just 7km outside the town, more Moorish splendours are to be seen among the ruins of the extravagant palace complex of **Medina Azahara**, which is undergoing fascinating reconstruction.

4

La Mezquita

Centro • Charge • http://mezquita-catedraldecordoba.es/en

The development of the **Mezquita** paralleled the new heights of confidence and splendour of ninth- and tenth-century Córdoba. Abd ar-Rahman III provided it with a new minaret (which has not survived but which provided the core for the later belfry), 80m high, topped by three pomegranate-shaped spheres, two of silver and one of gold and each weighing a tonne. But it was his son, **al-Hakam II** (r.961–76), to whom he passed on a peaceful and stable empire, who was responsible for the most brilliant expansion. He virtually doubled its extent, demolishing the south wall to add fourteen extra rows of columns, and employed Byzantine craftsmen to construct a new *mihrab*, or prayer niche; this remains complete and is perhaps the most beautiful example of all Moorish religious architecture.

Al-Hakam had extended the mosque as far to the south as was possible. The final enlargement of the building, under the chamberlain-usurper **al-Mansur** (r.977–1002), involved adding seven rows of columns to the whole east side. This spoiled the symmetry of the mosque, depriving the *mihrab* of its central position, but Arab historians observed that it meant there were now "as many bays as there are days of the year". They also delighted in describing the rich interior, with its 1293 marble columns, 280 chandeliers and 1445 lamps. Hanging inverted among the lamps were the bells of the pilgrimage Catedral of Santiago de Compostela. Al-Mansur made his Christian captives carry them on their shoulders from Galicia – a process that was to be observed in reverse after Córdoba was captured by Fernando el Santo (the Saint) in 1236.

Entering the Mezquita

As in Moorish times, the **Mezquita** is approached through the **Patio de los Naranjos**, a classic Islamic ablutions court that preserves its orange trees, although the fountains for ritual purification before prayer are now purely decorative. Originally, when in use for

Train & Bus Stations (500m)

0   200
metres

N

Medina Azahara

AVENIDA DE MEDINA AZAHARA

ABEL

AVDA. DE LOS MOZÁRABES

AVENIDA DE CERVANTES

FRAY L. DE GRANADA

ALHAKEN II

DOCE DE OCTUBRE

CANO

Jardines de
la Agricultura

AVENIDA DEL GRAN CAPITÁN

Ciudad
Jardín

ALBENIL

ALCALDE DE LA CRUZ CEBALLOS

ANTONIO   MAURA

Jardines de
la Victoria

ALONSO DE BURGOS

Colegiata de
San Hipólito

CABRERA

E. LUCENA

CRUZ CONDE

CONDE

PLAZA
A. GRILLO

DOCE · DM

JOSÉ ZORRILLA

GÓNGORA

Iglesia de
San Miguel

S. ZOILO

S. ÁLVARO

CAMINO DE LOS SASTRES

AVENIDA DE LA REPÚBLICA ARGENTINA

PASEO DE LA VICTORIA

DAVID

PÉREZ

RODOR DE FERNÁN NÚÑEZ

Iglesia de
San Nicolás
de la Villa

CONDE DE GONDOMAR

MOREIRA

V. RIVERA

BLOOM

ALFONSO XII

GLORIETA CRUZ ROJA

ALCALDE DE VELASCO NAVARRO

EDUARDO

LOPE DE HOCES

CASTRO

SAN FELIPE

SEVILLA

MÁLAGA

PLAZA DE
LAS TENDILLAS

CLAUDIO

CLOVERA

Airport

PUERTA DE
ALMODÓVAR

MARTÍN

FERLA

PLAZA
R Y CAJAL

PLAZA
DR. EMILIO
LUQUE

R. SÁNCHEZ

JESÚS MARÍA

MOLINO
TRIMBLE

ARGOTE

San
Juan

JUAN DE MENA

CÁRDENAS

MUNDA

MARÍA

TEJÓN

FERNÁNDEZ

RUANO

VALLADARES

L. DE AUSTRIA

BARROSO

SALVADORA

JUAN

VALERA

PLAZA DE
LA COMPAÑÍA

POMPEYO

REGO

MORALES

DE CÓRDOBA

AL MANZOR

LEIVA AGUILAR

LA
JUDERÍA

ÁNGEL

ALTA CANA

DIARIO

FERNANDO

MÁCCEL

La Casa Andalusí

Sinagoga

Museo
Taurino

BLANCO BELMONTE

PLAZA
5

6

4

5

PLAZA. DE
JERÓNIMO
PÁEZ

Museo
Arqueológico

AMBROSIO

CARDENAL

LÁZARO

ROMERO

CONDE DE LUQUE

Convento de
la Encarnación

CALLEJA DE
LAS FLORES

HORNO DEL
CRISTO

EULOGIO

CAIRUÁN

6

PLAZA
MAIMÓNIDES

PLAZA JUDÁ
LEVI

DEANES

CARDENAL

ENCARNACIÓN

REY HEREDIA

J. ROMERO
DE TORRES

9

SAN

FERNANDO

Iglesia
de San
Francisco

LUNA

ALBUCASISS

HERRERO

8

11

S. CLARA

CABEZAS

SAN

PLAZA DEL
POTRO

12 8

DR. MARAÑÓN

BARBAHOU

DOCTOR

M. ROA

13

TORRES

MANRÍQUEZ

CONDE

10

Hospital
de San
Sebastián

PLAZA
CAMPO DE
LOS
MÁRTIRES

REALES

TORRIJOS

La Mezquita

MAGISTRAL GLEZ.

FRANCÉS

DISO

LUIS DE LA CERDA

CAL DERÓN

PIMENTERA

LUCANO

9

14

E. R TORRES

CRUZ

RASTRO

CABALLERIZAS

SAN BASILIO

ENMEDIO

12

Alcázar
de los Reyes
Cristianos

AMADOR DE LOS RÍOS

CORREGIDOR

10 PLAZA
ALHÓNDIGA

13

PASEO DE L

Triunfo de
San Rafael

Puerta del
Puente

RONDA DE ISASA

Jardín Botánico, Seville & Granada

AVENIDA DEL ALCÁZAR

Puente
Romano

Río Guadalquivir

Torre de la Calahorra (200m)

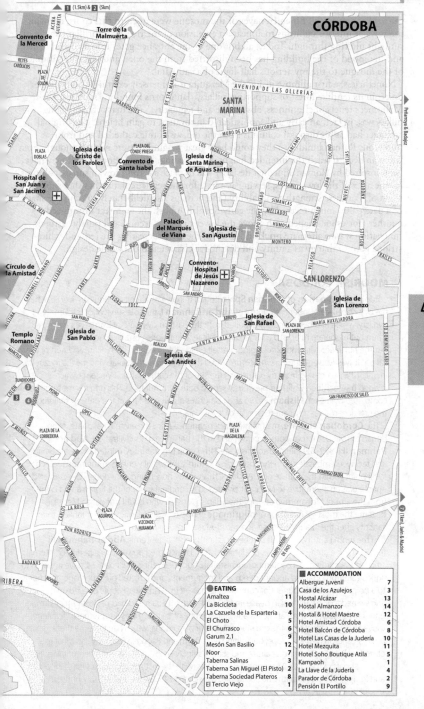

CÓRDOBA

● EATING

Amaltea	11
La Bicicleta	10
La Cazuela de la Esparteria	4
El Choto	5
El Churrasco	6
Garum 2.1	9
Mesón San Basilio	12
Noor	7
Taberna Salinas	3
Taberna San Miguel (El Pisto)	2
Taberna Sociedad Plateros	8
El Tercio Viejo	1

■ ACCOMMODATION

Albergue Juvenil	7
Casa de los Azulejos	3
Hostal Alcázar	13
Hostal Almanzor	14
Hostal & Hotel Maestre	12
Hotel Amistad Córdoba	6
Hotel Balcón de Córdoba	8
Hotel Las Casas de la Judería	10
Hotel Mezquita	11
Hotel Soho Boutique Atila	5
Kampaoh	1
La Llave de la Judería	4
Parador de Córdoba	2
Pensión El Portillo	9

the Friday prayers, all nineteen naves of the mosque were open to this court, allowing the rows of interior columns to appear an extension of the trees with brilliant shafts of sunlight filtering through. Today, all but one of the entrance gates is locked and sealed, and the mood of the building has been distorted from the open and vigorous simplicity of the mosque to the mysterious half-light of a cathedral.

Nonetheless, a first glimpse inside the Mezquita is immensely exciting. "So near the desert in its tentlike forest of supporting pillars," Jan Morris found it, "so faithful to Mahomet's tenets of cleanliness, abstinence and regularity." The mass of supporting pillars was, in fact, an early and sophisticated innovation to gain height. The original architect had at his disposal columns from the old Visigothic cathedral and from numerous Roman buildings; they could bear great weight but were not tall enough, even when arched, to reach the intended height of the ceiling. His solution (which may have been inspired by Roman aqueduct designs) was to place a second row of square columns on the apex of the lower ones, serving as a base for the semicircular arches that support the roof. For extra strength and stability (and perhaps also deliberately to echo the shape of a date palm, much revered by the early Spanish Arabs), the architect introduced another, horseshoe-shaped arch above the lower pillars. A second and purely aesthetic innovation was to alternate brick and stone in the arches, creating the red-and-white-striped pattern that gives a unity and distinctive character to the whole design.

MOORISH CÓRDOBA

Córdoba's **domination of Moorish Spain** began thirty years after its conquest – in 756, when the city was placed under the control of **Abd ar-Rahman I**, the sole survivor of the Umayyad dynasty, which had been bloodily expelled from the eastern caliphate of Damascus. He proved a firm but moderate ruler, and a remarkable military campaigner, establishing control over all but the north of Spain and proclaiming himself emir, a title meaning both "king" and "son of the caliph". It was Abd ar-Rahman who commenced the building of the Great Mosque (La Mezquita, in Spanish), purchasing from the Christians the site of the cathedral of St Vincent (which, divided by a partition wall, had previously served both communities). This original mosque was completed by his son **Hisham** in 796 and comprises about one-fifth of the present building, the first dozen aisles adjacent to the Patio de los Naranjos.

The **Cordoban emirate**, maintaining independence from the eastern caliphate, soon began to rival Damascus both in power and in the brilliance of its civilization. **Abd ar-Rahman II** (r.822–52) initiated sophisticated irrigation programmes, minted his own coinage and received embassies from Byzantium. He in turn substantially enlarged the mosque. A focal point within the culture of al-Andalus, this was by now being consciously directed and enriched as an alternative to Mecca; it possessed an original script of the Koran and a bone from the arm of Mohammed and, for the Spanish Muslim who could not get to Mecca, it became the most sacred place of **pilgrimage**. In the broader Islamic world, it ranked third in sanctity after the Kaaba of Mecca and the al-Alqsa mosque of Jerusalem.

In the tenth century, Córdoba reached its zenith under a new emir, **Abd ar-Rahman III** (r.912–61), one of the great rulers of Islamic history. He assumed power after a period of internal strife and, according to a contemporary historian, "subdued rebels, built palaces, gave impetus to agriculture, immortalized ancient deeds and monuments, and inflicted great damage on infidels to a point where no opponent or contender remained in al-Andalus. People obeyed en masse and wished to live with him in peace." In 929, with Muslim Spain and part of North Africa firmly under his control, Abd ar-Rahman III adopted the title of "caliph". It was a supremely confident move and was reflected in the growing splendour of Córdoba, which had become the largest, most prosperous city of Europe, outshining Byzantium and Baghdad (the new capital of the eastern caliphate) in science, culture and scholarship. At the turn of the tenth century, Moorish sources boast of the city's 27 schools, 50 hospitals (with the first separate clinics for the leprous and insane), 900 public baths, 60,300 noble mansions, 80,455 shops and 213,077 houses.

The mihrab

The uniformity was broken only at the culminating point of the mosque – the domed cluster of pillars surrounding the sacred **mihrab**, erected under al-Hakam II. The *mihrab* has two functions in Islamic worship: it indicates the direction of Mecca (and hence of prayer) and it amplifies the words of the imam, or prayer leader. At Córdoba, it is also of supreme beauty.

The inner vestibule of the niche (frustratingly fenced off) is quite simple in comparison, with a shell-shaped ceiling carved from a single block of marble. The chambers to either side – decorated with exquisite Byzantine mosaics of gold, rust red, turquoise and green – constitute the *maksura*, where the caliph and his retinue would pray.

The Catedral

Originally, the whole design of the mosque would have directed worshippers naturally towards the *mihrab*. Today, though, you almost stumble upon it, for in the centre of the mosque squats a Renaissance **Catedral coro**. This was built in 1523 – nearly three centuries of enlightened restraint after the Reconquest – and in spite of fierce opposition from the town council. The erection of a *coro* and *capilla mayor*, however, had long been the "Christianizing" dream of the Catedral chapter and at last they had found a monarch – predictably, Carlos V – who was willing to sanction the work. Carlos, to his credit, realized the mistake (though it did not stop him from destroying parts of the Alhambra and Seville's Alcázar); on seeing the work completed, he told the chapter, "You have built what you or others might have built anywhere, but you have destroyed something that was unique in the world." To the left of the *coro* stands an earlier and happier Christian addition – the Mudéjar **Capilla de Villaviciosa**, built by Moorish craftsmen in 1371 (and now partly sealed up). Beside it are the dome and pillars of the **earlier mihrab**, constructed under Abd ar-Rahman II.

The belfry and outer walls

The **belfry**, the **Torre del Alminar** at the corner of the Patio de los Naranjos, is contemporary with the Catedral addition and well worth a climb for the view of the patio and the Guadalquivir. Close by, the **Puerta del Perdón**, the main entrance to the patio, was rebuilt in Moorish style in 1377. It's worth making a tour of the Mezquita's **outer walls** before leaving; parts of the original "caliphal" decoration surrounding the portals (in particular, some exquisite lattice work) are stunning.

Torre de la Calahorra

Puente Romano s/n • Charge • http://torrecalahorra.es

At the eastern end of the Roman bridge over the Guadalquivir, the medieval **Torre de la Calahorra** houses a gimmicky, high-tech museum containing models of the pre-cathedral Mezquita, weird talking tableaux and a rather incongruous multimedia presentation on the history of man; there's a great panoramic **view**, though, from the top of the tower towards the city. As you cross the bridge you can see, near the western riverbank, the wheels and the ruined mills that were in use for several centuries after the fall of the Muslim city, grinding flour and pumping water up to the fountains of the Alcázar.

Alcázar de los Reyes Cristianos

Pza. Campo Santo de los Mártires s/n • Charge, free Thurs from 6pm (from noon June 16–Sept 15) • www.turismodecordoba.org/alcazar-de-los-reyes-cristianos

After the Christian conquest, the Alcázar was rebuilt a little to the west by Fernando and Isabel, hence its name, **Alcázar de los Reyes Cristianos**. The buildings are a bit dreary, having served as the residence of the Inquisition from 1428 to 1821, and later as a prison until 1951. However, they display some fine mosaics and other relics from Roman Córdoba, among which is one of the largest complete Roman mosaics in existence, and the wonderful **gardens** are a pleasant place to sit.

Plaza de la Corredera

To the northeast of the Mezquita, in an area that was once the *plateros* or silversmiths' quarter, you'll find **Plaza de la Corredera**, a wonderfully refurbished colonnaded square, much resembling Madrid's or Salamanca's Plaza Mayor. Unique in Andalucía, the square's complete enclosure occurred in the seventeenth century and presented the city with a suitable space for all kinds of spectacles. These included burnings by the Inquisition as well as bullfights, from which event the tiny **Callejón Toril** (Bull Pen) on the square's eastern side takes its name. Now bars and restaurants line the square, and their terraces are popular places to sit out on summer evenings.

La Judería

Between the Mezquita and the beginning of Avda. del Gran Capitán lies **La Judería**, Córdoba's old Jewish quarter, and a fascinating network of lanes – more atmospheric and less commercialized than Seville's Barrio Santa Cruz, though tacky souvenir shops are beginning to gain ground.

Sinagoga

C/Judíos 20 • Charge • http://turismodecordoba.org/synagogue

Near the heart of La Judería is a **sinagoga**, one of only three synagogues in Spain – the other two are in Toledo – that survived the Jewish expulsion of 1492. This one, built in 1316, is minute, particularly in comparison with the great Santa María in Toledo, but it has some fine stuccowork elaborating on a Solomon's-seal motif and retains its women's gallery. Outside is a statue of Maimónides, the Jewish philosopher, physician and Talmudic jurist, born in Córdoba in 1135.

Museo Taurino

Pza. de Maimónides s/n • Charge, free Thurs from 6pm (from noon June 16–Sept 15) • www.museotaurinodecordoba.es/ing

The small **Museo Taurino** (Bullfighting Museum) warrants a look, if only for the kitschy nature of its exhibits: row upon row of bulls' heads, two of them given this "honour" for having killed matadors. Beside a copy of the tomb of Manolete – most famous of the city's *toreros* – is exhibited the hide of his taurine nemesis, Islero.

Museo Arqueológico

Pza. de Jerónimo Páez • Charge • http://turismodecordoba.org/archaeological-museum

The **Museo Arqueológico** is now in two buildings, one completely new and the other its first refurbished home, the beautiful sixteenth-century mansion of Casa Páez, which has a basement viewing area that incorporates the *grados* (seats) of the Roman theatre both it and the mansion are built on top of. The museum exhibits an extensive Moorish collection, and well-presented Iberian and Roman sculptures as well as caliphal ceramics and *azulejos*.

Plaza del Potro

Near the river is **Plaza del Potro**, a fine old square named after the colt (*potro*) that adorns its restored fountain. This, as a wall plaque proudly points out, is mentioned in *Don Quixote*, and indeed Cervantes himself is reputed to have stayed at the inn opposite, the **Posada del Potro**, which has an atmospheric cattle yard within. The restored building is currently used as a centre for the study of flamenco and stages exhibitions and sporadic concerts (details from the *turismo*).

Palacio del Marqués de Viana

Pza. de Don Gome 2 • Charge • http://palaciodeviana.com

In the north of town are numerous Renaissance churches – some converted from mosques, others showing obvious influence in their minarets – and a handful of convents and palaces. The best of these, still privately owned although not by the family, is the **Palacio del Marqués de Viana**, whose main attraction for many visitors is its twelve flower-filled patios. The house itself – an ongoing work started in the fourteenth century – is mildly interesting and the guided tour (in Spanish only) leads you through drawing rooms, gaudy bedrooms (one with a telling Franco portrait), kitchens and galleries while pointing out furniture, paintings, weapons and top-drawer junk the family amassed over the centuries.

ARRIVAL AND DEPARTURE
CÓRDOBA

By train From the splendid combined train and bus station on Pza. de las Tres Culturas, on Avda. de América at the northern end of town, head east to the junction with broad Avda. del Gran Capitán; this leads down to the old quarters and the Mezquita (15min walk or bus #3 from outside the station).
Destinations Algeciras (2 daily; 3hr 10min); Cádiz (2 daily; 3hr 10min); Granada (6 daily; 2hr 5min); Jaén (4 daily; 1hr 40min); Madrid (22 AVE daily; 1hr 45min); Málaga (12 AVE daily; 55min); Ronda (2 daily; 1hr 50min); Seville (28 AVE daily; 45min).

By bus Buses arrive at the combined train and bus station on Pza. de las Tres Culturas. See train information above for details on getting to the centre.

Destinations Badajoz (1 daily; 5hr 15min); Écija (6 daily; 55min); Granada (6 daily; 2hr 45min); Jaén (4 daily; 2hr); Madrid (8 daily; 4hr 45min); Málaga (4 daily; 3hr); Málaga airport (1 daily; 3hr); Seville (3 daily; 2hr).

By car Arriving by car can be a pain, especially during rush hour in the narrow streets around the Mezquita. Parking in the centre is also a major headache, and it's worth considering staying somewhere that doesn't require traversing the old quarter. Better still is if you park up for the duration of your stay – Avda. de la República Argentina bordering the Jardines de la Victoria on the western edge of the old quarter, and across the river in the streets either side of the *Hotel Hespería Córdoba* are possible places – and then get around the city on foot, which is both easy and enjoyable.

INFORMATION AND TOURS

Turismo At the Palacio de Congresos y Exposiciones at C/ Torrijos 10, alongside the Mezquita (Mon–Fri 9am–7pm, Sat & Sun 9.30am–2.30pm; 957 355 179).

Municipal tourist office Córdoba's municipal tourist office (http://turismodecordoba.org) is located in Pza. de las Tendillas in the centre of the modern town, and on the main concourse of the train station.

Guided walks Guided walks around the old city are offered by Córdoba Visión and Konexión Tours (English spoken); buy tickets at tourist offices.

Opening hours Córdoba changes its monument timetables more than any other town in Andalucía – check with tourist offices for the latest information.

ACCOMMODATION
SEE MAP PAGE 294

The majority of **places to stay** are concentrated in the narrow maze of streets to the north and east of the Mezquita. Finding a room at any time of the year – except during Semana Santa and the May festivals (the city's busiest month) – isn't usually a problem. Note that Córdoba's high season is April to June, while July and August are low-season months, when upmarket rates often drop dramatically.

Albergue Juvenil Pza. Judá Levi, http://inturjoven.com. Excellent and superbly located modern youth hostel (with twin, triple and four-person en-suite rooms). It's a prime destination for budget travellers, so you may need to book ahead at busy periods. €

Casa de los Azulejos C/Fernando Colón 5, http:// casadelosazulejos.com. Stylish, small boutique B&B with distinctively furnished rooms, featuring iron bedsteads and artworks, ranged around a leafy patio, itself used for art shows. Also has pool and own car park. €€

★ **Hostal Alcázar** C/San Basilio 2, http://hostalalcazar. com. Comfortable and welcoming family-run B&B *hostal* with a nice patio and a range of en-suite rooms with a/c and TV. Also has some good-value apartments opposite (sleeping up to four people), and its own car park. €

Hostal Almanzor Corregidor Luís de la Cerda 10, http:// hostalalmanzor.es. East of the Mezquita, a pleasant refurbished *hostal*, with a/c, en-suite rooms with TV. Free

4

use of car park. €

★ **Hostal & Hotel Maestre** C/Romero Barros 4 & 16, http://hotelmaestre.com. Excellent *hostal*, between C/San Fernando and the Pza. del Potro, and neighbouring hotel with attractive a/c en-suite rooms with TV. Also has some good-value two-person apartments. €

Hotel Amistad Córdoba Pza. de Maimónides 3, http://nh-hoteles.com. Stylish upmarket hotel with comfortable rooms incorporating three eighteenth-century mansions, near the old wall in La Judería. Car park available. €€€€

★ **Hotel Balcón de Córdoba** C/Encarnación 8, http://balcondecordoba.com. Luxurious boutique hotel in a restored seventeenth-century convent. Features include plenty of original elements, a patio restaurant, rooftop terrace with close-up views of the Mezquita and comfy, spacious rooms, whose rates include breakfast. Parking can be arranged nearby. €€€€

★ **Hotel Las Casas de la Judería** C/Tomás Conde 10, http://lascasasdelajuderiadecordoba.com. This four-star hotel is an exquisitely charming restoration of an ancient *casa palacio* and rooms are arranged around patios with tinkling fountains and scented flowers. The elegant rooms are decorated with period furnishings and artworks and come with satellite TV and lots of frills. Also has a spa, restaurant and garage. €€€€

Hotel Mezquita Pza. Santa Catalina 1, http://hotel mezquita.com. Atmospheric and central hotel in a converted sixteenth-century mansion with excellent a/c rooms. €€€

Hotel Soho Boutique Atila C/Buen Pastor 19, www.sohohoteles.com. Bright and cheerful budget hotel, with a lovely courtyard and roof terrace overlooking the Mezquita. Rooms have a contemporary style which nods to the Moorish past. €€

Kampaoh Parque Los Villares, http://en.kampaoh.com. Córdoba's local glampsite offers a selection of bell tents and wooden "tiny houses". There's an outdoor pool, restaurant and grocery store. €

La Llave de la Judería C/Romero 38, http://lallavedela juderia.es. Elegant and welcoming nine-room hotel in La Judería. Entry is through a double patio, and rooms are classically furnished with chintz drapes and bedcovers, and some have terraces. Facilities include minibar, in-room internet and rooftop terrace/solarium. €€€€

Parador de Córdoba Avda. de la Arruzafa s/n, off Avda. El Brillante, http://parador.es. Córdoba's modern parador is located on the outskirts of the city 5km to the north of the Mezquita, but compensates with pleasant gardens, a pool and every other amenity (including a shooting range). €€€€

Pensión El Portillo C/Cabezas 2, http://pensionelportillo.com. Beautiful, refurbished and friendly old *hostal* with elegant patio, offering en-suite a/c singles and doubles. €

EATING

SEE MAP PAGE 294

Tapas bars and **restaurants** are on the whole reasonably priced – you need only to avoid the touristy places around the Mezquita. There are lots of good places to eat in La Judería and in the old quarters off to the east, above Paseo de la Ribera. Two celebrated specialities worth trying here are *rabo de toro* (slow-stewed bull's tail) and *salmorejo*, the delicious *cordobés* variant of gazpacho, made with bread, tomatoes, oil and chopped *jamón* often topped off with sliced hard-boiled eggs.

TAPAS BARS

La Bicicleta C/Cardenal González 1, 666 544 690. Small café-bar with bike-themed decor, serving salads, snacks, cheese boards, juices and yoghurts plus some delicious home-made cakes. €€

Garum 2.1 C/San Fernando 122, http://garum2punto1.com. This award-winning tapas bar specializes in sherry-spiked *salmorejo*, the local spin on *gazpacho*. That's not the only dish that chef Juan Luis Santiago and his team has mastered: try the squid croquettes in their own ink, salty Iberian pork, crispy trotters or oxtail churro. €€

Taberna San Miguel (El Pisto) Pza. San Miguel 1, www.casaelpisto.com. Known to all as *El Pisto* (the ratatouille), this is one of the city's legendary bars – over a century old – and not to be missed. Wonderful *montilla* and tapas: *rabo de toro, potaje de garbanzos con manitas* (chickpea stew with trotters) and ratatouille are house specials. €€

★ **Taberna Sociedad Plateros** C/San Francisco 6, http://tabernaplateros.com. This tapas bar, over a century old, serves a wide range of tapas – house specials include *arroz con bacalao* (cod paella) and *perdiz en escabeche* (marinated partridge). The bar is light and airy with a glass-covered patio complemented by a vibrant array of hanging plants dotted around the space and *azulejos*. €€

El Tercio Viejo C/Enrique Redel 17, 665 383 919. Handy for the Palacio de Viana, this local bar serves traditional tapas and *raciones* such as *rabo de toro* and *callos con chorizo* (tripe with chorizo) and the Córdoba delicacy, *caracoles* (snails, served in spicy broth in a large cup). €€

RESTAURANTS

★ **Amaltea** C/Ronda de Isasa 10, www.amaltea.es. Excellent organic restaurant with special veggie and coliac menus, run by a charming Wolverhampton-educated *cordobesa*. Specialities of the house include *couscous con verduras* (vegetables). Plenty of organic wines and a few special beers, too – try the Alhambra 1925. €€€

La Cazuela de la Esparteria C/Rodríguez Marín 16, http://lacazueladelaesparteria.es. Feast on traditional Andalucian cuisine alongside locals in this inviting taverna. Dishes may include fried aubergine chips in honey, Iberian pork cheek or oxtail stew, paired with excellent wines. €€

El Choto C/Almanzor 10, 957 760 115, http://restaurante

elchotocordoba.es. Attractive, small and serious restaurant with a little outdoor terrace offering a range of well-prepared rice (12 types), fish and meat dishes including its signature dish *choto asado* (roast kid). There's a good-value weekday lunch *menú de la casa*. €€

★ **El Churrasco** C/Romero 16 (not C/Romero Barros), http://elchurrasco.com. This renowned restaurant has attractive rooms and patio is famous for its *churrasco* (a grilled pork dish, served with pepper sauces) and Cordoban local dish *salmorejo*. €€

Mesón San Basilio C/San Basilio 19, 957 297 007. Good, unpretentious and busy local restaurant offering well-prepared fish and meat *raciones* and *platos combinados*, plus weekday menus for both lunch and dinner. €€

Noor C/Pablo Ruiz Picasso 8, http://noorrestaurant.es. Michelin-starred chef, Paco Morales, demonstrates his unique take on Andalusian cuisine. There's a set menu, but the two tasting menus take you on a journey to the city's gastronomic past where traditional ingredients such as aubergines, snails, lamb and almonds undergo a very modern transformation. €€€€

★ **Taberna Salinas** C/Tundidores 3, http://taberna salinas.com. Reasonably priced *taberna* established in 1879, with dining rooms around a charming patio. Good *raciones* place – try their *naranjas con bacalao* (cod with oranges) – and it serves a great *salmorejo*. €€€

Medina Azahara

Charge • http://turismodecordoba.org/medina-azahara-1

Seven kilometres to the northwest of Córdoba lie the vast and rambling ruins of **Medina Azahara**, a palace complex built on a dream scale by **Caliph Abd ar-Rahman III**. Naming it after a favourite, az-Zahra (the Radiant), he spent one-third of the annual state budget on its construction each year from 936 until his death in 961. Ten thousand workers and 1500 mules and camels were employed on the project, and the site, almost 2km long by 900m wide, stretched over three descending terraces. In addition to the palace buildings, it had a zoo, an aviary, four fish ponds, three hundred baths, four hundred houses, weapons factories and two barracks for the royal guard. Visitors, so the chronicles record, were stunned by its wealth and brilliance: one conference room was decorated with pure crystals, creating a rainbow when lit by the sun; another was built round a huge pool of mercury.

4

The Royal House

For centuries following its downfall the Medina Azahara continued to be looted for building materials; parts, for instance, were used in the Seville Alcázar. But in 1944 excavations unearthed the remains of a crucial part of the palace – the **Royal House**,

---

THE RISE AND FALL OF MEDINA AZAHARA

Medina Azahara was a perfect symbol of the western caliphate's extent and greatness, but it was to last for less than a century. Al-Hakam II, who succeeded Abd ar-Rahman, lived in the palace, continued to endow it, and enjoyed a stable reign. However, distanced from the city, he delegated more and more authority, particularly to his vizier Ibn Abi Amir, later known as **al-Mansur** (the Victor). In 976, al-Hakam was succeeded by his 11-year-old son Hisham II and, after a series of sharp moves, al-Mansur assumed the full powers of government, keeping Hisham virtually imprisoned at Medina Azahara, to the extent of blocking up connecting passageways between the palace buildings.

Al-Mansur was equally skilful and manipulative in his wider dealings as a dictator, retaking large tracts of central Spain and raiding as far afield as Galicia and Catalunya; consequently, Córdoba rose to new heights of prosperity. But with his death in 1002 came swift decline, as his role and function were assumed in turn by his two sons. The first died in 1008; the second, Sanchol, showed open disrespect for the caliphate by forcing Hisham to appoint him as his successor. At this, a popular revolt broke out and the caliphate disintegrated into civil war and a series of feudal kingdoms. Medina Azahara was looted by a mob at the outset, and in 1010 was plundered and burned by retreating Berber mercenaries.

where guests were received and meetings of ministers held. This has been meticulously reconstructed and, though still fragmentary, its main hall must rank among the greatest of all Moorish rooms. It has a different kind of stuccowork from that at Granada or Seville – closer to natural and animal forms in its intricate Syrian *Hom* (Tree of Life) motifs. Unlike the later Spanish Arab dynasties, the Berber Almoravids and the Almohads of Seville, the caliphal Andalucians were little worried by Islamic strictures on the portrayal of nature, animals or even people – the beautiful hind in the Córdoba museum is a good example – and it may well have been this aspect of the palace that led to such zealous destruction during the civil war.

The reconstruction of the palace gives a scale and focus to the site. Elsewhere, you have little more than foundations to fuel your imaginings, amid an awesome area of ruins, hidden beneath bougainvillea and rustling with cicadas. Perhaps the most obvious of the outbuildings yet excavated is the **Aljama mosque**, just beyond the Royal House, which sits at an angle to the rest of the buildings in order to face Mecca.

The gardens

After an extensive study of soil samples by biologists from Córdoba University to ascertain which plants and flowers would have originally been cultivated in the extensive **gardens**, reconstructive planting took place and the trees, shrubs and herbs are now maturing into a delightful and aromatic garden the caliphs would recognize.

ARRIVAL AND DEPARTURE   **MEDINA AZAHARA**

By car Follow Avda. de Medina Azahara west out of town, onto the road to Villarubia and Posadas. About 4km down this road, make a right turn (signed for the site), after which it's another 1km to the Centro de Interpretación. Note that you are obliged to park your car here and take the dedicated bus (€2.10 return) to the site. If you continue up the road to the site car park (for staff only) you will arrive at a locked gate forcing you to turn around and go back.

By bus City buses #01 and #02 from a stop on the Avda. de la República Argentina (at the northern end, near a petrol station) will drop you off at the intersection (cross the road with extreme care) from where it's a 1km walk to the Centro de Interpretación. Ask the driver for "El Cruce de Medina Azahara". A dedicated bus service also links the city with the site. The bus departs from a signed stop on the Glorieta (roundabout) Cruz Roja at the southern end of Paseo de la Victoria (confirm this at the tourist office), but tickets must be purchased in advance from any municipal tourist office kiosk (see page 299). Tickets cannot be purchased on the bus.

By taxi A taxi will cost you about €30 one-way for up to five people and there's a special round-trip deal ("Taxi-Tour Córdoba") for €55, which includes a 1hr wait at the site while you visit. A convenient taxi rank is located outside the *turismo* on the west side of the Mezquita.

Guided trips Córdoba Vision runs guided trips to the site (http://cordobavision.es, English spoken); buses leave from the same stop on Avda. del Alcázar as the bus service. The tour bus parks at the Centro de Interpretación and both you and the guide still use the bus service to the site.

Visiting the site Visitors must arrive at the Centro de Interpretación, a complex incorporating a museum, shop and *cafetería*; from here take a bus (every 10–20min) from the car park for the 2km journey to the site; once you have your ticket you can walk to the site but it is all uphill.

Jaén province

There are said to be over 150 million olive trees in the province of Jaén. They dominate the landscape as infinite rows of green against the orange-red earth, occasionally interspersed with stark white farm buildings. It's beautiful on a grand, sweeping scale, though it conceals a bitter and entrenched economic reality. The majority of the olive groves are owned by a mere handful of families, and for most residents this is a very poor area.

Sights may not be as plentiful here as in other parts of Andalucía, but there are a few gems worth going out of your way to take in. Fairly dull in itself, the provincial capital of **Jaén** merits a visit for its fine Catedral and Moorish baths, while farther to the northwest are **Baeza** and **Úbeda**, are two remarkable Renaissance towns jam-packed with architectural gems such as exuberant Renaissance palaces, richly endowed churches and fine public squares. Both were captured from the Moors by Fernando el Santo and stood for two centuries at the frontiers of the reconquered lands facing the Moorish kingdom of Granada. Extending northeast from the town of Cazorla, **Parque Natural de Cazorla**, Andalucía's biggest natural park, is a vast expanse of dense woodlands, lakes and spectacular crags.

Jaén

JAÉN, the provincial capital and by far the largest town, is an uneventful sort of place but there are traces of its Moorish past in the winding, narrow streets of the old quarter and in the largest surviving Moorish baths in Spain. Activity is centred on Pza. de la Constitución and its two arterial streets, Paseo de la Estación and Avda. de Madrid. The town is overlooked by the Cerro de Santa Catalina, a wooded hill topped by a restored Moorish fort, now partly transformed into a spectacular parador.

Catedral

Pza. de Santa María s/n • Charge • http://catedraldejaen.org

West of the focal Pza. de la Constitución is the imposing seventeenth-century Renaissance **Catedral**, by the great local architect Andrés de Vandelvira, whose design had the most influence over the building as it looks today. The spectacular **west facade**, flanked by twin sixty-metre-high towers framing Corinthian pillars and statuary by the seventeenth-century master Pedro Roldán, is one of the masterpieces of Andalucian Renaissance architecture.

Baños Árabes

Pza. Santa Luisa de Marillac • Free • www.bañosarabesjaen.es

To the north of the Catedral, between the churches of San Andrés and Santo Domingo, you'll find the painstakingly restored Moorish *hammam* in the **Baños Árabes**. Among the finest of their kind in Spain, the baths were originally part of an eleventh-century Moorish palace, and are now located inside the sixteenth-century Palacio de Villardompardo, which was constructed over it. On view are the various rooms (containing hot, tepid and cold baths), with pillars supporting elegant horseshoe arches and brickwork ceilings pierced with distinctive star-shaped windows.

ARRIVAL AND INFORMATION
JAÉN

By train The train station (912 320 320) is on Paseo de la Estación (bus #4 or #8 from the centre).
Destinations Cádiz (4 daily; 5hr); Córdoba (4 daily; 1hr 40min); Madrid (4 daily Mon–Sat, 3 daily Sun; 3hr 45min); Seville (4 daily; 3hr).

By bus The bus station (953 232 300) is at Pza. Coca de la Pinera, 300m northeast of Pza. de la Constitución.
Destinations Almería (2 daily; 4hr); Baeza/Úbeda (14 daily;

1hr 25min); Cazorla (3 daily; 2hr 30min); Córdoba (9 daily Mon–Fri, 6 daily weekend; 2hr); Granada (12 daily Mon–Fri, 11 daily weekend; 1hr 10min); Madrid (4 daily Mon–Sat, 3 daily Sun; 4hr 20min); Málaga (3 daily; 3hr 15min); Seville (5 daily; 4hr).

Turismo To the north of the Catedral on C/Maestra 8 (http://turjaen.org).

ACCOMMODATION

Places to stay in town are limited and – with the exception of *Albergue Inturjoven* – relatively expensive. There's usually no problem in finding accommodation at any time of the year and there are no seasonal rate changes. Mosquitoes can be a real problem in the town during the summer, at which time places with a/c come into their own.

★ **Albergue Inturjoven** C/Borja s/n, http://inturjoven. com. Behind the imposing facade of a former eighteenth-century hospital lies the youth hostel's excellent modern, if minimalist in style, en-suite a/c rooms and "apartments"

(which add a *salón* but no kitchen). There's also a pool. Somewhat incongruously the *albergue* also houses a full-blown spa with a variety of detox and anti-*edad* (ageing) cures costing much more than the rooms. €

Hostal Estación RENFE Pza. Jaén por la Paz, http:// hostalestacionjaen.com. RENFE's own B&B *hostal* at the front of the station is a rather swish affair with comfortable a/c rooms with TVs and a car park. €€

Hotel Europa Pza. de Belén 1, http://hoteleuropajaen.es. Perhaps the best of the more upmarket places in the centre,

4

where attractive a/c rooms come with safes and satellite TVs. €€

★ **Parador Castillo de Santa Catalina** Castillo, sited on a hill 3km from town, http://parador.es. For a truly memorable experience you could stay at this most spectacularly sited hotel. The comfortable rooms have fine balcony views with a sheer drop to the valley below; facilities include a pool, restaurant, bar and ample parking. €€€€

EATING AND DRINKING

Off the east side of Pza. Constitución, C/Nueva has a clutch of **places to eat** and there is a bunch of tapas bars in the streets to the north of the Catedral.

Casa Antonio C/Fermín Palma 3, north of the bus station, http://casantonio.es. This top culinary choice offers innovative *jiennense* and Basque-inspired dishes; house specials include *cochinillo* (suckling pig) and *paletilla de cabrito asada* (stewed goat). The *menú de degustación* is the best way to try a wide range. €€€€

Navas 13 C/Navas de Tolosa 13, 953 226 483. Popular tapas bar and *marisquería* with lovely anchovy, tuna and sardine dishes, as well as a great breakfast menu. Popular throughout the day, and justifiably. €€

Restaurante Támesis C/Maestro Sapena 9, http://restaurantetamesis.es. One of the best fine dining options in this part of Andalucía. Choose from tapas, sharing plates, some with a Mediterranean-Japanese twist, or the tasting menu that includes five types of olive oil to try. Steak tartare is a house special as is the *revuelto de habas con bacalao* (scrambled eggs with broad beans and cod). €€€

El Tostón C/Bernardo López 11, www.facebook.com/mesoneltoston. A reliable choice for tapas and *raciones*; serves a good *revuelto de bacalao y gambas* (scrambled eggs with cod and prawns). €€

Baeza

BAEZA is tiny, compact and provincial, with a perpetual Sunday air about it. At its heart is the Pza. Mayor – comprised of two linked plazas, Pza. de la Constitucíon at the southern end with a garden, and smaller Pza. de España to the north – flanked by cafés and very much the hub of the town's limited animation.

There are no charges to enter most of Baeza's monuments, but you may offer the guardian a small *propina* (tip).

Plaza de Leones

The **Plaza de Leones**, an appealing cobbled square enclosed by Renaissance buildings, stands slightly back at the southern end of Pza. de la Constitución. There's an ancient central fountain, while at its eastern flank is the former Audiencia (court house), now housing the *turismo*. Here, on a rounded balcony, the first Mass of the Reconquest is reputed to have been celebrated. The adjoining gate, the Puerta de Jaén, was a memento (or rebuke) left by Carlos V to the town that had opposed him and commemorates the Germanic ruler's procession through here in 1526, en route to marry Isabel of Portugal.

Palacio de Jabalquinto

C/Conde Romanones 1 • Free • 953 742 775

The finest of Baeza's mansions is the **Palacio de Jabalquinto**, now a seminary, which has an elaborate Gothic Hispano-Flemish (Isabelline) front showing marked Moorish influence in its stalactite decoration. Built in the fifteenth century by the Benavides family, the tranquil interior patio has a double tier of arcades around a central fountain and a superb Baroque **staircase** with fine carving.

Catedral de Santa María

Pza. de Santa María • Charge • 953 742 188

The rather squat sixteenth-century **Catedral de Santa María** is another design by Vandelvira (see opposite). Like many of Baeza and Úbeda's churches, it has brilliant painted *rejas* (iron screens) created in the sixteenth century by Maestro Bartolomé, the Spanish master of this craft. His work enclosing the choir, with depictions of a Virgin and Child accompanied by angels and cherubs, is stunning. In the cloister, part of the old mosque (which the church replaced) has been uncovered, but the Catedral's real novelty is a huge silver *custodia* – cunningly hidden behind a painting of St Peter, which whirls aside for a €1 coin.

ARRIVAL
BAEZA

By bus The bus station (953 740 469) is at the end of C/San Pablo and along C/Julio Burell.

By train The nearest train station is Linares-Baeza, 14km from Baeza and served by trains from Seville, Córdoba and Granada (note that there are few connecting buses; it's a €20 taxi ride). Most bus connections are via Úbeda.

INFORMATION AND ACTIVITIES

Turismo On Pza. de Leones, in the former Audiencia or court building (Mon–Fri 9am–7.30pm, Sat & Sun 9.30am–3pm; 953 779 982); you can pick up a map here, and they can also provide details of daily guided tours of the town.

Hiking There are some good walks around town; wandering up through the Puerta de Jaén on Pza. de los Leones and along the Paseo de las Muralla (aka Paseo de Don Antonio Machado) takes you round the edge of Baeza with fine views over the surrounding plains. You can cut back to Pza. Mayor via the network of narrow stone-walled alleys – with the occasional arch – that lies behind the Catedral.

ACCOMMODATION AND EATING

The town has a decent range of **places to stay**, some of which are architectural gems. There's usually no problem finding rooms in Baeza except during the summer *feria* in mid-August and even then you should have no trouble if you ring ahead. It's worth noting that many hotels have a weekend surcharge policy so if you can avoid a Friday-to-Saturday stay prices often fall considerably.

★ **Aznaitin** C/Cabreros 2, http://hostalaznaitin.com. Splendid *hostal* in the old quarter with stylishly decorated en-suite rooms. Friendly service, attractive pool and breakfast included adds up to an outstanding deal. Easy parking nearby or use their garage. Reduced rates Sun–Thurs. €€

Caseda Palacio de los Salcedo C/San Pablo 18, www.cetinahotels.com. Lovely converted sixteenth-century palace with slightly over-the-top Louis XV-style rooms with a/c, TVs, minibars and safes, with breakfast included. Interior rooms are gloomy but come with Jacuzzi. Reduced rates Sun–Thurs. €€

★ **Hotel Puerta de la Luna** C/Pintada Alta s/n, www.hotelpuertadelaluna.com. Beautiful four-star hotel situated in a refurbished seventeenth-century *casa palacio*. Facilities include two delightful patios, a restaurant, a library and a small pool. The comfortably furnished tiled-floor rooms are airy and well equipped, and it has its own car park. €€€€

Hotel TRH Ciudad de Baeza C/Concepción 3, http://en.trhbaeza.com. Well-equipped a/c rooms partly housed in a stylishly converted Renaissance monastery with a glassed-in patio. They do frequent cut-price deals so it's worth giving them a ring or checking the website. €€€€

K'Novas Pza. de España s/n, www.facebook.com/Knovas Baeza. This always-popular café is a great place to kick off your day with a lazy breakfast on the town's best terrace. Later on it serves good *tapas de autor* (signature tapas) such as *tortilla de gula* (eel omelette), *raciones* and *tostas* – try the partridge pâté toast with anchovies. €€

Palacio de Gallego C/Santa Catalina, http://palaciode gallego.com. Specializing in *asados* (roasted dishes) including meat, tuna and *almejas* (clams) on the barbecue, this is one of the best restaurants in town. Divided into a tapas bar and formal restaurant with pleasant terrace near the Catedral. €€

La Pintada C/Pintada Alta s/n, http://hotelpuertadelaluna.com. Part of the *Hotel Puerta de la Luna* (see page 305), the restaurant offers formal dining inside as well as on the patio. Traditional dishes include *espinacas baezanas* (Baeza-style spinach) and *solomillo de jabalí* (wild boar steak). €€€

Úbeda

ÚBEDA, 9km east of Baeza and built on the same escarpment overlooking the valley of the Guadalquivir, looks less promising when you reach it. Don't be put off by the modern suburbs, though, for hidden away in the old quarter is one of the finest architectural jewels in the whole of Spain, and perhaps even Europe. Follow the signs to the Zona Monumental and you'll eventually reach the **Plaza de Vázquez de Molina**, a tremendous Renaissance square and one of the most impressive of its kind on the peninsula. Most of the buildings around the square are the late sixteenth-century work of Andrés de Vandelvira, the architect of Baeza's Catedral and numerous churches in both towns. One of these buildings, the **Palacio de las Cadenas**, originally a palace for Felipe II's secretary, houses Úbeda's *ayuntamiento* and features a magnificent facade fronted by some monumental lions.

Capilla del Salvador

Pza. de Vázquez de Molina • Charge • 609 279 905

At the eastern end of Pza. de Vázquez de Molina, the **Capilla del Salvador**, erected by Vandelvira, though actually designed by Diego de Siloé, architect of the Málaga and Granada Catedrals, is the finest church in Úbeda. It's a masterpiece of Spanish Renaissance architecture with a dazzling Plateresque facade, its highlight a carving of the Transfiguration of Christ flanked by statues of San Pedro and San Andrés. Inside, the Transfiguration theme is repeated in a brilliantly animated *retablo* by Alonso de Berruguete, who studied under Michelangelo. Entry to the church is via a doorway on the south side.

San Pablo

Pza. del Primero de Mayo • Free • 953 750 637

The lovely square, Pza. del Primero de Mayo, is home to a bandstand and the superb arcaded sixteenth-century Ayuntamiento Viejo (Old Town Hall) from where councillors once watched heretics – denounced by the Inquisition – burn in fires located on the site of the modern bandstand. Here also is the idiosyncratic church of **San Pablo**, incorporating various Romanesque, Gothic and Renaissance additions and crowned by a Plateresque tower. It also boasts a thirteenth-century exterior and a superb portal.

ARRIVAL AND INFORMATION ÚBEDA

By bus The bus station (953 795 188) is on C/San José, west of the centre beyond the Hospital de Santiago.

By train The nearest train station is Linares-Baeza, 15km from Úbeda and served by trains from Seville, Córdoba and Granada (note there are few connecting buses; €25 taxi ride).

Turismo Housed in its own Renaissance mansion, the Palacio del Marqués de Contadero, C/Baja Marqués 4, just to the west of the Pza. de Vázquez de Molina; they can provide a town map.

ACCOMMODATION

You'll find the only budget **places to stay** within walking distance of the bus station, in the modern part of town. The *casco antiguo* (old quarter) has a choice of more upmarket places, some in stunning ancient palaces and mansions. Úbeda's high season is in April and May and thus hotel (but not *hostal*) rooms tend to be significantly cheaper in July and August. As in Baeza, many hotels apply a Friday-to-Saturday surcharge.

El Losal Cuesta El Losal 6–8, 686 644 963. Comfortable, clean and well-equipped apartments in a restored sixteenth-century mansion, a 5min walk north of the *ayuntamiento*. Guests have use of the lovely patio, gardens and pool. €

Hotel María de Molina Pza. del Ayuntamiento s/n, http://hotelmariamolina.com. In the heart of the old quarter, this hotel is housed in a magnificent sixteenth-century *casa palacio* with a superb patio. Rooms come with a/c, safe and satellite TVs, and some have balconies. €

Hotel El Postigo C/Postigo 5, http://hotelelpostigo.com. Located in the old quarter, this modern three-star hotel offers well-equipped rooms with satellite TVs, and a small pool in their terrace gardens with olive trees. Also has a library and huge log fire for winter days. €€

★ **Parador Condestable Dávalos** Pza. de Vázquez de Molina 1, http://parador.es. On arguably the most beautiful *plaza* in Andalucía, Úbeda's parador is housed in a fabulous sixteenth-century Renaissance mansion, with some of the well-appointed rooms overlooking the square. Call in for a drink if you're not staying. €€€€

EATING AND DRINKING

There are plenty of **places to eat** around Avda. Ramón y Cajal In the new town.

Asador Al-Andalus C/Los Canos 28, north of the old quarter, http://facebook.com/asador.alandalus. Just south of the bullring, this is a popular weekend venue serving local cuisine among Moorish decor. House specialities include *alcachofas salteadas* (braised artichokes) and *codillo de cerdo asado* (roast pork loin). €€€

Meson Gabino C/Fuente Seca 2, http://mesongabino.es. In a cave-like cellar with a wooden bar and earthenware pots, there's a rustic charm to this restaurant and a traditional menu to match. Highlights include the Andalusian blood sausage, the lamb chops, and the cheesecake. €€€

Navarro Pza. Ayuntamiento 2, 953 757 395. Overlooking the *ayuntamiento*, this bar serves tasty and reliably large portions of classic local dishes, such as *andrajos* (rabbit stew), *salmorejo* and *migas* (breadcrumbs with garlic and vegetables). €€

Parador Condestable Dávalos Pza. de Vázquez de Molina 1, http://parador.es. If you want to dine in style in the old quarter, try the parador's restaurant, which serves superbly prepared regional dishes such as *andrajos de Úbeda* (stew of cod, meat and vegetables) and *cordero guisado* (stewed lamb) that are available on a weekday menu. €€€€

Taberna Misa de 12 Pza. del 1a de Mayo 7, http://misade12.com. A square up from the Pza. del Ayuntamiento, this small bar serves tapas and *raciones* inside and on its pleasant shady terrace. Chargrilled meat is a speciality. €€

Cazorla

During the Reconquest of Andalucía, **CAZORLA** acted as an outpost for Christian troops, and the two castles that still dominate the town testify to its turbulent past – both were originally Moorish but later altered and restored by their Christian conquerors. Today, it's the main base for visits to the **Parque Natural de las Sierras de Segura y Cazorla**, a vast protected area of magnificent river gorges and forests. Cazorla also hosts the **Fiesta de Cristo del Consuelo**, with fairgrounds, fireworks and religious processions on September 16–21.

Cazorla itself is constructed around three main squares. Buses arrive in the busy, commercial **Pza. de la Constitución**, linked by the main C/Muñoz to the second square, **Pza. de la Corredera** (or *del Huevo*, "of the Egg", because of its shape). The *ayuntamiento* is here, a fine Moorish-style palace at the far end of the plaza. Beyond, a labyrinth of narrow, twisting streets descends to Cazorla's liveliest square, **Pza. de Santa María**, which takes its name from the old Catedral that, damaged by floods in the seventeenth century, was later torched by Napoleonic troops. Its ruins, now preserved, and the fine open square form a natural amphitheatre for concerts and local events as well as being a popular meeting place.

Museo de Artes y Costumbres
Pza. de Santa María • Charge

PARQUE NATURAL DE LAS SIERRAS DE SEGURA Y CAZORLA

Even casual visitors to **Parque Natural de las Sierras de Segura y Cazorla** are likely to see a good variety of wildlife, including *Capra hispanica* (Spanish ibex, a type of mountain goat), deer, mouflon, griffin and bearded vultures, and butterflies. Ironically, though, much of the best viewing will be at the periphery, or even outside the park, since the wildlife is most successfully stalked on foot, and walking opportunities within the park itself are surprisingly limited.

The main **information centre** inside the park is the Torre del Vinagre Centro de Interpretación (953 721 351). It's worth getting hold of a good **map** from here: the 1:100,000 map, *Parque Natural de las Sierras de Cazorla y Segura*, and the 1:50,000 version, *Cazorla*, are recommended, but best of all is the 1:40,000 set of map and guide packs to the Sierras de Cazorla and Segura (divided into two zones), published by Editorial Alpina, which are the most accurate maps available and detail *senderos* (footpaths), mountain-bike routes, refuges, campsites and hotels. In addition to the hiking routes marked on the maps above, Guy Hunter-Watts' *Walking in Andalucía* details six clearly described walks in the park of between 5km and 19km.

There's no public transport linking Cazorla with **Coto Ríos** in the middle of the park. Distances between points are enormous, so to explore the park well you'll need a car or to be prepared for long treks.

There are six official **campsites** plus seven designated camping areas throughout the park, which are accurately marked on the Editorial Alpina map. There's more accommodation at Coto Ríos, with three privately run campsites and a succession of *hostales*. Before setting out, you can also get the latest update on transport, campsites and accommodation from the *turismo* in Cazorla.

Cazorla's lower square, Pza. de Santa María, is dominated by **La Yedra**, an austere, reconstructed castle tower, which houses the **Museo de Artes y Costumbres**, an interesting folklore museum displaying domestic utensils, clothing, textiles and furniture from bygone times.

INFORMATION   CAZORLA

Turismo The *turismo* is at Pza. de Santa María s/n (http:// cazorla.es).

ACCOMMODATION

Outside August, finding a **place to stay** is usually no problem, as most visitors are either en route to, or leaving, the park. It's worth noting that outside the high summer months it can get quite chilly here in the evenings and while all the hotel rooms have heating, not all the *hostales* do.

Albergue Juvenil Pza. Mauricio Martínez 6, http://inturjoven.com. Cazorla's tidy youth hostel, housed in a former convent, has some double rooms and a pool, and is reached by following C/Juan Domingo (reached via steps) from Pza. de la Constitución. €

Camping Cortijo http://campingcortijo.com. Cazorla's campsite, with its stunning views of the town and surrounding mountains and plenty of shade, is located beyond the Castillo de la Yedra, 1km from the centre; to get there, follow the Camino San Isicio from the Pza. de Santa María. Closed Dec–Feb. €

Casa Rural Plaza de Santa María Callejón de la Pza. de Santa María, 630 435 663. Restored seventeenth-century mansion offering pleasant doubles with en-suite, a/c and heating. The house has several terraces with views of the castle and a garden courtyard with fountains. €

Hotel Guadalquivir C/Nueva 6, http://hguadalquivir.com. Central, charming and friendly small hotel offering comfy en-suite a/c rooms with TV. €

Hotel Puerta de Cazorla Avda. del Guadalquivir 49, http://hotelpuertacazorla.com. Just outside the centre (reached up a steep hill), this unassuming hotel comes with spotless en-suite rooms with a/c and TVs, and offers a wide range of park-based activities from guided hikes to 4WD excursions. €

Hotel Sierra de Cazorla 2km outside Cazorla, in the village of La Iruela, http://hotelspasierradecazorla.com. Modern complex comprising three- and four-star hotels plus a spa. The three-star option is particularly good value, with balcony rooms (best views from A10–A17) and scenic surroundings; there's also a restaurant, bar and great pool. It also produces its own walks guide for guests. €€

Parador El Adelantado 25km away in the park, http://parador.es. Somewhat featureless modern building made attractive by its wonderful woodland setting and swimming pool. Make sure to get a room with a view (rooms 4–11 and 18–22 are the ones to go for). It also has its own bar and restaurant. €€€

EATING AND DRINKING

Leandro C/Hoz 3, www.mesonleandro.com. Atmospheric and rustic restaurant awarded a Bib Gourmand by the Michelin Guide. The focus is on mountain game, with house specialities including venison grilled on a wood-fired range and a range of home-made burgers. €€

Mesón Don Chema Escaleras del Mercado 2, 953 710 529. Down steps off C/Muñoz, this is an economical restaurant specializing in *carnes de monte* (mountain game). Other specialities include *jamón ibérico* and *queso curado* (cured cheese). €€

Quinito Pza. Santa María 6, 853 890 268. This justifiably popular spot, overlooking a picturesque square, is an easy place to while away a couple of hours over generous tapas or *raciones* – the sherry-braised *guanciale* (pork cheek) is a house speciality. €€

★ **Restaurante La Yedra** C/Cruz de Orea 51, 953 710 292. One of the best restaurants in town, serving local dishes with a modern twist. Specialities include *pulpo con patata al ajo* (octopus with garlic potatoes) and *rin ran* (cream of vegetables with olives). €€€

Granada

If you see only one town in Spain, it should be **GRANADA**. For here, extraordinarily well preserved and in a tremendous natural setting, stands the **Alhambra** – the most exciting, sensual and romantic of all European monuments. It was the palace fortress of the Nasrid sultans, rulers of the last Spanish Moorish kingdom, and in its construction Moorish art reached a spectacular and serene climax. But the building seems to go further than this, revealing something of the whole brilliance and spirit of Moorish life and culture. There's a haunting passage, which the palace embodies:

"Life itself, which was seen elsewhere in Europe as a kind of probationary preparation for death, was interpreted [by the Moors] as something glorious in itself, to be ennobled by learning and enlivened by every kind of pleasure."

Jan Morris's book, *Spain*

Built on the slopes of three hills, the rest of the city basks in the Alhambra's reflected glory. Because the Moorish influence here was so ruthlessly extinguished following capitulation to the Catholic monarchs Fernando and Isabel, Granada tends to be more sober in character and austere in its architecture than Andalucía's other provincial capitals. Many visitors, once they've viewed the Alhambra, are too jaded or can't be fussed to take in the city's other sights, which is a pity, for Granada has much to offer. The hilltop **Albaicín**, the former Moorish town, is a fascinating quarter full of narrow alleyways and small squares, and a great place for an hour's stroll. Not far away, too, is the Catedral with the gem of the **Capilla Real** attached to it, the final resting place of the Catholic monarchs who ended Moorish rule in Spain. Add in **Moorish baths** and some fine churches, including the spectacular **La Cartuja** monastery, and you have more than enough to start you thinking about extending your stay.

The Alhambra

C/Real de le Alhambra • Charge • www.alhambra-patronato.es

The **Alhambra**, a treasure of Moorish Spain, is one of Spain's architectural wonders and its most-visited monument. There are three distinct groups of buildings on the Alhambra hill: the **Palacios Nazaríes** (Royal or Nasrid Palaces), the palace gardens of the **Generalife** and the **Alcazaba**.

Brief history

This Alcazaba, the fortress of the eleventh-century Ziridian rulers, was all that existed when the Nasrid ruler Ibn al-Ahmar made Granada his capital, but from its reddish walls the hilltop had already taken its name: *Al Qal'a al-Hamra* in Arabic means literally "the red fort". Ibn al-Ahmar rebuilt the Alcazaba and added to it the huge circuit of walls and towers that forms your first view of the castle. Within the walls he began a palace, which he supplied with running water by diverting the River Darro nearly 8km to the foot of the hill; water is an integral part of the

---

A WALK TO THE ALHAMBRA

The standard approach to the Alhambra is along the **Cuesta de Gomérez**, the semi-pedestrianized road that climbs uphill from Granada's central Pza. Nueva. The only traffic allowed to use this road are taxis and residents' vehicles. Should you decide to **walk** up the hill along the Cuesta de Gomérez (a pleasant 20min stroll from Pza. Nueva), after a few hundred metres you'll reach the **Puerta de las Granadas**, a massive Renaissance gateway erected by Carlos V. Here two paths diverge to either side of the road: the one on the right climbs up towards a group of fortified towers, the **Torres Bermejas**, which may date from as early as the eighth century. The left-hand path leads through the woods past a huge terrace fountain (again courtesy of Carlos V) to the main gateway – and former entrance – of the Alhambra. This is the **Puerta de la Justicia**, a magnificent tower that forced three changes of direction, making intruders hopelessly vulnerable. It was built by Yusuf I in 1340 and preserves above its outer arch the Koranic symbol of a key (for Allah the Opener) and an outstretched hand, whose five fingers represent the five Islamic precepts: prayer, fasting, alms-giving, pilgrimage to Mecca and the oneness of God. Enter here if you've got your ticket and want to visit the Alcazaba and Palacios Nazaríes. If you need to collect tickets or want to visit the Generalife first, note that the **entrance and ticket office** – at the eastern end, near to the Generalife – lie a further five-minute walk uphill, reached by following the wall to your left.

4

La Cartuja (1.2km) ◄   Hospital Clínico & 🚌 (9km)   Bus Station (2km), Jaén, Madrid,   Train Station (1km) ◄

Murcia ◄

ACCOMMODATION

AC Palacio de Santa Paula	15
Albergue Juvenil	20
Camping Granada	14
Camping Reina Isabel	18
Casa del Aljarife	8
Casa del Capitel Nazari	9
Casa Morisca	3
Hostal Costa Azul	16
Hostal Rodri	19
Hotel Albero	1
Hotel América	5
Hotel Casa 1800	6
Hotel Guadalupe	2
Hotel Los Angeles	13
Hotel Macía Plaza	12
Hotel Puerta de las Granadas	11
Parador de San Francisco	4
Pensión Landázuri	10
Santa Isabel la Real	7
U-Sense Granada Centro	17

EATING

Al Sur de Granada	8
Apecú	7
Bab Mansour	11
Bodegas Castañeda	10
El Carmen de San Miguel	6
Casa Cepillo	15
Casa de los Vinos	12
El Claustro	14
La Mimbre	1
Miss Sushi	13
Parador de San Francisco	2
Restaurante Las Tomasas	3
Restaurante León	9
Restaurante-Marisquería Cunini	16
Ruta del Azafrán	4
Sancho	17
El Trillo	5

SHOPPING

CNIG branch office (National Geographic Service)	1
El Corte Inglés	3
El Tiempo Perdido	4
Librería Dauro	2

SAN LUIS

ALBAICÍN

Casa del Chapiz

Iglesia del Salvador

Mirador de San Nicolás

S. Juan de los Reyes

Arco de las Pesas

San Bartolomé

Cvto. de la Concepción

Cvto. de Sta. Inés

San Cristóbal

MIRADOR DE ROLANDO

Palacio de Daralhorra

Cvto. de Sta. Isabel la Real

Casa de Porras

San José

PLAZA SAN MIGUEL BAJO

San Gregorio Bético

Iglesia de San Ildefonso

PLAZA DE LA MERCED

PLAZA DEL TRIUNFO

Puerta de Elvira

PLAZA DE LOS NARANJOS

ELVIRA

Jardines del Triunfo

GRAN VÍA DE COLÓN

PL. DE S. AGUSTÍN

Colegio de Niñas Nobles

SAN JUAN DE DIOS

MANO DE HIERRO

ARRIOLA

San Juan de Dios

Igl. de los Santos Justo y Pastor

S. Felipe Neri

SAN JERÓNIMO

Universidad

TRINIDAD

DUQUESA

PLAZA DE LA TRINIDAD

Colegio de San Bartolomé y Santiago

CONDE INFANTES

FÁBRICA VIEJA

PLAZA DE LOS LOBOS

Monasterio de San Jerónimo

0   200
metres

🚌 Airport (17km), ▼ Casa Museo Federico García Lorca (29km), Antequera & Málaga   20 ▼   13 & 14 ▼   ❹

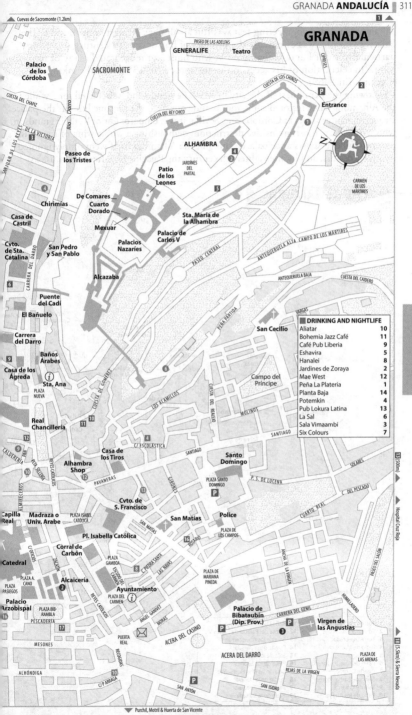

▲ Cuevas de Sacromonte (1.2km)

GRANADA

PASEO DE LAS ADELFAS

GENERALIFE **Teatro**

CUESTA DE LOS CHINOS

CIPRESES

P

Entrance

SACROMONTE

Palacio
de los
Córdoba

CUESTA DEL CHAPIZ

Río Darro

CUESTA DEL REY CHICO

DE LA VICTORIA

SAN JUAN DE LOS REYES

ALHAMBRA

JARDINES
DEL
PARTAL

**Paseo de
los Tristes**

**Patio
de los
Leones**

CARMEN
DE LOS
MÁRTIRES

Chirimías

De Comares
Cuarto Dorado

Mexuar

**Sta. María de
la Alhambra**

**Casa de
Castril**

**San Pedro
y San Pablo**

**Palacios
Nazaríes**

**Palacio de
Carlos V**

**Cvto.
de Sta.
Catalina**

CARRERA DEL DARRO

Alcazaba

PASEO CENTRAL

ANTEQUERUELA ALTA CAMPO DE LOS MÁRTIRES

**Puente
del Cadí**

El Bañuelo

ANTEQUERUELA BAJA

CUESTA DEL CAIDERO

PEÑA PARTIDA

VARGAS

**Carrera
del Darro**

San Cecilio

**Baños
Árabes**

**Casa de los
Ágreda**

Sta. Ana

PLAZA
NUEVA

CUESTA DE GOMÉREZ

LOS ALAMILLOS

CUESTA DEL REALEJO

**Campo del
Príncipe**

MOLINOS

SANTIAGO

■ DRINKING AND NIGHTLIFE	
Aliatar	10
Bohemia Jazz Café	11
Café Pub Liberia	9
Eshavira	5
Hanalei	8
Jardines de Zoraya	2
Mae West	12
Peña La Platería	1
Planta Baja	14
Potemkin	4
Pub Lokura Latina	13
La Sal	6
Sala Vimaambi	3
Six Colours	7

**Real
Chancillería**

CALDERERÍA

REYES CATÓLICOS

PEÑA SILLERA

ALMIRECEROS

C/ ESCOLÁSTICA

SANTIAGO

**Casa de
los Tiros**

GIRONÉS

SANTIAGO

**Santo
Domingo**

SOLARES

C. DEL PESCADO

**Alhambra
Shop**

PAVANERAS

PLAZA SANTO
DOMINGO
P

P. S. DE LUCENA

**Cvto. de
S. Francisco**

SAN MATÍAS

San Matías

Police

PLAZA DE
LOS CAMPOS

CUARTO REAL

**Capilla
Real**

**Madraza o
Univ. Árabe**

PLAZA ISABEL
CATÓLICA

Pl. Isabella Católica

ROSARIO

ANCHA DE LA VIRGEN

**Corral de
Carbón**

C/ PIEDRA SANTA

LAS NAVAS

Catedral

PLAZA
GAMBOA

Alcaicería

PLAZA A.
CANO

C/ CÓRDOVA

ZACATÍN

Ayuntamiento

PLAZA DEL
CARMEN

PLAZA DE
MARIANA
PINEDA

PASEO DEL SALÓN

PLAZA
PASIEGOS

**Palacio
Arzobispal**

PLAZA BIB-
RAMBLA

PESCADERÍA

REYES CATÓLICOS

ÁNGEL GANIVET

MORAS

**Palacio de
Bibataubín
(Dip. Prov.)**

CARRERA DEL GENIL

HUMILLADERO

**Virgen de
las Angustias**

MESONES

PUERTA
REAL

ACERA DEL CASINO

P

PLAZA DE
LAS ARENAS

ALHÓNDIGA

C/ P ARRIAGA

ACERA DEL DARRO

REJAS DE LA VIRGEN

SAN ANTÓN

SAN ISIDRO

▼ Purchil, Motril & Huerta de San Vicente

500m; Hospital Cruz Roja

(5.5km) & Sierra Nevada

4

Alhambra and this engineering feat was Ibn al-Ahmar's greatest contribution. The Palacios Nazaríes was essentially the product of his fourteenth-century successors, particularly Yusuf I and Mohammed V, who built and redecorated many of its rooms in celebration of his accession to the throne (in 1354) and the taking of Algeciras (in 1369).

Following their conquest of the city in 1492, **Fernando and Isabel** lived for a while in the Alhambra. They restored some rooms and converted the mosque but left the palace structure unaltered. As at Córdoba and Seville, it was **Emperor Carlos V**, their grandson, who wreaked the most insensitive destruction, demolishing a whole wing of rooms in order to build a Renaissance palace. This and the Alhambra itself were simply ignored by his successors, and by the eighteenth century the Palacios Nazaríes was in use as

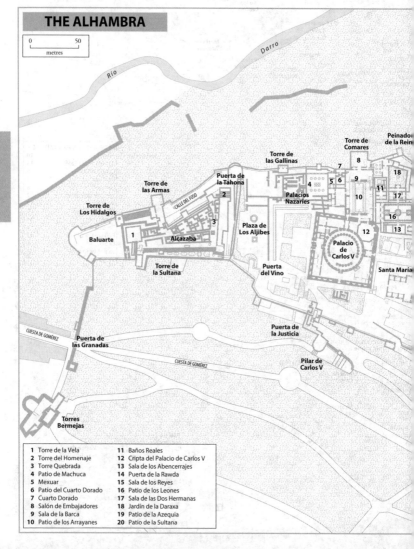

THE ALHAMBRA

1 Torre de la Vela	11 Baños Reales
2 Torre del Homenaje	12 Cripta del Palacio de Carlos V
3 Torre Quebrada	13 Sala de los Abencerrajes
4 Patio de Machuca	14 Puerta de la Rawda
5 Mexuar	15 Sala de los Reyes
6 Patio del Cuarto Dorado	16 Patio de los Leones
7 Cuarto Dorado	17 Sala de las Dos Hermanas
8 Salón de Embajadores	18 Jardín de la Daraxa
9 Sala de la Barca	19 Patio de la Azequia
10 Patio de los Arrayanes	20 Patio de la Sultana

a prison. In 1812, it was taken and occupied by **Napoleon's forces**, who looted and damaged whole sections of the palace, and on their retreat from the city tried to blow up the entire complex. Their attempt was thwarted only by the action of a crippled soldier (José García) who remained behind and removed the fuses; a plaque honouring his valour has been placed in the Pza. de los Aljibes.

Two decades later, the Alhambra's "rediscovery" began, given impetus by the American writer **Washington Irving**, who set up his study in the empty palace rooms and began to write his marvellously romantic *Tales of the Alhambra* (on sale all over Granada – and good reading amid the gardens and courts). Shortly after its publication, the Spaniards made the Alhambra a **national monument** and set aside funds for its restoration. This continues to the present day and is now a highly

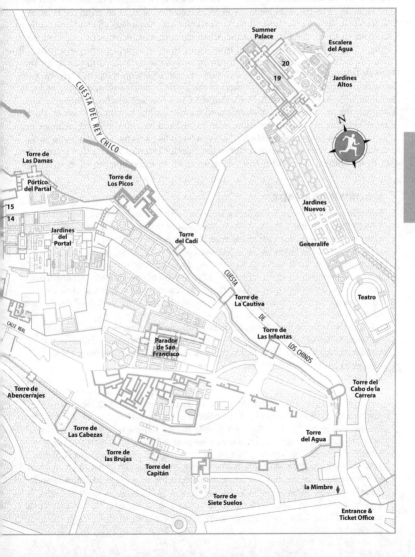

sophisticated project, scientifically removing the accretions of later ages in order to expose and meticulously restore the Moorish creations.

The citadel

Within the **citadel** stood a complete "government city" of mansions, smaller houses, baths, schools, mosques, barracks and gardens. Of this only the **Alcazaba** and the **Palacios Nazaríes** remain; they face each other across a broad terrace (constructed in the sixteenth century over a dividing gully), flanked by the majestic though incongruous **Palacio de Carlos V**.

The Alcazaba

The entrance to the Alhambra brings you into the complex at the eastern end, near to the Generalife gardens. However, as you will have a time slot for entering the Palacios Nazaríes (usually up to an hour ahead), it makes sense chronologically and practically to start your visit with the **Alcazaba** at the Alhambra's opposite, or western, end, entered through the **Puerta del Vino** – named from its use in the sixteenth century as a wine cellar.

The Alcazaba is the earliest and most ruined part of the fortress. At its summit is the **Torre de la Vela**, named after a huge bell on its turret, which until recent years was rung to mark the irrigation hours for workers in the *vega*, Granada's vast and fertile plain. It was here, at 3pm on January 2, 1492, that the Cross was first displayed above the city, alongside the royal standards of Aragón and Castile and the banner of St James. Boabdil, leaving Granada for exile in the Alpujarras, turned and wept at the sight, earning from his mother Aisha the famous rebuke: "Do not weep like a woman for what you could not defend like a man." To gain access to the Palacios Nazaríes you need to recross the **Pza. de los Aljibes**. In Nasrid times, this area was a ravine dividing the hill between the

---

MOORISH GRANADA

Granada's glory was always precarious. It was established as an independent kingdom in 1238 by **Ibn al-Ahmar**, a prince of the Arab Nasrid tribe that had been driven south from Zaragoza. He proved a just and capable ruler, but all over Spain the Christian kingdoms were in the ascendant. The Moors of Granada survived only through paying tribute and allegiance to Fernando III of Castile – whom they were forced to assist in the conquest of Muslim Seville – and by the time of Ibn al-Ahmar's death in 1275 theirs was the only surviving Spanish Muslim kingdom. It had, however, consolidated its territory (stretching from just north of the city down to a coastal strip between Tarifa and Almería) and, stimulated by refugees, developed a flourishing commerce, industry and culture.

By a series of shrewd manoeuvres Granada maintained its autonomy for two and a half centuries, its rulers turning for protection, in succession as it suited them, to the Christian kingdoms of Aragón and Castile and to the Merinid Muslims of Morocco. The city-state enjoyed a particularly confident and prosperous period under **Yusuf I** (r.1334–54) and **Mohammed V** (r.1354–91), the sultans responsible for much of the existing Alhambra palace. But by the mid-fifteenth century, a pattern of coups and internal strife became established and a rapid succession of rulers did little to stem Christian inroads. In 1479, the kingdoms of Aragón and Castile were united by the marriage of Fernando and Isabel, and within ten years they had conquered Ronda, Málaga and Almería. The city of Granada now stood completely alone, tragically preoccupied in a civil war between supporters of the sultan's two favourite wives. The Reyes Católicos made escalating and finally untenable demands upon it, and in 1490 war broke out. **Boabdil**, the last Moorish king, appealed in vain for help from his fellow Muslims in Morocco, Egypt and Ottoman Turkey, and in the following year **Fernando and Isabel** marched on Granada with an army said to total 150,000 troops. For seven months, through the winter of 1491, they laid siege to the city, and on January 2, 1492, Boabdil formally surrendered its keys. The Christian Reconquest of Spain was complete.

Royal Palace on one side, and the Alcazaba on the other. Following *la reconquista*, the ravine was filled in to hold two rainwater cisterns (*aljibes*) and the surface above laid out with fortifications. During the construction of Carlos V's palace in the sixteenth century, the area was cleared to create a parade ground, the rather desolate form it retains today.

The Palacios Nazaríes

It is amazing that the **Palacios Nazaríes** has survived, for it stands in utter contrast to the strength of the Alcazaba and the encircling walls and towers. It was built lightly and often crudely from wood, brick and adobe, and was designed not to last but to be renewed and redecorated by succeeding rulers. Its buildings show a brilliant use of light and space, but they are principally a vehicle for ornamental stucco decoration.

Arabic inscriptions feature prominently in the ornamentation. Some are poetic eulogies to the buildings and builders, others to various sultans (notably Mohammed V). Most, however, are taken from the Koran, and among them the phrase *Wa-la ghaliba illa-Llah* (There is no Conqueror but God) is tirelessly repeated. This became the battle cry (and family motto) of the Nasrids upon Ibn al-Ahmar's return in 1248 from aiding the Castilian war of Fernando III against Muslim Seville; it was his reply to the customary, though bitterly ironic, greetings of Mansur (Victor), ridiculing his role as a feudal puppet of the Christian enemy.

The palace is structured in three parts, each arrayed round an interior court and with a specific function. The sultans used the **Mexuar**, the first series of rooms, for business and judicial purposes. In the **Serallo**, beyond, they received embassies and distinguished guests. The last section, the **Harem**, formed their private living quarters and would have been entered by no one but their family or servants.

The Mexuar

The council chamber, the main reception hall of the **Mexuar**, is the first room you enter. It was completed in 1365 and hailed (perhaps formulaically) by the court poet and vizier Ibn Zamrak as a "haven of counsel, mercy, and favour". Here the sultan heard the pleas and petitions of the people and held meetings with his ministers. At the room's far end is a small oratory, one of a number of prayer niches scattered round the palace and immediately identifiable by their distinctive alignment (to face Mecca). This "public" section of the palace, beyond which few would have penetrated, is completed by the Mudéjar **Cuarto Dorado** (Golden Room), decorated under Carlos V, whose *Plus Ultra* motif appears throughout the palace, and the **Patio del Cuarto Dorado**. This has perhaps the grandest facade of the whole palace, for it admits you to the formal splendour of the Serallo.

The Serallo

The **Serallo** – the part of the complex where important guests were received – was built largely to the design of Yusuf I, a romantic and enlightened sultan who was stabbed to death by a madman while worshipping in the Alhambra mosque. Its rooms open out from delicate marble-columned arcades at each end of the long **Patio de los Arrayanes** (Patio of the Myrtles).

At the court's north end, occupying two floors of a fortified tower, is the royal throne room, known as the **Salón de Embajadores** (Hall of the Ambassadors). As the sultan could be approached only indirectly, it stands at an angle to the entrance from the Mexuar. It is the largest room of the palace, perfectly square and completely covered in tile and stucco decoration. Among the web of inscriptions is one that states simply "I am the Heart of the Palace." Here Boabdil signed the terms of his city's surrender to the Catholic kings, whose motifs (the arms of Aragón and Castile) were later worked into the room's stunning wooden dome, a superb example of *lacería*, the rigidly geometric "carpentry of knots". Here, too, so it is said, Fernando met Columbus to discuss his plans for finding a new sea route to India – which led to the discovery of the Americas.

4

The dome itself, in line with the mystical-mathematical pursuit of medieval Moorish architecture, has a complex symbolism representing the seven heavens. Carlos V tore down the rooms at the southern end of the court; from the arcade there is access (frequently closed) to the gloomy **Chapel Crypt** (*cripta*) of his palace, which has a curious "whispering gallery" effect.

The Harem

The **Patio de los Leones** (Court of the Lions), which has become the archetypal image of Granada, constitutes the heart of the **Harem**. The stylized and archaic-looking lions beneath its fountain (all now restored to their pristine marble glory) probably date, like the patio itself, from the reign of Mohammed V, Yusuf's successor; a poem inscribed on the bowl tells how much fiercer they would look if they weren't so restrained by respect for the sultan. The court was designed as an interior garden and planted with shrubs and aromatic herbs; it opens onto three of the palace's finest rooms, each of which looks onto the fountain.

The most sophisticated rooms in this part of the complex, apparently designed to give a sense of the rotary movement of the stars, are the two facing each other across the court. The largest of these, the **Sala de los Abencerrajes**, has the most startlingly beautiful ceiling in the Alhambra: sixteen-sided, supported by niches of stalactite vaulting, lit by windows in the dome and reflected in a fountain on the floor. This light and airy quality stands at odds with its name and history, for here Abu'l-Hasan (Boabdil's father) murdered sixteen princes of the Abencerraje family, whose chief had fallen in love with his favourite, Zoraya; the crimson stains in the fountain are popularly supposed to be the indelible traces of their blood, but are more likely to be from rust.

At the far end is the **Sala de los Reyes** (Hall of the Kings), whose dormitory alcoves preserve a series of unique paintings on leather. These, in defiance of Koranic law, represent human scenes; it's believed that they were painted by a Christian artist in the last decades of Moorish rule. The second of the two facing chambers on the court's north side, the **Sala de las Dos Hermanas** (Hall of the Two Sisters), is more mundanely named – from two huge slabs of marble in its floor – but just as spectacularly decorated, with a dome of over five thousand "honeycomb cells". It was the principal room of the sultan's favourite, opening onto an inner apartment and balcony, the **Mirador de Daraxa** (known in English as the "Eyes of the Sultana"); the romantic garden patio below was added after the Reconquest.

Beyond, you are directed along a circuitous route through **apartments** redecorated by Carlos V (as at Seville, the northern-reared emperor installed fireplaces) and later used by Washington Irving. Eventually you emerge at the **Peinador de la Reina**, or Queen's Tower, a pavilion that served as an oratory for the sultanas and as a dressing room for the wife of Carlos V; perfumes were burned beneath its floor and wafted up through a marble slab in one corner.

From here, passing the **Patio de la Lindaraja** (added in the sixteenth century – though the basin of its marble fountain was taken from outside the Mexuar), you reach the **Baños Reales** (Royal Baths). These are tremendous, decorated in rich tile mosaics and lit by pierced stars and rosettes once covered by coloured glass. The central chamber was used for reclining and retains the balconies where singers and musicians – reputedly blind to keep the royal women from being seen – would entertain the bathers. Entry is not permitted to the baths, though you can make out most of the features through the doorways. The visit route exits via the exquisite **Pórtico del Partal**, with the **Torre de las Damas** (Ladies' Tower) and elegant portico overlooking a serene pool. What appears no more than a garden pavilion today is in fact the surviving remnant of the early fourteenth-century Palace of the Partal, a four-winged structure originally surrounding the pool, the Alhambra's largest expanse of water. The **Jardines del Partal** lie beyond this, and the nearby gate brings you out close to the entrance to the Palacio de Carlos V.

Palacio de Carlos V

The grandiose **Palacio de Carlos V** seems totally out of place here, its austere stone-built architecture jarring with the delicate Oriental style and materials of the Moorish palace. Begun in 1526, it was never finished – the coffered ceilings of the colonnade were added only in the 1960s before which the Ionic columns had projected into open sky – as shortly after commissioning it, Carlos V left Granada never to return. Despite its incongruity the edifice is, however, a distinguished piece of Renaissance design in its own right, and the only surviving work of Pedro Machucha, a former pupil of Michelangelo.

Museo de Bellas Artes
Charge

On the palace's upper floor – reached by steps from a circular central courtyard where bullfights were once held – is a mildly interesting **Museo de Bellas Artes**. Here are displayed some notable examples of *andaluz* wood sculpture by seventeenth-century *granadino* Alonso Cano among others, as well as some vibrantly coloured abstract works by twentieth-century artist José Guerrero, who spent part of his life in New York and was influenced by American Expressionism.

Museo de la Alhambra
Free

The lower floor holds the **Museo de la Alhambra** (aka Museo Hispano-Musulman), a small but fascinating collection of Hispano-Moorish art, displaying many items discovered during the Alhambra restoration, including fine woodcarving and tile work. The star exhibit is a beautiful fifteenth-century metre-and-a-half-high **Alhambra vase** (Jarrón de las Gacelas), made from local red clay enamelled in blue and gold and decorated with leaping gazelles.

The Generalife

Paradise is described in the Koran as a shaded, leafy garden refreshed by running water where the "fortunate ones" may take their rest. It is an image that perfectly describes the **Generalife**, the gardens and summer palace of the sultans. Its name means literally "Garden of the Architect", and the grounds consist of a luxuriantly imaginative series of patios, enclosed gardens and walkways. It makes for an extremely interesting visit on your trip to the area.

By chance, an account of the gardens during Moorish times, written rather poetically by the fourteenth-century court vizier and historian Ibn Zamrak, survives. The descriptions that he gives aren't all entirely believable, but they are a wonderful basis for musing as you wander around the patios and fountains. There were, he wrote, celebrations with horses darting about in the dusk at speeds that made the spectators rub their eyes (a form of festival still indulged in at Moroccan *fantasías*); rockets shot into the air to be attacked by the stars for their audacity; tightrope walkers flying through the air like birds; and men bowled along in a great wooden hoop, shaped like an astronomical sphere.

Today, devoid of such amusements, the gardens are still evocative – above all, perhaps, the **Patio de los Cipreses** (aka Patio de la Sultana), a dark and secretive walled garden of sculpted junipers where the Sultana Zoraya was suspected of meeting her lover Hamet, chief of the unfortunate Abencerrajes. Nearby, too, is the inspired flight of fantasy of the **Escalera del Agua**, a staircase with water flowing down its stone balustrades. From here you can look down on the wonderful old Arab quarter of the Albaicín.

ARRIVAL AND DEPARTURE	THE ALHAMBRA
By bus A dedicated minibus service, the Alhambrabus (line #C3; daily 7am–11pm, every 5min; €1.20), departs from Pza. Isabel La Católica near the Catedral. This will drop you outside the Alhambra's entrance and ticket office.	**By car** To approach the Alhambra by car, use the signed route from the Puerta Real along the Paseo del Salón and the Paseo de la Bomba to the Alhambra's car park, close to the entrance and ticket office on the eastern edge of the complex.

On foot The standard approach to the Alhambra is along the Cuesta de Gomérez, the semi-pedestrianized road that climbs uphill from Granada's central Pza. Nueva (see box, page 309).

INFORMATION AND TICKETS

Information To check any changes to opening times, admission charges or booking procedures, visit the Alhambra's website www.alhambra-patronato.es.

TICKETS

Buying tickets in person To protect the Alhambra, only 6600 daily admissions are allowed. If you're buying tickets in person, you have three options: you can buy them at the Alhambra shop in town (C/Reyes Católicos 40; daily 9.30am–8.30pm), at the entrance (ticket office opens at 8am), where queues can be long, or by credit card from any ServiCaixa machine (several are located in a small building signed off the car park near the ticket office); insert your card into the machine and request a day and time. All tickets will state whether they are for morning (8.30am–2pm) or afternoon (mid-March to mid-Oct 2–8pm, mid-Oct to mid-March 2–6pm) sessions, and you must enter between the stated times (once inside, you may stay as long as you wish). However, you should bear in mind that tickets put on sale in the manners above are only what remain after prebooked ticket sales (see page 318), which could well mean in high season that no tickets are on sale at the entrance.

Buying tickets in advance To guarantee entry on a specific day it is strongly recommended you should book at least six weeks in advance, either online (http://tickets.alhambra-patronato.es) or by phone on 902 888 001 (24hr service). Tickets should then be collected at least 1hr before your time slot for the Palacios Nazaríes, allocated when booking (see page 315) from a ServiCaixa machine or the Alhambra ticket office. You will need your credit card and passport for identification. Concessionary tickets can only be collected from the Alhambra ticket office.

VISITING THE ALHAMBRA

The tickets have sections for each part of the complex – Alcazaba, Palacios Nazaríes, Generalife – which must be used on the same day. Note that you will not be allowed to enter the complex (even with pre-booked tickets) less than an hour before closing time. To alleviate the severe overcrowding that used to occur, tickets are stamped with a half-hour time slot during which you must enter the Palacios Nazaríes. You will not be allowed to enter before or after this time, but once inside the palace you can stay as long as you like: any waiting time can be spent in the Alcazaba, museums or the Generalife. Note, too, that the Museo de la Alhambra and the Museo de las Bellas Artes, both in the Palacio de Carlos V, have different hours and admission fees to those of the Alhambra. If you're planning to spend the day at the Alhambra, book a slot for the Palacios Nazaríes between 11.30am and 1.30pm. This allows you entry to the Alcazaba and Generalife at any time afterwards. An earlier or later time slot limits your access to the Alcazaba and Generalife to before 2pm or after 2pm respectively.

SPECIAL EVENTS

The Alhambra is also open for floodlit visits, limited to the Palacios Nazaríes, and occasional concerts are held in its courts (details from the *turismo*). Availability of tickets (which can be prebooked) is subject to the same terms as for daytime visits.

The Albaicín

The original Moorish town, where the first court was established in the eleventh century (and now a UNESCO World Heritage Site), the **Albaicín** stretches across a fist-shaped area bordered by the river, the Sacromonte hill, the old town walls and the winding C/Elvira (parallel to the Gran Vía de Colón). The best approach is along Carrera del Darro, beside the river. Coming from the Alhambra, you can make your way down the Cuesta de los Chinos – a beautiful path and a short cut.

Baños Árabes Al Andalus

C/Santa Ana 16 • Charge • http://hammamalandalus.com

Just to the east of Pza. Nueva behind the church of Santa Ana, the **Baños Árabes Al Andalus** gives you some idea of what a **Moorish bathhouse** would have been like when functioning. Here you can wallow in the graded temperatures of the re-created traditional baths – decorated with mosaics and plaster arabesques – or take tea in the peaceful *tetería* (tearoom) upstairs.

Casa de Castril

Carrera del Darro 43

Located on Carrera del Darro, the **Casa de Castril**, a Renaissance mansion, houses the town's **archeological museum**, currently closed indefinitely for restoration. To the side of the fine museum facade, C/Zafra ascends to the church of **San Juan** (which has an intact thirteenth-century minaret) and then, following a series of convoluted turnings, to the church of **San Nicolás**, whose square offers a stunning **view of the Alhambra**, considered the best in town.

El Bañuelo

Carrera del Darro 31 • Charge, free on Sunday • 958 027 900

The **Bañuelo** is a marvellous and little-visited Moorish public bath complex. Built in the eleventh century, the sensitively restored building consists of a series of brick-vaulted rooms with typical star-shaped skylights (originally glazed) and columns incorporating Visigothic and Roman capitals.

Sacromonte

To the east of the Albaicín is the gypsy cave-quarter of **Sacromonte**. Like many cities in Andalucía, Granada has an ancient and still considerable *gitano* population, from whose clans many of Spain's best flamenco guitarists, dancers and singers have emerged. They have traditionally lived in caves in this area, although these days the *barrio* is better known for its nightlife. If you wander up here in the daytime, take a look at the old **caves** on the far side of the old Moorish wall – most of them deserted after severe floods in 1962. There are fantastic views from the top. Sacromonte now has its own museum, the **Museo Cuevas del Sacromonte** (Barranco de los Negros s/n; charge; http://sacromontegranada.com) depicting the life and times of the *barrio*.

The Capilla Real

C/Oficios s/n • Charge • http://capillarealgranada.com/en/

In addition to Granada's Moorish legacy, it's worth the distinct readjustment and effort of will to appreciate the city's later Christian monuments, notably the **Capilla Real** (Royal Chapel), in the centre of town adjoining the Catedral at the southern end of Gran Vía de Colón. It's an impressive building, flamboyant late Gothic in style and built ad hoc in the first decades of Christian rule as a mausoleum for Los Reyes Católicos, the city's "liberators".

The tombs

The monarchs' **tombs** are as simple as could be imagined: Fernando (marked with a not-easily-spotted "F" on the left of the central pair) and Isabel, flanked by their daughter Joana ("the Mad") and her husband Felipe ("the Handsome"), resting in lead

---

PERSONAL SAFETY IN THE ALBAICÍN

Although you certainly shouldn't let it put you off visiting the atmospheric Albaicín quarter, it's worth bearing in mind that the area has been the scene of repeated **thefts** from tourists. To ensure that your visit is a happy one, take all the usual precautions: avoid carrying around large amounts of money or valuables (including airline tickets and passports – a photocopy of the latter will satisfy museums), and keep what you have in safe pockets instead of shoulder bags. If you do get something snatched, don't offer resistance; crime in these streets rarely involves attacks to the person, but thieves will be firm in getting what they want. Finally, try not to look like an obvious tourist (map/guidebook in hand is a dead giveaway) or flaunt expensive-looking photographic equipment or mobile phones, and keep to the streets where there are other people about, particularly at night.

coffins placed in a plain crypt. But above them – the response of their grandson Carlos V to what he found "too small a room for so great a glory" – is a fabulously elaborate **monument** carved in Carrara marble by Florentine Domenico Fancelli in 1517, with sculpted Renaissance effigies of the two monarchs; the tomb of Joana and Felipe alongside is a much inferior work by Ordoñez. In front of the monument is an equally magnificent **reja**, the work of Maestro Bartolomé of Jaén, and a splendid **retablo** behind depicts Boabdil surrendering the keys of Granada.

Isabel, in accordance with her will, was originally buried on the Alhambra hill (in the church of San Francisco, now part of the parador), but her wealth and power proved no safeguard of her wishes. The queen's final indignity occurred during the 1980s when the candle that she asked should perpetually illuminate her tomb was replaced by an electric bulb – it was restored in 1999 following numerous protests.

The Sacristy
In the Capilla's **Sacristy** is displayed the sword of Fernando, the crown of Isabel and her outstanding personal collection of **medieval Flemish paintings** – including important works by Memling, Bouts and van der Weyden – and various Italian and Spanish paintings, including panels by Botticelli, Perugino and Pedro Berruguete.

The Catedral
C/Gran Vila de Colón • Charge • 958 222 959

For all its stark Renaissance bulk, Granada's **Catedral**, adjoining the Capilla Real and entered from the door beside it, is a disappointment. It was begun in 1521, just as the chapel was finished, but was then left incomplete well into the eighteenth century. At least it's light and airy inside, though, and it's fun to go round putting coins in the slots to light up the chapels, where an El Greco *St Francis* and sculptures by Pedro de Mena and Martínez Montañés will be revealed.

LORCA'S GRANADA
One of the ghosts that walks Granada's streets and plazas is that of Andalucía's greatest poet and dramatist, **Federico García Lorca**, who was born in 1898 in Fuente Vaqueros, a village in the *vega*, the fertile plain to the west of the city. In the summer months the family – Lorca's father was a wealthy landowner – moved to the Huerta de San Vicente, now in the city suburbs but then a tranquil rural plot on the city's edge. Both sites can be visited.

HUERTA DE SAN VICENTE
C/Virgen Blanca s/n • Charge • http://huertadesanvicente.com • Southbound bus #C5 from Pza. Isabel La Católica or a taxi

Southwest of the centre, the **Huerta de San Vicente** comprises the house – with Lorca's bedroom – where he composed many of his best-known poems. The visit enables you to see the light and airy rooms and – in the poet's room – some original furniture including his work desk, bed and a poster of the Barraca theatre company which he helped to set up. When the Lorcas had it the house was surrounded by five acres of fruit trees and vegetable plots. Today it sits in the centre of what is claimed to be Europe's largest rose garden, Parque Federico García Lorca, the city's belated tribute.

CASA MUSEO FEDERICO GARCÍA LORCA
C/Poeta García Lorca 4 • Charge • http://patronatogarcialorca.org • Buses (hourly from 9am, last bus returns 9pm; 40min) leave from Avda. de Andaluces, fronting the train station

To the west of the city, in pleasant **Fuente Vaqueros**, is Lorca's birthplace, which has been transformed into a museum, the **Casa Museo Federico García Lorca**, and contains an evocative collection of Lorca memorabilia.

San Juan de Dios

C/San Juan de Dios s/n • Charge • 958 275 700

Northwest of the Catedral, ten minutes' walk along C/San Jerónimo, the Hospital of **San Juan de Dios**, with a pair of spectacular Renaissance patios, lies beyond a majestic portal. The inner patio has wonderful but sadly deteriorating frescoes depicting the San Juan's miracles. The hospital is still in use, but the porter will allow you a brief look. Next door, the hospital's church, a Baroque addition, has a Churrigueresque *retablo* – a glittering, gold extravaganza by Guerrero.

Monasterio de San Jerónimo

C/Rector López Argüeta 9 • Charge • http://realmonasteriosanjeronimogranada.com

The elegant Renaissance **Monasterio de San Jerónimo** was founded by the Catholic monarchs, though built after their death, with two imposing patios and a wonderful frescoed church. The largest of the patios (or cloisters in this context) is an elegant work by Diego de Siloé with two tiers of 36 arches. The church, also by Siloé, has been wonderfully restored after use as a cavalry barracks and has fabulous eighteenth-century frescoes.

La Cartuja

Pza. de Cartuja s/n • Charge • http://cartujadegranada.com • The monastery is a 10–15min walk from the Hospital of San Juan de Dios; bus line #C2, going north along the Gran Vía, also passes by

On the northern outskirts of town, **La Cartuja** is perhaps the grandest and most outrageously decorated of all the country's lavish Carthusian monasteries. It was constructed at the height of Baroque extravagance – some say to rival the Alhambra – and has a chapel of staggering wealth, surmounted by an altar of twisted and coloured marble.

ARRIVAL AND DEPARTURE | GRANADA

BY PLANE

The airport is 17km west of the city on the A92 *autovía*; buses connect with Pza. Isabel La Católica in the centre of town (10 daily; 30min). Buses run out to the airport from a stop on the east side of Gran Vía opposite the Catedral. Check with the website (http://siu.ctagr.es) for the latest timetable. Alternatively, a taxi costs about €25–30.

BY TRAIN

The train station (912 320 320) is 1km or so out on Avda. de Andaluces, off Avda. de la Constitución; to get into town, take bus #LAC, which runs direct to Gran Vía de Colón and the centre every 5min (€1.20). The most central stop is by the Catedral on the Gran Vía. Note that if you're travelling to Córdoba or Málaga the bus is much quicker and easier. Destinations Algeciras (3 daily, 4hr 30min); Almería (4 daily; 2hr 25min); Antequera (8 daily; 1hr 10min); 2hr 10min); Madrid (5 daily; 4hr); Ronda (3 daily; 2hr 50min); Seville (4 daily; 3hr 20min).

BY BUS

The city's main **bus station** is on Carretera de Jaén (958 185 480), some way out of the centre in the northern suburbs – bus #3 or #33 from outside will drop you near the Catedral (15min) – and handles all services except those to the Lorca museum at Fuente Vaqueros (see page 320). For departure information, check with the individual companies: Alsa (serving practically all destinations; http://alsa.es) and Empresa Tocina (serving the north side of the Sierra Nevada; http://autocarestocina.es). All terminals are on bus routes #SN1, #SN2 and #N5.

Destinations Alicante (5 daily; 5hr); Almería (7 daily; 2hr 15min); Cádiz (4 daily; 5hr); Cazorla (2 daily; 4hr); Córdoba (8 daily; 2hr 30min); Jaén (15 daily; 1hr 15min); Madrid (16 daily; 5hr); Málaga (15 daily; 1hr 45min); Mojácar (2 daily; 4hr 15min); Motril (14 daily; 1hr 15min); Seville (9 daily; 3hr); Lanjarón & Órgiva (3 daily; 1hr 30min; 2 daily to other villages in the Alpujarras); Pradollano (2 daily in winter, daily in summer; 45min); Valencia (5 daily; 5hr 45min); Úbeda/Baeza (9 daily; 2hr 30min).

BY CAR

Arriving by car you'll face the usual snarl-ups in the centre of town (try to time your arrival with the siesta) and the near-impossibility of finding on-street parking. You must also be careful not to enter the restricted-access central streets such as the Gran Vía, Recogidas and Reyes Católicos. If you ignore warning signs and enter these streets your number plate will be photographed and you will be fined at least €60 (unless your hotel is actually in one of these streets – no

4

exceptions are allowed).

Car parks are located at Puerta Real (down the right-hand side of the post office); La Caleta, near the train station; and on C/San Agustín, beneath the municipal market off the west side of Gran Vía near the Catedral. Long-term free street parking places are often to be found along Carrera del Genil and the Paseo del Salón, slightly southwest of the centre or across the bridges over the Genil to the southeast.

INFORMATION AND TOURS

Turismo The city's best and most efficient tourist office is the municipal tourist office at Pza. del Carmen s/n, inside the *ayuntamiento* (Mon–Sat 10am–8pm, Sun 10am–2pm; http://granadatur.com). They also have a sub-office in the Alhambra's ticket office (open same hours as the monument). The city's Junta de Andalucía *turismo*, C/Santa Ana 2 (Mon–Fri 9am–7.30pm, Sat & Sun 9.30am–3pm; 958 575 202), is up steps to the right of the church of Santa Ana off Pza. Nueva.

Granada City Tour A hop-on-hop-off electric train (http://granada.city-tour.com) takes in the main sights. The green route runs during the day and includes the Alhambra and Albaícin while the red nocturnal route excludes the Alhambra.

Guided walks Cicerone Granada's tours (English & Spanish; charge, under-14s free; book in high season; http://ciceronegranada.com) cover the city's major sights, including the Alhambra.

Listings The online *Guía Go* (http://laguiago.com/ granada) details most of what's happening on the cultural and entertainment front, as does the city's daily paper, *Ideal*, which is particularly good in its weekend editions.

ACCOMMODATION   SEE MAP PAGE 310

Granada has some of the most beautiful **hotels** in Spain, most noticeably in the atmospheric Albaícin but also along the Gran Vía, C/Reyes Católicos, in and around Pza. Nueva and Puerta Real and off Pza. del Carmen. The university zone, Pza. de la Trinidad (and east of here) is another good place to look, along with the semi-pedestrianized (taxis and residents only) Cuesta de Gomérez, which leads up from Pza. Nueva towards the Alhambra. In high season (April–June & Sept) and especially during Semana Santa (Easter Week), you should book as far ahead as possible.

All hotels have either their own **car park** or garage or can advise on finding a parking place. The main problem, almost anywhere, is **noise**, though the recently built road to the Alhambra, diverting traffic away from the centre, has made a big difference.

AC Palacio de Santa Paula Gran Vía de Colón 31, http:// marriott.com. Five-star hotel in three buildings including a fourteenth-century Moorish mansion and sixteenth-century convent. Some rooms include original stones, columns or Arabic inscriptions. Excellent restaurant and lovely patio that's part of the hotel bar, plus a sauna and all the trimmings you'd expect. €€€€

Albergue Juvenil Camino de Ronda 171, http:// inturjoven.com. Granada's youth hostel is conveniently close to the train station: turn left onto Avda. de la Constitución and left again onto Camino de Ronda. From the bus station, take bus #SN2 and get off at the stop after the railway bridge. It's efficiently run with facilities such as a laundry, lockers and towel hire, and all rooms are en-suite doubles; the staff are friendly but the food is institutional; it can also be booked up for days ahead in summer. €

Camping Granada Paraje, Cerro de la Cruz, http:// campinggranada.es. A restaurant, bar, laundry facilities and very welcome pool are among the amenities at this suburban campsite 8km north of central Granada, with pitches for tents and vehicles. €

Camping Reina Isabel 4km along the Zubia road to the southwest of the city, http://campingreinaisabel.es. This site, which has a pool, is less noisy and shadier than the *Sierra Nevada*, making a pleasant rural alternative. It can be reached by the Zubia-bound bus from the bus station. €

★ **Casa del Aljarife** Placeta de la Cruz Verde 2, http:// casadelaljarife.com. This welcoming upmarket Albaícin *hostal*, which occupies a restored sixteenth-century mansion near the heart of the *barrio*, has four lovely en-suite a/c rooms (two with Alhambra views) around a patio. The owner will meet you in nearby Pza. Nueva to guide you to the *hostal*. €€

★ **Casa del Capitel Nazari** Cuesta de Aceituneros 6, http://hotelcasacapitel.com. A beautiful sixteenth-century *palacio* transformed into an enchanting small hotel with elegant rooms overlooking a triple-tiered patio; superior doubles have an Alhambra view. Special offers in July, Aug and Nov–Feb can cut prices significantly. €€€

★ **Casa Morisca** Cuesta de la Victoria 9, http://hotelcasa morisca.com. Stunningly romantic small Albaícin hotel inside an immaculately renovated fifteenth-century Moorish mansion with exquisite patio; there are re-created Moorish furnishings throughout and room 15 (with Alhambra views) is the one to go for. Exterior rooms cost more. €€€

★ **Hostal Costa Azul** C/Virgen del Rosario 5, http:// hostalcostaazul.com. Friendly, central, small *hostal* with pleasant a/c en-suite rooms, and apartments for rent nearby. Has own restaurant next door. *Rough Guide* readers with this guide can claim a ten percent discount on rooms. €

Hostal Rodri C/Laurel de las Tablas 9, http://hostalrodri. com. Very comfortable, clean and quiet *hostal*, just off Pza. de la Trinidad near the Catedral. Owners can help with tourist information. €

Hotel Albero Avda. Santa María de la Alhambra 6, http://

hotelalbero.com. Excellent-value small hotel on the access road to the Alhambra to the south of the centre. Sparkling a/c rooms come with TV and some with balconies, and there's easy street parking. Ring if you have problems finding them (English spoken). €

Hotel América Real de la Alhambra 53, http://hotel americagranada.com. Charming one-star hotel in the Alhambra grounds; however, you're paying for location rather than creature comforts (a/c but no TVs) and prices are unjustifiably high. Booking essential. €€€

Hotel Casa 1800 C/Benalúa 11, http://hotelcasa1800. com. A stone's throw from the Paseo de los Tristes, this sixteenth-century restored mansion has a fine tiered patio. Romantic spacious rooms and deluxe suites have balconies with exceptional views of the Alhambra. Complimentary afternoon tea. €€€

Hotel Guadalupe Paseo de la Sabica s/n, http://eurostars hotels.co.uk/hotel-guadalupe.html. Comfortable and well-appointed hotel a stone's throw from the Alhambra's entrance – some of the a/c rooms have partial Alhambra views. Clients get reduced-rate parking in Alhambra car park, and the Alhambra bus from Pza. Nueva drops you nearby. Does frequent offers, and outside high season, rates drop by fifty percent. €€

Hotel Los Angeles Cuesta Escoriaza 17, http://hotel losangeles.net. Pleasant and good-value four-star hotel on a leafy, quiet avenue within easy walking distance of the Alhambra. All rooms come with a minibar and some with terrace balconies, and there's a garden, pool and car park. €€

Hotel Macía Plaza Pza. Nueva 4, http://maciahoteles. com. Centrally located hotel, with pleasant rooms overlooking an atmospheric square. If full, they can

recommend a couple of their other same-standard hotels nearby (see website for details). Exterior rooms cost more. €€€

Hotel Puerta de las Granadas Cuesta de Gomérez 14, http://hotelpuertadelasgranadas.com. Small, modern hotel on the way to the Alhambra with pleasant en-suite rooms with a/c, heating, TV and safe; the top two have Alhambra or Catedral views. €

Parador de San Francisco Real de la Alhambra, www. parador.es. Without question the most desirable – and most expensive – place to stay in Granada; a fifteenth-century converted monastery (where Isabel was originally buried) in the Alhambra grounds. We quote the cheapest standard room but suites (costing double this) have the best views. Booking (at least three months ahead) is essential. If you aren't staying, call in for a drink at the attractive terrace bar. €€€€

Pensión Landázuri Cuesta de Gomérez 24, http:// pensionlandazuri.com. Pleasant, good-value rooms, some en suite, plus its own bar and a roof terrace with a view of the Alhambra. €

Santa Isabel la Real Calle Sta. Isabel la Real 19, http:// hotelsantaisabellareal.com. This family-run hotel is set in a beautiful sixteenth-century casa in the heart of the Albaicín district. Just eleven rooms, many with original beams and terracotta tiled floors, are arranged around a typical Andalucian courtyard. €€

U-Sense Granada Centro Pza. de Bib-Rambla 4, www. urbansense.es. Inviting boutique hotel well located near the Catedral on an atmospheric square. A rooftop terrace looks out over the Alhambra and, beyond, the Sierra Nevada mountains. Within, rooms are modern and colourful, and the place generally has a vibrant, youthful atmosphere. €€

EATING
SEE MAP PAGE 310

When it comes to **restaurants**, Granada certainly isn't one of the gastronomic centres of Spain, possibly due in part to the *granadino* **tapas bars** that tempt away potential diners by giving out some of the most generous tapas in Andalucía – one comes "free" with every drink. A flavour of North Africa is to be found along **C/Calderería Nueva** and its surrounds in "Little Morocco", where you'll find health-food stores, as well as numerous Moroccan tearooms and eating places. This street is useful for assembling picnics for Alhambra visits, as is the ultramodern **Mercado Municipal** in Pza. San Agustín just north of the Catedral (Mon–Sat 8.30am–2pm). The warren of streets between **Pza. Nueva** and the **Gran Vía** has plenty of good-value places, particularly tapas bars, as does the area around **Plaza del Carmen** (near the *ayuntamiento*) and along C/ Navas. Another good location is the **Realejo**, home to lots of bars and restaurants with terraces, highly popular on summer nights.

TAPAS BARS
Al Sur de Granada C/Elvira 150, http://alsurdegranada. net. A thoroughly modern and very friendly bar-shop serving mostly organic breakfasts, sandwiches and salads. They stock over fifty local *granadino* wines and stage tastings plus exhibitions of work by local artists. Great stop for organic picnic food. €€

Bodegas Castañeda C/Almericeros 1, www.facebook. com/BodegasCastaNeda. Enjoyable – if very touristy these days – century-old tapas institution with some outdoor tables. Recommended tapas include pâté and cheese *tablas* ("boards" – on which they're served), *montaditos* (tapas on bread) and baked potatoes. €€

Casa de los Vinos C/Monjas del Carmen 2, http:// casadevinosgranada.es. Also known as "La Brujidera", this tiny establishment has one of Granada's best selection of Spanish wines. Sip your pick from over 150 while you sit in the all-wood interior or on the tiny outside terrace. *Tablas* of cold meat, cheese and pâté are decent value. €€

RESTAURANTS

CITY CENTRE AND ALBAICÍN

Apecú Pza. San Miguel Bajo 7, 623 177 053. This popular bar-restaurant is probably the best of the bunch on this atmospheric square. House specials include *lomo al Pedro Ximénez* (pork in sweet wine) and *albóndigas* (meatballs). €€

Bab Mansour C/Elvira 11, slightly west of Plaza Nueva, www.babamansour.com. In an atmospheric building characteristic of Calle Elvira's Little Morroco – stained-glass windows, low cushioned benches, lanterns and incense burners – this Moroccan restaurant serves delicious grilled shish kebabs, biryanis, and tagines. €€€

Casa Cepillo C/Pescadería 8, 615 059 368. Cheap and cheerful *comedor* with an excellent-value set menu; the soups are especially good. €

El Claustro Gran Vía 31, www.marriott.com. Part of the *Palacio de Santa Paula* hotel, this restaurant sits in the original sixteenth-century cloisters (outdoor dining in the courtyard also). The cuisine is ultramodern, however, giving a twist to local dishes. Try the *pulpo seco con setas* (dried octupus with wild mushroom) or the *lomo de ciervo* (venison fillet). Booking essential. €€€

★ **Restaurante Las Tomasas** Carril de San Agustín 4, http://lastomasas.com. Pricey restaurant with an international menu in a beautiful *carmen* with a stunning terrace view of the floodlit Alhambra at night. *Rodaballo a la bilbaína* (skate Bilbao-style) is a speciality. You can also nurse a *tinto de verano* and try the tapas if you don't want a full meal. €€€€

Restaurante León C/Pan 3, 958 225 143. This long-established restaurant serves many *carne de monte* (game) dishes, with a good-value set menu and mains. €€

★ **Restaurante-Marisquería Cunini** C/Pescadería 9, 958 250 777. One of Granada's most established and outstanding upmarket restaurants serving mainly fish. Also has a superb tapas bar attached. Booking advised. €€

El Trillo Callejón del Aljibe del Trillo 3, www.restaurante-eltrillo.com. Enchanting little mid-priced restaurant in an Albaicín *carmen* offering Basque-influenced cuisine: *arroz con jabalí y setas* (rice with wild boar and mushrooms) is their signature dish. The outdoor tables on a delightful garden patio are shaded by pear and quince trees. €€€

AROUND TOWN

★ **El Carmen de San Miguel** Pza. Torres Bermejas 3, http://carmensanmiguel.com. One of Granada's noted places to eat, with a fabulous terrace looking out over the city (book a frontline table). One of the restaurant's signature dishes, *cochinillo confitado a la vainilla* (suckling pig with vanilla), typifies its innovative approach (occasionally overdone) to *andaluz* cuisine. €€€

La Mimbre Paseo del Generalife s/n, http://restaurante lamimbre.es. With a delightful terrace shaded by willows (*mimbres*), this is one of the best of the restaurants on the Alhambra hill. The food – including *habas con jamón* (broad beans with ham) and braised oxtail – is good, but they are sometimes overwhelmed in high season. €€€

Miss Sushi Pza. del Padre Suárez 5, http://misssushi.es/ en. One of the city's most atmospheric restaurants is part of a Japanese-fusion chain, and forms part of the ground floor and basement of a fourteenth-century convent; some tables sit under the original water vats, and there's outdoor dining in the pleasant leafy square. Specialities include seared *tataki* tuna, yakitori burritos, and curry chicken gyozas. €€

Parador de San Francisco Alhambra, http://parador.es. The parador's restaurant is one of the best in an upmarket chain often noted for its blandness. There's a pleasant dining room plus a terrace with fine views, and regional specialities appear on a varied and not-too-bank-breaking menu. €€

Ruta del Azafrán Paseo del Padre Manjón 1, http:// rutadelazafran.com. Views of the Alhambra compete for diners' attention with the delicious food at this riverside restaurant. Moroccan dishes sit alongside Andalucian classics and Asian Fusion plates on the menu; don't miss the pork cheeks slow-cooked in red wine. €€€

Sancho C/Tablas 16, http://sanchooriginal.com. Reliable restaurant near Pza. de la Trinidad with a pleasant street terrace, and popular with locals. Serving hearty breakfasts and then grilled meat and salads later on. €€

DRINKING AND NIGHTLIFE
SEE MAP PAGE 310

When it comes to **flamenco**, finding anything near the real thing in Granada is not as easy as you might think. Shows in Sacromonte, traditionally the home of the city's flamenco performers, are generally shameless rip-offs and – unless you've heard otherwise from a knowledgeable source – to be avoided.

BARS AND CLUBS

Aliatar C/Recogidas 2, http://aliatar.es. Located in an old cinema, this is a huge dance venue where you can watch yourself on the giant screens while the DJs play the latest hits. Occasional live concerts and cocktail evenings on Friday and Saturday.

Bohemia Jazz Café Santa Teresa 17, http://facebook. com/bohemiajazzcafe. Relaxed jazz bar with cool sounds, and walls lined with photos and memorabilia.

Café Pub Liberia C/Duquesa 8, www.facebook.com/ liberiacafepub. Busy blues bar with live acts on Thursday evenings. Also has good pool tables.

Hanalei Piedra Santa 22. This popular place in the centre of town is a lively place for a cocktail, with a tiki theme, flaming drinks, and dancing.

Mae West C/Arabial s/n, http://maewestgranada.com. Nightclub in the Centro Comercial Neptuno with live gigs, stand-up comedians and disco music.

Planta Baja Horno de Abad, http://facebook.com/salaplantabaja. Long-established *discobar* – garage and lounge are big here – with plenty of live gigs.

★ **Potemkin** Pza. Hospicio Viejo s/n, http://facebook.com/potemkingranada. Great pint-sized *copas* bar with cool sounds (mainly first half of twentieth-century jazz) which also stages art exhibitions on its walls. A great feature here are the Japanese tapas and sushi nights (Wed & Sat).

Pub Lokura Latina C/Socrates 25, 644 926 635. *Discobar* popular with Latin American expats and tourists, with a focus on reggaeton, trap, salsa, and Latin music.

La Sal C/Santa Paula 11, 958 27 64 55. Originally a lipstick lesbian dance bar, this place is now attracting gay men too.

Six Colours C/Tendillas de Santa Paula 11, 958 203 995. With lots of action, this is probably the hottest LGBTQ+ venue in town, attracting a younger crowd than many of the other LGBTQ+ bars.

FLAMENCO

Eshavira C/Postiga de la Cuna 2, https://eshaviraclub.wordpress.com. Club and cultural association which specialises in flamenco fusion, with jazz a common point of crossover. A nice alternative to the touristy clubs.

Jardines de Zoraya C/de los Panaderos 32, http://jardinesdezoraya.com. Pretty good Albaicín café-restaurant that offers nightly flamenco shows often featuring big names. For the evening shows they offer a flamenco *cena* (dinner) which includes a three-course meal. Their terrace garden is also very attractive.

Peña La Platería Plazoleta de Toqueros 7, Albaicín, http://laplateria.org.es, http://facebook.com/plateriaflamenco. Private club devoted to the celebration of Andalucía's great folk art. There are frequent flamenco performances (Thurs or Sat are your best chances – check the club's Facebook page8), and visitors are generally welcomed so long as they show a genuine interest. You'll need to arrive between 9pm and 10pm, speak some Spanish and use a bit of charm.

Sala Vimaambi Cuesta de San Gregorio 30, Albaicín, http://vimaambi.com. A cultural and craft centre with frequent presentations of flamenco and *raíces* (roots) music from North Africa and South America. Concerts usually take place on Fri & Sat at 10pm, but not all are open to non-members. Ring or check their website for the current programme.

SHOPPING   SEE MAP PAGE 310   **4**

CNIG branch office (National Geographic Service) Avda. Divina Pastora 7. Sells a specialist selection of 1:500,000 and 1:25,000 maps.

El Corte Inglés Carrera del Genil 22, www.elcorteingles.es. Granada's branch of Spain's flagship department store has a good selection of Spanish food and wines in the basement supermarket.

El Tiempo Perdido C/Puentezuelas 49a, www.libreriaeltiempoperdido.com. "Lost Time" is a gorgeous antiques and bookshop, with a great selection of books on a wide variety of subjects, including a good English section.

Librería Dauro C/Zacatín 3, 958 224 521. This bookshop also sells maps of Granada and the surrounding area.

DIRECTORY

Hospital Cruz Roja (Red Cross), C/Escoriaza 8, 958 222 222; Hospital Clinico San Cecilio, Avda. del Doctor Olóriz, near the Pza. de Toros, 958 023 000.

Police For emergencies, dial 091 (national) or 092 (local). The Policía Local station is at Pza. de Campos 3, 958 808

502. There's also a property lost-and-found section in the *ayuntamiento* building on Pza. del Carmen (958 248 103).

Post office Puerta Real (Mon–Fri 8.30am–8.30pm, Sat 9.30am–1pm).

Parque Nacional Sierra Nevada

The mountains of the **Sierra Nevada**, designated Andalucía's second **national park** in 1999, rise to the south of Granada, a startling backdrop to the city, snowcapped for much of the year and offering good trekking and also skiing from late November until late April. The ski slopes are at **Pradollano**, an unimaginatively developed resort just 28km away from the city centre. From here, you can make the two- to three-hour trek up to **Veleta** (3400m), the second-highest peak of the range (and of the Iberian Peninsula); this is a perfectly feasible day-trip from Granada by bus.

The Sierra Nevada is particularly rich in **wild flowers**, with fifty varieties unique to these mountains. **Wildlife** abounds away from the roads; one of the most exciting sights is the Spanish ibex, *Capra hispanica*, that (with luck) you'll see standing on pinnacles, silhouetted against the sky. Birdwatching is also superb, with the colourful hoopoe – a bird with a stark, haunting cry – a common sight in the area.

The Veleta ascent

From the *Albergue Universitario*, 7.5km east of Pradollano ski resort (see below), the Capileira road (closed to vehicles) runs past the **Veleta**; asphalted, it is perfectly – and tediously – walkable. With your own transport, it's possible to shave a couple of kilometres off the walk to the summit by ignoring the no-entry signs at the car park near the *Albergue* and continuing on to a second car park farther up the mountain, from which point the road is then barred. Although the peak of the mountain looks deceptively close from here, you should allow two to three hours up to the summit and two hours down. There is no water en route so you'd be advised to take some along; the summit makes a great place for a picnic. Weather permitting, the **views** beyond the depressing trappings of the ski resort are fabulous: the Sierra Subbética of Córdoba and the Sierra de Guadix to the north, the Mediterranean and Rif mountains of Morocco to the south, and nearby to the southeast, the towering mass of **Mulhacén** (3483m), the Spanish peninsula's highest peak.

Pradollano

PRADOLLANO (aka Solynieve, "Sun and Snow"), which lies outside the boundaries of the national park, is a hideous-looking ski resort regarded by serious alpine skiers as something of a joke, but with snow lingering here so late in the year, it does have obvious attractions.

ARRIVAL AND DEPARTURE   PARQUE NACIONAL SIERRA NEVADA

By car To reach the Parque Nacional with your own transport, take the Acera del Darro and follow signs for the Sierra Nevada. Beyond the visitor centre, the route into the park continues for a further 10km to pass the Pradollano ski resort.

By bus Buses from Granada are operated by Autocares Tocina (http://autocarestocina.es) with a daily service to Pradollano

and the *Albergue Universitario*, where the bus terminates. Tickets should be bought in advance at the bus station, although you can pay on board if the bus isn't full. For the winter service (Oct–March), ring the bus company or check with the *turismo*.

INFORMATION

El Dornajo Parque Nacional Sierra Nevada Visitor Centre Ctra. de Sierra Nevada km 23 (http://sierranevada.es). Signposted just off the road, the main information centre sells guidebooks, maps and hats (sun protection is vital at this altitude), and has a permanent exhibition on the park's flora and fauna. They can provide hiking information (English spoken) and rent out horses and mountain bikes. The centre also has a stunning terrace view.

Maps The best map of the Sierra Nevada, including the lower slopes of the Alpujarras, is the one co-produced by the Instituto Geográfico Nacional and the Federación Española de Montañismo (1:50,000), generally available in Granada. A 1:40,000 map and guide set, *Sierra Nevada and La Alpujarra*, published in English by Editorial Alpina, is also good and comes with a booklet describing walks in the park and giving information on flora and fauna.

ACCOMMODATION

Albergue Juvenil C/Peñones 22, http://inturjoven.com. For budget accommodation, try the modern and comfortable *Albergue Juvenil*, on the edge of the ski resort, where you can get great-value (outside the Nov–March ski season) double and four-bed rooms, all en suite. They also rent out skis and equipment. €

Albergue Universitario Ctra de Sierra Nevada km 36, http://alberguesierranevada.com. In isolated Peñones de San Francisco, some 7.5km east of Pradollano, lies one

more (pricey) option: the *Albergue Universitario*, which has bunk rooms, doubles sharing bathrooms, and a restaurant. Ski and equipment hire also available. Half board (bed, breakfast and evening meal included). €€

Camping Las Lomas http://campinglaslomas.com. The only campsite in the area is at the Ruta del Purche, 15km out of Granada and halfway to Pradollano, with a supermarket and restaurant. The bus will drop you at the road leading to the site, from where it's a good 1km walk. €

Las Alpujarras

Beyond the mountains, farther south from Granada, lie the great **valleys of the Alpujarras**, first settled in the twelfth century by Berber refugees from Seville, and later the Moors' last stronghold in Spain.

The valleys are bounded to the north by the Sierra Nevada, and to the south by the lesser sierras of Lujar, La Contraviesa and Gador. The eternal snows of the high sierras keep the valleys and their seventy or so villages well watered all summer long. Rivers have cut deep gorges in the soft mica and shale of the upper mountains, and over the centuries have deposited silt and fertile soil on the lower hills and in the valleys; here the villages have grown, for the soil is rich and easily worked. The intricate terracing that today preserves these deposits was begun as long as two thousand years ago by Visigoths or Celtiberians, whose remains have been found at Capileira.

ARRIVAL AND DEPARTURE   THE ALPUJARRAS

By bus Buses are run by Alsa (http://alsa.es). There are four buses a day from Granada and one from Motril to Lanjarón and Órgiva, and one a day from Almería in the east. There are also buses from Granada (daily 8.30am, 2.30pm & 5pm) to Ugíjar (3hr 30min), in the "Low" Alpujarras, via a less scenic route through Lanjarón, Órgiva, Torvizcón, Cadiar, Yegen and Valor. A direct bus from Granada to the more spectacular "High" Alpujarras (noon & 4.30pm) runs via Trevélez to Bérchules (returns 5.50am & 5.05pm, passing Trevélez 6.15am & 5.30pm). The return buses arrive in Granada at 9.35am and 8.50pm respectively (there is another service from Trevélez to Granada at 4pm).

By car From Granada, the most straightforward approach to the Alpujarras is to take the Lanjarón turning – the A348 – off the Motril road (A44). Coming from the south, you can bear right from the road at Vélez de Benaudalla and continue straight along the A346 to Órgiva.

Lanjarón

The road **south from Granada to Motril** climbs steeply after leaving the city, until at 860m above sea level it reaches the **Puerto del Suspiro del Moro** – the Pass of the Sigh of the Moor. Boabdil, last Moorish king of Granada, came this way, having just handed

4

THE MOORS AND AFTER

When they came to occupy the Alpujarras, the **Moors** set about improving agricultural techniques and modified the terracing and irrigation in their inimitable way. They transformed the Alpujarras into an earthly paradise, and here they retired to bewail the loss of their beloved lands in **al-Andalus**, resisting a series of royal edicts demanding their forced conversion to Christianity. In 1568, they rose up in a final, short-lived revolt, which led to the expulsion of all Spanish Moors. Even then, however, two Moorish families were required to stay in each village to show the new Christian peasants, who had been marched down from Galicia and Asturias to repopulate the valleys, how to operate the intricate irrigation systems.

Through the following centuries, the land fell into the hands of a few wealthy families, and the general population became impoverished labourers. The Civil War passed lightly over the Alpujarras: the occasional truckload of Nationalist youth trundled in from Granada, rounded up a few bewildered locals and shot them for "crimes" of which they were wholly ignorant; Republican youths came up in their trucks from Almería and did the same thing. Under Franco, the stranglehold of the landlords increased and there was real hardship and suffering. Today, the population has one of the lowest per capita incomes in Andalucía, with – as one report put it – "a level of literacy bordering on that of the Third World, alarming problems of desertification, poor communications and a high degree of underemployment".

Ironically, the land itself is still very fertile – oranges, chestnuts, bananas, apples and avocados grow here – while the recent influx of **tourism** is bringing limited wealth to the region. The so-called "High" Alpujarras have become popular with Spanish tourists and also with migrants from northern Europe who have purchased property here; Pampaneira, Bubión and Capileira, all within half an hour's drive from Lanjarón, have been scrubbed and whitewashed. Though a little over-prettified, they're far from spoiled, and have acquired shops, lively bars, good, unpretentious restaurants and small, family-run **pensiones**. Other villages, less picturesque or less accessible, have little employment, and are sustained only by farming.

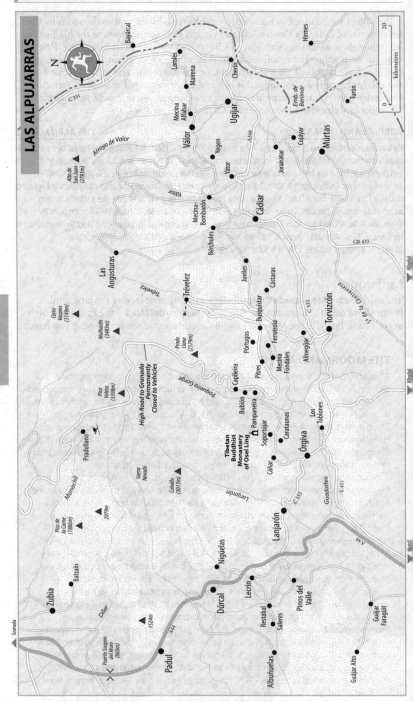

LAS ALPUJARRAS

over the keys of his city to the Reyes Católicos. From the pass you catch your last glimpse of the city and the Alhambra. Just beyond Béznar is the turning to **Lanjarón** and **Órgiva**, the market town of the region. **LANJARÓN** has been subject to tourism and the influence of the outside world for longer than anywhere else in the Alpujarras owing to the curative powers of its **spa waters**, sold in bottled form throughout Spain. However, the town itself is little more than a ribbon of buildings, mostly modern, flanking the road through the village, the Avda. Alpujarra, and its continuation, the Avda. Andalucía.

Balneario

http://balneariodelanjaron.com

Between February and December, the spa baths are open, and the town fills with the aged and infirm – should you wish to try a cure at the **Balneario** at the village's western end, note that a basic soak will cost €30, with add-ons for massage, mud baths and all kinds of other alarming-sounding *tracciones* and *inyecciones*.

The Moorish castle

Free

A ten-minute stroll below the main road – follow the signs down the hill from the main street and out onto the terraces and meadows below the town – and marking Lanjarón's medieval status as the gateway to the Alpujarras, is a **Moorish castle**, refurbished (although still in ruins) and with a dramatic setting.

ARRIVAL AND INFORMATION

LANJARÓN

By bus Buses stop at the two roundabouts at either end of the town and you can buy tickets on board or online from Alsa.

Turismo Opposite the Balneario, Avda. Andalucía s/n (Mon–Sat 10am–2pm & 4.30–8.30pm, Sun 10am–2pm; 958 770 462).

ACCOMMODATION AND EATING

Lanjarón has a good choice of **restaurants** and tapas bars, many attached to the hotels, which often offer good-value menus.

Asador Parque Avda. Alpujarra 44, http://asadorparque. com. Modern restaurant with pleasant terrace next to *Hotel España* set in the gardens of Palacete de la Duquesa de Santoña (in ruins). Specials include *habas con jamón* (broad beans with ham) and fried aubergines as well as salads and rice dishes. €€

★**Hotel Alcadima** C/Francisco Tarrega 3, http:// alcadima.com. The excellent *Hotel Alcadima* has the best pool and restaurant terrace in town, and many of the comfortable rooms boast stunning balcony views towards

the castle. €€

Hotel Castillo Alcadima C/Francisco Tarrega 3, http:// alcadima.com. Perhaps the best choice for dining out is the terrace restaurant of the hotel of the same name, which is a pretty perfect place to while away a summer evening with a superb view of the castle. Specialities include roast lamb and fish, though vegetarian possibilities include an *ensalada alpujarreña*. €€

Hotel España Avda. Alpujarra 42, http://hotelespana lanjaron.es. The grand-looking *Hotel España*, next door to the Balneario, has played host to Lorca and Manuel de Falla in its time. Slightly past its prime, it is nevertheless good value, very friendly and has a pool. B&B. €

WALKS FROM LANJARÓN

The countryside and mountains within a day's walk of Lanjarón are beyond compare. A track off the backstreets behind town takes you steeply up to the vast spaces of the **Reserva Nacional de la Sierra Nevada**. For a somewhat easier day's walk out of Lanjarón, go to the bridge just east of town and take the sharply climbing, cobbled track that parallels the **river**. After two to two and a half hours through small farms, with magnificent views and scenery, a downturn to a small stone bridge permits return to Lanjarón on the opposite bank. Allow a minimum of six hours and it would be wise to confirm with the *turismo* that the route is open before setting out.

Hotel Paris Avda. Alpujarra 23, http://hotelparislanjaron. com. A charming and very good value hotel B&B on the main street. Rooms come with TVs and there's a decent restaurant (guests only *menú del día* is great value) and a large pool. €

Órgiva

Heading east out of Lanjarón brings you after 11km to **ÓRGIVA** (also spelled Órjiva), the "capital" and market centre of the western Alpujarras. It is closer to the heart of the valley but is still really only a starting point; if the bus goes on to Capileira, you may want to stay on it. If you're **driving**, it's worth noting that petrol stations become scarcer from this point on.

Órgiva is a lively enough town, though, with plenty of bars and hotels and an animated **Thursday market** that draws in shoppers from far and wide. On the main street is an over-restored Mudéjar palace, now housing the *ayuntamiento*, and the sixteenth-century church of **Nuestra Señora de la Expectación**, whose towers add a touch of fancy to the townscape.

ACCOMMODATION AND EATING
ÓRGIVA

La Almazara C/González Robles 53, 958 784 628. Offers a range of hearty mountain dishes such as grilled meats and home-made burgers as well as excellent freshly made pizzas for €7–19. Also has a pleasant garden terrace. €€

Baraka C/Estación 12, http://teteria-baraka.com. An economical place worth seeking out in the upper town near the market, this is a pleasant small Moroccan-style café and *tetería* serving falafel, couscous, tagines and a variety of teas. €

Camping Órgiva Ctra. A348 km 18.9, http://camping orgiva.com. Órgiva's campsite, with ample shade plus a pool, bar and restaurant, lies 2km south of town, reached by continuing along the road where the bus drops you. It also rents out cabins and bungalows, has its own restaurant and pool, and can advise on walking routes and renting horses in the nearby Sierra de Lújar. €

Flor de Limonero at Taray Botánico Ctra A348 km18, http://ellimonerodelaalpujarra.com. Órgiva's best restaurant serves fusion food with the emphasis on local produce, particularly *carne a la brasa* (chargrilled meat) plus an excellent range of vegetarian and vegan options. €€

Posada Alpujarra Sol C/Veleta 11, 958 785 037. For budget accommodation, one of the nicest places is this self-catering option, opposite *Baraka*. You can rent the whole house (sleeps nine) or one of the clean and comfortable en-suite rooms. There's a roof terrace with a hot tub and barbecue. Minimum stay two nights. €

Taray Botánico Ctra A348 km18, http://hoteltaray.net/ en. Just over 1km along the A348 south of the town, this inviting three-star rural hotel is easier to get to with your own transport. The attractive rooms are surrounded by lovely gardens with a superb pool and there's also a bar-restaurant. They have frequent special offers. €€

The High (western) Alpujarras

The so-called High Alpujarras include the villages of Pampaneira, Bubión and Capileira, all picture-postcard places and hugely popular with Spanish and foreign visitors. The best way to experience the **High Alpujarras** (and get off the tourist track) is to walk, and there are a number of paths between Órgiva and Cadiar, at the farthest reaches of the western valleys. Equip yourself with a compass and the Instituto Geográfico Nacional/Federación Española de Montañismo 1:50,000 map or the Editorial Alpina map, which cover all the territory from Órgiva up to Bérchules (Alpina) and Berja (IGN/FEM) respectively. Alternatively, take a bus from Lanjarón (daily 11am and 1pm), which winds through all the upper Alpujarran villages. There are some excellent **walkers' guides** to the Alpujarras (see page 859).

Cánar, Soportújar and Carataunas

From Órgiva, the first settlements you reach, almost directly above the town, are **CÁNAR** and **SOPORTÚJAR**, the latter a maze of sinuous white-walled alleys. Like many of the High Alpujarran villages, they congregate on the neatly terraced mountainside, planted with poplars and laced with irrigation channels. Both villages are perched precariously on the steep hillside with a rather sombre view of Órgiva in the valley below, and the mountains of Africa over the ranges to the south.

Just below the two villages, the tiny hamlet of **CARATAUNAS** is particularly pretty and puts on a lively start to its Semana Santa on Palm Sunday, when an effigy of Judas is tossed on a bonfire.

Poqueira Gorge and around

Shortly after Carataunas the road swings to the north, and you have your first view of the **Poqueira Gorge**, a huge, sheer gash into the heights of the Sierra Nevada. Trickling deep in the bed of the cleft is the Río Poqueira, which has its source near the peak of Mulhacén. The steep walls of the gorge are terraced and wooded from top to bottom, and dotted with little stone farmhouses. Much of the surrounding country looks barren from a distance, but close up you'll find it's rich with flowers, woods, springs and streams.

A trio of villages – three of the most spectacular and popular in the Alpujarras – teeters on the steep edge of the gorge. The first is neat, prosperous and pretty **Pampaneira**. Nearby **Bubión** is backed for much of the year by snowcapped peaks. The village has a private **museum**, the Casa Alpujarreña (charge), just off Pza. de la Iglesia, the main square, displaying aspects of the folklore, daily life and architecture of the Alpujarras in a traditional house. Two kilometres north of Bubión, **Capileira** is the highest of the three villages and the terminus of the road – Europe's highest, but now closed to traffic – across the heart of the Sierra Nevada from Granada. The village's interesting **museum** (just downhill from the information kiosk; charge), contains displays of regional dress and handicrafts, as well as various bits and pieces belonging to, or produced by, Pedro Alarcón, the nineteenth-century Spanish writer who made a trip through the Alpujarras and wrote a (not very good) book about it.

Tibetan Buddhist Monastery of O Sel Ling

2km from Carataunas turn left (signed "Camino Forestal") and drive up the track for 6km • http://oseling.com

Between Soportújar and Pampaneira, on the very peak of the western flank of the Poqueira gorge, is the **Tibetan Buddhist Monastery of O Sel Ling** ("Place of Clear Light"), founded in 1982 by a Tibetan monk on land donated by the communities of Pampaneira and Bubión. The simple, stone-built monastery is complete with stupas and stunning **views** across the Alpujarras. Lectures on Buddhism are held regularly and facilities exist for those who want to visit for periods of retreat in cabins dotted around the site.

The Taha villages

Pitres and **Pórtugos**, 6km east of Pampaneira, are perhaps more "authentic" and less polished villages than in the High Alpujarras. Down below the main road (GR421) linking Pitres and Pórtugos are the three villages of Mecina Fondales (and its offshoot, Mecinilla), Ferreirola and Busquístar; along with Pitres, these formed a league of villages known as the *Taha* under the Moors. **Ferreirola** and **Busquístar** are especially attractive, as is the path between the two, clinging to the north side of the valley of the Río Trevélez. You're out of tourist country here and the villages display their genuine characteristics to better effect, while all around you is some of the best Alpujarran walking country.

Trevélez

TREVÉLEZ, at the end of an austere ravine carved by the Río Trevélez, is purportedly Spain's highest permanent settlement, with cooler temperatures year-round than its neighbours. In traditional Alpujarran style, it has lower, middle and upper quarters (*barrios bajo*, *medio* and *alto* – much more attractive names), overlooking a grassy, poplar-lined valley where the river starts its long descent.

Bérchules

Heading southeast from Trevélez, you come to **Juviles**, an attractive village straddling the road, followed, 5km further on, by **BÉRCHULES**, a high village of grassy streams and chestnut woods, also famous for its *jamón*. It is a large, abruptly demarcated settlement, three streets wide, on a sharp slope overlooking yet another canyon.

Cádiar

Just below Bérchules is **CÁDIAR**, the central town – or "navel" as the writer Gerald Brenan termed it – of the Alpujarras, more attractive than it seems from a distance, and a place that springs into life when a colourful **produce market** is held on the 3rd and 18th of every month. The annual **Fuente del Vino** wine and cattle fair (Oct 5–9) turns the waters of the fountain literally to wine.

ARRIVAL AND DEPARTURE

THE HIGH (WESTERN) ALPUJARRAS

By bus There are three daily buses to Capileira from Granada. In addition to this, anything going to Ugíjar and Berja will come very close to Capileira; buses to Granada and Órgiva pass by in the early morning with two in the late afternoon.

INFORMATION AND ACTIVITIES

PAMPANEIRA

Information and tours Nevadensis, on the main square, Pza. de la Libertad, is an information centre for the Natural and National Parks of the Sierra Nevada (http://nevadensis. com); they also sell large-scale topographical maps and offer guided treks, including an ascent of Mulhacén, and advice on weather conditions. Other activities include kayaking, climbing, canyoning and cross-country skiing.

BUBIÓN

Information Rustic Blue (http://rusticblue.com), a privately run information office on the main road to the right as you enter the village, can also book horseriding and walking tours and help with accommodation in fully equipped houses across the Alpujarras.
Horseriding For trips of five to seven days, contact the friendly Rancho Rafael Belmonte (http://ridingandalucia. com), at the bottom of the village near Rustic Blue, or the long-established Dallas Love (http://spain-horse-riding. com).

CAPILEIRA

Information A kiosk for the national park is at the centre of the village, near where the bus drops you. It hands out a village map and acts as an information office.
Hiking If you're thinking of doing any walking in this zone, this is probably the best village in which to base yourself.
Maps In addition to the information in the various villages, more fine walking routes are detailed in *34 Alpujarras Walks* by Charles Davis; *Landscapes of Andalucía* by John and Christine Oldfield; *Walking in Andalucía* by Guy Hunter-Watts; and *Holiday Walks in the Alpujarra* by Jeremy Rabjohns.

ACCOMMODATION

There are plenty of places to stay in the High Alpujarras but outside high summer make sure that the room heating is adequate as nights can be chilly.

PAMPANEIRA

Hostal Pampaneira C/José Antonio 1, http://hostal pampaneira.com. Homely B&B *hostal* above a bar-restaurant with functional en-suite rooms with TV and heating. €
Hotel Estrella de Las Nieves C/Huertos 21, 200m along the road climbing above the village, http:// estrelladelasnieves.com. This plush B&B hotel has well-equipped en-suite rooms, many with their own terrace balcony and spectacular views. Facilities include a garden pool and garage. €€

BUBIÓN

Las Terrazas Pza. del Sol 7, http://terrazasalpujarra.com. This is a comfortable and welcoming *hostal* with rustic tile-floored en-suite rooms with heating, many with views. It also rents out apartments and does a good-value breakfast. €
Los Tinaos C/Parras s/n, http://lostinaos.com. This option offers some excellent heated apartments that come with garden terraces, kitchens, satellite TVs and fine views. €

CAPILEIRA

Cortijo Catifalarga Ctra de Sierra Nevada s/n, http:// catifalarga.com. Some 500m beyond the *Ruta de Las Nieves* hotel and signed up a track on the left, this is a delightful hideaway with charming rooms and two apartments inside a traditional *alpujarreño cortijo*, along with fabulous views and a pool. Also has its own bar-restaurant. €
Finca Los Llanos Carretera Sierra Nevada s/n, http:// hotelfincaloslllanos.com. This is a relatively luxurious B&B option with spacious rooms with terraces; facilities include

a pool (at 1560m altitude) and good restaurant. €€
Hostal Atalaya C/Perchel 3, http://hostalatalaya.com.
To the right as you enter the village, this is a pleasant little
place with en-suite rooms with TVs and terrific views from
those at the front. €
Mesón-Hostal Poqueira C/Dr Castilla 11, http://
hotelpoqueira.com. Near the bus stop, this is a welcoming
option for en-suite heated rooms, some with terraces and
views, and there's also a pool and good restaurant with a
menu. It also has some attractive apartments sleeping up to
four for longer stays. €

PITRES
Balcón de Pitres Carretera Órgiva–Ugíjar km 51, http://
balcondepitres.com. Pitres' campsite, with restaurant and
pool, is located in a stunning position 1km west of the
village, with fine views. €
Cortijo Opazo Carretera Altarbéitar, Pórtugos, http://
cortijoopazo.com. This traditional farmhouse, 1.5km from
Pitres on the road to Pórtugos, has two cosy apartments
named after the mountain peaks opposite. Guests have
use of the large gardens and terrace, and owners can
offer advice on walks and activities in the area. Dinner is
available if booked 24 hours in advance. Minimum three
nights' stay. €€
Hotel San Roque C/Cruz 1, 958 857 528. On the east side
of the village, the B&B *Hotel San Roque* has decent rooms
with (on the south side) mountain views. €
Refugio Los Albergues Camino de Tavélez s/n, http://
refugiolosalbergues.weebly.com. Right on the eastern
edge of Pitres is this extremely charming low-slung stone
cottage, with a dormitory, one double room, and shared
bathroom and kitchen facilities. €

FERREIROLA
★ **Sierra y Mar** C/Albaycin 3, http://sierraymar.com.
A delightful Scandinavian-run B&B guesthouse in a
traditional mountain dwelling, with fine views and where
the owners – enthusiastic walkers – will advise on routes
in the area. €€

MECINA FONDALES
Hotel de Mecina Fondales C/La Fuente s/n, Mecina
Fondales, http://hoteldemecina.com. A delightful and
comfortable hideaway, where many rooms come with
terrace balconies and fine views. It also has an excellent
garden pool and can provide useful information about the
area and on renting horses and mountain bikes. €€

TREVÉLEZ
Camping Trévelez http://campingtrevelez.net. Trévelez's
campsite lies 1km out along the Órgiva road; conditions are
arctic in midwinter, but it also rents out some heated cabins. €
Hostal Fernando C/Pista del Barrio Medio s/n, 958 858 565.
Located in the *barrio medio*, this is a friendly place with good-
value heated en-suite rooms (useful outside of July & Aug). €
★ **Hotel La Fragua I, II** C/Antonio 4, barrio alto, http://
hotellafragua.com. With its pine-furnished en-suite heated
rooms, with TV and many with fine views, these two
hotels are the most pleasant places to stay in the village,
and there's also a pool. The place is popular with hiking
groups; check ahead to be sure of a room. The proprietors
can provide information on walking and other mountain
pursuits such as horseriding and mountain biking. They also
own a superb and justly popular restaurant (with veggie
options), see website for details. €

BÉRCHULES
Hotel Los Bérchules C/Bérchules, http://hotelberchules.
com. On the main road into the village, this two-star hotel
has comfortable rooms above its own restaurant, and
there's also a pool. €
El Mirador de Berchules Pza. de Zapata 1, 958 769 090.
In the upper village (ask for directions), this is an attractive
option for studios and apartments with terraces and views.
Also has its own good tapas bar, restaurant and pool. €€
El Vergel de Bérchules C/Baja de la Iglesia 5 y 14, http://
apartamentos-elvergeldeberchules.com. This new addition
is just below the church (as the street name implies) and
offers comfortable studios and apartments with kitchens,
salóns, TVs and woodstoves. Minimum two-night stay in
July & Aug. €

CÁDIAR
★ **Alquería de Morayma** 2km from Cádiar, http://
alqueriamorayma.com. The most tempting place to stay
here is an out-of-town option, 2km away along the A348
towards Torvizcón, where this excellent-value aparthotel
is housed in a converted *alpujarreño cortijo* (farmhouse)
sited in 86 acres of farmland. There are charmingly rustic
rooms and apartments (almost the same price), many with
patio terraces, and it has its own good restaurant (open to
nonguests). Guests can go mountain biking and horseriding,
and there are also plenty of hiking trails. The *Morayma's*
own organic farm and vineyard on the estate, the *bodega*
of which is open to visitors, also supplies the restaurant and
provides its virgin olive oil and bottled wine. €€

EATING AND DRINKING

PAMPANEIRA
Bar Belezmín Pza. Libertad 11, 958 763 102. On
Pampaneira's main square, this is one of the village's best

places to eat, with a menu filled with hearty *alpujarreño*
dishes such as *jabalí* (wild boar) and *perdiz* (partridge). €
Casa Julio Avda. de la Alpujarra 9, http://casa-julio.com.

4

Another place offering solid mountain fare accompanied with vegetables from its own *huerta* (vegetable garden). House specials include *potaje de hinojos* (fennel stew). €€

Ruta del Mulhacén Avda Alpujarra 6, http://rutadel mulhacen.es. At the entrance to the village, this restaurant has a marked Moorish theme in its Alhambra murals and a top terrace with exceptional views. *Potaje de hinojos* and *gachas pimentonas* (spicy "porridge") are house specials as is the *choto en salsa de almendra* (kid goat in almond sauce). €€€

BUBIÓN

Village fare includes *alpujarreño* specialities such as *migas* (breadcrumbs fried in garlic) and *plato alpujarreño* (a hefty fry-up).

Casa Angel C/Carretera 41, 649 155 001. A good option for solid mountain cooking (and home-made pizzas). €€

Teide C/Carretera s/n, http://restauranteteidebubion.com. This is the better of the two restaurants on the same side of the road here; there's a leafy terrace and a good-value weekday menu. €€

CAPILEIRA

Bar El Tilo C/Calvario 1, http://taberna-el-tilo.webnode. es. On the focal Pza. Calvario in the lower village, this is a decent place for *bocadillos* or *chacinería* (cured pork products) or simply for watching-the-world-go-by drinks on its tranquil terrace that's shaded by a lime tree. €

Bodega La Alacena C/Trocadero 1, 686 854 834. Downhill from *Bar El Tilo*, this is a popular option for *jamón* and cheese tapas and its shop also sells local products such as honey, wine, cheese and hams. €

El Jardin de los Sabores Carretera Sierra Nevada 16, 958 763 142. Cosy restaurant with well-prepared *alpurrajeño* specialities and Indian dishes – an unusual combination, but it works. Good vegetarian options. Has a pleasant garden terrace and a daily menu. €€

Restaurante Poqueira Near the bus stop, http://hotelespoqueira.es. This is a pleasant restaurant whose terrace has good views over the gorge, for *alpujarreño* specialities, such as soup and *choto al ajillo* (kid goat in garlic). €€

MECINA FONDALES

L'Atelier C/Alberca s/n, www.facebook.com/lateliervegrestaurant. Arguably the best place for food here is this French-run restaurant specializing in vegetarian/vegan cuisine, and located in the old village bakery in Mecinilla. Booking is advised at weekends. Also lets a couple of rooms, should you fancy staying after dinner. €€

TREVÉLEZ

Mesón La Fragua C/San Antonio s/n, http://hotellafragua. com. The hotel restaurant is Trevélez's best place to eat, serving well-prepared dishes in a rustic two-storey bar-restaurant. *Venao en salsa* (venison) and *cordero a la moruna* (lamb) feature among a wide range of specialities, and there are salads and vegetarian dishes, too. €€

Mesón Haraicel C/Real s/n just above the barrio bajo's main square, Pza. Francisco Abellán, www.facebook.com/mesonharaicel. Economical restaurant serving meat and fish dishes as well as salads; also offers tapas and *raciones* in its bar. Small outdoor terrace. €€

Mesón del Jamón C/Carcel 13, http://jamonestrevelez. com. Trevélez's *jamón serrano* is a prized speciality and an obsession throughout eastern Andalucía, and this is a good place to try it, along with *platos combinados*. €€

Mesón Joaquín C/Puente s/n, http://jamonestrevelez. com. In the lower *barrio*, this is another good bet for local *jamón*, which you can also purchase in larger quantities from its store opposite. The restaurant features *platos combinados*, and *solomillo de cerdo* (pork loin) is a house special. There's also a set menu. €€

BÉRCHULES

Abrasador Ctra A4130, on the way to Mecina Bombarón, http://elcercadoalpujarra.com. Part of the *El Cercado* apartment complex, this restaurant is one of the best places to eat in this part of the Alpujarras. The extensive menu includes local specialities plus grilled meats, including suckling pig; there's also a good-value tasting menu and weekday lunch *menú del día*. €€€

Eastern Alpujarras

Cádiar and Bérchules mark the end of the western Alpujarras, and a striking change in the landscape; the dramatic, severe but relatively green terrain of the Guadalfeo and Cádiar valleys gives way to open rolling and much more arid land. The villages of the eastern Alpujarras display many of the characteristics of those to the west, but as a rule they are poorer and much less visited by tourists. There are attractive places to visit nonetheless, among them **Yegen**, which Brenan wrote about, and the market centre of **Ugíjar**.

Yegen

In **YEGEN**, made famous by **Gerald Brenan**, some 7km northeast of Cádiar, there's a plaque on the house (just along from the central fountain) where the author lived during his ten or so years of Alpujarran residence. His autobiography of these times, *South from Granada*, is the best account of rural life in Spain between the wars, and describes the visits made here by Virginia Woolf, Bertrand Russell and the arch-complainer Lytton Strachey. Disillusioned with the strictures of middle-class life in England after World War I, Brenan rented a house in Yegen and shipped out a library of two thousand books, from which he was to spend the next eight years educating himself. He later moved to the hills behind Torremolinos, where he died in 1987, a writer better known and respected in Spain (he made an important study of St John of the Cross) than in his native England.

Brenan connections aside, Yegen is one of the most characteristic Alpujarran villages, with its two distinct quarters, cobbled paths and cold-water springs.

ACCOMMODATION AND EATING   YEGEN

Alojamientos Las Eras C/Carretera 39, http:// alojamientoslaseras.com. A reliable option for modern, fully equipped apartments decorated in typical local style. All feature an open fire in the living area, a TV and a terrace. €
Bar Pensión La Fuente Pza. de Fuente s/n, 958 851 067. Opposite the fountain in the square, this small B&B *hostal* offers rooms with bathrooms and has a bar decorated with some old photos of Brenan. Apartments are also available. The restaurant is a good breakfast option for nonguests too, and later in the day it serves tapas and *raciones* as well as

platos combinados and a daily menu. €
El Tinao C/Carretera 12, 616 644 677. Bright and airy en-suite rooms are on offer at this *hostal*, which is located on the main road; it also rents a couple of fully equipped houses in the village (three nights minimum). If you fancy eating here, Irish-born Loranne can cook whatever you fancy, but she specializes in local dishes, steaks with all the trimmings, and international dishes such as curries. Their set menu is very good value and varies day to day depending on seasonal ingredients. €

From the Alpujarras to Almería province

One way of entering Almería province from the Alpujarras is to take the A337 minor mountain road from Laroles (some 17k east of Yegen), which climbs dizzily and scenically to the **Puerto de la Ragua**, at 1993m Andalucía's highest all-weather pass. If you keep going straight on the **A92 autovía**, you'll meet the Almería–Sorbas road at what has become known as **Mini Hollywood** (see page 339), the preserved film set of *A Fistful of Dollars*. Alternatives are the winding A348 that eventually arrives at Almería city or the most straightforward route from Granada – and that followed by buses – via the *autovía*.

La Calahorra

Above La Calahorra • Charge

The main landmark, 16km beyond the town of Guadix, famous for its cave dwellings, is a magnificent sixteenth-century castle on a hill (15min hike) above the village of **La Calahorra**, one of the finest in Spain, with a remarkable Renaissance patio within. It's a private property and only available for viewing on Wednesday, but if you call the guardian the day before (avoiding siesta time, C/los Claveles 2, 958 677 098; Spanish only), he may be able to let you in.

ACCOMMODATION AND EATING   LA CALAHORRA

Hostal-Restaurante La Bella Carretera de Aldeire 1, http://hostallabella.com. In addition to en-suite rooms,

this place also has a decent restaurant with a good weekday menu. €

Almería province

The **province of Almería** is a strange corner of Spain. Inland, it has an almost **lunar landscape** of desert, sandstone cones and dried-up riverbeds. The coast to the east of the provincial **capital** is still largely unspoiled; lack of water and roads frustrated development in the 1960s and 1970s and even now, development is limited to small areas. This allowed the creation in the 1980s of the **Parque Natural de Cabo de Gata**, a haven for flora and fauna. To the west of Almería is another story, though, with a sea of plastic greenhouses spreading in a broad swathe for a good 30km across the Campo de Dalías, the source of much of Almería's new-found wealth.

A number of **good beaches** are accessible by bus, and in this hottest province of Spain they're worth considering during what would be the off season elsewhere, since Almería's summers start well before Easter and last into November. In midsummer, it's incredibly hot (frequently touching 38°C/100°F in the shade and often well above), while all year round there's an intense, almost luminous, sunlight. This and the weird scenery have made Almería one of the most popular **film locations** in Europe – much of *Lawrence of Arabia* was shot here, along with scores of spaghetti Westerns.

Almería

ALMERÍA is a pleasant, modern city, spread at the foot of a stark grey mountain in the heart of Almería province. Once you've seen the stunning Moorish Alcazaba, an austere Catedral and a wonderfully presented archeological museum there's not a lot left to do. Any time left over is probably best devoted to sampling the cafés, tapas bars and terrazas in the streets circling the Puerta de Purchena, the focal junction of the modern town, or strolling along the main Paseo de Almería down towards the harbour and taking day-trips out to the beaches along the coast. The city's own **beach**, southeast of the centre beyond the train lines, is long but nothing special.

The Alcazaba

C/Almanzor s/n • Charge • 950 801 008

At the summit of the stark, grey hill overlooking the city is a tremendous **Alcazaba**, probably the best surviving example of Moorish military fortification in Spain, with three huge walled enclosures, in the second of which are the remains of a mosque, converted to a chapel by the Reyes Católicos. In the eleventh century, when Almería was an independent kingdom and the wealthiest, most commercially active city of Spain, this citadel contained immense gardens and palaces and some twenty thousand people. Its grandeur was reputed to rival the court of Granada, but comparisons are impossible since little beyond the walls and towers remains, the last remnants of its stuccowork having been sold off by the locals in the eighteenth century.

From the Alcazaba, you get a good view of the coast, of Almería's **cave quarter** – the Barrio de la Chanca on a low hill to the left – and of the city's strange, fortified **Catedral**.

The Catedral

Pza. de la Catedral 8 • Charge • 669 913 628

Like the Alcazaba, the **Catedral**, in the heart of the old quarter, also has a fortress look about it. Begun in 1524 on the site of the great mosque – conveniently destroyed by the 1522 earthquake – it was designed in the late Gothic style by Diego de Siloé, the architect of the Catedral at Granada. Inside, the sober Gothic **interior** is distinguished by some superb sixteenth-century choir stalls carved in walnut by Juan de Orea and a stunning eighteenth-century altar. The church also contains a number of fine **pasos** of the Passion carried in the Semana Santa processions at Easter; among these, *El Prendimiento* (the Arrest of Christ) is outstanding.

Museo Arqueológico

Carretera de Ronda 91 • Charge • 950 016 256

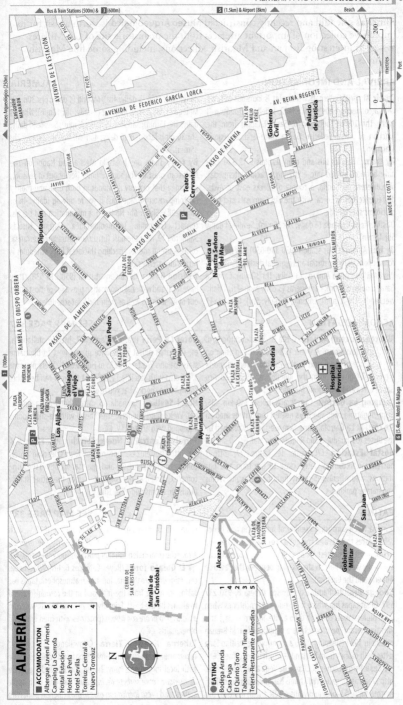

ALMERÍA

■ ACCOMMODATION
Albergue Juvenil Almería   5
Camping La Garrofa   6
Hostal Estación   3
Hotel La Perla   2
Hotel Sevilla   1
Torreluz Central &   4
Nuevo Torreluz

● EATING
Bodega Aranda   1
Casa Puga   4
El Quinto Toro   3
Taberna Nuestra Tierra   2
Tetería-Restaurante Almedina 5

Bus & Train Stations (500m) & 3 (600m)   5 (1.5km) & Airport (8km)   Beach

Museo Arqueológico (250m)
Gregorio Marañón

AVENIDA DE FEDERICO GARCÍA LORCA

Diputación

San Pedro

Teatro Cervantes

Gobierno Civil
Palacio de Justicia

PASEO DE ALMERÍA

RAMBLA DEL OBISPO ORBERA

Santiago el Viejo
Los Aljibes

Basílica de Nuestra Señora del Mar

PASEO DE ALMERÍA

Catedral

Ayuntamiento

Hospital Provincial

San Juan

Muralla de San Cristóbal

Alcazaba

Gobierno Militar

Port

Almería's splendid and recently constructed **Museo Arqueológico** is worth a visit for its impressive collection of important artefacts from the prehistoric site of Los Millares, as well as interesting Roman and Moorish collections, including some fine Moorish ceramics.

ARRIVAL AND INFORMATION

ALMERÍA

By air Almería's international airport is 8km out of town with a connecting bus service (#22, labelled "El Alquián") every 1hr 10min (between 6.45am–9.45pm) from the junction of Avda. Federico García Lorca and C/Gregorio Marañon.

By train Almería's bus and train stations (912 320 320) have been combined into a striking Estación Intermodal, on Carretera de Ronda, a couple of blocks east of Avda. de Federico García Lorca, with the bus terminals and train platforms side by side.

Destinations Granada (4 daily; 2hr 30min); Seville (4 daily; 5hr 45min).

By bus Almería's bus station (950 170 050) has frequent connections with provincial and regional destinations.

Destinations Agua Amarga (3 daily; 1hr 30min); Cabo de Gata (6 daily; 55min); Carboneras (3 daily Mon–Fri, 1 daily weekends; 1hr 15min); Córdoba (1 daily; 5hr); Granada (7 daily; 2hr); Jaén (3 daily; 4hr); Madrid (4 daily; 6hr 30min); Málaga (5 daily; 3hr); Mojácar (2 daily; 1hr 10min); Níjar (4 daily; 1hr 15min); San José (3 daily; 45min); Seville (4 daily; 5hr 30min); Tabernas (6 daily; 40min); Ugíjar (2 daily; 2hr 45min).

By ferry There are boats to Melilla and Nador on the Moroccan coast throughout summer (fewer out of season), a journey that can pay dividends in both time and money (in comparison to Algeciras) if you're driving (daily; 4h or 8hr Melilla, 5hr or 6hr Nador). For information and tickets, contact Compañía Trasmediterránea, Parque Nicolás Salmerón 19, near the port (http://armastrasmediterranea. com). A useful site for checking the latest ferry schedules is http://directferries.co.uk.

Turismo On Pza. de la Constitución (950 210 538). They have local and regional information plus a list of most buses out of Almería, as well as train and boat schedules.

ACCOMMODATION

SEE MAP PAGE 337

Albergue Juvenil Almería C/Isla de Fuerteventura s/n, http://inturjoven.com. A swish 150-double-room affair on the east side of town next to the Estadio Juventud sports arena; take bus #1 from the junction of Avda. Federico García Lorca and C/Gregorio Marañon. €

Camping La Garrofa Carretera Nacional 340 km 435, http://lagarrofa.com. The city's nearest campsite is sited on the coast at La Garrofa, some 5km west, easily reached by the buses to Aguadulce and Roquetas de Mar. €

Hostal Estación C/Calzada de Castro 37, http://hostalestacion.com. Situated close to the train and bus stations, and offering decently furnished en-suite rooms and garage parking. €

Hotel La Perla Pza. del Carmen 7, http://hotellaperla. es. The city's oldest hotel once played host to big-name stars making Westerns at Mini Hollywood. Offers pleasant a/c rooms with satellite TV; some at the rear can be rather cramped, so check what you're offered. €€

Hotel Sevilla C/Granada 25, http://hotelsevillaalmeria. net. Welcoming, modern, small hotel with en-suite rooms equipped with a/c and TV. €€

Torreluz Central & Nuevo Torreluz Pza. Flores 8 & 10, http://torreluz.es. One of the town's leading hotels contains good-value two- and four-star options in the same complex. Aimed at the corporate sector, the rather staidly furnished rooms underline this. €

EATING

SEE MAP PAGE 337

Almería has a surprising number of interesting and good-value places to **eat**, and you get a **free tapa with every drink**. Most of the best are around the Puerta de Purchena and in the web of narrow streets lying between the Paseo de Almería and the Catedral.

Bodega Aranda Rambla del Obispo Orbera 8, 950 237 597. Great tapas bar which fairly hums at lunchtimes when local professionals come to grab a bite. In former days this was the "sordid" *pensión* where a penurious Gerald Brenan put up in 1921 (sleeping six to a room) while waiting for a letter with money from England – which never came. €€

★ **Casa Puga** Corner of C/Lope de Vega and C/Jovellanos, http://barcasapuga.es. With hams hanging from the ceiling, marble-topped tables and walls covered with *azulejos*, this is an outstanding tapas bar – founded in 1870 – with a great atmosphere and loyal clientele; try the *atún en escabeche* (marinated tuna) or *pinchitos* (pork skewers). €€

★ **El Quinto Toro** C/Reyes Católicos 6, http://facebook. com/elquintotoroalmeria. Top-notch atmospheric tapas bar taking its name from the fifth bull in the *corrida* (reputed to always be the best). Friendly service and mouthwatering *patatas a lo pobre con huevo* (potatoes with fried egg) and other mains. €€

Taberna Nuestra Tierra C/Jovellanos 16, http://tabernanuestratierra.com. Great tapas and *raciones* made with local ingredients only; house specials include *tartar de arenque sobre sorbete de manzana* (herring with apple sorbet) and *presa ibérica con ajos negros* (Iberian pork with black garlic). €€

★ **Tetería-Restaurante Almedina** C/Paz 2, 697 932 911. Very friendly little Moroccan-run *tetería* which serves full meals later in the day, including couscous and chicken and lamb tagines. Stages live concerts of flamenco and North African music on Saturdays. €€

Mini Hollywood

Carretera Nacional 340A • Charge • http://minihollywoodoasys.com • Buses from Almería's Intermodal bus-train station to Tabernas stop at Mini Hollywood on the outward journey, but not on the return, so you need to get a taxi to Tabernas from Mini Hollywood

The N340a northwest from Almería towards Tabernas follows the Andarax riverbed before forking right into the badlands, an area which looks as if it should be the backdrop for a Hollywood Western. Just beyond the fork you discover that it has been just that: **Oasys Mini Hollywood** is a full-blown Western movie set, and a visit here is hard to resist – especially if you're travelling with kids. Once inside you can walk around the set of *A Fistful of Dollars* and various other spaghetti Westerns that were filmed here, and wander down Main Street into the *Tombstone Gulch* saloon for a drink. The fantasy is carried a step further with acted-out "**shows**" (noon & 5pm) – definitely the best times to visit – when actors in full cowboy rig blast off six-guns during a mock bank raid, or re-enact the "capture, escape and final shooting of Jesse James".

Further along the same road is another movie location, Fort Bravo (aka Texas Hollywood where an episode of *Doctor Who* was filmed in 2012), which has similar opening hours, prices and features (plus an Indian tepee village and Mexican town).

Níjar

Following the A7 east from Almería brings you, after 24km, to the turn-off for **NÍJAR**, famed throughout Andalucía for its pottery. A neat, white and typically Almerian town, with – in the upper *barrio* – narrow streets designed to give maximum shade, it makes for an interesting visit inland from the coast and Parque Natural de Cabo de Gata to the south.

Níjar is firmly on the tourist trail owing to the inexpensive **handmade pottery** manufactured in workshops and sold in the shops along the broad main street – Avda. García Lorca – and C/Real to the west, where many of the potters have their workshops. The more authentic artisans, however, are located in the **barrio alfarero**, along C/Real running parallel to the main street, where the workshops of Granados, El Oficio and the friendly, and cheaper, Angel y Loli (at no. 54, with traditional oven) are located; also, in a tiny street off the southern end of C/Real, is the studio-shop (named "La Tienda de los Milagros") of talented English ceramic artist Matthew Weir and his wife Isabel Soler, who dyes and weaves wool and silk. Níjar is known, too, for its *jarapas*: quilts, curtains and rugs made from rags, and widely on sale around the town.

INFORMATION

NÍJAR

Turismo At the junction of C/Real with Avda. García Lorca (June–Sept Mon–Sun 10am–2pm & 6–8pm; Oct–May Mon–Sat 10am–2pm & 4–6pm; 950 612 243, http://nijar. es); it can provide literature on the town and region.

ACCOMMODATION AND EATING

Bar La Glorieta Plaza de la Glorieta s/n, http://facebook. com/laglorietabarrestaurante. This friendly and popular little bar has an elevated terrace that offers decent tapas and an array of generous *raciones* – paella is also often on the menu here – as well as being a good place for a nightcap. €€
Cortijo La Alberca North of the town, Camino del Huebro, http://cortijolalberca.es. Homely B&B whose en-suite rooms have mountain views. €€
La Parada C/Lomas del Pilar, 636 379 612. A good stop for breakfast, lunch and sandwiches; it's on the right just as you start the climb to the upper square. They also offer a long list of tapas – you'll be spoilt for choice. €

The Costa de Almería

Almería's best **beaches** lie along its eastern coast, the Costa de Almería. Those to the west of the city, particularly surrounding the "ugly sisters" resorts of Aguadulce and Roquetas de Mar, have already been exploited, and what remains is rapidly being covered with *invernaderos*, or plastic tents, for fruit and vegetable production. In stark contrast, the eastern stretch of the Almerian coastline offers some of the most relaxing beaches left in Spain: half-abandoned fishing communities that have only begun to be promoted for tourists relatively recently. Outside the centres of **Mojácar** and **San José** development is low-key, and with a short walk along the coast you should be able to find plenty of relatively secluded spots to lay your towel.

El Cabo de Gata

The closest resort with any appeal is the modest **EL CABO DE GATA**, inside the **Parque Natural de Cabo de Gata**, where there is a long expanse of coarse sand. Six buses a day run between here and Almería. Arriving at El Cabo, you pass a lake, the **Laguna de Rosa**, protected by a conservation society and home to flamingos and other waders throughout the summer. Around the resort are plentiful bars, cafés and shops, plus a fish market. The beach gets windy in the afternoons, and it's a deceptively long walk eastwards to **Las Salinas** (The Salt Pans) for a couple of bar-restaurants and a café.

A few kilometres south, the **Faro de Cabo de Gata** (lighthouse) marks the cape's southern tip. There's also a **mirador** here from where you can get a great view of the rock cliffs and – on clear days – Morocco's Rif mountains.

INFORMATION   EL CABO DE GATA

Information In the lighthouse car park an information cabin has maps and information on the natural park.

ACCOMMODATION

Camping Cabo de Gata Carretera Cabo de Gata s/n, on the coast 2km northwest of the village, http://camping cabodegata.com. Decent campsite with reasonable, if not plentiful, shade and where facilities include a pool and restaurant. €

Hostal Las Dunas C/Barrio Nuevo 58, http://hostal lasdunas.com. Some 100m inland from the seafront, this friendly option has functional a/c en-suite rooms with TVs. €

San José

SAN JOSÉ is an established and popular family resort, set back from a sandy beach in a small cove, with shallow water. More fine **beaches** lie within easy walking distance and one of the best – Playa de los Genoveses – a kilometre-long golden strand, can be reached by a track to the southwest.

ARRIVAL AND INFORMATION   SAN JOSÉ

By bus San José is served by three daily buses to and from Almería, with a journey time of 45min.

By road Although it's possible to hike to the resort along a coastal track from the Faro de Cabo de Gata (lighthouse), this is now closed to vehicles. Going by road entails retracing your route to the resort of El Cabo de Gata and then following the inland road via the village of El Pozo de los Frailes.

Information On the main street, Avda. de San José, near the centre of the village, you'll find a Centro de Información for El Cabo de Gata natural park (http://cabodegata-nijar. com), which has lots of information on guided walks and horse treks, plus a complete list of accommodation.

ACCOMMODATION

Accommodation can be hard to come by in summer, but outside high season (July & Aug only) prices fall sharply.

Albergue Juvenil C/Montemar s/n, http://albergue sanjose.com. This privately run youth hostel has 86 places divided between rooms sleeping from two to six. It is usually booked solid at Easter and in August. €

Cortijo El Sotillo Carretera San José s/n, http://cortijo elsotillo.es. A kilometre from the centre, this refurbished eighteenth-century ranch house converted into a four-star country hotel has elegant rustically furnished rooms, an excellent mid-priced restaurant, bar, pool, tennis courts, and stables with horses for hire. €€€€

Hostal Brisa Mar C/Ancla s/n, http://hostalbrisamar.com. To the left of the main road as you come in, this is a bright and airy option with a/c en-suite balcony rooms with TVs and a small garden. €€

Hostal Sol Bahía C/Correos 5, http://solbahiasanjose.es. Near the main junction in the centre of the village, this is one of the better-value central places, offering spacious a/c en-suite balcony rooms with TV. €€

Hotel Doña Pakyta C/Correo s/n, http://playasycortijos. com. One of the swishest places in town, at the western end of the bay, offering light and airy terrace balcony rooms with four-star frills, stunning sea views and direct beach access. €€€€

Pensión Aloha C/Cala Higuera s/n, 950 611 050. Pleasant if spartan *hostal* with excellent a/c en-suite balcony rooms and the bonus of a fine palm-fringed pool at the rear; they also have a very good restaurant and tapas bar below. €€

EATING AND DRINKING

There are numerous **places to eat** around the beach and harbour zones, plus some well-stocked supermarkets. For fresh fish, try the restaurants overlooking the harbour.

4 Nudos Puerto Deportivo, http://4nudosrestaurante.com. This is a harbourside restaurant where rice dishes (e.g. *arroz con pulpo y almejas* – rice with octopus and clams) and fresh fish are house specials. It also does a few meat dishes and has a pleasant terrace. €€

Parroseta C/Correo 12, 611 679 688. Justifiably one of the most popular places in town, this laid-back restaurant specialises in rice in various forms, as is obvious from the vast paella dishes in a glass displau case, each containing one of the day's speicals. These include seafood mixes with clams and squid, classic rabbit paella, and vegertable dishes – you can order a small portion for one, or larger sharer servings. €€

Star of India C/Correo s/n, 602 110 105. Good Indian food is not always easy to find in Spain, but this place north of the town centre, near the roundabout, offers just that. There's a great selection of vegetarian food, with rich *dhals* and tasty *chana masala*, but there's also a good range of meat dishes, mainly focusing on familiar classics like chicken jalfrezi. €€

Los Escullos, La Isleta and Las Negras

The isolated and peaceful resort of **LOS ESCULLOS**, has a reasonable sandy beach fronted by a formidable eighteenth-century fort, the refurbished **Castillo de San Felipe**. Two kilometres farther east is **LA ISLETA**, another fishing hamlet, with a sleepy atmosphere and bags of charm. There's a rather scruffy village beach but a much better one a few minutes' walk away in the next bay to the east – the Playa la Ola.

LAS NEGRAS, 5km farther on, is another place with a decidedly Spanish feel, where there's a cove with a pebbly beach and a few bars and restaurants.

ACCOMMODATION — LOS ESCULLOS, LA ISLETA AND LAS NEGRAS

Arrecife C/Bahía 6, Las Negras, http://hotelesarrecife.es. This is an attractive and good-value *hostal* with a/c en-suite sea-view rooms and terrace balconies. €

Camping Los Escullos Los Escullos, http://losescullos cabodegata.com. Campsite set back from the sea with limited shade; facilities include bar-restaurant, pool and games courts. €

Casa Emilio Los Escullos, http://hostalcasaemilio.es. Close to the beach, this is a pleasant B&B *hostal-restaurante* offering a/c en-suite rooms with terrace balcony above a decent restaurant. €

Hostal Isleta de Moro La Isleta, http://laisletadelmoro. es. Overlooking the harbour, this *hostal* has reasonably priced en-suite balcony rooms with sea views, plus a popular bar-restaurant below for tapas and good fish meals. €

WeCamp Las Negras, https://wecamp.net. A glampsite set in a tranquil location with its own bay and reasonable shade, reached via a signed 1km road just outside the village. Facilities include mini-market, pool and bar-restaurant, and accommodation is in pre-erected bell tents with proper beds. €

Agua Amarga

AGUA AMARGA is a one-time fishing hamlet 10km north of Las Negras as the crow flies (though there's no direct road – you need to backtrack via the village of Fernan Pérez), that has transformed itself into a pleasant and easy-going resort. A fine sand EU-blue-flagged beach is the main attraction, and this is backed by a tasteful crop of villas. Agua Amarga is served by three daily direct **buses** from Almería.

ACCOMMODATION AND EATING — AGUA AMARGA

Apartamentos Caparrós C/Aguada 13, http:// apartamento-caparros.incostadealmeria.com/en. Four fully equipped apartments, sleeping up to five, around the resort, most only a few metres from the beach. Minimum

seven nights in July and August. €€
Family C/La Lomilla 6, http://familyaguaamarga.com.
The best-value place to stay is this welcoming French-run
B&B *hostal*, set back from the south end of the beach. It
has comfortable rooms (some small), a pool and a very
good French-Moroccan restaurant with an excellent-value
menu. €€
Hotel las Calas C/Desagüe 1a, 950 138 016, near *Hotel
Family*, http://hotellascalas.es. The restaurant of this hotel
offers pleasant dining on the beachfront terrace with a
selection of reasonably priced fish and rice-based dishes
such as *arroz con bogovante* (lobster) plus two menus. €€

Hotel El Tío Kiko C/Embarque 12, http://eltiokiko.com.
One of a clutch of luxury places here, this is a boutique
(adult-only mid-June to mid-Sept) B&B hotel with terrace
sea-view rooms arranged around a pool. €€€
Restaurante La Palmera C/Aguada 4, http://hostal
restaurantelapalmera.net/el-restaurante. With its terrace
fronting the beach this is another popular seafood
restaurant where paella features as a house special. €€
Los Tarahis C/Desagüe s/n, 950 138 235. With a sea-view
terrace, this is a decent place serving fish and *arroces* (such
as paellas) as well as salads. €€

Mojácar

MOJÁCAR is eastern Almería's main resort, hugely popular with Spaniards and foreign
visitors throughout summer. The coastal strip takes its name from the ancient hill
village that lies a couple of kilometres back from the sea – Mojácar Pueblo – a
striking agglomeration of white cubist houses wrapped round a harsh outcrop of
rock. In the 1960s, when the main Spanish *costas* were being developed, this was
virtually a ghost town, its inhabitants having long since taken the only logical step
and emigrated. The town's fortunes suddenly revived, however, when the local mayor,
using the popularity of other equally barren spots in Spain as an example, offered
free land to anyone willing to build within a year. The scheme was a modest success,
attracting one of the decade's multifarious "artist colonies", now long supplanted by
package-holiday companies and second-homers. The long and sandy **beach**, down
at the development known as Mojácar Playa, is excellent and the waters (like all in
Almería) are warm and brilliantly clear.

Mojácar Pueblo

MOJÁCAR PUEBLO is linked to the coastal resort 2km below by a road that climbs from
a prominent seafront junction called "El Cruce"; hourly **buses** also make the climb
from here until 11.30pm, after which it's a punishing hike or a taxi. The village is more
about atmosphere than sights, and once you've cast an eye over the heavily restored
fifteenth-century church of **Santa María**, the main diversion is to wander the narrow
streets with their flower-decked balconies and cascading bougainvillea, and call in at
the numerous boutiques and bars.

INFORMATION
MOJÁCAR

Turismo Pza. Fronton, opposite the church of Santa María
(Mon–Sat 9.15am–2pm & 4.30–7pm, Sun 9.15am–2pm;
902 575 130, http://mojacar.es). You'll need their free map
to negotiate the maze of narrow streets.

ACCOMMODATION AND EATING

Casa Minguito Pza. del Ayuntamiento s/n, 950 478 614.
This long-standing restaurant, with its pleasant terrace,
serves meat and fish dishes as well as a tasty paella for two;
their *menú del día* is very good. €€
La Ermita Pza.Nueva 1, http://facebook.com/www.
laermita.es. With a terrace and restaurant overlooking
the village, this is a friendly spot for salads, fresh fish (the
Garrucha prawns are particularly good) and grilled meats
including lamb chops and home-made burgers. €€
Hostal Arco Plaza Edificio Plaza, just off the main square,
http://hostalarcoplaza.es. Pleasant small *hostal* and a
reasonable deal for a/c en-suite rooms with TV. €

Hostal El Olivar C/Estación Nueva 11, http://hostalelolivar.
es. Clean and comfortable B&B *hostal* just round the corner
from the *turismo* offering en-suite rooms with a/c and TV.
The owners are friendly and helpful. €€
★ **El Palacio** Plaza del Cano s/n, southwest of the
church, http://alegria-hotels.com. Perhaps the *pueblo*'s
most creative restaurant combining Moroccan with
Mediterranean cuisine. The menu is reasonably priced
and includes signature dishes such as *pastela de ave* (fowl
pastela) and tagines. There's also a wonderful roof terrace
for alfresco dining and a charming, white-walled interior
room for cooler days. €€

Mojácar Playa

The beach resort of **MOJÁCAR PLAYA** is a refreshingly brash alternative to the upper village and caters to a mix of mainly Spanish tourists who fill its four-kilometre-long beach all summer. The busy road behind the strand is lined with hotels, restaurants and bars stretching north and south of the main junction, El Cruce, which is marked by a large *centro comercial*.

INFORMATION
MOJÁCAR PLAYA

Punto de información Small tourist office on the beach on El Cruce (http://mojacar.es). The *turismo*'s map also covers the coastal strip and is a useful aid to getting your bearings.

ACCOMMODATION AND EATING

There are plenty of *hostales* and hotels lining the seafront of Mojácar Playa and outside July and August prices fall by up to forty percent.

Camping El Quinto Carretera Mojácar-Turre s/n, 643 320 687. 2.5km or so inland, this is a good campsite with a pool, restaurant, live music, and comfortable bell tents. €

Casa Egea C/Las Ventanicas 127, 2km south of El Cruce, http://casaegea.com/en. On the seafront, this is a long-established and reliable restaurant specializing in fresh fish, seafood and local specialities such as stews. €€

Hostal El Palmeral Paseo Mediterráneo 433, http://hostalelpalmeral.com. Some 1.4km north of El Cruce. Clean en-suite rooms, cheerfully decorated although on the small side, with a/c and TV; most have sea views. Own parking. €€

Hotel El Puntazo Paseo Mediterráneo 257, http://hotelelpuntazo.com. One of the more established upmarket places for a/c sea-view terrace rooms, with minibars and safes. €€€€

Hotel Sal Marina Avda. del Mediterráneo 261, http://hotelsalmarina.com. South of El Cruce, this is a seafront hotel with very pleasant a/c balcony rooms with sea views. €€

4

Castilla y León and La Rioja

COVARRUBIAS

5 Castilla y León and La Rioja

The foundations of modern Spain were laid in the kingdom of Castile. Stretching north from Madrid, and incorporated within the modern *comunidad* of Castilla y León, it's a land of frontier fortresses – the *castillos* from which it takes its name – and a vast, fertile central plateau, the 700m to 1000m-high *meseta* that is given over almost entirely to grain. Beyond the historic cities, huge areas stretch to the horizon without a single landmark, not even a tree, though each spring a vivid red carpet of poppies decorates fields and verges. The Río Duero runs right across the province and into Portugal, with the river at the heart of one of Spain's great wine-producing regions, Ribera del Duero; another, more famous wine region lies to the north in the autonomous *comunidad* of La Rioja, whose vineyards line the banks of the Río Ebro.

It was Castile that became the most powerful force of the Reconquest, extending its domination through military gains and marriage alliances. By the eleventh century, Castile had merged with and swallowed León; through Isabel's marriage to Fernando in 1469 it encompassed Aragón, Catalunya and eventually the entire peninsula. The monarchs of this triumphant age were enthusiastic patrons of the arts, endowing their cities with superlative monuments, above which, quite literally, tower the great Gothic cathedrals of **Salamanca**, **León** and **Burgos**. These three cities are the major draws of the region, though in **Valladolid**, **Zamora** and even unsung **Palencia** and **Soria** you'll find outstanding reminders of the glory days of Old Castile. But equally in many lesser towns – notably **Ciudad Rodrigo**, **El Burgo de Osma** and **Covarrubias** – you'll be struck by a wealth of art, architecture and monuments.

Outside the main population centres, the sporadic and depopulated villages, bitterly cold in winter, burning hot in summer, are rarely of interest. That said, there are a few enclaves of mountain scenery, from the **Sierra de Francia** in the deep southwest to the lakeland of the **Sierra de Urbión** in the east. Moreover, the **wine region** of La Rioja has charms that go way beyond its famous product – the likeable provincial capital of **Logroño** is known for its lively tapas bars, while high in the Riojan hills are the little-known mountain villages and monasteries that reward the intrepid driver.

The final feature of the region is the host of Romanesque churches, monasteries and hermitages, a legacy of the **Camino de Santiago**, the historic pilgrim route from the Pyrenees to Santiago de Compostela. It cuts through La Rioja and then heads west across the upper half of Castilla y León, taking in the great cathedral cities of Burgos and León, but also many minor places of great interest, from **Frómista** in the central plains to **Astorga** and **Villafranca del Bierzo**.

Salamanca

SALAMANCA is the most graceful city in Spain. For four centuries it was the seat of one of the most prestigious universities in the world and at the intellectual heart of the burgeoning Spanish crown's enterprise – the *conquistador* Hernán Cortés and St Ignatius of Loyola were students, and Columbus came here in 1486 in an initially unsuccessful attempt to persuade a university commission of enquiry to back his exploration plans. City and university declined in later centuries, and

LA RIOJA

Highlights

❶ Universidad de Salamanca The graceful university buildings of Salamanca are an essential first stop in this most captivating of cities. See page 354

❷ Museo Nacional de Escultura, Valladolid The finest collection of Renaissance sculptures in Spain – housed in a magnificently restored monastic church. See page 369

❸ Logroño's lively tapas scene The capital of La Rioja has a tapas scene that rivals any of the big cities in Spain. See page 385

❹ La Rioja's monasteries Take a fantastic mountain drive to the wine region's peerless monasteries. See page 389

❺ Burgos Catedral The tourist crowds can't dull the appeal of this extraordinary masterpiece of Gothic art. See page 391

❻ Covarrubias The Gothic church, white half-timbered houses and numerous flower boxes make this small town quaint and very charming. See page 396

❼ León's architecture Marvel at the city's stunning array of architecture, from Gaudí's newly opened Casa Botines to the Convent of San Marcos. See page 401

❽ Las Médulas The devastation wreaked by Roman gold mining created an eerily captivating landscape. See page 412

HIGHLIGHTS ARE MARKED ON THE MAP ON PAGE 348

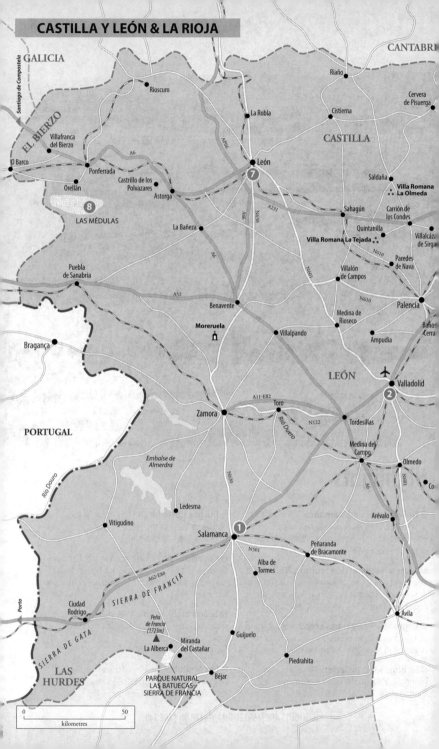

CASTILLA Y LEÓN & LA RIOJA

GALICIA

CANTABRI

EL BIERZO

CASTILLA

Santiago de Compostela

Rioscuro

Riaño

Cervera
de Pisuerga

Villafranca
del Bierzo

La Robla

Cistierna

O Barco

Ponferrada

León
7

Saldaña

Villa Romana
La Olmeda

Orellán

Castrillo de los
Polvazares

Astorga

Sahagún

Carrión de
los Condes

8

LAS MÉDULAS

La Bañeza

Quintanilla

Villalcázar
de Sirga

Villa Romana La Tejada

Paredes
de Nava

Puebla
de Sanabria

Villalón
de Campos

Palencia

A52

Benavente

Medina de
Rioseco

N610

Baños
Cerra

Moreruela

Villalpando

Ampudia

Bragança

LEÓN

PORTUGAL

Valladolid
2

A11-E82

Toro

Zamora

Río Duero

Tordesillas

N122

Medina del
Campo

Olmedo

Co

Embalse de
Almerdra

Ledesma

Arévalo

Vitigudino

Salamanca
1

N501

Peñaranda
de Bracamonte

Alba de
Tormes

Ávila

A62-E80

SIERRA DE FRANCIA

Ciudad
Rodrigo

Peña
de Francia
(1723m)

Guijuelo

Porto

SIERRA DE GATA

La Alberca

Miranda
del Castañar

Piedrahíta

Béjar

LAS
HURDES

PARQUE NATURAL
LAS BATUECAS-
SIERRA DE FRANCIA

0   50

kilometres

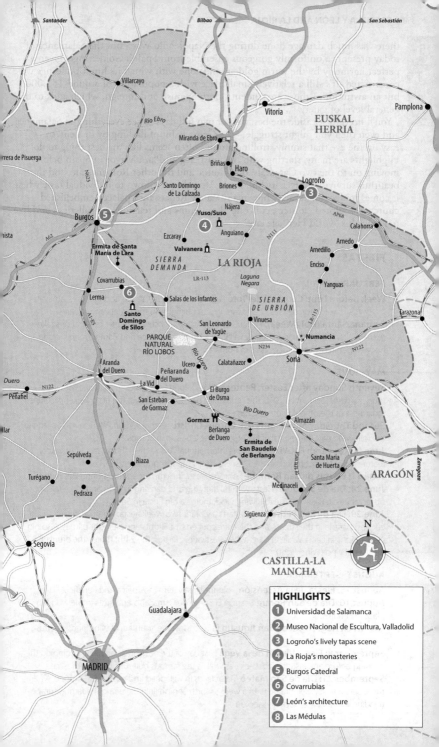

HIGHLIGHTS

1 Universidad de Salamanca

2 Museo Nacional de Escultura, Valladolid

3 Logroño's lively tapas scene

4 La Rioja's monasteries

5 Burgos Catedral

6 Covarrubias

7 León's architecture

8 Las Médulas

5

there was much damage done during the Napoleonic Wars, but the Salamanca of today presents a uniformly gorgeous ensemble from Spain's Golden Age, given a perfect harmony by the warm golden sandstone with which its finest buildings were constructed. It's still a relatively small place with a population of around 155,000 but an awful lot of those are students, both Spanish and foreign, which adds to the general level of gaiety.

You'll need to set aside the best part of two full days to see everything in Salamanca, and even then you might struggle – time has a habit of flashing by in a city so easy on the eye that simply strolling around often seems like the best thing to do. Highlights are many, starting with the most elegant Plaza Mayor in Spain before moving on to the two Catedrals, one Gothic and the other Romanesque, and the beautiful surviving university buildings. After this, it's down to individual taste when it comes to deciding exactly how many stately Renaissance palaces, embellished churches, sculpted cloisters, curio-filled museums and religious art galleries you'd like to see in this World Heritage city.

FIESTAS

FEBRUARY–APRIL

Week before Lent: Carnaval del Toro Particularly lively in Ciudad Rodrigo, the Carnaval (http://carnavaldeltoro.es) sees bull-running and bullfights in the streets and squares.
Semana Santa (Holy Week): Easter is enthusiastically observed here – celebrations take place in all the big cities, particularly Valladolid, León, Salamanca and Zamora, and include hooded penitents and processions of holy statues.

MAY–JUNE

Seventh Sunday after Easter: Pentecost Week-long Feria Chica in Palencia, with live music, art and food. Since 2016, the Feria Chica has been held over the first weekend in June, regardless of the official Pentecost day.
Second Thursday after Pentecost: Corpus Christi Celebrations in Palencia and Valladolid; the following day, the festival of El Curpillos is celebrated in Burgos.
June (dates vary): FÁCYL Salamanca's International Arts Festival (http://facyl-festival.com) features street concerts, urban art, DJ sets and neighbourhood events.
June 11: Fiestas de San Bernabé Logroño's festivities run for a week around this date.
June 24: Día de San Juan Fiesta with bullfighting and dancing in León and more religious observances in Palencia. The following week there's a big fiesta in Soria.
June 29: Día de San Pedro Burgos starts a vibrant two-week fiesta, when *gigantillos* (giant effigies) parade in the streets, and there are concerts, bullfights and all-night parties. Also big celebrations in León, while in Haro (where festivities start on the 24th) there's the drunken Batalla del Vino (Wine Fight).

AUGUST–SEPTEMBER

August 15: Fiesta de la Ascensión Colourful festivals in La Alberca and Peñafiel.
August 16: Día de San Roque Fiesta in El Burgo de Osma; also bullfights in the wooden plaza in Peñafiel.
Last week Aug: Fiesta de San Agustín In Toro, with the "fountain of wine" and *encierros* (bull-running).
September 8: Fiesta Virgen de la Vega First day of the fiesta in Salamanca, beginning the evening before and lasting two weeks, as well as the famous bull-running in Tordesillas.
September 21: Día de San Mateo Major *ferias* in Valladolid and especially Logroño, where the Rioja harvest is celebrated with a week's worth of high jinks including the famous grape-treading event in the Plaza de Espolón.

CASTILIAN CUISINE

5

It often seems like there's part of a pig, sheep or a cow on every plate in **Castile** – steaks can be gargantuan, the traditional roast meats, found everywhere, are *cochinillo* (suckling pig), *lechazo* (lamb) and *cabrito* (kid), while hearty Castilian appetites think nothing of limbering up first with a thick *sopa castellano*, usually containing chickpeas or white haricot beans, both staple crops from the *meseta*. In **Salamanca province**, *jamones* (hams) and *embutidos* (sausages) are at their best; in **Burgos** it's *morcilla* (black pudding) that's king. If you're feeling faint at the thought of so much meat – and Castilian menus can, truth be told, get a little monotonous – then the legendary tapas bars of **León** and **Logroño** ride to the rescue, where bite-sized morsels, from cuttlefish to mushrooms, offer a change of pace and diet. Only really in **La Rioja** does the traditional, heavy Castilian diet give way to something lighter and more varied. The rivers that irrigate the vines also mean freshwater fish, particularly trout, while La Rioja is the one part of the region where the contemporary Spanish foodie buzz has secured a real foothold.

Plaza Mayor

The grand **Plaza Mayor** is the hub of Salamantine life. Its vast central expanse is enclosed by a continuous four-storey building, broken only by the grand *ayuntamiento* (city hall) on its northern side. The building was the work of Andrea García Quiñones and of Alberto Churriguera, and nowhere is the Churrigueras' inspired variation of Baroque (see page 356) so refined as here. Cafés, restaurants and small shops ring the arcades, and some *pensiones* and hotels occupy parts of the upper storeys, but signs, advertising, lights and other modern clutter are not allowed to intrude upon the harmonious facades. Right around the arcades, facing out into the square, are medallion portraits of Spain's nobility and royalty through the ages, including the former Spanish king and queen Juan Carlos I and Doña Sofía.

Mercado Central

Pza. del Mercado

Arches from Pza. Mayor lead out into the surrounding shopping streets, including, on the east side, to Pza. del Mercado and the red-brick-and-iron **Mercado Central**. Housed in a protected building, the city's small two-tier market is a good place for picnic provisions, and it's surrounded on all sides by lively restaurants and tapas bars.

Convento y Museo de las Úrsulas

C/Las Úrsulas, entrance near Campo de San Francisco • Charge • 923 219 877

The unusual open-topped tower of the **Convento y Museo de las Úrsulas** rises above a charming quarter west of Pza. Mayor. Inside, sitting in the dark, cheery Franciscan nuns scrabble for change for the rare visitor and then turn on the lights so that you can inspect the primitive artworks, including the portrait of Úrsula herself – a Romano-British princess of the fourth century AD, martyred by the Huns while on pilgrimage to Rome. Look up for the greater treasure – the impressive, decorated, coffered ceiling – and on the way out examine the superb marble **tomb of Archbishop Alonso Fonseca**, founder of the convent.

Casa de las Muertes

C/Bordadores • No public access

Facing the east wall of the Convento de las Úrsulas is the impressive Plateresque facade of the **Casa de las Muertes** (House of the Dead), the mansion of leading Salamantine architect Juan de Álava, named for the four small skulls found at the base of the upper windows.

5

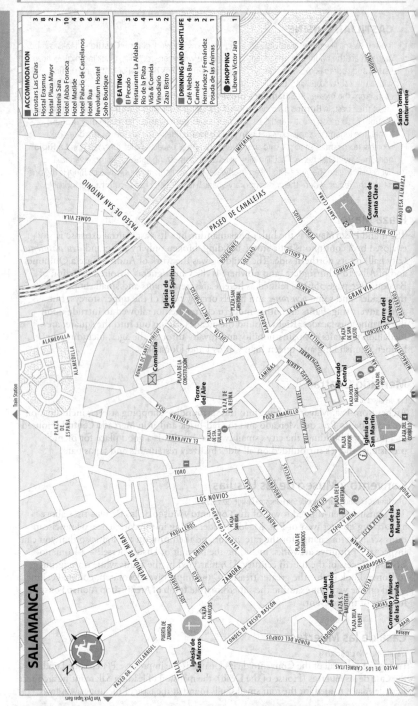

SALAMANCA

■ ACCOMMODATION	
Eurostars Las Claras	3
Hostal Erasmus	8
Hostal Plaza Mayor	2
Hosteria Sara	7
Hotel Abba Fonseca	10
Hotel Matilde	4
Hotel Palacio de Castellanos	9
Hotel Rua	6
Revolutum Hostel	5
Soho Boutique	1

● EATING	
El Pecado	3
Restaurante La Aldaba	6
Rio de la Plata	4
Vida & Comida	1
Vinodiario	5
Zazu Bistro	2

■ DRINKING AND NIGHTLIFE	
Café Niebla Bar	4
Camelot	3
Hernández y Fernández	2
Posada de las Ánimas	1

● SHOPPING	
Libreria Victor Jara	1

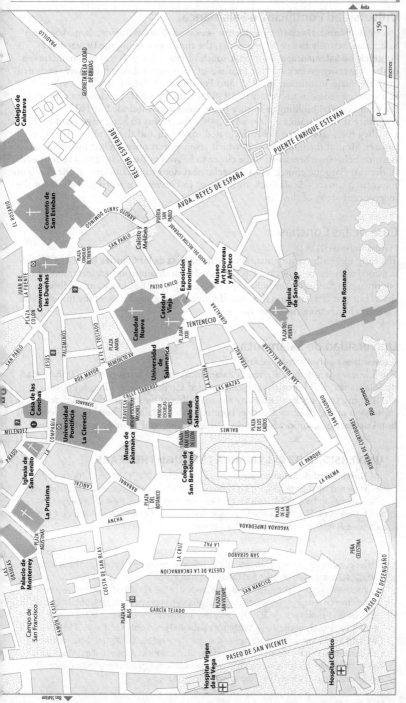

5

Universidad Pontificia de Salamanca

C/La Compañía • **Universidad Pontifíci** Charge for guided tours • www.upsa.es • **Scala Coeli** Charge • http://torresdelaclerecia.com

Salamanca actually has two universities, the minor one being the **Universidad Pontificia de Salamanca**, a short walk south of Pza. Mayor. It was originally linked to the university proper, but the faculties of theology and canon law were excluded from the main institution in 1852, and Pontificía was later formally established as a separate religious university in 1940 by Pope Pius XII. Guided tours around the grand central building, a former Jesuit college first founded in 1617, start at a magnificent stone staircase, *la escalera noble*, that seems to hang suspended in the air. They then take in the richly decorated main hall and the grandiose Baroque cloister, around the upper level of which Jesuit priests once walked meditational circuits, believing themselves to be closer to heaven at such a height. The tour ends in the vast Baroque church of **La Clerecía**, next door to the university. The climb up the church towers – **Scala Coeli**, or Stairway to Heaven – is worth the effort for the magnificent views of the city.

Casa de las Conchas

C/La Compañía 2 • Free • 923 269 317

The early sixteenth-century mansion called the **Casa de las Conchas** (House of Shells) is named after the rows of carved scallop shells that decorate its facade, symbol of the pilgrimage to Santiago. The building is now partly a public library and exhibition space, but you can look into the courtyard and enjoy a good view of the towers of La Clerecía church from the upper storey.

Universidad de Salamanca

C/Libreros • Charge, free for under-12s • http://usal.es

You'll know when you've arrived at Salamanca's central attraction, the **Universidad de Salamanca**, also known as the Universidad Civil, by the milling tour groups, all straining their necks to examine the magnificent facade. It's the ultimate expression of the Plateresque style, covered with medallions, heraldic emblems and floral decorations, amid which lurks a hidden frog, said to bring good luck and

UNIVERSIDAD DE SALAMANCA THROUGH THE YEARS

The **Universidad de Salamanca** was founded by Alfonso IX in 1218, and, after the union of Castile and León, became the most important in Spain. Its rise to international stature was phenomenal, and within forty years Pope Alexander IV proclaimed it equal to the greatest universities of the day. As at Oxford, Paris and Bologna, theories formulated here were later accepted as fact throughout Europe. The university continued to flourish under the Reyes Católicos, and in the sixteenth century it was powerful enough to resist the orthodoxy of Felipe II's Inquisition, but, eventually, freedom of thought was stifled by the extreme clericalism of the seventeenth and eighteenth centuries. Books were banned for being a threat to the Catholic faith, and mathematics and medicine disappeared from the curriculum. During the Peninsular War (1808–14), the French demolished 20 of the 25 colleges, and by the end of the nineteenth century there were no more than three hundred students (compared to 6500 in the late sixteenth century). The university saw a revival in the early part of the twentieth century, particularly under the rectorship of celebrated philosopher and man of letters Miguel de Unamuno. Today, numbers are higher than ever (around 30,000 students) and Salamanca University has a certain social cachet, though academically it ranks well behind Madrid and Barcelona. It does, however, run the highly successful Cursos Internacionales language school – nowhere else in Spain will you find so many young foreigners.

marriage within the year to anyone who spots it unaided. The centre of the facade is occupied by a portrait of Isabel and Fernando, surrounded by a Greek inscription commemorating their devotion to the university. There are several sections to visit – your ticket includes a tour of the main building's lecture rooms and library, as well as the Colegio Fonseca.

Aula Fray Luis de León and library

The university's old lecture rooms are arranged around a courtyard. The **Aula Fray Luis de León** preserves the rugged original benches and the pulpit where this celebrated professor lectured. In 1572, the Inquisition muscled its way into the room and arrested Fray Luis for alleged subversion of the faith; four years of torture and imprisonment followed, but upon his release he calmly resumed his lecture with the words, "As we were saying yesterday..."

An elegant Plateresque stairway leads to the upper storey, where you'll find the old university **library**, stuffed with thousands of antiquated books on wooden shelves and huge globes of the world. There's a faded magnificence here, which gives some idea of Renaissance Salamanca's academic splendour.

Museo de Salamanca

Patio de Escuelas 2 • Charge • https://museodesalamanca.org/visita/

Across from the university entrance is a small, enclosed square housing the **Museo de Salamanca**. This occupies an exquisite fifteenth-century mansion – originally the home of Isabel's personal physician – which is at least as interesting as the collection of Spanish religious paintings and sculpture contained within.

Cielo de Salamanca

Patio de Escuelas Menores • Free

At the back of the Patio de Escuelas, a beautifully sculpted double arch leads through to the cloistered Renaissance courtyard of the **Escuelas Menores**, which served as a kind of preparatory school for the university proper. A succession of weekend newlyweds pose here for photographs, while, on the far side of the courtyard, you'll find the entrance to the **Cielo de Salamanca**, a remarkable zodiacal ceiling that was once housed in the university chapel. As your eyes adjust to the light, centaurs, serpents and the Grim Reaper all come into focus amid the twinkling stars.

Catedral Nueva

Entrance on C/Benedicto XVI • Charge (for both Catedral Vieja & Nueva), free for two hours on Sundays • http://catedralsalamanca.org

You can't really tell from the outside, but Salamanca has two Catedrals – the earlier, Romanesque **Catedral Vieja**, or "old cathedral", is dwarfed by its **Catedral Nueva** ("new cathedral") neighbour. The latter, begun in 1513, was a glorious last-minute assertion of Gothic architecture. However, for financial reasons, construction eventually spanned two centuries and thus the building incorporates a range of styles. The main entrance on C/Benedicto XVI is contemporary with that of the university and equally dazzling in its wealth of ornamental detail. Inside, when you stand under the dome, you can clearly see the transition from plain Gothic at the bottom to colourful, exuberant late Baroque at the top. Alberto Churriguera and his brother José both worked here – the former on the choir stalls (fenced off, but lit by enough natural light to appreciate their beauty), the latter on the majestic dome.

Outside, **Pza. Anaya** is one of *the* great meeting places for Salamanca students, who lounge in the grass beds of the rose gardens; while from the slightly raised Catedral terrace you get a classic city view of domes, spires and sandstone facades.

5

Catedral Vieja

C/Benedicto XVI, enter through Catedral Nueva • Entrance and ticket kiosk inside Catedral Nueva • Charge (for both Catedral Vieja & Nueva), free for two hours on Sundays • http://catedralsalamanca.org

The chapels opening off the cloisters of **Catedral Vieja** were used as university lecture rooms until the sixteenth century and one, the **Capilla de Obispo Diego de Anaya**, contains the oldest organ in Europe (mid-fourteenth century). Otherwise, the old Catedral's most distinctive feature is its dome, known as the **Torre de Gallo** (Cock Tower) on account of its rooster-shaped weather vane. Fashioned like the segments of an orange, the dome derives from Byzantine models and is similar to those at Zamora and Toro; there's a good view of it from Patio Chico, the courtyard at the back of the Catedrals.

Ieronimus

Pza. Juan XXIII • Charge • http://ieronimus.es

The medieval towers of the Catedral Vieja provide a unique experience to learn about their 900-year-old history through a series of exhibitions and rooms, including dungeons and vaults. The route also takes you up along the battlements to see the Catedral's pinnacles and gargoyles. Be warned: there are two hundred steps to the top of the tower but you'll be rewarded with outstanding views of the city.

Museo Art Nouveau y Art Deco

C/Gibraltar 14 • Charge, free for under-14s and Thurs 11am–2pm • http://museocasalis.org

Explore the alleys behind the Catedral Vieja and you'll stumble upon Salamanca's quirkiest museum, the **Museo Art Nouveau y Art Deco**, contained within the Casa Lis. The mansion was built for an Art Nouveau enthusiast at the beginning of the twentieth century and is partly constructed from vibrantly painted glass (the best views of the house are actually from the ring road below). Winner of the Castilla y León Prize for the Arts in 2023, this museum holds a terrific miscellany of objects, from bronze statues and porcelain figures to jewellery and furniture, with notable pieces from the Fabergé and René Lalique workshops, and an exhibition that explores the origins of Casa Lis.

Convento de San Esteban

Pza. del Concilio de Trento • Charge • http://conventosanesteban.es

On the eastern edge of the historic quarter stands the vast **Convento de San Esteban**, whose facade portrays yet another faultless example of Plateresque art – the graphic central panel depicts the stoning of its patron saint, St Stephen. Paying for entry also allows you to see the lavish Baroque *retablo* by José Churriguera – a mighty 27m high, and one of the artist's first commissioned works in Salamanca – as well as the choir, the handsome cloister and the museum of sacred art. Closed Monday all day and Sunday afternoon.

SALAMANCA STYLE

Two great architectural styles were developed, and see their finest expression, in Salamanca. **Plateresque** is a decorative technique of shallow relief and intricate detail, named for its resemblance to the art of the silversmith (*platero*); Salamanca's native sandstone, soft and easy to carve, played a significant role in its development. Plateresque art cuts across Gothic and Renaissance frontiers – the decorative motifs of the university, for example, are taken from the Italian Renaissance but the facade of the Catedral Nueva is Gothic in inspiration. The later **Churrigueresque** style, an especially ornate form of Baroque, takes its name from **José Churriguera** (1665–1725), the dominant member of a prodigiously creative family, best known for their huge, flamboyant altarpieces.

Convento de las Dueñas

Pza. del Concilio de Trento • Charge • 923 215 442

The most beautiful cloisters in the city are at the **Convento de las Dueñas**, across the road from the Convento de San Esteban. Built in the sixteenth century on an irregular pentagonal plan, the imaginative upper-storey capitals are wildly carved with rams' heads, scallop shells, winged cherubs, mythical beasts and an extraordinary range of human faces. The nuns here sell boxes of delicious crumbly almond pastries (known as *amarguillos*) from a booth next to the entrance.

Convento de Santa Clara

C/Santa Clara 2 • Charge • https://museolasclaras.es

The thirteenth-century **Convento de Santa Clara** was found to be concealing unsuspected treasure when the whitewash was taken off the chapel walls in 1976. Underneath was an important series of frescoes from the thirteenth to the eighteenth century, while Romanesque and Gothic columns and a stunning sixteenth-century polychrome ceiling were also uncovered in the cloister. But the most incredible discovery was made in the church, where the Baroque ceiling was found to be false; rising above this, it's possible to see the original fourteenth-century beams, decorated with heraldic motifs of the kingdoms of Castile and León.

The Puente Romano

For a terrific city view up to the walls and spires of Salamanca, walk down below the Catedrals to the **Río Tormes** and cross the arched **Puente Romano**, built in the first century AD – try not to look back until you're most of the way across.

ARRIVAL AND INFORMATION
SALAMANCA

The compact *casco histórico*, with the Pza. Mayor at its heart, spreads back from the Río Tormes, bounded by a loop of avenues. The main bus and train stations are on opposite sides of the city, each about a 15min walk or a €5 taxi ride from the centre.

By train From the main train station on Paseo de la Estación, go left to Pza. de España, from where C/Azafranal or C/Toro lead directly to the Pza. Mayor. Salamanca's other train station – Salamanca-La Alamedilla – is closer to the centre but is for arrivals only. RENFE, http://renfe.com.
Destinations Ávila (8 daily; 1hr); Burgos (9 daily; 2–4hr); Madrid (13 daily; 2–3 hr); Valladolid (12 daily; 1hr 15min–3hr).

By bus The bus station is on Avda. Filiberto Villalobos (923 236 717, http://estacionautobusessalamanca.es). From here turn right and keep straight for 15min until you reach Pza. Mayor. Companies with ticket offices here include Alsa (Burgos and Portugal; 923 258 205, http://alsa.es); Auto-Res/Avanza (Valladolid/Madrid and Ávila; 923 232 266, http://avanzabus.com); El Pilar (Ciudad Rodrigo; 923 222

608, http://elpilar-arribesbus.com); Vivas (for León and Astorga/Ponferrada; 923 223 587, http://autocaresvivas.es); and Zamora-Salamanca (Zamora/León; 923 223 587, http://zamorasalamanca.es).
Destinations Astorga/Ponferrada (1–2 daily; 2hr 40min/3hr 30min); Ávila (4 daily; 1hr 30min); Burgos (4 daily; 3hr 30min); Cáceres (up to 9 daily; 3hr); Ciudad Rodrigo (up to 11 daily; 1hr); León (up to 3 daily; 3hr 30min); Madrid (every 30min–1hr; 2hr 30min); Palencia (up to 4 daily; 2hr 15min); Porto/Lisbon, Portugal (2–6 daily; 6hr/10hr); Valladolid (8 daily; 1hr 15min–2hr); Zamora (up to 17 daily; 1hr 10min).

By car As you drive into the centre, all the main hotels and car parks are clearly signposted. You can unload outside most hotels (though not on every street in the old centre), but street parking is usually restricted to 2hr, so it's best to use one of the garages or car parks (€16–20/day).

Turismo The *turismo* is on Pza. Mayor 32 (Mon–Fri 9am–7pm, Sat 10am–7pm, Sun 10am–2pm; 923 218 342, http://salamanca.es). There is also a seasonal office (July–Sept, variable hours) situated inside the train station.

ACCOMMODATION
SEE MAP PAGE 352

All the places reviewed below are in the *casco histórico*, and you'll be able to walk to everything in 5min or so. There are some splendid boutique and classy lodgings, but many budget *pensiones* are more or less permanently occupied by

students during the academic year. You may be approached at the train or bus station and offered private rooms, but these are best avoided.

Eurostars Las Claras C/Marquesa Almarza s/n, http://

5

eurostarshotels.com. Very comfortable, contemporary four-star hotel in a quiet corner of town – it's easy to find by car and has garage parking for a daily fee; free street parking is sometimes available in the "white zone". Spacious rooms in muted colours provide a tranquil base, the buffet breakfast is included and there's a good restaurant. Good rates are available online as prices change all the time. €€

Hostal Erasmus C/Jesús 18, http://erasmus-home. castile-leon-hotels.com/en/. A friendly hostel on a peaceful side street near the Casa de Conchas with bright, shared dorms. A simple coffee-and-toast breakfast is served in the *Cafeteria Maldeamores*, a 4min walk away on C/Quintana. €̄

Hostal Plaza Mayor Pza. del Corillo, http://hostal plazamayor.es. Despite the central location right next door to the Pza. Mayor, this is a surprisingly quiet and appealing budget option. The cosy rooms have private bathrooms and a/c, and there's a garage on site. €̄

Hostería Sara C/Meléndez, http://hosteria-sara-guest-house.castile-leon-hotels.com/en/. The best – and friendliest – budget option on this busy street, 100m from Pza. Mayor. Its eighteen rooms are comfortably furnished, and feature wood floors and tiled bathrooms. Internal rooms are nice and quiet. Six of the rooms also have a small kitchen. €̄

Hotel Abba Fonseca Pza. San Blas 2, http://abbafonseca hotel.com. A contemporary four-star hotel on a tranquil square a 10min walk from Pza. Mayor. Many rooms have lovely views across the city (though there are cheaper rooms without the views). There is also a small gym and hot tub. €€

Hotel Matilde C/Quintana 6, http://alda-plaza-mayor. castile-leon-hotels.com/en/. In the historic heart of Salamanca, a few steps from Pza. Mayor, this hotel is excellent value for money. Rooms are bright, modern and clean, some have great balcony views, and you'll be located well to explore many of the main sights on foot (and a good number of bars nearby). €€

Hotel Palacio de Castellanos C/San Pablo 58–64, http://nh-hotels.com. The glassed-in Renaissance cloister converted into a lobby lounge sets the tone in this lovely, marbled four-star hotel on the site of a former palace. Rooms are soft and romantic with lots of white. Breakfast is not included. €€

Hotel Rua C/Sánchez Barbero 11, http://hotelrua.com. The sparkling reception area, complete with chandeliers, is an attractive introduction to this four-star hotel. Although just a few steps away from Pza. Mayor, double glazing in the rooms does an excellent job of keeping out street noise. There's discounted parking a 5min walk away and breakfast is an added extra. Prices change frequently so best to look and reserve online. €€

★ **Revolutum Hostel** C/Sánchez Barbero 7, http:// revolutumhostel.com. There's nothing understated about this funky hostel that mixes 1960s retro style with antique furnishings, but the atmosphere is relaxed and inviting. Upstairs, there are double rooms as well as four- to five-bed dorms. The sleek glass bar serves flamboyant cocktails (noise can travel to some rooms at night). €̄

Soho Boutique Canalejas C/Grillo 18, www.sohohoteles. com. This four-star boutique hotel lies just a few minutes' walk from the old centre, and the famous Pza. Mayor. Spacious, contemporary rooms have polished wooden floors and colourful soft furnishings. There is also a café and breakfast buffet (not included). €€

EATING

SEE MAP PAGE 352

Salamanca is a great place for hanging out in bars and cafés. There are also many superb restaurants where you can eat really well for very little, although sitting outside to eat in the Pza. Mayor can attract a hefty mark-up. Just south of Pza. Mayor, the adjacent C/Meléndez and more touristy Rúa Mayor are packed with bars and restaurants, with enticing outdoor tables. There's another bunch of popular restaurants and tapas places near the market (around Pza. del Mercado and up C/Pozo Amarillo), but the best (and cheapest) **tapas bars** in the city are a 15min walk north of the old centre, along C/Van Dyck (follow Paseo Doctor Torres Villarroel, cross Avda. Portugal, and Van Dyck is two streets up on the right).

★ **El Pecado** Pza. Poeta Iglesias 12, http://elpecado restaurante.es. The funky townhouse interior of bare brick walls and wooden bookshelves filled with leather-bound volumes is the backdrop for some fusion cuisine – from pickled chicharro with lemon to veal sweetbread and passionfruit or smoked eel with citrus coconut. There are a few excellent tasting menus to try that range in price, served day and night. €€€

Restaurante La Aldaba C/Felipe Espino 6, 923 219 642. Traditional Spanish restaurant that serves hearty regional dishes such as *rabo del toro* (oxtail stew) and *pulpo* (Galician-style octopus). Choose either the formal dining area at the back or order *pintxos* in the lively bar full of locals at the front. €€

Río de la Plata Pza. Peso 1, http://restauranteriodelaplata. es. The well-regarded regional Castilian cuisine here is a real step up in quality from most places in the area – as are the prices. Hearty, rustic, feels-like-home-cooking dishes range from rabbit stew to hake casserole; fish is a speciality, as are seasonal *horta* (countryside) dishes using ingredients like asparagus, beans and mushrooms. €€

★ **Vida & Comida** Pza. de Santa Eulalia 11, http://viday comida.com. It's best to reserve a table at this popular restaurant, which serves *vanguardista* "gastrotapas". Choose from three *menús del día* (only available on weekdays) – dishes include a delicate octopus carpaccio, txangurro (spider crab) ravioli in almond cream and caramelized leeks in sauce. €€

★ **Vinodiario** Pza. de los Basilios 1, http://vinodiario. com. Terrific contemporary wine bar with food, just off the main tourist track in a nice square with outdoor tables. There are some great wines by the glass, plus superior tapas and *raciones*, including warm goat's cheese salad and a ground-beef-and-herb hamburger and a cheesecake that's quite possibly worth the flight to Spain alone. €€

Zazu Bistro Pza. de la Libertad 8, http://restaurantezazu. com. A classy French-Italian bistro with outside tables in an attractive plaza adjacent to Pza. Mayor. Inside, the restaurant serves French classics, such as *boeuf bourguignon* and cassoulet, and dishes with a Spanish twist, including Iberian pork ribs, plus Italian pastas and risottos. Don't forget to save room for their delicious desserts, including carrot cake and classic tarte tatin. €€

DRINKING AND NIGHTLIFE SEE MAP PAGE 352

There's a whole host of student-oriented **bars and clubs** on the southeast edge of the *casco histórico*, particularly in the arcades of the Gran Vía, in Pza. de San Justo and near the market (C/Varillas and C/Clavel). Another area for bars and clubs is around the Convento de las Úrsulas, though if you're looking for quantity over quality try the infamous **bars de litros** just to the north of here around Pza. de San Juan de Bautista, which sell drinks in litre "buckets". The café-bars in C/La Latina near the university are always bustling with students, day and night. C/Van Dyke is also a good spot.

BARS

Café Niebla Bar C/Bordadores 14, https://cafenieblabar. com. This cocktail and jazz bar is a real slice of life with a great atmosphere. With an extensive menu of classic cocktails and new, unique concoctions that use local flavours and aromas, this is a good place to start in the evening.

★ **Hernández y Fernández** Pza. de la Libertad 10, www.instagram.com/hernandezyfernandez_salamanca/. This tasteful café-bar is a dark and cosy place on a peaceful square just north of the Pza. Mayor. Stop for a coffee during the afternoon and you may find that you're still here late at night.

CLUBS

Camelot C/Bordadores 3, https://www.instagram.com/ camelot_salamanca/. Everyone in town knows this fun bar and *discoteca*, housed in part of the Convento de las Úrsulas. The interior, an ex-pilgrim's house, is a mix of medieval and industrial decor, with a bar on the first floor, above the dancefloor, and there are terraza seats outside.

Posada de las Ánimas Calle Toro 64, https://www. instagram.com/posadaanimas/. The shared terraza is a bit hidden away from the main drag, and don't miss the weird interior of cherubs, chandeliers and doll's houses.

SHOPPING SEE MAP PAGE 352

Librería Victor Jara C/Juan del Rey 6, has a reasonable selection of English language books.

DIRECTORY

Hospitals Hospital Clínico, Paseo San Vicente 182 (923 291 100); Hospital Virgen de la Vega, Paseo San Vicente 58 (923 291 200).

Language courses Courses offered by the Universidad de Salamanca (http://cursosinternacionales.usal.es) are heavily subscribed, but there are loads of other schools – see http://espanolensalamanca.com.

Laundry At Pza. Mercado 17 and Avda. Portugal 74.

Police Oficina de Denuncias y Atención al Ciudadano (ODAC) C/Jardines, 923 127 700. Report an incident at the ODAC office, then non-Spanish citizens must take their police report to the relevant embassy. Report lost property at Avda. de la Aldehueva, 923 279 195.

Post office Gran Vía 25.

Ciudad Rodrigo

The unspoiled frontier town of **CIUDAD RODRIGO** – 90km southwest of Salamanca, astride the road to Portugal – is worth a detour even if you don't plan to cross the border. It's an endearingly sleepy place which, despite destruction during the Peninsular War, preserves a rather austere castle (now a parador), a handsome Plaza Mayor and quiet old-town streets full of Renaissance mansions. It remains completely encircled by impressive walls and ramparts, and the thirty-minute walk around (and on top of) them is the best way to get an overview of the whole town. Given its history, it's perhaps surprising that there's much left to see at all. Ciudad Rodrigo was a crucial border point in the **Peninsular War**, guarding the route between Spain and Portugal. The town fell to the French after a fierce fight in 1810, but was later retaken by the

British in 1812 following a devastatingly rapid siege (cannonball dents are still visible above the doorway on one side of the Catedral). A triumphant rampage of looting followed, and the troops paraded out dressed in a ragbag of stolen French finery. A bemused Wellington muttered to his staff, "Who the devil are those fellows?"

ARRIVAL AND INFORMATION   CIUDAD RODRIGO

By train There is a train station, a fair walk north of the centre, though there haven't been any passenger services since 2020. The station used to be used exclusively for long-distance journeys, with trains to places such as Lisbon or Hendaye in France.

By bus From Salamanca, the bus is easily the most convenient way to get to Ciudad Rodrigo; the bus station is a 5min walk north of the old town.

By car Salamanca is under an hour's drive away. You can easily park outside the town walls, or try your luck with the limited spaces on Pza. Mayor.

Turismo Pza. Mayor 27 (opening times vary; 664 346 580, https://turismo.ciudadrodrigo.es).

Centro de Recepción de Visitantes Avda. Sefarad (opening times vary; 923 498 400).

ACCOMMODATION

★ **Hotel Conde Rodrigo I** Pza. de San Salvador 9, http://hotelesciudadrodrigo.com. An old sixteenth-century mansion loaded with character – check out the period-piece panelled bar. The rooms are nothing flashy, but perfectly decent and with good bathrooms, and it's very quiet at the rear. There's a gastro-bar for snacks and cocktails, and public parking nearby on Avda. Sefarad. €€

Parador de Ciudad Rodrigo Pza. Castillo 1, http://parador.es. The main historic hotel has an unrivalled location in the old castle, which has been beautifully restored. There are views to all sides, and some very grand rooms and public spaces, as well as a restaurant and a car park. €€€

Puerta del Sol C/Rúa del Sol 33, http://puerta-del-sol-guest-house.castile-leon-hotels.com/. This hotel offers trim little en-suite rooms by the Puerta del Sol gate, close to the Palacia de los Águila, and a cosy feel throughout. Public parking 1min away through the gate. €€

EATING AND DRINKING

★ **Estoril** C/General Pando 11, http://restaurante-estoril.com. The best place in town for modern interpretations of regional cuisine – grilled baby octopus, *rabo de toro*, truffle and partridge ravioli, etc. Meals are served in the formal, but unstuffy, restaurant to the rear; otherwise there's a terrace at the front for tapas and *raciones*. €€€

El Rodeo C/Gigantes 6, https://www.facebook.com/m.

carmenperezdeburgos. Simple, old-fashioned restaurant offering hearty local specialities, such as scrambled eggs with *farinato* (pork and bread sausage) and milk-fed lamb. €€

El Sanatorio Pza. Mayor 14, 923 461 054. Atmospheric little bar-restaurant whose walls are covered in bullfighting photos from decades of *corridas* and fiestas. €€

Sierra de Francia

The protected mountain region of the **Sierra de Francia** marks the southern region of Salamanca province, with captivating **La Alberca** the most obvious target. It's one of six "national monument" villages, along with the equally venerable **Mogarraz**, **Miranda del Castañar**, **San Martín del Castañar**, **Sequeros** and **Vilanueva del Conde**. La Alberca makes a good walking base for the surrounding hills and valleys, notably the stunning **Valle de Las Batuecas**, with its isolated monastery and ancient rock art. The area is best explored by car, in particular the stunning route along the Río Alagón: from the Monasterio San José de Las Batuecas, skirt the eastern edge of the *parque natural* to the viewpoint Riomalo de Abajo (just over the border in Extremadura) for a glorious view of the **Meandro Melero** – an almost complete oxbow lake. Complete the circuit by following the river east to the pretty village of **Sotoserrano**.

La Alberca

Seventy-six kilometres southwest of Salamanca, **LA ALBERCA** sits in the middle of the **Parque Natural Las Batuecas-Sierra de Francia**. The historic town is ringed by the trappings of mass tourism these days. However, the centre still maintains an extraordinary collection of late medieval, half-timbered houses. It's very pretty, and an obvious draw for weekenders and coach parties who trawl the rather-too-clean cobbled lanes shopping for basketware and other souvenirs. The smell and dirt of the farmyard may be long gone, but La Alberca is still known for its *embutidos* and *jamones*, and every second shop displays the rich, nutty hams, smoked pork and cured sausages.

ARRIVAL AND INFORMATION   LA ALBERCA

By bus Cosme buses (http://autocarescosme.com) run to La Alberca via Mogarraz (twice daily from Salamanca to Mogarraz, then a 15min bus to La Alberca). Buses aren't that frequent throughout the day, so check schedules in advance.

By car You should find somewhere to park on the main through-roads, though there's also a large car park a few hundred metres out on the Batuecas road, just past the *Hotel Antiguas Eras* and right next to the Casa del Parque information office.

Turismo Pza. Mayor 11 (Tues–Fri 10am–2pm & 4.30–6.30pm, Sat 10.30am–2pm & 4.30–6.30pm, Sun 10.30am–2pm; 923 415 291, http://laalberca.com); for information about walks in the region, visit Casa del Parque, Carretera Las Batuecas 22 (Feb to mid-June & Oct–Dec Fri & Sat 10am–2pm & 4–6pm, Thurs & Sun 10am–2pm; mid-July to mid-Sept Fri & Sat 10am–2pm & 5–7pm, Tues–Thurs & Sun 10am–2pm; 923 415 421, http://miespacionatural. es, http://patrimonionatural.org).

ACCOMMODATION AND EATING

Accommodation can be expensive for what you get, but there are some good deals around, both in the centre of town and on the Batuecas road, a few minutes' walk from the centre. There's also a terrific boutique hotel in nearby Mogarraz. Half a dozen **bars and restaurants** ring Pza. Mayor, and there are a few more down neighbouring streets serving tapas and meals: none particularly cheap, all agreeably rustic.

Al-Bereka 2km out on the Salamanca road (Km 76), http://albereka.com. The local campsite is more of a holiday complex, with rustic cabins and apartments to rent, as well as separate pools for adults and children, plus a café with a large peaceful terrace. Camping €, cabins €€

Hostal El Castillo C/Mogarraz, http://hostalelcastillo. com. This simple hotel next door to its sister hotel, *Hotel Doña Teresa*, is a pleasant retreat away from La Alberca's touristy town centre. Good budget rooms have great views of the sierra; there's a bar on the ground floor with a pool table. Breakfast is not included. €

Hotel Antiguas Eras C/Batuecas, http://antiguaseras.

com. This is an agreeable three-star hotel with spacious, cosy rooms, distant hill views, a peaceful garden and a family-friendly welcome. Staff have some really helpful recommendations for things to do in and around the area, and their website has information on nearby art, wine and nature trails. €€

Hotel Doña Teresa C/Mogarraz, http://hoteldeteresa. com. The smartest choice in town is this four-star hotel with spacious and elegant rooms and a good restaurant serving traditional cuisine. There's also use of a spa 1.5km away. €€

★ **Villa de Mogarraz** C/Miguel Angel Maillo 54, Mogarraz, 7km east of La Alberca, http://hotelspamogarraz. com. For the finest lodgings in the area, drive the short distance east to the equally ancient village of Mogarraz, where this restored mansion offers wonderfully stylish bedrooms featuring plenty of exposed stone, reclaimed wood and antique colonial furniture. The best rooms have Jacuzzis. There are spa facilities and a good restaurant too, known for its oak-grilled meats. €€

Parque Natural Las Batuecas-Sierra de Francia

The rolling hills, craggy peaks, deep valleys and dense forests of the **PARQUE NATURAL LAS BATUECAS-SIERRA DE FRANCIA** are a big draw for hikers and naturalists alike. Along the network of trails that crisscross the protected conservation area, walkers pass through a diverse landscape that teems with wildlife, where they may spot black vultures, owls, snakes, lizards and mountain goats. La Alberca is the obvious starting point for hikers: stop at the Casa del Parque information office to pick up maps to well-signposted trails of varying difficulty.

Peña de Francia

The most obvious route on a clear day is up to the summit of **Peña de Francia** (1728m), not quite the highest point in the range but the most panoramic. The trail is signposted

5

a couple of hundred metres outside La Alberca on the Batuecas road, across from the *Hotel Antiguas Eras*; it's 8.3km on foot (6hr round trip) or 17km by road. There's the church and sanctuary of Our Lady of the Peña de Francia at the windswept summit, and there are even lodgings at the *Hospedería del Santuario Peña de Francia* (https:// www.hospederiapenadefrancia.com), which has a welcome *cafetería* (closed in winter).

Valle de Las Batuecas

The Batuecas road out of La Alberca climbs 3.5km to the pass of **El Portillo** (1247m), surrounded by rugged hills. From here, the road drops sharply for another 9km, via a series of hairpin bends, into the **Valle de Las Batuecas**, where a signpost points you up a short track to a parking area outside the **Monasterio San José de Las Batuecas**. There's also a more direct 7km path (3hr 30min each way) from La Alberca, over the pass and down to the monastery. This sylvan retreat in a hidden valley was founded at the beginning of the seventeenth century, and is a closed Carmelite order (no public access). However, a signposted path around the side of the monastery leads along the babbling river to a series of three **rock-art** sites dating from between 5000 and 2500 BC, depicting hunting and pastoral scenes of goats and deer, and even human figures. The closest site, Cabras Pintadas, is an enjoyable half-hour's hike from the monastery gate.

Zamora and around

ZAMORA, 62km north of Salamanca and only 50km from the Portuguese border, is the quietest of the great Castilian cities, with a population of just 62,000. In medieval romances, it was known as *la bien cercada* (the well-enclosed) on account of its strong fortifications; one siege here lasted seven months. Its old quarters, still walled and medieval in appearance, are spread out along the top of a ridge that slopes down to the banks of the Río Duero, crossed at its widest point by a lovely sixteen-arched bridge and flanked by some restored medieval water mills, the Aceñas de Olivares (which are free to visit). The city's Romanesque churches are its most distinctive feature, while the old town's streets and squares make for an attractive overnight stay.

Romanesque churches

Opening times vary, consult tourist offices • Free

The joy of Zamora lies in its quiet, western old-town quarter – looking decidedly spruce and scrubbed these days – and, above all, in its 22 pale-stone **Romanesque churches**, with their unassumingly beautiful architecture, and towers populated by colonies of storks. The majority date from the twelfth century and reflect Castile's sense of security following the victorious campaigns against the Moors by Alfonso VI and El Cid. All are worthy of a closer look, though **San Juan de Puerta Nueva** (Pza. Mayor), **La Magdalena** (Rúa de los Francos) and **Santiago del Burgo** (C/Santa Clara) are considered the highlights.

Museo de la Semana Santa

Pza. de Santa María La Nueva • Charge, temporarily closed at the time of writing

One of several interesting museums in Zamora, the **Museo de la Semana Santa** is probably the most dramatic – although it has been closed for renovation since 2022. One large room is lined with *pasos* – elaborate statues and floats depicting the Passion of Christ – which are usually paraded through the streets during Zamora's famous Holy Week processions.

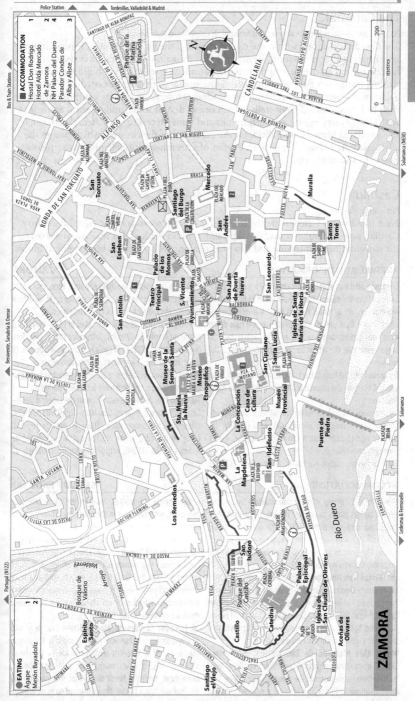

ZAMORA

ACCOMMODATION
Hostal Don Rodrigo ... 1
Hotel Alda Mercado
de Zamora ... 2
NH Palacio del Duero ... 4
Parador Condes de
Alba y Aliste ... 3

● **EATING**
Agape ... 1
Mesón Bayadoliz ... 2

Police Station
Tordesillas, Valladolid & Madrid

Bus & Train Stations

Benavente, Sanabria & Orense

Portugal (N122)

Ledesma & Fermoselle

Salamanca

Salamanca (N630)

0   200
metres

5

The Catedral

Pza. de la Catedral • Charge, free Mon afternoons and for under-12s • https://catedralzamora.com

The **Catedral**, enclosed within the ruined citadel at the far end of town, is now shining very brightly after restoration. Begun in 1151, its mainly Romanesque body is largely hidden behind an overbearing Renaissance facade, above which the building's most striking feature – a Byzantine-inspired dome similar to that of the Catedral Vieja at Salamanca – perches in incongruous splendour. However, it springs a surprise inside, with its famous carved **choir stalls**, which depict devout scenes and mystical animals as well as lusty carryings-on between monks and nuns. Access to the Catedral is through the associated **Museo Catedralicio**, on the other side of the cloisters, which houses the city's celebrated "Black Tapestries", a series of fifteenth-century Flemish masterpieces woven in stunning detail.

Castillo

Parque del Castillo • Free

Next to Zamora's Catedral are the impressive moated remains of the eleventh-century **Castillo**, now laid out as a shady park; wander round the back for majestic views over the surrounding countryside and Río Duero, along with Zamora's burgeoning suburbs.

ARRIVAL AND INFORMATION   ZAMORA

The **train and bus stations** are close to each other, but a fair way from the centre, 30min walk north of Pza. Mayor. Alternatively, it's a 10min ride on bus #4 (every 20min), which leaves from outside the bus station and runs down Avda. Tres Cruces, dropping you at Pza. Sagasta by Pza. Mayor; note that the return bus departs from outside the market.

By train From the train station on Ctra. de la Estación, walk straight out over the roundabout in front to join the Avda. Tres Cruces.

Destinations Madrid (6 daily; 1hr 30min); Santiago de Compostela (6 daily; 3hr 30min); Valladolid (3 daily; 1hr 30min); Vigo (3 daily; 3hr); A Coruña (8 daily; 3hr). Fewer trains run on weekends.

By bus The bus station is on Avda. Alfonso Peña (980 521 281); turn right out of the main entrance, then right again around the side of the terminal to reach the main road; turn left here and follow Avda. Tres Cruces into town.

Destinations León (8 daily; 2hr); Madrid (3–5 daily; 3hr); Palencia (3 daily; 2hr 20min); Salamanca (daily; 1hr); Toro (hourly; 30min); Valladolid (hourly; 1hr 30min); Burgos (2 daily; 3hr 30min). Fewer buses run on weekends.

By car Car parks in the centre are well signposted, but some of the old town is residents-only access and parking.

Turismo Pza. de Arias Gonzalo 5, near the Catedral (Mon–Sat 10am–2pm & 5–8pm, Sun 10am–2pm) 980 533 694, https://turismo-zamora.com). There is another regional office on the edge of the old town at Avda. Príncipe de Asturias 1 (980 531 845, http://www.turismocastillayleon. com).

ACCOMMODATION   SEE MAP PAGE 363

While there is plenty of **accommodation** in Zamora, decent budget places to stay are thin on the ground. Most hotels are within a short walk of the old quarter and it's usually easy to find a room, except over Easter week during the famous processions, when prices double and accommodation is booked solid.

★ **Hostal Don Rodrigo** C/Virgen de la Concha 5, http:// hostaldonrodrigo.es. This super-friendly two-star hostel is hands-down the best mid-range place to stay in town. The spic-and-span rooms have all the facilities that you'd expect at a good hotel, including memory-foam mattresses that make for a blissful night's sleep. Free parking. €

Hotel Alda Mercado de Zamora Pza. del Mercado 20, https://www.aldahotels.es/hoteles/castilla-y-leon/ zamora/hotel-alda-mercado-de-zamora. Handsome Art Deco boutique lodgings in a restored modernist mansion right opposite the market. Most of the rooms are nice and quiet, with some set in the eaves, and there's a good contemporary restaurant and garage parking (there's also restricted street parking outside in the market square). €

NH Palacio del Duero Pza. de la Horta, http://nh-hotels. com. Housed in a former convent and winery in a quiet residential area, this large hotel is easy to spot as a brick chimney still looms beside it. Some of its 49 rooms overlook the attractive Iglesia de Santa Maria de la Horta. Cheaper deals are available online. €€

★ **Parador Condes de Alba y Aliste** Pza. de Viriato 5, www.parador.es. Zamora's classy parador is a stunning conversion of a fifteenth-century palace in the heart of town, mixing lovely rooms with princely trappings throughout, from the heroic medallions surmounting the internal courtyard to the idly positioned suits of armour.

An elevated garden terrace and open-air summer pool have city views, while a fine restaurant serves updated regional cuisine. Sadly, the parador is due to close temporarily between Jan 2025 and July 2026 – dates may change so check the website. €€

EATING

SEE MAP PAGE 363

Zamora's most celebrated dishes are hearty affairs like *sopas de ajo* (garlic soup), *arroz de la Zamorana* (rice flavoured with pigs' trotters) and *habones Sanabreses* (broad beans cooked in a meaty paprika broth), as well as cod and octopus dishes. **Restaurants**, **cafés** and superb **tapas bars** are found in three main zones. In **Los Lobos**, there's a cluster of no-nonsense **tapas bars** in the alleys around Pza. del Maestro; bars line the streets around the **Pza. Mayor** and there's a lively run of music, tapas and drinking **bars** in the narrow C/los Herreros; the **New Zone** is also worth a look for tapas; its located east of Los Lobos, on C/Cervantes, C/Santa Teresa,

C/Lope de Vega and C/Pablo Morillo.

Ágape Pza. de San Miguel 3, http://restaurante agapezamora.com. A smart restaurant with tables on the Pza. Mayor that serves Italian pizzas, as well as a *menú del día*. They also do fresh pastas, as well as grilled meats and fish. €€

Mesón Bayadoliz C/Los Herreros 7, http://www. bayadoliz.es. At this hole-in-the-wall place, pork-filled or beef-filled baguettes, chicken wings and large glasses of beer are the order of the day. They don't take reservations. €

North of Zamora

To the north of Zamora, the baking wheat fields of the *meseta* extend to the horizon across the Tierra del Pan (The Land of Bread), historically one of Spain's key flour-producing regions. It's 140km from Zamora to León (or a 2hr bus ride) on a fast road (N630 then A66) and drivers can break the journey at a couple of interesting places.

Monasterio de Moreruela

Around 40km north of Zamora, look for a marked turn-off from the N630 (on the left) at the dusty roadside village of Granja de Moreruela. "Granja" means farm, meaning the village was originally an outlying property of the medieval **Monasterio de Moreruela**, which lies 3.7km from the highway down a paved country lane. It's now in ruins, and home to a large colony of storks, but is an evocative sight nonetheless, under a carpet of daisies and poppies, with rolling farmland to all sides.

Benavente

Thirty kilometres to the north of Monasterio de Moreruela, the town of **BENAVENTE** is rather charming once you penetrate the outskirts, with busy shopping streets set around two ochre-coloured stone churches. A broad landscaped *paseo* on a bluff offers extensive views over the surrounding countryside, while at the end of the gardens, the *Parador de Benavente* occupies the remains of the town's impressive castle.

Toro

TORO, 30km east of Zamora, looks dramatic seen from below: "an ancient, eroded, red-walled town spread along the top of a huge flat boulder", as Laurie Lee described it in *As I Walked Out One Midsummer Morning*. At closer quarters it turns out to be a rather ordinary provincial town, though embellished with one outstanding Romanesque reminder of past glory. Toro is also increasingly well known for its gutsy red **wines**, and the local tourist office can point you in the direction of local wineries open to the public. You're unlikely to want to stay the night, given the superior charms of nearby Zamora or Valladolid. Toro's a more realistic coffee or lunch stop – its Plaza Mayor is lined with characteristic red-brick houses and stone arcades, with many enticing **tapas bars** and **restaurants**.

Colegiata de Santa María la Mayor

Off Pza. Mayor • Charge • https://torosacro.com

5

THE BATTLE OF TORO

Toro – a historic military stronghold – played a role of vital significance in both Spanish and Portuguese history. The **Battle of Toro** in 1476 effectively ended Portugal's interest in Spanish affairs and laid the basis for the unification of Spain. On the death of Enrique IV in 1474, the Castilian throne was disputed: almost certainly his daughter Juana la Beltraneja was the rightful heiress, but rumours of illegitimacy were stirred up and Enrique's sister Isabel seized the throne. Alfonso V of Portugal saw his opportunity and supported Juana. In 1476 the armies clashed and the Reyes Católicos – Isabel and her husband Fernando – defeated their rivals to embark upon one of the most glorious periods in Spanish history.

Toro's pride and joy is the **Colegiata de Santa María la Mayor**, whose west portal (c.1240) inside the church is one of the most beautiful examples of Romanesque art in the region. Its seven recessed arches carved with royal and biblical themes still retain much of their colourful original paint. Also inspect *The Virgin of the Fly*, a notable fifteenth-century painting hanging in the sacristy – the eponymous insect perches on the Virgin's robes. Around the back of the church is a wide terrace with a famous view over the *meseta*, with the Río Duero far below.

ARRIVAL AND INFORMATION   TORO

By bus and car Buses to Toro are reasonably frequent (Zamora–Valladolid route; hourly service, fewer at weekends) and stop at the bus station. It's best to park outside town – walk through the big arch and straight

on for about 5min, through the clock tower, to reach Pza. Mayor, with the Colegiata immediately behind.
Turismo Pza. Mayor 1 (Tues–Sun 10am–2pm & 4–7pm; 980 694 747, https://www.toroayto.es).

Valladolid and around

VALLADOLID, at the centre of the *meseta* and capital of the Castilla y León region, ought to be dramatic and exciting. Many of the greatest figures of Spain's Golden Age – Fernando and Isabel, Columbus, Cervantes, Torquemada, Felipe II – lived in the city at various times, and for five years at the turn of the seventeenth century it vied with Madrid as the royal capital. It had wealth and prestige, yet modern Valladolid – a busy, working city of 301,000 – lost much that was irreplaceable, as many of its finest palaces and grandest streets were destroyed during the Peninsular War with France (1808–14). Nonetheless, much that remains is appealing in a city centre of restored squares and gleaming churches, with a series of excellent art museums including the Museo Nacional de Escultura, which holds the finest collection of religious sculpture anywhere in Spain. While it doesn't have the overriding beauty of Salamanca or the standout monumental presence of Burgos or León, Valladolid is an easy city to like – whether it's the pretty shaded gardens of the Campo Grande or the student bars lined up in the shadow of the majestic Santa María de la Antigua church. The best time to get a sense of the city's historic traditions is **Semana Santa** (Holy Week), when Valladolid is host to many extravagant and solemn processions.

Outside the city, there are easy side trips to the historic towns of **Tordesillas** and **Medina del Campo**.

Plaza Mayor

The heart of Valladolid is the spacious **Plaza Mayor**, a broad expanse surrounded by arcaded buildings painted a striking, uniform red. Originally laid out in the sixteenth century after a fire had devastated the city, it was the first plaza of its kind in the country, becoming the model for countless similar civic centrepieces in both Spain and its South American colonies. Though much rebuilt since, it's still one of the grandest urban spaces in Spain, scene of festival celebrations and concerts throughout the year. Its arcade cafés make a pleasant place to watch the world go by, while many of Valladolid's best tapas bars and restaurants can be found in the narrow streets just off its western edge.

Mercado del Val

C/Francisco Zarandona • http://mercadodelval.com

The main city **market** lies just north of Pza. Mayor, and clocks in at a rather impressive 112m long. The nineteenth-century cast-iron building was inspired by Les Halles in Paris and has undergone major renovations. It's now a traditional market with a number of "*gastropuestos*" – mini gastro bars for drinking and snacking. The market closes at 3pm most days, but the bars stay open til late.

Museo Patio Herreriano

C/Jorge Guillén 6 • Free • http://museopatioherreriano.org

The brilliant-white, restored Monasterio de San Benito houses the **Museo Patio Herreriano**. It's a beautiful space dedicated to contemporary Spanish art (from 1918 to the present day), with galleries on several floors wrapped around a Renaissance courtyard of luminous pale-gold stone. There's a permanent display of works by artists at the forefront of Spanish Cubism, Surrealism and abstract art, including Rafael Barradas, Joaquin Torres-García, Julio González and Ángel Ferrant, but also temporary exhibitions by young contemporary artists and sculptors.

Museo de Valladolid

Pza. de Fabio Nelli • Charge, free on weekends • 983 351 389

A classic piece of architecture from Valladolid's golden age, the city's finest Renaissance mansion holds the galleries of the **Museo de Valladolid**, containing the municipal archeological and art collections. The building – notably the impressive main staircase and internal courtyard – is magnificent; the old-fashioned displays less so, being the usual run of prehistoric bones, Bronze Age tools, Roman grave goods and medieval art.

The Catedral

Visitors' entrance on Pza. de la Universidad • **Museum** Charge • **Catedral** Free, charge to climb the tower • http://catedral-valladolid.com

The city's sixteenth-century **Catedral** is built right on top of the remains of its medieval predecessor. However, only half of it was ever built and what stands is something of a

---

FOOTSTEPS OF THE FAMOUS

Felipe II was born (1527) in Valladolid, and in other circumstances perhaps his home city and not Madrid might have become the permanent Spanish capital. As it was, Valladolid was only briefly the capital (1601–06), but Felipe's birthplace, the Palacio de los Pimentel (C/Angustias), has a memorial plaque, and his statue is over the way in Pza. San Pablo. Another surviving palace, Palacio de los Viveros (C/Ramon y Cajal), is where the royal teenagers **Fernando and Isabel** married in 1469, later to be the "Catholic Monarchs" of a new, triumphant Spain. The widely travelled **Miguel Cervantes** spent a few years in the city, too – what's thought to have been his house (Casa Cervantes, just off C/Miguel Iscar) is now a small museum. However, the city is perhaps proudest of **Christopher Columbus** (Cristóbal Colón), who died here in 1506 – there's a replica of the house he died in, known as Casa Colón, on C/Colón.

5

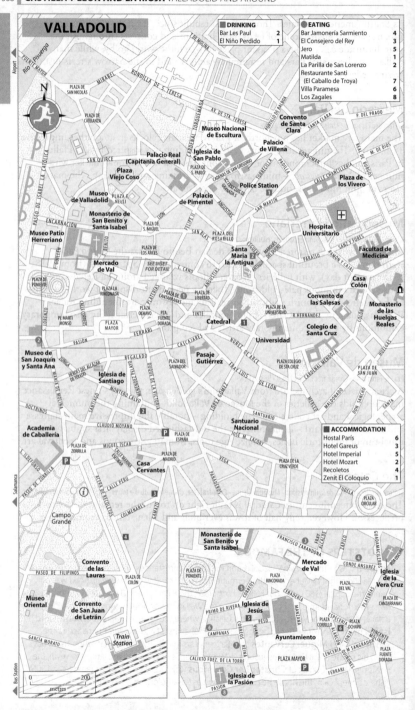

VALLADOLID

disappointment – rather plain, rather severe and rather hard to view as a whole. Inside, the highlight is the *retablo mayor* by Juan de Juni (and even this was actually made for the Gothic Santa María la Antigua in the plaza behind). Another addition to the Catedral is the ability to climb up its 70m-tall south tower to enjoy spectacular views over the city. The small **Museo Diocesano y Catedralicio** is more pleasing on the eye: the rooms of the former mortuary are packed full of treasures, including works by Baroque sculptors Gregorio Fernández and Juan de Juni.

Iglesia de San Pablo

Pza. de San Pablo • Open during services

If Valladolid's Catedral is no looker, you don't have to walk far to find a church that delivers. Protected by fourteen lions on pedestals brandishing heraldic plaques, the exuberant **Iglesia de San Pablo** – the sole surviving part of a Dominican convent destroyed in the nineteenth century – has an amazing facade that combines a wild mixture of styles in a froth of sculpted columns, expressive figures, and star and floral motifs. Added to by various regal and noble sponsors over a century or so, it's actually in two different styles, the lower part a lavish form of late Gothic known as Hispano-Flemish Gothic, the upper a confection of more classical style similar to the Catedral Nueva in Salamanca.

Museo Nacional de Escultura

C/Cadenas de San Gregorio 1–3 • Charge, free Sat afternoon & Sun morning • https://www.cultura.gob.es/mnescultura/

The most extraordinary sculpted facade of all in Valladolid is that of the **Colegio de San Gregorio**, adorned not just with coats of arms and crowned lions, but children clambering in the branches of a pomegranate tree and long-haired men carrying maces. Considered to be from the workshop of master sculptor Gil de Siloé, it's very much like icing on a cake. The building was constructed as a theological college by the Bishop of Palencia, Fray Alonso de Burgos – the Chancellor of Castile and confessor to Queen Isabel – and was richly endowed with Gothic Hispano-Flemish architecture, most obviously with a gleaming two-tier courtyard of twisted stone columns and an upper gallery that's a sculpted flight of fancy of heraldic, mythic and regal symbols. Inside, too, the building has been majestically restored and now contains the unmissable religious art and sculpture collection of the **Museo Nacional de Escultura**.

The stunningly presented collection from the thirteenth to eighteenth centuries includes some of the most brilliant works of the Spanish Renaissance and Baroque eras. Set in majestic galleries on two floors, arranged around the San Gregorio courtyard, the hugely expressive sculptures and other artworks were often commissioned directly for churches and monasteries.

The magnificent Renaissance works of sixteenth-century artists, such as **Alonso Berruguete** (1490–1561) and the Frenchman **Juan de Juni** (1507–77), are quite beautifully brutal: weeping crucifixion wounds, severed heads, agonized faces and rapt expressions. The dissolved Valladolid monastery of San Benito el Real also offers several pieces that are typical of the richness and power on display. The lower level houses some of the best examples of *pasos processionals* in northern Spain, with seventeenth-century masterpieces by Gregorio Fernández and Francisco de Rincón. The melodramatic – often comical – figures on floats, depicting scenes from The Passion, continue to be paraded through the streets of Valladolid every Easter to celebrate Semana Santa.

Palacio de Villena

C/Cadenas de San Gregorio 2 • Free • 983 250 375

Across the street from the San Gregorio facade stands the Renaissance **Palacio de Villena**, used as the **Museo Nacional de Escultura**'s centre for temporary exhibitions

5

and public events. It also contains one final, and extraordinary, flourish, namely the so-called **Belén Napolitano** or Nativity tableau – in an eighteenth-century Neapolitan street, between the hanging laundry, itinerant musicians and fruit sellers, the three Wise Men troop towards the manger on camels.

ARRIVAL AND INFORMATION
VALLADOLID

Arrival points are centred around Campo Grande park: the **train station** is at the foot of the park, and the **bus station** a few minutes' walk west.

By plane There's a small airport (983 415 500, https://www.aena.es/es/valladolid) 10km outside the city, served by domestic flights only. Buses and taxis run to the centre.

By train The train station is on C/Norte Recondo. It's a 15min walk up to town from the train station, or take one of the taxis outside. The AVE high-speed train service (reservations recommended) makes Valladolid just over an hour's jump from Madrid. It's also convenient by train from Valladolid to Palencia, Burgos, León and Medina del Campo. For information, consult RENFE http://renfe.com.

Destinations Burgos (up to 11 daily; 40min–1hr 30min); León (up to 14 daily; 1hr 30min–2hr); Madrid (33 daily; 1hr); Medina del Campo (hourly; 25–35min); Palencia (hourly; 30–50min); Salamanca (6 daily; 1hr 30min); Zamora (4 daily; 1hr 50min).

By bus The Estación de Autobuses is at C/Puente Colgante

2 (938 236 308). Bus companies include Auto Res/Avanza to Tordesillas/Salamanca (983 220 274, http://avanzabus.com) and La Regional to Tordesillas, Toro, Zamora, Palencia, Peñafiel (983 308 088, http://laregionalvsa.com).

Destinations El Burgo de Osma (4 daily; 2hr); Burgos (5 daily; 2hr); León (up to 9 daily; 2hr); Madrid (hourly; 2hr 30min); Palencia (Mon–Fri hourly, Sat & Sun 4 daily; 1hr 30min–2hr); Peñafiel (up to 7 daily; 1hr); Salamanca (up to 8 daily; 1hr 40min); Segovia (hourly; 2hr); Soria (4 daily; 3hr); Zamora (Mon–Fri hourly, Sat & Sun 4–6 daily; 1hr 30min).

By car Some of the signposted car parks offer all-day parking, such as the one opposite the bus station.

Turismo C/Acera de Recoletos, near the top of the Campo Grande (July to mid-Sept Mon–Sat 9.30am–2pm & 4.30–7.30pm, Sun 9.30am–2pm; rest of the year Mon–Sat 9.30am–2pm & 4–7pm, Sun 9.30am–2pm; 983 219 310, http://info.valladolid.es).

ACCOMMODATION
SEE MAP PAGE 368

The main concentration of **accommodation** – in all price ranges – is in the pleasant area around Pza. Mayor, though there are also some places down the east side of Campo Grande.

★ **Hostal París** C/Especería 2, http://hostalparis.com. The best mid-range place, with very agreeable rooms for the price. Some of the front ones have glassed-in street-facing balconies, though it's quieter at the back. Two cafés downstairs have good breakfast deals. €

★ **Hotel Gareus** C/Colmenares 2, http://hotelgareus.com. Stepping into the lobby at this terrific four-star boutique hotel is like entering a wonderful library, with a wall lined with books, marble floors, Chesterfield-style armchairs and ethnographic sculptures. The elegant style continues in the spacious bedrooms. There's also a fancy cocktail bar. €€

Hotel Imperial C/Peso 4, http://hotelimperial.es. Old-fashioned hotel in a beautiful Renaissance mansion right

by Pza. Mayor. Everything is a bit on the fussy side, but it's good value for money. The swish columned bar is certainly a talking point too. €

Hotel Mozart C/Mendez Pelayo 7, http://hotelmozart.net. This smart renovated three-star hotel occupies a very central location and offers spacious, modern rooms and a shiny bar with tables inside or outside on the sunny terrace. €

Recoletos C/Acera de Recoletos 13, https://www.valladolidrecoletos.com/. The city's finest boutique lodgings, opposite Campo Grande and not far from the train station, in a handsomely restored mansion. Upper-storey "loft" rooms have particularly good views. €€

Zenit El Coloquio Pza. de la Universidad 11, https://elcoloquio.zenithoteles.com/es/. The hotel is located right in the centre of town, close to the university and the Catedral. Sleek rooms offer views of one or the other. There's also an outdoor patio area with seating and a café. €€

EATING
SEE MAP PAGE 368

Pza. Mayor has the best outdoor **cafés** for a drink with views, while the streets around C/Correos, just to the west, are lined with largely upscale **tapas bars and restaurants** (though you'll still get a *menú del día* here for €15).

TAPAS BARS
Bar Jamonería Sarmiento C/Conde Ansúrez 11,

https://www.facebook.com/JamoneriaSarmiento/. A cross between a deli and a bar, this great little tapas bar presents a choice of cold cuts and simple tapas, from *morcilla* or *jamón* to *ventresca* tuna salad, accompanied by some fine regional wines. €

★ **Jero** C/Correos 11, http://jero.alacarta.site. Valladolid has an annual creative tapas competition and *Jero* often comes out on top, with its remarkable sculpted *canapés* called things like "Matrix", "Galactico" or "Mission Impossible" (a *bacalao*-and-mushroom *montadito* topped with tomato confit, prawn and almond crunch). €

Matilda C/Ebanistería 16–18, http://factoriamatilda. wordpress.com. This friendly café overlooking the regenerated Pza. de Cantarranas has large communal wooden tables and serves something a little different to the usual tapas plates. Think toast with grilled aubergines and tomatoes, hummus, nachos and Thai-style burritos. It's a good place for vegetarians. €

Villa Paramesa Pza. Martí y Monsó 4 http://villa paramesa.com. This well-regarded place, just off the Pza. Mayor, turns tapas-making into an artisanal craft, with elves in the kitchen turning out exquisite creations while the sommelier chooses wine from an extensive range. €€

RESTAURANTS

El Consejero del Rey C/Francisco Zarandona 6, http:// elconsejerodelrey.com. One of Valladolid's best restaurants, *El Consejero del Rey* serves beautifully presented mains, such as *robo del toro* in Pedro Ximénez wine sauce and grilled

octopus with chickpea foam. €€€

★ **La Parrilla de San Lorenzo** Pza. Pedro Niño 1, https://laparrilladesanlorenzo.es. To dine beneath the steady gaze of a Templar Knight in the cellar of a former convent is a unique experience. At this grandiose restaurant, you can admire the rich collection of gilt-framed art and museum pieces while tucking into the famous regional dish *lechazo* (suckling lamb). €€€

★ **Restaurante Santi (El Caballo de Troya)** C/Correos 1, http://restaurantesanti.es. Centrally located near the Pza. Mayor, this very atmospheric restaurant is set around a beautiful sixteenth-century courtyard. Mains include dishes such as lamb stew and grilled hake, they also offer a *menú del día*. The *Taberna Santi* next door offers more affordable dishes and tapas bites. €€€

Los Zagales C/Pasión 13, http://loszagales.com. This Valladolid institution, traditionally decked out with Spanish tiles, timber beams and barrels, has won numerous awards for its special tapas creations, while the normal menu includes the usual calamari, *croquetas* and *morcilla* (black pudding) from Burgos. €€

DRINKING SEE MAP PAGE 368

There are two good areas for late-opening **bars**: either in the Zona Coca – around the Pza. Martí y Monsó – or anywhere around the Catedral and the nearby Santa María de la Antigua church.

Bar Les Paul C/Empecinado 5, https://lespaulbar.com. An ambient rock and blues bar in the historic heart of Valladolid, named in honour of the legendary guitarist. Has

a pool table, a darts board, and also shows sports on TV.

★ **El Niño Perdido** C/Esgueva 16, https://www. instagram.com/elninoperdido_. This funky circus-themed bar is located very near the Catedral and has won numerous awards for its innovative cocktails. Sip your concoction while listening to smooth tracks of jazz and blues.

Tordesillas

The quiet riverside town of **TORDESILLAS**, 30km southwest of Valladolid, boasts an important place in Spain's (indeed, the world's) history. It was here, with papal authority, that the **Treaty of Tordesillas** (1494) divided "All Lands Discovered, or Hereafter to be Discovered in the West, towards the Indies or the Ocean Seas" between Spain and Portugal, along a line 370 leagues west of the Cape Verde Islands. Brazil went to Portugal – though it was claimed that the Portuguese already knew of its existence but had kept silent to gain better terms. The rest of the New World, including Mexico and Peru, became Spanish, with the consequences to play out across the generations.

Today's town is a low-key delight of faded red-brick buildings set around a charming, arcaded Plaza Mayor. There's a museum or two, and several timeworn churches, while a long medieval bridge extends across the wide Río Duero. There's a small beach on the other side, although swimming is not recommended, and a summer bar that's great for catching the evening breeze.

Real Monasterio de Santa Clara

Santa Clara • Charge • http://patrimonionacional.es

The town's most significant monument is the **Real Monasterio de Santa Clara**, which was originally built as a royal palace. It overlooks the Duero and is known as "The Alhambra of Castile" for its delightful Mudéjar architecture. The highlights here include the golden roof of the chancel and an organ that is thought to have belonged

5

to the unfortunate **Juana la Loca** (Joanna the Mad), daughter of Fernando and Isabel. She spent 46 years locked up in a windowless cell within a palace that once stood in the centre of Tordesillas. After Isabel's death, she had ruled Castile jointly with her husband Felipe I from 1504 to 1506 but was devastated by his early death, and for three years afterwards toured the monasteries of Spain, keeping the coffin perpetually by her side and stopping from time to time to inspect the corpse. In 1509, she reached Tordesillas, where first Fernando and, later, her son, Carlos V, declared her 'insane', imprisoning her for half a century and assuming the throne of Castile for themselves.

Several of the Convento's rooms and spaces are open to the public, including the pretty patio, with its horseshoe arches and Moorish decoration, while the former palace's fourteenth-century **Baños Árabes** (Arab baths) can also be visited – though they're closed during wet weather.

ARRIVAL AND INFORMATION   TORDESILLAS

By bus There are departures to Valladolid (daily; 30min) and Zamora (daily; 50min) with La Regional (http://laregionalvsa.com). The bus station is situated outside the old town centre.
By car Parking is easy near the bridge, beneath the old town.

Turismo Casas del Tratado, overlooking the river and signposted from the Pza. Mayor (June–Sept Tues–Sat 10am–1.30pm & 5–7.30pm, Sun 10am–2pm; Oct–May Tues–Sat 10am–1.30pm & 4–6.30pm, Sun 10am–2pm; 983 771 067, http://tordesillas.net).

ACCOMMODATION AND EATING

Hostal San Antolín C/San Antolín 8, http://hostalsan antolin.com. The best of the town's accommodation options, on a quiet old street in the centre. Rooms are nicely furnished, in vibrant colours, and non-guests are welcome at the decent grill-restaurant. €
Parador de Tordesillas Carretera Salamanca 5, 1km out

on the Salamanca road, http://parador.es. This tranquil parador is almost country club in feel, with grounds shaded by leafy pines, a sizeable outdoor pool and comfortable, rustic-style rooms. The regional Castilian restaurant is a treat. €€€

Medina del Campo

MEDINA DEL CAMPO, 23km south of Tordesillas and around 55km from Valladolid, stands below one of the region's great castles, the Moorish, brick-built Castillo de la Mota. The castle sits on one side of the train line, the town on the other, and it's also worth walking into the centre to see what's left of Renaissance Medina del Campo (Market of the Field), which in the fifteenth and sixteenth centuries was one of the most important market towns in Europe. Merchants came from as far afield as Italy and Germany to attend its *ferias* (fairs), and the handsome **Pza. Mayor de la Hispanidad** – ringed by cafés and restaurants – is still evocative of the days when the town's bankers determined the value of European currencies.

Castillo de la Mota

Avda. del Castillo • Charge, pre-booking essential (free entry to ground floor) • http://castillodelamota.es

A classic child's design if there ever was one – four square towers, battlements and a deep moat – the **Castillo de la Mota** often housed Queen Isabel's army, and later served as both prison and girls' boarding school. A visitor centre throws light on the castle's history, while areas open to the public include the main courtyard and lower rooms, including the impressive brick-vaulted chapel.

Museo de las Ferias

C/San Martín 26, near Pza. Mayor • Charge • http://museoferias.net

For the story of Medina's fifteenth- and sixteenth-century fairs, visit the **Museo de las Ferias**, which traces the history from their origins as simple trade gatherings to their later role as essential European money markets. Exhibits – from Flemish textiles to Italian silver – demonstrate the wealth that once poured into this now small town.

By train The quickest way here is by train from Valladolid; there's an hourly service and the journey takes 20–30min.

Turn right out of the station and keep walking for the castle and underpass to town.

Palencia and around

PALENCIA, 47km north of Valladolid, is Castile's least-known city, and capital of a small and equally unheralded province of the same name. Its outstanding Catedral hints at its rich past, especially in Roman and medieval times – Spain's oldest university was founded here in 1208 – however, today's city of 80,000 is a more modest place. There are pretty riverside gardens, famous Semana Santa processions and numerous restored plazas, most dominated by white-stone churches. In the wider province, Palencia also reveals its charms, especially in the north in the so-called Montaña Palentina – a region of peaks, lakes and Romanesque churches – but also along the Palencian section of the Santiago pilgrimage route (see page 398).

Catedral San Antolín

Pza. de la Inmaculada • Charge, free for under 12s and on Tues afternoons • http://catedraldepalencia.org

The older part of the city centre is at its most attractive near the Gothic **Catedral San Antolín**, which faces a large open square surrounded by restored buildings. The exterior is plain by Spanish standards; and as Palencia fell into decline soon after the Catedral's completion in 1219, there's an almost complete absence of Baroque trappings inside. However, this simply focuses attention on the highlights within, notably the stunning *retablo mayor*, which contains twelve beautiful little panels, ten of them painted by Juan de Flandes, court painter to Isabel – it's the best collection of his work anywhere. A staircase leads down into the atmospheric crypt, containing the worn, carved columns of the earlier Visigothic and Romanesque churches on this site, and an ancient well. The ticket also includes entry to the enclosed cloisters and the on-site **Museo Catedralicio**, featuring an early El Greco and some Flemish tapestries.

There are charming **riverside gardens** behind the Catedral, with two old stone bridges, while following the river further up, at the top of town, leads to more extensive parkland.

Plaza Mayor and around

Halfway along the main pedestrianized street of C/Mayor lies Palencia's principal square, **Plaza Mayor**, arcaded against the fierce Castilian summer sun and the biting winter winds. It's modest but attractive, like Palencia itself, with the old cast-iron market hall just visible off one side of the square and the thirteenth-century church of **San Francisco** off the other. If the church pricks your interest, then, with a map from the *turismo*, you can track down the other Romanesque and Gothic churches, all signposted on a walking route through town.

Palencia's adjacent **bus and train stations** are located at the north end of the city centre. The roundabout of Pza. León is over on the far side of the gardens to your left as you leave either terminal; from here the long, pedestrianized C/Mayor – the main shopping street – runs up to the Pza. Mayor (10min walk).

By train The train station is on Pza. de los Jardinillos.

Destinations Burgos (7 daily; 1hr 30 min); León (up to 18

daily; 1hr–1hr 30min); Valladolid (hourly; 30min).

By bus The Estación de Autobuses is on C/Pedro Berruguete (979 743 222).

Destinations Burgos (up to 3 daily; 1hr 15min); Carrión de los Condes (up to 3 daily; 45min); Madrid (4 daily; 3hr); Salamanca (up to 5 daily; 2hr 15min); Valladolid (hourly; 1hr); Zamora (up to 2 daily; 2hr 15min).

By car Short-term street parking is easy, or head for one

5

of the signposted car parks, like that at the Estación de Pequeña Velocidad on C/Juan Ramón Jiménez just east of the market.

Turismo C/Mayor 31 (July to mid-Sept Mon–Sat 9.30am–

2pm & 5–8pm, Sun 9.30am–5pm; mid-Sept to June Mon–Sat 9.30am–2pm & 4–7pm, Sun 9.30am–5pm; 979 706 523, http://palenciaturismo.es).

ACCOMMODATION

There aren't many exciting **accommodation** options in Palencia but hotels are at least reasonably priced and rarely full. If you prefer to see Palencia by day and stay outside the city, look no further than *Casa del Abad* in nearby Ampudia (see below).

Diana Palace Avda. de Santander 12, http://eurostarshotels.com. For a comfortable night in a four-

star business hotel, try the *Diana Palace*, opposite the train station – there are good web deals often available. €€

Hotel Don Rodrigo C/Los Gatos, https://www.hoteldonrodrigo.com. This three-star hotel near the Catedral is a good choice for a night or two in Palencia. The white-tiled rooms have everything you need, although they could do with updating. €

EATING AND DRINKING

Pza. Mayor comes into its own in the early evening, as families come out for a stroll and a drink. Later on, head for the tapas bars and restaurants on **Pza. Seminario** (off C/Cardenal Almaraz), C/Don Sancho and C/Los Soldados or to the bars on Paseo del Salón and Pza. San Pablo.

Asador La Encina C/Casañé 2, http://asadorlaencina.com.

Tortilla fans are in for a treat here, as this elegant restaurant with its bright-orange dining room is one of the best places to try this succulent dish in the whole of Spain. They also specialize in *lechazo churro*, a cut of lamb which has been slowly roasted in their brick oven. €€€€

Basílica de San Juan de Baños

Baños de Cerrato, near Venta de Baños, 7km south of Palencia • Charge (cash only), free Wed • https://ventadebanos.es/turismo/basilica-de-san-juan-de-banos/ • Roughly hourly buses from Palencia bus station (only three or four at weekends) run out to Baños in around 15min

A tucked-away village just outside Palencia contains the oldest church in the entire peninsula. The seventh-century **Basílica de San Juan de Baños**, established by the Visigoth King Recesvinto in 661, has tiny lattice windows and horseshoe arches, and incorporates materials from Roman buildings.

Ampudia

28km southwest of Palencia, along the P901

For a complete change of pace from the Castilian cities to all sides, make the quick drive from Palencia up onto the high farming plain, where the industrial suburbs soon give way to shimmering meadows, rippling cornfields and scores of wind turbines. The tiny town of **AMPUDIA**, with a population of well under a thousand, is a quiet gem, boasting two long porticoed streets whose seventeenth-century houses are supported by tree-trunk columns, some of which are several hundred years old. Once a serious feudal stronghold, Ampudia has a huge castle set on higher, grassy ground, with sweeping views, and an equally majestic Gothic church, though the somnolent streets, shuttered houses and dung-spattered farms at the town's edge are a more reliable indicator of its current status. That said, there is one magnificent place to stay here, ideal for a luxurious night out in the sticks.

ACCOMMODATION AND EATING   AMPUDIA

★ **Posada Real la Casa del Abad de Ampudia** Pza. Francisco Martin Gromaz 2, http://casadelabad.com. The former abbot's house is now a remarkable rustic-chic five-star hotel. A bright sun mural shines down from the entrance cupola, while gorgeous rooms feature bold colour washes on rough plaster walls, reclaimed-wood furniture

and designer bathrooms. Exposed stone and ancient beams abound and there's a retractable roof over the lounge-bar patio, while the classy restaurant – serving grilled hake to *chuletón* – occupies the old wine press. There's also a pool and some very elegant spa facilities. €€

Villa y Corte C/Reoyo 6, http://villaycorte.com. This cosy rural hotel feels more like an old-fashioned country home, with its warming fireplaces, oversized armchairs and comfortable living room. The welcoming restaurant serves local dishes such as *morcilla* (blood sausage), *sopa Castellana* (a traditional soup made from bread, garlic, chorizo or ham, and often eggs), *rabo del toro* and roasted lamb. €

The Ribera del Duero

The **Río Duero** long marked the frontier between Christian and Arab territory. It meanders right across central Castile, between Zamora and Soria, with the eastern section in particular, from Valladolid, marked by a series of spectacular castles and old market towns, some restored as tourist attractions, others crumbling to dust. This part of the river is also at the heart of one of Spain's greatest wine-producing areas, the **Ribera del Duero** (see page 375). It's a fine route to follow by car (N122), stopping off for lunch in rustic *posadas* and for walks in the beautiful surroundings. You can make the trip by bus, but if you do, realistically, you'll only be able to see the major towns of Peñafiel and El Burgo de Osma.

Peñafiel

The first stop along the Rio Duero from Valladolid is **PEÑAFIEL**, 60km to the east, whose fabulous castle is visible long before you reach the town. Standing on a narrow ridge, and at 210m long but only 23m across, it bears an astonishing resemblance to a huge ship run aground. At the edge of town and entirely surrounded by balconied wooden buildings, the other extraordinary sight is Pza. del Coso, which doubles as perhaps the most spectacular bullring in Spain during Peñafiel's Día de San Roque festival every August.

Castillo de Peñafiel

Charge, combined ticket available with Museo Provincial del Vino or wine-tasting tour • http://provinciadevalladolid.com

It's quite a hike up to the **Castillo de Peñafiel** (it's far easier to drive), which was built in the mid-fifteenth century out of the region's distinctive white stone. Guided visits around the castle take around forty minutes or so, after which you're encouraged to explore the **Museo Provincial del Vino**, where you can learn all about the Ribera del Duero wines – and even taste a few if you wish.

ARRIVAL AND INFORMATION   PEÑAFIEL

By bus From Valladolid, buses drop you on the west side of the Río Duratón – walk down to the river and cross the bridge, then turn right and walk up to the central Pza. de España. The street off the top of this square leads in 5min to Pza. del Coso.

By car Parking's not usually a problem, but if the town centre proves tricky, use the massive free car park a little way out on the road up to the castle.

THE WINES OF THE RIBERA DEL DUERO

Some of Spain's most celebrated red wine comes from the demarcated region of **Ribera del Duero** (http://rutadelvinoriberadelduero.es), including the country's best-known and most expensive wine, Vega Sicilia. Around 170 wineries are found along the Duero, with many of the *bogedas* concentrated between Peñafiel and Aranda del Duero, 40km to the east. If you'd like to make winery visits (not all are open for tours), the comprehensive website is a good place to start – some wineries require advance reservations, though many have shops that are open to casual buyers mornings and afternoons. **Bodegas Alejandro Fernandez** (http://grupopesquera.com) makes its fabulous Tinto Pesquera at Pesquera de Duero, 4km north of Peñafiel, while the acclaimed **Señorio de Nava** (http://senoriodenava.es) is based at Nava de Roa, 13km to the east.

5

ACCOMMODATION AND EATING

There are a couple of cheapish places to stay in the centre, but Peñafiel probably only warrants a night if you can run to one of the grander choices.

Azz Peñafiel Las Claras Pza. Adolfo Muñoz Alonso, https://www.azzhoteles.com/en/azz-penafiel-las-claras/. This seventeenth-century convent by the bridge, now a four-star riverside hotel and spa, retains its erstwhile elegance, with its cloister-lobby, tree-shaded terrace and garden pool. There's a good restaurant located in the former chapel, as well as a terrace café with a lunchtime *menú del día*. €€

Hotel AF Pesquera Paseo Estación 1, https://www.hotelpesquera.com. Another boutique option, this hotel and spa – a refurbished 1922 flour mill – is a grand, peaceful retreat in the heart of the wine region. Some rooms have stunning views of the castle. €€

Peñaranda del Duero

Whichever direction you come from you'll pass through rolling vineyards to reach the gorgeous, golden-hued town of **PEÑARANDA DEL DUERO**, whose restored historic heart sits beneath a battlemented castle. It's a popular weekend getaway, hence the rather upmarket accommodation and pristine houses, but nothing detracts from the first view of the picture-perfect Pza. Mayor – Renaissance palace on one side, bulky church on the other and flower-decked wooden houses.

With a day to spare, you might want to take the signposted local **walk** (21km) that leads up hill and down dale from Peñaranda, through the woods. Back at La Vid by the highway, marvel at how such a small village with such a small name has quite such a large monastery (guided visits available, check http://monasteriodelavid.org for times).

El Burgo de Osma and around

There's absurdly picturesque Río Duero scenery at **EL BURGO DE OSMA**, once a very grand place boasting both Catedral and university. Today, there are gleaming town walls, a lovely riverside promenade and ancient colonnaded streets overhung by houses supported on precarious wooden props. It's quaint and gorgeous in equal measure, and while the dominant Catedral is the only actual sight, the town rewards a leisurely stroll up the arcaded main street to Pza. Mayor. On summer nights, as the temperature drops, the families of El Burgo use the main square, with its lovely cafés and tree-shaded benches, as a playground, exercise yard and social space. Just out of town, there are easy drives to all sorts of fascinating destinations, from a canyon park to a mighty fortress, which makes El Burgo well worth a night's stay.

Parque Natural del Cañón del Río Lobos

Visitor centre 975 363 564 • https://www.cañondelriolobos.com; www.patrimonionatural.org

Don't miss the excursion north of El Burgo de Osma to the dramatically rocky landscape of **Parque Natural del Cañón del Río Lobos**. It's a quick 14km drive on a ruler-straight road to the small village of Ucero, just outside which (under the ruined castle) is the Casa del Parque **visitor centre**. From the visitor centre, the main road runs another kilometre or so up to the stone bridge over the source of the Río Ucero, where you've a choice. The signposted left turn here runs along the valley floor towards the Romanesque **Ermita de San Bartolomé**. There's a bar-restaurant near the turn, and plenty of parking and picnic places further in among the trees, from where paths run into the spectacular gorge – one of the walks from the visitor centre leads to the hermitage and back. The main road, meanwhile, twists up for 3km to the top of the canyon and the **Mirador de la Galiana** (1122m), affording mesmerizing views of the canyon walls and the circling eagles and vultures. It's worth noting that everything in the park is very busy in August, at Easter and on bank holidays, when it's not particularly *tranquilo* anywhere.

ARRIVAL AND INFORMATION

EL BURGO DE OSMA

By bus and car El Burgo is 60km east of Aranda del Duero and around 150km from Valladolid. The bus station is on the main Valladolid–Soria road through town, with free street parking along the road here, and Pza. Mayor just a minute or two's walk away.

Turismo Pza. Mayor, inside the former Hospital de San Agustín (Wed–Sun 10am–2pm & 4–7pm; 975 360 116, http://burgodeosma.es).

ACCOMMODATION

There is plenty of accommodation and at all three hotels (except *El Balcon*) you can park virtually outside.

El Balcon de la Catedral Pza. San Pedro 6, https://elbalcon delacatedral.es. These superb, charming apartments in the arcades of the Cathedral Square are rural and romantic, and can accommodate between two and five people. Location-wise, you can't get much better than this. €€

Castilla Termal Burgo de Osma C/de la Universidad 5, https://www.castillatermal.com. Housed in the old sixteenth-century Universidad de Santa Catalina, this elegant hotel and spa is well worth the extra splurge. Rooms are cosy and stylish and preserve all the old features of the university, such as arched windows and brick walls. There are lovely spa facilities and an excellent restaurant.

Better deals, which also include breakfast and a spa session, are available online. €€

Hospedería El Fielato Avda. Juan Carlos I, 1°, at C/Mayor, http://hospederiaelfielato.es. Decent rooms, if nothing glam, at a very reasonable hotel located in an old buiding right next door to the *Hotel II Virrey*. €

Hotel II Virrey C/Mayor 2, http://virreypalafox.com. The town's best hotel comes complete with baronial fittings that are virtually tourist attractions in their own right. The rooms are rather more modern, with contemporary fabrics and furnishings. There's a café at the hotel (which is entered from either the main road through town or Pza. Mayor); the restaurant (see below) is further up the main road, and website deals often include dinner. €

EATING AND DRINKING

El Burgo is a pork and steak town, and you can eat big, meaty meals at a number of *asadores*, including a couple of places along C/Mayor. The *Restaurante Virrey* is the local pig specialist – it even has a "pork museum" and an annual spring pig slaughter (*matanza*).

Casa Engracia C/Ruiz Zorrilla 3, 975 340 155. Good for a meal at modest prices – you can have tapas and drinks in the bar or meals in the small *comedor* at the back, where straightforward meat and fish grills are available, accompanied by decent local wine from ceramic jugs.

There's also a *menú del día*. €

Restaurante Virrey C/Universidad 7, https://virreypalafox. com/restaurante-virrey-palafox/. In an undistinguished building on the main road, this is the best restaurant in town, renowned for its regional cuisine. Pork in all guises is the *raison d'être* – especially at *matanza* weekends, when 22-dish tasting menus celebrate every cut of pork imaginable. There are also separate menus for vegetarians and children during these weekends. €€€

Calatañazor

Halfway between El Burgo de Osma and Soria, just off the N122, lies tiny **CALATAÑAZOR**, a sleepy medieval village overseen by skimpy castle ruins and some remarkable old houses, with their distinctive conical chimneys, decorative coats of arms and wooden balconies. It often seems deserted, though there's enough weekend and holiday trade to warrant several shops selling local honey, dried wild mushrooms and cheese.

ACCOMMODATION AND EATING

CALATAÑAZOR

Casa del Cura C/Real 25, http://posadarealcasadelcura. com. If you fancy a very quiet night, these rustic-chic lodgings make for a comfortable stay. There's also a rather

fancy restaurant, with an outdoor terrace overlooking the gorge. €€

Fortaleza de Gormaz

15km southeast of El Burgo de Osma, near Gormaz • Free

You'll see the stupendous **Fortaleza de Gormaz** fortress long before you climb to it, passing the nondescript village of Gormaz. It was originally built by the Moors in the tenth century, and two of their keyhole doorways survive, as well as a later medieval tower dating from after the castle was captured and modified by the Christians. The

5

fortress was once one of the largest fortified buildings in Spain – the inside is now a shell, albeit an enormous one, hundreds of metres across, and there are 28 towers in all, ruined but still mightily impressive. There are magnificent panoramas from here, down to the snaking Río Duero and the giant patchwork of fields in the cultivated plains below.

Berlanga de Duero

BERLANGA DE DUERO lies south of the N122 (Soria road), and a fair way south of the Río Duero as well, although it still takes the river's name. It's a quiet backwater that was rather more important in times past – the main sight is a **castle**, whose massive cylindrical towers and older double curtain-wall, reminiscent of Ávila, loom above the town. The way up is through a doorway in a ruined Renaissance palace, just a few minutes' walk from the centre. The **Pza. Mayor** is arcaded by precarious wooden posts sitting on stone pillars, while the other dominant monument is the **Colegiata de Nuestra Señora del Mercado**, one of the last flowerings of the Gothic style. Berlanga also has several fine mansions, some pretty arcaded streets, and **La Picota**, a "pillar of justice" to which offenders were tied (it's just outside the old town, on the El Burgo road). There are a few small hotels and restaurants, but little reason to stay overnight. The main square has a nice old café for coffee.

ARRIVAL AND INFORMATION   BERLANGA DE DUERO

By bus and car There's a bus service to Berlanga de Duero on Mondays and Fridays from Soria, which stops just out of the old centre, on the El Burgo road. The town stands just off the CL116 between El Burgo de Osma and Almazán (25km

from the former); coming from Gormaz (17km), follow the signs for Recuerda and then Morales.

Turismo Pza. del Mercado, Torre del Palacio (Daily 10am–2pm & 4–8pm; 975 343 433, http://berlangadeduero.es).

Ermita de San Baudelio de Berlanga

Casillas de Berlanga, 8km south of Berlanga de Duero; follow the pink signs from town • Charge, free Sat & Sun • 975 229 872

The thousand-year-old **Ermita de San Baudelio de Berlanga** is the best-preserved and most important example of Mozarabic style in Spain. Five years after being declared a national monument, in the 1920s, its marvellous cycle of frescoes was acquired by an international art dealer and exported to the US. After much fuss, the Spanish government got some of them back on indefinite loan, but they are now kept in the Prado in Madrid (see page 78). In spite of this loss, the simple hillside hermitage remains a beauty. Its ribbed interior vault springs from a central pillar, while much of the space is taken up by the tribune gallery of horseshoe arches. Some original frescoes do remain, including two bulls from the great sequence of animals and hunting scenes.

Centro de Interpretacion de San Baudelio de Berlanga

C/Bajada Dehesa 4 • Charge

The interpretation centre of the Ermita de San Baudelio de Berlanga is located in the main village and gives visitors an idea of the history of the **Ermita** and the surrounding area through audiovisual presentations, images, models and paintings. Ask at the *turismo* for access.

Soria and around

SORIA is a modest provincial capital of around 40,000 – an attractive place, despite encroaching suburbs, and the inspiration behind much of Antonio Machado's best-loved verse (the Seville-born poet lived here from 1907 to 1912). It stands between a ridgeback of hills on the banks of the Duero, with a castle ruin above and a medieval centre dotted with mansions and Romanesque churches. You can see all the sights

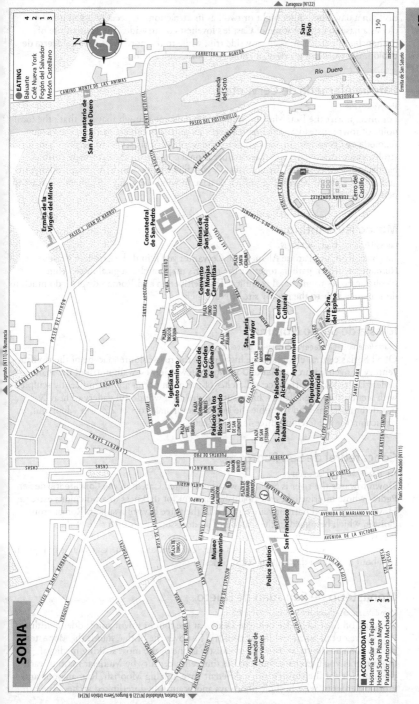

SORIA

Zaragoza (N122)

Ermita de San Saturio

Logroño (N111) & Numancia

Bus Station, Valladolid (N122) & Burgos/Sierra Urbión (N234)

Train Station & Madrid (N111)

EATING
Baluarte	4
Café Nueva York	2
Fogón del Salvador	1
Mesón Castellano	3

ACCOMMODATION
Hostería Solar de Tejada	1
Hotel Soria Plaza Mayor	2
Parador Antonio Machado	3

San Polo

Río Duero

Alameda del Soto

Monasterio de San Juan de Duero

Cerro del Castillo

Ermita de la Virgen del Mirón

Concatedral de San Pedro

Ruinas de San Nicolás

Convento de Monjas Carmelitas

Sta. María la Mayor

Centro Cultural

Ntra. Sra. del Espino

Iglesia de Santo Domingo

Palacio de los Condes de Gómara

Palacio de los Ríos y Salcedo

Palacio de Alcántara

Ayuntamiento

Diputación Provincial

S. Juan de Rabanera

Museo Numantino

Police Station

San Francisco

Parque Alameda de Cervantes

5

easily in a day, but a quiet night or two has its attractions, especially if you use the city as a base to explore some of Castile's loveliest countryside. The Roman site of **Numancia**, in particular, is an easy side trip, while to the northwest rises the **Sierra de Urbión**, the weekend getaway of choice for Soria's inhabitants.

Parque Alameda de Cervantes

Always open • Free

For once, it isn't the Pza. Mayor – quiet and handsome though that is – that's the focal point of town; instead Soria's best feature is its central botanical gardens, the **Parque Alameda de Cervantes**. In early evening, the whole of Soria seems to decamp here for strolls, games and chats, and there are occasional concerts in the extremely curious bandstand, the so-called "Tree of Music", which is wrapped entirely around a large tree, and far above head height; the musicians have to wind their way up a metal staircase to perform.

Museo Numantino

Paseo del Espolón 8 • Charge • 975 221 397

Just back from the Parque Alameda de Cervantes you'll find the excellent **Museo Numantino**, which gathers together the region's major archeological finds, from Neolithic bones to medieval ceramics. The Celtiberian and Roman displays do much to illuminate a visit to the nearby site of Numancia.

Iglesia de Santo Domingo

C/Santo Tomé, main entrance on Pza. del Vergell • Open only for services

Of all Soria's central churches, the highlight is the rose-coloured facade of the twelfth-century convent church of **Santo Domingo**, a few minutes' walk north of the main pedestrianized street. The recessed arches of the main portal are magnificently sculpted with scenes from the Life of Christ, surrounded by a wonderful gallery of heavily bearded musicians who resemble the lost medieval ancestors of ZZ Top – look out, in particular, for the fetching three-in-a-bed scene.

Concatedral de San Pedro

Pza. de San Pedro • Free, cloisters charge

Down towards the river is Soria's now rather isolated Catedral, the **Concatedral de San Pedro**, whose interior takes the Spanish penchant for darkness to a ridiculous extreme. However, light and harmony are restored in the three bays of a superb Romanesque cloister, which belonged to the Catedral's predecessor. The fourth side of the cloister is glassed in and contains the Catedral's best-preserved sculpture, a magnificent late twelfth-century work showing Christ's entry into Jerusalem. The Catedral is only open for about an hour a day, during Mass times.

Monasterio de San Juan de Duero

Paseo de las Ánimas • Charge, free Sat & Sun • 975 230 218

Standing on the old bridge over the Duero, at the foot of town, you suddenly realize that you're out of Soria and in the country. Just over the bridge stands the **Monasterio de San Juan de Duero**, whose ruined cloister is one of the most striking medieval monuments you'll ever see. Built in the thirteenth century by Mudéjar masons, each of the four sides of the cloister is in a different style, mixing Moorish, Romanesque and Gothic elements, with keyhole doorways and beautifully interlinked arches. The bare church, meanwhile, is now a museum, with two unusual freestanding temples inside boasting vivid, carved capitals.

Ermita de San Saturio

Camino San Saturio • Free • 975 180 703

The church of San Saturio, clinging to the edge of the rocks high above the River Duero, is quite a sight to behold. Legend has it that in the sixth century, a Sorian nobleman named Saturio decided to share out his wealth among the poor and go and live in a cave home next to the river. When part of the hermitage collapsed in 1694, it was replaced by a grand church that was completed in 1704. Today, the church features Gothic carvings, a beautiful Baroque alterpiece and intricate frescoes by the Baroque painter Juan Zapata Ferrer.

ARRIVAL AND INFORMATION   SORIA

By train The train station (912 320 320) is at the extreme southwest of the city, but limited services mean you're far more likely to arrive by bus.

By bus The bus station is on Avda. de Valladolid (975 225 160, https://www.estacionsoria.com) at the western side of the city, a 15min walk from the centre.

Destinations Burgos (1–3 daily; 2hr 15min); El Burgo de Osma (2–3 daily; 45min); Logroño (up to 8 daily; 1hr 30min); Madrid (8 daily; 2hr 30min); Medinaceli (6 daily; 1hr); Pamplona (5 daily; 2hr); Valladolid via Peñafiel (5

daily; 3hr); Vinuesa (2–3 daily; 25min); Zaragoza (2 daily; 2hr).

By car Street parking is easy to find, but is limited to 2hr in metered zones, so follow the signs to central car parks for overnight parking.

Turismo C/Medinaceli 2, near Parque Alameda de Cervantes (July to mid-Sept Mon–Sat 9am–2pm & 5–7.45pm, Sun 9.30am–2.30pm; mid-Sept to June Mon–Sat 9.30am–2pm & 4–6.45pm, Sun 9.30am–2.30pm; 975 212 052, http://sorianitelaimaginas.com).

ACCOMMODATION   SEE MAP PAGE 379

Soria's tourists are rarely great in number, so finding a place to stay shouldn't be a problem. There are plenty of centrally located budget options, and a reasonable choice of mid-range and four-star hotels.

Hostería Solar de Tejada C/Claustrilla 1, http://hosteria solardetejada.es. With its exposed wood and old stone walls, and charmingly decorated rooms all painted in different colours with coordinated fabrics, this is the best mid-range option in the city. €

Hotel Soria Plaza Mayor Pza. Mayor 10, https://hotelplazamayorsoria.com. This small boutique two-star townhouse has pride of place in Soria's prettiest old-town

square. Some rooms in the eaves retain their old beams, while decor, fabrics, bathrooms and public areas are all in the best contemporary style. €€

★ **Parador Antonio Machado** Parque del Castillo, www.parador.es. Soria's modern red-brick and glass parador has a beautiful hilltop location in the grounds of the ruined castle – there are steps down the hillside into the town centre (15min). Rooms are very spacious, with wooden floors and glassed-in balconies, and have stunning countryside views. Breakfast comes with the same glorious outlook, and the restaurant is a good choice for regional dishes. Check online for the best rates. €€

EATING   SEE MAP PAGE 379

Good **tapas** is the norm in Soria, while **restaurant** menus – here on the edge of Castile – show welcome Basque and Riojan influences, with fish and vegetables suddenly much more in evidence. The best selection of tapas bars is in Pza. Ramón Benito Aceña, at the end of the main drag, where the locals stand around outside at high circular tables and big wooden barrels. There's a grungier set of **bars** in nearby Pza. de San Clemente (just behind Citibank, off C/El Collado), while C/Manuel Vicente Tutot, behind the Museo Numatino, has a line of old-fashioned bars for Soria's cheapest eats.

Baluarte C/Caballeros 14, http://baluarte.info. This exciting, creative Michelin-star restaurant by chef Óscar

García offers a traditional or signature menu, with plates such as hake in a green tomato sauce or beef with local Sorian mustard. Reservations are essential. €€€€

Café Nueva York C/Collado 18, 975 212 784. The city's best *pastelería*, also nice for breakfast, with tables outside on old-town square Pza. San Blas y el Rosel. Some say it is the *Bettys* of Soria (those who are familiar with that highly esteemed café in York, UK). €

★ **Fogón del Salvador** Pza. Salvador 1, http://fogon salvador.com. An excellent *asador*, with tapas bar at the front and a more formal restaurant at the back, dominated by a huge wood-fired beehive oven and two mounted bulls' heads. The cuisine is typically meat-oriented – the steaks

5

and chops are *buey* (ox) rather than *vaca* (beef), thus are hung longer and are darker in colour and richer tasting, or there are things like roast *cabrito* (baby goat), a leg of lamb big enough for two, plus platters of smoked meats. €€€

Mesón Castellano Pza. Mayor 2, http://meson castellanosoria.com. Located in a cosy building of warm brick, with hams hanging from the wooden beams. You can hang out at the front with a cold beer, eat tapas at the bar or settle down for big meals in the *comedor*, enjoying meat and fish dishes (including trout from the Río Ucero). €€€

Numancia

Off the N111 to Logroño, just outside the village of Garray, 7km north of Soria • Charge • http://numanciasoria.es

Around 7km north of Soria lie the evocative ruins of **Numancia**, a hilltop Celtiberian (third to second century BC) and later Roman settlement. Numancia was one of the last towns to hold out against the Romans, falling to Scipio in 133 BC; its long and fierce resistance was turned into a tragic play by Cervantes and dubbed "a sort of Vietnam for Rome" by novelist Carlos Fuentes. It's a stunningly sited spot, with extensive remains of streets, drains, courtyards and public baths, some reconstructed houses and a stretch of wall. There's a good English-language interpretive leaflet available.

Sierra de Urbión

Summer weekends and holidays see locals flock to the tranquil slopes of the **Sierra de Urbión**, northwest of Soria, with its network of hiking and cycling trails, and even skiing at Santa Inés. Nearest Soria, the lower section of what is a protected *reserva nacional* is focused on the shores of an enormous reservoir, the Embalse de la Cuerda del Pozo, which has pine-wood and beachside picnic areas and plenty of watersports facilities. Just to the north is the main village of Vinuesa, while the real highlight of the range lies further north still – the lovely alpine glacial lake of Laguna Negra.

Vinuesa

VINUESA makes the most obvious base for the Sierra de Urbión. It's a pleasant village, attuned to tourists, with many restored old houses, a church adopted by nesting storks, a number of banks and ATMs, and even a late-night bar or two.

ARRIVAL AND DEPARTURE VINUESA

By bus The village is 33km from Soria (N234), and there are daily buses from Soria or Burgos.

ACCOMMODATION AND EATING

Half a dozen moderate **accommodation** options (mostly two-star-*hostal* standard) line the main road that leads down to the Laguna Negra turn-off. Nearly all the *hostales* have their own restaurants.

Camping Cobijo 2km along the Laguna Negra road, http://campingcobijo.com. The local campsite is a large pine-shaded resort-style affair, with swimming pool, bikes for rent, a restaurant and a little supermarket. It also has basic rooms (sleeps two) and bungalows (sleeps three to six). Only open from end March to end Oct. Camping €, bungalows €€

Virginia C/Castillo de Vinuesa 21, http://virginiarh.net. This is easily the pick of the local hotels, in the heart of the mountains, close to the bridge near the turn-off, with handsome rooms and a good-value restaurant of the same name just across the road. €

Laguna Negra

It's definitely worth the drive up to the **Laguna Negra**, a shining body of water hemmed in by a dramatic amphitheatre of granite cliffs. There's a lakeside boardwalk and several hiking trails, including the serious ascent from the lake to the summit of **Pico Urbión** (2229m), just over the border in La Rioja. To reach the lake follow the signs (18km) from Vinuesa until you reach a small upper car park just 300m from the *laguna*; at busy times, or if the barrier is closed, you'll have to park at the much larger car park, 1km back down the road (20min walk), near the seasonal café-restaurant.

La Rioja province

One of Spain's most famous wine regions, La Rioja takes its name from the Río Oja, which flows from the mountains down to the Río Ebro, the latter marking the northern border of **La Rioja province** (http://lariojaturismo.com). Confusingly, the demarcated wine region and province are not quite the same thing, since many of the best vineyards are on the north bank of the Ebro, in the Basque province of Araba – Alava in Castilian, the so-called Rioja Alavesa (see page 450). Nevertheless, the main wine towns are all in La Rioja proper, starting with the enjoyable provincial capital, **Logroño**, which is a great place to spend a couple of days eating and drinking. The province is traditionally divided further into two parts, with the busy little wine town of **Haro** being the mainstay of the **Rioja Alta**. This makes the best base for any serious wine touring, though there are *casas rurales* in many of the surrounding villages, too. It's also here, west of Logroño, that the Camino de Santiago winds on towards Burgos. East of Logroño is the **Rioja Baja**, the southeastern part of La Rioja province, which has quite a different feel – there are vineyards, but the main attraction is following in the footsteps of La Rioja's ancient dinosaurs. Logroño is the hub for all local bus and train services, but if you want to do any more than see the towns of Nájera, Haro and Calahorra, it's far better to have your own transport, as connections to the smaller villages are rarely convenient for day-trips.

Logroño

LOGROÑO, lying on the Río Ebro, is a prosperous city of around 153,000 – a pleasant place of elegant streets, open squares and riverside parkland. The wine trade is not as immediately apparent here as in, say, Haro, and there are few cultural attractions that demand attention. But the big draw is the city's lively old quarter, the so-called *casco viejo*, with its unparalleled selection of excellent tapas bars, for which it's worth making a considerable detour. The two main annual events – each fuelled by copious wine-drinking – are the **Fiestas San Bernabé** (June), a week's worth of enjoyably rowdy local festivities, from street fairs and *pelota* tournaments to folk concerts and costumed processions, and the even more exuberant **Fiesta de San Mateo** (September), which coincides with the annual *vendimia* (grape harvest).

Museo de la Rioja

Pza. de San Agustín • Free • http://museodelarioja.es

Housed in the Espartero Palace, a Baroque beauty dating from the eighteenth century, the engaging **Museo de la Rioja** tells the story of the La Rioja region – without the wine. Displays run from prehistory to the twentieth century and include religious and daily artefacts, Renaissance paintings and Roman murals. For anyone interested in the history of the area, this is a must-see.

Sala Amós Salvador

C/Once de Junio • Free • https://salaamossalvador.com

Located in a former medieval convent, the seat of the regional government – the **Parlamento de la Rioja** – faces a cobbled square which has several late-night cafés. There's no public access to the government offices, but part of the building also once served as a nineteenth-century tobacco factory, the **Fabrica de Tabacos**, and is now used as a contemporary art and exhibition centre, the **Sala Amós Salvador**; the tall red-brick factory chimney still stands around the back on C/Portales.

Iglesia de Santiago el Real

C/Barriocepo 6 • Free • http://santiagoelreal.org

Before the wine trade brought prosperity to Logroño, the town owed its importance for some six centuries to the Camino de Santiago, hence the church dedicated to

5

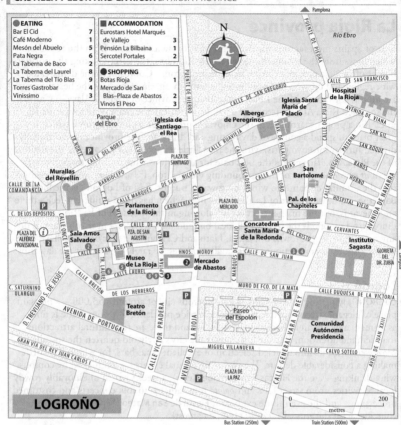

LOGROÑO

EATING		ACCOMMODATION	
Bar El Cid	7	Eurostars Hotel Marqués	
Café Moderno	1	de Vallejo	3
Mesón del Abuelo	5	Pensión La Bilbaina	1
Pata Negra	6	Sercotel Portales	2
La Taberna de Baco	2		
La Taberna del Laurel	8	SHOPPING	
La Taberna del Tío Blas	9	Botas Rioja	1
Torres Gastrobar	4	Mercado de San	
Vinissimo	3	Blas–Plaza de Abastos	2
		Vinos El Peso	3

0 — 200 metres

Bus Station (250m) ▼   Train Station (500m) ▼

the saint, which stands close to the iron bridge over the Río Ebro. High on the south side (ie not the side facing the river) of the lofty sixteenth-century church of **Santiago el Real**, above the main entrance, is a magnificent eighteenth-century Baroque equestrian statue of St James, mounted on a stallion that Edwin Mullins (in *The Pilgrimage to Santiago*) describes as "equipped with the most heroic genitals in all Spain, a sight to make any surviving Moor feel inadequate and run for cover". On the other side of the church is the landscaped Parque del Ebro gardens, which are good for a stroll.

Concatedral Santa María de la Redonda

C/Portales 14 • Free • 941 257 611

Logroño has many fine churches, principal among which is the **Concatedral Santa María de la Redonda**, which faces the old market square. The Catedral was originally a late Gothic hall church with a lovely, sweeping elevation that was extended at both ends in the eighteenth century – the twin-towered facade is a beautiful example of the Churrigueresque style. The evening *paseo*, meanwhile, fills the adjacent main street, C/Portales, packing out the bars and cafés under the arcades.

ARRIVAL AND INFORMATION   LOGROÑO

Logroño is some 100km north of Soria, and 115km east of Burgos. The bus and train stations lie in the modern part of town, south of the central gardens of the **Paseo del Espolón**.

By train The train station is 400m south of the bus station, down Avda. de España.

Destinations Burgos (2 daily; 2hr 30min); Haro (2 daily; 40min); Madrid (up to 10 daily; 4–8hr); Palencia (3 daily; 3hr); Valladolid (3 daily; 4–5hr); Vitoria (3 daily; 2hr); Zaragoza (3 daily; 2hr).

By bus Logroño bus station, Avda. Colón 44 (941 235 983).

Destinations Bilbao (4–6 daily; 2hr 30min); Burgos (up to 7 daily; 2hr); Calahorra (Mon–Sat 6–7 daily, Sun 3 daily; 1hr); Haro (up to 7 daily; 1hr); Nájera (hourly; 30min); Pamplona (up to 6 daily; 2hr); Soria (up to 5 daily; 1hr 30min); Vitoria (every 1–2hrs; 1hr).

By car Metered street parking and signposted garages are easy to find, though there's a large, free car park just opposite the surviving bit of medieval wall known as Murallas del Revellín, on the edge of the old town.

Turismo The *turismo* at C/Portales 50 (June–Sept Mon–Sat 10am–8pm, Sun 10am–2pm; end Sept to May Mon–Sat 9.30am–6.30pm, Sun 10am–2pm; 941 291 260, http://lariojaturismo.com) provides a free map of town and information on the whole Rioja region.

Online Cultural news and events are covered on http://culturalrioja.org.

ACCOMMODATION
SEE MAP PAGE 384

You shouldn't have trouble finding **accommodation**, except during the week-long Fiesta de San Mateo, which starts on September 21, for which rooms are booked months in advance. The lowest-priced accommodation is in the old town; business-class three- and four-star places line the avenues in the more modern parts of town.

Eurostars Hotel Marqués de Vallejo C/Marqués de Vallejo 8, https://www.eurostarshotels.com/eurostars-marques-de-vallejo.html. This four-star old-town hotel has been treated to a thorough makeover, giving it something of a boutique feel. Soundproofed rooms have polished wood floors and contemporary furnishings, and bathrooms are very swish. There's also adjacent private parking. €€

Pensión La Bilbaina C/Capitán Gallarza 10, 941 254 226. Smart en-suite rooms (including singles) at excellent prices. Everything is light, bright and clean, though furnishings are a bit ascetic (bed, wardrobe, chair). Street-facing rooms are apt to be noisy at weekends. €

Sercotel Portales C/Portales 85, https://www.sercotel hoteles.com/en/hotel-portales. Smart three-star hotel in contemporary style, right on the edge of the old town. Has garage parking. The website usually has some good deals. €€

EATING
SEE MAP PAGE 384

Logroño's old town is thick with bars and restaurants, and the local **cuisine** is celebrated for its potato and bean dishes, seasonal vegetables (particularly peppers, asparagus and mushrooms) and juicy steaks. But Logroño's masterpieces are its **tapas bars**, clustered in the bar-run alleys of **C/Laurel** and **Travesía de Laurel**, and the similar **C/San Juan**. In these two locales alone are dozens of different bars, each with their own advertised speciality, from grilled mushrooms to squid. Punters spill out in the alleys at the drop of a hat, washing it all down with a glass of the superb local Rioja wine. There are useful detailed bar guides on http://logropincho.com.

★ **Bar El Cid** Travesía de Laurel, 941 128 584. Logroño has a few different mushroom bars, but this one is definitely the best. Grilled *setas* (large flat mushrooms, similar to oyster mushrooms) are the only thing on the menu at this small traditional bar that has grape vines hanging from the ceiling. *Bar Soriano*, another mushroom-only bar opposite *Bar El Cid*, is also worth a stop. €

Café Moderno C/Francisco Martínez Zaporta 9, http://cafemoderno.com. A gloriously ornate café, established in 1916, with an antique bar full of old photographs, and locals playing board games inside. It's a good spot for breakfast, or a glass of *tinto* in the evening; there are reasonably priced meals. €

★ **Mesón del Abuelo** C/Laurel 12, 941 224 663. At bright, bustling "Grandad's House", the tapas specialities are *chipirones* (baby squid), *sepia* (cuttlefish strips) and thin pork steaks, plonked on the grill and then doused in garlic sauce, for a couple of euros a time. Sit at the counter and order dishes that take your fancy, perhaps langoustine or stuffed peppers. There's also a good wine list with plenty of decent Riojas at value-for-money prices. €

Pata Negra C/Laurel 24, 941 213 645. The mural of acorn-

WHAT'S YOURS?

Cosecha (which literally means "harvest"), when used on its own, refers to young wines in their first or second year, which tend to have a fresh and fruity flavour – you'll also see these wines advertised as the *vino de año*. **Crianzas** are wines that are at least in their third year, having spent at least one year in an oak cask and several months in the bottle. **Reservas** are vintages that have been aged for three years with at least one year in oak; and **gran reservas** have spent at least two years in oak casks and three years in the bottle.

rooting pigs on the wall is the clue, and this renowned *jamonera* (ham specialist) serves big cured meat platters, or you can snack on mini-sandwiches, mixing things like *jamón* and blue cheese or tuna and hot peppers, washed down with various grades of Rioja wine, which are all absurdly cheap. €

La Taberna de Baco C/San Agustín 10, 941 213 544. A truly excellent tapas bar, with a range of delicious specialities: try the *bombita* (potato-and-mushroom ball) or the *migas* (garlic and breadcrumb mixture with a fried egg) and brilliant fried green tomatoes. There are a few tables should you want to make a meal of it. €

La Taberna del Laurel C/Laurel 7, 941 220 143. Often bursting at the seams with patrons eagerly stuffing themselves with the famous house speciality, *patatas bravas*. €

La Taberna del Tío Blas C/Laurel 1, https://www.

tabernadeltioblas.es. A gastro-style *pintxo* bar, this modern place serves innovative bites including goat's cheese and berries, a mini chicken kebab with Padrón peppers and spinach *croquetas* with pine nuts. You can also get main meals such as grilled meats, and breakfast, too. €€

Torres Gastrobar C/San Juan 31, 941 102 115. This modern gastrobar serves a variety of creative tapas and *pintxos*, which are more like mini meals. Their most inventive offering is spider crab lasagne, while their most popular is the Kobe beef burger. €

★ **Vinissimo** C/San Juan 23, 941 258 828. Fantastically creative Spanish and Japanese tapas (*brochetas* of chicken, monkfish or even wild boar are a speciality), plus a carefully selected wine list add up to a more refined tapas bar than usual. A small dining room offers a good-value menu and various a la carte options. €€

SHOPPING

SEE MAP PAGE 384

Botas Rioja C/Sagasta 8, https://www.botasrioja.com. This shop, also known locally as *Félix Barbero* (after the craftsman who ran the place for many years, it's now continued by his son, Ivan), offers handmade traditional *botas de vino* (leather flagons filled with wine) that farmers used to carry their daily ration of wine out into the fields.

Mercado de San Blas–Plaza de Abastos C/Sagasta 1, https://www.mercadosanblas.com. The daily market is

definitely worth a visit for its traditional atmosphere and wide range of local produce. It's also right by many of the best tapas bars.

Vinos El Peso C/Peso 1, 941 226 120. Located on the corner of the Mercado de San Blas, this is a wine shop with a decent selection of regional wines and helpful staff who can help you to select from the dizzying array on offer.

Haro and around

The capital of Rioja Alta is **HARO**, a modern working town 44km northwest of Logroño. It's entirely devoted to the wine trade, but also has some lovely reminders of a grand past in an old centre that's worth at least a short stop – perhaps even overnight if the winery visits take their toll. Apart from harvest time (Sept), when everything shifts up a gear, the best time to be in Haro is in June, starting with the **Semana del Vino** (Wine Week, usually second week), when the bars and restaurants come together to offer *crianza* and *reserva* wine tastings at bargain prices. There's more of the same during the continuous **fiestas** of San Juan, San Felices (the town's patron saint) and San Pedro (June 24–29), when there are outdoor concerts, street parades and the climactic **Batalla del Vino** (June 29), when thousands of people climb the Riscos de Bilibio (a small mountain near the town) to be drenched from head to foot in wine.

Plaza de la Paz and around

At the centre of Haro is **Plaza de la Paz**, a sloping square whose glass-balconied mansions overlook an archaic bandstand. An antique sign on the arcade at the top of the square is entirely in keeping with the prevailing sepia tone, prohibiting carriages from entering the narrow streets beyond and threatening a one-peseta fine for transgressors. The very small old quarter off the square is attractive in a faded kind of way, with parallel lanes leading up to the landmark Renaissance church of **Santo Tomás**, with its 68m-high wedding-cake tower and richly carved portal.

Museo de la Cultura del Vino

Bodega Dinastía Vivanco, Briones, 6km southeast of Haro on the N232 • Charge for museum and *bodega* tour, combination tickets available • http://vivancoculturadevino.es

5

TOURING BODEGAS IN LA RIOJA

Wine is at the very heart of La Rioja's identity (http://riojawine.com), and few people will pass through without visiting a *bodega* and tasting a few *vinos*. If you can only visit one, make it **Bodega Dinastía Vivanco** in Briones (see page 386). In **Haro**, there are a dozen other *bodegas* within walking distance of town, most clustered around the train station – they offer daily tours (usually in English in the mornings), but you have to make a reservation (Haro *turismo* can advise about current tour times). Some are free, some charge €5–15 for tours and tastings lasting from ninety minutes to two hours. Scores of other wineries lie within half an hour's drive of Haro or Logroño, and tend to be open for drop-in visits without appointment. They've all got wine shops attached, and some have excellent restaurants. A good target is the striking village of **San Vicente de la Sonsierra** which has no fewer than sixteen wineries in the vicinity, while some of the most celebrated vineyards lie close to the town of **Laguardia** (see page 451), 19km northwest of Logroño or 26km east of Haro, in the Basque **Rioja Alavesa** region. **Cenicero** is also a good bet, with numerous big-name wineries located around the town.

Bodegas Bilbaínas http://bodegasbilbainas.com. One of the oldest *bodegas* in Haro, established in 1901, home of the classic Viña Pomal wines and their flagship contemporary label, La Vicalanda. Informative guided tours range from 1hr 30min–2hr.

Bodegas Muga http://bodegasmuga.com. Muga has a good visitor centre in Haro where you can learn about its painstaking traditional methods, such as using egg whites to clean the wine of impurities. On the €25 tour you'll also get to taste three wines. They also arrange segway tours of the vineyard and hot air balloon trips over the area.

López de Heredia http://lopezdeheredia.com. Standout attraction at this Haro winery is the eye-catching modernist wine shop designed by Zaha Hadid.

The best single visit for anyone interested in Rioja wine is the impressive **Museo de la Cultura del Vino** at the Dinastía Vivanco family *bodega* just outside Haro (you'll pass by on the drive from Logroño). It's a slick operation all round, with a comprehensive museum that covers every aspect of wine production, and guided tours of the associated winery that set off several times daily, taking you out into the vineyard and then down into the underground bowels of the operation. Add in a "tasting bar", with its automatic wine-dispensers, a well-stocked shop, café with vineyard views, fancy restaurant and vine-planted gardens, and you could easily spend half a day here.

ARRIVAL AND INFORMATION   HARO

By train The train station is a 15min walk from the centre, down over the bridge on the other side of the river, at Barrio de la Estación 1.

By bus Services from Logroño by bus are far more frequent than those by train and the bus station is slightly closer in, at Pza Castañares de Rioja 4, a 10min walk from the centre of town.

By car Haro is small, and finding free on-street parking isn't usually a problem.

Turismo Pza. de la Paz (June–Oct Tues–Sat 10am–2pm & 4–7pm, Mon & Sun 10am–2pm; Nov–May Tues–Sun 10am–2pm, Fri & Sat also 4–7pm, closed Mon; 941 303 580, http://haroturismo.org).

ACCOMMODATION

There are plenty of options available that are easier on the budget, but here are a couple (still relatively affordable) that offer a touch more luxury and historic charm.

Eurostars Los Agustinos C/San Agustín 2, https://www. eurostarshotels.com/eurostars-los-agustinos.html. This converted Augustinian convent founded in 1373, whose centrepiece is a magnificent glass-covered cloister, has rooms that mix traditional furnishings with up-to-date comforts. If you're staying, you're unlikely to eat anywhere

other than the fine restaurant, with dining among the stone walls of the hotel cloister. €€

★ **Hospedería Señorío de Briñas** C/Travesía de la C/Real 3, Briñas, 6km north of Haro, http:// hotelesconencantodelarioja.com. Magnificent baronial mansion in a charming riverside village. Rooms use the exposed stone and archaic features to ravishing effect, and there's a spa in the old wine cellar. A buffet breakfast is included. €€

5

EATING AND DRINKING

Even the humblest tapa is transformed by a glass of Rioja, and you'll get plenty – and very cheaply – in the dozen or so **bars and restaurants** that lie the short distance between Pza. de la Paz and Santo Tomás church.

Los Berones C/Santo Tomás 26, https://losberones.com. There's traditional Riojan tapas with Argentine influence here, and good-value meals, day and night, in this busy, rustic bar with a few wooden tables at the back. Plates include grilled lamb chops and salt cod drenched in a spicy tomato sauce. €€

Restaurante Terete C/Lucrecia Arana 17, http://terete.es. This traditional and historic restaurant opened back in 1877, and today is run by the fourth generation of the original family. They specialize in using seasonal vegetables in their dishes, such as artichokes, chard and wild mushrooms, and have a good selection of *tortillas*. €€€

Nájera

The Camino de Santiago sweeps through Logroño and on towards Burgos, passing to the south of Haro. At the small riverside town of **NÁJERA**, 15km south of Haro, dramatically sited below a pink, cave-riddled rock formation, you're ostentatiously welcomed to the "Capital of Furniture" (Nájera is known for its fixtures and fittings). Old and modern Nájera are separated by the grassy riverbanks of rippling Río Najerilla – there's plenty of free parking on either side – while just across the footbridge from the charming old town there's a riverside **market** every Thursday.

Monasterio Santa María la Real

Pza. de Santa María • Charge • http://santamarialareal.net

Dominating the old town is the stork-topped Gothic **Monasterio Santa María la Real**. This contains a royal pantheon of ancient monarchs of Castile, León and Navarra, though best of all is the attractive sixteenth-century cloister of rose-coloured stone and elaborate tracery.

ACCOMMODATION	NÁJERA

Duques de Nájera C/Carmen 7, http://hotelduques denajera.com. Charming hotel with just fifteen rooms, housed in an old seventeenth-century red-bricked building near the old town, also an ideal stop if you're walking the *camino*. Rooms are cosy and comforting with old wood-beamed ceilings and brightly coloured walls. There's also a bar and breakfast room. €€

Santo Domingo de la Calzada

The small town of **SANTO DOMINGO DE LA CALZADA**, 20km west of Nájera, owes its history and much of its livelihood to the Santiago pilgrim route, on which it is a stop. The Catedral, with its fourteenth-century Mudéjar cloister, is dedicated to town founder Domingo de la Calzada. There are plenty of inexpensive *menús del día* on offer at local restaurants to raise the strength and spirits of the pilgrims. The former medieval pilgrims' hospital is now a fine parador but, for all this, only the very centre of town around the Catedral is particularly attractive and, unless you're a foot-weary pilgrim or staying at the parador, there's no need to stay long in town – Ezcaray to the south (see page 389) is a better overnight stop.

ACCOMMODATION AND EATING	SANTO DOMINGO DE LA CALZADA

★ **Parador Santo Domingo de Bernardo de Fresneda** Pza. del Santo 3, http://parador.es. Only the wealthier sort of pilgrim gets to enjoy the luxurious comforts of the parador these days, in light rooms that occupy a modern annexe, grafted on to the old pilgrims' hospital. It's all nicely – if traditionally – done, though rooms are smaller than you'll get at some other paradors. A substantial breakfast is served in the lovely old restaurant until late morning (extra). €€

★ **Restaurante La Cancela** C/Mayor 51, 941 343 238. This fabulously friendly restaurant run by a father and son team serves up a delicious menu of high-quality Spanish dishes. Start with local aspargus before ordering juicy *entrecot* or *bacalao* and take advice on the extensive wine list – there are too many excellent vintages here to choose from. €€€

The mountain monasteries of Suso, Yuso and Valvanera

Around 18km from Nájera (a little further from Santo Domingo), the stone village of **San Millán de la Cogolla** serves as gateway to the magnificent twin mountain monasteries known as **Yuso** and **Suso**. You can see these easily as a half-day diversion from the main Rioja route, while a third monastery, **Valvanera**, lies further south, off the **LR113**, the trans-mountain road that provides a dramatic journey south and west between Nájera and Salas de los Infantes (90km; 2hr drive). This twists ever higher up the glorious, lush valley of the Río Najerilla, hugging the sides of the huge hydroelectric Mansilla dam, before careering across the bare uplands of the **Sierra de la Demanda** to cross into Castilla y León. The route makes a great roundabout approach to Burgos, and you'll emerge close to the equally magnificent monastery of Santo Domingo de Silos (see page 397).

Monasterio de Yuso

Charge • http://monasteriodeyuso.org

The immense lower **Monasterio de Yuso**, which dominates the valley, was built in the sixteenth and seventeenth centuries to house the relics of the crowd-pulling sixth-century saint, San Millán. It's at the centre of some fairly big tourist business, with one wing of the monastery housing a four-star hotel, a couple of big restaurants and enough parking to accommodate the entire Spanish nation, should it choose to all come at once.

ACCOMMODATION   **MONASTERIO DE YUSO**

Hostería del Monasterio Monasterio de Yuso, http:// hosteriasanmillan.com. Situated in one wing of the monastery, this is rather a grand place to spend the night – and many of the rooms have Jacuzzi baths. €€

Posada de San Millán C/Prestiño 3, http://laposadade sanmillan.es. Located in front of the Yuso complex, this simpler, rustic residence has just half a dozen inexpensive rooms. Minimum 3-night stay in August. €

Monasterio de Suso

Charge • http://monasteriodesanmillan.com

Much older than Monasterio de Yuso, the **Monasterio de Suso** lies a few hundred metres up in the hills, hidden from public view. You're taken up by shuttle bus to see the beautiful, haunting building, the original site of Millán's burial before he was sanctified in 1030 and later transferred down the hill into surroundings more in keeping with a patron saint.

Monasterio de Valvanera

No public access to monastery buildings • https://monasteriodevalvanera.es

The wonderfully situated monastery, the **Monasterio de Valvanera**, is 35km further south of San Millán de la Cogolla (and a 5km detour off the LR113 mountain road). If anything, the location is even more dramatic than that of Yuso and Suso – it's located 1000m above a steep-sided valley, with the tidy terraces of the Benedictine monks' vegetable gardens below. It's worth stopping briefly for the views – there's a bar and restaurant and some simple accommodation here – and to experience a monastic retreat with none of the crowds of its more renowned counterparts.

Ezcaray

For summer and winter escapes – hiking in the wooded valley of the Río Oja, skiing on the heights above – locals make a beeline up the LR111 to the pretty resort of **EZCARAY**, 15km south of Santo Domingo de la Calzada. This was a thriving textile centre in earlier centuries, which explains the mammoth former "royal factory" and dye shop you pass on the way into town (now partly converted into lodgings), while the ruined sixteenth-century bridge and the fortified medieval church in the centre also

5

speak of former grandeur. Tourism has led to a smartening-up of Ezcaray's landscaped riverside gardens, porticoed streets and ancient squares, and its big, solid stone houses, many supported on gnarled wooden pillars, have small, deep-set windows to help keep out the winter chill. Ezcaray is an attractive place to spend the night, particularly as it has acquired a reputation as a foodie destination, with some excellent local restaurants, including one of Spain's finest regional gastro-hotels.

ACCOMMODATION AND EATING   EZCARAY

Echaurren C/Padre José García 19, http://echaurren.com. Opposite the main church, this family-run gastro-hotel, now in its fifth generation, features some very comfortable and stylish guest rooms above three restaurants: *Echaurren Tradition, El Cuartito* and *El Portal*, and a tapas bar with a

terrace. €€€
Echaurren Tradition C/Padre José García 19, https:// echaurren.com/restaurante-echaurren-tradicion/. The seasonal menu here is based on traditional Riojan recipes from the current chef's mother. €€€€

La Rioja Baja

Forty kilometres from Logroño, **Calahorra** is the main town of **La Rioja Baja**, the southeastern part of the province. After the wine towns of the Rioja Alta it's a bit of a disappointment, and there's not really a pressing need to stop, though it does have an appealing old town. Calahorra also offers an attractive back-country route to Soria, via Arnedo, 12km southwest of town, where the scenery suddenly changes from cultivated flatland to vivid red rock, punctured by hundreds of caves, both natural and man-made, used in the past as houses and hermitages. From here – past attractive riverside **Arnedillo**, until reaching the tiny village of Yanguas, at the valley bottom village of Yanguas, 30km southwest – the LR115 makes a twisting journey through the narrow Río Cidacos gorge, before climbing up over the bare tops for the sweeping run into Soria, another 50km to the south. It takes a couple of hours all told from Calahorra to Soria, though it's a good idea to break in the middle at **Enciso** for some dinosaur-hunting. A hundred and twenty million years ago (in the early Cretaceous period), the southeastern part of La Rioja was a steamy marshland where dinosaurs roamed, leaving their footprints in mud that later fossilized, and you can spend an enjoyable day in the area following the tracks.

Calahorra

CALAHORRA, on the Cidacos river, was one of the most important cities in Roman Spain (known then as Calagurris) and today is known as the "city of vegetables" thanks to its fertile flood plains. Some remains from the Roman period can still be seen, including part of the original Roman walls, the remnants of a first-century villa called La Clinica and evidence of the Roman circus. A pleasant half-day can be spent strolling the old town.

ACCOMMODATION AND EATING   CALAHORRA

Coliceo 29 C/Coliceo 29, https://coliceo29.com. Opened in 2017 by chefs César and Patricia, this restaurant prides itself on fresh, top-quality local produce and inspiring dishes. €€
Parador de Calahorra Paseo del Mercadal, http:// parador.es. Comfortable red-brick hotel with simple wooden-floored rooms and an on-site bar and restaurant.

€€
Restaurant Parador de Calahorra Paseo del Mercadal, https://paradores.es/es/restaurante-del-parador-de-calahorra. Traditional Riojan cuisine that makes the most of seasonal regional produce. Try their specialties – the vegetable stew of La Rioja-style cod. €€€

Arnedillo

ARNEDILLO, 24km southwest of Calahorra, is a pretty spot, a minor spa set in a deep river valley beneath spiky crags, with its church at the very bottom by the river. From here it's an easy stroll off into the lovely surroundings, along the river and up the side valleys, past ruined water mills, restored hermitages and waterside allotments.

Hospederia   Las   Pedrolas http://laspedrolas.es. Although there's a *hostal* or two up on the main through-road, above the village, the best place to rest your head is this charming rustic house right outside the village church. Breakfast is also included. €

Enciso

The village of **ENCISO**, 11km from Arnedillo and 35km southwest of Calahorra, is La Rioja's main dinosaur centre and the easiest place to see some preserved footprints. You can either drive out to the main sites, or take the well-signposted 6km circular **walk** from Enciso's El Barranco Perdido. There are lots of other signposted dinosaur sites in the vicinity, at Munilla or Préjano, for example, though many are on 4WD dirt tracks. Pack your hiking boots.

El Barranco Perdido

Charge • http://barrancoperdido.com

Once just a small **Centre Paleontológico** giving information about the region's dinosaur sites, today Enciso is home to a greatly expanded and Disneyesque dinosaur-themed **El Barranco Perdido**. Rides, attractions and shows combine to make a full family-friendly day out, though those seeking an informative experience may be disappointed with its child-focused antics. For something quieter, follow the brown signposts from here which point you to the nearby sites of **Virgen del Campo** and **Valdecevillo**, both featuring lots of visible tracks in the stone as well as huge replica dinos to thrill the kids.

Burgos

BURGOS was the capital of Old Castile for almost five hundred years, the home of El Cid in the eleventh century, and the base, two centuries later, of Fernando III, the reconqueror of Córdoba and Seville. It was Fernando who began the city's famous Gothic Catedral, one of the greatest in all of Spain, and Burgos is a firm station on the pilgrim route. During the Civil War, Franco temporarily installed his Fascist government in the city and Burgos owes much of its modern expansion to Franco's "Industrial Development Plan", a strategy to shift the country's wealth away from Catalunya and the Basque Country and into Castile.

Burgos has been much scrubbed and restored over the last few years, every paving stone in the centre looks to have been relaid, and while it's no longer a clearly medieval city, the handsome buildings, squares and riverfront of the old town are an attractive prospect for a night's stay. Despite the encroaching suburban sprawl and a population of almost 200,000, when it comes down to it, Burgos really isn't that big. The Río Arlanzón bisects the city and neatly delimits the *casco histórico*, or old quarter, on the north bank. You can easily see everything here in a day, and while its lesser churches inevitably tend to be eclipsed by the Catedral, the two wonderful monasteries on the outskirts are by no means overshadowed.

The Catedral

Pza. del Rey San Fernando • Charge • http://catedraldeburgos.es

The *casco histórico* is totally dominated by the **Catedral**, one of the most extraordinary achievements of Gothic art. Its spires can be seen above the rooftops from all over town, and it's an essential first stop in Burgos. The Catedral has emerged from a lengthy period of restoration (1994 to 2015), looking cleaner than it has for centuries, and proving more popular too. There is also a separate visitor centre and a well-stocked gift shop.

5

The interior

Moorish influences can be seen in the Catedral's central **dome** (1568), which is supported on four thick piers that fan out into remarkably delicate buttresses – a worthy setting for the **tomb of El Cid** and his wife Jimena, marked by a simple slab of pink-veined marble in the floor below. Otherwise, perhaps the most striking thing about the vast interior is the size and number of its side chapels, with the octagonal **Capilla del Condestable**, behind the high altar, possibly the most splendid of all, featuring a ceiling designed to form two concentric eight-pointed stars. In the **Capilla de Santa Ana**, the magnificent *retablo* is by Gil de Siloé, a Flanders-born craftsman whose son Diego crafted the adjacent double stairway, the glorious **Escalera Dorada**.

Cloisters and Museo Catedralicio

The tourist route through the church leads out of the main body of the Catedral and into the spacious two-storey **cloisters**, and beyond this to a series of chapels that house the **Museo Catedralicio**, with its collection of religious treasures and two El Cid mementoes, namely his marriage contract and a wooden trunk. The light-filled lower cloister also has an audiovisual history of the church and its architecture, including a look at the various restoration projects.

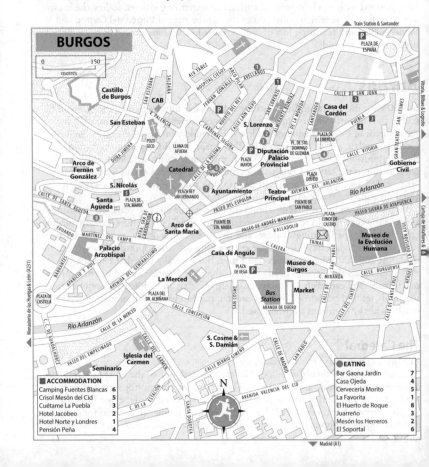

BURGOS

0 — 150 metres

▲ Train Station & Santander

Vitoria, Bilbao & Logroño ▶

Cartuja de Miraflores & ⑥ ▶

Monasterio de las Huelgas & León (A231) ◀

Madrid (A1) ▼

ACCOMMODATION
Camping Fuentes Blancas — 6
Crisol Mesón del Cid — 5
Cuétame La Puebla — 3
Hotel Jacobeo — 2
Hotel Norte y Londres — 1
Pensión Peña — 4

EATING
Bar Gaona Jardín — 7
Casa Ojeda — 4
Cervecería Morito — 5
La Favorita — 1
El Huerto de Roque — 8
Juarreño — 3
Mesón los Herreros — 2
El Soportal — 6

5

EL CID CAMPEADOR

Principal landmark along the leafy Burgos riverfront – right on the Puente de San Pablo – is the magnificent equestrian **statue of El Cid**, complete with flying cloak, flowing beard and raised sword. The city lays full claim to the Castilian nobleman, soldier and mercenary, born Rodrigo Díaz in the nearby village of Vivar in 1040 or thereabouts. Actually, his most significant military exploits took place around Valencia, the city he took back briefly from the Moors after a long siege in 1094, but no matter – El Cid (from the Arabic *sidi* or lord) is a local boy, whose heroic feats (not all strictly historically accurate) have been celebrated in Spain since the twelfth century. His honorific title, **Campeador** ("Supreme in Valour"), is some indication of the esteem in which he's always been held, though there's generally a veil drawn over his avarice and political ambition, not to mention the fact that, as an exiled sword-for-hire in the 1080s, El Cid turned out for Moorish princes as easily as for Christian kings. He died in Valencia in 1099, and the city fell again to the Moors in 1102, after which his wife Jimena took El Cid's body to the monastery of San Pedro de Cardeña, south of Burgos, where it rested for centuries. The body disappeared to France after the ravages of the Peninsular War, but husband and wife were reburied together in Burgos Catedral in 1921.

Arco de Santa María

Free • 947 288 868

The main approach to the old town and Catedral is across the **Puente de Santa María**, where you're confronted by the **Arco de Santa María**, a gateway that originally formed part of the town walls. There are temporary art exhibitions held inside, and you can also view its exquisite Mudéjar ceiling, but it's the exterior that really catches the eye. It was embellished with statues in 1534–36 to appease Carlos V after Burgos' involvement in a revolt by Spanish noblemen against their new Flemish-born king. Carlos' statue is glorified here in the context of the greatest Burgalese heroes: Diego Porcelos, founder of the city in the late ninth century; Nuño Rasura and Laín Calvo, two early magistrates; Fernán González, founder of the Countship of Castile in 932; and, above all, **El Cid Campeador**, who is surpassed in popular sentiment only by St James in his legendary exploits against the Moors.

Museo de la Evolución Humana

Paseo Sierra de Atapuerca • Charge • https://www.museoevolucionhumana.com

Housed in a modernist riverfront cube, the **Museo de la Evolución Humana** is one of Burgos' newer museums. It takes the important fossil finds and early human archeological sites at the local Atapuerca mountains as the starting point for an entertaining and informative tour through the history of human evolution. Wide-ranging displays cover subjects from the first use of fire to Darwin's expeditions aboard the *Beagle*. The museum also runs daily bus tours out to the Atapuerca archeological sites, where fossils and tools have been found dating back well over a million years.

Centro de Arte Caja de Burgos (CAB)

C/Saldaña • Free • http://cabdeburgos.com

CAB sits in a striking modern building right at the top of the steps by the church of San Esteban – it's a convenient stop on the way up to the castle. There are usually a couple of free exhibitions on at any one time – contemporary Spanish art and installations are its bread and butter – while CAB also puts on all sorts of other shows, events and workshops.

Castillo de Burgos

Charge, although closed for renovation until 2026 • 947 203 857

5

The highest point of town is marked by the **Castillo de Burgos**, a huge fortress that was largely destroyed by the French in 1813 – there are steps from opposite the church of San Esteban, which you can reach up C/Pozo Seco, behind the Catedral. The walls, battlements and staircases have been restored, and there's also a museum covering the history of the town, but even if you don't plan to go inside it's worth the short climb up the hill anyway, for the views from the *mirador* over the Catedral and town.

Monasterio de las Huelgas

Charge • http://patrimonionacional.es • Around 1.5km west of the city centre (20min walk): cross Puente de Santa María, turn right and follow the signs along the riverbank

The Cistercian **Monasterio de las Huelgas** is remarkable for its wealth of Mudéjar craftsmanship. Founded in 1187 as the future mausoleum of Alfonso VIII (who died in 1214) and his wife Eleanor, daughter of Henry II of England, it became one of the most powerful convents in Spain. It was popularly observed that "If the pope were to marry, only the abbess of Las Huelgas would be eligible!" A community of nuns still lives here (making pottery for sale), and though you can enter through the gatehouse into the impressive courtyard, you have to pay to go any further. It's very definitely worth it. The main **church**, with its typically excessive Churrigueresque *retablo*, contains the tombs of no fewer than sixteen Castilian monarchs and nobles, including Eleanor and Alfonso. Napoleon's troops paid their usual violent courtesy visit, and robbed the convent of its valuables, but remarkably, when the surviving tombs were later opened, many were found to contain regal clothes, embroidery and jewellery, now on display in a small **museum**. Other highlights include a set of delicate Romanesque cloisters, **Las Claustrillas**, and the ceiling of the main Gothic cloisters, which is adorned with patches of Mudéjar decoration. The **Capilla de Santiago** also has a fine Mudéjar ceiling and pointed horseshoe archway. Its statue of St James has an articulated right arm, which holds a wooden sword, used to bestow knighthood.

Cartuja de Miraflores

Free • www.cartuja.org • Around 4km east of the centre – follow the path along the south bank of the river (towards *Camping Fuentes Blancas*), bear right up the hill at the Fuente del Prior park (45min) and cross the road for the monastery; it's well signposted by road all the way from town

The second of the town's two notable monasteries, the **Cartuja de Miraflores**, famous for its three dazzling masterpieces by sculptor Gil de Siloé, lies in a secluded spot, a very pleasant hour's walk from the centre. The monastery buildings are still in use and you can visit only the **church** (1454–88), which is divided, in accordance with Carthusian practice, into three sections: for the public, for the lay brothers and for the monks. In front of the high altar lies the star-shaped carved alabaster tomb of Juan II of Castile (1405–54) and Isabel of Portugal, of such perfection that it forced Felipe II and Juan de Herrera to admit "We did not achieve very much with our Escorial". Isabel la Católica, a great patron of the arts, commissioned it from Gil de Siloé in 1489 as a memorial to her parents. The same sculptor carved the magnificent altarpiece, plated with the first gold shipped back from the Americas and featuring scores of figures with expressive faces, so delicately carved that even the open pages of a Bible and parchment rolls are depicted. Finally comes the smaller but no less intricate tomb of the Infante (Crown Prince) Alfonso, brother of Queen Isabel, through whose untimely death in 1468 she was later able to claim the throne of Castile.

ARRIVAL AND INFORMATION | BURGOS

By train Burgos Rosa de Lima station is on Avda. Príncipe de Asturias, 5km northeast of the centre, but bus #25 runs from right outside the entrance every 30min to Pza. España, a 20min journey. For current timetables and ticket information, consult RENFE (902 320 320, http://renfe. com).

Destinations Bilbao (3 daily; 2hr 40min); León (8 daily; 1hr 30min); Logroño (4 daily; 2hr 50min); Madrid (8 daily; 1hr

30min); Palencia (9 daily; 45min–1hr); Salamanca (7 daily; 2hr 30min); Valladolid (up to 13 daily; 1hr–1hr 20min); Vitoria (10 daily; 1hr 30min); Zaragoza (8 daily; 4hr).

By bus The bus station is on C/Miranda (947 288 855) on the south side of the river – it's a short walk up to cross the bridges into town.

Destinations Bilbao (up to 13 daily; 2–3hr); Covarrubias (Mon–Fri 2 daily; 30min); Donostia/San Sebastián (up to 10 daily; 3–5 hr); Frómista (1 daily; 1hr 30min); León (4–5 daily; 2hr direct); Logroño via Nájera (up to 9 daily; 2hr); Madrid (every 1–2 hr; 2hr 45min); Palencia (up to 3 daily; 1hr 15min); Salamanca (3 daily; 3hr 30min); Santander (4 daily; 3hr); Soria (up to 3 daily; 2hr 15min); Santo Domingo de Silos (Mon–Sat daily; 1hr 30min); Valladolid (5 daily; 2hr 30min); Vinuesa (2–3 daily; 2hr 15min); Zaragoza (4 daily; 4hr).

By car Short-term parking is available out of the centre along the river, though there are large central signposted car parks, including under Pza. Mayor, at Pza. de Vega (near the bus station), and at Pza. de España. Overnight parking available.

Turismo Pza. de Alonso Martinez 7 (July–Sept Mon–Sat 9am–2pm & 5–7.30pm, Sun 9.30am–2.30pm; mid-Sept to June Mon–Sat 9.15am–2pm & 4–6.30pm, Sun 9.30am–2.30pm; 947 203 125, http://turismocastillayleon.com).

CITUR Municipal Office C/Nuño Rasura 7, down an alley in a building off Pza. del Rey San Fernando, near the Catedral (June–Sept Mon–Sun 9am–8pm; Oct–May Mon–Sun 10am–2pm & 4–7.30pm; 947 288 874, https://turismo.aytoburgos.es/en/contacto/).

Trén Turistico A trolley-train rumbles around town (departures every 45min–1hr, between 10.30am–8pm), departing from outside the Catedral – it's €6.50 for adults, €4.50 for children, and runs between March and December. You can buy tickets at the train stop outside the Catedral or book online in advance (https://trainvision.es/tour/burgos/).

ACCOMMODATION
SEE MAP PAGE 392

It's generally nicest to stay over the river, closer to the old town, though many of the new three- and four-star hotels are on the outskirts or even further out.

Camping Fuentes Blancas Parque de Fuentes Blancas, http://campingburgos.com. Out along the river, a 45min walk or a bus ride from the centre (catch it from Avda. del Arlanzón, along the river by the Cid statue). Facilities are excellent, including a large sunny pool, a restaurant and café, bikes for rent, mini golf and bungalows. Camping and 2-person bungalows €̄

Crisol Mesón del Cid C/Fernán González 64, https://www.eurostarshotels.com/crisol-meson-del-cid.html. The best rooms to get here have balconies with great Catedral views. It's the most traditional hotel in the old town and has its own parking and a restaurant set apart from the main building. €€

Cuétame La Puebla C/Puebla 20, https://hoteles cuentame.com. This elegant townhouse is the best boutique choice in the city. Huge beds and striking wall coverings dominate the nineteen rooms, and while space is tight you can't fault black-marble designer bathrooms featuring twin sinks and rain showers. Helpful staff can organize bike rental and advise about parking. Good rates are available if you book online. €̄

Hotel Jacobeo C/San Juan 24, http://hoteljacobeo.com. Snazzy one-star outfit that offers small, trim rooms in muted, contemporary colours. There's a breakfast bar downstairs, though you're very close to all the cafés and restaurants. There are dorm rooms available at the pension next door. Dorms €̄, doubles €€

Hotel Norte y Londres Pza. Alonzo Martínez 10, https://www.hotelnorteylondres.es. A two-star hotel in a very attractive *belle époque* house, right in the centre. There's a traditional feel throughout, and rooms reflect the period but are cosy and comfortable; a fair few triples offer a bit more space and flexibility. Book online for the best rates. €€

Pensión Peña C/Puebla 18, 947 206 323. The top budget option in Burgos, this is a welcoming and immaculate *pensión*. It's right in the old town and popular with *camino* hikers, so advance reservations are essential. €̄

EATING
SEE MAP PAGE 392

You'll find plenty of **restaurants** in Burgos serving traditional Castilian dishes, including the local speciality, *morcilla* (a kind of black pudding or blood sausage, mixed with rice). Good **tapas bars** are legion, especially down the narrow bar-run of C/San Lorenzo (off Pza. Mayor), but also along C/Avellanos and near the Catedral around C/la Paloma. Many of the tapas bars here also act like nightspots where you can grab a drink, although there's a more stylish scene over on C/Puebla and C/San Juan.

best address in town for cakes, sweets and pastries – beautifully concocted, artisan-made chocs, *bombóns*, croissants and cakes from a masterful *pastelería*. There are seats on the main square too. They've opened a few more establishments at C/Vitoria 182, Pza. Alonso Martínez 7 and Pza. Santo Domingo de Guzmán 8. €̄

TAPAS BARS AND RESTAURANTS
Bar Gaona Jardín C/Sombrerería 29, 947 206 191. Pick your way into the interior, modelled on an *andaluz* garden, where beautifully sculpted bite-sized *pinchos* line the bar (specialities include the signature foie gras with

CAFÉ
Juarreño Pza. Mayor 25, http://juarreno.com. The

5

apple purée). It can be hard to find the first time – it's tucked down a dead-end alley, around the block from C/la Paloma (and is not to be mistaken for the *Gaonas*, a more mainstream tapas bar and restaurant on that street). €

Casa Ojeda C/Vitoria 5, http://restauranteojeda.com. One of the oldest and grandest places in town, dividing its efforts between deli, café, beer-house and restaurant. It's an ornately decorated space, with a smart Castilian restaurant upstairs and cheaper eats in the *comedor* or at the bar. Ask for wine recommendations to match your meal. €€€

★ **Cervecería Morito** C/Diego Porcelos 1, cnr C/ Sombrerería, 947 267 555. The best budget dining spot in town, permanently rammed with locals at meal times. It's a no-nonsense bar serving huge freshly cooked, meal-in-one platters (tuna *tortilla*, calamari and salad, say), or big stuffed sandwiches, *raciones*, salads and egg dishes, plus cheap drinks. €€

La Favorita C/Avellanos 8, http://lafavoritaburgos.com. The self-professed "urban tavern" reboots the genre, offering classic tapas and *pinchos* – *croquetas* to grilled foie gras, egg scrambles to tuna and chilli brochettes – or *raciones* and bigger dishes such as a plate of bellota ham, in

a rustic-chic city bar setting. €€

El Huerto de Roque C/Santa Agueda 10, https://elhuerto deroque.com. Elegant, yet laidback restaurant offering fusion Mediterranean mains and tapas with both Spanish and Greek influences. The *menú del día* includes creative dishes such as cherry *salmorejo* with olive oil ice cream and wild goat with creamy potatoes. Late at night, the restaurant turns into more of a bar-style atmosphere with cocktails and live music. €€€

★ **Mesón los Herreros** C/San Lorenzo 20, http://meson losherreros.es. At busy times, you have to perch around the barrel table-tops outside on the street at this classic old-town tapas bar. There's a famously wide range of tapas and *raciones* (snails to Galician octopus) and, like the other places along here, there's also an upstairs *comedor* for meals – with an excellent *menú del día*. €€

El Soportal C/Sombrerería 5, http://elsoportal.es. A rare find indeed – a tapas bar that is open for breakfast. Start your day with *tortillas* and *bocadillos* and come back later to feast on tapas and *raciones* from mini hamburgers to *huevos rotos*. The wine list is high quality and their other speciality is vermouth. €€

South and east of Burgos

South and east of Burgos lies a quartet of renowned sights – ancient hermitage, lavish abbey cloister and two very different restored towns – that are all easy excursions by car. They would make a fine, if busy, day's tour from Burgos, or can be seen en route to Soria, down the N234, though for an alternative overnight stop it's a hard choice between the dramatic parador at Lerma and the small-town charms of Covarrubias.

Ermita de Santa María de Lara

Quintanilla de las Viñas • Free

Down the N234 from Burgos towards Soria, past the first signposted turn-off for Covarrubias, there's a detour after 34km to the dusty village of Quintanilla de las Viñas, which retains a rare Visigothic church and hermitage, the **Ermita de Santa María de Lara**. It's a remarkable survivor, a simple stone building on a bare hillock outside the village, dating back to around AD 700. Only a third of its original size, it nonetheless packs an emotive punch, not least in the delicately carved exterior friezes depicting grapes, animals and a scallop shell over the door – centuries of pilgrims have left cruder scratched crosses on the walls. Inside, there's a stone arch with capitals representing the sun and moon, and a block that is believed to be the earliest representation of Christ in Spanish art.

Covarrubias

The small town – village really – of **COVARRUBIAS**, 40km south of Burgos, is superbly preserved, with many white half-timbered houses and an air of sleepy gentility throughout. Set by an old bridge overlooking the Río Arlanza, the *casco histórico* is arranged around three adjacent plazas of ever increasing prettiness. The late Gothic **Colegiata de San Cosme y San Damián** is the main church, crammed with tombs that give an idea of the grandeur of the town in earlier times. The whole ensemble is studiously quaint, and attracts weekend tourists in numbers, but it's not yet overwhelmed.

| ARRIVAL AND DEPARTURE | COVARRUBIAS |

By bus and car It's easiest to come by car, since the limited bus service from Burgos means that you'll probably have to stay the night. There's plenty of parking outside the village – you're not supposed to drive inside – and everything is within a 2–3min walk, and easy to find.

| ACCOMMODATION AND EATING |

Hotel Nuevo Arlanza Pza. de Doña Urraca 11, http://hotel nuevoarlanza.com. For views over the main square, ask for a front-facing room at the three-star *Hotel Nuevo Arlanza;* it also has its own restaurant, serving classic country Castilian cuisine, from *morcilla* to grilled trout. €€

Hotel Rural Princesa Kristina C/Fernán Gonzáles 8, https://hotelprincesakristina.com. Located in the historic heart of Covarrubias, this is a gorgeous little hotel in a refurbished nineteenth-century building. The rooms here are bright and cosy with wooden furniture and a rustic feel. €€

Pension Casa Galín Pza. de Doña Urraca 4, http:// casagalin.com. Brightly furnished budget rooms in the main square, above a homely tapas bar and restaurant where you'll get a straightforward meal at a reasonable price. The *menú del día* is usually available at night, too. €

Santo Domingo de Silos

The Benedictine abbey of **Santo Domingo de Silos**, 18km southeast of Covarrubias, is one of Spain's greatest Christian monuments. It's surrounded by the fawn stone buildings of a small village of the same name, which has half a dozen small hotels and a few cafés and restaurants, all rather overpriced – nearby Covarrubias is a far better overnight option.

Abadía de Santo Domingo de Silos

C/Santo Domingo • Charge • http://abadiadesilos.es

The defining feature of the **Abadía de Santo Domingo de Silos** is a double-storey, eleventh-century **Romanesque cloister**, with eight graphic sculpted reliefs on the corner pillars. They include *Christ on the Road to Emmaus*, dressed as a pilgrim to Santiago (complete with scallop shell), in solidarity with pilgrims who make a hefty detour from the main route to see the tomb of Santo Domingo, the eleventh-century abbot after whom the monastery is named. The same sculptor was responsible for about half of the **capitals**, which besides a famous bestiary include many Moorish motifs, giving rise to speculation that he may have been a Moor. Whatever the case, it is an early example of the effective mix of Arab and Christian cultures, which was continued in the fourteenth century with the vivid, painted Mudéjar wood-beamed ceiling. A quite different sculptor carved many of the remaining capitals, including the two that ingeniously tell the stories of the Nativity and the Passion in a very restricted space. Visits to the monastery also usually include entry to the eighteenth-century **pharmacy**, which has been reconstructed in a room off the cloister. The monks who sing at the abbey are considered one of the top three **Gregorian choirs** in the world – you may remember their 1994 platinum-selling CD *Chant* – and many visitors make a point to attend a service to hear the singing.

Lerma

The upper town of **LERMA**, high above the Río Arlanza, takes some beating as a piece of vanity building, constructed almost entirely between 1606 and 1617 at the behest of the Duke of Lerma, court favourite of the weak Felipe III. A pious man, Lerma established no fewer than six monasteries and convents in town, while on the site of the former castle he erected an enormous ducal palace, fronted by a sweeping, arcaded plaza. This is now a magnificent parador – well worth planning an itinerary around –while the restored town lends itself to a half-day visit in any case, particularly if you coincide with the weekly Wednesday market that takes up the entire main square.

5

ARRIVAL AND DEPARTURE

By bus and car There are daily buses from Burgos, 39km to the north, but realistically Lerma is a stop for drivers, overnight or otherwise, in combination with Covarrubias,

LERMA

23km to the east, and Santo Domingo de Silos beyond. You can park in the vast square, except during the day on Wednesdays (market day).

ACCOMMODATION

Parador de Lerma Pza. Mayor 1, http://parador.es. Everything is quite lovely in this beautifully restored ducal palace, with the tone set by the stunning central courtyard

around which are the public areas and restaurant. Rooms are palatial and look out over the burned countryside far below. €€€

EATING AND DRINKING

The pricey **restaurants** around the plaza all specialize in *lechazo asado* (roast suckling lamb), cooked in wood-fired ovens. For cheaper meals, walk straight down the steep

hill from the main plaza and out through the town gate to the main road, where there's a handful of less rarefied restaurants and *hostales*.

The Camino de Santiago: Burgos to León

The central section of the great pilgrim route, the **Camino de Santiago**, cuts across the northern plains of Castilla y León, with the stretch from Burgos to León seen as one of the most rewarding – not for the walking, which can be flat and dull, but in terms of the art and architecture encountered along the way. From Burgos the *camino* runs south of the main road, via the charming town of Castrojeriz and, more importantly, **Frómista**, before running up to **Carrión de los Condes** and **Sahagún**, the latter two towns both on the A231 Burgos–León road. With a car, rather than a rucksack and boots, there are also a couple of possible short detours off the main road to see the **Roman remains** on either side of Carrión de los Condes.

Frómista

FRÓMISTA still trades on the *camino*, but today's small crossroads of a town has only a fraction of the population of medieval times. Its undisputed highlight is the **church of San Martín**, which was originally part of an abbey that no longer exists. Carved representations of monsters, human figures and animals run right

---

THE CAMINO DE SANTIAGO IN CASTILLA Y LEÓN

With the vineyards and well-watered countryside of La Rioja behind you, the **Camino de Santiago** arrives at Burgos and the start of the plains of Castile. Pilgrims are sharply divided about the *meseta*. Fans praise the big skies and the contemplative nature of the unchanging views, while detractors bemoan the strong winds and the depressing way that you can see your destination hours before you reach it. It's certainly the flattest, driest part of the path and, if it's cold in winter, the lack of shade makes it uncomfortably hot in summer. The route often shadows the main road along a purpose-built gravel track, but there are many well-marked detours along isolated tracks crunchy with wild thyme.

Highlights are, of course, the glorious Gothic Catedrals of Burgos and León, after which the *meseta* ends at the town of Astorga, 50km southwest of León. From here you'll climb to the highest pass of the *camino* (1439m), where mist and fog can descend year-round and snow makes winter travel difficult. Good planning is therefore essential (see page 521). Traditionally, pilgrims bring a stone from home to leave on a massive pile at Cruz de Hierro, just before the pass. Things warm up considerably as you descend through gorgeous scenery to the Bierzo valley, 50km from Astorga, where the charming riverside town of Villafranca del Bierzo is an ideal place to rest before heading uphill into Galicia.

around the roof of the eleventh-century church, which was built in a Romanesque style unusually pure for Spain, with no traces of later additions. A couple of other churches in Frómista are also associated with the *camino*, and there's usually a steady trail of walkers and cyclists passing through, taking advantage of the simple accommodation here.

Villalcázar de Sirga

Thirteen kilometres along the *camino* from Frómista (the route shadows the road), **VILLALCÁZAR DE SIRGA** has a notable church, Santa María la Blanca, built by the Knights Templar in the heart of the village. The Gothic style here begins to assert itself over the Romanesque, as witnessed by the figure sculpture on the two portals and the elegant pointed arches inside. Meanwhile, as pilgrims strike onwards past the village they are confronted by surely one of the most dispiriting signposts along the whole route – "Carrión de los Condes, 6km" (oh good), "Santiago de Compostela, 463km" (oh heck).

Carrión de los Condes and around

If the stories are to be believed, quiet, conservative **CARRIÓN DE LOS CONDES**, 80km west of Burgos and 40km north of Palencia, has a sensational past. In typically inflammatory fashion, it was reputed to be the place where, before the Reconquest, Christians had to surrender one hundred virgins annually to the Moorish overlords – a scene depicted on the badly worn portal of the church of Santa María del Camino, situated at the edge of the old town (where the *camino* enters). Its pilgrim days have bestowed another dozen churches and monasteries upon Carrión, including the vast bulk of the Monasterio de San Zoilo, whose cloister contains the tombs of the counts (*condes*) of Carrión, from whom the town's name comes. On hot days, it's the riverside park that is most tempting, especially if you've just walked here in the height of summer, while quick car journeys take you to the region's remarkable Roman treasures.

ARRIVAL AND INFORMATION

CARRIÓN DE LOS CONDES

By bus and car Buses from Burgos and León stop outside the *Bar España* on the main road near the church of Santa María del Camino. Palencia buses stop in the square opposite. Ask in *Bar España* for tickets and times. There's plenty of free parking nearby.

Punto de Información Callejón de Santiago (Mon–Fri 9am–2pm; 979 880 932, http://carriondeloscondes.es) is inside the Museo Contemporaneo – it's up the passage by the church of Santiago, facing the main square.

ACCOMMODATION AND EATING

There are several simple *pensiones* and pilgrim-only *albergues* in town, and some lovely rural accommodation in the nearby countryside. Most cafés and restaurants – including one or two overlooking the main square – are aimed firmly at the passing pilgrim trade, so prices everywhere are reasonable.

★ **Estrella del Bajo Carrión** C/Mayor 32, Villoldo, CL615, 11km south of Carrión, http://estrellabajocarrion.com. The glam choice hereabouts is this delightful gastro-retreat in a nearby village. Spacious, all-in-white rooms are heavy with designer flair, and there's a sun deck outside under a spreading tree. Breakfast is really good, while the handsome restaurant (open to nonguests) serves creative regional cuisine using seasonal ingredients, from grilled

veg with a slug of estate-bottled olive oil to Palencian *lechazo* shanks. €€
Hostal La Corte C/Santa María 34, http://hostal restaurantelacorte.es. If you're on a budget, try these straightforward rooms right opposite Santa María del Camino church. The restaurant below is the place for good-value meals, from trout to *chuletón*. €
Hotel Real Monasterio San Zoilo C/San Zoilo, http://sanzoilo.com. By far the most historic accommodation in town is this resolutely traditional four-star hotel converted from part of the monastery – follow the signs, over the bridge, to find it. It also has Carrión's most notable restaurant, serving fancied-up regional cuisine, from lamb to fish. €€

5

Villa Romana La Olmeda

Pedrosa de la Vega, signposted 3km south of Saldaña, off CL615 • Charge, joint ticket with Villa Romana La Tejada available • http://villaromanalaolmeda.com

It's a quick 19km drive northwest of Carrión on a ruler-straight road to the well-signposted **Villa Romana La Olmeda**, which is considered one of the most important domestic Roman sites in Europe, boasting more than 1500 square metres of well-preserved mosaics. Founded as a country estate in the first century AD, but extensively remodelled on palatial lines in the fourth century AD, La Olmeda was more than a mere villa – rather a thriving centre of local agriculture and industry. But faced with the slow collapse of the Roman Empire, the estate gradually fell into disrepair, its buildings demolished, the villa's mosaic floors buried under farmland and its very existence forgotten. It was rediscovered in 1968 and has since been fully excavated, with the entire complex of buildings and the surviving mosaics now sheltered under a dramatic, modernist steel hangar standing in open countryside. Raised walkways lead you around the complex, past reception and dining rooms, bedrooms, storerooms, kitchens and baths, all radiating out from a central patio garden. Touch-screen monitors with computer-generated graphics show how the rooms might have looked, while the mosaics themselves are an impressive tour de force of polychromatic geometric designs, hunting scenes and more elaborate mythological sequences.

Saldaña and the Museo de La Olmeda

Iglesia de San Pedro • Free entrance with ticket for Villa Romana La Olmeda

For the archeological finds from Villa Romana La Olmeda, you have to continue 3km further north up the CL615 to the small town of **SALDAÑA**, whose medieval church of San Pedro has been pressed into service as the **Museo de La Olmeda**; follow the "Museo Arqueológico" signs from the central Pza. Mayor. Glass cases in the church nave present a snapshot of Roman country life 1600 years ago, with displays of coins, lamps, belt buckles, rings, necklaces, hunting weapons and cooking utensils, all of it recovered from the site excavations. Saldaña itself has a charming *casco histórico* of timber and brick houses ranged around its central square, near which you'll be able to park, and there are several cafés.

Villa Romana La Tejada

Quintanilla de la Cueza, 17km southwest of Carrión, off the N120 • Charge, joint ticket with La Olmeda available • https://www.villaromanalaolmeda.com/villa/tejada/presentacion

The other Roman villa site near Carrión is a bit harder to find than Villa Romana La Olmeda, and nowhere near as impressive, though it is just as rewarding in its own way. The **Villa Romana La Tejada** is just past the dead-end hamlet of Quintanilla de la Cueza; there's an easy-to-miss sign off the highway (on the left, coming from Carrión), from where a narrow 1km road leads to a parking area surrounded by a high green hedge. The villa itself is hidden within a vast, unsightly shed, but the surviving mosaics are another extraordinary reminder of the wealth that once characterized this now rather remote rural area, while La Tejada also shows off the hypocaust heating system that was de rigueur for any self-respecting Roman villa of the period.

Sahagún

From Carrión de los Condes the direct *camino* route west continues 35km to the small town of **SAHAGÚN**, once the seat of the most powerful monastery in all Spain. Although this is now little more than a ruined shell, several other churches in Sahagún repay the trip into town, particularly as the most interesting are built of red brick in characteristic Mudéjar style. A steady stream of pilgrims trudges into and out of Sahagún most days, but it really only warrants a quick stop for coffee and a tour of the churches before heading on to León.

5

Iglesia de San Tirso

C/San Tirso, by Parque San Benito, signposted through town • Free

The most delicate of Sahagún's churches is the beautifully restored twelfth-century **San Tirso**, a Mudéjar brick construction of great grace. If the beauty is all on the outside, it's still worth coinciding with the opening times, because inside the simple interior is a fascinating series of scale wooden models of all the town's famous churches – complete with doors that open and roofs that lift off to display minutely constructed interiors, complete with altars and pews.

Ruins of San Benito

Parque San Benito

Adjacent to San Tirso church is all that's left of the mighty twelfth-century monastery of **San Benito** (there's a model of the original inside San Tirso). Originally dedicated to San Facundo and San Primitivo, only one ruined, fenced-off chapel remains of the medieval complex – the more prominent bell tower and the freestanding arched gateway across the road, the so-called **Arco de San Benito**, both also in ruins, were much later additions.

Iglesia de San Lorenzo

Pza. San Lorenzo, signposted off Pza. Mayor • **Museo de Semana Santa** Free

Most imposing of the Mudéjar brick churches is thirteenth-century **San Lorenzo**, with its squat, square campanile – the church, open for Mass only, is currently propped up as the intricate brickwork has sagged over the centuries. In the adjacent building the small **Museo de Semana Santa** presents a fairly gory collection of life-sized, blood-spattered Christs either being led to the cross or crucified upon it. The museum is run by volunteers, so the hours are not always reliable.

ARRIVAL AND DEPARTURE	**SAHAGÚN**

By train Sahagún is an easy side trip from either Palencia or León (around 40min by train from either). The train station is a 10min walk from Pza. Mayor, down Avda. Constitución.
By bus Buses to León (1–2 daily; 1hr), Burgos (1 daily; 2hr 15min) and Carrión de Los Condes (1 daily; 50min) stop outside the *Hotel Puerta de Sahagún* on Carretera de Burgos (http://alsa.es), a 10min walk from the train station.
By car Signs through town lead you to San Tirso and San Benito, and there's convenient parking near the San Benito ruins.

León

Even if they stood alone, the stained glass in the Catedral of **LEÓN** and the Romanesque wall paintings in its Panteón Real would merit a very considerable journey, but there's much more to the city than this. An attractive provincial capital that welcomes *camino* pilgrims by the thousands, it also presents itself as a lively university town with one of the best tapas bar scenes in Spain. Handsome old- and new-town areas, set back from extensive riverside gardens, complement each other, and, while the city's major monuments are renowned, León is a fine place simply to spend a relaxed day or two. Large parts of the encircling medieval walls are still intact, and the tangle of narrow streets within is shabby in part, though the ramshackle buildings in faded ochre and rose pink give the **casco antiguo** a charm all of its own. By day, apart from the crowds around the Catedral and San Isidoro, it's much quieter in the pretty lanes and squares, though always with the accompanying footfall of arriving *camino* hikers making their way into town. At night, the old town bursts into life, with the streets thronged with people and the bars packed out. Things really take off during **Semana Santa**, and for the **fiestas** of San Juan and San Pedro in the last week of June. The celebrations, concentrated around the Plaza Mayor, get pretty riotous, with an enjoyable blend of medieval pageantry and buffoonery.

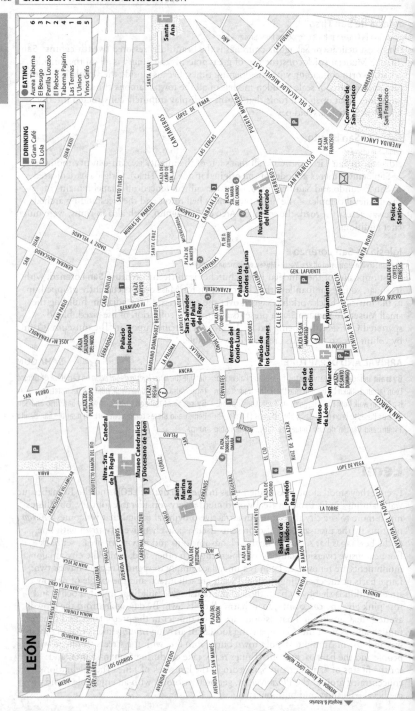

LEÓN

EATING
Aurea Taberna	6
El Besugo	3
Parrilla Louzao	7
El Rebote	2
Taberna Pajarín	4
Las Termas	1
L'Union	8
Vinos Grifo	5

DRINKING
El Gran Café	1
La Lola	2

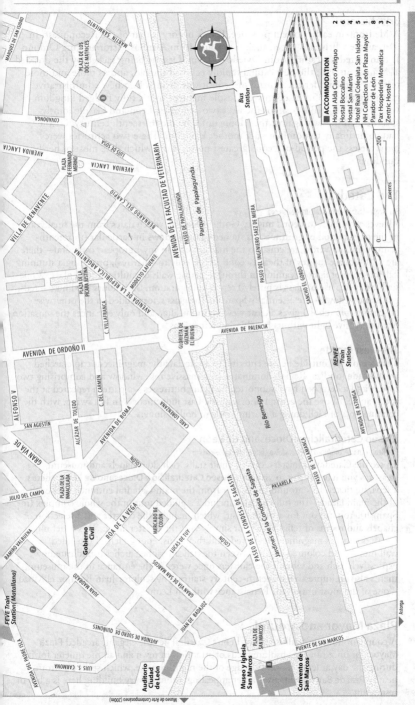

■ **ACCOMMODATION**

Hostal Alda Casco Antiguo	2
Hostal Boccalino	6
Hostal San Martín	4
Hotel Real Colegiata San Isidoro	5
NH Collection León Plaza Mayor	1
Parador de León	8
Pax Hospedería Monástica	3
Zentric Hostel	7

5

Brief history

Aside from an early Roman presence, León's history is that of the Reconquest. In 914, as the Christians edged their way south from Asturias, Asturian king Ordoño II transferred his capital from Oviedo to León. Despite being sacked by the dreaded al-Mansur in 996, the new capital rapidly eclipsed the old, and as more and more territory came under the control of León it was divided into new administrative groupings: in 1035, the county of Castile matured into a fully fledged kingdom with its capital at Burgos. For the next two centuries, León and Castile jointly spearheaded the war against the Moors until, by the thirteenth century, Castile had come finally to dominate her mother kingdom. These two centuries were nevertheless the period of León's greatest power, from which date most of her finest buildings.

The Catedral

Pza. Regia • Charge • http://catedraldeleon.org

All eyes are drawn to León's mighty Gothic **Catedral**, which dates from the final years of the city's period of greatness. Its stained-glass **windows** in particular (thirteenth-century and onwards) are equal to the masterpieces in any European cathedral – there are 1800 square metres of them (second in size only to Chartres), providing a stunning kaleidoscope of light streaming in through soaring walls of multicoloured glass. While such extensive use of glass is purely French in inspiration, the colours used here – reds, golds and yellows – are essentially Spanish. The glass screen added to the otherwise obscuring *coro* (choir) gives a clear view up to the altar, and only enhances the sensation of all-pervasive light with its bewildering refractions.

The west facade

Take a moment outside before entering to appreciate the magnificent triple-arched **west facade** (on Pza. Regia), dominated by a massive rose window and comprising two towers and a detached nave supported by flying buttresses – a pattern repeated at the south angle. Above the central doorway, the Last Judgement is in full swing, with the cooking pots of Hell doing a roaring trade in boiled sinners.

Museo Catedralicio y Diocesano de León

Pza. Regia • Charge, combined ticket available • http://catedraldeleon.org

To see the Catedral's cloisters, carved choir stalls, rich side chapels and museum treasures you have to pay to visit the **Museo Catedralicio y Diocesano de Léon**; there's a separate ticket desk around the corner from the main Catedral entrance to the left of the main facade. The full visit also includes a guided tour of the whole complex (in Spanish). You can opt for a partial visit, which includes the cloister and a selection of chapels and rooms of religious art, or simply visit the **cloister** alone. This is definitely worth doing: it's magnificently carved, and there's just enough left of the faded wall murals and coloured detail between the delicate ribbed arches to indicate how expressively rich and vibrant the cloisters once were. At the entrance to the museum, there's also an impressive sixteenth-century staircase by sculptor Juan Badajoz el Mozo – one of the most important Renaissance works in León.

Plaza Mayor and around

A couple of minutes' walk south of León's Catedral lies the elegant, arcaded **Plaza Mayor**, for once not the absolute focus of attention in town and all the quieter for it, during the day at least. It's on the edge of the nightlife zone, which spills out from nearby **Pza. de San Martín**, also rather appealing, though every building here is a bar or restaurant.

Plaza de Santa María del Camino

Hands-down plaza winner in León is **Plaza de Santa María del Camino**, a gorgeous cobbled square with two big shady trees, a surviving wooden arcade and the pretty Romanesque church of Nuestra Señora del Mercado – the name a reminder that the square was once the site of the city's grain market (it's still known as Plaza del Grano). The squat church tower (facing C/Herreros) is flanked by two dinky, if regal, stone lions.

Palacio de los Condes de Luna

Pza. del Conde Luna • Free • 987 216 794

Facing the Mercado del Conde Luna, the square's most historic building is the sixteenth-century **Palacio de los Condes de Luna**, former home of the counts (*condes*) of Luna, with its elegant facade and blind window arcade. It's now home to the **Centro de Interpretación y Museo de la Historia del Reino de León**, which was created to commemorate the 1100th anniversary of the Kingdom of León and houses pieces from the **Iglesia de San Salvador del Palat del Rey**, as well as replicas of the Bote de Braga (an intricately carved ivory container found in the Braga Cathedral in Portugal) and the Cristo de Carrizo (see page 407), both from the eleventh century.

Iglesia de San Salvador del Palat del Rey

C/Conde Luna, just off Pza. del Conde Luna • Free, temporarily closed at the time of writing

Possibly the oldest church in the city, **San Salvador** was founded by Ramiro II in the tenth century and served as an early pantheon for the Asturian kings (hence the "Palat del Rey" tag), until superseded by that of San Isidoro. There's virtually nothing left of the original church, or its Mozarabic successor, but this is another building that has been lovingly restored to serve as an exhibition hall, focusing on art, architecture and photography.

Plaza de Santo Domingo

The foot of the old town is marked by a series of striking buildings ranged around the traffic circle of **Plaza de Santo Domingo**. The modest **ayuntamiento** sits back in its own square, across the road from the Renaissance **Palacio de los Guzmanes**.

Casa Botines

Pza. San Marcelo 5 • Charge • http://casabotines.es

After 125 years, the mock-Gothic, exuberantly turreted **Casa de Botines** (1892–93) is finally open to the public. The house is the work of the celebrated Catalan *modernista* architect Antoni Gaudí and was built in just ten months in 1892. The exterior resembles a medieval fortress and features many of Gaudí's signature elements, such as stained glass, cast-iron columns and Catalan vaults. The new museum takes visitors on a journey through the house, and displays exhibits on the history of Casa Botines, the life and work of Gaudí, and living in the time of Gaudí. On the third floor, there is also a collection of nineteenth-century artwork.

Basílica de San Isidoro

Pza. de San Isidoro • Free

Founded by Fernando I, who united the two kingdoms of León and Castile in 1037, the mighty **Basílica de San Isidoro** was commissioned both as a shrine for the bones of San Isidoro and as a mausoleum for Fernando and his successors. Backing into the

5

very walls of the city, it's a beautiful construction, dating mainly from the mid-twelfth century and thus one of the earliest Romanesque buildings in Spain. Two adjacent doorways show fine sculpted reliefs, of the Descent from the Cross (right) and the Sacrifice of Abraham (left), the latter surmounted by a later Renaissance pediment topped by the horseriding San Isidoro himself. Inside, the saint's bones lie in a reliquary on the high altar. The attached Royal Collegiate Church has been turned into a lovely hotel (see page 407).

Panteón Real

Basílica de San Isidoro, entrance on Pza. de San Isidoro • Charge • http://museosanisidorodeleon.com

The royal bones (of eleven kings and twelve queens) were laid to rest in tombs in the adjacent **Panteón Real** (signposted "Museo"), essentially two crypt-like chambers constructed between 1054 and 1063 as a portico of the church. It's a deeply atmospheric space, with two squat columns in the middle of the Panteón carved with thick foliage, rooted in Visigothic tradition. Moreover, towards the end of the twelfth century, these extraordinarily well-preserved vaults were then covered in some of the most significant **frescoes** in Spanish Romanesque art. These present a vivid splash of colour, depicting not just biblical scenes and stories but also an agricultural calendar, for example. The central dome is occupied by Christ Pantocrator surrounded by the four Evangelists depicted with animal heads – allegorical portraits from the apocalyptic visions in the Bible's Book of Revelation. Your ticket also allows you to visit the cloister, as well as the small museum of glittering church treasures and the impressive library.

Convento de San Marcos and around

Pza. de San Marcos • 5min walk from the old town

The pilgrim route on to Astorga lies across the old bridge on the west side of town. Here, at the opulent **Convento de San Marcos**, and on presentation of the relevant documents, pilgrims were allowed to regain their strength before the gruelling Bierzo mountains west of León. The original pilgrims' hospital and hostel was built in 1168 for the Knights of Santiago, one of several chivalric orders founded in the twelfth century to protect pilgrims and lead the Reconquest. In the sixteenth century, it was rebuilt as a kind of palatial headquarters, its massive 100m-long facade lavishly embellished with Plateresque appliqué designs: over the main entrance, Santiago is depicted swatting Moors with ease. The monastery is now a parador hotel (see page 408), though the museum (see below) and church can still be visited.

Museo y Iglesia San Marcos

Pza. de San Marcos • Free • http://museodeleon.com

There's unimpeded access to the adjacent monastery church, the **Iglesia San Marcos**, which is vigorously speckled with the scallop-shell motif of the pilgrimage. However, the celebrated *coro alto* of the church, which has a fine set of carved stalls by Renaissance sculptor Juan de Juni, is out of bounds except on guided visits. Inside the church, there's a three-room annex housing the **Museo de León**, which tells the story of the monastery. Portraits of the Knights of Santiago hang from the old sacristy walls, while the Cloister Room contains sarcophagi of the bishops who lived in the monastery.

Museo de León

Edificio Pallares, Pza. de Santo Domingo 8 • Charge, free Sat & Sun • http://museodeleon.com

The headquarters of the **Museo de León** – the Edificio Pallares – was built in 2007 to provide a more spacious home to the large collection that had been displayed in the Iglesia San Marcos since 1869. The collection is dedicated to the history of the

5

province of León, from prehistory via the Roman Conquest and the Middle Ages to the present day, and contains archeological artefacts galore and church treasures, including a fourteenth-century processional cross made of rock crystal and the Cristo de Carrizo – a 33cm-high ivory figure of Christ on the cross.

Museo de Arte Contemporáneo

Avda. de los Reyes Leoneses 24 • Charge • http://musac.es • 15min walk north of San Marcos

The city's main centre for contemporary art and culture is the dazzling **Museo de Arte Contemporáneo (MUSAC)**, an attractive one-storey building built by the architects Emilio Tuñón and Luis Moreno Mansilla, who won the Mies van der Rohe Award – the EU Prize for Contemporary Architecture. The multicoloured glass facade was inspired by the stained-glass windows in the Catedral, and regularly changing exhibitions feature works and installations by Spanish and international artists.

ARRIVAL AND DEPARTURE
LEÓN

León's *casco antiguo*, which has most of the historic sights and the best bars and restaurants, lies east of the Río Bernesga, with the modern part of the city laid out in between. The main **train and bus stations** are on the river's west bank, from where it's a 20min walk up to the Catedral or a 5min taxi journey.

BY TRAIN
Train station Avda. de Astorga on the west bank of the river, just off Avda. Palencia (RENFE 902 320 320, http://renfe.com).
Destinations Astorga (4 daily; 40min); Bilbao (3 daily; 5hr); Burgos (6 daily; 1hr 30min); Logroño (1 daily; 4hr); Madrid (11 daily; 2hr); Oviedo (7 daily; 1hr); Palencia via Sahagún (up to 16 daily; 1hr–1hr 30min); Ponferrada (4 daily; 1hr 30min); Valladolid (up to 14 daily; 1–2hr); Vigo (1 daily;

6hr 30min).

BY BUS
Estación de Autobuses Paseo del Ingenero Saenz de Miera (987 211 000). Alsa (http://alsa.es) has services to Astorga, Burgos, Madrid, Carrion de los Condes, Sahagún, Salamanca and Zamora.
Destinations Astorga/Ponferrada (hourly; 50min); Burgos (4–5 daily; 2–3hr); Carrión de los Condes (1 daily; 2hr); Madrid (12 daily; 3hr 30min); Oviedo (hourly; 1hr 30min); Sahagún (1 daily; 1hr); Salamanca (up to 4 daily; 3–5hr); Valladolid (up to 11 daily; 2hr); Zamora (up to 17 daily; 2hr).

BY CAR
Parking is much easier in the modern district than in the old town.

GETTING AROUND AND INFORMATION

Turismo Pza. Regia, opposite the Catedral (July to mid-Sept Mon–Sat 9.15am–2pm & 5–7.30pm, Sun 9.30am–2.30pm; mid-Sept to June Mon–Sat 9.15am–2pm & 4–6.30pm, Sun 9.30am–2.30pm; 987 237 082, http://turismocastillayleon.com); Pza. San Marcelo, at the town

hall (Mon–Sun 9.30am–2pm & 5–7.30pm; 987 878 336, http://turismocastillayleon.com).
By taxi Radio Taxi León (987 261 415/987 070 305); Taxi Villaquilambe (622 451 070).

ACCOMMODATION
SEE MAP PAGE 402

In the **casco antiguo**, there's a cluster of budget places around the atmospheric Pza. Mayor, though anything without double-glazing close to the bars and restaurants can be very noisy at night. If you're on a bigger budget, you might prefer one of the decent mid-range options nearby.
★ **Hostal Alda Casco Antiguo** C/Cardenal Landázuri 11, https://www.aldahotels.es/hoteles/castilla-y-leon/leon/hostal-alda-casco-antiguo. This fantastic little secret is tucked away behind the Catedral, with super rooms – all wood floors and rustic furnishings – offering great value for money. There are a variety of different room types including triple and family rooms. €€
Hostal Boccalino Pza. de San Isidoro 1, https://www.

hotelboccalino.es. Sits on a lovely square overlooking San Isidoro church. The rooms are above a café-bar, and have parquet floors, good bathrooms with decent showers, double-glazing and church views; across the square is the associated restaurant, a good-value pizza and pasta place. €
Hostal San Martín Pza. Torres de Omaña 1, 2º, http://sanmartinhostales.com. An excellent *hostal* with simple but stylish rooms painted in pastel shades – though you can expect some noise from nearby bars if you're at the front. There's a fair choice of rooms, some with private or shared bathroom facilities. €
★ **Hotel Real Colegiata San Isidoro** Pza. Santo Martino 5, http://hotelrealcolegiata.es. Housed in the old

5

Royal Collegiate Church. Its 46 elegant rooms have period features and look out on to the inner courtyard. The hotel also has a fine restaurant and its own museum. €€€

NH Collection León Plaza Mayor Pza. Mayor 15, http://nh-hotels.com. Chic boutique style in a classy refit of one of the square's handsome arcaded buildings. Facilities and services are four-star standard, and include a restaurant and a bar. Best rates are online. €€

Parador de León Pza. de San Marcos 7, https://paradores.es. Housed in a renovated twelfth-century convent for pilgrims, this stunning five-star, avant-garde hotel is worth it if you really feel like treating yourself. It's absolutely beautiful, but very pricey, especially in high season. €€€€

★ **Pax Hospedería Monastica** Pza. Santa María del Camino 11, http://hospederiapax.com. The monastic, yet luxurious, rooms and the wonderful location overlooking the loveliest plaza in Léon make this a special place to stay. With a convent (and pilgrim-only *albergue*) right next door, it's more than likely that you'll see a nun wandering around the hotel building on her way to Mass. Note that there's only one double bedroom, all others are twin. €€

Zentric Hostel C/Legión VII, 6–2º Izda, 636 946 294, https://www.instagram.com/zentrichostel/. This stylish hostel feels more like a hotel with its dark wood-panelled walls, intricate ceiling work and large French doors, yet it has all the facilities of a hostel, such as a communal kitchen, washer/dryer and lounge area. Triple and quadruple rooms are also available. €

EATING

SEE MAP PAGE 402

The daily **Mercado del Conde Luna** sits in the middle of Pza. del Conde Luna, and offers a crash-course in Leónese cuisine, especially the meats which you'll see on every menu – not just the familiar chorizo, lamb and steak, but tripe and trotters, *morcilla* (blood sausage) and *costillas de cerdo* (smoked pork ribs). The liveliest **tapas bars and restaurants** are found around Pza. de San Martín – an area known as the **Barrio Húmedo** (the Wet Quarter) for the amount of liquid sloshing around.

TAPAS BARS

El Rebote Pza. de San Martín 9, 987 213 510. If you're a fan of Spanish *croquetas*, this is the place to come. They're particularly known for their innovative flavours such as pizza, *morcilla* (black pudding) and Mexican jalapeño. €

★ **Taberna Pajarín** Pza. Torres de Omaña, https://www.facebook.com/tabernapajarin. Vie for a position at the busy bar and order a traditional Leónese tapa, such as the knockout *morcilla* (a rich, garlicky purée of blood pudding) slathered onto crusty white bread, washed down with a great local wine. €€

★ **Vinos Grifo** Pza. Santa María del Camino 9, http://vinosgrifo.com. Sitting outside this relaxed café-bar beside a convent in the pretty "Plaza del Grano" is a memorable experience. You pay for the location with the slightly pricey menu but *platos combinados* are available and you get a free *pintxo* with every drink. There's also a wine bar, shop and attached hotel. €€€

RESTAURANTS

Aurea Taberna Pza. Santa María del Camino 2, https://aureataberna.es. Lunch here on the pretty cobbled square is a treat – choose from a selection of traditional or contemporary dishes, from "Grandmother's stew" to veggie noodles or Leónese-beef burgers, with *raciones* to share. €€€

El Besugo C/Azabacheria 10, 987 256 995. A good choice for a well-priced meal in the Barrio Húmedo – look beyond the spit-and-sawdust bar and head upstairs to the old-fashioned *comedor*, where hoary old waiters dispense a large range of *raciones* and simple meat and fish grills, with plenty of choice. €€

Parrilla Louzao C/Juan Madrazo 4, http://parrillalouzao.com. Fine-dining restaurant specializing in regional meat dishes, such as cured meats and melt-off-the-bone *costillas de cerdo* (pork ribs), alongside other provincial favourites, such as Sahagún-style grilled leeks. €€€

★ **Las Termas** C/Paloma 13, 987 264 600. A sleek little number serving creative regional cuisine. Menus change regularly, but seasonal salads and gutsy mains (like fresh anchovies with caramelized garlic and Padrón peppers) are typical. Their café next door has Catedral views, good cakes and home-made ice cream. €€

L'Union C/Flórez de Lemos 3, https://www.vegetariano launion.es. A vegetarian and vegan gem in the new town. Wholesome mains include tasty salads, a hearty lasagne and delicious burgers. €€

DRINKING AND NIGHTLIFE

SEE MAP PAGE 402

Bars here will give you a free *pincho* with every drink, so you can eat pretty well if you hop from bar to bar ordering *cortos* – small tumblers of beer for around €1.50 or so a pop. The other good area for bars is along C/Cervantes and the Pzas. de Torres de Omaña y el Cid – known as the **Barrio Romántico**, where there's a mix of traditional tapas places and more contemporary *copas* and music bars. Music **bars and clubs** tend to open Thursday to Saturday, between 11pm and 5am.

El Gran Café C/Cervantes 9, 987 272 301. Rock'n'roll bar with a regular diet of indie and rock gigs, plus a free Tuesday night jam session (from 9pm) that's a city stalwart.

La Lola C/Ruiz de Salazar 22, 987 224 303. This atmospheric bar, located near the *Basílica de San Isidoro*, is set in beautiful historic house with bare-brick walls and old wooden rafters. Run by the celebrated Latin rock legend Papá Quijano, it's filled with musical instruments, old photos, paintings and records. Live performances are held during afternoons.

DIRECTORY

Concerts Main city concert hall is the Auditorio Ciudad de León, Avda. Reyes Leoneses 4 (987 244 663, https://www.auditorioleon.com), for everything from symphony orchestras to Gregorian choirs.

Hospital Hospital de Léon, C/Altos de Navas (987 237 400).

Laundry El Lavadero, C/Obispo Almarcha 20 (https://lavanderiaellavaderoleon.weebly.com).

Police Policía Nacional, Villa Benavente 6 (987 218 900); Policía Local, Pza. San Marcelo (987 878 354).

Post office Main branch at the southern end of Avda. de Independencia, by Pza. de San Francisco (Mon–Fri 8.30am–8.30pm, Sat & Sun closed).

Astorga

The next major stop on the *camino*, southwest of León, is **ASTORGA**. The town has a long history – it was originally settled by the Romans (of whom many traces remain), was sacked by the Moors in the eleventh century, then rebuilt and endowed with the usual hospices and monasteries, but as the pilgrimage lost popularity in the late Middle Ages, Astorga fell into decline. These days it's a bustling, if small, provincial capital that once again places much emphasis on the pilgrimage, and is full of footsore hikers and souvenir shops, not to mention an incongruously grand Catedral and an even more out-of-place *modernista* bishop's palace, designed by Antoni Gaudí.

Catedral de Santa María

Pza. Catedral • Charge, free Tues 10.30am–12.30pm • https://catedralastorga.com

Astorga's **Catedral de Santa María** looks better than it has in centuries after a thorough restoration. Built between 1471 and 1693 (though on the site of a much older church), it has notable twin towers either side of the majestically carved main door, one in pink-tinged stone, one in green, colours that are repeated inside the nave on the soaring fluted columns. You can join worshippers and see the Catedral for free in the morning, but sightseers are encouraged to buy a ticket for the **Museo Catedralicio**, which in any case includes a visit to the church. Even if you're not normally interested in ecclesiastical treasures, the beautifully presented series of museum rooms is worth seeing. As well as the usual cases of robes, capes, mitres, crosses and chalices, there are some remarkable pieces here, including the Arcón de Carrizo – a beautiful painted twelfth-century wooden reliquary.

Palacio de Gaudí y Museo de los Caminos

Pza. Eduardo del Castro • Charge • https://www.palaciodegaudi.es/museo-de-los-caminos/

Standing across from the Catedral – and to many minds, upstaging it – is the **Palacio Episcopal**, or Bishop's Palace, which was designed by the celebrated Catalan architect Antoni Gaudí in 1886. It's quite an extraordinary building, more so inside than out,

---

MANTECADOS DE ASTORGA

Small traditional buttery sponge cakes called **mantecados** are Astorga's most famous treat. Legend has it that they were first created by the nuns in the **Convento de Sancti Spiritus** in the nineteenth century. A nun named Maria Josefa Gonzales Prieto marketed them to her congregation, and in 1805 the first official recipe for *mantecados* was recorded by Massimo Matheo and Francisco Calvo. Today, you'll find *mantecados* sold all over town, as well as a huge mural dedicated to the production of them, a few hundred meters before you reach the **Palacio de Gaudi**.

though even the exterior resembles a Disneyesque castle. Gaudí took the Gothic style as his inspiration and ran with it, resulting in a building of soaring brick and tile arches, intricate decorative work and luminous stained glass, culminating in an exquisite chapel that beats anything in the next-door Catedral hands down. The spectacular palace rooms now house the **Museo de los Caminos**, which traces the story of the pilgrimage through statues and artworks dating from its medieval origins, as well as examples of the documents issued at Santiago to certify that pilgrims had "travelled, confessed and obtained absolution". There's also a basement full of Roman altars and funerary statues and an attic devoted to contemporary regional art – together with a bird's-eye view down into the shining chapel.

Museo Romano

Pza. de San Bartolomé • Charge • 987 616 937

Astorga's Roman past is covered in the fascinating **Museo Romano**, which displays local archeological finds alongside changing exhibitions on various themes. However, the town also preserves a rich set of excavated remains, including a surviving "Bear and Birds" mosaic in a wealthy private Roman house, the **Casa Romana** – located just a few steps along the road from the museum.

Jardín de la Sinagoga

Pza. San Francisco • Free

Astorga is ringed by an almost complete circuit of **walls**, late Roman in origin and reconstructed over the centuries. It's only a short walk from the Roman museum to the **Jardín de la Sinagoga**, which retains a section of the old Roman sewer system and is also the best place for a view from the walls out over the plains to the Sierra de Teleno.

ARRIVAL AND INFORMATION
ASTORGA

By train The train station is a 15min walk from the town centre at Pza. de la Estación (912 320 320, https://www.adif.es).

Destinations León (up to 4 daily; 40min); Ponferrada (up to 4 daily; 1hr); Madrid (4 daily; 3hr).

By bus The bus station on Avda. de la Murallas (987 619 100) is right opposite the Palacio Episcopal; frequent services from León and Ponferrada (Alsa 987 619 100, http://alsa.es).

Destinations León (hourly; 1hr); Ponferrada (hourly; 1hr); Villafranca del Bierzo (3–4 daily; 1hr 40min).

By car Free parking is easy outside of the old town, either along the bus station road opposite the Palacio Episcopal, or in the large car park further down under the town walls.

Turismo Pza. Eduardo de Castro 5, across from the Palacio Episcopal (Tues–Sat 10am–2pm & 4–6.30pm, Sun 10am–2pm; 987 618 222, http://ayuntamientodeastorga.com).

ACCOMMODATION AND EATING

Astorga is an easy day-trip from León, but there's plenty of agreeable central accommodation if you fancy staying the night. Local **restaurants**, meanwhile, all advertise the delights of the *cocido Maragato* (stew featuring chickpeas and seven different kinds of sausage) – you eat the meats first, then the veg, then drink the broth, and good luck in finishing what tend to be gigantic portions. Astorga also has a reputation for its chocolate, production of which flourished here in the eighteenth and nineteenth centuries. The nicest places for a drink and a bite of tapas are the **cafés** and **bars** around Astorga's finest square, Pza. Mayor.

Aizkorri Pza. España 5, https://aizkorri.info. A Basque-style tavern right on Astorga's main square serving outstanding *pintxos*, such as a small but perfectly formed *bacalao* on

toast, braised scallops, and ratatouille and *alioli*. There are various menu options. €€

★ **Casa de Tepa** C/Santiago 2, http://casadetepa.com. The most atmospheric lodging in town is this handsome eighteenth-century townhouse with nine quiet, refined rooms (traditionally furnished, though with marble rain-shower bathrooms) and a sunny terrace garden where you can eat breakfast in summer. Private parking is available. €€

La Peseta Pza. de San Bartolomé 3, http://restaurante lapeseta.com. There's no quibbling among the locals when it comes to the town's best regional restaurant. Located just off Pza. Mayor, this restaurant has been in the hands of the same family for five generations (founded 1871). Specialities include the ubiquitous *cocido Maragato* and anything from stewed veal to *bacalao confitado* (cod in garlic sauce). There are also fifteen *hostal* rooms upstairs. €€€

Castrillo de los Polvazares

A fascinating side trip from Astorga takes in the improbably pretty village of **Castrillo de los Polvazares**, considered to be an archetypal settlement of the Maragato (a distinct ethnic group who crossed into Spain with the first Moorish incursions in the eighteenth century) and now zealously preserved as a local heritage showpiece. There's basically one long main cobbled street and a small church, with the rest being a charming collection of eighteenth-century, russet-coloured stone cottages flaunting window boxes and signs advertising honey (*miel*) for sale. Only residents can drive in (there's a car park by the bridge at the entrance to the village), so there's merely the cobbled footfall of pilgrims to disturb the timeless scene.

ARRIVAL AND DEPARTURE

CASTRILLO DE LOS POLVAZARES

By car Castrillo de los Polvazares is 5km west of Astorga on road LE142; by car, follow signs to Santa Colomba de Somoza out of Astorga, or on foot follow any backpacking pilgrim – the *camino* runs close to the village.

ACCOMMODATION AND EATING

Casa Coscolo C/La Magdalena 1, http://casacoscolo.com. It's not just hiking pilgrims who will fall gratefully into this little eatery. This Michelin-star restaurant is a village treasure, serving excellent regional cuisine – make sure you try their famous house specialty, the *cocido Coscolo*, their own take on the *cocido Maragato*. €€€

El Rincón Margato Pza. Concha Espín 9, http://el-rincn-maragato.castile-leon-hotels.com/es/. A budget-friendly guesthouse with peaceful, spacious rooms, some with views of the mountains and beautiful surroundings. There's also a restaurant a few minutes away. €

Ponferrada

At first sight, the heavily industrialized, bowl-shaped valley centred on the large town of **PONFERRADA** seems to have little to offer, but the mountainous terrain of the Bierzo has scenery as picturesque as any in Spain. The town itself is dominated by its outlying industrial suburbs, yet has an attractive old quarter, through which trudge weary pilgrims. Old and new towns are separated by the Río Sil, spanned by the iron bridge that gave Ponferrada its name, above which loom the high walls of the impressive castle. From the main square in the old town, **Pza. del Ayuntamiento**, pass through the quaint **Puerta del Reloj** (Clock Gateway) down to pretty **Pza. Virgen de la Encina**, which is overlooked by the town's finest Renaissance church and the curtain wall of the castle.

Castillo de los Templarios

Avda. del Castillo • Charge, free Wed • https://castillodelostemplarios.com

There are a couple of local museums in Ponferrada, but the only essential sight is the one you can hardly miss – the **Castillo de los Templarios**, which stands high above the river. Established by the Knights Templars in the thirteenth century, it's a textbook castle with fancy turrets and battlements, all gleaming after a handsome restoration.

ARRIVAL AND INFORMATION

PONFERRADA

By train and bus The train (Avda. Ferrocarril 15) and bus stations (Av. de la Libertad 222) are in the new town. Train connections include León, Madrid and Santiago de Compostela. The bus station is a 20min walk from the old town along C/General Gómez Nuñez (subsequently Avda. Pérez Colino) or 5min by taxi (Radio Taxi 987 087 087). Alsa routes include Villafranca del Bierzo and Astorga (http://alsa.es).

By car If you're driving from Astorga, you'll hit the old town first and can avoid the new section altogether. There's

5

parking on the edge of the old town, as well as under Pza. del Ayuntamiento, or free street parking on the bridge, below the castle.

Turismo C/Gil y Carrasco 4, by the castle (Mon–Sat 10am–2pm & 4.30–6.30pm, Sun 10am–2pm; 987 424 236, http://ponferrada.org/turismo).

ACCOMMODATION, EATING AND DRINKING

There are plenty of **hotels** and *hostales* in the new town, all signposted as you drive in (and detailed on the tourist office website). But it's nicest to stay in the old quarter, where there's a simple choice.

La Capricciosa Pza. Virgen de la Encina 1, 987 497 501. Prime position, with views over the pretty Pza. Virgen de la Encina, church and castle walls. It's an Italian place, with pizzas from the wood-fired oven – though they also use the traditional oven for pricier roast lamb and suckling pig dishes. €€

Hotel Aroi Bierzo Plaza Pza. del Ayuntamiento 4, https://www.aroihoteles.com/hotel-aroi-bierzo-plaza/. Charming rooms in a converted townhouse on the main square, with nice views. You can also grab an outdoor table for tapas and drinks from *La Taberna* (the former wine cellar), and there's contemporary regional cuisine in the hotel's *La Violeta* restaurant. €€

Hotel Los Templarios C/Flórez Osorio 3, https://hotellostemplarios.es. Straightforward rooms in this warmly decorated small hotel with its own restaurant. You'll find it just through the Clock Gateway from the main square. €

Las Médulas

Twenty-four kilometres southwest of Ponferrada lie **Las Médulas**, the jagged remains of hills ravaged by Roman strip-mining, which were declared a UNESCO World Heritage Site in 1997. Five tonnes of gold were ripped from the hillsides using specially constructed canals, leaving an eerie, mesmerizing landscape reminiscent of Arizona, peppered with caves and needles of red rock. Just outside Carucedo (on the N536) the road splits, with the right fork leading 3km up to the village of Las Médulas.

Las Médulas village

Aula Charge • 987 422 848 • **Las Médulas** Charge for guided walks • http://fundacionlasmedulas.info

This is a pretty place of restored stone houses, climbing roses and spreading chestnut trees set behind the largest rock outcrops, with a gaggle of rustic cafés that cater for day-trippers. There's information about old mining processes in the museum – the **Aula Arqueológica** – and guided walks from outside the **Centro de Recepción de Visitantes de Las Médulas**, located by the church, which has a visitor information centre, bike hire and a shop. From here, various signposted **trails** lead into the dramatic mine workings, the shortest being the hike to Somido lake (3km return; 50min) for great views of the outcrops, and the Las Valiñas trail (4km; 1hr 15min), which takes you partly inside the old mines themselves.

Mirador de Orellán

Charge • http://fundacionlasmedulas.info

The **Mirador de Orellán** offers the most spectacular panorama over the whole area of crumbling peaks. A detour of the Las Valiñas trail leads up here, or you can drive directly by taking the left fork out of Carucedo and winding up for 4.5km, through the village of Orellán. It's a steep 600m walk from the car park to the viewing platforms.

Villafranca del Bierzo

The last halt before the climb into Galicia, **VILLAFRANCA DEL BIERZO**, 22km from Ponferrada, was where pilgrims on their last legs could chicken out of the final trudge. Those who arrived at the Puerta del Perdón (Door of Forgiveness) at the simple Romanesque **church of Santiago** could receive the same benefits of exemption of years in Purgatory as in Santiago de Compostela itself. The town itself is quietly enchanting, with a jumble of old-town streets, slate-roofed houses, encircling hills, cool mountain air and the clear Río Burbia providing a setting vaguely reminiscent of the English Lake District. Look out for the famous **casas blasonadas** down C/del Agua – houses emblazoned with historic coats of arms, which show the lineage, and sometimes professions, of the families who lived there. The town's history and its pilgrim connection makes it a great place to stop for the night, with plenty of reasonably priced accommodation and a multitude of restaurants offering good-value pilgrim menus.

ARRIVAL AND DEPARTURE · VILLAFRANCA DEL BIERZO

By bus and car Regular buses from Ponferrada stop outside the tourist information centre on Avda. Díez Ovelar 10 (987 540 028, https://www.villafrancadelbierzo.org), where there are also some parking spaces.

ACCOMMODATION AND EATING

Hostal Puerta del Perdón C/Pza. de Prim 4, http://lapuertadelperdon.com. The family-run "micro-hostel" beside the Puerta del Perdón and its fine restaurant both have a reputation for outstanding quality. They offer seven cosy individually themed rooms, a pilgrim menu and local specialities from the a la carte menu, such as the chef's great-grandmother's recipe for *rabo de toro*. €̄

Hotel Las Doñas del Portazgo C/Ribadeo 2, http:// elportazgo.es. Probably Villafranca's finest accommodation, this boutique luxury hotel has seventeen rooms with country-chic decor. Located close to the tourist information centre. €€

Mesón Don Nacho Calle Troquelles, 987 540 076. If you want to eat like a local, this is the place to head for. Traditional cooking with excellent wine and a great ambience. €̄€

Euskal Herria: the País Vasco and Navarra

SAN SEBASTIÁN

Euskal Herria: the País Vasco and Navarra

The name that the Basque people give to their own land, Euskal Herria, covers the three Basque provinces that now form the *Comunidad Autónoma del País Vasco* (in Basque, "Euskadi") – Gipuzkoa, Bizkaia and Araba – as well as Navarra (Nafarroa) and part of southwestern France. Much of this region is immensely beautiful, and especially so along the coast, where green and thickly forested mountains, interspersed with stark solitary hills, seem in places to emerge from the sea itself. Yes, it often rains, and much of the time the countryside is shrouded in a fine mist, but so long as you don't mind the occasional shower, summer here offers a glorious escape from the unrelenting heat of the south.

Despite the heavy industrialization that has helped to make this one of the wealthiest areas in Spain, **Euskal Herria** is remarkably unspoiled – neat and quiet inland, rugged and wild along the coast. **San Sebastián** is a major resort city, with superb if crowded beaches and wonderful food, but lesser-known, similarly attractive villages line the coast all the way to **Bilbao**, home to the magnificent Museo Guggenheim. Inland, **Pamplona** boasts its exuberant Fiestas de San Fermín, while other destinations have charms of their own, from the drama of the **Pyrenees** to the laidback elegance of **Vitoria-Gasteiz**.

Look out especially for rural **accommodation** options, plentiful thanks to the **nekazalturismoa** (*agroturismo*) programme, which offers the opportunity to stay in traditional farmhouses and private homes, usually in areas of outstanding beauty, at a very reasonable cost. In Navarra, as in much of the country, these are known as **casas rurales**, or *landa exteak*. Pick up details from local **tourist offices** (which also handle bookings), or online at http://nekatur.net, and, for Navarra, http://casasruralesnavarra.com.

While a reasonable **bus** network connects the Basque Country's towns, the easiest way to get around is by car. If you want to follow the coast, though, the dramatic hills and cliffs mean there isn't always a shoreline road; with public transport especially you have to keep returning to the main roads way inland. **Train** services are relatively poor. San Sebastián lies on a major route to and from France, which also passes through Vitoria-Gasteiz, but Bilbao is off the main line on a minor spur, and direct trains between Bilbao and San Sebastián are much slower than the equivalent buses. Bilbao is, however, the eastern terminus of a separate narrow-gauge railway, now part of the national RENFE system, which follows the Atlantic coast west to Santander, Oviedo and beyond.

You're also more likely to see the Basque word for **street**, "kalea", rather than the Spanish, "calle".

Brief history

When the **Romans** invaded, they defeated the Aquitani, who inhabited large areas of southwestern Gaul and northern Iberia, and spoke an ancestral version of Basque. However, they allowed the more dominant group known as the Vascones, who lived in the mountains of Euskal Herria, to keep their language and independence in return for allowing free passage and trading rights.

Later rulers were less accommodating. Successive **Visigoth** kings tried and failed to eradicate the Basques. The **Moors** conquered the lowlands of Araba (Alava in Castilian)

Highlights

❶ **Playa de la Concha, San Sebastián** This graceful crescent strand, curving away from the delightful old town, has to rank among the world's greatest urban beaches. See page 426

❷ **Pintxos** The Basques prepare their pintxos with a genuine gourmet flair – especially in San Sebastián. See page 429

❸ **Mundaka estuary** Sublime scenery, world-class surfing, the beautiful seaside village of Mundaka, and Gernika, the Basque spiritual capital. See page 437

❹ **Museo Guggenheim, Bilbao** This swirling titanium edifice has become the symbol of the regenerated city. See page 441

❺ **Bodegas Ysios** An architectural extravaganza, designed to celebrate the rich red wines of Rioja. See page 451

❻ **Fiestas de San Fermín** Pamplona's famous fiesta is rowdy and dirty, but for once the bulls get a fair shot. See page 454

❼ **Olite** Delightful village of ochre-coloured stone mansions on the edge of the Navarran plains. See page 461

❽ **Bardenas Reales** This eerie Wild West desertscape is perhaps the last thing you'd expect to find in the Basque Country. See page 462

HIGHLIGHTS ARE MARKED ON THE MAP ON PAGE 418

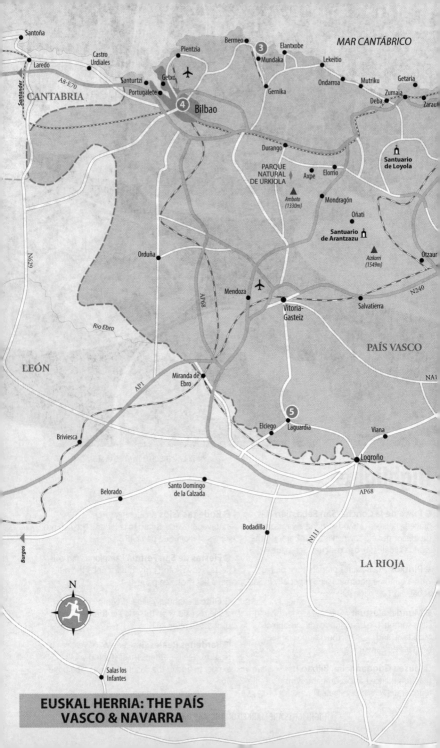

MAR CANTÁBRICO

Santoña

Laredo

Castro
Urdiales

CANTABRIA

Santander

A8-E70

Bermeo

Plentzia

Elantxobe

3

Mundaka

Lekeitio

Santurtzi
Getxo
Portugalete

Gernika

Ondarroa

Mutriku

Getaria

4 Bilbao

Deba

Zumaia

Zarau

Durango

PARQUE
NATURAL
DE URKIOLA

Axpe

Elorrio

Santuario
de Loyola

Amboto
(1330m)

Mondragón

Oñati

Orduña

Santuario
de Arantzazu

Aizkorri
(1549m)

Otzaur

Mendoza

N240

N629

AP68

Vitoria-
Gasteiz

Salvatierra

PAÍS VASCO

Río Ebro

LEÓN

Miranda de
Ebro

AP1

NA1

5

Briviesca

Elciego

Laguardia

Viana

Logroño

Belorado

Santo Domingo
de la Calzada

AP68

Bodadilla

N111

LA RIOJA

N

Salas los
Infantes

Burgos

EUSKAL HERRIA: THE PAÍS
VASCO & NAVARRA

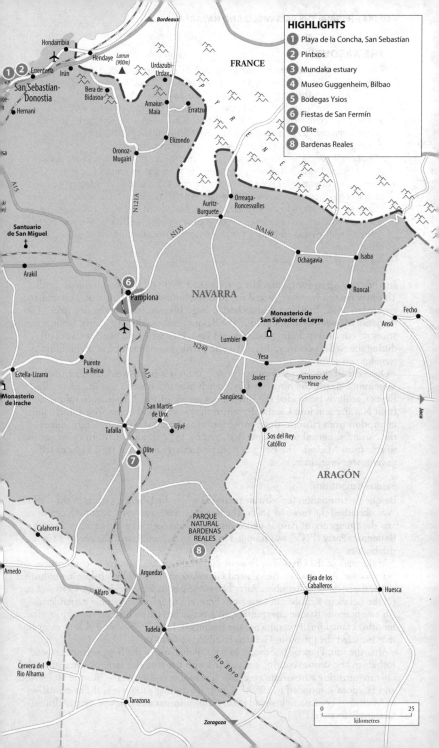

HIGHLIGHTS

1. Playa de la Concha, San Sebastián
2. Pintxos
3. Mundaka estuary
4. Museo Guggenheim, Bilbao
5. Bodegas Ysios
6. Fiestas de San Fermín
7. Olite
8. Bardenas Reales

FRANCE

Bordeaux

Hondarribia
Hendaye
Larrun (900m)
Urdazubi-Urdax
Errenteria
San Sebastián-Donostia
Irún
Bera de Bidasoa
Amaiur-Maia
Erratzu
Hernani
Elizondo
Oronoz-Mugairi

Santuario de San Miguel

Arakil

Auritz-Burguete
Orreaga-Roncesvalles
NA140
Ochagavía
Isaba
Roncal
Fecho

NAVARRA

Pamplona
Monasterio de San Salvador de Leyre
Ansó
Lumbier
Yesa
Pantano de Yesa
Jaca

Estella-Lizarra
Puente La Reina
Javier
Sangüesa
Monasterio de Irache
San Martín de Unx
Ujué
Sos del Rey Católico

Tafalla
Olite

ARAGÓN

Calahorra
PARQUE NATURAL BARDENAS REALES

Arnedo
Arguedas
Alfaro
Ejea de los Caballeros
Huesca
Tudela

Cervera del Río Alhama
Río Ebro

Tarazona
Zaragoza

0   25
kilometres

6

THE BASQUES

The origins of **the Basques** remain mysterious. They are a distinct people, generally with a different build from the French and Spanish and a different blood-group distribution from the rest of Europe. Their language, the complex **Euskara**, is unrelated to any other, and was already spoken in Spain when Indo-European languages began to arrive three thousand years ago. Written records were scarce until the first books in Euskara were published in the mid-sixteenth century. Language and culture survived instead through oral traditions, including that of the *bertsolariak* – popular poets specializing in improvised verse.

The Basque people have unquestionably inhabited the western Pyrenees for thousands of years. Archeologists and anthropologists used to argue that they might be the last surviving representatives of Europe's first modern human population, Cro-Magnon hunter-gatherers. More recently, however, **DNA analysis** has demonstrated clear affinities between 5500-year-old skeletons found in El Portalón cave, near Burgos, and modern Basques. The new suggestion is that the Basques are descended from early Neolithic farmers who became isolated – perhaps through a deliberate retreat into the mountains – from subsequent waves of migration.

and Navarra up to Pamplona, but never gained a grip on the mountainous north. This new enemy, however, forced the Basques, hitherto a collection of semi-affiliated groups, to unite. In 818, a Basque leader, Íñigo Íñiguez, became the first ruler of the **Kingdom of Navarre**. In due course, the Basques embraced Christianity, while retaining ancestral customs including their ancient laws. First written down (in Castilian) during the twelfth century, these laws and privileges, maintained as oral traditions, were known as **fueros**.

Once the Reconquest was complete and Spain was being welded into a single kingdom, Navarre (by now ruled by French monarchs) was a missing piece. The Reyes Católicos persuaded the Bizkaians, Gipuzkoans and Arabans to split away from Navarre and join Castile. In return the *fueros* would be respected, including exemption from customs duty, conscription and central taxation. Under duress, the Navarrese agreed to the same deal, and by 1512 all four territories were subject to rule from Madrid. The Basques have protectively defended their right to self-government ever since.

Basque nationalism

Basque determination for self-rule increased when the Liberals, victors in the Carlist War, abolished the *fueros* in 1876. The late nineteenth and early twentieth centuries saw the emergence of Basque nationalism as an ideology. The conservative **Basque Nationalist Party** (PNV) was founded in 1895 by Sabino Arana, the son of a Carlist shipbuilder.

At the start of the Civil War, Franco's Nationalists seized control of conservative Navarra and Araba, while Bizkaia and Gipuzkoa, dominated by left-leaning industrial cities, supported the Republic. After Navarrese troops captured Irún in 1936 and cut off the northern Republican zone from France, San Sebastián rapidly surrendered. An autonomous Basque government, in practice limited to Bizkaia, lasted just nine months. Franco finally conquered the Basques in June 1937, after a vicious campaign that included the infamous German bombing of **Gernika**.

After the war, Franco's boot went in hard. Public use of the Basque language was forbidden and central control was asserted with the gun. But state violence succeeded only in nurturing a new resistance, **ETA** (Euskadi ta Askatasuna – "Basque Homeland and Freedom"), founded in 1959. Its most spectacular success was the assassination in Madrid of Franco's right-hand man, prime minister and heir apparent, Admiral Carrero Blanco, in 1973.

Separatism today

The political situation started to change following the **transition to democracy**. The new constitution granted the Basques limited autonomy, with their own parliament and tax collection. There's now a regional police force, the red-bereted *ertzaintza*; the Basque language is taught in schools and universities; and the Basque flag (*ikurriña*) flies everywhere.

FIESTAS

6

JANUARY
19–20: Festividad de San Sebastián Twenty-four hours of festivities, including a *tamborrada*, a march with pipes and drums.

FEBRUARY
Weekend before Ash Wednesday: *Carnaval* throughout the region, but especially in Bilbao, San Sebastián and Tolosa.

MARCH/APRIL
March 4–12: A series of pilgrimages to the castle at Javier, birthplace of San Francisco Javier.
Semana Santa (Holy Week) Extensive Easter celebrations in Vitoria; also in Segura.
Easter Sunday: Aberri Eguna The Basque National Day, celebrated particularly in Bilbao.
April 28: Fiesta de San Prudencio Celebrated with *tamborradas* in Vitoria.

JUNE
24: Fiestas de San Juan In Lekeitio, Laguardia and Tolosa.
Last week: Fiesta de San Pedro In Mundaka, with Basque dancing.

JULY
First week: Fiesta at Zumaia with dancing, Basque sports and an *encierro* on the beach.
6–14: Fiestas de San Fermín In Pamplona, featuring the famous Running of the Bulls and the *gigantes y cabezudos* (giants and big heads).
22: Fiesta de la Magdalena In Bermeo, with torchlit processions of fishing boats and Basque sports.
24–28: *Encierro* in Tudela.

AUGUST
First weekend: Patron saint's celebration in Estella-Lizarra.
4–9: Fiesta de la Virgen Blanca In Vitoria, with bullfights, fireworks and *gigantones*.
Second weekend: Medieval festival in Olite.
14–17: Fiestas de Andra Mari In Ondarroa.
15: Semana Grande An explosion of celebration that lasts up to nine days, notably in Bilbao, with Basque games and races, and San Sebastián, where the highlight is an international fireworks competition.

SEPTEMBER
First week: Euskal Jaiak Basque games in San Sebastián.
4: Fiesta de San Antolín In Lekeitio, where the local youth attempt to knock the head off a (dead) goose.
9: Arrantzale Eguna (Día del Pescador) Fisherman's Day in Bermeo.
12: *Encierro* in Sangüesa.
14: Patron saint's day in Olite, with yet more bulls.
Last two weeks: International Film Festival In San Sebastián.

Basque demands for independence have not ended, however, and the violence continued. In the forty years from 1968, ETA killed around 850 people in various attacks, with targets ranging from members of the Spanish police and armed forces to Basque businessmen and politicians, academics, journalists, the tourist industry and random civilians. In 2017, however, following a long succession of ceasefires, ETA declared that it would permanently lay down arms and surrender all stockpiles of weapons. Currently, two-thirds of the elected Basque parliament could broadly be considered as separatists, but despite the new era of peace, the Spanish government has shown no willingness to negotiate over Basque self-determination.

San Sebastián (Donostia-San Sebastián)

Making the most of its glorious location, curving languidly around a magnificent semicircular bay lined with golden sand, **SAN SEBASTIÁN** ranks among the great resort cities of Europe. Although it's the capital of its region, Gipuzkoa, and has a reputation as a hotbed of Basque nationalism, it has never been a major port, or much of an industrial centre. Instead its primary identity, ever since the Spanish royal family first decamped here for the summer in 1845, has been as a summer playground. In July and August especially, it tends to be packed out, and its hotels are among the most expensive in Spain.

While the superb sheltered **beach** on its very doorstep is the biggest attraction of all, San Sebastián also boasts a charming old-town core, the **Parte Vieja**, squeezed up against the foot of verdant Monte Urgull and renowned for its high-quality **food**. The new town to the south, known as **Centro** and the city's commercial hub, holds a fine crop of *belle époque* edifices, though they're interspersed between dreary newer buildings.

The city's official name, **Donostia-San Sebastián**, is a tautology; Donostia is a Basque name for Saint Sebastian. Some say Sebastian was martyred in the Roman port of Ostia, and is thus the Don (saint) of Ostia; others that Ostia (or Osti) is simply an abbrevation of Sebastian. Getting around, you'll see signs and directions for Donostia-San Sebastián, or simply Donastia, the Basque name.

Parte Vieja

Although San Sebastián's old town, the **Parte Vieja**, stands on the site where the city first developed, almost nothing predates a disastrous fire, set by British troops, in 1813. With little trace of its original walls surviving either, it's a formal grid far removed from the typical old quarters of other Spanish cities. Nonetheless, it's a delight, its narrow streets and occasional pretty squares thronged in the daytime with shoppers and sightseers, and at night with revellers eager to sample its legendary *pintxos* bars and restaurants. Note that in other parts of Spain, the **old town** is often referred to as the Casco Viejo, but in San Sebastián this area is known as the Parte Vieja (old part).

THE FESTIVALS OF SAN SEBASTIÁN

San Sebastián's busy annual calendar of fiestas and festivals kicks off on the stroke of midnight at the start of January 20, the feast day of its namesake saint. Carnival too is celebrated in style, but the two biggest events of the year are the five-day, multi-venue **Jazz Festival** in late July (http://jazzaldia.com), which attracts well-known performers, not exclusively jazz, from all over the world, and the week-long **Film Festival** in the second half of September (http://sansebastianfestival.com).

Plaza de la Constitución

At the heart of the Parte Vieja, the **Plaza de la Constitución** makes a great arena for festivals. It even served as a bullring in the past; hence the numbers painted on the balconies to all sides. Amazingly, each window originally belonged to a separate apartment, each barely wider than a corridor; many dividing walls have now been removed, however, to make larger living spaces.

Museo San Telmo
Pza. Zuloaga 1 • Charge, free every Tues • http://santelmomuseoa.com

The **Museo San Telmo**, below Monte Urgull at the northeast edge of the Parte Vieja, sets out to trace the history of the Basque lands, and San Sebastián in particular. Some visitors, though, find it confusing, as it covers numerous themes and topics in a maze of buildings that incorporates a spectacular new extension. The original core, a deconsecrated convent, showcases vast monochromatic canvases by Catalan muralist Josep Maria Sert.

Exhibits cover everything from whaling to 1960s Basque pop music, by way of the regional intrigues of the Civil War, to an astonishing crude wooden wolf trap that forms the highlight of the section on rural life. Chronological displays of fine art start in the sixteenth century, including works by artists such as El Greco and Rubens, and well known Basque artists such as Jesús Olasgasti and landscape artist Darío Regoyos, with two outstanding works by María Paz Jiménez.

Basílica de Santa María
C/31 de Agosto 46 • Free • 943 423 124

The Baroque facade of the Basílica de Santa María is visible along the slender, arrow-straight C/Mayor, the main artery of the old town, all the way from the unremarkable Catedral in the new town. Although it dates from the eighteenth century, it only became a basilica following a papal visit in 1966; the pope's coat of arms can be seen along with a caravel of the kind used by Columbus, and an image of San Sebastián himself. You enter the main door to find that, thanks to the church's squashed-up position below Monte Urgull, the nave unexpectedly stretches not straight ahead of you but from side to side, with a huge altarpiece to your right and an alabaster Greek cross by Eduardo Chillida above the font to your left.

Monte Urgull
San Sebastián was originally a fishing settlement at the foot of the wooded **Monte Urgull**, a steep headland that until the connecting spit was built over was virtually an island in its own right. It takes barely twenty minutes to walk around the base of the hill, along a level path that offers tremendous sunset views, or a little longer to climb to its **summit** via the winding trails and stairways that lead up from the Parte Vieja. Topped by a massive statue of Christ (El Sagrado Corazón – "the Sacred Heart"), which towers over the Castillo de la Mota, the hillside intersperses formal gardens and wilder stretches, one of which, on the far side, cradles a small **cemetery** devoted to English soldiers who died during the First Carlist War, in the 1830s.

Castillo de la Mota
Monte Urgull • Charge • 943 428 417

The **Castillo de la Mota** atop Monte Urgull would be worth entering simply to enjoy the magnificent views across the city and bay, but this castle also holds an enjoyable **museum**. Its entertaining romp through local history begins with the eleventh century, but focuses especially on the growth of tourism, with some great photos and film footage from the 1920s and 1930s.

Aquarium
Pza. de Carlos Blasco Imaz 1 • Charge • http://aquariumss.com

6

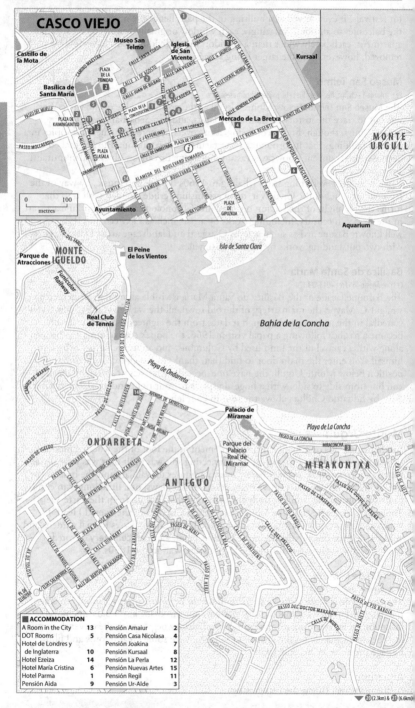

CASCO VIEJO

MONTE URGULL

MONTE IGUELDO

Parque de Atracciones

El Peine de los Vientos

Funicular Railway

Real Club de Tennis

Isla de Santa Clara

Bahía de la Concha

Playa de Ondarreta

ONDARRETA

ANTIGUO

Palacio de Miramar

Parque del Palacio Real de Miramar

Playa de La Concha

MIRAKONTXA

ACCOMMODATION			
A Room in the City	13	Pensión Amaiur	2
DOT Rooms	5	Pensión Casa Nicolasa	4
Hotel de Londres y		Pensión Joakina	7
de Inglaterra	10	Pensión Kursaal	8
Hotel Ezeiza	14	Pensión La Perla	12
Hotel María Cristina	6	Pensión Nuevas Artes	15
Hotel Parma	1	Pensión Regil	11
Pensión Aida	9	Pensión Ur-Alde	3

▼ 20 (2.3km) & 21 (6.6km)

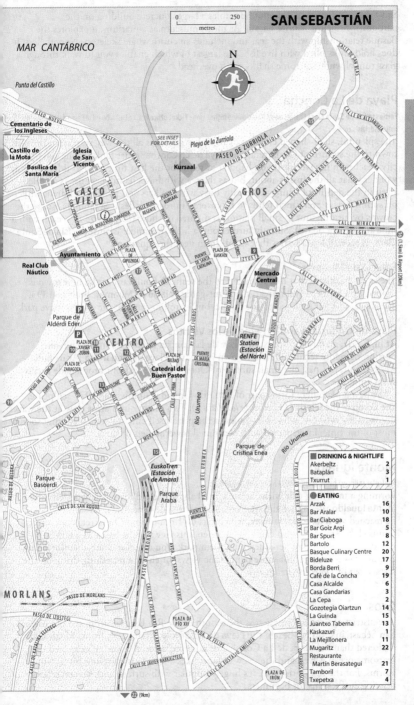

SAN SEBASTIÁN

MAR CANTÁBRICO

Punta del Castillo

Cementerio de los Ingleses

Castillo de la Mota

Iglesia de San Vicente

Basílica de Santa María

Kursaal

CASCO VIEJO

GROS

Playa de la Zurriola

Real Club Náutico

Ayuntamiento

Parque de Aldérdi Eder

CENTRO

Mercado Central

RENFE Station (Estación del Norte)

Catedral del Buen Pastor

Río Urumea

Parque de Cristina Enea

Río Urumea

EuskoTren (Estación de Amara)

Parque Araba

Parque Basoerdi

MORLANS

0   250   metres

SEE INSET FOR DETAILS

■ DRINKING & NIGHTLIFE	
Akerbeltz	2
Bataplán	3
Txurrut	1

● EATING	
Arzak	16
Bar Aralar	10
Bar Ciaboga	18
Bar Goiz Argi	5
Bar Sport	8
Bartolo	12
Basque Culinary Centre	20
Bideluze	17
Borda Berri	9
Café de la Concha	19
Casa Alcalde	6
Casa Gandarias	3
La Cepa	2
Gozotegia Oiartzun	14
La Guinda	15
Juantxo Taberna	13
Kaskazuri	1
La Mejillonera	11
Mugaritz	22
Restaurante Martín Berasategui	21
Tamboril	7
Txepetxa	4

San Sebastián's modern **aquarium** occupies a large concrete building on the harbourfront below Monte Urgull. As much museum as aquarium, it explores the Basque relationship with the sea, and includes an entire whale skeleton. Nonetheless, it does hold tanks filled with live fish, the largest of which enables you to walk through a glass tunnel while fearsome sharks swim overhead.

Playa de La Concha

Ferries to Isla de Santa Clara Charge, every 30min during high season • **Ticket office** Pza. La Lasta, board at Paseo del Muelle • http://motorasdelaisla.com

The splendid, shell-shaped crescent of sand that stretches all the way west from the old town to the suburb of Ondarreta, the **Playa de La Concha**, must rank among the finest city beaches in the world. If you happen to see it for the first time at high tide, you may wonder what all the fuss is about, but as the sea withdraws its full expanse is revealed. Even in the depths of winter it's usually busy with walkers and playing children, while on summer days every inch tends to be covered in roasting flesh. Swimmers escape the crowds by heading out to small platforms moored offshore (*los gabarrones* – each with a slide and diving board). Slightly further out, a little pyramidal island, the **Isla de Santa Clara**, is accessible via ferries that set off from near the aquarium.

Palacio de Miramar

The stony headland that marks an end to the seafront boulevard of the new town is topped by a former royal retreat, the avant-garde **Palacio de Miramar**, built in 1893. The mansion itself is closed to the public, but its rolling gardens are an attractive park.

Playa de Ondarreta and El Peine de los Vientos

At high tide, an outcrop splits the Playa de la Concha in two; its smaller western portion therefore technically has its own name, the **Playa de Ondarreta**. At its far western end, just past the small suburb of Ondarreta, the seafront promenade finally stops amid the rocks.

The paved plaza here forms part of Eduardo Chillida's unmissable 1977 sculpture, **The Comb of the Winds** (*El Peine de los Vientos*). Two mighty iron arms claw at the waves immediately offshore, while blowholes in the plaza itself emit an eerie breathing sound most of the time, interspersed with occasional towering jets of spray.

Monte Igueldo

Funicular railway Charge, every 15min • http://monteigueldo.es

Forming a matching pair with Monte Urgull above the old town, the wooded hill of **Monte Igueldo** rises above the west end of the Playa de Ondarreta. Its summit can be reached via a **funicular railway**, which sets off from behind Ondarreta's beachfront tennis club. At the top you can enjoy tremendous views of the bay and a rather wonderfully fading pay-per-ride amusement park. You can also climb the nineteenth-century tower (charge) for more panoramic views, or enjoy a refreshing drink on the terrace bar of *Hotel Monte Igueldo*.

Gros

The district of **Gros** lies just across the mouth of the Río Urumea from the old town. San Sebastián's "other" beach, the **Playa de la Zurriola**, stretches in front. Much less sheltered than the Playa de La Concha, its counterpart to the west, it's exposed to fearsome ocean waves, and the sea wall here takes a ferocious battering from winter storms. For the rest of the year, it's hugely popular with surfers, with several schools offering surf lessons for beginners.

Monte Ulia to Pasajes San Pedro

A gorgeous clifftop walk can be taken from Monte Ulia on the eastern side of Playa de la Zurriola all the way to the harbour town of Pasajes San Pedro. The walk (around 9km) begins behind the harbour via C/Navarra with a steep climb up C/Zemoria, then along lush, undulating wooded paths that offer some spectacular views of the sea and rugged coastline. There are painted red and white markings on trees and rocks along the way to guide you, and the route forms part of the Camino de Santiago (see page 518), so you may well pass some hiking pilgrims going the other way. You'll eventually drop down into Pasajes – passing Albaola, a Basque sea factory where the reconstruction of a sixteenth-century whaling boat is ongoing – and continue around to reach a couple of bars for a well-earned refreshment. It takes around three hours and there aren't any facilities along the way, so wear comfy walking shoes and take plenty of water. You can then walk a little further into San Pedro for a bus back to San Sebastián. For more information on the route, visit https://www.oarsoaldeaturismoa.eus/en/explore-oarsoaldea/nature/ulia-e.html.

Kursaal

http://kursaal.eus

Gros is dominated by the huge glass **Kursaal**, arrayed along the seafront promenade, which consists of two starkly angular blocks referred to by architect Rafael Moneo as "two beached rocks". Its main feature is a concert hall that's home to September's film festival, and it also holds substantial exhibition space.

ARRIVAL AND DEPARTURE   SAN SEBASTIÁN

By air San Sebastián's small airport, 22km east of the city, south of Hondarribia near the French border, is served only by a few domestic flights. It's easiest to fly to either Bilbao, then take a direct bus from outside the airport (hourly; 1hr 15min) or to Biarritz just over the border in France, then take a direct bus from there (hourly; 1hr).

By train San Sebastián has two train stations: RENFE (http://renfe.es) use the Estación del Norte in Gros, just across the river from the new town; while EuskoTren (http://euskotren.eus) services run east and west from the Estación de Amara, at the south end of Centro, a 20min walk from the Parte Vieja. Destinations from Estación del Norte Barcelona (2 daily; 6hr); Burgos (6 daily; 3hr 30min); Madrid (6 daily; 5–8hr); Pamplona (2 daily; 1hr 40min); Salamanca (5 daily; 6–8hr);

Vitoria (8 daily; 1hr 40min); Zaragoza (2 daily; 3hr 40min). Destinations from Estación de Amara Bilbao (hourly; 2hr 40min); Irún (every 30min; 35min).

By bus The main bus station is next to River Urmea on Paseo García Llorca (983 475 150, http://estaciondonostia.com). Destinations Bilbao (every 30min; 1hr 10min); Bilbao Airport (every hour; 1hr 15min); Hondarribia (every 20min; 30min); Irún (constantly; 30min); Lekeitio (5 daily; 1hr 20min); Bera (Vera) de Bidasoa (2 daily; 50min); and Vitoria (6 daily; 2hr 30min).

By car You can't drive into San Sebastián's Parte Vieja, and parking anywhere nearby can be extremely problematic. If your hotel doesn't have its own car park – and very few do – head straight for the underground garages nearby.

INFORMATION

Turismo Boulevard 8, on the edge of the Parte Vieja (Mon–Sat 9am–8pm, Sun 10am–7pm; 983 481 166, http:// sansebastianturismo.com).

ACCOMMODATION   SEE MAP PAGE 424

San Sebastián offers a fine crop of hotels, from *belle époque* beachfront palaces to charming old-town houses, but they charge some of the highest rates in Spain. For a summer stay, or the film festival in September, you can easily pay well over €100 even for a run-of-the-mill room (eye-wateringly more in the old part). It's essential to book as far in advance as possible, and some hotels offer discounts online.

PARTE VIEJA

★ **DOT Rooms** C/Puerto 15, 1º, https://sansebastian dotrooms.com. Welcoming guesthouse, upstairs in the

historic heart of the old town, just up from the harbour. Bright, attractive rooms abound in period charm, with exposed stonework and ancient beams. €€€€

Hotel Parma Paseo de Salamanca 10, http://hotelparma. com. It would be hard to pick a better location, at the edge of the old town and handy for the beach. The rooms, though, are a little bland and it can be noisy at night. The cheapest rooms face an internal courtyard, but those on the upper level enjoy great sea views. Friendly, helpful staff make a big difference. €€€€

Pensión Amaiur C/31 de Agosto 44, 2º, http://pension

6

amaiur.com. Classic old-style hotel, in a venerable house deep in the warren-like streets of the old town. Rooms differ in size – some sleep four – and are decorated in widely varying styles. Some have en-suite bathrooms and private balconies, others share bathrooms, and there are two communal kitchens. €€€

Pensión Casa Nicolasa C/Aldamar 4, 1º, http://pension casanicolasa.com. Impeccable and unusually large modern rooms, with spacious bathrooms, in a relatively peaceful location facing the market place in the old town. €€€€

Pensión Ur-Alde C/Puerto 17, 2º, http://ur-alde.com. Although it's in one of San Sebastián's older houses, this old-town hotel has minimal local flavour; for its modern en-suite bathrooms, spotless decor, and central location, though, it's not bad value. €€€

CENTRO

A Room in the City C/Easo 20, http://aroominthecity.eu. Much the best hostel in San Sebastián, with very helpful staff, lots of communal space and thoughtful touches everywhere you look. Just 5min walk from the beach, twice that to the old town, it spreads through two neighbouring buildings and sleeps up to 200 guests, in dorms for 4–12 people, or there is a twin option for two. You can't actually cook in the shared kitchen, just prepare drinks and snacks. Dorms €, twin with shared bathroom €€

Hotel de Londres y de Inglaterra C/Zubieta 2, http://hlondres.com. The very welcoming *grande dame* of San Sebastián hotels, this impressive white nineteenth-century edifice commands a superb position overlooking the beach, a short walk from the old town. Live it up in style in a spacious, comfortable room with huge seafront windows. €€€€

Hotel María Cristina Paseo Republica Argentina 4, http://hotel-mariacristina.com. Landmark five-star hotel, dominating the river-mouth near the edge of the old town, that's the epicentre of September's film festival. Its sumptuous *belle époque* rooms are the last word in old-style luxury, boasting huge beds and opulent bathrooms. €€€€

Pensión Joakina C/Camino 4, 4º, http://pensionjoakina.com. Long-established and very welcoming family-run

hotel, a short walk from the old town, where several of the bright, clean rooms have balconies, and guests share use of a small kitchen. €€

Pensión Nuevas Artes C/Urbieta 64, 1ºB, http://pension-nuevasartes.com. Welcoming upscale *pensión*, run by an exceptionally hospitable, English-speaking mother-and-daughter team. Large comfortable rooms with exposed brickwork, glassed-in balconies, and good en-suite facilities. €€€

★ **Pensión La Perla** C/Loiola 10, 1º, http://pension laperla.com. Great-value new-town *pensión*, handy for bus and train stations as well as the old town and beach. Friendly service and simple but spacious rooms, all en suite and some with balconies. €€

Pensión Regil C/Easo 9, 1º, http://pensionregil.com. Eight neat, tidy but rather small rooms, in a great location near the beach and old town, with extremely helpful management. €€€

GROS

Pensión Aida Iztueta 9, 1º, http://pensionesconencanto.com. Welcoming nine-room *pensión*, in a relatively quiet location near the main train station, Zurriola beach and old town. All rooms are brightly decorated, with exposed stone and en-suite facilities. For maximum peace, opt for an "interior" room, though those facing out are equipped with balconies. €€€

Pensión Kursaal C/Peña y Goni 2, 1º, http://pension kursaal.com. Very bright, large, modern rooms, just across the bridge from the old town and good for the surfing beach. They also offer rental bikes. €€€

ONDARRETA

Hotel Ezeiza Avda. Satrústegui 13, Playa de Ondarreta, http://hotelezeiza.com. This friendly hotel, facing the smaller of the bay's beaches, a long walk from the city centre, makes a good base for families looking for lower-key pleasures than the full-on city experience. All of the rooms are well maintained, with bright modern furnishings, and have en-suite facilities; most also enjoy lovely sea views. €€€€

EATING
SEE MAP PAGE 424

As the epicentre of the Basque culinary revolution, San Sebastián is a paradise for anyone who loves to eat. What's more, in addition to its world-famous gourmet restaurants an astonishing profusion of bars serve the latest concoctions in the form of **pintxos**. While it's very easy to sniff out your own favourites as you explore the Parte Vieja, it's worth joining one of the tourist board's guided tours, **Sabores de San Sebastián** (11.30am: April–June & Sept–Jan irregular Fridays, July & Aug Tues & Thurs, 983 481 166, http://sansebastianturismo.com), which for €18 buys you a drink and a *pintxo* in each of three old-town bars.

CAFÉS

Café de la Concha Paseo de La Concha s/n, http://cafede laconcha.com. The main draw of this café-restaurant, occupying prime position on the seafront, is the unmissable panorama of La Concha beach and the entire bay beyond. €€
Gozotegia Oiartzun C/Igentia 2, https://www.pasteleria oiartzun.com. Most customers drop in at this *pastelería*, facing from the edge of the Parte Vieja across to the ornate town hall, just to pick up one of the superb cakes – try the almond "Pastel Vasco". It also serves great coffee and has a few pavement tables if you don't mind paying a little extra to linger. €

BASQUE CUISINE

Basque cuisine has established a reputation as the finest in Spain. Cutting-edge chefs such as Martín Berasetegui, Juan Mari Arzak and Andoni Aduriz, the stars of the **nueva cocina vasca** (new Basque cuisine), delight in creating inventive new combinations and preparations, and restaurants throughout the region are crowded with eager diners happy to pay premium prices for superb food. As of 2024, a whopping nineteen Michelin stars have been awarded to restaurants across San Sebastián alone.

That said, Basque food doesn't have to be expensive. For visitors, the perfect way to sample it is in the form of **pintxos**, the Basque equivalent of tapas (though pintxos are generally smaller bites, held together by a cocktail stick). Bar counters throughout the region, and above all in San Sebastián, are piled high with fabulously enticing and utterly delectable goodies, freshly cooked, priced as a rule at €2–3, and almost invariably excellent. Most bars also prepare more substantial or complicated *pintxos* and *raciones* (sharing plates) to order. They're so irresistible that even if you never quite make it to a restaurant for a sit-down meal, you'll still come away raving about the Basque Country as one of the greatest foodie destinations on earth.

Seafood is a major ingredient of many Basque signature dishes. Look out especially for *bacalao* (cod) *a la vizcaina* or *al pil-pil* (a garlic-based sauce), *merluza a la vasca* (hake, Basque-style, usually in a green sauce with white asparagus and boiled eggs), *txipirones en su tinta* (squid cooked in its ink) or *txangurro* (spider crab).

La Guinda C/Zabaleta 55, http://laguindadelicoffee.com. With its whitewashed-wood aesthetic, this relaxed coffee bar/deli, a block back from the sea in Gros, wouldn't look out of place beside a New England beach. Call in for breakfast or a substantial lunchtime salad, or linger over the daily menu. €€

PINTXOS BARS

Bar Ciaboga C/Easo 9, 943 422 926. This small, unsuspecting bar with a relaxed vibe, just a couple of streets back from the beach, serves the best garlicky potatoes you'll ever eat. Their signature *raciones* – the "Platillo" – is served with an optional dusting of paprika and a couple of hunks of bread to mop up the olive oil. €

Bar Goiz Argi C/Fermín Calbetón 4, 943 425 204. Hugely popular Parte Vieja *pintxos* bar with a contemporary edge, no seating whatsoever, and an erratic attitude to its advertised opening hours. It's deservedly renowned for its prawn brochettes, but everything's good, with a fine mixture of hot and cold snacks. The restaurant in the basement is also recommended, but entirely separate. €

Bar Sport C/Fermín Calbetón 10, 943 426 888. Top-notch old-town *pintxos* bar, with slightly more room to squeeze in than usual, between the enticing snack-packed counter and the tables along the wall. Order full-size *raciones*, or opt for irresistible morsels like the *chipirone* (little squid) stuffed with crab. €

Bideluze Pza. de Gipuzkoa 14, https://www.bideluze donostia.com. Classy café-bar, facing an open garden square in the new town. Open around the clock, attracting an arty crowd with its gleaming wooden railway-carriage seats and general feel of an old apothecary, and of course their highly creative *pintxos*. €

Borda Berri C/Fermín Calbetón 12, 943 430 342. Rustic, inviting old-town *pintxos* place, with yellow walls, almost no seating, and eager crowds of in-the-know tourists. There's no food on display; everything on the changing blackboard menu is cooked to order. Fabulously tasty treats include a black-ink risotto with baby squid. €

Casa Alcalde C/Mayor 19, https://casaalcalde.com. This place is ideal for visitors who are just finding their feet, due to the numbered *pintxos* across the bar that make it easy for ordering. Settle in with your plate at the back, on one of the long wooden tables. €

La Cepa C/31 de Agosto 7, http://barlacepa.com. Bustling, old-fashioned bar in the heart of the old town, with hams festooning the bar and glass-topped tables displaying tiny trinkets such as casino chips and sweets. Inexpensive *pintxos* are listed on the blackboard, along with more substantial *raciones*. €

Juantxo Taberna C/Embeltrán 6, https://juantxo. com/taberna/. *Juantxo* serves the best *tortilla* sandwich (*bocadillo de tortilla*) in town. You can have simple *tortilla de patata*, or other delicious fillings such as *bacalao* or *jamón serrano*. You can also enter via the courtyard on C/Esterlines, where there are a few tables. €

La Mejillonera C/Puerto 15, https://cervecerias lamejillonera.es. This jam-packed, quick-fire Parte Vieja bar specializes, as the name suggests, in doling out platefuls of succulent mussels, with spicy tomato (*tigre*), lemon, or other toppings. It's fine if you don't like mussels, though – assuming you're partial to fried squid, the only other option. €

6

★ **Tamboril** C/Pescadería 2, 943 423 507, https://www. instagram.com/tambodonosti/. This tiny, lively, family-run bar, on the corner of Pza. de la Constitución, has a host of traditional pintxos on display, but it's really famed for its *champiñones* (mushrooms – "txampis" on the menu in Basque). €

Txepetxa C/Pescadería 5, http://bartxepetxa.com. While this old-town bar offers a full range of *pintxos*, almost everyone's here for just one thing – its out-of-this-world anchovies, served on toast. €

RESTAURANTS

★ **Arzak** Avda. Alcalde Elósegui 273, http://arzak.es. What might look like a typical family-owned *taberna*, on the lower slopes of Monte Ulia 3km east of the centre, is in fact the crucible of Basque *nueva cocina*, triple-starred by Michelin. Father-and-daughter team Juan Mari and Elena Arzak prepare a different selection of stunningly creative dishes each day – look out especially for pigeon or lamb. Behind the scenes, a fully fledged research lab is hard at work developing new concoctions. €€€€

Bar Aralar C/Puerto 10, http://bararalar.eus. The pleasant little dining room of this unpretentious old-town place, at the far end of a tapas bar that offers a spectacular array of *pintxos*, is a good place to come when you simply feel like eating a substantial plate of good food. €€

Bartolo C/Fermín Calbetón 38, http://bartoloetxea.com. A popular bar and restaurant, especially good for the fish – try the *merluza a la romana* (Roman-style hake) or *bacalao frito con pimientos* (fried cod with peppers). €€

Basque Culinary Centre Paseo Juan Avelina Barriola 101, http://bculinary.com. Attached to the local university, and housed in a showpiece building resembling a pile of plates, the Basque Culinary Centre is hard at work training the next generation of Basque chefs. A daily tasting menu enables visitors to sample their skills; you have to reserve ahead via the website, which also details occasional dinners and one-day courses. €€

Casa Gandarias C/31 de Agosto 23, http://restaurante gandarias.com. Very popular old-town restaurant, for once putting as much an emphasis on meat – from the cured hams hanging from the ceiling to chunky steaks – as fish. As usual, there's a big selection of *pintxos*, and people spill out into the street plates in hand, but head for a table at the back and settle down for a solid, well-cooked meal. €€€

Kaskazuri Paseo Salamanca 14, http://kaskazuri.com. A great option when you'd rather relax over a sit-down meal than fight the good fight in a *pintxos* bar, this good-value restaurant on the eastern edge of the old town, facing the Kursaal across the river-mouth, serves excellent local food on set menus. €€

Mugaritz Aldura Aldea 20, Errenteria, http://mugaritz. com. Consistently ranked among the top ten restaurants in the world and helmed by Andoni Aduriz, one of the great masters of molecular cuisine, *Mugaritz* represents contemporary Basque cuisine at its most outré. Inevitably, some ordinary diners find it pretentious, but visit with an open mind and you may well be blown away. There are, however, two significant drawbacks, one being that the restaurant is located in a rural hillside cottage 12km southeast of the centre, and the other being the pricey menu (changes daily, with up to 25 dishes). €€€€

Restaurante Martín Berasategui C/Loidi 4, Lasarte-Oria, http://martinberasategui.com. Contemporary rather than molecular, this three-star Michelin restaurant is housed in a bright modern structure in the hills 10km southwest of the city. Its eponymous chef remains rooted in traditional Spanish cuisine, while adding his own subtle twists. €€€€

DRINKING AND NIGHTLIFE

SEE MAP PAGE 424

It's hard to distinguish between venues for drinking and those for eating in San Sebastián, as several of the city's liveliest bars, especially in the Parte Vieja, also offer much of its finest food. *Pintxos* bars are the heart of the city's nightlife, but if you just want a coffee or cocktail, there are some stand-alone bars.

BARS

Akerbeltz C/de Mari 19, 943 451 452. Tiny little bar overlooking the harbour from the western side of the Parte Vieja, with exposed stone walls. Crowds of drinkers tumble out onto the steps outside; stay indoors for pounding music and a LGBTQ+-friendly vibe.

Txurrut Pza. de la Constitución 9, 943 429 181. With surprisingly few bars in the old town offering the chance to simply sit and enjoy an evening drink, this option in the attractive central pedestrian square is well-nigh irresistible, with the bonus of top-notch cocktails as well as the obvious drinks.

CLUBS

Bataplán Paseo de La Concha 10, http://bataplandisco. com. Very glitzy dance club overlooking the main beach, with a fabulous outdoor terrace for hot nights.

Hondarribia

The frontier town of **HONDARRIBIA**, just under 40km east of San Sebastián and across the mouth of the Bidasoa river from Hendaye in France, makes an appealing stopover. Down at water level, the broad boulevards back from the pretty harbour are lined with pavement cafés and traditional Basque architecture, but its fortified **Casco Antiguo**, a delightful little enclave higher up, offers a real sense of history. Filled with sturdily attractive medieval mansions, it centres on the **Pza. de Armas**, where the **Castille de Carlos V**, dating back to the tenth century, now houses an irresistible parador. The local beach, **Playa Hondartza**, lies a short walk north of the newer part of town.

ARRIVAL AND INFORMATION   HONDARRIBIA

6

By bus Regular buses connect Hondarribia with San Sebastián (every 20min; 30min), via the nearest train station at Irún.
Turismo Pza. de Armas 9 (July–mid-Sept daily 9.30am–

7.30pm, mid-Sept–Oct Mon–Sat 10am–7pm & Sun 10am–2pm, Nov–March Mon–Sat 10am–6pm & Sun 10am–2pm; 943 643 677, http://bidasoaturismo.com).

ACCOMMODATION

★ **Hotel Obispo** Pza. del Obispo, http://hotelobispo.com. Fourteenth-century palace with long-range sea views from the edge of the old town, converted into a hotel that offers a blend of modern furnishings and traditional rooms with balconies, plus free use of bicycles. €€€
Hotel Palacete Pza. de Gipuzkoa 5, http://hotelpalacete. net. Pleasant medieval mansion in the heart of the old town, with a nice little courtyard and tasteful modern rooms. Good rates in low season. €€
Hotel San Nikolas Pza. de Armas 6, http://hotel

sannikolas.es. Pretty townhouse in the Casco Antiguo, with pastel-blue balconies. Its sixteen en-suite rooms are relatively plain, but they have comfortable beds, and some enjoy sea views. €€€
Parador de Hondarribia Pza. de Armas 14, www. parador.es. While the entrance to the magnificent Castille de Carlos V is on the Casco Antiguo's main square, the lavishly appointed rooms of the so-called *Emperador* offer tremendous hilltop views across to France, and there's also an excellent restaurant. €€€€

EATING

While the Casco Antiguo is very short of restaurants and bars, the waterfront streets down near the harbour are packed with so many *pintxos* bars and restaurants that you can simply take the time to browse in search of whatever takes your fancy.
Hermandad de Pescadores C/Zuloaga 12, http://

hermandaddepescadores.com. Hondarribia's finest seafood restaurant stands just back from the harbour in the lower part of town, in a 750-year-old building. Crowds of eager diners squeeze onto wooden benches in its no-nonsense dining room to enjoy fresh fish. €€€

Inland from San Sebastián: Gipuzkoa

Gipuzkoa, the smallest province in Spain, is in many ways the heartland of Basque language and culture. Medieval towns such as **Tolosa**, with its traditional *Carnaval*, and Oñati, famous for its ancient university, are set in spectacular mountain scenery. In the nearby Sierra de Urkilla, the **Santuario de Arantzazu** is a prime pilgrimage destination for Basques.

Tolosa

TOLOSA, 24km south of San Sebastián, is famous for its **carnival**, celebrated with fervour over six days in February. Considered by Basques as superior to that in San Sebastián, this was the only carnival to maintain its tradition throughout the Franco era. Although fairly industrialized, Tolosa has an extensive **Casco Histórico** with an impressive square, Pza. Euskal Herria, and is also well known for its *pintxos*: be sure to try the *guindillas de Ibarra* (pickled green chilli peppers), and the *alubias de Tolosa* (kidney beans, served with blood sausage, cabbage and pork).

Tolosa has the largest **market** in the Basque Country, held on Saturday; activity centres on the distinctive, partly covered, Pza. Berdura in the old town.

Tolosa Puppets International Centre (TOPIC)

Pza. Euskal Herria • Charge • http://topictolosa.com

The hugely enjoyable **Tolosa Puppets International Centre**, in the imposing former law courts building on the main square, offers an entertaining romp through the world of puppetry. Modern displays, enhanced by tricksy lighting and mirrors and complemented by lots of video footage, illustrate puppets from around the globe, several of which are sold in the shop downstairs. Ideally, your visit would coincide with a performance or workshop; check the website for schedules.

ARRIVAL AND INFORMATION   TOLOSA

By bus Tolosa is served by direct buses from San Sebastián (5 daily; 30min) and Vitoria (up to 5 daily; 1hr 15min).

Turismo Pza. Zahara Parra 10, near the river in the old town (10am–2.30pm & 3.30–7pm; 943 697 413, http://tolosaldea.eus).

ACCOMMODATION AND EATING

Hotel Oria C/Oria 2, http://hoteloria.com. Business-oriented modern hotel, 500m south of the old town, with smart, comfortable rooms, plus its own restaurant and *asador*, offering a recommended cider-house set menu with an emphasis on local market produce. €€

Oñati and around

Without doubt the most interesting inland town in Gipuzkoa, **OÑATI**, 65km southwest of San Sebastián, was described by the Basque painter Zuloaga as the "Basque Toledo". Its many historic buildings include such fine specimens as the Baroque town hall and the parish church of **San Miguel**, facing each other across the arcaded Foruen Enparantz in full view of its café terraces. The church is only open during services, but can be visited on guided tours arranged by the tourist office – see page 432. Every count of Oñati from 988 until 1890 lies buried in its crypt, while its cloister is unusual for being built over the river.

Look out for various Navarran-style *casas torres*, as well as private family mansions, and the Plateresque-style sixteenth-century monastery of **Bidaurreta**.

University of Sancti Spiritus

Free

Active from 1548 until 1901, the **University of Sancti Spiritus** which dominates Oñati was for many centuries Euskal Herria's only functioning university. You are free to wander around the still-intact complex; the main facade, with its four pilasters adorned with figures, and the serene courtyard, are particularly impressive.

Santuario de Arantzazu

Free • http://arantzazu.org • Hourly buses from Oñati

Clinging dramatically to the mountainside above a gorge 9km south of Oñati, the **Santuario de Arantzazu** is a prime pilgrimage site for Basques, venerating **Our Lady of Arantzazu** (Santa María), the patron saint of Gipuzkoa. Built in 1950, its spiky monastery features contemporary work by the sculptors Eduardo Chillida (the doors) and Jorge Oteiza (part of the facade). The severe modernist architecture might not be to everyone's taste, but it's worth looking inside for the soaring stained-glass windows. The on-site visitor centre offers free guided tours (http://turismodebagoiena.eus).

ARRIVAL AND INFORMATION   OÑATI AND AROUND

Turismo C/San Juan 14, opposite Sancti Spiritus (June–Sept Mon–Sun 9.30am–2pm & 3.30–7pm; Oct–April Tues–Sun 10am–2pm & 4–6pm, Mon closed; May Tues–Fri 10am–2pm & 4–6pm, Sat–Sun 9.30am–2pm & 3–7pm, Mon closed; 943 783 453, http://onatiturismo.eus).

ACCOMMODATION AND EATING

Arregi C/Garagaltza 21, http://casaruralarregi.es. A rural *agriturismo*, run by a friendly family, located 2km northwest of Oñati, and holding chunkily furnished, good-value rooms. €€

Iraipe Ongi Hotel C/Zaharra 19, http://hotelongi. com. Simple but perfectly adequate lodging, behind the university. Rates for the eighteen en-suite rooms, which

include breakfast, drop significantly at weekends. €€

Torre Zumeltzegi C/Torre Zumultzegi, http://hoteltorre zumeltzegi.com. Monolithic medieval tower, out in the fields just 300m from the main square, that's been restored to hold a dozen opulent guest rooms, with exposed stone walls, as well as the town's best restaurant. €€€

6

The Costa Vasca

West of San Sebastián, both road and rail run inland, following the Río Oria, then turn towards the coast after 20km, at sprawling, overdeveloped Zarautz, which is also a popular surfing town. From here on, the **Costa Vasca** is glorious – a rocky and wild coastline, with long stretches of road hugging the edge of the cliffs – all the way to Bilbao. The hillsides, particularly around Getaria, are famous for the production of fizzy *txakoli* wine. The farther west you go, the less developed the resorts become.

Getaria

The tiny fishing port of **GETARIA**, 25km west of San Sebastián, lies not far beyond Zarautz. Founded in 1209, and sheltered by San Anton mountain, a humpbacked islet known as **El Ratón** (The Mouse) that was permanently joined to the mainland by a causeway in the fifteenth century, it later became a major whaling centre. These days it's much more of a resort, with a crescent beach thronged in summer with surfers and holiday-makers, and overlooked by fancy fish restaurants arrayed along terraces high above the harbour. Cheaper bars and cafés lurk in the lanes just inland, while the village preserves the magnificent fourteenth-century church of **San Salvador**.

The first man to sail around the world, **Juan Sebastián Elcano**, was born in Getaria in 1487 – his ship was the only one of Magellan's fleet to make it back home. Every four years, during the village's **fiestas** during the week of August 6, Elcano's landing is re-enacted at the harbour (last done in 2022).

Museo Cristóbal Balenciaga
Aldamar Parkea 6 · Charge · http://cristobalbalenciagamuseoa.com

A quite extraordinary museum dedicated to the life and work of the locally born fashion designer **Cristóbal Balenciaga** (1895–1972) opened on the hillside above Getaria in 2011. A classic example of Spain's breed of overblown architectural projects, consisting of a vast black-glass extension tacked on the hollowed-out nineteenth-century Palacio Aldamar, its completion was repeatedly delayed amid allegations of corruption and incompetence. The displays inside are on a much smaller scale, with a few dozen of Balenciaga's cocktail and wedding dresses displayed reverentially behind glass, each in its own dimly lit cage, rotating endlessly like a kebab on a spit.

ARRIVAL AND INFORMATION · GETARIA

By bus Getaria is served by direct buses from San Sebastián (daily, every 20–30min; 40min), which continue to Zumaia (15min).

Turismo The *turismo* is at Aldamar Parkea 2, immediately below the Balenciaga museum (Easter & June–Sept daily

10am–2pm & 3–7pm; Oct–Feb Tues–Sat 9am–1pm, Sun 10am–2pm, closed Mon; March–May Tues–Thurs 9am–3pm, Fri–Sat 9am–1pm & 4.15–6.15pm, Sun 9am–1pm, closed Mon; 943 140 957, http://getariaturismo.eus).

ACCOMMODATION

★ **Saiaz Getaria** C/Roke 25–27, http://saiazgetaria. com. Magnificent fifteenth-century mansion, topped by formidable stone towers, and stylishly converted to hold seventeen exceptionally comfortable bedrooms; pay a little bit extra to secure a full-on sea view. €€€

EATING AND DRINKING

Elkano C/Herrerieta 2, http://restauranteelkano.com. At his attractive restaurant in the heart of the old town, chef Aitor Arregui prepares truly excellent fresh fish and seafood meals. €€€

Mayflower Katrapuna 4, 943 140 658. Traditional *asador* grill with tables spreading across the harbour-view terrace, offering such delights as superb sardines, barbecued chicken, and *chipirones a lo Pelayo* (tiny cuttlefish with onion). €€€

Politena C/Nagusia 9, https://politenagetaria.com. Like several bars along Getaria's very pretty principal lane, this friendly spot sets out *pintxos* on the bar and serves full meals in a dining room further back, and also has a couple of outdoor tables. Its set menu is much better value than you'll find along the seafront. €€

Txoko Katrapuna 5, http://txokogetaria.com. Sea-view restaurant serving cutting-edge contemporary Basque cuisine, as seen on a particularly rainy day in the Steve Coogan/Rob Brydon TV series *The Trip to Spain*. As well as clams and two-person rice dishes, the speciality is grilled fresh fish, especially cod. €€

Ondarroa

The easternmost coastal town in Bizkaia, **ONDARROA** looks very different to the small resorts farther east towards San Sebastián. Squeezed in on either side of the mouth of a narrow, steep-sided river, it's a workaday place, with its seaward end dominated by a no-nonsense **fishing port** filled with an eclectic set of trawlers. However, it does make an interesting stopover, redeemed by an attractive **beach** within very easy walking distance east of the harbour, and the more substantial beach of **Saturrarán** around the headland beyond that.

ARRIVAL AND INFORMATION
ONDARROA

By bus Regular buses connect Ondarroa with the nearest train station at Deba, 8km east (hourly; 10min).

Turismo On the port at Kofradi Zaharra-Erribera 9 (mid-June to mid-Sept daily 10.30am–2.30pm & 4.30–8.30pm; mid-Sept to mid-June Tues–Sun 12am–2pm & 5–7pm; 946 831 951).

ACCOMMODATION

Camping Saturraran Saturraran, Mutriku, www.campingsaturraran.com. Summer-only campsite, 1km east of Ondarroa and set a 5min walk inland up the valley from the glorious sheltered beach at Saturraran. Camping €, apartments €€€

Pensión Patxi C/Artabide 21, 609 986 446. One of few accommodation options in Ondarroa, a simple but good-value *pensión* a couple of streets back from the fray near the harbour. €

Lekeitio

As one of Euskal Herria's nicest seafront towns, the lovely old port of **LEKEITIO**, on the west side of a broad rivermouth 10km west of Ondarroa, now welcomes plenty of pleasure boats to complement its active fishing fleet. Like many seafront towns hereabouts, it can get hit hard by winter storms, and the sea wall bears the scars of being patched up in a hurry.

Lekeitio is blessed with a fine and very central **beach** – half beside the harbour in the heart of town, and the rest, even better, across the river to the east. The little wooded island in the middle of the bay can be reached on foot at low tide.

Church of Santa María

Free • www.basilicadelekeitio.com

The **church of Santa María**, dominating Lekeitio from a high perch above the harbour, contains a magnificent sixteenth-century Flemish Gothic altarpiece, the third largest on the peninsula after those of the cathedrals of Seville and Toledo.

Santa Catalina Lighthouse

Charge • http://lekeitio.org

The only lighthouse in the region that's open to the public faces out to sea from a headland 2km north of the harbour. Displays inside the photogenic **Santa Catalina Lighthouse** explain the history of navigation along this stretch of coast, and allow visitors to pilot a virtual "boat" between Elantxobe and Lekeitio.

ARRIVAL AND INFORMATION   LEKEITIO

By bus Lekeitio is served by direct buses from the nearest station at Deba, 25km east (5 daily; 45min), as well as to Bilbao (hourly; 1hr 30min) and San Sebastián (4 daily; 1hr 20min).

By car Not only is there no parking east of the town centre,

there's nowhere even to turn around; park by the harbour if possible.

Turismo Santa Elena 2 (July & Aug daily 10am–3pm & 4–7pm, Sept–June Tues–Sun 10am–2pm; 946 844 017, http://lekeitio.org).

ACCOMMODATION

★**Hotel Palacio Oxangoiti** C/Gamarra 2, http://oxangoiti.net. Very central hotel, in a fine townhouse a few steps from the harbour. Seven comfortable en-suite rooms, most of which have balconies facing the church. €€€€
Hotel Zubieta Portal de Atea s/n, http://hotelzubieta.

com. Charming, very elegant hotel, set in the gardens of an old palace at the inland end of town, out in the fields but just 650m from the harbour. Bright, well-furnished en-suite rooms and excellent breakfasts. €€€

EATING AND DRINKING

Lekeitio is teeming with places to eat and drink, with a long line of harbourfront restaurants and *pintxos* bars.
Bar Marina Café Muelle Txatxo Kaia 1, 946 840 658. This large, bare-bones bar on the corner of the quayside nearest the church has a few harbourfront tables, a surprisingly green interior with murals of the old town, and a good

selection of inexpensive tapas. €
Oskarbi Muelle Txatxo Kaia 2, 946 243 859. The pick of several similar restaurants along the waterfront, serving good-value meals on its large, canopied terrace. The lunch menu includes salad or a hearty soup, a whole grilled fish, dessert and wine. €

Elantxobe

The well-preserved fishing village of **ELANTXOBE**, 10km west of Lekeitio, merits a detour back to the coast from the main road west. When the access road forks just before town, head left to reach the **upper village**, or right to drop down to the **harbour**, cradled within mighty concrete jetties and home to a handful of small bars. There's no beach here, but local kids hurl themselves into the sea from the quayside.

From the tiny roundabout at the end of the higher road – it's so small that buses have to park on a turntable and be spun around before they can leave – an incredibly steep cobbled street lined with attractive fishermen's houses, C/Nagusia, connects the village to the harbour below. A side turning from the same roundabout climbs 400m to a cemetery, from which a signposted track leads to **Mount Ogoño**, at 280m the highest cliff on the Basque coast.

ARRIVAL AND DEPARTURE   ELANTXOBE

By bus Buses to Bilbao (5 daily; 1hr 15min) and Lekeito (8 daily; 30min) stop in the main square.

By car There is limited parking just before the harbour, and along the upper road.

ACCOMMODATION

Casa Rural Arboliz C/Arboliz 12, http://arboliz.com. This conspicuous white-painted house, perched on the clifftop in Ibarrangelu, 1km southeast of Elantxobe, has been converted into a comfortable rural *agroturismo*, with kitchen facilities available, and a lovely sea-view garden. €€€

Itsasmin Ostatua C/Nagusia 32, 946 276 174. Simple *pension*, just beyond the end of the upper road, high above the port. All of its twelve rooms are en suite; half have little street-side balconies with harbour views. €

EATING AND DRINKING

Mentrame C/Portu 2, 946 739 250. Simple bar, down by   substantial *raciónes*. €
the port, with a decent selection of *pintxos* and some more

Gernika

GERNIKA, beside the Río Oka 25km northeast of Bilbao, is the traditional heart of Basque nationalism. It was here that the Basque parliament met until 1876, and here, under the **Tree of Gernika** (Gernikako Arbola), that their rights were reconfirmed by successive rulers. Somehow, although the rest of the town was destroyed by the infamous **bombing** of 1937 and had to be rebuilt, the parliament, church and tree remained miraculously unscathed. Although for Basques a visit to Gernika is something of a pilgrimage, for most outsiders it's not really a place to spend much time on a holiday, though the arcaded main street, **Artekalea**, has a certain appeal.

Gernika Peace Museum

Foru Pza, C/Artekalea • Free • www.museodelapaz.org

On a small, central open plaza, the **Gernika Peace Museum** sets out to commemorate the town's own tragedy and explore the very concept of peace. A reconstructed living room of a typical local house enables visitors to live through the bombing raid, complete with sound effects, while an extended section honours all the victims of the Basque conflict, listed according to whether they were killed by ETA, the security forces, or other groups.

Museo Euskal Herria

C/Allendesalazar 5 • Charge • https://bizkaikoa.bizkaia.eus

Housed in an eighteenth-century mansion, uphill near the Basque parliament building, the **Museo Euskal Herria** traces the history of the Basque Country from its earliest prehistoric inhabitants. Each of its component regions, including the Kingdom of Navarre and the areas now belonging to France, is examined in systematic detail. There's some interesting material, but with captions in Basque and Spanish only, it's liable to fall rather flat for English-speaking visitors.

The Batzarretxea and the Tree of Gernika

C/Allendesalazar • Free

THE BOMBING OF GERNIKA

The name of Gernika is famous the world over thanks to the nightmare painting by **Pablo Picasso**, which commemorated its **saturation bombing** during the Spanish Civil War. In one of the first such raids ever perpetrated on a civilian centre, on April 27, 1937, planes from the Condor Legion, which had been lent to Franco by Hitler and had taken off from Vitoria-Gasteiz, obliterated 71 percent of the buildings in Gernika in the space of three hours.

Gernika was chosen as the target largely for its symbolic importance. Around 250 people died, many of whom were attending the weekly market that's still held every Monday in the Pza. de Gernika. The nearby town of Durango had been bombed a few days earlier, but because there were no foreign observers, the reports were simply not believed. While the German government acknowledged its involvement in the bombing in 1997, to this day the Spanish government has never admitted its role.

Picasso started work on his painting the day that news of the bombing reached him in Paris. Finally brought "home" to Spain after the death of Franco, it is now exhibited in the Centro de Arte Reina Sofía in Madrid.

The **Batzarretxea**, or Casa de las Juntas, a short walk from the centre of Gernika, is home to the parliament of Bizkaia, which was reactivated in 1979. It's *not* the government of the Basque Country as a whole, though – that's in Vitoria-Gasteiz. While visitors can enter the building itself, the real attraction is what's left of the **Tree of Gernika** (Gernikako Arbola), the traditional meeting place of the Basque people. Now just a stump, protected in a little columned pavilion, it stands in the adjacent grounds, close to a replacement oak planted in 2005.

Europa Park and around

Stretching behind both the Batzarretxea and the Museo Euskal Herria, **Europa Park** contains ornamental gardens, a fast-flowing stream, and peace sculptures by Henry Moore and Eduardo Chillida. The Gothic church of **Santa María la Antigua** alongside is adorned with portraits of the various Bizkaian nobles who pledged allegiance to the *fueros*.

ARRIVAL AND INFORMATION   GERNIKA

By bus Frequent buses from Bilbao stop at C/ Iparraguirre 16 in the centre (every 30min; 40min).
By train Gernika's central station is a stop on the EuskoTren line between Bilbao and Bermeo (hourly; 1hr).

Turismo C/Artekalea 8, across from the Gernika Peace Museum (April–Oct Mon–Sat 10am–7pm, Sun 10am–2pm; Nov–March Mon–Fri 10am–6pm, Sat & Sun 10am–2pm; 946 255 892, https://gernikainfo.eus).

ACCOMMODATION

Hotel Gernika C/Carlos Gangoiti 17, http://hotel-gernika. com. Gernika's largest and most comfortable hotel is north of the centre, 500m along the road towards Bermeo. There's nothing remarkable about its forty en-suite rooms, but they're reasonably well kept and quiet. €€
Pensión Akelarre Ostatua C/Barrenkale 5, http://

hotelakelarre.com. Cheap central *pensión*, right behind the *turismo*, with seventeen plain but brightly painted rooms equipped with showers. The front desk is closed 1–6pm, and after 9pm, but you can check in by inserting a credit card next to the door. €€

EATING AND DRINKING

★ **Baserri Maitea** C/Atzondoa, Forua, http://baserri maitea.com. Whether you eat in the spacious dining room inside this beautiful 300-year-old Basque farmhouse, a couple of kilometres north of Gernika, or outdoors in the garden, it's a great spot to enjoy traditional dishes roasted in a wood-fired oven. €€€

Boliña El Viejo C/Adolfo Urioste 1, http://restaurante bolinaelviejo.com. Old-fashioned, very local bar-restaurant that's the best-value place to eat in the centre of Gernika. Traditional favourites in its simple *comedor* include grilled fish, beans and squid in ink. Not to be confused with the nearby *Boliña* restaurant. €€

Mundaka

Flowing north from Gernika, the Río Oka broadens into the Urdaibai estuary, fringed by hilly pinewoods and dotted with islets. A succession of sandy coves offer great swimming, but the best spots are at Sukarrieta and, especially, **MUNDAKA**. This lovely village remains amazingly unspoiled, despite having achieved legendary status for its magnificent **surfing**, which thanks to a unique rivermouth sandbar includes what's claimed to be the longest left break in the world.

Although Mundaka has frequently hosted surfing world championships, conditions vary considerably from year to year. Dredging operations to enable ships constructed upstream to reach the ocean have repeatedly affected its trademark "Wave", and even caused it to disappear altogether between 2003 and 2006. In time, though – so far, at any rate – the seabed sands return to their natural condition, and the surfers too return. In good years, during the peak winter season, it's possible to watch them riding the Wave from the plaza next to the church.

Playa de Laída

Charge for the ferry • https://izkiraurdaibai.com/en/activities/ferry-service/

In summer, swimmers leap into the water from all along the shoreline and quayside in Mundaka. The nearest proper beach, however, lies across the river. From the inlet slightly south of the port, a passenger ferry makes frequent trips to **Playa de Laída**, an enormous area of white sand, which at low tide stretches across the mouth of the bay in an unbroken crescent.

ARRIVAL, INFORMATION AND ACTIVITIES   MUNDAKA

By train Mundaka is served by half-hourly trains on the EuskoTren (http://euskotren.eus) line between Bilbao (1hr 10min), Gernika (20min), and Bermeo (5min).

Turismo Next to the harbour on C/Joseba Deuna (Easter & July–Aug Mon–Sat 10am–3pm & 4–7pm & Sun 10am–3pm, May–June & Sept–Oct Mon–Sat 10am–2pm & 4–6pm & Sun 10am–3pm, Nov–April Thurs–Sun 10am–2pm; 946 177 201, http://mundakaturismo.com).

Surfing The Mundaka Surf Shop, at Paseo Txorrokopunta 10 close to the port (daily 10am–9pm in summer; 946 177 229, http://mundakasurfshop.com), sells and rents equipment and offers surf lessons.

ACCOMMODATION AND EATING

Bar Los Txopos C/Duenaren 1, 946 088 621. Tapas bar with a full menu of *raciones* plus everything from *tortillas* to burgers. In truth, the food isn't exceptional, and the prices are relatively high, but the seafront location and expansive terrace seating make it all but irresistible anyway, even if just for a morning coffee. €€

Eco Hotel Mundaka C/Florentino Larriñaga 9, http://hotelmundaka.com. Attractive, surfer-friendly hotel, just off Mundaka's main square, with clean, comfortable rooms and an enthusiastic welcome. €€

★ **Hotel Spa El Puerto** C/Portu 1, http://hotelelpuerto. com. This delightful hotel faces out to sea from right beside the fishing port, and has a lovely shaded terrace. Several of its en-suite rooms have great sea views. Be warned that it's liable to be noisy at night in summer. €€

Portuondo 946 877 701, http://campingportuondo.com. A favourite with surfers, Mundaka's appealing campsite is perched high above the water a short walk south of town, with steps leading down to a rocky beach. There's a decent restaurant on site (closed Mon), and rental bungalow-style cabins are also available. Camping €, cabins €€

Bermeo

BERMEO, 3km north of Mundaka, is a venerable old fishing port that makes a good base for the estuary beaches nearby. Apart from the riot of red, green and blue boats in the harbour, which doubles as a marina, there's little to see, though both the harbour and the main square are fringed by the usual ranks of tapas bars and restaurants.

The spectacular island shrine of **San Juan de Gaztelugatxe**, 8km west of Bermeo, dates back to the tenth century. Sacked by Sir Francis Drake in 1593, it featured – topped by a digitally added castle – as "Dragonstone" in TV's *Game of Thrones*. It can only be reached by hiking downhill from car parks just off the main road, either on a direct 25min trail or a gentler 35min footpath. Either way, you access the shrine itself by crossing a little causeway and climbing 231 steep steps along a narrow ridge.

ARRIVAL AND INFORMATION   BERMEO

By train Bermeo is the northern terminus of a EuskoTren line (http://euskotren.eus), served by half-hourly trains from Bilbao (1hr 15min) via Gernika (20min) and Mundaka (5min).

Turismo Parque de Lamera, on the rivermouth (Mon–Sat 9am–7pm, Sun 9am–5.30pm; 946 179 154, http://bermeo. eus).

ACCOMMODATION

★ **Lurdeia** Artike Auzoa, s/n, http://lurdeia.com. Lovely rural *agriturismo*, attached to a hilltop organic farm, with large, tastefully decorated and very comfortable rooms with magnificent long-distance ocean views. It's reached by a convoluted but clearly signposted 9km drive south from the centre of Bermeo. €€€

Torre Ercilla Ostatua Talaranzko 14, 1º, 946 187 598. Inexpensive accommodation a few streets up from the port behind Santa María church. Ask for the spacious corner room, which has a balcony and glassed-in gallery as well as an en-suite bathroom. €€

Bilbao

Stretching for 14km beside the Río Nervión, **BILBAO** (Bilbo) is a large city that seldom feels like one. Even though its urban sprawl fills the narrow valley, you can always see the green slopes of the mountains to either side, beyond the high-rise buildings of the city centre. Bilbao's great achievement has been to reinvent itself since the collapse of its traditional industrial base at the end of the last century. The dramatic success of the **Museo Guggenheim**, which transformed a post-industrial wasteland in the city centre into a major tourist attraction, in turn triggered further visionary redevelopments including the construction of a new metro and airport.

With around 350,000 people in its urban core, and a total fast approaching one million in the metropolitan district, modern Bilbao is much the biggest city in the Basque Country, and serves as the capital of Bizkaia province. While no match for San Sebastián in terms of beaches or sheer prettiness, Bilbao still has plenty to offer, from its exuberant architecture and stimulating museums to the lively alleyways of its old town, the **Casco Viejo**, and its friendly inhabitants.

From the compact old town, on the river's right bank at the eastern edge of the centre, an easy and pleasant stroll leads all the way to the Guggenheim, crossed by way of the showpiece **Zubizuri** footbridge. Only when Bilbao industrialized in the nineteenth century did it expand back onto the left bank, to create the much larger new town, or **Ensanche**, with its broad avenues radiating from the central Pza. Moyúa. All but encircled by a huge loop in the river, this is still the commercial heart of the city.

The Casco Viejo

What's now known as the "old town", the **Casco Viejo**, is not in fact the oldest part of Bilbao. The city started out as a cluster of small fishing villages on the river's left bank, whereas the Casco Viejo grew up across the river between the fourteenth and nineteenth centuries. All Bilbao's oldest surviving buildings, however, are now concentrated here, and it's the most enjoyable area to explore on foot. A tight-knit labyrinth of old stone lanes, filled with bars and restaurants and cradling the delightful arcaded main square, the Pza. Nueva, it also holds some worthwhile museums.

Euskal Museoa Bilbao

Pza. Unamuno 4 • Charge • http://euskalmuseoa.eus

Devoted to Basque ethnology and history, the somewhat dour, old-school **Euskal Museoa Bilbao** is housed in the former Colegio de San Andrés. The cloister at its heart is a lovely retreat from the city bustle, and holds a stylized Iron Age stone figure known as the *Mikeldi*, depicting a hog with a disc in its belly, that's thought to have been used in ancient rituals. Displays in the museum itself trace ten thousand years of Basque fishing traditions, follow local shepherds as far as the western US, and explain the growth of Bilbao. There's also a huge relief model of the whole of Bizkaia. No captions are in English.

Arkeologi Museoa

Calzadas de Mallona 2, Pza. Unamuno • Charge • 944 040 990, https://www.facebook.com/arkeologimuseoa/

Bilbao's **archeology museum** stands across an old-town square from the Euskal Museoa, in a former train station that's been modernized to the point of being unrecognizable. Galleries on its three floors cover specific eras of human history in Bizkaia, from the Neanderthals onwards, with eye-catching displays but little detail. Exhibits include a surprising number of actual skeletons, plus a fishing vessel shipwrecked during the fifteenth century.

6

Mercado de la Ribera

C/de la Ribera • https://mercadodelaribera.biz/

Seven centuries since the first daily food market was established on the right bank of the Río Nervión, the **Mercado de la Ribera** remains the epicentre of life in Bilbao's old town. In its current form, it's an amalgam of a superbly elegant Art Nouveau building from 1929 with a modern revamp that has given it huge windows, more space, and greater ease of access. Venture in to relish its vast array of fresh produce and seafood.

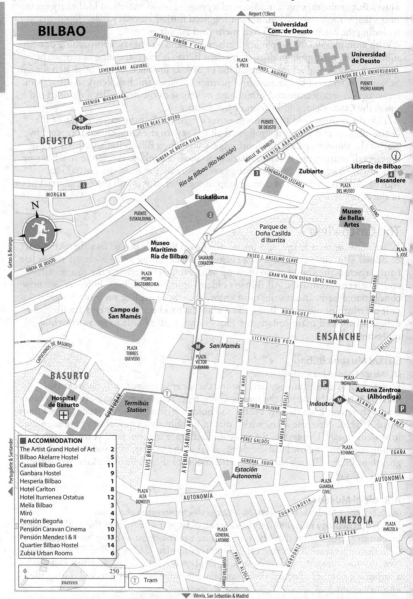

■ ACCOMMODATION	
The Artist Grand Hotel of Art	2
Bilbao Akelarre Hostel	5
Casual Bilbao Gurea	11
Ganbara Hostel	9
Hesperia Bilbao	1
Hotel Carlton	8
Hotel Iturrienea Ostatua	12
Meliá Bilbao	3
Miró	4
Pensión Begoña	7
Pensión Caravan Cinema	10
Pensión Mendez I & II	13
Quartier Bilbao Hostel	14
Zubia Urban Rooms	6

Museo Guggenheim

Charge • http://guggenheim-bilbao.eus

Frank Gehry's astounding **Museo Guggenheim** looms over the left bank of the Río Nervión, ten minutes' walk west of the Casco Viejo. Completed in 1997, it was hailed by architect Philip Johnson as "the greatest building of our time". The construction of such a showpiece project on a derelict industrial site represented a colossal gamble by the Basque government, which hoped to stimulate the revitalization of Bilbao.

6

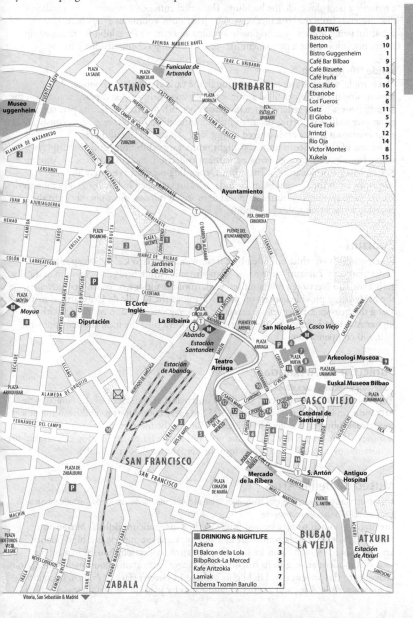

● EATING

Bascook	3
Berton	10
Bistro Guggenheim	1
Café Bar Bilbao	9
Café Bizuete	13
Café Iruña	4
Casa Rufo	16
Etxanobe	2
Los Fueros	6
Gatz	11
El Globo	5
Gure Toki	7
Irrintzi	12
Río Oja	14
Victor Montes	8
Xukela	15

■ DRINKING & NIGHTLIFE

Azkena	2
El Balcon de la Lola	3
BilboRock-La Merced	5
Kafe Antzokia	1
Lamiak	7
Taberna Txomin Barullo	4

Vitoria, San Sebastián & Madrid ▽

Amazingly enough, it worked. A gargantuan sculpture, whose sensual titanium curves glimmer like running water in the sun, it has inevitably overshadowed the artworks it contains.

The best way to approach the museum is along the river, either along the quayside, or by crossing the high Puente de la Salve road bridge from Deusto on the north bank. One of Louise Bourgeois' fearsome spindle-legged spiders, *Maman*, towers at the water's edge, while Anish Kapoor's column of glittering silver bubbles, *Tall Tree and the Eye*, stands in a reflecting pool alongside the building. The actual entrance, however, is via a walkway that descends from the structure's city side. Jeff Koons' enormous *Puppy* here, clad in colourful living flowers, was originally installed as a temporary exhibit for the opening ceremony, but became a permanent fixture after *bilbainos* clamoured for it to stay.

Inside the museum

Once inside, visitors flow seamlessly through the various galleries in no fixed order, crisscrossing the vast, light-filled atrium on walkways. Gehry called the largest room on the ground floor his "fish gallery"; stretching away beneath the road bridge, it's permanently given over to Richard Serra's disorienting sculpture series, *The Matter of Time*, consisting of eight enormous shapes of weathered orange steel, coiled and labyrinthine.

The rest of the museum hosts top-flight temporary exhibitions, and also displays works from its own ever-growing permanent collection, including pieces by Anselm Keifer, Mark Rothko and Cy Twombly. Depending on space, you may also see selections from the Guggenheim Foundation's unparalleled holdings of contemporary art. At various points en route it's possible to step outdoors, most notably onto the riverside terrace that holds Jeff Koons' *Tulips*.

Zubizuri

Resembling a vast white sail filled by a fresh wind, Santiago Calatrava's spectacular pedestrian-only **Zubizuri** – the name simply means "white bridge" – curves majestically across the Río Nervión a few minutes' walk from the old town. When first unveiled, the bridge only provided access on the left bank to the Muelle de Uribitarte, down along the quayside. Later on, an extended walkway was added to connect it with the higher Alameda Mazarredo; the infuriated Calatrava sued the local council, and won €30,000 compensation.

Funicular de Artxanda

Charge • https://funicularartxanda.bilbao.eus

Three blocks north of the river, the Pza. Funicular marks the foot of the **Funicular de Artxanda**, an inclined railway built in 1931 to carry commuters to and from the newer residential suburbs. It sweeps passengers 770m up the mountainside in less than five minutes. There are no views along the way, but a circular park at the top offers fabulous panoramas over the city and across into the verdant neighbouring valley.

Museo de Bellas Artes

Parque de Doña Casilda de Iturriza • Free entry to exhibitions via the old building while the museum is under construction, due to be completed mid-2025 • http://museobilbao.com

Inevitably doomed to play second fiddle to the Guggenheim, Bilbao's **Museo de Bellas Artes**, a short walk southwest in a very pleasant green park, is a high-quality art museum in its own right. Its sizeable permanent collection, housed in a bright, spacious modern annexe to its original core, ranges from anonymous medieval religious artworks to the present day. Highlights include El Greco's stark *St Francis*, Gauguin's *Washerwomen in Arles*, and a series of landscapes by Joaquin Sorolla, many of which were painted along the Basque coast. Basque artists are much better represented here than in the Guggenheim; look out for Anselmo Guinea's 1899 Art Nouveau panel *Back From the Pilgrimage*, and José Arrue's later depictions of idyllic village life.

Azkuna Zentroa (Alhóndiga)

Pza. Arriquabar 4 • Charge • https://azkunazentroa.eus

Entering the **Azkuna Zentroa**, a former wine warehouse in the new town that's popularly known as the **Alhóndiga**, you encounter a baffling space. The low ceiling is supported by 43 squat Philippe Starck-designed pillars in wildly differing styles and materials, while a fiery red sun hangs in the centre. Elements beyond include cafés and restaurants, a basement cinema, assorted performance and exhibition spaces, and a gym.

6

Itsasmuseum

Muelle Ramón de la Sota • Charge • www.museomaritimobilbao.org

The fancy **Itsasmuseum** (formerly the Museo Marítimo Ría de Bilbao) is at quayside level just west of the **Euskalduna** (an impressive edifice of rusty iron, glass, steel and concrete that hosts conferences and classical performances). The museum itself explains in intricate detail the city's maritime history and culture, and exactly how the *ría* between the city and the sea has been cleared over the centuries to deal with ever larger marine traffic. It's all very worthy, and you can clamber aboard assorted vessels in the old docks of the Euskalduna Shipyard outside.

Sopelana and Plentzia

For Sopelana, use ⓜ Larrabasterra; for Plentzia use ⓜ Plentzia

Fine **beaches** lie within easy reach of Bilbao, along the mouth of the estuary and around both headlands. Metro Line 1 makes those on the east bank the most accessible, for example at **Sopelana**, home to the nudist Playa de Arrietara. The beach at **Plentzia**, at the far end of the line, 15km out, is generally cleaner and less crowded.

Getxo and Portugalete

For Getxo use ⓜ Algorta; for Portugalete use ⓜ Aleeta

Getxo, 10km downstream at the head of the port and consisting of several distinct communities, makes a particularly nice excursion. Its ancient fishing-port core, set on a hilltop not far east of the river-mouth, remains pretty and lively, and stands just above two nice beaches, Ereaga and Arrigunaga.

Just before the river widens into the port, Getxo is connected with **Portugalete** on the west bank via the remarkable Vizcaya Bridge (http://puente-colgante.com). The little gondola that dangles from this preposterous late nineteenth-century "**transporter bridge**" carries passengers, and even half a dozen cars at a time, across the river every few minutes.

ARRIVAL AND DEPARTURE   **BILBAO**

BY PLANE

Aeropuerto de Bilbao Bilbao's airport (http://aeropuerto debilbao.net) is 12km north of town. Bizkaiabus services (every 30min; http://bizkaia.eus) take 20min to reach Pza. Moyúa in the centre of the new town (Ensanche), and continues to the Termibús station (ⓜ San Mamés); there are also hourly buses straight to Zarautz and San Sebastián.

BY FERRY

Bilbao's ferry port is at Zierbena, 21km northwest of the city centre, on the western side of the rivermouth. Brittany Ferries (http://brittany-ferries.co.uk) sail here from Portsmouth in the UK 1–3 times weekly. Regular buses and trains run from the docks to the centre.

BY TRAIN

Estación de Abando The main RENFE train station, on Pza. Circular, across the river from the Casco Viejo, sees services to Barcelona via Zaragoza (2 daily; 6hr 50min); Logroño (1 daily; 2hr 30min); Madrid (4 daily; 5–7hr); and Salamanca (3 daily; 5–6hr).

Estación de la Concordia Services along a separate narrow-gauge line, run by RENFE, head west along the coast from this highly decorative station, also known as the Estación de Santander, on the riverbank below the Estación de Abando, to Santander (3 daily; 3hr) and beyond.

BY BUS

Intermodal station Most long-distance and international bus companies use the Intermodal station (https://bilbaointermodal.eus), formerly known as Termibús, which fills an entire block between Luis Briñas and Gurtubay, 2.5km west of the Casco Viejo. To reach the town centre, change onto a local bus, head a block north to the San Mamés metro station or simply walk.

Destinations Barcelona (4 daily; 7hr); Bermeo, via Gernika and Mundaka (30 daily; 1hr 10min); Burgos (hourly; 3hr); Castro Urdiales (5 daily; 1hr); Elantxobe (3 daily; 1hr 45min); Lekeitio (hourly; 1hr 30min); León (1 daily; 5hr 30min); Madrid (hourly; 5hr); Oñati (3 daily; 1hr 10min); Ondarroa (hourly; 1hr 20min); Pamplona (6 daily; 2hr 15min); San Sebastián (every 30min; 1hr 15min); Santander (every 30min; 1hr 15min); Santiago (3 daily; 11hr); Vitoria (every 30min; 1hr 15min); Zaragoza (7 daily; 4hr).

BY CAR

Driving The motorways are very efficient at delivering drivers into the centre of Bilbao, but once there traffic is consistently dreadful; you're better off parking straight away in the car park nearest your accommodation, and walking from there.

INFORMATION

Turismo Bilbao has tourist offices (944 795 760, http://bilbaoturismo.net) at Pza. Circular 1, across the river from the old town and also next to the Museo Guggenheim (Easter to mid-Sept daily 9am–7.30pm, rest of the year 9am–5pm).

GETTING AROUND

By foot Central Bilbao is small enough to walk around comfortably; indeed, the riverside stroll between the Casco Viejo and the Guggenheim is a highlight for many visitors.

By taxi TeleTaxi 944 102 121, http://teletaxibilbao.com; Radio Taxi Bilbao 944 448 888, http://taxibilbao.com.

By metro The easy, efficient Metro Bilbao (www.metrobilbao.eus) runs every 4min between Plentzia (northeast of Getxo) and Extebarri, south of the centre; a second line runs out to Santurtzi at the western rivermouth. While the network is divided into three zones, all city-centre journeys (including in the Casco Viejo) lie within the same zone. If you're staying for any length of time, consider buying a *Barik* card, which can be topped up to any amount, and after an initial cost of €3 works out at €0.90 per journey.

By bus For parts the metro doesn't reach, there are red municipal buses with route maps at the green bus shelters, or for longer journeys (including to the airport) the green Bizkiabuses (http://bizkaia.eus).

By tram Green trams run along a single line, linking the Casco Viejo and the Museo Guggenheim with San Mamés and the bus station.

ACCOMMODATION
SEE MAP PAGE 440

The nicest area to stay has to be the **Casco Viejo**, though that's dominated by budget hotels and *pensiones*, and is liable to be very noisy at night. Bilbao's luxury hotels tend to be scattered across **Ensanche**; many feature hip contemporary architecture and highly regarded restaurants, and can offer amazingly good value. **Deusto** and **Castaños**, on the river's north bank, make good alternatives. The *turismo's* central **reservation** service can help with bookings (902 877 298, http://bilbaoreservas.com).

CASCO VIEJO

Casual Bilbao Gurea C/Bidebarrieta 14, http://casualhoteles.com. The simple, clean rooms in this well kept hotel are a great deal – and surprisingly peaceful – for such a central location, while the staff are exceptionally helpful. €€€

Ganbara Hostel C/Prim 13, 944 053 930. Modern hostel on the edge of the old town, with accommodation in four-, six- and eight-person dorms. The spacious communal areas make up for the somewhat cramped dorms. Rates include free breakfast plus all-day tea and coffee, and there's a laundry and kitchen. €

Hotel Iturrienea Ostatua C/Santa María 14, http://iturrieneaostatua.com. Clean, very friendly hotel, tucked away near the river in the Casco Viejo, with exposed stonework and antique furniture throughout; the walls are hung with quirky art and moody photos of Bilbao's industrial past. All nine rooms are en suite; many have plants trailing over balconies, and double-glazing to cut down noise. €€€

Pensión Caravan Cinema C/Correo 11, http://caravan-cinema.com. Each room in this comfortable little boutique hotel, just off the main square, celebrates a specific movie director, with all relevant films pre-loaded to the TV. Five, including "Pedro Almodóvar", are normal-sized doubles, but the real joy is the retro-furnished, two-room Hitchcock apartment, which sleeps up to seven guests. €€

Pensión Mendez I & II C/Santa María 13, 1º & 4º, 944 160 364. Comfortable rooms, simply but adequately furnished; they're hardly luxurious, but good value for anyone simply looking for a place to sleep. Those in *Mendez II* are slightly better, with en-suite bathrooms. The owners speak minimal English, and accept cash only. €

Quartier Bilbao Hostel C/Artekale 15, http://quartier bilbao.com. Modern and very central hostel, just up from the river, offering private doubles as well as dorms holding from two to ten beds; one storey is reserved for women only. There's also a communal kitchen and terrace. Dorms €, doubles €€

ENSANCHE

★ **The Artist Grand Hotel of Art** Alameda de Mazarredo 61, https://hoteltheartist.com. The work of designer Javier Mariscal, this is a wonderfully inspiring five-star hotel (previously named *Gran Hotel Domine*), appropriately close to the Guggenheim and sporting one of the most imaginative lobbies you'll ever see. Each floor has a unique design, while the luxurious rooms have bathrooms with transparent glass, and tubs designed by Philippe Starck. €€€€

Hotel Carlton Pza. Moyúa 2, http://hotelcarlton.es. The *grande dame* of Bilbao hotels, built in 1919 and still an atmospheric place to stay, with its abundant marble and dramatic stained-glass cupola. The rooms are tasteful and extremely comfortable, and several boast huge arched windows. €€€€

★ **Meliá Bilbao** C/Lehendakari Leizaola 29, http://melia. com. One of Bilbao's most distinctive buildings, a bold edifice inspired by Eduardo Chillida, utilizing Iranian pink marble and rusty garnet tones for the exterior, and green and white marble in the bathrooms. The stylish rooms are luxurious, with huge, incredibly comfy beds; there's also a pool. €€€€

Miró Alameda de Mazarredo 77, http://mirohotelbilbao. com. Attractive fifty-room hotel, with minimalist decor, bathrooms finished in black marble (and separated from the chic, white-toned rooms by a curtain), and a decent spa. €€€€

Pensión Begoña C/Amistad 2, 1º, http://hostalbegona. com. Solid mid-range option, near the narrow-gauge station and just a couple of minutes' walk over the bridge from the Casco Viejo. The colourful rooms have lino floors, good en-suite facilities, and comfortable beds, but no views. €€

Zubia Urban Rooms C/Amistad 5, http://pensionzubia. com. Veteran family-run hotel, near the left bank of the river across from the Casco Viejo, where the plain modernized rooms share bathrooms. The friendly staff are happy to share their local expertise; pets are welcome. €

CASTAÑOS AND DEUSTO

Bilbao Akelarre Hostel C/Morgan 4–6, http://bilbao akelarrehostel.com. Modern, well-run and well-equipped hostel near the university, a short walk from the Guggenheim. Some double rooms – albeit with individual bunks – plus dorms sleeping from four to twelve. Rates include breakfast, coffee and tea. Dorms €, doubles €€

Hesperia Bilbao Paseo Campo de Volantín 28, https:// hesperia.com. Smart, modern riverfront hotel, in a funky contemporary building fronted by pastel-coloured glassed-in balconies, near the Zubizuri bridge. The sizeable rooms have sleek minimalist furnishings, and there's on-site parking. €€€

EATING SEE MAP PAGE 440

While not quite on a par with San Sebastián, Bilbao ranks among the culinary capitals of Spain. Innovative **restaurants** and Michelin-star winners knock out everything from traditional Basque favourites to high-class *nueva cocina vasca* meals, while the **pintxos bars** are equally mouthwatering. Taking a high-speed *txikiteo* (*pintxos* crawl) through the Casco Viejo is an essential part of any visit – the best targets tend to be clustered in the *siete calles* (seven streets), bordered by C/de la Ronda and C/Pelota, but C/Diputación in Ensanche also holds good options. Bilbao's most famous dish is **cod** (*bacalao*), traditionally served with *salsa vizcaina* (a sauce of red onions and peppers) or *al pil-pil* (a garlic-based sauce).

faces the Catedral across a small square. Most locals drop in for coffee and a cake, or the *chocolate con churros*. €

★ **Café Iruña** C/Colón de Larreategui, https://www. cafeirunabilbao.net. Historic café and bar, facing the little Jardines de Albia park, and established in 1903. Elaborate murals and ornate Mudéjar decor and traditional grocery-style tiling make its three sections – a bar, a café, and a dining room – marvellously atmospheric. It's busy around breakfast time; later on it serves a set dinner menu, and it's also a great spot for a drink or a few *pintxos* – the *pinchos morunos*, or mini-kebabs, are especially worth trying. €€

PINTXOS BARS

Berton C/Jardines 11, http://berton.eus. This friendly Casco Viejo bar, a warm inviting space with some outside tables and lots of drinking space inside, has been such a success that it now has three neighbouring offshoots,

CAFÉS

Café Bizuete Pza. Santiago 6b, 944 794 278. The nicest spot for coffee in the Casco Viejo, this old-fashioned café

including a recommended restaurant. It offers fresh modern *pintxos*, including quails' eggs with prawns and mushrooms, and lots of ham options, plus *raciones* of prawns, anchovies and the like. €

★ **Café Bar Bilbao** Pza. Nueva 6, http://bilbao-cafebar. com. Exceptional anchovy, ham and *bacalao al pil-pil pintxos*, served by *simpático* staff, with everything labelled on the counter in the stylish old blue-tiled café interior, and some tables on the Casco Viejo's lovely main square. €€

Gatz C/Santa María 10, http://bargatz.com. Cosy late-night tapas bar in the old town, its blue walls festooned with vintage photos, where a mixed younger crowd enjoys exquisite *pintxos* such as delicious cod, or the Basque equivalent of ratatouille in a tiny tart. Good selection of wines and beers. €

El Globo C/Diputación 8, http://barelglobo.es. Creative, high-quality *pintxos* near Pza. Moyúa in the central Abando district. The interior decor is part wine bar, part upscale sandwich bar, and there's also outdoor seating – order through the hatch in the wall. Plentiful seafood options include baby squid with caramelized onions, or you can opt for goat's cheese. €€

Gure Toki Pza. Nueva 12, http://guretoki.com. Snuggled into the corner of the Casco Viejo's main square, this recently expanded tapas bar offers irresistible, eye-catching *pintxos ornamentales* including lovely langoustine and squid concoctions. You can also buy a more substantial salad to eat at the barrels out on the square itself. €

Irrintzi C/Santa María 8, http://irrintzi.es. Hip, buzzing old-town tapas bar, with groovy murals plus some of Bilbao's most creative *pintxos*, such as a monkfish lollipop served with strawberry gazpacho in a glass, or roast beef with spinach mousse. €

Xukela C/El Perro 2, 944 159 772. With its red panelling and checked linens, this perennially popular Casco Viejo tapas bar is oddly reminiscent of a French bistro, and serves substantial enough *raciones* to make a hearty meal; but it's best known for its wide range of snacks and top-class wine list. There's plenty of open space for drinkers who prefer to stand. €

RESTAURANTS
Bascook C/Barroeta Aldamar 8, http://bascook.com.

Among the most popular recent additions to Bilbao's dining scene, *Bascook* is the brainchild of chef Aitor Elizegi. His playful ideas include having a menu that's also a magazine, and offering a variety of cuisines. €€€

Bistro Guggenheim Guggenheim Museum, http://bistroguggenheimbilbao.com. The Guggenheim's in-house bistro serves a great-value set lunch menu and a dinner menu of zestful modern Basque cuisine, while its café and terrace bar sell simpler snacks. Either makes a perfect complement to visiting the museum itself. €€

Casa Rufo C/Hurtado de Amézaga 5, http://casarufo. com. Deservedly popular *cocina* in the Abando district, with three cosy, themed dining rooms specializing in three main items: cod and two types of unbelievably succulent steak (*chuleton*, priced by the kilo), the main reason you'll need a reservation. €€€

Etxanobe Euskalduna, Avda. Abandoibarra 4, https:// etxanobe.com. Enjoying tremendous views of the city from its open-air terrace, the Michelin-starred *Etxanobe* is run by celebrated Basque chef Fernando Canales. His innovative contemporary cuisine is available on set menus. €€€

Los Fueros C/Fueros 6, http://losfueros.com. Tucked in behind the back of Pza. Nueva, this small restaurant offers an escape from the usual old-town crowds. Order a la carte, with *raciones* of their signature grilled prawns, and plenty of cheaper options including half portions, or give yourself a real treat with a set menu. €€

★ **Río Oja** C/El Perro 6, 944 150 871. Cosy, old-fashioned, much-loved and exceptionally inexpensive Casco Viejo restaurant with an unusual emphasis on hearty stews (*cazuelas*) and sauces, arrayed along the bar for diners' inspection. With clams in green sauce or quail stew, this is a place to experiment a little; they also serve *raciones*. €

Victor Montes Pza. Nueva 8, http://victormontes.com. Atmospheric bar and dining room, lined with a collection of over 1600 wines, on the attractive main square of the old town. Traditional grills, special hams and fresh fish are served in the main, very popular dining room, and sumptuous *pintxos* in the bar; in summer they put out tables on the square. €€€

DRINKING AND NIGHTLIFE
SEE MAP PAGE 440

The city has a pulsating **nightlife**, especially at the weekends – and goes totally wild during the August **fiesta**, with open-air bars, live music and impromptu dancing everywhere and a truly festive atmosphere. The Casco Viejo is bursting with **bars**, almost all of which, of course, also serve *pintxos*. C/Barrenkale is the heart of the madness, but the outdoor tables in the beautiful Pza. Nueva make a great place for a more relaxed drink in the early evening. Ensanche, too, has plenty of pubs and bars. Bilbao also has a vibrant **club** scene, with the edgier San Francisco district south of the Casco Viejo, across the river and home to Bilbao's West African and Moroccan population, a hot area for dancing till dawn. Hard rock and punk fans tend

to congregate in the grungy bars along C/Iturribide, northeast of the Casco Viejo. For **live music** listings, check the local newspaper *El Correo* (http://elcorreo.com).

BARS
Lamiak C/Pelota 8, 944 159 642. Large, LGBTQ+-friendly café-bar with a cool gallery packed with tables upstairs, and a fashionable crowd at the weekends.

Taberna Txomin Barullo C/Barrenkale 40, 944 152 788. A great, laidback café-bar in the old town, with a friendly alternative crowd and a mural depicting Groucho Marx in a Basque beret.

CLUBS AND LIVE MUSIC VENUES

Azkena C/Ibañez de Bilbao 26, https://azkena.eus. Popular live music space and bar, with simple, minimalist decor and a dancefloor that tends to get busy late in the evenings.

El Balcon de la Lola C/Bailén 10, 635 757 763. Dance club, a short walk across the river from the Casco Viejo, which attracts an excited and very friendly mixed LGBTQ+-straight crowd.

BilboRock-La Merced Muelle de la Merced 1, 944 151 306. Large, retro-styled converted church, just across the Puente La Merced from the Casco Viejo, that's among the city's best live venues for rock and alternative music.

Kafe Antzokia C/Done Bikendi 2, http://kafeantzokia.eus. Cinema-turned-nightclub with an emphasis on live shows, and attracting big names, from world music and reggae to folk- and punk-influenced groups and Basque musicians. Resident DJs spin an eclectic mix Saturday nights, with plenty of local sounds. The restaurant is open at lunchtimes for drinks and light meals.

MUSIC AND THEATRE

Euskalduna Avda. Abandoibarra, http://euskalduna.eus. Ultramodern structure, built on the ruins of the city's last shipyard, which serves as home to the Bilbao Symphony Orchestra, with a programme of opera and classical music, and theatrical performances.

Teatro Arriaga Pza. Arriaga, http://teatroarriaga.eus. This magnificent old-town landmark hosts dance and music events, as well as theatre.

DIRECTORY

Football Athletico Bilbao (http://athletic-club.net), known for their red-and-white-striped shirts as *Rojiblancos*, are famous for only fielding Basque players or products of their own youth system. Watch them play at the Campo de San Mamés, at the western edge of the new town.

Hospital Hospital de Basurto, Avda. de Montevideo 18, 944 006 000 (ⓂSan Mamés). Call ambulances on 944 100 000 (24hr).

Post office Alameda Urquijo 19 (Mon–Fri 8am–9pm, Sat 9am–2pm; ⓂAbando or ⓂMoyúa). There's another post office near the Guggenheim main entrance, Alameda Mazarredo 13 (same hours).

Vitoria-Gasteiz

The capital of the entire País Vasco, as well as of the province of Araba (Alava), **VITORIA-GASTEIZ** is a fascinating and exceptionally friendly old city. All the better for lying off the tourist circuit, it's well worth a couple of days' visit. Sancho el Sabio, King of Navarre, built a fortress here in 1181, on the site of the Basque village of **Gasteiz**. He renamed it **Vitoria** to celebrate his victories over Alfonso VIII of Castille, who promptly captured it back in 1200. Stretching along a low ridge in the heart of a fertile plain, Vitoria subsequently prospered as a trading centre for wool and iron, and still boasts an unusual concentration of Renaissance palaces and fine churches.

The streets of the city's historic old town, the **Casco Medieval**, wrap themselves like a spider's web around either side of the central hill, while a neater grid of later

---

VITORIA'S FESTIVALS

Vitoria's largest annual festival, the **Fiesta de la Virgen Blanca**, is celebrated from August 4–9 each year. On the first day, head for the Pza. de la Virgen Blanca with a blue-and-white festival scarf, a bottle of cava and a cigar, and wearing old clothes. At 6pm, in the "Bajada del Celedón", a life-size, umbrella-toting doll dressed in traditional costume appears from the church tower and flies through the air over the plaza. This is the signal to spray champagne everywhere (hence the old clothes), light the cigar and put on your scarf – which the hard core don't take off until midnight on August 9, when Celedón returns to his tower, signalling the end of the fiesta. In between, the town is engulfed in a continuous party.

The city also hosts a **jazz festival**, in the middle of July, which attracts big-name performers (http://jazzvitoria.com), and it's also the scene of parades and celebrations in the days leading up to **Mardi Gras**.

developments, **Ensanche**, lies below on the plain. All Vitoria's graceful mansions and churches are built from the same greyish-gold stone, and many of the medieval buildings are amazingly well preserved. The pick of the bunch, on C/Fray Zacarías near the Catedral, include the **Palacio de Escoriaza-Esquibel**, with its sixteenth-century Plateresque portal, and the **Palacio de Montehermoso**, now run as a cultural and exhibition space. On the southern edge of the old town, the porticoed **Pza. de España** is a gem, while the neighbouring **Pza. de la Virgen Blanca** is more elegant, with glassed-in balconies. If you find the hill itself a bit of a challenge, note that Vitoria offers a remarkable feature: **moving stairways** climb it from both the east (Cantón de San Francisco Javier) and west (Cantón de la Soledad) sides.

Catedral de Santa María

Guided tours only • Charge, advance booking recommended • http://catedralvitoria.eus

After nine centuries of tottering precariously at the highest point of Vitoria's old town, at the north end of the ridge, the venerable **Catedral de Santa María** had to be closed for reconstruction in 1994. Work remains in progress to this day, but the building can be visited on **guided tours**, the precise schedule and content of which is constantly changing. Drop in at the **ticket office**, off Pza. de la Burullería, to pick up the latest details, or simply book online; most tours are in very rapid Spanish, but there's normally one in English daily.

The tours usually work their way up through the entire edifice, starting with displays in its ancient crypt, which include open tombs, continuing with a hard-hat expedition high above the nave, and culminating with a light show on the superbly carved fourteenth-century west doorway. Some also include the Catedral's tower and the city walls.

Museo Bibat de Naipes y Arqueología

C/Cuchillería 54 • Free • https://fourniermuseoabibat.eus

The word "Bibat", meaning "two in one", denotes the fact that this complex consists not only of two buildings fused together, but two distinct museums. The first and more unusual, housed in a grand medieval mansion, is devoted to **playing cards** (*naipes*). While many are rather beautiful, by their very nature they're also small and repetitive, and in the absence of much contextual material it's not as interesting as you might hope.

The modern interconnected annexe holds well-presented **archeological artefacts** found locally, ranging through prehistoric, Roman and early medieval times. One skull, dating from 2500 BC, has a neatly chipped stone arrowhead embedded in its base.

Artium

C/Francia 24 • Charge, free every afternoon and Sunday all day • https://artium.eus

The **Artium**, immediately east of the old town, is an attractive museum of contemporary art. Its subterranean galleries concentrate largely on temporary exhibitions of Basque and Spanish artists, for which the Artium is able to draw on the city's permanent collection of more than three thousand works.

Museo de Bellas Artes de Álava

Paseo de Fray Francisco de Vitoria • Free • https://arteederrenmuseoa.eus

A magnificent mansion on an attractive pedestrianized avenue in the Senda district, southwest of Vitoria's centre, holds the regional **Museo de Bellas Artes de Álava**. Its fine collection centres on the period from 1700 to 1950; highlights include *costumbrista* paintings, depicting Basque cultural and folk practices.

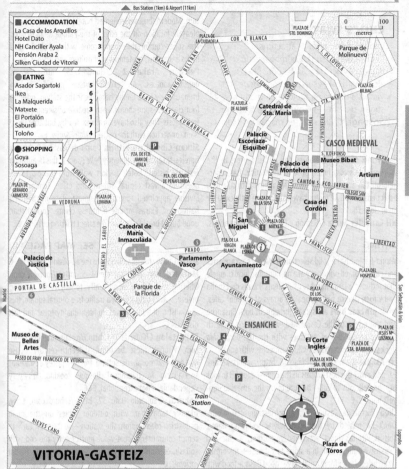

Bus Station (1km) & Airport (11km)

■ ACCOMMODATION
La Casa de los Arquillos	1
Hotel Dato	4
NH Canciller Ayala	3
Pensión Araba 2	5
Silken Ciudad de Vitoria	2

■ EATING
Asador Sagartoki	5
Ikea	6
La Malquerida	2
Matxete	3
El Portalón	1
Saburdi	7
Toloño	4

● SHOPPING
Goya	1
Sosoaga	2

VITORIA-GASTEIZ

ARRIVAL AND INFORMATION

By train Vitoria's RENFE train station is in the commercial district, a 10min walk south of the old town along the pedestrianized C/Dato.
Destinations Madrid (3 daily; 3hr); Miranda del Ebro (every 2hr; 20min); Pamplona (5 daily; 1hr).
By bus The bus station is at Pza. Euskaltzaindia, 2km northwest of the old town.

Destinations Bilbao (every 30min; 1hr); Laguardia (every 2hr; 50min); Logroño (every 2hr; 1hr 15min); Pamplona (10 daily; 1hr 30min); San Sebastian (every 1–2hr; 1hr 40min).
Turismo Pza. de España 1 (July–Sept daily 10am–8pm; Oct–June Mon–Sat 10am–7pm, Sun 11am–2pm; 945 161 598, http://turismo.vitoria-gasteiz.org).

ACCOMMODATION

SEE MAP PAGE 449

As Vitoria is not a major tourist destination, there's little accommodation within the old town; on the plus side, rates tend to be remarkably cheap. Budget hotels are concentrated near the train and bus stations, and more expensive options in Ensanche, south of the Casco Medieval.
★ **La Casa de los Arquillos** C/los Arquillos 1, http://lacasadelosarquillos.com. Lovely little boutique hotel in a

superb central location in a medieval building that's been converted to hold eight stylish en-suite bedrooms. They also offer eight larger but more expensive loft apartments in a nearby building. The one snag is that this area can get a little noisy, especially at weekends. Two-night minimum stay. €€
Hotel Dato C/Dato 28, http://hoteldato.com. Beyond the

6

> **CHOCS AWAY**
>
> Vitoria is famous for its attachment to **chocolates**. *Trufas, bombones* and *vasquitos y neskitos* can be purchased, along with cakes such as *chuchitos de Vitoria* (a bit like profiteroles) and other sugary delights, at **Goya**, C/Dato 6, and **Sosoaga**, C/Rioja 17 (see map page 449).

gaudy mix of classical statues and gilded mirrors in the stairwells, this cosy hotel, close to the station, has super-helpful staff and tastefully decorated rooms with colourful batik bedspreads. All rooms have baths; pay a little extra for an enclosed balcony. €

NH Canciller Ayala C/Ramón y Cajal 5, http://nh-hotels.com. Modern, business-oriented hotel in a convenient and pleasant location on the edge of the Parque de la Florida. The super-comfortable rooms come with polished wood floors and smart, contemporary furniture and fittings. €€

Pensión Araba 2 C/Florida 25, https://www.pensionaraba.es. An excellent-value *pensión* in an immaculately kept family home near the station, offering four clean en-suite rooms, each capable of sleeping up to four guests. They also have an annex nearby, but note there is no connection with the outlying *Hotel Araba*. €

Silken Ciudad de Vitoria Portal de Castilla 8, http://hoteles-silken.com. Opulently *belle époque*, this beautifully restored historic hotel, a short walk from the old town, opens to a vast central atrium, and offers comfortable, lavishly appointed rooms with immaculate marble-clad bathrooms. Extras include a fitness centre, cocktail bar, good buffet breakfasts, and free street parking outside. €€

EATING
SEE MAP PAGE 449

Vitoria-Gasteiz has a solid selection of quality **restaurants** and **cafés**, aimed principally at a no-nonsense local clientele that includes a large number of students. Plazas de España and Virgen Blanca hold appealing arrays of outdoor cafés, while **pintxos bars** are spread throughout both Ensanche and the edges of the Casco Medieval. Look out for such regional specialities as potatoes with chorizo, *porrusalda* (leek soup) and *perretxikos* (wild mushrooms with egg).

★ **Asador Sagartoki** C/Prado 18, http://sagartoki.com. Far and away the best *pintxos* in the city – beautiful to look at, and delicious to eat – be sure to try the amazing egg-yolk parcels. €

Ikea Portal de Castilla 27, http://restauranteikea.com. Don't be misled by the Scandinavian-sounding name; this is Vitoria's most acclaimed restaurant, a chic and expensive dining room in a stone townhouse transformed by architect Javier Mariscal. It serves good Basque food with a contemporary spin. €€€

La Malquerida C/Correría 10, http://lamalqueridavitoria.com. Hugely popular, hip, tapas bar, a few steps away from the Pza. de la Virgen Blanca. The chalked-up menu of innovative snacks and *raciones* can be enjoyed both indoors and out, with crowds spilling into the adjoining alleyways. €

Matxete Pza. del Matxete 4–5, http://matxete.com. Offering a welcome opportunity to enjoy the evening breeze, seated outdoors on a traffic-free central square, this specialist grill house serves up high-quality meat and fish dishes. €€

El Portalón C/Correría 151, http://restauranteelportalon.com. Vitoria's most beautiful sixteenth-century house makes an atmospheric setting for this pricey restaurant specializing in traditional Basque cooking. It's very dependable, if not exceptional. €€€

Saburdi C/Eduardo Dato 32, http://saburdi.com. Busy, friendly tapas bar, with outdoor tables on the main pedestrian road up from the station – so it's open early to tempt commuters. Great-value *pintxos* – try the cod with squash, or quail's egg with ham – plus more substantial *raciones*. €

Toloño Cuesta San Francisco 3, http://tolonobar.com. Determinedly modern tapas bar on the edge of the old town, with bright coloured lighting and brisk service, free nibbles with each drink, and a good changing menu of *pintxos*. Late-night DJs at weekends. €

Rioja Alavesa

Forty kilometres south of Vitoria-Gasteiz, across a range of high, little-populated hills, the wine-growing district of **Rioja Alavesa** feels like a rather incongruous appendage to the Basque Country. The north side of the Ebro valley does, however, belong to **Araba**, the same province as Vitoria-Gasteiz. As a result, so too do several of the richest and most famous **Rioja wineries**, even though the province of La Rioja, as well as the largest town hereabouts, Logroño (see page 383), lies immediately across the river.

Assuming you have your own transport, exploring the picturesque villages and **bodegas** of Rioja Alavesa makes a wonderful way to spend a day. The pick of the towns is lovely old **Laguardia**, while competition between the wineries is so fierce that several have invested quite astonishing amounts of money to attract attention, most notably **Bodegas Ysios** with its Santiago Calatrava-designed headquarters, and **Marqués de Riscal**, where Frank Gehry has created an amazing showpiece hotel.

If you drive down from Vitoria-Gasteiz, be sure to stop after 35km at the **Balcon de la Rioja**, a staggering hillside viewpoint that offers a panorama over the plains below.

Laguardia

Though little more than a village, **LAGUARDIA**, 15km northwest of Logroño, is the largest community in Rioja Alavesa. Stretching along the crest of a low ridge overlooking the vineyards, and still surrounded by its medieval walls, it's a gorgeous spot.

Within its stout gateways, a couple of slender cobbled lanes, lined with ancient mansions, connect the churches at either end. The finer of the two, **Santa María de los Reyes** to the north, boasts an ornately carved Gothic doorway. Much of the town itself is actually concealed from view; the hilltop is riddled with subterranean cellars, hollowed out to store wine.

Bodegas Ysios

Charge, reserve tours online • http://ysios.com

Framed by the hills that rise to the north, the mesmerizing **Bodegas Ysios** undulates through the vineyards 2km north of Laguardia, off the Vitoria-Gasteiz road. Its resemblance to an ancient temple is entirely deliberate; the name Ysios honours twin Egyptian deities Isis and Osiris, and no expense was spared when architect Santiago Calatrava, also responsible for Bilbao Airport (and, among other projects, the spectacular City of Arts and Sciences in Valencia), was commissioned to construct a new winery in 2001. The aluminium roof surmounts a wooden structure that on a more mundane level looks like a row of wine barrels.

Bodegas Marqués de Riscal

Charge, reserve in advance • http://marquesderiscal.com

Just outside the appealing village of **ELCIEGO**, 5km southwest of Laguardia, the **Bodegas Marqués de Riscal** is among the oldest and largest of the Rioja vineyards. Several tours each day provide the opportunity to learn about its history, and explore every stage of manufacture, from pressing to bottling. After seeing the cellars, used to store every vintage since 1858, you also get to taste a white and a red.

Although the *bodega* forms part of the so-called City of Wine, the major component of which is the extraordinary **hotel**, tours do not go into the hotel itself, but simply admire it from a distance of around 50m.

ARRIVAL AND INFORMATION — RIOJA ALAVESA

By bus Laguardia is served by regular buses from Vitoria-Gasteiz (every 2hr; 50min).

Turismo C/Mayor 52, Laguardia (Mon–Fri 10am–2pm & 4–7pm, Sat 10am–2pm & 5–7pm, Sun 10.45am–2pm; 945 600 845, http://laguardia-alava.com).

ACCOMMODATION AND EATING

LAGUARDIA

★ **Castillo el Collado** Paseo el Collado 1, https://castilloelcollado.com. Elegant hotel with ten antique-furnished rooms, individually styled on such themes as "Love and Madness", with vineyard views and an intimate, top-notch restaurant. €€€€

Hostal/Bar Biazteri Pza. San Juan 2, https://www.biazteri.es. Simple good-value en-suite rooms above a bar that serves good value weekday lunches that include a glass of Rioja, and also excellent tapas. €€

Los Parajes Pza. Mayor 46–48, http://hospederiade losparajes.com. One of two fancy restaurants in a luxury hotel (€€€€) in the heart of town, serving main courses like loin of venison or turbot with couscous. €€€

Silken Villa de Laguardia Hotel Paseo San Raimundo 15, https://www.hoteles-silken.com/es/hotel-villa-laguardia-rioja/. Large country-house hotel a short walk south of the town wall, with light, spacious rooms and a good restaurant. €€€

ELCIEGO

Hotel Marqués de Riscal C/Torrea 1, Elciego, https://

marriott.com. Designed by Frank Gehry and echoing his Guggenheim Museum, this extraordinary hotel, swaddled in a baffling tangle of multicoloured titanium ribbons, is an amazing structure for such a tiny village. Laid out to offer beautiful views of the ancient village nearby, it's breathtaking, albeit smaller than you might expect. The 43 rooms themselves are large and opulent, but only half are in the main structure; the rest are set into the adjacent hillside. There are also two very classy restaurants. €€€€

Pamplona

A prosperous city of just over 200,000 inhabitants, **PAMPLONA** (also known as **Iruña**) is a robust, visceral place, with a rough-hewn edge and a strong streak of macho self-confidence. Having started out as a powerful fortress town defending the northern approaches to Spain at the foothills of the Pyrenees (which took its name from the Roman general Pompey), it later became capital of Navarra – often a semi-autonomous state – and an important stop on the Camino de Santiago.

While tourism goes into a frenzied overdrive during the week in early July that sees the **Running of the Bulls** – officially, the **Fiestas de San Fermín** – Pamplona is an appealing year-round destination. Everything you're likely to want to see, including a massive citadel, fine churches and a beautiful park, lies within its remarkably compact **Casco Antiguo**. Centred on the **Pza. del Castillo**, and ringed with fashionable cafés, it's a glorious and very much lived-in jumble of buildings from all eras, where every twisting stone lane is worth exploring and intriguingly tatty old shops and bars lie concealed behind medieval shutters.

Catedral de Santa María

C/Curia s/n · Charge · http://catedraldepamplona.com

Built between the late fourteenth and the early sixteenth centuries, the **Catedral de Santa María** is basically Gothic. While it may not look promising at first, thanks to its unattractive eighteenth-century facade, it's worth paying to go inside. In the Catedral itself, the tomb of the recumbent Carlos III and his queen Eleanor, in the centre of the nave, dates from 1413. The fee also admits you to the appealing cloisters beyond, where you'll find several superbly sculpted doorways. The finest, the Puerta de la Preciosa, leads to what were originally the sleeping quarters, now home to an exhibition celebrating the Catedral's musical heritage. Another opens onto a chapel with a lovely star vault, and yet another into the **Museo Diocesano**, a collection of Navarran sacred art.

The city walls

Behind the Catedral, in one of Pamplona's oldest neighbourhoods, the most substantial remaining section of the **city walls** looks down over a loop of the Río Arga. Head out through the gate here, the Portal de Zumalacárregui (or de Francia), and you can follow paths down to the river, the perfect vantage point from which to admire the impregnability of these defences.

Museo de Navarra

C/Santo Domingo 47 · Charge, free Sat eve & Sun · https://museodenavarra.navarra.es

Although a magnificent medieval hospital just inside Pamplona's city walls serves as the entrance to the **Museo de Navarra**, most of its consistently beautiful treasures are

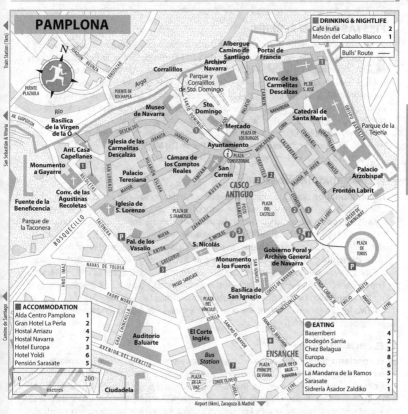

displayed in the light, uncluttered galleries of a modern annexe. Prehistoric relics in the basement include a dyed-green skull found in (or near) an ancient copper mine; higher up is a large mosaic floor taken from a Roman villa in Tudela. Other highlights include an ornately carved Muslim casket from 1004; a thirteenth-century ceiling fresco from a chapel in Olite; fourteenth-century Gothic murals from Pamplona's own Catedral; and, amid the extensive collection of paintings, Goya's full-length portrait of the Marqués de San Adrián, from 1804.

ARRIVAL AND DEPARTURE

PAMPLONA

By train Pamplona's train station is 1.5km northwest of the old city on Avda. San Jorge, served by local bus #9.

Destinations Barcelona (4 daily; 4hr); Madrid (up to 8 daily; 3–5hr); San Sebastián (2 daily; 2hr); Tudela (9 daily; 1hr 10min); Vitoria (5 daily; 50min–1hr 10min); and Zaragoza (8 daily; 2hr).

By bus The bus station is 250m south of the old town on C/ Yanguas y Mirando.

Destinations Bilbao (hourly; 2hr); Irún (3 daily; 2hr); Ochagavía (daily; 1hr 30min); Roncal (daily; 1hr 50min); San Sebastián (9 daily; 1–2hr); Zaragoza (2–3 daily; 2–4hr).

By car Drivers should leave their cars in the car parks at Pza. del Castillo, the bus station, or the bullring.

INFORMATION

Turismo Pamplona's main *turismo* is at C/ San Saturnino 2, adjoining Pza. Consistorial in the old town (July to mid-Sept Mon–Sat 10am–6pm, Sun 10am–2pm; mid-March to June & mid-Sept to Oct Mon–Sat 10am–2pm & 3–6pm, Sun 10am–2pm; Nov to mid-March Mon–Sat 10am–2pm & 3–5pm, Sun 10am–2pm; 948 420 700, https://www.pamplona.es/turismo).

6

FIESTAS DE SAN FERMÍN

Famous worldwide as the **Running of the Bulls**, thanks originally to Ernest Hemingway's 1926 *The Sun Also Rises*, Pamplona's **Fiestas de San Fermín**, or Sanfermines, lasts from noon on July 6 until midnight on July 14. The daily early-morning bull-run, or **encierro**, is just one component of nine days of riotous celebration, which also features bands, parades – the largest are on July 7 and July 10 – and 24-hour dancing in the streets. Almost everyone in Pamplona wears the official costume of white jeans, white T-shirt, and red neckerchief throughout the festival; you'll stick out like a sore thumb if you don't.

At the end of the week (midnight July 14), the festivities are officially wound up for another year with a mournful candlelit procession, the **Pobre De Mi** (Poor Me).

For detailed advice and schedules, see http://sanfermin.com.

ACCOMMODATION AND SECURITY

Accommodation during the fiesta should be booked far in advance – and be warned that many hotels triple their rates. If you arrive without a reservation, head for the *turismo*, where locals offer **rooms** at exorbitant prices. Many revellers simply sleep outdoors, on the ramparts, in the park or plaza. **Petty crime** soars, but valuables and luggage can be left at the bus station. In recent years, **sexual harassment** has also become a widely reported issue.

The **campsite**, *Ezcaba*, 7km east (http://campingezcaba.com), is large enough that spaces are always available, and it therefore does not accept reservations. It offers a cheap alternative and is connected to town by regular buses, as well as a straightforward cycle lane. Security is tight – admission is by pass only and a guard patrols all night.

ATMs frequently run out of money during the festival, while **banks** (and many shops) are closed over the weekend.

EL ENCIERRO

The **encierro**, the Running of the Bulls, takes place every morning from July 7 onwards. Six bulls are released at 8am, to run from the Corralillos near Pza. Santo Domingo to the bullring, where they will fight that evening. They take around four minutes to race a fenced-off course of just over 800m, through Pza. Consistorial and along C/Estafeta; official *pastores* (shepherds) armed with sticks make sure they keep going. In front, around and occasionally beneath the bulls run the hundreds of locals and tourists who are foolish or drunk enough to test their daring against the horns.

To **watch** the *encierro*, arrive early, by 6am. The best vantage points are near the start, or on the wall leading to the bullring. Try to get a spot on the outer of the two barriers – don't worry when the one in front fills up and blocks your view, as police move all these people on before the run.

ACCOMMODATION

SEE MAP PAGE 453

Much the most enjoyable area of Pamplona in which to stay is the Casco Antiguo, which has a reasonable selection of well-priced accommodation. Note that during San Fermin, rates below can triple.

Alda Centro Pamplona Pza. Virgen de la O 7, https://www.aldahotels.es. Cosy, welcoming hotel in a quiet corner of the old town. Its rooms are bright and en suite, albeit rather anonymous; some have balcony views overlooking the gardens to the south, and there's a bar in the basement. €€

Gran Hotel La Perla Pza. del Castillo 1, http://granhotellaperla.com. You simply can't beat Pamplona's grandest hotel for location, right on the main old-town square, or history – past guests include Hemingway and Chaplin. Spacious, well-restored rooms overlook either the square or lively C/Estafeta behind, with bargain rates for advance bookings. €€€€

Hostal Arriazu C/Comedías 14, http://hostalarriazu.com. Conveniently central and surprisingly quiet *hostal*, offering ageing but reasonably comfortable en-suite rooms just a few steps from the main square. €€

Hostal Navarra C/Tudela 9, 2º, http://hostalnavarra.com. Well-established *hostal* near the bus station. All of its clean if slightly small rooms, accessible by stairs only, have en-suite facilities and have been pleasantly refurbished, and there's a laundry room. €€

Hotel Europa C/Espoz y Miña 11, http://hoteleuropa

6

The event divides into two parts. First comes the actual running of the bulls, when the object is to run with the bull or whack it with a rolled-up newspaper. Even if you don't see the bulls amid the runners, you'll sense the terror and excitement; occasionally, if a bull manages to breach the wooden safety barriers, the fear spreads to the watching crowd.

Next, bullocks with padded horns are let loose on the crowd in the bullring. By then, the bullring is already too crowded for anyone who has watched the running to get in; to see both, you'll have to go on two separate mornings. Buy tickets for the bullring from the office outside, not from the touts inside.

TAKING PART

If you decide to **run** in the *encierro* – and we strongly advise you not to – remember that although it's generally less dangerous than it looks, at least one person gets seriously injured every year, while a total of sixteen have been killed in the last hundred years. Find someone who knows the ropes to guide you through the first time, and don't try any heroics. Don't get trapped hiding in a doorway, or come between a scared bull and the rest of the pack. Traditionally, bull-runs were male-only, but that law was overturned in 1974 amidst the feminist movement and since then increasingly more women have taken part each year. Under-18s are barred.

The only official way in is at the **starting point**, Pza. Santo Domingo, entered via Pza. San Saturnino. Shortly before the start, the rest of the course is cleared. Then, shortly before 8am, participants are allowed to make their own way to any point they choose. To mark the start, two rockets are fired: one when the bulls are released, and the second when they are all out. As soon as the first goes, you can start to run, though if you do so you'll probably reach the ring well before the bulls and be booed for your trouble. No one is allowed to stop altogether, and with plenty of **escape points** along the way, few of the typical daily quota of two thousand runners attempt to complete the entire course. A third rocket is fired when all the bulls are in the bullring, and a final fourth once they've all entered the corral within.

OTHER SAN FERMÍN EVENTS

Fireworks go off every evening in the Ciudadela park (about 11pm), and there's a **funfair** on the open ground alongside. Competing **bands** stagger through the streets all day playing to anyone who'll listen, and there's live **music** nightly from midnight in the bars and at Pza. del Castillo.

Bullfights take place daily at 6.30pm. Tickets can be bought at the Pza. de Toros, or online at http://feriadeltoro.com. Spain's main **opposition to bullfighting** is organized by ADDA (http://addaong.org), whose website has information about international campaigns and current actions.

Among **other Basque towns** where fiestas involve some form of *encierro* are Tudela (July 24–28), Estella-Lizarra (first weekend of Aug), and Tafalla (mid-Aug).

pamplona.com. Smart modern hotel just off the main square, offering compact, well-equipped rooms above one of the city's best restaurants. Breakfast works out much cheaper if reserved with the room. **€€**

Hotel Yoldi Avda. de San Ignacio 11, http://hotelyoldi.com. Old, three-star hotel with stylish rooms, a few hundred metres south of the Casco Viejo, near the bus station and not far from the bullring – this is where the bullfighters stay during San Fermín. Discounts on parking in nearby garages. **€€€**

Pensión Sarasate Paseo Sarasate 30, 946 304 890. Simple, central little *pension*, right on the edge of the old town, and nicely maintained in the finest old-school tradition. All rooms are en suite, some have balconies. **€**

EATING SEE MAP PAGE 453

Pamplona's greatest concentrations of **restaurants** and raucous little **bars** are along C/San Nicolás and its continuation C/San Gregorio, and along C/Estafeta on the *encierro* route. For good, inexpensive set menus and a wide range of **pintxos** and *bocadillos*, head for the streets around C/Mayor, in particular C/San Lorenzo. Navarra is noted for its fine asparagus, red peppers and red wines.

PINTXOS BARS

Baserriberri C/San Nicolás 32, http://baserriberri.com.

Highly acclaimed tapas bar, with a huge wine list and an innovative panoply of snacks, with various special deals on multiple creative *pintxos*, plus a set menu in the restaurant at the back. €€€

Bodegón Sarria C/Estafeta 50–52, http://bodegonsarria. com. Tapas bar and restaurant, where the *pintxos* taste as good as they look – try the artichoke plate – hams hang from the beams, and the glossy brick walls make an appealing backdrop. €€

Chez Belagua C/Estafeta 49–51, http://chezbelagua. com. Stylish, albeit intensely green-coloured, bar serving a mouthwatering array of *pintxos*, such as tune tataki, squid with onion, and black pudding, as well as set lunch and dinner menus. €€

★ **Gaucho** Traversa de Espoz y Mina 7, http://cafe bargaucho.com. Excellent tapas bar, just off Pza. del Castillo, where a tremendous range of *pintxos*, using ingredients like sea urchin roe and smoked eel, attracts a mixed crowd that spills out across the street at weekends. €

RESTAURANTS

★ **Europa** C/Espoz y Mina 11, http://hreuropa.com.

This hotel restaurant – Michelin-starred as of 2024 – is considered one of the best dining rooms in Navarra, under the direction of local culinary star Pilar Idoate, who knocks out a carefully crafted seasonal menu featuring traditional and *nouvelle* dishes. €€€€

La Mandarra de la Ramos C/San Nicolás 9 58, http:// lamandarradelaramos.com. There's a strong emphasis on meat and substance in this gleaming bar/restaurant, where the set menu bursts with hearty options like peppers stuffed with mince, plus abundant jams and cheeses. Most dishes are also available as *raciones*, and there's a long list of salads as well. €

Sarasate C/San Nicolás 19–21, http://restaurantesarasate. com. This great vegetarian restaurant, hidden away upstairs on a lively old-town street, was established in the 1950s, and has a set menu plus a good list of organic wines. €

Sidrería Asador Zaldiko C/Santo Domingo 39, http:// zaldiko.com. Close to the Museo Navarra, this typical Navarran grill and cider-house knocks out excellent steaks and lamb, grilled over a wood-fired *parilla*. €€€

DRINKING AND NIGHTLIFE   SEE MAP PAGE 453

★ **Café Iruña** Pza. del Castillo 44, http://cafeiruna.com. Elegant *belle époque* café and bar, with fine *pintxos* and a set menu. There's seating on the plaza or inside the grand old nineteenth-century dining room, with its huge mirrors and decorative pillars, and for once the TV is tiny, and dwarfed by its surroundings.

★ **Mesón del Caballo Blanco** C/Redín, 948 211 504, https://www.facebook.com/mesondelcaballoblanco. Arguably the most atmospheric bar in town, well away from the bustle in a converted medieval church, with a tree-shaded terrace at the top of the city walls giving fantastic views of Pamplona and the mountains beyond.

Southwest of Pamplona

Pamplona having long served as a gateway city to Spain, it's no surprise that the main route southwest towards the heart of the peninsula – by way of Logroño – holds some impressive medieval towns, including **Puente La Reina** and **Estella-Lizarra**.

Puente La Reina

Few towns so perfectly evoke the era of the great medieval pilgrimages as **PUENTE LA REINA** (known in Basque as **Gares**), 20km southwest of Pamplona. Its walled core consisting of three narrow pedestrian lanes, this long thin village is the meeting place of the two main Spanish routes: the Navarrese trail, via Roncesvalles and Pamplona, and the Aragonese one, via Jaca, Leyre and Sangüesa. From here on west, both sets of pilgrims followed the same path to Santiago.

The main historic thoroughfare, C/Mayor, is lined by tall buildings decorated with their original coats of arms. At its western end, the town's namesake **bridge**, sharply pointed and among the finest in Spain, crosses the Río Arga. Built by royal command at the end of the eleventh century, it's still in use, though now by pedestrians and animals only.

At the eastern edge of town is a twelfth-century Templar church, the **Iglesia del Crucifijo** (open for services only), which contains an unusual Y-shaped crucifix. In recent years, a pair of magnificent storks have nested atop its belfry.

INFORMATION	PUENTE LA REINA

Turismo C/Mayor 105, right by the bridge (Tues–Sat 10am–2pm & 4–7pm, Sun 11am–2pm, Mon closed; 948 341 301, www.puentelareina-gares.es).

ACCOMMODATION AND EATING

Albergue Puente Paseo de los Fueros 57, http://albergue puente.com. This spruce hostel has its front door beside the main road, and a back entrance opening within the old town. The dorm rooms hold four–ten beds, and there are a couple of bare-bones private doubles. Rates include a rudimentary breakfast, and there's a communal roof terrace. €

Hotel El Cerco C/Rodrigo Ximénez de Rada 20, https:// www.hotelelcerco.es/. Simple stone-walled hotel on the quietest lane of the old town, where arriving pilgrims are welcomed with cool home-made lemonade. €€

La Fonda de Tito C/Mayor 50, 948 340 075. The nicest place to eat in town, on the ground floor of a venerable house. It's excellent value – you can buy a huge seafood paella, or a set menu with a smaller plate of paella, followed by lamb chops and dessert, plus wine. €

Estella-Lizarra

The old town of **ESTELLA–LIZARRA**, 20km west of Puente La Reina, boasts a fine crop of monuments. While most of the old quarter, centred on **Pza. de los Fueros**, lies cradled within a loop of the Río Ega, several interesting buildings are across the river in Barrio San Pedro. The whole place is small enough to explore thoroughly on foot; be sure to seek out such churches as the fortified **San Pedro de la Rúa** and the long-abandoned **Santo Sepulcro**.

Palacio de los Reyes de Navarra

C/San Nicolás 1, Barrio San Pedro • Free • http://museogustavodemaeztu.com

Navarra's only large-scale Romanesque civil edifice, the twelfth-century **Palacio de los Reyes de Navarra**, is now open as an art gallery devoted to the Basque painter Gustavo de Maeztu (1887–1947). It also stages temporary exhibitions.

INFORMATION	ESTELLA-LIZARRA

Turismo Pza. San Martin 4 (Mon–Sat 10am–2pm & 3.30–6.30pm, Sun 10am–2pm; mid-Sept to mid-June Mon–Sat 10am–2pm; 848 420 485, https://www.visitnavarra.es/en/plan-your-trip/tourist-information-offices).

ACCOMMODATION

Hospedería Chapitel C/Chapitel 1, https://hospederia-chapitel.es. Comfortable and very friendly upscale hotel, in a beautifully and inventively restored seventeenth-century building, behind a modern brick facade in the heart of the old town. €€€

EATING AND DRINKING

La Cepa Pza. de los Fueros 15, http://www.restaurantecepa.com. Decent and very central restaurant with a stylish dining room, offering excellent meat and fish dishes and plenty of market-fresh vegetarian options. €€

La Moderna C/Mayor 54, 948 550 007. Despite the name, this is a deeply traditional café-bar, opening early for breakfast, and serving a good array of *pintxos* later on. €

The Navarran Pyrenees

East of Pamplona, the **Navarran Pyrenees** bite a hundred-kilometre-wide chunk out of France. While the frontier itself is lined with jagged 2000-metre peaks, most of this area consists of lush green uplands rather than impenetrable mountains. It's most readily explored as a driving day-trip from Pamplona, though several of the pretty and fundamentally similar villages along the way make appealing overnight stops. Each tends to have at least one hotel to cope with the steady trickle of **pilgrims** en route to Santiago.

Ever since the Middle Ages, the obvious route between Navarra and France has been to follow the **Roncesvalles** pass. As immortalized in the *Song of Roland*, Charlemagne was retreating this way in 778, after laying Pamplona to waste, when Basque warriors ambushed his forces and killed the noblest of his French knights, Roland himself.

Auritz-Burguete

Once it manages to break free from Pamplona's labyrinthine ring road, the N135 climbs steeply northeast along the Valle de Erro. With no need to huddle against the elements, each successive village straggles alongside the road and river. The first place it's worth pausing is **AURITZ-BURGUETE**, just after the road makes a sharp northwards turn to climb towards the pass. With their ornate gingerbread trimmings, its traditional houses epitomize the local architectural style.

ACCOMMODATION AND EATING · AURITZ-BURGUETE

Hostal Burguete C/San Nicolás 71, http://hotelburguete. com. After a century as the focal point for the village – Ernest Hemingway stayed here while writing *Fiesta* – this old-fashioned hotel is still very presentable, with its large, plain and shiny-floored en-suite rooms and a simple, good-value dining room. €

Loizu C/San Nicolás 13, http://loizu.com. Large gabled house at the south end of town, that has 27 very pleasant, modernized en-suite rooms. Its fine restaurant serves good-value contemporary cuisine with a set menu. Discounts for pilgrims. €€

Orreaga-Roncesvalles

Despite its fame as the traditional Spanish starting point of the Pilgrim Route to Santiago – road signs make it clear that the Gallego city lies a leg-aching 790km west

THE CAMINO DE SANTIAGO IN NAVARRA

The **Camino de Santiago** crosses into Navarra from France via the foothills of the Pyrenees, descending steeply to the historic monastery at **Orreaga-Roncesvalles**. As the mountains peter out, the path passes alongside trout-filled rivers lined with beech trees and through traditional whitewashed Basque villages graced with Romanesque churches.

Navarra has invested considerably in this section of the route, and its twenty or so *albergues* – all with comfortable, if basic, facilities – are among the best along the *camino* (see page 521). The path mainly follows dirt farm-tracks, although some stretches have been paved, which makes walking less messy but leaves pilgrims prone to blisters.

Traces of Charlemagne's tenth-century foray into Spain are everywhere in Navarra, from the pass before Roncesvalles by which he entered the country to a stone monument 20km farther on that depicts the massive Stride of Roland, his favourite knight. The region also contains some of Hemingway's much-loved haunts; the *camino* passes through his trout-fishing base at **Auritz-Burguete**, just 3km from Roncesvalles, and lively **Pamplona**, another 40km on.

There are a couple of stiff climbs, notably the 300m up to the **Alto de Perdón**, just outside Pamplona. Here, legend tells of an exhausted medieval pilgrim who stood firm against the Devil's offer of water in exchange for renouncing his Christian faith. The pilgrim was rewarded when Santiago himself appeared, and led him to a secret fountain.

Fine Romanesque architecture in Navarra includes the octagonal church at **Eunate**, 20km from Pamplona, thought to be the work of the Knights Templar, and the graceful bridge that gave its name to **Puente La Reina**, 4km farther on. The architectural highlight is undoubtedly **Estella-Lizarra**, where you can explore the Palacio de los Reyes de Navarra and many lovely churches. The route from Estella-Lizarra is lined with vineyards, and Bodegas de Irache's free Fuente del Vino (wine fountain), just outside town, is said to fortify pilgrims for the journey on through the Rioja region towards Santiago de Compostela.

– **ORREAGA-RONCESVALLES** is no more than a small cluster of buildings beside the N135. As you approach from Spain, neither the avenue of trees lining the 2km road from Auritz-Burguete nor the sloping hillside meadows around the hamlet itself hint at the peaks that soar to the east.

Colegiata de Santa María

Free, charge for cloister and museum • http://roncesvalles.es

Orreaga-Roncesvalles centres on a venerable monastery complex that stretches northwards away from the road. Its various elements can be visited in different combinations, with free access to the brooding church known as the **Colegiata de Santa María**. You have to pay to see its elegant Gothic cloisters, however, while to learn more about the history of the pilgrimage, visit the small adjoining museum.

Silo de Carlomagno

A roadside chapel near the church, named the **Silo de Carlomagno** for its resemblance to a granary, is said to mark the spot decreed by Charlemagne for the burial of Roland and his other fallen heroes. This site, however, only rose to prominence after the bishop of Pamplona built a pilgrimage hospital here in 1127.

INFORMATION	ORREAGA-RONCESVALLES
Turismo In the monastery complex (Mon–Sat 10am–2pm & 4–7pm, Sun 10am–2pm; 948 760 301, http://	roncesvalles.es).

ACCOMMODATION AND EATING

Casa Sabina Carr. de Francia http://casasabina.roncesvalles.es. Four spartan but adequate en-suite rooms, above a welcoming little mountain restaurant/bar just in front of the tourist office. On weekdays, a set menu is served (with a cheaper version for pilgrims), or you can buy a plate of pasta and a glass of wine for a similarly affordable price. €

La Posada de Roncesvalles Carr. de Francia http://laposada.roncesvalles.es. Large hostel run under the auspices of the monastery, with comfortable en-suite rooms for two to four people. Pilgrims get discounted accommodation. €€

Ochagavía

If, rather than heading north into France from Orreaga-Roncesvalles, you turn east from Auritz-Burguete, you'll find yourself on the remote and rather lovely NA140, which undulates from valley to valley. Though each is separated from the next by steep and densely wooded hills, the road never climbs above the treeline.

Just over 30km along, at the confluence of the Zatoia and Anduña rivers, the ancient settlement of **OCHAGAVÍA** makes the ideal spot to break a day-trip from Pamplona. The Anduña cuts a broad swathe through the heart of town, with a pleasant promenade stroll along both its banks, forested slopes looming to either end, and a fine old church on the hillside just above. For details of longer hikes hereabouts – especially in the **Irati Forest** immediately north – pick up a trail map from the tourist office.

INFORMATION	OCHAGAVÍA
Turismo C/Labaria 21, on the north bank of the river (Mon–Sat 10am–2pm & 4.30–7.30pm, Sun 10am–2pm;	948 890 641, https://www.visitnavarra.es/es/planifica-viaje/oficinas-de-turismo).

ACCOMMODATION AND EATING

Hostal Orialde C/Urrutía 6, http://hostalorialde.es. Sturdy farmhouse, facing a footbridge on the river's south bank, that's now a hotel with ten antique-furnished, en-suite rooms. €€

Hotel Rural Auñamendi C/Urrutía 23, http://hotel

ruralaunamendi.com. Slightly pricey but comfortable en-suite rooms, on an open square set slightly back south of the river. The pub-like restaurant on the ground floor (closed Sat eve & Sun) serves main courses such as local trout with ham. €€

Roncal

Twenty kilometres southeast of Ochagavía, the **Valle de Roncal** is arguably the prettiest in the Navarran Pyrenees. In high summer it can get a bit too busy for comfort, but come spring or autumn its villages and meadows, wild flowers and trees, are a delight. The nicest place to get your bearings and grab a meal is the little community of **RONCAL** itself, clustered beside the NA137, 6km south of its junction with the NA140 at Isaba.

INFORMATION   RONCAL

Turismo Carr. Del Roncal (Mon–Sat 10am–2pm & 4.30–7.30pm, Sun 10am–2pm; 948 475 256, https://www.visitnavarra.es/es/planifica-viaje/oficinas-de-turismo). Doubles as a Nature Interpretation Centre, with details of hiking and other activities.

Monasterio de San Salvador de Leyre

Charge • http://monasteriodeleyre.com

The **Monasterio de San Salvador de Leyre**, set amid mountainous country 50km southwest of Roncal and 4km northeast of **YESA**, grew as the first stop in Navarra on one of the many pilgrim routes from France to Santiago. To reach it from Roncal, dip briefly southwards into the province of Aragón, then head west back into Navarra on the A21, the main road between Pamplona and Jaca.

Although the convent buildings date from the sixteenth to eighteenth centuries, the church is largely Romanesque; its tall, severe apses and belfry are particularly impressive. After languishing in ruins for over a century, it was restored by the Benedictines in the 1950s and is now in immaculate condition. The crypt, with its sturdy little columns, is the highlight. You can also access the church by attending **services**, at all except the earliest of which the twenty or so white-robed monks employ Gregorian chant.

ACCOMMODATION AND EATING   MONASTERIO DE SAN SALVADOR DE LEYRE

Hospedería de Leyre http://monasteriodeleyre.com. Housed in the monastery's former hospice, this smart hotel has a mix of double and single (half-rate) rooms, all en suite, as well as a handful capable of accommodating three or four guests. Its restaurant serves a good-value dinner menu. €€€

Javier

Although tiny **JAVIER**, 5km south of Yesa, never had anything to do with the Pilgrim Route, it's a place of pilgrimage in its own right, as St Francis Xavier was born in its redoubtable **castle** in 1506. Javier itself, 500m beyond the castle, is predominantly modern, and holds nothing of interest.

Castillo de Javier

Charge • https://www.castillodejavier.es

The patron saint of Navarra, the Jesuit missionary St Francis Xavier, travelled all over the Far East, and died in China in 1552. The restored **castle** that was his birthplace, originally built as a Moorish stronghold in the ninth century, now serves as an absorbing **museum** dedicated to the saint's life; labels are in Spanish only. Coachloads of pilgrims arrive daily, and the castle's spacious grounds hold a large cafeteria as well as plenty of room for picnics.

ACCOMMODATION AND EATING   JAVIER

Hotel Xabier Pza. de Santo, http://hotelxabier.com. Grand but nonetheless relaxing hotel, facing the main entrance to Javier's castle, with comfortable, well-equipped rooms, a terrace with sunset views and a restaurant that serves a good-value set menu. €€

Sangüesa

Once a major pilgrim halt, run-down little **SANGÜESA**, 8km southwest of Javier, still boasts a number of significant monuments, including several churches from the fourteenth century and earlier. Many of its streets have changed little in centuries, and still hold handsome mansions, the remains of a royal palace and a medieval hospital, as well as the seventeenth-century Palacio de Ongay Vallesantoro.

Santa María La Real

C/Mayor 1 • Charge • 948 870 132

The Romanesque church of **Santa María La Real**, pressed up against the Río Aragón at the west end of Sangüesa, dates from the twelfth century. Its finest feature is its southern facade, with a richly carved doorway and sculpted buttresses: God, the Virgin and the Apostles are depicted amid a chaotic company of warriors, musicians, craftsmen, wrestlers and animals.

Southern Navarra

South of Pamplona, the country changes rapidly; the mountains are left behind and the monotonous plains of central Spain begin to open out. The people are different, too – more akin to their southern neighbours than to the Basques. Regular buses and trains run south to **Tudela**, Navarra's second city, passing through Tafalla and **Olite**, while attractive smaller towns and villages dot the area.

Olite

OLITE, 42km south of Pamplona, is as gorgeous a small town as you could ever hope to stumble across, all the more unexpected in that its larger neighbour Tafalla is quite unremarkable, and even Olite is surrounded by ugly modern developments. Its dominant feature is a former royal palace, the **Palacio Real de Olite**, but it also has a couple of fine old churches, Romanesque **San Pedro** and Gothic **Santa María**.

Olite's exuberant **Fiesta del Patronales** takes place from September 13 to 19, and there's a **medieval festival** on the second weekend in August leading up to the saint's day of Olite's patron, the "Virgin of the Cholera" on August 26, which commemorates a cholera epidemic of 1885.

Palacio Real de Olite

Charge • http://guiartenavarra.com

The magnificent **Palacio Real de Olite**, which rambles along most of Olite's eastern flank, was commissioned in 1387 by Carlos III, the French-born king of Navarre. All fairy-tale turrets and grand halls, keeps and dungeons, it's a colossal structure that takes a couple of hours to explore properly – and that's despite the fact that only its so-called "New Palace" section is open to visitors, as the oldest parts now house the local parador. The entire complex was originally sumptuously decorated and painted in bright colours, but few fixtures and trappings now remain; the appeal instead is largely architectural, supplemented by the tremendous views over the old town.

Galerías Medievales

Pza. Carlos III • Charge, temporarily closed at the time of writing • 948 741 885

Olite's central square, Pza. Carlos III, sits atop a series of impressive **Medieval Galleries**, unearthed in the 1980s. Their original purpose is a mystery; they could have been a market or crypt, or even part of a secret tunnel linking Olite with Tafalla. Accessed via a spiral stairway that drops from the square, they now hold displays on the costumes and cuisine of the Navarran court that are aimed largely at schoolchildren.

Museo del Vino

Pza. de los Teobaldos 10 • Charge, combined ticket with the Palacio available • http://guiartenavarra.com

Housed, along with the *turismo*, in one of Olite's abundant spare seventeenth-century palaces, facing the parador, the well-presented **Museo del Vino** celebrates the town's central role in the Navarran wine industry. Visitors who make their way through its three floors of high-tech displays are rewarded with a complimentary glass of wine.

ARRIVAL AND INFORMATION   OLITE

By train The station is on the northern edge of town, 450m from the palace.
Destinations Pamplona (3 daily; 32min); Tudela (2 daily; 40min).
By bus Regular buses head to Pamplona (12 daily; 50min) and Tudela (2 daily; 50min).

Turismo Pza. de los Teobaldos 4 (mid-March to mid-Oct Mon–Sat 10am–2pm & 4–7pm, Sun 10am–2pm; mid-Oct to mid-March Mon–Thurs & Sun 10am–2pm, Fri & Sat 10am–2pm & 3–6pm, Sun 10am–2pm; 848 423 222, http://olite.es).

ACCOMMODATION AND EATING

Hotel Merindad de Olite C/ Judería 11, https://hotel merindaddeolite.com. Cosy hotel in a reconstructed house kitted out in medieval style, with parking nearby immediately outside the town walls. Ten individually themed rooms with balconies and en-suite facilities, plus a reasonable restaurant. €€
★ **Parador de Olite** Pza. de los Teobaldos 2, www. parador.es. Olite's fabulous fifteenth-century *parador* makes

the most of its superb setting inside the Palacio Viejo, with stone staircases and ancient hallways leading to lavishly comfortable rooms, some of which are in a newer wing and have glassed-in balconies. €€€€
Restaurante Casa Zanito C/Mayor 10, https://casazanito restaurante.es. Atmospheric townhouse restaurant in the heart of Olite, with a great dinner menu. €€

Ujué

Twenty kilometres northeast of Olite, a lonesome road winds off eastwards from San Martín de Unx to bring you, after 8km, to tiny, hilltop **UJUÉ**. This perfect medieval defensive village perches high on the terraced hillside above the harsh, arid landscape; it's inconceivably narrow to drive into, and all but impossible to park once you're in.

Ujué is dominated by the thirteenth-century Romanesque church of **Santa María**, where the heart of King Carlos II of Navarra is supposedly preserved inside the altar. Views from its balconied exterior extend over the whole region of La Ribera. It's also the destination of a notable **romería** (pilgrimage), on the first Sunday after St Mark's Day (April 25), when half the populace of Tafalla walk through the night to celebrate Mass here and commemorate their town's reconquest from the Moors in 1043.

From Ujué's main square, a couple of pedestrianized cobbled streets plunge down to the beautiful little Pza. Mayor, where you'll find a ramshackle old bar with a balcony terrace.

Parque Natural Bardenas Reales

Free • http://bardenasreales.es

The further south you travel in Navarra, the drier the landscape becomes, until it's hard to believe you're still in the Basque Country. Indeed, the extraordinary **Parque Natural Bardenas Reales** (Bardenas Reales Natural Park), 70km south of Pamplona, looks more like the deserts of the Wild West than anything you'd expect to find in Spain.

To reach these desolate, eerily beautiful badlands, detour east of the main north–south roads to reach the village of Arguedas, 20km north of Tudela, then follow signs east. An **information centre**, 6km along, offers maps and advice. With an hour to spare, drivers can complete a short dirt-road loop to admire spectacular formations including stark mesas, jagged striated hills, and bizarre isolated rock columns. If you have more time you can venture further off the beaten track, or explore various clearly marked hiking trails.

Tudela

Thousand-year-old **TUDELA**, on the banks of the Ebro 90km south of Pamplona, lies at the heart of the region known as La Ribera. Its old town, stretching north of the richly decorated **Pza. de los Fueros**, is a jumble of cobbled lanes little changed since Alfonso I of Aragón ended the Moorish occupation of the city in 1119. The thirteenth-century **Puente Sobre** over the Ebro looks as if it could never have carried the weight of an ox cart, let alone seven centuries of traffic on the main road to Zaragoza.

The Catedral and the Museo de Tudela

C/Roso • Charge • http://palaciodecanaldetudela.com

The main doorway of Tudela's sturdy twelfth-century Gothic **Catedral** only offers access to a small portion of the interior. To see the rest, pay for admission to the adjoining **Museo de Tudela**, in the former dean's palace, where assorted polychrome statues, paintings and altarpieces are nicely displayed without being all that interesting. This leads to impressive Romanesque cloisters, adorned on all sides with deft primitive carvings. Large placards explain the city's Muslim and Jewish traditions.

ARRIVAL AND INFORMATION TUDELA

By train The train station is 850m southeast of the old town.

Destinations Madrid (5 daily; 2–3hr); Pamplona (hourly; 1hr 20min); Zaragoza (every 3 hr; 40min–1hr).

By bus Tudela's bus station is alongside the train station, with departures for Pamplona (9 daily; 1hr 30min).

Turismo Pza. de los Fueros 5–6 (Mon–Sat 10am–2pm & 4–7pm, Sun 10am–2pm; 948 848 058, http://tudela.es).

ACCOMMODATION AND EATING

AC Ciudad de Tudela C/Misericordia, https://www.marriott.com/en-us/. Tudela's classiest accommodation, part of the *Marriott* chain, is located in an imposing eighteenth-century mansion at the edge of the old town and has smart, plushly furnished rooms, aimed primarily at business travellers, plus a restaurant. €€€

Hotel Remigio Pza. de los Fueros 2, http://hostalremigio. com. Plain, light, en-suite rooms at reasonable prices, just off Pza. de los Fueros close to the old town, with a good modern restaurant downstairs. €€

Cantabria and Asturias

PICOS DE EUROPA

Cantabria and Asturias

While the northern provinces of Cantabria and Asturias are popular holiday terrain for Spaniards and the French, they remain little touched by the mass tourism of the Mediterranean coast. That's largely due to their unreliable weather, but the sea is warm enough for swimming in summer, and the sun does shine, if not every day. It's the warm, moist climate, too, that's responsible for the forests and rich vegetation that give this region its nickname – Costa Verde, the Green Coast. The provinces also boast elegant old seaside towns, and a dramatic landscape that features tiny, isolated coves along the coast and, inland, the fabulous Picos de Europa, with peaks, sheer gorges and spectacular montane wildlife.

7

Centred on the city of Santander and formerly part of Old Castile, **Cantabria** was long a conservative bastion amid the separatist leanings of its coastal neighbours. **Santander** itself, the modern capital, is an elegant if highly conventional resort, served by direct ferries from Britain. To either side lie attractive, lower-key resorts, crowded and expensive in August especially, but quieter during the rest of the year. The best are **Castro Urdiales**, to the east, and **Comillas** and **San Vicente de la Barquera** to the west. Perhaps the pick of the province's towns, though, is the beautiful **Santillana del Mar**, overloaded with honey-coloured mansions and, at times, with tourists, too. Nearby, the world-famous **prehistoric cave** paintings of **Altamira** are no longer open to most visitors, but they are explained by a great museum, and another set of caves can be seen at **Puente Viesgo**, near Santander.

To the west loom the towering cliffs and rugged coves of **Asturias**, a land with its own idiosyncratic traditions, which include status as a principality (the heir to the Spanish throne is known as the Príncipe de Asturias), and a distinctive culture that incorporates bagpipes and cider. Asturias has a base of heavy industry, especially mining and steelworks – and a long-time radical workforce – but for the most part, the coastline is a delight, with wide rolling meadows leading down to the sea. Tourism here is largely local, with a succession of old-fashioned and very enjoyable **seaside towns** such as **Ribadesella**, **Llanes** and **Cudillero**. Asturias also holds three sizeable cities: **Oviedo**, its delightful capital; **Avilés**, at its best during the wild *Carnaval* celebrations; and nearby **Gijón**, which enjoys a vibrant nightlife and cultural scene as well as good beaches.

Inland, everything is dominated by soaring mountains known as the **Picos de Europa**, which take in parts of León, as well as Cantabria and Asturias, though for simplicity the whole national park is covered in this chapter. A quiet pleasure on the peripheries is the wealth of Romanesque, and even rare pre-Romanesque, churches found in odd corners of the hills. These reflect the history of the old Asturian kingdom – the embryonic kingdom of Christian Spain – which had its first stronghold in the mountain fastness of **Covadonga**, and spread slowly south with the Reconquest.

Santander

Much the largest city in Cantabria, with a population approaching 200,000, **SANTANDER** is an elegant, refined resort that's also a major transport hub. While its setting on the narrow Bahía de Santander is beautiful – from the heart of the city, you

SANTA MARÍA DEL NARANCO, OVIEDO

Highlights

❶ Playas From El Sardinero in Santander all the way west through Asturias, the region has two hundred beaches to choose from. See page 471

❷ Santillana del Mar Wander the narrow streets of this chocolate-box village, with its picturesque houses and stunning Romanesque church. See page 477

❸ Picos de Europa With its soaring peaks, verdant hillsides, remote villages, medieval towns and nearby coast, this compact mountain range should not be missed. See page 482

❹ Cares Gorge The finest hiking trail in the Picos: a horizontal walk through the vertical world of the Desfiladero de Cares. See page 489

❺ Sidra Asturias's national drink must be poured from a great height to attain optimum fizz. See page 495

❻ Avilés Carnaval Experience Spain at its most vibrant during the Mardi Gras celebrations. See page 501

❼ Santa María del Naranco, Oviedo An enigmatic, jewel-like pre-Romanesque church. See page 503

❽ Cudillero This lovely little fishing port might have been airlifted straight from a Greek island. See page 506

HIGHLIGHTS ARE MARKED ON THE MAP ON PAGE 468

THE NARROW-GAUGE RAILWAY

Communications in Cantabria and Asturias are generally slow, with the one main road following the coast along the foothills of the Picos de Europa. If you're not in a hurry, try using the narrow-gauge **rail line** which was formerly known as **FEVE**. You may well still see that name in use, but it's now run by the main national **RENFE**, and timetables are listed in a separate section of the RENFE website (https://www.renfe.com/EN/viajeros/horarios.html).

Broadly speaking, the line consists of three separate routes: Bilbao to Santander; Santander to Oviedo (where local services serve the triangle of Gijón, Avilés and Oviedo); and Oviedo to Ferrol in Galicia. All are often breathtakingly beautiful, skirting beaches, crossing *rías* and snaking through limestone gorges, but it takes several days to see the network in its entirety.

can enjoy clear views across the bay to rolling green hills and high mountains that seem to glow at sunset – the city centre lost most of its finest buildings to a massive fire in 1941. Nonetheless, the narrow lanes of the **old town** still abound in atmospheric bars and restaurants, while the central waterfront has been re-landscaped, and adorned with the showpiece museum **Centro Botín**.

Thanks to its superb sandy **beaches** – the best is **El Sardinero**, facing the open sea a couple of kilometres east of the old town – Santander rivals Biarritz and San Sebastián as a favourite summer retreat for sophisticated holiday-makers from the interior. Still home to the namesake Santander bank, this prosperous city has a much more bourgeois identity than its earthier northern neighbours – and away from the beaches, there's not all that much to see or do – but it's a pleasant place to while away a day or two.

CANTABRIA & ASTURIAS

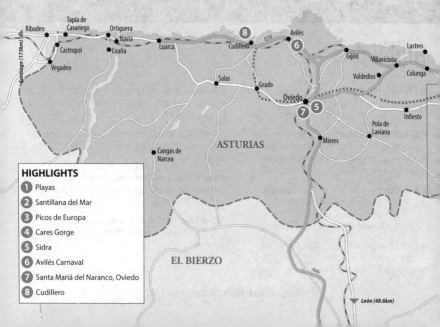

HIGHLIGHTS

1. Playas
2. Santillana del Mar
3. Picos de Europa
4. Cares Gorge
5. Sidra
6. Avilés Carnaval
7. Santa Mariá del Naranco, Oviedo
8. Cudillero

Centro Botín

Jardines de Pereda • Charge • http://centrobotin.org

Santander's long-neglected waterfront was transformed in 2017 with the unveiling of a gleaming cultural centre, the **Centro Botín**. Designed by Renzo Piano, architect of Paris's Pompidou Centre, it's a beautiful building. One of its two dazzling white sections holds **gallery** space plus a restaurant and shop, the other houses an **auditorium**. Both are propped 7m above ground level on pillars artfully sited to avoid obscuring the view across the bay, and clad in opalescent ceramic discs that reflect the shimmering play of the adjacent waters. Better still, the ugly multilane highway that previously cut the city centre off from the sea has been pleasantly re-routed underground, allowing the Centro Botín to stand in attractive open-air gardens.

As for the gallery itself, it has no permanent collection, so whether you pay to visit rather than simply admiring the whole edifice from outside will probably depend on the current temporary exhibition – check the website for details.

7

Old town Santander

Most of what's known as the **old town** in Santander, a compact grid of streets that stretches parallel to the shoreline of the bay, is not very old at all, as the neighbourhood had to be entirely rebuilt after the fire of 1941 destroyed its medieval core. Not that it looks particularly modern, either, just slightly faded. As you stroll around, the only area that really holds any great appeal and worth a look lies just a block back from the waterfront, along the parallel lanes that connect the colonnaded **Pza. Porticada** in the west to the **Pza. de Pombo** and the **Pza. Matías Montero**.

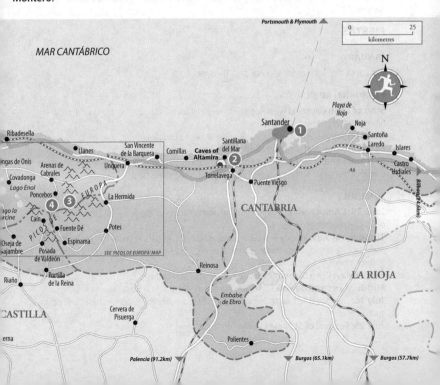

Museo de Prehistória y Arqueologia de Cantabria (MUPAC)

C/Hernán Cortés 4 • Charge • https://museosdecantabria.es

The basement of the attractive Mercado del Este, in the heart of the old town, houses the **Museo de Prehistória y Arqueologia de Cantabria (MUPAC)**, a cavernous modern space that follows a timeline through regional history from the earliest human inhabitants up to the Roman occupation. At first, it feels oddly empty, but once you get used to the tiny scale of its most ancient artefacts, such as complex bone tools and knapped flints, you'll see that they're absolutely exquisite. The standout is an ibex head carved during the Magdalenian area, 16,000–19,000 years ago. As you continue through the museum, the exhibits grow ever larger, first with the advent of metal and pottery, then with the creation of substantial stone monuments and statues.

MAS – Museo de Arte Moderno y Contemporáneo

C/Rubio 6 • Free • www.museosantandermas.es

Santander's free art museum, the **Museo de Arte Moderno y Contemporáneo (MAS)**, underwent a recent restoration. Its collection consists of an eccentric mishmash, leavened by a handful of Goya portraits.

Museo Marítimo

Av. de Severiano Ballesteros s/n • Charge • http://museosdecantabria.es

Ten minutes' walk east of the old town, beyond the **Puerto Chico** where the pleasure boats dock, the **Museo Marítimo** traces the history of Cantabria's involvement with the sea. If you don't read Spanish, you'll find that enough captions are translated into

---

FIESTAS

JANUARY

22: Saint's day fiesta at San Vicente de la Barquera.

FEBRUARY–APRIL

Start of Lent: Carnaval Week-long festivities in Avilés, Gijón, Oviedo, Mieres, Santoña – fireworks, fancy dress and live music.
Good Friday: Re-enactment of the Passion at Castro Urdiales.
Easter Sunday and Monday: Bollo Cake festival at Avilés.
First weekend after Easter: La Folia Torchlit procession at San Vicente de la Barquera; a statue of the Virgin Mary is carried through town on a fishing boat.

JUNE/JULY

June 29: L'Amuravela Cudillero enacts an ironic review of the year – and then proceeds to obliterate memories.
Throughout July: Weekly fiestas in Llanes, with Asturian dancers balancing pine trees on their shoulders and swerving through the streets. Also, tightrope walking and live bands down at the harbour.
First Friday: Coso Blanco Nocturnal parade at Castro Urdiales.
Mid-July: Festival de Folk Cultural fiesta at San Vicente de la Barquera.
July 16: Traditional festival at Comillas, with greased-pole climbs, goose chases and other such events.
July 25: Festival of St James Cangas de Onis.

English to provide a general overview, but you'll miss a lot of detail, and may prefer to gravitate to the aquarium that fills most of the basement.

Palacio de la Magdalena

Gardens free, tourist train and palace tours charge • http://palaciomagdalena.com • Bus #1 from Jardines del Pereda

Perched on its eponymous headland at the eastern tip of the city, the **Palacio de la Magdalena** affords magnificent views of the golden coastline. Built at the end of the nineteenth century by Alfonso XIII, whose presence here did much to make Santander fashionable, the palace itself is not desperately exciting, but the grounds make a popular retreat for families keen to escape the crowded beaches.

The beaches

Buses #1, #3, #4, #7, #13 and #15 shuttle between the Jardines de Pereda in the city centre and El Sardinero beach; #4 and #15 start from the train station, and call at Magdalena beach en route

The first of Santander's beaches, **Playa de la Magdalena**, lies on the southern side of the Magdalena headland. A beautiful yellow strand, sheltered by cliffs and flanked by a summer **windsurfing** school, it is deservedly popular. Around the headland to the north, two smaller and often slightly quieter beaches, **Camello** and **La Concha**, precede the main event, **El Sardinero**, which stretches for two magnificent kilometres, and is itself divided at high tide into two sections, Primera to the south and Segunda to the north.

Somo

Water taxi departs from alongside the Palacete del Embarcadero every 30min • Charge • http://losreginas.com

---

AUGUST

Throughout August: Festival Internacional Music and cultural festival, featuring prestigious performers, at Santander.

First or second weekend: Descenso Internacional del Sella Mass canoe races from Arriondas to Ribadesella down the Río Sella, with fairs and festivities in both towns.

First Sunday: Asturias Day Celebrated above all at Gijón.

12: Fiesta at Llanes.

15: El Rosario The fishermen's fiesta at Luarca, when the Virgin is taken to the sea.

Last Friday: Battle of the Flowers At Laredo.

Last week: San Timoteo Riotous festivities at Luarca, with fireworks over the sea, people being thrown into the river and a Sunday *romería*.

SEPTEMBER

7–9: Running of the bulls at Ampuero (Santander).

19: Americas Day In Asturias, celebrating the thousands of local emigrants in Latin America; at Oviedo, floats, bands and groups represent every Latin American country. The exact date varies.

21: Fiesta de San Mateo At Oviedo, usually a continuation of the above festival.

Last Sunday: Campoo Day Held at Reinosa, and featuring a parade in traditional dress.

29: Romería de San Miguel At Puente Viesgo.

NOVEMBER

First or second weekend: Orujo Local-liquor festival in Potes.

30: San Andrés Saint's day fiesta, celebrated with a small regatta at Castro Urdiales, plus samplings of sea bream and snails.

7

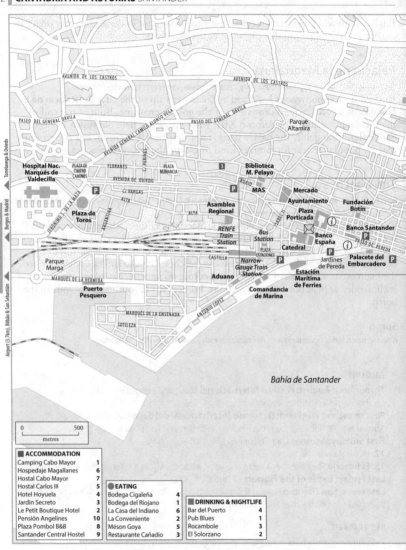

■ ACCOMMODATION	
Camping Cabo Mayor	1
Hospedaje Magallanes	6
Hostal Cabo Mayor	7
Hostal Carlos III	5
Hotel Hoyuela	4
Jardin Secreto	3
Le Petit Boutique Hotel	2
Pensión Angelines	10
Plaza Pombol B&B	8
Santander Central Hostel	9

● EATING	
Bodega Cigaleña	4
Bodega del Riojano	1
La Casa del Indiano	6
La Conveniente	2
Méson Goya	5
Restaurante Cañadío	3

■ DRINKING & NIGHTLIFE	
Bar del Puerto	4
Pub Blues	1
Rocambole	3
El Solorzano	2

If you find the city beaches too crowded, catch a **water taxi** across the bay to the long stretches of dunes at **Somo** – a major **surfing** destination where you'll find boards to rent and a summer **campsite** – with a stop at **Pedreña** en route.

ARRIVAL AND DEPARTURE
SANTANDER

By plane Ryanair flights from London Stansted, Edinburgh and Dublin, as well as domestic flights, land at Santander–Seve Ballesteros airport, 4km south at Parayas on the Bilbao road, across the bay in full view of the city. There are taxis into town, or buses run nonstop to the bus station.

By train The mainline and narrow-gauge train stations

stand side by side on the Pza. Estaciónes, just back from the waterside 500m west of the old town.

Destinations Bilbao (3 daily; 3hr); Llanes (2 daily; 2hr 20min); Madrid (3 daily; 4hr), change at Palencia for east–west routes including León; Oviedo (2 daily; 4hr 50min).

By bus A largely subterranean bus station (942 211 995)

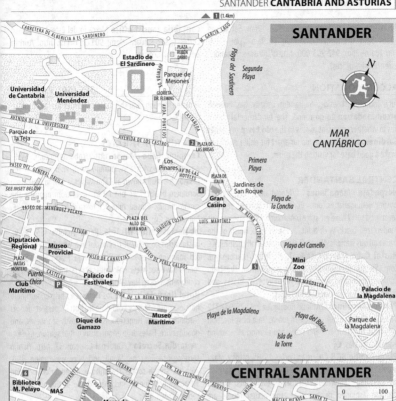

Ferries to Pedreña (3km) & Somo (5km)

faces the train stations across Pza. Estaciónes.

Destinations Barcelona (3 daily; 9hr); Bilbao (every 30min; 1hr 30min); Oviedo (15 daily; 2hr 15min); Potes via San Vicente and Unquera (3 daily; 2hr 30min); Santillana (9 daily; 40min).

By ferry Brittany Ferries (http://brittany-ferries.co.uk) from England dock in the heart of the city, a short walk from either the old town or the train and bus stations.

GETTING AROUND

By bus An extensive network of city buses, run by TUS (942 200 771, www.tusantander.es), covers all areas. Almost all routes pass alongside the Jardines de Pereda. Individual journeys cost €1.30.

INFORMATION

Santander tourist office The municipal *turismo* stands in the Jardines de Pereda near the ferry port and Centro

Botín (mid-June to Sept Mon–Fri 9am–9pm, Sat & Sun 10am–5pm; Oct to mid-June Mon–Fri 9am–7pm, Sat & Sun 10am–2pm; 942 203 000, https://turismo.santander.es/en/tourist-offices).

Cantabria tourist office Mercado del Este 4, C/Hernán Cortés (daily 8.30am–9pm; 901 111 112, http://turismodecantabria.com).

ACCOMMODATION
SEE MAP PAGE 472

July and August aside, Santander usually has enough **accommodation** to go round. The fundamental choice lies in whether you want to stay in the **old town** or near **El Sardinero** beach; they're too far apart for either district to make a good base for visiting the other.

CENTRAL SANTANDER

Hospedaje Magallanes C/Magallanes 22, http://hospedajemagallanes.com. Plain, neat rooms, recently revamped so all have en-suite bathrooms, in an anonymous modernized block, with a lift, a 15min walk north of the train and bus stations. The staff are exceptionally helpful. €€

Hostal Cabo Mayor C/Cádiz 1, 2°, http://hcabomayor.com. Six spotless en-suite rooms across from the train stations, decorated in a modern palette of blacks and whites, with friendly management. €€

Pensión Angelines C/Atilano Rodríguez 9, 1° 25, 942 312 584. Basic but scrupulously clean rooms, in a busy location very near the train, bus and ferry, and sharing all washing and WC facilities. €€

Plaza Pombo B&B C/Hernán Cortés 25, 3°, https://plazapombo.com. Attractive central B&B in an ideal position for enjoying Santander's bars and restaurants. Behind the old-fashioned public areas, the actual rooms are surprisingly modern and bright, though not all have en-suite bathrooms. €€€

Santander Central Hostel C/Calderón de la Barca 4, http://santandercentralhostel.com. As the name suggests, this hostel is hugely convenient for the old town and its transport connections. Its sixteen-bed dorms can feel crowded, though, and the shared facilities are rather basic. Dorms €

THE REST OF THE CITY

Camping Cabo Mayor http://cabomayor.com. Well-equipped site with a swimming pool, 2km north of the casino on a bluff known as Cabo Mayor, a 10min walk from Sardinero beach. Take bus #9 to Cueto from opposite the *ayuntamiento*. Closed mid-Oct to mid-April. Camping €, bungalows €€

★ **Hostal Carlos III** Avda. Reina Victoria 135, www.hostalcarlos3.com. Well-run *hostal* in a wonderful turreted old mansion overlooking Playa de la Magdalena. Some rooms have sea-view balconies, others their own private courtyards. Closed Nov–April. €€

Hotel Hoyuela Avda. de los Hoteles 7, https://sardinerohoteles.com/. Stately old-school hotel, perfect for El Sardinero beach. Huge rooms, many with sea views, and good service. Rates drop enormously out of season. €€€€

★ **Jardin Secreto** C/Cardenal Cisneros 37, http://jardinsecretosantander.com. Small and very welcoming B&B, with six stylish rooms featuring exposed brickwork and attractive bed linens, and sharing use of the eponymous secret garden. €€

Le Petit Boutique Hotel Avda. de los Castros 10, http://lepetithotelsantander.com. Rather exquisite B&B, housed in an unexpected little cottage just a few metres up from the centre of El Sardinero beach. The seven tastefully decorated bedrooms are named for different world cities, and vary considerably in size; the breakfasts are excellent. €€

EATING
SEE MAP PAGE 472

Santander's old town holds the largest selection of **cafés**, tapas **bars** and **restaurants**, though plenty more lie close to El Sardinero.

Bodega Cigaleña C/Daoiz y Velaverde 19, http://cigalena.com. Beyond its gorgeous tiled exterior, this atmospheric, museum-like bar, decorated with old bottles, is a lovely spot to enjoy tapas and a glass of wine, or linger over the traditional set dinner menu, or signature meat and fish mains. €€€

Bodega del Riojano C/Río de la Pila 5, http://bodegadelriojano.com. Traditional *bodega* in a sixteenth-century wine cellar, serving good *raciones*, with a flagstone floor, beautifully painted casks and antique furniture. €€

La Casa del Indiano Mercado del Este, C/Hernán Cortés 4, 942 074 660. Popular South American-style bar that fills half the flagstone-floored former market. Open from breakfast onwards for drinks and snacks, with patio seating as well as along the fine old counter, and a full restaurant menu plus a good spread of *pintxos*. There always seems to be a special deal of some kind, like the €1 *pintxos* on Thursdays. €

★ **La Conveniente** C/Gómez Oreña 19, 942 212 887. Very old-fashioned and very atmospheric nineteenth-century *bodega* serving fried fish and other delicious, but pricey, snacks. Live piano music, too. €€

Méson Goya C/Daoiz y Velaverde 25, http://mesongoya.com. Restaurant in a fine old house in the heart of the old town, serving a good range of *raciones*, including a delicious langoustine and mushroom *revueltos*, plus set menus. To best appreciate the setting, ask for a table on the mezzanine. €€

Restaurante Cañadio Pza. Cañadio, http://restaurante

canadio.com. The city's most famous restaurant, known far and wide for the sublime fish and regional cooking of Paco Quirós, Michelin-starred in 2023. There are typical main

dishes and a tasting menu, or you can join the foodies in the more modest bar, snacking on delicious *raciones* or *pintxos*. **€€€**

DRINKING AND NIGHTLIFE

SEE MAP PAGE 472

As both a university town and an upscale resort, Santander offers lively nightlife, especially on summer weekends. In the summer, the city welcomes students from all over the world to what it calls an "international university" of short courses, augmented by a music and cultural festival throughout August (http://festivalsantander.com).

Bar del Puerto C/Hernán Cortés 63, http://bardelpuerto. com. Swish bar and restaurant popular with the sailing set.
Pub Blues Pza. Cañadio 15, https://canadioblues.es. Popular blues and jazz music bar, with an expensive

restaurant attached.
Rocambole C/Hernán Cortés 35, 646 795 089. A twenty-year veteran of the late-night scene, this old-town club attracts a young and trendy crowd, with DJs every night and live comedy on Thursdays. Things tend not to get going before 3am.
El Solórzano C/de la Peña Herbosa 17, http://bar solorzano.com. This stylish but relaxed bar, decorated with *belle époque* flair and always packed, is renowned for its vermouths and fine wines, but also serves excellent *pintxos*.

7

East to Castro Urdiales

Easily accessible by car but still appealingly rural, the coast east of Santander is becoming ever more developed for tourism. The best-known resort is **Laredo**, with its enormous beach, but lower-key alternatives include the fishing ports of **Santoña** and **Castro Urdiales**.

Laredo

From its old core, sheltered behind a rocky promontory, **LAREDO**, poised 50km both east of Santander and west of Bilbao, has expanded westwards along the sandspit at the mouth of the Río Asón to become one of Cantabria's most popular resorts. In summer, the beaches and profusion of pubs, clubs and discos attract a young crowd, while there's enough of an interest during the rest of the year to keep most of the hotels and restaurants open.

Laredo was Cantabria's capital for a spell in the nineteenth century. Set well back from the overdeveloped beachfront, the village-like old town, the **Puebla Vieja**, stills retains the odd trace of its former walls and gates, climbing up towards a splendid thirteenth-century parish church, **Santa María de la Asunción**. Beyond that, you can climb quickly to the cliffs and grand open countryside.

A five-minute walk from the old town leads down to the best **beach** this side of San Sebastián, the **Playa de Salvé**. A gently shelving crescent of sand, well protected from the wind, it stretches for a full 5km.

INFORMATION AND ACTIVITIES

LAREDO

Turismo On Alameda Miramar at the west end of the old town, near the bus terminal (Easter & July to mid-Sept daily 9am–9pm; April–June & mid-Sept to Oct daily 9.30am–2pm & 4–7pm; Nov–March Mon–Sat 9.30am–2pm & 3–6pm, Sun 9.30am–2pm; 942 611 096, http://laredo.es).

Scuba diving Mundo Submarino offers dives and training (942 611 861, http://mundosubmarino.es).
Boat trips Boats from the end of the harbour nearest the old town cross to Santoña and set out on hour-long sea cruises (637 584 161, http://excursionesmaritimas.com).

ACCOMMODATION

Camping Laredo C/República de Filipinas 2, http:// campinglaredo.com. Conveniently located 700m back from the beach, not far west of the town centre, with separate adults' and kids' pools and some wooden "eco-bungalows". Closed mid-Sept to April. Camping **€**, bungalows **€€€**

Hotel el Cortijo C/González Gallego 3, http://hotelcortijo. com. Clean, simple hotel, a block back from the beach, a short walk from the old town. Nothing fancy, but the rates are as good as you'll find in high season for such a central location. **€€€**

EATING AND DRINKING

Guti C/Mayor 7, 942 605 674. The pick of several options along the old town's main street, serving good-value local cooking in a little dining room; mixed grills are the speciality. €

El Pescador Avda. Cantabria 2, http://restaurantepescador. es. Good seafood restaurant, with a prime position on the beachfront not far from the old town; their catch of the day is always excellent. €€

Santoña

West across the mouth of the estuary from Laredo, compact little **SANTOÑA** is still a working fishing port, shielded from the open ocean by the mighty wooded hill of Monte Ganzo, and famous for its **anchovies**. You can watch the catch being unloaded before sampling it in the tiny bars grouped around the streets leading up from the port, particularly C/General Salinas.

Turismo C/Santander 5 (Mon–Sat 10am–2pm & 5–8pm, Sun 11am–2pm; 942 660 066, http://turismosantona.es).

ACCOMMODATION AND EATING

Hotel Juan de la Cosa Playa de Berria 14, http://hotel juandelacosa.com. Modern hotel with large sea-view rooms and apartments, across from Berria beach on the ocean side of the headland 2km west of central Santoña. €€€

Napoleon C/Alfonso XII 34, 942 662 347. This good fish restaurant on the eastern edge of old-town Santoña is a great place to try the succulent local anchovies, they also have a set menu. €€

Castro Urdiales

The congenial, handsome resort of **CASTRO URDIALES**, 20km east of Laredo, is only a short drive west from the huge conglomeration of Bilbao. Both hotel rooms and space on the beaches are at a premium in high season and at weekends.

Castro Urdiales retains a considerable fishing fleet, gathered around a beautiful natural **harbour**. Above this looms a massively buttressed Gothic church, **Santa María**, and a lighthouse, built within the shell of a Knights Templar castle. These are linked to the remains of an old hermitage by a reconstructed medieval **bridge**, known locally as the Puente Romano, under which the sea roars at high tide. The old quarter, the **Mediavilla**, is relatively well preserved, with arcaded streets and tall, glass-balconied houses.

Flaviobriga

C/Ardigales 5–7 • Free • https://turismo.castro-urdiales.net

Castro Urdiales stands on the site of the Roman town of **Flaviobriga**, and a short stretch of ancient Roman street has been unearthed on C/Ardigales. You can simply admire it from the pavement outside, or enter to take a closer look at the foundations of assorted buildings.

The beaches

In high season, the main "town beach", **Playa del Brazomar**, a small strip of sand hemmed in by a cement esplanade, can be very busy. However, the crowds can be left behind by heading farther east to more secluded coves, or west to **Playa Ostende**, with its rough, dark sand. From this latter beach, an unusual walk leads back to town along the cliffs, with the sea pounding the rocks beneath you. In a tiny bay en route, the sea comes in under a spectacular overhang.

By bus The local bus terminal is a half-hour walk east of the centre on C/Leonardo Rucabado, but town buses, and services to Bilbao, stop outside *Café-Bar Ronda* on Paseo Menendez Pelayo.

By car Finding a parking space is appallingly difficult in season; spare yourself a lot of hassle by settling for the first roadside space you see.

Turismo On the esplanade alongside C/de la Constitución, immediately south of the harbour (July to mid-Sept daily 9am–8pm, mid-Sept to June Mon–Sat 9am–2.30pm & 4.30–6.30pm; 942 871 512, https://turismo.castro-urdiales.net).

ACCOMMODATION

Pensión La Mar C/La Mar 27, http://lamarcastro.es. Clean and presentable, if far from distinguished, en-suite rooms, on a little shopping street just back from the sea in the heart of town. €€

Hotel Las Rocas C/Flaviobriga 1, http://lasrocashotel.com. Imposing, classy, pastel-yellow four-star hotel, facing the beach in the newer part of the town. Comfortable upscale rooms with sea views, plus private parking. €€€

EATING AND DRINKING

Places to **eat** are clustered beneath the arches at the castle end of the harbour. Lively **C/Ardigales**, a block inland from the Paseo del Mar and packed with *mesones* and *tabernas*, is the centre of the nightlife scene.

La Cierbanata C/La Correría 15, 942 871 562. The best of several old-fashioned tapas bars under the arcades just back from the harbour, with a colourful tiled interior and a few wooden benches outside. *Pintxos* heaven, with *raciones* of mussels, razor-shell clams and the like. €

★ **Mesón Marinero** C/La Correría 19, http://meson marinero.com. Top-notch fish restaurant, with harbour-facing tables beneath the arches of a huge white waterfront building. Main courses are pricey, but you can dine well and cheaply on the *pintxos* set out along the bar. €€

Sidrería Marcelo C/Ardigales 12, 942 782 310. Traditional cider-house across from the Roman ruins, with standing room at the barrels outside as well as great snacks or a good set menu – and fresh cider. €€

Santillana del Mar and around

The picturesque village of **SANTILLANA DEL MAR** is the first major tourist destination west of Santander. No less an authority than Jean-Paul Sartre, in *Nausea*, hailed Santillana as "*le plus joli village d'Espagne*" (the prettiest village in Spain). The crowds that flock here in summer have unquestionably dented its appeal, but on a quiet day it remains as beautiful as ever. Its cobbled lanes abound in gorgeous sandstone churches and mansions with flowery overhanging balconies, while the farms and fields that climb the adjacent hillsides give it a lovely rural atmosphere. Strolling is a delight, even if most of the ochre-coloured buildings now hold restaurants, hotels or souvenir shops.

Despite consisting of little more than two pedestrianized streets and a couple of plazas, Santillana feels more like a sizeable medieval town that never grew beyond its original core than it does a village. Many of the fifteenth- to eighteenth-century **mansions** clustered close to the Pza. Mayor still belong to the original families, but their noble owners have rarely visited in the last couple of centuries. Among the finest is the **Casa de los Hombrones**, on C/Cantón, named after the two moustached figures that flank its grandly sculpted escutcheon.

La Colegiata

Pza. Las Arenas • Charge, combined ticket with Museo Diocesano • www.santillanamuseodiocesano.com

Jutting into the fields at the north end of the village, Santillana's elegantly proportioned village church, **La Colegiata**, is dedicated to Santa Juliana. Her recumbent tomb is in the central aisle of the church itself, which also holds a magnificent *retablo*. The most outstanding feature of the complex, however, is its ivy-drenched twelfth-century **Romanesque cloister**, where the squat, paired columns and lively capitals are carved with images of animals and hunting, as well as ornate patterns and religious scenes.

Museo Diocesano Regina Coeli

El Cruce • Charge, combined ticket with La Colegiata • www.santillanamuseodiocesano.com

The seventeenth-century **Altamira Convento de Regina Coeli**, on the main road across from the village entrance, houses the **Museo Diocesano Regina Coeli**. This exceptional museum holds painted wooden figures and other religious art, brilliantly restored by the nuns. They're displayed with great imagination to show the stylistic development of certain images, particularly of San Roque, a healing saint always depicted with a dog who licks the plague sore on his companion's thigh.

The Caves of Altamira

Museum Charge • http://museodealtamira.mcu.es

The **Caves of Altamira**, which burrow into the hillside 2km west of Santillana, consist of an extraordinary series of caverns, adorned by prehistoric human inhabitants fourteen thousand years ago with paintings of bulls, bison, boars and other animals. No one knows exactly why the murals were created, but archeologists say that they were not primarily related to hunting; the specific animals depicted were not eaten any more than other species. Etched in red and black with confident and impressionistic strokes, and sealed by a roof collapse a thousand years later, they remained in near-perfect condition when rediscovered in the 1870s, their colours striking and vigorous; as Picasso put it, "After Altamira, everything is decadence". During the 1950s and 1960s, however, the caves seriously deteriorated due to the moisture released in the breath of visitors, and they were subsequently **closed** to prevent further damage. Since 2015, they have been reopened to a single group of five adults each week – there is a waiting list, but at the time of writing they weren't accepting new applications.

Most visitors have to content themselves with the fascinating **Museo de Altamira** alongside, which centres on a large and very convincing replica of a portion of the caverns that gives a spine-tingling sense of how the paintings look *in situ*. Comprehensive displays trace human history all the way back to Africa, with three-dimensional replicas and authentic finds from Altamira and other Spanish sites, and plentiful captions in English.

ARRIVAL AND INFORMATION
SANTILLANA DEL MAR

By bus Local buses, including to the nearest train station, 9km southeast in Torrelavega, stop on the main road near the tourist office.
Destinations Santander (7 daily; 40min); Torrelavega (hourly; 20min).

Turismo C/Jesús Otero 20, just off the main road and adjoining the largest car park (July to mid-Sept daily 9am–8pm; April–June & mid-Sept to Oct daily 9.30am–7pm; Nov–March Mon–Sat 10am–6pm, Sun 9.30am–2.30pm; 942 818 812, http://santillanadelmarturismo.com).

ACCOMMODATION

Santillana is not really a destination for budget travellers. If you're going to spend a night here, it's worth paying to stay in one of its many gorgeous luxury **hotels**, which uniquely include two **paradores**. The highest room rates tend to apply for just two or three weeks in mid-August.
Casa del Marqués C/Canton 26, http://hotelcasa delmarques.com. Grand and very luxurious historic hotel, with sumptuous public spaces and tasteful, well-appointed rooms. **€€€€**
★ **Casa del Organista** C/Los Hornos 4, http://casadel organista.com. This beautiful eighteenth-century B&B, just up from the central square, has very comfortable rooms, some with balconies, as well as nice public spaces, and also serves great breakfasts. **€€**

Hotel Altamira C/Canton 1, http://hotelaltamira.com. Fine hotel opening off the corner of the main square, with 32 plush antique-furnished rooms and suites, lots of wood panelling, and several dining rooms. The front courtyard makes a delightful breakfast venue. **€€€**
★ **Parador de Santillana Gil Blas** Pza. Ramón Pelayo 11, http://parador.es. Housed in a splendid mansion adjoining the main square, this definitive parador features a delightful terrace restaurant. **€€€€**
Posada Santa Juliana C/Carrera 19, http:// santillanadelmar.com. While ranking among Santillana's cheaper *posadas*, this still maintains high standards, and offers six attractive, beamed en-suite B&B rooms. Three-night minimum stay in summer. **€**

EATING AND DRINKING

Santillana is disappointingly short on tapas bars, and although it has plenty of conventional **restaurants**, most tend to be expensive and relatively ordinary.

Los Blasones Pza. de la Gandara 8, 942 818 070. Reliable restaurant, in a fine old building near the main car park, with good-value set menus featuring clams followed by steak or duck. €€

Restaurante Castillo Pza. Mayor 10, 942 818 377. Well

located on the main square, with a couple of stone benches for soaking up the early-morning sun, this place is busy with locals year-round. It acts as a *sidrería* near the front and a more formal restaurant further back, with a great-value daily set menu. €

Puente Viesgo: prehistoric caves

Las Monedas & El Castillo Charge • http://cuevas.culturadecantabria.com

The attractive village of **PUENTE VIESGO**, set in a river gorge amid forested escarpments on the N623 to Burgos, 15km southeast of Santillana or 24km southwest of Santander, stands close to some remarkable **prehistoric caves**. Guided tours (in Spanish only) depart from an informative visitor centre located 1.5km up a winding mountain road from the village bus stop (served by SA Continental buses from the main station in Santander). Two of the four caves, 700m apart, are open to the public, **Las Monedas** and the even more impressive **El Castillo**, but places are limited, and in summer it's best to book at least 24 hours in advance. Both caves are magnificent, with weirdly shaped stalactites and stalagmites, and bizarre organ-like lithophones – natural features used by Paleolithic peoples to produce music – while the astonishing paintings, depicting animals from mammoths to dogs, are clear precursors to the later developments at Altamira. The visitor centre has an excellent digital exhibit enabling 360-degree views and interactive "tours".

7

ACCOMMODATION   PUENTE VIESGO

La Anjana Corrobarceno 8, http://posadalaanjana.es. Spacious, well-equipped rooms at the south end of Puente Viesgo, where rates include breakfast in the excellent restaurant. €€

Gran Hotel Balneario C/Manuel Pérez Mazo, 942 598 061, http://balneariodepuenteviesgo.com. Luxurious four-star hotel with its own lavish spa, set in superb grounds

overlooking the glorious valley, and very close to the caves. €€€

La Terraza C/General 18, 942 598 102, http://laterraza depuenteviesgo.es. Squat little yellow-painted hotel, typical of several cheaper alternatives in Puente Viesgo, where the simple but attractive rooms share bathrooms. €€

South of Santander: Reinosa and the Ebro

South of Santander, a large area of quiet Cantabrian countryside is dominated by an extensive reservoir, the Pantano del Ebro. The N611 to Palencia brushes its shores en route to the pleasant old town of **Reinosa**. To the east, the **Río Ebro** trails a lovely valley, passing unspoiled villages, Romanesque architecture and cave churches.

Reinosa

REINOSA is a pretty, characteristically Cantabrian town with glass-fronted balconies and *casonas* – seventeenth-century townhouses – that display the coats of arms of their original owners.

On the last Sunday in September – "**Campoo Day**" – the people of the Alto Campoo region, of which Reinosa is the capital, celebrate their unique folklore and traditions. Locals parade in distinctive alpine-style costume, complete with unusual stilted clogs known as *albarcas*, and enjoy displays of traditional dance, typical foods and late-night festivities.

INFORMATION   REINOSA

Turismo Avda. Puente Carlos III 25 (Tues–Sat 10.30am–2.30pm & 4–7pm, closed Sun & Mon; 942 755 215, http:// aytoreinosa.es).

ACCOMMODATION

Hotel San Roque Avda. Cantabria 3, https://www.hotel-sanroque.com. Simple but comfortable en-suite rooms in an appealing restored building, a short walk from the liveliest part of town; it also has a decent restaurant. €€

Posada Fontibre El Molino 23, Fontibre, http://posada fontibre.com. Rambling old mill, full of bizarre knick-knacks, near the source of the Ebro in a pretty little valley 5km west of Reinosa, with six quirky, rather lovely bedrooms. €€

EATING AND DRINKING

For a small town, Reinosa has a wide range of traditional **bodegas** and **mesones**, concentrated around the central Pza. de la Constitución.
Meson Cantabria Travesía Avda. Naval 12, 942 286 687. This side-alley tavern fully deserves its sky-high reputation

for making the best *tortillas* in the region, with all sorts of fillings, but also serves a decent range of other *raciones*. €
Pepe el de los Vinos Avda. Puente Carlos III 29, 942 750 588. Central bar that makes a good venue for a glass of wine and a snack, and also offers more substantial meals. €

The western Cantabrian coast

West of Santillana, the coast is dotted with successive low-key resorts as far as drab little Unquera on the border with Asturias. Both the main towns, **Comillas** and **San Vicente de la Barquera**, are well worth a visit. While the narrow-gauge rail line runs inland along this stretch, the towns are linked by regular buses.

Comillas

COMILLAS, 16km west of Santillana del Mar, is a curious rural town with pretty cobbled streets and squares, which in its centre seems almost oblivious to the proximity of the sea. It nonetheless boasts a pair of superb beaches: **Playa de Comillas**, the closest, has a little anchorage for pleasure boats and a few beach cafés, while the longer and less developed **Playa de Oyambre** is 4km west out of town towards the cape.

El Capricho
Barrio de Sobrellano • Charge • http://elcaprichodegaudi.com

Comillas is the unlikely location of the first house ever designed by architect **Antoni Gaudí**. Built in 1883, the villa known as **El Capricho** stands an easy walk from the centre. With its whimsical tower, adorned like most of the exterior with glazed handmade sunflower tiles, it has the incongruous air of a Hansel and Gretel gingerbread house. Visitors wander at will through both the gardens and the house itself, which curves around a greenhouse that may well predate Gaudí's commission.

Palacio de Sobrellano
Gardens Free • **Palace** Charge • 942 720 339, http://centros.culturadecantabria.com

The enormous **Palacio de Sobrellano**, all but next door to El Capricho but most readily accessed from the main road below, is another nineteenth-century *modernista* extravaganza. Designed by Gaudí's associate, Juan Martorell, it was home to the Marqués de Comillas, a nineteenth-century local boy who made good in the Americas, and whose statue overlooks the beach from a nearby hillside. Reverential guided tours, in quick-fire Spanish, offer more information than you could possibly need about the furniture in the palace's downstairs rooms, then release you to explore contemporary sculpture upstairs at your own pace.

ARRIVAL AND INFORMATION   COMILLAS

By bus Frequent buses use the main coast road through Comillas.
Destinations San Vicente (up to 7 daily; 15min); Santander (5 daily; 1hr 15min); Santillana (5 daily; 20min).

Turismo In the town hall, C/Joaquín del Piélago 1 (mid-June to mid-Sept daily 9am–9pm; mid-Sept to mid-June Mon–Sat 9am–2pm & 4–6pm, Sun 9am–2pm; 942 722 591, http://comillas.es).

ACCOMMODATION

The basic choice in Comillas tends to lie between paying extra to stay right by the **beach**, or settling for a cheaper option up in **town**, which is where you'll probably spend your evenings anyway.

Camping Comillas C/Manuel Noriega, www.camping comillas.com. Attractive campsite in a great position, right above the beach on the headland at the east side of town. Closed Oct–June. €

Hotel Josein C/Manuel Noriega 27, 942 720 225. Custard-yellow hotel spilling down the hillside immediately above the Playa de Comillas; the lovely rooms have floor-to-ceiling sea-view windows and galleries that literally overhang the beach. The old town is an easy 10min walk away. Rates include breakfast. €€€

★ **Hotel Marina de Campios** C/General Piélagos 14, http://marinadecampios.com. Very charming hotel in a nineteenth-century house, up a few steps south of the old centre, with twenty antique-furnished rooms. A/c costs extra. €€€

EATING AND DRINKING

Gurea C/Ignacio Fernández de Castro 11, 942 722 446. Good local cuisine in a large indoor dining room, with set menus. €€

Restaurant El Carel C/Infantas 2, 636 619 822. Small restaurant with a homely interior and some seating outdoors, serving carefully prepared, delicious local food. €€

San Vicente de la Barquera

The approach to **SAN VICENTE DE LA BARQUERA**, marooned on both sides by the sea 12km west of Comillas, is dramatic. If you're following the coast road, you reach the town via a long causeway across the Río Escudo, the Puente de la Maza. Local lore maintains that if you manage to hold your breath all the way across the bridge, your wish will come true. Inland, dark green, forested hills rise towards the Picos de Europa, strikingly silhouetted as the sun goes down.

The town itself is functional rather than pretty, with little left of its historic core. On the other hand, it's a thriving fishing port with a string of locally famed seafood restaurants – San Vicente is usually packed with day-trippers in summer, here to spend serious money on eating and drinking. There's a good sweep of **beach** fifteen minutes' walk away, across the causeway on the east side of the river and flanked by a small forest.

A hot climb up from the waterfront soon brings you to the remnants of the hilltop medieval town, which despite its intriguing setting and spectacular views turns out to be somewhat humdrum. At either end of the ridge, you'll find an impressive Renaissance **ducal palace** and a sturdy Romanesque-Gothic church, **Santa María de los Ángeles**.

ARRIVAL AND INFORMATION

SAN VICENTE DE LA BARQUERA

By train The nearest station on the narrow-gauge railway is 4km south at La Alcebasa.

By bus Buses stop at the bottom of Avda. Miramar near the west end of the causeway.

Destinations Comillas (7 daily; 15min); Potes (2 daily; 1hr 20min); Santander (11 daily; 1hr 10min).

Turismo Avda. Generalísimo 20 (March–June & Oct Mon–Sat 10am–2pm & 4–7pm, Sun 10.30am–2pm; July–Sept daily 10am–2pm & 5–8pm; Nov–Feb Mon–Sat 10am–4.30pm, Sun 10.30am–2pm; 942 710 797, http://sanvicentedelabarquera.es).

ACCOMMODATION AND EATING

Hotel Azul de Galimar Camino Alto Santiago 11, http://hotelazuldegalimar.es. Good-value villa hotel, perched on the hillside 400m above the west end of the causeway and less than 10min walk from the centre, where the bright modern rooms have broad estuary views and spotless bathrooms. €€€

Hotel Luzón Avda. Miramar 1, 942 710 050. A refined hotel close to the seafront, alongside the main square, with 36 pleasant rooms with large windows. €€

★ **El Pescador** Avda. Generalísimo 26, 942 710 005. It's not immediately obvious when you peer into its cavernous interior from this street, but this large, rough-and-ready tapas-bar-cum-restaurant also offers waterfront open-air tables on the quayside around the back. There's something to suit every budget, with a wonderful-value set lunch menu, or a fabulous array of seafood such as a plate of anchovies, the big local speciality, and all sorts of pricier seafood platters and paella-type feasts. €€

7

The Picos de Europa

The **PICOS DE EUROPA** may not be the highest mountains in Spain, but they're the favourite of many walkers, trekkers and climbers. Designated a national park in its entirety, the range is a miniature masterpiece: a mere 40km across in either direction, shoehorned in between three great **river gorges**, and straddling the provinces of Asturias, León and Cantabria. Asturians see the mountains as a symbol of their national identity, and celebrate a cave-shrine at **Covadonga** in the west as the birthplace of Christian Spain.

Hikes in the Picos are amazingly diverse, with trails to suit all levels, from a casual morning's stroll to two- or three-day treks. The most spectacular and popular routes are along the 12km **Cares Gorge**, and around the high peaks reached from the cable car at Fuente Dé and the subterranean funicular railway at Poncebos, but dozens of alternative paths explore the river valleys or climb into the mountains. Take care if you go off the marked trails: the Picos can pose extreme challenges, with unstable weather and treacherous terrain.

The Picos have become a major tourist destination, and the most accessible areas get very crowded in July and August. If you have the choice, and are content with lower-level walks, spring is best, when the valleys are gorgeous and the peaks still snowcapped, although the changing colours of the beech forests in autumn give some competition.

You can **approach** – and leave – the Picos along half a dozen roads: from León, to the south; from Santander and the coast, to the north and northeast; and from Oviedo and Cangas de Onís, to the northwest. Public transport serves much of the park, but services are generally infrequent, even in summer.

The east: the Cantabrian Picos

If you're driving along the coast and want to dip briefly into the Picos, the Asturian portion of the range (see page 490) is the most readily accessible. It takes little more effort, however, to reach the **Cantabrian** section of the mountains, where following the valley of the Río Deva from **Potes** to **Fuente Dé** takes you into the very heart of the Picos. Villages such as **Espinama** make superb overnight stops, and there are endless opportunities for **hiking**.

From the coast to Potes

The N621 heads inland at **Unquera**, at the mouth of the Deva on the Cantabria–Asturias border. Decision time comes 12km along, at sleepy little **PANES**, where the C6312 forks west into Asturias, towards Cangas de Onís, while the N621 continues south towards Potes.

Immediately south of Panes, you enter the eerily impressive gorge of the Río Deva, the **Desfiladero de La Hermida**, whose sheer sides are high enough to deny the village of **LA HERMIDA** any sunlight from November to April. From nearby **Urdón**, a path leads west to Sotres (see page 492); it's a pleasant few hours' walk, with mountains looming up around you.

Around 6km south of La Hermida, in the village of **Lebeña** lies amid beautiful countryside, a short detour east of the main road. Its church, **Santa María**, built in the tenth century by "Arabized" Christian craftsmen, is considered the supreme example of Mozarabic architecture, with its thoroughly Islamic geometric motifs and repetition of abstract forms.

Potes

POTES, the main road junction and travellers' base on the east side of the Picos, is still just 500m above sea level, but it's beautifully situated, at the confluence of the

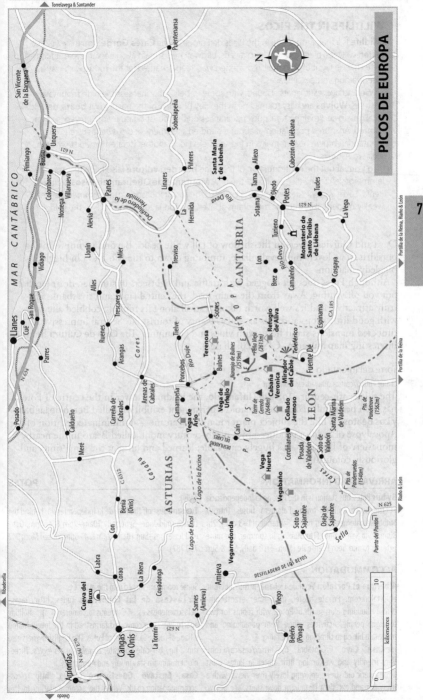

7

WILDLIFE IN THE PICOS

Wildlife is a major attraction in the Picos de Europa. In the **Cares Gorge**, you may well see griffon vultures, black redstarts and ravens; birdwatchers should also keep an eye out for the butterfly-like flight of the small, red-winged wallcreeper, named for the mouse-like way it creeps along vertical cliff faces.

Wild and domestic goats abound, with some unbelievably inaccessible high mountain pastures. **Wolves** are easy to imagine in the grey boulders of the passes, but **bears**, despite local gossip and their picturesque appearances on the tourist-board maps, are very seldom spotted. An inbred population of about a hundred specimens of *Ursus arctos pyrenaicus* (Cantabrian brown bear) remains in the southern Picos; another isolated group survives in western Asturias.

To learn about the reintroduction of the huge **bearded vulture** (also known as the lammergeyer) to the Picos, call in at the new **Montañas de Quebrantahuesos** centre in Benia, 16km west of Arenas de Cabrales (http://quebrantahuesos.org). In summer, staff lead weekly guided hikes into the mountains above Covadonga to see the birds in the wild.

Deva and Quiviesa rivers in the shadow of tall white peaks. Beyond its unpromising outskirts, it's a lovely medieval village, tumbling down to the Río Deva in higgledy-piggledy abandon.

Although Potes does get clogged with traffic and sightseers in summer, don't let that put you off visiting. Away from the main road, the central lanes and riverbanks are truly attractive, and it's well worth taking a stroll along its roughly cobbled alleyways, with good little shops and bars as well as plenty of tourist tat. Several impressive timbered mansions stand hung with vines and geraniums. The **Casa de Cultura** holds an interesting **map museum** (C/Sol 20; charge).

Torre del Infantado

Charge • http://centros.culturadecantabria.com

The thirteenth-century **Torre del Infantado**, the landmark tower in the centre of Potes, has been beautifully converted to hold a permanent exhibition called **Beato de Liébana y Los Beatos**. While the subject matter may seem arcane – an illuminated edition of the Apocalypse of St John produced by a ninth-century monk called Beato in the nearby monastery of Liébana – it's hugely enjoyable; learned and lurid at the same time, and gloriously colourful.

ARRIVAL AND INFORMATION   POTES

By bus Potes' bus station is in the Pza. de la Independencia at the west end of town. Palomera buses (http://autobusespalomera.com) run to Santander (1–3 daily, 2hr 30min) via San Vicente (1hr 30min); in summer, the route extends to and from Fuente Dé (Mon–Fri 3 daily, Sat & Sun daily).

Turismo Just off the Pza. de la Independencia, behind the church (mid-June–Sept daily 10am–2pm & 4–8pm; Oct–mid June Tues–Sun 10am–2pm & 4–6pm, closed Mon; 942 730 787).

ACCOMMODATION

Albergue el Portalón Vega de Liébana, http://albergueelportalon.com. Private hostel, in a fine seventeenth-century building 8km south of Potes, with rooms for two to eight people. Activities range from paragliding and mountain biking to climbing and trekking. €
★ Casa Cayo C/Cántabra 6, http://casacayo.com. Very friendly and welcoming little hotel in Potes' most atmospheric old street, enjoying lovely river views, with a lively bar and excellent restaurant downstairs, see below.

Some rooms are tucked into the attic. €€
★ La Casa de las Chimeneas Tudes, http://lacasadelaschimeneas.es. Gorgeous complex of holiday apartments, in a converted farmstead in the lovely hilltop village of Tudes, 9km south of Potes. The English owners also run a tiny bar-café opposite, *La Taberna del Inglés*. Three-night minimum stay in July and August. €€
Casa Gustavo Guesthouse Aliezo, http://picos-accommodation.co.uk. While the accommodation in this

friendly farmhouse B&B, 3km east of Potes, is pretty basic, the English owners are a great source of Picos advice for visitors who don't speak Spanish, and arrange activities like skiing and canoeing. Allergy suffers be warned; the house is full of cats and dogs. €€

EATING AND DRINKING

Asador Llorente C/San Roque 1, 942 738 165. The wooden balcony of this busy bar/grill, renowned for its good, cheap *raciones* and substantial cheese platters, hangs high above the Quiviesa. €€

Casa Cayo C/Cántabra 6, http://casacayo.com. Very nice hotel and restaurant with a river-view dining room; portions are healthy and prices are reasonable. The *Lebaniego* stew is a huge meal in itself. €

Sidrería La Majada C/Independencia, 629 434 627. Bar-restaurant in an irresistible setting, with outdoor tables spreading out from an old cottage down by the river. It's better for a drink, really, than for its run-of-the mill-food – snacks, dishes like chicken with apple, or a set menu. €

The Deva valley

A lovely minor road, the CA185, heads west into the mountains from Potes, running beside the **Río Deva** below a grand sierra of peaks known as the Macizo Oriental. En route to the cliff-walled natural amphitheatre at Fuente Dé, it passes through several delightful villages.

Monasterio de Santo Toribio de Liébana

Free • http://santotoribiodeliebana.es

Close by Turieno, above the main road on the south bank of the river, is the much-reconstructed eighth-century **Monasterio de Santo Toribio de Liébana, which** preserves fine Romanesque and Gothic details, and the largest claimed piece of the True Cross. It was here during the ninth century that one monk, Beato, produced illustrations of the Apocalypse that inspired the creation of similar works – all known as "Beatos" – all over medieval Europe. A few reproductions of Beato's works are on show, but there's a much better exhibition to be found in Potes (see page 482).

Turieno

TURIENO, across the river from the main road 3km west of Potes, is a quiet village where, once you're off the highway, you're as likely to share the road with a donkey as a car. Narrow mule tracks run to nearby hamlets that scarcely see a tourist from one year to the next; the walk to **Lon** and **Brez** is especially worthwhile, through a profusion of wild flowers and butterflies.

Cosgaya

The quiet and pretty village of **COSGAYA** lies 13km southwest of Potes and 6km east of Espinama. No more than a brief riverside strip, it remains idyllic despite the presence of two large hotels, one either side of the road.

Espinama

Located twenty kilometres from Potes – far enough to feel that you're deep into the mountains – **ESPINAMA** is a charming village, spilling down the hillside at the mouth of a slender gorge cut by the tiny Río Nevandi. Like Cosgaya, it straddles a busy road, but when the traffic dies down after dark it's a magical spot, while in the daytime there are plenty of walks (see page 488) in the nearby woods and meadows.

Fuente Dé

Teleférico Charge • https://telefericodefuentede.com

The CA185 comes to a halt 4km past Espinama, hemmed in on three sides by towering sheer-sided walls of rock. This is the source of the Río Deva; debate as to whether its name should be Fuente de Deva or Fuente de Eva has left it called simply **FUENTE DÉ**. Most visitors to this lonely spot are here to ride the **teleférico**, a cable car that climbs

7

PICOS PRACTICALITIES

ACCOMMODATION

While accommodation of all kinds abounds in the more popular villages, it's essential to book in advance, especially in summer. Alpine **refugios**, high in the mountains, range from organized hostels to free unstaffed huts where you'll need to bring your own food. They provide blankets or hire out sleeping bags. In many places, guests have to leave their rucksacks outside the dorm, so remember to bring a small padlock. **Camping** beside the *refugios* is accepted, and about half a dozen more campsites are scattered around the villages. However, camping outside these sites is officially prohibited below 1600m, and subject to on-the-spot fines, but unofficially you won't be disturbed once away from populated areas.

ACTIVITY OPERATORS

Companies arranging activities of all kinds, from canoeing and canyoneering to horseriding and mountain biking, include:

Cangas Aventura Avda. Covadonga 17, Cangas de Onís, http://cangasaventura.com.

Jaire Aventura El Merediz, Cangas de Onís, http://jairecanoas.com.

Montañas del Norte C/Pico 7 and C/Marqueses de Argüelles 26, Ribadesella, http://montanasdelnorte.com.

Picos Tour C/San Roque 6, Potes, http://picostour.com.

Turaventura C/Manuel Caso de la Villa 50, Ribadesella, https://www.turaventura.com.

CLIMATE

Good days for walking in the valleys turn up even in the depths of winter, but at high altitudes the **walking season** lasts from late June to September, varying according to the preceding winter's snowfall. All year round, the weather is unstable, with brilliant sunshine rapidly turning to clouds, cold rain or dense mist; in summer, cloud often descends on the valleys, while higher up conditions remain bright and clear.

EQUIPMENT

Most trails in the Picos are stony, rugged and steep; **hiking boots** are necessary on all but the easiest routes. Reliable water sources are sporadic, so carry your own. The routes given in this guide, unless mentioned otherwise, are straightforward and well marked; for walks at high altitude or off the marked trails, proper equipment and experience are essential.

almost vertically up 753m of cliff. It's an extremely popular excursion throughout the year, and though the cars set off every twenty minutes, carrying twenty passengers each time and taking under five minutes for the trip, you may well have a long wait to ascend due to queues, especially in the middle of the day when it is particularly popular. No reservations are accepted. What's more, at busy times you'll probably find yourself queuing again to come down, which in the mountain chill, 1900m above sea level, is not nearly so congenial.

The cable car provides easy access to an extraordinary mountainscape, well worth seeing even if you don't have time to **hike** any distance from the top. Many day-trippers simply wander around close to the upper station, known as **El Cable**, where they make an incongruous spectacle in their bathing suits and with toddlers in tow. The views back down to the valley are amazing, while an enticing track immediately sets off higher into the wilderness. Within a few minutes' walk there may not be another soul around, and it's easy to tailor a walk to your energy levels, or the prevailing weather conditions.

There's a simple café at the upper station, and the restaurant at the *Refugio de Aliva* (see page 488) is less than 4km along the main trail.

GUIDED WALKS

Between July and September, the national park service runs a weekly programme of free daily **guided walks** of easy to moderate standard, lasting 3–5hr and leaving from various points around the park's perimeter. These make an excellent way for novice walkers to get to know the Picos, although guides don't necessarily speak any English. The national park offices also have lists of **guiding companies** operating in each province.

MAPS

Adrados publish the best Picos maps, in two 1:25,000 sheets, one covering the western massif, the other the central and eastern massifs, plus good walking and climbing guides.

MOUNTAIN FEDERATIONS

For information on trekking and climbing in the Picos, contact:
Federacíon de Montañismo de Asturias Oviedo 684 624 667, http://fempa.net.
Federacíon de Deportes de Montaña de Castilla

y León Valladolid 983 360 295, http://fclm.com.
Federacíon Cántabra de Montaña y Escalada Reinosa 942 755 294, http://fcdme.es.

NATIONAL PARK OFFICES

For **online information** on the Picos, including guided walks and updates on route closures and access, see https://parquenacionalpicoseuropa.es. The huge **visitor centre** (daily 9am–6pm; 942 738 109) at **Sotama**, 6km south of **Lebeña** in Cantabria, offers comprehensive audiovisual displays and exhibitions, plus information on guided walks. Two additional **provincial offices** provide information on routes, activities and wildlife within the park, although each tends to be short of information on the other regions: Casa Dago, Avda. Covadonga 43, Cangas de Onís, Asturias (see page 494), and Posada de Valdeón, León (see page 489). **Information centres** also operate between July & mid-September in Poncebos, Fuente Dé, Los Lagos, Oseja de Sajambre and Panes, while the park headquarters is at C/Arquitecto Reguera 13, Oviedo (Mon–Fri 8am–3pm; 985 241 412).

TRANSPORT

No drivable **roads** cross the Picos, apart from a 4WD-only track from Espinama to Sotres, and circuits are long and slow; if you plan to trek across the range, allow sufficient time to get back to your starting point. **Buses** on the main roads are limited to one or two a day, and are very sketchy out of season. **Bikes** can be rented in Potes and other main towns.

ACCOMMODATION AND EATING   DEVA VALLEY

Camping La Isla Turieno, http://campinglaislapicos deeuropa.com. Very attractive campsite, tucked close to the river behind an orchard in Turieno, with a swimming pool and pony-trekking. €
Camping El Redondo Fuente Dé, http://camping fuentede.com. A 240-place campsite hidden away in a lovely wooded spot on the slopes beyond the end of the road, and equipped with a shop and bar. Horseriding available. €
Camping San Pelayo Baró, http://campingsanpelayo. com. Pleasant family-oriented campsite, in a tiny village 10km up the valley west of Potes. The site has its own restaurant serving local specialities, and there's a sizeable pool. €
Hotel Cosgaya Cosgaya, https://hotelcosgaya.com. The smaller of Cosgaya's two roadside hotels, housed in a sturdy

alpine-looking stone-built mansion, offers 24 tasteful en-suite doubles, all with views, plus a pool. €€
Hostal Nevandi Espinama, https://hostalnevandi.es. In the heart of Espinama village, this *hostal* has ten plain but reasonably comfortable en-suite doubles, with large beds; the owners also offer a few larger self-catering apartments (see https://apartamentosnevandi.com) in the ravishing, even smaller hamlet of Pido across the valley. Hostel €, apartments €€
★**Hotel del Oso** Cosgaya, http://hoteldeloso.com. Rather grand but extremely welcoming hotel, in a fine old house beside both road and river. The spacious terrace is a great place to lounge over a coffee or drink. There are fifty well-furnished rooms, plus a good dining room and an outdoor pool surrounded by lawns. €€
Hotel Rebeco Fuente Dé, http://www.hotelrebeco.

7

HIKING IN THE EASTERN PICOS: FROM ESPINAMA AND FUENTE DÉ

The best starting point for hikes into the mountains from the Picos' eastern side has to be **Espinama**, though if you're pressed for time, taking the cable car up from **Fuente Dé** and then hiking back down to Espinama (10km; 3–4hr) makes a quick and relatively pain-free alternative.

A superb trek from Espinama follows a dirt track (passable in 4WD vehicles) to **Sotres**, 8km east of Poncebos (12.5km; 5hr). Setting off north, it climbs stiffly, winding past hay fields, until tall cliffs on either side form a natural gateway, and you enter a landscape of rocky summer pasture and small streams. Near the highest point, 4.5km along, the track divides; the left-hand path leads up to the *Refugio de Aliva* and the top of the cable car, but for Sotres continue straight ahead, up to the ridge forming the pass.

Over the divide the scenery changes again, into a mass of crumbling limestone. In spring and winter, the downhill stretch of track here is slippery and treacherous. Next you climb slightly once again to the east, to reach Sotres itself, which clings to a cliff edge above a stark green valley. A zigzag climb to the west leads in 5km (around 2hr) to the even more appealing village of **Bulnes** (see page 492).

Accommodation is available in both Sotres and Bulnes, but you can also stay higher up in the mountains in the hotel-like rooms of the remote *Refugio de Aliva* (942 730 999; closed Oct–April; €), which has a restaurant. That stands 3.5km northeast of the top of the Fuente Dé cable car, along the clearly signposted PR24 trail, which then continues down another 2km to meet the track up from Espinama at the junction described above.

es. Perched at road's end in Fuente Dé, this modern hotel resembles a mountain lodge. Eleven of its thirty en-suite rooms are family-sized, and its good-value restaurant stretches onto a nice mountain-view terrace. €€
Parador de Fuente Dé http://paradores.es. Modern parador set in a stunning mountain amphitheatre, near the foot of the cable car. The comfort inside belies the uninspiring exterior, there's a good restaurant, and bargain off-season rates are frequently available. €€€
Posada Javier Turieno, http://posadajavier.com. Pretty little rural hotel, set amid the fields well away from the main road, and equipped with eight very pleasantly decorated (and centrally heated) en-suite rooms. €€

★ **Puente Deva** Espinama, http://hostalpuentedeva. com. The en-suite rooms belonging to this inviting little inn are actually in a separate building, 50m away; they're clean and correct, with valley views, but can get very cold out of season. The *Vicente Campo* restaurant in the inn itself serves absolutely delicious food year-round, with set menus, fabulous steaks and specials such as succulent roast kid. €€
Remoña Espinama, http://turismoruralremona.es. Cosy en-suite rooms above an old tavern on the main road, where the dining room serves a decent traditional set menu, as well as self-contained apartments in a newly built structure nearby. €

The south: the Leonese Picos

Although the southern flanks of the Picos de Europa lie in the region of **León**, visitors naturally experience the national park, and the mountains themselves, as a single unit. Exploring the southern side of the Picos from the north coast requires considerable effort, but those who do take the time, or simply approach from the south, are rewarded with some stunning towns and villages, leading up to the hike along the **Cares Gorge**.

Posada de Valdeón

Whether you're heading north from León, or touring the perimeter of the mountains, only one route leads into the heart of the Picos from the south. It starts from the village of **POSADA DE VALDEÓN**, in a delightful setting at the junction of two minor roads. Surrounded by soaring mountain slopes, it makes an ideal base for hikers.

Coming **from the east**, you'll get here by way of tiny **Portilla de la Reina**, a hamlet on the N621 that's served by León–Potes buses and lies 10km southeast of the high mountain pass known as the **Puerto de San Glorio**, a total of 38km southeast of Potes. The minor and quite enchanting LE243 runs 20km north from Portilla de la Reina to Posada, its last three ravishing kilometres as a narrow single-lane track. For those coming from the west, note that LE244 leaves the N625 just south of another pass, the **Puerto del Pontón**, and a total of 45km south of Cangas de Onís; it remains broad and easy for its entire 23km run to Posada. Finally, it's also possible to reach the village on foot from Fuente Dé, in about four hours, over a mix of dirt tracks and footpaths.

Cordiñanes and Caín

The **Río Cares** runs through Posada del Valdeón, and its gorge begins just north of the village. Over its first section, as far as Caín, it remains relatively wide, running past brilliant green meadows at the base of the cliffs, and paralleled on its eastern side by a narrow paved road. The village of **CORDIÑANES**, 2km along – and also accessible on foot, via a dirt track on the western side of the river – makes for an especially peaceful night's stop. In summer, the one main street of the pretty village of **CAÍN** itself, 6km further north, can get uncomfortably full of hikers and day-trippers; a grocery sells basic supplies.

7

INFORMATION   THE LEONESE PICOS

National Park office A short way up a side road just south of the centre in Posada del Valdeón (July–Sept Mon–Fri 9am–2pm, Sat & Sun 9am–2pm & 4–6.30pm; Dec to mid-March daily 9am–2pm & 4–6.30pm; rest of year Mon–Fri 8am–3pm; 987 740 549, https://parquenacionalpicoseuropa.es).

ACCOMMODATION AND EATING

Albergue Cuesta-Valdeón C/San Sebastián, Los Llanos de Valdéon, http://alberguelacuesta.org. Simple, clean hostel just north of Posada, offering dorm beds with shared kitchen and bathrooms. €
Casa Cuevas Travesía del Cares, Caín, http://casacuevas.es.

Friendly hotel/café/grill, facing the river at the final bend in the road in the centre of Caín, serving grilled meats like succulent chicken, plus a set menu, on its large terrace, and also offering decent en-suite rooms. Rates include breakfast. €

HIKING IN THE SOUTHERN PICOS: THE CARES GORGE

Deservedly the most popular walk in the Picos takes hikers into the heart of the central massif, along the **Cares Gorge** (**Desfiladero de Cares**). Its most enclosed section, between Caín and Poncebos – a massive cleft more than 1000m deep and 12km long – bores through awesome terrain along an amazing footpath hacked out of, and at times right through, the cliff face. Maintained in excellent condition by the water authorities, it's perfectly safe. Many day-trippers simply get a taste of it by walking as far as they choose to and from Caín, but with reasonable energy, it's perfectly possible to hike its full length – in both directions – in well under a day.

The **gorge** proper begins immediately north of Caín, where the valley briefly opens out, then suddenly disappears when a solid mountain wall blocks all but a thin vertical cleft. In its early stages, the trail burrows through the rock, before emerging onto a broad footpath. During busy periods, the first few kilometres are thronged with day-trippers thrilling at the dripping tunnels and walkways. If you're prone to a fear of heights, you may not get more than a kilometre or so from Caín, but that in itself makes a lovely walk.

Around 4km out from Caín, the crowds usually thin out. The mountains rise pale and jagged to either side, with griffon vultures circling the crags. The river drops steeply, some 150m below you at the first bridge, but closer to 300m by the end. Just over halfway along, the canyon bends to the right and widens to descend to Poncebos. Enterprising individuals run makeshift, summer-only refreshments stands. For its final 3km, the main route climbs a dry, exposed hillside.

It is, of course, equally possible to walk all or part of the gorge from the north, starting at Poncebos (see page 491).

★ **Desván Valdeón** Travesía de Prada 10, Posada de Valdeón, http://desvanvaldeon.com. Stylish, top-quality restaurant that serves exceptional food at affordable prices, including great salads and desserts, and delicious, delicate blue-cheese croquettes. All seating is indoors, in a well-lit upstairs dining room that also has a mountain-view balcony. The opening hours can be erratic outside summer. €̄

Hotel Cumbrés Valdeón Travesía de Soto, Posada de Valdeón, 987 742 710. Smart modern inn on the western edge of the village, where several of the comfortable rooms have mountain-view balconies. Closed Nov–March. €̄€̄€̄

★ **Pensión Begoña** Pza. Cortina El Concejo 8, Posada de Valdeón, 987 740 502. Clean, homely and friendly place in the village centre, with simple rooms (with shared bath) in the main building, and slightly smarter en-suite rooms in an annexe; prices for both are great value. The downstairs restaurant, open for all meals daily, has outdoor tables, and serves inexpensive local food like wild-boar stew and ultra-strong cheese. €̄

The Sella valley

The N625 between Riaño and Cangas de Onís, the road along the western end of the Picos, is arguably as spectacular as the Cares Gorge. Mountains rear to all sides and for much of the way the road traces the gorge of the **Río Sella**. The central section of this, the **Desfiladero de los Beyos**, is said to be the narrowest driveable gorge in Europe – a feat of engineering rivalling anything in the Alps, and remarkable for the 1930s.

Not far south of the road's highest pass, the frequently foggy 1290-metre **Puerto del Pontón**, the exceptionally pretty village of **OSEJA DE SAJAMBRE** stands high on the steep slope of a broad and twisting valley.

The north: the Asturian Picos

The most striking thing about the northern flanks of the Picos de Europa is just how near the mountains are to the sea. Spectacular scenery begins barely a dozen kilometres inland from resorts such as Ribadasella and Llanes. The AS114 highway runs parallel to the coast through the foothill area known as **Cabrales**, providing easy access to the mountains to the south, beyond **Poncebos** and **Covadonga**.

Arenas de Cabrales

The main village of this region, **ARENAS DE CABRALES** (shown on some maps as Las Arenas), might seem unremarkable if you simply scoot through, but stop for a while and you'll find it a cheerful, friendly little place. Not too commercialized, it holds a good selection of restaurants and inexpensive accommodation. On the last Sunday in August, Arenas hosts the **Asturian Cheese Festival**, a great excuse for dancing and music that's, oddly enough, not adorned with all that much cheese.

Cueva el Cares
Charge, advance reservation recommended • http://fundacioncabrales.com

The Cabrales area is famed for its exceptionally strong cheese. Gastronomes will want to check out the **Cueva el Cares**, a cheese-making museum beside the river a short way down the road towards Poncebos. Guided tours lead visitors into a series of natural caves, kitted out with displays and dioramas. You get the odd glimpse of pungent cheeses fermenting in various nooks and crannies, and there's a free tasting at the end.

ARRIVAL AND INFORMATION	ARENAS DE CABRALES
By bus Regular buses run from outside the *turismo* towards Cangas del Onís and Oviedo. **Turismo** On the main street near the bridge (Weds–Sun	10am–2pm & 4–7pm; 985 846 484, https://www.cabrales.es).

ACCOMMODATION

Camping Naranjo de Bulnes Carratera Cangas-Panes, https://www.campingnaranjodebulnes.com. Decently equipped campsite, with nicely shaded pitches and rental bungalows amid the woods and meadows on the south

bank of the river, 1km east of town. Closed Oct–March. €
Hotel Picos de Europa C/Mayor s/n, http://hotelpicos deeuropa.com. Large hotel, by the river in the middle of town, painted an unmissable shade of orange, and offering well-equipped en-suite rooms plus a pool and a pleasant mountain-view terrace. €€
Torrecerredo Barrio de Vega s/n, http://hoteltorrecerredo.com. Cheerful hotel with an appealing hostel-like atmosphere, enjoying great mountain views from its perch

in the fields on the hillside, a few hundred metres along a narrow lane from the west end of town. The English owners can arrange a wide range of mountain activities. €€
Villa de Cabrales C/Mayor s/n, http://hotelcabrales.com. Prices at this elegant hotel, at the west end of town, drop considerably out of season, but it's good value even in summer. En-suite rooms (no. 31 is the best), a good bar, and a garden terrace with mountain views. €€

EATING AND DRINKING

Chigre el Orbayu 31 Barrio del Casteñeu, 985 536 251. This is part *sidrería*, part café, with outdoor tables on a cobbled backstreet and an inexpensive daily set menu. They even offer a cider-based *sangría*. €
Restaurante La Panera C/Sublayende 1, 985 846 810. Garden restaurant, a short climb up from the highway just east of the main intersection and enjoying fine mountain views.

The local beans, *fabadas Asturianas*, are the speciality. €€
★ **Sidrería Calluenga** Pza. Castañeu, http://calluenga.com. Highly recommended village restaurant, on a little square set well back from the main road and open on one side to a little stream. Fabulous local dishes include clams with wild mushrooms or cod with potatoes, plus good vegetarian options. €

Poncebos

The dead end AS264 branches south off AS114 at Arenas, climbing alongside the Cares river into the mountains. Most visitors simply go the first five, easy, kilometres to

---

HIKING IN THE NORTHERN PICOS: FROM PONCEBOS AND SOTRES

The best starting points for hikes on the northern flanks of the Picos are Poncebos and Sotres. Besides being the northern trailhead for the Cares Gorge, **Poncebos** lies at the foot of the path up to Bulnes. Allow 1hr 30min for that climb, which branches east from the gorge trail 1km south of Poncebos, across the medieval bridge of Jaya. If you have problems with vertigo, you're better off taking the funicular.

   Sotres, accessible by road 9km east of Poncebos, marks the northern end of the ravishing 12.5-kilometre hike from Espinama (see page 488), and makes a good overnight halt for walkers heading across the central Picos. A hugely enjoyable 2hr loop trail circles the valley slopes surrounding the village itself, while a direct trail connects Sotres with Bulnes in 5km. Once you've crossed the broad, windy pass of **Pandébano**, an old, steep, cobbled path drops down into Bulnes.

   From both Bulnes village and the pass at Pandébano, well-used paths lead up to the **Vega de Urriello**, a high pasture at the base of the Picos' trademark peak, the **Naranjo de Bulnes** (2519m) – an immense slab of orange-hued rock that stands aloof from the jagged grey sierras around it. The approach from Pandébano is easier, a two- to three-hour hike along a track that passes the small *refugio* of **Terenosa** (635 552 016, https://www.reservarefugios.com/en/shelters/terenosa; closed Oct–April; €). The direct path up from Bulnes is heavy going, and takes up to six hours in bad conditions, with a slippery scree surface that's dangerous when wet. Once up on the plateau, you'll find another *refugio*, the **Vega de Urriello**, at 1953m (984 090 981, http://refugiodeurriellu.com; €), and a permanent spring, as well as large numbers of campers and rock climbers.

   Experienced trekkers only, equipped with the appropriate maps and gear, can continue beyond the Vega de Urriello across the central massif, through an unforgiving roller-coaster landscape, to the **Cabaña Verónica** *refugio*, which is for emergency use only, and has just three bunks. An easy descent from there leads to the top of the **Fuente Dé** cable car. Alternatively, you can continue west through further challenging terrain to another *refugio* at **Collado Jermoso** (636 998 727, http://colladojermoso.com; €), then drop down the ravine of Asotín to Cordiñanes at the top of the **Cares Gorge**.

7

PONCEBOS, a gloomy little spot, too small to be considered even a village, that's home to an antiquated power plant and three unattractive and somewhat institutional hotels.

If you have your own transport, you're better off staying in Arenas or further afield, but for hikers Poncebos offers the twin advantages of lying at the northern end of the **Cares Gorge**, which ranks among the Picos' very best trails, as well as at the foot of the steep, hour-and-a-half trek up the gorge of the Tejo stream to lovely little **Bulnes**.

Funicular de Bulnes

Charge • https://www.alsa.es/regionales/asturias/funicular-de-bulnes

A bizarre **funicular railway** takes around twelve minutes to burrow 2km upwards through a long round hole in the rock from Poncebos, and emerge at a point 400m higher, just below **Bulnes**. You don't have to be a die-hard mountaineer to feel there's something not quite right about an underground railway that tunnels through a beautiful mountain landscape without so much as a glimpse of light. For the casual visitor, however, it provides easy access to the inner recesses of the Picos massif, in a much less forbidding, and more picturesque, spot than the desolation encountered at the top of the Fuente Dé cable car.

Bulnes

The tiny but delightful stone-built mountain village of **BULNES** nestles in a cleft cut by the Río Tejo between two high peaks. Long the exclusive preserve of hardy hikers, it now also handles a daily influx of nonchalant sightseers on the funicular from Poncebos – when you emerge from the railway tunnel, it lies just a couple of hundred metres up and to the left, along an easy footpath. Many visitors now bring baby-buggies, and romping infants contrast strangely with exhausted trekkers in the two streamside cafés in the heart of the village.

Sotres

SOTRES, 5km east of Bulnes on foot and also accessible by road, 9km east of Poncebos along the dramatic CA1, is a small, relatively modern village that's cupped in a superb high-mountain valley. As the trailhead for several notable hikes (see page 491), it's a popular walkers' base.

ACCOMMODATION	BULNES AND SOTRES

★ **La Casa del Chiflon** Bulnes, http://lacasadelchiflon. com. Lovely B&B, offering simple en-suite rooms for two, three or four guests, a few metres from a cosy streamside bar and restaurant in the middle of Bulnes, where the owners serve hearty and very tasty mountain food. Open Easter & June to mid-Oct. €

Hotel Peña Castil Sotres, https://www.hotelpenacastil. com. Welcoming stone-built inn, on the right as the road enters Sotres, where one of the en-suite rooms can sleep a family group of up to five people. There's a good restaurant and bar, with outdoor tables. €€

Hotel Rural Casa Cipriano Sotres, https://www. casacipriano.com. Good-value village hotel, with fourteen en-suite rooms. They can also arrange hiking and 4WD expeditions, while the dining room is open for all meals daily, and serves good pizzas. €€

Covadonga

Cave Free • Museum Charge • http://santuariodecovadonga.com

The pilgrimage site of **COVADONGA**, high in the northern Picos, is renowned as the place where the **Reconquest of Spain** began. Squeezed between enormously steep slopes, it's a stupendous spot, centring on a cave set into a high cliff face, from immediately below which a powerful waterfall spurts forth. It lies 5km up a spur road that parallels the Río Reinazo south into the mountains, 4km east of Cangas de Onís.

According to Christian chronicles, the Visigothic King Pelayo and a group of 31 followers repelled a 400,000-strong Moorish army here in 718. While the reality was slightly less dramatic, the Moors being little more than a weary and isolated expeditionary force, the symbolism of the event lies at the heart of Asturian, and

Spanish, national history, and the defeat allowed the Visigoths to regroup, slowly expanding Christian influence over the northern mountains of Spain and Portugal.

Despite being overwhelmed with tourists in summer, Covadonga remains a serious religious shrine. There's no village, just a cluster of buildings dominated by a grandiose nineteenth-century pink-granite **basilica** that's more impressive from the outside than in. Alongside, the **Museo de Covadonga** displays assorted paintings and engravings.

A short walk leads through cliff-face shrines to the **cave** itself. Daily Mass is celebrated in the stone chapel at the far end, next to Pelayo's sarcophagus.

ACCOMMODATION COVADONGA

Gran Hotel Pelayo Real Sitio de Covadonga, http:// granhotelpelayo.com. This large hotel, next to the cave, is in all honesty something of an eyesore, but once you're inside the views are tremendous. The rooms are reasonably comfortable, but the wi-fi is very poor. €€€

Lago de Enol and Lago de la Ercina

Beyond Covadonga, the road climbs sharply to reach the placid **mountain lakes** of **Enol** and **La Ercina** after 12km. To no specific schedule, however, it's often closed to all private traffic in summer, at which time visitors have to catch shuttle buses, which start from Cangas de Onís and pick up passengers at successive car parks along the route up to Covadonga. Just to complicate matters further, the lakes are also liable to be completely shrouded by mist, at which times the road closes and the buses stop running.

The **Mirador de la Reina**, a short way before the lakes, gives an inspiring view of the assembled peaks. From the higher Lago de la Ercina, a good path leads east within three hours to the **Vega de Ario**, where there's a **refugio** (650 092 000, http:// refugiovegadeario.es; closed Nov–April), camping on the meadow, and unsurpassed **views** across the Cares Gorge to the highest peaks in the central Picos.

Most walkers, however, trek south from the lakes to the **Vegarredonda** *refugio* (€; 985 922 952, http://refugiovegarredonda.com). This popular route initially follows a dirt track but later becomes an actual path through a curious landscape of stunted oaks and turf. Vegarredonda, about three hours' walk, overlooks the very last patches of green on the Asturias side of the Cornión massif. From here the path continues west for another hour up to an overlook, the **Mirador de Ordiales**.

Cangas de Onís

The busy market town of **CANGAS DE ONÍS** stands at the junction of the main routes between the Picos and central Asturias. The surrounding peaks provide a magnificent if distant backdrop to its big sight – the so-called **Puente Romano** (Roman Bridge), splashed across many a tourist brochure. In truth this high-arched bridge, with its cross dangling beneath, has been rebuilt many times, but it's a fine spectacle nonetheless.

As an early residence of the fugitive Asturian-Visigothic kings, Cangas lays claim to the title of "First Capital of Christian Spain". Today, however, it belies such history; only a small area of town, well east of the river, retains its medieval architecture. Instead it's a somewhat scruffy, workaday place, specializing in activity tourism, that's nonetheless ideal for a comfortable night, a drink in a nice bar, and a solid meal after a spell in the mountains. It also abounds in stores selling souvenir packages of delicious local drinks and food products, including cabrales cheese, cured meats, cider and multicoloured *fabadas* (beans).

Capilla de Santa Cruz

Free

The curious little **Capilla de Santa Cruz** is a fifteenth-century rebuilding of an eighth-century chapel that counts as one of the earliest Christian sites in Spain. It was founded over a Celtic dolmen, now visible through an opening in the floor. To get there from the bridge, take the first left off the main road eastwards, the Avenida de Covadonga, and cross Río Güeña.

ARRIVAL AND INFORMATION   CANGAS DE ONÍS

By bus Alsa buses (http://alsa.es) stop in the centre of Cangas.

Destinations Arenas de Cabrales (5 daily; 35min); Covadonga (hourly; 15min); Llanes (1 daily in Aug; 50min); Oviedo (hourly; 1hr 20min); Posada de Valdeón (2 daily in summer; 1hr 40min); Ribadesella (1 daily; 30min).

Turismo Avda. de Covadonga 21, immediately east of the bridge (July to mid-Sept daily 9am–9pm; mid-Sept to June Tues–Sat 10am–2pm & 4–7pm, Sun 11am–1.30pm; 985 848 005, https://turismocangasdeonis.com).

National Park office Casa Dago, Avda. de Covadonga 43 (Easter, summer and national holidays daily 10am–6pm; 985 848 614, https://parquenacionalpicoseuropa.es).

Tours The many activity operators in Cangas (see page 486) can arrange tours and adventures of all kinds. Jaire Aventura, El Merediz (985 841 464, http://jairecanoas.com) offers guided hikes along Cares Gorge, plus a shuttle service that drops hikers off at Caín and picks them up in Poncebos after the gorge hike.

ACCOMMODATION

Hotel Los Lagos Nature Pza. Camile Beceña 3, http://loslagosnature.com. Smart, well-maintained hotel behind the town hall in the heart of Cangas, where the bright, large rooms are a little anonymous but have good bathrooms. €€€

Hotel Nochendi Constantino González 4, https://www.hotelnochendi.com. Just off the main road in the middle of Cangas, overlooking a stream, this modern hotel offers crisp, neat rooms with stylish bathrooms, and a decent restaurant. €€

★ **Hotel Puente Romano** Puente Romano 8, http://hotelpuenteromanocangas.com. Ochre-coloured villa, with 27 sizeable, comfortable, good-value rooms and very friendly management, in a convenient location just short of the bridge on the west bank of the river. €€

Parador de Cangas de Onís Villanueva, Cangas de Onís, http://parador.es. Plush, spacious parador, in a verdant setting in the sumptuously restored monastery of La Vega, 2km north of town towards Arriondas. €€€€

Pensión Covadonga Avda. de Castilla 38, http://hotel-covadonga.com. Simple but welcoming hotel, a 5min walk south of the centre, offering plain rooms with river views. €€

EATING AND DRINKING

El Polesu C/Ángel Tarano 3, https://llagarelpolesu.es. The pick of several classic sidrerías in this small alleyway, just east of Pza. Ayuntamiento. Lots of outdoor tables (equipped with nifty cider-pouring devices), and a great range of snacks, like patatas con cabrales or stuffed squid. €

★ **La Sifonería** C/San Pelayo 28, http://lasifoneria.net. Small sidrería and tapas bar, kitted out with a great collection of antique soda siphons, not far south of Avda. de Covadonga. With its attractive tiled decor and hearty mountain food, it's always packed with locals; be sure to try a delicious sartén, a single-pan melange of, for example, ham, eggs and potatoes. The same owners run a fully fledged restaurant two doors away, A La Sombra d'Un Sifón. €€

The Asturian coast: Llanes to Lastres

The wild and rugged coast of eastern Asturias runs parallel to the **Picos de Europa**, which towers just 20km inland. The **narrow-gauge line** hugs the shoreline as far as **Ribadesella**, an attractive little fishing port, before turning inland towards Oviedo. Beyond Ribadesella, towards Gijón, there are fewer appealing towns, though the fishing village of **Lastres** makes a pretty stop.

Llanes

Asturias's easternmost resort, **LLANES**, is a delightful seaside town, crammed between the foothills of the Picos and a particularly majestic stretch of the coast. To both east and west stretch sheer cliffs, little-known beaches and a series of beautiful coves, yours for the walking.

In the centre of town, a tidal stream lined with cafés and seafood restaurants runs down into a small harbour. In the **old town** itself, a tangle of lanes twists around a small hill to the west, while tall medieval walls shelter impressive buildings in various stages of decay. Among them are the **Torre Medieval**; the semi-ruined and overgrown Renaissance palaces of the **Duques de Estrada** and the **Casa del Cercau** (both closed to the public); and the **Basílica de Santa María**, built in the plain Gothic style imported from southern France.

The three town beaches are small but pleasant and very central. Immediately beyond the western beach, the little **Playa del Sablón**, steps climb to the top of a dramatic die-straight cliff, where a long *rambla*, the **Paseo de San Pedro**, offers a superb walk with wonderful views. In the opposite direction from town, the excellent **Playa Ballota** lies 3km to the east, with its own supply of spring water down on the sand (and a nudist stretch).

ARRIVAL AND INFORMATION

LLANES

By train Llanes' narrow-gauge railway station is a short walk southwest of the centre.

Destinations Oviedo (2 daily; 2hr 40min); Ribadesella (2 daily; 40min); Santander (2 daily; 2hr 30min).

By bus The bus terminal is at the bottom end of C/Pidal, not far southeast of the stream.

Destinations Gijón (3 daily; 1hr 40min); Ribadesella

(hourly; 30min); San Vicente (6 daily; 30min).

Turismo C/Marqués de Canillejas 1, in the former fish market, an attractive Art Deco structure on the east side of the port (July to mid-Sept daily 10am–2pm & 4.30–7.30pm; mid-Sept to June Mon–Sat 10am–2pm & 4–6.30pm, Sun 10am–2pm; 985 400 164, http://llanes.es).

ACCOMMODATION

Camping La Paz Playa de Vidiago, http://campinglapaz.com. Wonderful ocean-view campsite, located on a dramatic headland overlooking a lovely, undeveloped sandy beach, 5km east of Llanes and a 10min walk from Vidiago station. €

El Habana Hotel de Campo La Pereda s/n, Llanes, 985 402 526, http://elhabana.net. Large, very welcoming country-house hotel in a peaceful little village 3km inland from Llanes, set against the foothills of the Picos. Spacious and nicely furnished rooms, plus a pool and a dining room

for guests only. Closed Oct–April. €€€€

Hotel Sablón C/La Moria 1, http://hotelsablon.com. Long-established hotel in an irresistible location, perched on the bluff just above the Playa del Sablón, a minute's walk west of the old town. Most, but not quite all, of the spacious tiled-floor rooms have large sea-view windows. €€

Posada del Rey C/Mayor 11, http://laposadadelrey.es. This attractive little hotel, in a lively and thus potentially noisy lane in the heart of old Llanes, offers comfortable, pleasantly furnished en-suite rooms. €€

EATING AND DRINKING

El Almacén C/Posada Herrera s/n, 985 403 007. Cosy *sidrería*, tucked away in a very quiet spot just inside the

ASTURIAN FOOD AND DRINK

Asturian food is not for the faint-hearted, and, traditionally, not for vegetarians. The signature dish is **fabada**, a dense haricot-bean stew floating with pungent chunks of meat: black pudding, chorizo and ham. It's served in a round terracotta dish, from which you mop up the juice with a hunk of bread. **Seafood** is another feature, from sea urchins – particularly popular in Gijón – to sea bream and squid.

The region is also renowned for producing a huge range of **handmade cheeses**, most notably the pungent, blue-veined and totally delicious cabrales, which, in its purest form, is made with cow, sheep, and goat's milk combined. Another variety is a small cone-shaped cheese known as *afuega'l pitu*, which sometimes has a wrinkled exterior as a result of being hung in cloth.

Everywhere you go, you'll see waiters pouring **sidra** (cider) – which you can only order by the bottle – from above their heads into wide-rimmed glasses. It's considered rude to refill your own glass; you're supposed to allow the waiter to top you up, then knock back the frothing brew in one go. As it's a point of honour for the waiters to stare straight ahead rather than look at the glasses, and any residue that you haven't drunk within a minute or two is summarily discarded on the floor, the entire region tends to reek of stale cider.

walls near the Torre Medieval, with outdoor tables and a wide selection of tapas and small plates, including all sorts of mushrooms and bottles of wine. €

★ **El Bodegón** Pza. de Siete Puertas, 985 400 185. This characterful old-style tavern, spilling out onto benches in a pretty tree-shaded square just up from the harbour, is good for *sidra* and Asturian *raciones* and seafood specialities. €€

Confitería Vega C/Mercaderes 10, http://confiteria vegallanes.com. This old-fashioned bakery and cake shop is a great place for takeaway goodies. €

Ribadesella

The unaffected old port of **RIBADESELLA**, 18km west of Llanes, at the mouth of the Sella river, is linked by a bridge to a sedate resort area that faces one of the finest **beaches** in Asturias. The attractive **old town**, crammed against the hillside to the east, consists of successive, long stone alleyways, running parallel to the **fishing harbour** and bursting with great little bars and *comedores*.

Across the bridge to the west, ten minutes' walk from the old town, the excellent town beach, **Playa Santa Marina**, is lined with impressive nineteenth-century mansions built by returning emigrants who'd prospered in the Americas. The seafront itself is a pleasant pedestrian promenade.

Cueva Tito Bustillo

Charge for cave and museum, both free Wed • http://centrotitobustillo.com

Sealed by a landslide around 12,000 years ago, and only rediscovered in the late 1960s, the **Cueva Tito Bustillo** on the west side of the river is adorned with a remarkable collection of **prehistoric paintings**, created between 25,000 BC and 10,000 BC. Best known for its vivid depictions of horses, it's also a natural wonder, with mighty stalactites hanging from the ceiling, and was declared a World Heritage Site in 2008.

The cave is a short walk from the old town – turn left along the riverbank from the west end of the bridge. Tickets are sold in a modern **museum** a couple of minutes' further walk from the cave entrance, but you can only see the cave itself on guided tours, restricted to 150 visitors per day. **Reserve** far in advance, by phone or online, or, barring last-minute no-shows, you're unlikely to get inside, and will have to settle for the museum's excellent displays on ancient art.

If you are lucky enough to join a cave tour, the experience is more akin to entering a long tunnel than a cave, particularly since the current entrance is a man-made passageway. There's no elevation change, you simply penetrate for around half a mile into the hillside to reach the main chamber. A quick-fire Spanish guide points out the intricacies of the paintings, many of which are superimposed one atop the other and thus hard for the uninitiated to decipher.

ARRIVAL AND INFORMATION

By train Ribadesella's narrow-gauge railway station is a stiff climb up from the old town on C/Santander.
Destinations Llanes (2 daily; 40min); Oviedo (2 daily; 3hr); Santander (2 daily; 3hr).
By bus The bus station is near the tourist office, at the east end of the bridge.

Turismo In the old town, on Paseo Princesa Letizia at the east end of the bridge (July & Aug daily 10am–2pm & 4–7pm; Sept–June Tues–Sat 10am–2pm & 4–6pm, Sun 11am–2pm; 985 860 038, http://ribadesella.es).

ACCOMMODATION

Camping Ribadesella C/Sebreño, http://camping-ribadesella.com. Ribadesella's best campsite is several hundred metres from the sea, just south of the main road 2.5km west of the centre, beyond the west end of the beach, but has a great outdoor pool and a covered indoor one. Rental bungalows are available in high season only. Camping €, bungalows €€

Hotel Ribadesella Playa C/Ricardo Cangas 3, http://hotelribadesellaplaya.com. While it may not be the most spectacular of the beachside villas, this affordable option offers pleasant rooms – many with great sea views – for reasonable rates, which include an excellent buffet breakfast. The old town is within easy walking distance. €€€

★ **Hotel Villa Rosario** C/Dionisio Ruizsánchez 6,

http://hotelvillarosario.com. A gingerbread confection of pyramidal turrets and enamelled chrome tiles, this grand seafront mansion includes a wooden-decked terrace and a covered beach-view restaurant. The lovely light rooms in the villa proper, known as "El Palacete", are slightly less luxurious, but preferable to the more expensive alternatives in the modern extension alongside, *Villa Rosario II*. €€€€

Pensión Arbidel C/Oscura 1, http://arbidelpension.com.

Inexpensive, cheerful little option, back from the sea at the south end of the old town, offering pleasant en-suite rooms. €€

Puente del Pilar C/Puente del Pilar, 985 860 446. The best-value hotel west of the river, set 200m back from the sea beside a muddy stream, 1km west of the bridge. Sixteen very tasteful rooms, peaceful gardens, and a restaurant serving traditional Asturian food. €€

EATING AND DRINKING

Sidrería La Marina C/Manuel Caso de la Villa, 985 861 219. Big, buzzy place, facing the port on a busy road and offering anything from full meals to steaks and tasty snacks. €

Sidrería El Tarteru C/Marqueses de Argüelles 5, 985 857 639, http://sidreriaeltarteru.blogspot.com. Welcoming cider-house restaurant, across from the fish market as the main road curves around the waterfront, where the servings are so huge that a *ración* of local specialities like *cachopo* (veal cutlets with ham and cheese) or squid comfortably feeds two people. €

Lastres

LASTRES, off the Santander–Gijón highway 25km west of Ribadesella, below larger **Colunga**, is a tiny fishing village built dramatically on a steep and very verdant cliffside. Day-trippers huff and puff their way down its precipitous pedestrian lanes to the modern harbour, but it's a nice enough place to consider spending a night or two, with the bonus of a couple of good beaches on its outskirts.

ACCOMMODATION AND EATING   LASTRES

Casa Eutimio C/San Antonio s/n, http://casaeutimio.com. Very nice en-suite rooms, comfortably furnished in warm colours, in a great location above the port. Good seafood restaurant, serving all meals daily. €€

Costa Verde Playa de la Griega, Colunga, https://camping costaverde.es. Large, well-maintained campsite, with grassy pitches set close to an excellent beach, 2km east of Llastres. Closed Oct to mid-May. €

Gijón

With 275,000 inhabitants, the port of **GIJÓN** (Xixón) is the largest city in Asturias. Despite its industrial reputation, it remains largely surrounded by open green countryside, and it's a genuinely enjoyable place to visit, with its dynamic old core flanked by huge curving **beaches** to either side. Much of the city had to be rebuilt after suffering intensive bombardment during the Civil War; when miners armed with sticks of dynamite stormed the barracks of the Nationalist-declared army, the beleaguered colonel asked ships from his own side, anchored offshore, to bomb his men rather than let them be captured.

Gijón fans back along the coast in both directions from the stark rocky headland known as **Cimadevilla**, with the modern marina of the pretty **Puerto Deportivo** to the west (and the commercial port out of sight beyond that), and the town beach to the east. War damage has left little to see on Cimadevilla itself, though high up at the tip of the promontory a grassy park enjoys great views of the Cantabrian Sea, framed by Eduardo Chillida's sculpture *Elogio del Horizonte* (Eulogy to the Horizon). The epicentre of today's city lies at the narrow "neck" of the peninsula, immediately south of Cimadevilla. On its western side, the **Pza. del Marqués** holds a statue of Pelayo, the eighth-century king who began the Reconquest.

In the second week of July, Gijón hosts the **Semana Negra** arts festival (http://semananegra.org) in tents set up in an old shipyard in the Natahoyo neighbourhood, which incorporates readings and recitals, art displays and concerts, and involves plentiful partying too.

Museo Casa Natal de Jovellanos

Pza. de Jovellanos • Free • http://museos.gijon.es

While few non-Spanish visitors may be familiar with the politician and writer Gaspar Melchor de Jovellanos (1744–1811), it's well worth dropping into the spacious and very central house where he was born, which has been turned into a museum. As well as exhibits on the man himself, the **Museo Casa Natal de Jovellanos** holds an enjoyable collection of Asturian art and photography, including a fascinating self-portrait by the stylish Julia Alcayde (1885–1939), and, upstairs, the glossy hardwood sculptures of José María Navascués (1934–79), in which human figures blend into machines.

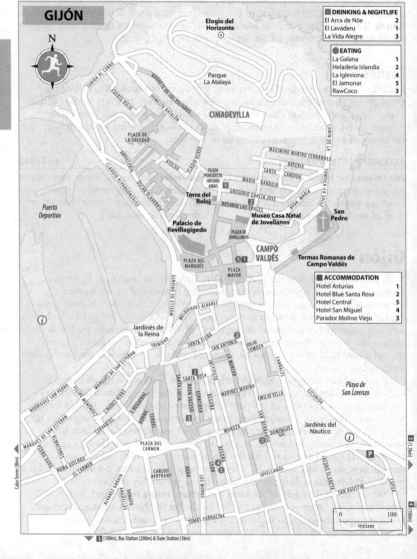

GIJÓN

DRINKING & NIGHTLIFE
El Arca de Nöe	2
El Lavaderu	1
La Vida Alegre	3

EATING
La Galana	1
Heladería Islandia	2
La Iglesiona	4
El Jamonar	5
RawCoco	3

ACCOMMODATION
Hotel Asturias	1
Hotel Blue Santa Rosa	2
Hotel Central	5
Hotel San Miguel	4
Parador Molino Viejo	3

Palacio de Revillagigedo

Pza. del Marqués 2 • Free • 985 346 921

Dominating the seafront Pza. del Marqués, the **Palacio de Revillagigedo** is a splendid mix of neo-Baroque and neo-Renaissance styles, with a light modern interior that's every bit as striking as the eighteenth-century facade. It's regularly used for temporary exhibitions, as well as concerts and performances.

Termas Romanas de Campo Valdés

Charge • http://museos.gijon.es

An inconspicuous entrance from the seafront promenade immediately north of San Lorenzo beach, on the east side of the peninsula, leads to the remarkable **Termas Romanas** (Roman Baths) of ancient Gigia. Uncovered during an aborted attempt to build an underground car park, they lie beneath an open park in front of the San Pedro church. A subterranean museum displays their history and use, while walkways allow you to crisscross the actual ruins.

7

Playa de San Lorenzo

The sands of **Playa de San Lorenzo**, a lengthy golden beach reminiscent of the one at San Sebastián, curve 2km westwards from Campo Valdés. On summer afternoons and weekends, the whole city seems to descend here, while it's the focus of the evening *paseo* all year round, and even on the gloomiest winter day some hardy surfer is usually braving the waves. At the far eastern end of the beach, the tranquil Parque Isabel La Católica stretches back along the east bank of the Río Piles.

The one snag with San Lorenzo is that the strand dwindles to almost nothing at high tide. That's not a problem at the extensive beaches immediately west of central Gijón, such as **Playa de Poniente**.

Parque Arqueológico-Natural Campa Torres

Charge • http://museos.gijon.es

For a dramatic coastal panorama, and insights into Gijón's origins, follow the shoreline 8km northwest of the centre to the **Cabo Torres** headland. At road's end, just past a large chemical plant, you can't yet see what lies over the brow of the next hill. A museum explains what's in store; this ancient site was occupied by Iron Age metalworkers during the eighth century BC, and later by a Roman settlement.

A delightful trail then leads into the **Parque Arqueológico-Natural Campa Torres**, where various ancient sites have been excavated and in some instances reconstructed. The magnificent views extend over the modern port below, and far beyond Gijón to verdant fields and tiny villages tucked into exquisite coves.

ARRIVAL AND INFORMATION | GIJÓN

By train All trains, including local and long-distance RENFE services as well as those on the narrow-gauge line formerly known as FEVE – on which passengers using coastal services both east and west have to change at El Berrón, 20km south – use the Estación de Sanz Crespo on C/Sanz Crespo, 1.2km southeast of the centre.

Destinations León (5 daily; 1hr 40min); Madrid (4 daily; 4hr); Oviedo (hourly; 30min).

By bus The wonderful Art Deco bus station (http://alsa. es) is just south of the narrow-gauge station, between C/ Ribadesella and C/Llanes.

Destinations Avilés (every 30min; 30min); Oviedo (every 15min; 30min–1hr).

Turismo Gijón's *turismo* is on a broad jetty in the middle of the marina, off Pza. Fermín García (mid-May to Oct daily 10am–8pm; Aug 10am–9pm; Nov to mid-May 10am–2.30pm & 4.30–7.30pm; 985 341 771, www.gijon.info). There's a summer-only office alongside the Playa de San Lorenzo (May to mid-July & Sept daily 10am–2pm & 4–8pm; mid-July to Aug daily 10am–9pm). Both sell the Gijón Card, which gives free admission to the city's museums, free use of public transport, and many other discounts.

ACCOMMODATION

SEE MAP PAGE 498

Hotel Asturias Pza. Mayor 11, http://hotelasturiasgijon. es. Friendly if pricey hotel, in a great location on the attractive main square between the beach and port, with a choice between "modern" and "classic" rooms. €€

Hotel Blue Santa Rosa C/Santa Rosa 4, http://blue hoteles.es. Modern hotel in a very central location near the old town, which rather extraordinarily manages to have its own underground car park, as well as a little café – rates include breakfast – and street-level terrace. The bedrooms are small, but they're dazzlingly bright and clean, with a/c and blue linens; some have galleried windows. €€€

Hotel Central Pza. del Humedal 4, http://hotel centralasturias.com. Comfortable and well-maintained little hotel, handily poised between the bus and train stations ten minutes' walk from the old town, and offering smart but simple rooms. €€

Hotel San Miguel C/Marqués de Casa Valdés 8, http:// hsanmiguel.com. Small, friendly hotel, in an unremarkable building one block inland from San Lorenzo beach and a short walk from the old town, where the bright wood-panelled rooms resemble freshly decorated spare bedrooms. €€

Parador Molino Viejo Parque de Isabel La Católica, http://parador.es. The usual luxurious standard of parador accommodation, set in a converted water mill in an attractive park, 500m inland from the east end of San Lorenzo beach. €€€€

EATING

SEE MAP PAGE 498

The streets along and immediately behind the seafront contain a mass of **café-restaurants**, all reasonably priced and most offering a set menu. If in doubt, head to any of the *sidrerías* around Pza. Mayor.

La Galana Pza. Mayor 10, http://restauranteasturiano lagalana.es. This great big bar-restaurant on the central square is Gijón's best-known rendezvous for cider and food, from snacks to full meals. Packed out every night, it's very friendly and welcoming, with tapas, *raciones*, a substantial set dinner menu and a big selection of *cazuelina* stews. €€

Heladería Islandia C/San Antonio 4, 985 350 747. Inventive ice-cream café offering (among other flavours) *sidra*, *fabada* and cabrales cheese. €

La Iglesiona C/Begoña 34, 985 171 417. This place, among the larger of the enticing tapas bars that line "La Ruta", has a fine array of hams hanging from the ceiling, and a few outdoor tables on the pedestrian C/Espaciosa around the back. Order a glass of wine and you'll be given some free snacks. You can buy a sizeable, great-value *racion* of local sausage, chorizo or other meat, and plates of melt-in-your mouth *jamón iberico*. €

El Jamonar C/Begoña 38, https://eljamonar.es. Atmospheric old-school tapas bar, which despite its ham-oriented name serves *raciones* of all kinds, including all the classic seafood options – mussels, squid and octopus, available in half portions – plus cod with various sauces. €

RawCoco C/San Bernardo 36, http://rawcoco.es. A healthy counterpoint to Gijón's prevailing cider-and-fried-food ethos, this bright, friendly juice bar serves wonderful smoothies, plus wholesome breakfasts and wraps, sandwiches and salads, not necessarily vegetarian. €

DRINKING AND NIGHTLIFE

SEE MAP PAGE 498

At the weekend, a lively **nightlife** scene kicks off around the area known as **La Ruta**, a grid enclosed by C/Santa Lucía, C/Buen Suceso and C/Santa Rosa, just east of Pza. del Carmen. Revellers also head to Cimadevilla, whose bars are crammed in summer, and to C/Rufo Rendueles and its extensions along the beach. **Clubbing** is focused around **El Náutico** farther north, and along the streets nearby, especially lively C/Jacobo Olañeta and C/San Agustín.

El Arca de Nöe C/Esculto Sebastián Miranda 1, 985 351 437. When you've had your fill of raucous *sidrerías*, get a cool taste of Montmartre at this arty jazz bar, with its open shuttered windows and fine wines; there's no food, though.

El Lavaderu Pza. Periodista Arturo Arias 1, http:// sidreriaellavaderugijon.com.es. On summer evenings, youthful crowds – and copious quantities of cider – spill out from this charming old-fashioned bar, just up from the port, to fill the wide square outside, which as well as large tables holds a broad staircase ideal for soaking up the sun. Come at a quieter moment, and it's a great spot for an outdoor meal, with all the usual *raciones* and a daily menu.

La Vida Alegre C/Buen Suceso 8, 984 068 218. The most laidback bar on La Ruta, with fairy lights and exposed brick walls and a cool mambo soundtrack.

Avilés

Determined to consign its gritty industrial reputation to the past, the city of **AVILÉS**, 23km west of Gijón, has invested heavily in cleaning up its act. While its arcaded **old town** is looking spruce, though, the futuristic **Centro Niemeyer**, immediately across the Ría de Avilés from the centre, is an architectural showpiece that is struggling to survive.

The old town

As well as abounding in shops, bars and places to stay, Avilés' likeable **old town** holds the pretty, walled **Parque de Ferrera**, and is strewn with fourteenth- and fifteenth-century churches and palaces. Churches worth a closer look include the Romanesque **San Nicolás de Bari**, on C/San Francisco, and the thirteenth-century **Santo Tomás. La Iglesia de los Padres Franciscanos** contains the tomb of Don Pedro Menéndez de Avilés, the first governor of Spanish Florida, who founded the first European city in what is now the United States, St Augustine, in 1565.

The finest of the palaces are the Baroque **Camposagrado**, in Pza. Camposagrado, built in 1663 and now serving as an art school, and the seventeenth-century **Palacio de Marqués de Ferrera** in Pza. de España, these days an expensive hotel. Look out for the seventeenth-century **Fuente de los Caños** around the corner on C/San Francisco, with its six grotesque heads spouting water.

Centro Niemeyer

Charge • https://www.centroniemeyer.es

Great hopes for Avilés' twenty-first-century regeneration were pinned on the **Centro Niemeyer**, a multipurpose cultural complex constructed on a former industrial site directly across the river from the old town. Designed by the late Brazilian architect Oscar Niemeyer, it opened on his 103rd birthday in 2010. Consisting of three stark geometric buildings – a dome, a tower encircled by a spiral staircase, and a long sinuous S-curve – set atop an enormous dazzling-white platform that's ideal for public events, it was intended as a year-round venue for performances and exhibitions. As it's turned out, though, the open-air platform stages occasional events, and the temporary exhibitions open up only in summer, so the Centro looks like it's becoming one of the most embarrassing white elephants in a land of pallid pachyderms.

ARRIVAL AND INFORMATION   **AVILÉS**

By plane Asturias airport, 14km west of Avilés, has all the usual car-rental outlets, and is connected to the city by express buses (http://alsa.es).

By train Mainline and narrow-gauge RENFE trains share a station on Avda. Telares, a short walk north of the old town, across Parque Muelle.

By bus The bus terminus is alongside the train station on Avda. Telares.

Turismo C/Ruiz Gómez 21, off Pza. de España (July to mid-Sept daily 10am–7pm; mid-Sept to June Mon–Fri 10am–2pm & 4.30–6.30pm, Sat & Sun 10.30am–2.30pm; 985 544 325, http://avilescomarca.info).

CARNAVAL IN ASTURIAS

Carnaval, the Mardi Gras week of drinking, dancing and excess, usually takes place over late February and early March. Spanish celebrations are reckoned to be at their wildest in Tenerife, Cádiz and Asturias – and, in particular, **Avilés**. Events begin in Avilés on the **Saturday before Ash Wednesday**, when virtually the entire city dons fancy dress and takes to the streets. Many costumes are veritable works of art, ranging from toothbrushes to mattresses and packets of sweets. By nightfall, anyone lacking a costume is liable to be drenched in some form of liquid. The festivities, which include live music and fireworks competitions, last till dawn.

The celebrations continue throughout Asturias over the following week. Sunday is a rest day before *Carnaval* continues in **Gijón** on the **Monday** night. On **Tuesday** night, the scene shifts to **Oviedo**, where the crowds tend to be smaller and the events less frantic. Finally, on the **Friday after Ash Wednesday**, **Mieres**, a mining town just southeast of Oviedo, plays host to celebrations in an area known as C/Vicio. Be aware that it's virtually impossible to find accommodation across the region during this time.

ACCOMMODATION

Casa del Puente Azud C/Acero 5, http://hostal puenteazud.com. In truth, the small en-suite rooms of this simple *pensión*, 500m southeast of the centre, are no more exciting than its drab blue exterior, but the rates are unbeatable. €€

Hotel Alda Palacio Valdes C/Ponte Llano 4, http://hotel palaciovaldes.com. Pleasant, good-value hotel, alongside the old town facing the bridge to the Centro Niemeyer, and offering tasteful modern bedrooms, some with turquoise balconies. €€

Hotel La Serrana C/Fruta 9, http://hotel40nudos.com. Comfortable and stylish modern hotel, on a pedestrian street in the heart of town, where the well-equipped rooms have excellent bathrooms. €€

Palacio de Avilés Pza. de España 9, https://www.palacio deaviles.com. Smart, central hotel, housed in a grand seventeenth-century mansion, that's the most luxurious option in town, with spacious modernized rooms. €€

EATING AND DRINKING

Casa Alvarin C/las Alas 2, http://casaalvarin.com. Good old-fashioned restaurant, tucked down an alleyway just off the main square, and serving a full range of hearty *raciones*, from beans with clams to octopus or juicy ham, plus set dinner menus. €€

★ **Casa Tataguyo** Pza. Carbayedo 6, http://tataguyo. com. This very charming 1840s *mesón*, one of several on the same square, is the oldest in town. Hearty traditional cuisine, with clam and cod dishes a speciality. €€

Oviedo

As the Asturian capital, **OVIEDO** has long been relatively wealthy, and its bourgeois culture contrasts sharply with the working-class ethos of the region's other cities. Its history can be traced through the grand, lovingly restored administrative and religious buildings that render it among the most attractive cities in northern Spain.

Enclosed by scattered sections of the medieval town walls, and centring on the Catedral, a compact, attractive quarter preserves the remains of **Old Oviedo**. All the better for being largely pedestrianized, it's a knot of squares and narrow streets built in warm yellow stone, while the newer part is redeemed by the huge public park in its centre. Excellent bars and restaurants, many aimed at the lively student population, pepper the entire city.

Three small **churches** in Oviedo, built in a style unique to Asturias, rank among the most remarkable in Spain. All date from the first half of the ninth century, a period of almost total isolation for the Asturian kingdom, which then extended just 65km by 50km, and was the only part of Spain under Christian rule. Oviedo became the centre of this outpost in 810, as the base for King Alfonso II, son of the victorious Pelayo.

The Catedral

Pza. Alfonso II el Casto • Charge • http://catedraldeoviedo.com

During the ninth century, King Alfonso II built a chapel, the **Cámara Santa** (Holy Chamber), to house holy relics rescued from Toledo when it fell to the Moors. Remodelled in the twelfth century, it now forms the inner sanctuary of Oviedo's unusually uncluttered Gothic **Catedral**. With its primitive capitals, the innermost of the Cámara Santa's pair of interconnecting chapels is thought to be Alfonso's original building. The antechapel is a quiet little triumph of Spanish Romanesque; each of the six columns supporting the vault is sculpted with a pair of superbly humanized Apostles.

Built around the attractive Gothic cloister, itself built on pre-Romanesque foundations, the **Diocesan Museum** holds a high-quality collection of devotional art and artefacts.

Museo de Bellas Artes

C/Santa Ana 1 • Free • http://museobbaa.com

Oviedo's **Museo de Bellas Artes** is immediately south of the Catedral. Its original core, the eighteenth-century Palacio de Velarde, concentrates on older works, including a couple of portraits by Goya and a sombre collection of the twelve Apostles that are credited to El Greco with "an unequal intervention of his painting school". A gleaming modern extension, with an open design that also reveals vestiges of the Roman city, displays contemporary Spanish art. Pride of place goes to Picasso's *Mosquetero con Espada y Amorcillo* and Dalí's lyrical *Metamorfosis de Ángeles*, with its unusually muted palette of browns and blues, while an entire room is given over to the twentieth-century Asturian artist Aurelio Suárez.

Museo Arqueológico

C/San Vicente 3 & 5 • Free • http://museoarqueologicodeasturias.com

Oviedo's **Museo Arqueológico** occupies an impressively modern structure behind the Catedral, built around the former convent of San Vicente and affording views of otherwise inaccessible parts of the building. Its comprehensive run-through of several thousand years of Asturian history is of most interest to locals, but it does hold some beautiful ancient artefacts. Ask for a booklet of translations, as few captions are in English. The section on the region's prehistoric caves is especially interesting.

Santa María del Naranco

Exterior accessible at all times (free); interior on guided tours only (charge, ticket with San Miguel de Lillo) • https://www. santamariadelnaranco.es

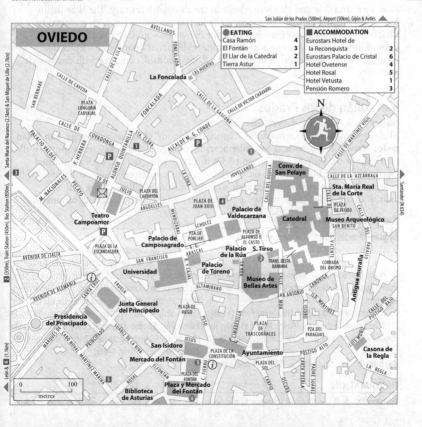

The greatest Asturian church, **Santa María del Naranco**, is set majestically amid the fields on a wooded slope 3km above the city. It's an easy signposted drive, or a 45-minute walk from the train station through the quiet suburb of Ciudad Naranco. Even if you drive, you still have to walk the final 200m to the visitor centre and ticket office along a deeply furrowed hedgerow path, so in principle this is a gloriously peaceful spot, although huge tour groups do descend upon it in summer.

The initial glimpses of the warm stone and simple bold outline, in perfect harmony with its surroundings, led Jan Morris to describe it as "formidable beyond its scale". If you think it doesn't look like a church, there's a good reason for that – it wasn't built as one. Instead it was designed as a palatial hunting lodge for Alfonso's successor, Ramiro I (842–52), and only converted into a church at the end of that century. Architecturally, the open porticoes at both ends predate later innovations in Byzantine churches, while thirty or so distinctive decorative medallions skirt the roof.

San Miguel de Lillo

Exterior accessible at all times (free); interior on guided tours only (charge, ticket with Santa María del Naranco)

King Ramiro's palace chapel, **San Miguel de Lillo**, stands a couple of hundred metres beyond Santa María. Built with soft golden sandstone and red tiles, it's generally assumed to be by the same architect – Tiodo – but its design is quite different. Less than half of the original ninth-century church remains, the rest having been swept away by a landslide and clumsily rebuilt in the thirteenth century. The altar sits in Santa María del Naranco, and much of the interior sculpture has been removed to Oviedo's Museo Arqueológico, but look for the window grilles carved from single slabs of limestone, and the superb Byzantine-style carved door frames depicting, incongruously enough, the investiture of a Roman consul, complete with circus-style festivities.

San Julián de los Prados

C/Selgas 2 • Charge • https://www.sanjuliandelosprados.com

The nearest of Oviedo's remarkable "Asturian-Visigoth" churches to the city, **San Julián de los Prados**, also known as **Santullano**, stands alongside a highway ten minutes' walk northeast of the centre. Built around 830, it is large and spacious, with an unusual "secret chamber" built into the outer wall. The original frescoes inside, still remarkably colourful, are executed in similar style to those of Roman villas – along with architectural motifs, you'll see two Latin crosses hung with the letters alpha and omega.

ARRIVAL AND DEPARTURE   OVIEDO

By plane Asturias airport, near the coast 50km northwest of Oviedo, is connected to the city by express buses (http://alsa.es).

By train The conventional and narrow-gauge train lines share a station on Avda. de Santander, 750m northwest of the centre.

Destinations Barcelona (2 daily; 9hr 20min); Ferrol (1 daily; 7hr 15min); León (6 daily; 1hr 10min); Madrid (3 daily; 3hr 30min); Ribadesella (2 daily; 2hr 30min); Santander (2 daily; 5hr).

By bus Oviedo's bus terminal (985 969 696, www.estaciondeautobusesdeoviedo.com) is a short walk northeast of the train station, on C/Pepe Cosmen.

Destinations Avilés (every 15min; 30min); Cangas de Onís (hourly; 1hr 35min); A Coruña via Betanzos (5 daily; 3hr 30min–6hr); Covadonga (3 daily; 2hr); Gijón (every 30min; 30min); León (hourly; 1hr 45min); Lugo (2 daily; 4hr 15min–5hr); Madrid (14 daily; 5–6hr); Pontevedra (up to 4 daily; 7hr); Ribadeo via Luarca (5 daily; 3hr); Ribadesella (4 daily; 1hr 10min); Santander (12 daily; 2hr 15min–3hr 45min); Santiago (4 daily; 4–6hr).

INFORMATION

Turismo Pza. de la Constitución 4 (mid-June to mid-Sept   daily 9am–7pm; mid-Sept to mid-June Mon–Fri 9am–

5.30pm, Sun 10am–5pm; 984 493 563, https://www. oviedo.es/); there's also a booth, "El Escorialín", at Marqués de Santa Cruz 1 (Mon–Fri 8am–2.30pm & 3.30–5pm, weekends 10am–2pm & 3.30–5pm; 985 227 586).

ACCOMMODATION
SEE MAP PAGE 503

Oviedo has a good supply of **accommodation**, with cheaper *hostales* concentrated along C/Uría, opposite the train station, and along C/Nueve de Mayo and its continuation, C/de Caveda.

Eurostars Hotel de la Reconquista Gil de Jaz 16, http://hoteldelareconquista.com. A very comfortable accommodation with top-notch service and a price tag to match, in a magnificent eighteenth-century building near Parque de San Francisco and the train station. €€€

Eurostars Palacio de Cristal C/Policarpo Herrero s/n, https://www.eurostarshotels.com. This gleaming architectural showpiece, 1km southwest of the old town, forms part of a complex designed by Santiago Calatrava that also includes the city's conference centre and a high-end shopping centre. While it's not the greatest of locations, prices can be quite reasonable in high season. €€

Hotel Ovetense C/San Juan 6, http://hotelovetense.com. Plain but great-value en-suite rooms, near the Catedral in the old town. The friendly management also run the lively, similarly recommended *sidrería* downstairs, which is open for breakfast. €

Hotel Rosal C/Cabo Noval 2, https://hotelrosaloviedo.es. Restored nineteenth-century building, a short walk south of the old town, offering twelve bright, sizeable en-suite rooms and with exceptionally helpful staff; the quietest rooms are on the top floor. €€

Hotel Vetusta C/Covadonga 2, http://hotelvetusta.com. Stylish modern hotel, with galleried upper storeys, on the northern edge of the old town near the cider lanes. Sixteen pleasant rooms, half of which have mini-saunas. €€

Pensión Romero C/Uría 36–38, https://hostalromero oviedo.wordpress.com. Simple hotel on the edge of the old town, 5mins' walk from the station, with very plain en-suite rooms at bargain rates. It's on a main road, so ask for a room at the back. €€

EATING
SEE MAP PAGE 503

Old Oviedo is packed with eating options, including plenty of restaurants as well as *sidrerías*, or cider-houses, most of which serve substantial meals.

Casa Ramón Pza. Daoiz y Velarde & Pza. Del Fontán, http://casaramonoviedo.com. Hugely popular with local families, this bustling, busy restaurant is open on two sides, and thus has outdoor tables on two separate old-town squares. Come to savour Asturian specialities of all kinds. €

El Fontán C/Fierro 2, 985 222 360. This café-restaurant on the upper floor of the market, with large windows overlooking the square outside but also the stalls within, makes an excellent breakfast or lunch spot, with everything from *chocolate con churros* to a substantial set menu and meat or fish mains. €

El Llar de la Catedral C/Alfonso III El Magno, 984 104 270. Top-notch restaurant in a prime setting in the cathedral square; the perfect spot for a leisurely lunch of Asturian favourites. €€

★ **Tierra Astur** C/Gascona 1, http://tierra-astur.com. At the top of "El Bulevar de la Sidra", this bustling place is the best and most salubrious *sidrería* hereabouts, with a large indoor dining room and an enclosed wooden terrace as well as its own deli. Run by the best-known local food distributor, it's unbeatable for quality and serves enormous platters of local cheeses and meats, rich Asturian cuisine and, of course, large quantities of cider. The all-day, seasonally changing set menu is superb. Live music Thurs & Fri. €€

DRINKING & NIGHTLIFE

Oviedo's most renowned area for **drinking** lies immediately north of the Catedral, just outside the pedestrian district, where lively **C/Gascona** is festooned with a large neon sign proclaiming it "El Bulevar de la Sidra". The area is known for its spit-and-sawdust *sidrerías*, or **cider bars**, and with so many similar establishments to choose from, there's no great need to recommend one above the rest. On weekend nights, the city is liable to fill up with huge crowds of teenage revellers, who commandeer many of its public spaces. If you prefer a less raucous atmosphere, head for the bars around graceful arcaded **Pza. de Fontán** near the old market.

West to Galicia

The coast west of Avilés, as far as the Río Navia, is rugged, with scarcely more than a handful of resorts carved out from the cliffs. The most appealing are pretty little **Cudillero** and the old port of **Luarca**. West again from the Río Navia, the coast becomes marshy and largely unexceptional.

Cudillero

The delightful fishing village of **CUDILLERO** is squeezed so tightly into a narrow, corkscrewing valley 25km west of Avilés that none of its buildings manage to face directly out to sea. Nonetheless, the brightly coloured arcaded houses that rise, one above the other, up the steep horseshoe of cliffs that surround the port give it the feel, and appeal, of a Greek island village, and it's usually thronged with visitors in summer.

As you climb the twisting main street away from the water, the architecture becomes grittier, but the whole town still oozes character. Climb the steep staircase that branches left just beyond the town hall, 150m up from the sea, to reach a viewpoint that perfectly frames the port, cradled in its natural amphitheatre.

Cudillero doesn't have a beach – the nearest is the lovely cove at **Playa Aguilar**, 3km east – so its most obvious attractions are the **fish tavernas** in the cobbled plaza just above the seafront. On weekday afternoons, from 3pm onwards, returning fishing boats sell their fresh catch beside the harbour.

ARRIVAL AND INFORMATION

By train The narrow-gauge station is atop the cliffs, 2km above town.
Destinations Avilés (every 3hr; 1hr), Gijón (12 daily; 1hr 50min), Oviedo (12 daily, via Pravia; 2hr), and Viveiro (1 daily; 3hr 50min).
By bus Cudillero is connected with Avilés (8 daily; 50min) and Gijón (8 daily; 1hr 30min).
By car The most direct route to the village is a hair-raising and very narrow road that twists its way down from the main road. Motorists would do better to follow the longer road that leaves the N632 a couple of kilometres further west, and approaches Cudillero along the coast; there's seafront parking, a couple of hundred metres west of the harbour.

Turismo Puero del Oeste, beside the harbour, just west of the centre (July & August daily 10am–2pm & 4–7.30pm; June & Sept daily 11am–2pm & 4–6pm; 985 591 377, http://cudillero.es); or, out of season, in the town hall on Plaza San Pedro (Oct–May Mon–Sat 10am–3pm, Sun closed).

ACCOMMODATION

Camping Cudillero C/Playa Aguilar, http://camping cudillero.com. Rural campsite, set well back from the clifftops east of town, a steep 1.4km walk above gorgeous Aguilar beach, with a snack bar and shop, plus rental bungalows and a heated pool. Cash only. Closed mid-Sept to mid-April. Camping €, bungalows €€
★ **La Casona de Pio** C/Riofrío 3, http://lacasonadepio. com. Cudillero's nicest hotel, set just back from the main seafront square. Lovely, very comfortably furnished en-suite rooms with galleried windows (though not quite sea views), room service and a good restaurant downstairs. €€€
Hotel Sol de la Blanca C/Suárez Inclán 84, http:// hotelsoldelablanca.es. Small, simple *pensión*, halfway up the hill on the main street up from the port, and offering good-value en-suite doubles. €€

EATING AND DRINKING

Los Arcos C/Fuente de Abajo 2, 985 590 086. While the restaurants that squeeze cheek by jowl into Cudillero's pretty seafront plaza look universally irresistible, the quality of the food itself varies widely. This is the most dependable option, with three separate components, including an outdoor café, a *sidrería* and a more formal upstairs dining room. €€

El Pescador C/Tolombredo de Arriba, https://www.hotel restauranteelpescador.com. This elegant seafood restaurant with terrace seating serves some spectacular caught-on-the-day fish plates, and an extensive menu featuring *fabada asturiana*, local seafood paella and the like. €€€

Luarca

Beyond Cudillero, the N632 leaps over viaducts that span deep, pine-wooded gorges. A side road dips down steeply after 50km to reach the attractive port of **LUARCA**, a mellow place that's built around an S-shaped cove surrounded by sheer cliffs. Down at sea level, the town is bisected by a winding stream, and knitted together by numerous narrow bridges.

A modest seaside resort, Luarca has defiantly retained its traditional character, including a few *chigres* – old-fashioned Asturian taverns – where you can be initiated into the art of *sidra* drinking. The town **beach** is divided in two: the nearer strip is narrow but more protected, while the broader one beyond the jetty is subject to seaweed litter.

From the *turismo*, C/de la Carril leads up to the cliffs overlooking the port, which has an unusual decorative cemetery, a hermitage chapel and a lighthouse.

ARRIVAL AND INFORMATION LUARCA

By train The narrow-gauge station is 2km east of town.

By bus The bus station, just off C/Crucero on the river, is connected with Oviedo (6 daily; 1hr 30min) and Ribadeo (6 daily; 1hr 30min).

By car Central Luarca is very short on parking; park on the perimeter as soon as you arrive.

Turismo Palacio de Gamoneda, Pza. Alfonso X (daily 10.30am–1.45pm & 4–6.45pm; 985 640 083, http://turismoluarca.com).

ACCOMMODATION AND EATING

Hotel Rico Pza. Alfonso X 6, http://hotelrico.com. Small, modern, good-value hotel in the very centre of town, where the rather minimal en-suite rooms do at least have large galleried windows. €€

Villa La Argentina Villar s/n, www.villalaargentina. com. Very comfortable rooms, in a sumptuous *belle époque* mansion with spacious formal gardens, 15min walk east of the centre in the hillside Villar district. No restaurant. €€€

Villa Blanca Avda. de Galicia 25–27, 985 641 079. Smart, formal gourmet restaurant, just up from the west bank 800m inland, with a hard-earned reputation for serving fine traditional Asturian cuisine; the emphasis, naturally, is on seafood. The weekday lunch menu is a real bargain. €€

7

Galicia

PILGRIMS WALKING ALONG THE WAY OF ST JAMES

Galicia

Passionately entangled with the Atlantic Ocean at the northwest corner of the Iberian Peninsula, Galicia feels far removed from the rest of Spain. Everywhere is green, from the high forested hills to the rolling fields, a patchwork of tiny plots still farmed by hand. Indeed, with its craggy coast and mild, wet climate, Galicia is more like Ireland than Andalucía. Its people take pride in their Celtic heritage, and cherish the survival of their language, Galego. It's hardly off the beaten track, however. Santiago de Compostela ranked during the Middle Ages as the third city of Christendom, and pilgrims have been making their way here along the Camino de Santiago for well over a thousand years.

Santiago itself remains the chief attraction for visitors. Still focused around its unspoiled medieval core, an enticing labyrinth of ancient arcades and alleyways, it should be on every itinerary. Galicia's other major selling point is its endlessly indented **shoreline**, slashed by the powerful sea into the deep narrow estuaries known here as *rías*, and framed by steep green hillsides. Sadly, a lack of planning controls has meant that much of the coast is depressingly overbuilt, albeit with dreary villas and apartments rather than high-rise hotels. With each town merging into the next, those few resorts that remain recognizable as medieval fishing villages, such as **Cambados**, **Muros** and **Baiona**, come as welcome highlights. Pretty, secluded sandy beaches do exist, but they take a bit of finding these days, and often require a drive away from the built-up areas.

Of the distinct coastal stretches, the **Rías Altas** in the north are generally wilder and emptier, while the picturesque **Rías Baixas**, closer to Portugal, are warmer and more developed, and attract many more visitors. In between the two lie the dunes and headlands of the more rugged **Costa da Morte**. Only a couple of the seafront towns have grown to become cities: the modern ports of **A Coruña**, with its elegant glass-encased balconies, and **Vigo**, perched alongside a magnificent bay. Further inland, the settlements are more spread out, and the river valleys of the Miño and the Sil remain beautifully unspoiled, while the attractive provincial capitals of **Pontevedra**, **Ourense** and **Lugo** seem little changed since the Middle Ages.

The Galegos are renowned for having **emigrated** all over the world. Between 1836 and 1960, around two million Galegos – half the total population – left the region, thanks largely to the limited availability of agricultural land. Half of them ended up in Argentina, where Buenos Aires is often called the largest city in Galicia. An untranslatable Galego word, *morriña*, describes the exiles' particular sense of homesick, nostalgic longing. That Celtic melancholy has its counterpart in the exuberant devotion to the land, its culture and its produce that you'll encounter in Galicia itself, as evinced in its music – they even play the bagpipes (or *gaita galega*) – literature and festivals. Above all, Galegos view their **food** and **wine** almost as sacraments: share in a feast of the fresh local seafood, washed down with a crisp white Albariño, and the *morriña* may get a hold on you, too.

Santiago de Compostela

The ancient pilgrimage centre of **SANTIAGO DE COMPOSTELA** ranks among the most beautiful cities in all of Spain. A superb ensemble of twisting stone lanes, majestic squares and historic churches, interspersed with countless hidden nooks and crannies,

PONTEVEDRA

Highlights

❶ Santiago de Compostela The goal of pilgrims for over a thousand years, this ravishing cathedral city is a labyrinth of ancient lanes and dramatic squares. See page 510

❷ Sunset at Fisterra Fantastic views over the Atlantic, from the very edge of the world. See page 534

❸ Pimientos de Padrón Once tasted, these randomly piquant green peppers, fried in hot oil and sprinkled with sea salt, are never forgotten. See page 537

❹ Seafood and white wine Galicia is renowned for its delicious *mariscos* and unique Ribeiro and Albariño wines. See page 539

❺ Pontevedra Pontevedra's sleepy *zona monumental* metamorphoses into a lively party zone after dark. See page 542

❻ The Illas Cíes The pristine sands of these three islets make for an irresistible day-trip. See page 548

❼ The parador at Baiona This fabulous hotel enjoys an unsurpassable setting; look for special offers on rooms. See page 549

❽ Cañón de Río Sil A truly staggering gorge, carved by the Romans into still-functioning vine-growing terraces. See page 553

HIGHLIGHTS ARE MARKED ON THE MAP ON PAGE 512

its medieval core remains a remarkably integrated whole, all the better for being very largely pedestrianized. Hewn from time-weathered granite, splashed with gold and silver lichen and sprouting vegetation from the unlikeliest crevices, the buildings and plazas, arcades and flagstones seem to blend imperceptibly one into the other. Warrens of honey-coloured streets wind their way past a succession of beautiful monasteries and convents, culminating in the approach to the immense **Pza. do Obradoiro**, flanked by the magnificent **Catedral**, the supposed resting place of the remains of St James. To enjoy an overall impression of the entire ensemble, take a walk along the promenade of the **Paseo da Ferradura**, in the spacious **Alameda** just southwest of the old quarter.

To this day, locals and visitors alike flock to Santiago for its round-the-clock vitality, making it far more than a mere antiquarian curiosity. Modern tourists are attracted as much by its food, drink and history as by religion, but pilgrims still arrive in large numbers, sporting their *vieira* (scallop shell) symbol. Each year at the **Festival of St James** on July 25, a ceremony at his shrine re-dedicates the country to the saint. Years in which the date falls on a Sunday – the next is 2027 – are designated "Holy Years", and the activity becomes even more intense.

HIGHLIGHTS

1. Santiago de Compostela
2. Sunset at Fisterra
3. Pimientos de Padrón
4. Seafood and white wine
5. Pontevedra
6. The Illas Cíes
7. The parador at Baiona
8. Cañon de Río Sil

GALICIA

GALEGO FOOD

Galegos boast that their **seafood** is the best in the world, and for quality and sheer diversity it's certainly hard to match. Local wonders to look out for include *vieiras* (the scallops whose shells became the symbol of St James), *mejillones* (the rich orange mussels from the *rías*), *cigallas* (Dublin Bay prawns, though often inadequately translated as shrimp), *anguilas* (little eels from the Río Miño), *zamburiñas* (little scallops), *xoubas* (sardines), *navajas* (razor-shell clams), *percebes* (barnacles), *nécoras* (shore crabs) and *centollas* (spider crabs). *Pulpo* (octopus) is so much a part of Galego eating that there are special *pulperías* cooking it in the traditional copper pots, and it's a mainstay of local fiestas. In the province of Pontevedra alone, Vilanova de Arousa has its own mussel festival (first Sun in Aug), Arcade has one devoted to oysters (first weekend in April) and O Grove goes all the way, with a generalized seafood fiesta. When eaten as tapas or *raciones*, seafood is not overly expensive, but be wary of items like *percebes* that are sold by weight – a small plateful can cost as much as €50. Superb **markets** can be found everywhere; the coastal towns have their rows of seafront stalls with supremely fresh fish, while cities such as Santiago hold grand arcaded market halls, piled high with produce from the surrounding countryside.

Another speciality, imported from the second Galego homeland of Argentina, is the **churrasquería** (grill house). Often unmarked and hard to find, these serve up immense *churrascos* – a term that in Galicia usually refers to huge portions of beef or pork ribs, cooked on an open grill (*parrilla*). While Galegos don't normally like their food highly spiced, *churrascos* are usually served with a devastating garlic-based *salsa picante*.

Other common dishes are *caldo galego*, a thick stew of cabbage and potatoes in a meat-based broth; *caldeirada*, a filling fish soup; *lacon con grelos*, ham boiled with turnip greens; and the ubiquitous *empanada*, a flat light-crusted pie, often filled with tuna and tomato. Should you be around during the summer months, be sure to try *pimientos de Padrón*, sweet green peppers fried in oil and sprinkled with salt, served as a kind of lucky dip with a few memorably spicy ones in each serving.

For all its fame, however, Santiago remains surprisingly small. Its population stands at around 100,000, of whom, amazingly, 40,000 are students at its venerable university. Almost everything of interest is contained within the densely packed historic core, known as the *zona monumental*, which takes fifteen minutes to cross on foot but several days to explore thoroughly. Most of the commercial activities and infrastructure lie a short distance south, in the less appealing modern quarter, which is also where the students tend to live.

Uniquely, Santiago is a city at its best in the rain; situated in the wettest fold of the Galego hills, it suffers brief but frequent showers. Water glistens on the facades, gushes from the innumerable gargoyles and flows down the streets.

The Catedral

Charge, tours available • http://catedraldesantiago.es

All roads in Santiago lead to the **Catedral**. You first appreciate its sheer grandeur upon venturing into the vast expanse of Pza. do Obradoiro. Directly ahead stands a fantastic Baroque pyramid of granite, flanked by huge bell towers and everywhere adorned with statues of St James in his pilgrim guise with staff, broad hat and scallop-shell badge. This is the famous **Obradoiro facade**, built between 1738 and 1750 in the efflorescent style known as Churrigueresque by an obscure Santiago-born architect, Fernando de Casas. No other work of Spanish Baroque can compare with what Edwin Mullins sublimely called its "hat-in-the-air exuberance".

Behind the facade, the main body of the Catedral is Romanesque, rebuilt in the eleventh and twelfth centuries after a devastating raid by the Muslim vizier of Córdoba,

FIESTAS

MARCH

1: San Rosendo Celanova's big festival, at the monastery.
Pre-Lent: *Carnavales* throughout the region.

APRIL/MAY

Semana Santa (Holy Week) Celebrations include a symbolic *descendimiento* (descent from the Cross) at Viveiro on Good Friday and a Resurrection procession at Fisterra. On Palm Sunday, there are Stations of the Cross at Monte San Tecla, near A Guarda.
Sunday after Easter: Fiesta de Angula Elver gastronomic festival at Tui.
Second Monday after Easter: Fiesta San Telmo At Tui.
Late April to early May (dates vary) Festival at Ribadavia celebrating and promoting Ribeiro wines.
May 1: *Romería* at Pontevedra marks the start of a month-long festival.

JULY

First weekend: Rapa das Bestas The capture and breaking in of wild mountain horses at Viveiro.
11: Fiesta de San Benito At Pontevedra, with river processions, and folk groups, and a smaller *romería* at Cambados.
Second weekend: Feira Franca Medieval de Betanzos Three-day fair at Betanzos, reliving the town's time under Andrade rule.
Second weekend: International Festival of the Celtic World Ortigueira hosts Galicia's most important music festival (http://festivaldeortigueira.com); pipe bands from all Celtic lands perform, alongside musicians from around the world, and every event is free.
16: Virgen del Carmen Sea processions at Muros and Corcubión.
24–25: St James (Sant Yago) Two days of celebration in many places, with processions of bigheads and *gigantones* on the 24th and spectacular parades with fireworks and bands through the following evening.
25: Santiago Galicia's major fiesta, at its height in Santiago de Compostela. The evening before, there's a fireworks display and symbolic burning of a cardboard effigy of the mosque at Córdoba. Also designated "Galicia Day", the festival has become a nationalist event, with political and cultural events for a week on either side.

AUGUST

First Sunday Albariño wine festival at Cambados (https://fiestadelalbariño.com); bagpipe festival at Ribadeo; Virgen de la Roca observances outside Baiona; pimiento festival at Padrón; *navaja* (razor shell) festival at Fisterra.
16: Fiesta de San Roque Festivals at all churches that bear his name: at Betanzos, there's a Battle of the Flowers on the river and the launching of the Fiesta del Globo.
24: Fiesta (and bullfights) at Noia.
25: Fiesta de San Ginés At Sanxenxo.

SEPTEMBER

6–10: Fiestas del Portal At Ribadavia.

OCTOBER

First two weekends: Fiesta do Marisco Seafood festival at O Grove.

NOVEMBER

Early Nov: Magosto castaña Chestnut festival at Ourense.

al-Mansur, in 977. Although, perhaps not surprisingly, he failed to find the body of the saint, he forced the citizens to carry the bells of the tower to the mosque at Córdoba – a coup that was later dramatically reversed (see page 293).

Pórtico de Gloria

The acknowledged highlight of Santiago's Catedral – indeed, one of the great triumphs of medieval art – is the **Pórtico de Gloria**, the original west front, now installed just inside the main doors, immediately behind the Obradoiro facade.

Completed in 1188 under the supervision of **Maestro Mateo**, the Pórtico represented both the culmination of all Romanesque sculpture and a precursor of the new Gothic realism, each of its host of figures being strikingly relaxed and quietly humanized. Above the side doors are representations of Purgatory and the Last Judgement, while Christ presides in glory over the main door, flanked by his Apostles, and surrounded by the 24 Elders of the Apocalypse playing celestial music.

So many millions of pilgrims have given thanks at journey's end, by praying with the fingers of one hand pressed into the roots of the Tree of Jesse below the saint, that five deep and shiny holes have been worn into the solid marble. Finally, for wisdom, they would lower their heads to touch the brow of Maestro Mateo, the humble squatting figure on the other side.

The High Altar

The spiritual climax of each pilgrimage to Santiago comes when pilgrims climb the steps that lead up behind the **High Altar** – an extraordinary gilded riot of Churrigueresque – in order to embrace the Most Sacred Image of Santiago, and kiss his bejewelled cape. The process is rounded off by confession and attending a High Mass.

The Botafumeiro

Thanks to an elaborate pulley system in front of the altar, operated by eight priests (*tiraboleiros*), the Catedral's immense "**Botafumeiro**" (incense burner) is swung in a vast thirty-metre ceiling-to-ceiling arc across the transept. Originally designed to fumigate bedraggled pilgrims, it's now used only at certain services – ask whether there's one during your visit.

The crypt

A steady procession of pilgrims also visits the bones of St James, which are kept in a **crypt** beneath the altar. Lost for a second time in 1700, after being hidden before an English invasion, these relics were rediscovered in 1879. In fact, building workers found three skeletons, which were naturally held to be St James and his two followers. The only problem, identifying which was the Apostle, was fortuitously resolved as a church in Tuscany possessed a piece of Santiago's skull that exactly fitted a gap in one of them.

The Pazo de Xelmírez and the Catedral Museum

Charge, various combination tickets including guided tours available • http://catedraldesantiago.es

The **Pazo de Xelmírez**, immediately adjoining the Catedral and entered to the left of the main stairs, holds the ticket office for Catedral tours, as well, on its lower floor, as temporary exhibits under the aegis of the Catedral museum. The *pazo* was originally the opulent palace of the twelfth-century Archbishop Xelmírez, who rebuilt the Catedral, raised the see to an archbishopric and "discovered" a ninth-century deed that gave annual dues to St James's shrine of one bushel of corn from each acre of Spain reconquered from the Moors – a decree that was repealed only in 1834.

The entrance to the **Catedral Museum** itself is on the right of the main Catedral facade. Displays on its ground floor focus especially on Maestro Mateo, with a reconstruction of the cathedral's original choir, while the second floor features artefacts from throughout its history, potentially including the Botafumeiro when it's not in use.

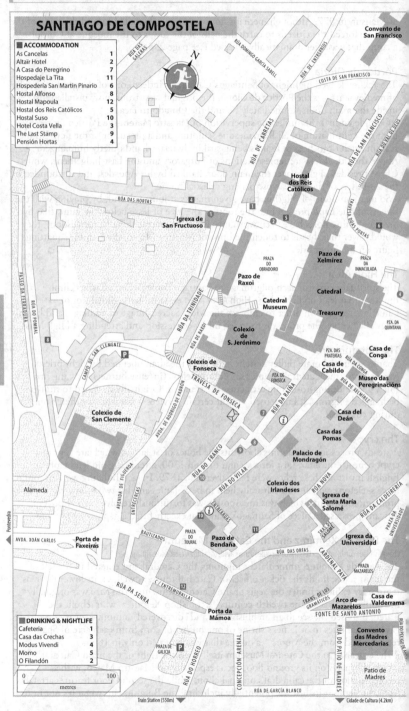

SANTIAGO DE COMPOSTELA

ACCOMMODATION

As Cancelas	1
Altaïr Hotel	2
A Casa do Peregrino	7
Hospedaje La Tita	11
Hospedería San Martín Pinario	6
Hostal Alfonso	8
Hostal Mapoula	12
Hostal dos Reis Católicos	5
Hostal Suso	10
Hotel Costa Vella	3
The Last Stamp	9
Pensión Hortas	4

DRINKING & NIGHTLIFE

Cafeteria	1
Casa das Crechas	3
Modus Vivendi	4
Momo	5
O Filandón	2

0 — 100 metres

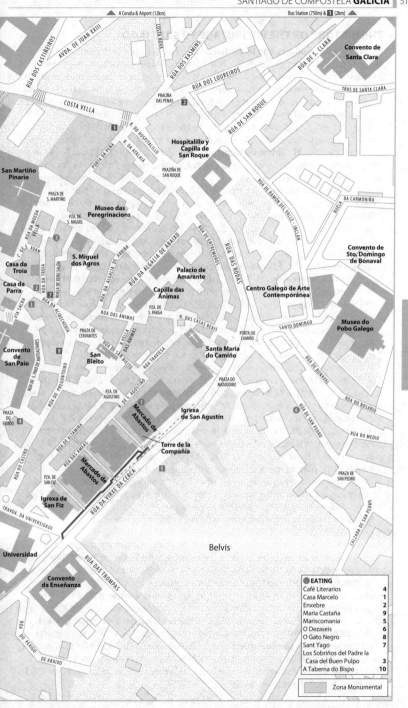

EATING

Café Literarios	4
Casa Marcelo	1
Enxebre	2
Maria Castaña	9
Mariscomania	5
O Dezaseis	6
O Gato Negro	8
Sant Yago	7
Los Sobriños del Padre la Casa del Buen Pulpo	3
A Taberna do Bispo	10

Zona Monumental

THE HISTORY OF THE PILGRIMAGE TO SANTIAGO

The great medieval **pilgrimage to Santiago** was arguably Europe's first exercise in mass tourism, an extraordinary phenomenon in an age when few people ventured beyond their own town or village. Home to the shrine of St James the Apostle (Santiago to the Spanish, Saint Jacques to the French), the city became the third holiest site in Christendom, after Jerusalem and Rome. Following in the footsteps of Godescale of Puy, who arrived in 951, half a million pilgrims turned up each year during the eleventh and twelfth centuries.

Although the shrine was visited by the great – Fernando and Isabel, Carlos V, Francis of Assisi – you didn't have to be rich to come. The roads that led here through France and northern Spain, collectively known as **El Camino de Santiago** (The Way of St James, or the Pilgrim Route), were lined with monasteries, villages and charitable hospices, and an order of knights was founded for the pilgrims' protection. There was even a guidebook, written by the French monk Aymery Picaud, who recorded such facts as the bizarre habits of the Navarrese Basques (said to expose themselves when excited, and to protect their mules from their neighbours with chastity belts).

Why did the pilgrims come? Though some, like Chaucer's Wife of Bath, were lured by social fashion, adventure, or the opportunities for marriage or even crime, it was for most a question of faith. Thanks to the miraculous power of **St James**, the journey guaranteed a remission of half their time in Purgatory. Few doubted that the tomb beneath Santiago's cathedral altar held the mortal remains of James, son of Zebedee and Salome and first cousin of Jesus Christ. It seems scarcely credible that the whole business was an immense **ecclesiastical fraud**.

Yet the legend has no apparent basis in fact. It begins with the claim that St James visited Spain after the Crucifixion, to spread the gospel. He is said, for example, to have had a vision of the Virgin in Zaragoza. He then returned to Jerusalem, where he was undoubtedly beheaded by Herod Agrippa. But the legend relates that two of James's followers removed his corpse to Jaffa, where a boat appeared, without sails or crew, and whisked them in just seven days to Padrón, 20km downstream from Santiago.

The body was then buried, lost and forgotten for 750 years, before being rediscovered at Compostela in 813. That was a time of great significance for the Spanish Church. Over the preceding century, the Moors had swept across the Iberian Peninsula, gaining control over all but the mountain kingdom of Asturias. The **discovery** of the bones of St James, beneath a buried altar on a site traditionally linked with his name, was singularly opportune. It occurred after a bishop was led to the site with the help of a local hermit, who was attracted to the hillside by visions of stars; the hill was known thereafter as Compostela, "field of stars". Alfonso II, king of Asturias, travelled along the coastline to pay his respects and built a chapel, thus establishing the **pilgrimage**, and the saint was adopted as the champion of Christian Spain against the infidel. In a historic discovery in the 1950s, a tomb thought to hold the remains of the bishop was found on the floor of the cathedral – the remains were confirmed by DNA testing in 2024, following further scientific investigation.

St James soon appeared on the battlefield. Ramiro I, Alfonso's successor, swore that James fought alongside him at the Battle of Clavijo (844), personally slaughtering sixty thousand Moors. Over the next six centuries Santiago Matamoros (Moor-killer) manifested himself at some forty battles, assisting, for example, in the massacre of the Inca armies in Peru. While that may seem an odd role for the fisherman-evangelist, it presented no problems to the Christian propagandists who portrayed him as a knight on horseback in the act of dispatching whole clutches of swarthy, bearded Arabs with a single thrust of his long sword. (With consummate irony, when Franco brought his crack Moroccan troops to Compostela to dedicate themselves to the overthrow of the Spanish Republic, all such statues were discreetly hidden under sheets.)

Only half of modern pilgrims describe their journey as prompted by religious faith. Others may be following their own **spiritual quest**, or simply keen to immerse themselves in Spanish history and culture. Whatever the motivation, its popularity has exploded in recent decades: while a mere handful of people walked to Santiago in the 1960s, the route now attracts well over 400,000 pilgrims a year, half of whom are Spanish.

Up on the third floor, it comes as a surprise to step out into the open air, in the form of the late Gothic **cloisters**, the courtyard of which offers a wonderful prospect of the riotous mixture of the exterior. Upstairs again, the tapestry rooms on the topmost floor include pieces based on Goya paintings, and open onto a long open-air gallery with similarly good views over the Pza. do Obradoiro.

Doors from both the cloisters and the cathedral itself (in which case you have to pay the museum an admission fee) lead into the **Treasury**, where the highlight is a huge carved altarpiece depicting the legend of St James.

Las Cubiertas

Charge • http://catedraldesantiago.es

Taking a guided tour of the **roof** of Santiago's Catedral, known as **Las Cubiertas**, is an experience not to be missed. The tours start from the **Pazo de Xelmírez**, and offer the only access to the vaulted twelfth-century kitchen and thirteenth-century synodal hall on the palace's higher storeys.

From there, the climb up leads through the upper floors of the Catedral interior (when no service is taking place), while the roof itself, which consists of shallow granite steps, offers superb views over the rest of the city, as well, of course, as the Catedral's own towers and embellishments. Every way you turn, it's crawling with pagodas, pawns, domes, obelisks, battlements, scallop shells and cornucopias.

Note that the standard tour features a quick-fire Spanish commentary that may well leave you floundering. To be sure of a place on an English-language tour, at no extra charge, contact them five days in advance in summer, or two days in low season.

8

Praza do Obradoiro

You could easily spend several hours exploring the squares around the Catedral. The **Praza do Obradoiro**, in front of the main facade, is Santiago's most formal and impressive public space. Its northern side is dominated by the elegant Renaissance **Hostal dos Reis Católicos** (Hostal de los Reyes Católicos). As late as the thirteenth century the Catedral was used to accommodate pilgrims, but slowly its place was taken by convents around the city. Fernando and Isabel, in gratitude for their conquest of Granada, added to these facilities by building this superb hostel for the poor and sick. Now a parador (see page 522), it's very much *the* place to stay, though particularly expensive in high season. Even if you can't afford it, stroll in to take a look at its four lovely courtyards or the chapel with magnificent Gothic stone carvings, or simply to enjoy a drink or meal.

Praza da Quintana

Just as large as the Pza. do Obradoiro, but somehow more intimate, the **Praza da Quintana** holds a flight of broad steps that join the back of the Catedral to the high walls of the **Convento de San Paio**, and serve around the clock as impromptu benches for students and backpackers. The "Porta Santa" doorway here is only opened during Holy Years (see page 512).

Praza das Praterías

The **Praza das Praterías**, the Silversmiths' Square, centres on an ornate fountain of four horses with webbed feet, and features the seventy-metre-high Berenguela, or **clock tower**. On its south side is the extraordinarily narrow **Casa del Cabildo**, which was built in 1758 to fill the remaining gap and ornamentally complete the square – you'd never know to look at it, but it's little more than a facade.

San Martiño Pinario

Pza. San Martiño • Charge • http://espacioculturalsmpinario.com

The **Pza. da Inmaculada**, on the Catedral's northern side, is dominated by the grand Baroque frontage of the Benedictine monastery of **San Martiño Pinario**. At 20,000 square metres, this ranks among the largest religious buildings in Spain. Its left flank, as you face it, is now run as a hotel, while the monastery church to the right, entered via the nearby Pza. San Martiño, holds a quite extraordinary **museum**. The church itself is filled with magnificent Baroque altarpieces, while the various chapels and rooms to the side display bejewelled treasures and sculptures. Upstairs, things take a surprising twist: the monks' natural history collection includes a grotesque stuffed sloth, sharing space with an echidna and a pangolin, and there's also an apothecary they put together to treat pilgrims.

Museo das Peregrinacións

Rúa de San Miguel and Pza. das Praterías • Free • http://mdperegrinacions.com

Santiago's superb **Museo das Peregrinacións**, which relates the story of pilgrimage not only here but also to religious shrines the world over, is housed in a large modernized building in the Pza. das Praterías. Excellent displays, spreading through several floors, trace the parallel development of the legend of St James, the Camino de Santiago, the Catedral, and the city itself. A fascinating section explores how depictions of St James himself reflect his changing image over the centuries. English translations are provided throughout and the topmost storey gives views out over the rooftops.

Museo do Pobo Galego

C/San Domingos de Bonaval • Charge • http://museodopobo.gal

In the convent of **Santo Domingo**, immediately northeast of the old quarter, the **Museo do Pobo Galego** provides a diverse overview of Galego crafts and traditions. Many aspects of the way of life depicted haven't entirely disappeared, though you're today unlikely to see *corozas*, straw suits worn into the last century by mountain shepherds. The account of the annual cycle of the seasons is interesting, and there's also a moving account of Galicia's history of emigration. Look out, too, for the unique seventeenth-century triple stairway, each spiral of which leads to different storeys of a single tower. If several of you set off up different flights, you may lose each other for hours.

The convent chapel, known as the **Panteón de Galegos Ilustres**, holds the mortal remains of such local heroes as the poet Rosalía de Castro and the essayist and caricaturist Castelao. Gardens and orchards stretch up the hillside behind, offering a wonderful spot for a break from sightseeing.

Centro Galego de Arte Contemporánea

Rúa Valle Inclan • Free • http://cgac.xunta.gal

The modern **Centro Galego de Arte Contemporánea**, opposite Santo Domingo convent, is a gloriously light and large exhibition space. It generally stages temporary shows of contemporary art and sculpture.

Cidade da Cultura

Monte Gaiás • Free • http://cidadedacultura.gal

An architectural showpiece, perched on a hillside 2km southeast of the centre – a circuitous 4km route few visitors would choose to walk – the **Cidade da Cultura** (City of Culture) was another product of Spain's economic over-exuberance. Its first sections, a museum and performance centre, opened in 2011, but plans to build other components have been abandoned, and no further exhibitions or events are scheduled.

PRACTICALITIES OF THE CAMINO DE SANTIAGO

Few modern pilgrims walk from their homes to Santiago de Compostela and back; most follow one of the half-dozen standard routes through Spain and France. The most popular, the 750-kilometre **Camino Francés**, heads westward across northern Spain from Roncesvalles (Orreaga-Roncesvalles in Basque) in the Pyrenees.

Most pilgrims stay in hostels, called **albergues** or **refugios**. Conveniently spaced at intervals ranging from 10km to 20km, these provide simple dormitory accommodation, are usually equipped with hot showers, sometimes have kitchen facilities and charge either a nominal fee of a few euros or ask for a donation. *Albergues* can get crowded in summer, so pilgrims sometimes have to sleep on mattresses on the floor. More expensive choices are often available. Pilgrims also receive special treatment at restaurants – most offer a pilgrim menu for around €10 – and meals are served earlier than the Spanish norm, at about 8pm.

To prove your pilgrim status, you'll need a **credencial** (pilgrim passport); it's best to get one in advance from your local pilgrim association (see below), although you can also pick one up at the *albergue* in Roncesvalles. You then collect *sellos* (stamps to prove your progress) from *albergues*, churches and even some cafés, and finally show your stamped *credencial* in Santiago to receive a *compostela* (certificate of pilgrimage). According to the official rules, you need only walk the final 100km, or cycle the last 200km, to be entitled to a *compostela*. If your motives are not strictly religious, apply for a *certificado* rather than a *compostela*.

It's hard to lose your way. The *camino* sticks to good tracks and minor roads, is clearly marked with yellow arrows, and generally passes through populated areas where locals can steer you in the right direction. Spring and autumn are the **best seasons**: the route is quieter than in summer, most *albergues* are open, and you'll miss the weather extremes of the *meseta* and the mountains. If you're fit and healthy, you can walk from Roncesvalles to Santiago de Compostela in about a month, covering around 25km a day. Nevertheless, allow extra time for rest days, unforeseen injuries or simply the urge to linger in the lovely towns en route.

The most useful *camino* website, offering route guides and advice, is https://www.csj.org.uk, run by the UK-based **Confraternity of St James**.

8

ARRIVAL AND DEPARTURE SANTIAGO DE COMPOSTELA

By plane Santiago's airport, 13km east of the city in Lavacolla, is connected by Ryanair with London Stansted and several Spanish cities, and by easyJet with London Gatwick. Several outlets offer car rental, but avoid Goldcar, which has very poor service. Frequent local buses (every half-hour) connect the airport with the bus and train stations, and Pza. de Galicia (Rúa Doctour Teixeiro), the closest stop to the old town.

By train The train station is a 10min walk south of the old town at Rúa de Horreo 75.

Destinations A Coruña (up to 28 daily; 30min); Burgos (2 daily; 7hr); Donostía/San Sebastian (3 daily; 10hr); León (3 daily; 5hr); Madrid (9 daily; 3hr); Ourense (14 daily; 40min); Pontevedra (18 daily; 40min); Vigo (up to 10 daily; 1hr 30min).

By bus Santiago's bus station is in an inconvenient and very urbanized location, a 10min walk northeast of the old town.

For schedules see http://monbus.es.

Destinations A Coruña (16 daily; 1hr–1hr 30min); Barcelona (daily; 15hr); Betanzos (7 daily; 1hr 30min); Camariñas (2 daily; 3hr); Cambados (3 daily; 1hr 30min); Fisterra (4 daily; 3hr); León (daily; 6hr); Lugo (9 daily; 1hr 30min–2hr); Madrid (3–6 daily; 9hr 30min); Muros (10 daily; 1hr 30min); Muxía (2 daily; 2hr); Noia (hourly; 50min); Ourense (5 daily; 2hr); Padrón (hourly; 40min); Pontevedra (hourly; 1hr); Sobrado dos Monxes (1 daily; 1hr 15min); Vigo (hourly; 1hr 30min).

By car As almost all the streets in the old quarter are pedestrianized, and very few hotels offer parking facilities, drivers have little choice but to use one of the large car parks (http://tussa.org) on the periphery. The closest to the Catedral is the huge Xóan XXIII car park, a short way north, which is also where all coach tours pull in.

INFORMATION

Turismo Rúa do Vilar 63 (May–Oct daily 9am–9pm; Nov–April daily 10am–6pm; 981 555 129, http://santiago turismo.com) in the old town. Another office nearby at

Rúa do Vilar 1 (all year Mon–Fri 10am–5pm; 881 866 397, http://turismo.gal) provides information on Galicia as a whole.

ACCOMMODATION

SEE MAP PAGE 516

Santiago offers an enormous array of **accommodation** to suit all budgets, ranging from its gorgeous parador down to the many inexpensive *hostales* aimed at pilgrims and young travellers. Make a priority of staying in the old quarter, which is in any case where most places are concentrated. Even during the July festival, this is rarely a problem, as half the bars rent out rooms.

Altaïr Hotel Rúa dos Loureiros 12, http://altairhotel. net. Classy little hotel in a quiet street immediately north of the old town, where the eleven rooms with their walls of exposed stone, are decorated according to a soothing, Japanese-influenced modern aesthetic. Discounted rates at nearby car park. €€€

A Casa do Peregrino Rúa Azabachería 2, http://acasado peregrino.com. You might not expect it from the ice-cream shop downstairs, but this ancient house, in the heart of the old town, has eleven attractive rooms, with exposed stonework including moulded basins. Modern features include soundproofing and walk-in showers. €€

Hospedaje La Tita Rúa Nova 46, http://latitacompostela. com. Pleasant, bare-bones and very inexpensive rooms, sharing a bathroom and WC, above a bar in the old quarter. With single rooms half-price, it's a real bargain for solo travellers. €

Hospedería San Martin Pinario Pza. da Inmaculada, http://sanmartinpinario.es. This stylish modern hotel has an austere, monastic feel that's hardly surprising given its location in a colossal (and very central) medieval monastery. The rooms are still recognizably cells, with bathrooms, minimal furnishings and no TVs, but the beds are extremely comfortable, with luxurious linens. Hugely atmospheric and remarkably quiet, it also offers simple meals in its cavernous ancient dining rooms, which is open to nonguests as well. €€

Hostal Alfonso Rúa Pombal 40, http://hostalalfonso.com. Pleasant family-run hotel, across from the Parque Alameda on the edge of the old town, where the rooms are small and simply furnished; those at the back have fabulous Catedral views. Rates include a decent breakfast. €€

Hostal Mapoula Rúa do Entremurallas 10, http://mapoula. com. Clean, friendly, third-storey *hostal*, with spacious, en-suite rooms; some sleep three or four guests. Tucked just inside the old town, near Pza. de Galicia, it's close to the heart of the action, so don't be put off by the slightly dingy alleyway. €€

★ **Hostal dos Reis Católicos** Pza. do Obradoiro 1, http:// parador.es. Santiago's magnificent parador – also known as Parador de Santiago de Compostela – facing the Catedral, is one of the world's most famous – and possibly oldest – hotels. Its 136 irresistibly luxurious rooms are arranged around four separate tranquil courtyards, and there are also two restaurants and a plush bar. It's worth every penny, especially if you get a pilgrims' or multi-day discount. €€€€

Hostal Suso Rúa do Vilar 65, http://hostalsuso.com. A neat, comfortable *hostal*, run by four friendly brothers, and consisting of ten attractively renovated en-suite rooms above a good bar-restaurant in a lively arcaded street. €€

★ **Hotel Costa Vella** Rúa da Porta da Peña 17, http:// costavella.com. Welcoming, very comfortable and beautifully furnished hotel on the northern edge of the old

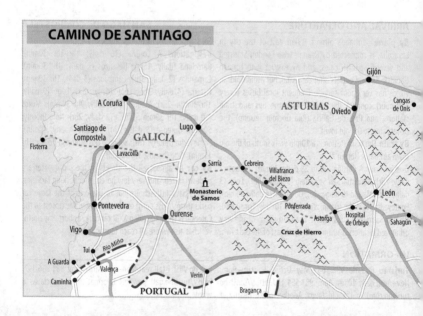

CAMINO DE SANTIAGO

THE CAMINO DE SANTIAGO IN GALICIA

For the thousands who walk the **Camino de Santiago** every year, its final section through Galicia still echoes the medieval pilgrimage. On this last leg, the *camino* is naturally at its most crowded. It passes few tourist sights, meandering instead through tiny villages. Pilgrims have to work hard, as the route clambers up and down steep hills and valleys, but the scenery, green with oak forests and patchworked fields, provides gorgeous recompense. The downside, of course, is that Galicia gets a lot of rain, and you can get caught in a storm even in summer. The Galego government makes huge efforts to promote the *camino*, maintaining an extensive network of pilgrim hostels along the eight separate routes that converge on Santiago – all are listed on http://caminodesantiago.gal.

The **Camino Francés** enters Galicia at the Pedrafita do Cebreiro pass, a desolate spot where hundreds of English soldiers froze or starved to death during Sir John Moore's retreat towards A Coruña in 1809. The mountain village of **O Cebreiro** is reached by a fierce climb of 30km from Villafranca del Bierzo in León, up cobbled paths often slick with mud and dung. There can be snow here in winter, and fog often obscures the spectacular views, but it's a magical place, with round, thatched-roof *pallozas* (stone huts) and intricate *horréos* (granaries).

The volume of pilgrims peaks at **Sarría**, 115km from Santiago and the last major town where you can start walking and still earn a *compostela*. The closer you get to Santiago, the more pilgrim rituals you'll encounter. Medieval pilgrims would wash themselves in the river at **Lavacolla**, 12km east of the city, to prepare for their arrival. During this ritual cleansing – often the first bath since leaving home – they'd pay extra attention to their private parts; *lavacolla* is said to mean scrotum-washing. From there, they'd race 5km to **Monte de Gozo** (Mount of Joy), where the first to cry "*mon joie*" on spotting Santiago's Catedral spires was declared the king of the group.

Although most pilgrims stop at **Santiago de Compostela**, some continue another 75km west to Fisterra (Finisterra), a Celtic route towards the setting sun that predates the medieval pilgrimage by at least a millennium. The quiet, well-marked rural route ends at **Cabo Fisterra**, the westernmost point of mainland Europe (see page 534).

8

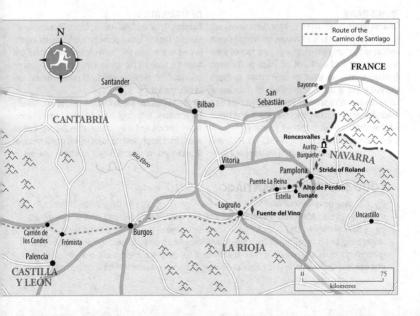

quarter, with views over the rooftops. Paying a little extra gets you a larger room with a delightful balcony. Breakfast with coffee and delicious toast is available in the all-day café/bar, which is open to nonguests; in summer you can eat or drink in the lovely flower-filled garden. €€€

The Last Stamp Rúa Preguntoiro 10, http://thelaststamp. es. Bright no-curfew hostel, in a historic building in the heart of town, that's named to signify the last stamp (*el último sello*) on the special pilgrims' passport. Each guest gets a dorm bed, with its own lockable cupboard, while each room has its own bathroom and can be configured to suit from two to eight guests, and there's a communal kitchen and laundry. €

Pensión Hortas Rúa Hortas 30, 881 359 018. Tasteful conversion of a typical townhouse, a short walk from the Catedral down a quiet street, into a seven-room hotel. Sparkling modern bathrooms, plus a café downstairs. €€

CAMPING

As Cancelas Rúa de 25 de Julio 35, http://camping ascancelas.com. Located well outside the old town, a half-hour walk uphill northeast from the Catedral – or 800m from the bus station – this year-round campsite has tent pitches and some four-person rental bungalows. Served by buses #8 and #9, as well as the airport bus, it's reached via the road to A Coruña, branching off at the Avda. del Camino Francés. Camping €, bungalows €€€

EATING SEE MAP PAGE 516

Santiago has a plethora of great **places to eat**. The two main concentrations lie along the parallel rúas Franco and Raiña, which get very busy in summer, and northeast of the Catedral on the quieter rúas da Troia and Porta da Peña, where there's much more outdoor seating. Traditional **tapas bars**, with small dishes spread out on the counter, are outnumbered by informal *mesones*, serving substantial and consistently superb seafood *raciones*. There are also plenty of more formal **restaurants**.

CAFÉ

Café Literarios Pza. da Quintana, 981 882 912. The terrace of this popular café, perched at the top of the broad stairs in the square behind the Catedral, makes a perfect venue for peaceful people-watching. €

TAPAS BARS

Casa Marcelo Rúa Hortas 1, https://casamarcelo.net. Adding Asian flavours to Spanish tapas has brought crowds flocking to this buzzy one-room restaurant, located down the stairs that lead northwest off Praza de Obradoiro. Reservations are only taken for large groups, so there's always a queue at opening time; diners sit at communal tables, one of which is squeezed into the kitchen. The food is delicious – such as *dim sum*, spicy raw tuna or steak tartare – but portions are small, so costs quickly soar. €€

O Gato Negro Rúa da Raiña s/n, 981 583 105. Jostle with the good-natured crowds at the plain white bar, or if you're lucky grab one of the five tables at the back, then enjoy classic Galego specialities such as *empanada* or peppers, or shellfish of all kinds, with local Ribeiro wine by the jug or by the bowl. €

Sant Yago Rúa da Raiña 12, 981 582 444. Smoked hams and cheese are the speciality at this friendly, stylish tapas bar, which also has an upstairs dining room, but the *tortillas* (made to order for one to three people) and seafood are every bit as good, and very well priced, plus a great-value three-course *menú del día* including wine. €

A Taberna do Bispo Rúa do Franco 37, http://ataberna dobispo.com. This smart, busy tapas bar on the main tourist thoroughfare stands out for its brightly lit counter display of appetizing goodies, with lots of cheese, meat snacks and seafood offerings. €

RESTAURANTS

Enxebre Hostal dos Reis Católicos, Pza. do Obradoiro 1, 981 582 200. The less formal of the parador's two restaurants, housed in the attractive former cellars and entered just down the slope off the square, serves tasty variations on traditional Galego cuisine, with tapas-sized portions as well as daily specials. €€

★ **Maria Castaña** Rúa da Raiña 19, 981 560 137. This cosy bar-restaurant, with rough-hewn tables and exposed stone, serves delicious food at reasonable rather than rock-bottom prices, from simple seafood tapas or soft cheese wrapped in anchovies, via scrambled-eggy *revoltos* or seaweed, to

FOOD SHOPPING IN SANTIAGO

If you're shopping for your own food, or simply enjoy ogling ultra-fresh produce, don't miss the large covered **Mercado de Abastos**, held daily until 3pm in and around the venerable stone halls of the Pza. de Abastos, on the southeast edge of the old city. Thursday is the main market day, but it's also bustling on Saturdays. As well as wonderful seafood and vast piles of green vegetables, the market is packed with local specialities like the traditional breast-shaped **cheese**, *queso de tetilla*, and flat *tarta de Santiago* almond cakes, adorned with crosses in honour of the Apostle.

paella-like fish *cazolos*, designed to share, plus affordable bottles of fine Galego wine. €

Mariscomania Mercado de Abastos, http://mariscomania. com. You need a spirit of adventure, and time to spare, to make the most of this intriguing, daytime-only restaurant, inside the market. The idea is, you tour the market by yourself, buying whatever fresh seafood or meat takes your fancy (but not whole fish), and they then cook it for you for a small charge (cash only), plus the cost of bread, drinks and dessert. You don't get a table until your food is cooked. €

O Dezaseis Rúa San Pedro 16, http://dezaseis.com.

Friendly rustic restaurant, near what was traditionally the main entry point for pilgrims reaching Santiago, where the good-value menu of local specialities – octopus gets its own special twist – includes a weekday set lunch, with wine and coffee. €€

★ **Los Sobriños del Padre la Casa del Buen Pulpo** Fonte de San Miguel 7, 981 583 566. The long-winded name belies the simplicity, and quality, of the *pulpo*, *tortilla* and other *raciones* at this very plain little local restaurant, which has pavement tables and serves white china jugs full of wine. If you only eat *pulpo* once in your life, make it here. €€

DRINKING & NIGHTLIFE

SEE MAP PAGE 516

With all those students to keep the city buzzing, countless bars remain alive with drinkers long into the night. Santiago is also the best place in Galicia to hear Celtic **music**, played either by solo performers on *gaitas* (bagpipes), or by student ensembles known as *tunas,* who stroll the streets in historic garb at night, especially in summer, playing assorted guitars, mandolins and fiddles.

Cafetería Hostal dos Reis Católicos Pza. do Obradoiro 1. On a summer evening, the outdoor terrace at the parador, with views back towards the Catedral and out to the green hills, is the ideal spot to linger over a sunset cocktail.

Casa das Crechas Via Sacra 3, 607 772 279, http:// facebook.com/casadascrechas. Art Nouveau bar with a slightly boho edge just behind the Pza. da Quintana, with an emphasis on Galego, Breton and Celtic sounds, along with world music in general.

Modus Vivendi 1 Pza. de Feixóo, 981 576 109. The longest-standing pub in the city still offers a warm welcome to every wandering pilgrim. Sip a craft beer or whisky to the sound of live music, and admire the eccentric trinkets in the display cabinets.

Momo Virxe da Cerca 23, http://pubmomo.com. A popular hangout with wide-ranging appeal, full of students during termtime. Fantastic and varied decor includes Parisian-style mini café-bars, an outdoor terrace and a jungle-themed dancefloor playing retro sounds.

O Filandón Rúa da Azabachería 6, 981 572 738. Thread your way through the simple cheese and wine shop to reach the narrow, bustling bar in the cave-like space at the back, where students and wine-lovers enjoy cheap, high-quality local *vinos* and free meaty morsels.

8

The Rías Altas

Galicia's north coast has been raked by the ocean into a series of dramatic bays and estuaries known as the **Rías Altas** (High Estuaries). As you head westward from Asturias, the coastline becomes noticeably more desolate, the road twisting around rocky inlets where wind-lashed villages cling to the shore, backed by eucalyptus forests and wild-looking hills. Driving is slow, though the final stretch of the **narrow-gauge railway**, from Luarca to Ferrol, is arguably the most picturesque of the entire route.

Ribadeo

RIBADEO, the easternmost Galego town and *ría*, is a charming enough little place, with plenty of bars and restaurants tucked into the lanes that surround its lively central square, the Pza. de España. The **Palacio del Marquès de Sargadelos** here, with its unusual decorative tower, is the most prominent monument.

Thanks to a succession of fine beaches, the coast immediately west of Ribadeo has seen almost continuous low-level strip development. It's well worth stopping at the **Praia As Catedrais**, however, 6km along, where low tide reveals some extraordinary natural arches, towering from a stark sandscape. The waves are usually too strong for swimming, but it's an unforgettable spot for coastal hiking, along a network of boardwalks.

ARRIVAL AND INFORMATION

RIBADEO

By train Ribadeo is served by trains along the coast, east | towards Cudillero (2 daily; 2hr 10min) and west towards

Viveiro (3 daily; 1 hr 5min).

Turismo Rúa Gamalo Fierros 7 (Mon–Sat 10am–2pm & 4–7pm, Sun closed; 982 128 689, https://turismo.ribadeo. org), near the parador.

ACCOMMODATION, EATING AND DRINKING

Mediante Pza. de España 16, http://hrmediante.com. The best-value alternative to the parador, on a central pedestrian street that holds lots of retsaurants and cafés. Half a dozen of its twenty rooms have balconies facing the Palacio del Marquès across the main square. €€

Parador de Ribadeo Rúa Amador Fernández 7, http:// parador.es. Ribadeo's modern parador, a short way south of the centre, faces the green fields of Asturias across the Eo estuary. Its rooms spill down the riverbank in successive sunny tiers, each with its own glassed-in gallery. €€€€

★ **San Miguel** Porto do Porcillán, http://restaurante sanmiguel.org. Superb, albeit expensive, seafood restaurant, down by the port beneath the main road bridge across from Asturias, a short walk from Ribadeo's tiny and somewhat faded harbour. Fabulous views and great food, with delights such as Galician cod, huge paellas and hearty *zarzuelas*. €€€

Viveiro

Now much more of a tourist centre than a port, **VIVEIRO**, 60km west of the Asturian border, has holiday homes spreading up the hillsides of the *ría* and along its many **beaches**. The old town, however, remains protected by the vestiges of its Renaissance walls. Largely closed to traffic, its narrow streets are lined with glass-fronted houses in delicate wooden frames.

The large **Praia de Covas** is a good ten minutes' walk from town across a causeway, while the pick of several more peaceful beaches around the bay is the **Praia de Faro**, further up towards the open sea.

ARRIVAL AND INFORMATION   VIVEIRO

By train and bus Both the bus station and the narrow-gauge railway station (2–3 trains daily in each direction to Ribadeo and Ferrol) are across the harbour from the old town, 5mins' walk apart.

Turismo Avda. Ramón Canosa (mid-June to mid-Sept Mon–Fri 10am–2pm & 4.30–7pm, Sat 11am–1.30pm, Sun closed; mid-Sept to mid-June Mon–Wed & Fri 11am–2pm & 4.30–7pm, Thurs 11am–2pm; 982 560 128, http:// viveiroturismo.com).

ACCOMMODATION

With no hotels in the heart of the old town, there's something to be said for staying near the beaches, across the harbour.

Camping Vivero Praia de Covas, http://campingvivero. com. Viveiro's spacious, well-shaded campsite is located just behind the largest local beach. Closed Oct–May. €

Hotel As Areas I Rúa Granxas 84, http://hotelesasareas.es. This comfortable hotel is one of a chain of three within a few metres of each other, all set just back from the long Praia de Covas beach and a 20min walk west of town. Free parking. €€

Hotel Vila Rúa Nicolás Montenegro 57, http://hotel-vila. es. Plain but clean and perfectly adequate hotel, in a drab street just outside the walls at the Porta del Vallado, on the inland side of town. €

EATING AND DRINKING

O Muro Rúa Margarita Pardo de Cela 28, 982 560 823. This busy, functional *pulpería* and grill serves a wide menu of fish and meats, and even pizzas. €

La Quinta Rúa Pastro Diaz 66, http://asadorlaquinta. es. Very good little grill house/bar one block back from the waterfront in the old town, with some tables on the pedestrian street outside. Daily specials include squid stuffed with chopped-up octopus. €€

Porto do Barqueiro and Ortigueira

West of Viveiro, shorefront development finally thins out, and the scenery grows ever more dramatic. The first train stop is 16km along at the tiny and very picturesque fishing village of **PORTO DO BARQUEIRO**, near Spain's northernmost point. Set amid a dark mass of pines another 14km farther on, the much larger town of **ORTIGUEIRA** spreads back from a large waterfront plaza, and hosts a musical extravaganza each July, the International Festival of the Celtic World (http://festivaldeortigueira.com).

★**El Castaño Dormilón** O Baleo 15, Ortigueira, http://elcastanodormilon.es. Former school, a short way inland 4km east of Ortigueira, which has been exquisitely converted into a bright, great-value and exceptionally comfortable rural inn. Rates include breakfast. €€

Hotel Porto do Barqueiro Porto do Barqueiro, 981 414 098, http://hotelportodobarqueiro.com. The best value among a handful of hotels dotted around the tiny harbour at Porto do Barqueiro; the rooms are undeniably plain,

but the views are great, and €10 extra gets you a private balcony. The cheaper little *Marina* hotel nearby is run by the same management. €

A Sobreposta Porto do Barqueiro, http://asobreposta.es. That this huge terrace restaurant, with its sweeping sea views, is always crowded may be partly because it's the one place where you can't see the ugly modern structure it's set upon; the food itself, though, is excellent, with wonderful fresh-caught fish at reasonable prices. €€

San Andrés de Teixido

While the narrow-gauge railway heads inland after Ortigueira, drivers can make a worthwhile side trip to the hermitage at **SAN ANDRÉS DE TEIXIDO**, the so-called "Mecca of the Galegos". The tortuous road up leaves the main AC862 at **Mera**, 9km west of Ortigueira, and climbs for a magnificent 12km farther, high above the coast, threading in and out of the pine forests into rolling clifftop meadows and bare heathland. The cliffs at **Vixía de Herbeira**, just short of the sanctuary, are said to be some of the tallest in Europe, at over 600m, while the church itself perches high above the ocean. Like so many of Galicia's sanctuaries, it is based on a pre-Christian religious site, but a monastery was already in place by the twelfth century. It now welcomes coachloads of Galego pilgrims, so the adjoining hamlet holds a café as well as plenty of souvenir stalls.

Cedeira

CEDEIRA, 12km southwest of San Andrés in its own attractive little *ría*, is a graceful port where elegant glass-balconied houses line the shaded, canalized mouth of a small stream. For once its old quarter has not become commercialized; instead you'll find restaurants and tapas bars strung along the northern quayside, towards the fishing port.

To the south, the huge Magdalena beach sweeps along the curve of the bay. In truth, it's more of a cluster of sand dunes than a real beach, so the sea feels slightly cut off from town, and kids tend instead to wade and swim in the river-mouth.

Hotel Herbeira Lugar de Cordobelas, http://hotelherbeira. com. This startling modern hotel, on a hillside 1km south of town, looks like a stack of boxes; each holds a bright, beautifully equipped room with great views of both beach and town, and there's a large pool. €€€

Mesón Muíño Kilowatio Rúa do Marineiro 9, 981 482 690. Friendly little bar near the river-mouth, serving fresh seafood or meat at bargain prices. Local families drop in to fill up on inconceivably large plates of fried squid. €

Betanzos

As the navy-dominated port of Ferrol, birthplace of General Franco, is best avoided, the final stop worth making in the Rías Altas is the ancient town of **BETANZOS**. Twenty kilometres southeast of A Coruña, at the head of the **Ría de Betanzos**, it's built on a pre-Roman site so old that what was once a steep seafront hill now stands well inland at the confluence of the Mendo and Mandeo rivers. Fragments of medieval walls are peppered around the base of the hill.

Betanzos' attractive main square, **Plaza dos Irmáns García Naveira**, is just below its hilltop old quarter. A short walk up brings you to the smaller Plaza da Constitución, home to the Gothic church of Santiago. Within the mass of twisting and tunnelling narrow streets below stands the twelfth-century church of **Santa**

8

María do Azougue, while the tomb of Conde Fernán Perez de Andrade "O Boo" (The Good), who commissioned its construction, lies in the Gothic Igrexa de San Francisco opposite.

If you're in Betanzos on August 16, don't miss the Fiesta del Globo, the highlight of which is the midnight launch, from the Torre de Santo Domingo in the main square, of the world's largest paper balloon, daubed with political slogans. There is also a medieval festival in the second weekend of July, when the town is transported back to the times of the Andrade lords.

Museo das Mariñas

Rúa Emilio Romay 1 • Charge, temporarily closed for renovations at the time of writing • 981 773 693

Just behind Betanzos' main square lies the excellent Museo das Mariñas, which provides a fascinating insight into the history of the town and neighbouring *mariñas* (sea-facing villages), and includes a colourful collection of period costumes.

ARRIVAL AND DEPARTURE
BETANZOS

By train and bus The Betanzos Ciudad RENFE train station, a 10min walk south of the centre, is only used by 4–6 daily trains between Ferrol and A Coruña. Other trains use the Betanzos Infesta station, 2.5km away at the top of a steep climb. Buses from A Coruña pull up just behind the square. By car The construction of a massive underground car park beneath the main square has made it easy to drive into and out of central Betanzos.

INFORMATION

Turismo Pza. de Galicia 1, just off the main square (Mon–Thurs 9.30am–2.30pm, Fri 9.30am–2.30pm & 4–6pm, Sat 11am–1pm, Sun closed; 981 776 666, http://betanzos.net).

ACCOMMODATION, EATING AND DRINKING

Eating and drinking possibilities in Betanzos centre on the row of attractive bars under the stone arcades of the main square, and the two tiny alleys that drop down between them.
Café Versalles Rúa Ferradores 9, 981 772 910. Modernist café, right on the main square, with decorative dark-wood panelling. Ideal for morning coffee, or fine wines later in the day. €
★ Casa Carmen Rúa da Fonte de Unta 12, 667 534 642. Delightful old *mesón*, with several tables beneath the venerable stone arches that lead down from the central square. There's a great range of seafood *raciones* and an set lunch menu, while the speciality is *tortilla de Betanzos*, an omelette that sandwiches layers of spinach and tomato. €€
Hotel Garelos Rúa Afonso IX 8, http://hotelgarelos.com. A short walk west of the main square, just outside the hilltop centre, this jazzed-up town hotel offers smart, modernized en-suite rooms at slightly inflated prices. €€
O Pote Travesía do Progreso 9, http://mesonopote.com. Betanzos' finest tapas bar, the pick of half a dozen somehow crammed into this narrow alleyway off the main square. Serves a wide range of tasty snacks rooted in traditional Galician cooking with a modern culinary twist, all to be enjoyed in a buzzy atmosphere. €€

A Coruña

The handsome port of A CORUÑA centres on a narrow peninsula that juts from Galicia's northern coast, 64km north of Santiago. A broad headland curves in both directions from the end of that peninsula to create two large bays: one faces across to Ferrol, and shelters a large harbour, while the other lies open to the Atlantic, and is lined by a long sandy beach. In the dynamic city in between, a five-minute walk takes you from a bustling modern port to a relaxed resort, by way of old stone alleyways where tantalizing restaurants, tapas bars and nightspots jostle for attention.

The distinctive glass-fronted galleries of the sea-facing buildings, rising six storeys high along the Avenida da Marina in front of the port, form a magnificent ensemble. They were originally designed so that local residents, whose lives were intertwined with the ocean, could watch the activity of the harbour in shelter.

Praza de María Pita

The heart of A Coruña, poised between the old city and its modern sprawl just inland from the port, is the colonnaded **Praza de María Pita**, home to the huge Palacio Municipal. The city's role as the departure point for the Spanish Armada in 1588 earned it a retaliatory visit from Sir Francis Drake the following year. His attack was only repelled when local heroine María Pita killed the English standard-bearer; her spear-brandishing statue now stands in the square.

The old town

The narrow streets of the **old town** wind around the Romanesque churches of **Santiago** and **Santa María del Campo**, and are shielded from the sea by a high wall. A small walled garden, the **Xardín de San Carlos**, holds the tomb of English general Sir John Moore, killed nearby in 1809 during the British retreat from the French during the Peninsular Wars. A wall nearby holds poet Charles Wolfe's contemporary lines describing Moore's original hasty battlefield burial – "Not a drum was heard, not a funeral note" – along with a similarly melancholic offering by Galicia's most famous poet, Rosalía de Castro.

Museo de Belas Artes

Rúa Zalaeta 2 • Charge, free Sat pm & Sun am • http://museobelasartescoruna.xunta.es

Conveniently located in the old city core, A Coruña's fine arts museum, the **Museo de Belas Artes**, concentrates largely on religious art of the seventeenth and eighteenth centuries. Its pride and joy are a couple of small Rubens canvases, on themes taken from Greek mythology. Twentieth-century pieces include some surrealist sea-themed paintings by Urban Lugrís and some interesting abstract works by painter and lithographer Luis Seoane.

Museo Arqueolóxico e Histórico

Castelo San Antón • Charge • 981 189 850

The Castelo San Antón, on what was once an island at the port entrance, started out as a garrison and was a military and political prison until the 1960s. It now houses the **Museo Arqueolóxico e Histórico**, which, as well as fascinating ancient finds including pre-Christian gold jewellery, holds a replica of an Iron Age wicker-and-leather boat.

The beaches

The sweeping golden arc of the city's main beaches, **Praia do Orzán** and the contiguous **Praia de Riazor**, line the opposite side of the peninsula from the port. Considering how close they are to the city centre, they're surprisingly clean and unpolluted. Arrive early in summer to grab a prime spot.

Casa Museo Picasso

Payó Gómez 14 • Free • 981 189 854

Pablo Picasso lived in A Coruña between the ages of 9 and 13, and produced his first oil paintings here. The **Casa Museo Picasso**, his former home near the city centre, is a typical galleried townhouse. It's of interest mainly for its authentic (but not original) period furnishings rather than the few reproduced paintings by both Pablo and his father.

Casa das Ciencias

Parque de Santa Margarita • Charge • http://casaciencias.org

8

Arteixo, Fisterra & Carballo

A CORUÑA

■ ACCOMMODATION

Alda Alborán Rooms	5
Hostal Carbonara	4
Hotel Avenida	1
Hotel Lois	3
Hotel Nido	2
NH Collection A Coruña Finisterre	6

● EATING

Pulpeira de Melide	2
El Serrano	1

■ DRINKING & NIGHTLIFE

Cova Céltica	1

Bus Stations (1.2km); Train Station (1.4km) • 1 (1.8km); Madrid & Santiago

Casa das Ciencias

Palacio de Congresos

CALVO SOTELO

PRAZA DE PORTUGAL

CIUDAD DE LUGO

AVDA. DE FISTERRA

AVDA. RUBINE

ALFREDO VICENTI

AVDA. B. AIRES

AVENIDA DE PEDRO

JUAN FLÓREZ

PRAZA DE VIGO

FONTÁN

EL FERROL

BETANZOS

PRAZA DE OURENSE

COMPOSTELA

FONSECA

RÚA PAYO GÓMEZ

AVDA. LINARES RIVAS

SÁNCHEZ BREGUA

C. JUANA DE VEGA

DURÁN LORIGA

PRAZA DE PONTEVEDRA

Casa Museo Picasso

Praia do Riazor

PIERAO UNIFICADO SANTA LUCÍA Y LINARES RIVAS

Rosaleda

PIERAO DE LA BATERÍA

LOS CANTONES

ESTRELLA

RÚA ALTA

RÚA NUEVA

JUAN CANALEJO

BARRIE DE LA MAZA

La Coraza

Enseada do Orzán

Praia do Orzán

Z

PEIRAO DE CALVO SOTELO

La Terraza

Xardíns de Méndez Núñez

Kiosko Alfonso

Estación Marítima

Gobierno Civil

OLMOS

GALERA

REAL

DE SAN ANDRÉS

RÚA DA BARRERA

SOL

DEL ORZÁN

CORRALÓN

C. DEL HOSPITAL SAN ROQUE

Igrexa de S. Andrés

ROTONDA DO MATADERO

DE ZALAETA

Museo de Belas Artes

Museo Domus (550m) & Aquarium Finisterrae (1km)

Porto da Coruña

PEIRAO DE TRANSATLÁNTICOS

Dársena da Marina

AVDA. DA MARINA

RIEGO DE AGUA

DO. RIEGO DE AGUA

Galerías Coruñesas

Puerta Real

FRANXA

S. NICOLÁS

S. Nicolás

PZA. DE S. AGUSTÍN

Mercado

PAN-ADEIRAS

S. Jorge

PZA. DE ESPAÑA

PRAZA DE MARÍA PITA

Palacio Municipal

Torre de Hercules (1.5km)

PASEO MARÍTIMO

PASEO DE LA DÁRSENA

TABERNAS

SANTIAGO

Igrexa de Santiago

Colegiata de Santa María del Campo

P. DEL PARROTE

Casa de la Cultura

Xardín de San Carlos

Hospital Militar

Museo Militar

S. FRANCISCO

Xardíns da Maestranza

NTRA. SRA. DEL ROSARIO

M. ASTRAY

HERRERÍAS

LAPATERÍA

MAESTRANZA

CORTADURA

Convento de Santo Domingo

VERAMAR

PASEO MARÍTIMO

Enseada de San Amaro

OLD TOWN

Museo Arqueolóxico e Histórico

Casino Club Náutico

PASEO SIR JOHN MOORE

0 —— 100
metres

At the inland end of the peninsula, southwest of the centre, a tower atop a hill in the lovely little Parque de Santa Margarita holds the **Casa das Ciencias**, or House of Science. Filled with gadgets to play with, this enjoyable science museum is intended mainly for kids, and also features a **planetarium**.

Torre de Hercules

Charge, free Mon • http://torredeherculesacoruna.com

During the Iron Age, the site of A Coruña was home to the Artabri tribe, one of whose hillforts can still be seen at nearby Elviña. It was the Romans, however, who built the landmark **Torre de Hercules**. Said to be the oldest active lighthouse in the world, it dominates the northern tip of the headland, 2km from the city centre, amid a sweeping expanse of grass and heather. It's an impressive spectacle, though it was re-clad in the eighteenth century, with an outer skin wrapped around the frail original tower. Visitors now enter via the foundations, where archeologists have exposed the Roman stonework. Only thirty people at a time can climb to the top, for superb views out over the Atlantic, so during busy periods you can expect a long wait.

Aquarium Finisterrae

Paseo Alcalde Francisco Vázquez 34 • Charge • http://casaciencias.org

Far more than just a series of fish tanks, **Aquarium Finisterrae**, on the headland immediately west of the Torre de Hercules, will delight adults and children alike. Its highlight, the 4.5-million-litre *Nautilus* tank, plunges visitors into a watery world filled with the marine life of the Atlantic coast.

Museo Domus

Rúa Santa Teresa 1 • Charge • http://casaciencias.org

Situated just above the Paseo Marítimo, the modern **Museo Domus**, or Museum of Mankind, takes visitors on an educational trip around the workings of the human body. Aimed more at local schoolkids than tourists, many of its displays lack English captions. Besides models explaining pregnancy and childbirth, and even a pair of fluid-preserved conjoined twins, it holds some fascinating interactive exhibits, including "mindball", a counter-intuitive game in which you beat your opponent by being more relaxed. Films in its 3D cinema cost extra.

ARRIVAL AND DEPARTURE

A CORUÑA

By train A Coruña's train station is south of the city on Av. Ferrocarril 2, where Avda. Alcalde Alfonso Molina meets the ring road, Ronda de Outeiro; it's a half-hour walk to the centre, or you can take buses #5 or #11.

Destinations Barcelona (7 daily; 7hr 30min); Betanzos (10 daily; 25min); Bilbao (3 daily; 10hr 30min); Burgos (daily; 7–8hr); León (3 daily; 6hr); Lugo (4 daily; 1hr 45min); Madrid (9 daily; 3hr 30min); Ourense (14 daily; 1hr); Santiago de Compostela (hourly; 30min); Vigo (8 daily; 2hr); Zaragoza (1 daily; 11hr 30min).

By bus The bus station is 2km south of the centre at Rúa Cabelleros 21, a short walk from the train station.

Destinations Betanzos (every 30min; 45min); Camariñas

(daily; 2hr); Fisterra (4 daily; 2hr); Laxe (2 daily; 1hr 30min); Lugo (8–14 daily; 1hr 30min); Madrid (4 daily; 7–9hr); Ourense (3 daily; 2–3hr); Oviedo (4 daily; 3–6hr); Pontevedra (10 daily; 2hr); Santiago de Compostela (16 daily; 1hr 20min); Vigo (9 daily; 2hr 15min); Viveiro (1 daily; 3hr 30min).

By car Driving in A Coruña is extremely difficult and unrewarding; no map could do justice to the tangle of dead-end and one-way streets in the old quarter. Drive out to the Torre de Hercules, but otherwise it's best to park as soon as possible; practically the entire city centre is underpinned by vast underground car parks.

INFORMATION

City turismo Pza. de María Pita 6 (Feb–Oct Mon–Fri 9am–6.30pm, Sat 10am–5pm, Sun 10am–3pm; Nov–Jan

Mon–Fri 9am–5.30pm, Sat 10am–5pm, Sun 10am–3pm; 661 687 878; http://turismocoruna.com). You can also pick up tourist information at the Torre de Hercules on C/Doctor Vázquez 1.

ACCOMMODATION
SEE MAP PAGE 530

Whatever your budget, the pedestrian streets that approach Pza. María Pita and the old town are the best hunting grounds for **accommodation**, though if you're driving you won't be able to park nearby.

Alda Alborán Rooms Rúa Riego de Agua 14, https://aldahotels.es. Excellent location near Pza. María Pita, with thirty comfortable rooms, all with baths and some with balconies overlooking the attractive pedestrianized street. €€

Hostal Carbonara Rúa Nueva 16, http://hostalcarbonara.com. Simple en-suite rooms, some with balconies, in a friendly central location, with discounted parking in the nearby Orzan-Riazor car park. €

Hotel Avenida Rúa Alvaro Cunqueiro 1, www.hotel avenida.com. Stylish modern hotel, in a not especially attractive neighbourhood south of the centre that's very handy for the train station. Surprisingly quiet, it offers a high standard for the price. €€€

Hotel Lois Rúa Estrella 40, http://loisestrella.com. Up-to-the-minute little hotel deep in the pedestrian lanes, where the dozen rooms have been revamped with a soothing modern cream-and-grey palette. Four of the rooms are small singles, and the larger doubles have local-style glass balconies. €€

Hotel Nido Rúa San Andrés 146, http://hotel-nido-coruna.com. This place is housed within a pink-tinged modern block on central A Coruña's main street, close to all the action, with fifty gleaming if unexciting rooms; for a quieter night, ask for one facing the courtyard. €

NH Collection A Coruña Finisterre Paseo del Parrote 2, https://nh-hotels.com. The top option in town, this vast orange waterfront five-star, in easy reach of everything, comes complete with tennis courts, an Olympic-size swimming pool and every conceivable luxury. All rooms have sea views. €€€€

EATING
SEE MAP PAGE 530

The small streets leading west from Pza. de María Pita, from Rúa da Franxa through to Rúa La Galera, Rúa Los Olmos and Rúa Estrella, are crowded with bars that offer some of Spain's tastiest **seafood**.

Pulpeira de Melide Pza. de España 16, http://pulpeirademelide.com. Sit outdoors on a large if not especially attractive square, and grapple with eight-armed beauties at a classic Galego octopus restaurant. They offer a wide range of regional specialities, except on Sunday evenings, when they only sell octopus. €€

El Serrano Rúa la Galera 23, http://elserrano.es. A cornucopia for carnivores, this fine old *jamonería* serves ham platters plus all kinds of sausage as well, and there's also a full menu of *raciones*, including excellent squid. €€

DRINKING AND NIGHTLIFE
SEE MAP PAGE 530

In summer, the beachfront **bars** across the peninsula do a roaring trade, while bar-filled Rúa Orillamar is a good place to start the evening.

Cova Céltica Rúa do Orzán 82, 981 915 140. Celtic pub with exposed stone walls that's a popular rendezvous for folky students. Besides microbrewed local beers, they sell Anti-Imperial.

The Costa da Morte

Wild, windy and at times desolate, the **Costa da Morte**, west of A Coruña, is often passed over by tourists heading for the Rías Baixas. That's a great shame; while it's far less "developed" than the regions to the south, it boasts similarly beautiful coves, tiny fishing villages huddled against the headlands, and forested mountain slopes aplenty.

Its fearsome name – "Coast of Death" – stems from the constant buffeting it receives from the Atlantic waves. The most notorious of countless **shipwrecks** that litter the seabed is the oil tanker *Prestige*, which snapped in two following a ferocious storm in 2002, releasing 77,000 tonnes of crude oil that were swiftly mopped up.

The coast from **Camariñas** to **Fisterra** is the most exposed and westerly stretch of all. Ever since a Roman expedition under Lucius Florus Brutus was brought up short by what seemed to be an endless sea, it has been known as *finis terrae* (the end of the world). This is prime territory for hunting the expensive seafood delicacy *percebes* (barnacles), which have to be scooped up from the very waterline. Gatherers are commonly swept away by the dreaded "seventh wave", which appears out of nowhere from a calm sea.

Even where the isolated coves do shelter fine beaches, you rarely find resort facilities, and braving the splendid-looking waters is only recommended for the strongest of swimmers.

Malpica de Bergantiños

Few potential stopping points lie immediately west of A Coruña. The first seaside village within easy reach is **MALPICA DE BERGANTIÑOS**, 45km from the city. A working, and rather forbidding,

> ### GETTING AROUND THE COSTA DA MORTE
> While it's well worth following the coastal road west around the Costa da Morte all the way to Fisterra, you'll need to allow plenty of time. **Driving** is slow, and, with no train lines, **buses** offer the only public transport. They're predominantly operated by Monbus (http://monbus.es), whose routes include Muxía to Fisterra (3 daily; 50min), and Fisterra to Santiago via Cée, Carnota, Muros and Noia (6 daily; 3hr).

fishing port, it nonetheless has a marvellous, though exposed, beach hardly 100m away from the harbour.

To reach the sheltered **Praia de Niñons**, 10km west, head for **Corme**, then turn right at Niñons and follow narrow lanes that thread through the cornfields. A granite church stands guard just above the beach itself, a crescent of thick sand that stretches to either side of a little stream.

ACCOMMODATION AND EATING   **MALPICA DE BERGANTIÑOS**   **8**

Hostal Casa da Vasca Porto de Bariza 42, https:// casadavasca.com. Seafront inn, on a gloriously isolated headland between Malpica and the Niñons beach, with six comfortable modern rooms and a restaurant. €€
San Francisco Rúa Eduardo Pondal 5, http://sanfrancisco malpica.com. Good seafood restaurant in a tiny fishing village, where you can choose your dinner from a crowded fishtank. Typical mains are reasonably priced, but watch out – a plate of *percebes* can work out to be pretty expensive. €€

Laxe

After crossing the River Anllóns via an ancient bridge at **Ponteceso**, the coast road reaches **LAXE** (pronounced "la-shay"), 24km southwest of Malpica and a much better bet for an overnight stop. A formidable sea wall protects a small harbour, while the café-lined waterfront street faces a broad expanse of fine sand. Closest to town, it's heaped up in dunes, but soon it levels out to become a long beach that offers the area's safest swimming.

Just outside Laxe, the somewhat exposed **Praia de Soesto** is even better than the town beach, while a perfect cove, the **Praia de Arnado**, lies just beyond. There's yet another massively long beach, the **Praia de Traba**, 6km south and backed by dunes and a jigsaw of mini-fields.

ACCOMMODATION AND EATING   **LAXE**

Casa do Arco Pza. de Ramón Juega 1, 981 706 904. Fine hotel and restaurant offering meat and fish dishes, with weekday and tasting set menus, housed in an ancient archway that leads off an attractive little seafront square. They also run a cheaper *méson* and tapas bar, and offer simple rooms. €
Hostal Residencia Bahía Avda. Besugueira 24, http:// bahialaxe.com. Good-value hotel, right in the port above a burger bar. Several of its en-suite rooms have spacious balconies with sea views, costing extra. €€
Hotel Playa de Laxe Avda. Cesareo Pondal 27, http:// playadelaxe.com. Very comfortable modern hotel, close to the beach at the southern end of town, 800m from the centre, and offering good buffet breakfasts. €€
★ **Mar de Fondo** Rúa Rosalia de Castro 4, 981 735 474. The pick of several waterfront restaurants between the plaza and the church, this cosy but very stylish little place has black tablecloths and black-clad waiters, and serves wonderful fresh-caught fish, plus melt-in-your-mouth ham and superb wine. €€

Camariñas

Although the seafront buildings of **CAMARIÑAS**, 25km southwest of Laxe, are almost entirely modern, it's still an attractive village, curled around a harbour that's home to a fishing fleet. Everything has visibly spruced up in recent years, thanks to a busy tourist season that sees the quayside lined in summer with the yachts of well-heeled visitors.

Camariñas marks the start of Galicia's wild west, at the region's westernmost extremity. Notice boards in town detail excellent walking in the vicinity, including the five-kilometre trek to the lighthouse at **Cabo Vilán**, guarding the treacherous shore on a rocky outcrop; climb the adjacent rocks for a stunning sea view. Winds whip viciously around the cape, and the huge, sci-fi propellers of the adjacent wind farm spin eerily, lit by the searchlight beam of the lighthouse once darkness falls.

ACCOMMODATION AND EATING   CAMARIÑAS

Café Bar Playa Avda. Ambrosio Feijoo 3, 981 736 141. This simple bar, with outdoor tables across from the harbour, is the main village rendezvous, and serves great tapas and *raciones* at rock-bottom prices; even their bread is wonderful.

★ **Hotel Puerto Arnela** Pza. del Carmen 20, https://hotelpuertoarnela.com. This lovely little flower-bedecked hotel, in one of Camariñas' few ancient houses, faces the sea from the far end of the port. The nicest rooms have their own balconies; there's also a small restaurant, and the owners are exceptionally friendly. Rates include breakfast. €€

Muxía

On the tip of a rocky promontory, across the *ría* from Camariñas, the small fishing port of **MUXÍA** stretches languidly along the shoreline. Make your way up to the Romanesque church on the hill above, though, and there's a fabulous view to either side of the headland. Paths lead either down from there, or for 600m along the waterfront from town, to the eighteenth-century **Santuario da Virxe da Barca**, where a massive sea-level church marks what was once an important site of Galicia's pre-Christian animist cult. The cult centred on the misshapen granite rocks at the farthest point of the headland, some of which are precariously balanced and said to make wonderful sounds when struck correctly; others supposedly have healing power. In later times, the rocks were reinterpreted as the remains of the stone ship that brought the Virgin to the aid of Santiago, an obvious echo of the saint's own landing at Padrón.

ACCOMMODATION AND EATING   MUXÍA

Casa de Lema Morpeguite, http://casadelema.com. Lovely rural inn, inland 8km south of Muxía, with very comfortable rooms with exposed-stone walls, nice gardens, and fresh home-cooked meals. €€

Lonxa d'Álvaro Rúa Marina 22, http://restaurantedalvaro.com. Welcoming little restaurant in the town harbour, with outdoor seating overlooking the sea and good prices on meat and seafood, with the option of a more expensive seafood blow-out for two. €€€

Fisterra

Famed, until Columbus told Europe differently, as the western limit of the world, the town of **FISTERRA** (**Finisterre**) still looks like it's about to drop off the end of the earth. On a misty, out-of-season day, it can feel like no more than a grey clump of houses wedged into the rocks, but it puts on a cheerier face in the summer sunshine, when crowds of day-trippers fill the quayside restaurants.

Just beyond the southern end of Fisterra's long harbour wall, a tiny bay cradles an appealing beach, overlooked by the pretty little eighteenth-century **Castelo de San Carlos**. Originally an artillery post, this now holds a museum of fishing (charge). The exceptionally friendly curator (a published poet) provides a quick-fire history of local lore and traditions.

Santa María das Areas, beside the road south out of town, is a small but atmospheric church. Its beautiful carved altar, like the strange weathered tombs left of the main door, is considerably older than the rest of the building.

ACCOMMODATION AND EATING FISTERRA

Casa Velay Pza. Cerca 14, 981 740 127. Poised above the northern end of Fisterra's little in-town beach, this friendly establishment offers bargain-priced rooms, and also has a good-value bar-restaurant, with outdoor sea-view tables. €
Hostal Praia de Estorde Praia de Estorde 217, http://restauranteplayadeestorde.wordpress.com. Delightful if somewhat isolated *hostal*/restaurant, commanding a fine white-sand beach that nestles in a small cove 7km east of Fisterra, 1km beyond the village of Sardiñeiro. They also run a small summer-only campsite, *Ruta de Finisterre*, in the

woods across the road. Camping €, double €€
Hotel Rural Prado da Viña Camino Barcia, 981 740 326, http://pradodavina.es. Comfortable little purpose-built B&B, on the hillside just north of central Fisterra, with nice en-suite rooms and a small swimming pool. Rates include breakfast. €€
Lorca Calafigueira Paseo da Ribeiro, 661 460 719. One of several similar restaurants that sprawl onto Fisterra's broad main harbourfront, serving individual dishes or a three-course lunch menu, and mixed seafood plates. €€

Fisterra Lighthouse

Thanks to the shape of the headland, the **Fisterra Lighthouse**, which marks the final point of the Camino de Santiago, is 4km south (rather than west) of Fisterra itself. The road there leads first along a heather-clad mountainside, then through a pine-forest plantation, before stopping at a little plaza named in honour of Professor Stephen Hawking, who came here in 2008. The squat, square lighthouse perches high above the waves at the very tip of the cape. When, as so often, the whole place is shrouded in thick mist and the mournful foghorn wails across the sea, it's an eerie spot, and when the sun sets over the western horizon it's positively magnificent. Traditionally, this is where pilgrims would burn their clothes, signalling the end of the pilgrimage, and also collect their scallop shell; the wearing of a scallop throughout the journey is a relatively recent phenomenon. Prominent notices now forbid any such fires, but the blackened rocks tell a different story.

8

ACCOMMODATION AND EATING FISTERRA LIGHTHOUSE

★ **Semaforo** Faro de Fisterra, http://hotelsemaforo defisterra.com. Small hotel/restaurant, a few metres before the lighthouse and the only place to stay right at the cape itself, which charges somewhat over the odds for its five

upscale guest rooms. The smart restaurant serves pricey seafood specials on its panoramic terrace, or you can get cheaper tapas at *O Refuxio*, the bar below. €€€€

Ezaro, O Pindo and Carnota

Around **EZARO**, where the Río Xallas meets the sea 30km east of Fisterra, the scenery is marvellous. The rocks of the sheer escarpments above the road are so rich in minerals that they are multicoloured, and glisten beneath innumerable tiny waterfalls. Drive around 500m inland along the west bank of the river, then walk another 400m, passing a small hydraulic power station, to reach an impressive waterfall.

Another couple of kilometres on, the little (though far from picturesque) port of **O PINDO**, beneath a stony but thickly wooded hillside, has a small beach. Towards Carnota, another 12km south, the series of short beaches finally joins together into one long, unbroken line of dunes, swept by the Atlantic winds. The village of **CARNOTA** stands a couple of kilometres from the shore, but its palm trees and old church are still thoroughly caked in salt. To reach the beach, follow a long wooden boardwalk across the marshes.

ACCOMMODATION O PINDO

Pensión Sol E Mar Carr. General 316, Praia do San Pedro, O Pindo, 981 760 298. Good-value sea-view hotel on the

coast road, a short walk from the beach and with eight comfortable en-suite rooms. €€

Ría de Muros e Noia

South of the Costa da Morte, the coastline is pierced repeatedly by the huge fjord-like bays known as the **Rías Baixas**, much the most touristed portion of Galicia's seashore. The northernmost of these, the **Ría de Muros e Noia**, remains relatively underdeveloped, but unspoiled little **Muros** is well worth visiting.

Muros

Some of the best traditional Galego architecture outside Pontevedra can be found in the old town of **MUROS**, enhanced by a marvellous natural setting at the widest point of the Ría de Muros, just before it meets the sea. The town rises in tiers of narrow streets from the curving waterfront, where fishing boats unload their catch, to the Romanesque **Iglesia de San Pedro**. Everywhere you look are squat granite columns and arches, flights of wide steps, and benches and stone porches built into the house fronts. There's also a nice – though small – **beach** on the edge of town beside the road to Fisterra.

ARRIVAL AND INFORMATION   MUROS

By bus Monbus services from Santiago (hourly; 1–2hr) stop on the waterfront.

Turismo The seasonal *turismo* is in the central square, where the coast road bends (July to mid-Sept Tues–Sat 10am–3pm & 4–6pm, Mon 10am–2pm, Sun closed; mid-Sept to June Mon–Fri 10am–3pm; 981 826 050, http://muros.gal).

ACCOMMODATION

★ **Hostal Ría de Muros** Rúa Castelao 53, 981 826 056. An unexpected gem; behind its unprepossessing exterior on the coast road, this eight-room central hotel offers fantastic value. The six rooms away from the road are smart but unexceptional, but the seafront doubles on the top storey, which cost extra, are breathtaking: spacious and tastefully furnished, with glorious balconies facing the harbour and bay. €

★ **Jallambau Rural** Lugar de Miraflores, http://jallambau rural.com. Commanding a majestic panorama of the bay from the hillside above town, and reached via a ferociously steep, narrow road, this superbly equipped and positioned four-room B&B can also be rented in its entirety as a holiday home. Three-night minimum in high season. €€€€

ACCOMMODATION AND EATING

Casa Sampedro Pza. Del Ayuntamiento, https://casasampedromuros.com. Very friendly, very good restaurant, with tables on the main square at the big curve in the coast road. Huge helpings of superb fresh seafood as well as salads, desserts and fine wines. They also offer four nicely converted rooms. €€

Pulpería Pachanga Rúa Castelao 29, 981 826 048. Right on the seafront, with outdoor seating in its own little precinct, this excellent *raciones* bar-restaurant has a stone-vaulted interior, and serves fresh seafood and grilled meats. €

Noia

NOIA (Noya), 25km east of Muros near the head of the *ría*, is, according to a legend fanciful even by Galego standards, named after Noah, whose Ark supposedly struck land nearby. Its claim to be a "Little Florence" is scarcely less absurd, but there's still a lot to like about Noia. Once Santiago's port, now connected to the city by a motorway, it centres on a medieval core where the impressive church of **San Martino** dominates a delightful ancient square.

ACCOMMODATION AND EATING   NOIA

Hospederia Valadares Rúa Egás Móniz 1, http://hospederiavaladares.es. Clean modern hotel beside the main promenading square, at the edge of the old core, offering simple rooms plus a restaurant serving all meals. €

Tasca Típica Rúa Cantón 15, 881 863 954. Atmospheric tapas bar, spreading from a fourteenth-century mansion onto tables tucked beneath imposing stone arches, and serving, as promised, the typical array of Galego specialities. €

Baroña

To trace the southern side of the Ría da Noia, sometimes called the "Cockle Coast", follow the C550 as it winds past dunes that serve in good weather as excellent beaches. From the roadside *Castro de Baroña* (*O Castro*) restaurant, just outside **BAROÑA** (Basonas) 18km along, a fifteen-minute walk down through the woods leads to a lovely little beach. Built atop a rocky outcrop that juts into the sea, and somehow spared by the mighty Atlantic waves for two millennia, is the **Castro de Baroña** itself, or rather its remains. The once-impregnable pre-Roman settlement consists of the circular stone foundations of several thatched dwellings that were in turn enclosed behind a fortified wall.

Ría de Arousa

Tourism has made a significant impact on the **Ría de Arousa**. The most popular destination is the old port of **O Grove** – linked by bridge to the island of **A Toxa**, which holds a very upscale enclave of luxury hotels – while much the nicest historic town is **Cambados**, renowned for its beautiful central plaza.

Strip development mars much of the coast, but the hillsides just inland are a patchwork of tiny fields, primarily planted with the grapes that go into delicious **Albariño wine**.

Padrón

According to legend, St James completed his miraculous posthumous voyage to Galicia by sailing up the Ría de Arousa as far as **PADRÓN**. Accumulated silt from the Río Ulla having left it stranded 12km inland, Padrón is no longer on the sea, and the old town now consists of a handful of narrow pedestrian lanes squeezed between two busy roads. There's surprisingly little to show for the years of pilgrimage, except an imposing seventeenth-century church of Santiago, where the actual *padrón* (mooring post) to which the vessel was tied supposedly resides under the high altar.

Padrón is best known as the source of the small green peppers known as **pimientos de Padrón**, served whole, shallow-fried in oil and liberally sprinkled with sea salt. Most are sweet, but around one in ten is memorably hot.

Casa Museo Rosalía de Castro
A Matanza • Charge • http://rosalia.gal

Just east of old Padrón, across the tracks from the pink ADIF train station, sits the house of nineteenth-century Galego poet **Rosalía de Castro**, now a museum. The jumble of texts, photographs and bric-a-brac may hold most appeal for fans, but the low-ceilinged rooms furnished in period style have character, and the gardens are pleasant.

INFORMATION   **PADRÓN**

Turismo Avda. de Compostela (Tues–Sat 10am–2pm & 4.15–7pm, Sun 10am–1.30pm; 646 593 319, http:// padron.gal).

ACCOMMODATION AND EATING

Pensión Jardín Avda. del Estacion 3, http://pensionjardin. com. The best-value place to stay in Padrón offers antique-furnished rooms in an eighteenth-century house, overlooking the park on the edge of the old town. €

Pulpería Rial Pza. das Travesas 13, http://pulperiarial. com. Friendly and attractive octopus and seafood restaurant, on a tiny little square in the heart of the old town. Try a plate of their signature *pulpo*. €€

Illa de Arousa

The first two towns on the *ria*'s southern shore, **Vilagarcía de Arousa** and **Vilaxoán**, just over 20km southwest of Padrón, are too industrialized to make worthwhile

8

stops. A little further south, however, a 2km bridge crosses to the wooded **Illa de Arousa**, which holds great beaches. Effectively part of the mainland, the island has a sizeable population, concentrated in the eponymous fishing port at its northern end. Turn south as soon as you're over the bridge to reach a small "natural park", the **Parque Carreirón**. If you're driving, you'll have to leave your car when the island narrows to a mere 50m wide, but you can walk on to reach half a dozen

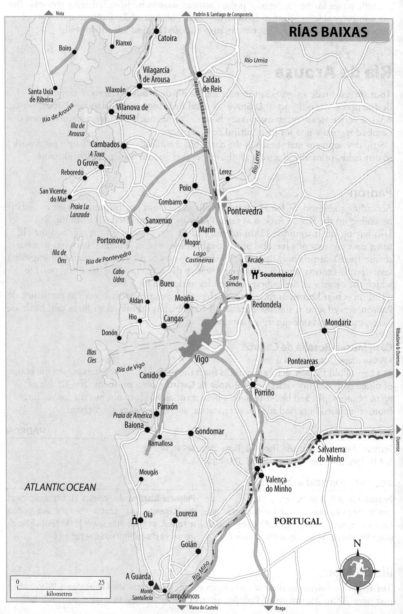

RÍAS BAIXAS

8

ATLANTIC OCEAN

PORTUGAL

N

0   25
kilometres

THE WINES OF GALICIA

Thanks to the international success of its crisp, dry **Albariño**, the best-known Spanish white wine, Galicia is a premium wine-producing region. The Romans first introduced vines two thousand years ago, growing them on high terraces sculpted by slaves into the banks of rivers like the Miño and Sil. With its mild climate and high rainfall, Galicia is more akin to Portugal than to the rest of Spain, and Galego wines, and especially Ribeiro, were much exported to Britain during the seventeenth and eighteenth centuries, before declining relations between Britain and Spain led the Portuguese to develop their own wineries, which produce similar wines to this day.

Albariño is a grape variety, introduced to Galicia by monks who followed the Camino de Santiago here from the Rhine during the twelfth century – it translates literally as "white wine from the Rhine". Albariño cultivation centres around the **Rías Baixas** (http://doriasbaixas.com), where around five thousand farmers grow grapes on tiny, scattered plots, often banding together to bottle and market their wine. The largest cooperative winery, **Condes de Albarei**, on the main road 2km south of Cambados, is open for guided tours and visits (https://condesdealbarei.com).

The best-selling wine in Galicia itself is **Ribeiro**, produced around **Ribadavia** on the Río Miño. It comes in both white and red, from such grape varieties as Treixadura, Torrontés and Loureira. The success of Albariño has spurred greater quality control, and white Ribeiro has now lost its previous trademark cloudiness, and is seen as the closest Spanish approximation to the dry Muscadet of France. Ribadavia's tourist office (http://ribadavia.net) organizes guided tours, and provides maps and listings for free, self-guided winery visits.

Only the **Ribeira Sacra** region, concentrated along the stunning canyon of the Río Sil (see page 553), produces more red than white wine. That it's not better known is largely because two-thirds of it never reaches the market but is drunk by the producers themselves. There are no large wineries or even cooperatives, but the three thousand farmers who create it have instigated a tourist route through the region and its vineyards (http://ribeirasacrata.com).

8

fine, isolated beaches, which are backed by trees and saltwater marshes loved by migratory water birds.

ACCOMMODATION   ILLA DE AROUSA

Camping El Edén Praia do Concerrado, http://eleden campingplaya.com. The nicest campsite on the island, just before the end of the road to the Parque Carreirón, with rental bungalows and its own tapas bar. Closed mid-Sept to Easter. Camping €, bungalows €€

Cambados

By contrast with most of its neighbours, the village of **CAMBADOS**, 5km south of the Illa de Arousa bridge, is exquisite. Only its historic core, however, set a couple of hundred metres back from the waterfront and easily missed if you're driving along the coast road, deserves such praise. The paved stone **Pza. de Fefiñáns** here is an idyllic little spot, overlooked by a seventeenth-century church and lined with beautiful buildings, several of which house wine shops and *bodegas*. As the vines crammed into its every spare square centimetre testify, Cambados is the production centre for Galicia's excellent **Albariño wine**. There's a **wine museum** in the old town, but it's too rudimentary to be of much interest.

The seafront itself is unremarkable, though a small island at its southern end holds the vestiges of a watchtower erected to look out for Viking raiders, while the vast seaweed-strewn flats exposed at low tide play host to legions of redoubtable freelance clam- and cockle-pickers known as *mariscadoras*.

INFORMATION   CAMBADOS

Turismo Pza. do Concello (Mon–Fri 8.30am–2.30pm, Sat & Sun closed; 986 520 902, http://cambados.es).

ACCOMMODATION

Hotel Real Cambados Rúa Real 8, http://hotelreal cambados.com. Thoughtfully decorated rooms in a very friendly, very comfortable little hotel, just steps from the square in the heart of the old town. €€€

Parador de Cambados Pza. Clazada, http://parador.es. Centred on a much-expanded seventeenth-century *pazo*, or manor house, just off the waterfront road at the edge of the old town, Cambados' fine parador (also known as Parador del Albariño) offers very comfortable rooms and some lovely suites, plus a courtyard bar and a very good restaurant. €€€€

EATING AND DRINKING

Bar Laya Pza. de Fefiñáns, https://barlaya.com. With lots of tree-shaded tables out on the main square, this *bodega* makes a great place to stop for a liquid lunch, and to sample the local wines.

Brothers Café Cervecería Pza. Alfredo Brañas 2, 986 520 827. On summer weekends, the old lanes just inland from Cambados' marketplace fill with young revellers; this pub, on a tiny square, is right in the thick of things, and often features late-night DJs and/or live music.

Restaurante María José Rúa San Gregorio 2, 986 542 281. Excellent little restaurant, on the seafront across from the parador. Downstairs, the separate *Taberna da Calzada* is a good tapas bar that also sells ice cream. Up above, María José adds a creative twist to Galego staples, with set lunch and dinner menus that include half a bottle of Albariño per person. €€

O Grove and A Toxa

O GROVE, at the northern tip of the peninsula that lies across the bay from Cambados, is primarily a family resort. Inexpensive bars and restaurants compete to attract summer visitors, while hotels line waterfront Rúa Teniente Domínguez and Rúa Castelao. The town plays host to a huge Fiesta do Marisco (Shellfish Festival) early in October, one of the longest-running food festivals in Galicia.

Across the bridge, the pine-covered islet of **A TOXA** (La Toja) caters for a completely different clientele. It's very explicitly a playground for the wealthy, with luxury holiday homes and three huge and very expensive hotels set in the forest clearings, plus a nine-hole golf course.

Acuario do Grove

Punta Moreiras s/n • Charge • http://acuariodogrove.es

In the port area of Punta Moreiras, just before the village of **Reboredo** 3km southwest of O Grove, the **Acuario de O Grove** displays a huge array of Atlantic marine life, and explains the fishing traditions of Galicia.

INFORMATION

O GROVE AND A TOXA

Turismo A kiosk by the port in O Grove on Rúa do Corgo (Tues–Sat 10am–2pm & 4–6pm, Sun 11am–2pm; 986 731 415, http://turismogrove.es).

ACCOMMODATION

O Grove holds plenty of hotels, with its pricier options along the seafront. Even more exclusive and expensive hotels lie across the bridge on **A Toxa**, while the pretty village of **San Vicente do Mar**, 8km southwest at the opposite end of the peninsula, offers cheaper and quieter alternatives.

Casa Angelina Rúa Torre Cacheiras 4, San Vicente, http://casaangelina.com. Attractive modern house, near the beach at the peninsula's western tip, where the nicest of the ten comfortable en-suite rooms have sea-view balconies. €

Hotel Puente de la Toja Rúa Castelao 206, O Grove, http://hotelpuentedelatoja.com. The smartest waterfront hotel in O Grove, facing the bridge to the island, can be great value in low season. €€€

CAMPING

Moreiras Rúa Reboredo 26, Moreiras, http://camping moreiras.com. Well-shaded year-round beachfront campsite, with its own restaurant and shop, near the tip of a little inlet 3km west of O Grove, close to the aquarium. Camping €, bungalows €€€

Paisaxe II Praia de Area Grande, http://camping playapaisaxe.com. Large campsite, just back from the beach near San Vicente, 8km west of O Grove, with a restaurant. Closed Nov–March. Camping €, bungalows €€

EATING AND DRINKING

Although the waterfront by the port in O Grove is full of the inevitable *marisquerías*, it holds disappointingly few tapas places.

★ **Balcón de Floreano** Pza. de Arriba 11, O Grove, 662 252 270. Very friendly tapas bar-*meson*, with a few tables on a tiny square just up from the seafront, a cosy interior, and polka-dot

flowerpots up on the balcony. As well as a great-value, all-day set menu, they offer good sandwiches and snacks. €

Taberna Lavandeiro Rúa Hospital 2, O Grove, 986 731 956. Fancy fishy restaurant, set slightly back from the port, offering a *mariscada* (seafood platter) for two as well as typical individual dishes. €€

Ría de Pontevedra

Of all the Rías Baixas, the long, narrow **Ría de Pontevedra** is the archetype, its steep and forested sides closely resembling a Scandinavian fjord. **Pontevedra** itself is a lovely old city, set just as the Río Lérez starts to widen into the bay. Though it lacks a beach of its own, it makes a good base for excursions along either shore. The **north coast** is the most popular with tourists, with **Sanxenxo** its best-known resort; to avoid the built-up sprawl, though, head for the **south coast**, which stretches out past secluded beaches towards the rugged headland.

Praia La Lanzada and the north-shore beaches

The southern side of the narrow neck of the peninsula that holds O Grove is adorned with the region's largest beach, the vast golden arc of **Praia La Lanzada**. Packed with sun-worshippers in summer and a favourite of windsurfers in winter, the whole strand is best admired from the sloping hillside of the peninsula at its western end. The mainland to the east holds several more excellent **beaches**, often far less crowded than La Lanzada. Most have campsites nearby.

Sanxenxo

The coastal resort of **SANXENXO** (Sanjenjo) lies 10km southeast of La Lanzada, or 17km west of Pontevedra. Together with the barely distinguishable suburb of **Portonovo**, 3km west, it forms the heart for Galicia's one real exercise in mass tourism: not that there's any large-scale development, just a long succession of little beaches, each with its own crop of largely seasonal small **hotels**. Individually they're nice enough, but cumulatively they're overwhelming; as the major attraction for Spanish visitors is the summer **nightlife**, they're interspersed with bars and clubs that stay open until long after dawn.

INFORMATION SANXENXO

Turismo In the marina at the east end of the main Praia de Silgar beach (July to mid-Sept Mon–Sat 9am–9pm, Sun 10am–2pm; mid-Sept to June Tues–Sat 10am–2pm & 4–7pm; 986 720 285, http://sanxenxo.es).

ACCOMMODATION

Hotel Farsund Praia de Areas 54, www.hotelfarsund. es. Friendly little hotel, with simple but perfectly adequate rooms and a restaurant, in a quiet area a very short walk from the beach west of central Sanxenxo. Closed Nov–April. €€

Illa de Ons

The beautiful **Illa de Ons** lies out on the ocean at the mouth of the Ría de Pontevedra. Wilder and more windswept than the nearby Illas Cíes, it's home to a community of fishermen and some interesting birdlife. Good walking tracks provide terrific views of coast and sea; you can hike round the entire island in three hours, or climb to the lighthouse and back in just over an hour.

Although the Praia das Dornas where the boats arrive is pretty enough, you may prefer to find your own patch of paradise – the eastern shore is indented with half a dozen small but very sandy **beaches**. The best of the lot is the **Praia de Melide**, a gorgeous stretch of white sand near the northern tip. There are no hotels or other facilities, but it is possible to **camp** for free, within a designated area.

ARRIVAL AND DEPARTURE   ILLA DE ONS

By ferry Several ferry companies serve Illa de Ons; broadly speaking, they run daily between June and late September, and less frequently in May. Naviera Mar de Ons sail from Sanxenxo, Portonovo and Bueu (986 225 272, http:// mardeons.com); Cruceiros Rías Baixas from Sanxenxo and Portonovo (986 731 343, http://crucerosriasbaixas.com); and Pirates de Nabia depart from Bueu (986 320 048, http:// piratasdenabia.com).

Combarro and Poio

The fishing village of **COMBARRO**, 7km west of Pontevedra, boasts Galicia's largest collection of **hórreos** (stone granaries), which line the waterfront and look across the *ría* to Marín. A path cut into the rocks leads from the main square behind the *hórreos*; it's littered with souvenir shops as well as bars and tavernas, many with outdoor tables. During Combarro's **sardine festival**, on June 23, fish are grilled in the open air on the shore. Inland, the tight streets are lined with little houses, each with its Baroque stone balcony and gallery, winding towards the chapel of San Roque.

Monasterio de San Xoán de Poio
Rúa Convento • Charge • https://turismopoio.com

Above the modern town of **POIO**, 2km east of Combarro, the seventeenth-century Benedictine **Monasterio de Poio** is a haven of calm. Its cloister features a million-piece mosaic mural of the Camino de Santiago, created between 1989 and 1992 by Czech artist Anton Machourek, and there's an eccentric museum of tiny books.

ACCOMMODATION AND EATING   COMBARRO AND POIO

Casa Solla Avda. Sineiro 7, http://restaurantesolla.com. Very fancy, expensive modern restaurant, on the main road through Poio, offering delicious gourmet food and good views over the fields, with set tasting menus with several courses featuring *percebes* to tuna with Padrón peppers and Norway lobster. €€€€

Monasterio de Poio 986 770 000. The stately monastery of Poio contains a wonderful *hospedaría*, modern and efficient despite the age and beauty of its setting, and with a *cafetería* that serves all meals daily, 8am–8pm. €€

Pontevedra

Compact, charming and very tourist-friendly, **PONTEVEDRA** is the quintessential old Galego town. Located just back from the open sea at the head of its namesake *ría*, at the last bend in the Río Lérez, it was supposedly founded by a Greek hero returning from the Trojan War, and prospered as a medieval fishing port. Although it has lost its ancient walls, it still centres on an attractive *zona monumental*. A maze of pedestrianized, flagstoned alleyways, interspersed with colonnaded squares, granite crosses and squat stone houses with floral balconies, the old quarter is always lively, making it perfect for a night out enjoying the regional food and drink.

Prazas da Peregrina and da Ferrería

Two adjoining squares connect Pontevedra's old and new quarters. On the **Praza da Peregrina** there's a pilgrim chapel, the **Santuario de la Peregrina**, a tall, eye-catching Baroque structure with a floor plan in the shape of a scallop shell, while the **Praza da Ferrería** is a paved square lined by arcades on one side and rose trees on the other. On its eastern side, the town's main church, **San Francisco**, is best admired from outside.

Amid the fountains, gardens, and open-air cafés that surround the Praza de Ferrería, all the daily rituals of life in a small town take place, especially during the Sunday *paseo*, when the entire population hits the streets. It's also the prime location for the city's many festivals, the busiest of which, **Os Maios**, lasts through the whole of May.

To reach the **zona monumental**, follow any of the narrow lanes that lead north from Praza da Ferrería. Rúa Figueroa swiftly reaches the attractive little complex of old stone houses adjoining the picture-postcard **Pza. da Leña**.

The Alameda and around

Leading down from Pza. de España towards the sea, the **Alameda** is a grand promenade dotted with monuments commemorating largely naval achievements.

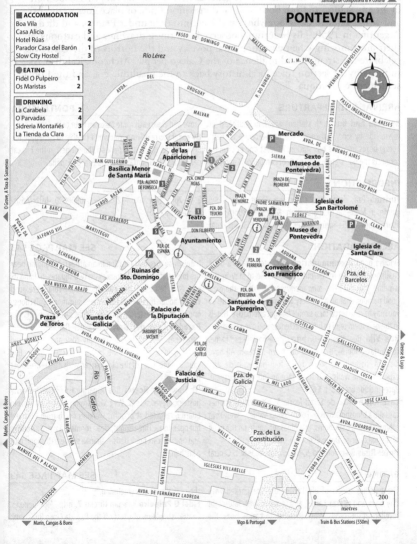

A **statue of Christopher Columbus** stands slightly off the Alameda. His flagship, the *Santa María*, was built in Pontevedra and is also known, here at any rate, as *La Galega*; some locals even claim that the navigator was a native son who passed himself off as Genoese.

Museo de Pontevedra

Pza. da Leña & nearby • Free • https://museo.depo.gal

The ambitious **Museo de Pontevedra** spreads through half a dozen buildings in the old town. Its original core was a couple of old stone houses, linked by a little bridge, in the gorgeous Pza. da Leña. Its newest and largest component, a vast complex 100m east, consists of the **Sexto** (Sixth) and the converted Sarmento convent. Typical products of Spain's recent, short-lived boom, and now as a rule disconcertingly short of visitors, the galleries here display an extensive collection of art and sculpture from both town and province. Pride of place goes to the artist and writer **Alfonso Castelao**, who was driven into exile under Franco, and died in Argentina in 1950. His beautifully observed paintings, drawings and cartoons, at their most moving when depicting rural poverty and the horrors of the Civil War, celebrate the strength and resilience of the Galego people. Archeological displays in the convent section trace local history back to the Neolithic era, and the Roman settlement of Turoqua.

ARRIVAL AND DEPARTURE

PONTEVEDRA

By train and bus Both stations are 1km southeast of town, side by side, and connected to the centre by half-hourly buses from the bus station. At least one bus hourly connects the bus station with each of Cambados, Cangas, O Grove and Vigo; each route takes an hour or less.

By car If you're driving, you won't be able to penetrate the historic core; it's best to park on the fringes, in the big car parks under Rúa Santa Clara and Pza. de España.

INFORMATION

Turismo Pza. de España s/n corner Montero Ríos Av. (summer Mon–Sat 9.30am–2pm & 4.30–8.30pm, Sun 10am–2pm & 5–8pm; winter Mon–Sat 9.30am–2pm & 4–7pm, Sun 10am–2pm; 986 090 890, http://visit-pontevedra.com).

ACCOMMODATION

SEE MAP PAGE 543

Finding good **accommodation** in Pontevedra is a little challenging. While it's definitely preferable to stay in the winding streets of the *zona monumental*, where there's a good parador, that area has very few mid-range options, so you may have to settle for a simple budget alternative. Hotels in the new town tend to be characterless and overpriced.

Boa Vila Rúa Real 4–6, http://hotelboavila.es. Large, comfortable rooms, in a good old-town location. All have modern bathrooms, some have four-poster beds and exposed-stone walls, and some face an internal courtyard. Rates include breakfast. €€

Casa Alicia Avda. de Santa María 5, http://habitaciones casaalicia.blogspot.co.uk. Four good-value, well-kept rooms, sharing bathrooms, in a pleasant house on the edge of the old quarter. Dorm €, double €€

Hotel Rúas Rúa Figueroa 5, http://hotelruas.net. Central

hotel, in an excellent location in an attractive building near the tourist office with entrances on two squares, holding its own good restaurant and café. Its en-suite rooms are good value, though they can get noisy on a summer night; choose one without an external window if that's a concern. €€

Parador Casa del Barón Rúa del Barón 19, http://parador.es. Elegant but delightfully cosy and well-priced parador, in a historic stone mansion tucked into a tiny square in the heart of the old quarter, with a little off-street parking. €€€

★ **Slow City Hostel** Rúa Amargura 5, http://slowcity hostelpontevedra.com. Very welcoming hostel in the old quarter, targeted at pilgrims walking north from Portugal but open to all. Three bright, clean rooms – a twin, a double, and one with six bunk beds – share a single bathroom, plus a kitchen. €

EATING

SEE MAP PAGE 543

The twisting streets of old Pontevedra are packed with tiny **bars** and **restaurants**, and jammed with late-night revellers at weekends. When it comes to **tapas bars**, the choice is almost overwhelming.

Fidel O Pulpeiro Rúa San Nicolás 7, http://opulpeiro.es. Central, simple *mesón*, just off the Pza. da Cinco Rúas, with glaring lights and white tables but big helpings of fabulous fresh octopus and seafood. €

★ **Os Maristas** Pza. da Verdura 5, 986 053 893. Busy bar with a lot of outdoor seating, that serves a full menu of *raciones* but is renowned for the astonishing liqueur, Tumba Dios, a fearsome blend of *aguardiente* (firewater) and *vino de pasas* (raisin wine), laced with coffee plus secret herbs and spices. €€

DRINKING

SEE MAP PAGE 543

The five spoke-like streets that run from the central **Pza. da Cinco Rúas** are busy with bars, as is the arcaded **Pza. da Verdura** with its open-air tables. The elegant **Pza. Teucro**, with its orange trees, holds grown-up wine bars.

La Carabela Pza. da Ferraría, https://carabelarestaurante. es. Named for Columbus's flagship, this handsome old café has been the favourite rendezvous on Pontevedra's central square for generations; huddle over breakfast at the picture windows inside, or savour evening drinks and free peanuts at the numerous outdoor tables, under the arcades and spilling into the flowery gardens.

★ **O Parvadas** Rúa González de Zúñiga 4, 986 864 710. This wonderfully atmospheric bar, tucked away in a little cottage behind the Peregrina church, is also known as *Casa Fernandes*. Besides serving delicious, ultra-cheap Ribeiro wine in a white ceramic bowl with a tapa, they offer a full menu of *raciones*. Join the local elders indoors, or head for the tiny vine-covered courtyard at the back.

Sidreria Montañés Rúa González de Zúñiga 6, https:// sidreriamontanes.com. Asturian-style cider is something of a rarity in Galicia, but this lively bar, with an extensive outdoor patio, is a welcome exception, and it also serves great Asturian stews and cheeses.

La Tienda da Clara Pza. do Teucro 8, 986 860 556. Classy wine shop that also serves fine wines and beer, plus well-priced snacks, to be relished at outdoor tables that spread from under the arcades onto the attractive Pza. de Teucro.

The southern shore

Though the first stretch of the Ría de Pontevedra's southern side is ugly, those who press on beyond the military town of **Marín**, 7km southwest of Pontevedra and home to an exceptionally smelly paper factory, are rewarded with some gorgeous and largely deserted little bays. **Buses** from Pontevedra's Pza. de Galicia run right around the headland and along the southern shore of the *ría*.

Praia de Mogor

Beyond Marín the bay broadens into a series of breathtaking sandy coves. A narrow side road drops away from the main coast road immediately beyond the naval academy outside Marín, leading to three beaches. The second of these, the **Praia de Mogor**, is perfect, with fields of green corn as the backdrop to a crescent of fine, clean sand, one end of which is shielded by a thick headland of dark green pines. There are a couple of seasonal bar-cum-restaurants overgrown with vines, and the villagers' rowing boats are pulled up in the shade of the trees.

Ría de Vigo

The **Ría de Vigo** ranks among the most sublime natural harbours in the world. Its narrowest point is spanned by a vast suspension bridge that carries the Vigo–Pontevedra highway; its twin towers are visible from all around the bay. On the inland side, the inlet of **San Simón** is effectively a saltwater lake. The road and railway from Pontevedra run beside it to **Redondela**, separated from the sea by a thin strip of green fields, and pass close to the tiny San Martín islands, once a leper colony and an internment centre for Republicans during the Civil War. Beneath these waters lies a fleet of Spanish bullion galleons, sunk by a combined Anglo-Dutch force at the Battle of Rande in 1703.

The city of **Vigo** looks very appealing, spread along the waterfront, but although it makes a good base for trips along the south shore to **Baiona**, across the bay to **Cangas**, and out to the wonderful **Illas Cíes**, it holds few attractions of its own worth visiting.

Cangas

The prime reason to visit the ever-growing resort of **CANGAS** is to enjoy the superb twenty-minute **ferry** ride across the *ría* from Vigo. During the crossing, watch out for the *mexilloneiras* – ramshackle rafts resting like water-spiders and used for cultivating mussels.

Cangas is at its most lively during its Friday **market**, when the seafront gardens are filled with stalls. Otherwise, make for the **Praia de Rodeira**, a beautiful sandy beach with majestic views that's a ten-minute walk from the ferry jetty (turn right as you get off).

The beaches and hills west of Cangas are stunning and all but deserted. The best target is the **Praia de Melide**, at the tip of the peninsula 2km beyond **Donón**. An isolated cove backed by woods and a lighthouse, it offers tremendous walks along the cape.

ARRIVAL AND INFORMATION   CANGAS

By bus and ferry Frequent ferry services between Cangas and Vigo operate daily (from Vigo 7.20am–10.30pm; from Cangas 7am–10pm; http://mardeons.com). The bus station alongside the jetty is used by buses to and from Pontevedra and Vigo.

Turismo The *turismo* is at the ferry dock (Easter–Sept daily 11am–2pm & 4–6pm; 986 300 875, http://cangas.gal).

ACCOMMODATION AND EATING

A considerable cluster of **bars and restaurants** surrounds the port in Cangas.

Hostal Prado Viejo Rúa Ramón Cabanillas 16, Moaña, https://hotelpradoviejo.com. Pleasant hotel in Cangas' closest neighbour, Moaña, 5km east; it has stylish en-suite rooms with floor-to-ceiling windows, a smart seafood restaurant and private parking. €€€

Hotel Airiños Avda. Eugenio Sequeiros 30, Cangas, 986 304 000. This modern hotel offers comfortable sea-view rooms from the inland side of Cangas' waterfront public park, and also has a decent restaurant. €€

Hotel Playa Avda. Ourense 78, Cangas, http://hotel-playa.com. Good-value hotel, on the beach in the middle of the Praia de Rodeira, and open year-round. As well as tasteful, well-equipped rooms, they also offer self-catering apartments of various sizes. €€

Castillo de Soutomaior

Charge • https://castelodesoutomaior.com

A worthwhile detour 2km east of the village of Arcade, north of Vigo on the old road to Pontevedra, leads to the twelfth-century hilltop **castle of Soutomaior**. The rambling halls and towers of the castle itself are used for temporary exhibitions, while its superb landscaped grounds are planted with mighty sequoias and other exotic species. One former inhabitant travelled to Samarkand early in the fifteenth century, as ambassador to the court of Tamerlane the Great.

Vigo

Few cities enjoy such a magnificent natural setting as **VIGO**. Arrayed along the sloping southern shoreline of its namesake estuary, it enjoys views not only of the bay itself, surrounded by green forest ridges, but also out towards the ocean. While it's undeniably impressive when seen from a ship entering the harbour, however, once you're ashore it fails to live up to that initial promise, and few visitors use it as more than an overnight stop.

Although Vigo is now the largest city in Galicia, home to 300,000 people, Baiona, nearer the mouth of the *ría*, was the principal port hereabouts until the nineteenth century. Then the railways arrived, and Vigo became the first Galego town to industrialize, opening several sardine canneries. It's now Spain's chief fishing port – indeed, some claim it's the largest in the world – with wharves and quays stretching almost 5km along the shore.

Pride of place in the middle still belongs to the passenger port where generations of Galego emigrants embarked for the Americas. These days, cruise passengers mingle with tourists arriving at the **Estación Marítima de Ría** off the Cangas ferry, and most of them set off to explore the steep cobbled streets that climb up into the old city, which is known as **O Berbés** and is crammed with shops, bars and restaurants.

Along the seafront, early in the morning, kiosks revive fishermen with strong coffee, while their catch is sold both there and in the lively daily market hall nearby, the **Mercado da Pedra**. Immediately below, on the aptly named **Rúa da Pescadería**, women set out plates of fresh oysters on permanent granite tables to tempt passers-by. On **Rúa Carral**, shops sell marine souvenirs.

Castro hill

A stiff but enjoyable climb up from the old town, mostly along stone staircases, brings you to the top of the **Castro hill**. So named for the circular ancient ruins still visible on one side, and also the site of a seventeenth-century castle, the hill provides comprehensive views.

Museo Quiñones de León

Free • http://museodevigo.org

The **Museo Quiñones de León** is the focal point of the **Parque de Castrelos**, the extensive formal gardens and woodlands that start 2km southwest of Castro hill. Set in an attractive old manor house, it's one of Galicia's widest-ranging museums, covering the archeology and history of Vigo and its region. It also boasts a fine collection of Galego art.

Museo do Mar de Galicia

Avda. Atlantida 160 • Charge • http://museodomar.xunta.gal

The **Museo do Mar de Galicia**, 5km southwest along the waterfront from the centre of Vigo, tells the story of Galicia's relationship with the sea, with hugely detailed material on the fishing industry leavened by film posters, toys, and other entertaining ephemera. Circular walls from an ancient *castro* (pre-Roman village) that stood on this site are exposed outside, and there's also a rather rudimentary aquarium.

The beaches

Most of the **beaches** near Vigo are crowded and unappealing. Farther south, however, the beach at **Samil** is better, while those at **Vao** and **Canido**, further on, are also quite reasonable, and are equipped with campsites.

ARRIVAL AND DEPARTURE — VIGO

By plane Vigo's airport, served by Ryanair flights from London, is 9km east of the city on bus route #9A.

By train Vigo's RENFE station is 500m southeast of the old town on Rúa Vía Norte.

Destinations A Coruña (hourly; 1hr 30min); Barcelona (3 daily; 10hr 30min–14hr); Burgos (daily; 7–8hr); Irún (daily; 12hr); León (daily; 6hr); Madrid (3 daily; 4–5hr); Ponferrada (2 daily; 4–5hr); Pontevedra (hourly; 15min); Oporto (2 daily; 2hr 20min); Santiago de Compostela (12 daily; 1hr).

By bus Vigo's bus station is 500m south of the RENFE station, making it 1km southeast of the old town. Local buses #12A and #12B (http://vitrasa.es) run via the train station to the Porta do Sol in the old town.

Destinations A Coruña (9 daily; 2hr 15min); Baiona (hourly; 1hr); Cangas (20 daily; 1hr); Lugo (5–6 daily; 3hr); Madrid (3 daily; 8hr); O Grove via Pontevedra (9 daily; 2hr); Oporto and Lisbon (3 weekly; 3hr 30min/6hr); Ourense (13 daily; 2hr); Oviedo (daily; 6hr); Pontevedra (every 30min; 30min–1hr); Ribadavia (13 daily; 1hr 30min); Santiago de Compostela (hourly; 1hr 30min); Tui (every 30min; 45min).

By car The most convenient central car parks are on the seafront at Rúa das Avenidas – where an extraordinary elevator system whisks your car away from you – and beneath the Porta do Sol.

By boat Boats from the Estación Marítima, immediately below the old town, cross the *ría* to Cangas (see page 546), and head out in season to the Illas Cíes (see page 548).

INFORMATION

Turismo López de Neira 8 (daily 10am–5pm; 986 224 757, http://turismodevigo.org).

ACCOMMODATION

Vigo's **hotels** are concentrated in two main areas: around the old town, down by the port, which is close to the best restaurants and bars; and in the less atmospheric streets up by the train station.

Hostal Casais Rúa Lepanto 16, 886 112 956. Simple and very friendly budget hotel, offering small en-suite rooms in a surprisingly quiet location near the train station. Rates include breakfast. €

Hostal Continental Rúa Baixada Fonte 3, 986 223 403. Great-value little hotel, with friendly owners and simple en-suite rooms, on a lively (well, potentially noisy) street 100m up from the ferry terminal. €

Hotel Alda Puerta del Sol Rúa Porta do Sol 14, https://aldahotels.es. Clean, very central hotel that offers small but pleasant en-suite rooms, plus a couple of five-person apartments. Good off-season and weekend discounts. €€

★ **Hotel Puerta Gamboa** Rúa Gamboa 12, http://hotelpuertagamboa.com. Very friendly family-run hotel, set in a charming nineteenth-century house in the old town, just a few steps from the ferry port; it also has a decent restaurant. All eleven rooms are en suite, with good facilities; some have large balconies. Rates drop considerably in low season. €€€

EATING AND DRINKING

Virtually all the **bars** in Vigo's old quarter serve great tapas. Rúa da Pescadería is the liveliest place for **lunch**, at the outdoor tables among the oyster sellers.

El Mosquito Pza. da Pedra 4, http://elmosquitorestaurante.com. Crowds flock to this intimate family-run restaurant immediately above the fish market, for the city's finest Galego cuisine. Seafood is of course the speciality; just be prepared to pay significantly more than you would in a typical *raciones* place. €€€

La Pintxoteca Rúa Sombrereiros, 637 259 604. This bustling little tapas bar has two locations in the same old-town street; this one specializes in seafood, the other, on the edge of the Praza de Constitución, in ham and other meat. Both places serve substantial *raciones* and tapas. €

Taverna da Curuxa Rúa dos Cesteiros 7, 986 436 526. Top-quality *raciones*, from *pimientos* to squid in all forms, in a deliberately rustic setting just off Pza. de Constitución in the heart of the old town. €

Illas Cíes

The most irresistible sands of the Ría de Vigo adorn the three islands of the **Illas Cíes**, which can be reached by boat from Vigo, and (less regularly) from Baiona and Cangas. Sprawling across the entrance to the *ría*, battered by the open Atlantic on one side but sheltering delightful sandy beaches where they face the mainland, the islands were long used by raiders such as Sir Francis Drake as hideouts from which to ambush Spanish shipping, but are now a nature reserve. The most southerly, **Illa de San Martiño**, is an off-limits bird sanctuary; the other two, **Illa do Monte Ayudo** and **Illa do Faro**, are joined by a narrow causeway of sand, which cradles a placid lagoon on its inland side.

Most visitors stay on the sands, where you'll find a sprinkling of bars and a campsite in the trees. If you want to escape the crowds, it's easy to find a deserted spot, particularly on the Atlantic side. From the beach, a long climb up a winding rocky path across desolate country leads to a lighthouse with a commanding ocean view. The islands' campsite has a small shop and restaurant, but if you're on a budget you're better off taking your own supplies.

ARRIVAL AND DEPARTURE   ILLAS CÍES

Only a certain number of visitors are allowed to visit the Cíes on any one day, so aim for an early boat.

By ferry Mar de Ons ferries (40min; 986 225 272, http://mardeons.com) run from Estación Marítima in Vigo from July until the second Sunday of September (8 daily; first leaves Vigo at 9am, last leaves Cíes at 8.30pm), and less frequently around Easter, on weekends in May, and in June, and during the second half of September (4 daily; first leaves Vigo at 10.45am, last leaves Cíes at 7.15pm). Services also operate from Cangas and Baiona, less frequently but following the same seasonal pattern; in summer, the first boat leaves Cangas at 8.40am, and the last Cangas boat leaves Cíes at 8.30pm, while the corresponding times for Baiona are 9.30am and 7.45pm.

ACCOMMODATION

Camping Islas Cíes http://campingislascies.com. This gloriously sited campsite is the islands' only accommodation option; if you want to stay in mid-season, book ahead to make sure there's space. It has its own shop, café and restaurant, and tents are available for rent if you don't have your own. Closed late Sept to late May. €

Baiona

BAIONA (Bayona), 21km southwest of Vigo, is situated just before the open ocean at the head of a miniature *ría*, the smallest and southernmost in Galicia. This small and colourful port, which nowadays makes a healthy living from its tourist trade, was the first place in Europe to hear of the discovery of the New World. On March 1, 1493, Columbus's *Pinta* made its triumphant return to Spain, an event commemorated by numerous sculptures scattered around town. An exact replica of the *Pinta* (charge) is moored in the harbour, which these days contains pleasure yachts rather than fishing boats.

The **medieval walls** that surround the wooded promontory adjoining Baiona enclose an idyllic parador (see page 549). It's definitely worth paying the small fee to walk around the parapet, which provides changing, unobstructed views across the *ría* to the chain of rocky islets that leads to the Illas Cíes. Another hugely enjoyable footpath circles beneath the walls at sea level, and provides access to several diminutive beaches. These are not visible from the town proper, which despite its fine esplanade has only a small, if attractive, patch of sand.

Praia de América

Galicia's best-known **beach** lies 2km east of Baiona, across the mouth of the bay. The **Praia de América** is a superb long curve of clean sand that remains surprisingly underdeveloped considering its reputation, and is lined at a discreet distance by imposing suburban villas, only a few of which hold hotels or other businesses. A coastal footpath leads north to the beach from the village of **Ramallosa**, on the seafront Vigo–Baiona highway, near the spot where a splendid little Roman bridge crosses the Río Miñor.

8

ARRIVAL AND INFORMATION BAIONA

By bus Buses between Vigo and A Guarda stop near the seafront, close to the tourist office and parador.

Turismo Baiona's seafront *turismo* is on Rúa Arquitecto Jesús Valverde, alongside the gate that leads up to the parador (Mon–Wed, Fri & Sat 10.30am–2pm & 3.30–6.30pm, Thurs 10.30am–2pm, Sun 11am–2pm & 4–6pm; 986 687 067, http://baiona.org).

ACCOMMODATION

Hotel Tres Carabelas Rúa Ventura Misa 61, 986 355 133. Good-value hotel on a narrow pedestrianized street one block inland, where each of the seventeen en-suite rooms honours a particular sea legend, from Robinson Crusoe to Moby Dick. €

★ **Parador Conde de Gondomar** Monte Real, http://parador.es. It's hard to imagine any better location than Baiona's gorgeous parador, which, though totally surrounded on the headland by genuine medieval walls, is actually a modern version of a traditional Galego manor house. The rooms are spacious and comfortable, with superb views, and as well as two restaurants, it has a couple of bars, both open to non-residents, one of which stands alone in the grounds. €€€€

CAMPING

Bayona Playa Praia Ladeira, Sabaris, 986 350 035, http://campingbayona.com. While the beach itself isn't as good as Praia de América, the waterfront setting of this year-round campsite, 1km east of town on a long spit of land with the sea to one side and an inland lagoon to the other, is magnificent, and it has a large waterslide too. Camping €, bungalows €€

Playa América Nigran, http://campingplayaamerica.com. Huge campsite beside Baiona's best beach, 2km across the bay, which has abundant rental bungalows as well as tent pitches. Closed Oct to mid-April. Camping €, bungalows €€

EATING AND DRINKING

Seafood **restaurants** abound on Pza. Pedro de Castro and along Rúa Ventura Misa, most with tanks stuffed full of doomed marine creatures. Ventura Misa is also the hub of the town's **nightlife**, with several bars and pubs staying open late.

Casa Rita Carabela La Pinta 17, https://casarita.eu. You have to trust the owner at this top-notch seafood restaurant, on the edge of the old town near the market; there's no menu, he just brings you whatever his wife happens to have bought in the morning market. €€€

Jaqueyvi Rúa de Reloxo 4, 986 356 773. Smart little restaurant that specializes in rice with fish. €€
La Micro Rúa Carabela la Pinta 11, 607 925 164. This little bar-brewpub, upstairs in the entrance lobby of the town market, sells all sorts of intriguing beers from Galicia and beyond, as well as bar snacks. €

Oia

The C550 highway continues due south for 30km from Baiona to the mouth of the Río Miño, the frontier with **Portugal**. This windswept stretch of coastline is scattered with hotels; there are no beaches, but the sight of the ocean foaming through the rocks is mightily impressive.

A massive granite statue known as the **Virgen de la Roca** towers above the first curve south of Baiona; on solemn occasions, devotees climb inside it to reach the boat she holds in her right hand. Farther on, beneath **OIA** – little more than a tight bend in the road – the sheer stone facade of a Baroque **monastery** somehow withstands the constant battering of the sea.

A Guarda

The workaday port of **A GUARDA** (La Guardia), just short of the Miño, is largely the modern creation of emigrants returned from Puerto Rico. However, this is an ancient site, and home to some remarkable prehistoric ruins.

Monte Santa Trega

Charge for the archeological museum

The extensive remains of a **celta** – a pre-Roman fortified hill settlement – set amid the pine woods of **Monte Santa Trega**, can be reached by a stiff thirty-minute climb or an easy drive up from A Guarda. Occupied between 600 and 200 BC, the *celta* was abandoned when the Romans arrived. The site consists of the foundations of well over a hundred circular dwellings, crammed tightly inside an encircling wall. A couple have been restored as full-size thatched huts; most are excavated to a metre or so, though some are still buried. On the north slope there's also a large **cromlech**, or stone circle, while if you continue upwards you reach an avenue of much more recent construction, which is lined with the Stations of the Cross, and best seen looming out of the mist. At the summit, five minutes on, there's a church, a small **archeological museum** of Celtic finds, two restaurants and a hotel.

Camposancos

While A Guarda itself has a couple of small **beaches**, there's a better stretch of sand at the village of **Camposancos** about 4km south, facing Portugal and a small islet capped by the ruins of a fortified Franciscan monastery.

ARRIVAL AND INFORMATION | A GUARDA

By bus Buses arrive at Pza. Avelino Vicente, well above the port.
By ferry Camposancos is connected by river ferry with Caminha in Portugal, but at the time of writing the ferry service was temporarily out of operation until further notice.
Turismo Rúa Pza. do Reloxo 1 (May–Sept Tues–Sat 10am–2pm & 4.30–6.30pm; Oct–April Mon–Fri 10am–2pm; 986 614 546, http://turismoaguarda.es).

ACCOMMODATION AND EATING

Alda Santa Trega Monte Santa Trega, https://aldahotels. es. Hotel poised above the *celta* at the top of Monte Santa Trega, boasting glorious, incomparable views along the coast and the Río Miño; all rooms are en suite. €€
Casa Chupa Ovos Rúa A Roda 24 58, 986 611 015. Cosy, friendly restaurant, a couple of streets up from the harbour, run by a local fishing family and specializing in fresh, inexpensive seafood, with typical *raciones*. €€
Hotel Convento de San Benito Pza. San Benito, http:// hotelsanbenito.es. This is much the best hotel in A Guarda, located in the beautiful old Benedictine convent by the port, and with a couple of dozen antique-furnished rooms that enjoy great sea views. €€

Tui

TUI (Tuy, pronounced *twee*), 24km inland from A Guarda and roughly the same distance south of Vigo, is the principal Galego frontier town on the Miño, staring across to the neat ramparts of Portuguese **Valença do Minho**. The old town stands back from the river, tiered amid trees and stretches of ancient walls above the fertile riverbank. Sloping lanes, paved with huge slabs of granite, climb to the imposing fortress-like **Catedral** dedicated to San Telmo, patron saint of fishermen, while a pair of enticing little river beaches lie on the far side of the old town from the main street.

A fifteen-minute walk out of town leads to the Portuguese border, by way of an iron bridge designed by Gustave Eiffel (creator of the famous Parisian landmark). Ravishing little **VALENÇA DO MINHO**, dwarfed behind its mighty walls and a much more compelling destination than Tui, lies a similar distance beyond. There's no border control at the bridge: just stroll (or drive) across and head up the hill to the centre.

ARRIVAL AND INFORMATION   TUI

By train If you're coming by train from Ribadavia or Ourense, it's much quicker to go to Guillarei station, a taxi ride 3km east from the town, than to wait for a connection to Tui itself.

By bus Tui has regular buses to Vigo and A Guarda.
Turismo Paseo da Corredera 16 (Tues–Sun 10.30am– 1.30pm & 4–7pm; 677 418 405, https://tui.gal).

ACCOMMODATION

Hotel Colón Rúa Colón 11, www.hotelcolontuy.com. Modern hotel with large, comfortable rooms, a good restaurant, a pool and great views across to Valença. €€
Parador San Telmo Avda. Portugal s/n, http://parador.es.

Tui's imposing parador, out near the border with Portugal, features extensive landscaped grounds with a good swimming pool and tennis courts. €€€€

EATING AND DRINKING

O Novo Cabalo Furado Pza. do Concello 3, https://onovo cabalofurado.es. Next to the cathedral, the more formal offshoot of the *Vello Cabalo* is the best of Tui's surprisingly small handful of restaurants. If money's no object, this is the

place to sample a plate of the local speciality, *angulas*, baby eels from the river. €€€
O Vello Cabalo Furado Rúa Seixas 2, 986 603 800. Good and very affordable *raciones*, a block down from the cathedral. €€

Inland Galicia

While most visitors to Galicia concentrate their attentions on Santiago and the coast, what lies inland can be both spectacular and intriguing. The **Romans** were always more interested in mining gold from inland Galicia than they were in its coastline, and remarkable vestiges of their ancient occupation still survive, including terraced vineyards along the stupendous **canyon of the Río Sil**, and the intact walls of unspoiled **Lugo**. The obvious route for exploring is the one used by the Romans, following the beautiful **Río Miño** upstream, via towns such as **Ribadavia** and **Ourense**, and through the wine regions of **Ribeiro** and **Ribeira Sacra**.

Ribadavia

Roughly 60km east of either Vigo or Tui along the A52 motorway, but more pleasantly approached by following the N120 highway or the train line up the Miño valley – which tends to fill with mist every morning – the riverside town of **RIBADAVIA** is grander than its size might promise. Centre for a thousand years of the Ribeiro wine industry, it's home to several fine churches and a sprawling **Dominican monastery**.

Ribadeo also holds an interesting **Barrio Xudeo** (Jewish Quarter), dating back to the eleventh century, when its first Jewish immigrants arrived. By the fourteenth century,

Jews constituted half the local population, and this ranked among the most important Jewish communities in Spain.

Head for the tiny square behind the Iglesia de la Magdalena for a wonderful view of the hillside terraces. Immediately above the central Pza. Maior, home to several good bar-restaurants, look out for the remains of the small but quaint **Castillo de los Condes de Ribadavia**.

INFORMATION   RIBADAVIA

Turismo Pza. Maior 7, in a Baroque former palace (summer   10.30am–2.30pm; 988 471 275, http://ribadavia.es).
Mon–Fri 9.30am–3.30pm, Sat 10am–2pm & 4–6pm, Sun

ACCOMMODATION

Hostal Plaza Pza. Maior 15, 988 470 576. The only hotel in   its own restaurant. €
the old town, this hostal has good en-suite rooms as well as

Celanova

Monastery Charge • 988 432 201

Little **CELANOVA**, 35km southeast of Ribadavia and best reached along the high and winding road that follows the south bank of the Miño, is hardly more than a village. Its long, narrow main square is appealingly overshadowed by a vast and palatial **Benedictine monastery**, officially known as the Monasterio de San Salvador. Felipe V retired into monastic life here, having spent much of his reign securing the throne in the War of the Spanish Succession (1701–13). The monastery is now a school, but you can explore its two superb cloisters – one Renaissance, the other Baroque – and the cathedral-sized church. Most beautiful of all is the tiny, tenth-century Mozarabic chapel of **San Miguel** in the garden.

Ourense

Set slightly back from the Miño atop a low hill, the historic core of **OURENSE** (Orense), one of Galicia's four provincial capitals, is more engaging than you might expect from the dispiriting urban sprawl that surrounds it. While not a place to spend more than one night – and not a place to break a train or bus journey, as both stations are a considerable way out, across the river – the old quarter does at least offer a handsome and lovingly restored tangle of stepped streets, patrician mansions with escutcheoned doorways, and grand little churches squeezed into miniature arcaded squares. Its centrepiece is a squat, dark **Catedral**, modelled on the one in Santiago.

A bewildering number of bridges cross the River Miño as it curves through Ourense. The oldest is the thirteenth-century **Ponte Romana**, with its iconic arches, but the most impressive is the modern **Ponte Milenio**, a futuristic road bridge with an undulating pedestrian loop that provides great views. Ourense is also known for its hot springs, with several thermal areas across the city.

ARRIVAL AND INFORMATION   OURENSE

By train Ourense's train station is north of the river, 2.5km   2.5km from the old town; change to a local bus to reach the
from the old town and served by local buses.   centre.
Destinations A Coruña (14 daily; 1hr 10min); Burgos (4   Destinations A Coruña (3 daily; 2hr 30min); Celanova
daily; 5hr 30min); León (4 daily; 4hr); Madrid (10 daily; 2hr   (2 daily; 1hr); Lugo (6 daily; 1hr 40min); Santiago de
15min); Monforte de Lemos (5 daily; 40min); Pontevedra   Compostela (7 daily; 2hr); Vigo (13 daily; 2hr).
(15 daily; 1hr); Ribadavia (daily; 20min); Santiago de   **Turismo** Isabela la Católica 2 (Mon–Fri 9am–2pm &
Compostela (15 daily; 40min); Vigo (8 daily; 2hr).   4–8pm, Sat & Sun 11am–2pm; 988 366 064, https://www.
By bus The long-distance bus station is north of the river,   turismodeourense.gal).

ACCOMMODATION

Barceló Ourense Rúa Curras Enriquez 1, https://barcelo. com. Ourense's most luxurious hotel is a smart modern high-rise near the river in an unexciting part of town, a few minutes' walk from the old quarter. Spacious and very comfortable rooms at good rates. €€

Hotel Zarampallo Rúa Hermanos Villar 19, http://zarampallo.es. Stylish, albeit small doubles, with either shower or bath, in the heart of the old town, plus a restaurant downstairs. €

EATING AND DRINKING

Casa do Pulpo Rúa Juan de Austria 15, 988 238 308. This nice little tapas bar, facing the cathedral, sells all kinds of seafood and meat dishes as well as its signature octopus. €
Casa María Andrea Pza Eironcino dos Cabaleiros 1,

http://casamariaandrea.com. Spacious, good-value old-town restaurant, with balcony seating above a pretty little square. €

Cañon de Río Sil

It's only practicable to explore the area northeast of Ourense by car – and as you admire inland Galicia's most spectacular scenery, you can expect the driving to be slow. Follow the N120 out of the city, alongside the Río Miño, then head east after 20km at the confluence of the Miño with the lesser **Río Sil**. For the next 50km, the final stretch of the Sil is quite extraordinarily picturesque and dramatic, flowing through a stunning canyon known as the **Gargantas del Sil**.

The gorge is the heartland of the **Ribeira Sacra wine region**, the only part of Galicia that produces more red than white wine. Even where they're all but vertical, the river cliffs are almost always terraced with grape vines. That phenomenal landscaping project was started by the Romans, and has continued for two millennia. A high mountain road climbs east from the N120 just before the confluence, then winds along the topmost ridge of the canyon's southern flank, passing through several lovely villages.

Castro Caldelas

The village of **CASTRO CALDELAS** surmounts a small hilltop 50km east of Ourense, a few kilometres south of the canyon itself. The medieval castle at the very top (charge) gives tremendous views over the town and surrounding countryside.

Just before the village, a side road drops back down to the river, where a small **jetty** is the base for **boat trips** on the Sil (schedules vary; 988 215 100, www.riosil.com).

Doade

A steep and precipitous winding road, LU903, climbs 4km up the northern slopes of the Sil gorge from the boat jetty, to reach the village of **DOADE**. Shortly before the village, a dirt road leads an amazing viewpoint over the canyon and its ancient vineyards. A statue of a woman grape harvester, officially entitled the **Spatium Interpretationis Riveyra Sacrata**, commemorates nine centuries of viniculture.

INFORMATION   CAÑON DE RÍO SIL

Turismo Castro Caldelas has a useful *turismo* in its hilltop castle (daily 10am–2pm & 4–8pm; 988 203 358, www. castrocaldelas.es).

ACCOMMODATION AND EATING

Casa da Eira Lugar Albuergeria 31, http://acasadaeira. com. This is an amply comfortable B&B in a Galego farmhouse 10km west of Parada do Sil, with extensive views out over the canyon and a couple of rental apartments too. Not only do they encourage you to explore on foot, but they also supply hiking maps and personal GPS systems. Rooms €€, apartments €€€

Parador de Santo Estevo de Ribas de Sil Nogueira de Ramuín, http://parador.es. One of Spain's newest and nicest paradors stands 8km east of the main road, within a magnificently converted tenth-century monastery. The ancient cloisters remain intact, but it also boasts ultramodern spa facilities, including a whirlpool bath set on an outdoor terrace, and a beautifully styled contemporary restaurant. €€€€

Pousada Vicente Risco Rúa Grande 4, Castro Caldelas, www.pousadavicenterisco.com. A very pleasant little hotel in the heart of the village, with eight attractive and good-value en-suite rooms, and a good restaurant. €€

★ **Reitoral de Chandrexa** Parada do Sil, 988 208 099, http://chandrexa.com. Higgledy-piggledy old farmhouse, with magnificently uneven oak floors and exposed beams, tucked away down a very rural lane 6km north of the village of A Teixeira. All its three delightful B&B rooms are similarly priced though only some have en-suite facilities. The friendly owner prepares fabulous dinners when requested, with produce from his own fields, and also offers canoe rental. €

Monforte de Lemos

A dozen kilometres north of Doade, or 66km south of Lugo along the C546, the rail junction of **MONFORTE DE LEMOS** makes a satisfyingly unspoiled and ancient overnight stop. The town proper, which is home to an incongruously gigantic yet elegant Renaissance **Colegio**, encircles a hill of largely tumbledown old houses. The surprisingly rural area at the top of the hill holds a rambling ensemble which includes the **Torre de Homenaxe** and a 400-year-old monastery that's home to an imposing parador.

INFORMATION
MONFORTE DE LEMOS

Turismo Monforte's *turismo*, alongside the Colegio (Tues–Sun 10am–2pm & 5–9pm; 982 404 715, http://
monfortedelemos.es), can advise on tours of the Ribeira Sacra wine region and its Romanesque monuments.

ACCOMMODATION AND EATING

★ **O Grelo** c/Campo de la Virgen s/n, 609 603 046. This fabulous restaurant, a short way down the hillside from the parador, with outdoor terrace views, offers an inventive if expensive take on traditional Galego cuisine. You can enjoy a full meal, and on Friday evenings you can sample the food in the form of tapas. €€€

Parador de Monforte de Lemos Pza. Luis de Góngora y Argote, http://parador.es. Stately parador, housed in a grand Benedictine monastery, on the highest point not only in town but for a considerable distance around. Fifty spacious rooms, with tiled floors and huge comfortable beds, plus a pool and restaurant. €€€€

Lugo

The oldest city in Galicia, and as "Lucus Augusti" the region's first capital, two thousand years ago, **LUGO** is these days a small town that's chiefly remarkable for its stout **Roman walls**. Rated as the finest late Roman military fortifications to survive anywhere in the world, the walls with which the Romans enclosed this hilltop, overlooking the Miño river, still form a complete loop around the old town. Few traces remain of the 71 semicircular towers that once punctuated the perimeter; instead, a broad footpath now runs atop the full 2.5-kilometre length of the ramparts, so a thirty-minute walk takes you all the way around, to admire the city core from every angle.

Sadly, insensitive building and a busy loop road make it impossible to appreciate the walls from any distance outside, but the road does at least keep traffic out of the centre, which maintains an enjoyable if slightly neglected medley of medieval and eighteenth-century buildings. The most dramatic of the old city gates, the **Porta de Santiago**, in the southwest, offers access to an especially impressive stretch of wall, leading past the **Catedral**.

Catedral de Santa María

Charge • https://catedraldelugo.es

The large and very mossy **Catedral de Santa María**, tucked into a corner of the walled city, was originally Romanesque when built in the twelfth century. Since then, it has been repeatedly rebuilt, with flamboyant Churrigueresque flourishes still conspicuous despite the more recent Neoclassical facade. The interior is remarkable for being entirely split down the middle, its two separate aisles running either side of a succession of chapels and altars.

Museo Provincial
Rúa Nova • Free • http://museolugo.org

Lugo's excellent **Museo Provincial** holds a well-displayed collection of Galego art, contemporary Spanish work swiped from the Prado, and an early collection of Galicia's Sargadelos china, alongside the more predictable Roman remains and ecclesiastical knick-knacks.

Porta Mina
Rúa do Carme 3 • Charge • 982 250 962

The exhibition space at the **Porta Mina**, 200m northwest of the Catedral, is the best of several little museums devoted to different aspects of Lugo's Roman history. It tells the saga of the life and death of the settlement of Lucus Augusti, from its founding as a military camp until the invading Suevi razed it to the ground on Easter Day, AD 460.

ARRIVAL AND INFORMATION   LUGO

By train Lugo's train station is 600m northeast of the old town. Destinations A Coruña (6 daily; 2hr); Madrid (5 daily; 4hr 15min).

By bus The bus station is just south of the walls, on Pza. da Constitucíon.

Destinations A Coruña (hourly; 2hr); Ourense (4 daily; 1hr 40min); Pontevedra (daily; 2hr 30min); Santiago de Compostela (9 daily; 2hr); Vigo (5 daily; 3hr); Viveiro (3 daily; 2–3hr).

Turismo Pza. do Campo 11, in the old town; its three upper storeys hold good displays on the history of the walls (June to mid-Oct daily 10am–8pm; mid-Oct to May daily 10am–6pm; 982 251 658, http://lugoturismo.com).

ACCOMMODATION

Hotel España Rúa Vilalba 2, http://hotelespanalugo.com. Simple budget hotel, outside the walls not far from the cathedral. Its decent en-suite rooms have been spruced up with tree murals; the quietest face a courtyard rather than the street. €

Méndez Núñez Rúa Raiña 1, http://hotelmendeznunez. com. Upscale four-star hotel, in a modern building with large balconies, within the walls immediately north of the central Pza. Maior. Crisply minimal furnishings but a good standard of comfort. €€€

EATING AND DRINKING

Mesón O Castelo Rúa Nova 23, http://pulperiaocastelo. com. Among the very best of the many bar-restaurants on the old town's busiest lane, facing the provincial museum. A great range of inexpensive tapas and *raciones*: *pulpo*, a substantial meat dish, or a delicious local sausage. €

Sobrado dos Monxes
Charge • http://monasteriodesobrado.org

The twelfth-century Cistercian monastery of **Sobrado dos Monxes** makes a highly worthwhile detour en route between Lugo and Santiago. The range of the abbey buildings proclaims past royal patronage, their scale emphasized by the tiny village below, while the huge church itself sprouts flowers and foliage from every niche and crevice, its honey-coloured stone blossoming with lichens and mosses. Within, all is immensely grand – long, uncluttered vistas, mannerist Baroque, and romantic gloom; there are superb, worm-endangered choir stalls (that were once in Santiago's cathedral) and, through an arch in the north transept, a tiny, ruined Romanesque chapel. A community of monks maintains the monastery and operates a small shop.

Aragón

ZARAGOZA

9

Aragón

Politically and historically Aragón has close links with Catalunya, with which it formed a powerful alliance in medieval times, exerting influence over the Mediterranean as far away as Athens. Locked in on all sides by mountains, it has always had its own identity, with traditional *fueros* (jurisdictions) like the Basques and a written Aragonese language existing alongside Castilian. The modern *autonomía* – containing the provinces of Zaragoza, Teruel and Huesca – is well out of the Spanish political mainstream, especially in the rural south, where Teruel is Spain's least populated region. Coming from Catalunya or the Basque Country, you'll find that the Aragonese pace of life is noticeably slower.

It is the **Pyrenees** that draw most visitors to Aragón, with their sculpted valleys, stone-built farming villages and excellent trekking. Some valleys have been built up with expensive ski resorts, but they still reveal the stunning wilderness of the **Parque Nacional de Ordesa** and the **Parque Natural de Posets-Maladeta**, with their panoply of canyons, waterfalls and peaks. Aragón's Pyrenean towns are also renowned for their sacred architecture; **Jaca** has one of the country's oldest Romanesque cathedrals.

The most interesting monuments of central and southern Aragón are, by contrast, Mudéjar: a series of churches, towers and mansions built by Muslim workers in the early decades of Christian rule, which are included on UNESCO's World Heritage list. In addition to its absorbing Roman remains, **Zaragoza**, the Aragonese capital and the only place of any real size, sets the tone with its remarkable Aljafería palace.

Other examples are to be found in a string of smaller towns, in particular **Tarazona**, **Calatayud**, **Daroca** and – above all – the southern provincial capital of **Teruel**. This region is extremely remote and even its capital doesn't see too many passing visitors. It is unjustly neglected, considering its superb Mudéjar monuments, and there are some wonderful rural routes to explore. In southern Aragón, the captivating walled village of **Albarracín** is incredibly picturesque, while to the east lies the isolated region encompassing the **Sierra de Gúdar** and **El Maestrazgo**, a rugged countryside stamped with dark peaks and gorges. This area is largely untouched by tourism, so transport of your own is a big help here, if not essential.

The languid **Cinco Villas**, northwest of Zaragoza, make for an interesting and laidback couple of days of touring; the most interesting are **Sos del Rey Católico** and **Uncastillo.**

Zaragoza

The city of **ZARAGOZA** is home to about half of Aragón's 1.3 million population and the majority of its industry. It's a sizeable but immensely enjoyable place, with a lively zone of bars and restaurants tucked in among remarkable monuments, and it's a handy transport nexus, too, for both Aragón and beyond. Highlights include the spectacular Moorish **Aljafería**, an impressive collection of **Roman ruins** and an awesome basilica, devoted to one of Spain's most famous incarnations of the Virgin Mary, **Nuestra Señora del Pilar**.

The city's **fiestas** in honour of the revered saint Virgen del Pilar – which take place throughout the week closest to October 12 – are well worth planning a trip around, as long as you can find accommodation. In addition to the religious processions (which occur on October 12), the local council lays on a brilliant programme of cultural events, featuring top rock, jazz and folk bands, floats, bullfights and traditional *jota* dancing.

CAÑÓN DE ORDESA

Highlights

❶ Basílica de Nuestra Señora del Pilar, Zaragoza The majestic shrine of one of the most revered patron saints of Spain. See page 561

❷ The Aljafería, Zaragoza Step into the Moorish past at this magnificent palace. See page 566

❸ Cinco Villas Experience small-town Aragón as it once was in these lovely "five villages", where you might go all day hearing nothing but pealing church bells in the mountain stillness. See page 570

❹ Teruel Not only does this historic provincial capital feature majestic Mudéjar architecture,

but you can often have it all to yourself – Teruel is refreshingly off the tourist trail. See page 574

❺ Albarracín Wander medieval lanes past balconied houses in this postcard town. See page 577

❻ Monasterio de San Juan de la Peña Built right into a craggy mountain, it's hard to tell where the rock face ends and the monastery begins. In a word – stunning. See page 590

❼ Parque Nacional de Ordesa Located in the Pyrenees, this dramatic, canyon-slashed landscape offers fine high-altitude hiking. See page 592

HIGHLIGHTS ARE MARKED ON THE MAP ON PAGE 560

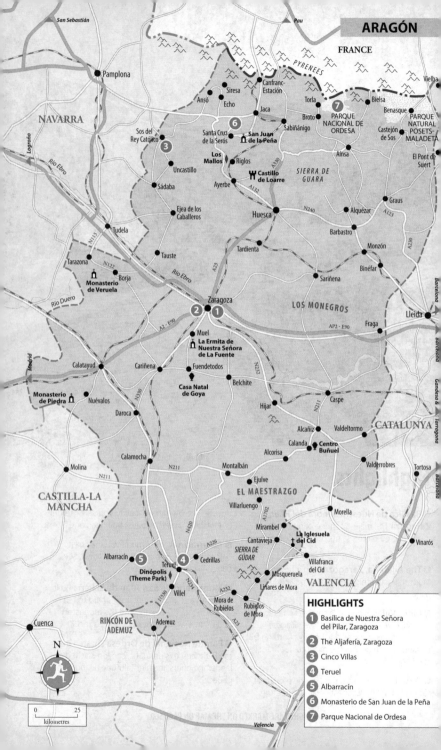

ARAGÓN

FRANCE

PYRENEES

San Sebastián

Pau

Pamplona

NAVARRA

Logroño

Río Ebro

Ansó

Siresa

Echo

Canfranc-Estación

Jaca

Torla

Bielsa

Broto

Sabiñánigo

7

PARQUE NACIONAL DE ORDESA

Benasque

PARQUE NATURAL POSETS-MALADETA

Vielha

Castejón de Sos

Sos del Rey Católico

3

6

Santa Cruz de la Serós

San Juan de la Peña

El Pont de Suert

Los Mallos

Riglos

Uncastillo

Castillo de Loarre

Ayerbe

SIERRA DE GUARA

Aínsa

Sádaba

Ejea de los Caballeros

Huesca

A132

N240

Alquézar

Graus

A123

Barbastro

A130

Tudela

N113

Tarazona

N122

Borja

Monasterio de Veruela

Tauste

Río Ebro

A23

Tardienta

Monzón

Binéfar

Sariñena

Río Duero

2

1

Zaragoza

LOS MONEGROS

Lleida

A2 - E90

AP2 - E90

Fraga

Barcelona

Madrid

Calatayud

Muel

La Ermita de Nuestra Señora de La Fuente

Cariñena

Fuendetodos

N330

Belchite

N232

Caspe

Gandesa & Tarragona

Monasterio de Piedra

Nuévalos

Casa Natal de Goya

Híjar

N211

Alcañiz

Valdeltormo

CATALUNYA

Daroca

Calamocha

Alcorisa

Calanda

Centro Buñuel

Valderrobres

Tortosa

Molina

N211

Montalbán

Valderrobres

Barcelona

CASTILLA-LA MANCHA

N211

Ejulve

EL MAESTRAZGO

Morella

Villarluengo

A1702

Mirambel

Vinarós

A226

Cantavieja

La Iglesuela del Cid

Albarracín

5

Teruel

4

Cedrillas

SIERRA DE GÚDAR

Villafranca del Cid

Dinópolis (Theme Park)

N330

N234

Mosqueruela

VALENCIA

Villel

A232

Linares de Mora

Cuenca

Mora de Rubielos

Rubielos de Mora

A23

RINCÓN DE ADEMUZ

Ademuz

N

Valencia

0 ——— 25
kilometres

HIGHLIGHTS

1 Basílica de Nuestra Señora del Pilar, Zaragoza

2 The Aljafería, Zaragoza

3 Cinco Villas

4 Teruel

5 Albarracín

6 Monasterio de San Juan de la Peña

7 Parque Nacional de Ordesa

FIESTAS

MAY

First Friday: Battle of Vitoria Commemorated in Jaca with processions and folkloric events.
Monday of Pentecost: Romería Nuestra Señora de Valentuñana At Sos del Rey
Católico.

JUNE

25: Fiesta de Santa Orosia In Jaca.

JULY

First Saturday: Feria de la brujería y plantas medicinales Witchcraft and medicinal herb
festival in Trasmoz (the only town to have been excommunicated by the Church)
First and second week: Vaquilla del Ángel One of Aragón's major festivals sees Teruel
burst into ten days of festivities.
Last two weeks: Pireneos Sur World music festival at Sallent de Gallego and Lanuza (http://
pirineos-sur.es).

AUGUST

Early August: Fiesta de San Lorenzo In Huesca.
14–15: Fiestas del Barrio Street markets and parties in Jaca.
27–28: *Encierros* – local bull-running – at Cantavieja.

SEPTEMBER

4–8: Fiesta at Barbastro includes *jota* dancing, bullfights and sports competitions.
8: Virgin's birthday prompts fairs at Echo and Calatayud.
8–14: Bull-running and general celebrations at Albarracín.
17–20: Fiestas de Los Mozos Unique festival in Rus dating back to times of plague, with
processions and dancing.

OCTOBER

Week closest to October 12: Aragón's most important festival, in honour of the Virgen del
Pilar. Much of the province closes down around October 12, and at Zaragoza there are floats,
bullfights and *jota* dancing.

The **Pza. del Pilar** is the obvious point to start exploring Zaragoza. The square,
paved in a brilliant, pale stone, provides a vast, airy expanse that extends from **La
Seo**, past the great Basílica de Nuestra Señora del Pilar, and over to Avda. César
Augusto. The plaza spans the city's entire history: Roman ruins at both ends;
between the churches, a Renaissance exchange house, the **Lonja**; and, at the centre,
some modern statuary and the **Fuente de la Hispanidad**, a giant waterfall shaped like
a section of Central America and the Caribbean to commemorate the Columbus's
arrival there in 1492.

Basílica de Nuestra Señora del Pilar

Pza. del Pilar • Free • https://catedraldezaragoza.es

Majestically fronting the Río Ebro, the **Basílica de Nuestra Señora del Pilar** is one of
Spain's greatest and most revered religious buildings. It takes its name from a **pillar** –
the centrepiece of the church – on which the Virgin Mary is said to have descended
from heaven in an apparition before St James the Apostle. This monumental shrine,
with towers and a central dome flanked by ten brightly tiled cupolas, was designed

9

ZARAGOZA

Pamplona (A68) ▲

▲ Expo Zaragoza & Acuario de Zaragoza (1.6km)

PLAZA DE LAS
COMUNIDADES
EUROPEAS

PASEO DE ECHEGARAY Y CABALLERO

SANTA LUCÍA

SANTA INÉS

PLAZA DE
SANTO
DOMINGO

PREDICADORES

CASTA ÁLVAREZ

AGUADORES

ARMAS

Aljafería

SAN BLAS

SAN PABLO

BASILIO BOGGIERO

CONDE DE ARANDA

AVENIDA DE MADRID

PLAZA
DEL
PORTILLO

**San
Pablo**

MARIANO CEREZO

CONDE DE ARANDA

**Plaza de
Toros**

RAMÓN PIGNATELLI

PLAZA
DE LA
VICTORIA

FUENTERRABÍA

S. MARTÍN

PLAZA SAN
LÁMBERTO

MADRE RAFOLS

RAMÓN Y CAJAL

SANTIAGO

**San
Ildefonso**

AVENIDA DE CÉSAR AUGUSTO

PASEO MARÍA AGUSTÍN

DOCTOR FLEMING

JOSÉ LUIS

PLAZA DE
NTRA. SRA. DEL
CARMEN

Train & Bus Stations (1.7km)

JOSÉ ANSELMO CLAVÉ

MANUEL ESCORIAZA Y FABRO

**IAACC
Pablo
Serrano**

ALBAREDA

CALLE DE BILBAO

MADRE SACRAMENTO

**Puerta del
Carmen**

CALLE DE CANFRANC

PASEO DE PAMPLONA

CALLE DE PONCANO PONZANO

PLAZA DE
ARAGÓN

PASEO DE TERUEL

HERNÁN CORTÉS

PIZARRO

ALMAGRO

AVDA. PINTOR FRANCISCO GOYA

ACCOMMODATION	
Albergue Juvenil Baltasar Gracián	8
Catalonia El Pilar	1
Hotel Palafox	7
Hotel Reino de Aragón	5
Hotel Sauce	3
Hotel Zentro Zaragoza	6
INNSiDE Meliá Zaragoza	4
Zaragoza Camping	2

DRINKING & NIGHTLIFE	
La Boveda del Albergue	1
Bull McCabe's	6
La Casa del Loco	5
La Cucaracha	3
Da Luxe	4
Oasis	2

● EATING	
Bodegas Almau	4
Bodegón Azoque	8
El Calamar Bravo	7
El Champi	3
El Fuelle	6
Gran Café Zaragoza	2
Montal	1
Restaurant Triana	5

**Antigua Facultad
de Medicina
y Ciencias**

PLAZA DE
BASILIO
PARAÍSO

GRAN VÍA

▼ 8 (1km) & Teruel (A23)

Teruel (A23) & La Romareda (1km) ▼

in the late seventeenth century by Francisco Herrera el Mozo and built by Ventura Rodríguez in the 1750s and 1760s.

The pillar, encased in a marble surround and topped by a diminutive image of the Virgin, is constantly surrounded by pilgrims, lining up to touch an exposed (and thoroughly worn) section. Elsewhere, the main artistic treasure of the basilica is a magnificent sixteenth-century alabaster reredos on the high altar.

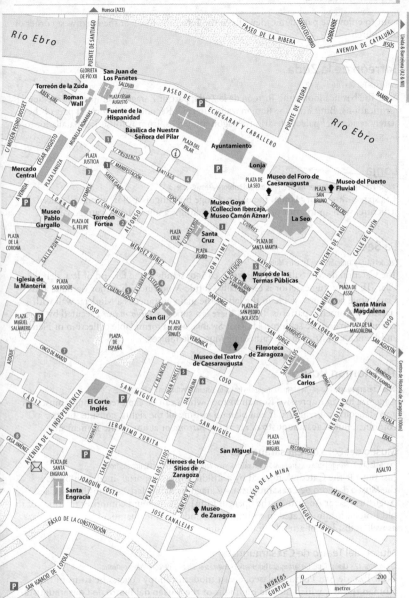

Museo Pilarista and Torre

Museo Charge • **Torre** Charge

Off the church's north aisle is the **Museo Pilarista**, which displays the original sketches for the decoration of the domes by Goya, Velázquez, and Francisco and Ramón Bayeu. Your ticket also admits you to the **Sacristía Mayor**, off the opposite aisle, which has a collection of religious paintings and tapestries. You'll have to pay extra, however, if you

9

want to enjoy the panoramic views from the **Torre**, the tower at the northwest corner of the church.

Torreón de la Zuda

Glorieta de Pío XII • Free

Near the basilica looms the **Torreón de la Zuda**, part of Zaragoza's impressive medieval fortifications. Built atop the **Roman walls**, after the Reconquest it formed part of the stately residential palace of various Aragón monarchs, from Alfonso I el Batallador to Jaime I.

Lonja

Pza. del Pilar • Usually only open for art exhibitions and temporary shows • Free

The sixteenth-century **Lonja**, the old exchange building, is a Florentine-influenced structure, with an interior of elegant Ionic columns and a soaring, vaulted ceiling.

La Seo

Pza. del Pilar • Charge, includes Tapestry Museum

The Catedral de San Salvador, known as **La Seo**, stands at the far end of Pza. del Pilar. The gleaming exterior is essentially Gothic-Mudéjar with minor Baroque and Plateresque additions, while to the left of the main entrance is a Mudéjar wall with elaborate geometric patterns. Inside, there is a superb *retablo mayor* executed by German Renaissance sculptor, Hans of Swabia, and a formidable collection of Flemish and French tapestries in the cathedral's **Museo de Tapices**.

The Roman Route

Ruta Caesaraugusto Charge • See http://zaragoza.es for up-to-date information on the Roman sites

Zaragoza has an impressive Roman history, which can be explored through museums and archeological remains. If you plan on visiting all the sights, consider buying a combined **Ruta Caesaraugusto** ticket at the *turismo* or at any of the Roman sites.

Museo del Foro de Caesaraugusta

Pza. de la Seo 2 • Charge (Ruta Caesaraugusto ticket valid) • www.zaragoza.es/sede/portal/museos/foro/

Just outside the Catedral, marked by a striking entrance portal lined with onyx, is the **Museo del Foro de Caesaraugusta** – Zaragoza's name derives from that of Caesar Augustus (César Augusto in the Spanish form). The museum comprises the ruins of the old Roman forum, located in an impressive underground chamber beneath the plaza, as well as displays of artefacts found on site.

Museo del Teatro de Caesaraugusta

C/San Jorge 12 • Charge (Ruta Caesaraugusto ticket valid) • www.zaragoza.es/sede/portal/museos/teatro/

Near Pza. de San Pedro Nolasco, a vast modern canopy covers the ruins of the Roman theatre, which are the highlight of the **Museo del Teatro de Caesaraugusta**. The exhibit features audiovisual displays, collections of archeological finds and a walk through the theatre and its vaulted galleries, which gives you a sense of its former grandeur.

Museo de las Termas Públicas and Museo del Puerto Fluvial

Museo de las Termas Públicas C/San Juan y San Pedro 3–7 • Charge (Ruta Caesaraugusto ticket valid) • www.zaragoza.es/sede/portal/museos/termas/ • **Museo del Puerto Fluvial** Pza. San Bruno 8 • Charge (Ruta Caesaraugusto ticket valid) • www.zaragoza.es/sede/portal/museos/puerto/

The **Museo de las Termas Públicas** displays the remains of the city's Roman baths, along with a scale model, while the **Museo del Puerto Fluvial** preserves the vestiges of the Roman river-port buildings.

Museo Goya (Coleccion Ibercaja, Museo Camón Aznar)

C/Espoz y Mina 23 • Charge • https://museogoya.fundacionibercaja.es/

A block south of the Pza. del Pilar, in the impeccably restored Palacio de los Pardo, the **Museo Goya (Coleccion Ibercaja, Museo Camón Aznar)**, houses the private collections of José Camón Aznar, a distinguished scholars of Spanish art. Highlights include a permanent display of most of Goya's prints – the artist was born at nearby Fuendetodos (see page 569).

Museo Pablo Gargallo

Pza. San Felipe 3 • Charge • www.zaragoza.es/sede/portal/museos/pablo-gargallo

On the western side of the *casco viejo* (old town), the **Museo Pablo Gargallo**, dedicated to the work of the celebrated Aragonese sculptor, is housed in the Renaissance Palacio Argillo. Some of Gargallo's sculptures use Cubist techniques, while others are more traditional renderings in bronze and marble.

Santa María Magdalena

Pza. de Magdalena • Charge

The handsome church of **Santa María Magdalena**, which dates back to the mid-fourteenth century, features the finest of Zaragoza's several Mudéjar towers. You can visit the interior on guided visits organized by the Alma Mater museum (www.almamatermuseum.com).

Centro de Historia de Zaragoza

Pza. San Agustín 2 • Free • www.zaragoza.es/ciudad/museos/es/chistoria

The **Centro de Historia de Zaragoza**, housed in the old convent of San Agustín, has innovative galleries on Zaragoza's history, and is also often used for contemporary art exhibitions, both local and international.

Museo de Zaragoza and around

Museum Pza. de los Sitios 6 • Free • www.museodezaragoza.es/ • **San Miguel** C/San Miguel • **Santa Engracia** Pza. de Santa Engracia

The well-curated **Museo de Zaragoza** features works by famous Aragonese artist Goya, along with other exhibits that span the city's Iberian, Roman and Moorish past. Nearby is a pair of interesting churches: **San Miguel**, which has a minor *retablo* by Forment and a Mudéjar tower, and **Santa Engracia**, with a splendid Plateresque portal.

IAACC Pablo Serrano

Paseo María Agustín 20 • Free • http://iaacc.es

The **Instituto Aragonés de Arte y Cultura Contemporáneos** (Aragón Institute of Contemporary Arts and Cultures), or **IAACC**, occupies an eye-catching building designed, in part, by acclaimed Aragonese architect José Manuel Pérez Latorre. Displays include contemporary art, architecture, design and sculpture, as well as works by well-known Aragonese abstract sculptor after whom the institution is named.

9

The Aljafería

C/ de los Diputados s/n • Charge, includes guided tour, free first Sun of the month • https://reservasonline.aljaferia.com/

From the tenth to the eleventh century Zaragoza was the centre of an independent dynasty, the Beni Kasim. Their palace, the **Aljafería**, was built in the heyday of their rule in the mid-eleventh century and, as such, predates the Alhambra in Granada and Seville's Alcázar. Much, however, was added later, under twelfth- to fifteenth-century Christian rule, when the palace was adapted and used by the *reconquista* kings of Aragón. Since 1987, the Aragonese parliament has met here.

The foremost relics from the original design are a tiny and beautiful **mosque**, and an intricately decorated court, the **Patio de Santa Isabella**. From here, the **Grand Staircase** (added in 1492) leads to a succession of mainly fourteenth-century rooms, remarkable for their carved *artesonado* ceilings; the most beautiful is in the Throne Room. Book guided visits online at https://reservasonline.aljaferia.com.

Expo Zaragoza

On and around Avda. de Ranillas

In 2008, Zaragoza hosted the splashy **Expo Zaragoza**, based around the theme of water and sustainable development. The gleaming Expo site, unfolding along the river just northwest of the city centre, featured plenty of intriguing architecture, some of which is still standing, including the iconic **Water Tower**, looming at nearly 76m tall; and a sleek bridge pavilion designed by Zaha Hadid. The Expo site now functions as a business district, where occasional conferences are hosted.

Acuario de Zaragoza

Avda. de José Arterés • Charge • http://acuariodezaragoza.com

The Expo site is also home to the **Acuario de Zaragoza** (Zaragoza Aquarium), the largest freshwater aquarium in Europe, with more than three hundred river species from around the world. It's very kid-friendly, and often packed with schoolchildren.

ARRIVAL AND DEPARTURE | ZARAGOZA

By air Zaragoza's airport (www.aena.es/en/zaragoza) is 10km northwest of the city centre; an airport bus (#505) takes about 20min to reach the city centre (times line up with arrivals and departures: see www.consorciozaragoza.es). Taxis cost around €30.

By train Trains use the intermodal Estación Delicias (http://estacion-zaragoza.es), just over 3km from the centre. Local buses #34, #36 and #52 link the station with the city centre. Destinations Regular and AVE trains zip throughout the day to Barcelona (13–20 daily; 4–5hr; AVE 1hr 45min), Madrid (12–15 daily; 3hr; AVE 1hr 25min) and Tarragona (5–10 daily; 3hr; AVE to Tarragona Camps 1hr 10min). There are also services (some may require a change) to Bilbao (4 daily; 4hr 30min); Burgos (7 daily; 4hr); Cáceres (5 daily; 6hr); Cádiz (4 daily; 9hr); Córdoba (5 daily; 3–5hr); Girona (10 daily; 3hr); Huesca (4–7 daily; 50min–1hr); Jaca (2 daily; 2hr 20min); León (9 daily; 6hr); Lleida (10–12 daily; 2h); Logroño (5 daily; 2hr); Málaga (10 daily; 4hr 30min); Pamplona (7 daily; 2–3hr 30mins); Salamanca (4 daily; 4hr 30min–7hr); San Sebastián (3 daily; 4–6hr); Seville (4 daily; 4-5hr 30min); and Teruel (4 daily; 2hr 30min).

By bus Buses arrive at the main bus station (www.estacion-zaragoza.es), next to the train station. There are Avanza (www.avanzabus.com), and Alsa (www.alsa.com) services from Asturias, Barcelona, Bilbao, Galicia, León, Madrid and several destinations in Old Castile. Agreda (www.agredabus.es) and Hife (www.hife.es) operates services to Huesca, Jaca, Daroca, Cariñena (45min), Muel (30min) and Belchite.

Destinations A Coruña (daily; 11hr); Barcelona (hourly; 3hr 45min); Belchite (3–4 daily; 1hr); Bilbao (9 daily; 3hr 30min); Burgos (3 daily; 3hr 15min); Huesca (every 30min; 1hr); Jaca (6 daily; 2hr 15min); León (3 daily; 5hr 30min–7hr); Lleida (5 daily; 1hr 45min–3hr); Logroño (3 daily; 2hr 15min); Madrid (hourly; 3hr 30min); Salamanca (2 daily; 6hr 45min); Santiago de Compostela (daily; 11hr); Sos del Rey Católico (daily; 2hr 15min); Tarragona (10 daily; 2hr 45min); and Valladolid (5 daily; 5–6hr).

By car Car rental is available from Enterprise, Estación AVE, C/Rioja 33 (976 322 221, www.enterprise.es); Avis, Estación AVE, C/Rioja 33 (902 090 321, www.avis.es); and Hertz, C/ Hernán Cortés 31 (976 320 400, www.hertz.es/).

By taxi Radio-Taxi Aragón (976 383 838, www.radiotaxi aragon.com/); Radio-Taxi Zaragoza (976 424 242, https://taxizaragoza.com).

INFORMATION AND TOURS

Turismo The main *turismo* is opposite the basilica on Pza. del Pilar (www.zaragoza.es/sede/portal/turismo). This caters for the city, while a well-equipped office on Pza. España 1 (http://turismodearagon.com) has information on the Zaragoza province. There's also a *turismo* booth at the train station.

Tours The *turismo* offers several different walking tours around town from €5.50 (also available in English). The Bus Turístico (Tourist Bus) travels between all the main sights every 35–40min, departing from C/Don Jaime, next to the Lonja (summer daily; winter weekends only; €8). The full journey takes about 1hr 45min.

Discount card The *turismo* sells a Zaragoza Family pass (www.zaragoza.es/sede/portal/turismo/post/zaragoza-family), which offers discounts on the Tourist Bus, the Aquarium and many other attractions.

ACCOMMODATION   SEE MAP PAGE 562

Zaragoza has a decent range of accommodation, from simple *pensiones* to well-appointed hotels. The central, atmospheric *casco viejo* houses many of the *pensiones*, both around Pza. del Pilar and the small streets off C/Méndez Núñez. You'll also find a good number of hotels dotted around the area east of Pza. de España.

Albergue Juvenil Baltasar Gracián C/Franco y López 4, https://reaj.com/albergues/juvenil-baltasar-gracian. This well-run hostel, about 500m from the train station, has basic but clean rooms sleeping two, four or eight people on bunk beds, and breakfast in the simple dining room included. Discount for under-26s. €̄

Catalonia El Pilar C/Manifestación 16, https://www.cataloniahotels.com/es/hotel/catalonia-el-pilar. Located inside a lovely *modernista* building on the edge of the old town, this hotel blends contemporary design with traditional features such as a wrought-iron lift. Rooms feature designer furnishings and a simple, understated colour scheme. €€

Hotel Palafox C/Marqués de Casa Jiménez, https://palafoxhoteles.com. One of the closest five-stars to the *casco viejo*, this sleek spot sports a blend of contemporary, Aragonese and Mudéjar design by Pascua Ortega. Excellent facilities, including parking, a fine restaurant (closed Sun & Aug) and an outdoor pool. €€€

Hotel Reino de Aragón C/Coso 80, https://hotelreinodearagon.com. Smart Silken chain hotel with a boutique feel. Rooms combine classical and contemporary style with satellite TV and marble-clad bathrooms. Often offers good online deals in low season. €€

Hotel Sauce C/Espoz y Mina 33, https://hotelsauce.com. Along with its great name, this hotel has a central location – 100m from Pza. del Pilar – and well-maintained, attractively furnished rooms. There's also a 24hr bar. The best prices are online. €€

Hotel Zentro Zaragoza C/Coso 86, www.vinccizaragozazentro.com. This upmarket hotel reveals a *modernista* facade and an elegant, cool-toned lobby (from which you can peer down at the underground Roman remains) that gives way to handsome rooms. Check the website for good last-minute or low-season offers. €€

★ **INNSiDE Meliá Zaragoza** Avda. Cesar Augusto, 13, www.melia.com/en/hotels/spain/zaragoza/innside-zaragoza. Smart, centrally located hotel within a few minutes walk of El Tubo. Rooms are vast, with separate seating and desk areas and the plush decor exudes a homely feel. There's a decent gym and a buffet breakfast, plus complimentary access to a nearby swimming pool. €€€

Zaragoza Camping C/San Juan Bautista de la Salle, about 7km southwest of the city, https://zaragozacamping.com. This well-tended campsite, on the city's outskirts, has good facilities, including a pool, organized kids' activities, a hostal (dorms with bunks for four or six) bungalows (sleeps four), glamping tents and a café/restaurant. Dorms €̄, bungalows/glamping €€

EATING   SEE MAP PAGE 562

The *casco viejo* features an array of economical restaurants, *comedores* and bars. As you'd expect in a place of this size, you'll also find upmarket restaurants scattered throughout the rest of the city. For tapas – and plenty of late-night drinking – head to **El Tubo**, the series of narrow streets near Pza. de España, particularly Estébanes, Cuatro de Agosto and La Libertad; also try the areas around Pza. de Santa Marta or Pza. de San Pedro Nolasco.

Bodegas Almau C/Estébanes 9, www.bodegasalmau.es. Spirited tapas bar established in 1870, with a handsome, tiled interior that gives way to a bustling outdoor courtyard area strewn with pebbles and barrel-tables. A range of tasty tapas includes their speciality of *dulce de anchoa* (sweet anchovy), an award-winner. €̄

Bodegón Azoque C/Marqués Casa Jiménez 6, https://bodegonazoque.com/. Upmarket tapas bar, catering to a smart business crowd sipping quality wine at the rustic, wood-encased bar. Barrels of wine stand at the door, while diners graze on sardines and the celebrated *jamón de Jabugo*, or dine on elegantly presented regional cuisine (including a good set lunch). €€

El Calamar Bravo C/Cinco de Marzo 14, 976 794 264. A popular and inexpensive tapas bar with outstanding *calamares* sandwiches and *patatas bravas*, all smothered in mayonnaise and spicy salsa. A few tables line one side of the fish-and-chip-shop-esque interior. €̄

★ **El Champi** C/La Libertad 16, www.instagram.com/elchampizgz21. Lively tapas joint that's known for its

9

9

signature (and only) tapa – succulent mushrooms topped with one prawn and a powerful garlic sauce. Organic wines and beer. €

El Fuelle C/Mayor 59, https://el-fuelle.com/. Earthy local *cocina*, specializing in no-frills Aragonese cuisine, especially meat dishes. Great atmosphere and value for money. €€

Gran Café Zaragoza C/Alfonso I 25, 976 290 882. Historic, genteel café; the nineteenth-century interior features dark-wood ceilings, a burnished wooden bar and large windows overlooking the street. There's no kitchen but it does serve simple *bocadillos*. €

Montal Torre Nueva 29, 976 298 998, http://montal.es. An old shop dating from 1919, full of delicious gourmet delights, that also has an alluring restaurant. Relax on a Renaissance balcony for an elegant dinner of regional cuisine or their excellent set lunch. Reservations essential. €€

Restaurant Triana C/Estébanes 7, www.instagram.com/eltriana_zgz. Friendly family-run restaurant and *taberna* serving a full range of tapas and raciones, which change according to what's in season. Good, locally focused wine list. €

DRINKING AND NIGHTLIFE

SEE MAP PAGE 562

The *casco viejo* has several hopping *zonas* of music-and-tapas bars and nightclubs, including the area around C/Contamina and C/Temple, which hits its stride at the weekends after midnight.

BARS

Bull McCabe's C/Cádiz 7, https://bullmccabes.net. One of the most popular of Zaragoza's Irish bars, with two floors and reasonably priced pints of the black stuff.

La Cucaracha C/Temple 25. Raucous place in the heart of *casco viejo*'s bar district, especially popular for its range of mind-numbing shots. Tends to get busy well after midnight.

CLUBS AND LIVE MUSIC

La Bóveda del Albergue C/ Predicadores 70, http://

campanadelosperdidos.com. Wonderfully unique bar with an old-time, traditional decor in a cave-like cellar and a great line-up of local performers, from jazz and blues to folk.

La Casa del Loco C/Mayor 10, https://facebook.com/lacasadellocozaragoza. Rock pub with plenty of live acts, and a mix of the latest English and Spanish sounds, along with the occasional Ibiza-style foam party. Cover €7–10 for live shows.

Da Luxe Pza. del Pilar 12, https://daluxe.es. Plush *discoteca*, home to the late-night party crowd, just behind the main *turismo*.

Oasis C/Boggiero 28, https://salaoasis.com. Combined club and live music venue that's been going for well over a century. Good cocktails and a small stage featuring a wide range of performers.

DIRECTORY

Cinema Filmoteca de Zaragoza, Pza. de San Carlos 4, https://filmotecazaragoza.com. City-run film archive, showing arthouse and classic films, including original-language movies.

Football Real Zaragoza (www.realzaragoza.com) plays at La Romareda stadium in the south of the city.

Hospital Miguel Servet, Pza. Isabel la Católica 1–3, 976 76 55 00, https://sectorzaragozados.salud.aragon.es.

Post office The main *Correos* is at Paseo de la Independencia 33 (Mon–Fri 8.30am–8.30pm, Sat 9.30am–1pm).

Shops The big shopping street is Paseo de la Independencia, south of Pza. de España, and is lined with chain stores, including a branch of El Corte Inglés. Northwest of the city lies the Gran Casa (www.grancasa.es), one of Zaragoza's largest shopping centres.

ARAGONESE CUISINE

Aragonese cuisine in many ways reflects the region: rugged, hearty, traditional. In a word: meat. Popular dishes include roast lamb (**ternasco**, derived from the word *tierno*, or tender); plump coils of pork sausages, such as **longaniza**; and, of course, **ham**, particularly from Teruel, whose dry but cold winds create an ideal climate for curing. The region is also known for its stews, such as **chilindrón**, which gets its name from the heavy pot in which it is cooked. Multiple varieties exist – the traditional version is a fragrant mix of bell peppers, chicken and cured ham. **Migas** ("breadcrumbs"), based on day-old bread cooked with garlic, peppers and other ingredients, is a popular dish throughout central Spain; the Aragón recipe calls for sausage and grapes. As for fish, fresh river **trout** from the Pyrenees often appears on menus, while sweets include the region's famous **frutas de Aragón**: candied fruits covered in chocolate. Aragón also has several **wine-growing regions**, including Somontano, Campo de Borja, Cariñena and Calatayud.

South of Zaragoza

Few tourists spend much time exploring the sights and towns to the south of Zaragoza. However, wine buffs might want to follow the **Ruta de los Vinos** through **Cariñena**. There are vineyards dotted all over Aragón, but some of the best wines – strong, throaty reds and good whites – come from this region, which is best explored with your own transport.

Goya enthusiasts will be interested in **Muel**, and his birthplace in **Fuendetodos**. Nearby lies **Belchite**, one of Spain's most poignant reminders of the Civil War.

Buses travel from Zaragoza to several towns in this area, including Cariñena, Muel and Belchite.

Muel and La Ermita de Nuestra Señora de la Fuente

Hermitage Free

MUEL, the northernmost point of the region, was once a renowned pottery centre but has seen much better days. However, it still retains a Roman fountain and a hermitage, **La Ermita de Nuestra Señora de la Fuente**, with some early frescoes of saints by Goya painted in 1772.

Fuendetodos

Buses run three times daily (twice on Saturdays) from Zaragoza to Fuendetodos (1hr 5min)

Francisco Goya, who became court painter to Carlos IV, spent his early childhood in the pretty village of **FUENDETODOS**, 24km southeast of Muel. Among the stone houses, with flowers sprouting on balconies, is Goya's home, now a charming museum.

Casa Natal de Goya and Museo del Grabado de Goya

C/Zuloaga • Charge • http://fundacionfuendetodosgoya.org

The **Casa Natal de Goya** is the eighteenth-century labourer's house where Goya was born in 1746; it has been faithfully restored, complete with rustic, period decor. Entry is included with tickets to the **Museo del Grabado de Goya**, 100m farther along C/Zuloaga at no. 3, which exhibits four of the artist's print series: *Caprichos* (Caprices), *Desashres* (Disasters), *Tauromaquia* (Bullfighting) and *Disparates* (Absurdities). *Caprichos* and *Disparates* represent a savage attack on the follies Goya perceived in Spanish society at the time, while *Tauromaquia* reflects the artist's genuine passion for bullfighting.

Belchite

Autocares Hife buses (http://hife.es) run from Zaragoza (one–three daily)

The old town of **BELCHITE**, 20km east of Fuendetodos and 50km southeast of Zaragoza, was left untouched after it was bombed by Franco's forces and is perhaps the most haunting reminder of the horrors of the Spanish Civil War.

The sign at the entrance reads simply "*Belchite, Pueblo Viejo*". Abandoned houses, with twisted wrought-iron balconies, peeling shutters and crumbling walls pocked with bullet holes, line the streets The church is especially affecting, with its gaping ceiling, and crushed rocks where the pews used to be. The only signs of life are the occasional shepherd and his flock, weaving through the silent ruins to the green fields beyond. The new town of Belchite town, constructed after the war, is 1km away.

Cariñena

Twenty-seven kilometres west of Fuendetodos, just off the main A23 highway, **CARIÑENA** is the capital of the Campo de Borja *comarca* (region). The town was named

9

after the Cariñena grape and is home to a small wine museum and a clutch of **bodegas**, where you can taste and buy wine. Buses arrive here twice a day from Zaragoza.

Museo del Vino
Camino de la Platero 1 • Charge • http://elvinodelaspiedras.es/museo-del-vino

This well-run **Museo del Vino** (closed for renovation until early 2025) explores the Cariñena wine region through a variety of exhibits, from old wine-making instruments to photos of ancient *bodegas* and vineyards. It also provides recommendations for touring the local vineyards.

North of Zaragoza

For a real taste of rural Spanish life, head north from Zaragoza to the delightful **Cinco Villas**, a collection of hill towns which stretches for some 90km along the border with Navarra and comprises **Tauste**, **Ejea de los Caballeros**, **Sádaba**, **Uncastillo** and **Sos del Rey Católico**. Each has its own charm and all are set in beautiful, scarcely visited countryside. The title of Cinco Villas is owed to Felipe V, who awarded it for their services in the War of the Spanish Succession (1701–14). For those en route to the Pyrenees (the road past Sos continues to Roncal in Navarra) or to Pamplona, the Cinco Villas make a pleasant stop-off. **Sos** and **Uncastillo** are the most interesting of the five and attract most visitors – but you could easily still have the streets to yourself.

Tauste, Ejea de los Caballeros and Sádaba

TAUSTE, closest of the towns to Zaragoza, has an interesting parish church built in the Mudéjar style. Nearby **EJEA DE LOS CABALLEROS** retains elements of Romanesque architecture in its churches. Twenty kilometres northwest, remote, tranquil **SÁDABA** boasts an impressive thirteenth-century castle, as well as the remains of an early synagogue.

Uncastillo

As its name suggests, **UNCASTILLO**, 15km northwest of Sádaba, is arranged around an imposing castle. This dates from the twelfth century and houses the small **Museo de la Torre** (charge; http://fundacionuncastillo.com), which has simple exhibits on the castle and local history.

Sos del Rey Católico

SOS DEL REY CATÓLICO, 120km from Zaragoza, derives its name from Fernando II, El Rey Católico, born here in 1452 and as powerful a local-boy-made-good as any Aragonese town could hope for. His reputed birthplace, the **Casa Palacio de Sada** (charge), now displays exhibits on the history of the impressive Aragonese monarchy and also houses the *turismo*. The narrow, cobbled streets of the *centro histórico*, like so many in Aragón, are packed with marvellously grand mansions. Sos also features the lovely Romanesque **Church of San Esteban**, with beautifully preserved fourteenth-century frescoes, and the ruined **Castillo de la Peña Felizana**, which offers magnificent views over the village's terracotta rooftops and surrounding countryside. The excellent parador has memorable vistas and might entice you to spend at least one night.

ARRIVAL, INFORMATION AND TOURS

By bus Only one bus a day makes it up from Zaragoza to Sos (2hr 30min), leaving at 5pm from Monday to Friday and returning at 7am. You'll need your own transport if you want to explore this area in any depth.

Turismo Casa Palacio de Sada, Sos (June to mid-Sept daily 10am–2pm & 4–8pm; mid-Sept to May Wed–Fri 10am–1pm & 4–6pm, Sat & Sun 10am–2pm & 4–7pm; 948 888 524, www.oficinaturismososdelreycatolico.com); Iglesia de San Martin de Tours, Uncastillo.

Tours In addition to the tour of the Palacio de Sada, the Sos tourist office also offers a guided walk through the village (charge).

ACCOMMODATION AND EATING

The best base for the area is the parador in Sos, but the other villages have a few choices, while the surrounding countryside features a number of quaint *casas rurales*. The local *turismos* can help with recommendations.

UNCASTILLO

★ **Posada la Pastora** Behind the Santa María church, https://lapastora.net/. This lovingly renovated, excellent-value *posada* has contemporary, country-house-style rooms and friendly owners who can help you explore the area. Some rooms have balconies and there's an excellent, hearty breakfast. €

SOS DEL REY CATÓLICO

Hotel Triskel C/las Afueras 9, www.aldahotels.es/hoteles/ aragon/zaragoza/hotel-alda-triskel. This comfortable though otherwise characterless hotel overlooks the old town, with a lovely view – get one with a balcony. €

★ **Parador Sos del Rey Católico** C/Arquitecto Sainz de Vicuña, www.parador.es. This superb hotel is well worth a splurge and makes a great base for touring the area. In the finest parador tradition, it's a lovely blend of historic and modern architecture – and also has spectacular panoramic views across the surrounding unspoiled countryside. Rooms have character and are reasonably spacious, while the elegant restaurant serves Aragonese specialities, such as *ternasco*, or young lamb, and wine from the Campo de Borja region. Service can be a little laidback, though. €€

West of Zaragoza

The Aragonese plains are dotted with reminders of the Moorish occupation, and nowhere more so than at **Tarazona**, an atmospheric old town loaded with Mudéjar architecture. If you're en route to Soria or Burgos, it's an ideal place to break the journey. Don't miss out, either, on the tranquil Cistercian monastery of **Veruela**, 15km southeast, and the magnificent **Monasterio de Piedra**, 20km south of the attractive Moorish town of **Calatyud**. Further south, **Daroca** is another imposing town well worth a visit.

Tarazona

TARAZONA's most absorbing sights lie in the old upper town, incorporating the **Judería** and **Morería** (Jewish and Moorish quarters, respectively), which stands on a hill overlooking the river, its medieval houses and mansions lining the *callejas* and *pasadizos* – the lanes and alleyways.

Ayuntamiento

Pza. de España

At the heart of the old town is **Pza. de España**, which is flanked by a magnificent sixteenth-century **ayuntamiento**, with a facade of coats of arms, sculpted heads and figures in high relief. A frieze, representing the triumphal procession of Carlos V after his coronation as Holy Roman Emperor runs the length of the building.

Santa María Magdalena and around

C/Conde • Charge

The Mudéjar tower of the church of **Santa María Magdalena** dominates the town. Within the church, look for the interesting fifteenth-century wooden lectern, carved in a geometric pattern. From the entrance there are especially good views of the eighteenth-century **Pza. de Toros** below – an octagonal terrace of houses, with balconies from which spectators could view the *corrida*.

9

Catedral

C/la Verónica • Charge • www.catedraldetarazona.es/

In the lower town, the principal sight is the **Catedral**, which was built mainly in the fourteenth and fifteenth centuries. It's a typical example of the decorative use of brick in the Gothic-Mudéjar style, with a dome built to the same design as that of the old Catedral in Zaragoza, and Mudéjar cloisters.

Monasterio de Veruela

Charge • 976 649 025

The **Monasterio de Veruela**, isolated in a fold of the hills 15km to the southeast of Tarazona, and standing within a massively fortified perimeter, is one of Spain's great religious houses. Now uninhabited, you can visit the magnificent twelfth-century church, fourteenth-century cloisters and convent buildings. It also houses a well-run **Museo del Vino**, with snazzy exhibits that trace Campo de Borja wine, wine tastings and a well-stocked shop.

ARRIVAL AND INFORMATION   TARAZONA

By bus Regular daily buses with Therpasa (https:// therpasa.es/) travel between Zaragoza and Tarazona (1hr 5min).
Turismo Pza. de San Francisco (Mon–Fri 9.30am–1.30pm & 4–7pm; Sat 10am–2pm & 4–7pm, Sun 10am–2pm &

4–6pm; 976 640 074, http://tarazonamonumental.es). The *turismo*, in the main square below the Catedral, runs guided tours (check website for times) of the cathedral, the Palacio Episcopal, the Iglesia de Santa Magdalena and the town.

ACCOMMODATION

La Fonda C/Marrodán 17, http://lafondatarazona.es. This friendly inn offers style on a budget in the historic centre. The simple, minimalist rooms have crisp white linens and clean lines, and the delicious breakfasts (extra charge) will set you up for a day of sightseeing. €€
Hostal Santa Agueda C/Visconti 26, http://santaagueda. com. This welcoming *hostal* is set in a lovingly restored historical home, with lovely period furnishings. A buffet breakfast is included and the *hostal* also houses a small exhibit on Tarazona 1920s singer and vaudeville performer

Raquel Meller. €
★ **La Merced de la Concordia** Pza. de la Merced 2, http://lamerced.info. Handsome hotel in a 1501 *palacete* with modern flourishes that juxtapose nicely with the historical interior: pale-wood floors, recessed lights and sleek furnishings meet stone walls and restored rustic ceilings. Some of the rooms are suites and very spacious. Enjoy creatively prepared regional fare in the elegant, soft-toned restaurant (closed Sun dinner & Mon). €€

EATING AND DRINKING

El Caserón 2 Reino Aragón 2, 976 642 312. Located just north of the old town, this friendly bar has haunches of ham dangling over the bar, and serves up traditional cuisine. €

El Galeón Avda. La Paz 1, 976 642 965. In the lower town, this mid-priced restaurant serves good traditional food, including grilled *ternasco* (lamb) and seafood. €€

Calatayud

Like Tarazona, **Calatayud** is a town of Moorish foundation. It's worth climbing up to the old upper town where, amid a maze of alleys, stand the church of **San Andrés** (generally closed to visitors; enquire at *turismo*) and **Colegiata de Santa María** (open most Saturdays; enquire at *turismo*) both of which have ornate Mudéjar towers. Santa María, the collegiate church, also has a beautifully decorative Plateresque doorway, while towards the river, at C/Valentín Gómez 3, **San Juan el Real** (free; http://facebook. com/sanjuancalatayud) features paintings attributed to the young Goya. The ruins of a Moorish castle (open access; free) survive on high ground at the opposite end of town from the train station, and offer lovely views. The **Museo de Calatayud** (free; www. calatayud.es/contenido/museo-calatayud), set in the historic Convento de la Orden del Carmelo, explores Calatayud's culture and history.

ARRIVAL AND INFORMATION

By bus Regular daily buses travel between Zaragoza and Calatayud (www.monbus.es, 1hr 10min).
Turismo Museo del Calatayud, Pza. de Santa Teresa 3 (Mon–Sat 9.30am–1.30pm & 4–8pm; 976 886 322, www.calatayud.es/turismo).
By train There are regular AVE trains between Zaragoza and Calatayud (25min).

ACCOMMODATION

Hospedería Mesón la Dolores Pza. Mesones 4, http://mesonladolores.com. Comfortable hotel in a rustic eighteenth-century building with stone arches, tiled floors and dark wood ceilings. The restaurant serves a hearty *menú del día*, which includes gazpacho and grilled meats. €̄

Hotel Castillo de Ayud Avda. de la Diputación 8, http://hotelcastillodeayud.com. This stylish, complex offers spacious, modern rooms in a *belle époque* building, with superior rooms and suites in an adjoining contemporary extension. There's a soothing spa, plus a pair of restaurants, one offering simple, traditional cuisine and a well-priced weekly lunch menu and a more upmarket option with a creative tasting menu. €̄€̄

Monasterio de Piedra

Charge • http://monasteriopiedra.com

The **Monasterio de Piedra** – "The Stone Monastery" – lies 20km south of Calatayud, 4km from the village of **NUÉVALOS**. The monastic buildings, once part of a grand Cistercian complex, are a ruin, but they stand amid lush park-like **gardens**, with waterfalls, grottoes and lakes. The entrance fee includes a guided tour of the monastery's cloisters, church, wine cellar, refectory and kitchens.

ARRIVAL AND DEPARTURE

By bus A bus runs from Zaragoza to Nuévalos and the Monasterio de Piedra (https://www.monbus.es/; 2hr 15min) at 9am on Tues, Thurs, Sat and Sun. The same bus departs at 10.30am from Calatayud.

ACCOMMODATION

Hotel Monasterio de Piedra Near the gardens' entrance, https://monasteriopiedra.com/hotel/. This handsome abbey-turned-hotel is part of the Monasterio de Piedra and allows you to sleep in the Cisterian monks' rooms, which have been plushly renovated and have views of the cloisters, monastery or park. There is also a spa, and guests enjoy reduced admission to the park. €̄€̄€̄€̄

Hotel Río Piedra Carretera del Monasterio de Piedra, Nuévalos, www.hotelriopiedra.com. This family-run hotel, at the foot of the road up to the monastery, has a range of rooms, some with terraces. The restaurant serves well-prepared regional cuisine. €̄€̄

Hotel Las Truchas Carretera del Monasterio de Piedra, Nuévalos, www.hotellastruchas.com. This family-run, reasonably priced hotel has simply furnished but clean rooms, tennis courts, a kids' playground, and a pool and a simple restaurant serving local cuisine. €̄

Daroca

DAROCA, 38km southeast of Calatayud, is a charming old town, set within an impressive run of **walls** that includes no fewer than 114 towers. Though largely in ruins today, they are still striking. You enter the town through its original gates, the **Puerta Alta** or stout **Puerta Baja**, which are linked by the C/Mayor. The appeal of Daroca lies more in the whole ensemble, although the maze of ancient streets is dotted with Romanesque, Gothic and Mudéjar **churches**. Foremost among them is the Renaissance **Basilica de Santa María** (https://updaroca.com/basilica/visitas/; charge for museum), off Pza. de España, which has a small museum of religious artefacts.

ARRIVAL AND INFORMATION

By bus Daroca is connected to Calatayud, Teruel and Cariñena/Zaragoza by a couple of daily bus services.
Turismo C/Mayor 44 (www.daroca.es/turismo/). The small *turismo* offers guided visits.

9

ACCOMMODATION AND EATING

Hotel Cien Balcones C/Mayor 88, http://cienbalcones. com. As the name suggests, this welcoming hotel has balconies galore, many fronted by wrought-iron handiwork, and overlooking a breezy patio. Ask about their creative packages, one of which includes a horse ride into the countryside. The elegant *Ruejo* restaurant serves regional cuisine. Breakfast included. €

La Posada del Almudí C/Grajera 7, http://posadadel almudi.es. Near Pza. Santiago, this place has two types of room: those in the restored fifteenth- to sixteenth-century mansion house; or those in a modern, stylish annexe across the street. There's also a bar and good restaurant (best to reserve). €€

Teruel

The provincial capital of **TERUEL** offers an appealing glimpse into this rugged and sparsely populated wedge of Aragón. Because it's often overlooked, the region came up with the playful slogan *Teruel existe* ("Teruel exists"). This high, remote corner of Spain, with its back-of-beyond villages and medieval sights that haven't been prettified, has the coldest winters in the country.

The impressive and appealing town of Teruel was an important Moorish city and retained significant Muslim and Jewish communities after its Reconquest by Alfonso II in 1171. It contains some of the finest **Mudéjar** work in Spain, including the spectacular towers, built by Moorish craftsmen over three centuries, which, like the fabulous Mudéjar ceiling in the Catedral, should not be missed.

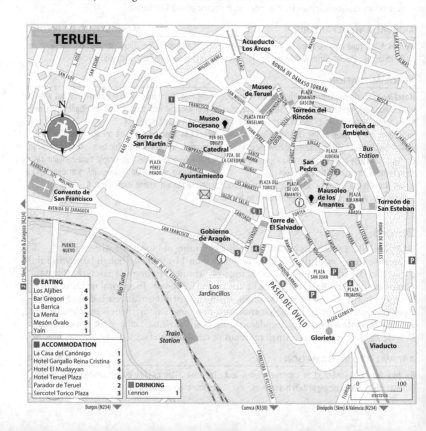

> ## EL RINCÓN DE ADEMUZ
>
> **El Rincón de Ademuz** (http://rincondeademuz.es), 30km due south of Teruel, is a strange little region: a Valencian province enclosed within Aragonese territory. It's a very remote corner of Spain, with a bleak kind of grandeur, and sees scarcely a tourist from one year to the next.
>
> The place to head for – and if you're bussing it, the only realistic place to get to from Teruel – is **ADEMUZ** itself, without doubt Spain's tiniest and least significant provincial capital. Strung along a craggy hill at the confluence of two long rivers, this could make a beautiful base for walking, and there's a fascination just in wandering the streets with their dark stone cottages and occasional Baroque towers.
>
> For energetic **trekking** there's Torre Baja, which lies to the north along the Río Turia, and beyond it the beautiful village of Castielfabib. The most interesting of these little Ademuz hamlets, Puebla de San Miguel, is to the east, in the Sierra Tortajada, easily accessible by road from Valencia, but also from a minor road just out of Ademuz in the Teruel direction, east over the Río Turia bridge and signposted to Sabina, Sesga and Mas del Olmo.

The **centro histórico**, located on a hill above the Río Turia, has the Pza. del Torico at its heart and is enclosed by the remains of fortified walls, with a viaduct linking it to the modern quarter to the south. Leading off to the north is a sixteenth-century aqueduct, **Los Arcos**, a slender and elegant piece of monumental engineering.

La Escalinata

Facing the train station is **La Escalinata**, a flight of steps decorated with bricks, tiles and turrets that is pure civic Mudéjar in style – note the iron gap in the wall to the left, where a lift (free) shoots up to the *paseo*.

Torre de El Salvador and Torre de San Martín

Torre de El Salvador Charge • Torre de San Martín Not open to the public • http://teruelmudejar.com

The **Torre de El Salvador** is the finest of Teruel's four Mudéjar towers and is thought to have been built in the fourteenth century. It is covered with intricately patterned and proportioned coloured tiles to stunning effect, echoed closely in its more modest sister tower, **Torre de San Martín** (exterior only), best reached via C/los Amantes and said to predate it. A common feature of all the towers is that they stand separate from the main body of the church to which they belong, a design that was almost certainly influenced by the freestanding minarets seen in Muslim architecture.

Catedral de Santa María de Mediavilla

Pza. de la Catedral • Charge • www.diocesisdeteruel.org/catedral-de-teruel

The **Catedral de Santa María de Mediavilla**, built in the twelfth century but gracefully adapted over subsequent years, boasts a fine Mudéjar tower, incorporating Romanesque windows and a lantern with Renaissance and Mudéjar features. The interior follows a more standard Gothic-Mudéjar pattern and at first sight seems unremarkable, save for its brilliant Renaissance *retablo*. Climb the stairs by the door, however, and put money in the illuminations box, and the fabulous **artesonado ceiling** is revealed. Completed between 1260 and 1314 by Moorish craftsmen, it's a fascinating mix of geometric Islamic motifs and medieval paintings of courtly life.

Museo de Arte Sacro

Pza. de la Catedral • Charge • www.diocesisdeteruel.org/museo-de-arte-sacro-de-teruel

9

Standing next to the Catedral is the sixteenth-century Palacio Episcopal, which houses the **Museo de Arte Sacro**. Inside, look out for the *Calvario*, a beautiful woodcarving of Jesus (whose arms are missing), St John and the Virgin Mary, carved in the fifteenth century but for many years hidden behind a wall in a church in Sarrón, where it was discovered in 1946. Another highlight is the *Arbol de la Vida*, a striking seventeenth-century ivory carving of Christ.

Museo de Teruel

Pza. Fray Anselmo • Free • https://www.museodeteruel.es/

The well-run **Museo de Teruel** is worth a peek for its range of exhibits on local folklore and traditional rural life, including pottery, silverwork, clothing and a reconstructed interior of an eighteenth-century chemist shop. The museum also has interesting temporary exhibitions, including contemporary photography.

San Pedro and Mausoleo de los Amantes

San Pedro Charge • Mausoleo de los Amantes Charge • http://amantesdeteruel.es

Just beyond Pza. del Torico, which is flanked by a trio of *modernista* houses, is the church of **San Pedro**, endowed with a lovely thirteenth-century Mudéjar tower that you can visit. Its claim to fame, however, relates to the nearby **Mausoleo de los Amantes**, a chapel containing the alabaster tomb of the Lovers of Teruel, Isabel de Segura and Juan Diego Martínez de Marcilla. This pair's tale of thwarted love is a legend throughout Spain. The story goes that Diego, ordered by his lover's family to go away and prove himself worthy, left Teruel for five years, returning only to find that Isabel was to be married that same day. He asked for a last kiss, was refused and died, heartbroken; Isabel, not to be outdone, arranged his funeral at San Pedro, kissed the corpse and died in its arms. The lovers' (reputed) bodies were exhumed in 1955 and now lie illuminated for all to see – a macabre yet popular pilgrimage for newlyweds.

Dinópolis

Charge • www.dinopolis.com

Teruel, as the location of the first Spanish dinosaur discovery, the Aragosaurus, is an important place for paleontology. Loosely based on this heritage is **Dinópolis**, a lively dinosaur theme park with rides, guides dressed as mad professors and oodles of dinosaur exhibits. Dinópolis also runs a number of similarly themed parks in the region, including the Bosque Pétreo (Petrified Forest); see the website for details.

ARRIVAL AND INFORMATION | TERUEL

By train Trains run regularly from Zaragoza (2hr 30min) and Valencia (2hr 40min). The station is on the fringes of the *centro histórico*; from the train station, walk up La Escalinata and C/Nueva into town.

By bus The bus station is also on the eastern edge of town; walk north a short way up the ring road, taking the first left to Pza. Judería. There are a number of bus companies, so check the timetables in the windows before buying a ticket, as some buses are considerably slower than others.

All services are reduced on Sundays.

Destinations Ademuz (Mon–Sat; 55min); Albarracín (Mon–Sat; 2hr); Barcelona (6 daily; 6hr 45min); Valencia (5 daily; 2hr 15min); Zaragoza (7 daily; 2hr 15min).

Turismo Pza. de los Amantes 6 (daily 10am–2pm & 4–8pm; Aug daily 10am–8pm; 978 624 105, https://turismo.teruel.es)

Regional tourist office C/San Francisco, near the La Escalinata (www.sienteteruel.es).

ACCOMMODATION | SEE MAP PAGE 574

La Casa del Canónigo C/San Martín, https://lacasadelcanonigo.com/. Well-preserved *casa* in the middle of the old town, set in a seventeenth-century mansion that was acquired by the *canónigo* (canon) of the Teruel Catedral in 1698. It offers rooms, suite and apartments, and serves breakfasts and dinners prepared with local specialities. **€€€**

Hotel Gargallo Reina Cristina Paseo del Óvalo 1, www. hotelreinacristinateruel.com. This attractive hotel by the Torre del Salvador has modern if unexciting rooms, as well as an excellent restaurant (€€) that serves regional cuisine with a creative twist, including some veggie options. €€€
Hotel El Mudayyan C/Nueva 18, https://elmudayyan. com/. Lovely hotel set in two adjoining buildings where you can – quite literally – explore underground Teruel: medieval tunnels, once used by priests to travel to and from the sacristy, extend below the hotel. The rooms are snug but individually and attractively decorated with Mudéjar touches, while a small Moroccan-style tearoom makes for a relaxing afternoon. €€
Hotel Teruel Plaza Pza. Tremedal 3, http://hotelteruel

plaza.com. This smart modern hotel near Pza. San Juan has contemporary rooms with wooden floors and king-size beds. There's a café and TV room. €€
Parador de Teruel Carretera Sagunto-Burgos, 2km out of town, www.parador.es. This modern hotel, on a wooded hillside overlooking the town and towers 2km from the centre, has a swimming pool, tennis courts and a large garden. Rooms are fresh and spacious and many have fine views over the countryside. €€€
Sercotel Torico Plaza C/Yagüe de Salas 5, http:// hoteltoricoplaza.com. Centrally located contemporary hotel with understated, simple rooms and suites. A breakfast buffet is included and there's convenient parking close by. €€

EATING SEE MAP PAGE 574

The town's most celebrated gastronomic creation is **Jamón de Teruel**. You'll find the tasty, fat-streaked *jamón* in shops and served up in tapas bars and restaurants all over town and trying it is an experience not to be missed. The main areas for restaurants are on the eastern side of the old town, principally Pza. Judería, C/Bartolomé Esteban, C/Abadía and C/San Esteban, though you'll also find lively cafés on Pza. del Torico.
Los Aljíbes C/Yagüe de Salas 3, www.losaljibes.com/. A buzzing café and *bodega* specializing in Aragonese and Navarran cuisine such as *migas a la Pastora* and juicy lamb, with a well-stocked tapas counter and an extensive wine list featuring local vintages. €€
Bar Gregori Paseo del Óvalo 6, 978 600 580. This friendly tapas bar serves all the favourites, including Teruel's famous *jamón* and pigs' ears. Outside tables, plus good, keenly priced wine and *sangría* make for a chilled place to pass the evening. €
La Barrica C/Abadia 5, 978 618 235. Cosy, inventive tapas bar serving a variety of dishes and an extensive list of wines.

Try the *patatas* with *jámon* and truffle mayonnaise. €
La Menta C/Bartolomé Esteban 10, 978 605 804. One of the city's top restaurants, with a carefully constructed menu that changes weekly, and sumptuous dishes of Aragonese classics (including local truffle). €€
Mesón Óvalo Paseo del Óvalo 2, https://mesonovalo.es. A very popular *mesón* with warm, tangerine-coloured walls, quality cooking (the trout dishes are excellent) and a range of Maestrazgo specialities. €€
★ **Yaín** Pza. de la Judería 9, www.yain.es. Proof that creative, gourmet fare has a place in Teruel. The sleek restaurant (named after the Hebrew word for "wine", because of its location on Pza. de la Judería) reveals gleaming dark wood, alabaster lamps and an impressive wine cellar. Regional dishes with a twist include *pimiento del piquillo* (bright-red peppers shaped like a *piquillo*, or "little beak") stuffed with cod, and quail with a *garbanzo* puree. The eight-course gastronomic menu makes for a memorable splurge. €€€

DRINKING SEE MAP PAGE 574

Teruel is a quiet little town, but you'll find a cluster of bars on the streets around Pza. Judería and Pza. Bolamar.
Lennon C/San Andrés 23, www.instagram.com/

salapublennon.teruel. A vast, laidback bar with several rooms, comfy chairs and sofas, occasional live music and a pool table.

Albarracín

ALBARRACÍN, 38km west of Teruel, is one of the more accessible targets in rural southern Aragón – as well as one of the most picturesque towns in the province, poised above the Río Guadalaviar and retaining, virtually intact, its medieval streets and tall, balconied houses. There's a historical curiosity here, too, in that from 1165 to 1333, the town formed the centre of a small independent state, the kingdom of the Azagras.

Despite its growing appeal as a tourist destination, Albarracín's dark, enclosed lanes and ancient buildings adorned with splendid coats of arms still make for an intriguing wander. Approaching from Teruel, you may imagine (wrongly) that you're about to come upon a large town. The **medieval walls** swoop back over the hillside, protecting, within the loop of the river, a far greater area than the extent of the town, past or present.

9

Moving on from Albarracín, if you have transport, you could take a pleasant route west to Cuenca through beautiful countryside, by way of Frías de Albarracín and the source of the Río Tajo (see page 173).

Catedral and Museo Diocesano

C/Catedral • Charge • http://fundacionsantamariadealbarracin.com

The **Catedral**, a medieval building remodelled in the sixteenth to eighteenth centuries, rises over a small square, and features an eye-catching gilded altarpiece. The **Museo Diocesano**, housed in the attached Palacio Obispal, displays religious and sacred art from around the region, including paintings, sculpture, metalwork and musical instruments.

Museo de Albarracín

C/San Juan 18 • Charge • http://fundacionsantamariadealbarracin.com

The well-curated **Museo de Albarracín** is housed in an eighteenth-century hospital that was also used as a prison after the Civil War. It features a range of exhibits and audiovisual displays on the history, art and culture of Albarracín, including rare archeological finds such as a series of eleventh-century ceramics.

Castillo de Albarracín

Charge • http://fundacionsantamariadealbarracin.com

The crumbling but atmospheric **castle**, in the southern part of town on an impressive clifftop, forms part of Albarracín's impressive early remains, and dates from the ninth century when the town was a fortified Islamic outpost. Among its remains are parts of a tenth-century Moorish palace, a hammam and various lookout points along the ancient walls as well as several murals from the Christian era.

Torre Blanca and Torre del Andador

Torre Blanca Charge • **Torre Andador** Free • http://fundacionsantamariadealbarracin.com

The **Torre Blanca**, near Albarracín's castle, has been extensively renovated and houses temporary changing exhibitions. You can also climb up to a lookout point for sweeping views over the surrounding landscape. The **Torre del Andador** looms over the northern part of town.

ARRIVAL AND INFORMATION   ALBARRACÍN

Bus One bus a day (Mon–Sat) runs from Teruel to Albarracín (45min).

Turismo C/San Antonio, next to the main bridge (Mon–Sat 10am–2pm & 4–8pm, Sun 10am–2pm & 4–7pm; 978 710 262), has information on the town and the surrounding region.

Centro de Información C/Catedral, next to the Catedral (daily: summer 10am–2pm & 4–8pm; winter 10am–2pm & 4–6.30/7pm; 978 704 035, http://fundacion santamariadealbarracin.com). The centre offers guided tours of Albarracín and the Catedral (see page 578).

ACCOMMODATION AND EATING

★ **Casa Santiago** Subida a las Torres 11, https://casade santiago.es. This inviting, family-run hotel is set in a

restored country house at the top of a stone staircase near the Pza. Mayor. The nine cosy, individually decorated rooms

have colourful quilts and wood-beamed ceilings – some even have four-poster beds. There is also a sun-lit sitting room where you can look out over the brightly tiled roofs of Albarracín. The simple restaurant serves local cuisine. €€
El Hostal Los Palacios C/Los Palacios, beyond the Portal de Molina, https://www.lospalacioshostal.es. This welcoming hotel features sixteen warm, well-cared-for rooms, some with

rustic brick walls, and a casual terrace restaurant-bar serving hearty regional cuisine with good value set lunch. €
Posada del Adarve C/Portal de Molina 23, https://posada deladarve.com. Relax in handsome, carefully renovated rooms and suites, some with wood-beam ceilings, tiled floors and rustic wooden furniture, in a historic townhouse that is part of the town's medieval walls. €€

Sierra de Gúdar

The mountains of the **SIERRA DE GÚDAR** and nearby El Maestrazgo (see page 580), to the east and northeast of Teruel, offer striking, often wild, beauty, with severe peaks, deep gorges and lush meadows. Just a century ago, this now impoverished region had four times the number of inhabitants it does today. Defeated in their attempts to make a living from agriculture, many left to seek their fortunes in the cities, leaving behind the crumbling remains of the once grand, honey-hued farmhouses that dot the landscape and the stone-walled terraces etched into the steep-sided hills.

A landscape of sharp, rocky crags, Sierra de Gúdar is easy to access by following the N234 southeast from Teruel and then heading northeast into the mountains along the A232, to the lovely medieval villages of **Mora de Rubielos**, 42km from Teruel, and its even lovelier twin, **Rubielos de Mora**. Head north for **Linares de Mora** and Mosqueruela, also charming and remote mountain villages. Your own transport is essential in this region.

Mora de Rubielos and Rubielos de Mora

These confusingly named villages both have fine collections of medieval houses, with small, wrought-iron balconies, bedecked with flowers. Both are lovely places to while away an afternoon. **MORA DE RUBIELOS** has an impressive castle, while **RUBIELOS DE MORA**, 14km from Mora de Rubielos, features handsome *palacios* with finely carved wooden eaves, a small art museum and the **Ex Colegiata de Santa María la Mayor**, which is on Pza. de Marqués de Tosos and has an ostentatious tiered bell tower. If you want to see inside, enquire at the *turismo*.

Castillo de Mora de Rubielos
Mora de Rubielos • Charge • https://castillomoraderubielos.com

For such a small place, Mora de Rubielos has an extremely grand **castle**, built in a luminous pinkish-gold stone, which during the Middle Ages served as both a defensive fort and noble residence, and was the heart of town life. It hosts a small **Museo Etnológico**, a motley collection of rustic antiquities. If it's open, it's worth having a peek inside the bulky, Gothic Ex Colegiata de Santa María below the castle.

Fundación Museo Salvador Victoria
Rubielos de Mora • Free • www.museosalvadorvictoria.com

Housed in the eighteenth-century Hospital de Gracia, the **Fundación Museo Salvador Victoria** features an in-depth collection of work by Salvador Victoria (1928–1994), from lithographs to luminous paintings. It also has a collection of contemporary Spanish art from the second half of the twentieth century, including works by Lucio Muñoz, Rafael Canogar, Manuel Rivera and Antonio Saura.

Linares de Mora

The vegetation becomes scrubbier and the views more dramatic as the road climbs north 25km from Rubielos to **LINARES DE MORA**, a beguiling place, with houses piled higgledy-

9

piggledy up the mountainside and glorious views. Its ruined castle is situated, rather precariously, on a jutting rock above the village, while another promontory hosts a church.

ARRIVAL AND DEPARTURE · MORA DE RUBIELOS AND RUBIELOS DE MORA

By bus Buses are infrequent in this area, but most villages are connected with each other and/or Teruel once a day. A bus (Mon–Fri) leaves Teruel in the afternoon for Mosqueruela via Mora de Rubielos, Rubielos de Mora and Linares de Mora, returning in the early morning.

INFORMATION

Mora de Rubielos C/Diputación 2 (Tues–Fri 10am–2pm & 5–7.30pm, Sat & Sun 5–8pm; 978 806 132, www. moraderubielos.com).

Rubielos de Mora C/Hispanoamérica 1 (daily: July–Sept 10am–2pm & 5–8pm; Oct–June 10am–2pm & 4–7pm; 978 804 096, www.rubielosdemora.es).

ACCOMMODATION AND EATING

MORA DE RUBIELOS

Hotel Jaime I Pza. de la Villa, www.hoteljaime.com. This attractively restored hotel has 28 elegantly rustic rooms in an old mansion, some with wooden beams and large balconies, as well as two charming apartments. The restaurant serves good regional cuisine. €€

Hotel La Trufa Negra Avda. Ibañez Martín 10, www. latrufanegra.com. This swanky hotel has stylish rooms full of amenities, a luxurious spa and an upmarket restaurant (€€€) serving excellent local cuisine. This area of the Maestrazgo is famous for its truffles and the hotel offers trips out into the countryside with truffle-hunters and their dogs; you can then enjoy the truffles on the tasting menu. €€€€

RUBIELOS DE MORA

Hotel de la Villa Pza. del Carmen, www.hoteldelavilla. com. This handsome hotel in a sixteenth-century castle has fourteen elegant rooms with wooden furnishings and beamed ceilings, and a fine restaurant with a great value set lunch menu. €€

Los Leones Pza. Igual y Gil 3, https://losleones.info/. A well-restored seventeenth-century palace near the church, complete with antique bedsteads and heavy wooden doors. Also has a smart restaurant serving an excellent array of regional specialities. €€€

LINARES DE MORA

El Portalico C/Portalico, https://elportalico.hotelsby. es. Situated on the edge of the old quarter, this basic but clean *hostal* is set in a historic mansion and has pleasant, simply furnished rooms. There's also a traditional bar and restaurant serving classic local dishes. €

El Maestrazgo

Unfolding northeast of Teruel, the **MAESTRAZGO** is dry, windswept, rugged terrain dominated (and named after) the Maestrazgo mountain range. This sparsely populated region can often seem to be stuck in time, particularly if you wander the quiet, cobbled streets of its ancient mountain villages. In the southern Maestrazgo, **Cantavieja** makes a useful base for exploring and hiking, while well-preserved **La Iglesuela del Cid** lies to the southeast. The northern limits of the Maestrazgo edge into Tarragona province in Catalunya, and can be approached from Tarragona/Gandesa, or from Zaragoza via Alcañiz, where the N232 forks: east to the lovely town of **Valderrobres**, with its superb castle and elegant Gothic church, and south to **Calanda** and a centre dedicated to film-maker Luis Buñuel.

Cantavieja

CANTAVIEJA, dramatically situated by the edge of an escarpment at an altitude of 1300m, is a little livelier and larger than most Maestrazgo villages, though its population is still under a thousand. The beautiful, porticoed **Pza. de Cristo Rey**, halfway up C/Mayor from Pza. de España, is typical of the region, and the escutcheoned *ayuntamiento* bears a Latin inscription with suitably lofty sentiments: "This House hates wrongdoing, loves peace, punishes crimes, upholds the laws and honours the upright".

Museo de las Guerras Carlistas de Cantavieja
C/Mayor 15 • Charge • https://museovirtualmaestrazgo.com/museo-de-las-guerras-carlistas/

The small **Museo de las Guerras Carlistas de Cantavieja** documents the nineteenth-century Carlist Wars in Cantavieja via audiovisual displays, scale models, old uniforms, newspaper clippings and weapons.

Mirambel

The best views of Cantavieja can be found on the rough and narrow road to **MIRAMBEL**, 15km to the northeast and walkable in about four hours. The village preserves a timeless atmosphere, with its ancient walls, gateways and stone houses. It was temporarily thrown into a whirl of excitement when Ken Loach filmed *Land and Freedom* (1995) here, but these days it's back to its usual, sleepy self.

La Iglesuela del Cid

LA IGLESUELA DEL CID, 11km to the southeast of Cantavieja, is a fine walk along a rough country road. The village's name bears witness to the exploits of **El Cid Campeador**, who came charging through the Maestrazgo in his fight against the infidel. Other than the El Cid *romería*, a fiesta organized by the village forty days after Easter (usually in May), there's nothing else to commemorate the legendary hero.

The village's ochre-red, dry-stone walls, ubiquitous coats of arms and stream – now little more than a trickle – are picturesque, but there's not much else to see. The central, compact Pza. de la Iglesia is enclosed by the old *ayuntamiento*, the attractive **Iglesia Parroquial de la Purificacíon** and a restored eighteenth-century *palacio*, now an upmarket hotel (see page 582).

Villarluengo and beyond

A dramatic, almost alpine, route is in store if you head 30km northwest from Cantavieja, past Cañada de Benatanduz to **VILLARLUENGO**, an enchanting village of ancient houses stacked on a terraced hillside.

Continue 6km farther north on the A1702, over the Villarluengo Pass (1132m), and you'll come to the wonderfully atmospheric *Hostal de la Trucha*. A further 19km, over another pass and past the striking jagged limestone ridges known as **Los Órganos de Montoro**, the road drops down to the small village of **Ejulve**, and then 11km north to the N211 between Montalbán and Alcañiz.

Calanda and Centro Buñuel

C/Mayor 48, on the edge of town • Charge • www.bunuelcalanda.com

CALANDA is home to the excellent **Centro Buñuel**, dedicated to surrealist film-maker Luis Buñuel, who was born here in 1900. Buñuel left Spain in the 1930s, spending his most creative periods in France and then Mexico, where he died in 1983, but he remained fond of his hometown throughout his life. The centre houses a series of innovative displays on the man and his movies, and also has an extensive film library.

Valderrobres

VALDERROBRES is one of the Maestrazgo's most attractive towns. It stands 50km from Calanda, near the border with Catalunya and astride the Río Matarraña, whose crystal waters, flanked by lush valleys, teem with trout. The old quarter sits north of the river, connected to the new town by Avda. Hispanidad and the Puente de Piedra, with the unassuming seventeenth-century **ayuntamiento** on Pza. España just over the bridge.

9

Dominating the town is the **Castillo** (www.castillodevalderrobres.com/; charge), once owned by the archbishops of Zaragoza and restored in the 1980s. Today it hosts an array of cultural events and exhibitions. There is also a fourteenth-century church worth visiting here, the **Santa María La Mayor,** which has a fine rose window and is one of the most impressive examples of Levantine Gothic architecture in the region.

ARRIVAL AND INFORMATION   EL MAESTRAZGO

By bus The main approaches to El Maestrazgo are from Teruel, and there are daily buses to Cantavieja and La Iglesuela del Cid, or from Morella in the province of Castellón. Bus schedules tend to vary widely, so it's best to confirm with the *turismo* in Teruel. The main bus route to northern Maestrazgo is between Valderrobres and Alcañiz (50min) and Tortosa (1hr); buses run Monday to Friday and stop next to the iron bridge in Valderrobres.

Turismos In Cantavieja the *turismo* is at C/Mayor 15 (mid-July to mid-Sept daily 10am–2pm & 4–7pm; mid-Sept to mid-July usually Sat & Sun only; 678 340 228, https:// cantaviejaturismo.com/). Valderrobres' *turismo* is at Avda. Cortes de Aragón 7, near the iron bridge (July & Aug Tues–Sat 9.30am–2pm & 5–7.30pm, Sun 9.30am–2pm; Sept–June Wed–Sat 10am–2pm & 4–6pm, Sun 10am–2pm; 978 8500 01, www.valderrobres.es/turismo).

ACCOMMODATION AND EATING

CANTAVIEJA

★ **Hotel Balfagón** Avda. Maestrazgo 20, https:// hotelspabalfagon.com. This stylish and modern hotel, on the main road at the southern edge of town, has comfortable rooms and a spa with sauna and Jacuzzi. There's also an excellent restaurant that serves traditional cuisine and more than eighty different wines, and a lounge bar with expansive terrace. €€

LA IGLESUELA DEL CID

Casa Amada C/Fuente Nueva 10, 964 443 373. This simple *hostal*, on the main road through the village, has basic rooms and a restaurant serving well-priced, substantial country cooking. €
Hospedería Palacio Matutano Daudém, C/Ondevila 4, https://palaciomatutanodauden.com. Elegant boutique hotel, set in an eighteenth-century *palacio*, with luxurious, antique-filled rooms and a small spa. The restaurant serves regional cuisine and offers a *menú del día*. Breakfast included. €€

VILLARLUENGO AND AROUND

Fonda Villarluengo C/Castel 1, Villarluengo, 613 876 512.

Friendly *hostal* with well-maintained rooms above a bar and a *comedor* serving simple meals. €
Hostal de la Trucha C/Las Fábricas, 6km north of Villarluengo, http://hostallatrucha.com. Set in an old farmhouse on the banks of the tranquil Río Pitarque, this wonderfully atmospheric *hostal* has 54 simple rooms with Castilian furniture and tiled floors. There's also an outdoor swimming pool and a restaurant that serves trout caught in the fish farm a few metres away. €€

VALDERROBRES

Fonda La Plaza Pza. España 8, opposite the ayuntamiento, www.fondalaplaza.es. Long-time *fonda* in the old quarter, which has atmospheric, rustic rooms set in a medieval mansion. The restaurant serves a *menú del día*. €
Hostal Querol Just up Avda. Hispanidad from the bridge, www.hotelquerol.com. This plain but adequate *hostal* has simple, clean rooms and a bar and *comedor* serving local cuisine. Half- and full-board packages are available. €
El Salt C/Elvira Hidalgo 14, www.hotelelsalt.com. In the new town, this is one of the more comfortable options. It's not far from the river, and has well-maintained rooms and a simple restaurant. €€

Huesca

HUESCA, the provincial capital, is a pleasant mix of urban and rustic, with modern apartment buildings lining its perimeter and an atmospheric old quarter with outdoor cafés and drinking dens. Huesca's history is impressive: the Romans settled here first, calling it Osca, followed by the Moors who took Huesca in 718, just seven years after their arrival in Spain, and ruled it for almost four hundred years. In 1096, it became the capital of the Aragón kingdom until power was transferred to Zaragoza in the early twelfth century. Huesca is also a good jumping-off point for the splendid castle of **Loarre**.

Catedral and Museo Diocesano

Pza. de la Catedral • Charge • www.huescaturismo.com/es/monumental-detalle/7/catedral-museo-diocesano/

The **Catedral**, standing majestically at the centre of the old town, beautifully reveals the city's past, featuring every architectural style from brick Mudéjar to soaring Gothic. It features a superb sixteenth-century alabaster *retablo* by Renaissance artist Damián Forment, with a triptych detailing scenes from the Crucifixion. A spiral staircase (180 steps) leads up the fourteenth-century bell tower to a terrace affording sweeping views over the city and to the Pyrenees beyond. The **Museo Diocesano** exhibits sacred art, from medieval to Baroque, culled from across the region.

Ayuntamiento

Pza. de la Catedral 1 • Charge • www.huesca.es

The **Ayuntamiento** features a Baroque staircase and a nineteenth-century painting, *The Bell of Huesca*, which depicts one of the more macabre moments in Huesca's history. As the legend goes, in the twelfth century King Ramiro II ordered the beheading of a group of noblemen who had apparently committed treason. He then had their heads laid out in a circle, forming the base of the bell, and suspended one of the heads on a rope over the circle, as the bell's clapper. It is this Ramiro II who is buried in San Pedro el Viejo.

Museo de Huesca

Pza. de la Universidad • Free • http://museodehuesca.es/

The **Museo de Huesca** showcases a wide variety of archeological and artistic items from around the province, including the ruins of a Roman necropolis, lithographs by Goya and paintings by Aragonese artists, including Huesca native Ramón Acín. The museum is built around the octagonal courtyard of the Palacio de los Reyes de Aragón.

San Pedro el Viejo

Pza. de San Pedro • Charge • www.sanpedroelviejo.com

Founded as a Benedictine monastery in the eleventh century, the church of **San Pedro el Viejo** houses the tombs of Aragonese royalty King Alfonso I and his son Ramiro II. It also features a lovely, well-maintained Romanesque cloister with beautifully carved capitals.

ARRIVAL AND INFORMATION

HUESCA

By train and bus The intermodal train and bus station is on C/Zaragoza, south of town. Huesca is well connected by bus and train to the region and beyond: regular Avanza buses (https://aragon.avanzagrupo.com) connect the town with Zaragoza (just over 1hr), Jaca (1hr 15min), Barbastro (45min), Lleida (2hr 30min) and Barcelona (3hr 30min–

4hr). Numerous trains run daily to Zaragoza (55min) and Teruel (3hr 45min). AVE trains also run to Zaragoza (45min) and Madrid (just over 3hr).
Turismo Pza. López Allué (daily 9am–2pm & 4–8pm; 974 292 170, http://huescaturismo.com).

ACCOMMODATION

Hostal Un Punto Chic - Joaquín Costa C/Joaquín Costa 20, www.hostaljoaquincosta.com. Central, amiable *hostal* with 23 diminutive rooms decorated in a white-and-grey colour scheme and with bathrooms revealing designer flair. €
Hostal San Marcos C/San Orencio 10, https://hostal sanmarcos.es. Friendly *hostal* with no-frills but well-maintained en-suite rooms. Within easy walking distance of Huesca's main sights and just 500m from the bus and train station. €

Hotel Sancho Abarca C/Coso Alto 52, www.hotel sanchoabarca.com. A notch above the other accommodation in town, this hotel has modern, crisp rooms with decently sized, modern bathrooms, a spa and fitness centre with a sauna, and a restaurant serving Aragonese cuisine. €€€
La Posada de la Luna C/Joaquín Costa 10, https:// posadadelaluna.com. Petite, colourful, boutique-style hotel with cosy rooms and good bathrooms. €

9

EATING AND DRINKING

Hervi C/Santa Paciencia 2, 974 240 333. A lively restaurant with an outdoor seating area, a local crowd, hearty dishes, including grilled meats and seafood, and nicely priced regional wines. The set lunch is great value. €€

Meson Doña Taberna Avda Juan XIII 13, https://donataberna.es. This warm and welcoming restaurant serves a wide range of Aragonese produce, including delicious steaks and grilled fish. There are a series of set menus: the *menu ejecutivo* is recommended. €€

★ **Restaurante Venta del Sotón** Ctra. A-132 Huesca, www.ventadelsoton.com. This unusual restaurant is arranged around a circular fireplace that is not just a decorative feature, but also used for cooking. They offer a special tasting menu that showcases typical Aragonese dishes which changes according to what is in season

accompanied by local wine. There is also a stylish tapas area with a terrace, where you can enjoy dishes such as goat's cheese and truffle terrine and grilled lamb chops. €€€

La Taberna de Lillas Pastia Pza. Navarra 4, https://lillaspastia.es. Dine on gourmet Aragonese cuisine, from suckling pig to *arroz negro* (rice cooked in squid ink) topped with tender octopus. The speciality is truffle (*la trufa*) and the wine selection is chosen from local vineyards, including the Somontano region. Splurge on the nine-course tasting menu. €€€€

Las Torres C/María Auxiliadora 3, https://lastorres-restaurante.com. Innovative cuisine finds inspiration in the local bounty, from freshwater fish to pig's trotters to aromatic herb sauces. The dining room is grandly elegant, with white linen tablecloths and sparkling crystal glasses. €€€

Around Huesca

The mountainous terrain around Huesca reveals several eye-catching sights, including the imposing Castillo de Loarre and Los Mallos, a surreal series of rock formations.

Castillo de Loarre

36km northwest of Huesca and 4km beyond the village of Loarre • Charge • https://castillodeloarre.es/

From afar, the scene looks like little more than rocky outcrops punctuating the Aragonese landscape but as you draw closer, the eleventh-century **Castillo de Loarre** comes into magnificent focus, glowering from its hilltop perch. The castle was constructed in the eleventh century by Sancho Ramírez, king of Aragón and Navarra, and its dark and mysterious, maze-like interior makes for great exploring: tunnels lead down to dark cellars, and narrow stairs wind up to lookout towers that command wonderful views over the far-reaching fields. The castle's two main **towers** are the imposing Torre de la Reina, and the Torre del Homenaje, which features a huge fireplace. You can also peer into a quiet Romanesque **church**, which has detailed, carved capitals in the apse.

ARRIVAL AND DEPARTURE   CASTILLO DE LOARRE

By foot The castle is a 2km (1hr) walk from the village. Take the PR-HU105 footpath.

By bus During the week, two buses (www.avanzabus.com) run daily from Huesca to Loarre (35min), with one service on Sat.

By train Ayerbe, 7km southwest of Loarre, has the closest train station, with services from Huesca (30min), though schedules vary; check ahead. Two buses a day (weekdays only, www.avanzabus.com) make the 10min trip between Ayerbe and Loarre.

ACCOMMODATION

Camping La Banera 1.5km out of Ayerbe on the road to Loarre, https://campingayerbe.com. This decent, well-maintained campsite has hot water in the bathrooms, and a small bar-restaurant (open to campers only). Open Easter to October. €

Hospedería de Loarre Pza. Miguel Moya, https://hospederiadeloarre.es. Restored seventeenth-century *hospedería* with warmly decorated, comfortable rooms and a respected restaurant serving Aragonese cuisine. €€

Los Mallos and Riglos

About 45km from Huesca, the village of **Riglos** is a good base for the otherworldly towering rock formations of **Los Mallos** (The Mallets), popular with rock climbers.

ACCOMMODATION

Refugio de Riglos At the entrance to Riglos, http://refugioderiglos.es. Catering to climbers and trekkers, this *refugio* has two-, six- and eight-bed rooms and a fitness room with a climbing wall, so you can warm up before doing the real thing. There's also a communal kitchen with fridge and microwave, and an on-site restaurant serving hearty Aragonese food. €

Sierra de Guara

The bird's-eye view of the relatively under-the-radar **SIERRA DE GUARA** shows an arid, almost desolate terrain cleaved by over two hundred sculpted canyons and gorges that look like giant, angry slashes in the earth. This is canyoning (*barranquismo*) country: the eastern half of Sierra de Guara is the most popular section for outdoor activities, and the pleasant town of **Alquézar**, in the southeastern corner, functions as the Guara's hub.

Alquézar

Tackling the great outdoors and brushing up your Aragonese history are prime draws in small but well-preserved **ALQUÉZAR**, which lies about 45km from Huesca and 20km northwest of Barbastro. In town the streets are dotted with outdoor operators and tour companies that specialize in canyoning, mountain climbing and hiking excursions (see page 585).

Colegiata de Santa María del Mayor

Charge • http://somontano.org/alquezar

Keeping watch over Alquézar is the imposing **Colegiata de Santa María del Mayor**, which was originally built as a Moorish citadel in the eighth century. It was later conquered by the Christians, who adapted it into a monastery and fortress complex in the twelfth century. Reflecting its long and varied history, the Romanesque cloister has detailed capitals and frescoes depicting the New Testament that were created in the fifteenth to eighteenth centuries, while the Gothic-Renaissance church is heavy on Baroque art, but also has a simple yet powerful wooden Crucifixion dating back to the thirteenth century.

ARRIVAL AND INFORMATION

ALQUÉZAR

By bus One bus (www.avanzabus.com) runs on weekdays from Alquézar from Barbastro (40min).

Turismo C/Arrabal, on the edge of the old town (daily 9am–1.30pm & 4.30–8pm; Aug daily 9am–8pm; sometimes limited hours in winter; 974 352 916 or 638 295 807, https://turismoalquezar.es).

ACCOMMODATION

Albergue Rural de Guara C/Pilaseras, https://albergue ruraldeguara.com. Sturdy, simple *refugio* above town with

---

CANYONING IN THE SIERRA DE GUARA

Alquézar has a range of quality canyoning operators who cater to all levels, and offer everything from thrilling descents into dark, echoing caves to treks along gaping gorges to river rafting. Average cost is around €55–70 per person per day, with prices varying depending on the level of difficulty and size of tour group.

OUTDOOR OPERATORS IN ALQUÉZAR
Avalancha C/Arrabal s/n, www.avalancha.org. This well-regarded operator organizes canyoning, rafting, hiking and *via ferrata* trips plus accommodation in its comfortable hotel (www.hotel-santamaria.com).

Guías Boira Paseo San Hipólito, www.guiasboira.com. This friendly operator offers a wide range of guided trips, including canyoning, *via ferrata*, rafting and *escalada en hielo* (ice climbing). They can also help with accommodation.

9

views over the countryside and simple double rooms and dorms with six to eight beds. Half-board packages available. €
Hotel Castillo C/Pedro Arnal Cavero 11, www.hotelcastillo alquezar.com. This traditional Aragonese farmhouse was converted into a hotel in 2013 and features stone walls, wooden beams and cool, modern decor. Rooms are spacious and many have private terraces overlooking the town. €€
Hotel Maribel C/Arrabal, www.hotelmaribel.es. This colourful, quirky – and slightly kitsch – boutique hotel has nine opulent rooms, each one named (and individually decorated) after different types of grape. The Moscatel room

has a canopied bed and Swarovski crystal lamp, while the Moristel features a forged-iron headboard and wallpaper in a colour "inspired by the tones in the water of the river Vero". €€€
Hotel Villa de Alquézar C/Pedro Arnal Cavero 12, www.villadealquezar.com. A stone arch graces the front door at this artfully renovated hotel, which has wood-beam ceilings and a terrace with views of the Colegiata and the Río Vero canyon. Some rooms have their own private terraces; all have comfortable beds and en-suite bathrooms. There's also a spa and a small outdoor pool in the courtyard. €€

EATING AND DRINKING

Casa Pardina C/Medio, http://casapardina.com. Handsome, rustic restaurant with modern touches, and a lovely terrace that overlooks the Guara countryside. It offers two set menus featuring seasonal produce: a gastronomic tasting menu featuring creative renditions of Aragonese dishes and a 'Casa Pardina' menu that focuses on classic local cuisine. €€€

Restaurante Cueva Reina C/Baja 42, https://cuevareina restaurante.wordpress.com. This contemporary restaurant has a comfortable dining room with views over the Río Vero and serves dishes such as pork in local Somontano wine and roast Aragonese lamb shoulder. It offers a good set lunch on weekdays, plus a more ambitious gastronomic menu at weekends, along with their à la carte offerings. €€€

Barbastro

BARBASTRO's formidable history put it on the map, but it's the rich local wines that have given this small town its staying power as a tourist destination. For more than three centuries, the Moors ruled Barbastro as one of their chief outposts in the far north. In 1137, it was here that the marriage of Petronia, daughter of Ramiro of Aragón, to Count Ramón Berenguer IV of Barcelona established the union of Aragón and Catalunya. As for the *vino*: Barbastro is capital of the **Somontano** wine region, and makes for an ideal jumping-off point for tastings at the thirty-plus *bodegas* and vineyards clustered around town (see page 587).

Barbastro's old town exudes a certain faded glory and is presided over by a sturdy Gothic Catedral. In **Pza. de la Constitución** sits the fifteenth-century *ayuntamiento*. Nearby are the arcaded **Pza. del Mercado** and the shaded **Paseo del Coso**, where you can ease into the evening over a drink or three at the outdoor bars.

The Catedral

Pza. Palacio • Charge • https://museodiocesano.es

The handsome sixteenth-century **Catedral** features an alabaster *retablo* by Damián Forment. He left the work unfinished when he died in 1540, and the remainder was completed by his student, Liceire, two decades later. The Catedral bell tower has been well preserved (you may not be able to visit if there are storks nesting), while inside the building are elegant ribbed vaults and a nave with carved columns. The **Museo Diocesano** features a sacred art from Aragón's rural medieval churches, archeological remains from the Moorish era, and an array of Gothic and Romanesque murals.

ARRIVAL AND INFORMATION

By bus Multiple daily Avanza buses (www.avanzabus.com) operate to Huesca (50min), where you can make connections to Jaca and Zaragoza. Buses also travel to Lleida (1hr 35min), Benasque (1hr 45min) and Alquézar (40min).

Turismo Avda. de la Merced 64 (July & Aug Mon–Sat 10am–2pm & 4–7.30pm, Sun 10am–2pm & 5–7pm; Sept–June Tues–Sat 10am–2pm & 4–7.30pm; 974 308 350, https://barbastro.org).

9

SOMONTANO WINE

Somontano has become one of Aragón's most distinguished D.O. – Denominación de Origen – wine regions, with more than thirty vineyards producing superb red, white and rosé wines from a variety of local and international grapes.

The organization **Ruta del Vinos Somontano** (Somontano Wine Routes; https://rutadelvinosomontano.com) lists the local bodegas, and offers myriad tours, including the wine bus, which runs every third Saturday of the month from Zaragoza, Huesca and Barbastro (974 30 83 50, bus@rutadelvinosomontano.com; charge) taking in a range of wineries and including some free time in either Barbastro or Alquézar.

Many of the vineyards are also individually open to visitors (generally Mon–Sat, morning to early evening), and offer tours. The Barbastro *turismo* has a wealth of information on routes, vineyards and itineraries.

ACCOMMODATION

La Alcoba de Baco C/Mayor, 974 316 342. Next to the Palacio de los Argensola, these handsome, central apartments have full kitchens, and cater to those visiting Somontano for *enoturismo* (wine tourism). €€

Hostal Pirineos C/General Ricardos 13, 974 310 000. Simple *hostal* with basic, well-maintained rooms. The restaurant serves good food, with a set-price lunch menu every day. €

Hotel San Ramón del Somontano C/Academia Cerbuna 2, www.hotelsanramonsomontano.com. This beautiful four-star hotel is set in a 1903 modernist *hostal* that has hosted everyone from George Orwell to Miguel de Unamuno. The elegant original design has been artfully incorporated into the modern hotel. There's a spa and some rooms have Jacuzzis. The restaurant (see page 587) serves Aragonese cuisine. €€

EATING AND DRINKING

El Placer C/Goya 5, 974 308 983, www.facebook.com/restaurantelplacer. A bright, modern restaurant serving both local and fusion dishes, from slow-cooked pork with potatoes and chilled *salmorejo* soup with ham to tuna tataki or squid-infused rice with a lime emulsion. €€

San Ramón del Somontano Hotel San Ramón del Somontano, www.hotelsanramonsomontano.com. The well-appointed restaurant in this historic hotel serves tasty regional cuisine based on locally sourced ingredients, plus an array of Somontano wines. €€

The Aragonese Pyrenees

The **ARAGONESE PYRENEES** exemplify all the superlatives associated with the soaring Pyrenean mountains: the peaks here are the highest, the wildest and, in the eyes of many, the most beautiful of the Spanish Pyrenees. From the snowy mountain tips piercing the deep-blue sky to lushly forested valleys and thundering rivers, the Aragonese Pyrenees are one of the country's national treasures. So lace up your ski or hiking boots, and take to the verdant valleys or snow slopes – the mountains offer adventure throughout the seasons.

Jaca, the biggest city in the Aragonese Pyrenees, has plenty of bus connections into the mountains. It also boasts a formidable Catedral and a decent array of hotels and *hostales*, making it a popular base, particularly for the busy **ski resorts** to the north, including Astún and Candanchú. As for summer activities, hiking trails traverse the entire range, including in the gorgeous **Ansó** and **Hecho** valleys and the magnificent **Parque Nacional de Ordesa y Monte Perdido** – a real must-visit.

Jaca

The busy industrial town of **JACA** is one of the main crossroads and transport hubs of northern Aragón, and first impressions are not great. Venture into the city centre, however, and you'll find a bevy of sights that powerfully evoke the town's long history,

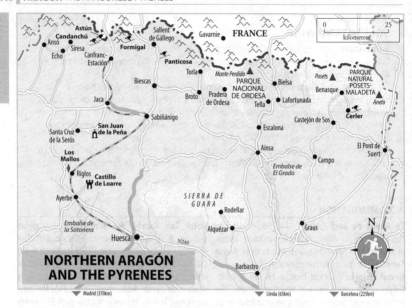

including the magnificent Catedral. Extending south of the Catedral is Jaca's *casco antiguo*, which includes atmospheric plazas and streets, and the fifteenth-century Torre de Reloj (watchtower).

Jaca was founded by the Romans and then conquered by the Moors in the early eighth century. Later in the century it was won back by the Christians, in a victory that's celebrated annually on the first Friday in May. In an interesting twist, the Moorish armies were driven back thanks to an immense – and brave – effort by the town's women, and the festival includes a parade that pays homage to these brave Jaca citizens. In the eleventh century, the town became the first capital of the Aragón kingdom, though by the end of the century the power had shifted to Huesca.

Jaca makes for a good jumping-off point for outdoor adventure in the Pyrenees, including skiing at Astún and Candanchu, just 30km away (see page 589). During the **Festival Folklórico de los Pirineos** (http://jaca.es/festival), held in late July and early August every odd-numbered year, people stream in from all over the Pyrenees to show off their cultural traditions with religious dances, performances and food. Also in August, over a two-week period, is the annual **Festival Internacional en el Camino de Santiago** (www. festivalcaminosantiago.com) featuring religious and classical music concerts at different venues, including the famous Catedral, as well as a medieval market in the city centre.

Catedral and Museo Diocesano

Pza. de San Pedro • Charge • www.diocesisdejaca.org

The jewel of Jaca is its eleventh-century **Catedral de San Pedro Apóstol**, one of the oldest in Spain, and perhaps the city's finest reminder of its years as the seat of the Aragonese kingdom. The Catedral's incredible history and staying power is revealed through its gorgeous amalgam of styles, from French Romanesque to Gothic. And, while the original Romanesque design has been largely built over – the original ceilings were in wood, which were replaced by double-barrel vaults – you can still find vestiges of it, such as the simple main door. Within the Catedral are elegant carvings gracing the capitals, a sixteenth-century statue of Santiago and a central apse painted in 1792 by Aragonese artist Manuel Bayeu, who was Francisco Goya's brother-in-law. A highlight is the shrine of Santa Orosía, the patron saint of Jaca. Adjoining the Catedral

HIT THE SLOPES IN ARAGÓN

Skiing in the Aragon Pyrenees matches that of Catalunya and, increasingly, of France. Overall, the **ski resorts** are well maintained and cater to all levels, from downhill daredevils to wobbly first-timers. Note that, as in the Catalan Pyrenees, some of the best discounts are via pre-trip package deals offered by hotels, agencies or the resorts themselves. But even if you don't book a package ahead of time, you can often find deals once you've arrived, offered by the *turismos* as well as the hotels and the resorts.

In the west are **Candanchú** (www.candanchu.com), which has a well-known ski school, and **Astún** (https://100k.astun.com), with a wide range of pistes, including plenty for beginners. The main hub for accommodation and other services is **Jaca**.

Partly funded by the Aragón government, Aramón (http://aramon.com) now manages a group of formerly independent ski resorts. **Formigal-Panticosa**, with 187 skiable kilometres, is the largest in Spain, and has 147 runs and 37 lifts. It caters to all levels. In the Pyrenees' easternmost section, sleek **Cerler** attracts seasoned skiers, with several ski centres totalling about 100km, altitudes up to 2730m, 74 runs and 39 lifts. Cerler also offers equipment rental and ski and snowboard schools. **Benasque** (see page 596) is a popular hub for Cerler.

is the **Museo Diocesano**, which displays an extensive collection of religious art, artefacts and frescoes from mountain churches throughout the area.

Ciudadela

Avda. del Primer Viernes de Mayo • Charge • https://ciudadeladejaca.es

The impressive star-shaped **Ciudadela** (also known as the Castillo de San Pedro) looms just east of the centre of town, and is still partly used by the military. Wander along the fortified walls for lovely views of the surrounding mountains and countryside. The **Museo de Miniatura Militares** (Museum of Military Miniatures) within is mesmerizing collection of over 35,000 toy soldiers, dioramas, models and more. The tiny lead soldiers, measuring 2cm in height, are depicted in historical battles from around the world, from the Crusades to the Crown of Aragón era.

Puente San Miguel

The fifteenth-century **Puente San Miguel** arches across the river west of the Ciudadela. It was the main entrance to Jaca used by pilgrims on the Camino Aragonés, a branch of the Camino de Santiago.

ARRIVAL AND INFORMATION

JACA

By bus Regular buses travel daily from the central bus station, on Avda de la Jacetania, to Huesca (1hr 15min) and Zaragoza (2hr 15min), both served by Avana (www.avanzabus.com) and Pamplona (1hr 45min), served by La Brundesa (https://laburundesa.com).

By train The train station, on C/Estación, is about a 15min walk from the town centre. Regular trains run to Zaragoza (3hr 20min) and other regional towns.

Turismo Pza. de San Pedro (summer Mon–Sat 9am–9pm, Sun 9am–3pm; winter Mon–Fri 9am–1.30pm & 4.30–7pm, Sat 10am–1pm & 5–7pm; 974 360 098, www.jaca.com/turismo).

ACCOMMODATION

SEE MAP PAGE 590

★ **Barrose** C/Estiras 4, Barós, www.barosse.com. This wonderfully unique adults-only *casa rural*, in a village 2km south of Jaca, blends designer style with rustic, romantic appeal. Each of the five rooms is named after traditional edifices, such as the Romanesque-style Ermita (hermitage), with stone, gleaming woods and elegant drapes, and there's a sauna and spa. €€€€

Hotel Conde Aznar Paseo de la Constitución 3, www. condeaznar.com. This welcoming and great value family-run three-star hotel has elegant rooms and suites with cosy, traditional decor. Some feature jacuzzis. €€

Hotel Mur C/Santa Orosía 1, https://hotelmur.com. Famed writers and artists from Pío Baroja to Santiago Ramón y Cajal have warmed the beds at this large, historic hotel, which first opened its doors in 1875. Rooms are a bit dated in their decor, but are handsomely maintained. €

JACA: CASCO ANTIGUO

EATING
Lilium   2
Mountain House   1
Restaurante Biarritz   3
Restaurante Cobarcho   4
La Tasca de Ana   5

ACCOMMODATION
Barrose   4
Hotel Conde Aznar   3
Hotel Mur   1
Maison de l'Arc   2

Maison de l'Arc C/San Nicolás 4, https://maisondearc.com. Handily located next to the Catedral, this offers simple but stylish and well-equipped rooms, with exposed stone walls, private bathrooms and a small kitchen area with a fridge and microwave to prepare your own snacks. €€

EATING

SEE MAP PAGE 590

Lilium Av. del Primer Viernes de Mayo 8, 974 355 356. This popular restaurant is spread over three levels and serves home-style Alto-Aragonese dishes such as lamb *al estilo de mi madre* (in the style of my mother), washed down with an extensive wine list of Somontanos and Riojas. €€

Mountain House Avda. De Francia 34, www.lacasadelamontana.com. A delightful, family-run café-bar which serves simple tapas, burgers, sandwiches, salads and homemade cakes – and includes good selection of vegan and vegetarian options. €

Restaurante Biarritz Avda. Primer Viernes de Mayo 12, www.restaurantebiarritz.com. The speciality at this refined restaurant is *carnes a la brasa* (grilled meats), from thick, juicy steaks to tender veal. Pair your meat with fresh salads

of goat's cheese and *bacalao* (cod). €€

Restaurante Cobarcho C/Ramiro I 2, www.restaurantecobarcho.com. Aragón is meat country – and you can get a hearty taste of it at this friendly spot: grilled and roasted lamb chops and T-bone steaks, suckling pig, duck and more are on the menu. They offer several set menus, including one which showcases classic dishes from Alto Aragon. €€

La Tasca de Ana C/Ramiro I 3, 974 364 726, http://latascadeana.com. It can get crowded and loud, but if you're going to do tapas in Jaca, this long-running spot is the place to go. It draws a healthy mix of locals and visitors, all here to chow on the delicious small bites, from grilled squid, pungent cheeses and cured hams to the perennially popular *langostinos* (prawns). €

San Juan de la Peña and around

Charge • www.monasteriosanjuan.com/

The **Monasterio de San Juan de la Peña**, set amid protected natural parkland 21km south of Jaca, is one of the most stunning sacred buildings in Aragón, if not in Spain. Tucked protectively under the overhang of a massive boulder, it's built right into a rocky mountain: from certain angles, it's hard to tell where man-made structure ends and nature begins. Dating from the ninth century, the monastery is named after a hermit who lived in solitude atop the towering cliff (*peña*). The monastery features a Romanesque church with twelfth-century murals and the Gothic San Victorián chapel, but the real standout is the elegant twelfth-century cloister, shaded by the bulging rock face that looms over it. The cloister has ornate capitals, depicting Bible scenes.

In 1675, a fire in the monastery forced the monks to leave and build a newer one, which sits further up the hill. The **Monasterio Nuevo** (same hours as old monastery) features a helpful visitors' centre and two interpretation centres, which chronicle the history of the monastery and the eventful lives of Aragón's kings and queens.

Church of Santa María

Charge (or included in admission to San Juan de la Peña)

From San Juan de la Peña, a series of trails fans out through the forest, including a popular path to the nearest village, **Santa Cruz de la Serós**, 7km away, which is home to the elegant eleventh-century Romanesque church of **Santa María**, formerly a monastery.

ARRIVAL AND DEPARTURE   SAN JUAN DE LA PEÑA AND AROUND

By bus There is no scheduled bus from Jaca, but in high season a bus occasionally connects Santa Cruz de Serós to the monastery; call the monastery to confirm.

ACCOMMODATION

Hospedería Monasterio de San Juan de la Peña http://hsanjuanpena.com. Forming part of the Monasterio Nuevo, this handsome four-star hotel features elegant rooms, lovely gardens, a rustic restaurant and a spa. Temporarily closed for renovations at the time of writing, expected to re-open mid-2025. €€

Valles de Echo and Ansó

Wild and beautiful, the **Ansó and Echo valleys**, northwest of Jaca, burrow deep into the Pyrenees. The terrain is by turns desolate and fecund and the tiny mountain villages are as quaint as they come. But perhaps the main allure is that this region gets fewer visitors than elsewhere in the Pyrenees and although the summer can get busy, in the off season you can often have an entire trail (if not an entire valley) largely to yourself. In fact, if there is activity on the slopes, it's usually the local **wildlife** – the forested mountains, especially in the Valle de Echo, are home to creatures large and small, from chamois to red squirrels to a small population of brown bears. Keep an eye out too for all sorts of birds, including the lammergeier bearded vulture. The valley's main towns are the charming Echo and Ansó, while elsewhere, natural wonders abound, including **La Selva de Oza** (about 5km from Siresa), a spruce and pine forest crossed by the rushing Río Aragón Subordán, which is thick with Pyrenean trout.

Echo and around

Lovely **ECHO** – or **Hecho**, in Spanish – the main town of the valley of the same name, is the very definition of rustic Aragón. Stone houses with wrought-iron balconies cast shadows on cobbled streets, the scene framed by vivid green valleys and elegant peaks. The village made its mark in history as the *sede* (seat) of the young Aragonese kingdom, and is also where King Alfonso I was born. Here, locals speak "Cheso", a dialect of Aragonese.

Museo del Arte Contemporáneo al Aire Libre

Ctra. Oza • Free

Echo also has an arty angle: until the mid-1980s, the town hosted an annual symposium on contemporary sculpture, founded by artist Pedro Tramulas. One of its legacies is the **Museo del Arte Contemporáneo al Aire Libre**, an open-air sculpture park near the entrance to town, featuring striking contemporary stone pieces – the juxtaposition of modern art and historic town makes for a memorable scene.

9

ARRIVAL AND INFORMATION

By bus Buses from Jaca service Echo and Siresa (both around 1hr) generally once a day Monday to Friday (974 360 508, www.autocaresescartin.es).

ACCOMMODATION

Albergue Siresa C/Reclusa, Siresa, 2km north of Echo, https://reaj.com/albergues/juvenil-siresa/. This basic, friendly *albergue*, in the heart of small Siresa, has comfortable bunk-bedded dorms and plenty of information on exploring the surrounding mountains, including books and mountain gear rental; they can also arrange guided hikes. Breakfast included; half- and full-board packages are also available. **€**

Borda Bisaltico Carretera Gabardito, 6km north of town, http://bordabisaltico.com. This well-tended complex features a campsite, an *albergue* with four-person dorms, and basic apartments. Dorms **€**, apartments **€€**

Camping Valle de Hecho Carretera Puenta la Reina, http://campinghecho.com. This well-run campground has a range of amenities, including an outdoor pool, a restaurant,

ECHO AND AROUND

Turismo In the Museo de Arte Contemporáneo al Aire Libre (July–Oct daily 10am–1.30pm & 5.30–8pm; usually closed mid-Oct to mid-June; https://turismovalledehecho.com).

a *cafetería* and organized activities, including hiking excursions. They also have wooden bungalows (minimum two nights). Camping **€**, apartments **€€**

Casa Blasquico Pza. Palacio de la Fuente 1, http://casa blasquico.es. Lovingly cared for rooms, each named after a flower or herb, feature comfortable beds, hardwood floors and clean bathrooms. The hotel also has the acclaimed *Restaurante Gaby* where breakfast is served for an extra fee. **€**

Hotel Castillo d'Acher Pza. Mayor, Siresa, 974 375 313, http://castillodacher.com. Basic, well-maintained but somewhat dated rooms in the centre of the village. The restaurant serves decent regional cuisine, including *conejo con caracoles* (rabbit with snails), tripe with chickpeas and grilled meats. **€**

EATING AND DRINKING

Restaurante Gaby Casa Blasquico, http://casablasquico. es. This lovely restaurant is a town institution – and for good reason. It's the model of mountain charm: low, wood-beamed ceilings; walls hanging with old photos; and

excellent regional cuisine, including grilled *conejo* (rabbit), crêpes with mushrooms and a superb wine list, with a particular focus on Aragón's Somontano wines. **€€**

Ansó

ANSÓ rivals Echo for rustic, alpine appeal: red-roofed stone houses stand out against a backdrop of lush greenery, with the big, blue sky opening above. As with many mountain villages in the Pyrenees, the pleasure here is to just wander the cobbled streets and Pza. Mayor, and perhaps to take some shade along the banks of the river, the Río Veral.

ARRIVAL AND INFORMATION

By bus One bus service a day from Jaca serves Ansó Mon–Sat (just over 2hr).

ANSÓ

Turismo Pza. Domingo Miral 1 (974 370 225, https://valledeanso.es/).

ACCOMMODATION

El Pajar de Pierra Avda. Pedro Cativiela 3a & 3b, https://www.elpajardepierra.com. This *casa rural*-style house is done up as an elegant farmhouse and features cosy interiors and lovely mountain views throughout, especially from the breezy garden. Groups and families can rent out the full house (five bedrooms, three bathrooms and a fully equipped kitchen) by the day or the weekend. They also rent out rooms

if you call within a week before your arrival date. **€**

Posada Magoria C/Milagro 32, https://posadamagoria. com. This inviting *posada* has been beautifully restored, with wood-beam ceilings, solid furniture and comfortable beds. The restaurant (reserved for guests) serves organic vegetarian cuisine using vegetables grown in the garden, including squash and aubergine. **€€**

Parque Nacional de Ordesa y Monte Perdido and around

The best of Aragón's natural wonders all seem to converge with glory in the **PARQUE NACIONAL DE ORDESA Y MONTE PERDIDO**. Presiding over the park's greenery is the Monte Perdido (Lost Mountain) range, the largest limestone chain in Western Europe. Verdant valleys blanketed in beech, fir and pine cut through the terrain, and clear blue streams and gushing waterfalls keep the fields lush and green. After the snow melts, honeysuckle, primroses and irises bloom in rocky crevices and on sun-speckled slopes. As for wildlife, the park is teeming with it: Egyptian vultures and golden eagles soar overhead; Pyrenean chamois scamper up hillsides; and trout dart through ice-cold streams.

Many of the deep valleys were created by massive glaciers, at the heads of which are cirques: basins shaped like an amphitheatre with steep walls of rock. Elsewhere, tiny alpine villages, with stone houses crowned with sandstone-tile roofs and conical chimneys, dot the mountainsides and make for pleasant stops.

The park is divided roughly into three main sections: **Ordesa** (to the west), **Añisclo** (to the south) and **Escuaín** (to the east). The town of **Torla**, 3km south of the park's southwest border, is the most popular gateway.

Torla

TORLA in many ways exemplifies the modern-day Pyrenean town: turn down one cobbled street in the old town, and you're rewarded with the alluring sight of stone houses prettily framed by bright-green valleys and naked peaks; turn the other way, and you run smack into a high-rise hotel or a belching tour bus. It is, however, this very mix of low-key village life and tourist-friendly amenities that makes Torla a good base for exploring the park.

Hikes in the park

The park offers a wide range of hikes, from where you can see crashing waterfalls, gaping canyons and vivid-green valleys. You can access the park on foot from Torla on the well-marked GR15 path from town, which eventually links up with the GR11, a right fork of which goes to **Pradera de Ordesa**, entrance to the **Cañón de Ordesa** and the starting point for most of the popular hikes further into the park. The whole trek from Torla to Pradera takes about two hours.

Circo de Soaso

The **Circo de Soaso** trek is one of the park's main crowd-pleasers. It offers a lovely overview of the park's natural highlights – gorgeous greenery, tumbling waterfalls – but it's not too challenging, and it can be completed in a day. From Pradera de Ordesa the route leads through forest, followed by a steep climb up the **Senda de los Cazadores** (Hunters' Path), which then flattens out as the Faja de Pelay path to the beautiful **Cola de Caballo** (Horsetail Waterfall). The journey takes about three to four hours each way (around 6–7hr round trip).

Circo de Cotatuero

This trek has a lovely waterfall as a reward, and takes you along the northern crest of the impressive **Valle de Ordesa**. The full round-trip hike takes about 5 to 6 hours. The hike should only be done in the summer or early autumn due to the risk of avalanches. From Pradera de Ordesa, the hike starts steeply and eventually leads to a lookout point below the thundering **Cascada de Cotatuero.** To return from the Cascada, head downhill and then continue on the Cotatuero *circo* back to the Pradera de Ordesa.

Refugio Góriz and Monte Perdido

From Pradera de Ordesa, trek along the GR11 to Circo de Soaso (about 3hr) and then up to the *Refugio Góriz* at 2169m (see page 595), the traditional jumping-off point to climb **Monte Perdido** (3355m). The trek up Monte Perdido (about 5hr) requires intermediate mountaineering skills, crampons and other professional equipment.

Brecha de Rolando and Refuge des Sarradets

If you have a head for heights, try this memorable onward route from the Cascada de Cotatuero: from the waterfalls, on the Cotatuero cirque, you can climb, via a series of iron pegs in a wall, the **Clavijas de Cotatuero**. Note that you don't need any special climbing equipment but you should be fit and like heights. Once you've done the climb, it's about a two- to three-hour trek to the **Brecha de Rolando**, a large natural gap in the Cirque de

9

Gavarnie on the French border. From the Brecha, it's then a steep climb (about 500m) to the *Refuge des Sarradets* at 2587m (see page 596), across the border in France.

Parc National des Pyrénées and Gavarnie village

The northern section of the park is adjacent to France's **Parc National des Pyrénées**, which in total runs for about 100km along the Spain–France border. The French side offers more of the same wild Pyrenean landscape, and a popular trek with hikers is to cross northwest into the French park and on to the pretty village of **Gavarnie**. Many will do this hike over the course of a couple of days. From Torla, hike along the GR15.2 to **Puente de los Navarros** and then continue on the GR11 to San Nicolás de Bujaruelo (roughly 7km from Torla), which is marked by a medieval bridge. Here you'll find the *Refugio Valle de Bujaruelo* (see page 596). From the San Nicolás bridge, you can trek over mountains and into France and Garvarnie – about a six- to eight-hour hike.

Cañón de Añísclo and Garganta de Escuaín

The canyons of **Añísclo** and **Escuaín** dramatically carve up the terrain in the southeast corner of Ordesa. These canyons draw considerably fewer tourists than the Cañón de Ordesa, in part because it can be a tough area to penetrate, with no public transport and minimal accommodation. With your own transport, it is well worth a stop.

Cañón de Añísclo

From the north, the **Cañón de Añísclo** – filled with jagged cliffs, quiet forests of looming trees and gurgling brooks – is a day-hike from *Refugio Góriz*. If you have your own transport, you can reach it from the south. About 13km from tiny **Escalona**, 10km north of Aínsa in the direction of Sarvisé, is a trail that leads into the canyon; it's a five-hour round-trip trek through the most verdant section of the gorge to the clearing, **La Ripareta**.

Garganta de Escuaín

The **Garganta de Escuaín**, in the Río Yaga valley, may be smaller than Añísclo but it is just as spectacular. It's best accessed from the village of **Lafortunada**, 20km north of Aínsa. From Lafortunada, you can trek the GR15 trail for the two-hour trip to the pretty village of **Tella**, which has a **park information office** (C/Iglesia, Tella; https://www. miteco.gob.es/es/parques-nacionales-oapn/red-parques-nacionales/parques-nacionales/ ordesa/guia-visitante.html). Just beyond the village, a trail leads to tiny **Escuaín**, from where it's about an hour into the gorge. With your own transport, you can also reach Escuaín from a small road off the Escalona–Sarvisé road.

Aínsa and around

In certain lights of day, the medieval stone village of **Aínsa** looks like it has sprouted from the earth itself. The village is perched on a hill and views of the surrounding looming mountains greet you around every turn. Aínsa also has a decent selection of accommodation and makes an ideal base for exploring the park, as it lies about 10km from the trail into the **Cañón de Añísclo**.

Iglesia de Santa María

Pza. Mayor • Charge for belfry • https://villadeainsa.com/iglesia-de-santa-maria-de-ainsa

The exceptional Romanesque **Iglesia de Santa María** rises over the Pza. Mayor, and features a simple entryway with four archivolts (decorative arches). Inside are a triangular cloister and a fortified four-storeyed belfry, which you can ascend for far-reaching views from the top.

Bielsa

Some 33km north of Aínsa lies the small town of **BIELSA**, west of which sits the gorgeous *Parador de Bielsa* (see page 596), the most comfortable jumping-off point for exploring the park. Bielsa sits at the confluence of the Cinca and Barrosa rivers, and northeast of town, in the park, unfolds the lush Valle de Pineta and the glassy Lago de Marboré. From the parador, which sits at the park's edge, you can trek – 4 to 5 hours one-way – through the valley to Marboré Lake, and there are numerous shorter walks in the area.

ARRIVAL AND DEPARTURE   PARQUE NACIONAL DE ORDESA Y MONTE PERDIDO

By bus One bus (https://www.avanzabus.com/) every day from Sabiñánigo, a transport hub for the area, to Aínsa stops at Torla (1hr) and Barbastro. There are additional weekday services in July and August between Sabiñánigo and Torla and three times a week (daily in summer) there's also a service to Bielsa (just under 1hr). Several daily buses operate from Jaca to Sabiñánigo. In the summer, a shuttle runs from Torla to the park entrance (Easter week, June–Nov: https://ordesabus.com/) and no cars are allowed to drive in.

By car Outside of high season (Easter week and July to mid-Sept) you can drive to the park border, northwest from Torla. Otherwise you'll have to leave your vehicle in the Torla car park and board the shuttle to the park (see page 595).

INFORMATION

Centro de Visitantes The park is well served by tourist information offices, including a gleaming centre in the car park at Torla (summer daily 9am–1pm & 4.15–7pm; winter Mon–Fri 9am–3pm, Sat & Sun 9am–2pm & 3.15–6pm; 974 486 472, https://www.miteco.gob.es/es/parques-nacionales-oapn/red-parques-nacionales/parques-nacionales/ordesa/guia-visitante/cvtorla.html) with permanent displays on the ecology of the park and an ascending ramp that simulates climbing a mountain, featuring a different rock face on each floor. A lookout point at the top offers views of the Aragonese landscape.

Turismos There are tourist offices in several towns near the park. You can get info on park conditions, trails and maps here but don't expect English to be spoken. In Torla the *turismo* is on Pza. Aragón, in the old town (mid-June to mid-Sept daily 9.30am–1.30pm & 5–9pm; www.turismo-ordesa.com). Aínsa's *turismo* is at Avda. Ordesa 5 (daily 10am–2pm & 4–7.30pm; shorter hours in winter; 974 500 767, https://villadeainsa.com). Bielsa's is on Pza. Mayor (daily 10am–2pm & 4–7.30pm, shorter hours in winter; 974 501 010, https://www.bielsa.com).

Maps and guides Editorial Alpina (www.editorialalpina.com) has good maps of the park. Cicerone (www.cicerone.co.uk) publishes in-depth trekking guides, including one on the Spanish Pyrenees and the GR11 trail.

ACCOMMODATION AND EATING

The towns around the park have a decent mix of hotels and budget beds (book ahead in high season). The park has a number of basic stone refuges (€15–30/person), where you can stay when on longer treks. Note that refuges will often be closed for a part of the low season; enquire before setting out. Camping is prohibited inside the park.

TORLA

Camping Río Ara 300m from Torla, on the road to Ordesa, signposted from road, 974 486 248, www.campingrioaraordesa.com. Set in a verdant riverside area close to town, this leafy campsite has a café-bar, supermarket and wi-fi. There is also information on trekking into the park. €

Camping y Refugio Valle de Bujaruelo 7km north of Torla, off the A-135, in the Valle de Bujaruelo, 974 486 348, https://campingvalledebujaruelo.com. Well-maintained alpine complex, surrounded by the leafy Valle de Bujaruelo, with a range of accommodation, including camping (most plots with electricity), dorms for two to five people in the refuge and bungalows with kitchenettes. Dorms €, bungalows €€

Hotel Villa Russell C/Principal s/n, https://hotelvillarussell.com. This established, amiable spot, on Torla's main drag, offers basic (and rather dated) but well-cared-for rooms with an alpine feel, wooden furnishings and cosy blankets. Some rooms come with a small kitchenette, so you can self-cater. €€

Refugio Lucien Briet C/Francia, 974 486 221, https://refugiolucienbriet.com. Long-running, stone-walled refuge-style hostel with well-maintained dorm rooms and double en suites. They also run the nearby restaurant, *La Brecha*, with simple, local cuisine from Navarran trout to grilled rabbit. €

Villa de Torla Pza. Aragón 1, www.hotelvilladetorla.com. This handsome alpine hotel has fairly straightforward rooms with the occasional rustic touch (hardwood floors, old-fashioned furniture) but it's the outdoor pool – surrounded by mountain greenery – that makes it a notch above the others. €€

REFUGES IN THE PARQUE NACIONAL DE ORDESA

Refuge de la Brèche De Roland – Les Sarradets https://refugebrechederoland.ffcam.fr/. Simply furnished, well-run refuge on the French side of the mountains with great views that gets busy in summer. Generally staffed Easter–Oct only. €

Refugio Góriz www.goriz.es. This refuge has a well-

9

maintained interior, comfortable mattresses and a restaurant. It's always a good idea to book ahead in summer, though if the refuge is full and you have a tent, you can camp nearby and eat at the hut. Note that in high season you must make reservations online at least two days in advance of your stay; otherwise, you can call to book a space. €

Refugio Valle de Bujaruelo www.refugiodebujaruelo. com/. Comfortable refuge with meal service and camping. There are dorms and simple private doubles. Open weekends from mid-March to the end of summer; limited opening times rest of year. €

AÍNSA AND AROUND

Albergue Mora de Nuei Portal de Abajo 2, https:// moradenuei.com. Top-notch hostel, featuring dorms with sturdy wooden bunks, clean bathrooms and a snack bar. They also have comfortable doubles. €

Casa Alfonso C/Mayor, Aínsa 2, 974 500 981, https:// restaurantecasaalfonso.com/. This charming spot has thick stone walls and wooden beans. The house speciality is hearty Aragonese meat dishes, including the famous

chuletón de ternera del Pirineo, a thick steak produced from locally raised livestock. It offers good-value set menus featuring Spanish and Aragonese specialities. €€

Casa Vidaller C/Calvario 4, Bielsa, www.vidaller.com. A delightful, family-run guesthouse in the old centre of Bielsa, this offers a handful of individually decorated, cosy rooms with lots of rustic charm. There's a café for breakfasts and simple snacks and they can provide picnics for hiking trips. €€

Parador de Bielsa Valle de Pineta, 14km northwest of Bielsa, www.parador.es. This inviting, rustic parador has handsome rooms with lovely mountain views. It sits on the eastern slopes of the park and makes a comfortable base for exploring the area, with numerous hikes starting from its front door. The restaurant serves regional cuisine, including Aragón's version of migas, with sausage and grapes. Note that there is no public transport between the parador and Bielsa, but taxis are available between the two. €€€€

Los Siete Reyes Pza. Mayor 27, Aínsa, https:// lossietereyes.com. Wonderfully rustic hotel right on the Pza. Mayor, with inviting rooms that blend old and new – stone walls, colourful art, crisp linens. €€€

Benasque and around

East of Bielsa lies the small town of **BENASQUE**, spectacularly set in the spacious green Ésera valley and ringed by rocky mountains. Much of the surrounding area is protected as the **Parque Natural Posets-Maladeta**, and numerous trails snake through the valleys and up the mountains. A lively crossroads, the town of Benasque itself is hardly untouched – it's often crammed with adventure-seeking tourists in high season – but this also means that it has plenty of outdoor sports services and tours, mountaineer-friendly accommodation and decently priced restaurants where you can refuel over robust meals.

Benasque is especially popular with avid climbers and trekkers who wish to ascend the Pyrenees' highest peaks, **Aneto** (3404m) and **Posets** (3371m). To do this you'll need all the proper equipment: crampons, ice axe, rope and a helmet to guard against falling rocks. If you're less experienced, your best bet is to go on a trek with one of the many operators in town (see page 597). Either way, the tourist office has simple maps and can update you on weather and trail conditions. There's a popular ski hub at **Cerler** (see page 589).

ADVENTURE ACTIVITIES IN BENASQUE

Benasque is filled with a wide variety of adventure operators and gear shops; the turismo can direct you to recommended outfits. The prices for guided outdoor trips, from mountain treks to snowboarding courses, are similar to other Pyrenean destinations, ranging from around €50 per person per day, with prices varying depending on the level of difficulty and size of tour group.

OUTDOOR OPERATORS

All Radical Mountain Avda. Francia, 675 72 01 84 (shop), https://allradical.com. This well-run outfit specializes in snowboarding and other winter sports; they rent out skis, snowboards and other gear and equipment, and offer ski and snowboard classes.

Barrabés Avda. Francia, 974 551 351, www.barrabes. com. Large, well-regarded adventure retailer that rents

out gear, guidebooks, maps and more. Keep an eye out for their ongoing rebajas (sales).

Compañía de Guías Valle de Benasque Based in the All Radical Mountain shop, Avda. Francia, 974 551 690, www.guiasbenasque.com. This long-running operator offers all manner of guided climbs, treks and hikes through all the seasons – and for all levels.

HIKES AND REFUGES AROUND BENASQUE

Benasque falls more or less in the middle of the trans-Pyrenean GR11 trail, making the town a popular resting spot for hikers, whether for one or more nights. One of the best ways of exploring the surrounding wilderness is to use the many refuges dotted around Benasque as your base.

One of the more popular treks is northwest of Benasque, along the Estós valley to the **Refugio de Estós**, a three-hour trek. You can then continue over the Puerto de Gistaín to the **Refugio de Viadós**, which takes another 5 hours. Viadós is a base for treks up Posets, but again, this is a serious undertaking, and you'll need all the proper equipment to do this climb.

An alternative to this route (though best if you're in tip-top shape, because it can be challenging) is northwest up the Eriste valley, 4km southwest of Benasque, and then over the **Collado de Eriste** before descending to Viadós. Along this route, you can stop at the **Refugio Ángel Órus**.

North of Benasque lies the lush **Upper Esera valley** and massive **Maladeta massif**. A small hub is **La Besurta**, about 16km northeast of Benasque (and linked by buses in summer), which has parking and a small hut/bar with food and supplies (summer only) and is a gateway to hikes in the area. A good base is *Hotel-Spa Hospital de Benasque* (see below), about 3km before you reach La Besurta. In the summer, buses connect Benasque to La Besurta (€13.50 round-trip) and also to Valle de Vallibierna and the **Refugio Pescadores**, 11km northwest of Benasque.

REFUGES AROUND BENASQUE

Refugio Ángel Órus http://refugioangelorus.com. Located in the Valle del Forcau at a height of 2148m. Open year-round. €

Refugio de Biadós www.viados.es. Located in Chistau valley, with wonderful mountain views. Open at Easter, weekends between Easter and the summer, and daily from July to September. €

Refugio Estós www.refugiodeestos.com. Beautifully situated hostel with lake and mountain views. Open year-round. They offer breakfast, lunch and dinner as well as picnics for hikes. €

ARRIVAL AND INFORMATION

BENASQUE AND AROUND

By bus Two buses (www.avanzabus.com) daily (one on Sunday) run from Barbastro (1hr 45min) and Huesca (2hr 45min). Buses from other towns in the region, including Aínsa, also run to Benasque but via connections in Barbastro.

Turismo C/Horno 10, (daily in summer 9.30am–1pm & 4.30–7.45pm; may have limited hours in winter; 974 551 289, https://turismobenasque.com).

ACCOMMODATION

Hotel Aneto Carretera de Francia 4, www.sommoshoteles. com. One of the first four-star hotels in the area, *Hotel Aneto* has spacious rooms, fetching mountain views and pools. They can also help arrange hiking and ski trips. €€€

Hotel Aragüells Avda. Los Tilos, www.hotelaraguells. com. Simple rooms with wooden floors and a restaurant serving regional cuisine; they also offer apartments. €€

Hotel Ciria Avda. Los Tilos, www.hotelciria.com. Long-time, family-run hotel in the middle of town that has cosy rooms with sturdy furnishings. They can also arrange for guided treks into the mountains. The popular restaurant *El Fogaril* (see below) serves hearty mountain cuisine. €€

Los Llanos del Hospital Camino Real de Francia, Los Llanos del Hospital, about 3km from La Besurta, http:// llanosdelhospital.com. This mountain resort is anchored by a large, handsome alpine lodge with an excellent spa. It's a great jumping-off point for exploring the Parque Natural Posets-Maladeta, with a range of activities throughout the year, from skiing in winter to hiking in summer. Regular buses run from La Besurta. €€

EATING AND DRINKING

El Fogaril Hotel Ciria, www.hotelciria.com. The Ciria brothers, avid hunters and fishermen, bring back their catch to this well-regarded restaurant. It's known for serving original game and meat dishes, from wild boar to partridge to *sarrio* (Pyrenean mountain goat). €€

La Llardana Camino de San Anton, at the entrance to Benasque, http://lospirineos.info/lallardana. This amiable *casa rural* has a top-notch restaurant, with beautiful views and local cuisine cooked over a wood-fired grill. €€

Restaurante La Parrilla Ctra. Francia, 974 551 134. Enjoy traditional mountain cuisine, from wild rice to rich Magret duck to grilled meats at this friendly restaurant. €€

Barcelona

CASA COMALAT

Barcelona

Barcelona vibrates with life and is a firm favourite. No other city in Spain can touch it for sheer style, looks or energy. Its art museums are world-class and its football team sublime, while its designer restaurants, bars, galleries and shops lead from the front. And in Antoni Gaudí's extraordinary church of the Sagrada Família, the winding alleys and ageing mansions of the picture-postcard Gothic Quarter, and the world-famous boulevard that is La Rambla, it has three sights that rank high on any Spanish sightseeing list. As a thriving port, prosperous commercial centre and buzzing cultural capital of 1.7 million people (metropolitan population of nearly six million), Barcelona is almost impossible to exhaust – even in a lengthy visit you can barely scrape the surface.

Every visitor starts on **La Rambla**, then dives straight into the medieval nucleus of the city, the **Barri Gòtic** (Gothic Quarter), but there are plenty of other central old-town neighbourhoods to explore, from **La Ribera** – home to the **Museu Picasso** – to funky **El Raval**, where cool bars, restaurants and boutiques cluster around the striking contemporary art museum, the **MACBA**. Even if you think you know these heavily touristed neighbourhoods well, there's always something new to discover – tapas bars hidden down alleys little changed for a century or two, designer boutiques in gentrified old-town quarters, bargain lunches in workers' taverns, unmarked gourmet restaurants, craft outlets and workshops, *fin-de-siècle* cafés, restored medieval palaces and neighbourhood markets.

But endlessly fascinating as these districts are, Barcelona is much more than just its old-town areas. The fortress-topped hill of **Montjuïc**, for example, contains the Olympic stadium as well as some of the city's finest art museums, notably the **MNAC**, the Museu Nacional d'Art de Catalunya – note that word "*nacional*", a testament to Catalunya's unshakeable sense of identity – and the Fundació Joan Miró. Other museums explore the work of internationally famous Catalan artists, from Joan Miró to Antoni Tàpies. The **Eixample** – the nineteenth-century, uptown extension of Barcelona – abounds in *modernista* architectural wonders, from private houses to Gaudí's peerless **Sagrada Família**, as well as modern creations such as the colour-changing **Torre Glòries** and cantilevered **Disseny Hub**, home to the city's applied art collections.

If all that sounds like too much cultural hard work, look instead to the harbour, parks, gardens and beaches for entertainment. Sometimes, it's remarkably easy to forget you're in a big city at all – walking from the **Port Vell** harbour, for example, takes you along the marina, through the old fishing and restaurant quarter of **Barceloneta**, past the leafy **Parc de la Ciutadella**, and out along the beachside promenade to the bar-and-restaurant zone of the **Port Olímpic**. Other easy jaunts include the trip to the distinctive neighbourhood of **Gràcia**, with its small squares, lively bars and the amazing **Park Güell**. If you're saving yourself for just one aerial view of Barcelona, wait for a clear day and head for **Tibidabo**, a hillside amusement park backed by the Collserola forest, while beyond the city limits the one day-trip everyone should make is to the mountain monastery of **Montserrat**, 40km northwest.

Along La Rambla

La Rambla may be the most famous street in the city, but little remains today of what made it so popular. The poet Federico García Lorca once said "it's the only

PARK GÜELL

Highlights

① La Boqueria If you're not hungry when you visit the city's – arguably Spain's – greatest market, you soon will be. See page 605

② Sagrada Família The *modernista* works of Antoni Gaudí define Barcelona – his breathtaking basilica is a virtuoso masterpiece. See page 622

③ MNAC A thousand years of Catalan art is contained within the superb Museu Nacional d'Art de Catalunya, the flagship gallery on the slopes of Montjuïc. See page 627

④ Fundació Joan Miró The life's work of the iconic Catalan artist is housed in Barcelona's best-looking gallery. See page 628

⑤ Park Güell If you visit only one city park, make it Gaudí's extraordinary flight of fancy. See page 632

⑥ FC Barcelona at Camp Nou The world's greatest football team? Only *madrileños* will argue with you. See page 633

⑦ Las Golondrinas Jump on a sightseeing boat around the harbour and along the coast to see Barcelona at its best. See page 639

⑧ Bar hopping, El Raval The city's coolest neighbourhood is the best place for a night on the tiles. See page 646

HIGHLIGHTS ARE MARKED ON THE MAP ON PAGE 602

street in the world which I wish would never end", but sadly today it's much less appealing, and mostly filled with tourist traps and chain fast food joints. That being said, it's still lined with magnificent buildings and a handful of interesting attractions and is always busy. In August of 2017, a devastating **terrorist attack** occurred here.

La Rambla forms the dividing line between the Barri Gòtic to the east and El Raval to the west. It actually comprises five separate sections (rambles) strung head

to tail – from north to south, Rambla Canaletes, Estudis, Sant Josep, Caputxins and Santa Mònica – though you'll rarely hear them referred to as such. Visit to see its main sights, then swiftly move on.

Plaça de Catalunya

Ⓜ Catalunya

SHOPPING
Fantastik	1

EATING
Agua	1

ACCOMMODATION
Barcelona Urbany	1
Hotel Arts Barcelona	2
W Barcelona	3

DRINKING & NIGHTLIFE
Bikini	4
Gimlet	3
Sala Razzmatazz	1
Universal	2

HIGHLIGHTS
1. La Boqueria
2. Sagrada Família
3. MNAC
4. Fundació Joan Miró
5. Park Güell
6. FC Barcelona at Camp Nou
7. Las Golondrinas
8. Bar hopping, El Raval

FIESTAS

FEBRUARY

Festes de Santa Eulàlia http://bcn.cat/santaeulalia. A week's worth of music, dances, parades of *gegants* (giants), *castellers* (human tower-builders) and fireworks in honour of one of Barcelona's patron saints, culminating on her saint's day, February 12.

Llum BCN http://bcn.cat/llumbcn. Held in conjunction with the **Festes de Santa Eulàlia** is the city's light festival. It typically lasts over a long weekend and is situated in the Poblenou district. Light installations are set up across the neighbourhood, drawing large crowds.

EASTER

Setmana Santa (Holy Week) Starting at around 5pm on Good Friday, a procession from the church of Sant Agustí on C/l'Hospital (El Raval) leads to La Seu and back, while Palm Sunday sees the blessing of the palms at La Seu and Sagrada Família.

APRIL

23: Día de Sant Jordi St George's Day, dedicated to Catalunya's dragon-slaying patron saint – the city fills with roses and books, exchanged by sweethearts as gifts.

MAY

Last week: Primavera Sound http://primaverasound.com. The city's hottest music festival, a massive five-day bash, attracts top names in rock, indie and electronica.

JUNE

23/24: Revetlla/Dia de Sant Joan The "eve" and "day" of St John is the city's wildest annual celebration, with bonfires and fireworks (particularly on the beach), drinking and dancing, and going for a dip in the sea at midnight. The day itself (June 24) is a public holiday.

JULY

1–31: Les Nits de Barcelona nitsdebarcelonapedralbes.com. A season of big-name concerts in the lush Jardins del Palau de Pedralbes; recent headliners have included the Pretenders and Patti Smith.

1–31 Festival de Barcelona Grec http://barcelonafestival.com. The summer's foremost arts and music festival, with performances at Montjuïc's open-air Greek theatre (see page 627).

AUGUST

Mid-month: Festa Major de Gràcia http://festamajordegracia.cat. Decorated streets, music, dancing, fireworks and *castellers* around the neighbourhood.

SEPTEMBER

11: Diada Nacional The Catalan national day is a public holiday in Barcelona.

24: Festes de la Mercè http://bcn.cat/merce. The city's biggest festival lasts for a week, featuring costumed giants, firework displays, street theatre and competing teams of *castellers*.

OCTOBER/NOVEMBER

End October to November: Festival Internacional de Jazz http://jazz.barcelona. The city's major annual jazz festival spotlights big-name solo artists and bands.

Ciutat Vella http://ciutatflamenco.com. Ten days of guitar recitals, singing and dancing, plus DJ sessions and a chill-out zone.

DECEMBER

1–22: Fira de Santa Llúcia A Christmas market and crafts fair outside La Seu.

Plaça de Catalunya lies at the heart of the city, with the old town and port below it, and the structured Eixample district above and beyond. Laid out in its present form in the 1920s, and centred on a formal arrangement of statues, circular fountains and trees, it's the focal point for events and demonstrations. It's also the site of the main tourist office, while the principal landmark is the massive **El Corte Inglés** department store behemoth – half Art Deco, half Fascist – where the ninth-floor café has stupendous views.

Església de Betlem and around

10

La Rambla 107 • Free • Ⓜ Liceu

The **Església de Betlem** was built in 1681 in Baroque style for the Jesuits, but was completely gutted in 1937 as anarchists sacked the city's churches at will. It seems hard to believe, but this part of La Rambla was a war zone during the Spanish Civil War. As recounted in *Homage to Catalonia*, **George Orwell** was caught in the crossfire between the nearby *Café Moka* (La Rambla 126) and the Poliorama cinema opposite, now the **Teatre Poliorama** (La Rambla 115).

Palau de la Virreina

La Rambla 99 • Free • http://lavirreina.bcn.cat • Ⓜ Liceu

The graceful eighteenth-century **Palau de la Virreina** is used by the city's culture department, and holds a useful ground-floor **information centre** and ticket office, "Tiquet Rambles". Under the overall name of **Centre de la Imatge**, various galleries and studios present interesting temporary **exhibitions**, with an emphasis on culture and photography. Duck into the courtyard to see the city's two 5m-high **Carnival giants** (*gegants vells*) representing the thirteenth-century Catalan king Jaume I, and his wife Violant.

Mercat de la Boqueria

La Rambla 91 • http://boqueria.barcelona • Ⓜ Liceu

Barcelona's glorious main **food market**, officially the Mercat Sant Josep but invariably known as **La Boqueria**, stands immediately west of La Rambla, at the point where a sudden profusion of flower stalls marked the switch to **Rambla Sant Josep** (also known as Rambla de les Flors). It was established outside the city's medieval walls in the thirteenth century for farmers to bring produce fresh from the fields. Today's cavernous hall was erected between 1836 and 1840, and stretches back from a wrought-iron entrance arch facing La Rambla. Today, the stalls at the front of the market sell more novelty chocolates, sweets and smoothies than traditional Spanish and Catalan

---

ON THE MIRÓ TRAIL

Halfway down La Rambla, just past the Boqueria, a large round mosaic by **Joan Miró** is set in the middle of the pavement. The Catalan artist, whose namesake museum on Montjuïc is one of Barcelona's major highlights, was born just a couple of minutes' walk away, in the Barri Gòtic; a plaque marks the relevant building on Passatge del Crèdit, off C/Ferran.

Once you've seen one Miró in Barcelona, you start to spot them everywhere. There's another large ceramic mural on the facade of Terminal B at the **airport**, for a start, while he also designed the starfish logo for the **Caixa de Pensións** savings bank and the **España logo** on Spanish National Tourist Board publications. Then there's his towering *Dona i Ocell* ("Woman and Bird") in the **Parc Joan Miró**, near Barcelona Sants train station, while a smaller *Dona* stands in the courtyard of the **Ajuntament** (city hall). In many ways, Barcelona is a Miró city, whatever Picasso fans might think.

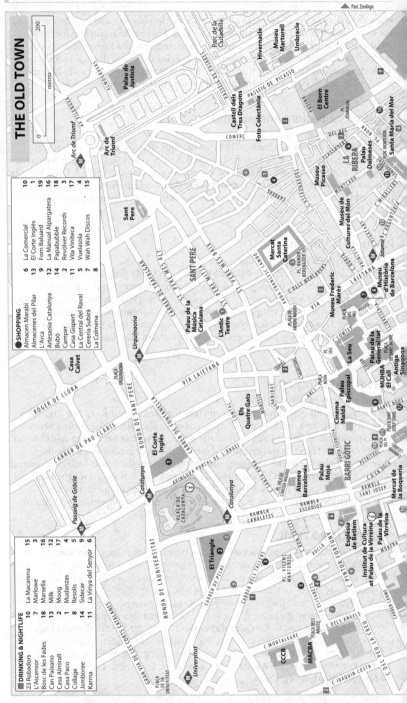

THE OLD TOWN

0 _____ 200
meters

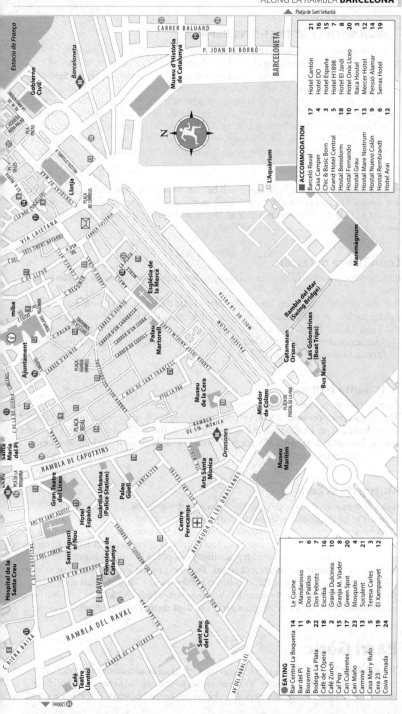

10

HIGH SOCIETY AT THE HOTEL ESPAÑA

A hidden gem is tucked around the back of the Liceu opera house, on the otherwise fairly shabby C/Sant Pau, where some of the most influential names in Catalan architecture and design came together at the start of the twentieth century to transform the **Hotel España** (see page 639) into one of the city's most lavish addresses. With a wonderfully tiled dining room designed by Lluís Domènech i Montaner, a bar with an amazing marble fireplace by Eusebi Arnau, and a bathing area with glass roof (now the breakfast room) whose marine murals were executed by Ramon Casas, the hotel was the fashionable sensation of its day. A century later it's back in vogue, following a remarkable restoration, and lunch or dinner in the original *modernista* dining room (known as the *Fonda España*) is a real in-the-know treat.

produce, but head to the back and you'll be met with a riot of noise and colour, from the central fish and seafood stands to stalls laden with bunches of herbs, pots of spices, baskets of wild mushrooms, mounds of cheese and sausage, racks of bread, hanging hams and overloaded meat counters.

Gran Teatre del Liceu

La Rambla 51–59 • See website for current schedule of tours, which varies seasonally and with each production • liceubarcelona.cat • Ⓜ Liceu

Barcelona's celebrated opera house, the **Gran Teatre del Liceu**, was first founded as a private theatre in 1847. Tours of the lavish interior depart from the modern extension, the Espai Liceu. There's also a longer in-depth backstage tour. Highlights include the classically inspired **Saló dels Miralls** (Salon of Mirrors) and the impressive gilded auditorium containing almost 2,300 seats.

Arts Santa Mònica

La Rambla 7 • Free • http://artssantamonica.gencat.cat • Ⓜ Drassanes

The Augustinian **convent of Santa Mònica** dates originally from 1626, making it the oldest building on La Rambla. It was remodelled in the 1980s as a contemporary **arts centre**, known as **Arts Santa Mònica**, and hosts regularly changing exhibitions in its grand, echoing galleries.

Museu de la Cera

La Rambla 4–6, entrance on Ptge. de Banca • Charge • http://museocerabcn.com • Ⓜ Drassanes

Housed in an impressive nineteenth-century bank building at the foot of La Rambla, Barcelona's wax museum, the **Museu de Cera**, is no Madame Tussaud's – it's something stranger and more unsettling than that, and in its way it's rather wonderful. In recent years, an effort has been made to replace dusty old politicians and historical figures with current celebrities, singers and actors. Pose next to the Beatles as they sit side by side, or gaze into the eyes of Billie Eilish or Leonardo de Caprio. Whole rooms are given over to *Star Wars* or to Spanish TV show *Money Heist*. Make sure you don't miss its extraordinary neighbouring grotto-bar, the **Bosc de les Fades** (see page 645).

Barri Gòtic

The **Barri Gòtic**, or Gothic Quarter, forms the very heart of the old town, spreading from the east side of La Rambla. It's a remarkable concentration of medieval buildings principally dating from the fourteenth and fifteenth centuries, when Barcelona reached the height of its commercial prosperity before being absorbed into the burgeoning kingdom of Castile. It takes the best part of a day to see everything here, with the Catedral – **La Seu** – a particular highlight, and you certainly won't want to miss the archeological remains at the **Museu d'Història de Barcelona**, the **Gaudí Exhibition Center** in the Museu Diocesà, or the eclectic **Museu Frederic Marès**. That said, sauntering through the atmospheric alleys or simply sitting at a café table in one of the lovely squares is just as much an attraction.

The picture-postcard images of the Barri Gòtic are largely based on the streets north of C/Ferran and C/Jaume I, where tourists throng the boutiques, bars, restaurants, museums and galleries. South of here – from Pl. Reial and C/Avinyó to the harbour – the Barri Gòtic is less gentrified.

10

La Seu

Pl. de la Seu • Charge • http://catedralbcn.org • Ⓜ Jaume I

Barcelona's Catedral, **La Seu**, is one of the great Gothic buildings of Spain. Located on a site previously occupied by a Roman temple and then an early Christian basilica, it was begun in 1298 and finished in 1448, save for the neo-Gothic main facade, added in the 1880s.

The Catedral is dedicated to the city's co-patroness, **Santa Eulàlia**, martyred by the Romans for daring to prefer Christianity, and her tomb rests in a crypt beneath the high altar. The rest of the interior is typically ornate, with no fewer than 29 side chapels, but the Catedral's most magnificent component is its fourteenth-century **cloister**, which looks over a lush garden complete with soaring palm trees and – more unusually – a gaggle of honking geese. White geese have been kept here for over five hundred years, either, depending on which story you believe, to reflect the virginity of Santa Eulàlia, or as a reminder of the erstwhile Roman splendour of Barcelona, as geese were kept on the Capitoline Hill in Rome.

The obligatory admission charge includes entry to the interior, the choir, cloister and **museum**, which is filled with glittering church treasure, and various chapels not otherwise open to the public.

Museu Diocesà / Gaudí Exhibition Center

Pl. de la Seu 7 • Charge • http://museudiocesa.esglesia.barcelona • Ⓜ Jaume I

Barcelona's **Museu Diocesà**, housed in the ancient tower immediately left (east) of the Catedral's main facade, is now almost entirely devoted to celebrating the life, works and spirituality of Antoni Gaudí, and brands itself the **Gaudí Exhibition Center**. Even those ecclesiastical treasures that it continues to display are now cast in terms of their influence on Gaudí.

In many ways it has become the Gaudí museum that Barcelona needed, providing a readily accessible overview of the architect's inspirations and achievements. As well as items

---

BOHO BARCELONA AND THE FOUR CATS

There's not much to see in the shopping zone north of the Catedral, but a century or so ago a tavern called **Els Quatre Gats** (The Four Cats; C/Montsió 3, http://4gats.com) burned brightly as the heart of Barcelona's bohemian in-crowd. Opened by Pere Romeu and other *modernista* artists in 1897 as a gathering place for artists and literary types, the building itself was gloriously decorated in exuberant Catalan Art Nouveau style.

Els Quatre Gats soon thrived as the scene of poetry readings and the venue for cultural debate, while a young Picasso designed the menu. Today, a modern restoration displays something of its former glory, with the – frankly overpriced – bar-restaurant overseen by a copy of Ramon Casas' famous wall painting of himself and Romeu on a tandem bicycle (the original is in the MNAC).

he owned, including his wooden workbench and tools, it displays photos, newspapers and black-and-white footage of Barcelona a century ago. Successive galleries upstairs explain and illustrate Gaudí's "Masterpieces", culminating of course with the Sagrada Família.

Plaça del Rei

Ⓜ Jaume I

10 The harmonious enclosed square of **Plaça del Rei**, behind the Catedral apse, was once the courtyard of the palace of the counts of Barcelona, later the residence of the count-kings of Aragón. The palace buildings are steeped in history, and include the romantic Renaissance **Torre del Rei Martí**, the main hall known as the **Saló del Tinell**, and the fourteenth-century **Santa Agata chapel**, both now part of the Museu d'Història de Barcelona. The square itself was the scene of one of Barcelona's greatest historic set pieces, since it was from the steps of the exterior stone staircase that Ferdinand and Isabella received Christopher Columbus on his triumphant return from the New World in 1493.

Museu d'Història de Barcelona (MUHBA)

Pl. del Rei, entrance on C/Veguer • Charge • http://museuhistoria.bcn.cat • Ⓜ Jaume I

The excellent **Museu d'Història de Barcelona** (Barcelona History Museum) not only extends through the labyrinth of buildings that surround the Pl. del Rei but also, crucially, burrows beneath them, to reveal the extensive site of the Roman city of Barcino.

The remains date from the first to the sixth centuries AD and reflect the transition from Roman to Visigothic rule. Not much survives above chest height, but explanatory diagrams show the extent of the streets, walls and buildings, while models, mosaics, murals and displays of excavated goods help flesh out the reality of daily life in Barcino.

While the displays on the upper levels inevitably lack the visceral impact of actually seeing the ancient city laid out at your feet, they do illuminate Barcelona's subsequent history, including its spell as a Muslim city under the caliphate of Damascus, and explore its medieval growth as a major trading port. The complex also incorporates the beautiful **Capella de Santa Agata** (also known as the Capella Palatina) and the impressive **Saló del Tinell**, in which temporary exhibitions may incur an extra admission charge.

Museu Frederic Marès

Pl. de Sant Iu 5–6, off C/Comtes • Charge • www.museumares.bcn.cat • Ⓜ Jaume I

The fascinating **Museu Frederic Marès**, in a wing of the old royal palace behind Pl. del Rei, celebrates the diverse passions of sculptor, painter and restorer Frederic Marès (1893–1991). His beautifully presented collection of ancient, religious medieval

A TOUR OF JEWISH BARCELONA

Barcelona's medieval Jewish quarter lay in the shadow of the Catedral – under the Church's careful scrutiny. It was centred on C/Sant Domènec del Call, where you'll find the most notable surviving landmark, the **Antiga Sinagoga** (C/Marlet 5, corner with C/Sant Domènec del Call; Charge; http://sinagogamayor.com; Ⓜ Liceu). Not many people stop by, and if you do, you'll get a personalized tour of the small room. The prosperous settlement persisted until the pogrom and forced conversion of 1391, after which most of the buildings used by the Jews were torn down. However, a plaque further down C/Marlet (junction with C/Arc Sant Ramon del Call) marks the site of the former rabbi's house, while in nearby Plaçeta Manuel Ribé another house – originally belonging to a veil-maker – now serves as a small museum, the **MUHBA El Call** (Pl. Manuel Ribé; Charge; http://museuhistoria.bcn.cat; Ⓜ Liceu).

sculpture does little to prepare visitors for his true obsession, namely a kaleidoscopic array of curios and collectibles. These present an incredible retrospective jumble gathered during fifty years of travel, with entire rooms devoted to keys and locks, cigarette cards and snuff boxes, fans, gloves and brooches, playing cards, walking sticks, doll's houses, toy theatres and archaic bicycles, to name just a sample. The museum's summer café occupies the romantic courtyard, with seats under the orange trees.

Església de Santa María del Pi and around

10

Pl. Sant Josep Oriol • Charge • http://basilicadelpi.com • ⓂLiceu

The **Església de Santa María del Pi**, an eleventh-century church rebuilt three hundred years later in the Catalan-Gothic style, stands at the centre of three delightful little squares, five minutes' walk from the Catedral. Daily guided tours lead visitors up the 260 steps of its octagonal bell tower, which doubled in the Middle Ages as a watchtower and defensive refuge.

The church stands on the prettiest square, **Pl. Sant Josep Oriol**, which hosts an **artists' market** at the weekend, and is overhung with balconies and scattered with seats from the *Bar del Pi* (see page 642). A **farmers' market** spills across Pl. del Pi on the first and third Friday, Saturday and Sunday of the month, selling honey, cheese, cakes and other produce.

Palau de la Generalitat

Pl. de Sant Jaume, entrance on C/de Sant Honorat • Free • http://presidencia.gencat.cat/es/ambits_d_actuacio/palau-de-la-generalitat • ⓂJaume I

On the north side of **Pl. de Sant Jaume** – the square that marks the very centre of the Barri Gòtic – rises the **Palau de la Generalitat**, traditional home of the Catalan government, from where the short-lived Catalan Republic was proclaimed in April 1931. There's a beautiful cloister on the first floor, opening off which are the chapel and salon of Sant Jordi (St George, patron saint of Catalunya as well as England) and an upper courtyard planted with orange trees and peppered with presidential busts. Aside from the guided tours on alternate weekends, the Generalitat opens to the public on **Dia de Sant Jordi**, or Saint George's Day (April 23; expect a 2hr wait) – when the whole square is festooned with bookstalls and rose sellers – as well as **Diada Nacional de Catalunya** (National Day, September 11) and **La Mercè** (September 24).

Ajuntament de Barcelona

Pl. de Sant Jaume • Public admitted Sun 10am–1.30pm, entrance on C/Font de Sant Miquel • Free • http://bcn.cat • ⓂJaume I

Although parts of Barcelona's City Hall, the **Ajuntament** on the south side of Pl. de Sant Jaume (also known as Casa de la Ciutat), date from as early as 1373, its Neoclassical facade was added when the square was laid out in the nineteenth century. On Sundays, you're allowed into the building for a self-guided tour around the splendid marble halls, galleries and staircases. The highlights are the magnificent restored fourteenth-century council chamber, the **Saló de Cent**, and the dramatic historical murals by Josep María Sert in the **Saló de les Cròniques** (Hall of Chronicles), while the ground-floor courtyard features sculptural works by celebrated Catalan artists.

Plaça Reial and around

ⓂLiceu

Of all the old-town squares, perhaps the least typical of Barcelona but the most popular with visitors is the grand, arcaded **Plaça Reial**, hidden behind an archway, just off La Rambla. Laid out in around 1850 in a deliberate echo of the great *places* of France, this

10

elegant square is studded with tall palm trees and decorated iron lamps (made by the young Antoni Gaudí), bordered by high, pastel-coloured buildings, and centres on a fountain depicting the Three Graces. It used to be a bit dodgy here, but most of the unsavoury characters have been driven off over the years and predatory menu-toting waiters are usually the biggest nuisance these days.

The alleys on the south side of Plaça Reial emerge on C/Escudellers, which now teeters on the edge of respectability despite its lingering air of late-night seediness. Bars and restaurants hereabouts, especially on funky **Pl. de George Orwell** at the eastern end of C/Escudellers, attract a youthful crowd.

To the south, down **Carrer d'Avinyó**, the harbourside **La Mercè** neighbourhood was formerly home to merchants enriched by Barcelona's maritime trade, while Carrer de la Mercè and the surrounding streets are still home to old-style **taverns**.

Palau Martorell

C/Ample 11 · Charge · http://palaumartorell.com · ⓂDrassanes

This grand neoclassical building, sitting on the Plaça de Mercè, has opened to the public as an art museum. Its stated aim is to house temporary exhibitions by international artists, such as Alphonse Mucha, Basquiat, Alexander Calder and Tamara de Lempicka. The three-storeyed interior, lit by a vast stained-glass skylight, is worth a visit in its own right.

Sant Pere

The Barri Gòtic is bordered on its eastern side by Via Laietana, which was cut through the old town at the start of the twentieth century. Across it to the east stretches the quiet neighbourhood of **Sant Pere**, home to two remarkable buildings, the Palau de la Música Catalana concert hall and the Mercat Santa Caterina.

Palau de la Música Catalana

C/Sant Pere Més Alt · Guided tours charge · http://palaumusica.cat · ⓂUrquinaona

Lluís Domènech i Montaner's stupendous **Palau de la Música Catalana** barely seems to have enough space to breathe in the narrow C/Sant Pere Més Alt. Built in 1908, its bare brick structure is lined with tiles and mosaics, the highly elaborate facade resting on three great columns, like an elephant's legs. The stunning interior, meanwhile, incorporates a bulbous stained-glass skylight that caps the second-storey auditorium – something that contemporary critics claimed to be an engineering impossibility. Successive extensions and interior remodelling have opened up the original site – to the side, an enveloping glass facade provides the main public access to the box office, terrace restaurant and foyer bar.

To see the Palau at its best, try to join the 2000-plus audience at a performance in the main auditorium, ideally in daylight – the concert season runs from September until June (see page 648). Otherwise, it's well worth taking a daytime **guided tour** of the interior – visitor numbers are limited, so you'll almost certainly have to book a day or two in advance.

Mercat Santa Caterina

Av. de Francesc Cambò 16 · http://mercatsantacaterina.com · ⓂJaume I

The splendid restoration of Sant Pere's **Mercat Santa Caterina** has retained its original nineteenth-century balustraded market walls while adding slatted wooden doors and windows and a dramatic multicoloured undulating roof. This is one of Barcelona's best places to shop for food or grab a snack, and is actually a lot more authentic nowadays than the **Boqueria**. The foundations of a medieval convent discovered here during the renovation work are visible at the rear.

La Ribera

South of Sant Pere, across C/Princesa, **La Ribera** (the two neighbourhoods together are better known as El Born) sports Barcelona's biggest single tourist attraction, the **Museu Picasso**. The sheer number of visitors in this neighbourhood rivals the busiest streets of the Barri Gòtic, and has had a knock-on effect in attracting bars, shops and restaurants. La Ribera is at its most hip, and most enjoyable, around the Passeig del Born, the elongated square leading from Santa María church to the El **Born Centre de Cultura I Memòria**, in the stunningly restored iron-and-glass Antic Mercat del Born.

10

Museu Picasso

C/Montcada 15–23 • Charge • http://museupicasso.bcn.cat • Ⓜ Jaume I

Although the celebrated **Museu Picasso** ranks among the world's most important collections of Picasso's work, some visitors are disappointed to find that it contains few of his best-known pictures, and few in the Cubist style. Nonetheless, the permanent collection holds almost four thousand works, displayed in five adjoining medieval palaces, which provide a fascinating opportunity to trace Picasso's development from his early paintings as a young boy to the major works of later years. The whole place is extremely well laid out, with abundant space and natural light.

The highlights

Particularly fascinating are the **early drawings**, in which Picasso – still signing with his full name, Pablo Ruíz Picasso – attempted to copy the nature paintings in which his father specialized. Paintings from his art-school days in Barcelona (1895–97) show tantalizing glimpses of the city that the young Picasso was beginning to know well – the Gothic old town, the cloisters of Sant Pau del Camp, Barceloneta beach – and even at the ages of 15 and 16 he was producing serious work.

Paintings from the **Blue Period** (1901–04), ranging from moody Barcelona roofscapes to the cold face of *La Dona Morta*, burst upon you. Subsequent galleries only make the barest nods to Picasso's Cubist (1907–20) and Neoclassical (1920–25) stages, though his return to the city with the Ballets Russes in 1917 is commemorated by *Harlequin*. Another large jump brings us to 1957, and the 44 interpretations of **Las Meninas**, brilliantly deconstructing the individual portraits and compositions that make up Velázquez's masterpiece, which Picasso completed between August and December that year.

PICASSO IN BARCELONA

Although born in Málaga, **Pablo Picasso** (1881–1973) spent much of his youth – from the age of 14 to 23 – in Barcelona, and there are echoes of the great artist at various sites throughout the old town. Not too far from the museum, you can still see many of the buildings in which Picasso lived and worked, notably the Escola de Belles Arts de Llotja (C/Consolat del Mar, near Estació de França), where his father taught drawing and where Picasso himself absorbed an academic training. The apartments where the family lived when they first arrived in Barcelona – Ptge. d'Isabel II 4 and C/Reina Cristina 3, both opposite the Escola – can also be seen, though only from the outside. Less tangible is to take a walk down C/Avinyó, which cuts south from C/ Ferran to C/Ample. Large houses along here were converted into brothels at the turn of the twentieth century, and Picasso used to haunt the street, sketching what he saw – women at one of the brothels inspired his seminal Cubist work, *Les Demoiselles d'Avignon*.

Museu de Cultures del Món

C/Montcada 12 • Charge • http://museuculturesmon.bcn.cat • ⓂJaume I

Housed in two medieval palaces directly across from the Picasso museum, the **Museu de Cultures del Món** – Museum of World Cultures showcases objects of phenomenal beauty and power from the world beyond Europe, not necessarily ancient but mostly imbued by their creators with deep spiritual significance. It's a somewhat haphazard assortment, but there's no disputing its overall quality or impact.

Downstairs, the African section ranges from the Christian art of Ethiopia to reliquary statuettes, helmets and masks, some credited to specific twentieth-century sculptors. On the higher levels, the Oceania segment includes actual remodelled human skulls from New Guinea, belonging to enemies and revered ancestors alike, and carved *moai* figures from Easter Island, while the extensive Asian galleries hold everything from Japanese Noh theatre masks and Korean ceramics to jewelled knives from Indonesia and bronze Krishna statuettes from India, with touch-screen displays to explain whatever catches your eye.

Basílica de Santa Maria del Mar

Pl. de Santa María • Charge • http://santamariadelmarbarcelona.org • ⓂJaume I

La Ribera's flagship church of **Santa Maria del Mar** is the city's most exquisite example of pure Catalan-Gothic architecture. Conceived as thanks for the Catalan conquest of Sardinia in 1324, work on the church began in 1329 and was finished in just over half a century, which is pretty rapid for medieval church construction (and also explains its consistency of style). Its wide nave, narrow aisles, massive buttresses and octagonal, flat-topped towers are all typically Catalan-Gothic features, while its later Baroque trappings were destroyed during the Civil War, which is probably all to the good. Subsequent restoration work has concentrated on showing off the simple bare spaces of the interior and the stained glass, especially, is beautiful.

Rather than exploring the church itself, the **guided tours** of Santa Maria del Mar, conducted in Catalan and English, take visitors up to a small platform that has been erected on the rooftop, for views over the city.

Passeig del Born

Ⓜ Jaume I/Barceloneta

Once the site of medieval fairs and tournaments – *born* means jousting tournament – the fashionable **Passeig del Born** fronting the church of Santa María del Mar is now an avenue lined with plane trees shading a host of classy bars and shops. Shoppers scour the narrow medieval alleys on either side for boutiques and craft workshops, while at night the Born becomes one of Barcelona's best bar areas.

El Born Centre de Cultura I Memòria

Pl. Comercial 12, at Pg. del Born • Charge for exhibitions and guided tours • http://elborncentrecultural.cat • Ⓜ Jaume I/Barceloneta

The handsome **Antic Mercat del Born** (1873–76), the biggest of Barcelona's nineteenth-century market halls, spent a century as the city's main wholesale fruit and veg market before closing in 1971. Spared demolition thanks to local protest, it languished empty for decades, and finally reopened in 2013. Now, beneath a renovated canopy of sparkling glass and intricate wrought iron, **El Born Centre de Cultura I Memòria** looks back over three centuries of Catalan history, from the siege of 1714 to the present day. The transformation took so long partly because excavations revealed that the market stood directly on the remains of eighteenth-century shops, factories, houses and taverns that predate the Ciutadella fortress and the Barceloneta district – a fascinating discovery that's on full display.

Foto Colectània

Pg. de Picasso 14 • Charge • http://fotocolectania.org • Ⓜ Jaume I/Barceloneta

A non-profit photography gallery that houses small but high-quality exhibitions from Catalan, Spanish and international photographers. Run by a foundation that promotes local photographers abroad, it also houses a library comprising thousands of images.

Parc de la Ciutadella

Park entrances on Pg. de Picasso (Ⓜ Barceloneta, or a short walk from La Ribera) and Pg. de Pujades (Ⓜ Arc de Triomf) • Free

The **Parc de la Ciutadella**, east of La Ribera, is the largest green space in the city centre. It's also the meeting place of the Catalan parliament (no public access), occupying part of a fortress-like structure that's the only surviving portion of the star-shaped Bourbon citadel that gave the park its name. After la Ciutadella was chosen to host the Universal Exhibition in 1888, *modernista* architects left their mark in eye-catching buildings and monuments, not least the giant brick Arc de Triomf at the park's inland end.

10

El Raval

The old-town area west of La Rambla takes its name, **El Raval**, from the Arabic word for "outskirts". Until the fourteenth century, when a new circuit was added to Barcelona's medieval walls, it was primarily agricultural. Once enclosed, it became the site of hospitals, churches, monasteries and various noxious trades, while later still it acquired a reputation as a red-light district, known as the Barri Xinès – Chinatown. Even today the backstreets around C/Sant Pau and C/Nou de la Rambla hold pockets of sleaze, while a handful of old bars trade on their former reputations as bohemian hangouts. El Raval has changed markedly, particularly in the "upper Raval" around the contemporary art museum, the **MACBA**, and these days cutting-edge galleries, designer restaurants and fashionable bars all form part of the scene.

Museu d'Art Contemporani de Barcelona (MACBA)

Pl. dels Àngels 1 • Charge • http://macba.cat • Ⓜ Catalunya

The huge, luminous **Museu d'Art Contemporani de Barcelona**, known as the **MACBA**, anchors the upper Raval. Inside, a series of swooping ramps from the ground floor to the fourth floor afford continuous views of the square below – usually full of careering skateboarders. The collection represents the main movements in art since 1945, mainly in Catalunya and Spain but with a smattering of foreign artists as well. The pieces are shown in rotating exhibitions, so you may catch works by Joan Miró, Antoni Tàpies, Eduardo Chillida, Alexander Calder, Robert Rauschenberg or Paul Klee. Joan Brossa, leading light of the Catalan avant-garde "Dau al Set" group, has work here, too, as do contemporary conceptual and abstract artists.

Centre de Cultura Contemporània de Barcelona (CCCB)

C/de Montalegre 5 • Charge • http://cccb.org • Ⓜ Catalunya

Adjoining MACBA is the **Centre de Cultura Contemporània de Barcelona**, or **CCCB**, which hosts temporary art and city-related exhibitions as well as supporting a cinema and a varied concert and festival programme. At the back of the building is *Terracccita* café-bar, which has a sunny terrace on the modern square joining the CCCB to the MACBA.

Hospital de la Santa Creu

Entrances on C/Carme and C/de l'Hospital • Free • http://lacapella.bcn.cat • Ⓜ Liceu

El Raval's most historic relic, the large **Hospital de la Santa Creu**, is an attractive complex of Gothic buildings that was founded as the city's main hospital in 1402, and retained that role until 1930. The fifteenth-century hospital wards were subsequently converted for cultural and educational use, and now hold the Royal Academy of Medicine, an art and design school, and two libraries, including the Catalan national library, the Biblioteca de Catalunya. Visitors can wander freely through the charming medieval cloistered **garden**, while the former chapel, **La Capella** (entered separately from C/l'Hospital) is an exhibition space for contemporary artists.

10

Rambla del Raval

Ⓜ Liceu

The most obvious manifestation of El Raval's changing character is the **Rambla del Raval**. Striking through the centre of the district, this palm-lined boulevard has a distinct character all its own – its signature landmark, halfway down, is the massive Botero cat sculpture, *El Gato de Botero*, while on either side are kebab joints, restaurants, cafés and bars. A weekend **street market** (selling anything from samosas to hammocks) brings the *rambla* to life.

Filmoteca de Catalunya

Pl. Salvador Seguí 1–9 • **Cinema** Charge • **Exhibition** Free • http://filmoteca.cat • Ⓜ Liceu

The 2012 opening of the Josep Lluís Mateo-designed **Filmoteca de Catalunya**, a colossus of concrete and glass in Pl. Salvador Seguí (long known for its pickpockets and prostitutes) marked yet another step in the push to revitalize El Raval. As well as two below-ground cinemas, the building holds a film library, a bookshop and spaces for cinema-related exhibitions. All films are shown in their original language, with Spanish or Catalan subtitles.

Palau Güell

C/Nou de la Rambla 3–5 • Charge; includes audioguide • http://palauguell.cat • Ⓜ Liceu

Between 1886 and 1890, the young **Antoni Gaudí** designed the extraordinary **Palau Güell** as a townhouse for the wealthy shipowner and industrialist **Eusebi Güell**. Commissioned as an extension of the Güell family's house on La Rambla, to which it's connected by a corridor, it was the first modern building to be declared a World Heritage Site by UNESCO. Restored, complete with remarkable roof terrace, to its original state, it's now one of Barcelona's major architectural showpieces.

Steered by a helpful audioguide, visitors explore the Palau Güell from top to bottom, at their own pace. At a time when architects sought to conceal the iron supports within buildings, Gaudí turned them to his advantage, displaying them as decorative features in the grand rooms on the **main floor**. Columns, arches and ceilings are all shaped, carved and twisted in an elaborate style that became the hallmark of Gaudí's later works. The vast **central hall** is topped with a parabolic dome that's pierced with holes to let in natural light, and it echoes to a thunderous organ that's played throughout the day. Meanwhile, the spectacular **roof terrace** culminates in a fantastical series of chimneys decorated with swirling patterns made from fragments of glazed tile, glass and earthenware.

Port Vell

Perhaps the greatest transformation in Barcelona has been along the waterfront, where harbour and Mediterranean have been returned to their rightful prominence. The glistening harbourside merges seamlessly with the old town, with the tourist attractions of **Port Vell** (Old Port) just steps from the bottom of La Rambla.

Mirador de Colom

Pl. del Portal de la Pau • Charge • 932 853 834 • Ⓜ Drassanes

At the foot of La Rambla, in the middle of swirling traffic, stands the striking **Mirador de Colom**, which commemorates the visit made by Christopher Columbus (known locally as Cristòfoll Colom) to Barcelona in 1493. A lift whisks you up to the enclosed *mirador* at Columbus's feet for terrific 360-degree city views.

10

Museu Marítim

Avda. de les Drassanes • Charge • http://mmb.cat • Ⓜ Drassanes

Barcelona's medieval shipyards, or **Drassanes**, date back to the fourteenth century, and were originally used as a dry dock to fit and arm Catalunya's war fleet in the days when the Catalan-Aragonese crown was vying with Venice and Genoa for control of the Mediterranean. The unique stone-vaulted buildings make a fitting home for the city's **Museu Marítim** (Maritime Museum), which celebrates the city's role as a naval base, trading centre, and port of passage for generations of migrants and visitors.

The permanent collection uses seven vessels, starting with a Greek merchant ship from the fourth century BC, to trace the history of navigation. Delicate model boats and gorgeous antique maps illuminate the story, with actual shipping containers serving as display cases. The vast central gallery holds a full-size replica of the magnificent, 60m-long *Royal Galley*, which was built right here in 1568, and fought as the Spanish flagship in the Battle of Lepanto three years later.

The huge, high-ceilinged halls offer plenty of space for high-tech temporary exhibitions, and also hold a good shop and café, while the admission fee also provides access to the **Santa Eulàlia** on the nearby waterfront, a three-masted ocean schooner that once made the run between Barcelona and Cuba.

Rambla del Mar and Maremàgnum

Moll d'Espanya 5 • Free • http://maremagnum.es • Ⓜ Drassanes

The old wharves and warehouses of the inner harbour have been replaced by an entertainment zone reached via the wooden **Rambla del Mar** swing bridge. This stretches across the harbour to **Maremàgnum**, two floors of restaurants, gift shops and boutiques, plus outdoor seating and park areas that provide fantastic views. The 2024 addition of the *Bus Nàutic*, a zero-emissions catamaran designed to ferry commuters and visitors to and from the breakwater, has been hugely successful.

L'Aquàrium

Moll d'Espanya • Charge • http://aquariumbcn.com • Ⓜ Drassanes/Barceloneta

L'Aquàrium drags in families and school parties to see 11,000 fish and sea creatures in 35 themed tanks representing underwater caves, tidal areas, tropical reefs, the planet's oceans and other maritime habitats. It's somewhat overpriced, and offers few new experiences, save perhaps the 80m-long walk-through underwater tunnel, which brings you face to face with rays and sharks.

Museu d'Història de Catalunya

Pl. de Pau Vila 3 • Charge • http://mhcat.net • Ⓜ Barceloneta

The absorbing **Museu d'Història de Catalunya** (Catalunya History Museum) occupies the upper levels of the one surviving warehouse on the Port Vell harbourside, the beautifully restored **Palau de Mar**. This exhaustive museum traces the history of Catalunya from the Bronze Age to the present day, with its spacious exhibition areas wrapped around a wide atrium, and a dramatic section on the Civil War.

10 The Eixample

The vast nineteenth-century street grid north of Pl. de Catalunya, now Barcelona's main shopping and business district, was designed as part of a revolutionary urban plan – the **Eixample** in Catalan (pronounced ey-sham-pla, the "Extension" or "Widening") – that divided districts into regular blocks, whose characteristic wide streets and shaved corners survive today. It's not a neighbourhood as such – and, in fact, is further split into two distinct sections, either side of the two central parallel avenues, Passeig de Gràcia and Rambla de Catalunya – the **Dreta de l'Eixample** (i.e., the right-hand side)

THE EIXAMPLE

and **Esquerra de l'Eixample** (left-hand side). It's on and around Passeig de Gràcia, above all, that the bulk of the city's show-stopping *modernista* (Catalan Art Nouveau) buildings is found, along with classy galleries and hotels, shops and boutiques.

Museu del Modernisme Barcelona

C/Balmes 48 • Charge • http://mmbcn.cat • Ⓜ Passeig de Gràcia

Barcelona's traditional "gallery district", just off Rambla de Catalunya, makes a fitting location for the *modernista* treasures of the small **Museu del Modernisme Barcelona**. Of the two exhibition floors in this former textile warehouse, the grand vaulted basement contains paintings and sculpture, while the ground floor holds *modernista* furniture, from screens to sofas. There are paintings and works by many famous names, whether oils by Ramon Casas, or sinuous mirrors and tables made by Antoni Gaudí for the *Casa* Batlló (see page 620) and Casa Calvet (see page 644). A rare opportunity to examine extraordinary Art Nouveau fixtures, fittings and furniture, it provides an invaluable crash course in the varied facets of Catalan *modernisme*.

10

EATING
Cinc Sentits	3
Disfrutar	1
La Flauta	4
Lasarte	2
Tapas24	5

ACCOMMODATION
Almanac Barcelona	3
Casa Bonay	4
Hostal Girona	5
Hotel Axel	1
Mandarin Oriental	2

DRINKING & NIGHTLIFE
Aire Chicas	3
Dry Martini	2
Punto BCN	4
Velódromo	1

SHOPPING
Altaïr	7
Antonio Miró	4
Arenas de Barcelona	6
Cubiña	3
Estanc Duaso	2
L'Illa	1
Mango	5
Mango Outlet	8

Casa Amatller

Fundació Amatller, Pg. de Gràcia 41 • Charge • http://amatller.org • ⓜ Passeig de Gràcia

Josep Puig i Cadafalch's striking **Casa Amatller** apartment block (c.1900) was designed for Antoni Amatller, a chocolate manufacturer, art collector, photographer and traveller. It's a triumph of decorative detail, particularly the facade, which rises in steps to a point, studded with ceramic tiles and heraldic sculptures. Inside, the hallway's twisted stone columns are interspersed with dragon lamps. Parts of the house are open to the public, who can admire its original *modernista* furniture and interior design, take a peep at Amatller's photographic studio, and even, at certain times, sample hot chocolate in the kitchen.

10

Casa Batlló

Pg. de Gràcia 43 • Charge • http://casabatllo.es • ⓜ Passeig de Gràcia

The most extraordinary creation on the "Block of Discord", Antoni Gaudí's **Casa Batlló** (pronounced *by-o*) was designed for industrialist Josep Batlló. The original apartment

---

BUILDING A DESIGNER CITY

As Barcelona grew more prosperous throughout the nineteenth century, it was clear that the city had to expand beyond the Barri Gòtic. The winning plan in a contest to design the city's new quarters was that of utopian engineer and urban planner **Ildefons Cerdà i Sunyer**, who drew up a grid-shaped town marching off to the north, intersected by long, straight streets and cut by broad, angled avenues. Work started in 1859 and the Eixample immediately became the fashionable area in which to live, as the moneyed classes moved into luxurious apartments on the wide new avenues. As the money in the city moved north, so did a new class of architects who began to pepper the Eixample with ever more striking examples of their work, inspired by *modernisme*, the Catalan offshoot of Art Nouveau. Three **architects** in particular came to prominence and introduced a style that has given Barcelona a look like no other city.

ANTONI GAUDÍ I CORNET

Born in Reus, near Tarragona, to a family of artisans, **Antoni Gaudí i Cornet** (1852–1926) produced work that was never strictly *modernista* in style, but the imaginative impetus he provided was incalculable. Fantasy, spiritual symbolism and Catalan pride are evident in every building he designed, while his architectural influences were Moorish and Gothic, embellished with elements from the natural world. Gaudí rarely wrote a word about the theory of his art, preferring the buildings to demand reaction – no one stands mute in front of an Antoni Gaudí masterpiece.

LLUÍS DOMÈNECH I MONTANER

While Gaudí may be in a class of his own, arguably the greatest pure *modernista* architect was **Lluís Domènech i Montaner** (1850–1923). Drawing on the rich Catalan Romanesque and Gothic traditions, his work combined traditional craft methods with modern technological experiments, seen to triumphant effect in his masterpieces, the Palau de la Música Catalana and the Recinte Modernista de Sant Pau.

JOSEP PUIG I CADAFALCH

The work of **Josep Puig i Cadafalch** (1867–1957) is characterized by a wildly inventive use of ceramic tiles, ironwork, stained glass and stone carving. His first commission, the Casa Martí, housed the famous *Els Quatre Gats* tavern for the city's avant-garde artists and hangers-on, while in various Eixample mansions Puig i Cadafalch brought to bear distinct Gothic and medieval influences.

building, built in 1877, was considered dull, so Gaudí was hired to give it a face-lift, and completed the work by 1907. This time, the result was very far from dull, with the most conspicuous feature being the undulating street facade, adorned with balconies that might be carnival masks or the teeth-laden jaws of fish, and pockmarked higher up with circular ceramic buttons laid on a bright mosaic background. The interior, however, is every bit as compelling, meaning that despite the crowds and high prices, the **self-guided tours** should absolutely not be missed.

For once, the audioguides are excellent, pointing out details you might otherwise overlook, and offering "augmented-reality" views of how the place looked when new and first lived in. They culminate when you emerge on the rooftop to find yourself surrounded by colourful **chimneys**, crusted with mosaics and broken tiles.

10

Fundació Antoni Tàpies

C/Aragó 255 • Charge • http://fundaciotapies.org • Ⓜ Passeig de Gràcia

The definitive collection of the work of Catalan abstract artist **Antoni Tàpies** (1923–2012) is housed in Lluís Domènech i Montaner's first important building, the **Casa Montaner i Simon** (1880). Converted in 1990 to house the **Fundació Antoni Tàpies**, it's now capped by Tàpies's own striking sculpture, *Núvol i Cadira* ("Cloud and Chair"; 1990), a tangle of glass, wire and aluminium.

While the building itself is a beauty, with its Moorish-style flourishes, cast-iron columns and lack of dividing walls, Tàpies's art is not immediately accessible, and tends to polarize opinion. Expect to see a selection from the permanent collection, plus temporary exhibitions highlighting works and installations by contemporary artists.

Museu Egipci de Barcelona

C/València 284 • Charge • http://museuegipci.com • Ⓜ Passeig de Gràcia

Half a block east of Passeig de Gràcia, the **Museu Egipci de Barcelona** holds an exceptional collection of artefacts from ancient Egypt, ranging from the earliest kingdoms to the era of Cleopatra. The emphasis is on the shape and character of Egyptian society, and a serendipitous wander is a real pleasure, turning up items such as a wood and leather bed from the First and Second Dynasties (2920–2649 BC), and cat mummies from the Late Period (715–332 BC).

La Pedrera

Pg. de Gràcia 92, entrance on C/Provença • Charge • http://lapedrera.com • Ⓜ Diagonal

Gaudí's weird and wonderful apartment building, universally known as **La Pedrera** or the Stone Quarry but constructed as the Casa Milà between 1905 and 1911, is simply not to be missed. Its rippling facade is said to have been inspired by the mountain of Montserrat, while the apartments themselves, whose balconies of tangled metal drip over the facade, resemble eroded cave dwellings.

Declared a UNESCO World Heritage Site in 1984, La Pedrera is always hugely in demand; at peak periods it's essential to book in advance. Visitors only get to see a small proportion of the building, as most of the apartments are still privately occupied. Entering the complex, you step first into the larger of two oval interior courtyards, from which you're directed instead into an elevator that climbs straight to the extraordinary **terrat** or roof terrace. Those among the bizarre structures up here that most resemble chimneys, albeit crusted with broken tiles and/or shattered champagne bottles, tend to stand atop ventilation shafts, while others mark the top of stairwells; by and large it's what look like clusters of helmeted sentinels or warriors that truly are chimneys. An excellent exhibition on Gaudí's life and work has been installed beneath the 270 curved brick arches of the **attic** immediately below.

10

ANTONI GAUDÍ AND THE SAGRADA FAMÍLIA

Begun in 1882 by public subscription, the **Sagrada Família** was intended by its progenitor, Catalan publisher Josep Bocabella, as an expiatory building to atone for the revolutionary ideas then at large in Barcelona. Original architect Francesc de Paula Villar planned a modest church in an orthodox neo-Gothic style. Two years later, however, the 32-year-old **Antoni Gaudí** took over, and changed the direction and scale of the project almost immediately.

Initial work was slow. It took four years, until 1901, to finish the crypt, while the first full plan was only published in 1917. Gaudí himself vowed never to work on secular projects again, and devoted the rest of his life to the Sagrada Família. The more rigid his devotion to his **Catholic faith** grew, however, the more unfettered his architectural imagination became, while always rooted in functionality and strict attention to detail.

Antoni Gaudí was run over by a tram on the Gran Via on June 7, 1926. Initially unrecognized, he **died** in hospital three days later. All of Barcelona turned out for his funeral procession, after which he was buried in the Sagrada Família crypt. Only one facade of the Sagrada Família was then complete. Work stalled during the Civil War, with most of Gaudí's plans and models lost in the turmoil. Construction finally restarted, amid great controversy, during the 1950s, and is financed by private funding and ticket sales. Gaudí's own plans have been followed wherever possible, but critics accuse his successors of infringing his original spirit. Computer-aided design and high-tech construction techniques have so greatly speeded up the processes involved, however, that the debate is effectively over. Even if the builders fail to meet their current target of finishing the church to mark the centenary of Gaudí's death in **2026**, no doubt remains that the Sagrada Família will be completed in the near future.

The whole place reopens in the evening for various after-dark tours and events, including occasional jazz concerts on the rooftop. Other ways to visit La Pedrera include a tour with VR glasses, access to "unseen" spaces with a paid supplement, a joint ticket with the Recinte Modernista de Sant Pau, and other ideas are constantly added – check the website for details.

Sagrada Família

C/Mallorca 401 • Charge • http://sagradafamilia.org • Ⓜ Sagrada Família

Encountering the **Basílica de la Sagrada Família** for the first time has a breathtaking visceral impact. As work on Gaudí's masterpiece races towards completion, and its extraordinary towers climb ever closer towards the heavens, the glorious, overpowering church of the "Sacred Family" is now more than ever a symbol for Barcelona, and even the coldest hearts find the Sagrada Família inspirational in both form and spirit.

The Sagrada Família passed a crucial milestone in 2010, when it was consecrated as a **basilica** by Pope Benedict. While now a fully functioning church, complete with altar, pews, organ, stained-glass windows and regular Masses, it's not necessarily a peaceful place to visit – it's also a **building site**, with all the cacophony that suggests. At the time of writing, out of its planned eighteen spires, all but the central spire of Jesus Christ had been completed. Surmounted by a giant cross, this is slated for completion in 2026 and at 173m will be the highest of all, thereby making the Sagrada Família the tallest church in the world.

Visiting the Basilica

All Sagrada Família tickets are for a specific date and time. Buy yours online as far in advance as possible; in summer, you've very little chance of simply turning up and being able to get in. Aim to visit early in the day, to beat the crowds. If you're lucky, you may coincide with an English-language tour, though the audioguides provide substantially the same information. However you visit, you'll start by circling the exterior. The eastern **Nativity facade**, facing C/Marina, was the first to be completed and is alive with fecund detail, its very columns resting on giant tortoises. Contrast this with the Cubist austerity of the western **Passion facade** (C/Sardenya), where the brutal story of the Crucifixion is played out across the harsh mountain stone.

The **interior** of the Basilica is an immense, peaceful and uncluttered space. Every bit as "luminous" as Gaudí dreamed, it's a forest, filled with the light that streams through its stained-glass windows, where the columns are the trees that bear the weight of the structure. Separate elevators climb the **towers** on the Passion and Nativity facades. As well as a close-up look at the spires themselves, you'll be rewarded by views of the city through an extraordinary jumble of latticed stonework, ceramic decoration, carved buttresses and sculpture.

10

The museum
Sagrada Família tickets also cover the excellent **museum** that extends through its lower level, and traces Gaudí's career, with models and diagrams to explain the symbolism of the church. You can also peer down at his actual tomb in the crypt, and watch sculptors at work in the plaster workshop.

Recinte Modernista de Sant Pau
C/Sant Antoni María Claret 167, at C/Independència • Charge • http://santpaubarcelona.org • Ⓜ Sant Pau Dos de Maig

Lluís Domènech i Montaner's *modernista* **Hospital de la Santa Creu I de Sant Pau** is possibly Barcelona's one piece of architecture that can rival the Sagrada Família for size and invention. A huge precinct of dazzling Art Nouveau imagination, devoted to secular rather than spiritual ends, it's best approached by walking up the four-block Avinguda de Gaudí from the Sagrada Família, which gives terrific views back over the church.

Domènech i Montaner started work on the project in 1902, to replace the medieval Santa Creu hospital in the Raval. He created an astonishing complex of pavilions, at once practical and playful, topped by golden-tiled domes, festooned with turrets and towers, and covered with sculpture, mosaics, stained glass and ironwork. The hospital finally closed in 2009, with its patients moving to an adjoining new hospital, and the complex reopened in 2014. Of the 48 pavilions Domènech i Montaner originally envisaged, 27 were completed; twelve now constitute a World Heritage Site, of which eight have so far benefitted from a €100 million restoration programme. While still primarily noteworthy for their exterior decoration, they're being filled with display panels and exhibits, some of which explain the details and history of the ensemble. The pick of the bunch, the main administration building, has an ornate Gothic-style chapel upstairs, kitted out with Art Nouveau tiles and floral mosaics.

Plaça de les Glòries Catalanes
Ⓜ Glòries

Barcelona's major avenues all meet at the **Plaça de les Glòries Catalanes**, a former roundabout dedicated to the "Catalan glories", from architecture to literature. In the final phase of extension renovation, it has seen traffic rerouted underground and a greening of the whole area, with deckchairs, tables and a 'games zone', where users can borrow board games to play on site. Signature buildings hereabouts include that of the anvil-shaped **Museu del Disseny**, and Jean Nouvel's cigar-shaped **Torre Glòries** (142m), a highly distinctive aluminium-and-glass tower with no fewer than four thousand windows, housing the headquarters of the local water company.

Museu del Disseny
Pl. de les Glòries Catalanes 37–38 • Charge • http://dissenyhub.barcelona • Ⓜ Glòries

10

Barcelona's showpiece **Museu del Disseny** (Design Museum) gathers the former collections of its decorative arts, ceramics, textile and clothing, and its graphic arts museums, into a single, stunning new building, the **Disseny Hub**, which, thanks to its distinctive shape, is widely known as "The Stapler". Of its four floors, the first most closely corresponds to what you might expect of a design museum, displaying everyday objects, largely of Catalan origin, that range from chairs, tables and bicycles to toilets and, yes, staplers. The second holds a random but beautiful assortment of decorative arts from the third century onwards, starting with Coptic textiles from Egypt and winding up with ceramic works by Picasso and Miró. Next comes a floor devoted to fashion, illustrating how clothing has successively increased, reduced, accentuated and revealed various body shapes over the past five centuries, while the top floor traces the history of graphic design in twentieth-century Barcelona.

Teatre Nacional de Catalunya

Pl. de les Arts 1 • Charge for guided tours • visites@tnc.cat, http://tnc.cat • Ⓜ Glòries or tram T4

Designed by local architect Ricardo Bofill and inaugurated in 1997, the **Teatre Nacional de Catalunya** – Catalunya's national theatre, southwest of Glòries – is a soaring, postmodern glass box, encased within a faux-Greek temple. Reserve ahead, and you can take an hour-long guided backstage **tour**, while a summer evening's drink on the open-air *terrassa* is a nice way to take in the grandiose surroundings.

L'Auditori and the Museu de la Música

L'Auditori C/Lepant 150 • http://auditori.cat • Museu de la Música C/de Padilla 155 • Charge • http://visitmuseum.gencat.cat/es/museu-de-la-musica-de-barcelona • Ⓜ Glòries/Marina

Forming a sort of cultural enclave, **L'Auditori** is the city's contemporary city concert hall, within which is housed the **Museu de la Música**. It's all very impressive, with soaring glass-walled display cases, and yet it struggles to engage, partly because of the sheer number and variety of instruments and partly because of the impenetrable commentary, with sections called things like "The humanist spirit and the predominance of polyphony".

Parc Joan Miró

C/de Tarragona 74 • Free • Ⓜ Tarragona

Laid out on the site of Barcelona's nineteenth-century municipal slaughterhouse, on the left-hand side of the Eixample, the **Parc Joan Miró** features a raised piazza marked only by Joan Miró's gigantic mosaic sculpture *Dona i Ocell* ("Woman and Bird"), towering above a shallow reflecting pool. The rear of the park is given over to games areas and landscaped sections of palms and firs, with a kiosk café and outdoor tables among the trees.

Arenas de Barcelona

Gran Via de les Corts Catalanes 373–385, at Pl. d'Espanya • http://arenasdebarcelona.com • ⓂEspanya

The **Arenas de Barcelona**, a fabulous Moorish-style bullring, was built in 1900 but was reimagined as a shopping centre in 2011. Conceived by architect Richard Rogers, and preserving its beautiful brick exterior, the retail levels at Arenas are hung in sweeping, circular galleries, while on top a wide walk-around promenade circles the dome, offering 360-degree views of the city's western side and an array of restaurants.

10

Montjuïc

It takes at least a day to see **Montjuïc**, the steep hill and park that rises over Barcelona to the southwest. There's been a castle on the heights since the mid-seventeenth century, but since being chosen to host the **International Exhibition** of 1929, Montjuïc has effectively become a cultural leisure park, anchored around the unsurpassed national collection of Catalan art in the **Museu Nacional d'Art de Catalunya (MNAC)**. This is complemented by two other superb galleries, namely the international contemporary art in the **CaixaForum** and the showcase for Catalan artist Joan Miró in the **Fundació Joan Miró**. In addition, Montjuïc holds separate archaeological, ethnological, military and sports museums, as well as structures and stadiums from the 1992 Olympics.

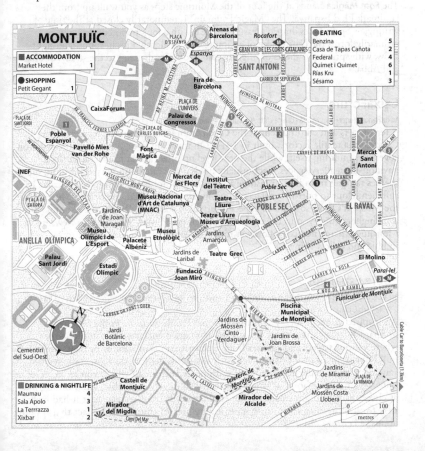

10

By metro For easy access to CaixaForum, Poble Espanyol and MNAC, use Ⓜ Espanya (follow exit signs for "Fira/Exposició").

By funicular The Funicular de Montjuïc departs from inside the metro station at Ⓜ Paral·lel and takes a couple of minutes to ascend the hill (every 10min; charge; http://tmb.cat). From the upper station on Avda. de Miramar, you can switch to the Montjuïc cable car or bus services, or walk in around 5min to the Fundació Joan Miró, 20min to the MNAC.

By Telefèric de Montjuïc Starting from Avda. de Miramar across from the higher Funicular de Montjuïc station, this separate cable car serves as a complement to the funicular, carrying passengers in eight-seater gondolas up to the castle (daily: March–May & Oct 10am–7pm; June–Sept 10am–9pm; Nov–Feb & Nov & Dec 10am–6pm; charge; http://tmb.cat).

Telefèrico del Puerto The cross-harbour Telefèrico del Puerto cable car, crosses high above Barcelona's harbour, all the way from Barceloneta to the Jardins de Miramar (every 15min; daily: March–May & mid-Sept to Oct 10.30am–7pm; June to mid-Sept 10.30am–8pm; Oct–Feb 11am–5.30pm; charge; http://telefericodebarcelona.com). From there it's a 10min walk to the Montjuïc cable car and funicular stations, another 5min to the Fundació Joan Miró.

Bus City bus #150 (transport tickets and passes valid) loops around the main Montjuïc attractions, departing from Avda. de la Reina María Cristina, outside Ⓜ Espanya. The sightseeing, hop-on-hop-off Bus Turístic follows a similar route.

Font Màgica

Pl. de Carles Buïgas • Free • http://bcn.es/fontmagica

The **Font Màgica** stands at the foot of the Montjuïc steps as you walk up from the landmark Pl. d'Espanya. The "Magic Fountain" is temporarily closed at the time of writing, as Spain takes drastic measures to deal with a long period of drought, but ordinarily forms the centrepiece of an impressive, if slightly kitsch, sound-and-light show, with sprays and sheets of brightly coloured water dancing to the strains of Holst and Abba.

CaixaForum

Av. de Francesc Ferrer i Guàrdia 6–8 • Charge • http://caixaforum.es/barcelona • Ⓜ Espanya

A terrific arts and cultural centre, the **CaixaForum** is set within the former Casamarona textile factory, built in 1911. On the main floor, a permanent exhibition covers the building itself, while the next level up offers access to several distinct pavilion-like gallery spaces. Each usually holds a separate temporary exhibition, on themes ranging from film or fashion to medieval history. The Fundació La Caixa has sufficient clout to borrow artefacts from big-name outfits like the British Museum or the Musée d'Orsay, so you can expect a very high standard. Riding the elevators one level higher brings you to the undulating brick-paved **roof**, which offers views up to Montjuïc. There's no access however to its tall, emblematic Casaramona **tower**, etched in blue and yellow tiling.

Poble Espanyol

Avda. de Francesc Ferrer i Guàrdia 13 • Charge • http://poble-espanyol.com • Ⓜ Espanya and 800m walk, or bus #150 or #13 from Avda. de la Reina María Cristina

An inspired concept for 1929's International Exhibition, the **Poble Espanyol**, or Spanish Village, is a homogenous self-contained enclave, built in old stone, where various streets and squares hold reconstructions of famous or characteristic buildings from all over Spain. Each little district is dedicated to a specific region, starting with the fairy-tale medieval walls of Ávila through which you enter. "Get to know Spain in one hour" is the promise; it's all hugely enjoyable, and nothing like as cheesy as you might imagine. You could easily believe, in fact, that it had been here for hundreds of years, an impression helped, of course, by the fact that it's now almost a century old.

Museu Nacional d'Art de Catalunya (MNAC)

Palau Nacional • Charge • http://mnac.cat • Ⓜ Espanya/Poble Sec, or bus #150 from Avda. de la Reina María Cristina, or bus #55 from C/Lleida

The towering, domed **Palau Nacional**, set proud on Montjuïc at the top of the long climb up from the Font Màgica, was the flagship building of Barcelona's 1929 International Exhibition. It's now home to one of Spain's greatest museums, the **Museu Nacional d'Art de Catalunya (MNAC)**, which showcases a thousand years of Catalan art in stupendous surroundings.

In such a wide-ranging museum it can be hard to know where to start. If your time is limited, be sure not to miss the **medieval** collection, which is split into two main sections, one dedicated to **Romanesque** art, the other to **Gothic**. MNAC also has impressive holdings of European **Renaissance and Baroque** art, as well as an unsurpassed collection of **nineteenth- and twentieth-century Catalan art**. In addition, there's a changing roster of blockbuster exhibitions.

Romanesque collection

From the eleventh century, great numbers of sturdy Romanesque churches were built in the high Catalan Pyrenees, decorated with extraordinary biblical frescoes. By the nineteenth century, however, many of them lay abandoned. Today, the frescoes are magnificently presented at MNAC, in nest-like reconstructions of the original church interiors. The highlight of the whole astonishing collection comes in room 7, where the extraordinary Christ in Majesty, painted by the so-called Master of Taüll for the twelfth-century church of Sant Climent in Taüll, combines a Byzantine hierarchical composition with the imposing colours and strong outlines of contemporary manuscript illuminators.

Gothic collection

The evolution from the Romanesque to the **Gothic** period was marked by a move from murals to painting on wood, and by the depiction of more naturalistic figures in scenes of the lives of saints and royalty. By the time of fifteenth-century Catalan artists like **Jaume Huguet** and **Lluís Dalmau**, works showed the strong influence of contemporary Flemish painting, in the use of denser colours, the depiction of crowd scenes and a concern for perspective. The last Catalan-Gothic-era artist of note is the so-called **Master of La Seu d'Urgell**, who is responsible for a fine series of six paintings that once formed the covers of an organ.

Renaissance and Baroque collections

Major European artists displayed include Rubens, Goya, El Greco, Zurbarán and Velázquez, though the museum is of course keen to play up Catalan works of the period, which largely absorbed the prevailing European influences – thus Barcelona artist **Antoni Viladomat** (1678–1755), whose twenty paintings of St Francis, executed for a monastery, are shown here in their entirety. However, more familiar to most will be the masterpieces of the Spanish Golden Age, notably Velázquez's *Saint Paul*.

TEATRE GREC AND THE BARCELONA FESTIVAL

Montjuïc takes centre-stage during Barcelona's annual summer cultural festival (http://barcelona.cat/grec), known as the Grec, when arias soar from the open-air stage of the **Teatre Grec**, a Greek theatre cut into a former quarry on the Poble Sec side of the hill. Running from late June until the end of August, the festival incorporates drama, music and dance, with the opening sessions and many atmospheric events staged in the theatre, from Shakespearean productions to shows by avant-garde performance artists. These can be magical nights, but you'll need to be quick off the mark for tickets, which usually go on sale in May.

10

Modern art collection

MNAC ends on a high note with its **modern Catalan art** collection, which is particularly good on *modernista* and *noucentista* painting and sculpture, the two dominant schools of the nineteenth and early twentieth centuries. Rooms highlight individual artists and genres, shedding light on the development of art in an exciting period of Catalunya's history, while there are fascinating diversions into *modernista* interior design (with furniture by Gaudí), avant-garde sculpture and historical photography.

Fundació Joan Miró

Parc de Montjuïc • Charge • http://fmirobcn.org • ⓜ Paral·lel, then Funicular de Montjuïc and 5min walk, or bus #150 from Avda. de la Reina María Cristina, or #55 from C/Lleida

Montjuïc's highlight for many is the **Fundació Joan Miró**, Barcelona's most adventurous art museum, opened in 1975 and set among gardens overlooking the city. Joan Miró (1893–1983) was one of the greatest Catalan artists, establishing an international reputation while never severing his links with his homeland. He showed a childlike delight in colours and shapes and developed a free, highly decorative style – the paintings and drawings, in particular, are instantly recognizable, and are among the chief links between Surrealism and abstract art. Miró had his first exhibition in 1918, and after that spent his summers in Catalunya (and the rest of the time in France) before moving to Mallorca in 1956, where he died.

Inside the museum

Miró's architect friend Josep Lluís Sert designed the beautiful museum building. Largely donated by Miró himself, its huge collection of paintings, graphics, tapestries and sculptures ranges from 1914 up to 1978. Most of the paintings are drawn from Miró's later years, as he only started to set works aside for the museum in the 1960s. However, they do include early Realist works dating from before he decided to "assassinate art" and abandon figurative painting in the mid-1920s, like the effervescent *Portrait of a Young Girl* (1919).

Other gaps are filled by donations from Miró's widow, Pilar Juncosa, which demonstrate Miró's preoccupations during the 1930s and 1940s. This was the period when he started his **Constellations** series, introducing the colours, themes and symbols that, eventually pared down to the minimalist basics, came to define his work: reds and blues; women, birds and tears; the sun, moon and stars.

THE OLYMPICS ON MONTJUÏC

The main road through Montjuïc climbs around the hill and up to the city's principal Olympic area, centred on the **Estadi Olímpic**. Built originally for the 1929 exhibition, the stadium was completely refitted to accommodate the 1992 opening and closing ceremonies, while a vast terrace to one side provides one of the finest vantage points in the city. Long water-fed troughs break the concrete and marble expanse, and the confident, space-age curve of Santiago Calatrava's **communications tower** dominates the skyline. Around the other side, just across the road from the stadium, the history of the Games themselves is covered in the **Museu Olímpic i de l'Esport** (Av. de l'Estadi 60; charge; http://museuolimpicbcn.cat).

The 1992 Olympics were the second planned for Montjuïc's stadium. The first, in 1936 – the so-called "People's Olympics" – were organized as an alternative to the Nazis' infamous Berlin Games of that year, but the day before the official opening Franco's army revolt triggered the Civil War and scuppered the Barcelona Games. Some of the 25,000 athletes and spectators who had turned up stayed on to join the Republican forces.

Elsewhere you'll find several of Miró's enormous, dense and very shaggy **tapestries**, and his **pencil drawings**, particularly of misshapen women and gawky ballerinas. His **sculptures** are displayed outdoors, both in the gardens and on the spacious roof terrace. There's also a contemporary art **library**, a **bookshop** and a pleasant open-air **café** that's accessible whether or not you pay to get into the museum itself.

Castell de Montjuïc

Carretera de Montjuïc 66 • Charge • http://bcn.cat/castelldemontjuic • Direct access by Telefèric de Montjuïc, or bus #150 from Avda. de la Reina María Cristina

The best way to reach the **castle** at the very top of Montjuïc is via the Telefèric de Montjuïc (see page 626), which tacks up the hillside before depositing you just outside the forbidding red-brick walls of the eighteenth-century fortress. It's worth coming up here simply to admire the dramatic location, and to enjoy the views from the grounds, which are free to enter.

Paying admission to the castle buys you marginally better views, especially from its broad ramparts, but more importantly gives access to fascinating displays on its history. Finally handed over to the city in 2008, the fortress had long been a symbol of Barcelona's occupation by a foreign power – the Spanish state. After all, it had served for decades as a military base and prison, with its mighty cannon trained on the city below, and it was here that the last president of the prewar Generalitat, **Lluís Companys**, was executed on Franco's orders on October 15, 1940.

Below the castle walls, a pathway cut from the cliff edge, the **Camí del Mar**, provides great views out to sea. The path is just over 1km long and ends at the back of the castle battlements near the **Mirador del Migdia**.

Jardí Botànic de Barcelona

C/Dr Font i Quer 2 • Charge • http://museuciencies.cat • Ⓜ Espanya, then 20min walk via escalators, or bus #150 from Avda. de la Reina María Cristina or #55 from C/-Lleida

Principal among Montjuïc's many gardens is the **Jardí Botànic de Barcelona**, which is laid out on terraced slopes that offer fine views across the city. It's a beautifully kept contemporary garden, where wide, easy-to-follow paths wind through landscaped zones representing the flora of the Mediterranean, Canary Islands, California, Chile, North and South Africa and Australia.

Cascada

Parc de la Ciutadella • Ⓜ Arc de Triomf

The first major project undertaken inside the park was the **Cascada**, in its northeast corner. The young Antoni Gaudí, then a student, assisted the principal architect, and the Baroque extravagance of this monumental fountain hints at the flamboyant decoration that later became his trademark. He's also thought to have had a hand in designing the iron park gates.

Castell dels Tres Dragons and Museu Martorell

Pg. de Picasso • Ⓜ Arc de Triomf

The whimsical red-brick **Castell dels Tres Dragons** (Three Dragons Castle) at the park's northwest corner was designed by Lluís Domènech i Montaner. Home for many years to the local zoology museum, after being left empty for years, it's currently being reformed. It's a similar story with the neoclassical **Museu Martorell**, which long housed the city's geological collections and reopened in 2023 to house temporary scientific exhibitions.

10

10

THE CROSS-HARBOUR CABLE CAR

Barcelona's most thrilling ride has to be the **Telefèrico del Puerto** cable car, which sweeps across the inner harbour between the top of the Torre de Sant Sebastiá, near the tip of Barceloneta, and the hill of Montjuïc (every 15min; charge; http://telefericodebarcelona. com). As you dangle high above the water, you can enjoy superb views over the city. There's an additional stop in the middle, at the hundred-metre-tall Torre de Jaume I in Port Vell. As the cable car only carries nineteen passengers at a time, expect queues – and potential disappointment – in summer and at weekends, while strong winds will close the ride altogether.

Umbracle and Hivernacle

Pg. de Picasso • Not open to the public • Ⓜ Arc de Triomf

The twin unsung glories of Ciutadella are its plant houses: the handsome **Umbracle** (palm house), with a barrelled wood-slat roof supported by cast-iron pillars, and the larger **Hivernacle** (conservatory), the enclosed greenhouses of which are separated by a soaring glass-roofed terrace. The Hivernacle lay in ruins for many years but in 2023 was spectacularly renovated, although the new plants will take a few years to become fully established.

Barceloneta

An eighteenth-century neighbourhood of tightly packed streets, **Barceloneta** squeezes between the harbour on one side and the **beach** on the other. It was laid out on bare mudflats in 1755, primarily to rehouse inhabitants of the Ribera district, whose homes had been destroyed to make way for the Ciutadella fortress. Its long, narrow streets, punctuated by small squares, are lined with small, tall and abundantly windowed houses, designed to give the sailors and fishing folk who lived here plenty of sun and fresh air.

Though this remains very much a workaday community, some original houses feature decorative flourishes, while an eighteenth-century fountain and the Neoclassical church of **Sant Miquel del Port** survives in **Plaça de la Barceloneta**. A block over, in Pl. de la Font, the beautifully refurbished local food market, **Mercat de la Barceloneta** (Mon–Thurs 7am–2pm, Fri 7am–8pm, Sat 7am–3pm), is home to some good bars and restaurants.

Barceloneta is famous for its **seafood restaurants**. They're especially concentrated along the harbourside Passeig Joan de Borbó, where for most of the year you can eat at an outdoor table, however the ones inside the Barceloneta neighbourhood or by the marina are better quality.

Platja de Sant Sebastià and Passeig Marítim

Ⓜ Barceloneta

Barceloneta's beach, **Platja de Sant Sebastià**, is the first in the series of sandy **city beaches** that stretches northeast from here along the coast. It curves out to the landmark, sail-shaped *W Barcelona* hotel (see page 641), which was designed by Catalan architect Ricardo Bofill. Meanwhile, at the Barceloneta end there are beach bars, outdoor cafés and public sculptures, while a double row of palms backs the **Passeig Marítim** esplanade that runs above the sands as far as the Port Olímpic (a 15min walk). Sunbathers sprawl on the sands, swimmers venture into the water, and there's a surfing break immediately offshore. The foreshore is busy with strolling pedestrians, and itinerant vendors patrol the strands offering snacks and drinks.

Port Olímpic

Ⓜ Ciutadella/Vila Olímpica

As you approach **Port Olímpic** along the Passeig Marítim, a shimmering golden mirage slowly resolves itself into a **huge copper fish**, courtesy of Frank Gehry, architect of Bilbao's Guggenheim. The emblem of the huge seafront development constructed for the 1992 Olympics, it's backed by the city's two tallest buildings, the **Torre Mapfre** and the steel-framed **Hotel Arts Barcelona**, both 154m high.

The bulk of the action is contained within two wharves: the **Moll de Mestral** and the **Moll de Gregal.** For years these have sported two tiers of fairly tacky bars and seafood restaurants, and been a hotspot for crime, but the whole area was overhauled for the 2024 America's Cup, and now houses upmarket restaurants and various maritime enterprises.

Northeast along the coast from Port Olímpic, the **city beaches** are split into separate named sections (Nova Icària, Bogatell, Mar Bella, Nova Mar Bella and Llevant), each with showers, playgrounds and open-air café-bars. It's a pretty extraordinary leisure facility to find so close to a city centre – the sands are regularly swept and replenished, while joggers, cyclists and bladers have one of the Med's best views for company.

Diagonal Mar

Ⓜ El Maresme Fòrum, or tram #T4 to Fòrum via Glòries and Avda. Diagonal

The waterfront convention and business district of **Diagonal Mar**, 4km along the coast northeast of Port Olímpic, was developed in the wake of the Universal Forum of Cultures expo, held here in 2004. Everything is on a grand scale, starting with Jacques Herzog's dazzling **Museu Blau**, which hovers – seemingly unsupported – above the ground. Beyond that stretches the vast **Parc del Fòrum**, a showpiece urban leisure project.

Museu Blau

Pl. Leonardo da Vinci 4–5, Parc del Fòrum • Charge • http://museuciencies.cat • Ⓜ El Maresme Fòrum, or tram T4 to Fòrum

To unravel the mysteries of life, the universe and everything, you need travel no further than the Natural Science Museum's bold reboot of its heritage collections in the visually stunning **Museu Blau** (Blue Museum). The permanent Planeta Vida (Planet Life) exhibition here plots a journey through nothing less than the history of life on earth. Starting with the Big Bang, it draws on a million-strong array of rocks, fossils, plants and animals, ranging from the smallest microbe to a giant whale skeleton. It's heavily focused on evolutionary, whole-earth, Gaia principles, with plenty of entertaining, interactive bells and whistles to guide you through topics as diverse as sex and reproduction and environmental conservation.

Parc del Fòrum

Ⓜ El Maresme Fòrum, or tram T4 to Fòrum via Glòries and Avda. Diagonal

Diagonal Mar's main open space, the **Parc del Fòrum**, is an immense, undulating expanse that spreads out towards the sea, culminating in a giant solar-panelled canopy that overlooks the marina, beach and park areas. The space can seem a bit soulless at times, but bars, dancefloors, an open-air cinema and chill-out zones are set up in summer, while the authorities have shifted some large music festivals and events down here in order to inject a bit of life into the place outside convention time.

Gràcia

Before it was finally annexed as a city suburb in the late nineteenth century, **Gràcia**, the closest neighbourhood to the Eixample, had long maintained its identity as a village. It still retains a genuine small-town atmosphere, distinct from the old-town neighbourhoods, while its vibrant cultural scene and nightlife counters the notion that Barcelona begins and ends on La Rambla. That said, there's not that much to see, but wander the narrow, gridded streets, catch a film or hit one of the excellent local bars or restaurants, and you'll soon get the feel of a neighbourhood that still has a soul. Most of the boutiques, galleries, cinemas and cafés are near pretty **Plaça de la Virreina**, with **C/Verdi** in particular always worth a stroll. A short walk southwest, **Pl. del Sol** is the beating heart of much of the district's nightlife, while **Plaça Vila de Gràcia**, the "clock-tower square", a couple of minutes south, is another popular place to meet for brunch. However, the one unmissable attraction is just on the neighbourhood fringe, namely Antoni Gaudí's breathtaking **Park Güell**.

Park Güell

Set on the hillside above Gràcia, Antoni Gaudí's extraordinary **Park Güell** was, apart from the Sagrada Família, his most ambitious project. It was originally planned as a private housing estate, but only two of the proposed sixty houses were actually built, and the park was opened to the public instead in 1922. It's now one of Barcelona's most popular tourist attractions, and admission to the **Zona Monumental** that holds

SHOPPING
Entre Latas 2
Hibernian Books 1

ACCOMMODATION
Generator Hostel and Hotel 1

DRINKING & NIGHTLIFE
Bobby Gin 5
Cafè del Sol 3
Canigó 2
Heliogàbal 4
Otto Zutz 1

EATING
Flash, Flash 2
Goliard 3
La Pepita 4
San Kil 1

its most iconic sites is by timed ticket only. Access to the rest of the park, where the wooded, landscaped gardens make a nice spot for a picnic, remains free.

Zona Monumental

Charge · http://parkguell.barcelona

Sealed off as the **Zona Monumental** and looking down across the city to the Mediterranean, the core of Park Güell is a hallucinatory swirl of ideas and excesses. Up to 400 visitors are allowed in every half-hour, and each ticket is only valid for a specific half-hour time slot (once inside, you can stay as long as you like, although the area is very big, so it's likely it won't be for long). Reserve online as far ahead as possible, though tickets are also sold when available – unlikely in high summer – at ticket offices or ATMs in the park itself. Directly ahead of the main entrance, on C/ Olot, a monumental stairway climbs past a giant mosaic salamander known as **el drac** (the dragon) to reach the vast **Hall of Columns**, where 84 Doric columns soar at disconcertingly irregular angles to enclose a space Gaudí intended to be the estate's market. A long meandering **ceramic bench** snakes along the edge of the terrace that forms the roof of the Hall of Columns. Entirely covered with a brightly coloured, broken tile-and-glass mosaic (a technique known as *trencadís*), it forms a dizzying sequence of abstract motifs, symbols, words and pictures.

Casa Museu Gaudí

Park Güell, outside Zona Monumental · Charge · http://asamuseugaudi.org

One of Gaudí's collaborators, Francesc Berenguer, designed a turreted house for the architect, now known as the **Casa Museu Gaudí**, which stands immediately east of the Zona Monumental. Gaudí lived here from 1906 until 1925, when he de-camped to the Sagrada Família. The downstairs rooms celebrate Gaudí's work as a designer, while upstairs his ascetic study and bedroom have been kept much as he knew them.

ARRIVAL AND DEPARTURE   GRÀCIA AND PARK GÜELL

By metro and train For Gràcia, the best metro stations are Ⓜ Diagonal (south), Ⓜ Fontana (north) or Ⓜ Joanic (east); each is around 500m walk from Gràcia's central squares. If you're heading straight for Park Güell use Ⓜ Vallcarca; walk a few hundred metres down Avda. de Vallcarca until you see the escalators on your left, which climb to the western park entrance (15min).

By bus Bus #24 from Pl. de Catalunya or Pg. de Gràcia stops on Carretera del Carmel at the eastern gate of Park Güell. The Bus Turístic stops at the bottom end of C/Larrard.

Les Corts and Pedralbes

West of Barcelona city centre, what was once the village of **Les Corts** is now seamlessly integrated into the modern city, and noteworthy primarily for holding the hallowed precincts of Camp Nou, FC Barcelona's stupendous football stadium. Nearby, across Avinguda Diagonal, the Palau Reial de Pedralbes is home to serene public gardens, while a half-day's excursion can be made by walking up past the Gaudí dragon gate at Pavellons Güell to the calm cloisters of the Gothic monastery of **Pedralbes**.

Camp Nou and FC Barcelona

Football in Barcelona being a genuine obsession, support for the local giants **FC (Futbol Club) Barcelona** has been raised to an art form. *Més que un club* ("More than just a club") is the proud boast, and certainly during the dictatorship years the club stood as a symbol around which Catalans could rally. Arch-rivals Real Madrid, on the other hand, were always seen as Franco's club. In recent years, the swashbuckling players in the *blaugrana* (claret and blue) shirts have won hearts worldwide to become every football fan's second favourite team.

10

Museum and stadium tour

Entrance on Avda. Aristides Maillol • Temporarily closed • http://fcbarcelona.com • Ⓜ Palau Reial

Together, the stadium and museum – billed as the "Camp Nou Experience" – provide a magnificent celebration of Spain's national sport. This, Europe's largest stadium, was built in 1957, enlarged for the 1982 World Cup semi-final to accommodate 98,000 people, and is currently undergoing a face-lift, scheduled for completion in 2026, that will increase its capacity to around 105,000. At the time of writing, matches are being played in the smaller Estadi Olímpic on Montjuïc, but due to move back to the Camp Nou in early 2025.

Tracing the history of the club from its foundation in 1899, the **museum** shifts from black-and-white photos and battered old boots and balls to a relentless succession of silverware, although ongoing renovations promise to make this a more dynamic, high-tech experience. Beyond the museum, the **self-guided tour** winds through the visitors' changing rooms and players' tunnel out onto the pitch, and then leads up to the press gallery and directors' box for stunning views. While it's a poor substitute for attending an actual game, it does give the chance take a selfie alongside a life-size photo of Lionel Messi.

Palau de Pedralbes

Avda. Diagonal 686 • Free • Ⓜ Palau Reial or tram #T1, #T2 or #T3

Set in formal grounds opposite the university on Avinguda Diagonal, the Italianate **Palau de Pedralbes** is closed to the public, but its **gardens** – a breezy oasis of Himalayan cedars, strawberry trees and bougainvillea – are a lovely way to spend an afternoon. Hidden in a bamboo thicket is an early work by Antoni Gaudí, the *Hercules fountain* (1884). In June and July each year, a music festival (http://almafestival.info) takes place in the gardens.

Pavellons Güell

Avda. de Pedralbes 7 • Charge • http://rutadelmodernisme.com • Ⓜ Palau Reial

As an early test of his capabilities, Antoni Gaudí was asked by his patron, Eusebi Güell, to rework the entrance, gatehouse and stables of the Güell summer residence, which was sited on a large working estate well away from the filth and the unruly mobs of downtown Barcelona. The brick-and-tile stables and outbuildings – known as the **Pavellons Güell** – survive as Gaudí created them, though it's the **gate** that's the most famous element (which you can still see even if the rest is currently closed for renovations). An extraordinary winged dragon made of twisted iron snarls at the passers-by, its razor-toothed jaws spread wide in a fearsome roar.

Monestir de Pedralbes

Bxda. del Monestir 9 • Charge • http://monestirpedralbes.barcelona • Ⓜ Palau Reial and 20min walk, or FGC Reina Elisenda (frequent trains from Pl. de Catalunya) and 10min walk, or bus #64 from Pl. Universitat

Founded in 1326 for the nuns of the Order of St Clare, the Gothic **Monestir de Pedralbes** is, in effect, an entire monastic village preserved on the outskirts of the city, within medieval walls that completely shut out the clamour of the twenty-first century. After 600 years of isolation, the monastery was sequestered by the Generalitat during the Civil War; when it opened as a museum in 1983, a new convent was built alongside as part of the deal.

The triple tiers of the magnificent **cloisters** are supported by the slenderest of columns, with the only sound the tinkling water from the fountain. Side rooms and chambers give a clear impression of medieval convent life, from the chapterhouse and austere refectory to a fully equipped kitchen and infirmary. Treasures acquired by the monastery over the centuries include Gothic furniture, paintings by Flemish artists, and some outstanding illuminated choir books. In the adjacent **church** the foundation's sponsor, **Elisenda de Montcada**, wife of Jaume II, lies in an ornate marble tomb.

Tibidabo and Parc de Collserola

The views from the heights of **Tibidabo** (550m), the peak that signals the northwestern boundary of Barcelona, are legendary. On a clear day you can see across to the Pyrenees and even as far out to sea as Mallorca. However, while many visitors make the tram and funicular ride up to Tibidabo's wonderfully old-fashioned amusement park, few realize that the **Parc de Collserola** stretches beyond, peppered with peaks, wooded river valleys and hiking paths. Meanwhile, families en route to or from Tibidabo won't want to miss the CosmoCaixa science museum.

CosmoCaixa

C/Isaac Newton 26 • Charge • http://cosmocaixa.org • FGC Avda. del Tibidabo (trains from Pl. de Catalunya) and 10min walk, or Tramvia Blau (see page 635) or Bus Turístic stop close by

For anyone travelling with children in tow, Barcelona's enormous, up-to-the-minute science museum, **CosmoCaixa**, is a must-see attraction. Hands-on experiments and displays investigate everything "from bacteria to Shakespeare", with the two big draws being the 100 tonnes of "sliced" rock in the **Mur Geològic** (Geological Wall) and, best of all, the **Bosc Inundat** – nothing less than a thousand square metres of real Amazonian rainforest, complete with croc-filled mangroves, anacondas and giant catfish.

Parc d'Atraccions Tibidabo

Pl. del Tibidabo • Charge • http://tibidabo.cat • Tibibus and Cuca de Llum funicular (both included in ticket price – see website for instructions) from Ⓜ Vall d'Hebron or FGC Avda. Tibidabo

Barcelona's self-styled "magic mountain" amusement park – the **Parc d'Atraccions** – has been thrilling the citizens for over a century. It's a mix of traditional rides, plus an influx of high-tech roller coasters and free-fall drops, laid out around several levels of the mountaintop and connected by landscaped paths and gardens. Some famous historic attractions are grouped under the discounted "Emblematic Rides" ticket, like the aeroplane – spinning since 1928 – the carousel, and the quirky Museu d'Autòmates, a fully functional collection of coin-operated antique fairground machines. Summer weekends finish with parades, concerts and a noisy *correfoc* fireworks display.

ARRIVAL AND DEPARTURE   **TIBIDABO**

By train, tram and funicular Take the FGC train (Tibidabo line #7) from Pl. de Catalunya to Avda. Tibidabo (the last stop), then cross the road to the tram/bus shelter. An antique tram, the Tramvia Blau (temporarily closed) or Bus 196 then run you uphill to Pl. del Doctor Andreu. The Tramvia Blau recently underwent renovations, and there's a bus service that also runs the route. By the tram and bus stop on Pl. del Doctor Andreu, you change to the Funicular del Tibidabo, with connections to Tibidabo at the top. This underwent a

massive renovation project recently and turned into a new ride called the Cuca del Llum or Glow Worm, which allows for panoramic views and interactive electronic screens.
By bus The Bus Turístic stops at Avda. del Tibidabo, to connect with the Tramvia Blau or Bus 196. Alternatively, the special Tibibus (T2A) runs direct to Tibidabo from Pl. de Catalunya. Local bus #111 runs on a circuit (every 30min; city passes and transport tickets valid) between Tibidabo park and Vallvidrera village.

Parc de Collserola

http://parcnaturalcollserola.cat • FGC Bxda. de Vallvidrera (on the Sabadell or Terrassa line from Pl. de Catalunya or Gràcia; 15–20min)

Given a half-decent day, local bikers, hikers and outdoors enthusiasts all make a beeline for the city's ring of wooded hills beyond Tibidabo, the **Parc de Collserola**. The **park**

information centre lies in oak and pine woods, an easy, signposted ten-minute walk up through the trees from the train station. There's a bar-restaurant here with an outdoor terrace, plus an exhibition on the park's history, flora and fauna, while the staff hand out English-language leaflets detailing walks that range from a fifteen-minute stroll to the Vallvidrera dam to a couple of hours circling the hills.

ARRIVAL AND DEPARTURE   BARCELONA

10

All Barcelona's main points of arrival, including the airport, are reasonably convenient, with train and metro stations for onward travel. In most cases, you can be off the plane, train, bus or ferry and in your hotel room within the hour.

BY PLANE

Barcelona Airport Barcelona's airport (902 404 704, http://aena.es) is 15km southwest of the city at El Prat de Llobregat. A taxi to the city centre costs about €35, including an airport surcharge.

Airport train The R2 Nord train route departs from Terminal T2 (connected to T1 by free shuttle buses). Trains run every 30min to Barcelona Sants, the city's main railway station (departures from airport, daily 5.42am–11.38pm; departures to airport, 5.13am–11.14pm; journey time 20min; €4.90), and continue on to Pg. de Gràcia (best stop for Eixample, Pl. Catalunya and La Rambla). The T-Casual ticket and Barcelona Cards are valid.

Metro The airport is connected to Barcelona's metro system by the L9 Sud line, which only runs as far as Zona Universitària, rather than the city centre. To get to the Catalunya station, for example, you have to change on to the L1 line at Torrassa. A single ticket from the airport to any other metro station costs €5.50; the T-Casual ticket (see page 638) is not valid.

Aerobús The Aerobús (daily 5.35am–1.05am, every 10min; €7.25 one-way, €12.50 return; http://aerobusbarcelona. es) from both T1 and T2 stops in the city at Pl. d'Espanya, Gran Via–Urgell, Pl. Universitat and Pl. Catalunya. It takes 35–40min to reach Pl. Catalunya, longer in the rush hour. Services to the airport from Pl. Catalunya leave from in front of El Corte Inglés department store; separate buses run to either Terminal T1 or T2.

Local bus City bus #46 connects both T1 and T2 with Pl. d'Espanya for a one-way fare of just €2.55; if you're staying in the city centre you'll need to catch a connecting bus or metro onwards from there.

Other regional airports Some budget airlines offer "Barcelona" flights that in fact fly to airports elsewhere in Catalunya. Thus Ryanair fly to Reus, near Tarragona 110km south of Barcelona (see page 726), with connecting buses to Barcelona Sants train station.

BY TRAIN

Barcelona Sants The main station for national and international arrivals, including high-speed AVE trains to and from Madrid, is Barcelona Sants (Ⓜ Sants Estació), 3km

west of the centre. From Sants, metro line 3 runs direct to Drassanes and Liceu (for La Rambla), Catalunya (for Pl. de Catalunya) and Pg. de Gràcia (Eixample), while line 5 runs to Diagonal (Eixample and Gràcia).

Estació de França Some inter-city services and regional trains also stop at Estació de França, in La Ribera, near Ⓜ Barceloneta.

Regional and provincial trains Other possible arrival points by train are Pl. de Catalunya, at the top of La Rambla (for trains from coastal towns north of the city, and towns on the Puigcerdà–Vic line), and Pl. de Gràcia (Catalunya provincial destinations).

Destinations Figueres (at least hourly; 1hr–2hr 40min); Girona (at least hourly; 40min–2hr 10min); Lleida (at least hourly, 58min–3hr 5min); Madrid (at least hourly; 2hr 30min–9hr); Portbou (at least hourly; 2–3hr); Puigcerdà (7 daily; 3hr 15min); Ripoll (hourly; 2hr 10min); Sitges (every 10–30min; 30–40min); Tarragona (around 2 hourly; 30min–1hr 20min); Valencia (up to 15 daily; 3hr–5hr 15min); Vic (hourly; 1hr 15min); Zaragoza (around 2 hourly; 1hr 20min–5hr 20min).

BY BUS

Barcelona Nord The main bus terminal is on C/Ali-Bei (372 065 366, http://barcelonanord.cat; Ⓜ Arc de Triomf), four blocks north of Parc de la Ciutadella. There's a bus information desk on the ground floor (daily 7am–9pm), with ticket offices above at street level (reserve ahead for long-distance routes). Some inter-city and international services also stop at the bus terminal behind Barcelona Sants station on C/Viriat (Ⓜ Sants Estació). Either way, you're only a short metro ride from the city centre.

Destinations Andorra (9 daily; 3hr 15min–4hr 30min); Cadaqués (1–2 daily; 2hr 45min); Girona (2–3 daily; 1hr 50min); Lleida (10–12 daily; 2hr 30min–3hr); Lloret de Mar (26 daily; 1hr); Madrid (8 daily; 8hr); Palafrugell (12 daily; 2hr 15min); Tarragona (4 daily; 1hr 30min); Tossa de Mar (23 daily; 1hr 20min); Valencia (12 daily; 4hr 30min); Zaragoza (9 daily; 3hr 30min).

BY FERRY

Estació Marítima Ferries from the Balearics dock at the terminal in Port Vell, at the bottom of Avda. Paral·lel (Ⓜ Drassanes), not far from La Rambla. Offices inside the terminal sell tickets to Palma de Mallorca, Mahón, Ibiza and Formentera (July & Aug are very busy), with Trasmediterranea (http://trasmediterranea.es) and

10

SIGHTSEEING DISCOUNT CARDS

If you're planning to do a lot of sightseeing, you can save money by buying one or more discount cards. It's up to you which suits your needs, but the Barcelona Card is likely to be the best deal, as it includes public transport.

Barcelona Card (3 days €49.50, 4 days €58.50 or 5 days €69.30, details on http://barcelonaturisme.com). Free public transport, plus free admission to most major museums, plus discounts at other museums as well as shops and restaurants. The two-day version, the €24.30 Barcelona Card Express, covers transport but no free museum admissions, only discounts. All are available online, or for slightly more, at points of arrival, tourist offices and kiosks, and other outlets.

Articket (€38, valid one year; http://articketbcn.org). Free admission into six major art centres and galleries (MNAC, MACBA, CCCB, Museu Picasso, Fundació Antoni Tàpies and Fundació Joan Miró). Buy at participating galleries, at Barcelona tourist offices and kiosks, or online.

Ruta del Modernisme (€18, valid one year; http://rutadelmodernisme.com). English-language guidebook, map and discount-voucher package that covers 116 *modernista* buildings in Barcelona and other Catalan towns. Accompanying adults who pay €7 can benefit from the same discounts without buying a separate copy of the book. If you plan to visit several such sites, this is worth having as well as a Barcelona Card.

Balearia (http://balearia.com). Navi Grandi Veloci (http://gnv.it) sails to Nador and Tangiers in Morocco. Grimaldi Ferries (http://grimaldi-lines.com) also serves the Balearics, plus Civitavecchia and Sardinia in Italy.

BY CAR

Driving into Barcelona Head for the Ronda Litoral, the southern half of the city's ring road. Following signs for "Port Vell" takes you towards the main exit for the old town; exits for Gran Vía de les Corts Catalanes (C31) and Avda. Diagonal will suit better if uptown Barcelona is your destination.

Parking City-centre garages and car parks (1hr from around €4, 24hr from €24) are linked to display boards showing where spaces are available. There are cheaper BSM (Barcelona Serveis Municipals, http://aparcamentsbsm.cat) long-term car parks for residents and visitors; the best option is the large Pl. Fòrum car park at Diagonal Mar (ⓂEl Maresme-Fòrum). Closer to the centre, the 24-hour BSM car park at Barcelona Nord bus station (C/d'Ali-Bei 54; ⓂArc de Triomf) is a little more expensive. Otherwise, the city's ubiquitous Área Verda meter zones allow pay-and-display parking for visitors (from around €3/hr, 1 or 2hr maximum stay).

INFORMATION

The city tourist board, Turisme de Barcelona, has a useful website (http://barcelonaturisme.com), plus offices in the city centre as well as at the airport and Barcelona Sants station. There are also staffed kiosks in main tourist areas, such as on La Rambla and outside the Sagrada Família, which sell discount passes and entrance tickets for popular attractions.

Turisme de Barcelona The main tourist office, at Pl. de Catalunya 17, opposite El Corte Inglés, ⓂCatalunya, offers an accommodation desk plus tour and ticket sales, and a gift shop, but it's always busy – frustrating if you just want a quick answer to a question. There's a Barri Gòtic office on Pl. de Sant Jaume, entrance at C/Ciutat 2, ⓂJaume I.

Institut de Cultura Palau de la Virreina, La Rambla 99, ⓂLiceu (http://barcelonacultura.bcn.cat). Cultural information office and ticket sales for events, concerts, exhibitions and festivals.

Centre d'Informació de Catalunya Palau Robert, Pg. de Gràcia 107, Eixample, ⓂDiagonal (http://palaurobert.gencat.cat). Information about travel in Catalunya, plus exhibitions and events relating to all matters Catalan.

Barcelona Informació (Oficina d'Atenció Ciutadana) Pl. de Sant Miquel 3, Barri Gòtic, 010, http://ajuntament.barcelona.cat; ⓂJaume I. Citizens' information office, around the back of the Ajuntament. While not targeted at tourists, it's invariably helpful with all aspects of living in Barcelona (though English isn't necessarily spoken).

GETTING AROUND

Most of the central sights can be reached on foot in under 20min from Pl. de Catalunya. Barcelona also has an excellent integrated **public-transport** system, comprising the metro, buses, trams and local trains plus funicular railways and cable cars. Route and ticket information is posted at major bus stops and all metro and tram stations, and the local transport authority, **Transports Metropolitans de Barcelona** (TMB; http://tmb.cat), has a useful website. A transit plan divides the province into six zones, but as the entire metropolitan area of Barcelona (except the airport)

10

falls within Zone 1, that's the only zone you'll need to worry about on a day-to-day basis.

TICKETS AND TRAVEL PASSES

Tickets On all the city's public transport (including night buses and funiculars) you can buy a single ticket every time you ride (€2.55).

Targetes It's much cheaper to buy a T-Mobilitat reusable *targeta* (50¢) and load it up with a discount ticket. The most useful of these is the T-Casual (€12.15), which is valid for ten separate journeys other than to or from the airport on metro line L9 Sud, with changes between methods of transport allowed within 75 minutes. It can only be used by one person at a time, so you have to buy a separate one for each person travelling. There's also a single-person, one-day T-Día at €11.20 for unlimited travel within Zone 1, plus Hola Barcelona Card combinations (2–5 days' travel, including to and from the airport; €17.50–€40.80). These let you pass through the metro or train barrier, or slot in the machine on the bus, tram or funicular; they're sold at metro, train, tram and funicular stations, but not on the buses.

Out of town Heading for Sitges, Montserrat and other out-of-town destinations, you'll need to buy a specific ticket or relevant zoned *targeta*.

METRO, BUSES AND TRAMS

Metro The metro runs on eight lines, from 5am to midnight on Monday to Thursday, plus Sunday and public holidays; 5am to 2am Friday and the eves of public holidays; and 24hr on Saturday.

Buses Bus routes operate daily, roughly from 4/5am until 10.30pm, though some lines stop earlier and some run until after midnight. Night buses (*Nit bus*) fill in the gaps on all main routes, with services every twenty minutes to an hour from around 10pm to 4am. Many bus routes (including all night buses) stop in or near Pl. Catalunya.

Trams Lines #T1, #T2 and #T3 (daily 5am–midnight, Fri & Sat until 2am, every 8–20min) depart from Pl. Francesc Macià and run along the uptown part of Avda. Diagonal to suburban destinations in the northwest – useful tourist stops are at L'Illa shopping centre and the María Cristina and Palau Reial metro stations. Lines #T4 , #T5 and #T6 run

from Ciutadella-Vila Olímpica (where there's also a metro station), up to Glòries, down Avda. Diagonal to Diagonal Mar and the Parc del Fòrum, and to Badalona up the coast.

TRAINS

FGC The city's commuter train line – Ferrocarrils de la Generalitat de Catalunya (FGC; http://fgc.cat) – has its main stations at Pl. de Catalunya and Pl. d'Espanya, to destinations including Montserrat and Tibidabo.

RENFE The national rail service, RENFE (902 320 320, http://renfe.com), runs all other services out of Barcelona, with local lines – north to the Costa Maresme and south to Sitges – designated as *Rodalies/Cercanías*. The hub is Barcelona Sants, with services also passing through Pl. de Catalunya (heading north) and Pg. de Gràcia (south).

TAXIS

Black-and-yellow taxis turn on a green roof light when available for hire – typical short journeys across town cost around €12. After a minimum charge of €2.55, they charge €1.23/km (€1.51 after 8pm, and on Sat, Sun & hols), with surcharges for picking up from Barcelona Sants station (minimum fare €2.50 and the airport (€4.50). Taxis have meters, so prices are transparent; ask for a receipt (*rebut*) if necessary. Firms include Barna Taxi (933 222 222, http://barnataxi.com) and Radio Taxi 033 (933 033 033, http://radiotaxi033.com). Uber and Lyft do not currently operate in Barcelona.

CYCLING AND BIKE RENTAL

Although the city council has invested heavily in the "Bicing" pick-up and drop-off scheme (http://bicing.cat) – you'll see the red bikes and bike stations everywhere – it's aimed at encouraging locals to use bikes for short trips, rather than at tourists. Plenty of bike-rental outfits are more geared to tourist requirements, typically charging €6–7 for two hours, €15–17 for a full 24 hours, and double that for an electric bike.

Bike rental outfits Biciclot, Pg. Marítim 33, Port Olímpic (ⓂCiutadella-Vila Olímpica), http://biciclot.net; Bicicleta Barcelona, C/Esparteria 3, La Ribera (ⓂBarceloneta), http://bicicletabarcelona.com.

TOURS

You can see the sights of Barcelona on anything from a bike to a helicopter. Walking and bike tours are especially popular, while other operators offer tapas-bar crawls, party nights and out-of-town excursions. Highest profile are the open-top sightseeing bus tours, whose board-at-will services stop outside every attraction.

Baja Bikes http://biketoursbarcelona.com. Three-hour tours start in the Pl. de Sant Jaume in the Barri Gòtic, and visit various places in the Born, followed by some of Gaudí's buildings in the Eixample.

Barcelona Walking Tours http://barcelonaturisme. com. The tourist office coordinates popular walks and tours, including a 2hr tour of the Barri Gòtic, a 2hr Picasso tour, and a 2hr *modernisme* tour. Advance booking essential.

Bus Turístic barcelonabusturistic.cat. The city's official sightseeing service offers three distinct but interconnecting routes for a single ticket, linking all the main tourist sights and making over forty stops (departures every 5–25min). Northern (red) and southern (blue) routes depart from Pl. Catalunya (daily: April–Sept 9am–8pm; Oct–March 9am–

7pm), and a full circuit on either route takes 2hr. The green Fòrum route (daily April–Sept 9.30am–8pm) runs from Port Olímpic to Diagonal Mar and back via the beaches, and takes 40min. Tickets are available on board, online, or at Sants station or tourist offices.

Las Golondrinas http://lasgolondrinas.com. Daily sightseeing boats from Pl. Portal de la Pau, behind the Columbus monument, heading either around the port (40min), or along the coast as well, including Port Olímpic and Diagonal Mar (90min).

My Favourite Things http://myft.net. Highly individual, 4hr English-language tours on themes like where and what locals eat, Art Nouveau discoveries or forgotten neighbourhoods. Advance bookings essential.

Spanish Civil War Tours http://thespanishcivilwar.com. Long-time resident Nick Lloyd's absorbing half-day tours weave gripping human stories with the historical events that shaped the city between 1936 and 1939. Delivered in English, tours must be booked in advance.

10

ACCOMMODATION

Finding accommodation in Barcelona can be very difficult, so it's always best to book in advance, especially at Easter, in summer and during festivals or trade fairs. **Prices** are high for Spain – absolute cheapest rooms in a simple family-run hotel, sharing a bathroom, cost around €60 (singles from €40), though for private facilities €80–90 a night is more realistic. Places with a bit of boutique styling start at around €120, while for Barcelona's more fashionable hotels, count on €250–400 a night. In youth hostels, or cheap hotels with dorms, a bed goes for €15–35 a night, depending on the season.

You can **reserve** hotel accommodation online with the city tourist board or make same-day bookings in person only at their **tourist offices** (see page 637). For apartments, try Sh Barcelona (http://shbarcelona.com) or Inside-BCN (http://insidebarcelona.com).

Pau 2, http://hostalmarenostrum.com; ⓜLiceu. A cheery La Rambla *pensión* whose English-speaking management offers comfortable double, triple and family rooms with satellite TV and a/c. The updated rooms – all are en suite – are modern and double-glazed against the noise, and some come with balconies and street views. Breakfast included and a glass of cava upon arrival if booked directly. €€

★ **Hotel H1898** La Rambla 109, entrance on C/Pintor Fortuny, http://hotel1898.com; ⓜCatalunya. The former HQ of the Philippines Tobacco Company has four grades of eye-popping boutique rooms (the standard is "Classic") in deep red, green or black. Public areas are similarly dramatic, like the neo-colonial lounge and bar, and the tropics-kissed terrace *La Isabela*. There's also a Catalan restaurant *El Nido*, as well as outdoor and indoor pools and a glam spa. €€€€

LA RAMBLA, SEE MAP PAGE 606

★ **Hostal Benidorm** La Rambla 37, http://hostal benidorm.com; ⓜDrassanes. Refurbished *pensión* opposite Pl. Reial that offers clean and functional rooms. All offer bathrooms, however the economic ones are very small. Some also have a balcony and La Rambla view if you're prepared to pay a bit more. €€

Hostal Mare Nostrum La Rambla 67, entrance on C/Sant

BARRI GÒTIC, SEE MAP PAGE 606

Hostal Fernando C/Ferran 31, http://hfernando.com; ⓜLiceu. Light, modern rooms all with a/c and private bathroom. They also offer family rooms with bunk beds for kids. Breakfast is included. €€

Hostal Rembrandt C/Portaferrissa 23, http://hostal rembrandt.com; ⓜLiceu. A safe, old-town budget *pensión*. Simple tile-floored rooms (a bit cheaper without private

---

WHAT'S THE NEIGHBOURHOOD LIKE?

First things first: if you hanker after a **La Rambla** view, you'll pay for the privilege – generally speaking, there are much better deals to be had either side of the famous boulevard, often just a minute's walk away. It can also be a noisy area to stay, so you may want to stay in the side streets anyway. Most of Barcelona's cheapest accommodation (as well as some classy boutique choices) is found in the **Barri Gòtic** and **El Raval** neighbourhoods, which can both still have their rough edges – be careful (without being paranoid) when coming and going after dark. East of the Barri Gòtic, in **Sant Pere** and **La Ribera**, there are a number of safely sited budget, mid-range and boutique options, handy for the Picasso museum and Born nightlife area. North of Pl. de Catalunya, the **Eixample** has some of the city's most fashionable hotels, often housed in converted palaces and mansions and located just a few minutes' walk from the *modernista* architectural masterpieces. For waterfront views look at **Port Vell** at the end of La Rambla, and at the **Port Olímpic** southeast of the old town. If you prefer neighbourhood living, then **Gràcia** is the best base, as you're only ever a short walk away from its bars, restaurants and clubs.

10

bathroom) have a street-side balcony or little patio, while larger rooms are more versatile and can sleep up to four. €€
Hotel Arai C/Avinyó 30, http://hotelarai.com; ⓜLiceu. Gothic quarter charm meets modern luxury in this renovated eighteenth-century palace turned aparthotel. Original details are preserved and fine art from a private collection lines the walls. The 31 small apartments reveal ancient bricks and stonework and there is even a hotel museum. €€€€
Hotel Cantón C/Nou de Sant Francesc 40, http://hotelcantonbarcelona.com; ⓜDrassanes. A modest one-star hotel that's only two blocks off La Rambla and close to the harbour and Port Vell. Forty-seven rooms feature uniform blue-and-white trim curtains and bedspreads, central heating and a/c, fridge and wardrobe. €€
★ **Hotel DO** Pl. Reial 1, 934 813 666; ⓜLiceu. Renowned Catalan architect Oriol Bohigas led the renovation of this nineteenth-century Neoclassical building on the city's emblematic Pl. Reial. The result is a gastronomic boutique hotel with eighteen impeccably appointed rooms, most overlooking the square, which seamlessly blends the contemporary with the timeless. On top of this, quite literally, is the rooftop lounge and blue-tiled plunge pool, plus spa with sauna, steam room and heated bench. Out of season it can be a bargain. €€€€
Hotel El Jardí Pl. Sant Josep Oriol 1, http://eljardi-barcelona.com; ⓜLiceu. The hotel's location, overlooking the charming Pl. del Pi, is what sells this place – and explains the steepish prices for rooms that can seem a bit bare and poky. Some of the rooms are also interior, so have no outside windows. But the best (the top ones have terraces or balconies) do look directly onto the square. €€
Itaca Hostel C/Ripoll 21, http://itacahostel.com; ⓜJaume I. Bright and breezy converted house close to the Catedral, offering spacious hostel dorms (sleeping six, eight or ten) with balconies. Dorms are mixed, though you can also reserve a private double or triple (private toilets, but shared showers). €
Mercer Hotel C/Lledó 7, http://mercerbarcelona.com; ⓜJaume I. Parts of this jewel of a hotel are ancient (including some Roman wall), and architect Rafael Moneo highlighted a huge mix of architectural styles when restoring the building: medieval arches, wooden coffered ceilings and ornate Gothic columns found in the rooms and public areas marry with contemporary designer furnishings. Rooms are elegant, spacious and silent. A restaurant, and rooftop bar and pool, with a garden of aromatics such as lavender and rosemary offer options for relaxation. €€€€
Pensió Alamar C/Comtessa de Sobradiel 1, http://pensioalamar.com; ⓜLiceu/Jaume I. If you don't mind sharing a bathroom then this makes a convenient and great value base. There are twelve rooms (singles, doubles and triples), most with little balconies and, while space is tight, there's a friendly welcome, laundry service and use of a kitchen, but street noise can be a bit of an issue. No credit cards. €

PORT VELL, SEE MAP PAGE 606
★ **Serras Hotel** Passeig de Colom 9, http://serrashotel.com; ⓜBarceloneta. A breezy, elegant hotel that manages to be smart but relaxed. Rooms feature vast beds and lots of crushed velvet – book a room at the front for a view across the port. The rooftop restaurant is great for a Mediterranean lunch, and you can slide into the small pool afterwards. €€€€

EL RAVAL, SEE MAP PAGE 606
Barceló Raval Rambla del Raval 17–21, http://barcelo.com; ⓜLiceu/Sant Antoni. This glow-in-the-dark tower is a neighbourhood landmark and has sophisticated, open-plan rooms and quirky decor, plus a 360-degree top-floor terrace with plunge pool and sensational city views. €€€
Casa Camper C/d'Elisabets 11, http://casacamper.com; ⓜUniversitat/Liceu. Synonymous with creative, comfy shoes, *Camper* took a bold step into the hospitality business with this striking hotel. Rooms are divided by a corridor: the "sleeping" side faces a vertical garden; the other part is a "mini-lounge" with TV, hammock and balcony. €€€€
★ **Hostal Grau** C/Ramelleres 27, http://hostalgrau.com; ⓜCatalunya. A homely and friendly eco *pensión* with attractive rooms on several floors; you'll pay around €40 more for superior rooms with balconies, while two private apartments in the same building (sleeping two to six) offer a bit more independence. €€€
★ **Hotel España** C/Sant Pau 9–11, http://hotelespanya.com; ⓜLiceu. The *modernista* icon has been sumptuously restored as a four-star-plus hotel, and the gem-like interior – colourful tiles, bright mosaics, sculpted marble, iron swirls and marine motifs – has no equal in Barcelona. Guest rooms are a perfectly judged blend of earth tones and designer style, and there's a plunge pool and chill-out deck on the roof terrace. The house restaurant – known as *Fonda España* – offers contemporary Catalan bistro dishes overseen by hot chef Martín Berasategui. €€€€
Hotel Onix Liceo C/Nou de la Rambla 36, http://onixhotels.com; ⓜLiceu/Drassanes. Steps from Palau Güell, this four-star hotel features minimalist decor that melds nicely with the building's older architectural elements. There's a tropical patio and big-for-Barcelona pool on the ground floor. €€

MONTJUÏC, SEE MAP PAGE 625
★ **Market Hotel** C/Comte Borrell 68, at Ptge. Sant Antoni Abat, http://hotelmarketbarcelona.com; ⓜSant Antoni. The designer-budget Market makes a definite splash with its part-Japanese, part-neocolonial look. It's a feel that flows through the building and down into the restaurant, while the hotel's vintage Asian-style *Bar Rosso* has become a bit of a local hipsters' haunt. €€€

SANT PERE, SEE MAP PAGE 606
★ **Grand Hotel Central** Via Laietana 30, http://grandhotelcentral.com; ⓜJaume I. A wham-glam designer

hotel beloved of all the style mags. Spacious, ever-so-lovely rooms hit all the right buttons – hardwood floors, Egyptian cotton sheets, high-end toiletries – and up on the roof there are amazing views from the sundeck and infinity pool. Tapas and Catalan cuisine are on the menu in the hotel's plush restaurant. €€€€

LA RIBERA, SEE MAP PAGE 606

★ **Chic & Basic Born** C/Princesa 50, http://chicandbasic. com; ⓜ Jaume I. Punchily boutique and in-your-face, from the open-plan, all-in-white decor to laugh-aloud conceits like adjustable mood-lighting, sashaying plastic curtains and mirrored walls. There are other *Chic & Basic* outlets in the city centre as well as apartments. €€€

★ **Hostal Nuevo Colón** Avda. Marquès de l'Argentera 19, 1º, http://hostalnuevocolon.es; ⓜ Barceloneta. Well-kept *pensión* with simple, yet comfortable rooms – you'll save if you share a bathroom. Sunny front rooms, lounge and terrace all have side views to Parc de la Ciutadella. €€

BARCELONETA, SEE MAP PAGE 602

★ **W Barcelona** Pl. Rosa dels Vents 1, http://w-barcelona. com; ⓜ Barceloneta. The signature building on the Barceloneta seafront is the stupendously cool, wave-shaped *W Barcelona*. There's a hip, resort feel, with direct beach access, the open-plan designer rooms have fantastic views through floor-to-ceiling windows, and facilities are first-rate, from the "whatever you want" concierge to the infinity pool and various restaurants of different stripes. €€€€

PORT OLÍMPIC, SEE MAP PAGE 602

★ **Hotel Arts Barcelona** C/Marina 19–21, Port Olímpic, hotelartsbarcelona.com; ⓜ Ciutadella-Vila Olímpica. A city benchmark for five-star designer luxury, service and standards. The hotel's thirty-three floors offer fabulous views of the port and sea, with rooms featuring floor-to-ceiling windows and enormous marble bathrooms. Seafront gardens encompass an open-air pool and hot tub, a two-Michelin-star restaurant and a 43rd-floor spa. €€€€

EIXAMPLE, SEE MAPS PAGES 602 AND 618

Almanac Barcelona Gran Vía de les Corts Catalanes 619–621, http://almanachotels.com/barcelona; ⓜ Passeig de Gràcia. This five-star luxury hotel is a grey-and-gold temple of luxury built around a soaring, oak-slatted atrium, with 61 designer rooms and thirty suites featuring details including Ibizan marble bathrooms and antique mirrors, and the usual

details you'd expect at this level – spas, restaurants and rooftop pool – are all present and correct. €€€€

★ **Barcelona Urbany** Avda. Meridiana 97, http://urbany hostels.com/barcelona; ⓜ Clot. Huge steel-and-glass four hundred-bed hostel that's on handy metro and airport train routes (it's an easy ride in to Pl. de Catalunya). The rooms are boxy en suites with pull-down beds (sleeping two to eight) that are just as viable for couples on a budget as backpackers. Bar and terrace, plus free health club and pool entry in the same building. €

Casa Bonay Gran Vía de les Corts Catalanes, http://casa bonay.com; ⓜ Girona. Calling this renovated, Neoclassical nineteenth-century building a "hotel" is to sell it short. It's also an event space, book store, artisanal coffee bar and artist's hangout. The *Bodega Bonay* restaurant serves superb Italo-Catalan dishes and a range of natural wines. There's a rooftop bar, cocktail lounge, DJs, live music – and even some beautifully tasteful, eco-friendly rooms to stay in. The vibe is very much like plugging into the local community. €€€€

Hostal Girona C/Girona 24, 1º, http://hostalgirona.com; ⓜ Urquinaona. Delightful, family-run *pensión* with a wide range of cosy, traditional rooms (not all en suite), plus corridors laid with rugs, polished wooden doors, antique paintings and restored furniture throughout. €€

Hotel Axel C/d'Aribau 33, http://axelhotels.com; ⓜ Universitat. Located in the Gayxample, The *Axel's* snazzy "heterofriendly" boutique stylings are a real hit with the LGBTQ+ community. It's a hip space with designer rooms (featuring eco-friendly toiletries), a bar and restaurant that are part of the local scene, plus fabulous terrace pool and "Skybar". €€€€

Mandarin Oriental Pg. de Gràcia 38–40, http://mandarin oriental.com/barcelona; ⓜ Passeig de Gràcia. This designer addition to Barcelona's most prestigious avenue fills the premises of a former bank building with a soaring white atrium and a serene selection of gorgeously light rooms. There's the obligatory superstar restaurant, *Moments*, while bar, spa, mimosa garden and rooftop "dipping pool" combine oriental tranquillity and Euro cool. €€€€

GRÀCIA, SEE MAP PAGE 632

Generator Hostel and Hotel C/Corsega 373, http:// generatorhostels.com/hostels/barcelona; ⓜ Diagonal. Big, bright and abuzz with people having fun, the *Generator* lounge frequently features live music, DJ sets and art performances, as well as a pool table and big-screen TV. The clean, modern rooms range from budget dorms up to a penthouse. There's 24hr reception. €

EATING

You'll probably do most of your **eating** where you do most of your sightseeing. However, if you venture no farther than La Rambla, or the streets around the cathedral, you are not going to experience the best of the city's cuisine – in

the main tourist areas, food and service can be indifferent and prices high. Instead, explore the backstreets of neighbourhoods like Sant Pere, La Ribera, El Raval and Poble Sec, where you'll find excellent restaurants, some little

10

WHAT'S COOKING IN BARCELONA?

The minimalist, food-as-chemistry approach, pioneered by Catalan super-chef Ferran Adrià (of *El Bulli* fame), has Barcelona in a vice-like grip. The best local chefs continue to reinterpret classic Catalan dishes in innovative ways, and while prices in these gastro-temples are high there's a trend towards more economic, bistro-style dining even by the hottest chefs. The current fad is the fusion of Mediterranean and Asian flavours – a so-called **"Mediterrasian" cuisine**. It rears its head especially in the world of tapas, and in Barcelona these days, you're as likely to get shrimp tempura or a yucca chip as you are to get a garlic mushroom.

more than hole-in-the-wall taverns, others surprisingly funky and chic. Most of the big-ticket, destination-dining restaurants are found in the Eixample, while Gràcia is a pleasant place to spend the evening, with plenty of good mid-range restaurants. For fish and seafood, you're best off in the harbourside Barceloneta district or at the Port Olímpic.

Most cafés are open from 7am or 8am until midnight, or much later – so whether it's coffee first thing or a late-night nibble, you'll find somewhere to cater for you. Restaurants generally open 1pm to 4pm and 8.30pm to 11pm, though in tourist zones like La Rambla and Port Olímpic, they tend to stay open all day.

LA RAMBLA, SEE MAP PAGE 606

CAFÉS

Cafè de l'Òpera La Rambla 74, http://cafeoperabcn. com; m Liceu. If you're going to pay through the nose for a Rambla seat, it may as well be at this famous old café-bar opposite the opera house, which retains its fin-de-siècle feel. There's a handful of sought-after pavement tables. €€€
Café Zurich Pl. Catalunya 1, 933 179 153; m Catalunya. This is the most famous meet-and-greet café in town right at the top of the La Rambla underneath El Triangle shopping centre. Sit inside if you don't want to be bothered by endless rounds of buskers and beggars. €€
Escribà La Rambla 83, http://escriba.es; m Liceu. Many rate this classy pastry shop in the historic *modernista* Antiga Casa Figueras building near the Boqueria market as the best pâtisserie in Barcelona. €

TAPAS BARS

Bar Central La Boqueria Mercat de la Boqueria, La Rambla 91, 933 011 098; m Liceu. This gleaming, chrome stand-up bar in the market's central aisle is the venue for ultra-fresh market produce, served by snazzy staff who work at a fair lick. Breakfast, snack or lunch, it's all the same to them – salmon cutlets, sardines, calamari, razor clams, hake fillets, sausages, pork steaks, asparagus spears and the rest, plunked on the griddle and sprinkled with salt. Breakfast costs just a few euros or it's not much more than that for some tapas or a main dish and a drink. €

BARRI GÒTIC, SEE MAP PAGE 606

CAFÉS

Bar del Pi Pl. Sant Josep Oriol 1, http://bardelpi.com; m Liceu. Best known for its terrace tables on one of Barcelona's prettiest squares. Linger over drinks, tapas and sandwiches as the old town reveals its charms, especially during the weekend artists' market. €
Granja Dulcinea C/Petritxol 2, http://granjadulcinea. com; m Liceu. One of the old town's age-old treats is to come here for a thick hot chocolate, slathered in cream. It's a bygone-era kind of place, with dickie-bow-wearing waiters patrolling the beamed and panelled room. €

TAPAS BARS

★**Bodega La Plata** C/Mercè 28, http://barlaplata. com; m Drassanes. A classic taste of the old town, with a marble counter open to the street and dirt-cheap wine served straight from the barrel. They only do five types of tapas here, but they do them well, from *butifarra* (a type of Catalan sausage) sandwiches to tomato and onion salad. You can also do a dish of the speciality anchovies, either marinated or deep-fried like whitebait. €

RESTAURANTS

★**Can Culleretes** C/Quintana 5, http://culleretes.com; m Liceu. Barcelona's oldest restaurant (founded in 1786) serves straight-up Catalan food (*botifarra* sausage and beans, salt cod, spinach and pine nuts, wild boar stew) in cosy, traditional surroundings. Local families come in droves, especially for celebrations or for Sun lunch, and there are good-value set meals available at both lunch and dinner. €€

EL RAVAL AND MONTJUÏC, SEE MAPS PAGES 606 AND 625

CAFÉS

Federal C/Parlament 39, http://federalcafe.es; m Poble Sec. Effortlessly cool brunch bar and café, squished into a corner townhouse with a great little roof-garden on top. The Australian owners have imported classic brunch options from avocado toast with poached egg, eggs Benedict and banana pancakes. They also serve excellent coffees and cakes. They also have a second branch at Ptge. de la Pau 11 in the Barri Gòtic). €€

Granja M. Viader C/Xuclà 4–6, http://granjaviader.cat; ⓂLiceu. The oldest traditional *granja* (milk bar) in town has a pavement plaque outside for services to the city. The signature drink is their own invention, "Cacaolat" (a popular bottled chocolate milk), or try *mel i mató* (curd cheese and honey) or *llet Mallorquina* (fresh milk with cinnamon and lemon rind). €

TAPAS BARS

★ **Dos Palillos** C/Elisabets 9, http://dospalillos.com; ⓂCatalunya. This hipster hangout, run by former *El Bulli* chefs, is a flag-waver for Asian fusion tapas, which offers à la carte *dim sum* in the front bar (Cantonese caramelized walnuts to steamed dumplings) and a back-room, counter-style Asian bar where tasting menus feature all the highlights. €€€

RESTAURANTS

Cera 23 C/Cera 23, http://cera23.com; ⓂSant Antoni. Start your meal at this charming Galicia-meets-the-Mediterranean bistro with an effervescent blackberry mojito, and then tuck into market-fresh dishes like wild mushroom and truffle risotto, coconut milk veg curry or a black rice-and-seafood "volcano". €€€

★ **Dos Pebrots** C/Doctor Dou 19, dospebrots.com; ⓂCatalunya. Around the corner from *Dos Palillos* is Albert Raurich's love letter to Mediterranean cuisine. Once a favourite bar for poets and off-duty chefs, *Dos Pebrots* now uses historical dishes such as Roman garum (anchovy sauce) as the basis for contemporary tapas and small dishes. Don't miss the pigs' nipples. €€

Suculent Rambla de Raval 45, http://suculent.com; ⓂLiceu. This restaurant puts prime, seasonal produce – often home-grown – in the spotlight. Some dishes include animal ingredients in supporting roles but it's the vegetables you'll applaud, in dishes such as pumpkin parmesan cream and black truffle and grilled artichoke with mantis shrimp. €€€

SANT PERE, SEE MAP PAGE 606

TAPAS BARS

Mosquito C/Carders 46, http://mosquitotapas.com; ⓂJaume 1. A funky Asian tapas bar, festooned with hanging paper lanterns, which pours artisan beers and offers an authentic, made-to-order *dim sum* menu, from shrimp dumplings to tofu rolls. It's so popular that you'll almost always have to queue for a table. €

RESTAURANTS

Casa Mari y Rufo C/Freixures 11, 933 197 302; ⓂJaume I. A great place for no-frills but high-quality market cooking, with a busy family turning out lots of fresh seafood such as grilled clams and squid, barbecued octopus and oysters. €€€

Le Cucine Mandarosso C/Verdaguer i Callís 4, http://lecucinemandarosso.com; ⓂUrquinaona. Naples meets Barcelona in this cosy country kitchen-like restaurant near the Via Laietana. It's crowded and cramped but the top-value southern-Italian comfort food here is the real deal. The home-made cakes are so good you'll buy more to take away. Dishes change daily, depending on ingredients. €€

LA RIBERA, SEE MAP PAGE 606

TAPAS BARS

Cal Pep Pl. de les Olles 8, http://calpep.com; ⓂBarceloneta. You may have to queue for this famous tapas bar (there are no reservations for the bar), and prices are high, but it's definitely worth it for the likes of impeccably fried squid, grilled monk fish, Catalan sausage and beans, and baby squid and chickpeas. There's also a small dining room and a handful of tables outside. €€€

El Xampanyet C/Montcada 22, http://elxampanyet.es; ⓂJaume I. Traditional blue-tiled bar doing a roaring trade in sparkling cava, cider and tapas (anchovies are the speciality, but there's also marinated tuna, spicy mussels, sun-dried tomatoes, sliced meats and cheese). Be prepared to queue. €€

RESTAURANTS

Carmina C/Argenteria 37, http://carminarestaurante.com; ⓂJaume I. A gorgeous renovation of an eighteenth-century building has been artfully blended with neon, artsy ceramics and oversized lamps and is now the home of *Carmina*. The speciality is superb Italian food with nods to Spanish cuisine, such as oxtail croquettes with pecorino. The pasta dishes are especially good. €€

BARCELONETA, SEE MAP PAGE 606

TAPAS BARS

★ **Cova Fumada** C/Baluard 56, 932 214 061; ⓂBarceloneta. Behind brown wooden doors on Barceloneta's market square (there's no sign), this rough-and-ready tavern may not look like much but the food's great – tapas made with ingredients fresh from the market, from griddled sardines to the house speciality *bomba* (spicy potato-meatball). €€

RESTAURANTS

★ **Can Maño** C/Baluard 12, 933 193 082; ⓂBarceloneta. This old-fashioned diner is packed with noisy locals around formica tables. Expect fried or grilled fish, basic wine and absolutely no frills, but it's an authentic experience, and a cheap one. Payment is cash only. €

Green Spot C/Reina Cristina 12, http://encompaniadelobos.com/the-green-spot; ⓂBarceloneta. Vegetarian and vegan restaurants good enough to keep omnivores happy too are rare in Barcelona. *Green Spot* fits the bill, even though its fun,

10

fresh, international dishes, embracing all the latest trends, aren't quite as refined as its oak-panelled decor. €€

PORT OLÍMPIC, SEE MAP PAGE 602

RESTAURANTS

Agua Pg. Marítim 30, http://somosesencia.es; Ⓜ Ciutadella-Vila Olímpica. By far the nicest boardwalk restaurant on the beachfront strip, perfect for brunch, with a seasonal, contemporary Mediterranean menu – grills, *risotti*, pasta, salads and tapas. €€

POBLE SEC AND MONTJUÏC, SEE MAP PAGE 625

TAPAS BARS

Casa de Tapas Cañota C/Lleida 7, http://casadetapas. com; Ⓜ Poble Sec. This colourful, family-friendly tapas bar is an ideal spot to refuel over-tired children after a visit to Montjüic's Magic Fountain. Adults can unwind with a fresh, cold beer pulled from pressurized copper tanks. The tapas are above average in both quality and price. €€

★ **Quimet i Quimet** C/Poeta Cabanyes 25, http://quimet quimet.com; Ⓜ Paral·lel. In Poble Sec's cosiest tapas bar, little plates of classy finger-food are served reverently from the minuscule counter – things like roast onions, marinated mushrooms, stuffed cherry tomatoes and anchovy-wrapped olives. €€

PARAL·LEL, SEE MAP PAGE 625

RESTAURANTS

★ **Benzina** Passatge de Pere Calders 6, http://benzina. es; Ⓜ Poble Sec. Down a wide pedestrianized alleyway off the hipster drag of C/deParlament is this industrially chic Italian restaurant, serving some of the best food around. The convivial atmosphere and upbeat seventies and eighties soundtrack provide a joyful backdrop to *linguine aglio e olio* with lobster and avocado, a heavenly carbonara and much more. €€€

Rías Kru C/Lleida 7, http://riaskru.com; Ⓜ Poble Sec. This creative if expensive seafood restaurant gives deep-sea delicacies a more contemporary context. Expect cocktails, oysters and first-rate sashimi plus a handful of equally impressive meat dishes. €€€

EIXAMPLE, SEE MAP PAGE 618

TAPAS BARS

★ **Tapas24** C/Diputació 269, http://carlesabellan.com; Ⓜ Passeig de Gràcia. Star chef Carles Abellan gets back to his roots at this basement tapas bar. There's a reassuringly traditional feel that's echoed in the menu – *patatas bravas*, Andalucian-style fried fish, meatballs, chorizo sausage and

fried eggs. But the kitchen updates the classics too, so there's also *calamares romana* (fried squid) dyed black with squid ink, or a burger with foie gras. There's always a rush and a bustle at meal times, so be aware that you might have to queue. €€

RESTAURANTS

★ **Cinc Sentits** C/Aribau 58, http://cincsentits.com; Ⓜ Universitat. Contemporary Catalan cuisine that touches the "Five Senses" and has earned chef Jordi Artal two Michelin stars. The tasting menus use rigorously sourced wild fish, mountain lamb, seasonal vegetables, farmhouse cheeses and so on in elegant, pared-down dishes that are all about flavour. €€€€

★ **Disfrutar** C/Villaroel 163, http://disfrutarbarcelona. com; Ⓜ Hospital Clinic. The hottest restaurant in Barcelona, and arguably the world, currently belongs to three former head chefs of the legendary but now-closed *El Bulli*. The creativity here is off the charts. Tasting menus are an endless procession of tiny delights that will make you smile and groan with pleasure, at least until the bill arrives. €€€€

La Flauta C/Aribau 23, 933 237 038; Ⓜ Universitat. One of the city's best-value lunch menus sees diners queuing for tables early – get there before 2pm to avoid the rush. Meals are served tapas-style, day and night, based on seasonal market produce, from wild mushrooms to locally landed fish. €€

★ **Lasarte** C/Mallorca 259, http://restaurantlasarte.com; Ⓜ Diagonal. One of the best restaurants in Spain, with three Michelin stars to prove it. Basque gastronomic superstar Martín Berasategui has his name on the door but it's Paolo Casagrande who runs the kitchen, turning out a complex tasting menu that's strong on perfectionism and clean flavours. Send a message of apology to your bank manager before you reach for the wine list. €€€€

GRÀCIA, SEE MAP PAGE 632

TAPAS BARS

La Pepita C/Còrsega 343, http://lapepitabcn.com; Ⓜ Diagonal/Verdaguer. There's usually a queue out the door here, and deservedly so. The tapas, such as carabinero prawn croquettes with romesco sauce, or smoked aubergine fritters with goat's cheese, honey and apples, are fantastic, and the atmosphere is chatty and convivial. Hundreds of "love notes" scrawled by customers on the white-tiled walls attest to its popularity. €€

RESTAURANTS

Flash, Flash C/Granada del Penedès 25, http://flashflash barcelona.com; Ⓜ Diagonal. A classic 1970s' survivor, *Flash, Flash* does *tortillas* served any time you like, any way you like, from plain and simple to elaborately stuffed, with sweet ones for dessert. Chances are you'll love the original white leatherette booths and monotone "models-with-

BARCELONA'S VEGETARIAN RESTAURANTS

Vegetarians will find themselves pleasantly surprised by the choice available in Barcelona if they've spent any time in other areas of Spain. The restaurants listed below are reliable places for a good veggie meal, but you'll also be able to do pretty well for yourself in tapas bars and modern Catalan brasseries and restaurants.

Biocenter C/Pintor Fortuny 25, http://restaurante biocenter.es; Liceu; see map page 606. One of the longest-running strictly veggie places in town, with a popular fixed-price lunch menu. For dinner, they dim the lights, add candles and sounds, and turn out a few more exotic dishes, from seitan in a white-wine reduction to ginger tofu. €€

Sésamo C/Sant Antoni Abat 52, 934 416 411; Sant Antoni; see map page 625. Classy tapas place (bar at the front, restaurant tables at the back) that offers up a heavily vegetarian-orientated chalkboard menu of innovative dishes – think strawberry-basil gazpacho,

slow-roast tomato tart, or a daily risotto and pasta dish, all reasonably priced. €€

Teresa Carles C/Jovellanos 2, http://teresacarles.com; Catalunya; see map page 606. Stylish vegetarian and vegan cuisine served in a hip – but most certainly not "hippy" – space with soaring ceilings, exposed-brick walls and soft, white lighting. The lunch menu is a great bargain, while a la carte offerings like artisanal pastas, a hearty seitan burger and vegan ceviche don't cost much more. Their second Barcelona outpost, *Flax & Kale*, is located nearby at C/Tallers 74. €€

10

cameras" cutouts – very Austin Powers. €

Goliard C/Progrés, http://goliard.cat; Diagonal. Smart but casual *Goliard* offers a pared-down dining experience in a contemporary foodie bistro that looks like it should cost three times as much. Although the menu is divided into starters and mains, there are smaller portions available if you want to mix and match. €€

DRINKING AND NIGHTLIFE

Whatever you're looking for from a night out, you'll find it somewhere in Barcelona – bohemian boozer, underground club, cocktail bar, summer dance palace, techno temple, or Irish pub, you name it. Best known of the city's **nightlife haunts** are its hip designer **bars**, while there's a stylish **club and music scene** that goes from strength to strength fuelled by a potent mix of resident and guest DJs, local bands and visiting superstars. Local listings magazine *Time Out Barcelona* (http://timeout.com/barcelona) covers up-to-date openings, hours and club nights, and most bars, cafés and music stores carry flyers and free magazines containing news and reviews. For the Barcelona music scene, check out the website http://atiza.com.

ESSENTIALS

Opening hours and closing days Most bars stay open until 2am, or 3am at weekends, while clubs tend not to open much before midnight and stay open until 5am, or even later at weekends – fair enough, as they've often barely got started by 3am. Unlike some restaurants, bars and clubs generally stay open throughout August.

Admission charges Some clubs are free before a certain time, usually around midnight. Otherwise, expect to pay €10–20, though this usually includes your first drink (if there is free entry, don't be surprised to find that there's

San Kil C/Legalitat 22, http://instagram.com/restaurante_ san_kil; Joanic. There's no shortage of Korean restaurants in Barcelona, but *San Kil* has a place in the hearts of locals as the original. Family-run and super friendly, it's a no-nonsense affair, but the *bulgogi* (spicy beef wrapped in lettuce leaves), dumplings and seafood omelette are all excellent. €€

a minimum drinks' charge of anything up to €15). Tickets for gigs run from €24 to €60 depending on the act, though there are cheaper gigs (from €6) almost every night of the year at a variety of smaller clubs and bars.

BARS

LA RAMBLA, SEE MAP PAGE 606

Bosc de les Fades Ptge. de la Banca 5, http:// museocerabcn.com; Drassanes. Tucked away in an alley off La Rambla, by the wax museum, the "Forest of the Fairies" is festooned with gnarled plaster tree trunks, fountains and stalactites. It's a cheesy, but atmospheric location for a beer or sangria.

BARRI GÒTIC, SEE MAP PAGE 606

★ **L'Ascensor** C/Bellafila 3, 933 185 347; Jaume I. Sliding, antique wooden elevator doors announce the entrance to "The Lift", but it's no theme bar – just an easy-going cosy hangout that's great for a late-night drink.

Collage C/Consellers 4, http://collagecocktailbar.com; Jaume I. A stylish vintage place with a relaxed, pleasant atmosphere. The knowledgeable bartenders will mix you a creative drink and offer insightful advice on mixing. If that piques your interest you can even go to their cocktail-

THE GIN AND TONIC CRAZE

In Barcelona, they don't let anything come between their gin and their tonic – not even the word "and". The **gintonic**, as it's known, has always been a favourite drink. In recent years, however, there's been a surge in bars specializing in the classic cocktail and its star ingredient, **ginebra**, with spots such as *Bobby Gin* in Gràcia (see page 647), *Dry Martini* in Esquerra de L'Eixample (see page 646) and *Xixbar* in Poble Sec (see page 646) stocking a long list of brands. And the tonic component has not been forgotten, with bars pouring a dizzying array of premium varieties. It's a refreshing trend worthy of a glass-clinking *salut*.

making class for a well-spent afternoon.

★ **Milk** C/Gignàs 21, milkbarcelona.com; ⓜ Jaume I. Irish-owned bar and bistro (nothing like an Irish pub) that's carved a real niche as a welcoming neighbourhood hangout. Get there early for the famous brunch (daily 9am–4.30pm); there's also dinner and cocktails every night to a funky soundtrack.

EL RAVAL, SEE MAP PAGE 606

23 Robadors Robador 23, http://23robadors.wordpress. com; ⓜ Liceu. The tapas are lukewarm but the live jazz, blues and flamenco performances in this underground bar are red hot. It gets packed quickly, so arrive early or sharpen your elbows.

★ **Casa Almirall** C/Joaquin Costa 33, http://casaalmirall. com; ⓜ Universitat. Dating from 1860, Barcelona's oldest bar is a *modernista* design classic – check out the doors, counter and stupendous glittering bar. They serve a range of drinks and some great cocktails, but absinthe and vermouth are the order of the day.

★ **Marsella** C/Sant Pau 65, 934 427 263; ⓜ Liceu. Authentic, enjoyably atmospheric 1930s bar – named after the French port of Marseilles – that featured in Woody Allen's *Vicky Cristina Barcelona*, so you can expect a spirited mix of film fans, oddball locals, young dudes and various others.

★ **Resolis** C/Riera Baixa 22, http://resolisbar.com; ⓜ Sant Antoni. A cool hangout with decent tapas, where punters spill out of the door, drinks in-hand, on to a street famous for its vintage clothes shops, and where a good time is had by all.

SANT PERE, SEE MAP PAGE 606

Casa Paco C/d'Allada Vermell 10, 935 073 719; ⓜ Jaume I. This tiny bar is great for tapas (try the spicy *patatas bravas*) and late night drinks out on the terrace, which is set out in an atmospheric square.

LA RIBERA, SEE MAP PAGE 606

Marlowe C/Rec 24, http://marlowe.bar; ⓜ Barceloneta. There's a slightly noir atmosphere in this small, elegant cocktail bar – yes, the bar is named after the famous Chandlerian character. There is no set drinks menu, just talk

to the creative bartenders, let them know what you're in the mood for, and their professional hands will mix something just for you.

Mudanzas C/Vidrería 15, barmudanzas.com; ⓜ Barceloneta. A recent change in ownership means that this much beloved local haunt is now popular with a young, international, cocktail crowd but during the day it's still a relatively peaceful place for a beer off the main drag.

La Vinya del Senyor Pl. Santa María 5, lavinyadelsenyor. es; ⓜ Jaume I. A great wine bar with front-row seats onto the lovely church of Santa María del Mar. The wine list is really good and there are classy tapas available.

PORT VELL, SEE MAP PAGE 606

★ **Can Paixano** C/Reina Cristina 7, http://canpaixano. com; ⓜ Barceloneta. This crowded backstreet joint where the drink of choice – all right, the only drink – is cava is a must on everyone's itinerary. Don't go thinking sophistication – the drinks might come in traditional champagne coupes, but this is a counter-only joint where there's fizz, basic tapas and sausage butties and that's your lot.

POBLE SEC AND MONTJUÏC, SEE MAP PAGE 625

Xixbar C/Rocafort 19, http://xixbar.com; ⓜ Poble Sec. "Chicks" is an old *granja* (milk bar) turned candlelit and atmospheric, but completely unstuffy, cocktail bar. Gin is the big drink to enjoy here (they claim over one hundred varieties), and they even have their own specialist gin shop on site.

EIXAMPLE, SEE MAP PAGE 618

Dry Martini C/Aribau 166, http://drymartinibcn.org; ⓜ Diagonal. White-jacketed bartenders, dark wood and brass fittings, a self-satisfied air – it could only be the city's legendary uptown cocktail bar. Best drink to order? The clue's in the bar's name.

Velódromo C/Muntaner 213, http://barvelodromo.com; ⓜ Hospital Clínic. Renovated by the Barcelona beer company Moritz, this superbly glam Art Deco gem has a lofty, Parisian feel, equipped with a swooping staircase and a gleaming bar. It's ideal for swish drinks and cocktails, though with fancy breakfasts, brunch bites and a tapas-and-bistro menu it's also made for early starts and later dinners.

GRÀCIA, SEE MAP PAGE 632
Bobby Gin C/Francisco Giner 47, http://bobbygin.com; Ⓜ Diagonal. A sign inside says "El gintonic perfecto no existe" (the perfect gin and tonic does not exist). Perhaps. But the sizeable G&Ts here come very, very close.

Cafè del Sol Pl. del Sol 16, 932 371 448; Ⓜ Fontana. The granddaddy of the Pl. del Sol scene sees action day and night. On summer evenings, when the square is packed, there's not an outdoor table to be had.

★ **Canigó** C/Verde 2, http://barcanigo.com; Ⓜ Fontana. Family-run neighbourhood bar now entering its third generation and second century. It's not much to look at, but the drinks are cheap and it's a real Gràcia institution, packed out at weekends with a young, hip and largely local crowd.

SARRIÀ-SANT GERVASI, SEE MAP PAGE 602
Gimlet C/Santaló 46, http://gimletbcn.com; FGC Muntaner. Especially popular in summertime, when the street-side tables offer a great vantage point for watching the party unfold. There are also two or three other late-opening bars on the same stretch.

CLUBS AND LIVE MUSIC

BARRI GÒTIC, SEE MAP PAGE 606
Jamboree Pl. Reial 17, http://masimas.com; Ⓜ Liceu. Nightly gigs pull in the crowds. There's everything from jazz, funk and hip-hop to jam sessions. The club kicks off after midnight, playing funky sounds until the small hours.

Karma Pl. Reial 10, http://karmadisco.com; Ⓜ Liceu. Old-school studenty basement place spinning indie, Brit pop and US college, while a lively crowd gathers at the square-side bar and terrace.

La Macarena C/Nou de Sant Francesc 5, http://macarenaclub.com; Ⓜ Drassanes. Once a place where flamenco tunes were offered up to La Macarena, the Virgin of Seville – now a tiny heaving temple to all things electro. Live gigs and DJ sessions.

★ **Sidecar** Pl. Reial 7, http://sidecar.es; Ⓜ Liceu. The old town's hippest concert space has nightly gigs and DJs championing rock, indie, roots, electronica and fusion acts.

EL RAVAL, SEE MAP PAGE 606
★ **Moog** C/Arc del Teatre 3, http://moogbarcelona.com; Ⓜ Drassanes. It's tiny, but one of the most influential clubs around for electronic sounds, playing techno, electro, drum 'n' bass and trance to a cool but up-for-it crowd.

POBLENOU, SEE MAP PAGE 602
Sala Razzmatazz C/Pamplona 88, http://salarazzmatazz.com; Ⓜ Bogatell. *Sala Razzmatazz* hosts the biggest in-town rock gigs, while at weekends the former warehouse turns into "five clubs in one", spinning indie, rock, pop, techno, electro, retro and more, in variously named music bars like "The Loft", "Pop Bar" or "Lolita". Admission gets you entrance to all the bars.

POBLE SEC AND MONTJUÏC, SEE MAP PAGE 625
★ **Maumau** C/Fontrodona 35, http://maumaunderground.com; Ⓜ Paral·lel. A great underground lounge-club, cultural centre and chill-out space with nightly film and video projections, exhibitions, and a roster of guest DJs playing deep, soulful grooves. Strictly speaking it's a private club, but they tend to let foreign visitors in for free.

Sala Apolo C/Nou de la Rambla 113, http://sala-apolo.com; Ⓜ Paral·lel. Old-time ballroom turned hip-concert venue with gigs on two stages (local acts to big names) and an eclectic series of club nights with names to reckon with (Nasty Mondays, Crappy Tuesdays, etc).

La Terrrazza Avda. Francesc Ferrer i Guàrdia, Poble Espanyol, http://laterrrazza.com; Ⓜ Espanya. Open-air summer club that's *the* place to be in Barcelona. Non-stop dance, house and techno – though don't get there until at least 3am, and be prepared for the style police.

GRÀCIA, SEE MAP PAGE 632
★ **Heliogàbal** C/Ramon y Cajal 80, http://heliogabal.com; Ⓜ Joanic. Not much more than a boiler room given a

---

LGBTQ+ BARCELONA

There's a vibrant local **LGBTQ+** crowd in Barcelona, not to mention the lure of nearby Sitges (see page 717), mainland Spain's biggest LGBTQ+ resort. There's a particular concentration of bars, restaurants and clubs in the so-called **Gaixample**, the "Gay Eixample", an area of a few square blocks just northwest of the main university in the Eixample. The biggest event of the year is Carnaval in Sitges, while the main city party is Barcelona's annual LGBTQ+ **Pride** festival (http://pridebarcelona.org), which has events running over ten days each June, from street parades to Tibidabo funfair parties.

Aside from *Time Out Barcelona* (http://timeout.cat, in English), you'll find info on http://travelgay.com/destination/gay-spain/gay-barcelona. Also worth a look is Patroc (http://patroc.com), a guide for LGBTQ+ travellers to European destinations including Barcelona and Sitges.

10

lick of paint, but filled with a cool, twenty-something crowd here for the live poetry and music. Recent licensing issues have meant that they have only been able to host small, acoustic sessions, which are always special, intimate events. Admission and drinks are inexpensive.

Otto Zutz C/Lincoln 15, http://ottozutz.com; FGC Gràcia. It first opened in 1985 and has since lost some of its glam cachet, but this three-storey former textile factory still has a shedload of pretensions.

LES CORTS, SEE MAP PAGE 602

★ **Bikini** Avda. Diagonal 547, http://bikinibcn.com; Ⓜ Les Corts/María Cristina. This traditional landmark of Barcelona

ARTS AND CULTURE

As you would expect from a city of its size, Barcelona has a busy entertainment calendar – throughout the year there'll be something worth catching, whether it's a contemporary dance performance, cabaret show or night at the opera. Classical and contemporary music, in particular, gets an airing in some stunning auditoriums, while the city boasts a long tradition of street and performance art, right down to the human statues plying their trade on La Rambla. A useful first stop for tickets and information is the **Palau de la Virreina** (La Rambla 99; http://bcn.cat/cultura; Ⓜ Liceu). BCN Shop (http://bcnshop. barcelonaturisme.com) and Eventbrite (http://eventbrite.es) are the main advance booking agencies for music, theatre, cinema and exhibition tickets.

The city council's Institute of Culture website, http://lameva. barcelona.cat/barcelonacultura, covers every aspect of art and culture in the city. Otherwise, the best listings magazine is *Time Out Barcelona* (http://timeout.cat), online or found in cafés, restaurants and around town.

CLASSICAL MUSIC AND OPERA

Most of Barcelona's classical music concerts take place in the extravagantly decorated Palau de la Música Catalana or at the purpose-built, contemporary L'Auditori, while opera is performed at its traditional home, the Gran Teatre del Liceu on La Rambla. Notable festivals include the Festival de Barcelona Grec (July), and there are free concerts in Barcelona's parks each summer, the so-called Música als Parcs.

★ **Ateneu Barcelonès** C/Canuda 6, Barri Gòtic, http:// ateneubcn.org; Ⓜ Catalunya. This 150-year-old cultural association presents a variety of intellectually stimulating events throughout the year, including conferences, film screenings and workshops, as well as concerts and recitals (from Baroque to contemporary), some of which take place in its verdant garden.

L'Auditori C/Lepant 150, Glòries, http://auditori.cat; Ⓜ Marina/Glòries. The city's main concert hall is home to the Orquestra Simfònica de Barcelona i Nacional de Catalunya (OBC), whose weekend concert season runs from October to June. Also featured are other orchestral and chamber works,

nightlife offers a regular diet of great indie, rock, roots and world gigs, followed by club sounds.

LGBTQ+ BARS AND CLUBS, SEE MAP PAGE 618

Aire Chicas C/Diputació 233, Eixample, http://airechicas. com; Ⓜ Passeig de Gràcia. The hottest, most stylish lesbian bar in town is a relaxed place for a drink and a dance to pop, house and retro sounds.

Punto BCN C/Muntaner 63–65, Eixample, http:// grupoarena.com; Ⓜ Universitat. A Gaixample classic that attracts a lively crowd for drinks, chat and music. Wednesday happy hour is a blast, while Friday night is party night.

jazz and world gigs, and music for families.

Gran Teatre del Liceu La Rambla 51–59, http://liceu barcelona.cat; Ⓜ Liceu. Hosts a wide-ranging programme of opera and dance productions, plus other concerts and recitals. The season runs from September to July – note that sales for the next season go on general sale in mid-May.

★ **Palau de la Música Catalana** C/Palau de la Música 4–6, off C/Sant Pere Més Alt, Sant Pere, http://palaumusica. cat; Ⓜ Urquinaona. This is home to the Orfeó Català choral group, and the venue for concerts by the Orquestra Ciutat de Barcelona, among others, though throughout the year you can catch anything here, from *sardanes* (see page 649) to pop concerts.

DANCE

Barcelona is very much a contemporary dance city, with its own dedicated dance venue, Mercat de les Flors, as well as regular performances by regional, national and international artists and companies at theatre venues like the TNC, Teatre Lliure and Institut del Teatre.

Mercat de les Flors C/Lleida 59, Montjuïc, http:// mercatflors.cat; Ⓜ Poble Sec. The city's old flower market serves as the "national centre for movement arts", with dance the central focus of its varied programme – from Asian performance art to European contemporary dance.

FILM

At most of the larger cinemas and multiplexes films are usually shown dubbed into Spanish or Catalan, though several cinemas do screen mostly original-language ("*VO*") foreign films. Tickets cost around €7–9, and most cinemas have one night (usually Mon or Wed) when entry is discounted, usually to around €5–6.

Cinema Maldà C/Pi 5, Barri Gòtic, http://cinemamalda. com; Ⓜ Liceu. Hidden away in a little shopping centre, just up from Pl. del Pi, the Maldà is a great place for independent movies and festival winners, all in *VO*.

FilmoTeca de Catalunya Pl. Salvador Seguí 1–9, El Raval, http://filmoteca.cat; Ⓜ Liceu. Run by the Catalan

CELEBRATING CATALAN-STYLE

Catalunya's national folk dance, the **sardana**, is danced every week in front of La Seu, in Pl. de la Seu (every Sun at 11.15 from February to July). Mocked in the rest of Spain, the dance is, the Catalans claim, very democratic. Participants (there's no limit on numbers) all hold hands in a circle, each puts something in the middle as a sign of community and sharing, and since it is not overly energetic (hence the jibes), old and young can join in equally.

The main event in a **traditional Catalan festival** is usually a parade, either promenading behind a revered holy image (as on saints' days or at Easter) or a more celebratory costumed affair that's the centrepiece of a neighbourhood festival. At the main Santa Eulàlia (Feb), Festes de Gràcia (Aug) and La Mercè (Sept) festivals, and others, you'll encounter parades of *gegants*, 5m-high giants with papier-mâché heads based on historical or traditional figures. Also typically Catalan is the **correfoc** ("fire-running"), where brigades of drummers, dragons and devils with spark-shooting flares fitted to pitchforks, cavort in the streets. Perhaps most peculiar of all are the **castellers**, the human tower-builders who draw crowds at every traditional festival, as they pile person upon person, feet on shoulders, to see who can construct the highest, most aesthetically pleasing tower (ten human storeys is the record).

10

government, the FilmoTeca shows three to five different films (often foreign-language, and usually in VO) every day – the programme changes every couple of weeks. Tickets are around half the price of those at commercial cinemas.

Sala Montjuïc Castell de Montjuïc, http://salamontjuic. org. During summer there's a giant-screen open-air cinema at Montjuïc castle – bring a picnic or buy food there. Screenings are in the original language, with Spanish subtitles, and deckchairs are available for hire. Catch the Telefèric de Montjuïc cable car (see page 626), or the cinema bus from Pl. d'Espanya (Ⓜ Espanya; departures from 8.30pm, returns when film finishes).

Verdi C/Verdi 32, and **Verdi Park** C/Torrijos 49, Gràcia, http://cines-verdi.com; Ⓜ Fontana. Sister cinemas in adjacent streets showing independent, art-house and VO movies.

THEATRE AND CABARET

Barcelona's two big theatrical projects are the Teatre Nacional de Catalunya (Catalan National Theatre), which promotes Catalan productions; and the Ciutat del Teatre (Theatre City) on Montjuïc, which incorporates the progressive Teatre Lliure and the Institut del Teatre theatre and dance school. Local productions draw on the city's strong cabaret tradition – more music-hall entertainment than stand-up comedy, and thus more accessible to non-Catalan/Spanish speakers. For last-minute tickets visit the Palau de la Virreina (La Rambla 99), which offers same-day half-price tickets from 3hr before the show.

L'Antic Teatre C/Verdaguer i Callis 12, Sant Pere, http:// lanticteatre.com; Ⓜ Urquinaona. Independent theatre with a wildly original programme of events, many free, from video shows to offbeat cabaret performances. In the end, though, the best bit may just be the garden bar.

★ **Cafè Teatre Llantiol** C/Riereta 7, El Raval, http:// llantiol.com; Ⓜ Sant Antoni. Idiosyncratic cabaret café-theatre offering a mix of mime, song, clowning, magic and dance. Shows normally begin at 8.30pm and 10.30pm, with late-night specials on Friday and Saturday.

El Molino C/Vila i Vilà 99, Avda. Paral·lel, Poble Sec, http:// elmolinobcn.com; Ⓜ Paral·lel. One of Barcelona's most famous old cabaret theatres – the self-styled "Little Moulin Rouge" – has a classy new look for its burlesque and music stage shows.

Teatre Lliure Pl. Margarida Xirgu 1, Montjuïc, http:// teatrelliure.cat; Ⓜ Poble Sec. The "Free Theatre" performs the work of contemporary Catalan and Spanish playwrights, as well as reworkings of the classics, from Shakespeare to David Mamet (some productions have English subtitles).

Teatre Nacional de Catalunya (TNC) Pl. de les Arts 1, Glòries, http://tnc.cat; Ⓜ Glòries. Features major productions by Catalan, Spanish and European companies, including translated classics (such as Shakespeare in Catalan), original works and productions by guest companies. Also hosts smaller-scale plays, experimental works and dance productions.

SHOPPING   SEE MAPS PAGES 602, 606, 618, 625 AND 632

While not on a par with Paris or the world's other style capitals, Barcelona still leads the way in Spain when it comes to **shopping**. It's the country's fashion and publishing capital, and there's a long tradition of innovative *disseny*

(design), from clothes and accessories to crafts and household goods. The annual sales (*rebaixes*; *rebajas* in Castilian) follow the main fashion seasons – mid-January until the end of February, and throughout July and August.

10

ANTIQUES, ARTS, CRAFTS AND GIFTS

The best area for antiques browsing is around C/Palla, between La Seu and Pl. del Pí, combined with the antique market on Thursdays in front of La Seu. The Tallers Oberts, or Open Workshops (http://tallersobertsbarcelona.cat), are usually held over the last two weekends of May, when there are studio visits, exhibitions and other events.

★ **Almacen Marabi** C/Flassaders 31, La Ribera, http://almacenmarabi.blogspot.com; Ⓜ Jaume I. Mariela Marabi makes handmade felt finger dolls, mobiles, puppets and animals of extraordinary invention. Her eye-popping workshop also has limited-edition pieces by other selected artists and designers.

Almacenes del Pilar C/Boqueria 43, Barri Gòtic, http://adelpilar.com; Ⓜ Liceu. A world of frills, lace, cloth and materials used in the making of Spain's traditional regional costumes – pick up a decorated fan for just a few euros.

L'Arca C/Banys Nous 20, Barri Gòtic, http://larca.es; Ⓜ Liceu. Catalan brides used to fill up their nuptial trunk (*arca*) with embroidered bedlinen and lace, and this shop is a treasure trove of vintage and antique textiles.

Artesania Catalunya C/Banys Nous 11, Barri Gòtic, http://bcncrafts.com; Ⓜ Liceu. Changing exhibitions in the showroom of the local government's arts and crafts promotion board, from contemporary basketwork to colourful glassware.

Cereria Subirà Bxda. Llibreteria 7, Barri Gòtic, http://cereriasubira.cat; Ⓜ Jaume I. Barcelona's oldest shop (since 1760) has a beautiful interior, selling hand-crafted candles.

Estanc Duaso C/Balmes 116, Esquerra de l'Eixample, www.duaso.com; Ⓜ Diagonal/FGC Provença. Owned and run by Jordi Duaso, president of Barcelona's Tobacconist's Guild, this cigar-smoker's paradise features a huge walk-in humidor, expert advice and regular workshops by international cigar-makers, who roll stogies in store by hand.

★ **Fantastik** C/Joaquin Costa 62, El Raval, http://fantastik.es; Ⓜ Universitat. You'll never know how you lived without such beguiling gifts, whether it's Chinese robots, African baskets, Russian domino sets or Vietnamese kitchen scales.

Vuelasola C/Zamora 103-105, Poblenou, http://vuelasola.com; Ⓜ Jaume I. A shop-cum-workshop tucked away on one of La Ribera's quietest streets, this is a great place for an unusual gift, with stylish bowls and serving dishes, mugs, mobiles and hand-painted ceramic fish in cream and pastel shades. You can watch the artists at work and join in one of their regular ceramic workshops if you'd like to have a go yourself.

BOOKS

Altaïr Gran Vía de les Corts Catalanes 616, Eixample, http://altair.es; Ⓜ Universitat. This travel superstore has a massive selection of travel books, guides, maps and world music, plus a programme of travel-related talks and exhibitions.

★ **La Central del Raval** C/Elisabets 6, El Raval, http://lacentral.com; Ⓜ Catalunya. Occupying a unique space in the former Misericordia chapel, La Central is a fantastically stocked arts and humanities treasure trove, with books piled high in every nook and cranny.

Hibernian Books C/Verdi 66, Gràcia, http://hibernianbooks.com; Ⓜ Fontana. Barcelona's best secondhand English bookstore has around forty thousand titles in stock – they're not particularly cheap, but you can part-exchange, and there are occasionally giveaway bargains available.

CLOTHES, SHOES AND ACCESSORIES

New designers can be found in the medieval streets and alleys of La Ribera, around Pg. del Born, but also down C/Avinyó in the Barri Gòtic, between C/Carme and MACBA in El Raval, and along C/Verdi in Gràcia. For secondhand and vintage clothing, stores line the whole of C/Riera Baixa (El Raval), with others nearby on C/Carme and C/l'Hospital, and on Saturdays there's a street market there.

Antonio Miró C/Enric Granados 46, Eixample Esquerra, http://antoniomiro.com; Ⓜ Passeig de Gràcia. Barcelona's most innovative designer, especially good for classy suits, though now also branding accessories and household design items.

Camper Passeig de Gràcia 4, Eixample Dreta, http://camper.com; Ⓜ Catalunya. Spain's favourite shoe store opened its first shop in Barcelona in 1981. Providing hip, well-made, casual city footwear at a good price has been the cornerstone of its success. There are several other branches throughout the city.

La Comercial C/Rec 73, La Ribera, http://lacomercial.info; Ⓜ Jaume I. Three boutiques – all clustered around C/Rec – comprise the fabulous La Comercial, which carries a carefully curated selection of on-trend men's and women's fashion and fragrances.

Mango Pg. de Gràcia 65, Eixample, http://mango.com; Ⓜ Passeig de Gràcia. Mango, now available worldwide, began in Barcelona and prices here are generally a bit cheaper than in North America or other European countries.

Mango Outlet C/Girona 37, Eixample, http://mangooutlet.com; Ⓜ Girona. Last season's Mango gear at unbeatable prices, with items starting at just a few euros. The shop is in the city's "garment district" and there are other outlet stores in the same neighbourhood.

★ **La Manual Alpargatera** C/d'Avinyó 7, Barri Gòtic, http://lamanual.com; Ⓜ Liceu. Traditional workshop making *alpargatas* (espadrilles) to order, as well as other straw, rope and basketwork.

Petit Gegant C/Parlament 65, Sant Antoni, http://petitgegant; Ⓜ Poble Sec. Located on what is currently Barcelona's coolest street, this small boutique, hung with bunting and balloons, is a yummy mummy's dream. Kit out your tot in colourful, stylish designs (age range 0–8), with funky T-shirts, sleepsuits and leggings, plus bibs, muslins and organic lotions.

DEPARTMENT STORES AND MALLS

Note that cafés and leisure outlets in malls often open later than the shop hours given below, and on Sunday, while the normal shops don't.

Arenas de Barcelona Gran Via de les Corts Catalanes 373–385, Eixample, http://arenasdebarcelona.com; ⓂEspanya. This designer mall is a glam refit of a former bullring, and while it's bigger on leisure facilities than shops and boutiques, you won't want to miss the view from the circular rooftop promenade.

El Corte Inglés Pl. de Catalunya 14, Eixample, http://elcorteingles.es; ⓂCatalunya. The city's largest department store has outlets all over the city – visit the flagship Pl. de Catalunya branch for nine storeys of clothes, accessories, cosmetics, household goods, toys and the top-floor café.

L'Illa Avda. Diagonal 557, Les Corts, http://lilla.com; ⓂMaría Cristina. The landmark uptown shopping mall is stuffed full of designer fashion (including the local Beatriz Furest), plus Camper (shoes), FNAC (music, film and books), Decathlon (sports), El Corte Inglés (department store), Caprabo (supermarket), gourmet food hall and much more.

DESIGN AND STYLE

Cubiña C/Mallorca 291, Eixample, http://cubinya.es; ⓂVerdaguer. The building itself is stupendous – Domènech i Montaner's *modernista* Casa Thomas – while inside holds the very latest in household design, from slinky CD racks to €5,000 dining tables.

FOOD AND DRINK

One of the best local supermarket chains is Mercadona (http://mercadona.es), which has a useful branch on Ronda de Sant Pere 31, and there are lots of others dotted throughout the city. The most convenient downtown supermarket is that in the basement of El Corte Inglés (Pl. de Catalunya), and there are also Carrefour markets at La Rambla 113 and Via Laietana 48 in Sant Pere.

Bubó C/Caputxes 10, La Ribera, http://bubo.es; ⓂJaume I. There are chocolates and then there are Bubó chocolates – jewel-like creations and playful desserts by pastry maestro Carles Mampel.

★ **Casa Gispert** C/Sombrerers 23, La Ribera, http://casagispert.com; ⓂJaume I. Roasters of nuts, coffee and spices for over 170 years. It's a truly delectable store of wooden boxes, baskets, stacked shelves and tantalizing smells.

La Colmena Pl. Àngel 12, Barri Gòtic, http://pastisseria lacolmena.com; ⓂJaume I. Established in 1849, "the hive" has a huge range of traditional Catalan cakes, pastries and sweets prettily displayed in wooden cabinets in its carefully preserved interior. In autumn, try the *panellets* (marzipan balls, often covered with pine nuts), or choose a bag of daintily wrapped sweets that have been handmade to the same recipe for well over a century.

★ **Entre Latas** C/Torrijos 16, Gràcia, http://entrelatas-bcn.com; ⓂJoanic. A truly charming shop, with beautifully arranged displays of stylishly packaged gourmet tinned goods, from smoked sardines from Riga to razor clams from Galicia. To accompany them, pick up a box of artisan crackers and a bottle of vermouth, all with equally attractive packaging.

Forn Baluard C/Baluard 38–40, Barceloneta, http://baluardbarceloneta.com; ⓂBarceloneta. There are scores of bakeries in Barcelona, but when push comes to shove, foodies pick the Baluard, right next to Barceloneta market (they also have several other shops throughout the city), whose passion for artisan bread, cakes and pastries knows no bounds.

Papabubble C/Banys Nou 3, Barri Gòtic, http://papa bubble.com; ⓂLiceu. Groovy young things rolling out home-made candy to a chill-out soundtrack. Come and watch them at work, sample a sweetie, and take home a gorgeously wrapped gift.

Vila Viniteca C/Agullers 7 & 9, La Ribera, http://vilaviniteca. es; ⓂBarceloneta. A very knowledgeable specialist in Catalan and Spanish wines. Pick your vintage and then nip over the road for the gourmet deli part of the operation.

MUSIC

Independent music and CD stores are concentrated around C/Tallers (El Raval), off La Rambla.

Revólver Records C/Tallers 11, El Raval, http://revolverrecords.es; ⓂCatalunya. Revólver sells the city's best selection of vinyl at the lowest prices. Defiantly old-school, it's a record shop like they used to make them. It's next door to its near-identically named but separately run sister shop, Discos Revólver. Mon–Sat 10am–8.30pm.

★ **Wah Wah Discos** C/Riera Baixa 14, El Raval, www.wah-wahsupersonic.com; ⓂLiceu. Vinyl heaven for record collectors – rock, indie, garage, 1970s punk, electronica, blues, folk, prog, jazz, soul and rarities of all kinds.

10

DIRECTORY

Banks and exchange For exchange offices, look down La Rambla, or go to Barcelona Sants station; El Corte Inglés, Pl. de Catalunya; or Turisme de Catalunya tourist office, Pl. de Catalunya 17.

Consulates Australia, Avda. Diagonal 433, Esquerra de l'Eixample, 933 623 792, http://spain.embassy.gov.au; ⓂDiagonal; Canada, Pl. de Catalunya 9, 932 703 614, http://canadainternational.gc.ca/spain-espagne, ⓂCatalunya; Republic of Ireland, Gran Vía Carles III 94, Les Corts, 934 915 021, http://embassyofireland.es, ⓂMaría Cristina/Les Corts; New Zealand, Travessera de Gràcia 64, ⓂGràcia, 932 090 399, http://mfat.govt.nz, FGC Gràcia; UK, Avda. Diagonal 477, Eixample, 933 666 200, www.ukinspain.fco. gov.uk, ⓂHospital Clínic; USA Pg. de la Reina Elisenda 23,

10

Sarrià, 932 802 227, http://barcelona.usconsulate.gov, FGC Reina Elisenda.

Hospitals For emergency hospital treatment, call 061 or go to one of the following central hospitals, which have 24hr accident and emergency (*urgències*) services: Centre Perecamps, C/Pieyre de Mandiargues 5, El Raval, ⓂDrassanes; Hospital Clínic i Provincial, C/Villaroel 170, Eixample, ⓂHospital Clínic; Hospital del Mar, Pg. Marítím 25–29, Vila Olímpica, ⓂCiutadella-Vila Olímpica; Hospital de la Santa Creu i Sant Pau, C/Sant Quintí, Eixample, ⓂHospital de Sant Pau.

Laundries LavaXpres, at eighteen locations, including C/ Junta de Comerç 10, El Raval, ⓂLiceu, and C/Nou de Sant Francesc 5, Barri Gòtic, ⓂLiceu, http://lavaxpres.com.

Left luggage There are left-luggage offices (*consigna*) at Barcelona Sants train station and Barcelona Nord bus station. Locker Barcelona, near Plaça Catalunya at C/ Estruc 36, Barri Gòtic, lockerbarcelona.com, ⓂCatalunya/ Urquinaona, lets you access your belongings throughout the day free of charge, and offers other services such as luggage weighing, boarding pass printing, a changing room and internet access.

Pharmacies Usual hours are weekdays 9am–1pm and 4–8pm. At least one in each neighbourhood is open daily 24hr (and marked as such) – a convenient central option is Farmàcia Clapés, La Rambla 89 (http://farmalarambla24h. com).

Police Guàrdia Urbana station at La Rambla 43, opposite Pl. Reial (932 562 477; ⓂLiceu; 24hr; English spoken). To get a police report for your insurance, go to the Mossos d'Esquadra (Catalan police force) station at C/Nou de la Rambla 76–80, El Raval (933 062 300; ⓂParal·lel) – take your passport as proof of ID. Contact the police on: Mossos d'Esquadra 112, Policía Nacional 091, Guàrdia Urbana 092.

Post offices The main post office (*Correus*) is on Pl. Correus, Barri Gòtic, http://correos.es, ⓂBarceloneta/Jaume I (Mon–Fri 8.30am–9.30pm, Sat 8.30am–2pm).

Swimming pools The city's most spectacular pool is the open-air Piscina Municipal de Montjuïc, Avda. Miramar 31, Montjuïc, Funicular de Montjuïc. Indoor and outdoor beachside pools at Club Natació Atlètic Barceloneta, Pl. del Mar, ⓂBarceloneta.

Telephone offices There are a handful of *locutorios*, which specialize in discounted overseas connections, scattered through the old city, particularly in El Raval.

Montserrat

The mountain of **Montserrat**, with its strangely shaped crags of rock, its monastery and ruined hermitage caves, stands just 40km northwest of Barcelona, off the road to Lleida. It's the most popular day-trip from the city, reached in around ninety minutes by train and then cable car or rack railway for a thrilling ride up to the monastery. Once there, you can visit the basilica and monastery buildings, and complete your day with a walk around the woods and crags, using the two funicular railways that depart from the monastery complex. Inevitably, both monastery and mountain are ruthlessly advertised as a tourist trip from the city or the Costa Brava, while the main **pilgrimages** take place on April 27 and September 8, but don't be put off – the place itself is still magical and well worth a visit.

Monestir de Montserrat

Legends hang easily upon Montserrat. Fifty years after the birth of Christ, St Peter is said to have deposited an image of the Virgin carved by St Luke in one of the mountain caves. The so-called Black Virgin (La Moreneta) icon was subsequently lost in the early eighth century, after being hidden during the Muslim invasion, but reappeared in 880, accompanied by the customary visions and celestial music. A chapel was built to house it, superseded in 976 by a Benedictine monastery, the Monestir de Montserrat, set at an altitude of nearly 1000m. Miracles abounded and the Virgin of Montserrat soon became the chief cult image of Catalunya and a pilgrimage centre second in Spain only to Santiago de Compostela. Its fortunes declined in the nineteenth century, though in recent decades Montserrat's popularity has again become established. Today, in addition to the tourists, tens of thousands of newly married couples come here to seek La Moreneta's blessing.

The monastery's various outbuildings – including hotel and restaurant, post office, souvenir shop, self-service cafeteria and bar – fan out around an open square, and there are extraordinary mountain views from the terrace.

MONTSERRAT BOYS' CHOIR

Montserrat is awash in spirituality – but never more so than when the Montserrat's world-famous **boys' choir** sings. Time your visit to hear the boys' soaring voices fill the basilica (Mon–Fri 1pm). The choir belongs to the Escolania (http://escolania.cat), a choral school established in the fourteenth century and unchanged in musical style since its foundation. One of the oldest boy's choirs in Europe, the Escolania is comprised of boys aged 9 to 14 who receive a rigorous music-focused education at Montserrat. Unlike its famous European counterparts, the choir has rarely toured abroad – that is, until recently. After performing in the US for the first time in 2014, the choir returned in 2017, making appearances on both coasts.

10

Basílica

Free

Of the religious buildings, only the Renaissance **Basílica** is open to the public. **La Moreneta** stands above the high altar, and the approach to this beautiful icon reveals the enormous wealth of the monastery, as you queue along a corridor leading through the back of the basilica's rich side chapels. The best time to visit the basilica is when Montserrat's world-famous **boys' choir** sings (see page 653).

Museu de Montserrat

Charge • http://museudemontserrat.com

The **Museu de Montserrat** presents a few archeological finds brought back by travelling monks, together with paintings and sculpture dating from as early as the thirteenth century, including works by Old Masters, French Impressionists and Catalan *modernistas*. There's also a collection of Byzantine icons, though other religious items are in short supply as many of the monastery's valuables were carried off by Napoleon's troops, who sacked the complex in 1811.

Mountain walks

Funicular departures vary by season, but mostly every 20min, 10am–5pm • Charge

Following the mountain tracks to the nearby caves and hermitages, you can contemplate Goethe's observation of 1816: "Nowhere but in his own Montserrat will a man find happiness and peace." One funicular drops to the path for **Santa Cova**, a seventeenth-century chapel built where the La Moreneta icon is said to have been found. It's an easy walk there and back, which takes less than an hour. The other funicular rises steeply to the hermitage of **Sant Joan**, from where it's a tougher 45-minute walk to the **Sant Jeroni** hermitage, and another fifteen minutes to the **Sant Jeroni summit** at 1236m.

ARRIVAL AND INFORMATION   MONTSERRAT

There are two ways to reach Montserrat by public transport: either by cable car or mountain railway, but in the first instance you need to take the **FGC train** (line R5, direction Manresa), which leaves Barcelona's Pl. d'Espanya (Ⓜ Espanya) daily at hourly intervals.

By cable car Get off the train at Aeri de Montserrat (50min) for the connecting cable car (http://aeridemontserrat.com). You may have to queue for 15min or so, but then it's an exhilarating 5min swoop up the sheer mountainside to a terrace just below the monastery.

By mountain railway The Montserrat mountain railway, the Cremallera de Montserrat (http://cremallerade montserrat.cat), departs from Monistrol de Montserrat (the next stop after Aeri de Montserrat, another 5min) and takes 20min to complete the climb.

By car Take the A2 motorway as far as the Martorell exit, and then follow the N11 and C55 to the Montserrat turn-off – or park at either the cable-car or the mountain-railway station and take the rides up instead. All-in cable-car/*cremallera*/Montserrat attraction combo tickets are available at the station for drivers who park-and-ride.

Visitor Centre http://montserratvisita.com. You can pick up maps of the complex and mountain here, and staff can also advise about the accommodation options.

Catalunya

CADAQUÉS

Catalunya

Barcelona may make the biggest splash with visitors, but it's the rest of Catalunya that defines the region's distinct – and proud – identity. From the soaring Pyrenees to the Mediterranean-licked coast, from fragrant vineyards to tiny stone villages, this is a region that, perhaps more than anywhere else in Spain, feels like a country unto itself. You'll hear Catalan – and only Catalan – on the streets of many inland communities. And, though Barcelona leads the way in Catalan dining, it's beyond the city where you'll find even purer (and dare we say better) versions of the cuisine, rooted in Catalunya's natural bounty, from wild mushrooms to sun-warmed tomatoes. Catalan towns are generally very well-maintained – and often surprisingly prosperous – a relic of the early industrial era when Catalunya developed more rapidly than most of Spain. There's a confidence in being Catalan that dates back to its fourteenth-century Golden Age, when it was part of the large Kingdom of Aragon, which ruled the Balearics, Valencia, the French border regions, and even Sardinia. Times have changed, of course, but the Catalan flag continues to exert a certain power that you'll feel in all corners of the region.

Catalunya (Cataluña in Castilian Spanish, Catalonia in English) is, above all, a spectacular study in contrasts, from the snowy peaks of the Pyrenees to the sparkling blue water of the coast's shallow coves. The showy swagger of Costa Brava's mega-resorts, meanwhile, mixes alluringly with the stillness of ancient monasteries hidden in the heartland. Despite this diversity, however, Catalunya is relatively compact, so it's possible – as many a local will proudly point out – to ski in the morning and sunbathe on the beach in the afternoon.

On the whole everything is easily reached from Barcelona; the city is linked to most main centres by excellent bus and train services. The obvious targets are the **coasts** north and south of the city, and the various **provincial capitals** (Girona, Tarragona and Lleida), all of which make for comfortable day-trips. Even on a short trip, you can take in the medieval city of **Girona** and the surrounding area, which includes the lush **Empordà wine** region, as well as the best of the beach towns on the **Costa Brava**, which runs up to the French border. This was one of the first stretches of Spanish coast to be developed for mass tourism, and though that's no great recommendation, the large, brash resorts are tempered by some more isolated beaches and lower-key holiday and fishing villages, such as **Cadaqués**. Just inland from the coast, **Figueres** contains the Teatre-Museu Dalí, Catalunya's biggest tourist attraction.

With more time, you can head for the **Catalan Pyrenees**, which offer magnificent and relatively isolated hiking territory, particularly in and around the **Parc Nacional de Aigüestortes**, and good skiing in winter. South of Barcelona, the **Costa Daurada** features a fine beach at **Sitges** and the attractive coastal town of **Tarragona**; inland, the appealing **cava vineyards** around Sant Sadurní d'Anoia or the romantic monastery of **Poblet** figure as approaches to the enjoyable provincial capital of **Lleida**.

Brief history

The **Catalan people** have an individual and deeply felt historical and cultural identity, seen most clearly in the language, which takes precedence over Castilian on street names and signs. Despite being banned for over thirty years during the Franco

Highlights

❶ Empordà wine country Sip your way through the scenic vineyards of the up-and-coming wine region of Empordà, where new, small-batch wineries are turning out award-winning vintages. See page 677

❷ Cadaqués Experience the Costa Brava as it once was at this lovely, quirky seaside town. See page 679

❸ Girona This beautiful, labyrinthine city boasts a two-thousand-year-old history, including one of the best-preserved medieval Jewish quarters in the country. See page 682

❹ El Celler de Can Roca Feast on elevated Catalan cuisine at this gastronomical heavyweight helmed by the Roca brothers, or try their latest culinary venture – *Restaurant Normal* – which opened in Girona in July 2021. See page 687

❺ Teatre-Museu Dalí Explore the life and work of the flamboyant artist at this shrine to Surrealism. See page 689

❻ Skiing Baqueira-Beret Grab the ski poles: this premiere ski resort offers the finest skiing in the Pyrenees, if not in Spain. See page 713

❼ Sitges Sample the frenetic nightlife or, better still, the *Carnaval*, of chic Sitges. See page 717

HIGHLIGHTS ARE MARKED ON THE MAP ON PAGE 658

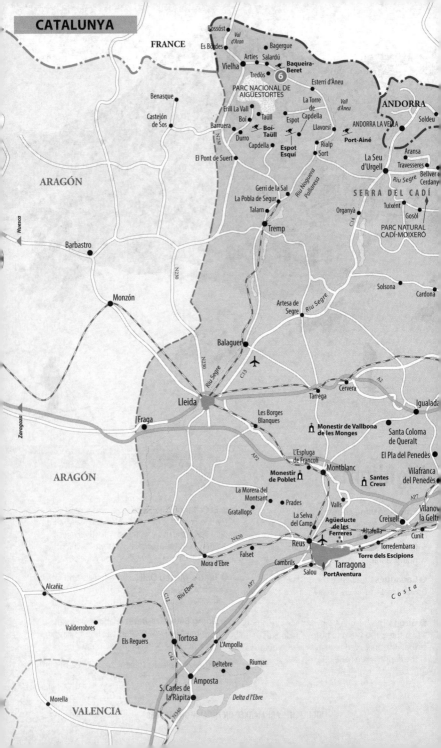

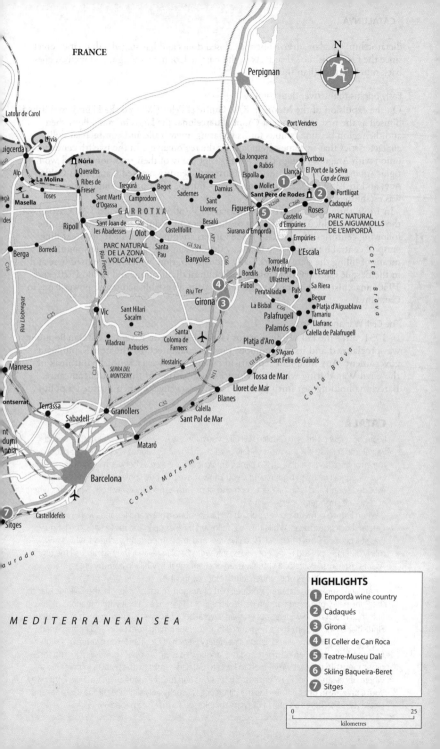

FRANCE

MEDITERRANEAN SEA

HIGHLIGHTS

1. Empordà wine country
2. Cadaqués
3. Girona
4. El Celler de Can Roca
5. Teatre-Museu Dalí
6. Skiing Baqueira-Beret
7. Sitges

0 ————————————— 25
kilometres

N

dictatorship, Catalan survived behind closed doors and has staged a dramatic comeback since the Generalísimo's death. As in the Basque Country, though, regionalism goes back much farther than this.

Early origins to the twentieth century

On the expulsion of the Moors in 874, Guifré el Pelós (Wilfred the Hairy) established himself as the first independent **Count of Barcelona**; the lands he ruled flourished and the region became famous for its seafaring, mercantile and commercial skills, characteristics that to some extent still set the region apart. In the twelfth century came union with Aragón, though the Catalans kept many of their traditional, hard-won rights (*usatges*). From then until the fourteenth century marked Catalunya's **Golden Age**, and in 1359 the Catalan Generalitat – Europe's first parliamentary government – was established.

In 1469, through the marriage of Fernando V (of Aragón) to Isabel I (of Castile), the region was added on to the rest of the emergent Spanish state. Throughout the following centuries the Catalans made various attempts to secede from the stifling grasp of central bureaucracy, which saw the Catalan enterprise as merely another means of filling the state coffers. Early industrialization, which was centred here and in the Basque Country, only intensified political disaffection, and in the 1920s and 1930s anarchist, communist and socialist parties all established major power bases in Catalunya.

The Civil War and Franco

In 1931, after the fall of the dictator General Primo de Rivera, a **Catalan Republic** was proclaimed and its autonomous powers guaranteed by the new Republican government. Any incipient separatism collapsed, however, with the outbreak of the Civil War, during which Catalunya was a bastion of the Republican cause, Barcelona holding out until January 1939. In revenge, Franco pursued a policy

---

CATALÀ

Learning a few phrases in Catalan will take you a long way. Few visitors realize that outside Barcelona, at least, it is the most widely used language in Catalunya and sometimes commit the error of calling it a dialect. On paper, *Català* looks like a cross between French and Spanish and is generally easy to understand if you know those two but, spoken, it has a distinct, rounded sound and is far harder to come to grips with, especially away from Barcelona, where accents are stronger.

When Franco came to power, publishing houses, bookshops and libraries were raided and Catalan books destroyed. While this was followed by a let-up in the mid-1940s, the language was still banned from the radio, TV, daily press and, most importantly, schools, which is why many older people today cannot necessarily write Catalan (even if they speak it all the time). As for Castilian, in Barcelona virtually everyone can speak it, while in country areas, many people can sometimes only understand it but not speak it.

Catalan is spoken in Catalunya proper, part of Aragón, much of Valencia, the Balearic Islands, the Principality of Andorra and in parts of the French Pyrenees, albeit with variations of dialect (it is thus much more widely spoken than several better-known languages such as Danish, Finnish and Norwegian). It is a Romance language, stemming from Latin and, more directly, from medieval Provençal and *lemosi*, the literary French of Occitania. The grammar is slightly more complicated than Castilian, and the language has eight vowel sounds (including three diphthongs). In the text we've tried to keep to Catalan names (with Castilian in parentheses where necessary) – not least because street signs and *turisme* maps are in Catalan. Either way, you're unlikely to get confused as the difference is usually only slight: ie Girona (Gerona) and Lleida (Lérida). There's a Catalan glossary to help you further (see page 865).

FESTIVALS AND EVENTS

FEBRUARY/MARCH/APRIL

Lent: Carnaval Sitges has Catalunya's best celebrations.
Easter: Setmana Santa (Holy Week) Celebrations at Besalú, Girona, Tarragona and La Pobla de Segur.
April 23: Setmana Medieval de Sant Jordi St George is celebrated throughout Catalunya, with a week of exhibitions, dances and medieval music in Montblanc, among other places.

MAY/JUNE

Throughout May: Festival Jazz In Vic.
First fortnight of May: Festa de la Llana Annual wool fair in Ripoll.
May: Fires i Festes de la Santa Creu Processions and music in Figueres.
Corpus Christi (variable): Festa de Corpus Christi Big processions in Sitges, plus the massive **Patum** festival in Berga.
Mid-May: Temps de Flors Flower festival in Girona.
End May: L'Aplec del Caragol Annual snail festival in Lleida.
June 21–23: Festa de Sant Patllari In Camprodon.
June 24: Dia de Sant Joan Celebrated everywhere.

JULY/AUGUST

Early July to late August: Ripoll International Music Festival Classical music in Ripoll.
Early July: Cantada de Havaneres Sea shanties in Calella de Palafrugell.
Third week of July: Festa de Santa Cristina At Lloret de Mar.
July/early August: Festival Internacional de Música In Torroella de Montgrí.
Mid-July to late August: Cap Roig Festival In Calella de Palafrugell.
Late July: Festa del Renaixement (Renaissance Festival) In Tortosa.
Late July to late August: Festival de Música de Begur In Begur.
Mid-August: Festa de Sant Magi In Tarragona.

SEPTEMBER

22: Sant Maurici At his *ermita* in the national park above Espot.
Second week: Mercat de Música Viva Festival in Vic.
Mid Sept: Festa de Vielha Annual fair.
Third week: Festa de Santa Tecla Human castles (*castells*) and processions of *gegants* (giant puppets) in Tarragona.
Nearest weekend to 24th: Festa de Sant Prim i Felicià At Besalú.

OCTOBER

Third weekend: Sant Ermengol Celebrations in La Seu d'Urgell.
Last week: Fires i Festes de Sant Narcis In Girona.

DECEMBER

Early December: Mercat Medieval de Vic Re-creation of a medieval market.

11

of harsh suppression, attempting to wipe out all evidence of Catalan cultural and economic primacy. Among his more subtle methods was the encouragement of immigration from other parts of Spain in order to dilute regional identity. Even so, Catalunya remained obstinate, the scene of protests and demonstrations throughout the dictatorship, and after Franco's death a **Catalan government** was formally reinstated in 1979. This, the semi-autonomous **Generalitat**, enjoys a high profile and continues to extend its power.

11

The independence movement

The years from 2012 to 2018 saw a powerful resurgence in the pro-independence movement. In 2012, there were mass demonstrations of 1.5 million people in Barcelona on September 11, Catalunya's national day. On September 11, 2013, hundreds of thousands formed a human chain, from the northern to southern borders of the region, to promote Catalan autonomy. In November 2015, Catalan politicians voted for a resolution aimed at developing an independent nation by 2017. On September 11, 2016, hundreds of thousands rallied to support Catalunya's secession from Spain. On October 1, 2017, Catalunya held unofficial referendum on independence. The Madrid government, with legal support from the Spanish courts, had pronounced the referendum to be unconstitutional. It turned into a day of reckoning: the Spanish national police launched a crackdown across the region, resulting in violent clashes. The country was submerged into a political plight with no clear outcome. The leaders of the movement were jailed, and sentencing finally came two years later in October 2019, when it was announced that some would be imprisoned for up to thirteen years. This resulted in massive violent protests both in Barcelona and across the region, which lasted for several weeks. Since then, and with the arrival of a Socialist Party government, under prime minister Pedro Sánchez, the nationalist fervour has quieted somewhat. After an inconclusive general election in the summer of 2023, Sánchez offered an amnesty to the architects of the 2017 insurrection if Catalan separatist parties lent their support to return him to power, and for now relative stability appears to have returned.

The Costa Brava

Stretching from Blanes, 60km north of Barcelona, to the French border, the **Costa Brava** (Rugged Coast) is often maligned for its droves of visitors – and attendant mass-tourism infrastructure. But north of the main resorts, the Costa Brava still reveals the "rugged" in its name: wooded coves, high cliffs, gorgeous beaches and deep-blue water. Though it continues to struggle under its image as the first developed package-tour coast in Spain, the Costa Brava is very determinedly moving on to new horizons. Today, in most of the **Costa Brava**, there is a greater focus on the area's natural beauty and fascinating cultural heritage.

Broadly, the coast is split into three areas: **La Selva** at the southern tip, clustered around brash **Lloret de Mar**, and the medieval walled town of **Tossa de Mar**; the stylish central area of **Baix Empordà** between Sant Feliu de Guíxols and Pals, popular with the chic Barcelona crowd, which boasts some wonderfully scenic stretches of rolling coastline around Palamós, the beaches and villages of inland Palafrugell and hilltop Begur; and the more rugged **Alt Empordà** in the north. This area is marked by the broad sweep of the Golf de Roses, site of a nature reserve, the Parc Natural dels Aiguamolls de l'Empordà, and the alluring peace of the ancient Greek and Roman settlement of Empúries, and extends to the bohemian Cadaqués, which attracts an arty crowd paying tribute to Salvador Dalí; the artist lived most of his life in the labyrinthine warren of converted fishermen's huts in a neighbouring cove, now a fabulous museum.

GETTING AROUND   COSTA BRAVA

By car Driving is the easiest way to get around and gives you access to some of the more remote parts of the coast, though expect the smaller coastal roads to be very busy in summer and parking to be tricky in the major towns.

By bus Buses in the region are almost all operated by Moventis (http://compras.moventis.es), which has offices in the bigger towns and offers an efficient service the length of the coast. Teisa (http://teisa-bus.com) also operates

some routes in the area. You could consider using Girona or Figueres as a base for lateral trips to the coast, as both have big bus termini and are within an hour of the beach.

By train The train from Barcelona to the French border runs inland most of the time, serving Girona and Figueres, but emerging on the coast itself only at Llançà. The AVE train, which is faster but pricier, operates from Perpignan in France to Figueres and on to Barcelona.

By boat Between Easter and September, there are daily boat services (*cruceros*), which cover short hops along the coast; there are generally services between Lloret de Mar, Tossa de Mar and Sant Feliu de Guíxols, among other coastal towns. Tourist offices have up-to-date information on companies and schedules; timetables and routes can vary yearly.

By foot You can access some of the lovelier coves by walking all or just parts of the fabulous Camí de Ronda necklace of footpaths that runs along the whole of the coastline.

Lloret de Mar

Brash, tourist-magnet **LLORET DE MAR**, some 66km northeast of Barcelona, is everything you've ever heard about it – and more. Yet underneath its undeniable beach-driven commercialism and gaudy nightlife is a centuries-old town trying to make itself known. The result is a mix of hedonism and history, with music-pumping clubs clustered around a delightful fifteenth-century church, anonymous high-rises alongside genteel mansions and a packed main beach that belies some splendid rocky coves tucked away on either side of town. Lloret's main **beach** and neighbouring Fenals beach is where many of the hotels are grouped; the south end of Fenals, backed by pine woods, is somewhat less crowded. Farther afield are a number of tiny **coves** favoured by local bathers. Cala Santa Cristina and the adjacent Cala Treumal are the best, while the lovely Cala Boadella is popular with nudists; all are off the Blanes road. Any sightseeing in Lloret is centred on the warren of streets in the **old town**, amid the hustle of T-shirt shops and tourist paraphernalia.

11

Church of Sant Romà and Capella del Santíssim
Pl. de l'Església

Holding court over the old town is the colourful church of **Sant Romà** (open for services only), originally built in Gothic style in 1522. A *modernista* renovation was begun in 1914, but much of this work was destroyed in the Civil War; only the adjacent **Capella del Santíssim**, with its Byzantine cupolas, Mudéjar and Renaissance influences, remains.

Museu del Mar
Pg. Camprodon i Arrieta • Charge • 972 364 454

Explore Lloret's maritime legacy – illustrated by ship models, a replica of an 1848 figurehead and photos and mementoes – as well as other aspects of the town's history in the well-run **Museu del Mar**. The museum shares space with one of the town's *turisme* in Can Garriga, a beautifully restored nineteenth-century mansion on the town's stately promenade.

Jardins de Santa Clotilde
Charge • patrimoni.lloret.cat/ca/moll-museu-obert-de-lloret/jardins-de-santa-clotilde

On a headland above the coast, southwest of town, are the surprisingly tranquil **Jardins de Santa Clotilde**, ornamental gardens laid out in *modernista* style in 1919 and offering fabulous views over the Mediterranean. In spring and summer, you can sometimes catch live jazz on the weekends in the gardens; ask at the *turisme* for details.

Cementiri Modernista de Lloret de Mar
Camí del Repòs • Free • patrimoni.lloret.cat/en/moll-open-museum-of-lloret/modernist-cemetery

Head beyond the thronged beaches and noisy bars, and your reward is the quiet **Cementiri Modernista de Lloret de Mar** just west of the town centre. Created in 1901, this impressive cemetery features funerary art by an astonishing line-up of *modernista* greats, including Josep Puig I Cadafalch (see box, page 620), Antoni M. Gallisà i Soqué and Eusebi Arnau. Many of the lavish mausoleums were commissioned by *Indianos*, which is the term for locals who left the Costa Brava in the 1800s to seek fortune in the Americas – mostly Cuba. While many didn't find riches abroad, those who did often returned to build grand mansions and, in the case of this cemetery, mausoleums.

ARRIVAL AND INFORMATION

By bus The bus station is north of the town centre, on Carretera de Blanes. As well as frequent services from nearby Tossa, there are regular buses from Barcelona (hourly; 1hr 5min), Girona (2 hourly; 40min), Palafrugell (2 daily; 1hr 50 mins) and Platja d'Aro (4 daily; 1hr 15min), among others.

By boat *Cruceros* and other coastal boats dock at the beach, which is where the ticket offices are too. In summer there are around a dozen daily services up and down the coast.

Turisme The most central *turisme* is on the seafront at Pg. Camprodon i Arrieta 1 (March to mid-June Mon–Sat 9am–1pm & 4–7pm, Sun 10am–1pm & 4–7pm; mid-June to mid-Sept daily 9am–8pm; mid-Sept to Oct Mon–Sat 9am–1pm & 4–7pm, Sun 10am–1pm & 4–7pm; Nov–Feb Mon–Sat 9am–1pm & 3–6pm, Sun 9am–2pm; http://lloretdemar.org).

ACCOMMODATION AND EATING

Lloret is undeniably a tourist town, with a slew of large hotel-resorts. But gone are the days of noisy pools and bland rooms. Thanks to stiff competition, Lloret's high-rise hotels have been improving over the years, with an enhancement in services, amenities and decor. Plus, you'll also find decent smaller spots in the old part of town, not far from the beach.

Though Lloret may be the domain of fast-food joints and fish and chips, there's still a reasonably good choice of places to **eat** in the old town. **Clubs** are mainly centred around Avda. Just Marlés, the main road into town running perpendicular to the seafront, while lively **bars** dot the streets around Pl.

CUINA CATALANA

Catalunya has a fantastic climate, a rich plurality of products and diverse geography – the sea, the mountains, and the plains. There are few parts of the world this fertile.

Ferran Adrià

That's how the famous Catalan chef describes his home region's geographical bounty, source of its rich *cuina catalana*. Culled from **"mar i muntanya"** (sea and mountain), Catalunya's cuisine matches fresh seafood on the coast with hearty meats (particularly sausages) inland, while fragrant fruits and vegetables provide ballast to every meal.

The **seafood** variety is impressive, and includes plump shrimp and langoustine; eel from the Ebro delta; trout from Pyrenean rivers; and the ever-present *bacallà* (cod). **Sausages**, most using pork as a base, include *botifarra*, *fuet* (a thin, dried sausage) and *llonganissa* (cured sausage). Catalunya has taken **mushrooms** to a high art, not least aromatic *bolets* (wild mushrooms), which are picked and prepared in autumn. In late winter and early spring, *calçots* (large, tender, sweet spring onions) are roasted over coals and dipped in **romesco** sauce, which is made with tomatoes, peppers, onions, almonds, garlic and olive oil.

Perhaps Catalunya's best-loved export is **pa amb tomàquet**, bread rubbed with tomato and drizzled in olive oil, which is not only ubiquitous throughout the region, but in the rest of Spain. As for dessert: Catalunya's answer to crème brûlée is the custard-style *crema catalana*. And when it comes time to celebrate, do so with **cava** (see box, page 716).

CATALAN CHEFS

Contemporary Catalan cuisine has become synonymous with **Ferran Adrià**, who transformed (and transfixed) the culinary world with his famous scented *espumas* (foams) and "molecular gastronomy" (or, as Ferran prefers to describe it, *cocina de vanguardia*). The effects have gone far beyond the dazzling laboratory of a kitchen in his former restaurant **El Bulli** on the Costa Brava. Ferran closed *El Bulli* in July 2011 to launch a nonprofit culinary foundation (see box, page 678). Chefs across the region have been inspired by Ferran, each adding their own spin, including (in Barcelona) Carles Abellán, as well as Albert Adrià who, with older brother Ferran, opened the excellent tapas bar *Tickets* (see page 644) in 2011, followed by several other restaurants in the city, adding to the Adrià empire. Elsewhere in the region, you'll find restaurants serving elevated Catalan cuisine, including at *Compartir* (see page 680) in Cadaques, helmed by three former *El Bulli* chefs; *El Motel* (see page 691), considered the birthplace of modern Catalan cuisine; and the legendary three-Michelin-starred *Celler de Can Roca* (see page 687), twice voted best restaurant in the world.

d'Espanya and Pl. del Carme, just behind the beach.

Aqua Hotel Bertran Park Avda. del Mar 16, http://
aquahotel.com. Straightforward, well-maintained all-
inclusive hotel that's in a quieter section of the town centre
– away from the party crowds, but close enough to stroll to
the beach. Sizeable rooms are comfortable and clean, plus
there's a swimming pool and buffet restaurant. €€€

Hotel Santa Marta Platja de Santa Cristina, http://
hstamarta.com. A tranquil escape, this luxurious hotel
sits above a quiet beach and the Ermita de Santa Cristina,
between Lloret and Blanes, with elegant rooms, a spa and
lovely views of the sea. 3-night minimum stay in summer. €€€

Sant Pere del Bosc Hotel & Spa Paratge de Sant Pere
del Bosc, 5km inland from Lloret de Mar, http://hotel
santperedelbosc.com. For an elegant change of pace, relax
at this historic Catalan *modernista* boutique hotel. Handsome
individually decorated rooms, named after flowers, poets
and singers, have lovely views – some of the Mediterranean,
and others of the leafy gardens. Ease into the evening at the
inviting restaurant, which serves stellar traditional Catalan
cuisine with a twist, like spinach cannelloni with romesco
sauce and cod with chickpea puree. €€€€

Tossa de Mar

Tossa de Mar is quite a sight upon arrival by boat: medieval walls and the turrets of the
old quarter, **Vila Vella**, rise pale and shimmering on the hill above the modern town.
Tossa has managed to escape the full-blown tourism of Lloret, 13km to the south,
and balances comfortably between restful holiday hub and working town. Founded
originally by the Romans, the town has twelfth-century walls that surround the old
quarter – a maze of cobbled streets, whitewashed houses and flower boxes – and climb
the headland, offering terrific views over beach and bay.

Tossa's best beach is the **Platja de la Mar Menuda**, around the headland away from
the old town and very popular with divers; look for a natural pink cross in the rock,
supposedly marking where Sant Ramon de Penyafort gave a dying man his absolution
in 1235. The central **Platja Gran**, though pleasant, gets crowded; if you have your own
transport, make for the tiny coves north and south of the town, which are much more
rewarding. Booths on the main beach sell tickets for **boat trips** (Easter–Oct) around the
surrounding coastline, including to Sant Feliu.

Far de Tossa and around
Pg. de la Vila Vella

Towering over the Vila Vella is a nineteenth-century lighthouse, the **Far de Tossa**, home to
an innovative exhibition on Mediterranean lighthouses. Just below here, not far from the
ruins of the town's fifteenth-century Gothic church, stands a **statue of Ava Gardner**, who
made the town famous in the 1950 film, *Pandora and the Flying Dutchman*.

Museu Municipal
Pl. Roig i Soler 1 • Charge • 972 340 709

Located in the old quarter, the **Museu Municipal** features a Roman mosaic and
remnants, including ceramic vases, from a nearby excavated Roman villa, and a
Chagall painting, *Celestial Violinist*. Chagall spent summers here for four decades, and
evocatively called Tossa the "blue paradise".

ARRIVAL AND INFORMATION   **TOSSA DE MAR**

By bus The bus station is at Avda. del Pelegrí, behind the
turisme. To reach the centre, and the beaches, head straight
down the road opposite the bus station and turn right along
Avda. Costa Brava. Tossa is an easy day-trip from Barcelona
(16 daily; 1hr 20min) and Lloret (generally every 30min;
40min).

By boat *Crucero* boats stop right at the centre of the beach,

with the ticket offices nearby. Boats travel to Lloret de Mar (up
to 7 daily; 30min), and Platja d'Aro/Sant Antoni de Calonge/
Palamós (up to 5 daily; 1hr 15min/1hr 25min/1hr 45min).

Turisme Avda. del Pelegrí 25, in front of the bus station
(March–May & Oct Mon–Sat 9.30am–1.30pm & 4–7pm;
June–Sept Mon–Sat 9am–9pm; Nov–Feb Mon–Sat
9.30am–4pm; http://infotossa.com).

ACCOMMODATION

There's plenty of accommodation in the warren of tiny   streets around Sant Vicenç church and below the old city

11

walls. There are also a handful of local campsites, all within 2–4km of the centre.

Gran Hotel Reymar Platja de Mar Menuda, http://ghreymar.com. Elegant beachfront hotel across the bay from the Vila Vella. Modern rooms come with marble-clad bathrooms and terraces overlooking the sea. The Reymar Spa offers soothing massages and aromatherapy treatments. Closed Nov–April. €€€€

Hotel Cap d'Or Pg. del Mar 1, http://hotelcapdor.com. Relaxed, friendly, ivy-clad *pensió* on the seafront – in the home of the family who has managed it since 1954 – nestled beneath the walls of the old town. Rates include breakfast. Closed Nov–April. €€

Hotel Delfín Avda. Costa Brava 2, http://hotelesdante.com. Take in the sun from your balcony at this inviting hotel that has spacious, modern rooms with marble bathrooms. It

also has a rooftop pool and restaurant, and the beach is just a 5min saunter away. €€€

Hotel Diana Pl. d'Espanya 6, http://hotelesdante.com. Handsome hotel set in a *modernista* mansion on an attractive square. It has a bar on the seafront and you can also use the facilities at sister hotel *Hotel Delfín*. Large rooms have sea or *plaça* (cheaper) views and tiled floors. Rates include breakfast. Closed Nov–Easter. €€€€

Sea Green, Cala Llevadó 3km out of town, off the road to Lloret, http://calallevado.com. This is one of the better local campsites, with good facilities – swimming pool, bar-restaurant – plus plenty of outdoor activities, from windsurfing to mini-golf. They also have a range of other options, including bungalows, cabins made with natural woods and insulated with the wool from local sheep and cottages. Closed Oct–April. €

EATING AND DRINKING

Tossa offers a plethora of restaurants, from top-notch seafood spots to simple *sangría*-and-tapas joints. Pg. del Mar and the road behind it, C/Portal, are brimming with alfresco options. Come evening, C/Sant Josep gets lively with revellers hitting the bars.

Bahía Pg. del Mar 19, http://restaurantbahiatossa.com. A welcoming interior and breezy terrace are the comfortable setting for tasty seafood meals. €€

Bar La Lluna C/Abat Oliba 10, 972 342 523. Settle in to the outdoor garden patio at this small family-run tapas restaurant that's tucked into a quiet alley in the old town.

The menu is rustically traditional – meatballs in cider, *patatas bravas*, garlic shrimp – along with fresh *sangría*. Note that it is only open April to October. €€

★ **La Cuina de Can Simon** C/Portal 24, http://cuinacansimon.com. This venerable joint turns out classic regional dishes in an elegant dining room of linen-topped tables, stone walls and oil paintings. The menu features a *mar i muntanya* (sea and mountain) section, including suckling lamb and lobster *suquet*, a local stew that originated on the Costa Brava. €€€

Baix Empordà

Baix Empordà, which unfolds north of La Selva, reveals a local flavour – medieval villages, quiet coves, inland countryside that seems to stretch on forever – that's sometimes overshadowed by the splashy tourist infrastructure on other parts of the coast. **Platja d'Aro** is a smarter version of Lloret – with a particularly lively summer nightlife, popular with weekenders from Barcelona – while the working fishing ports of **Sant Feliu de Guíxols** and **Palamós** remain largely (and thankfully) aloof from their boisterous neighbours. Farther north, the area around **Palafrugell** boasts some fabulous cove towns, while hilltop **Begur** stands over a string of lovely little coves. **Inland** lures include the medieval towns of Pals and Peratallada, atmospheric Iberian ruins at Ullastret and the pottery industry of La Bisbal.

Sant Feliu de Guíxols and around

Separated from Tossa by 22km and, reputedly, 365 curves of stunning corniche, **SANT FELIU DE GUÍXOLS** is a bustling town with a decent beach and a cluster of handsome *modernista* buildings, evidence of its prosperous nineteenth-century cork industry. Its origins go back to the tenth century, when a settlement grew up around a Benedictine **monastery**, whose ruins, including the arched Porta Ferrada, still stand in Pl. Monestir.

Sant Feliu's old-world style is at its most apparent in the *modernista* **Casa Patxot** (built in 1917 and now home to the Chamber of Commerce) at Pg. del Mar 40, on the corner of Rambla Portalet, and the curious Moorish-style **Nou Casino La Constància** nearby at Pg. dels Guíxols 1–3, which was begun in 1851 and later adorned with *modernista* touches and brightly coloured swooping arches. The *passeig* follows the sweep of the coarse sand **beach** and yachting marina, while the streets back from the sea are great for a stroll past the shops and bars and the eighteenth-century **Pl. del Mercat**, with its bustling daily market.

Church of Sant Feliu es la Mare de Déu dels Àngels and Museu d'Història de la Ciutat

Pl. del Monestir • Charge • http://museu.guixols.cat

The **Church of Sant Feliu es la Mare de Déu dels Àngels** has a Romanesque facade and beautifully crafted crucifix dating from the same period as the Benedictine monastery, though it was rebuilt in Gothic style in the fourteenth century. The church is open for services only, while the rest of the complex is part of the **Museu d'Història de la Ciutat**, which contains absorbing exhibitions on the history of the town, including local archeological finds, as well as temporary exhibitions on everything from local painters to photographers.

S'Agaró

On a headland north of Sant Feliu is the curious village of **S'AGARÓ**, created in the 1920s, where every house was built in the *modernista* style by Rafael Masó, a student of Antoni Gaudí. The short Camí de Ronda leading to the fabulous **Platja Sa Conca** is the best way to explore and take in a swim.

11

ARRIVAL AND INFORMATION   SANT FELIU DE GUÍXOLS

By bus Teisa bus services to and from Girona stop opposite the monastery, while the Sarfa bus station (for buses to and from Palafrugell, Girona and Barcelona) is a 5min walk north of the centre on the main Carretera de Girona, at the junction with C/Llibertat.

Destinations Barcelona (8 daily; 1hr 25min); Girona (at least hourly; 55mins); Palafrugell (hourly; 55min); Palamós

(hourly; 35min); Platja d'Aro (hourly; 15min).

By boat *Cruceros* (boats) dock on the main beach, where you'll also find the various ticket offices.

Turisme La Rambla 22, 972 820 051 (June–Sept daily 10am–8pm; Oct–May Mon–Sat 9.30am–6pm, Sun 10am–2pm; http://guixols.cat).

ACCOMMODATION AND EATING

Can Segura C/Sant Pere 11, http://cansegurahotel.com/en/restaurant. A cheerful maritime-themed dining room opening on to a sidestreet terrace forms part of a decades-old family-run hotel. The seafood is excellent, as are the various rice dishes. €€€

Cau del Pescador C/Sant Domènec 11, http://caudel pescador.com. This atmospheric spot has a generous choice of seafood, from Sant Feliu anchovies to shrimp and squid, at mid-range prices. €€€

Hostal de la Gavina Pujada de l'Hostal, S'Agaró, http://lagavina.com. Sitting in peaceful grounds overlooking Platja Sant Pol at the southern end of S'Agaró, this five-star hotel features elegant but unpretentious marble-floored rooms adorned with hand-carved vintage furniture and fine antique rugs and lamps; the luxury continues with wood-panelled dining rooms, bars, terraces, a saltwater pool and spa. One of the most famous hotels in the area, it has had a list of famous guests, including Elizabeth Taylor. €€€€

Hostal del Sol Carretera de Palamós 194, http://

hostaldelsol.cat. Take a breather from the beachside bustle at this colonial-style hotel, which rises up near S'Agaró, and has airy rooms that all face out, with lovely views. Plus, there are two pools, as well as a decent complimentary breakfast. Closed mid Oct to Easter. €€

Hotel Barcarola C/Pablo Picasso 1–19, http://hotel barcarola.es. Large, well-run hotel, just north of Sant Feliu, near S'Agaro and Sant Pol Beach. Kick back in comfortable rooms, some with ample terraces with sunbeds. Plus, there's a swimming pool and free parking. €€€

El Trinquet C/Sant Pere 26, http://facebook.com/eltrinquet menjaribeure. With traditional tiled floors and dark wood furniture, this low-key tapas bar is an atmospheric spot for dinner. The menu is regularly updated and may include *gambes amb oli de coco i gingebre* (prawns cooked in coconut oil and ginger), *seitons del Cantàbric* (fresh anchovies with lemon) or *bacalao amb pebrot de piquillo* (salt cod with piquillo peppers). Nab a stool at the bar counter or sit at one of the handful of tables spilling onto the pavement outside. €€

Platja d'Aro and around

A few kilometres to the north of S'Agaró, **PLATJA D'ARO** is a neon strip of bars and shops running parallel to, but hidden from, a long sandy beach. It's by no means picturesque, but it does offer good **nightlife**, a great **beach** and some stylish **shopping**.

Beyond Platja d'Aro, the road leads to the more family-oriented but not terribly pretty town of **Sant Antoni de Calonge**; more enticing are the **coves** and beaches strung out between the two towns, all of which can be reached on foot by the serpentine and at times tricky **Camí de Ronda** or by a number of footpaths descending from the main road.

ARRIVAL AND INFORMATION   PLATJA D'ARO AND AROUND

By bus Regular Sarfa buses travel to Platja d'Aro from around the Costa Brava, including Girona (45min–1hr).
Turisme C/Mossèn Cinto Verdaguer 4, on the junction with

central Avda. S'Agaró (July & Aug 8am–9pm, rest of year daily 9am–1pm & 4–7pm; http://platjadaro.com).

ACCOMMODATION

Platja d'Aro is filled with an array of hotels, from small family-run spots to larger tourist-driven resort hotels.
Hotel Bell Repòs C/Nostra Senora del Carme 18, http://

hotelbellrepos.com. This long-running hotel, with clean, basic rooms, is near the main beach. A hearty buffet breakfast is included. €€

Palamós and around

Immediately northeast of Sant Antoni de Calonge, **Palamós** was founded in 1277 and sacked by Barbarossa in 1543. The town's pleasant old quarter, set apart from the new on a promontory at the eastern end of the bay, makes for a pleasant afternoon wander and an evening at one of the breezy outdoor restaurant terraces.

Accessible from Palamós by road or along the Camí de Ronda are two fabulous **beaches**. The first, the idyllic **Cala S'Alguer**, is framed by nineteenth-century fishermen's huts, while the larger **Platja de Castell** was rescued from the clutches of property developers thanks to a local referendum. Perched on the headland at the northern tip of Platja de Castell are the tranquil ruins of an Iberian settlement.

Museu de la Pesca

Edifici del Tinglado, Port de Palamós • Charge • http://museudelapesca.org

The working fishing port here is home to the interesting **Museu de la Pesca**, which chronicles the town's fishing and maritime history via audiovisual exhibits and historic fishing equipment and other archeological finds. The museum also organizes a variety of activities, many targeted at kids, including sailing, seafood cooking classes and visits to local fish auctions.

ARRIVAL AND INFORMATION   PALAMÓS AND AROUND

By bus Regular Sarfa buses travel to Palamós from around the Costa Brava, including Girona (1hr 25min).
Turisme Pg. del Mar (summer daily 9am–9pm; winter

Mon–Sat 9.30am–2pm & 3–6.30pm, Sun 9.30am–2pm; http://palamos.cat).

EATING

The town features a variety of good traditional restaurants. For **after-dark fun**, the best places are between the old town and the port in the area called La Planassa (towards the end of the promontory).
Maria de Cadaqués C/Tauler i Servià 6, http://

mariadecadaques.cat. This popular restaurant, just off the marina, has an impressive history: it was founded in 1936 as a fishermen's tavern, and continues to serve excellent shellfish and *calamares*. €€€

Palafrugell

A cluster of streets and shops around a sixteenth-century church and the bustling Pl. Nova, **PALAFRUGELL** lies 5km north of Palamós, and 4km inland from the breezy coastline. It's at its liveliest during the morning produce market (Tues–Sun), which on Sunday expands to include clothing, toys and other items. In the summer (July to early Sept), Palafrugell hosts an evening handicrafts market (Thurs–Sat). For accommodation, go for one of the surrounding beach towns, including Llafranc and Tamariu, which have a wider choice of hotels.

Museu del Suro
Plaçeta del Museu del Suro • Charge • http://museudelsuro.cat

Set in a handsome former *modernista* cork factory, this museum delves into one of Palafrugell's most important historic industries – cork. Exhibits include factory machinery once used to manufacture cork and old large-scale photos that depict the history and evolution of cork-making in Palafrugell. The museum also exhibits a wide variety of changing art shows, including contemporary local artists and photographers.

Fundació Josep Pla
C/Nou 51 • Charge • http://fundaciojoseppla.cat

While relatively unknown beyond Catalunya, within the region Pla is considered one of the greatest writers in the Catalan language. Born in Palafrugell in 1897, Pla's literary output was tremendous. As the *Paris Review* eloquently summed up his long career, "If Barça is more than just a football club, then Pla – a political and cultural journalist, travel writer, biographer, memoirist, essayist, novelist, and foodie, whose collected works clock in at more than thirty-thousand pages and thirty-eight volumes – was more than just a writer." The **Fundació Josep Pla**, which encompasses the house where Pla was born, features permanent and temporary exhibits that chronicle Pla's life of letters, including photographs, books, clippings and more.

11

ARRIVAL AND INFORMATION   PALAFRUGELL

By bus Buses arrive at Palafrugell's Sarfa bus terminal at C/Lluís Companys 2, a 10min walk from the town centre. Palafrugell is also well connected by bus to other cities in the region, including to Barcelona (8–10 daily; 2hr 15min); Figueres (2–5 daily; 1hr); Girona (14 daily; 1hr 20min); L'Escala (3 daily; 45min); Palamós (hourly; 15min); Pals (9 daily; 25–45min); and Sant Feliu (hourly; 55min).

Turisme Avda Generalitat 33 (May, June & Sept Mon–Sat 10am–1pm & 5–7pm, Sun 9.30am–1.30pm; July & Aug Mon–Sat 10am–1pm & 4–7pm, Sun 9.30am–1.30pm; Oct–April Mon–Sat 10am–1pm & 4–7pm, Sun 10am–1pm; http://visitpalafrugell.cat).

EATING

Palafrugell features a range of restaurants, from casual to elegant.

Mas Oliver Avda. d'Espanya (outside town on the ring road), 972 301 041. Tuck into praised Catalan cuisine, including excellent grilled fish and meats. The atmospheric dining room is strewn with bric a brac, and there's an outdoor terrace for warmer weather. €€

Pa i Raim C/Torres i Jonama 56, http://pairaim.com. Inviting, elegant restaurant featuring excellent Catalan cuisine with a twist, including monkfish with sautéed artichoke, and steak with wild mushroom cream. €€€

Around Palafrugell

The area around Palafrugell boasts tranquil, pine-covered slopes, which back three of the most alluring villages on the Costa Brava – **Calella**, **Llafranc** and **Tamariu** – each with a distinct character and all with scintillatingly turquoise waters. With no true coastal road, the beach development here has been generally mild – low-rise, whitewashed apartments and hotels – and although a fair number of foreign visitors come in season, it's also where many of the better-off Barcelonans have a villa for weekend and August escapes. All this makes for one of the most appealing (though hardly undiscovered) stretches of the Costa Brava.

Calella de Palafrugell
Captivating **Calella de Palafrugell** possesses a gloriously rocky coastline punctuated by several tiny sand and rocky **beaches** with a backdrop of whitewashed arches and *fin-de-siècle* villas. From the charming area around the minuscule main beaches, the town stretches southwards along a winding Camí de Ronda to the hidden **El Golfet** beach.

Jardí Botanic de Cap Roig
Charge • http://fundacionlacaixa.org/ca/jardins-cap-roig

> ## CHEERS TO CREMAT
>
> Catalan sailors returning from Cuba and the Antilles in the nineteenth century brought back more than soulful *havaneres* songs. They also brought back Caribbean rum, which forms the basis for **cremat**, a typical drink of the fishing villages in this region, particularly Calella and neighbouring Llafranc.
>
> The potent concoction contains rum, sugar, lemon peel, coffee grounds and sometimes a cinnamon stick. The ritual of drinking *cremat* is a big part of the experience: it's brought out in an earthenware bowl and you have to set fire to it, occasionally stirring until (after a few minutes) it's ready to drink. Also part of the ritual is to sing *havaneres* while drinking.
>
> Calella hosts a **Cantada de Havaneres** in July, with groups performing *havaneres*. Check in with the *turisms* in Palafrugell (see page 668) or Calella (see page 669).

11

Above the El Golfet beach, the Cap Roig headland is home to the **Jardí Botanic de Cap Roig**, a clifftop botanical garden and castle begun in 1927 by an exiled colonel from the tsar's army and his aristocrat English wife. This is also the site of the superb music event **Festival Jardins de Cap Roig** (mid-July to late Aug; http://caproigfestival.com), which features everything from jazz to rock, and has in the past hosted such big names as Bob Dylan, Diana Ross and Elvis Costello.

Llafranc

A gentle, hilly twenty-minute walk from Calella de Palafrugell, high above the rocks along the Camí de Ronda, brings you to **Llafranc**, tucked into the next bay from Calella de Palafrugell, and with a good (if packed) stretch of **beach** and a glittering **marina**. A little more upmarket than Calella, it's a self-consciously opulent place with expensive beachside restaurants and hillside villas glinting in the sun. Steps lead up from the port for the winding climb through residential streets to the **Far de Sant Sebastià**, a lighthouse where you'll be rewarded with some terrific views.

Tamariu, Platja d'Aiguablava and Fornells

Tamariu, 4km north of Llafranc, is quieter and a great favourite with well-heeled Catalan families. The town's action is focused on the small seafront, and the **promenade** – lined with tamarind trees, the source of the town's name – has a hushed but inviting atmosphere, with small shops, pavement restaurants and neighbours sitting on their front porches. Geared more towards the summer-home crowd, the town has fewer hotels than other towns on the coast, but most are good.

It's a pleasant drive along the coast from here to Begur, passing **Platja d'Aiguablava**. Just 1km north of Aiguablava is the tiny and exclusive cove of **Fornells**, home to the lovely *Hotel Aiguablava*.

ARRIVAL AND INFORMATION   AROUND PALAFRUGELL

By bus From June to Sept, buses run regularly from Palafrugell to Calella and then on to Llafranc (July & Aug every 30min; June & Sept roughly hourly), reducing to around four times daily from October to May. A less frequent service runs to the more distant beach at Tamariu (June–Sept; 3–4 daily).

Turisme C/Voltes 6, Calella de Palafrugell (July & Aug Mon–Sun 10am–1pm & 5–8pm; Easter–June & Sept to mid-Oct Mon–Sat 10am–1pm & 4–7pm, Sun 10am–1pm; http://visitpalafrugell.cat).

ACCOMMODATION

CALELLA DE PALAFRUGELL

Hotel Garbi Pg. de les Roques 3–5, http://hotelgarbi.com. Take in the sea air from your balcony at this inviting hotel run by the Cardona family. Rooms are simple but pleasant and light-filled, with large windows, plus have comfy beds and well-equipped bathrooms. Splash in the outdoor pool or walk to the beach, which lies a 10min stroll away. €€

Hotel Sant Roc Pl. Atlàntic 2, http://santroc.com. This

plush hotel sits perched over the sea, with superb views of the coves. The restaurant, *El Balcó del Calella*, serves tasty Mediterranean cuisine. €€€

LLAFRANC

★ **Hotel Blau Mar Llafranc** C/Farena 36, http://hotel blaumarllafranc.com. Perched above town, and flooded with Mediterranean light, this hotel offers sweeping views of the sea. The interior is equally inviting, with natural wood furnishings, plenty of pastels and florals, and access to a sun-speckled garden. 4-night minimum stay in summer. €€€€

Hotel Casamar C/Nero 3, http://hotelcasamar.net. This friendly hotel has cool-toned rooms, and some have balconies that feature lovely views of the bay. The restaurant (see page 671) is a destination unto itself, serving inventive Catalan-inspired cuisine. Closed in winter until April. €€€

Hotel El Far Muntanya de Sant Sebastià, http://hotelelfar. com. This sumptuous hotel sits on a cliff, and the elegant rooms each have a balcony with panoramic views. The alluring restaurant serves fresh seafood and a good selection of paella, rice and *fideuà* (like paella with noodles) dishes. Breakfast included. €€€€

Hotel Terramar Pg. Cipsela 1, http://hterramar.com. On the seafront, this comfortable family-run hotel has simple yet elegant rooms overlooking the beach. €€€

TAMARIU

Hotel Hostalillo C/Bella Vista 22, http://hotelhostalillo. com. Perched above the sea, and surrounded by pines, this inviting hotel features gorgeous views of the beach and bay. Relax in airy rooms, all with mini-fridges and most with balconies. €€€

Hotel Tamariu Pg. del Mar 2, http://tamariu.com. The seafront *Tamariu*, originally a fishermen's tavern in the 1920s, has basic but comfortable rooms with terraces, as well as well-equipped apartments. There's also a good restaurant with lots of salads, grilled fish and a good selection of vegetarian dishes. €€€

PLATJA DE FORNELLS

Hotel Aiguablava Platja de Fornells, http://hotel aiguablava.com. The Costa Brava may have changed drastically from its early days of deserted coves and fishing villages. But some hotels have stood the test of time, like the charming, family-run *Hotel Aiguablava*, which opened in 1934. Spacious rooms with wood floors feature garden or sea views. Feast on traditional Catalan dishes at the restaurant, while taking in views of the Mediterranean through arched windows. €€€

11

EATING

CALELLA DE PALAFRUGELL

Tragamar Platja de Canadell, http://tragamar.com. This stylish seaside restaurant focuses on fresh seafood, from manta ray to lobster stew. They also serve meat dishes such as local Girona steak. €€€

LLAFRANC

Casamar Hotel Casamar C/Nero 3, http://hotelcasamar. net. This Michelin-starred restaurant, helmed by progressive chef Quim Casellas, overlooks the sea and features a seasonal menu of creative cuisine, including dishes like sautéed artichoke with quail's egg and filet of sole perfumed with passion fruit. €€€€

Begur and around

In the lee of a ruined hilltop castle, chic **BEGUR**, about 7km from Palafrugell and slightly inland, stands at the centre of a web of winding roads twisting down to its tranquil and equally stylish **beaches**. Narrow lanes lead to the simple exterior and surprisingly ornate Gothic interior of the **Església Parroquial de Sant Pere**; most remarkable is the odd contrast between statuary and architecture, especially the simplicity of the alabaster *Madonna and Child* compared with the busy altarpiece. Winding streets are lined with multi-coloured houses and grand Cuban-style mansions, built during the nineteenth century when residents returned from making their fortunes on the island. Watching over it all, the thrice-destroyed **Castell de Begur** offers fabulous perspectives of the rocky coves to the south and the curving swathe of the Golf de Roses to the north. The annual **Festival de Música de Begur**, generally from late July to late August, features everything from classical music to swing and jazz, while the **Fira d'Indians** festival in early September celebrates the town's connection with Cuba.

From here roads lead east to the **Cap de Begur**, with its spectacular *mirador*, the coves of **Sa Tuna** and **Aiguafreda**, linked by a scenic footpath (1km), and the pretty hamlet of **SA RIERA**, where you can walk to **Platja del Raco** and **Platja Illa Roja**, some of the best beaches on the coast.

ARRIVAL AND INFORMATION

By bus Sarfa buses travel to Begur from around the Costa Brava, including nearby Palafrugell (10–25mins). The beaches are connected to the town by summer minibus services.

ACCOMMODATION AND EATING

There are a few fairly expensive hotels at the beaches, while beyond the pleasant *Fonda Caner* you'll find further options for a meal or a drink at plenty of beachside spots and in town around the Pl. del la Villa.

Aiguaclara Sant Miquel 2, http://hotelaiguaclara.com. There's good reason this hotel receives so many accolades. Set in an 1866 Cuban-style mansion, with just ten rooms, it is a wonderfully charming respite. The beautifully renovated rooms feature plump beds, tiled floors and balconies and terraces, with views of the village, castle and the Pyrenees rising far beyond. Minimum stays of 2–3 nights in summer. **€€€**

Can Climent Platillos C/Pi i Ralló 8, http://canclimentplatillos.com. This tiny bar-restaurant punches well above its weight in culinary prowess. The menu is creative

BEGUR AND AROUND

Turisme Avda. Onze de Setembre 5, just south of Begur's main square, Pl. de la Vila (daily: spring and autumn 9am–2pm & 4–7pm; summer 9am–9pm; winter 9am–2pm; http://visitbegur.cat).

and season-led with a focus on fish and seafood – tuna carpaccio with wasabi ice cream, sea urchin, wild Alaska salmon – though the likes of suckling pig or crispy oxtail caters to the carnivores. There's plenty of tapas too. Great atmosphere but always busy, so book ahead. **€€€**

Cluc Hotel Begur C/Metge Pi 8, http://cluc.cat. This boutique hotel, set in an 1800s colonial house, rivals the best of boho-chic Paris – tiled floors, stone walls, distressed wood, gauzy curtains, quirky light fixtures. Buffet breakfast of local produce is included. **€€€**

Hotel Rosa C/Pi i Ralló 19, http://hotelrosabegur.com. This family-owned spot has comfortable rooms and a cheerful atmosphere. They also have a relaxing spa and a sunny roof terrace to enjoy breakfast on. Ask about their off-season discounts. **€€€**

Pals

Turisme C/Creu 7 • http://visitpals.com

The 7km journey north from Palafrugell to Torroella de Montgrí can be broken at **PALS**, also 7km from Begur. This fortified medieval village was long neglected until it was painstakingly restored by a local doctor after the Civil War, which has resulted in the rather unfortunate side effect of being invaded by scores of day-trippers. Even so, its fourteenth-century streets and hilltop setting make it an enjoyable place for a stroll. The golden-brown buildings cluster around a stark tower, all that remains of the town's Romanesque **castle**; below is the beautifully vaulted Gothic **Església de Sant Pere** and Romanesque **Torre de les Hores**.

La Bisbal

LA BISBAL, 12km northwest of Palafrugell on the main road to Girona, is a medieval market town in an attractive river setting. Since the seventeenth century, La Bisbal has specialized in the production of **ceramics**, and pottery shops line the main road through town (C/Aigüeta); these are great for browsing and picking up some terrific local pieces.

Ceramics apart, La Bisbal is a pleasant stop anyway, as its handsome old centre retains many impressive mansions, the architectural remnants of a once thriving Jewish quarter and the fortified medieval **Castell Palau de la Bisbal**.

Castell Palau de la Bisbal

Charge • 972 645 500

La Bisbal's most important historical building is the fortified **Castell Palau**, built for the bishops of Girona. The sturdy castle, which dates back to the eleventh and twelfth centuries, has been in continuous use since it was built, including a spell as a prison during the Spanish Civil War. Inside, you'll learn about medieval Catalunya while touring its various sections.

ACCOMMODATION AND EATING

LA BISBAL

Arcs de Monells C/Vilanova 1, Monells, http://hotelarcsmonells.com. This lovely hotel, set in a fourteenth-

century hospital in Monells, 3km northwest of La Bisbal, is an elegant base for exploring the area. It has a beautifully renovated interior and comfortable rooms, as well as a large garden and pool. €€€

★ **Hotel Castell d'Empordà** http://hotelcastellemporda. com. This 800-year-old castle, perched on top of a hill 3km north of the town with beautiful views of the surrounding countryside, is now a sumptuous hotel. You're in good company: a captain for Christopher Columbus stayed here, and Dalí once tried to buy it. There are also 2 restaurants, which celebrate the local bounty, and serve creative Catalan cuisine and excellent regional wines. Hotel €€, restaurant €€€€

Peratallada and Ullastret

Five kilometres northeast of La Bisbal is the medieval walled town of **PERATALLADA**, which has preserved a rustic feel with the help of its tiny cobbled streets, stone arches and shaded squares. An influx of small hotels and restaurants has proved to be surprisingly in keeping with their thirteenth-century Romanesque setting, making it a fabulous base away from the beach. The focal point is the **Castell de Peratallada** (closed to visitors), whose origins have been dated to pre-Roman times.

Museu d'Arqueologia de Ullastret

Puig de Sant Andreu d'Ullastret • Charge • http://macullastret.cat

Six kilometres northeast lie the remains of the Iberian settlement of **Puig de Sant Andreu d'Ullastret**, a lovely, peaceful ruin with an archeological **museum** that has excavated artefacts from the area. The site is just north of the friendly, historic village of **Ullastret**, signposted off the main road.

11

INFORMATION	PERATALLADA AND ULLASTRET
Turisme The *turisme* is on Pl. del Castell, in front of the Castell de Peratallada (summer daily 10.30am–1.30pm	& 4.30–8.30pm; winter generally Sat & Sun only; http://visitperatallada.cat).

ACCOMMODATION	
Hostal Restaurant La Riera Pl. les Voltes 3, Peratallada, http://lariera.es. Cosy *hostal*, comfortably housed in a seventeenth-century building – and one of the area's more	economical options. The restaurant serves good Catalan cuisine. €€

Torroella de Montgrí

TORROELLA DE MONTGRÍ, 8km from Ullastret and 9km beyond Pals, was once an important medieval port, but today has been left high and dry by the receding Mediterranean. It now stands 5km inland, beneath the shell of the huge, crenellated **Castell de Montgrí** (at 302m, a stiff 30min walk away), built by King Jaume II between 1294 and 1301 but never completed. The town itself remains distinctly medieval in appearance with its narrow streets, fine mansions and the fourteenth-century parish church of **Sant Genís**. The **Festival de Torroella de Montgrí** (http://festivaldetorroella. cat), held each July and August in the main square and church, features an excellent line-up of classical music.

ARRIVAL AND INFORMATION	TORROELLA DE MONTGRÍ
By bus Three buses a day travel between Torroella and Barcelona (just under 3hr), and there are regular buses to L'Estartit (10min). **Turisme** Centre Cultural, C/Ullà 27 (July & Aug daily	10am–2pm & 5.30–9pm; Sept–June Mon–Sat 10am–2pm & 5–8pm, Sun 10am–1.30pm; http://torroellademontgri. com/en).

ACCOMMODATION	
Palau Lo Mirador Pg. de l'Església 1, http://hotel palaulomirador.com. This handsome, historic hotel features	a palatial interior, with spacious rooms and well-appointed bathrooms. €€

L'Estartit and the Illes Medes

The nearest beach to Torroella is 6km to the east at **L'ESTARTIT**, an otherwise unexceptional resort town. Call into the *turisme* for information about the nearby

Illes Medes, Catalunya's only offshore islands – kiosks in the area sell boat trips in the summer. The tiny islands form a protected nature reserve, hosting the most important colony of herring gulls in the Mediterranean, numbering some eight thousand pairs, and offer some of the best **diving** and snorkelling on the coast.

ARRIVAL AND INFORMATION	L'ESTARTIT AND THE ILLES MEDES
By bus Hourly buses travel between here and Torroella de Montgrí (10min).	along the seafront (summer daily 9.30am–2pm; rest of year Mon–Fri 9am–6pm, Sat & Sun 10am–2pm; http://
Turisme At the northern end of Pg. Marítim, which runs	visitestartit.com).

EATING

Restaurant Bravo Pg. Marítim 82–86, http://restaurant-bravo.com. You'll find plenty of bars and restaurants along the seafront, like this restaurant, which specialises in rice | dishes and paellas. It also serves fresh seafood, including fresh mussels and grilled fish, on a breezy terrace. €€€

11

Alt Empordà

Beyond Torroella de Montgrí, the scenery changes quite abruptly as you move into the fertile plains and wetlands of the southern part of the **Alt Empordà**, dominated by the broad swathe of the **Golf de Roses**. Coves give way to long stretches of sand as far north as **Roses**, which nestles in its own closed-in bay. The gulf is backed for the most part by flat, rural land, well watered by the Muga and Fluvià rivers. Having been left to its own quiet devices for centuries, this section of coast is distinct from the otherwise touristy Costa Brava, and has really only suffered the attentions of the developers in towns at either end of the bay, most notably in the few kilometres between Roses and the giant marina resort of Empuriabrava.

At the southern end of the gulf is the pleasant old fishing port of **L'Escala**, made more remarkable by the presence of **Empúries**, a ruined Greek and Roman settlement and one of Spain's most important archeological sites. Beyond Roses, the familiar crashing rocks and deeply indented coves return with a vengeance in the wild Cap de Creus headland. The jewel in the crown here is **Cadaqués**, eternally linked to **Salvador Dalí**, who lived for years in the neighbouring fishermen's village of **Portlligat**, now home to an absorbing museum in his bizarre former residence. For the final run to the French border, the road swoops along the coast through quieter villages such as whitewashed **El Port de la Selva**.

L'Escala

At the southernmost end of the sweeping billhook of the Golf de Roses, **L'ESCALA** is split between its shabby but picturesque *nucli antic*, or **old town**, favoured by local holiday-makers, and the more commercial **Riells** quarter, which has a beach and is the haunt of foreign visitors. Infinitely more appealing, the narrow pedestrianized streets of the old town huddle around the ancient port, where you'll find medieval mooring posts

---

THE ART OF ANCHOVIES

There are anchovies, and then there are **Catalan anchovies**. Most think of anchovies as oily, limp little items, but here on the Catalan coast, and most famously in **L'Escala**, *anchoas* (*anxoves* in Catalan) are succulent, pale in colour and plump – almost double the size of what you may be used to. L'Escala is widely known for its canning factories where Catalunya's best anchovies are packaged.

You can sample them in most bars and restaurants – and there may be nothing better than a plate of anchovies, a hunk of bread (the better to soak up the aromatic olive-oil-laced juices) and a *cerveza* or three, enjoyed at a seaside *terraza*. And bring the taste home with you: plenty of grocery shops around town sell little jars and cans that you can pack into your bags.

and a cannonball, fired from a ship in May 1809, embedded in the wall of the house at C/Joan Massanet 2 (close to the seafront at the end of C/Pintor de Massanet).

A further enticement is L'Escala's proximity to the ancient site of Empúries, which lies just a couple of kilometres out of town.

ARRIVAL AND INFORMATION   L'ESCALA

By bus Buses stop on Avda. Girona, just down the road from the *turisme*. Regular services travel to and from Barcelona (3 daily; 3hr); Figueres (10 daily; 45min–1hr); Girona (7 daily; 1hr); Palafrugell (3 daily; 45min); and Pals (3 daily; 25min).

Turisme Pl. de las Escoles 1, on the edge of the old town (mid-June to mid-Sept Mon–Sat 9am–8.30pm, Sun 10am–1pm; mid-Sept to mid-June Mon–Fri 9am–1pm & 4–7pm, Sat 10am–2pm, Sun 10am–1pm; http://lescala.cat).

ACCOMMODATION AND EATING

Freshly caught fish and seafood, particularly **anchovies**, are the speciality of the town's **restaurants**, with a good choice in the port and the old town. For a **drink**, head to the *nucli antic*, where you'll find a range from fishermen's taverns and bars.

Hostal Spa Empúries Platja de Portitxol s/n, http://hostalempuries.com. This lovingly run hotel places a premium on sustainability – using biodegradable products and sourcing all its electricity from renewable resources. It also has an excellent location, near the beach and the main entrance to Empúries. Many of the sleek rooms have terraces overlooking the sea. The attached *Villa Teresita*

restaurant serves tasty local organic cuisine. €€€
Restaurant l'Avi Freu Passeig Lluís Albert 7, http://restaurant-avi-freu.com. This established restaurant serves quality fish and rice dishes such as black rice with squid and typical L'Escala fish stew. €€€
Villa Teresita Hostal Empúries, http://hostalempuries.com. This light-filled restaurant follows *Hostal Empúries'* eco-friendly philosophy, serving what they call "eco-Mediterranean" cuisine. Feast on crayfish and prawns sourced from Palamós and Roses, grilled squid, and cod with pig's ears and beans. €€€

Empúries
C/Puig i Cadafalch • Charge • http://mac.cat • You can enter the site via the beach in summer, but at other times the main entrance and car park lie on the road farther inland

The archeological site of **Empúries**, which lies behind a sandy bay about 2km north of L'Escala, has immense historical significance, being the first entry point of classical Mediterranean culture into Iberian Spain – its fascination derives from its distinct Greek and Roman quarters showing how one culture steadily usurped the other. You can see the ruins in a leisurely afternoon, spending the rest of your time on the pleasant duned stretch of sand nearby.

Empúries was the ancient Greek Emporion (literally "trading station"), founded in the early sixth century BC by merchants who, for three centuries, conducted a vigorous trade throughout the Mediterranean. In 218 BC, their settlement was taken by Scipio, and a Roman city – more splendid than the Greek, with an amphitheatre, fine villas and a broad marketplace – grew up above the old Greek town. The Romans were replaced in turn by the Visigoths, who built several basilicas, and Emporion disappears from the records only in the ninth century when, it is assumed, it was wrecked by either Saracen or Norman pirates.

The Greek colony
The remains of the original **Greek colony**, destroyed by a Frankish raid in the third century AD – at which stage all inhabitants moved to the Roman city – occupy the lower part of the site. Among the ruins of several **temples**, to the south on raised ground is one dedicated to Asklepios, the Greek healing god whose cult was centred on Epidauros and the island of Kos. The temple is marked by a replica of a fine third-century-BC statue of the god, the original of which (along with many finds from the site) is in the Museu Arqueològic in Barcelona. Nearby are several large water filters: Emporion had no aqueduct so water was stored here to be filtered and purified and then supplied to the town by means of long pipes, one of which has been reconstructed. Remains of the town gate, the **agora** (or central marketplace) and several

streets can easily be made out, along with a mass of house foundations, some with mosaics, and the ruins of Visigoth basilicas. A small **museum** stands above, with helpful models and diagrams of the excavations, as well as a variety of archeological finds, and a digital and audiovisual display giving a brief history of the settlement.

The Roman town

Beyond the museum stretches the vast but only partially excavated **Roman town**. Here, two luxurious villas have been uncovered, and you can see their entrance halls, porticoed gardens and magnificent mosaic floors. Farther on are the remains of the **forum**, **amphitheatre** and outer walls.

Parc Natural dels Aiguamolls de l'Empordà

Ctra Sant Pere Pescador a Castelló d'Empúries, Castelló d'Empúries • Free

Halfway around the Golf de Roses, in two parcels of land on either side of the resort of Empuriabrava, is one of Spain's more accessible nature reserves. The **Parc Natural dels Aiguamolls de l'Empordà** is an important wetland reserve, created by the Catalan government in 1983 to save what remained of the Empordà marshland, which once covered the entire plain here but gradually reduced over the centuries as a result of agricultural developments and cattle raising. The park attracts a wonderful selection of birds to both its coastal terrain and the paddy fields typical of the area.

The park

There are two main **paths** around the lagoons and marshes: the first takes around two hours, while a second five-hour trek crosses more open land and can be cycled. Hides have been created along the way; morning and early evening are the best times for **birdwatching** and you'll spy the largest number of species during the migration periods (March–May & Aug–Oct). You'll almost certainly see marsh harriers and various waterfowl, and might spot bee-eaters and the rare glossy ibis.

Sant Pere Pescador

The nearest village to the visitors' centre at El Cortalet is **Sant Pere Pescador**, 6km south, pleasant enough but surrounded by a glut of sprawling, extremely busy campsites. You can rent bikes here, handy given the flat countryside, but the hordes of tourists make Castelló d'Empúries, 8km farther on, a more attractive base.

ARRIVAL AND INFORMATION   PARC NATURAL DELS AIGUAMOLLS DE L'EMPORDÀ

By bus Sarfa buses travel daily to Sant Pere Pescador from Castelló d'Empúries, L'Escala and Figueres.

Visitor centre Centre Informació el Cortalet (http://

emportaturisme.com). Here you can pick up a brochure marking the recommended routes in the park.

ACCOMMODATION

Nautic Almatà In the Parc Natural dels Aiguamolls de   l'Empordà, http://almata.com. This massive campsite is one of

---

OLIVE OIL TOURS AND TASTINGS

Empordà has made a name for itself with its excellent wines. And now the region's olive oils are sharing the spotlight. For a tasting and tour, head to **Oli de Ventalló** (C/Bassa 20; http://oliventallo.com), in the small stone town of Ventalló (9km west of L'Escala), where olive oil groves unfold in all directions. This family-run olive oil producer offers an array of tours, including a sunrise and sunset tour (charge), where you'll stroll the olive groves, visit the mill and sample olive oils – Empordà's soil is rich in slate, which lends a tartness to the oil. The tour also includes a feast of local fare, like *pa amb tomàquet* with nutty cheese. Call ahead to book – tours generally run on Tuesdays and Thursdays in July and August; for the rest of the year, it's by appointment.

SIP YOUR WAY THROUGH EMPORDÀ

The vineyards in the **Empordà** wine region (http://doemporda.cat) aren't just old. They're ancient. This lush wine region, which unfolds inland from the Costa Brava, has been producing wine since the fifth century, when the Phoenicians first settled in the area. While primarily known for its naturally sweet Garnatxa, the region is going through a renaissance, with new, progressive small-batch winemakers developing a wide variety of blends. Over fifty wineries populate the Empordà, which is flanked by the Pyrenees on one side and the Mediterranean on the other, extending from Figueres north to the French border, and south through Baix Empordà. Rich soils and a mild Mediterranean climate ensure a flourishing harvest, but there's also something else that's unique to the region: the strong Tramuntana winds, which help protect the vines from disease and frost. Turisme Costa Brava Girona has launched a **DO (Denominació d'Origen) Empordà Wine Route** (http://costabrava.org/what-to-do/wine-and-gastronomy/wine-route), which features a range of recommended wineries, hotels and restaurants. Top picks in the region include Perelada (http://perelada.com), Celler Martin Faixó (http://cellermartinfaixo.com) and Vinyes Olivardots (http://olivardots.com).

the best for access to the park. It has well-maintained facilities, including two pools and bike rental, and can organize outdoor excursions. Also available are a range of accommodation, including bungalows and villas for four or five. **€**

Castelló d'Empúries

Formerly the capital of the counts of Empúries, the delightful small town of **CASTELLÓ D'EMPÚRIES**, halfway between the beach at Roses and Figueres, is also midway between the two halves of the Parc Natural dels Aiguamolls. A five-minute walk from where the bus stops takes you into a small medieval conglomeration that's lost little of its genteel charm. The town's narrow alleys and streets conceal some well preserved buildings, a medieval bridge and a handsome church.

Church of Santa María

Museum Charge • basilicasantamaria.com

The towering thirteenth-century church, **Santa María**, has an ornate doorway and alabaster altarpiece which alone are reward enough for the trip. Known as the Catedral de l'Empordà, the church was intended to be the centre of an episcopal city, but opposition from the bishopric of Girona meant that this was never to be, thus leaving Castelló with a church out of proportion to the town.

ARRIVAL AND INFORMATION

CASTELLÓ D'EMPÚRIES

By bus Sarfa buses service Castelló d'Empúries from Figueres (15 daily, 15min), Cadaqués (6 daily, 45 min) and Barcelona (1 daily, 2hr). It's a 10min walk from the bus stop into town.

Turisme Pl. dels Homes, 972 156 233 (Jul & Aug daily 9am–9pm; winter Mon–Thurs 10am–4pm, Fri & Sat 10am–2pm & 4–8pm, Sun 10am–2pm, http://castelloempuriabrava.com).

ACCOMMODATION AND EATING

Hotel Canet Pl. Joc de la Pilota 2, http://hotelcanet.com. Relax at this lovely, historic hotel with views out over the tawny roofs of the village; there's also a restaurant that serves Catalan cuisine, including seafood, grilled meats and local produce. **€€**

Hotel de la Moneda Pl. de la Moneda 8–10, http://hotel delamoneda.com. Well-run hotel set in an eighteenth-century home, with comfortable, brightly painted rooms. **€€€**

Hotel Palau Macelli C/Carbonar 1, http://palau-macelli.com. A stunning seventeenth-century building houses this elegant and spacious hotel. The garden, spa and pool mean that guests are happy to stay all day. **€€€**

Roses

ROSES, 9km from Castello, enjoys a lovely situation beneath medieval fortress walls at the head of the grand, sweeping bay. It's a site that's been inhabited for over three thousand years – the Greeks called the place Rhoda when they set up a trading colony around the excellent natural harbour in the ninth century BC – but apart from the ruined **Castell de la Trinitat** and the Citadel, which contains the absorbing **Museu de la Ciutadella**, there's little in present-day Roses to hint at its long history. Instead, Roses is a full-blown package resort that trades exclusively on its 4km of sandy beach, which has fostered a large and popular watersports industry. If you're staying, don't skip a day-trip to Cadaqués, which you can reach via a short bus ride over the hill.

Citadel and the Museu de la Ciutadella

Charge • http://rosescultura.cat/ca/la-ciutadella

You can walk around the **Citadel**, which contains the remains of the Greek settlement of Rhoda, an ancient Roman villa and the **Museu de la Ciutadella**, which explores the Citadel's history – and its role in the evolution of Roses – via exhibits and photographs.

ARRIVAL AND INFORMATION
ROSES

By bus The bus station is on the corner of C/Gran Vía Pau Casals and Rambla Ginjolers. Sarfa buses travel to and from Barcelona (1 daily, 2hr 15min) and Figueres (2 hourly, 30min).

Turisme Av. De Rhode 77 near the seafront promenade (Mon–Sat 10am–2pm & 3–6pm, Sun 10am–1pm; http://visit.roses.cat/en).

ACCOMMODATION AND EATING

Almadraba Park Hotel Avda. Díaz Pacheco 70, Platja de l'Almadraba, http://almadrabapark.com. Open since 1969, is this large hotel sitting along the clifftops. The hotel features pretty views of the sea and stylishly comfortable

---

THE EVOLUTION OF EL BULLI – AND FERRAN ADRIÀ

In 2011, the most famous chef in the world closed his restaurant at the height of its popularity. Why? The answer to that explains who Catalan chef Ferran Adrià is.

Adrià's legendary "molecular gastronomy" restaurant **El Bulli**, near the town of Roses, was voted best restaurant in the world numerous times by *Restaurant* magazine. At its apex, there were two million reservation requests per year – and eight thousand granted. The land on which it sat was originally purchased by a German couple, who opened a restaurant, which they named after their pet French bulldogs – *El Bulli*. Adrià joined the staff in 1984, guiding it to culinary heights until its closing.

Adrià is perhaps best known for his "foams" (*espumas*), scented with everything from carrot to pine nuts to smoke. One of his culinary signatures has been to re-create traditional Mediterranean flavours via very non-traditional methods, his wizardry yielding such concoctions as liquid ravioli; spherified olives; parmesan ice cream; and "caviaroli" – caviar made with *allioli*. As Adrià has said of his cuisine: "Nothing is as it seems." Adrià is also famous for his deconstruction of Spain's comfort dishes, like *tortilla de patatas*. Hot potato is transformed into foam, onion made into a thick purée and egg white becomes a whipped sabayon. It's served in a tiny sherry glass with a spoon: the flavours fill the mouth – intense, warm and startlingly familiar.

Adrià closed *El Bulli* in July 2011, and in its place has set up a culinary foundation and centre, the ever-evolving El Bulli Foundation, which occupies the same space as did the restaurant, perched over the quiet cove of **Montjoi** at the end of a long and winding road above Roses. The foundation includes elBulli 1846, a culinary lab and exhibition space. But this is just the tip of his multi-project empire: Adrià launched Bullipedia (a type of culinary Wikipedia), taught a class at Harvard and has been featured in the documentary film *Eating Knowledge*. For the latest information, check the website: http://elbullifoundation.org.

Adrià is sometimes compared to another famous native son of Catalunya: Salvador Dalí. One is a surrealist on canvas, the other a surrealist in the kitchen. Adrià, in eloquent fashion, summed up the relationship between art and cuisine like this: The dialogue between art and cuisine is still young. But in the end, it's not that important if cuisine is art, but if it changes the way you look at the world.

rooms, as well as a great restaurant, serving seasonal produce. Restaurant closed mid-Oct to March. €€
★ **Hotel Perelada** C/Robertí, 22km west of Roses, http://hotelperelada.com. Empordà wine is the inspiration for this handsome hotel. This is a place for the full R&R

experience: kick back under stone arches in the WineSpa; dine on local cuisine at *Restaurant L'Olivera* and then retire to the soothing rooms, which feel like an extension of the surrounding earthy landscapes, with wooden floors, woven baskets and muted creams and greys. €€€

Cadaqués

The Costa Brava is hardly undiscovered, but if there's one place that still holds the hidden, quirky allure of the coast's early days, it's **CADAQUÉS**. This is thanks, in part, to its accessibility (or inaccessibility, as the case is): this northern Costa Brava town is reached only by the winding road over the hills from either Roses (16km) or Port de la Selva (12km), which gives it an air of isolation. With whitewashed and bougainvillea-festooned houses lining narrow, hilly streets, a tree-lined promenade and craggy headlands on either side of a working fishing port, it's genuinely picturesque. Already by the 1920s and 1930s the place had begun to attract the likes of Picasso, Man Ray, Lorca, Buñuel, Thomas Mann and Einstein, but Cadaqués really "arrived" as an **artistic-literary colony** after World War II when Surrealist painter **Salvador Dalí** and his wife Gala settled at nearby Portlligat, attracting for some years a floating bohemian community. Today, a seafront statue of Dalí provides the town's physical and spiritual focal point, haughtily gazing on the artists, well-heeled Barcelonans and art-seeking foreigners who have rolled up in his wake.

With its art galleries and studios, smart restaurants and trendy clothes shops, Cadaqués makes for an interesting stroll. At the top of the hill is the austere-looking sixteenth-century **Església de Santa María**, containing an ornate eighteenth-century altarpiece and a side chapel on the left painted by Dalí. Local **beaches** are all tiny and pebbly, but there are some enjoyable walks around the harbour and nearby coves; the helpful *turisme* has further information and maps.

ARRIVAL AND INFORMATION   CADAQUÉS

By bus Sarfa buses arrive at the little bus office on C/Sant Vicenç, on the edge of town, next to a large pay car park. From here, you can walk along C/Unió and C/Vigilant to the seafront or climb up through the old streets to reach it. Buses run to Barcelona (2 daily; 2hr 45min); Castelló d'Empúries (6 daily; 45min); Figueres (4 daily; 1hr) and

Roses (7 daily; 30min).
Turisme C/Cotxe 2, just back from Pl. Frederic Rahola on the promenade (summer Mon–Sat 9am–9pm, Sun 10am–1pm & 5–8pm; winter Mon–Sat 9am–1pm & 3–6pm, Sun 10am–1pm; http://visitcadaques.org).

ACCOMMODATION

Cadaqués can get very busy in the peak season, and it's a good idea to book in advance. Note that many hotels close in low season, from November to February, so call ahead if you're visiting in winter.
Hostal La Residència C/Caritat Serinyana 1, http://laresidencia.net. Handsome building, built in 1904 (the year that Dalí was born) and loaded with character, though the rooms are relatively ordinary – the suites are elaborately decorated with Dalí in mind, however, and the balconies have stunning views. €€
★ **Hostal Vehí** C/Església 6, http://hostalvehi.com. Friendly and family-owned, this excellent-value *pensió* has a lovely central location near the church and well-tended rooms, and is consequently very popular. Closed Nov–Feb. €€
Hotel Blaumar C/Massa d'Or 21, http://hotelblaumar. com. If you've come to Cadaqués for some quiet afternoons

of sprawling poolside, *Blaumar* delivers. It's about a 10min walk from the centre of town, but that gives it an intimate, tucked-away feel. Rooms are simple but well kept, most with terraces, and the staff is helpful and accommodating. Closed Oct to April. €€
Hotel Calina Avda. Salvador Dalí 33, Port Lligat, http://hotelcalina.com. Near Port Lligat beach, about a 20min walk from town, this well-maintained hotel offers tidy rooms with terraces as well as self-catering studio apartments that are ideal for families. Plus, you can splash in two swimming pools surrounded by gardens. €€
Hotel Horta d'en Rahola C/Sa Tarongeta, http://hortacadaques.com. This eighteenth-century family home has been charmingly transformed into an adults-only boutique hotel, with a lovely garden, and seven breezy rooms with local art on the walls and views over the old town. €€

Llané Petit C/Dr Bartomeus 37, http://llanepetit.com. Friendly, relaxing hotel at the southern end of the town. Most rooms have terraces with sea views, and there is a well-maintained pool. Closed Jan–Feb. €€

Playa Sol Platja Pianc 3, http://playasol.com. Set in a curve of the seafront, this quiet, charming hotel offers simply furnished with blue and white sea-themed décor, and affording superb views of the town or over tranquil gardens. Closed Dec. €€

★ **Tramuntana Hotel** C/Torre 9, http://hotel-tramuntana-cadaques.com. This light-filled boutique hotel offers a lovely mix of design, comfort and easy access to the sea, which is a short walk away. The eleven rooms, splashed with cool whites, tans and greys, each have a balcony with waterfront views. €€

EATING AND DRINKING

Moderately priced seafood **restaurants**, any of which are worth trying, are strung along the seafront, while dotted about the old town and along C/Miquel Rosset are places to suit a wide range of tastes and budgets. **Nightlife** is a pleasurable blend of laidback idling at the beachside terraces and stylish hobnobbing around the bars and restaurants on C/Miguel Rosset.

Es Balconet C/Sant Antoni 2, http://restaurantesbalconet.com. Trek up a small winding street from the seafront to this cosy nook, where seafood reigns supreme. Go for the generous fixed menus, like monkfish with scallops, which includes a starter of superb tuna carpaccio or a salad and dessert. €€€

El Barroco C/Nou 10, http://elbarroco.net. This long-running restaurant represents all that's unique about Cadaqués: Surrealist-tinged artwork lines the walls, while the sunny courtyard spills over with flowers and crawling vines. The menu is equally creative, with a focus on Lebanese cuisine, like meze platters of hummus, falafels and tabbouleh. There are also whole vegan and vegetarian menus. Dalí used to dine here with Gala, and the owner is happy to share anecdotes of the restaurant's formidable history. €€

Casa Anita C/Miquel Rosset 16, 972 258 471. Cadaqués marches to the beat of its own drum, and this quirky institution is a good example. Seating is at communal tables and there are generally no menus – just the family staff rattling off the day's specials of superb Catalan cuisine. Best to reserve ahead. €€€

Casa Nun Pl. de Portitxó 6, http://casanun.com. This lovely restaurant offers top-notch regional fish and meat dishes, which you can enjoy on the small, sunny terrace perched above the Pl. des Portitxó. €€

Compartir Riera Sant Vicenç, http://compartircadaques.com. Founded by three former *El Bulli* chefs, this award-winning restaurant features multi-course meals that are designed for diners to share ("compartir"). Inventive dishes include ribs of rabbit with an apple *allioli*. The setting matches the cuisine: the spacious restaurant is awash in the colours of Cadaqués – white and blue – as well as a sun-dappled terrace. They also have cute apartments sleeping from 1–3 people (€€). €€€€

La Sirena C/Es Call, http://restaurantelasirena.com. Tucked away in the old town, this appropriately named restaurant – "sirena" means "mermaid" – serves some of the best seafood in town, as well as excellent paellas. €€€

Casa-Museu Salvador Dalí

Charge • http://salvador-dali.org

A well-signposted twenty-minute walk north of Cadaqués and 3km by road is the tiny harbour of **PORT LLIGAT**, former home of Salvador Dalí. The artist had spent much of his childhood and youth in Cadaqués, and later, with his wife and muse, Gala, he converted a series of waterside fishermen's cottages in Port Lligat into a sumptuous

---

THE DALÍ TRIANGLE

There are three museums in the Costa Brava devoted to the life and work of **Salvador Dalí** and they're known locally as the Dalí Triangle. The **Teatre-Museu Dalí** in Figueres (see page 689) provides a display of the breadth of his art and his consummate creative skill, whereas the **Casa-Museu Castell Gala Dalí** (see page 688), northwest of Girona, reveals the artist's complex personal relationship with his Russian wife and muse, Gala. Famously, he was only allowed to enter her home with permission; he repaid her with mischief by painting false radiators on the covers she had insisted he install to hide the real ones. You can also gain insight into the artist at **Casa-Museu Salvador Dalí** (see page 680) in Port Lligat, next to Cadaqués, which was his only fixed home from 1930 until 1982, when he moved into Gala's castle. The *casa* is a tortuous maze of a home made up of fishermen's huts that were successively acquired and strung together.

home that has all the quirks you would expect of the couple, such as speckled rooftop eggs and a giant fish painted on the ground outside. The house is now open to the public as the **Casa-Museu Salvador Dalí**, and although there's not much to see in the way of art, it's worth the visit to see first-hand how the two of them lived until Gala's death in 1982, after which Dalí moved to Figueres. Visitor numbers are strictly controlled and you have to **book a visit** beforehand.

Tours take in most of the house, and include Dalí's studio, the exotically draped model's room, the couple's master bedroom and bathroom, a secondary workshop in an olive grove and, perhaps best of all, the oval-shaped sitting room that Dalí designed for Gala, which, apparently by accident, boasts stunning acoustics. You'll also see the garden and swimming pool where the couple entertained guests – they didn't like too many strangers trooping through their living quarters. The phallic-shaped pool and its various decorative features, including a giant snake and a stuffed lion, are a treat.

Cap de Creus

Museum Free • **Creuers Cadaqués** http://creuerscadaques.com

A road winds 8km from Casa-Museu Salvador Dalí past glimpses of wave-plundered coves to the wind-buffeted **Cap de Creus** headland, the easternmost tip of the Iberian Peninsula, which provides breathtaking views of the coast and is topped by a lighthouse built in 1853. It's now occupied by the **Museu Espai Cap de Creus**, with a small exhibition on the surrounding nature reserve. If you fancy viewing the Cap de Creus from the sea, you'll find a few **boats** along the seafront that do excursions, including those run by Creuers Cadaqués. The nature reserve (http://parcsnaturals.gencat.cat) itself is also definitely worth exploring, filled with enchanting rock formations that inspired many of Dalí's paintings. It's best discovered on foot via the numerous coastal paths and hiking trails.

El Port de la Selva and around

Thirteen kilometres northwest of Cadaqués, **EL PORT DE LA SELVA** is centred on its fishing and pleasure **ports**, while either side is a ribbon of lovely **coves** with some of the cleanest water in the Mediterranean: those to the north are far more rugged and reached on foot or by sea, while the ones to the west are easier to get to and, therefore, more popular.

Sant Pere de Rodes

Charge

It's 8km up the paved **road** from El Port de la Selva, via Selva de Mar, to the Benedictine monastery of **Sant Pere de Rodes**, just below the 670m-high summit of the Serra de Roda; approaching **by foot**, use the marked trail (1hr 30min) through the Vall de Santa Creu, which begins at Molí de la Vall.

The first written record of the monastery dates back to 879, and in 934 it became independent, answerable only to Rome: in these early years, and thanks especially to the Roman connection, the monks became tremendously rich and powerful. As the monastery was enlarged it was also fortified against attack, starting a period of splendour that lasted four hundred years before terminal decline set in. Many fine treasures were looted when it was finally abandoned in 1789, and it was also pillaged by the French during the Peninsular War; some of the rescued silver can be seen in Girona's Museu d'Art.

Once one of the most romantic ruins in all of Catalunya, its central church universally recognized to be the precursor of the Catalan Romanesque style, the monastery was robbed of a great deal of its charm by overzealous restoration. No original columns or capitals remain in the cloister and some of the work looks too clinical. The redeeming feature, apart from the view, is the **Catedral**, which retains its original stonework from the tenth to fourteenth centuries, including eleventh-century column capitals carved with wolves' and dogs' heads. Nearby is the peaceful pre-Romanesque church of **Santa Elena**, all that remains of the small rural community that grew up around the monastery.

Castell de Sant Salvador

Above the monastery (and contemporary with it) stands the much more atmospheric, ruined **Castell de Sant Salvador**, a thirty-minute scramble up a steep, narrow path. This provided the perfect lookout site for the frequent invasions (French or Moorish) which normally came from the sea; in the event of attack, fires were lit on the hill to warn the whole surrounding area.

ARRIVAL AND DEPARTURE	**EL PORT DE LA SELVA AND AROUND**
By bus Six daily buses traves from Figueres to El Port de la Selva (35min), though there's currently no public transport	to Sant Pere de Rodes.

Girona and around

Beautifully preserved **Girona**, which is accessible within an hour from the sea, offers a refreshing change from the sun-and-sand hedonism of the Costa Brava. This elegant, provincial capital features a walled medieval quarter, **Barri Vell**, perched on a hill – a delight to explore, with narrow cobbled alleyways, balconied houses and shady little *plaças*. Clinging to the banks of the Ríu Onyar, as it meanders through the centre of town, is a long row of picturesque pastel-hued houses, the **Cases de l'Onyar**.

Historically, Girona has seen it all – at least by Spanish standards. The Romans settled here, and called the town Gerunda. Girona then became an Islamic town after the Moors conquered Spain. A vibrant Jewish community also flourished here for more than six centuries, and Girona's **Call**, the medieval Jewish quarter, remains one of the best preserved in Spain. Elsewhere, you'll spy a fetching mix of architectural styles, from Romanesque to *Modernisme*. Girona also features a range of excellent museums, a lovely cathedral and lively arts and music festivals. **Rambla de la Llibertat**, running along the river, is the city's grand promenade, where locals take their daily *paseo* past a bustling strip of shops and restaurants.

Northwest of Girona, in the town of Púbol, rises the **Casa-Museu Castell Gala Dalí**, a medieval castle-turned-museum, which used to belong to surreal master Salvador Dalí and his wife Gala.

Catedral

Pl. de la Catedral • Charge • http://catedraldegirona.cat

Looming majestically over the old quarter, Girona's **Catedral** is an elegant amalgamation of architectural styles. The Romanesque cloister and tower are the only parts remaining from the original eleventh-century building, and the Catedral was continually rebuilt and expanded up to and throughout the eighteenth century. The splendid Gothic nave, dating from the fifteenth and sixteenth centuries, is the second widest of its kind in the world (after St Peter's in Rome). Also impressive are the fourteenth-century silver altarpiece and Gothic tombs.

It's well worth visiting the twelfth-century **cloister** (same hours as the Catedral), and the Tresor Capitular (Chapter Treasury), which features a wealth of religious artefacts, including medieval gold pieces, a fifteenth-century bible and the ornate sixteenth-century *retablo* of Santa Elena. The main attraction is a splendid Italian tapestry, which dates back to the twelfth century and depicts the Creation. The Catedral was also one of the filming locations for the popular *Game of Thrones* series.

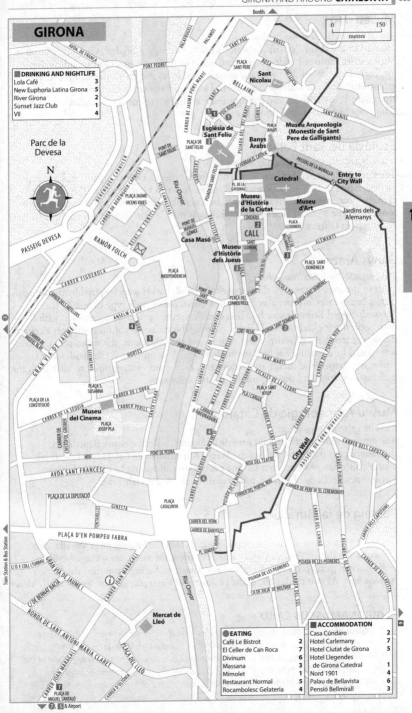

GIRONA

DRINKING AND NIGHTLIFE
Lola Café	3
New Euphoria Latina Girona	5
River Girona	2
Sunset Jazz Club	1
VII	4

Parc de la Devesa

EATING
Café Le Bistrot	2
El Celler de Can Roca	7
Divinum	6
Massana	3
Mimolet	1
Restaurant Normal	5
Rocambolesc Gelateria	4

ACCOMMODATION
Casa Cúndaro	2
Hotel Carlemany	7
Hotel Ciutat de Girona	5
Hotel Llegendes de Girona Catedral	1
Nord 1901	4
Palau de Bellavista	6
Pensió Bellmirall	3

11

Museu d'Art

Pujada de la Catedral 12 • Charge • http://museuart.cat

Housed in the Palau Episcopal (Bishop's Palace) near the Catedral, Girona's five-storey **Museu d'Art** features a wide-ranging collection of Romanesque, Gothic and modern art, including beautifully preserved murals from local churches, fifteenth-century embroidery and rare stained-glass tables. Don't miss the tenth-century portable altar from Sant Pere de Rodes and the impressive collection of modern Catalan art, such as sculptures by Olot artist Miquel Blay.

Església de Sant Feliu

Pl. de Sant Feliu • Charge, includes Catedral • http://catedraldegirona.cat

The large **Església de Sant Feliu** is one of Girona's most iconic churches, and it reveals an interesting transition between the Romanesque and Gothic styles. The thirteenth-century Romanesque interior is topped by a grand Gothic nave, and a Baroque tower looms over the western facade. The highlight is the Catalan Gothic statue, *Crist Jacent* (Recumbent Christ).

Banys Àrabs

C/Ferran el Catòlic • Charge • http://banysarabs.cat

Built in the twelfth century, the **Banys Àrabs** (Arab baths) were inspired by the Romans' public bathhouses, and are among the best preserved of their type in Spain. The Moorish-tinged Romanesque building contains several graceful rooms, each with its own pool: the frigidarium (cold-water room), whose elegant columns support a central dome; the tepidarium (warm-water room); and the caldarium, the steam room, which was heated by a roaring fire burning underneath. Also on view is the apodyterium (changing room), and there's an outdoor terrace, a good vantage point to view both the building's exterior and the surrounding Girona cityscape.

Museu Arqueologia de Catalunya

C/Santa Llúcia 8 • Charge • http://mac.cat

The impressive **Monestir de Sant Pere de Galligants**, a Romanesque Benedictine monastery near the baths, houses the **Museu Arqueologia de Catalunya**. It features a large collection of finds from Girona excavations, including beautiful Hebrew tombstones, sections of Roman pillars and Bronze Age metalworks.

Passeig de la Muralla

Free

One of the finest vantage points over Girona is from the **Passeig de la Muralla**, also known as the Passeig Arqueològic, a walkway along the ramparts and medieval city wall. You can gain access to it from various points, including from near the Museu Arqueologia. As you trudge along the perimeter of the walls, you can enjoy lovely views

---

GIRONAMUSEUS CARD

The **GironaMuseus card** (http://gironamuseus.cat) offers discounted entry to six of Girona's museums – the Museu d'Arqueologia de Catalunya, Museu d'Art, Museu d'Història de la Ciutat, Museu d'Història dels Jueus, Museu del Cinema and Casa Masó. Pay regular entry at any of the six, pick up the card and then you'll receive fifty percent discount to the other museums. You can get the card at any of the museums covered by the card, or at the *turisme* (see page 686).

of Girona – over the colourful rooftops to the river snaking through the centre – and the surrounding Ter valley. The walkway has several exits along the way, and it ends at Pl. Catalunya, where you can descend and amble back into the old town.

Carrer de la Força and the Jewish Quarter

Girona's Jewish community, known as the **Call** or the **Aljama**, existed for more than six hundred years, and the warren of narrow streets and alleyways around **Carrer de la Força** is widely regarded as one of the finest preserved Jewish neighbourhoods in Europe.

Centre Bonastruc ça Porta and Museu d'Història dels Jueus
C/Força 8 • Charge • http://girona.cat/call

The well-run **Centre Bonastruc ça Porta**, housed in a former synagogue, is home to the **Museu d'Història dels Jueus**, which does an excellent job of curating archeological and ethnological finds from Girona's Jewish heritage. The exhibition covers themes such as festivals and tradition; the synagogue and cemetery; the diaspora; and the Inquisition, which features a display of original documents ordering the expulsion of all Jews from Spain. Other highlights include a gilded seal used for making Passover bread; a fourteenth-century limestone slab inscribed with Jewish law from a local synagogue; and a unique belt buckle, dating to between the thirteenth and fifteenth centuries, engraved with what is believed to be the mythical Leviathan, which features in the Hebrew Bible.

11

Museu d'Història de la Ciutat
C/Força 27 • Charge • http://girona.cat

Girona's history is formidable, and the excellent **Museu d'Història de la Ciutat** offers a well-organized overview under one roof. There's a wide range of Roman remains and modern arts and crafts on show, and the museum includes exhibits on the old fortified walls, and those who attacked them to plunder Girona; the history of the Catalan *sardana* dance and other folkloric traditions; and contemporary paintings by regional artists.

Casa Masó
C/Ballesteries 29 • Charge • http://rafaelmaso.org

Step into early twentieth-century Girona at the superbly restored home of acclaimed Girona architect Rafael Masó (1880–1935), who formed a key part of the Catalan *noucentisme* cultural movement. *Noucentisme*, which took its name from the "1900s" (in Catalan, *noucents*), was both a continuation of *modernisme* and a reaction to it, with a style that was characterized by elegant classicism as well as a renewed civic and Catalan pride. **Casa Masó** is the only one of the famous houses on the Ríu Onyar that is open to the public, and the beautifully designed interior features period furnishings, as well as paintings, sculpture, ceramics and drawings from the eighteenth to twentieth centuries.

Museu del Cinema
C/Sèquia 1 • Charge • http://museudelcinema.cat

The top-notch **Museu del Cinema**, based on an extraordinary private collection, is less a museum and more of what the curators call "cinema before cinema", with an utterly intriguing array of the gadgets and artefacts that provided popular entertainment before cinema itself came along, from Indonesian shadow puppets to eighteenth- and nineteenth-century devices like phantasmagoria, fantascopes and magic lanterns. It's all rounded up with movie memorabilia, including costumes from *Tootsie* and *Hello Dolly*.

11

JEWISH GIRONA

A Jewish community first settled in Girona in the late ninth century; by the tenth century, the Jews had become a prosperous and influential sector of the city's society, but this all changed in the thirteenth century, when Gironan Jews became the victims of severe and unrelenting persecution. The entire Jewish quarter became a constant target of racist attacks and eventually became an isolated ghetto, in which the residents were virtually imprisoned, confined within neighbourhood limits and banned from the rest of the city. This continued until 1492, when all Jews were expelled from Spain. Life in the Call was bleak and presented an immense daily challenge: out of desperate necessity, residents created an underground community of tiny alleys and courtyards within which to survive.

ARRIVAL AND INFORMATION

GIRONA

By train The train station is near Pl. d'Espanya, a 15–25min walk southwest from the Barri Vell. Girona is well connected by train; it's on the train line between Barcelona (39min or 1hr 30min), Figueres (40min) and Portbou (1hr). The Barcelona–Paris high-speed train (2–4 trains daily) stops in Girona and Figueres, as does the high-speed Madrid–Marseille.

By bus The bus station is next to the train station. Teisa buses operate regularly to regional cities, including Besalú (50min) and Olot (a little over 1hr). Sarfa runs several buses in the summer from the airport to the coast, including Roses (1hr 15min) and Tossa de Mar (1hr 15min).

Turisme Rambla de la Llibertat 1 (April–Oct: Mon–Fri 9am–8pm, Sat 9am–2pm & 3–7pm, Sun 9am–2pm; Nov–March: Mon–Fri 9am–7pm, Sat 9am–2pm & 3–7pm, Sun 9am–2pm; http://girona.cat/turisme).

ACCOMMODATION

SEE MAP PAGE 683

Girona has a wide variety of accommodation, from well-maintained hostels to historic hotels, many of which are central and within an easy stroll to the old quarter. In the surrounding countryside, you'll also find a range of comfortable **cases de pagés** (*casas rurales*), including in the rustic hamlet of **Bordils**, which lies 10km northeast of town.

THE CITY

Casa Cúndaro Pujada de la Catedral 7, http://casacundaro.com. Top off your experience of medieval Girona by staying at this family-run hotel, which features restored rooms and apartments in a historic Jewish home a short stroll from the Catedral. It may lack a contemporary shine, but it has history in spades, with wooden beams to stone walls. €€

Hotel Carlemany Pl. Miquel Santaló, http://hotel carlemanygirona.com. Modern hotel, geared more towards business travellers, but handily within walking distance of the train station. €€

Hotel Ciutat de Girona C/Nord 2, http://hotel ciutatdegirona.com. This simple hotel in the centre of town has modern rooms in muted greys and red. The owners also operate the Apartaments Plaça del Vi, comfortable, amenity-rich apartments that are ideal for longer stays or for groups. €€

Hotel Llegendes de Girona Catedral Portal de la Barca 4, http://llegendeshotel.com. Set in a magnificently restored eighteenth-century building, this handsome hotel is smack in the centre of town, near the Catedral and the Banys Àrabs. The comfortable rooms balance sleek amenities and crisp white bed linen with earthy touches like exposed brick walls and pine ceilings. Couples take note: the Eros Room is curated for couples, with furnishings like a tantric chair. €€

Nord 1901 C/Nord 7–9, http://nord1901.com. This lovely boutique hotel offers the best of all worlds. It's central, in

FEAST ACROSS CATALUNYA AT MERCAT DEL LLEÓ

Barcelona has the famous La Boquería; Girona's version is the Mercat del Lleó (Mon–Fri 7am–2pm, Sat until 2.30pm; http://mercatlleo.cat), a colourful, aromatic market that unfolds just east of the river on Pl. Calvet i Rubalcaba. The 60-plus stalls reflect the natural diversity of Catalunya – apples and pears from fragrant Girona orchards, mushrooms pulled from Pyrenean soil, pungent goat's cheeses from the Garrotxa region and vast displays of freshly caught seafood from the Mediterranean. Take a twirl through the market for a whiff of local flavour, and then refuel over a *café* at the market bar. For a deeper exploration of the market and Girona's culinary heritage, check out Girona Food Tours (http://gironafoodtours.com; tours and fees vary), launched by two long-time Girona residents.

the heart of Girona. It's housed in a historic building, with plenty of luxurious and contemporary amenities, and it has one of the only gardens with private swimming pool in this part of town. Choose between handsome rooms or spacious apartments. Doubles €€

Palau de Bellavista Pujada Polvorins 1, http://urhbellavistagironahotel.com. The short trek uphill to this stylish, glass-wrapped hotel is worth it for the view alone. Take in panoramic vistas of Girona's medieval quarter and beyond, and then relax in the sleek rooms, done up in bright whites and caramel browns. €€

Pensió Bellmirall C/Bellmirall 3, http://bellmirall.cat. Housed in a renovated fifteenth-century building, with comfortable rooms, a communal living room and a hearty continental breakfast. It's right near the Catedral, so light sleepers may be woken up by the bell chimes. €€

EATING

SEE MAP PAGE 683

Girona has a diversity of **restaurants**, including a top-notch selection serving Catalan cuisine, most famously at the *Celler de San Roca* (see box, page 687) and most recently at the latest culinary venture by the Roca brothers –*Restaurant Normal* (see page 687). The Old Town is sprinkled with restaurants and bars, while you'll find breezy outdoor cafés along Rambla de la Llibertat and Pl. del Vi.

Café Le Bistrot Pujada Sant Domènec 4, http://cafelebistrot.com. Inviting restaurant with a *belle époque* interior and tables outside, where you can fill up on their speciality – *pizzes de pagès* (Catalan pizzas on thick bread) and crepes. €€

★ **El Celler de Can Roca** Can Sunyer 48, about 2.5km northwest of Girona, off the Taialà road, http://cellercanroca.com. The menu showcases Ferran Adrià-style renderings of Catalan cuisine. Among the 20-plus courses: a tiny olive tree hung with melting balls of olive oil ice cream; langoustine enveloped in a cocoa-bean sauce, served in a bowl the shape of a cocoa bean; and sea bream capped with a patchwork quilt of *samfaina* (Catalonia's answer to ratatouille). Your best bet is to book online – reservations are accepted up to 11 months in advance; a new month becomes available at midnight on the 1st day of every month. €€€€

Divinum C/Albereda 7, http://divinum.cat. Feast on creative contemporary Catalan cuisine at this sleek restaurant, with dishes like succulent veal with port wine and apples, and sardines with strawberries and yogurt.

Don't miss the superb array of artisanal cheeses. This is a place where it's well worth going for the tasting menu, which shows off the best of the kitchen. €€€

Massana C/Bonastruc de Porta 10, http://restaurantmassana.com. This elegant, deservedly celebrated restaurant takes locally sourced cuisine to a high art, serving such dishes as juicy lamb shoulder with rosemary and vegetables and roasted wild turbot with truffles. €€€

Mimolet C/Pou Rodó 12, http://mimolet.cat. Classy, welcoming restaurant with a Catalan menu built around local produce, including rabbit with turnip cream, hazelnuts and cacao. €€€

Restaurant Normal C/Plaça de l'Oli 1, http://restaurantnormal.com. The Roca brothers opened this gourmand destination in 2021, putting head chef Elisabet Nolla in charge of the kitchen. The focus is on homemade, seasonal food rooted in place, made from recipes passed down the generations. Expect a more relaxed vibe than that of *Normal*'s older sibling, *El Celler de Can Roca*. €€€€

Rocambolesc Gelateria C/Santa Clara 50, http://rocambolesc.com. A Willy Wonka-esque ice-cream and sweets shop by celebrated pastry chef Jordi Roca. It serves freshly churned, all-natural ice cream – try the ever-popular baked apple flavour – with toppings like cotton candy and guava jam. €

DRINKING AND NIGHTLIFE

SEE MAP PAGE 683

Girona's nightlife caters to the sizeable university crowd, with rustic **bars** in Pl. de la Independencia and across the river along Rambla de la Llibertat, and splashier **clubs** (like *Blau Club*) further afield. The suburb of Pedret, about 700m north of the old town, also heats up at night with a string of clubs, while in the summer, everyone heads to the open-air bars,

---

DINING WITH THE ROCA BROTHERS

Every year, kitchens around the world vie for first place in *the* World's 50 Best Restaurants list. And in 2013 and 2015, that honour went to the three-Michelin-starred **El Celler de Can Roca** (see page 687) in Girona. The Roca brothers – Joan, Josep and Jordi – had already been household names in Spain, but nabbing the top spots – twice – catapulted them onto the worldwide culinary stage. Their win was well-deserved, and each brother continues to work his speciality within the restaurant – Joan as the head chef, Jordi on desserts, and Josep on wine. If you don't get a reservation at the restaurant, you can still sample the Roca magic in Girona – at their **Rocambolesc Gelateria** (see page 687) or at their latest venture *Restaurant Normal* (see page 687).

Les Carpes, which operate in the Parc de la Devesa, on the west side of the river in the modern part of town.

Lola Café C/Força 7, 629 794 360. This lively bar, in the middle of the old town, serves tasty tropical cocktails – mojitos, caipirinhas – and heats up with occasional live music, from Catalan rumba to salsa and more.

New Euphoria Latina Girona Camp de les Lloses 8. About 2km south of town, this is where the cool kids come to groove and flirt, with DJs spinning tracks all night long on the weekends.

River Girona C/Barca 2, http://instagram.com/rivergirona_. This casual bar and café, with a large, sun-dappled terrace, is at the foot of the lovely Església de Sant Feliu. Enjoy cocktails, chilled beer, local wine and other beverages, from fresh-squeezed juice to coffee, as well as hearty sandwiches and burgers.

Sunset Jazz Club C/Jaume Pons i Martí 12, http://sunsetjazz-club.com. Near the old town, this lively joint hosts regular jazz concerts and jam sessions featuring musicians from around the country – and the world. You can enjoy potent cocktails poured with top-shelf alcohol, plus a good assortment of whiskies.

VII Pl. del Vi 7, viigirona.com. Ease into the evening at this charming wine bar that has an apt location: Pl. del Vi (Wine Square). The bar's well-curated wine list crisscrosses the globe, but ask for the day's selection of local wine (from from the surrounding Empordà wine region (see page 677).

Púbol

Salvador Dalí had many obsessions, but none quite like Gala, his beloved wife and lifelong muse, who he met when she was visiting Cadaqués in 1929 with her husband, French poet Paul Éluard. Dalí and Gala fell in love and married in 1934. Dalí lavished many gifts on her, including, in 1969, the medieval castle of Casa Púbol, which rises near the small village of **Púbol**, about 20km northeast from Girona. Gala lived here, and rumour has it that she entertained a string of lovers all the while, and imposed strict rules on Dalí, who supposedly had to get permission before he could visit. She stayed here until her death in 1982, when **Dalí** moved in. The artist made this his permanent base until 1984 when fire struck parts of the castle, prompting him to move to Figueres.

Castell Gala Dalí

Charge • http://salvador-dali.org • Regular Sarfa-run Girona–Palamós buses stop in La Pera, from where it's 2km to Púbol (you'll need to walk or take a taxi); the Barcelona–Portbou train stops in Flaçà, which is 4km from Púbol

The castle, which is now the **Castell Gala Dalí**, is decorated in vintage Dalí style, though parts of it are considerably more understated than other Dalí sights – it is one of three in the region (see box, page 680). Stuffed animal heads protrude from walls, and dome ceilings are painted in quasi-religious motifs, but there are also quietly stark rooms with simple wood floors. Exhibits feature a supremely entertaining array of Dalí photos, particularly from his 1930s–40s heyday, while outside is an atmospheric swimming pool and garden, populated by sculptures of Richard Wagner, one of Dalí's favourite composers. One of the most important rooms is the mausoleum in the basement, where Gala is buried.

Figueres

It is a testament to **Dalí**'s enduring popularity that his eponymous museum, in the middle of **FIGUERES**, 35km northeast of Girona, is one of the most visited sites in the region. There's more to Figueres, of course, but you wouldn't immediately know it from the crowds tripping over themselves to get to the museum. Native son Dalí returned to Figueres specifically to create this homage to Surrealism, and what an homage it is: wonderfully bizarre and cheekily interactive, the museum is all you'd expect from the world's most celebrated Surrealist.

By all means make the museum your first stop – but leave yourself some time to roam Figueres afterwards. Cutting a wide swathe through the centre of town is **La Rambla de Figueres**, a graceful, leafy pedestrian street lined with modern houses and outdoor cafés. The **Museu de l'Empordà** features local archeological finds and the nearby **Castell de Sant Ferran** is a massive fortification on sprawling grounds.

Teatre-Museu Dalí

Teatre-Museu Dalí Pl. Gala i Salvador Dalí • **Dalí Joies** Corner of C/María Àngels Vayreda and Pujada del Castell • Charge • http://salvador-dali.org

One thing is certain: you won't have trouble spotting the **Teatre-Museu Dalí**. Just look for a roof topped with giant eggs and a red facade with protruding bread loaves. Housed in a former theatre – which is particularly apt, for this most theatrical of artists – the museum is designed around a large courtyard with white ceramic sinks and gold mannequins inspired by Oscar statues. Light streams into the building through a transparent, geodesic dome ceiling that resembles the eye of a fly, in a nod to Dalí's fixation with insects. Incidentally, the artist had no problem with flies, but was supposedly repulsed by ants, which he depicted crawling out of eyeballs and such in his paintings.

Dalí created the museum to be an all-round sensory – and surreal – experience. Look through binoculars to see *Gala Nude Looking at the Sea Which at Twenty Metres is Transformed into a Portrait of Abraham Lincoln*, or revive a "dead" body in a coffin made of circuit boards. And check out *The Face of Mae West That Can Be Used as a Drawing Room*, in which Mae's giant nose has a fireplace (complete with logs) built into each nostril, and her fleshy red lips are a couch.

Inside the **Sala de Tresor** are housed many of Dalí's better-known works, including *The Spectre of Sex Appeal*, which explores the artist's famous sex phobia. Other emblematic works include *Soft Self-Portrait with Fried Bacon*, in which Dalí's dripping visage is held up by little sticks, and *Venus de Milo with Drawers*.

The museum also features a terrific line-up of changing temporary exhibitions, which have included everything from Dali self-portraits to the artist's three-dimentional art.

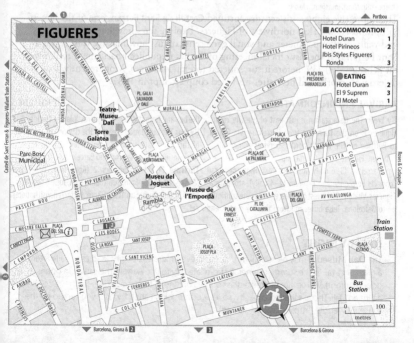

Dalí, fittingly, is buried in his fantastical museum. By 1984, he had moved to the nearby **Torre Galtea**, where he died in 1989. His body now lies behind a simple granite slab in a basement gallery of the museum. The museum ticket includes entry to the nearby **Dalí Joies** exhibit, featuring jewels designed by Dalí.

Museu de l'Empordà

La Rambla 2 • Charge • http://museuemporda.org

The **Museu de l'Empordà** explores the region's history, with exhibits covering Greek and Roman archeological remains, frescoes, sacred art and medieval sculpture. It also features a well-curated collection of nineteenth- and twentieth-century art by an assortment of well-known Catalan and Spanish artists, from Sorolla and Miró to Tàpies to Dalí.

Museu del Joguet de Catalunya

C/Sant Pere 1 • Charge • http://mjc.cat

From ancient toy wooden tops and bronze Roman rattles to candy-red cars, miniature circuses and twentieth-century optical-illusion games, the **Museu del Joguet de Catalunya** (Toy Museum of Catalunya) offers a playful glimpse into the history of having fun. Particularly curious are the religious items, which include altar boys' clothes from 1905 and mini-churches with tiny moveable priest figures. Don't miss the traditional *caganers*, little figurines of squatting peasants taking a break to "fertilize the earth", who are cheekily hidden in the back of Catalan nativity scenes. The museum also hosts lively temporary exhibitions.

Castell de Sant Ferran

Charge • http://castillosanfernando.org

The impressive eighteenth-century fortified **Castell de Sant Ferran**, one of the largest in Europe, stands 1km northwest of Figueres. Explore the sprawling castle grounds and walk its 4km perimeter and you'll get a sense of just how massive it is. It was at Sant Ferran that the last official meeting of Spain's Republican parliament took place, on February 1, 1939, before it surrendered to Franco's forces. More recently, Colonel Tejero was imprisoned here after his failed coup attempt in 1981.

ARRIVAL AND INFORMATION

FIGUERES

By train The train station is just east of the city centre. Figueres is on the train line from Barcelona, via Girona, to Portbou on the French border. Services run regularly between Figueres and Girona (up to 20 daily; 40min), and Barcelona (3–6 daily; just over 2hr). High-speed rail connects Perpignan and Figueres (2–4 daily), stopping at Figueres-Vilafant, 2km west of Figueres; the route continues on to Barcelona. Teisa buses run from the city centre, and the bus and train stations, to Figueres-Vilafant station.

By bus The bus station is east of the city centre, just south of the train station. Buses operate regularly to regional cities, including Girona (1hr) and Barcelona (2hr 30min).

Turisme Pl. de l'Escorxador 2 (April–May, Oct–March Mon–Sat 9.30am–6pm, Sun 10am–3pm; June & Sep Mon–Sat 9.30am–7pm, Sun 10am–3pm; http://en.visitfigueres.cat).

DALÍ BY NIGHT

The **Dalí Museum** may be surreal by day, but is even more so at night (and especially after a glass of cava). In the summer, generally from late July to late August, the museum opens its doors at night. Visitors are offered a glass of cava on one of the terraces, where they also show a film on Dalí. There is limited capacity, so it's worth booking ahead, which you can do on the museum website (http://salvador-dali.org).

ACCOMMODATION
SEE MAP PAGE 689

Hotel Duran C/Lausaca 5, http://hotelduran.com. Long-running hotel – Dalí and Gala were frequent visitors – that has been sparsely updated, with gleaming polished wood floors and muted colours enlivened by striped curtains and bedspreads. Keep an eye out for original Dalí works displayed throughout. The restaurant serves tasty Catalan cuisine. €€

Hotel Pirineos Avda. Salvador Dalí 68, http://hotelpirineospelegri.com. Central, comfortable and pristine, *Hotel Pirineos* has spacious, handsome rooms with well-equipped bathrooms. €€

Ibis Styles Figueres Ronda Avda. Salvador Dalí 17, http://hotelronda.com. It looks a bit antiseptic from the outside, but this modern hotel has elegant rooms and a friendly restaurant with terrace. €€

EATING
SEE MAP PAGE 689

Figueres is crammed with casual restaurants, many of which cater to the crowds visiting Museu Dalí. You will find some good choices, though, slightly beyond the centre.

El 9 Suprem C/Llobregat 4, http://facebook.com/elsuprem. With bright and airy interiors, *El 9 Suprem* offers consistently good food at affordable prices. The menu features classics like paella, *fideuá de carne* (a fried pasta dish with pork) and *canelons de bolets i trufa* (mushroom and truffle cannelloni). €€€

Hotel Duran C/Lausaca 5, http://hotelduran.com. You're in good company: Dalí used to have his own dining room here, where creative regional cuisine has been prepared by the Duran family for generations. *Dishes* might include *suquet* (fish stew) or duck with pears. €€€

★ **El Motel** Hotel Empordà, Avda. Salvador Dalí i Domènech 170, 1km northwest of Figueres, http://elmotelrestaurant.com. Before the foams of Ferran Adrià and the "emotional cuisine" of the Roca brothers, there was the *Hotel Empordà* (originally called the *Motel Ampurdan*, in part because it sits on a busy roadway), where chef Jaume Subirós is credited with elevating traditional cooking from home kitchen to restaurant quality. Considered the birthplace of modern Catalan cuisine, *El Motel* (as the restaurant is now called in homage to its roots) continues to serve some of the finest and most innovative food in the region. The chefs find inspiration in the sea, with dishes like wild sea bass from Cadaqués with lime leaves and polenta, and rock lobster from Cap de Creus with fragrant rice, shrimp from Roses and sea cucumbers. €€€€

La Garrotxa

The fertile landscape of **La Garrotxa**, which unfolds west of Girona and Figueres, is anchored by the historic capital of **Olot**. To the east lies lovely, quiet **Besalú**; to the north, mountain peaks march along the French border; and to the south extends the **Parc Natural de la Zona Volcànica**, a verdant, hilly terrain punctuated by volcanic cones and craters.

Besalú

Medieval **BESALÚ**, about 50km north of Girona, is a captivating sight: the impressive eleventh-century Romanesque **Pont Fortificat** spans the River Fluvià at the entrance to the town, beyond which rise church towers amid stone houses. These days, Besalú is a small, humble town, but its beautifully preserved core, with dark little streets, arcaded shops and elegant historic architecture, is testament to its formidable past. Roman, Visigothic and Muslim rulers all passed through, but Besalú's most important role came between the tenth and twelfth centuries, when it served as the capital of the region until power was transferred to Barcelona.

Església de Sant Pere and around

The thirteenth-century **Casa de la Vila**, which now houses the *Ajuntament*, rises over Pl. de la Llibertat. To the west of Llibertat lies a spacious *plaça*, the Prat de Sant Pere, which is presided over by the tenth-century Benedictine monastery **Església de Sant Pere**. Keep an eye out for the beautiful Gothic window on the west facade. The nearby Romanesque **Església de Sant Vicenç** features impressive Gothic capitals. Both churches are usually only open for services, but guided tours are sometimes organized by the *turisme*.

Miqvé

Baixada de Mikwe • Charge for guided tours

Similar to Girona, Besalú had a Jewish community from the ninth century onwards, until the Jews were forced out of town in 1436 due to Christian persecution. Their **Miqvé**, said to be the only existing Jewish ritual bath in Spain, sits near the river and features a barrel-vaulted underground stone room. The bath was also once connected to the town's **synagogue**, the remains of which were discovered nearby.

ARRIVAL AND INFORMATION   BESALÚ

By bus The bus stop is on the main Olot–Girona road; there are regular buses to and from Figueres (25min) and Girona (50min).

Turisme C/Pont 1 (daily 10am–2pm & 4–7pm; http://

besalu.cat). In addition to guided tours of the churches and Miqvé, the *turisme* also offers tours encompassing all of Besalú's sights.

ACCOMMODATION AND EATING

★ Cúria Reial Pl. de la Llibertat 8, http://curiareial.com. Enjoy the twin pleasures of top-notch local cuisine and the beautiful outdoors at this friendly, mid-priced restaurant, where you can dine alfresco on the terrace overlooking the historic bridge. €€

Els Jardins de la Martana Pont 2, http://lamartana. com. For a feel of Besalú's history, bed down in this antique mansion, with its faded but graceful rooms and leafy

gardens, that sits across from the Pont Fortificat. €€

Pont Vell C/Pont Vell 24, http://restaurantpontvell. com. Named after the bridge that it overlooks, this rustic restaurant with a lovely outdoor terrace offers traditional Catalan cuisine with a modern twist, including squid stuffed with wild mushrooms; *escudella*, a typical Catalan stew of meat and vegetables; and the *Pont Vell* speciality – sweet and sour rabbit. €€€

Beget

The tiny village of **BEGET**, about 30km northwest of Besalú, is nestled so deeply in a valley that you don't see it until you're almost upon it. And when you do, it's a handsome sight: Beget looks much as it did centuries ago, with narrow cobbled streets, little bridges and stone houses. A stillness fills the graceful twelfth-century church, **Sant Cristòfor**, which rises over the village. The church (sporadic opening times; enquire in the village) is notable for its *Majestat*, a carved-wood figure of Christ in a full-length tunic, arms outstretched.

ARRIVAL AND DEPARTURE   BEGET

By bus and taxi It's hard to reach Beget without your own transport. If you don't have your own wheels, the best

option is to take a bus to Camprodon (see page 698), and then hire a taxi.

EATING

Can Jeroni C/Bellaire 17–19, http://canjeroni.net. Friendly, family-run restaurant serving seasonal Catalan cuisine such as roast lamb or chicken with plumes and

prunes. Seating is available near an old bridge and with views of the church. €€€

CYCLING THE CARRILET

Where trains once rumbled down tracks, cyclists can now pedal amid quiet greenery. The **Ruta del Carrilet** (http://viesverdes.cat) are traffic-free trails for pedestrians and cyclists that follow unused train lines, offering the chance to ride or stroll through the rolling Catalan countryside, passing small towns and villages along the way. Among the most popular is the 54km Olot-to-Girona route. In Olot, the trail starts at Fonts Sant Roc (Sant Roc Springs), just southwest of the city, near the Fluvià River; enquire at the *turisme* for further information and directions. The route is relatively flat and therefore appropriate for all levels, and is especially popular with families.

Olot

La Garrotxa's provincial capital, **OLOT**, is an amiable, mid-sized town with busy shopping streets and a breezy Pl. Mayor. Passeig d'en Blay, the central *rambla*, is flanked by lovely historic buildings and dotted with lively cafés. Olot's varied countryside, marked by sheer cliffs, verdant valleys and extinct volcanic cones and craters, inspired the highly respected nineteenth- and twentieth-century **Olot School** of landscape painters, whose works you can view in the town's Museu de la Garrotxa.

Museu de la Garrotxa

C/Hospici 8 · Charge · http://museus.olot.cat

Nature was at the core of the Olot School of painters, who explored Garrotxa's unique landscape on canvas, from rolling, pastoral hills to desolate terrain punctuated by stark trees. The school, founded by Joaquim Vayreda i Vila, was also influenced by the French Impressionists. You can view many of its striking works in the well-curated **Museu de la Garrotxa**, housed in a renovated eighteenth-century hospital. The museum also features *modernista* sculptures by Miquel Blay and Josep Clarà, and exhibits on the history of Olot and Catalan arts and crafts.

Parc Nou

Avda. Santa Coloma, 1km southwest of town centre · Jardí Botànic Free · http://museus.olot.cat

Parc Nou is a nine-acre municipal park that encompasses the leafy **Jardí Botànic** and the **Casal dels Volcans**, a Palladian building that houses the helpful Centro d'Informació del Parc Natural de la Zona Volcànica, where you can pick up park maps and other information. The park also hosts a variety of open-air musical concerts and festivals.

ARRIVAL AND INFORMATION
OLOT

By bus The bus station is at the east end of C/Bisbe Lorenzana, the main thoroughfare. Teisa runs regular buses to and from Barcelona (2hr 25min) and Girona (just over 1hr).
Turisme C/Francesc Fàbregas 6 (summer Mon–Sat 10am–

2pm & 4–7pm, Sun 10am–2pm; winter Mon–Sat 10am–1pm & 4–8pm, Sun 10am–1pm; http://turismeolot.com). The *turisme* has up-to-date lists of local accommodation and transport timetables, and also sells a joint ticket to the museums in the area.

ACCOMMODATION AND EATING

Olot has a range of decent **hotels and hostels** in town, but some of the most appealing accommodation options are the **manors and B&Bs** in the surrounding countryside, many of which make the most of their proximity to the Parc Natural de la Zona Volcànica, with terraces, hearty breakfasts to fuel your hiking, and bikes for hire.
Ca l'Enric Carretera de Camprodon, Vall de Bianya, 7km northwest of Olot, http://restaurantcalenric.cat. Locally sourced Catalan cuisine is taken to a high art at this long-running restaurant that's set in a beautifully renovated nineteenth-century country house. Dishes range from beef tartare with herbs to rabbit with wild mushrooms. The restaurant also features a variety of tasting menus. €€€€
★ **Les Cols** Carretera de la Canya, on the northern outskirts of Olot, http://lescols.com. Fresh produce reigns supreme at this elegant Michelin-starred restaurant, where

the menu might include locally sourced crayfish salad or asparagus grown in their own garden. €€€€
Hotel Borrell C/Nonet Escubós, Olot, http://hotelborrell.com. Near the centre of town, next to Pl. Catalunya, this small hotel has simple rooms with hardwood floors and decently sized bathrooms. €€
Mas El Guitart Vall de Bianya, 7km northwest of Olot, just above Sant Andreu de Socarrats village, http://guitartrural.com. Comfortable country house, with farmyard-themed hardwood-floor rooms and cabins. There's also a soothing spa that offers therapies including hot-stone massages and reflexology. Minimum stay at certain times of the year. €
Olot Xanascat Pg. de Barcelona 15, Olot, http://xanascat.cat. This central, well-kept youth hostel with simple dorms is housed in a nineteenth-century tower set amid gardens. €

Parc Natural de la Zona Volcànica

The sprawling **Parc Natural de la Zona Volcànica** makes up much of the **Baixa Garrotxa** region. You won't see lava flows and smoke-snorting volcanoes, though – the last

VOLCANIC CUISINE

The volcanic fields of the Garrotxa region aren't just an intrinsic part of the landscape – they're also an intrinsic part of the local cuisine. Garrotxa is famed for its fertile soil, which has given way to an equally fertile and rich **Cuina Volcànica** (http://cuinavolcanica.cat – volcanic cuisine). Traditional ingredients – all locally produced – include Santa Pau haricot beans, black radishes, mushrooms and sheep's cheese. Olot, Besalú and Santa Pau have a variety of top-notch *cuina volcànica* **restaurants**, such as La Deu (see page 694). If you're in the area in January, head to Santa Pau (see page 694) for its Fira de Fesol, which celebrates the region's famous beans.

eruption was almost 11,000 years ago, and the park is in fact largely green and verdant, with a remarkably fertile soil. The volcanic landscape comes in the shape of the park's forty cones, which vary widely in size, the bigger ones topping 170m.

There are numerous trails through the park – if you're short on time, you can opt to take shorter trails to several of the volcanoes that start at car parks around Olot. Posted signs point out those that lead to the two easiest cones to access from town: **Volcà del Croscat**, the youngest cone in the park, and **Volcà de Santa Margarida**.

ARRIVAL AND INFORMATION PARC NATURAL DE LA ZONA VOLCÀNICA

Accessing the park You'll need your own wheels to access the park; there is a regular Teisa bus service between Girona and Olot.

Centro d'Informació del Parc Natural de la Zona Volcànica Casal del Volcans, Olot (http://gencat.cat/parcs/garrotxa). The main park information office is in Parc Nou in Olot, where you can pick up helpful hiking maps.

Turisme Av. De Volcans 14, Santa Pau (Wed–Sun 10am–2pm; http://santapau.com).

ACCOMMODATION AND EATING

Cal Sastre C/Cases Noves, near Plaçeta dels Balls, Santa Pau, http://calsastre.com. For a taste of the famous Santa Pau *fesols* (haricot beans), dine at this established Catalan restaurant, which also doubles as a handsome hotel (price includes breakfast). **€€€**

Can Blanc Ptges de la Deu, around 1.5km north of Olot, http://canblanc.es. The location here is the big draw: it's in the Parc Natural, and surrounded by greenery, yet still within easy reach of town (around 30min on foot, should you want to walk). Rooms are comfortable, and nearby is the historic *La Deu Restaurant*. **€€**

La Deu Restaurant Carretera de la Deu s/n, near Can Blanc, about 1.5km south of Olot, http://ladeu.es. This established restaurant, which sits in the Parc Natural and dates back to 1885, is helmed by the fourth and fifth generations of the Reixac family. The menu is rooted in *cuina volcànica*, and includes their signature La Deu potatoes, typical Catalan cannelloni; and grilled wild seabass. **€€€**

Santa Pau

Medieval **Santa Pau**, 9km southwest of Olot, sits right in the middle of the volcanic region, and is a great jumping-off point for exploration. The beautifully preserved village features stone houses, narrow lanes, ancient archways and the thirteenth-century **Pl. Mayor**, once the Firal dels Bous (Cattle Market). Santa Pau is also known for its *fesols* (haricot beans), which figure prominently in the local cuisine. The village celebrates its beloved bean in the Fira de Sant Antonic, also known as the **Fira de Fesol** (Fesol Festival), in mid- or late January.

Vic

The Serra del Montseny, a towering granite mountain range with lushly forested slopes, looms southwest of Girona. On the west of the range, 34km southwest of Olot and easily accessible as a day-trip from Barcelona, is the likeable, well-preserved town of

Vic. Vic is considered one of the more quintessential Catalan centres, both because the locals have especially strong Catalan pride, and also because it's near the Ripoll area, cradle of Catalan history. Vic was once the capital of an Iberian tribe, and in the second century became a Roman settlement – you'll spy various Roman remains, including parts of a temple, scattered around town.

Vic also hosted a prosperous medieval market, and the town has a yearly **Mercat Medieval de Vic** (http://vicfires.cat) in its old quarter in early December, celebrating its medieval past. Vic is defined by its elegant, enormous **Pl. Mayor**, ringed by historic, porticoed buildings, which features a colourful **food market** twice a week (Tues & Sat) – and if there's one thing to buy, it's Vic's famous sausages (*llonganissa* or *fuet*), which are heralded throughout Catalunya and perfect for tossing into the suitcase to bring home.

The Catedral and Museu d'Art Medieval

Catedral Pl. de la Catedral • Charge for cloister and crypt • **Museu d'Art Medieval** Pl. Bisbe Oliba 3 • Charge • http://museuepiscopalvic.com

Vic's Neoclassical **Catedral** looms over the centre of town; inside, striking murals depict scenes from the Bible by Catalan artist Josep Maria Sert. The nearby **Museu d'Art Medieval** features a superb collection of sacred art from the eleventh to thirteenth centuries, including an alabaster altarpiece depicting the Passion, Resurrection and Ascension of Christ. The museum also showcases an array of art and religious artefacts culled from Pyrenean churches, making it one of the most important collections of Catalan Romanesque art outside of the Museu d'Art de Catalunya in Barcelona.

ARRIVAL AND INFORMATION

VIC

By train and bus Trains and Sagalés buses run regularly to and from Barcelona (1hr 20min). It's a short walk east from the (adjacent) train and bus stations to the centre of town.

Turisme Pl. del Pes (Mon–Fri 9am–2pm & 4–7pm, Sat 10am–2pm & 4–7pm, Sun 10am–4pm; http://victurisme.cat).

ACCOMMODATION AND EATING

Estació del Nord Pl. de l'Estació 4, http://estaciodelnord.com. It's hard to get any more convenient than the sleek little boutique hotel on the upper level of Vic's train station. The fully refurbished hotel has well-maintained rooms, with lots of white and pale, earthy colours. €

El Jardinet C/Corretgers 8, http://eljardinetdevic.com. Dine on seasonal Mediterranean cuisine at this welcoming restaurant with a cute outdoor garden. It offers a well-priced weekday lunchtime *menú del día*. €€€

Seminar Allotjaments Ronda Camprodon 2, http://seminarivic.cat. This converted seminary, which lies a 5min stroll north of the old town, offers basic but comfortable rooms with private baths, as well as a *cafetería* that serves Catalan cuisine and breakfasts. €€

Up Rooms Vic Ptge. Can Mastrot, http://uproomsvic.com. This four-star contemporary hotel, in the heart of town, has comfortable rooms with hardwood floors and modern artwork. €€

The Catalan Pyrenees

Looming gracefully over northern Catalunya, the snow-tipped Pyrenees form a mighty barrier between the Iberian Peninsula and the rest of Europe. You can ski and hike throughout these mountains, making use of a range of ski centres and vast stretches of natural parkland. Imposing peaks reach more than 3400m, while fierce rivers cleave the green valleys; tucked away in the valleys and clinging to the mountains are centuries-old alpine villages, each with its own Romanesque church, collectively forming an open-air rural museum of early medieval architecture, particularly in the beautiful **Vall de Boí**.

The Pyrenees are easy to reach from Barcelona – **Ripoll**, a gateway town to the mountains, is accessible in less than three hours. The ski scene dominates the mountains northwest of Ripoll, while summer draws hikers and trekkers. North of Ripoll is the village of **Ribes de Freser**, where you can board the famous **cremallera** railway which snakes its way up to the small ski town and pilgrimage site of **Núria** – one of the most magnificent journeys in the Pyrenees.

West of here stretches the formidable **Serra del Cadí**, which offers superb hiking and trekking around one of Catalunya's most recognizable peaks, the **Pedraforca**. To the north, along the French border, is **La Cerdanya**, a lush, sunny Pyrenean valley that's especially popular in the summer with outdoor enthusiasts. Cerdanya's capital is the lively town of **Puigcerdà**, while just across the border sits the geographical oddity of **Llívia**, a Spanish town fully enclosed by France. In winter, skiers flock to **La Molina** and **Masella**, the two big ski resorts in the area.

The mountainous terrain around **La Seu d'Urgell**, still further west, offers some of the best trekking in the Pyrenees. Whitewater aficionados get their adrenalin rush in the **Noguera Pallaresa** valley, where churning rivers offer the best rafting in the region. Finally, in the far northwest unfolds the rugged **Parc Nacional d'Aigüestortes i Estany de Sant Maurici**, and lush **Val d'Aran**, one of Spain's top ski resorts.

11

Ripoll

The quiet mountain town of **RIPOLL**, which serves as a good starting point for exploring the Pyrenees, is known as the cradle of Catalunya, as it was here that founding father Guifré el Pélos (Wilfred the Hairy) staked his claim to what became the Autonomous Community of Catalunya. The chief reason to visit is to view the impressive Benedictine Monestir de Santa Maria. Ripoll also holds an international **music festival** in July and August in the fourteenth-century church of Sant Pere, and is the starting point for a beautiful Via Verde (Green Way; http://viesverdes.cat) – trek or cycle the 15km La Ruta del Ferro i del Carbó (Iron and Coal), which starts near the train station, to Sant Joan de les Abadesses (see page 697).

Monestir de Santa Maria

Pl. Abat Oliba • Charge • http://monestirderipoll.cat

One of the few parts of the building to survive a tragic fire, the splendid twelfth-century facade of the west portal of the **Monestir de Santa Maria**, which was founded some four hundred years earlier, is considered one of Spain's great works of Romanesque art. The portal showcases a series of sculptures depicting the Creation and other biblical scenes in gorgeous detail – singing angels, the stories of Moses and Solomon and mythical beasts representing the Apostles, among other scenes – giving it its nickname as the "Stone Bible" or "Ripoll Bible". The cloister has also aged beautifully, while the nave is a replica of the original structure that was built over Guifré el Pélos' tomb.

LONG-DISTANCE HIKING IN THE PYRENEES

Running roughly parallel to the GR10, which runs on the French side, the **GR11** is a network of long-distance hiking trails which traverses the Spanish Pyrenees from one end to the other. Estimated to be about 850–900km in length, it runs from the Golfo de Vizcaya (Bay of Biscay) in the Basque region to the west to Cap de Creus, near Cadaqués in the east. For seasoned trekkers, there is also the **HRP** (Haute Randonnée Pyrénéenne), which follows a higher and wilder course in the Pyrenees, crisscrossing the Spanish–French border along the way. It runs largely through the Parc National des Pyrénées in France but also takes in parts of the Parc Nacional d'Aigüestortes i Estany de Sant Maurici. In Spain, you can get more general information about the GR routes from the Federación Española de Deportes de Montaña y Escalada (FEDME; Spanish Mountain Sports Federation; http://fedme.es), though the website is mostly in Spanish only. Tourist offices, refuges and many hotels in the Pyrenees can also supply maps, information on accommodation along the route and more.

DRAGONS AND DEVILS

Pleasant **Berga**, 30km west of Ripoll, has the usual historical draws – an old town, the remains of a castle – but the reason that it's on the map, so to speak, is as host of one of Catalunya's most famous festivals, the **Festa del Patum**. During Corpus Christi week, Berga's otherwise staid streets fill with parade floats of pagans and fantasy creatures – the famous *gegants*, devils, dragons spewing fireworks and dragon-slayers – while revellers dance on the sidelines and behind the floats. The festival is said to be named after the sound of the drum, and you'll hear the crowd chanting "pa-tum, pa-tum!" throughout. During Patum, you must book accommodation at least a month in advance.

Museu Etnogràfic de Ripoll

Pl. Abat Oliba • Charge • http://museuderipoll.org

The **Museu Etnogràfic de Ripoll**, one of Catalunya's first ethnographic museums, explores the history of Ripoll and inland Catalunya through its culture, society, religion and trades, with exhibits on everything from farming methods to folklore. Ripoll had a thriving metalworking industry in the Middle Ages, and later became a production centre for weapons and firearms, and exhibits include ancient keys, forged ironwork and early rifles and other weapons.

ARRIVAL AND INFORMATION

RIPOLL

By train and bus The train and bus stations are near each other, a 10min walk from the centre of town. Regular trains from Barcelona stop in Ripoll (2hr) en route to Puigcerdà.

Turisme Pl. Abat Oliba, near the monastery (Mon–Sat 10am–1.30pm & 3.30–6pm (7pm July & Aug), Sun 10am–2pm; http://visit.ripoll.cat).

ACCOMMODATION AND EATING

Hostal del Ripollès Pl. Nova 11, http://hostal-del-ripolles.cataloniatophotels.com. Comfortable if a bit faded – a convenient spot for those who just want to bed down after a day of hiking and cycling. Plus, the family-style restaurant serves hearty local fare. €

La Trobada Pg. Compositor Honorat Vilamanyà 4, http://latrobadahotel.com. This family hotel is perfectly central – near the monastery, the train and bus stations and the Via Verde (see page 696). Quiet, nature-inspired rooms offer a variety of views, from the Pyrenees to the towering monastery. €€

Sant Joan de les Abadesses

Sitting in the verdant Ríu Tur valley 1km northeast of Ripoll, the petite town of **SANT JOAN DE LES ABADESSES** was built around the monastery of the same name, which was founded by Guifré el Pélos in 887 and named after his daughter. Sant Joan is a pleasant place for a stroll, particularly through the Pl. Mayor to the Gothic bridge over the Ríu Ter.

The monastery and museum

Charge • http://monestirsantjoanabadesses.cat

The twelfth-century **monastery** features an elegant single-nave church, a Gothic cloister and a thirteenth-century wooden sculpture depicting Christ's descent from the cross. Also a highlight is the beautiful alabaster Gothic altarpiece of Santa María la Blanca, which dates from the fourteenth century. The **Museu de Monestir** offers a well-curated overview of the town's formidable religious history, with sacred artefacts and detailed embroidery and silverware.

ARRIVAL AND INFORMATION

SANT JOAN DE LES ABADESSES

By bus Teisa buses run regularly to Sant Joan de les Abadesses (3–5 times daily, sometimes less often on weekends) on the Girona–Olot–Ripoll route.

Turisme Palau de l'Abadia, next to the Museu del Monestir (Mon–Sat 10am–2pm & 4–7pm, Sun 10am–2pm; http://santjoandelesabadesses.cat).

ACCOMMODATION

Sant Joan has a couple of welcoming options – or venture into the countryside, where you'll find a variety of excellent rustic houses.

★ **Hotelet de Sant Joan** C/Mestre Andreu 3, http://hoteletdestjoan.com. A wonderful find in this rustic wedge of Spain, this casual boutique hotel has simple yet stylish rooms, with wood floors, snow-white bed linen and elegant lights. €€

Camprodon

CAMPRODON, 12km east of Sant Joan de les Abadesses, is where you really start to feel like you're in the mountains: the peaks loom in the distance, the air is crisp and the streets are dotted with ski- and outdoor-gear shops. Camprodon also has an upscale, alpine-holiday air to it, particularly along the broad promenade of **Passeig Maristany**, where many well-off Catalans have mountain villas. Camprodon's handsome centrepiece is the sixteenth-century **Pont Nou**, which spans the Ríu Ter in the middle of town. From here, the main street leads to the lovely Romanesque **Sant Pere church**, open generally for services only.

ARRIVAL AND INFORMATION

By bus Regular Teisa buses from Ripoll stop at a shelter at the southeast edge of town.

Turisme The *turisme* is on C/St. Roc 22 (Tues–Sat 10am–2pm & 4–8pm, Sun 10am–2pm; http://valldecamprodon.org).

ACCOMMODATION AND EATING

Camprodon gets busy in the peak season, when it's advisable to make reservations. You'll also find some good accommodation out of town in the Ter valley.

Cal Marquès C/Catalunya 11, http://restaurantcalmarques.cat. Feast on local Catalan cuisine at this spacious restaurant, which serves top-notch grilled meats and game – beef, rabbit, duck – as well as seasonal vegetables and well-crafted desserts. €€€

Hotel Camprodon Pl. Dr Robert 3, http://hotelcamprodon.com. This well-run hotel, in a *modernista* building, has a graceful interior and clean if slightly faded rooms. €€

Hotel Sant Roc Pl. Carme 4, http://hotelsantroc.info. A family hotel set in the heart of town. Warmly rustic rooms have alpine-style wood ceilings and comfy beds. €€

El Pont 9 Cami Cerdanya, http://restaurantelpont9.com. Enjoy lovely views of the bridge, and market-fresh Catalan cuisine, from pungent sheep cheeses to rice with wild mushrooms and artichokes. €€€

Around Camprodon

Beyond Camprodon, appealing mountain villages and trekking trails dot the peaks and **Ter valley**. This is hiking territory, and many visitors come to this area for outdoor adventure, whether on the trails in summer, or on the slopes of **Vallter 2000** in winter. The best way to explore is with your own wheels, though a few buses do crawl through the valley. **Villalonga de Ter**, 5km from Camprodon, makes for an agreeable stopover in your explorations of the valley; it has a Romanesque church, Sant Martí, on the main *plaça*. Another pleasant stop is the hilltop **Tregurá de Dalt**, 6km beyond Villalonga, where stone houses line cobbled streets and there are lovely views of the valley and peaks. Both have good accommodation options.

Vallter 2000

http://vallter2000.com

If you're looking to ski in the area, try the well-run **Vallter 2000**, which overlooks the Ter valley and has a decent range of pistes, as well as a variety of offerings for kids, from a good ski school to a Jardí de Neu (snow garden), where the wee ones can play in the snow. The resort also offers plenty of summer activities, from hiking to horseriding.

Ribes de Freser, Núria and around

The Freser valley extends north of Ripoll to the mountain village of **Ribes de Freser** and Queralbs before unfolding eastward through a stunning gorge. Ribes de Freser sits at the confluence of three rivers, hemmed in by verdant valleys, and features a small old town and the **church of Santa María**, which dates back to the eleventh century but was then rebuilt in the 1900s in a modernist style. The village is best known as the starting point for the famous rack-and-pinion **cremallera** train (see page 699), which snakes up the mountain to the sanctuary of **Núria** and its neighbouring ski centre, offering tantalizing views along the way. Ribes de Freser also makes for a pleasant Pyrenean base, thanks to its proximity to the mountains and decent array of accommodation.

Santuari de la Mare de Déu

The Núria valley has long been visited by pilgrims, and the **Santuari de la Mare de Déu** had its beginnings in a visit by **Sant Gil of Nîmes**, who came here on retreat in the seventh century. Gil left behind a wooden statue of the Virgin Mary, which became an object of veneration, and eventually a patron saint among local shepherds. The sanctuary consists basically of a parochial **church** (built in 1911) and a hermitage – a small, ancient-looking mountain church, built in 1615 and refurbished over the years. The overall complex itself is rather plain – it includes the sanctuary, plus several straightforward bars, restaurants and self-catering apartments. Pilgrims still come to visit, and the church holds daily Mass for locals, but the devout are usually outnumbered by skiers in winter and hikers in summer.

ARRIVAL AND INFORMATION

By train Regular trains on the Barcelona–Puigcerdà line stop at the Ribes de Freser (2hr 30min), where you can catch the *cremallera* train (see page 699).

Turisme Ctra. de Bruguera 2, Ribes de Freser (Tue–Thurs

RIBES DE FRESER, NÚRIA AND AROUND

10am–2pm & 4–6pm, Fri 10am–2pm & 4–7.30pm, Sat 10am–2pm & 4–8pm, Sun 10am–2pm; http://valldribes.cat).

ACTIVITIES

Hiking The area abounds with good hikes, including the popular trek along the river gorge from Núria to the village of Queralbs (2hr 30min). Those with more stamina can go on a full-day hike through the Gorges of Freser, trekking on the GR11.7 and then returning on another signposted trail.

You can take a break along the way at *Refugi Coma de Vaca* (see page 700).

Skiing The Vall de Núria ski centre (http://valldenuria.cat) has plenty of activities for kids, so is popular with families.

ACCOMMODATION AND EATING

RIBES DE FRESER

Hotel Resguard dels Vents Cami de Ventaiola 1km north of town, http://hotelresguard.com. Stylish rooms in a mountain chalet-like hotel with views of the surrounding quiet mountains and a small, peaceful spa. €€€

Hotel Restaurante Els Caçadors C/Balandrau 24–26, http://hotelsderibes.com. This hotel has good-sized rooms

in an earthy colour scheme. The restaurant serves tasty, mid-priced Catalan cuisine with a creative twist – and hearty portions. €€

NÚRIA

Alberg Núria Xanascat Pic de l'Àliga, http://xanascat.cat. Location is the big draw at this youth hostel, which sits at

---

THE CREMALLERA

The journey of the Cremallera de Vall de Núria, most often just known as the **cremallera** railway ("zip" in Catalan), built in 1931, is spectacular: the little train follows the rushing Ríu Freser and then, quite suddenly, begins to scale steep mountainsides along stomach-churning switchbacks, from where you're rewarded with beautiful views of the river and valley far below. Trains depart from the Ribes-Enllaç station, in the southern part of Ribes, daily year-round except November, when it runs only at weekends. In high season (July to mid-Sept, plus winter hols), trains run 10–13 times a day; in low season, it's around 6–7 times. One-way journey time is thirty-five minutes. For the latest information, visit http://valldenuria.cat or call 972 732 020.

the top of the cable-car line of the ski centre. Basic dorms, large communal spaces, and they can help arrange outdoor activities. They also have private rooms with bath. €

GORGES OF FRESER
Refugi Coma de Vaca http://comadevaca.com. This well- maintained refuge has bunk-bed dorms, a common room with wooden tables, and mountain views. Staffed Easter and mid-June to mid-September, but call ahead to confirm. They also offer half board and picnics. €

The Serra del Cadí

Unfolding in the eastern section of the Western Pyrenees, the verdant **Parc Natural Cadí-Moixeró** encompasses the massive **Serra del Cadí**, which has the area's best hiking and trekking around one of Catalunya's most recognizable mountains, **Pedraforca**. The village of **Bagà** houses the park's tourist office. The park has a number of staffed refuges, which you can access via treks from the surrounding mountain villages. There are also superb birding opportunities. It's best to have your own transport, as buses pass only intermittently through the outer villages.

Bagà makes for a good base in the area. It has a tidy little medieval quarter, centred on Pl. Porxada, and a pretty Romanesque-Gothic church. Surrounded by the leafy Gòsol valley, the village of **Gòsol**, 10km to the west of Saldes (see page 700), is also a good base. The remains of an eleventh-century castle loom over the village, which is dotted with a few places to stay and a good campsite nearby. Gòsol celebrates its popular annual festival on August 15, with local folk dances, music and cuisine.

ARRIVAL AND INFORMATION   THE SERRA DEL CADÍ

By bus Alsa buses travel three times daily from Barcelona via Berga to Bagà (2hr 30min); buses drop you off near the centre of Bagà.
Park information office C/Vinya 1, Bagà (July & Aug

Tue–Sati 10am–1pm & 5–8pm, Sun 10am–2pm; rest of year Sat 10am–1pm & 5–8pm, Sun 10am–2pm; http://parcsnaturals.gencat.cat). You can pick up maps and a list of refuges here.

PEDRAFORCA: HIKING THE MIGHTY PITCHFORK OF CATALUNYA

Gaze up at **Pedraforca**, which rises east of Gòsol, and it's easy to see why it has become one of Catalunya's most iconic peaks. Its name means "stone pitchfork" because the looming mountain appears cleaved down the middle, resulting in two impressive peaks. The Pedraforca also appears in the coat of arms for Berguedà, the surrounding *comarca* (region). The mountain is a boon for hikers; most people access it from **Saldes**, a village at the foot of the mountain. A number of hiking outfits lead treks up Pedraforca, including Pyrenees Trail, which does a full day-hike, covering 15km and a total ascent of 1000 metres.

Pedraforca is also dotted with a variety of refuges. A ninety-minute trek from Saldes brings you near **Refugi Lluís Estasen** (1647m; important to reserve ahead in summer), from where you can ascend the 2491m Pedraforca (the full trek up and down takes about 5–6hr). The hike up the mountain reaches the divide between the two summits, where you'll connect with the path coming up from Gòsol. You'll find a number of refuges on the mountain; the tourist office in Bagà has up-to-date information on all of them. One popular day-hike from the *Refugi Lluís Estasen* is to the **Refugi Sant Jordi** (1570m; staffed generally only in summer) to the east, with the mountain peaks rising up all around you.

REFUGES
Refugi Lluís Estasen http://refugipedraforca.com. Generally staffed only in summer; call ahead or enquire at park information office. €

Refugi Sant Jordi http://refugisantjordi.com. Generally staffed only in summer; call ahead or enquire at park information office. €

ACCOMMODATION AND EATING

Cadí Vacances Southwest of Gòsol, off the road to Tuixént, http://cadivacances.com. This well-maintained complex has both a camping area and bungalows, as well as a swimming pool, playgrounds and restaurant with fireplace. €

Cal Triuet Pl. Major 4, Gòsol, http://lacuinetadeclatriuet. com. This long-time hotel and restaurant has decent rooms; they can offer information on hikes into the surrounding mountains. The restaurant serves good mid-priced regional cuisine. €

Hotel Ca L'Amagat C/Clota 4, Bagà, http://hotel calamagat.com. Near the centre of town, this cosy spot has comfortable rooms and a stone-and-wood-walled restaurant with hearty Catalan cuisine. €€

La Cerdanya

The verdant **Cerdanya valley**, hemmed in by looming peaks to the north and south, has long shared a geo-cultural affinity with France. The border snakes its way through the middle of the valley, but you can hardly tell where Spain ends and France begins. Catalan is spoken on both sides of the border and, in many ways, Cerdanya seems to function as an independent entity, with customs all its own. As the locals say, it's not quite Spain, and it's not quite France – it's simply La Cerdanya. The only Pyrenean valley running east–west, the Cerdanya is showered with more sunlight than any other part of the range, and is therefore a popular summer spot for hikers and mountain bikers. In winter, skiers flock to **La Molina** and **Masella**, the two big ski resorts. **Puigcerdà**, the capital of Cerdanya, is the transport hub for the area, from where you can catch a train that continues into France – the only still-running trans-Pyrenean rail route, and offering lovely views along the way.

Toses

The small village of **TOSES**, about 18km west of Ribes de Freser, is perched at 1450m. Its highlight is the church of **San Cristòfol**, dating from the tenth to twelfth century (open usually for services only). The church is modest but well restored, with a handsome nave, rectangular belfry and reproduction frescoes.

La Molina and La Masella

La Molina http://lamolina.com • **La Masella** http://masella.com

The combined ski resorts of **La Molina** and **La Masella** comprise one of the larger ski areas in the Spanish Pyrenees, with pistes on **Tosa d'Alp** (2537m; 15km south of Puigcerdà) and a total of 101 runs. If you're new to skiing, try La Molina, which caters to beginners and has a good ski school. La Masella also has a ski school, and offers extensive runs that appeal to more skilled skiers.

ARRIVAL AND ACCOMMODATION

LA MOLINA AND LA MASELLA

By bus It's easiest to get around with your own transport, though in the ski season there is an intermittent bus from Puigcerdà (generally departing once in the morning to the resort, and twice in the afternoon back to Puigcerdà).

There's also a combined Skitren ticket to La Molina from Barcelona, which includes the train, bus and your lift pass for €53.

ACCOMMODATION

You'll find a few options in the area. Many skiers, if they have their own transport, opt to stay in Puigcerdà or other villages in the region.

Hotel Adserà La Molina, http://hoteladsera.com. This alpine hotel has simple but comfortable rooms, an on-site restaurant with regional food and views of the Cerdanya valley. Ask about discounts and packages, which they offer for ski classes and lift passes. €€

Puigcerdà

Perched above the breezy union of the rivers Segre and Querol (*puig* is Catalan for "hill"; *cerdà* comes from Cerdanya), with the Pyrenees looming grandly above, hilltop **PUIGCERDÀ** is one of the prettier border towns you'll come across. With its cluster of

SKIING THE CATALAN PYRENEES

There's a good reason that the Spanish royal family and other luminaries choose to ski in the Catalan Pyrenees – it's home to some of the best resorts in Spain. As with most ski regions, often the best way to save is through the **package deals** offered by many hotels, which include discounts on lift tickets. General prices are €15–25 a day for ski gear (skis, boots, poles), and €28–50 daily for lift passes, with prices varying with the length of time you buy passes for, whether it's a weekday or the weekend, and the quality of the resort. Note, also, that it's well worth checking ahead to find out the level of snow, especially in the spring.

The Catalan Pyrenees offer a surprising variety of resorts, catering both to first-timers and advanced skiers. Intermediate skiers will find plenty of thrilling terrain at **La Masella** in La Cerdanya, which now also offers skiing at night on Fridays and Saturdays along 10km on thirteen slopes. Also popular for expert skiers is **Boí-Taüll** on the western boundary of Aigüestortes and the premiere **Baqueira-Beret** in the Val d'Aran. The best resorts for newbies and families are **Espot Esquí** on the eastern boundary of the Parc Nacional de Aigüestortes i Estany de Sant Maurici, and **La Molina** near La Masella.

budget lodgings and proximity to ski resorts, the town is a busy stopover for skiers, hikers and mountain bikers.

Founded in 1177, Puigcerdà has a rich history, but sadly most of its old buildings were destroyed in the Civil War, and its aged roots are best reflected in the layout and design of its narrow streets and *plaças*. Among the monuments that were spared is the *campanaria* (bell tower) in graceful **Pl. de Santa Maria**, while the well-preserved Pl. Cabrinetty (near Pl. de l'Ajuntament) has beautiful balconies and porticoes.

Church of Sant Domènec and around

Pg. 10 d'Abril

The **church of Sant Domènec** was built in 1291 and restored after the Civil War. The church features an elegant portal, while inside is a series of fourteenth-century Gothic paintings. Next door sits the convent of Sant Domènec, which now houses a library, a historical archive and sacred artefacts.

ARRIVAL AND INFORMATION   PUIGCERDÀ

By train and bus The train and bus stations sit at the bottom of the hill, from which a free funicular (daily 5.30am–midnight) travels up to Pl. de l'Ajuntament in the middle of town. Several trains daily connect Puigcerdà with Barcelona (3hr), via Vic and Ripoll. *Rodalies* (local) trains also run 4–5 times daily from Puigcerdà to Latour de Carol in France (10min), from which there are connections to Toulouse (2hr 30min–3hr).

Turisme Pl. Santa Maria, (Mon–Fri 10am–4pm, Sat 9.30am–2pm & 3.30–7.30pm, Sun 9.30am–2pm; 972 880 542).

ACCOMMODATION

Hotel del Lago Avda. Dr Piguillem 7, http://hotellago. com. Blessed with a breezy garden, this hotel features alpine-style rooms, and a small spa offering massages and facials. €€

Hotel Villa Paulita Avda. Pons i Gasch 15, http://villa paulitahotel.com. This charming boutique hotel, housed in a nineteenth-century summer villa, has cheery rooms and a good restaurant serving regional cuisine. Hearty breakfast included. €€

Mercer Hotel Torre del Remei Camí del Remei 3, about 5km southwest of Puigcerdà, http://hoteltorredelremei. com. For a taste of the good life in the Catalan Pyrenees, stay at this modernist palace-turned-upscale hotel, surrounded by rolling gardens. The 24 rooms are sleek and modern with original touches on the bare brick walls. The Suite even has its own elegant fireplace and sweeping views of the grounds. The handsome restaurant features superb Catalan cuisine. Try the speciality Gaig Cannelloni. €€€

Park Hotel Puigcerdà Crtra. Barcelona-Andorra, http:// hotelparkpuigcerda.com. Well-run hotel with spacious rooms, all with balconies and mountain views. Relax at the outdoor pool or at the soothing spa, and top off the day in the restaurant, which has a good menu of Catalan dishes. €€

EATING AND DRINKING

Puigcerdà has a range of restaurants, most tending towards homely regional cuisine; take a twirl around Pl. de Santa Maria, which has plenty of eating spots.

La Cava Taberna Miguel Bernades 14, http://lacava tabernapuigcerda.com. Feast on grilled octopus with *papas arrugàs* (wrinkled potatoes) or suckling pig at this laid-back haunt, tucked away down a backstreet off the main square. Alternatively, order plates of tapas to share – *bacalao* with squid ink aioli, *pa amb* tomàquet (tomatoes on bread with olive oil), *anxoves* (anchovies) with a squeeze of lemon, fried *calamars* (squid). €€€

Tap de Suro C/Querol 21, 678 655 928. This lively restaurant features a tasty selection of tapas, from silky slivers of *iberico* ham to pungent sheep's cheeses, as well as an excellent line-up of local wines. €€

La Taverna del Call Pl. del Call, latavernadelcall.cat. Fill up on tasty, mid-priced regional food, including grilled fish and meats, at this popular, welcoming *taberna*, which has a terrace overlooking the *plaça*. €€

Llívia

In 1659, the town of **LLÍVIA** officially became a Spanish enclave within France, a geographical oddity that has garnered a mention in guidebooks ever since. Though the Spanish ceded 33 villages to France that year, tiny Llívia, deemed a town, remained Spanish. Just 6km from Puigcerdà, it's easy to reach on foot, or you can take a bus. Either way, Llívia makes for a lovely day-trip, if only to lose yourself in the town's medieval aura, which becomes increasingly apparent the higher you climb the steep streets.

11

Mare de Déu dels Àngels

C/Forns 13 • Charge • http://llivia.org

This sturdy **church**, dating from the fifteenth century, features Doric columns and a Baroque *retablo*. The best time to visit is during the long-running Llívia **music festival** (since 1982), which is held in and around the church on August weekends, and features orchestras, choirs and sometimes big-name stars (Catalan opera great Montserrat Caballé once performed here).

Museu Municipal

C/Forns 12 • Charge • http://museullivia.net

The **Museu Municipal** features sections of what is thought to be the oldest pharmacy in Europe, founded in the early fifteenth century. Look out for the ancient pharmaceutical implements, as well as an impressive collection of Renaissance coffers, with portraits of saints.

ARRIVAL AND INFORMATION

LLÍVIA

By bus Buses leave for Llívia from in front of Puigcerdà's train station at least twice daily on weekdays, and once daily on weekends.

Turisme C/Forns 10 (Wed–Fri 9.30am–2pm, Sat 10am–2pm & 3.30–7pm, Sun 9.30am–2.30pm; Aug Daily 10am–2pm & 3.30–7pm; http://llivia.org).

ACCOMMODATION AND EATING

★**Can Ventura** Pl. Major 1, http://canventura.com. *Can Ventura* excels at seasonal Catalan fare that is rooted in local produce. The rustic restaurant, set in a beautifully renovated seventeenth-century townhouse, serves tender steak cooked over hot stones; mountain rice with *butifarra* sausage and wild mushrooms; and traditional ratatouille with poached egg. Top it off with a dessert of *crema catalana* along with a brisk Cerdanya white wine. €€€

La Formatgeria de Llívia Pla Ro, Gorguja, http:// laformatgeria.com. This inviting restaurant on the town's eastern edge is housed in a former cheese factory, and accordingly serves gooey fondues and raclettes, as well as seasonal Catalan cuisine. They also have their own wine cellar. €€€

Hotel Bernat de So C/Cereja 5, http://hotelbernatdeso. com. Just north of town, this handsome hotel is a lovely blend of the rustic and the elegant, with a breezy outdoor garden, a pool and a comfortable living room with a fireplace. €€

Set Terres C/Puigcerdà 8, http://setterres.com. This beautifully refurbished 1772 farmhouse is now an adults-only boutique B&B with seven lovely rooms, filled with natural light and earthy colours, each named after one of the fields in the surrounding Cal Estorc estate. €€

Bellver de Cerdanya

The Pyrenean atmosphere is very evident in the historic village of **BELLVER DE CERDANYA**, where rustic, slate-roofed chalets line the cobbled streets. About 25km west of Puigcerdà, Bellver overlooks the rushing Ríu Segre; and trout fishing was once a major local industry. The elegant **Pl. Major** is graced with impressive porticoes, while nearby rises the Gothic church of **Sant Jaume**. South of town is the twelfth-century Romanesque church of **Santa Maria de Talió**, presided over by a wooden Virgin.

ARRIVAL AND INFORMATION
BELLVER DE CERDANYA

By bus Bellver is one of the first stops on the bus route between Puigcerdà (25min) and La Seu d'Urgell (35min).

Turisme Pl. de Sant Roc 9 (Sat 10am–1pm & 4–7pm, Sun 10am–2pm; 973 510 229).

La Seu d'Urgell

Known to locals simply as Seu, the pleasant town of **LA SEU D'URGELL**, capital of the *comarca* of Alt Urgell, sits amid looming peaks, with Andorra just 10km to the north and the valleys of the rocky Serra del Cadí nearby. As the seat (*seu*) of the regional archbishopric since the sixth century and home to an outdoor market held continuously since 1029 (on Tues and Sat), Seu has a formidable history, which is revealed in its well-preserved medieval quarter, twisting alleys and imposing Catedral.

The pleasantly mysterious medieval quarter is a small warren of narrow, arcaded streets. **Carrer dels Canonges**, the oldest street, cuts through its heart, and is lined with centuries-old buildings like **Cal Roger**, believed to have been a pilgrim's hostel, and which reveals wooden ceiling beams and some fourteenth-century Gothic carvings (enquire at the *turisme* about visiting).

Catedral de Santa Maria
Pl. dels Oms • Charge • http://museudiocesaurgell.org

Seu's twelfth-century **Catedral de Santa Maria**, just off Pl. dels Oms, is a wonderfully preserved example of Romanesque architecture, with a thirteenth-century cloister which has columns topped with sculpted figures from medieval mythology, and the adjoining eleventh-century chapel of San Miquel. The **Museu Diocesà** features superbly preserved reliquaries and fragments of the sarcophagus of Bishop Abril Pérez.

Espai Ermengol–Museu de la Ciutat
C/Major 8 • Free • http://espaiermengol.cat

Next to the Catedral, the small **city museum** features four floors of exhibits on La Seu's history. Exhibits include archeological remains, videos and interactive maps and an in-depth look at local products such as the region's well-known Cadí cheese. On the top floor, you can enjoy lovely views over the rooftops of town.

ARRIVAL AND INFORMATION
LA SEU D'URGELL

By bus The bus station is on C/Joan Garriga Massó, just north of the old town. Alsina Graells runs buses to Barcelona (10 daily; 3hr 30min), Puigcerdà (10 daily; 1hr) and Lleida (1 daily; 2hr 30min).

Turisme Helpful, well-stocked *turisme* on C/Major 8 (summer Mon–Fri 10am–2pm & 4–7pm, Sat 10am–2pm & 4–7pm, Sun (summer only) 10am–1pm; http://turismeseu.com).

ACCOMMODATION AND EATING

Seu has a number of decent hotels scattered about town. If you have your own wheels, try one of the many *casas rurales* in the area, as most are reasonably priced and have an inviting homespun ambience. The *turisme* also has a list of recommended country hotels in the area.

Arbeletxe C/Sant Ermengol 22, http://arbeletxe.com. The

Basque Country meets Catalunya at this stylish restaurant that serves a classic menu with contemporary touches, like a squid salad with caviar lentils; cod cheeks; vegetable lasagne; succulent duck; and a dessert of pear tart. €€

El Castell de Ciutat 1.5km west of La Seu, at the foot of the Castellciutat citadel, http://hotelelcastell.com.

This luxurious Relais & Châteaux hotel and spa is set in an ancient castle, and features elegant rooms, sumptuous spa treatments and excellent Mediterranean cuisine, which you can enjoy on the breezy terrace overlooking the Urgellet valley. €€€

El Menjador C/Major 4, 612 432 860. This inviting, quirky restaurant, set in a former inn and decorated with flowers and colourful local art, features market-fresh cuisine, including melted local Argelia cheese fondue with asparagus, vegetarian cannelloni or beef burger, as well as tapas. €€

Parador Seu d'Urgell C/Sant Domènec 6, https://paradores.es/es/parador-de-la-seu-durgell. This welcoming parador has a blend of old and new – the spacious ground floor incorporates a Romanesque cloister strewn with sofas, while rooms are modern with pale woods. €€€

Restaurant 3 Portes Avda. Joan Garriga i Massó 7, http://restaurant3portes.com. Mid-priced grilled meats, such as pork tenderloin with mushrooms, and well-prepared seafood served in a breezy garden. €€

The Noguera Pallaresa valley

Catalunya's most famous whitewater-rafting river, the **Noguera Pallaresa**, churns through the lush valley of the same name. The river has long been an important source of hydroelectric power, and large power plants sit at various points along its banks. The *raiers* (logger-raftsmen) of **La Pobla de Segur** used to ride rafts of logs from the Pallars Forest all the way south to the lowlands.

The town of **Sort**, north of La Pobla de Segur, has become the region's whitewater-rafting hub, with a host of aquatic-adventure shops. If you're using public transport, you'll likely arrive or depart from La Pobla de Segur, which has most of the valley's connections to and from Barcelona and Lleida.

La Pobla de Segur

The amiable town of **LA POBLA DE SEGUR** is one of the largest in the Vall de la Noguera, and a good base for river rafting or relaxing amid valley scenery for a few days. You'll find a decent selection of simple accommodation, plus regular train and bus services.

ARRIVAL AND INFORMATION   **LA POBLA DE SEGUR**

By train Regular trains connect La Pobla de Segur with Lleida (1hr 50min) and Barcelona (4hr; via Lleida).

WHITEWATER ADRENALINE RUSH

The **Noguera Pallaresa**'s mighty flow is legendary, and draws thrill-seekers from around Spain and further afield. The original rafts were primitive – logs lashed together – but could withstand the frothy waters, and were ridden by *raiers* (rafters) to the sawmills of La Pobla de Segur. These days, the rafts are of the inflatable variety, and exciting whitewater trips are offered by operators throughout the region.

The most popular section of the river is between **Llavorsí** and **Rialp**, but tour companies offer a range of trips, each more rugged and scenic than the last. The rafting **season** is from April to early September; some outfitters also offer rafting programmes in March and October. In season, trips are run daily, usually in the late morning and lasting 1–2 hours on the water. The tourist office has a list of recommended **rafting operators**, including those listed below. Most offer other activities as well:

ACTIVITIES OPERATORS

Rafting Llavorsí Camí de Riberies, Llavorsí, http://raftingllavorsi.cat. This established operator offers rafting, kayaking and multiple other aquatic adventures as well as canyoning; in the winter, they can arrange snowshoe treks.

Roc Roi Pl. Nostra Senyora de Biuse, Llavorsí, http://rocroi.com. This friendly operator runs a multitude of

river sports, including kayak beginner's classes plus trekking and horseriding.

Rubber River Avda Diputación 14, Sort, http://rubber-river.com. The town of Sort is filled with rafting and adventure shops, including this reputable outfitter, which offers everything from rafting and canoeing to bungee-jumping and horseriding.

11

11

> ## TREN DELS LLACS
>
> Never underestimate the allure of nostalgia. This historic **Tren dels Llacs** (Lake Train, 1hr 50min one way) comprises refurbished old-fashioned steam and diesel locomotives. On its 90km journey between Lleida and La Pobla de Segur, the quaint train chugs over 31 bridges and through 41 tunnels, along cliffs, mountain passes and, of course, lakes. The train) operates from April to October, generally only on the weekends or on holidays. You can buy tickets only at the tourist offices in Lleida or in La Pobla de Segur, or La Tienda de FGC in Barcelona on Carrer Pelai. For details, check the website: http://trendelsllacs.cat.

By bus Regular buses run between La Pobla de Segur and Lleida and Barcelona. Buses also head west to El Pont de Suert, Boí and Capdella, where you can access the Parc Nacional d'Aigüestortes i Estany de Sant Maurici; as well as north to Sort and Llavorsí, from where you can also access

the park.
Turisme Pl. del Ferrocarril, at the north end of town, near the train station (Mon–Sat 9am–2pm & 4.30–8pm, Sun 9am–1pm, Aug Tues–Fri 5–8pm; http://lapobladesegur. cat).

ACCOMMODATION AND EATING

Fonda Can Frasersia C/Major 4, http://canfasersia.com. This former boarding house in the middle of the old town is one of several simple *fondas*, and has a range of economical rooming options, from double rooms with or without private bathroom. They can also organize lots of activities

from hiking to cycling. €€
Hotel Solé Avda. de l'Estació 44, http://hotelsole.es. Kick back at this straightforward but well-maintained hotel, with ample rooms and bathrooms, and a pool. Apartments are also available. €

Gerri de la Sal

Thirteen kilometres north from La Pobla de Segur toward Sort, you'll come to the petite village of **GERRI DE LA SAL**, named after the nearby salt mines. Next to the village, an old stone bridge leads to the beautiful twelfth-century **Monasterio de Sant Maria**. Though it's closed to the public, the area around it is lovely for a wander. Just beyond Gerri de la Sal is a tunnel, alongside which the old road hugs the rocky side of the mountain and is open to hikers and bikers.

Museu Gerri

Pl. Àngel Esteve 10 • Charge • http://baixpallars.ddl.net/museu-de-gerri

This small but growing **museum** explores the history of salt mining in Gerri de la Sal, an industry that dates back to the ninth century. The museum, which forms part of the European Route of Industrial Heritage, features photos, tools and implements and a video that traces the evolution of salt in Gerri de la Sal, from the salt springs to the advent of salt mines to transport – salt was carried by mules to be grinded and packed into sacks.

Sort

The capital of the *comarca* of Upper Pallars, **SORT** is a pleasant mix of old and new, with an ancient core and modern facilities catering to the outdoor adventurers (see page 705) who descend in the spring and summer. Every year in early July, the town hosts the **Raiers (Rafters) Festival**, celebrating the log-rafters of the past.

ARRIVAL AND INFORMATION   SORT

By bus One Alsina Graells bus departs Barcelona daily for Sort, Rialp, Llavorsí and Esterri d'Àneu. Buses stop at a shelter north of town.
Turisme Camí de la Cabanera (July, Aug & Easter Mon–

Sat 9am–2pm & 4–7pm; Sept–mid-June Tue–Thurs 10am–2pm, Fri & Sat 10am–2pm & 4–7pm, Mon & Sun 10am–2pm; http://pallarssobira.cat).

EATING

El Fogony Avda. Generalitat 45, http://fogony.com. This   is a wonderful surprise in Sort: a handsome restaurant, run by a husband-and-wife team, that serves superlative 0km slow food Catalan cuisine, including pig trotters with mushrooms, truffles and bacon, and rabbit with tomato *allioli*. €€€

Rialp and Port-Ainé

Tiny **RIALP**, which lies just 3km north of Sort, is an atmospheric jumble of old houses and new chalets. **Port-Ainé**, 15km northeast of Rialp, features good beginner and intermediate skiing on its thirty-plus runs, and also has a dedicated children's slope. Snow conditions are generally top-notch, even in the spring.

ACCOMMODATION   RIALP AND PORT-AINÉ

Hotel Condes del Pallars Avda. Flora Cadena 2, Rialp, http://hotelcondesdelpallars.com. This long-running resort-style hotel is a favourite with families. It can be a bit faded in places, but it serves its purpose as a place to base yourself for winter sports, with plenty of amenities, including a restaurant (guests only), a small gym and a kids' activity centre. Rate includes breakfast. €€

Llavorsí

A rugged mountain landscape surrounds the riverside **LLAVORSÍ**, 10km north of Rialp. With an attractive mix of stone houses, modern accommodation and established outdoor operators, the town makes for a good base. Sports operators offer a wide range of activities, including rafting, mountain biking, canyoning and rock climbing. Regular buses run from Barcelona to Llavorsí (5hr 30min) via Sort and Rialp.

ACCOMMODATION AND EATING   LLAVORSÍ

Camping Aigües Braves 1km north of Llavorsí, http://campingaiguesbraves.com. This campsite has a variety of facilities, including pool, bar and arranged activities. They also offer weekend deals in wooden bungalows, sleeping up to four. €
Hotel de Rei Avda. Pallaresa 10, http://hotelderei.top. This well-run hotel has an array of comfortable rooms, from doubles to triples to sizeable family rooms, many of which have views of the mountains. The restaurant serves up good breakfasts and Catalan dinners. €
Hotel Riberies Camí de Riberies, http://riberies.cat. This four-star hotel features alpine-style rooms, a spa with Jacuzzi and a good restaurant serving regional cuisine, from baked sea bass with capers and lemon to duck with red berries. €€

Vall d'Àneu and Esterri d'Àneu

The **Vall d'Àneu** stretches north of Llavorsí, sitting at the head of the Noguera Pallaresa river. The rugged valley is well placed for access to the region's great outdoors, from hiking in the Parc Nacional d'Aigüestortes i Estany de Sant Maurici to skiing at the Espot resort to the west and Baqueira-Beret to the north. The Vall d'Àneu is made up of a smattering of villages and towns, most comprising a mix of modern chalets catering to the ski crowd and traditional homes and restaurants.

Esterri d'Àneu

Once a rustic mountain community, **Esterri d'Àneu** is now angled as an alpine resort, with both contemporary apartment buildings and hotels. It has a well-restored **old town**, over which rises the elegant **Sant Vicenç** church. A lovely Romanesque bridge, dating to the early thirteenth century, arches over the river, along whose banks you can walk and take in the surrounding mountain scenery.

ARRIVAL AND INFORMATION   ESTERRI D'ÀNEU

By bus Regular buses travel between Esterri d'Àneu and Barcelona (5hr 30min) and Lleida (3hr).
Turisme C/Major 6 (Tues–Thur, Sun 10am–1pm, Fri & Sat 10am–1.30pm & 5–8pm; http://vallsdaneu.org). Has information on the valley and outdoor activities.

ACCOMMODATION AND EATING

Hotel Apartamentos Trainera C/Major 54, http:// hoteltrainera.com. Amenity-filled aparthotel with clean

11

rooms and apartments. Relax at the spa (which offers massages and other treatments) or check out the games room. The on-site restaurant serves decent dishes, plus vegan and vegetarian choices. €€

Parc Nacional d'Aigüestortes i Estany de Sant Maurici

http://gencat.cat/parcs/aiguestortes

One of nine in Spain, Catalunya's largest national park, the **Parc Nacional d'Aigüestortes i Estany de Sant Maurici**, encompasses soaring peaks topping 3000m and lush meadows irrigated by more than four hundred lakes, streams, waterfalls and impressive glacial valleys. Established in 1955, the park comprises valleys blanketed in pine and fir forests, while wild animals like the isard, a small antelope also known as the chamois, roam the terrain. You might even spot a golden eagle or black woodpecker, both common here.

Hiking and trekking opportunities abound, from easy walks around sparkling lakes to serious treks up the mountain. The **Sant Nicolas valley** in the west features numerous glacial lakes, as well as the meanders of **Aigüestortes** (Twisted Waters). In the east lies the massive **Estany de Sant Maurici** (Sant Maurici Lake), at the head of the Escrita valley. In the winter, you can also **cross-country ski** through the park, though there are no marked trails.

The park's western sector is best reached from the **Vall de Boí** – to explore Aigüestortes, the approach is generally from Boí via **El Pont de Suert**; the eastern portion, including Lake Sant Maurici, is accessed via **Espot**, which lies just beyond the eastern border of the park. The easiest starting point for the higher mountains is **Capdella**, south of the park. If you'll be hiking for several days at a time between June and September, you can stay at any of the **refuges** throughout the park (see page 708). Either visitor centre can give you a list.

ARRIVAL PARC NACIONAL D'AIGÜESTORTES I ESTANY DE SANT MAURICI

By car and taxi Private cars are not allowed in the park, but 4WD taxis travel from the main square in Boí to the information booth at the entrance; taxis operate during daylight hours. The closest you can get to the park in your car is La Molina car park, near the boundary. When this fills up, try the La Farga car park, about 1.5km east. You can arrange for a 4WD taxi to take you from either car park further uphill. When you arrive at the park entrance from Boí (3.5km) it's then about another 3.5km to the crashing waterfalls of Aigüestortes. It's important to keep track of the weather, as it can greatly affect accessibility. In the cold season, it can be difficult to access certain roads.

INFORMATION

Visitor centres There are park information booths at the entrance and also above the waterfalls. You can also pick up trail guides and park maps at the visitor centres in Boí (see page 710) and Espot (see page 709).

Maps Editorial Alpina (http://editorialalpina.com) has excellent, detailed topographical maps of the park.

Entrance Entry to the park is free.

Safety It's always a good idea to alert the refuge staff before you set out on treks, any time of year.

ACCOMMODATION

Refuges Accommodation in and around the park encompasses around twenty refuges, both in the park and in the park's peripheral zone. The refuges usually open in the summer (when most are staffed), Easter and sometimes Christmas, as well as on selected weekends and school holidays during the rest of the year. Refuges are usually equipped with bunk beds and have a basic meal service. Most refuges are fully booked during July and August, so you'll need to reserve ahead, which you can do via http://lacentralderefugis.com or by calling 973 641 681.

Camping Camping in the park is officially forbidden, though you can camp in the peripheral zone.

Vall de Fosca

The verdant **Vall de Fosca**, which extends just south of the park, received its name Fosca ("dark") because it's surrounded by steep slopes that obscure the sun. Tiny **Capdella** is perched at its northernmost point and, at 1420m, is the highest of the fifteen or so tiny villages and settlements that are sprinkled south through the valley, including **Espui** and **La Torre de Capdella**. Capdella makes for a good jumping-off point into the park, and is the village closest to the **teleférico** (see page 709).

ARRIVAL AND INFORMATION · VALL DE FOSCA

By bus Buses travel from La Pobla de Segur to Capdella (30min).
Turisme The Vall de Fosca *turisme* is in the *ajuntament* of

Torre de Capdella on the Pl. Major (Mon–Fri 9am–3pm, Mon & Thurs also 4.30–8.30pm; http://vallfosca.net), 4km south of Espui.

Espot, Espot Esquí and around

ESPOT is a cosy mountain town hemmed in by a lovely green valley, which has increasingly been built up as a tourist centre. In the winter, skiers pass through on their way to **Espot Esquí** (http://espotesqui.cat), just south of town, which has nearly thirty alpine trails.

You can access the park from Espot, which lies about 7km from the **Estany de Sant Maurici**. Upon arrival at the *estany* (lake), you'll want to get your camera out: it's a beautiful scene, the lake fringed by wilderness and dominated by the spires of **Els Encants** ("The Enchanted Ones"; 2700m).

11

ARRIVAL AND INFORMATION · ESPOT, ESPOT ESQUÍ AND AROUND

By bus and taxi The daily buses from Barcelona, Lleida and La Pobla de Segur to Esterri d'Àneu stop at the Espot turn-off. From there, it's a steep 8km uphill walk to Espot, and then another similar distance to get to the park.
By taxi The quickest and easiest way to the park is by taxi, which travel from Espot to Estany de Sant Maurici. Taxis

generally depart from the park information offices).
Casa del Parc information office C/Sant Maurici 5, at the edge of Espot (daily 9am–2pm & 3.30–5.45pm; 973 624 036). Has maps of the park and up-to-date weather reports.

ACCOMMODATION AND EATING

Camping La Mola Carretera Estany de Sant Maurici, 3km east of Espot, http://campinglamola.com. Located outside of Espot, this quality campsite features an excellent range of amenities, including a pool, tennis court, games room, bar and a small supermarket. They also have bungalows. €
Cal Juquim Pl. Sant Martí 1, 626 894 041. This popular restaurant in the centre of Espot, serves filling mountain

fare, including grilled meats, from lamb and wild boar to juicy sausages. €€
Casa Felip C/Felip, http://casafelip.com. Located in the middle of Espot, this long-established place has comfortable rooms, a small front garden and a storage area for skis and bikes. They can also help arrange outdoor activities, in summer and winter. €

Vall de Boí

Extending just west of the national park is the lush **Vall de Boí**, anchored by the mountain village of **Boí**. The highlights of the valley are its lovely **Romanesque churches**, the most remarkable of their kind in Catalunya. In 2000, the churches were designated a World Heritage Site by UNESCO, who described them as "an especially pure and consistent example of Romanesque art in a virtually untouched rural setting".

HIKES AND RIDES FROM CAPDELLA

There are a number of popular **treks** from Capdella, including the half-day hike to the inviting *Refugi Colomina*, set amid mountain lakes (see page 710). You'll find various treks around the *Refugi Colomina*, including to Estany Llong, by way of Estany Tort. You can also access the park on the **teleférico** (cable car; July–Sept; around 9 departures daily, 8am–6pm). The cable car travels from the Saliente reservoir (about 7km north of Capdella) to the Estany Gento, which is near an entrance of the park – on its fifteen-minute trip, the cable car climbs 450m. It was originally constructed in 1981 to transport materials and workers while the Saliente power station was being built, and it's said to be one of the cable cars with the greatest transport capacities in Europe; it was opened to the public in 1991.

And it is this setting that leaves the lasting impression – the beautiful simplicity of the early Romanesque architecture is magnified by the utter alpine stillness surrounding them. The churches, all built between the eleventh and fourteenth centuries, were constructed of local materials, like stone, slate and wood – and their most striking features are their elegant belfries which, in the case of **Taüll**, rises an impressive six storeys. Note that many of the church frescoes are reproductions – though excellent ones, to be sure – because the originals have been moved to MNAC in Barcelona. In addition to the valley's two finest churches in Taüll, other Romanesque beauties worth a visit are Sant Feliu in **Barruera**, Nativitat in **Durro** and Santa Eulàlia in **Erill la Vall**.

Boí

The pleasant town of **BOÍ** serves as a good starting point for exploring the surrounding region, both for the Romanesque churches – you can walk a variety of signposted trails from Boí to neighbouring churches – and also the national park, an entrance to which lies 3.5km from town. Boí also has a helpful park information office, and its own Romanesque church, the twelfth-century **Sant Joan**: parts of the original belfry are still intact, and the church has three naves. As with other churches in the area, the frescoes are reproductions but nonetheless eye-catching, and include images of mythical animals.

Estany de Cavallers

Five kilometres north of Boí is the **Estany de Cavallers** reservoir, where you can pick up trails towards the lake-filled landscape in the northwest section of the park, which are presided over by the Besiberri and Montrarto peaks. A good refuge in the northwest of the park is *Ventosa i Calvell* (see box, page 710).

Taüll

TAÜLL, 3km east of Boí, is home to two of the valley's best-known Romanesque churches. **Sant Climent**, consecrated in 1123, features an exquisite six-storey square belfry that rises gracefully above the town. The church's emblematic Romanesque murals were created

---

POPULAR HIKES AND REFUGES

One of the most popular (though challenging in parts) hikes is to traverse the park from east to west, starting at the **Estany de Sant Maurici**. The full trek, all the way to **Boí**, takes about 9–10 hours, but you can shorten it by hopping in a taxi for the last part from the park entrance to Boí. Roughly halfway along it sits the **Refugi de Estany Llong**.

The northern section of the park offers a wealth of treks for the adventurous and well-equipped – the Espot park information office has detailed maps of trails – as well as refuges, including the top-notch **Refugi de Colomèrs**, the **Refugi de Restanca** and the **Ventosa i Calvell**, near Estany Negre.

Another good hike from the east is to **Refugi Josep Maria Blanc**, which lies southwest of Espot and is surrounded by lush valleys. The hike from Espot to the refuge takes 3–4 hours. From here, the hike continues to the **Colomina** refuge, which you can reach in another 3–4 hours.

REFUGES

The refuges are all very similar – usually sturdy, stone houses with simple rooms and basic beds. For all, see http://lacentralderefugis.com/refugios.

Refugi de Colomèrs. Daily Easter & mid-June to late Sept, weekends Feb & March. €

Refugi Colomina. Early Feb, mid-March to mid-April & mid-June to mid-Sept; call ahead to confirm. €

Refugi de Estany Llong. Late Feb, Easter & June to mid-Oct. From €

Refugi Josep Maria Blanc. Late May to mid-Oct. Breakfast included. €

Refugi de Restanca. Weekends most of the year, plus daily Easter week & mid-June to late Sept. €

Refugi Ventosa i Calvell. Mid-June to late Sept & some winter weekends. Breakfast included. €

ROMANESQUE CHURCHES IN THE VALL DE BOÍ

Pick up information on all the Romanesque churches at the **Centre d'Interpretació del Romànic**, on C/Batalló in **Erill la Vall** (http://vallboi.cat/en/romanesque-centre), in the centre of the valley. All churches have the same general hours: July to early Sept daily 10am–2pm & 4–8pm; rest of the year daily 10am–2pm & 4–7pm and most have a small entrance fee; Santa Maria de Taüll is free.

---

by the so-called Master of Taüll, and transferred to Barcelona in 1922. Particularly striking is the image of Christ Pantocrator (Christ in Majesty) in the apse. Taüll's second Romanesque icon is the church of **Santa Maria**, with its four-storey belfry.

Boí-Taüll
http://boitaullresort.es

The valley is also home to a ski centre, **Boí-Taüll**, which lies 11km southeast of Taüll. The resort has nearly fifty pistes and lifts that reach up to 2750m, and covers an area of about 45km. They offer an array of classes for beginners, and a good family ski programme. Call ahead, as the resort may be undergoing some changes and may therefore have limited hours.

ARRIVAL AND INFORMATION
VALL DE BOÍ

By bus Buses from Barcelona to La Pobla de Segur run up to three times daily throughout the year. From July to mid-September, a connecting bus travels from La Pobla de Segur to El Pont de Suert and from there to Barruera and the Boí turn-off, about 1km before Boí.

Park information office C/Graieres 2, Boí (daily 9.30am–2pm & 3.30–6pm; 973 696 189). Has route information, maps and a list of the refuges in the park. There are also information booths both at the park entrance and above the Aigüestortes waterfalls (see page 708).

ACCOMMODATION AND EATING

BOÍ
Hotel Pey Pl. Treio 3, http://hotelpey.com. This welcoming, family-run hotel has a range of alpine, wood-panelled rooms. They also have a friendly restaurant, where you can refuel over *escudella* stews and grilled meats, from rabbit to beef. €€

CALDES DE BOÍ
Caldes de Boí 5km north of Boí, http://caldesdeboi.com. If you'd like some pampering, head to this lovely spot, considered one of the best spas in the Spanish Pyrenees; it has a wide range of treatments, from natural springs to massages, and several accompanying hotels, including *Manantiel*, which is comfortable and well maintained. Usually closed Jan–March. €€

TAÜLL
★ **Hotel el Rantiner** C/Trestaüll 5, http://hotel elrantiner.com. This wonderfully cosy mountain hotel features ample rooms rustically done up with wood floors and sturdy furniture. Wake up to mountain views and a hearty breakfast, included in the price. €€
Hotel Santa Maria Relax Cap del Riu 3, http://hotel santamariarelax-ardanue.com-hotel.com. This beautifully renovated house features cosy, wood-beamed rooms, a dining room with a fireplace, and a breezy garden. €€€
El Xalet de Taüll C/El Como 5, http://elxaletdetaull.com. This inviting chalet has wood-panelled rooms, mountain views and a summer garden. May be closed for part of winter so call ahead. €€

Val d'Aran

Nudging the French border in the far northwest of the Catalan Pyrenees, the lush **Val d'Aran** has long been geographically and culturally distinct from the rest of the Pyrenees. You can see the disparity of its architecture – French-style chalets dot the mountains – and you can hear it on the streets: the language here is Aranés, a mix of Gascon French and Catalan. The valley drains towards the Atlantic and splits into the Garonne River, whose waters eventually feed the vineyards of Bordeaux.

The Val d'Aran joined Catalunya-Aragón in the twelfth century and was fully given over to Catalunya in 1389. Completely ringed by high peaks, however – some reaching over 3000m – it has always been difficult to access. For most of the valley's history, the only routes in from the Spanish side crossed the tricky **Bonaigua** or Bossòst passes, both accessible only in summer. This changed only in 1948, when the first Vielha Tunnel opened on the N230 highway.

The valley's capital and commercial centre is **Vielha**, a beautiful alpine town with one foot in the past and the other in the very contemporary present, as a luxury resort. In winter, the Val d'Aran becomes upscale **skiing** country, drawing folks from all over Spain and France. While the area still reveals pockets of traditional life, it has undergone a massive shift in the last several decades, with upmarket apartments replacing family dwellings, and much of the retail catering to slick skiers. The Spanish royal family, along with the fit and fabulous, frequent **Baqueira-Beret**, one of Spain's premier ski resorts.

The Val d'Aran is divided into three sectors: **Vielha e Mijaran** (Middle Aran), **Baish Aran** (Lower Aran; northwest of Vielha near the French border) and **Nau Aran** (Upper Aran; east of Vielha). Both Upper and Lower Aran are ripe for exploration, each of their mountain villages more lovely than the last. You'll find plenty of hiking and trekking opportunities – trails meander all over the valley. You could easily spend a day or two hiking from one tiny village to the next, enjoying a country meal at one, and bedding down in a rustic farmhouse in the next. **Salardú** and **Arties** make for pleasant stopovers in Nau Aran.

Vielha

The valley centres on the bustling town of **VIELHA**, which goes through a metamorphosis in winter: when the snow descends, so too do the slickly outfitted skiers, who crowd the slopes, gear shops and restaurants. After the snow melts, Vielha reverts to its small-town self, when the hilly streets get quiet, and the bars are again the domain of the locals. The tiny old quarter features the parish church of **Sant Miquèu**, with a twelfth-century wooden *Crist de Mijaran*, a superb example of Romanesque art.

Musèu dera Val d'Aran

C/Major 26 • Charge • 973 641 815

The small **Musèu dera Val d'Aran**, housed in a seventeenth-century building in the old town, features an overview of Aranese history, folklore and ethnology, from prehistoric times to today, including exhibits of old photographs, period furnishings and more.

ARRIVAL AND INFORMATION   **VIELHA**

By bus Seven Alsina Graells buses travel daily between Barcelona and Vielha (5hr 30min), via Lleida and El Pont de Suert. From June to September, one to two daily buses also run from Barcelona to Vielha via La Pobla de Segur, Llavorsí

GO WILD

The Val d'Aran has long drawn the crowds for its alpine activities. These days, it's also drawing crowds for its alpine animals. Wildlife-watching has been growing in popularity in the Val d'Aran, with the tourist office (see page 713) expanding its wildlife coverage, and with tour companies, such as **WildWatching Spain** (http://wildwatchingspain.com) and **Aran Experience** (http://aranexperience.com), offering a variety of wildlife treks, including springtime photo treks and summer birding. Among the animals you might spot are, in spring and summer, the Pyrenean capercaillie, black woodpecker, brown bear, bearded vulture and marmot; and in winter, the spotted woodpecker, mountain passerines and golden eagle. The wildlife park **Aran Park** in Bossòst (Cha; http://aran-park.es) features a wide range of animals in a natural setting, including deer and bears; in 2017, the park introduced more wild animals, including grey wolves.

and Salardú.
Turisme C/Sarriulera 6 (daily 10am–1.30pm, 4.30–8pm; http://visitvaldaran.com). This office has up-to-date lists of accommodation in the valley.

ACCOMMODATION

Hotel El Ciervo Pl. de San Orenç 3, http://hotelelciervo.net. This cheerful, family-run hotel has well-maintained rooms, each individually decorated, and an excellent breakfast buffet with local specialities. Closed June & Nov. €€
Hotel Vielha Val d'Arán C/Aneto 1, http://tryp-vielha-baqueira.h-rez.com. Wake up to views of the Pyrenees from this well-run hotel, with spacious rooms, as well as pool, sauna and spa. The restaurant offers buffet breakfasts and dinners, or enjoy a cocktail on the bar's outdoor terrace. €€
Parador de Vielha Carretera del Túnel, http:/paradores. es/es/parador-de-vielha. The draw at this modern parador is the lovely view of the mountain peaks. The granite building is very contemporary-looking – no historic charm here – but the rooms are warmly done up in the trademark parador style, with wooden furniture. There's also a pool and spa and a good restaurant. €€

EATING AND DRINKING

Casa Turnay 2km east, in the village of Escunhau, http:// instagram.com/casaturnay. Rustic, stone-walled Aranese restaurant with hearty local food, from grilled rabbit to trout fished from local rivers to *butifarra negra* (Catalan sausage). €€
★ **Era Coquela** Avda. Garona 29, http://eracoquela.com. This deservedly popular restaurant serves hearty, lovingly prepared local cuisine in a cosy dining room, from wild boar cannelloni and grilled fish with romesco sauce to duck with cassis sauce and pear tart with ice cream. €€€
Eth Cornèr C/Sant Nicolau 2, http://ethcorner.com. After a day on the slopes, there's no better spot to fill up on hearty tapas and wine than this long-time local's favourite. Try the *truita de ceps* (mushroom omelette), *torrades* (large toasts with different toppings), and huevos rotos (scrambled eggs with ingredients such as ham and potatoes). €€
Saxo Blu C/Marrec 6, https://www.instagram.com/ saxoblu. Long-running, amiable bar with cocktails and occasional live music.

Baqueira-Beret
http://baqueira.es

The massive **Baqueira-Beret** ski resort has more development than any other in the area and imbues the valley with a stylish sheen. It's one of Spain's choicest resorts, and has the crowd to match. Discerning skiers, most famously Spain's king himself, flock to its 70-plus pistes, which cover up to 105km – making it one of Spain's largest resorts. The resort amenities – groomed pistes, numerous chairlifts, a top-notch ski staff – rival the Pyrenean scenery of frosted peaks piercing the bright-blue sky. If you don't want to go for the pricey resort accommodation, do what many do: stay for considerably less at a nearby village, such as Salardú or Vielha.

Salardú

The Val d'Aran contains over thirty hillside villages, most with their own Romanesque church. **SALARDÚ**, which lies just west of Baqueira-Beret, is one of the valley's larger settlements, with the thirteenth-century **church of Sant Andreu** (open for services; enquire at *turisme* about other times) standing tall in its centre. Take a look at the detailed portal and, inside, the carefully restored frescoes.

Salardú has a decent tourist infrastructure – several options for lodging and food – but also a rugged alpine personality. Call ahead to your hotel in the non-snow season, as they sometimes close.

ARRIVAL AND INFORMATION   SALARDÚ

By bus From June to Sept, one daily service runs from Barcelona to Vielha via La Pobla de Segur, Llavorsí and Salardú (about 5hr 30min).
Turisme C/Balmes 2 (daily 9.30am–1.30pm & 4.30–7.30pm; http://visitvaldaran.com).

ACCOMMODATION AND EATING

Albergue Era Garona Carretera de Vielha, http:// peretarres.org. Basic but fairly spacious youth hostel in a stone-and-slate building. Rooms, which have up to four beds, come with either private or shared bathroom. €

Hotel Deth Pais Pl. Dera Pica, http://hoteldethpais.com. This small, comfortable, slate-roofed hotel in the village centre has clean rooms with balconies. Buffet breakfast included in the price, and they can help arrange outdoor activities in the surrounding mountains. €

Hotel Mauberme Carretera Bagergue 3, http://hotelmauberme.com. Small, home-away-from-home hotel with wonderfully cosy rooms with slanted wood ceilings, a charming sitting room with fireplace and an included hearty buffet breakfast. €€

Prat Aloy Dera Mola, http://prataloy.gahan.com.ar. This place serves meaty dishes, like grilled steak, lamb and sausages. €€€

Refugi Rosta Pl. Major 1, http://refugirosta.com. Comfortable if faded refuge in a three-hundred-year-old building on the main plaça, catering to trekkers and skiers on a budget. It also doubles as the PyrenMuseum, which features old photographs and maps of the region. Refugi Rosta also runs PyrenHab (http://pyrenhab.com), a casa rural just to the west of Salardú, which is ideal for groups (€€). Sometimes closed March, Oct and Nov. €

Arties

ARTIES, 3km west of Salardú, offers a charming mix of Pyrenean history and the chance to join the locals in dining (and drinking) out. Its old town is pleasant for a stroll, featuring the signature slate-roof houses of the valley, and you can take in the Romanesque-Gothic **Santa Maria** (open for services), which has a barrel-vaulted nave and a five-storey belfry.

ACCOMMODATION AND EATING ARTIES

Casa Irene C/Major 3, http://hotelcasairene.com. This well-regarded restaurant serves mountain cuisine, from grilled rabbit to thick Aranese stews. They also have an adjoining hotel, with elegant, individually decorated wood-floored rooms. €€

★ **Casa Rufus** C/Sant Jaume 8, in Gessa, 1.5km east of Arties, casarufus.com. When it comes to alpine cuisine, this place looks the part: a stone facade gives way to a warmly wood-panelled dining room. This is food made for trekking the mountains: big bowls of steaming Aranese stew, grilled beefs, sausages and the ubiquitous but excellent cod. €€

Eth Restilhè Pl. Carrera 2, in Garos, 2km west of Arties, http://restilhe.com/en/restaurante-eth-restilhe. Fill up on mountain cuisine, from the exquisite house pâté to grilled sausages to trout with herbs, at this long-running family restaurant. €€€

Urtau Arties Pl. Urtau 12, http://urtau.com/tabernas/#arties. There's a good reason that this local tapas chain pulls in the crowds. The diverse menu is flavourful, filling and fun, including a huge array of tapas and pintxos, from croquettes to grilled shrimp. Other locations are in Vielha and Bossòst. €€

Bossòst

An enticing blend of history, alpine beauty and local cuisine, the village of **BOSSÒST** lies roughly equidistant to Vielha (15km to the southeast) and the French border, just to the north. Bossòst's Romanesque highlight is the beautiful twelfth-century church, crowned by a well-preserved bell tower, and with apses designed in the Lombard (early Romanesque) style. Bossòst is near the gorgeous Portilhon mountain pass – accessible via driving and hiking – which reveals one of the finest viewpoints in the area: **Còth de Baretja**, looking out over the majestic Val D'Aran.

ARRIVAL AND INFORMATION BOSSÒST

By bus From June to Sept, a bus runs regularly in the valley, connecting Bossòst and Vielha (20min); in winter, the bus runs on a reduced schedule, if at all.

EATING

★ **Er Occitan** C/Major 66, http://eroccitan.com. Sample the best of Catalan alpine "slow food" cuisine at this elegantly rustic restaurant, with stone walls and white bed linen. Among the dishes are elderflower tempura; suckling pig with four types of garlic; lamb with potatoes stuffed with goat's cheese and bacon; and a dessert rooted in a traditional Val d'Aran mulled wine. For the finest sampling, go for the tasting menu or the "surprise menu", selected by the chef. €€€

El Portalet C/Sant Jaume 32, http://restaurantportalet.com. The mountain landscape doesn't just unfold outside of this charming restaurant, but inside too. The dining room reflects the earthy colours of the surrounding valley, incorporating elements of nature like tree trunks and branches. The hyper-seasonal menu also reflects the local environment, with dishes like lamb with sweetbreads and cucumber tartare; suckling pig with maple syrup; and monkfish with black sausage. €€€€

Southern Catalunya

The great triangle of land south of Barcelona may be one of the lesser-visited wedges of Catalunya – but it shouldn't be. This wonderfully varied area encompasses a sun-speckled coast, a trinity of medieval monasteries and the historically rich provincial capitals of Tarragona and Lleida.

West of Barcelona lies **cava country**, where you can tour Catalunya's best-known cava producers, especially around **Sant Sadurní d'Anoia**. On the coast, just south of Barcelona, sits vibrant **Sitges**, a major LGBTQ+ summer destination that's also home to some fine *modernista* architecture. Beyond this is the **Costa Daurada** – the coastline that stretches from just north of Tarragona to the Delta de l'Ebre – which suffered less exploitation than the Costa Brava. It's easy enough to see why it was so neglected – the shoreline can be drab, with beaches that are narrow and characterless, backed by sparse villages – but there are exceptions, and if all you want to do is relax by a beach for a while, there are several down-to-earth and perfectly functional possibilities.

The Costa Daurada really begins to pay dividends, however, if you can forget about the beaches temporarily and spend a couple of days in **Tarragona**. It's a city with a solid Roman past – reflected in an array of impressive ruins and monuments – and makes a handy springboard for trips inland into Lleida province. South of Tarragona, Catalunya peters out in the lagoons and marshes of the **Delta de l'Ebre**, a riverine wetland rich in birdlife – perfect for slow boat trips, fishing and sampling the local seafood.

Inland attractions are fewer, and many travelling this way are inclined to head on out of Catalunya altogether, not stopping until they reach Zaragoza. It's true that much of the region is flat, rural and dull, but nonetheless it would be a mistake to miss the outstanding monastery at **Poblet**, only an hour or so inland from Tarragona. A couple of other nearby towns and monasteries – notably medieval **Montblanc** and **Santes Creus** – add a bit more interest to the region, while by the time you've rattled across the huge plain that encircles the provincial capital of **Lleida** you'll have earned a night's rest. Pretty much off the tourist trail, Lleida is the start of the dramatic road and train routes into the western foothills of the Catalan Pyrenees, and is only two and a half hours from Zaragoza.

Vilafranca del Penedès

Pleasant **VILAFRANCA DEL PENEDÈS**, capital of the *comarca* of Alt Penedès, lies about 45km southwest of Barcelona, and offers the twin pleasures of history and wine. It was founded in the eleventh century in an attempt to attract settlers to land retaken from the expelled Moors and in time became a prosperous market centre. This character is still in evidence today, with a compact old town with narrow streets and arcaded squares adorned with restored medieval mansions. In the centre, around Pl. de Sant Joan, a Saturday market sells everything from farm-fresh produce to clothes, household goods and handicrafts. The **vineyards** of Vilafranca are all scattered in the countryside out of town – one of the closest (and most famous) is Torres (see page 716).

The **Festa Major** (http://festamajor.info), at the end of August and the first couple of days in September, brings the place to a standstill. Dances and parades clog the streets, while the festival is most widely known for its display of *castellers* – teams of people competing to build human towers (see page 723).

Vinseum

Pl. Jaume I 5 • Charge • http://vinseum.cat

Opposite the much-restored Gothic church of Santa Maria, the **Vinseum** features an impressive collection, including antique casks, wine-themed art through the ages and historic *porrons*, a traditional Catalan wine pitcher with a thin spout, designed to pour *vino* in a stream directly into your mouth, so that it can be shared around a table.

(In George Orwell's *Homage to Catalonia*, he humorously recounts his experience in drinking from one.) Rivalling the museum's exhibits is the building itself, a thirteenth-century royal palace that was once the seat of the Catalan-Aragon crown. After your visit, sample local wines at the *Vinmuseum Tavern*.

ARRIVAL AND INFORMATION

VILAFRANCA DEL PENEDÈS

By train Regular trains travel from Barcelona to Vilafranca (50min).

Turisme C/Hermenegild Clascar 2 (Mon & Sun 10–1pm,

Tues–Sat 9.30am–1.30pm & 3–6pm; http://turismevila franca.com).

ACCOMMODATION, EATING AND DRINKING

Cal Ton C/Casal 8, http://restaurantcalton.com. This Michelin-listed restaurant has been winning fans since opening in 1982. A series of dining spaces creates a cosy, intimate feel; ask for a table in the glass-roofed, tiled-floor

conservatory. The menu showcases traditional Catalan cuisine, best washed down with excellent local wines. €€€

Casa Torner i Güell Rambla de Sant Francesc 26, http:// casatorneriguell.com. This graceful *modernista* boutique

CAVA COUNTRY

Cava – Spain's answer to champagne – is grown largely in the Penedès region, which also produces quality white wines and robust reds. "Cava" simply means cellar, and was the word chosen when the French objected to the word champagne. The eminently drinkable, and very affordable, sparkling wine is usually defined by its sugar content: *seco* (literally "dry") has around half the sugar of a *semi-seco* ("semi-dry"). In addition to selling bottles of bubbly, the region's famous *bodegas* often offer informative tours and tastings, and are located in stunning properties, attractions in themselves. Most can be found in the Penedès region near the town of **Sant Sadurní d'Anoia**, about 30km west of Barcelona, and in the countryside around **Vilafranca de Penedès**, 15km southwest of Sant Sadurní. And, while the Penedès continues to be dominated by the big names – **Codorníu**, **Freixenet** and **Torres** – a wave of small-batch wineries are beginning to present strong competition, many of them offering organic bubbly, like **Parés Baltà**. There are regular trains from Estació-Sants Barcelona to Sant Sadurní (40min) and Vilafranca de Penedès (50min). Also, Codorníu offers bus service to and from Barcelona; see their website for details.

THE WINERIES AROUND PENEDÈS

Bodegas Torres Finca el Maset, Pacs del Penedès, 3km northwest of Vilafranca de Penedès, http://torres. es. Torres, one of Spain's leading wine producers, leads well-organized tours, which include trundling through the fragrant vineyards in a small tourist train, slick audiovisual presentations, and a tasting at the end. Oenophiles can opt for a more in-depth experience with wine-tasting classes on Saturdays.

Codorníu Avda. Jaume Codorníu, just outside Sant Sadurní d'Anoia, http://codorniu.com. Codorníu, one of Spain's best-known cava brands, is credited with bringing sparkling wine production to Spain in 1872. On a tour, you'll explore the cellars, view the beautiful *modernista* premises designed by Josep Maria Puig i Cadafalch and enjoy a tasting at the end. Reservations are essential – you can call or book online. The winery is about 2km from the highway and well signposted. The winery also offers a range of culinary and cava

experiences, including a full Mediterranean lunch paired with cavas.

Freixenet C/Joan Sala 2, visible from the highway, http://freixenet.com. This celebrated producer offers interesting tours which include a visit to their oldest cellars, originally excavated in 1922, a ride on a tourist train around the winery and samples of bubbly. There's also a well-stocked shop. Tours must be booked in advance, either by phone or the website.

Parés Baltà C/Masia Can Baltà, Pacs del Penedès, just west of Vilafranca, http://paresbalta.com. L'Alt Penedès is dotted with smaller family-run wineries, which offer a unique alternative to the biggies. Parés Baltà, helmed by two women winemakers, focuses on organic wines, and offers a variety of tours around its lovely property. In some parts, the vineyards grow amid wild parkland – Parés Baltà is one of the few producers in Spain with vineyards in a natural park, the Parc del Foix. Pick up a bottle of the award-winning rosé Parés Baltà Ros de Pacs.

hotel is in the heart of the charming old town. The stylish rooms feature gleaming woods and sleek furnishings. Take in breezes in the leafy garden and sip local wines in the handsome cocktail lounge. €€

Inzolia C/Palma 21, just off C/Sant Joan, http://inzolia. com. An agreeable place in town to wine taste: a range of cavas and wines are sold by the glass, and there's a good wine shop attached.

Sitges

SITGES, 40km from Barcelona, is definitely the highlight of this stretch of coast. Established in the 1960s as a holiday town, whose liberal attitudes openly challenged the rigidity of Franco's Spain, it has now become the great weekend escape for young Barcelonans, who have created a resort very much in their own image. It's also a noted LGBTQ+ holiday destination, with the nightlife to match. Indeed, if you don't like vigorous action of all kinds, you'd be wise to avoid Sitges in the summer – staid it isn't. Finding a place to stay in peak season can be a challenge, unless you arrive early in the day or book well in advance. None of this deters the varied and generally well-heeled visitors, however – nor should it, since Sitges as a sort of Barcelona-on-Sea is definitely worth experiencing for at least one night.

The town itself is appealing and attractive: a former fishing village whose well-maintained houses and narrow streets have attracted artists and opted-out intellectuals for a century or so. But, it's the **beach** that brings most people to Sitges, and it's not hard to find, with two strands right in town, to the west of the church. From here, a succession of *platjas* of varying quality and crowdedness stretches west for a couple of kilometres down the coast. A long seafront promenade flanks the beach, and all along there are beach bars, restaurants, showers and watersports facilities. Towards the end of the western stretch of beach, you'll reach nudist beaches, a couple of which are exclusively LGBTQ+.

Museu Cau Ferrat

C/Fonollar • Charge, includes Museu Maricel • http://museusdesitges.cat

This gorgeous renovated mansion overlooks the sea and contains the **Museu Cau Ferrat**, which served from 1891 onwards as the home and workshop of artist and writer **Santiago Rusiñol i Prats** (1861–1931). Rusiñol organized five *modernista* festivals in Sitges between 1892 and 1899, and the town flourished as a major *modernista* centre under his patronage. Magnificently tiled rooms display an extraordinary array of paintings, artefacts and decorative ironwork gathered by Rusiñol, including works by Rusiñol himself, contemporaries such as Picasso, and even a couple of minor El Grecos that he bought when the painter's reputation was much less elevated than it is today.

CARNAVAL AND FANTASY IN SITGES

Carnaval in Sitges (Feb/March) is outrageous, thanks largely to the LGBTQ+ community. The official programme of parades and masked balls is complemented by an unwritten but widely recognized schedule of events. The climax is the Tuesday late-night parade, in which exquisitely dressed drag queens swan about the streets in high heels, twirling lacy parasols and coyly fanning themselves. Bar doors stand wide open, bands play, and processions and celebrations go on until four in the morning.

If you're a fan of fantasy, don't miss the annual **Sitges Film Festival** (http:// sitgesfilmfestival.com), one of the world's premiere fantasy and horror film festivals. The festival has also expanded to embrace other genres and attracts some big-name actors and directors. It takes place over ten days in late October at venues around the town (information and venues from the *turisme*). In the summer, the city government usually hosts **outdoor concerts** at the various museums and gardens, including opera, jazz and classical guitar. Enquire at the tourist office.

Museu Maricel de Mar

C/Davallada 12, adjoining Museu Cau Ferrat • Charge, includes Museu Cau Ferrat • http://museusdesitges.cat

Browse the timeline of Catalan art from the tenth century on, including richly detailed medieval art and the nineteenth-century Luminist School of Sitges, a group of landscape artists who were inspired by the town's beautiful seaside light and open skies.

Fundació Stämpfli Art Contemporani

Pl. de l'Ajuntament 13 • Charge • http://fundacio-stampfli.org

Housed in Sitges' former fish market and a similarly venerable adjoining building, the **Fundació Stämpfli** is home to the wide-ranging contemporary art collection of Swiss-born artist Peter Stämpfli and his wife, Anna Maria, who have been active members of the local art scene since the 1970s. The works – some eighty paintings, sculptures and more by international artists such as Erró, Gérard Fromanger and Stämpfli himself – offer a sweeping view of various art movements from the past fifty years. The renovated space in which the collection is presented is simple but beautiful, with a vaulted, wood-beamed ceiling and gleaming floors.

Casa Bacardi

Pl. Ajuntament 11 • Charge • http://casabacardi.es

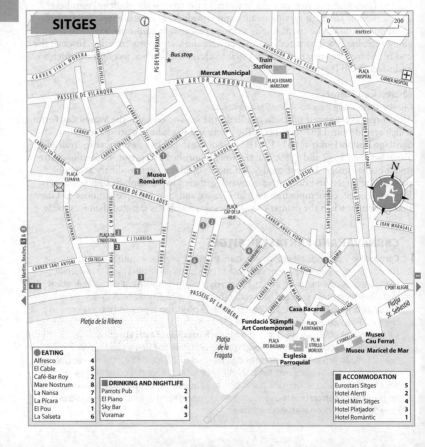

●EATING	
Alfresco	4
El Cable	5
Café-Bar Roy	2
Mare Nostrum	8
La Nansa	7
La Pícara	3
El Pou	1
La Salseta	6

■ DRINKING AND NIGHTLIFE	
Parrots Pub	2
El Piano	1
Sky Bar	4
Voramar	3

■ ACCOMMODATION	
Eurostars Sitges	5
Hotel Alenti	2
Hotel Mim Sitges	4
Hotel Platjador	3
Hotel Romàntic	1

The founder of Bacardi rum, Facundo Bacardí Massó, was born in Sitges and raised here until his mid-teens, when he emigrated to Cuba in 1830. The **Casa Bacardi**, housed in the historic Mercat Vell, explores the history of Bacardi rum – and its connection to Sitges – culminating in a rum tasting. Casa Bacardi also offers cocktail-making classes on weekday evenings at 6pm and 9pm.

ARRIVAL AND INFORMATION
SITGES

By train Trains to Sitges leave Barcelona's Estació-Sants every 30min throughout the day (trip length 25–40min). The train station is a 10min walk from the town centre and seafront. For current timetables and ticket information, consult RENFE (902 240 202, http://renfe.es).

By bus Buses stop in front of the train station, except those to and from Barcelona, which stop outside the main *turisme*.

MonBus (938 937 511, http://monbus.cat) runs throughout the day (until about 10.30pm) from Sitges to Barcelona airport and the city centre.

Turisme Pl. Eduard Maristany 2 (June–mid-Oct Mon–Sat 10am–2pm & 3–7pm, Sun 10am–2pm; Jan–June & mid-Oct–Dec Mon–Sat 10am–2pm & 3–6pm, Sun 10am–2pm; http://visitsitges.com).

ACCOMMODATION
SEE MAP PAGE 718

There are dozens of hotels of all types and prices in Sitges, but it's a good idea to reserve in high season as they fill up quickly. If you arrive without a reservation, a short walk through the central streets and along the front (particularly Pg. de la Ribera) reveals most of the possibilities. Come out of season (after Oct and before May) and the high prices tend to soften a little.

Eurostars Sitges Cami del Miralpeix 12, http://eurostars hotels.com/eurostars-sitges. As far as resorts go, this is a good one. Though sprawling, with plenty of conference amenities, it still feels personalized, with warmly decorated rooms and an intimate spa. Plus, the resort is equipped with several pools; a range of breezy restaurants, most specializing in Mediterranean cuisine, along with bars and lounges; and a free shuttle bus to the beach in high season. €€€

Hotel Alenti C/1er de Maig, http://hotelalenti.com. Sleek hotel, in an all-white, cube-shaped building, with plenty of pale wood and picture windows that let in the Sitges sunshine. Restaurant with a terrace directly onto the "Street of Sin". €€€

★ **Hotel Mim Sitges** Avda. Sofia 12, http://mimhotels. com/en/sitges/hotel-mim-sitges. This gleaming contemporary hotel ticks all the boxes: it's central and near the beach, environment friendly and rich with amenities, including a spa and a rooftop pool and *Sky Bar* (see page 720). Rooms are filled with natural light and bathrooms have rain showers. €€€€

Hotel Platjador Passeig de la Ribera, 35, http:/ hotelplatjadorsitges.com-hotel.com. Relax in colourful rooms, some with sun-warmed balconies with views of the sparkling Mediterranean, at this inviting hotel. Plus, splash in the well-maintained pool and enjoy a hearty buffet breakfast, included in the rate. €€€

Hotel Romàntic C/Sant Isidre 33, http://mediumhoteles. com/en/hotel-medium-romantic. Attractive converted nineteenth-century villa in the quiet streets away from the front, not far from the train station, with ornate, *modernista* touches and rooms with plenty of character; some have a terrace overlooking the palm-shaded gardens. It's a favourite with LGBTQ+ visitors. Breakfast included. Closed Nov–March. €€€

EATING
SEE MAP PAGE 718

Most of the **restaurants** along the promenade feature sea-view terraces and serve paella and seafood, while the side streets are dotted with inviting spots. You can get picnic supplies at the town's **market**, the Mercat Municipal, near the train station, on Avda. Artur Carbonell.

Alfresco C/Pau Barrabeig 4, http://alfrescorestaurante.es. This welcoming restaurant serves superb Catalan cuisine with Asian touches, like Thai marinated lamb salad and grilled octopus with spinach. €€

El Cable C/Barcelona 1, http://elcable.cat. With its lively social scene, Sitges is a tapas town – and the long-running, amiable *El Cable* is one of the best. Feast on *patatas bravas*, ham croquettes and spicy sausage. €

Café-Bar Roy C/Parellades 9, http://casaroysitges.com. An old-fashioned café with dressed-up waiters and marble

tables. Watch the world go by from its prime streetside perch, over a glass of cava or a fancy snack. €€

Mare Nostrum Pg. de la Ribera 60, http://restaurant marenostrum.com. Long-established fish restaurant on the seafront, with a menu that changes according to the catch and season. €€€

La Nansa C/Carreta 24, http://restaurantlanansa.com. A *nansa* (fishing net) hangs in this amiable, family-run restaurant, which has wood-panelled walls, brass lanterns and maritime paintings. The top-notch seafood- and fish-focused menu includes the regional favourite, *arroz a la Sitgetana* (rice with meat, prawns, clams and a generous splash of Sitges Malvasia wine). €€€

La Pícara C/Sant Pere 3, http://lapicarasitges.cat. Graze on top-notch tapas at this cheerful restaurant, from calamari

SITGES' LGBTQ+ SCENE

The frenetic and ever-changing **LGBTQ+ scene** in Sitges is chronicled on a LGBTQ+ map and guide available from *Parrots Pub*, as well as from several other bars and clubs, including the sing-along bar *El Piano* (see page 720). Most of the bars and clubs are centred around Pl. Indústria and in the triangle made up by Carrer Espalter, Carrer Sant Francesc and Carrer Parellades. Sitges' clubs are liveliest in the summer, when they're open Friday and Saturday nights and sometimes during the week; in winter, hours vary and may be limited. Most clubs open no earlier than midnight and stay hopping until the wee hours.

For more information, check out http://gaysitgesguide.com.

to juicy shrimp to *albondigas* (meatballs) to croquettes. The wine list is also strong, featuring a superb selection of Catalan vintages. €€

El Pou C/Sant Bonaventura 21, http://elpoudsitges.com. Stylish, welcoming tapas bar, where the Catalan-Japanese fusion menu includes duck carpaccio and meatballs with squid. €€€

La Salseta C/Sant Pau 35, http://lasalseta.com. Classic, unpretentious Catalan dishes (cod with garlic confit, seafood paella and plenty of vegetarian options), cooked with slow-food attention and using locally sourced ingredients, keep this cosy little dining room filled with tourists and locals alike. €€€

DRINKING AND NIGHTLIFE

SEE MAP PAGE 718

Late-opening **bars** centre on pedestrianized Carrer 1er (Primer) de Maig (popularly known as *Carrer del Pecado*, or "Street of Sin") and its continuation, C/Marqués de Montroig, while Carrer de les Parellades and Carrer Bonaire complete the block. In summer, this is basically one long run of **disco-bars**, pumping music out into the late evening, interspersed with the odd restaurant or fancier cocktail bar, all with outdoor tables vying for your euros.

Parrots Pub Pl. de la Indústria, http://parrots-sitges.com. One of the town's best-known LGBTQ+ bars, at the top of C/1er de Maig, and a required stop for practically everyone at some point; it's just one place where you can pick up the

free LGBTQ+ map of Sitges.

El Piano C/Sant Bonaventura 37, http://elpianositges. com. Join the crowd in singing show tunes at this friendly LGBTQ+ bar.

Sky Bar Av. Sofia 12, http://mimhotels.com. Toast the night at this soaring bar that crowns *Hotel Mim Sitges*. The star here is the spectacular view, but the cocktails also hold their own, including potent mojitos, as well as sparkling cava.

Voramar C/Port Alegre 55, http://pub-voramar.com. Charismatic, old-school seafront bar, away from the main crowds, just right for an ice-cold beer or sundowner cocktail.

Tarragona

Sited on a rocky hill, sheer above the sea, **TARRAGONA** has a formidable ancient past. Settled originally by Iberians and then Carthaginians, it was later used as the base for the Roman conquest of the peninsula, which began in 218 BC with Scipio's march south against Hannibal. The fortified city became an imperial resort and, under Augustus, **Tarraco** was named capital of Rome's eastern Iberian province – the most elegant and cultured city of Roman Spain, boasting at its peak a quarter of a million inhabitants. Temples and monuments were built in and around the city and, despite a history of seemingly constant sacking and looting since Roman times, it's this distinguished past which still asserts itself throughout modern Tarragona.

Time spent in the handsome upper town quickly shows what attracted the emperors to the city: strategically – and beautifully – placed, it's a fine setting for some splendid Roman remains and a few excellent museums. There's an attractive medieval section, too, while the rocky coastline below conceals a couple of reasonable beaches. If there's a downside, it's that Tarragona is today the second-largest port in Catalunya, so the views aren't always unencumbered – though the fish in the Serrallo fishing quarter is consistently good and fresh. Furthermore, the city's ugly outskirts to the south have been steadily degraded by new industries – chemical and oil refineries and a nuclear power station – which do little for Tarragona's character as a resort.

Orientation

The city divides clearly into two parts: a predominantly medieval, walled upper town (where you'll spend most of your time) known as **La Part Alta**, and the prosperous modern centre below, referred to as **Eixample**, or the Centre Urbà. Between the two cuts is the **Rambla Nova**, a sturdy provincial rival to Barcelona's, lined with fashionable cafés and restaurants, culminating at its southern end with the lovely

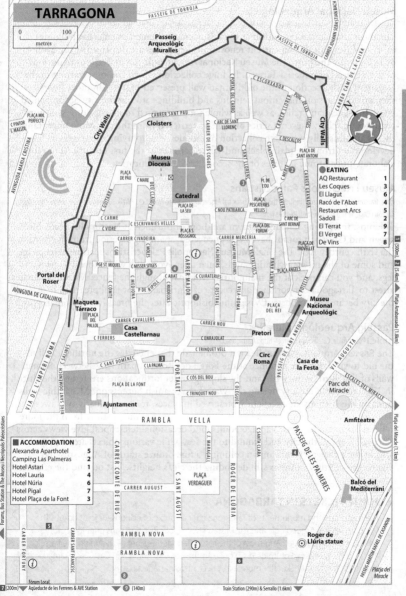

TARRAGONA

0 — 100 metres

EATING

AQ Restaurant	1
Les Coques	3
El Llagut	6
Racó de l'Abat	4
Restaurant Arcs	5
Sadoll	2
El Terrat	9
El Vergel	7
De Vins	8

ACCOMMODATION

Alexandra Aparthotel	5
Camping Las Palmeras	2
Hotel Astari	1
Hotel Lauria	4
Hotel Núria	6
Hotel Pigal	7
Hotel Plaça de la Font	3

11

Balcó del Mediterràni, overlooking the sea. Parallel, and to the east, lies the **Rambla Vella**, marking – as its name suggests – the start of the old town. To either side of the *rambles* are scattered a profusion of relics from Tarragona's Roman past, including various temples and parts of the forum, theatre and amphitheatre. Note that some of the most impressive monuments are a fair way out, but there's enough within walking distance to occupy a good day's sightseeing and to provide a vivid impression of life in Tarragona in imperial Roman times.

Museu Nacional Arqueològic
Tinglado 4, Moll de la Costa • Charge (includes the Museu i Necròpolis Paleocristians) • http://mnat.cat

The most stimulating exhibition in town is normally housed in adjacent buildings off Pl. del Rei, but during current renovations key pieces are displayed at the Moll de la Costa by the port. The **Museu Nacional Arqueològic** is a marvellous reflection of the richness of imperial Tarraco. Its huge collection is well laid out, starting in the basement with a section of the old Roman wall preserved *in situ*. On other floors are thematic displays on the various remains and buildings around the city, accompanied by pictures, text and relics, as well as whole rooms devoted to inscriptions, sculpture, ceramics, jewellery – even a series of anchors retrieved from the sea. More importantly, there's an unusually complete collection of mosaics, exemplifying the stages of development from the plain black-and-white patterns of the first century AD to the elaborate polychrome pictures of the second and third centuries.

Museu i Necròpolis Paleocristians
Avda. Ramón i Cajal 78 • Charge (includes the Museu Nacional Arqueològic) • http://mnat.cat • Walk 20min out of the centre down Avda. Ramón i Cajal, which runs west off Rambla Nova

The most interesting remains in town are those of the ancient **Necropolis**. Here, both pagan and Christian tombs have been uncovered, spanning a period from the third to the sixth century AD. The small **Museu i Necropolis Paleocristians** features sarcophagi and some of the most fascinating finds, such as an ivory doll with moveable arms and legs, and you can peek at the main burial grounds through the fence. Most of the relics attest to Tarragona's importance as a centre of Christianity: St Paul preached here, and the city became an important Visigothic bishopric after the break-up of Roman power.

Passeig Arqueològic Muralles
Portal del Roser, Avda. Catalunya • Charge • http://tarragona.cat

The **Passeig Arqueològic Muralles** is a promenade that encircles the northern half of the old town. From the entrance at the Portal del Roser, a path runs between **Roman walls** of the third century BC and the sloping, **outer fortifications** erected by the British in 1709 to secure the city during the War of the Spanish Succession. Megalithic walls built by the Iberians are excellently preserved in places, too, particularly two awesome gateways; the huge blocks used in their construction are quite distinct from the more refined Roman additions. Vantage points (and occasional telescopes) give views across the plain behind the city and around to the sea, while various objects are displayed within the *passeig*: several Roman columns, a fine bronze statue of Augustus and eighteenth-century cannons still defending the city's heights. Just beyond the entrance

---

JOINT TICKETS IN TARRAGONA

The museums and monuments of Tarragona offer a couple of options for joint tickets. The Museu Nacional Arqueològic and the Museu i Necròpolis Paleocristians offer joint entry (http://mnat.cat; charge). And most of the rest of Tarragona's sights – including the Passeig Arqueològic Muralles, Forum de la Colonia, Amfiteatre, Circ Roma and Casa Castellarnau – also have their own joint ticket (for more info, check http://tarragona.cat).

HUMAN CASTLES

It's not often that you'll come across a group of grown men and women who willingly climb onto each other's back to form a tall, if a bit wobbly, human tower. But when you do, it's a sight to behold. Catalunya's famous *castellers* – teams of people competing to build human towers – originated in **Valls**, near Tarragona, at the end of the eighteenth century. Over time, the rest of Catalunya embraced the tradition, and *castells* now form a part of festivals throughout the region. The impressive *castells* can loom up to ten human storeys tall, and are completed by a small child scrambling to the very top.

Castells are a feature of Tarragona's annual **Festival of Santa Tecla** in mid-September. The Festa Major of Vilafranca del Penedès in late August (see page 715) also showcases *castells*.

on the right, a small doorway leads up to the battlements from where you get fine views of the old city.

Fòrum

Pl. del Forum • Charge • http://tarragona.cat

In the centre of town, the Roman forum, or rather forums, have also survived, since – as provincial capital – Tarragona sustained both a ceremonial **Fòrum Provincial** (the scant remnants of which are displayed on Pl. del Fòrum) and a **Fòrum de la Colonia** on C/ Lleida, whose more substantial remains are on the western side of Rambla Nova, near the Mercat Central. Located on the flat land near the port, this was the commercial centre of imperial Tarraco and the main meeting place for locals for three centuries. The site, which contained temples and small shops arranged around a porticoed square, has been split by a main road: a footbridge now connects the two halves where you can see a water cistern, house foundations, fragments of stone inscriptions and four elegant columns.

Amfiteatre

Parc del Miracle • http://tarragona.cat

A group of Tarragona's tangible Roman remains lie close to each other at the seaward end of the Rambla Vella. Most rewarding is the **Amfiteatre**, built into the green slopes of Parc del Miracle. The tiered seats backing onto the sea are original, and from the top you can look north, up the coast, to the headland; the rest of the seating was reconstructed in 1969–70, along with the surviving tunnels and structural buildings.

Circ Romà and Pretori

Rambla Vella, Pl. del Rei • Charge • http://tarragona.cat

The **Circ Romà**, or Roman Circus, was the site of chariot races. The visible sections encompass vaults that are set back from the street under the gloom of the surrounding buildings. You can exit through the Roman **Pretori** tower on Pl. del Rei.

Casa Castellarnau

C/Cavallers 14 • Charge • http://tarragona.cat

Strolling the old town's streets will also enable you to track down one of Tarragona's finest medieval mansions and lesser-known museums, the **Casa Castellarnau**. The interior courtyard alone rewards a visit, with its arches and stone coats of arms built over Roman vaults. Otherwise, the small-scale collections are largely archeological and historical (Roman jars and the like), rescued from banality by some rich eighteenth-century Catalan furniture and furnishings on the upper floor. At the time of writing, it was closed for renovation – check the website for details.

Catedral

Pl. de Palau 2 • Charge • http://catedraldetarragona.com

The central C/Major climbs to the quarter's focal point, the **Catedral**, which sits at the top of a broad flight of steps. This, quite apart from its own grand beauty, is a perfect example of the transition from Romanesque to Gothic forms. You'll see the change highlighted in the main facade, where a soaring Gothic portal is framed by Romanesque doors, surmounted by a cross and an elaborate rose window. Except for services, entrance to the Catedral is through the **cloisters** (*claustre*; signposted up a street to the left of the facade), themselves superbly executed with pointed Gothic arches softened by smaller round divisions. The cloister also has several oddly sculpted capitals, one of which represents a cat's funeral being directed by rats. Note that the Catedral has been undergoing renovations, so parts of it may be closed to the public, and the entry fee may therefore be reduced. The ticket also gives access to the **Museu Diocesà**, which is piled high with ecclesiastical treasures.

Serrallo

A fifteen-minute walk west along the industrial harbourfront from the train station (or the same distance south from the Necropolis) takes you to the working port of **Serrallo**, Tarragona's so-called "fishermen's quarter". Built a century ago, the harbour here isn't particularly attractive, though it's authentic enough – fishing smacks tied up, nets laid out on the ground for mending. The real interest for visitors is the line of **seafood restaurants** which fronts the main Moll dels Pescadors. The warehouses nearby, back towards town, have been given a face-lift, as has the Estació Marítima (cruise-ship terminal).

ARRIVAL AND DEPARTURE

TARRAGONA

By train The train station is on Pg. de Espanya (902 432 343), from which it's an easy walk into town. In addition to the regular trains, there are high-speed AVE trains from Barcelona, Madrid and other main cities which arrive at the Camp de Tarragona AVE station, a 10min taxi ride from the centre.

Destinations Barcelona (every 30min; 1hr); Cambrils (12 daily; 20min); Lleida (12 daily; 2hr, Talgo 1hr, AVE 30min); Sitges (direct every 30min; 1hr); Tortosa (13 daily; 1hr); Valencia (16 daily; 4hr, Talgo 2hr 15min); Zaragoza (12

daily; 3hr 30min).

By bus The bus terminal is at the end of Rambla Nova, at Pl. Imperial Tarraco.

Destinations Barcelona (18 daily; 1hr 30min); Berga (July & Aug daily, rest of year Sat & Sun only; 3hr 10min); La Seu d'Urgell (daily at 8am; 3hr 45min); Lleida (6 daily; 1hr 45min); Montblanc (3 daily; 50min); Poblet (Mon–Sat 3 daily; 1hr 5min); Tortosa (Mon–Fri 1 daily; 1hr 30min); Valencia (7 daily; 3hr 30min); Zaragoza (4 daily; 4hr).

INFORMATION

Turisme C/Major 39 (July–Sept Mon–Sat 9am–9pm, Sun 10am–2pm; Oct–June Mon–Sat 10am–2pm & 3–6pm, Sun 10am–2pm; http://tarragonaturisme.cat). There are a few other information booths/offices, including on Rambla Nova (summer daily 10am–8pm; winter Mon–Sun

10am–2pm).

Regional tourist office C/Fortuny 4, just south of Rambla Nova (Mon–Fri 9am–2pm & 4–6.30pm, Sat 9am–2pm; http://tarragonaturisme.cat). Especially good if you're travelling farther afield.

ACCOMMODATION

SEE MAP PAGE 721

Alexandra Aparthotel Rambla Nova 71, http:// alexandra-aparthotel.tarragona.top-hotels-es.com/en. Outside the hotel, you're in the thick of things, right on busy Rambla Nova. Inside, the airy *Alexandra* offers a quiet retreat, with generously sized rooms and studios, many with fully equipped kitchens and dining rooms, making this an ideal spot for families and groups of friends. €€

Camping Las Palmeras http://laspalmeras.com. There are a number of campsites east of town including this well-maintained site at Platja Llarga, 3km northeast along the coast. Also on offer are spacious bungalows, which are ideal

for families and groups. €

Hotel Astari Vía Augusta 95–97, http://hotelastari.com. Friendly hotel with modern rooms, a decent swimming pool and pleasant garden. It's a 15min walk from the old town, and less than a 10min stroll from the nearest beach. €

Hotel Lauria Rambla Nova 20, http://hotel-lauria.com. Well-located just off the main *rambla* with modern if functional rooms and a small outdoor pool. €

Hotel Núria Vía Augusta 145, http://hotelnuria.com. Pleasant hotel near Arrabassada beach, 1km northeast of Tarragona – the *playa* stretches right nearby, and town is about a 25min walk away (or you can opt for one of the regular buses). The decor tends towards minimalist, and there's a restaurant-café, with a weekday lunchtime menu. €

Hotel Pigal Cardenal Cervantes 6, http://hotelpigal.com. Proof that even budget digs can be stylish, this cheery little

hotel, with a blue facade fronted by cute balconies, has simple rooms with wood furnishings and tiled floors. €

Hotel Plaça de la Font Pl. de la Font 26, http://hotelpdelafont.com. Central, cosy hotel with simple, well-scrubbed rooms and a small restaurant with a cheery terrace on the *plaça*. €

EATING

SEE MAP PAGE 721

There are plenty of good **restaurants** in the centre of Tarragona; many – particularly in and around Pl. de la Font – have outdoor seating in the summer. Alternatively, you could try the fish and seafood places down in Serrallo – not cheap, but the food is fresh and you can find some menus for around €18–25 in the narrow street behind the main Moll dels Pescadors. Tarragona's marina (Port Esportiu) features several **clubs and bars**, which generally heat up in the summer – though note that they come and go with great regularity. It's in town – around the old quarter and the Catedral and in the streets between the train station and Rambla Nova – that you'll find spots with more historical, local appeal.

★ **AQ Restaurant** C/Coques 7, http://aq-restaurant.com. Glossy restaurant – the sky-lit dining room sports honey-hued walls and sleek furnishings – with impressive cuisine to match. Husband-and-wife team Quintín and Ana (after whom the restaurant is named) serve up seasonal food with flair including superb fresh fish and shellfish. €€€

Les Coques C/Sant Llorenç 15, http://les-coques.com. Top-notch Catalan fare in a comfortable restaurant near the Catedral. €€€

El Llagut C/Natzaret 10, http://elllagut.com. Rice and seafood are the stars of the menu at this handsome tavern. Try *arròs negre* (rice with squid ink) and a huge array of fresh seafood, from monkfish to mussels to cuttlefish. The well-curated wine list showcases superb vintages from around Catalunya. €€€

Racó de l'Abat C/Abat 2, http://instagram.com/restaurantdelabat. Beamed ceilings and crimson plaster walls give this Catalan restaurant – located in a former

palace dating from the sixteenth century – an intimate, heritage vibe. €€

Restaurant Arcs C/Misser Sitges 13, http://restaurantarcs.com. Ancient, graceful stone arches – hence the name – preside over a cosy dining room. Fresh Mediterranean dishes include cod with a cabrales cheese sauce and duck with sweet-and-sour cherry preserves. €€€

Sadoll C/Mare de Déu de la Mercè 1, http://sadoll-restaurant.com. Inviting restaurant tucked away in a quiet corner near the Catedral and featuring fresh, creative dishes in an elegant Art Nouveau dining room. €€€

El Terrat C/Pons d'Icart 19, http://elterratrestaurant.com. Delve into the wonderfully varied menu, from tapas to traditional to avant-garde, at this established restaurant with a large terrace. Dishes may include delectable croquettes with ceps and foie; duck with an orange and vanilla emulsion; and cod with a compote of tomato and raisins. €€€

El Vergel C/Major 13, http://elvergeltarragona.com. Excellent vegetarian and vegan restaurant with an inventive menu that changes often. Dishes may include vegan "chorizo" with chimichurri, mushroom croquettes, and lemon and eggplant risotto – all washed down with organic wines or cold-pressed juices. The dining space is as inviting as the food: whitewashed walls accented with green-painted shutters and patterned tiles. €€€

De Vins C/Mendez Núñez 10, http://devins.es. Perennially popular restaurant with an excellent seasonal menu of traditional dishes – *jamón iberico*, clams in a marinara sauce, steak tartare. Go for the weekday lunchtime menu or the tapas tasting menu. €€€

Around Tarragona

The coast between Tarragona and the historic town of **Altafulla**, 11km east, is littered with Roman remains, well worth checking out, though for all but the Roman **aqueduct** you'll need your own transport. West of Tarragona, the pleasant town of **Reus** features an entertaining museum on master Catalan architect Antoni Gaudí.

Aqüeducte de les Ferreres

Free • http://tarragona.cat • Parking on site; check with *turisme* about bus transport to the site

Perhaps the most remarkable (and least visited) of Tarragona's monuments stands 4km outside the original city walls, reached via a small, signposted road off the main Lleida highway. This is the Roman **Aqüeducte de les Ferreres**, which brought water from the Ríu Gayo, some 32km away. The most impressive extant section, nearly 220m long and 27m high, lies in an overgrown valley in the middle of nowhere: the utilitarian beauty of the aqueduct is surpassed only by the one at Segovia and the Pont du Gard, in the south of France. Popularly, it is known as El Pont del Diable (Devil's Bridge) because, remarked Richard Ford, of the Spanish habit of "giving all praise to 'the Devil', as Pontifex Maximus".

Reus

Gaudí aficionados might want to take a spin through the small, handsome city of **Reus**, 14km west of Tarragona, where the *modernisme* master, Gaudí, was born in 1852. While Reus has no Gaudí buildings – he left at the age of 16 – it does feature a smattering of other *modernista* structures, all of which form part of the town's **Ruta del Modernisme**. Besides Gaudí, Reus is popular for its good shopping, especially clothing, thanks in part to the town's once-thriving textile industry.

Gaudí Centre

Pl. del Mercadal 3 • Charge • http://gaudicentre.com

11

The sleek **Gaudí Centre** offers an engaging overview of the great artist via three floors of tactile and sensory exhibits. The first floor focuses on young Gaudí and his connection with Reus; look for what is believed to be the only handwritten notebook by Gaudí still in existence. The second floor, called "Gaudí the Innovator", focuses on his progressive designs. The top floor shows a film on Gaudí and covers his influence on architecture around the globe.

ARRIVAL AND INFORMATION   REUS

By bus Regular trains and buses connect Reus with Tarragona (15min) and Barcelona (1hr 40min). Buses also travel regularly between the Barcelona airport and Reus airport, which lies about 6km east of Reus and handles various budget European airlines.

Turisme Inside the Gaudí Centre (Mon–Sat 9.30am–2pm & 4–7pm, Sun 10am–2pm; http://reus.cat/turisme). You can pick up a map at the helpful *turisme*, and they also offer a variety of good guided tours of the city, which sometimes include access to *modernista* buildings otherwise closed to the public.

ACCOMMODATION AND EATING

El Círcol de Reus Plaça del Prim 4, http://elcircoldereus. cat. The grand El Círcol, in the heart of town, is a Reus landmark, home to a cultural society founded in 1852. Acclaimed chefs Joan Urgellès and Xavi Martí Macarrilla serve up excellent Mediterranean cuisine with classic French touches. €€

Mas Passamaner Camí de la Serra 52, La Selva del Camp, 5km northwest of Reus, http://maspassamaner.com. For a further taste of *modernisme*, consider staying at this hotel designed by the master architect Lluís Domènech i Montaner in 1922, and converted into a five-star hotel, with elegant rooms, a pool and a spa. €€€€

WINE TOURING IN THE PRIORAT

Around 35km west of Tarragona lies one of Catalunya's top wine regions, the **Priorat**, which was awarded its DOC in 2001. The red wine produced here, and in the adjacent Montsant DOC, is highly sought after, and the *cellers* have started to follow their more established competitors in La Rioja by cashing in with wine tours and tastings. The *turisme* in Tarragona has up-to-date information, or you can try the local office in Falset (Mon–Sat 10am–2pm, Sun 11am–2pm; http://turismepriorat.org). Many tours have English-speaking guides – reservations are essential.

La Conreria de Scala Dei C/Mitja Galta 32, Scala Dei, just south of La Morera de Montsant, http:// vinslaconreria.com. This established winery, named after the Carthusian monks of Scala Dei, offers tours through its cellars and vineyards followed by tastings.

Costers del Siurana Camí Manyetes, Gratallops, http:// costersdelsiurana.com. This highly regarded winery offers tours through the cellars, and also runs the charming, small *Cellers de Gratallop* restaurant nearby, which serves regional cuisine – and Priorat wine, of course.

Altafulla

ALTAFULLA makes a reasonable stop. Take a wander about the old town, where there's a 400-year-old castle (privately owned), the Baroque **Església Parroquial de Sant Martí** (open for services only), which was completed in 1705 and has a distinctive octagonal dome, and a pair of gateways left standing from the original medieval walls.

Vil·la Romana dels Munts

C/Vil·la Romana • Charge • http://mnat.cat

Surrounded by a sleepy estate of holiday homes, the **Vil·la Romana dels Munts** is one of the more important finds in the region, primarily because of the exceptional mosaics and paintings that decorated its rooms and thermal baths – indicating an owner of high standing. The mosaics are preserved in the Museu Nacional Arqueològic in Tarragona and today the villa is worth a look chiefly for the ruins of its thermal baths, which include a remarkably well-preserved arch and water tank.

ARRIVAL AND INFORMATION	**ALTAFULLA**
By bus and train Regular buses and trains connect Altafulla with Tarragona (10min).	**Turisme** Pl. dels Vents (Mon–Sat 10am–1pm & 5–8pm, Sun 10am–2pm; 977 651 426, http://altafulla.cat).

11

Tortosa

The only town of any size in Catalunya's deep south is **TORTOSA**, slightly inland astride the Ríu Ebre. In the Civil War the front was outside Tortosa for several months until the Nationalists eventually took the town in April 1938. The battle cost 35,000 lives, and is commemorated by a gaunt metal monument on a huge stone plinth in the middle of the river in town. The fighting took its toll in other ways, too: there's little left of the medieval quarter, the *barri antic*, which lies on the east bank of the Ebro, north of the modern commercial district. Nonetheless, Tortosa still throws a boisterous and popular Festa del Renaixement (Renaissance Festival; http://festadelrenaixement.org) in late July, which celebrates the city's history, with thousands turning out in period costumes, along with theatre, street entertainment, live music, free-flowing wine and more.

Catedral de Santa Maria

C/Portal del Palau • http://cataloniasacra.cat/llocs/catedral-de-santa-maria-de-tortosa

The **Catedral de Santa Maria** is worth a look. Founded originally in the twelfth century on the site of an earlier mosque, it was rebuilt in the fourteenth century, and its Gothic interior and quiet cloister – although much worn – are both lovely.

La Suda and the Jardins del Príncep

Jardins del Príncep • Charge • http://tortosaturisme.cat

Tortosa's brightest point is also its highest. **La Suda**, the old castle, sits perched above the Catedral, glowering from behind its battlements at the Ebre valley below and the mountains beyond. Like so many in Spain, the castle has been converted into a luxury parador, but there's nothing to stop you climbing up for a magnificent view from the walls, or from going into the plush bar and having a drink.

The **Jardins del Príncep**, which sit at the base of the castle, feature an impressive collection of sculptures of the human figure by Santiago de Santiago.

ARRIVAL AND INFORMATION	**TORTOSA**
By train Tortosa is connected by regular trains to Barcelona (2hr) and Tarragona (1hr). **By bus** Buses run from Tortosa to Vinaròs (in Castellón province to the south), from where you can reach the wonderful inland mountain town of Morella; and to	Tarragona and the Delta de l'Ebre area. **Turisme** Jardins del Príncep (May to Sept Mon–Sat 10am–2pm & 4–7pm, Sun 9.30am–1.30pm; Oct to April 10am–1.30pm & 3.30–6.30pm, Sun 9.30am–1.30pm; http://tortosaturisme.cat).

11

THE WINE CATHEDRAL

The name says it all: The **Catedral del Vi** (Wine Cathedral; C/Pilonet, http://catedraldelvi.com; charge) rises over Pinell de Brai, roughly 30km north of Tortosa, in the Terra Alta region, which is Catalunya's southernmost wine region. Designed by Gaudí disciple Cèsar Martinell, the winery is a magnificent tribute to *modernisme*, revealing its architectural hallmarks, from soaring stone arches to colourful tiling. The winery offers self-guided audio tours and wine and olive-oil tastings, as well as free guided visits at noon and 5pm on the weekends. Make a day of it, and sample local cuisine – and Pagos de Híbera wine – at the stately restaurant (open Sat & Sun for lunch only), which serves an excellent menu. Dishes include grilled octopus and traditional Catalan sausage, followed by choice desserts – try the luscious *crema catalana*. Northwest of Pinell de Brai lies the town of Gandesa, the capital of the Terra Alta wine region, and home to the **Celler Cooperatiu de Gandesa** (Avda. Catalunya 28, http://coopgandesa.com), another magnificent building also designed by Martinell.

ACCOMMODATION AND EATING

Parador de Tortosa http://parador.es. For a splurge, it's well worth opting for this historic parador, where you'll feel like you've stepped into the medieval era. It also has one of the better restaurants in town, open to non-guests and specializing in fish from the Ebro delta. €€

La Torreta de Remolins C/David Ferrando 4, http://latorretaderemolins.cat. Dine on traditional Catalan cuisine, from grilled meats and fish to rice dishes and salads. The wine list is culled from the Terra Alta region, including superb reds. €€

The Delta de l'Ebre

In the bottom corner of Catalunya is the **Delta de l'Ebre** (Ebro Delta), 320 square kilometres of sandy delta constituting the biggest wetland in Catalunya and one of the most important aquatic habitats in the western Mediterranean. Designated a natural park, its brackish lagoons, marshes, dunes and reed beds are home to thousands of wintering birds and provide excellent fishing; around fifteen percent of the total Catalan catch comes from this area. The scenery is unique in Catalunya, with low roads running through field after field of rice paddies, punctuated by solitary houses and small villages, before emerging onto dune-lined beaches. Since much of the area of the **Parc Natural de Delta de l'Ebre** is a protected zone, access is limited, and it's best to visit with your own transport. Check in with the well-stocked tourist office about birdwatching opportunities and other nature tours and treks.

Deltebre

The best place to start to get a good sense of Delta de l'Ebre is the town of **DELTEBRE**, at the centre of the delta, 30km from Tortosa. There's also an interesting **Ecomuseum**, in the park information centre (http://turismodeltadelebro.com; charge), which has an aquarium displaying species found in the delta.

Riumar

The town of **RIUMAR**, 10km east of Deltebre, also makes for a good base to explore the area. It has a couple of restaurants and good, if windy, bathing on a sandy beach, connected to the road by duckboards winding through the dunes, and more remote beaches accessible to the north.

INFORMATION AND TOURS   DELTA DE L'EBRE

Park information centre Martí Buera 22, on the main highway, on the edge of Deltebre (http://deltebre.net). The well-signposted information centre can provide you with a

map of the delta and has information about tours and local walks.

River cruises A river cruise is a good way to experience the delta. Several boat companies, including Creuers Delta de l'Ebre (http://creuersdeltaebre.com), the Santa Susanna (http://santasusana.es) and Olmos (http:// crucerosdeltadelebro.es) operate trips of an hour or so on the river. Enquire at the tourist office or call ahead, because the boats sometimes only operate for groups.

ACCOMMODATION AND EATING

Casa Núri Final Goles de Ebre, Riumar, http://restaurant nuri.com. Dine on a wide range of seafood, from shrimp to mussels, as well as the local speciality, *arròs a banda* – similar to paella except that the rice is brought before the seafood. €€€

Delta Hotel Avda. del Canal, on the outskirts of Deltebre towards Riumar, http://deltahotel.net. This comfortable hotel has well-cared-for, rustic rooms, some with wood-beam ceilings, as well as a breezy garden. €€

Montblanc

The walled medieval town of **MONTBLANC**, 8km before the turning to the monastery at Poblet, is a surprisingly beautiful place to discover in the middle of nowhere. The Pl. Major is picturesque, and livens up for the evening *passeig*, while there are many fine little Romanesque and Gothic monuments contained within the town's tight circle of old streets; all are marked on the map in front of the town's medieval gateway, the **Torre-portal de Bové**, which is just 100m or so up from the train station. On the southern side of the walls, the **Torre-portal de Sant Jordi** marks the spot where San Jordi, or St George (patron saint of Catalunya as well as England), slew the dragon, an event commemorated with a fiesta on April 23.

Santa Maria la Major

Pl. Major • Free • http://santamariamontblanc.cat

Just above the central Pl. Major, stands the grand Gothic parish church of **Santa Maria la Major**; its elaborate facade has lions' faces on either side of the main doorway and cherubs swarming up the pillars. There's a fine view from the once fortified mound that rises behind the church (known as the Pla de Santa Bàrbara) over the rooftops, defensive towers and walls, and away across the plain.

Sant Miquel

Pl. St Miquel • Free, open only as part of a guided tour • http://montblancmedieval.cat

East from Santa Maria along C/Major is the church of **Sant Miquel**, which dates from the fourteenth century, and has Romanesque and Gothic elements, an impressive coffered ceiling and lovely Gothic lateral chapels. The church was the seat of the Catalan courts from 1307 to 1370.

Museu Comarcal de la Conca de Barberà

Just off Pl. Major • Free or nominal fee (varies) • http://mccb.cat

This fine local **history museum**, set in a medieval home dating from the thirteenth century, has well-curated exhibits on the history and culture of the region, including on the art of glassmaking, and features a reproduction of an old chemist's shop.

ARRIVAL AND INFORMATION   MONTBLANC

By bus Regular trains and buses connect Montblanc to Tarragona (50min) and Lleida (50min).

Turisme At the eastern end of C/Major (Mon–Sat 9am–5pm, Sun 10am–2pm; http://montblancmedieval. cat). Helpful *turisme* in the old church of Sant Francesc, just outside the walls. They offer guided tours of medieval Montblanc.

ACCCOMMODATION

Fonda Cal Blasi C/Alenyà 11–13, http://fondacal blasimontblanc.es-hotel.com. This warm and friendly *fonda* is in a restored nineteenth-century stone townhouse, just a short walk from Pl. Major. They also serve home-cooked meals rooted in seasonal produce, along with local wines from Conca de Barberà. €€

Santa Coloma de Queralt

This well-preserved pocket of history, hidden amid the plains of the *comarca* of Conca de Barbarà, lies 29km north of Montblanc. **SANTA COLOMA DE QUERALT** is a town made for meandering – and soaking up the medieval past. The best way to explore is via guided tours (see page 730) run by the tourist office, which include a variety of sights: the lovely porticoed squares, the Pl. de l'Església and Pl. Major; the fourteenth-century **Ermita de Santa Maria de Bell-lloc**, home to a 1370 alabaster sepulchre of the Counts of Queralt; and the **Cal Jaume Punto**, a perfectly preserved general store from 1848.

El Castell dels Comtes
Pl. del Castell • Open only as part of a guided tour

Santa Coloma's most iconic building is the formidable eleventh-century El Castell dels Comtes, crowned by a handsome defence tower that you can ascend for gorgeous views of the surrounding countryside. The grand interior houses government offices, the tourist office and an exhibition space that features changing exhibits, from historic photos to sculptures.

11

ARRIVAL AND INFORMATION   SANTA COLOMA DE QUERALT

By bus Regular buses connect Santa Coloma de Queralt to Tarragona (1hr) and Barcelona (2hr).
Turisme Castell dels Comtes de Santa Coloma (Tues–Sun 10am–2pm; http://stacqueralt.altanet.org). Helpful, info-packed *turisme* within the Castell dels Comtes, with an adjoining exhibition space. They offer excellent guided tours with a variety of themes, including one that focuses on the historical buildings of town and a culinary tour, which celebrates local produce and wine. Times vary for tours; contact tourist office to enquire and book.

EATING

★ **Hostal Colomí** C/Raval de Jesús 12, http://hostal colomi.com. Catalunya is justly famous for its wildly progressive cuisine, exemplified by the Roca Brothers (see page 687) in Girona. But, this culinary stardom is rooted in the region's traditional dishes, many of which reveal Catalunya's natural bounty. For a taste, turn to *les germanes Camps* – the Camps sisters – who helm *Hostal Colomí*, founded in 1948. For many, this isn't just the best traditional Catalan cuisine in the Tarragona region – it's the best in the country. The meal starts with two large *porrons* (pitchers) of wine – one white, one red – and a platter of *pa amb tomàquet* (bread smeared in tomato and drizzled in olive oil). The feast continues, including warm ham croquettes, cod and platters of grilled meat and asparagus from the open-air grill, culminating in dessert – *crema catalana*, of course. **€€€€**

The Monestir de Poblet
Charge • http://poblet.cat

There are few ruins more stirring than the **Monestir de Poblet**, lying in glorious open country, vast and sprawling within massive battlemented walls and towered gateways. Once *the* great monastery of Catalunya, it was in effect a complete manorial village and enjoyed scarcely credible rights, powers and wealth. Founded in 1151 by Ramón Berenguer IV, who united the kingdoms of Catalunya and Aragón, it was planned from the beginning on an immensely grand scale. The kings of Aragón-Catalunya chose to be buried in its chapel and for three centuries diverted huge sums for its endowment, a munificence that was inevitably corrupting. By the late Middle Ages Poblet had become a byword for decadence – there are lewder stories about this than any other Cistercian monastery – and so it continued, hated by the local peasantry, until the Carlist revolution of 1835 when a mob burned and tore it apart. Italian Cistercians repopulated the monastery in 1940 and over the decades since then it's been subject to continual – and superb – maintenance and restoration.

The cloisters

As so often, the **cloisters**, focus of monastic life, are the most evocative and beautiful part. Late Romanesque, and sporting a pavilion and fountain, they open onto a series of rooms: a splendid Gothic **chapterhouse** (with the former abbots' tombs set in the floor), wine cellars, a parlour, a **kitchen** equipped with ranges and copper pots, and a sombre, wood-panelled **refectory**.

The chapel

Beyond, you enter the **chapel** in which the twelfth- and thirteenth-century tombs of the kings of Aragón have been meticulously restored by Frederic Marès, the manic collector of Barcelona. They lie in marble sarcophagi on either side of the nave, focusing attention on the central sixteenth-century altarpiece.

The dormitory

You'll also be shown the vast old **dormitory**, to which there's direct access from the chapel choir, a poignant reminder of Cistercian discipline. From the dormitory (half of which is sealed off since it's still in use), a door leads out onto the cloister roof for views down into the cloister itself and up the chapel towers.

11

ARRIVAL AND INFORMATION   MONESTIR DE POBLET

By bus Two to three buses a day (Mon–Sat) run to Poblet from Tarragona or Lleida, passing right by the monastery. It's an easy day-trip from either city.

By train By train, you get off at the ruined station of L'Espluga de Francolí, from where it's a beautiful 3km walk to the monastery, much of it along a signposted country track. Since it lies on the same line, it's easy enough to combine a trip to Poblet with a stop-off at Montblanc.

Turisme Pg. Abat Conill 9, Poblet (summer Tues–Sat 10am–1.30pm & 3–6pm, Sun 10am–2pm; winter Tues–Fri 10am–3.30pm, Sat 10am–3pm; 977 871 247).

ACCOMMODATION AND EATING

Staying overnight at **Poblet** is an attractive proposition if you have your own transport, since it makes a good base for an excursion into the surrounding countryside. A kilometre up the road from Poblet, around the walls, the hamlet of **Les Masies** has a couple of hotels and restaurants, while **L'Espluga**, 2km northwest, also has a few places to stay.

★ **Hostatgeria de Poblet** 977 871 201. For the full monastic experience, stay at the lovely *Hostatgeria de Poblet*, which rises up alongside the monastery. Designed by Spanish architect Mariano Bayón, the building blends harmoniously with its surroundings, featuring honey-hued stone, a cloister and a courtyard planted with olive trees. The monastic philosophy extends to all parts of the property, which is quiet and soothing, with no TVs in the simply furnished rooms. Guests are invited to participate in the monastery's liturgy and services. The restaurant serves seasonal dishes, some inspired by historical monastic menus. €€

Sercotel Villa Engràcia Carretera de les Masies, Les Masies, http://villaengracia.com. This attractive former spa built in 1888, set in pleasant, leafy grounds, has elegant, well-outfitted rooms, an outdoor pool and tennis courts. €€€

Prades

If you have time and transport, a couple of excursions into the countryside surrounding Poblet are well worth making. The red-stone walled village of **PRADES**, in the Serra de Prades, 20km from the monastery, is a beautifully sited and tranquil place that needs no other excuse for a visit. It's also the place to be during the second weekend of July, when they replace the water in the fountain with cava, and you can join in and help yourself – or order a bottle of bubbly at a terrace bar in the porticoed *plaça* and enjoy the scene. The area around Poblet is also home to two more twelfth-century Cistercian monasteries.

Reial Monestir de Santes Creus

Charge • http://larutadelcister.info

The **Reial Monestir de Santes Creus** lies 7km north of the Barcelona–Lleida highway, and is clearly signposted. It's built in Transitional style, with a grand Gothic cloister and some Romanesque traces, and you can explore the dormitory, chapterhouse and main church.

Monestir de Vallbona de les Monges

Charge • http://larutadelcister.info

The **Monestir de Vallbona de les Monges** is about 16km north of Poblet, and reached via Montblanc. This monastery of *monges* (nuns) has been occupied continuously for over 800 years. The church, built over the twelfth to fourteenth centuries, is a particularly noteworthy example of the transition between Romanesque and Gothic, and has a rectangular nave and elegant cloisters.

Lleida

LLEIDA (Lérida), at the heart of a fertile plain in inland Catalunya, has a rich history. First a *municipium* under the Roman Empire and later the centre of a small Arab kingdom, it was reconquered by the Catalans and became the seat of a bishopric in 1149. Little of those periods survives in today's city but there is one building of outstanding interest, the splendid Catedral, which is sufficient justification in itself to visit. Several interesting museums and a steep set of old-town streets will easily occupy any remaining time. Rooms are easy to come by, and the students at the local university fill the streets and bars on weekend evenings, including at the breezy Pl. de Sant Joan, in good-natured throngs.

Seu Vella and Castillo del Rey

Charge for Catedral and castle • http://turoseuvella.cat

The **Seu Vella**, or old Catedral, is enclosed within the walls of the ruined Castillo del Rey (also called La Suda), high above the Riu Segre, a twenty-minute climb from the centre of town. It's a peculiar fortified building, which in 1707 was deconsecrated and taken over by the military, remaining in their hands until 1940. Enormous damage was inflicted over the years but the church remains a notable example of the Transitional style, similar in many respects to the Catedral of Tarragona. The Gothic cloisters – among the largest cloisters in the world – are masterly, each walk comprising arches different in size and shape but sharing delicate stone tracery. They served the military as a canteen and kitchen. You can also visit parts of the reconstructed **castle**, such as the fortified walls – the views from the walls over the plain are stupendous. Note: From the old town, there is an elevator that you can enter at Pl. de Sant Joan, which will whisk you to the Seu Vella complex.

Seu Nova

Free

You can climb back down from the old Catedral towards the river by way of the new Catedral, **La Seu Nova**. It's an austere eighteenth-century building with Neoclassical doorways, a main facade topped by a large crest of the Casa de Borbón and a series of minuscule, high stained-glass windows.

Museu de Lleida

C/Sant Crist 1 • Charge • http://museudelleida.cat

The spacious **Museu de Lleida** is the city's flagship museum. Two floors show off ancient finds from throughout Lleida and Catalunya, including Romanesque altarpieces, a Visigoth baptismal font and stone sculptures from the Seu Vella.

ARRIVAL AND INFORMATION   LLEIDA

By train Trains regularly connect Lleida to Barcelona via Valls or Reus/Tarragona (17 daily; 2hr–4hr 15min, AVE 1hr). There are also services to: La Pobla de Segur (3 daily; 2hr 10min); Tarragona (8 daily; 1hr 30min–2hr); and Zaragoza (20 daily; 1hr 50min). For current timetables and ticket information, consult RENFE (902 240 202, http://renfe.es). It's a 15–20min walk east of the train station to Pl. de Sant Joan.

By bus Lleida has regular buses to Barcelona (Mon–Sat 10 daily, Sun 4 daily; 2hr 15min); Huesca (5 daily; 2hr 30min);

THE SNAIL TRAIL IN LLEIDA

You don't need to visit France for the finest escargot. Lleida's snails – *caragols* – rival their neighbours to the north. This small capital of inland Catalunya is one of Spain's most famous snail cities. With snails, simpler is better: the most delicious preparation is *caragols a la llauna* –grilled, and seasoned with olive oil, salt, pepper and garlic. On the side? A generous dollop of *allioli*. This being Spain, there is of course a dedicated festival – the **Aplec del Caragol** in late May is one of the largest snail festivals in the country, with more than twelve tons (yes, tons) of snails served. But, you don't need to wait until then to feast on snails: Lleida is filled with restaurants that serve the delicacy.

La Seu d'Urgell (2 daily; 3hr); Montblanc (6 daily; 1hr 30min); La Pobla de Segur (daily; 2hr); Poblet (Mon–Sat 3 daily; 1hr 15min); Tarragona (3 daily; 2hr); Vielha, via Túnel de Vielha (2 daily; 3hr); and Zaragoza (Mon–Sat 6 daily, Sun 2; 2hr 30min). It's a 15–20min walk west of the bus station, down Avda. de Blondel, to Pl. de Sant Joan.

By plane The Lleida-Alguaire airport (973 032 700, http://aeroportlleida.cat), 15km northwest of Lleida, is a regional hub. UK charter flights also occasionally fly here, ferrying skiers to the Pyrenees.

Turisme C/Mayor 31 (Mon–Sat 10am–2pm & 4–7pm, Sun 10am–2pm; http://turismedelleida.cat).

11

ACCOMMODATION AND EATING

Lleida is dotted with a variety of accommodation, including near the train station; along Rambla Ferran, which leads into the centre; and on central Pl. Sant Joan. The streets north of the church of Sant Martí hold a range of restaurants; this is where the students come to eat and hang out at the loud **music-bars** along the block formed by C/Sant Martí, C/Camp de Mart, C/Balmes and Avda. Prat de la Riba.

El Celler del Roser C/Cavallers 24, http://cellerdelroser.cat. One of the better spots to sample the celebrated snails is at this cosy, mid-priced restaurant, with wood tables and exposed brick walls. There's a strong local wine list. €€
Ferreruela C/Bobalà 8, http://ferreruela.com. Showcasing *cuina de la terra* (local cuisine), this convivial restaurant

serves an excellent range, including Lleida's signature snails with *allioli*, grilled cod with *samfaina* (ratatouille) and juicy lamb. Plus, as part of the dessert menu, they offer an excellent assortment of local cheeses. €€€
Hotel Zenit Lleida C/General Brito 21, http://zenithoteles.com. This central hotel – you're within easy walking distance to train station and city centre – has modern, simple and clean rooms. €€
La Huerta Avda. Tortosa 7, http://lahuerta-restaurant.com. Dive into platters of succulent snails and other traditional Catalan fare at this Lleida institution, which was established in the mid-1960s. €€€

Valencia and Murcia

MORELLA

Valencia and Murcia

Named "El Levante" after the rising sun, this lush region is the part of
Spain that wakes up first. Valencia has the Mediterranean Sea as its
front yard, while the inland *huerta* (garden) is one of the most fertile in
Europe, crowded with orange and lemon groves, date-palm plantations
and rice fields still irrigated by systems devised by the Moors. Paella
originated in these parts, and a juicy orange is named after Valencia.
Evidence of the lengthy Moorish occupation can be seen throughout,
in the castles, crops and place names – Benidorm, Alicante and
Alcoy are all derived from Arabic. The region also encompasses the
historical Murcia, which offers a fascinating contrast to the sun-and-
sand debauchery on the water. Explored from one end to the other,
this is a land of ancient and modern, of beauty and beastliness.

The growing self-assurance of the region is evident in the increasing presence of
Valenciano – a dialect of Catalan – which challenges Castilian as the main language of
education and broadcasting in the area.

Murcia's province is quite distinct, a *comunidad autónoma* in its own right, and there
could hardly be a more severe contrast with the richness of the Valencian *huerta*. This
southeastern corner of Spain is virtually a desert and is some of the driest territory
in Europe. It was fought over for centuries by Phoenicians, Greeks, Carthaginians
and Romans, but there survives almost no physical evidence of their presence, and
it then fell under Moorish rule for five hundred years. The province's capital city of
Murcia, with its lovely Catedral and terrace tapas bars, makes for a comfortable base for
exploring the region.

Much of the **coast** of the Valencia region is marred by heavy overdevelopment,
with concrete apartment blocks and sprawling holiday complexes looming over
many of the best beaches. However, away from the big resorts, particularly around
Denia and **Xàbia** (Jávea), there are some attractive isolated coves, while the historic
hilltop settlements of **Altea** and **Peñíscola** are undeniably picturesque, if touristy. In
Murcia, the resorts of the **Mar Menor** are reasonably attractive and very popular with
Spanish families in high season; the best beaches are in the extreme south, around
Águilas, where you'll find some dazzling unspoiled coves. The increasingly vibrant
cities of **Valencia** and **Alicante** are the major urban centres, and there are several
delightful historic small towns and villages a short way inland, such as **Morella**,
Xàtiva and **Lorca**.

The Valencia area has a powerful tradition of **fiestas**, and there are a couple of
elements unique to this part of the country. Above all, throughout the year and more
or less wherever you go, there are mock battles between Muslims and Christians
(*Moros y Cristianos*). Recalling the Christian Reconquest of the country – whether
through symbolic processions or re-creations of specific battles – they are some of
the most elaborate and colourful festivities to be seen anywhere, especially in Alcoy
(see box, page 768). The other recurring celebrations are the *fallas* festivals, in which
giant, colourful papier-mâché sculptures are displayed in the streets, before being
ceremoniously burned.

Getting around by public transport is relatively straightforward as there are frequent
train and bus services, though you'll need your own transport to really explore the area.
The motorway network is excellent, but tolls are quite pricey so do keep this in mind
when travelling here.

Highlights

❶ La Ciudad de las Artes y las Ciencias
Europe's largest cultural centre and the architectural definition of Valencia: progressive, playful, breathtaking. See page 741

❷ Las Fallas Witness giant effigies going up in an explosion of flames – this is one of Spain's most famous festivals. See page 746

❸ Barrio del Carmen Valencia's most atmospheric *barrio* is full of history, charming plazas and hip bars and cafés. See page 752

❹ Paella Feast on Spain's most iconic dish in its birthplace. See page 754

❺ Festival Benicàssim Huge annual music festival featuring the biggest names in alternative pop. See page 759

❻ Morella Step into medieval Spain in this fortified town crowned by a fairy-tale castle. See page 761

❼ Alicante A city that seems to capture the Mediterranean: elegant esplanades, *sangría* at terrace cafés and silky-sand beaches. See page 768

❽ Cuatro calas Águilas' gorgeous cove beaches offer an inviting blend of sun, sea and, on some stretches in low season, solitude. See page 784

HIGHLIGHTS ARE MARKED ON THE MAP ON PAGE 738

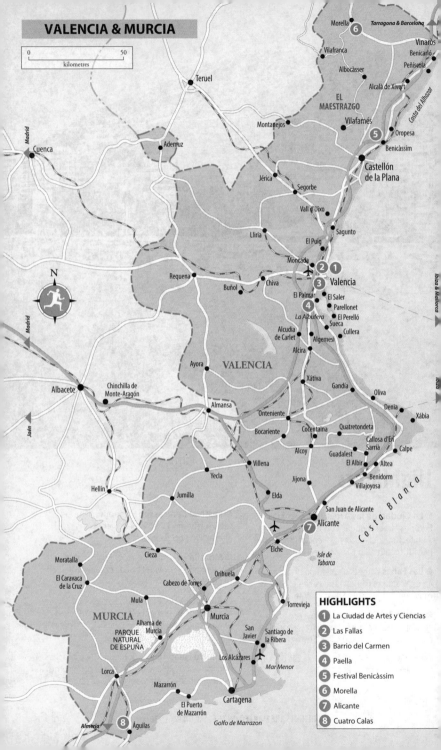

VALENCIA & MURCIA

0 ——— 50
kilometres

HIGHLIGHTS

1 La Ciudad de Artes y Ciencias
2 Las Fallas
3 Barrio del Carmen
4 Paella
5 Festival Benicàssim
6 Morella
7 Alicante
8 Cuatro Calas

VALENCIAN CUISINE

Gastronomy is of great cultural importance to the Valencians. Rice is the dominant ingredient in dishes of the region, grown locally in paddy fields still irrigated by the Moorish canal system (*acequias*). Gourmets tend to agree that the best **paellas** are to be found around (but not *in*) Valencia, where the dish originated. The genuine version doesn't mix fish and meat – it typically contains chicken, rabbit, green beans, *garrofón* (large butter beans), snails, artichokes and saffron – and should be prepared fresh and cooked over wood (*leña*), not scooped from some vast, sticky vat; most places will make it for a minimum of two people.

Other **rice-based dishes** vary around the region: *arroz negro* is rice cooked with squid in its own ink, which gives the dish its black colour. This is typically served with *allioli*, a strong garlic mayonnaise. *Arroz al horno* is drier, baked with chickpeas. *Fideuà* is seafood and noodles cooked paella-style. The most famous, *arroz a banda*, is found on the south coast around Denia – it's rice cooked with seafood, served as two separate dishes: soup, then rice. Around Alicante, you can try *arroz con costra*, which is a meat-based paella topped with a baked egg crust. To learn more about the region's most popular ingredient and the way it's processed, visit the **Museo del Arroz** (C/del Rosario 3, Valencia; 963 676 291), Valencia's rice museum, housed in an old rice mill. Apart from rice, **vegetables** (best *a la plancha*, brushed with olive oil and garlic) are always fresh and plentiful.

The sweet-toothed should try **turrón** (see box, page 772), a nuts-and-honey nougat, or a cooling *horchata*, or *orxata* (see box, page 752), a rich drink made from tiger nuts (*chufas*).

Valencia

12

For many, **VALENCIA**'s enviable perch on the Mediterranean would be enough of a draw. Not so for the city itself: Valencia has been reinventing itself at a heady pace, and shows no signs of slowing down. Well on the way to equalling – indeed, eclipsing in some instances – the cosmopolitan vitality of Barcelona and the cultural variety of Madrid, Spain's third-largest city has finally shaken off its slightly provincial former reputation. The vast, iconic **La Ciudad de las Artes y Ciencias** cultural complex was completed in 2005, the state-of-the-art metro is still expanding and dozens of trendy bars, restaurants and boutiques have injected new life into the historic centre and, just to the south, in the hip Russafa district. Valencia also fully redeveloped its beach and port area, in part sparked by its hosting of the prestigious yachting jamboree, the America's Cup, in 2007. More recently, the city was designated World Design Capital in 2022, cementing its reputation is a destination creativity and design. The old fisherman's quarter of El Cabañal, once a no-go area, has had a face-lift, and is now filled with renovation projects, colourful restored houses and new bars and restaurants popping up all the time. Despite the city's size and *stylista* cachet, Valencia retains an unpretentious if tangibly charged air.

Always an important city, Valencia was fought over for the agricultural wealth of its surrounding *huerta*. After Romans and Visigoths, it was occupied by the Moors for over four centuries with only a brief interruption (1094–1101) when **El Cid** recaptured it. He died here in 1099, but his body, propped on a horse and led out through the gates, was still enough to cause the Moorish armies – previously encouraged by news of his death – to flee in terror. It wasn't until 1238 that Jaime I of Aragón permanently wrested Valencia back. It has remained one of Spain's largest and richest cities ever since.

Valencia has long boasted some of the best **nightlife** in mainland Spain. *Vivir Sin Dormir* (Live Without Sleep) is the name of one of its bars, and it could be taken as a Valencian mantra. The city is alive with noise and colour throughout the year, with explosions of gunpowder, fireworks and festivities punctuating the calendar. Valencia's **fiestas** are some of the most riotous in Spain and the best is Las Fallas (see box, page 746).

FIESTAS

FEBRUARY

Week before Lent: Carnaval Águilas' *Carnaval* is one of the wildest in the country. Vinaròs also has good *Carnaval* celebrations.

MARCH/APRIL

March 12–19: Las Fallas Valencia's Las Fallas (see box, page 746) is by far the biggest of the *fallas* festivals, and indeed one of the most important fiestas in all Spain. The whole thing costs over €1 million, most of which goes up in smoke (literally) on the final *Nit de la Cremà*, when the huge papier-mâché caricatures are burned.

March 19: Día de San José Smaller *fallas* festivals in Xàtiva, Benidorm and Denia.

Third Sunday of Lent: Fiesta de la Magdalena Castellón de la Plana celebrates the end of Moorish rule with pilgrimages and processions of huge floats.

Semana Santa (Holy Week) In Elche, there are, naturally, big Palm Sunday celebrations making use of the local palms, while throughout the week there are also religious processions in Cartagena, Lorca, Orihuela and Valencia. The **Easter processions** in Murcia are particularly famous, and they continue into the following week with, on the Tuesday, the Bando de la Huerta, a huge parade of floats celebrating local agriculture, and, on the Saturday evening, the riotous "Burial of the Sardine" which marks the end of these spring festivals.

April 22–24: Moros y Cristianos After a colourful procession in Alcoy, a huge battle commences between the two sides in the main square.

MAY

1–5: Fiestas de los Mayos *Fiesta* in Alhama de Murcia, and Moros y Cristianos in Caravaca de la Cruz.

Second Sunday: La Virgen de los Desamparados The climax of this celebration in Valencia is when the statue of the Virgin is transferred from her basilica to the Catedral.

Third Sunday: Moros y Cristianos In Altea.

JUNE

23–24: Hogueras de San Juan Magnificent festival in Alicante with processions and fireworks, culminating as huge effigies and bonfires are burnt in the streets at midnight. It's celebrated on a smaller scale on the beaches of Valencia (Malvarossa, Cabañal and Aloboraya)

The most atmospheric area of the city is undoubtedly the maze-like **Barrio del Carmen** (in Valenciano "de Carmé"), roughly north of the Mercado Central to the Río Turia, extending up to the Torres de Serranos and west to the Torres de Quart. Filled with old-style townhouses housing stylish cafés, tapas bars and boutiques, it's an incredibly vibrant neighbourhood to explore. The **city walls**, which, judging from the two surviving gates, must have been magnificent, were pulled down in 1871 to make way for a ring road, and the beautiful church of **Santo Domingo**, in Pza. de Tetuan, has been converted into a barracks – it was from here that General Milans del Bosch ordered his tanks onto the streets during the abortive coup of 1981. This incident, however, isn't representative of the city's political inclination, which has traditionally been to the left – Valencia was the seat of the Republican government during the Civil War after it fled Madrid, and was the last city to fall to Franco.

The oldest part of Valencia is almost entirely encircled by a great loop of the **Río Turia**, which is now a landscaped **riverbed park**. In 1956, after serious flooding damaged much of the old town, the river was diverted. The ancient stone bridges remain, but the riverbed now houses cycle ways, footpaths and football pitches, as well as the astonishing Ciudad de las Artes y Ciencias, Europe's largest cultural complex. As further proof that

with bonfire-jumping. Altea also celebrates with a popular tree-bearing procession and a bonfire in the old town.

JULY
Early July: Fiestas de la Santísima Sangre Dancing in the streets of Denia, plus music and mock battles.
15–20: Moros y Cristianos In Orihuela.
Second week: Feria de Julio Valencia hosts music, bullfights and above all fireworks, ending with the Battle of the Flowers in the Alameda.
Penultimate weekend: FIB Benicàssim's international music festival, a massive party bringing together some of the biggest names in both the Spanish and international music scenes.
25–31: Moros y Cristianos Villajoyosa sees battles by both land and sea.

AUGUST
4: Festa del Cristo de la Salut Festival in El Palmar with processions by boat into the lake.
Mid-August: Misteri d'Eix Elche presents a mystery play, based on a drama dating back to medieval times.
14–20: Feria de Agosto Xàtiva's fair has a very extensive cultural dimension including concerts, plays and exhibitions, plus bullfights and barrages of fireworks.
15: Local festivities in Denia.
Last week: La Tomatina (see box, page 755) A riotous free-for-all of tomato-throwing takes place in Buñol on the last Wednesday of the month. There's also a music festival in Morella.
Last Wednesday: Local fiesta in Sagunto, and at the same time the great Moros y Cristianos festival and a mystery play in Elche.

SEPTEMBER
4–9: Moros y Cristianos In Villena.
Second week: Bull-running through Segorbe's streets.
8–9: Les Danses Celebrations in Peñíscola's old quarter include a human tower construction.
22: Fiesta de Santo Tomás In Benicàssim with bands and a "blazing bull".

OCTOBER
Second Sunday: La Virgen de Suffrage Benidorm celebrates its patron saint's day.

Valencia is ever reinventing itself, Central Park, a 57-acre space for promenades, gardens and an art centre, is one of the city's largest redevelopment projects to date.

Valencia's main beach is the **Playa de la Malvarrosa** to the east of the city centre, which becomes **Playa El Cabañal** at its southern end.

La Ciudad de las Artes y las Ciencias

Avda. Autopista del Saler • Charge • https://cac.es • Ⓜ Alameda (15min walk); bus #13 from Carrer Roger de Lloria, just south of the Pza. del Ayuntamiento, or bus #95 at the Torres de Serrano; if you drive, you can park at the Umbracle car park

More than any other project, the breathtaking **Ciudad de las Artes y las Ciencias** (City of Arts and Sciences, or CAC), rising from the riverbed, symbolizes the autonomous government's vision for Valencia and its quest to establish the city as a prime tourist destination. The giant complex consists of a series of futuristic edifices designed mainly by Valencian architect Santiago Calatrava.

The architecture itself is simply stunning. Even if you only have a day or two in the city, it's well worth the effort getting here to take in the eye-catching buildings surrounded by huge, shallow pools. Calatrava's designs adopt an organic form, his technical and

Museo del Gremio de Artistas Falleros, Tarragona & Barcelona

Casa-Museo de Vicente Blasco Ibáñez, Castellón, Tarragona & Barcelona

Playa Levante

Balearic Ferry Terminal, Playa Malvarrosa & Las Arenas

12

La Ciudad de las Artes y Ciencias (200m) & El Saler & Alicante

& Alicante

PZA STA. MÓNICA

Pont de Fusta

ALBORAYA

BACHILLER

AVENIDA DEL PRIMADO REIG

PLAZA ALCALDE DOMINGO TORRES

ALVARO DE BAZAN

Jardines del Real (Los Viveros)

BOTÁNICO

Real Monasterio de la Trinidad

MENENDEZ PELAYO

N

PTE. TRINIDAD

GENERAL ELIO

Museo de Bellas Artes

PLAZA LEGION ESPAÑOLA

AVENIDA DE BLASCO IBÁÑEZ

Facultats

C/ ALFONSO DE CORDOBA

ARTES GRAFICAS

DOCTOR MOLINER

AVELLOS

Palacio de Benicarló

PINTOR

PZA SAN LORENZO

Basílica Virgen de Los Desamparados

LOPEZ

Almudín

PZA DE LA VIRGEN

C/ ALMUDIN

San Esteban

Catedral

PZA NÁPOLES Y SICILIA

Palacio Monaterio del Temple

Jardines del Turia

MICER MASCO

AVENIDA SUECIA

AVENIDA DE ARAGÓN

PTE. DEL REAL

Museu de la Ciudad

Santo Domingo

PLAZA DE TETUÁN

PASEO DE LA CIUDADELA

AMADEO DE SABOYA

PZA DE LA REINA

PZA S. VICENTE FERRER

C/ GOBERNADOR VIEJO

San Martín

Museo Nacional de Cerámica

Colegio del Patriarca

C/ DEL MAR

PASARELA EXPOSICIÓN

ALAMEDA

PASEO

SERRANO FLORES

Aragón

C/ MARQUES DE DOS AGUAS

La Glorieta

LA PAU

PLAZA PORTA DEL MAR

Alameda

PLAZA ALFONSO MAGNÁNIMO

EL QUINTANA

San Juan de la Cruz

Universidad

El Parterre

PLAZA PATRIARCA

NAVARRO REVERTER

EL PONTO

R. CEPEDA

BARCAS

Palacio de Justicia

GRANADOR ESTEVE

PLAZA DE AMÉRICA

PLAZA DE ARAGÓN

PINTOR SOROLLA

SORNI

PTE. DE ARAGÓN

Colón

COLÓN

JORGE JUAN

A. VDA. DEL PUERTO

PASCUAL Y GENIS

ISABEL LA CATÓLICA

H. CORTES

Horchateria Daniel

C/ SEBERO MORALES

SALAMANCA

Xàtiva

C/ FELIX PIZCUETA

C/ CIRILO AMORÓS

Mercado Colón

PLAZA CÁNOVAS DEL CASTILLO

Plaza de Toros

Museo Taurino

CIRILO AMORÓS

GRAN VIA MARQUÉS DEL TURIA

M. GOZALVO

CONDE DE ALTEA

BURRIANA

AVENIDA JACINTO BENAVENTE

CUSCAR

Palau de la Música y Congresos

GRAN VIA GERMANIAS

ALMIRANTE CADARSO

REINA DOÑA GERMANA

A.VDA. EDUARDO BOSCÁ

EIXAMPLE

Buses to El Saler & El Palmar

AVENIDA ANTIGUO REINO DE VALENCIA

PINTOR SALVADOR ABRIL

DOCTOR

PEDRO III EL GRANDE

SUMSI

MATIAS PERELLÓ

PTE. ANGEL CUSTODIO

CADIZ

REINA DOÑA MARIA

CENTELLES

ESCULTOR JOSÉ CAPUZ

ALCALDE REIG

C/ DE PUERTO RICO

RUZAFA

LITERATO AZORÍN

SUECA

CENTELLES

AVENIDA PERIS Y VALERO

ZAPADORES

OBISPO JAIME PÉREZ

LUIS OLIAG

GENERAL URRUTIA

Museu Fallero

engineering brilliance providing the basis for his pioneering concrete, steel and glass creations. However, despite near-universal acclaim for its architecture, the complex has not completely escaped criticism. Some feel that with the vast cost of constructing it should have been used to tackle the city's pressing social issues, while others have been less than overwhelmed by some of the content inside the Ciudad's startling structures.

In your explorations, stroll through the **Umbracle**, a series of 18m-high arches towering over a landscaped walkway shaded with vegetation from throughout the region, including palms, honeysuckle, bougainvillea and, of course, orange trees.

Hemisfèric

Charge • https://cac.es

The **Hemisfèric**, one of the more astonishing buildings of the complex, is a striking eye-shaped concrete structure – complete with lashes, and an eyeball that forms a huge concave screen used to project IMAX movies, laser shows, nature documentaries and more.

Museo de las Ciencias

Charge • https://cac.es

The colossal **Museo de las Ciencias** (Science Museum), whose protruding supports make the building resemble a giant sun-bleached carcass, contains interactive exhibits about science, sport and the human body. Visitors can test their physical strength and their mental agility or look at a colourful 3D representation of DNA or a Foucault Pendulum, which at 34m is one of the longest in the world.

Parque Oceanográfico

Charge • https://cac.es

The **Oceanogràfic**, designed by Félix Candela, is one of the world's largest aquariums. It's divided into multiple zones, with beluga whales in the Arctic area, Japanese spider crabs in the temperate zone and a kaleidoscopic collection of reef fish, sharks and turtles in the 70m tunnel that forms the tropical zone. The dolphin show is included in the ticket price and, in the summer, the aquarium opens for night visits. The restaurant is a sleek underwater space where you dine with fish darting past your table.

Palau de les Arts Reina Sofía and L'Ágora

Charge for a guided tour • https://lesarts.com

The majestic pistachio-nut-shaped **Palau de las Artes** is a high-tech performing arts palace with renowned conductor David Livermore at the helm. Stages and halls of varying sizes – all with splendid acoustics – host ballet, opera and classical music concerts, among others. Performances are staged throughout the year, and it's well worth snagging a ticket to see one. The equally impressive 80m L'Àgora, inaugurated in November 2009 to host the Valencia 500 Open tennis tournament, is now the CaixaForum cultural centre (https://fundacionlacaixa.org/es/caixaforum-valencia) which features excellent temporary art exhibitions, talks, film screenings, concerts, family activities and more.

Plaza del Ayuntamiento

In the heart of Valencia, just north of the train station, is the **Plaza del Ayuntamiento**, a handsome central square lined with flower stalls, an impressive floodlit fountain and the surprisingly attractive post office headquarters. The *ayuntamiento* itself houses the **Museo Histórico Municipal** (free; 963 525 478), whose library has an impressive eighteenth-century map of Valencia showing the city walls intact.

Estación del Norte

Built in 1917, the **Estación del Norte**, just south of the Pza. del Ayuntamiento on C/Xàtiva, is another of the city's lovely, and surprisingly well preserved, *modernista* buildings. Its facade is covered in detailed images of oranges, and its interior is filled with intricate ceramic mosaics, tiled ceilings and carved wooden doorways.

Museo Nacional de Cerámica

Poeta Querol 2 • Charge, free Sat after 4pm • www.cultura.gob.es/mnceramica/home.html

The distinctive feature of Valencian architecture is its elaborate Baroque facades, the most extraordinary being the entrance to the **Palacio del Marqués de Dos Aguas**. Hipólito Rovira, who helped to design its amazing alabaster doorway complete with revolving statue of the Virgin del Rosario, died insane in 1740, which should come as no surprise to anyone who sees it. Inside the *palacio* is the **Museo Nacional de Cerámica**, with a vast collection of ceramics from all over Spain, and particularly Valencia, itself a major ceramics centre, largely owing to the size of its *Morisco* (Moorish people who converted or were forced to convert to Christianity) population. Apart from an impressive display of ceramic tile works (*azulejos*), the collection contains some stunning plates with gold and copper varnishes (*reflejos*) and a trio of evocatively ornate eighteenth-century carriages.

12

Plaza Patriarca

Rising over the **Plaza Patriarca** is the Neoclassical former **Universidad**, with lovely cloisters where free classical concerts are sometimes held in the summer, and the beautiful Renaissance **Colegio del Patriarca** (guided visits only, book online at https://patriarcavalencia.es) filled with intricate frescoes, works by El Greco, gleaming religions relics and detailed sixteenth-century Flemish tapestries. The university **library** contains the first book printed in Spain, *Les Trobes*, in 1474.

The Catedral and around

Pza. de la Reina • Charge (combined admission for cathedral and museum, separate admission for Miguelete) • https://catedraldevalencia.es

The café-rich **Pza. de la Reina** is overlooked by the florid spire of the church of Santa Catalina and octagonal tower of Valencia's **Catedral**. Founded in the thirteenth century, the Catedral embraces an eclectic combination of architectural styles (apparently including, interestingly, Jewish iconography), with the lavishly ornate Baroque main entrance leading to a largely Gothic-built interior. It's an exhausting climb up the tower, known as the **Miguelete**, but the spectacular views of the city and its many blue-domed churches more than compensate. The **museum** contains more paintings and

---

THE VALENCIA CARD

If you plan on exploring the city extensively, consider buying a **Valencia Card** (€15/20/25 for one, two or three days, discounts when bought online; https://valenciatouristcard.com), which gives you unlimited access to the entire transport system, free entry to many museums and money off your bill at bars and restaurants. There are also various 72-hour options available, which include entrance to the top attractions of the City of Arts and Sciences.

also a 2300-kilo tabernacle made from gold, silver and jewels donated by the Valencian people. Above the structure's crossing, the Catedral's fourteenth-century lantern is another fine feature, as are its soaring windows that are glazed with thin sheets of alabaster to let in the Valencian light.

Many visitors, however, come just for the Catedral's most celebrated religious icon: a gold-and-agate chalice (the Santo Cáliz), said to be the one used by Christ at the Last Supper – the **Holy Grail** itself, and no mean asset in a post-*Da Vinci Code* era. It's certainly old and, hidden away throughout the Dark Ages in a monastery in northern Aragón, it really did inspire many of the legends associated with the Grail. Other treasures include the two Goya paintings of the San Francisco chapel, one of which depicts an exorcism (the corpse was originally naked, but after Goya's death a sheet was painted over it).

Plaza de la Virgen

The famous meeting point of the Tribunal de las Aguas is in the **Plaza de la Virgen**, just behind the Catedral. Here, the black-clad regulatory body of Valencia's water users meets at noon every Thursday to judge grievances about the irrigation system of the *huertas*. The practice dates back to Moorish times, and Blasco Ibáñez (1867–1928) describes their workings in detail in his novel *La Barraca*, which is about peasant life in the Valencian *huerta* and remains the best guide to the life of the region at that time.

Real Basílica de Nuestra Señora de los Desamparados

Pza. de la Virgen • Free • https://basilicadesamparados.org

Two footbridges allow the clergy (only) to go straight from Valencia's Catedral into the archbishop's palace and on to the domed basilica of **Nuestra Señora de los Desamparados**, also on the Pza. de la Virgen, where thousands of candles constantly burn in front of the image of the Virgin, patron of Valencia.

Museo de la Seda

C/ Hospital 7 • Charge (ticket price includes entrance to Iglesia de San Nicolás) • www.museodelasedavalencia.com

This important silk museum is housed in the old fifteenth-century **Colegio del Arte Mayor de la Seda** (College of the Art of Silk Making) and is filled with beautifully restored frescoes, colourful *azulejo* tiles and gilt-edged ceilings. The displays take visitors on a journey of the history of silk, from how it's made to its important role in

---

FALLAS: VALENCIA ON FIRE

Valencia erupts in a blaze of colour and noise for the Fiesta de las Fallas, March 12 to 19. During the year, each *barrio* or neighbourhood builds satirical caricatures or *fallas*, some as tall as buildings. These begin to appear in the plazas at the beginning of March and are judged and awarded prizes before being set alight at midnight on March 19, the **Nit de la Cremà** – traditionally, carpenters celebrated the beginning of spring by decorating the torches they used over winter and adding them to a ritual bonfire. The *fallas* are ignited all at once – with the last to go up being the prizewinner. Each *falla* features *ninot*s (individual characters), the best of which is saved from the flames and displayed in the Museu Fallero (see page 748).

During the fiesta, **processions** of *falleros*, dressed in traditional costume and accompanied by bands, carry flowers to the Pza. de la Virgen, where they are massed to create the skirt of a huge statue of La Virgen. The daily Las Mascaletas **firecracker display** (2pm in the Pza. del Ayuntamiento) sees the whole city racing to this central square for a ten-minute series of body-shuddering explosions. There are also nightly fireworks, bullfights, paella contests in the streets and *chocolate y buñuelos de calabaza* (hot chocolate and deep-fried pumpkin doughnuts) stalls. Finally, around 1am on March 20, the *falla* of the Pza. del Ayuntamiento goes up in flames, followed by the last thunderous fireworks display of the festival.

Valencia's past. End your visit in the room next to the gift shop for a fascinating live silk weaving demonstration using one of the college's original looms.

La Lonja

Pza. del Mercado • Charge • 962 084 153

If you tire of Baroque excesses, you could head for the wonderfully sombre interior of the Gothic **La Lonja** (also known as La Lonja de la Seda, or the Silk Exchange). The main focus of this UNESCO-listed building is its superb main hall, with its elegant rib-vaulted ceiling supported by slender, spiralling columns; the orange trees in the central courtyard pay testament to Valencia's diverse heritage.

Mercado Central

Pza. del Mercado • www.mercadocentralvalencia.es

The enormous **Mercado Central**, a *modernista* iron, girder and glass structure built in 1928, is embellished with a collage of tiles and mosaics, and crowned with swordfish and parrot weather vanes. It's one of the biggest markets in Europe –fitting for *huerta* country – with almost a thousand stalls selling fruit and vegetables, meat and seafood.

Mercado Colón

C/Jorge Juan 19 • https://mercadocolon.es

About 1km southeast of the Mercado Central, Valencia's other market, the renovated **Mercado Colón** is an even more impressive *modernista* building. Its open-sided rectangular design loosely resembles a church, with slim wrought-iron columns supporting a steep pitched roof, and monumental arched facades at either end. However, it's the building's detail that's really outstanding, combining two-tone brickwork with broken-tile mosaic chimneys, features that reveal the influence of *modernista* architect Antoni Gaudí – indeed, the market's architect, Francisco Mora, was a close friend of the Catalan genius. In recent years, the Mercado Colón has become a lively and atmospheric place to go at night, housing many upmarket restaurants, bars and *horchaterías*. Music concerts are also sometimes held here.

Museu de Bellas Artes and the Jardines del Real

C/San Pío V 9 • Free • https://museobellasartesvalencia.gva.es

The **Museu de Belles Artes**, on the far side of the river, has one of the best general collections in Spain, with works by Bosch, El Greco, Goya, Velázquez, Ribera and Ribalta, as well as large quantities of modern Valencian art. The museum takes up the southwest corner of the **Jardines del Real** (also called Los Viveros). The lovely gardens – the largest of Valencia's parks – are well worth a stroll, and host various outdoor concerts in the summer.

Torres Serranos

Pza. de los Fueros • Charge, free Sun • https://cultural.valencia.es/es/museu/torres-de-serranos

The fourteenth-century **Torres Serranos**, once part of Valencia's fortified walls, is an impressive gateway defending the entrance to town across the Río Turia. Climb up to the top for panoramic views over the old city; to the west, you can pick out another gateway, the Torres de Quart, which dates from the fifteenth century.

Instituto Valenciano de Arte Moderno

C/Guillém de Castro 118 • Charge, free Wed 4–7pm & Sun • https://ivam.es

The **Instituto Valenciano de Arte Moderno (IVAM)** features a permanent display of works by sculptor Julio González and painter Ignacio Pinazo, as well as many excellent temporary exhibitions by mainly Spanish contemporary artists.

Casa-Museo José Benlliure

C/Blanquerias 23 • Charge, free on Sun & holidays • https://cultural.valencia.es/es/museu/casa-museo-benlliure

Set in the beautifully renovated home of Valencian painter and sculptor José Benlliure, the **Casa-Museo José Benlliure** displays historical and religious works, from paintings and drawings to sculptures and ceramics. Pieces by his son, Pepino, are also on show, as are works by his brother, established sculptor Mariano Benlliure, and there's a lovely garden with flowers and palms.

Museo Fallero

Pza. Monteolivete 4 • Charge • www.valencia.es/-/infociudad-museo-fallero-de-valencia

The **Museo Fallero** offers a fascinating insight into Valencia's Fiesta de las Fallas. On display is a wacky array of *ninots* that have been voted the best of their year, and consequently saved from the flames.

Bombas Gens Centre d'Art

Avda. de Burjassot 54–56 • Free • https://bombasgens.com

Valencia's newest contemporary arts centre, located inside an old bomb factory used during the Civil War. Exhibits change regularly and it's also home to Ricard Camarena's Michelin-starred restaurant (see page 752).

Bioparc

Avda. Pío Baroja 3 • https://bioparcvalencia.es • Metro lines #3, #5 and #9 to Nou d'Octubre (10min walk) or buses #26, #67 and #98 from various points

If you're travelling with kids, the city's expansive **Bioparc**, an open-air zoo west of the city centre, might entice. As far as zoos go, this well-maintained specimen tries to be a

---

THE PORT AND THE PLAYAS

Barcelona famously transformed its waterfront from drab to dazzling, and Valencia has done something similar to its city coastline, having significantly spruced up its beaches and boardwalk over the last decade. In 2007, Valencia became the first European port since 1851 to host the America's Cup (which was staged here again in 2010), and to celebrate the event, parts of the forgotten waterfront were redeveloped, with a gleaming new **marina** and the eye-catching **Veles e Vents** ("Sails and Winds") structure designed by British architect David Chipperfield helping to transform the area. In the last couple of years the area of El Cabañal near the beach has been completely reformed with lots of new options for accommodation and dining.

As for **beaches**, you can catch some rays on the soft sand of the broad and breezy *playas* Malvarrosa and Cabañal, which are backed by the Paseo Marítimo and extend along the waterfront. The outdoor cafés, bars and clubs here are particularly popular in the summer months. Check out the Marina Beach Club (Paseo Neptuno; https://marinabeachclub.com) right next to the water, offering a restaurant, café, pool, sun loungers, bar and a nightclub.

There are a number of ways to get to Malvarrosa and Playa Cabañal, but one easy route is to take the line #5 metro from the central Colón station to Marítim Serrería, then switch to line #8, to Marina Real Juan Carlos I. You can also catch buses from Pza. del Ayuntamiento, often supplemented during the summer by buses from various points in the centre; ask at the *turismo*.

THE FRESCOES OF THE PARROQUIA DE SAN NICOLÁS

Hidden down a tiny alleyway in the Barrio del Carmen, you'll find the **church of San Nicolás** (C/Caballeros 35; www.sannicolasvalencia.com; charge). Once blackened and covered by hundreds of years of smoke from candles and incense burners, its intricate frescoes now gleam and sparkle once more after extensive renovation. Painted by Dionis Vidal between 1697 and 1700, they cover almost 2000 square metres of the church's interior and have even been likened by experts to those by Michelangelo in Rome's celebrated Sistine Chapel. Today, San Nicolás is one of the best examples of Gothic architecture mixed with Baroque decoration in Spain.

---

different sort of place. The creators have made serious attempts to be as eco-aware and animal-friendly as possible, with re-created African savanna and Malagasy landscapes that are home to roaming rhinos, giraffes, antelopes, gorillas, leopards, elephants and lions.

Casa-Museo de Vicente Blasco Ibáñez

C/Isabel de Villena 159 • Charge • www.casamuseoblascoibanez.es

The **Casa-Museo de Vicente Blasco Ibáñez** explores the life of the celebrated Valencian author, journalist and political activist Vicente Blasco Ibáñez (1867–1928). An outspoken antimonarchist, he was best known in the English-speaking world for his World War I novel *Los Cuatro Jinetes del Apocalipsis* (The Four Horsemen of the Apocalypse), which was later made into a film. His renovated home, just off Malvarrosa beach, has been turned into an in-depth museum featuring personal mementoes, photographs, documents and more, all of which offer insight both into Blasco Ibáñez himself and the political history of Valencia and Spain during his time.

ARRIVAL AND DEPARTURE   **VALENCIA**

BY PLANE

Valencia airport The airport (961 598 500, www.aena. es/en/valencia.html) is 8km west of town, and served by metro lines #3 & #5; the most convenient stop for the centre is Colón. Bus #150 also links the airport with the city centre (€1.45). Alternatively, a taxi will set you back around €20.

BY TRAIN

Estación del Norte Situated close to the town centre and used for local and regional trains (www.renfe.com); walk north along Avda. Marqués de Sotelo to the Pza. del Ayuntamiento, the central square.

Destinations Alicante (7 daily; 1hr 30min–2hr 15min); Benicàssim (9 daily; 1hr 10min); Castellón de la Plana (8 daily; 38min–1hr); El Puig (every 20min; 20min); Gandía (every 30min; 58min); Madrid (7 daily; 4hr–7hr 30min); Málaga (1 daily; 8hr 30min); Murcia (5 daily; 3hr 20min); Orihuela (5 daily; 3hr); Peñíscola (10 daily; 1hr 30min); Sagunto (9 daily; 35min); Segorbe (4 daily; 1hr); Teruel (4 daily; 2hr 25min); Xàtiva (every 30min; 35min); and Zaragoza (3 daily; 5hr).

Estación Joaquín Sorolla Just south of Estación del Norte, this is the station (902 432 343, www.renfe.com) for the high-speed AVE trains. There are free shuttles from

Estación del Norte to Sorolla for AVE ticket holders. There's also a metro stop, Joaquín Sorolla Station, nearby, and a taxi rank just outside.

Destinations Madrid (around 15 daily; 1hr 40min); Barcelona (7 daily; 3hr 15min).

BY BUS

Valencia's bus station The station is some way out on the north side of the river at Av. Menéndez Pidal 11 (963 466 266); take local bus #L1, L2, L3 or #94 or the metro to Turia, or allow 30min to walk.

Destinations Alicante (20–25 daily; 2hr 30min–4hr 30min); Barcelona (13–16 daily; 4–5hr); Benidorm (18–23 daily; 2hr 30min–3h 45min); Cuenca (3 daily; 4hr); Denia (10–11 daily; 1hr 45min); Gandía (11–14 daily; 1hr); Madrid (16–20 daily; 4hr); Murcia (11–14 daily; 3hr 15min); and Sagunto (25 daily; 45min).

BY FERRY

Puerto de Valencia The Balearic ferry terminal connects with Pza. del Ayuntamiento via bus #4, #30 or #95 and with Estación del Norte train station via bus #2. Ferries are operated by Trasmed (www.trasmed.com) and Baleària (www.balearia.com).

Destinations Palma de Mallorca (June–Sept 2 daily; 8hr; Oct–May weekly; 9hr); Ibiza (June–Sept daily; 6hr 45min; Oct–May weekly; 6hr 45min); Maó, Menorca (1 weekly; 15hr).

GETTING AROUND

By metro, bus and on foot Most of Valencia's sights are centrally located and can be reached on foot, but the city also has an efficient, well-maintained public transport system – metro, trams and buses – which are helpful for reaching outlying neighbourhoods and sights (including the Ciudad de las Artes y Ciencias) and the beaches. Metro stations in the city centre include Xàtiva and Colón, where you can connect with several metro lines. Local EMT buses (http://emtvalencia.es) cost €1.50/journey, and they also sell various discount multi-use tickets; trams and metro are €1.50 for inner zone A, which covers central Valencia (more info on the metro system at http://emtvalencia.es). You can also get a Bono ticket of 10 journeys in zone A for €8.50. If you plan on using public transport regularly, a Valencia Card (see page 745) is a good way to save.

By tourist bus The hop-on-hop-off Valencia Bus Turístic (https://valenciabusturistic.com; €22/24hr, €24/48hr, children 7–16 €11/24hr, €12/48hr) tours all the city's major sights, as well as a separate route (€22) to Albufera (see page 754).

By car Rental companies in Valencia include Avis (airport & Gran Vía de Ramón y Cajal 2, among other locations; www.avis.es); Hertz (airport & C/Dr. Ferran, among others; www.hertz.es); and Enterprise Rent-A-Car (airport & Estación Joaquín Sorolla; www.enterprise.es).

By taxi Radio Taxi 963 703 333; Tele Taxi 963 571 313.

By bike Valencia is a great city for cycling, with many specialized cycle lanes. Use the city's **public bike scheme**, ValenBiSi (www.valenbisi.es); €13.30 for a seven-day subscription. Another option is to hire a bike from ValenciaBikes (C/de Tapinería 14, www.valenciabikes.com).

INFORMATION AND TOURS

Turismo The main *turismo* is at Pza. del Ayuntamiento (Mon–Sat 9am–6.50pm, Sun 10am–1.30pm; 963 524 908, www.visitvalencia.com). There are also branches at the airport and at the Joaquín Sorolla train station. Valencia has helpful regional offices including at C/Paz 48 (Mon–Sat 9am–6pm & Sun 10am–2pm; 963 986 422, www.comunitatvalenciana.com).

Tours Valencia Guías on C/Turia 67 (963 851 740, https://valenciaguias.com) offers a range of excellent tours, including by bike, in many languages.

ACCOMMODATION
SEE MAP PAGE 742

Valencia boasts a huge range of **accommodation**, from historical hotels to hip hostels and sunny beachfront properties. The city centre, between the train station and the Río Turia, is sprinkled with budget hotels and hostels.

THE CITY CENTRE AND AROUND

★ **ABCyou Bed & Breakfast** C/Taquígrafo Martí 10, www.abcyou.es. With modern white decor contrasting with old Spanish tiled floors, this cool Dutch-owned B&B has individually decorated rooms and apartments for up to four people. There is also a small garden haven. Don't miss out on the home-baked goodies and freshly squeezed juice for breakfast. €€

Casual Vintage C/Barcelonina 1, www.casualhoteles.com. Funky, vintage-themed hotel with bright, stylish rooms and views over Pza. del Ayuntamiento. They also have four more sister hotels in town – see the website for details. €€

Hôme Youth Hostel & Hôme Backpackers C/La Lonja 4 & Pza. Vicente Iborra, https://homehostelsvalencia.com. These lively hostels are located in the historic quarter and feature retro-chic furnishings and clean dorms, plus double rooms. Dorms €, doubles €€

Hospes Palau de Mar Avda. De Navarro Reverter 14, www.hospes.com/en/palau-mar. Set in a nineteenth-century baronial mansion, this handsome hotel exudes a lovely blend of old and new, from the renovated historic facade to the sleek, white interior that borders on minimalist. Get pampered at the Bodyna Spa, and then dine on Mediterranean dishes at the restaurant. Deals are available on the website. €€€€

Hostal Antigua Morellana C/d' En Bou 2, www.hostalam.com. Homely, colourful rooms in a cheerful, well-maintained hotel close to the Barrio del Carmen. Book ahead. €€

Hostal Venecia Pza. del Ayuntamiento 3, www.hotelvenecia.com. Don't be fooled by the *hostal* tag: this is a stylish, well-managed, central hotel. Some rooms come with views over the Pza. del Ayuntamiento, while others are interior-facing. All are clean and comfy. Special parking discounts available. €€

Hotel Ad Hoc Monumental C/Boix 4, www.adhochoteles.com. One of Valencia's first boutique hotels, this is suitably comfortable and elegant, with exposed brick walls and textile wall-hangings, in a building with plenty of period character. Cheaper no-refund rates are available online. €€€

Hotel Dimar Gran Vía del Marqués del Turia 80, www.hoteldimar.es. Comfy and elegant individually decorated rooms, featuring black and white photos and illustrations of the city. Its location on the edge of the old town is ideal. €€€

Hotel One Shot Colón 46 C/ de Colón 46, www.hoteloneshotcolon46.com. Sleek, modern hotel close to the

Plaza del Toros, the Estación del Norte and the hip bars of the Russafa district. €€

★ **Hotel Palacio Marqués de Caro** Almirall 14, www.carohotel.com. This luxury boutique hotel, in a thirteenth-century palace, reveals a gorgeous blend of history and *haute* style. The owners (one of whom is a descendant of the last Moorish King of Valencia) discovered a large section of Moorish wall when renovating the building and incorporated it into the design of the hotel; the result is a bewitching glimpse into the Valencia of the past, with upscale amenities that are very much from the present. €€€€

Red Nest C/de la Paz 36 & Pza. Tetuan 5, https://nesthostelsvalencia.com. Cheery, bright backpacker hostels with dorms, a bar and games room. While doubles are available, you'll get a lot more value for money at one of the hotels instead. The busy social calendar features walking tours and pub crawls. Dorms €, doubles €€

room00 Hostel C/Samaniego 18, www.room00hostel.com. Just about as central as you can get, this stylish and friendly hostel sits in Barrio del Carmen, just a stumble away from a slew of fashionable bars and cafés. Check online for the best rates. Dorms €, doubles €€

★ **Vincci Palace** La Paz 42, www.vinccihoteles.com. Well-heeled hotel with the history to match, housed in a former *palacete* that offered safe lodging to intellectuals during the Civil War, with a lovely facade fronted by wrought-iron balconies. Comfortable rooms, soft beds, spic-and-span bathrooms and all the amenities. €€€€

EATING

As befits Spain's third-largest city, Valencia's foodie scene is wonderfully varied and suits all budgets. For **tapas** and cheap eats, head to the area around the Mercado Central, where there are plenty of places offering set menus for under €15; Barrio del Carmen is also sprinkled with lively tapas bars. The once-gritty, now-hip Russafa, just south of the centre, has evolved into one of Valencia's coolest neighbourhoods, where you can find everything from Arabic tearooms to vegan and vegetarian restaurants. Valencia has also marched into the gourmet culinary echelons with style and swagger: witness such standouts as *Ricard Camarena*. And while the city is the home of **paella**, the finest places to eat it are, in fact, out of town, in Perellonet or El Palmar (see page 754), or along the city beach – Paseo Neptuno is lined with small paella and *marisco* restaurants.

RESTAURANTS

La Barra de Kaymus Avda. del Mestre Rodrigo 44, www.labarradekaymus.com. This classy restaurant just north of the city centre fuses modern and traditional and is headed up by chef Nacho Romero. Try the superb *arroces* (rice dishes), like monkfish and artichoke. €€

★ **LaLoLa** C/ Subida del Toledano 8, https://lalola restaurante.com. This kitsch flamenco-themed restaurant,

THE PORT AND THE BEACHES

Hotel Balandret Paseo de Neptuno 20, https://balandret.com. Trendy boutique hotel with cool cream-coloured rooms and sea views. There's also an excellent restaurant (€€) serving classic Valencian cuisine. €€€

Hotel El Coso Paseo Neptuno 12, https://elcoso.es/hotel-el-coso. If you're in Valencia for the *playa*, then you'll like the location of this beachside hotel, with easy access to Playa Malvarrosa. Rooms are decent; ask for one with a beachside view when booking. They also have an excellent beachside restaurant. It's about 30min into town, walking to, and hopping on, the tram. €€€

Hotel El Globo Paseo de Neptuno 44, www.hotelelglobo.com. Friendly place with simple rooms – some with great views – near the beach. They also run the long-established bar *Vivir Sin Dormir* (see page 753). €€

Hotel Las Arenas Eugenia Viñes 22–24, www.hotel valencialasarenas.com. Valencia's only five-star beachside hotel maximizes its proximity to the sea: the morning light fills the cream and dark-wood rooms, sun-speckled terraces face the sea and it's a short stroll to the beach. There's also a spa and several restaurants. €€€€

Hotel Neptuno Paseo de Neptuno 2, www.hotel neptunovalencia.com. Light-flooded hotel with a minimalist, modern look: white furnishings, a glass lift, hardwood floors and a beach-facing terrace, strewn with low sofas and plump red pillows. The top-notch *Tridente* restaurant (€€) serves up creative Valencian cuisine. €€€€

12

SEE MAP PAGE 742

hidden down a tiny side street in the Barrio del Carmen, serves classic Valencian and Andalusian cuisine with a twist. Think watermelon gazpacho with mandarin sorbet or prawns with red berries and mango, not to mention tasty traditional paellas. They also have good options for vegetarians and coeliacs. They also run the colourful little *La Colmada de Lola* tapas bar (see page 754). €€

Ocho y Medio Pza. Lope de Vega 5, http://elochoymedio.com. Named after the Fellini film, this bi-level restaurant with brightly coloured murals on the walls and views of the Santa Catalina church excels at classic Mediterranean fare, including aromatic paellas or *arroces melosos* (creamy rice dishes). €€

★ **Palace Fesol** Hernán Cortés 7, https://restaurante palacefesol.es. Feast on plump sardines, fragrant *arroces* and superb wines at this graceful restaurant which is over a century old – proof that things do get better with age. The rustic dining room boasts a colourful mosaic, beamed ceiling and stone walls, while the gracious owner is the consummate host. €€

La Pepica Paseo Neptuno 6, https://lapepica.com. Founded in 1898, this inviting, spacious paella restaurant has undeniable staying power: over the decades, it has hosted plenty of the rich and famous, from Hemingway and Orson Welles to swaggering bullfighters and the Spanish

12

HORCHATA

Valencia is known for its **horchata** – a kind of ice-cold milky drink made from *chufas* (tiger nuts), which is sometimes accompanied by long, thin cakes called *fartons*. Legend has it that the name *horchata* was coined by Jaime I, shortly after he conquered Valencia. He was admiring the *huerta* one hot afternoon, and an Arab girl offered him a drink so refreshing that he exclaimed, "*Això es or, xata*" (this is gold, girl).

HORCHATERÍAS

There are **horchaterías** all over Valencia city; traditionally, however, the best *horchata* comes from **Alboraya**, formerly a village in the Valencian suburbs, now absorbed into the city – to get there take metro line #3.

La Casa de l'Orxata Mercado de Colón, www.casaorxata. com; see map page 742. In the historic Mercado de Colón, try the excellent *La Casa de l'Orxata*, who make their smooth *horchata* with traditional methods and organic ingredients, and sell it from street carts around town.

Horchatería Daniel Mercado de Colón, https:// horchateria-daniel.es; see map page 742. Another of the excellent spots to cool your throat in the Mercado de Colón. Going since 1949, they also have two other branches in the city.

Santa Catalina Pza. Santa Catalina, www. horchateriasantacatalina.com; see map page 742. Minutes from the Catedral, this iconic *horchateria* and *chocolatería* has over a hundred years of history and is the most famous in the city.

Subies Carretera de Barcelona, Alboraya, https:// subies.es; see map page 742. One old-time spot in the Almássera neighbourhood of Alboraya where three generations have been honing their craft.

royal family. Settle in on the sun-speckled terrace and tuck into fresh fish and seafood or aromatic paellas. €€

Restaurante La Marítima Veles e Vents, Muelle de la Aduana, https://veleseventsvalencia.es/restaurante/ restaurante-la-maritima. Located on the first floor of the large Veles e Vents complex with views of the marina, this modern seafood restaurant is part of the Sucursal Group, who also run three other award-winning restaurants in the building. €€

Ricard Camarena Bombas Gens, Avd. de Burjassot 54, https://ricardcamarena.com. Valencian cuisine is taken to a high art at this Michelin-starred restaurant, the latest project by chef Ricard Camarena, housed in the new Bombas Gens cultural centre. There are two set menus to choose from – the *Camino Oxalis*, which is vegetarian and the *Recorrido Ricard Camarena* (a pescatarian version is available). You can also choose a starter, main course and dessert from their other, slightly less expensive, menu. Reservations are essential. €€€€

La Salvaora C/Calatrava 19, https://lasalvaora.com. This slender Andalucian restaurant, with high, dark-wood tables and white marble floors, pays homage to flamenco singers and stars via black-and-white photos on the walls. The creative fare includes baked salmon with an orange and Parmesan crust, and beetroot risotto with mushrooms and goat's cheese. €€

TAPAS BARS

La Bodeguilla del Gato C/Catalans 10, 963 918 235. Yes, it can sometimes seem like there are more tourists than locals, but this is an authentically lively tapas bar nonetheless, with exposed-brick and mustard walls hung with bullfighting posters. Munch on tapas options such as *chorizo in red wine* and baked Camembert with blueberries. €€

★ **Casa Montaña** C/José Benlliure 69, www. emilianobodega.com. This vintage, cheery tapas bar in the Cabañal fishermen's quarter is one of the oldest (and best) in the city, with one of Valencia's most impressive wine cellars to boot. Graze on a wonderful array of tapas from anchovies and *michirones* (broad beans) to cod croquettes. There's also a restaurant with two set menus. €€

★ **Colmado LaLola** C/Bordadores 10, https://lalola restaurante.com/portfolio/colmado-lalola. This funky deli and tapas bar serves up a tasty array of local cheeses with home-made jams and chutneys, cured meats and seafood plates such as deep-fried sea urchins. €€

La Pilareta C/Moro Zeit 13, www.barlapilareta.es. This boisterous joint, which has been around since 1917, gets packed most nights, with the beer-happy crowd spilling out onto the pavement. The speciality is *clóchinas* (mussels), which you can slurp at the bar, tossing the shells into buckets on the floor. €

DRINKING AND NIGHTLIFE

SEE MAP PAGE 742

The heady days of *La Ruta del Bacalao* (when people drove hundreds of kilometres to party in Valencia's out-of-town warehouses) may be long gone, but the city still takes its

nightlife seriously. The **Barrio del Carmen** is one of the liveliest areas at night, especially around C/Caballeros, with scores of small cafés, bars and restaurants. The whole area between Pza. de la Reina, Pza. Santa Ursula and Pza. Portal Nueva is heaving at the weekend. Calle Juan Llorenç, west of the city centre, is another popular area to bar- and club-hop, with lively Latin and salsa-style clubs. Meanwhile Russafa, southeast of the city centre, is full of funky cafés and bars and hipster hangouts. Across the Río Turia, near the **university**, particularly on and around C/Blasco Ibáñez, and just north, around Pza. Benicamlet, you'll find a more studenty, alternative-music-style nightlife, especially during the school year.

In **summer**, the bars lining the **Malvarrosa beach** are the places to be. Many Valencian bars serve *Agua de Valencia*, the classic Valencian cocktail, made with orange juice, cava and vodka, and served by the jug.

To get a grip on **what's going on**, you can check out https://valenciasecreta.com, which offers updated overviews of nightlife and restaurants. Note that the big nightclubs are generally open Thursday to Saturday, and usually get going after midnight. A good resource for clubs is https://xceed.me/en/valencia, which tells you what's on each night.

BARS

Café de las Horas Conde de Almodóvar 1, https://cafedelashoras.com. Baroque-tinged, LGBTQ+-friendly bar with a gurgling fountain, tiled floors and a marble bar. Drop in early evening for a romantic glass of wine, or later in the night join the crowds getting tipsy on chilled jugs of *Agua de Valencia*. They also serve breakfast, cakes and tapas.

Café del Negrito Pza. del Negrito 1, 963 914 233. This sociable spot, in one of Valencia's loveliest plazas, is perfect for an outdoor cocktail. Come evening, a bohemian crowd gathers for conversation and *cervezas al aire libre*.

★**Café Sant Jaume** C/Caballeros 51, https://cafe santjaume.com. Of the many bars on this main drag, the characterful *Sant Jaume*, set in a small, converted pharmacy with aged mirrors and tiles, is one of the most popular, with a great terrace that packs in the crowds nightly.

Café Tocado C/Cádiz 44, 650 390 232. Enjoy cocktails and conversation at this fun, long-standing Russafa café, with a decor inspired by Paris cabarets.

Destino 56 Paseo Neptuno 56, https://destino56.es. Ease into the Valencia night over cocktails with views of Playa de las Arenas, followed by grooving on the dancefloor. They also serve traditional food during the day.

★**La Fabrica de Hielo** C/Pavia 37, www.lafabrica dehielo.net. Set in an old ice factory (hence the name), this quirky vintage-style bar is filled with 70s-inspired furniture and odd knick-knacks. As well as the bar, it acts as an arts space for everything from concerts and workshops to movie nights. Check the website for details.

Johnny Maracas C/Caballeros 39, www.instagram.com/johnnymaracas53. Stylish locals, salsa steps and strong cocktails come together at this funk, Latin, house music lounge.

Radio City C/Santa Teresa 19, https://radiocityvalencia.es. This veteran drinking den hosts poetry, films and live music, with full-on flamenco on Tues.

★**Ubik Café** C/Literato Azorín 13, https://ubikcafe. blogspot.com. Housed in a library-cum-bookshop, this lively bar offers a great atmosphere, cosy sink-down chairs, a range of martinis, beers and tapas bites, as well as lots of vegan and vegetarian options such as burgers and cauliflower tart. They also offer a menu of the day.

L'Umbracle Terraza L'Umbracle, La Ciudad de las Artes y las Ciencias, https://umbracleterraza.com. Sexy lounge where you can sip tasty cocktails under palm trees and the twinkling stars, and then head to the downstairs dance club *Mya* to finish off the night.

Vivir Sin Dormir Paseo Neptuno 42, www.vivirsindormir. com. Once a legend, and now a lively pub-club with a long bar and an outdoor terrace, particularly popular with travellers. They also serve brunches and meals.

CLUBS

Akuarela Playa C/Eugenia Viñes 152, https://akuarela playa.es. This chic alfresco summer club next to Malvarrosa Beach plays a host of Latin, reggaeton and Afro-Caribbean rhythms, which you can dance to by the light of the moon.

Indiana C/San Vicente 95, https://discotecaindiana.com. This vibrant club is one of the most popular in the city and attracts a young student crowd.

Jimmy Glass C/Baja 28, www.jimmyglassjazz.net.

12

LGBTQ+ VALENCIA

The city has a robust **LGBTQ+ scene**, with plenty of bars clustered in the Barrio del Carmen, and especially along C/Quart. In general, though, much of Carmen's nightlife is LGBTQ+-friendly, including amiable café-bars such as *Café de las Horas*. A general LGBTQ+ resource is **Col-lectiu Lambda de lesbianes**, **gais**, **transsexuals i bisexuals** (https://lambdavalencia. org), whose focus is on Pride events, outreach and local news.

Deseo 54 C/Pepita 15, www.deseo54.com; see map page 742. North of the centre, this lively club sees plenty of revellers decked out in wild outfits (or lack thereof) – that is sequins on some nights, shirtless on others.

The Muse C/Ruaya 48, www.instagram.com/the_muse_valencia; see map page 742. Large, popular LGBTQ+ bar with a lively outdoor terrace, best for pre-clubbing drinks and tunes.

Authentically smoky, shoebox-shaped jazz club putting on quality live acts. Entrance fees vary. Visit website to find out concert schedule.
Play Club C/Cuba 8, https://xceed.me/es/valencia/club/play-club. Cool hipster club in the heart of the Russafa neighbourhood. The club is split into two rooms – one playing a mix of electronic and R&B, and the other, all the latest modern hits. There are also live concerts on Fridays and Saturdays, as well as karaoke.

DIRECTORY

Hospital Hospital General, Avda. Tres Cruces (963 131 800, https://chguv.san.gva.es).
Police Pg. de l'Albareda 17, 963 600 350.

Post office Pza. del Ayuntamiento 24 (Mon–Fri 8.30am–8.30pm, Sat 9.30am–1pm, www.correos.es).

Around Valencia

There are a number of good **day-trips** to be made from Valencia, including a visit to the monastery at **El Puig** or a meal at some of the region's very best **paella** restaurants at El Palmar, El Perelló or El Perellonet.

Real Monasterio del Puig de Santa María

Guided visits only • Charge • https://www.monasteriodelpuig.org/ • Trains (every 30min; 20min) and buses (hourly; 30min) from Valencia

Eighteen kilometres north of Valencia on the road to Sagunto is the small town of **El Puig** (pronounced "pooch"), where it's well worth spending a couple of hours visiting the impressive **Real Monasterio del Puig de Santa María**, a huge fort-like structure flanked by four towers that dominates the town and surrounding countryside. The Orden de la Merced – the order that acts as guardians of the sanctuary – was founded by Pedro Nalaso in 1237 after he'd seen a vision of the Virgin Mary on the nearby hill. It is a favourite pilgrimage destination for Valencians and royalty alike, from Jaime I to the present monarchs Juan Carlos I and Doña Sofía, although in Franco's time it was put to a rather different use – as a prison.

Museum of Print and Graphics

Closed for renovation • Free • www.elpuigturistico.net

In the lower cloister, the **Museum of Print and Graphics** (one of the most important in Europe) contains a wealth of artefacts, including the former smallest book in the world – the size of a thumbnail. Looking at it through a magnifying glass reveals the Padre Nuestro (Lord's Prayer) in half a dozen languages. Other star exhibits include a copy of the Gutenberg Bible and a wonderful pictorial atlas of natural history, both from the sixteenth century. In the upper cloister are its real treasures – fourteenth-century plates, bowls and jars recovered from the seabed close to El Puig.

La Albufera and the paella villages

La Albufera, just 12km south of Valencia, is a vast lagoon separated from the sea by a sandbank and surrounded by rice fields. Being one of the largest bodies of fresh water in Spain, it constitutes an important wetland, and attracts tens of thousands of migratory birds – a throng composed of 250 species, of which ninety breed here regularly. In the Middle Ages, it was ten times its present size but the surrounding paddies have gradually reduced it. Whether you're into birdwatching or not, the lagoon area makes a relaxing change from the city.

It's possible to "hop on, hop off" the Valencia Bus Turístic and tuck into a lunch of **paella**, or eels with *all i pebre* (piquant sauce), in the lakeside village of **El Palmar**, which is packed with restaurants. In July and August, El Palmar celebrates its **fiesta**; on the middle Sunday the image of Christ on the Cross is taken out onto the lake in a procession of boats

ALL PULPED OUT: LA TOMATINA

La Tomatina – the tomato-throwing festival of Buñol – is about as wild and excessive as Spanish fiestas get. Picture this: 30,000 people descend on a small provincial town at the same time as a fleet of municipal trucks, carrying 120,000 tonnes of tomatoes. Tension builds. "To-ma-te, to-ma-te" yell the crowds. And then the truckers let them have it, hurling the ripe, pulpy fruit at everyone present. And everyone goes crazy, hurling the pulp back at the trucks, at each other, in the air … for an hour. It's a fantasy battle made flesh: exhausting, not pretty and not to everyone's taste. But it is Buñol's contribution to fiesta culture, and most participants will tell you that it is just about as much fun as it is possible to have with your clothes on. After the fight the local fire brigade arrives to hose everything down, and a lull comes over the town. And then, miraculously, within the hour, everyone arrives back on the street, perfectly turned out, to enjoy the rest of the fiesta, which, oddly enough, includes such refined pursuits as orchestral concerts in the town's open-air auditorium.

La Tomatina has been going since 1944 but has become a lot bigger in recent years. The novelist Louis de Bernières was one of the first foreign writers to cover the event: he wrote a superb account that is reprinted in *Spain: Travelers' Tales*, and concluded that, if he planned his life well and kept his health, he could attend another nineteen Tomatinas, before he would be too enfeebled for the occasion.

If the idea appeals, then you'll need to visit Buñol on the **last Wednesday of August** (but call the Valencia tourist office just to check). You can get there from the city by train or bus in around an hour, but try to arrive early, with a spare set of clothing that you should leave at a bar. For more information, check out the festival website https://latomatina.info, or try the town's website www.bunyol.es.

As Buñol's **accommodation** options are limited, most people take in the fiesta as a day-trip from Valencia; but if you want to stay, try *Hotel Condes de Buñol*, Avda. Blasco Ibañez 13 (962 504 852, https://sites.google.com/view/hotel-condes-de-bunol/inicio; €̄ but prices rise during Tomatina).

12

and hymns are sung. Another 2km farther along the road to El Perelló is the village of **El Perellonet**, where you can also sample some of the best paella in Spain.

ARRIVAL AND DEPARTURE

LA ALBUFERA AND THE PAELLA VILLAGES

By bus One of the easiest ways to see La Albufera is to jump aboard the Valencia Bus Turístic (https://valenciabusturistic. com), which leaves from various points in the city (€22 for a two-hour trip, including a short boat ride on the lake). Additionally, buses #24 and #25 regularly run to El Palmar and El Perellonet.

EATING AND DRINKING

Blayet Avda. Gaviotas 17, El Perellonet, https://blayet. com. This inviting spot, including a hotel with sea views, has been ladling out fragrant paellas and fresh seafood since 1935. Book ahead on weekends. They also have an attached hotel with bright cosy rooms and outdoor terraces. €̄€̄

Nou Raco Del Palmar 21, El Palmar, https://nouraco.com. Traditional cuisine meets modern sensibility (and decor) at this welcoming restaurant where seafood is the speciality, along with paella, of course. €̄€̄

North of Valencia and the Costa del Azahar

Within an hour's drive from Valencia are the fine Roman ruins at **Sagunto** as well as sweeping mountain scenery and good hiking around **Segorbe** and **Montanejos**. All three are perfect destinations for day-trips from the city. Towards the sea, the coast north of Valencia, which runs up to the pleasant port town of **Vinaròs** on the regional border, is known as the Costa del Azahar. It is dotted with **beach resorts**; sun-seekers should head to **Benicàssim** and provincial capital **Castellón de la Plana** for the best sandy spots. Culture-lovers will appreciate the historic walled city of **Peñíscola** and its spectacular clifftop location, plus the fortified town of **Morella**, which features a castle and Gothic architecture and is about an hour's drive west of Vinaròs.

Sagunto

Twenty-four kilometres north of Valencia are the fine Roman remains of **SAGUNTO** (Sagunt). This town passed into Spanish legend when, in 219 BC, it was attacked by Hannibal in one of the first acts of the war waged by Carthage on the Roman Empire. Its citizens withstood a nine-month siege before burning the city and themselves rather than surrendering. When belated help from Rome arrived, the city was recaptured and rebuilding eventually got under way. Today, Sagunto has several restored buildings to explore, especially in the well-preserved Jewish quarter, where you'll find medieval houses lining the cobbled alleyways.

Teatro Romano

C/Castillo • Free • 962 617 267, www.saguntoturismo.com

Chief among Sagunto's ruins is the second-century Roman amphitheatre, the **Teatro Romano**, the basic shape of which survives intact. After years of (occasionally controversial) renovation, it's now recognized as a *Bien de Interés Cultural* national monument. In the summer (usually Aug) you can take in plays and concerts and the views from its seats are wonderful, encompassing a vast span of history – Roman stones all around, a ramshackle Moorish castle on the hill behind, medieval churches in the town below and, across the plain towards the sea, the black smoke of modern industry.

Museu Històrico de Sagunto

C/Castillo • Free • www.saguntoturismo.com

The **Museu Històric de Sagunto**, which occupies two storeys of a fourteenth-century medieval house, features archeological finds from Sagunto and around, including Latin and Hebrew inscriptions and sculptures, detailed mosaics, vases and ceramics.

ARRIVAL AND INFORMATION   **SAGUNTO**

By train and bus There are trains every 30min and frequent buses between Sagunto and Valencia; the town centre is a 25min walk from the train station.

Turismo The main office is at Pza. Cronista Chabret (962 655 859, www.saguntoturismo.com).

ACCOMMODATION

Hotel Barú C/Felisa Longás 1, 962 608 067, http://elsarenals.com. This spacious beachfront hotel has modern rooms, a pool with sun terrace, restaurants and a gym. Ask at reception for local tours such as kayaking, go-karting and paddleboarding. **€€€**

Coves de Sant Josep

Charge • https://covesdesantjosep.es • Frequent buses from Sagunto pass through Vall d'Uixo

Twenty-eight kilometres north of Sagunto, at **Vall d'Uixo**, is the underground river of San José, featuring caves with astonishing stalactites. Along with boat trips through the caves, the attendant tourist complex also has a swimming pool (only open in summer), picnic area, restaurant and an auditorium which holds summer concerts.

Segorbe

About 30km inland from Sagunto is **SEGORBE**, which is worth a visit for its tranquil surrounds and ruins. It lies in the valley of the Río Palancia, among medlar and lemon orchards. Segorbe has its **fiesta** in September, including the Entrada de Toros y

Caballos where bulls are run through the town by horses. One kilometre outside town on the road to Jérica, the so-called **fountain of the provinces** has fifty spouts, one for each province of Spain, each labelled with the coat of arms.

Catedral and Museo Catedralicio

C/Santa Maria 12 • Charge • https://catedraldesegorbe.com

Segorbe's **Catedral** was begun in the thirteenth century, but suffered in the Neoclassical reforms, and only the cloister is original. Its **museum** contains a few pieces of Gothic Valencian art, with *retablos* by Vicente Maçip and his son; Flemish artwork; and a Madonna with Child in marble by the Italian master Donatello.

ARRIVAL AND INFORMATION   SEGORBE

By train and bus There are daily trains and buses between Valencia and Segorbe.

Turismo The tourist office is in Pza. Alto Palancia (Mon–

Fri 9am–2pm & 4–6pm, Sat 10am–2pm & 4–6pm, Sun 10am–2pm; summer evening opening times until 7pm, except Sun; 964 713 254, https://turismo.segorbe.es).

ACCOMMODATION

Hotel Spa Martín el Humano C/Fray Bonifacio Ferrer 7, https://hotelmartinelhumano.es. Accommodation options are limited in Segorbe, but this handsomely renovated historic building is now a comfortable hotel with spacious rooms, a good restaurant and a spa. **€€€**

Montanejos

Thirty-eight kilometres from Segorbe, tiny **MONTANEJOS** (not to be mistaken for Montan, the village just before) is popular with visitors for its hot springs, **Fuente de Baños**, where the water emerges at 25°C and has medicinal properties. **Walks** around the village join up with the nationwide GR (Gran Recorrido) network of trails.

ARRIVAL AND INFORMATION   MONTANEJOS

By bus Regular buses travel from Segorbe.

Information Visit www.visitmontanejos.com for information.

ACCOMMODATION

Hotel Rosaleda del Mijares Carretera de Tales 28, www. hotelrosaledadelmijares.com. Well-appointed hotel with a gym and a spa that provides a range of therapies. **€€€**

Castellón de la Plana

CASTELLÓN DE LA PLANA is a provincial capital and one of the main cities in the Costa del Azahar area. Important sights are mostly around Pza. Mayor, which contains a fine seventeenth-century **ayuntamiento**, the sixteenth-century **El Fadrí** bell tower and the neo-Gothic **Concatedral de Santa María** – the original eleventh-century building was destroyed in the Civil War.

The **Parque Ribalta**, dedicated to local Baroque painter Francisco Ribalta, is well worth a stroll but perhaps the main reason to visit are the nearby **beaches**, including at Castellón's *grau* (port), 5km east of the centre – and along the coastal road north to Benicàssim.

Museo de Bellas Artes

Avda. Hermanos Bou 28 • Free • https://mbacas.ivc.gva.es

The impressive contemporary premises of the **Museo de Bellas Artes** features some valuable works by Francisco Zurbarán, José Benlliure and Vicente Salvador Gómez, such as ceramics and sculptures, and other paintings and works by a variety of regional and Spanish artists.

ARRIVAL AND INFORMATION

By train and bus Buses and trains arrive at the combined station on Avda. Pintor Oliet. Buses for the port and the beaches leave regularly from Pza. Borrull, and from nearby Pza. Farrell to Benicàssim.

CASTELLÓN DE LA PLANA

Turismo The *turismo* on Pza.de la Hierba (Mon–Sat 10am–6pm; 964 229 813, www.castellonturismo.com) has a wealth of information about the city and district.

ACCOMMODATION

Hotel Herreros Avda. del Puerto 28, http://hotelherreros. com. This well-run hotel, about 2km from the beach, has

simple, comfy rooms. €

Vilafamés

VILAFAMÉS, 24km inland from Castellón, is an attractive hill town that successfully mixes the medieval, Renaissance and modern. In the highest part of town, there's an ancient ruined castle, conquered by Jaime I in 1233.

Museo de Arte Contemporáneo

Vincente Aguilera Cerni Diputación Provincial 20 • Charge • www.macvac.es

The fifteenth-century Palau del Batlle houses the **Museo de Arte Contemporáneo**, a collection of over five hundred sculptures and paintings, from the late 1920s onwards, including works by Miró, Lozano, Chillida and Barjola.

ACCOMMODATION AND EATING

VILAFAMÉS

El Jardin Vertical C/Nou 15, www.eljardinvertical.com. This welcoming *casa rural,* in a five-storey seventeenth-century stone-walled house, has lovely, rustic rooms and views of the rolling countryside. €€€

El Rullo C/la Fuente 2, www.elrullo.es. Clean, colourful, wood-beamed rooms and a restaurant that does a daily lunch and dinner, right in the heart of the old town. €€

Benicàssim and around

It's music that draws the masses to **BENICÀSSIM**, a few kilometres north of Castellón, which hosts the annual, highly acclaimed alt-music **Festival Internacional de Benicàssim (FIB)**. Aside from the festival, Benicàssim is also a popular summer resort for Spaniards, with its sun-kissed beaches and well-oiled tourist infrastructure.

Bodegas Carmelitano

C/Bodolz 12, off Avda. Castellón • Charge (book in advance) • https://carmelitano.com

The Benicàssim area was well known as a centre for the production of Moscatel wine; very few vineyards remain today, but you can take a wine-tasting tour at **Bodegas Carmelitano**, named after the local Carmelite monks who produced an acclaimed aromatic herb liqueur here in the late seventeenth century. The *bodegas* continue to make the liqueur, using the same process and recipes as the monks, as well as Moscatel and other wines. Tours include the history of the *bodega*, a visit to the cellar and wine and liqueur tasting.

Aquarama

Ctra. Nacional 304km • Charge • www.aquarama.net

As befits a vacation spot, Benicàssim boasts the massive **Aquarama** water park just south of town, with all the usual pools, water slides, overpriced snacks and screaming (but happy) kids.

Desierto de las Palmas

Six kilometres inland from Benicàssim, the **Desierto de las Palmas** is a nature reserve with a scattering of ruins (including the atmospheric *monasterio antiguo*, abandoned in

FESTIVAL INTERNACIONAL DE BENICÀSSIM (FIB)

The annual **Festival Internacional de Benicàssim** (https://fiberfib.com) in late July draws tens of thousands to hear the world's biggest names in alternative pop and rock. Over the years, it has pulled in everyone from Vampire Weekend to Kaiser Cheifs and Red Hot Chili Peppers and Kasabian. The dance tents are as buzzing as the live music stages, with DJs playing all night long.

the late eighteenth century) and walking circuits. The name was coined by Carmelite monks whose presence in the area dates back to 1697.

ARRIVAL AND INFORMATION | BENICÀSSIM

By train Trains for both Vinaròs and Castellón leave fairly regularly from the small station, 10min walk north of the *turismo*.

By bus There's a regular bus service between Castellón and Benicàssim: buses leave from the bus stop on Avda. Pintor Oliet roughly every 15min in summer, every 30min in winter. There are also five daily buses to and from Vinaròs, two of which stop at Peñíscola en route.

Turismo C/Santo Tomás 74–76 (June–Sept Mon–Fri 9am–2pm & 5–8pm, Sat & Sun 10.30am–1.30pm Oct–May Mon–Fri 9am–2pm & 4–7pm, Sat & Sun 10.30am–1.30pm & 4–7pm; 964 300 102, https://turismo.benicassim.es).

ACCOMMODATION

Although Benicàssim is heavily developed for package tourism, budget accommodation is fairly easy to come by in the streets around the *turismo*.

Camping Azahar Partida Vilaroig, www.azaharcamping.com. Well-run campsite close to Voramar Beach, with a pool and restaurant. Pitches and caravan site available. €̄

Hotel Montreal C/Les Barraques 5, https://hotelmontreal.es. Comfy, polished-floor rooms near Terrers Beach, plus a swimming pool, sun-dappled garden terrace and a buffet-style restaurant. €€€

Hotel Residencia Canada C/La Pau 1, www.hotelcanadabenicasim.com. Sunny, well-kept rooms in the city centre, about a 20min stroll to the beach. €€

Hotel Voramar Paseo Pilar Coloma 1, https://voramar.net. This friendly, family-run hotel occupies an enviable perch right on Vormar Beach. The restaurant serves international dishes such as sandwiches and burgers, as well as tapas, and looks out at the sea. Vegetarian dishes available. €€

EATING AND DRINKING

There are plenty of restaurants in the town centre, particularly on and around C/Tomás. As for nightlife, Benicàssim has its fair share of party spots: C/los Dolores is dotted with pubs, and for *discotecas* head to Avda. Gimeno Tomás.

★**La Suculenta** C/Mestre J. Segarra 4, https:// lasuculentalatremenda.es. Young chef, Jorge Lengua, who trained at several Michelin-starred restaurants, is at the helm of this airy, central dining spot. Classic Mediterranean dishes are given a modern spin, and include excellent paella and rice dishes. There's a great-value weekend menu. €€

Peñíscola

Apart from the gorgeous town of **Alcalà de Xivert**, which has a Baroque church and an Arab-Christian hilltop castle, there's not too much north of Benicàssim until you reach **PEÑÍSCOLA**, 60km away. The setting is one of Spain's most stunning: a fortified promontory jutting out into the Mediterranean, zealously shielding its warren of alleys and lanes with perfectly preserved medieval walls. From here, it's easy to see why Peñíscola is called the "The City in the Sea" – the spur is surrounded by water everywhere except its northeast corner.

The breezy Paseo Marítimo is a pleasant place from which to take in views of the sea, and the resort's slender **beach** is well kept, if busy. The farther north you get from the castle, the quieter it becomes. There's also a smaller cove beach, Playa Sur, 200m west of the old town.

Castillo

Charge • https://castillodepeniscola.dipcas.es

Peñíscola's **castle**, where part of *El Cid* was filmed, is well worth a visit to admire the colossal vaulted guards' quarters, basilica and the views from its roof. There was once a Phoenician settlement here, and later it was occupied by Greek, Carthaginian, Roman and Moorish rulers, but the present castle was built by the Knights Templar, with alterations by Pedro de la Luna. Pope Benedict XIII (Papa Luna) lived here for six years after he had been deposed from the papacy during the fifteenth-century church schisms.

Museo del Mar
C/Principe • Free • www.peniscola.org/ver/875/Museu-de-la-Mar.html

Peñíscola's **Museo de Mar** explores the town's rich maritime history in three sections: ancient seafaring and archeological finds, including anchors, old bronze diving helmets and pottery; the fishing industry and its evolution; and the area's underwater flora and fauna, comprising aquariums filled with local fish species and more.

ARRIVAL AND INFORMATION   PEÑÍSCOLA

By bus Buses shuttle between Peñíscola and Vinaròs every 30min between 7.30am and 11pm, stopping at various points along Avda. Papa Luna. For points south, you'll have to change bus at Benicarló (C/San Francisco). There is also a bus route to Alcañiz (1 daily Mon–Fri).

Turismo Paseo Marítimo (July & Aug daily 10am–8pm; Easter week, April–June & Sept daily 10am–7pm; Oct–March Mon–Sat 9.30am–5.30pm, Sun 10am–2pm; 964 480 208, www.peniscola.es). They provide good maps and accommodation information.

ACCOMMODATION

Pension Casa Juanita C/Escuela 4, https://pension casajuanita.es. Comfortable en-suite rooms with balconies, right in the middle of the old town – it's in the same block as the *ayuntamiento* building. €€

EATING AND DRINKING

The area just below the old town is thick with **restaurants**, many serving local dishes such as *suquet de peix* (fish stew). **Mandarina** Avda. Papa Luna 1, www.mandarinaclub.net. This restaurant-lounge gets crowded in summer, but if you can nab a seat on the breezy terrace, you can enjoy their Asian-inspired menu, as well as burgers and salads – and then ease into the warm evening over cocktails. They also do tasty rice and paella dishes. €€

El Peñón C/Santos Mártires 3, www.restauranteelpenyon. es. This classic restaurant has been serving quality seafood and local specialities since 1982, and the paella is widely considered one of the best in the region. €€

Vinaròs

The **beaches** of **VINARÒS**, next along the coast, are small but rarely packed, and in town there's an elaborate Baroque church, with an excellent local produce market nearby. In the early evening, visit the dockside **market** to watch the day's catch being auctioned and packed off to restaurants; the *langostinos* are reputedly the best in Spain. In mid-August, Vinaròs celebrates the **Fiestas del Langostino**, with plenty of outdoor seafood feasts.

ARRIVAL AND INFORMATION   VINARÒS

By train The train station, 2km west of the centre, has twelve daily services to and from Valencia via Castellón and eleven connecting to Barcelona via Tarragona.

By bus There are two buses to Morella (Mon–Fri 2 daily), leaving from Pza. de Sant Esteve. Both the half-hourly service to Peñíscola and the six daily buses to Castellón (three of which stop at Benicàssim) leave from the corner of

Avda. de Leopold Querol and Pg. del 29 de Setembre. **Turismo** Near the seafront, the *turismo* (Pg. de Colom; summer Mon–Sat 10am–2pm & 5–8pm, Sun 11am–2pm; winter Mon–Fri 10am–2pm & 5–7pm, Sat 10am–2pm, Sun 11am–2pm; 964 453 334, https://turisme.vinaros.es) has decent maps and will help to locate accommodation.

ACCOMMODATION AND EATING

El Faro Puerto de Vinaròs, 678 246 903. This converted lighthouse serves fresh, quality seafood dishes, and a creative array of tapas, as well as grilled meat and rice dishes. They also have a great *menú del día*. €€

12

Hotel Nou Casablanca C/Santa Ana 30, 964 450 425. Central, family-run hotel with cosy, colourful rooms and a lounge area. Quadruple rooms are available for families. €€

Morella

MORELLA, 62km inland on the road from the coast to Zaragoza, is one of the most attractive – and possibly most friendly – towns in the Castellón province. A medieval fortress town, it rises from the plain around a small hill crowned by a tall, rocky spur and a virtually impregnable **castle** that dominates the surrounding countryside. A perfectly preserved ring of ancient walls defends its lower reaches. The city was recovered from the Moors in the thirteenth century by the steward of Jaime I. He was reluctant to hand it over to the Crown, and it's said that the king came to blows with him over possession of the town. Today, Morella hosts an annual **festival of classical music** in the first two weeks of August.

Basílica de Santa María la Mayor

Pza. de la Iglesia • Charge • https://basilicademorella.org

Chief among the town's monuments is this beautiful **basílica**, a fourteenth-century Gothic construction with carved doorways and an unusual raised *coro* reached by a marble spiral stairway, with detailed reliefs that depict the different stages in the life of Christ.

El Castillo

Charge • www.morella.net/morellaturistica/descubre-morella/monumentos/el-castillo

Morella **castle** itself is now in ruins, but the view up to its imposing walls from the town below is still impressive, as is the view down from the crumbling courtyard at the top – down over the monastery, bullring and town walls to the plains. In the distance are the remains of the peculiar Gothic **aqueduct** that once supplied the town's water. The splendid restored Palacio del Gobernador features an exhibit on the history of the castle and of Morella.

12

Museo Tiempo de los Dinosaurios

Pza. de San Miguel • Charge • www.morella.net/morellaturistica/descubre-morella/museos-y-espacios-culturales/museo-de-dinosaurios

The curious **Museo Tiempo de los Dinosaurios** features a wide array of dinosaur fossils, from carnivores to herbivores, discovered in the area, along with audiovisual displays (mainly in Spanish) and exhibits on geological finds. Look out especially for the full-scale replica of an iguanodon.

ARRIVAL AND INFORMATION   MORELLA

By bus Buses run between Morella and Vinaròs (Mon–Fri 2 daily) and Castellón (Mon–Fri 2 daily, Sat daily). Morella is one possible approach to the Maestrazgo region of southern Aragón – buses leave for Alcañiz (Mon & Fri 1 daily) and Cantavieja/Villafranca del Cid (Mon–Fri daily, early evening departure).

Turismo Pza. de San Miguel (summer Mon–Sat 10am–2pm & 4–7pm, Sun 10am–2pm; winter Tues–Sat 10am–2pm & 4–6pm, Sun 10am–2pm; 661 425 294, www.morella.net/morellaturistica).

ACCOMMODATION

La Fonda Moreno C/Sant Nicolau 12, www.lafonda moreno.es. Pleasant, colourful rooms, along with an inviting restaurant serving regional cuisine. €€
Hostal La Muralla C/Muralla 12, www.hostalmuralla.net. Relax in clean, well-kept rooms with views of the hills. €
Hotel El Cid Puerta San Mateo 3, www.hotelelcidmorella.

com. Good-value, modern, comfortable rooms, some with views and balconies. They also have a restaurant with good value menus. €
Hotel del Pastor Sant Juliá 12, http://hoteldelpastor.com. Welcoming hotel with elegantly carved wooden beds and colourful tiles in the bathrooms. Rates include breakfast. €€

EATING AND DRINKING

Calle Sant Juliá, between the church and *ayuntamiento*, and its neighbouring streets are Morella's main destination for

food, with bars, bakeries and cafés. Ask for *flaons*, a local pastry made from cinnamon, cheese and almonds. Morella is prime **truffle** country – the best time to try them is between February and early March, when many of the restaurants serve truffles, and the town hosts a gastronomic festival celebrating this aromatic delicacy.

Casa Roque Cuesta San Juan 1, www.casaroque.com. For local *trufa negra* and other gourmet-rustic delicacies, head to this inviting restaurant where the traditional menu showcases what's in season. €€

Mesón del Pastor Cuesta Jovani 7, www.mesondelpastor. com. Fill up on robust Basque-style dishes of grilled meats, wild mushrooms (Nov) and the region's famous truffles (Feb). They even have a whole truffle menu with truffle breakfasts and mains. €€€

The Costa Blanca

Stretching south of Valencia, the **Costa Blanca** (White Coast) boasts some of the **best beaches** in the region, especially between Gandía and Benidorm. Much of it, though, suffers from the worst excesses of **package tourism**, with concrete building projects looming over the sand. It pays to book ahead in summer, particularly in August. Campers have it somewhat easier – there are hundreds of campsites – but driving can be a nightmare unless you stick to the toll roads (which are nearly always deserted). If you're taking the inland route as far as **Gandía**, you'll get the opportunity to see the historic town of **Xátiva**.

Xàtiva

The ancient town of **XÀTIVA** (Játiva), 50km south of Valencia, was probably founded by the Phoenicians and certainly inhabited by the Romans. Today, it's a scenic, tranquil place and makes a great day-trip. Medieval Xàtiva was the birthplace of Alfonso de Borja, who became Pope Calixtus III, and his nephew Rodrigo, father of the infamous Lucrezia and Cesare Borgia. When Rodrigo became Pope Alexander VI, the family moved to Italy.

Xàtiva has a fine collection of mansions scattered around town, but most are private and cannot be entered. Many of the churches, though, have been renovated, and the **old town** is a pleasant place to wander. **Fiestas** are held during Semana Santa and in the second half of August, when the Feria de Agosto is celebrated with bullfights and livestock fairs.

Museo del Almodí
Corretgeria 46 • Charge, free on Mon • https://xativaturismo.com/en/the-almodi-museum

In the centre of town, the **Museo del Almudín** features both an archeological collection and an art museum. The latter includes several pictures by José Ribera (who was born here in 1591) and engravings by Goya – *Caprichos* and *Los Proverbios*. A portrait of Felipe V is hung upside down in retribution for his having set fire to the town in the War of the Spanish Succession and for changing its name (temporarily) to San Felipe.

The castle
Charge, includes entrance to municipal museums • https://xativaturismo.com/en/xativa-castle

From town, it's a steep uphill walk (there's the option of a tourist train for €4.20) to Xàtiva's tenth-century **castle** – follow signposts from the main square, Pza. del Españoleto. It's worth the ascent, though; the castle has been renovated with exhibition rooms and leafy gardens, and there are stunning lookout points over the surrounding town and vast countryside, plus a chapel that houses the tomb of the Count of Urgell.

Església de Sant Feliu
Free • https://xativaturismo.com/en/sant_feliu

On the hill leading to the castle is the thirteenth-century **Església de Sant Feliu**, a hermitage built in transitional Romanesque-Gothic style, and the oldest church in

Xàtiva. The interior boasts ancient pillars, fine capitals and a magnificent Gothic *retablo*.

ARRIVAL AND INFORMATION	XÀTIVA

By bus and train Xàtiva is served by buses and trains to and from Valencia; the train (1hr) is cheaper, and leaves every 30min. There are also connections with Gandía (by bus) and Alicante (by train).

Turismo Av. De Selgas 2 (Tues–Thurs 10am–5pm, Fri 10am–6pm, Sat & Sun 10.15am–2pm; 962 273 346, https://xativaturismo.com).

ACCOMMODATION AND EATING	

In the bakeries, keep an eye open for **arnadí** – a local speciality of Moorish origin, it's a rich (and expensive) sweet made with pumpkin, cinnamon, almonds, eggs and pine nuts. **Hotel & Restaurante Montsant** Subida al Castillo de Xàtiva s/n, https://mont-sant.com. If you'd like to go the deluxe route, opt for this ancient country house on the way up to the castle, which has gorgeous jasmine gardens, a pool and an excellent restaurant. €€€

Gandía and around

GANDÍA, 65km south of Valencia, is a historical town and lively resort area. The town centre features the impressive Borja palace, a quiet old quarter including the attractive Colegiata de Santa María church, and plenty of shops and restaurants. The long, sun-splashed **Gandía Playa** sprawls along the coast 4km away, and draws crowds of vacationing Spaniards in the summer.

Palacio Ducal de los Borja

Charge • www.palauducal.com

The main testimony to Gandía's heyday is the **Palacio Ducal de los Borja**, built in the fourteenth century, with Renaissance and Baroque additions and modifications later. Duke Francisco de Borja was largely responsible for the golden age of the town (late fifteenth to early sixteenth century) in terms of urban and cultural development. Learned and pious, the duke opened colleges all over Spain and Europe, and was eventually canonized. The palace contains his paintings, tapestries and books, but parts of the building itself are of equal interest, such as the *artesonado* ceilings and the pine window shutters. There are also several beautiful sets of *azulejos*, but these are outshone by the fourteenth-century Arabesque wall tiles, whose brilliant lustre, should it become damaged, would be irreparable as it was derived from pigments of plants that became extinct soon after the Muslims left. The palace also occasionally hosts excellent contemporary and international arts and theatre programmes.

ARRIVAL AND INFORMATION	GANDÍA

By train and bus The joint bus and train station is on Avda. Marqués de Campo. Trains and buses run regularly to and from Valencia. The AVE train connects Gandía with Madrid (via Valencia) in just over 3hr; trains run a couple of times a day in each direction. Schedules may be limited in winter; contact RENFE (www.renfe.com) for current updates.

Turismo The main *turismo* is opposite the station (summer Mon–Fri 9.30am–1.30pm & 4–8pm, Sat 9.30am–1.30pm; winter Mon–Fri 9.30am–1.30pm & 3.30–7.30pm, Sat

9.30am–1.30pm; 962 877 788, www.visitgandia.com). There are two more offices on Paseo Neptuno, Gandía Playa, housed in buildings made to look like mini lighthouses (July–mid-Sept Mon–Sat 9.30am–8.30pm, Sun 9.30am–1.30pm; mid-Oct–March Tues & Thurs 9.30am–2.30pm, Fri 9.30am–2.30pm & 3.30–6.30pm, Sun 9.30am–1.30pm; March–June & mid-Sept–mid-Oct Mon–Fri 10am–2.30pm & 4–7.30pm, Sat & Sun 9.30am–1.30pm; 962 842 407).

GETTING AROUND	

By bus Buses run every 15–20min (6am–11.30pm) from the tourist office in town to Gandía Playa.

ACCOMMODATION	

Albergue Mar i Vent C/ Dr. Fleming 61, 10km south of Gandía town, 962 826 550, https://ivaj.gva.es. This

12

exceptionally pleasant hostel with dorms is on the beachfront at Playa de Piles. In summer, about six daily buses run there from the train station; in winter, there are fewer buses, and they drop you off about 1km from the hostel. €

Hotel Bayren & Spa Paseo de Neptuno 62, www.

hotelrhbayren.com. Big, glossy four-star beach hotel and spa – if you're in Gandía for the sun and sand, then this place delivers. Most of the rooms have balconies, plus there's a pool, restaurant/terrace and plenty of activities for kids. €€€

EATING

Gandía town has a range of restaurants, from traditional spots with a *menú del día* to tapas, while the beach zone is a good place for **seafood** and paellas; don't miss *fideuà*, a seafood paella cooked with vermicelli instead of rice.

Casa Sanchís La Tulipa C/Forn 10, 962 965 114. Going strong for almost a century, this delightfully old-fashioned bar serves all the classic tapas favourites, along with main dishes prepared with whatever is in season. Try the *tellines*

(clams) cooked with parsley and garlic or the delicious *fideuà*. €

Restaurante Telero C/Sant Ponç 7, https://telero.es. This charming little restaurant with bare-brick walls and lemon-yellow hues serves delicious tapas, as well as mains such as *arroz meloso*, cod with honey mayonnaise and roasted lamb. €€

DRINKING AND NIGHTLIFE

For **nightlife**, head just slightly inland to Pza. del Castell for cocktails at one of the busy bars, then make for the beach area clubs, most of which are liveliest on summer weekends; some open in the low season for events and parties.

CocoLoco Camí Vell de Valencia 120, https://cocoloco.es. The crowds at this flashy club get hot and sweaty, dancing to everything from Latin beats to techno. The owners also

run several other nightspots, including poolside beach club *Agua de Coco* on Paseo Neptuno.

Discoteca Bacarra C/Legazpi 7, www.instagram.com/bacarragandia. Groove to DJ-spun tunes surrounded by fresh-off-the-beach locals. Entrance fee varies depending on the event.

Around the cape: Gandía to Altea

A string of attractive little towns and beaches stretches from **Gandía** to **Altea**, before you reach the developments of Benidorm and Alicante, but your own transport is essential to enjoy the best of them, and accommodation can be pricey. The least expensive option along this coast is to camp – there are scores of decent **campsites**, and a useful booklet listing them is available from local *turismos*.

Denia

DENIA, at the foot of Parque Natural Montgó, is a sizeable, sprawling town even without its summer visitors. Beneath the wooded capes beyond, bypassed by the main road, stretch probably the most beautiful **beaches** on this coastline – it's easier if you have a car to get to most of them, though there are a couple of buses that make the trip from the port.

ARRIVAL AND DEPARTURE   DENIA

By train and bus Trains depart regularly for Benidorm, where you can then connect to a tram to Alicante. Buses also run hourly to and from Alicante, departing from Pza. Archiduque Carlos, among other spots.

By ferry Ferries service Mallorca, Ibiza and Formentera: for

information, contact Baleària (www.balearia.com).

Departures Sant Antoni, Ibiza (1 daily; 2hr); Ibiza Town (1 daily; 3hr); Palma (1 daily; 7hr 45min); Formentera (2 daily; 2hr 30min).

ACCOMMODATION

Hostal Loreto C/Loreto 12, www.hostalloreto.com. Simple and slightly dated place, though the rooms have a certain rustic style with wooden beams. You can sun yourself on the loungers on the roof terrace, relax in the games room and enjoy breakfast in a pretty, colourfully

tiled patio garden. €€

La Posada del Amar Pza. Drassanes, https://laposada delmar.com. Set in a nicely renovated thirteenth-century building that was a former customs house at the port, this hotel blends old and new with elegant aplomb. €€€

Xàbia

At the heart of this area, very near the easternmost Cabo de la Nao, is **XÀBIA** (Jávea), an attractive, prosperous town surrounded by hillside villas, with a fine beach and a very pleasant old town. In summer, both Denia and Xàbia are lively in the evenings, especially at weekends, as they're popular with *valencianos*. There are plenty of idyllic cove beaches close to Xàbia; one of the best is **Cala Portitxol** (also known as Playa la Barraca), a wonderful sand-and-pebble bay backed by high cliffs.

ACCOMMODATION   XÀBIA

Hotel Javea Pío X 5, https://hotel-javea.com. This place by the port has rooms with modern bathrooms with a touch of a maritime theme and balmy sea views. €€

EATING AND DRINKING

Nightlife is centred on the beach bars. Later in the evening, the crowds move to the out-of-town clubs on the road to Cabo de San Antonio.

Bohemians Av. Ultramar 2, https://bohemiansjavea.com. This local classic has been around for years, but has recently moved to elegant new premises overlooking the sea. The Mediterranean dishes have international touches – such as the Thai-style fish curry or beef stroganoff – and the views are heavenly. €€

La Fontana Paseo Amanecer 1, www.restaurante lafontana.es. Specializing in traditional paellas and *fideuàs* since 1963, this large and airy beachside restaurant will please everyone with its wide offering of pizzas, pastas, seafood and grilled meats. €€

Altea

Heading southeast from Xàbia, you pass the dramatic rocky outcrop known as the **Peñón de Ifach**, its natural beauty offering a stark contrast to the concrete towers of the neighbouring package resort of **Calpe** (Calp). If you'd like to enjoy the coast for a night or two, you'll find that **ALTEA**, just 11km to the south, is a more attractive proposition: a small resort set below a historic hilltop village, with views overlooking the whole stretch of coastline. Tourist development is centred on the seafront, where there's a pebble beach and an attractive promenade of low-rise apartment buildings interspersed with tottering old fishermen's houses.

The old village, or *poble antic*, up the hill, is even more picturesque, with its steep lanes, white houses, blue-domed church and profuse blossoms. In summer, the entire quarter is packed with pavement diners and boutique browsers.

If you need a sandy shore, head just south again to El Albir, which also has great hikes up to a lighthouse on a craggy outcrop.

INFORMATION   ALTEA

Turismo C/Sant Pere 14 (summer usually Mon–Sat 10am–2pm & 4.30–7pm, Sun 10am–2pm; rest of the year reduced hours; 965 844 114, https://visitaltea.es).

ACCOMMODATION

It's a good idea to book ahead in the summer. Beyond town, the verdant environs reveal a number of comfortable and unique *casas rurales*.

Hotel Altaia C/Sant Pere 28, https://hotelaltaia.es. This friendly, family-run place on the seafront has prime sea views from balustraded balconies. €€€

El Naranjal Cami dels Morers 15, www.campingelnaranjal. com. Well-run campsite 1.5km south of Xàbia with facilities including a pool and bar and, in the summer, live music and other events. Minimum one-week stay for bungalows in summer. Camping €, bungalows €€

★ **Refugio Marnes** Sierra de Bernia, Benissa, www. refugiomarnes.com. Some 15km northwest of Calp, this rural *finca* (country estate), covering 50 acres, has three types of accommodation: a restored farmhouse B&B, two private cottages and a luxurious Bedouin tent (both available for weekly rentals only). Cheaper rates out of summer season. B&B €€, cottages/tent €€€

EATING AND DRINKING

It's a treat to **eat** in the old town, with most of the alfresco dining centred on Pza. de la Iglesia; there are also plenty of cafés and restaurants along the seafront. The best places to **drink** are to be found around the main square of the old

12

village.

Oustau C/Mayor 5, http://oustau.com. A French-influenced quality restaurant and one of the better-known old-town options. Dishes are named after Hollywood stars and movies. Think DiCaprio roasted leg of lamb and Mr. Bean aubergine tart. €€€

Restaurante La Capella C/Sant Pau 1, www.lacapella-altea.com. This lovely place is set in a historic building with stone walls and a breezy terrace. Traditional, if pricey, cuisine, from *arroz a la banda* to salads bursting with local produce. €€€

Restaurante Frotón Playa C/Sant Pere 24, 966 881 655. By the seafront, this relaxed spot serves up breakfasts, as well as a good selection of old school tapas dishes from *gambas al ajilo* (garlic shrimps) to *pulpo* (octopus) and fried fish platters. €

Benidorm

Hugely high-rise, vaguely Vegas and definitely dodgy, **BENIDORM** is the beach resort that everyone loves to hate. Nonetheless, the crowds keep coming. Fortunately, the reason it was so popular during the boom of the 1970s and 1980s is still present – sun-drenched sandy beaches and crystal-clear sea – so the British, German and Scandinavian holiday-makers who are lobster-red from the sun (and, often, the drink) still arrive in their hordes.

Decades ago, British writer Rose Macaulay described Benidorm as a small village "crowded very beautifully round its domed and tiled church on a rocky peninsula". The old part's still here, serving up fresh mojitos, delicious tapas and Mediterranean leisure, but you may need to walk past the "English" pubs screening football and rugby and the pulsating discos and bar-clubs to find it.

The connection to Benidorm from Alicante via tram is quick and easy so it's possible to do a day-trip if you want to just enjoy the beach and the bars, and then avoid the boisterous atmosphere in Avenida de Mallorca – but, when in Rome…

12

ARRIVAL AND INFORMATION

By train, bus and tram Trains arrive at the top of town, off Avda. de Beniarda, while the main bus stop is at the junction of Avda. de Europa and C/Gerona. Moving on to Alicante, you can either take the FGV tram or a bus, but the tram is quicker and more convenient. There's also a night-train service ("TRAMnochador", www.tramalacant.es/en/

tramnochador) that runs along the coast to Alicante in July and August. Regular buses travel to and from Valencia.

Turismo Pza. Canalejas, in the old town (Mon–Fri 9am–9pm, Sat & Sun 10am–5.30pm; 965 851 311, https://en.visitbenidorm.es).

ACCOMMODATION

With tens of thousands of hotel beds and hundreds of apartments, finding a **place to stay** isn't a problem (except perhaps in July and Aug – when you may need to commit to a minimum of three nights or more). Budget places are clustered around the old town, and out of season many of the giant hotels slash their prices drastically, making Benidorm a cheap base from which to explore the surrounding area.

Asia Gardens Hotel & Thai Spa Glorieta del Fuego Mítica, www.asiagardens.es. If you're looking to splurge in Benidorm, this elegant, five-star hotel which was recently

voted the best hotel in Spain at the World Travel Awards, is the place to do it. Set back from the sea (2km from the beach) in massive grounds on the slopes of the Sierra Cortina, it boasts Balinese-style furnishings, a Thai spa and two good Asian-themed restaurants. There's a two-night minimum stay in summer. €€€€

Camping Raco Avda. Doctor Ochoa 35, www.campingraco.com. One of the best – and greenest – of Benidorm's myriad campsites. Camping €, bungalows €€€

Gran Hotel Bali C/Luís Prendes 4, www.granhotelbali.

BENIDORM'S WATER PARKS

If you're travelling with kids (or just want to get in touch with your inner child), you're spoilt for choice in Benidorm, where each amusement park seems to eclipse the next: there's the "mythical" theme park **Terra Mítica** (Mythic Land; www.terramiticapark.com); the wildlife theme park **Terra Natura** (https://benidorm.terranatura.com); and the **Aqualandia** water park (www.aqualandia.net); to name just three and, well, you get the idea.

com. It's hard to miss this towering deluxe landmark, one of Europe's highest hotels – and the preferred choice of visiting rock royalty. Prices can plummet by half in the low season. €€€€

Hotel Irati C/Condestable Zaragoza 5, http://hotelirati. com. Cosy family-run hotel, close to the old town and the beach, with a small restaurant, bar and bicycle hire. €€

Hotel El Palmeral C/Santander 12, https://hotel palmeral.com. Set away from the hustle and bustle of central Benidorm, this lovely hotel sits just 30 metres from Poniente Beach. It offers everything you could need, from simple, bright bedrooms to a large pool and restaurant. €€€

Hotel Rocamar C/Cuatro Esquinas 18, www.hotel rocamarbenidorm.es. Smack in the heart of the old town, with simple rooms boasting touches of boutique style.

There's also a charming library, living room, gym and relaxing terrace. €€€

INNside by Meliá Avda. Alcoy, www.melia.com. An adults-only resort with a funky bar area and a pool 10m from the beach. It offers stylish summery rooms with balconies, and a restaurant serving, among other things, an indulgent breakfast spread. €€€€

Villa del Mar Avda. Armada Española 1, www.hotel villadelmar.com.es. This beachfront hotel has a spa, restaurant and brilliant rooftop bar where you can snuggle up on a huge sunbed and watch the world of Poniente beach go by, plus modern, airy rooms with sea views and rain showers. Spa and restaurant do breakfast, lunch and dinner daily. Its sister hotel *Villa Venecia* (Pza. San Jaume 1) is a five-star gourmet boutique hotel located nearer to the centre. €€€€

EATING AND DRINKING

Fish and chips and fried breakfasts can dominate in Benidorm, but local cuisine is available and surprisingly authentic if you eat in the old town around C/Santo Domingo.

Club Náutico Benidorm Paseo Colón, www.cnbenidorm. com. For a departure from the Benidorm crowds and cacophony, amble down to this quiet waterfront restaurant

south of the centre, where you can sample fresh seafood on a breezy terrace. €€

La Picaeta de Matias C/L'Alt 3, 687 239 466, www. instagram.com/la_picaeta_maties. Basic and friendly spot – just as popular with locals as it is with tourists, offering tasty tapas and seafood. €€

Inland from Benidorm

In total contrast to the coastal strip, the remote mountainous terrain **inland from Benidorm** harbours some of the most traditional and isolated villages in the Valencia region. Better roads and local government grants (which encourage the conversion of rural properties into guesthouses) are beginning to open up this area to tourism, but for now the austere *pueblos* retain a fairly untouched character, Castilian is very much a second language, and the main visitors are hikers. The area is rich in **birdlife**, with golden eagles, and, in autumn, griffon vultures are often spotted soaring over the limestone ridges. There's no bus or train service, other than links to Alcoy and **Guadalest** (generally only once daily to and from Benidorm), so you'll need your own wheels to get around – and a leisurely drive to take it all in is well worth it. Head to the **Amadorio Reservoir**, a staggering aquamarine expanse, for a swimming experience that is nothing like that on the beach.

Continue west along the well-maintained highway to Sant Vicent del Raspeig **then travel north to Alcoy**, for a memorable contrast between hedonistic sun-and-sand coast and quiet, rural inland.

Guadalest

Twenty-one kilometres west of Benidorm, **GUADALEST** is one of the most popular tourist attractions in the area. The sixteenth-century Moorish castle town is built into the surrounding rock, and you enter through a gateway tunnelled into the mountain. If you can put up with the slew of tourists and gift shops, it's worth visiting for the view down to the reservoir (accessible via the village of Beniarda just to the west) and across the valley.

Museo Ethnològico

C/Iglesia 1 • Free, but donations requested • https://guadalest.es

Set in an eighteenth-century house on the main street, **Museo Ethnològico** explores local history via exhibits of antique tools and agricultural methods, plus audiovisual accompaniments and displays that explain the production process of local foods, "from olives to olive oil".

INFORMATION AND TOURS

GUADALEST

Turismo The office on Avda. de Alicante (Mon–Sun: March–June & Oct 10am–2pm & 3–8pm; July–Sept 10am–2pm & 3–7pm; Nov–Feb 10am–2pm & 3–5pm; 965 885 298, https://guadalest.es) has maps of the town and can arrange trips on a solar-powered tourist boat which centre on the local flora and fauna.

Alicante

In the minds of many, **ALICANTE** (**Alacant**) is often lumped together with the other brash Costa Blanca resorts. It shouldn't be. Valencia's second-largest city, the thoroughly Spanish Alicante has a decidedly elegant Mediterranean air. Seafront *paseos* and wide, breezy esplanades, such as the Rambla Méndez Núñez, are peppered with cosy bars and terrace cafés; a series of well-curated museums feature everything from ancient archeology to contemporary art; the city's culinary scene is making a name for itself, just as its healthy nightlife did long ago; and its long, sandy beaches are sun-kissed for much of the year. The city's well-maintained beach – **Playa del Postiguet** – has some nice *chiringuitos* but gets very crowded in summer. The beaches at **San Juan de Alicante**, about 6km out (take bus #22 or #28 from the Pza. del Mar, or the FGV line 3 tram to Costa Blanca or line 4 to Avd. Benidorm, Londres or Pza. Corua), are also quite built up, while **Playa Arenales**, backed by sand dunes, is more pleasant; it's 12km south of the city and reachable by an hourly bus from the main bus station.

Founded by the Romans, who named it Lucentum (City of Light), and dominated by the Arabs in the second half of the eighth century, Alicante was finally reconquered by Alfonso X in 1246 for the Castilian Crown. In 1308, Jaime III incorporated Alicante into the kingdom of Valencia.

Today, the main **fiesta**, Las Hogueras de San Juan, is at the end of June, and ignites a series of cracking celebrations, second only to Las Fallas in Valencia, including over fifty individual bonfire spots around the city.

FIESTAS DE MOROS Y CRISTIANOS

Fiestas de Moros y Cristianos are some of the most important fiestas in the region, and the three-day Fiesta de Moros y Cristianos in **Alcoy**, about 60km from Alicante, is perhaps the biggest of the lot. It's held for three days around St George's Day (Día de San Jordi); usually April 23 but this can vary slightly according to when Easter falls. Magnificent processions and mock battles for the castle culminate in the decisive intervention of St George himself – a legend that originated in the Battle of Alcoy (1276), when the town was attacked by a Muslim army. New costumes are made each year and prizes are awarded for the best, which then go into the local museum, the **Museo Alcoyano de la Fiesta**, at C/San Miquel 60–62 (charge; www.asjordi.org/museo).

On the first day, the Christians make their entrance in the morning before the Moors in the afternoon; day two is dedicated to St George, with several religious processions; day three sees a gunpowder battle, leading to the saint's appearance on the battlements. Access from Alicante is easy, with five buses a day. If you decide to stay in town, you can try *Hostal Savoy*, C/Casablanca 9 (www.hostalsavoy.com; €€), or the *Hotel Reconquista*, Puente San Jorge 1 (https://hotelreconquista.es; €€€). The *turismo* on Pza. d'Espanya 14, next to the *ayuntamiento* (Mon–Fri 10am–2pm & 4–6pm, Sat & Sun 11am–2pm; www.alcoyturismo.com), can also offer suggestions for accommodation. After Alcoy's fiesta, the Moros y Cristianos fiestas in **Villena** (beginning of Sept) and **Elche** (Aug) are two of the best.

Castillo de Santa Bárbara

Charge • https://castillodesantabarbara.com

The rambling **Castillo de Santa Bárbara**, an imposing yet grand medieval fortress located on the bare rocky hill above the town beach, is Alicante's main historical sight. It's best approached from the seaward side where a 205m shaft has been cut straight up through the hill to get you to the top; the **lift** entrance is on Avda. Juan Bautista Lafora. Almost opposite are the Iberian and Roman remains that have been found on the site, but most of the present layout dates from the sixteenth century. The castle itself is home to the **Museo de la Ciudad de Alicante (MUSA)** which explores the history of Alicante and the surrounding region via a variety of exhibits. The grounds, or **Parque de la Ereta**, are attractively landscaped, with olive groves, renovated pathways, a café and tremendous views of the city. There's also a viaduct-style path which passes Ermita de Santa Cruz, a cute traditional whitewashed chapel.

Museo de Arte Contemporáneo Alicante (MACA)

Pza. de Santa María 3 • Free • https://maca-alicante.es/

North of the impressive *ayuntamiento* and next to the Santa María basilica, the **Museo de Arte Moderno** is housed in the city's oldest surviving civil building, a Baroque affair dating back to 1685. The renovated museum houses an important collection of contemporary (especially twentieth-century) art, including works by Chillida, Picasso, Dalí and Miró.

Museo Arqueológico

12

Charge, combined admission tickts with El Tossal de Manises and Illeta de Banyets available • www.marqalicante.com • Bus routes #9, #21 and #22 pass the museum and trams L1, L3 and L4 stop nearby

The impressive, stylish **Museo Arqueológico (MARQ)** features locally found relics from the Iberian to medieval periods and a video on Alicante's development. The museum also manages **El Tossal de Manises**, the remains of the ancient Roman settlement of Lucentum, in the suburb of Albufereta and the **Illeta dels Banyets** archaeological site, and can arrange visits to the site.

Illa de Tabarca

Charge for boats with Kontiki • https://cruceroskontiki.com

Illa de Tabarca, a small island and Mediterranean Marine Reserve off the south coast of the city, makes a great day-trip from Alicante. You can relax on the decent, sunny beach, which has basic facilities, including snorkelling centres, but it does tend to get very cramped during the summer. Weather permitting, the 50min boat rides leave from the Explanada de España; call to clarify sailing times.

Museu de Fogueres

Rambla Méndez Núñez 29 • Free • https://alicanteturismo.com/museo-de-fogueres-de-alicante

The exhibits at the **Museu de Fogueres** delve into the history of the raucous Hogueras de San Juan bonfire festival (around June 24), which is similar to Valencia's Las Fallas celebration. Exhibits include impressively detailed satirical effigies that are burned during the festivities, plus elaborate costumes and photographs documenting the festival's history.

ARRIVAL AND DEPARTURE   ALICANTE

By plane The airport (www.aena.es/es/alicante-elche-miguel-hernandez.html) is 12km south of the centre, in El Altet. The C6 shuttle bus, which departs every 20min from 5am–midnight and hourly from midnight–5am; (daily €3.85) travels into town, dropping off at Pza. del Mar, La Rambla and other city-centre spots.

By train Estación de RENFE, Avda. Salamanca, has direct connections to Madrid, Albacete, Murcia and Valencia,

12

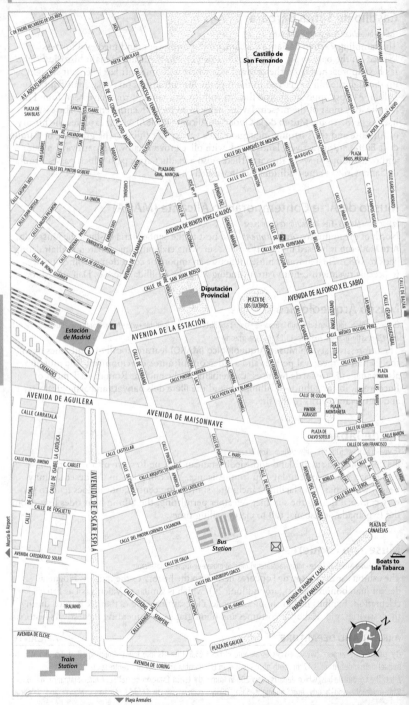

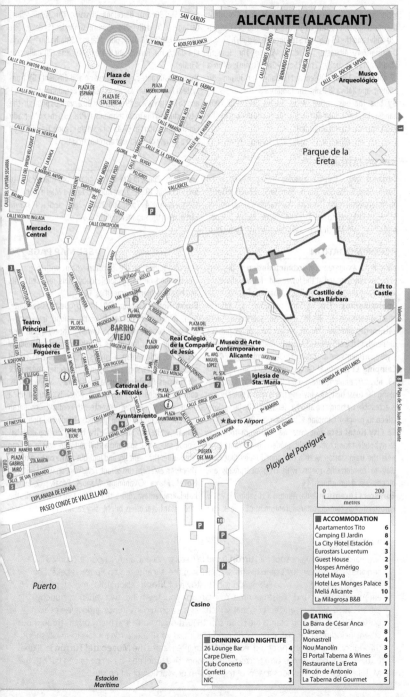

ALICANTE (ALACANT)

SAN CARLOS
C. ADOLFO BLANCH
E. Y MINA
CALLE DEL PINTOR MURILLO
CALLE TORRES QUEVEDO
BERNARDO LÓPEZ GARCÍA
GARCÍA GUTIÉRREZ
CALLE DEL DOCTOR SAPENA
Museo Arqueológico
Plaza de Toros
PLAZA DE ESPAÑA
CUESTA DE LA FÁBRICA
PLAZA MISERICORDIA
CALLE DEL PADRE MARIANA
PLAZA DE STA. TERESA
CALLE NUEVA BAJA
CALLE NUEVA ALTA
M. CALBE
CALLE DE LA HUERTA
CALLE JUAN DE HERRERA
CALLE PARAÍSO
GLORIA
CALLE DE LABRADOR
CALLE DE LA ESPERANZA
CALLE DEL CAPITÁN SEGARRA
DÍAZ MOREU
OLVIDO
CALLE DEL PINTOR VELÁZQUEZ
C MANUEL ANTÓN
CALDERÓN
CALLE DE LA BANCA
PELIGROS
CALLE DEL PINO
CALLE DE SAN VICENTE
EMPECINADO
DESENGAÑO
VALCÁRCEL
Parque de la Ereta
BALMES
CALLE DE LA
PLATOS
CALLE VICENTE INGLADA
GALLO
CALLE CONCEPCIÓN
P
Mercado Central
NVDA. CONSTITUCIÓN
TOMÁS LÓPEZ TORREGROSA
GRAL. PRIMO DE RIVERA
TENIENTE DAÓIZ
DIPUTADO
AUSSET
SAN BARTOLOMÉ
ÁLVAREZ
JIMÉNEZ
PL. DEL CARMEN
S. ROQUE
PLAZA DEL PUENTE
Castillo de Santa Bárbara
Lift to Castle
Teatro Principal
PL. DE S. CRISTÓBAL
ARGENSOLA
RAMBLA DE MÉNDEZ NÚÑEZ
BARRIO VIEJO
CARMEN
TOLEDO
Real Colegio de la Compañía de Jesús
PLAZA QUIJANO
Museo de Arte Contemporáneo Alicante
LUCEUM
Museo de Fogueres
C/SANTO TOMÁS
C/SAN ANDRÉS
SAN PASCUAL
VIRGEN DE BELÉN
SAN AGUSTÍN
CALLE MALDONADO
PL. ARQ. MIGUEL LÓPEZ
FRAY JUAN RICO
S. ILDEFONSO
SONSOLES
VILLEGAS
OBISPO
C/SAN JOSÉ
CALLE MONJAS
PL. STA. MARÍA
Iglesia de Sta. María
AVENIDA DE JOVELLANOS
CALLE DE BALÉN
MIGUEL SOLER
S. NICOLÁS
CALLE VILLAVIEJA
Catedral de S. Nicolás
PLAZA STA.FAZ
CALLE JORGE JUAN
Pº RAMIRO
DE FINESTRAT
CALLE MAYOR
Ayuntamiento
PLAZA AYUNTAMIENTO
CALLE DE GRAVINA
★ Bus to Airport
PASEO DE GOMIZ
MÉDICO MANERO MOLLÁ
PORTAL DE ELCHE
CALLE RAFAEL ALTAMIRA
JUAN BAUTISTA LAFORA
Playa del Postiguet
VIEJO
PLAZA GABRIEL MIRÓ
STA. MARTA
CALLE ISLAO
PUERTA DEL MAR
CALLE DE SAN FERNANDO
EXPLANADA DE ESPAÑA
PASEO CONDE DE VALLELLANO
Puerto
P
P
P
Casino
Estación Marítima

0   200
metres

ACCOMMODATION

Apartamentos Tito	6
Camping El Jardín	8
La City Hotel Estación	4
Eurostars Lucentum	3
Guest House	2
Hospes Amérigo	9
Hotel Maya	1
Hotel Les Monges Palace	5
Meliá Alicante	10
La Milagrosa B&B	7

EATING

La Barra de César Anca	7
Dársena	8
Monastrell	4
Nou Manolín	3
El Portal Taberna & Wines	6
Restaurante La Ereta	1
Rincón de Antonio	2
La Taberna del Gourmet	5

DRINKING AND NIGHTLIFE

26 Lounge Bar	4
Carpe Diem	2
Club Concerto	5
Confetti	1
NIC	3

12

Valencia

8 & Playa de San Juan de Alicante

including the high-speed AVE service to Madrid. Alicante is the starting point for the C1 service to Murcia del Carmen (20 daily) and the C3 route to San Vincente (8 daily).

Destinations Albacete (11 daily; 55min–1hr 30min); Madrid (12–14 daily; 2hr 15min–2hr 40min); Murcia (5 daily; 1hr 15min); Valencia (12 daily; 1hr 30min–2hr 15min); and Xàtiva (8 daily; 1hr 15min).

By bus The bus station, Avda. Loring (965 130 700), handles local and long-distance services, mostly run by the ALSA operator (www.alsa.com).

Destinations Albacete (8 daily; 2hr 15min); Almería (5 daily; 5hr 30min); Barcelona (8 daily; 7hr 30min–9hr); Cartagena (6 daily; 2hr 45min); Granada (5 daily; 5hr 30min); Madrid (9 daily; 6hr); Málaga (5 daily; 8hr); Murcia (14 daily; 1hr 10min–2hr 30min); Valencia (20 daily; 2hr 45min).

By tram Alicante's ever-expanding and efficient FGV tram system (www.tramalacant.es) zips to Benidorm via line #1 and to Denia via line #9, picking it up at various points in the city including the main terminus at Pza. Luceros or Mercado Central; fares start at €1.45 for a single in zone 1, and there's also a variety of multi-use discount tickets.

INFORMATION

Turismo Avda. Rambla Méndez Núñez 41 (Mon–Fri 10am–6pm, Sat & Sun 10am–2pm; 965 200 000, https://alicanteturismo.com). There are also branches at Estación de RENFE (mid-March to mid-Oct daily 10am–2pm & 5–8pm; mid-Oct to mid-March Mon–Sat 10am–2pm & 4pm–7pm,

Sun 10am–2pm), in Pza. del Ayuntamiento (mid-March to mid-Oct daily 10am–2pm; mid-Oct to mid-March Mon–Sat 10am–2pm & 4–7pm, Sun 10am–2pm) and at Playa de San Juan in the summer months.

ACCOMMODATION
SEE MAP PAGE 770

Alicante has a wide range of **accommodation**, with plenty of hotels concentrated at the lower end of town, above the attractively tiled seafront walk, Explanada de España.

Apartamentos Tito C/San Augustín 1, https://apartamentostito.es. Bright colourful apartments with kitchenettes and living rooms, perfect for couples, families or friends in the old town of Alicante. Another eight studio-style apartments are available at C/San Nicolás 10. €€€

Camping El Jardín El Campello C/Doctor Severo Ochoa 39, https://campingeljardin.com. One of many campsites along the coast here, this inviting site is near a quiet beach, is accessible by tram and also has fetching little bungalows (sleep six people). Camping €, bungalows €€€

La City Hotel Estación Avda. de Salamanca 16, www.lacityhotelestacion.com. Bright, modern, good-value hotel near the train station, with a cool-toned lobby that gives way to comfortable rooms with crisp bedspreads and blonde-wood furnishings. €€

Eurostars Lucentum Avda. Alfonso X El Sabio 11, www.eurostarshotels.com/eurostars-lucentum.html. Sleek and central addition to the *Eurostars* chain, with plenty of blonde wood, gleaming marble lobby floors, recessed lights and business-friendly amenities. €€€

Guest House C/Segura 20, https://guesthousealicante.com. A perennial budget favourite among travellers – and with good reason – this inviting, cheery guesthouse is lovingly cared for by the amiable owner. Individually decorated, spic-and-span rooms and apartments reveal personal touches, such as complimentary coffee and tea. €€

★ **Hospes Amérigo** C/Rafael Altamira 7, www.hospes.com/es/amerigo. This upmarket hotel is housed in a magnificently restored seventeenth-century Dominican convent. The rooms reveal gleaming hardwood floors and delicate white curtains, while the breezy rooftop deck has a pool, sauna and spa, and a chill-out zone where you can relax under the night sky and look out to the castle and sea. There's an excellent restaurant, *Fondillón*, on site. €€€€

Hotel Maya C/Canónigo Manuel Penalva 2, www.hotelalicantemaya.com. Sitting at the foot of the castle, this three-star hotel offers bright, airy rooms, an outdoor pool

---

TURRÓN

Spaniards have a sweet spot for **turrón** (*torró* in Catalan/Valenciano), a nougat candy with almonds and honey that's perhaps most popular in the Alicante region. *Turrón* is believed to have originated as a Moorish delicacy in the town of **Jijona** (Xixona). It is most typically eaten and sold around Christmas time. You can sink your teeth into two varieties: crunchy (often called Alicante) and soft (Jijona), which has a smooth consistency almost like peanut butter. The two leading brands are Lobo and 1880, though you'll find many others throughout Spain, including small-batch boutique producers; and you'll see *turrón* for sale in sweet shops throughout the region, including along C/Mayor in Alicante. The **Museo del Turrón** in Jijona (https://museodelturron.com) traces turrón's impressive timeline – it can be traced back to the Middle Ages – and includes a view of the modern production plant on site.

and a restaurant. €€

★ **Hotel Les Monges Palace** C/San Agustín 4, https://hotellesmongespalace.com. Named after the convent of cloistered nuns (*monges*) that sits across the street, this is one of the better – and more original – deals in Alicante, with lovely, strikingly styled rooms. Some are antique-chic, while others are Japanese-influenced, and are accessed from corridors lined with vibrant *azulejos*, oddball curios and unlikely paintings – and there's a chill-out area and a roof terrace. Ask for an upstairs room if you're a light sleeper. €€

Meliá Alicante Pza del Puerto 3, www.melia.com/es/hoteles/espana/alicante. Smack-bang in between the port

and Postiguet Beach, this hotel has spacious sea-view rooms with red or black hardwood decor, and a pool area with bar for seaside snacks. The charming restaurant serves modernized local food and the lounge bar has some of the best maritime panoramas in the city. €€€€

La Milagrosa B&B C/Villavieja 8, www.lamilagrosabealicante.com. Efficiently run, often busy bed & breakfast with great-value rooms that are simple, spotless and inviting. A well-kept roof terrace, seemingly nestled just under the imposing castle silhouette, seals the deal. They also have apartments. €€

EATING SEE MAP PAGE 770

Alicante boasts a rich variety of restaurants, and is now as much a culinary destination as a seaside town: uniquely, a good number of the city's well-known chefs are women, such as María José San Román of *Monastrell* (see page 773), who is nicknamed the "Saffron Queen" for her prowess with rice dishes. Restaurants are concentrated in and around the old town, with **tapas** places on C/San Francisco. If you want to fashion your own meals, there's no better place than the enormous **Mercado Central**, housed in a wonderful old *modernista* building on Avda. Alfonso X El Sabio. Another market (a major outdoor event) is held by the Pza. de Toros (Thurs & Sat 9am–2pm).

La Barra de César Anca C/Ojeda 1, www.cesaranca.com. Sleek tapas bar where the innovative César Anca reinvents the modern tapas bites. Plates include crunchy parmesan taco filled with steak and langoustine bruschetta with brie. €€

Dársena Muelle de Levante 6, https://darsena.com. This handsome nautical-themed restaurant on the waterfront, complete with porthole windows, serves aromatic paellas and top-notch seafood in a genteel setting. The paella here is the real deal and must be ordered by two or more. €€

★ **Monastrell** Av. Almirante Julio Guillen Tato 1, http://monastrell.com. Local super-chef María José San Román creates delicious Spanish cuisine with a twist, from red prawns in saffron-infused olive oil to a superb variety of rice dishes, including one with smoked moray eel. Three tasting menus are available. €€€€

Nou Manolín C/Villegas 3, https://grupogastronou.com/en/nou-manolin. Feast on market-fresh regional fare, including superb shellfish and paella in the curved terracotta restaurant space. Desserts are excellent too. €€€

El Portal Taberna & Wines C/Bilbao 2, www.elportaltaberna.es. This trendy tapas joint, restaurant and wine bar is filled with low-level lighting, shiny brass and living plant-covered walls. Dishes include rice with baby cuttlefish and mushrooms and lemon clove steamed mussels. They also serve excellent-value plates of the day (weekday lunchtime), a couple of vegetarian dishes and cocktails. €€

Restaurante La Ereta Parque de la Ereta, https://laereta.es/. The memorable city views are matched by the remarkable cuisine, presented in a single gourmet tasting menu featuring the freshest seasonal produce. Halfway up to the castle and surrounded by the greenery of Parque de la Ereta, the attractive wood-and-glass restaurant offers a refreshing change from the bustle of the city. €€€€

Rincón de Antonio C/San Rafael 13, 965 202 688. Local family-run restaurant, located in an atmospheric setting just down from the castle. The menu includes everything from traditional paellas and calamari to fish stews. Good value *menú del día* on weekdays. €

La Taberna del Gourmet C/San Fernando 10, https://latavernadelgourmet.com. Stylish modern haunt with an eye-catching rocky facade, which serves some excellent tapas and organic wines, including artichoke flowers, sea bass ceviche and scrambled eggs with peppers, potatoes and sausage. Great value set lunches, including on Saturdays. €€

12

DRINKING AND NIGHTLIFE SEE MAP PAGE 770

For hitting the bars and **drinking** with locals, the old town – or El Barrio, as it's called – still rules, with everything from dark, cosy bars to jazz joints. Alicante also has a decent number of **LGBTQ+ clubs and bars**, both in the old town and just south of it, around C/San Fernando. For a slightly more Ibiza-style night, with large bars and clubs in a small vicinity, head to the port area past the casino. This designated party village never fails to be lively even for midweek, out-of-season drinking and dancing – often until sunrise.

BARS
26 Lounge Bar Pza. Portal de Elche 26, https://26cocktailroom.com. This stylish lounge bar is filled with wall art and natural wood, and serves a wide array of exotic cocktails. They also have an outdoor terrace and serve light lunches and snacks.

NIC C/Castaños 22, https://nicalicante.com. One of the best cocktail spots in the city, this place has become well-known for their creative gin and tonics.

CLUBS

Carpe Diem C/Santo Tomás 5, 678 156 612. Busy pub and nightclub serving beers and a dangerously tempting selection of *chupitos* (shots). Very popular with students including foreigners on exchange from American universities.

Club Concerto C/San Fernando 31, https://grupoconcerto. com. This stylish club is the place to be seen on Friday and Saturday nights and attracts a lively, youngish crowd.

Confetti C/Médico Pascual Pérez 8, www.confetti classics.e/. This popular, colourful club is a staple on the Alicante club circuit and has both DJs and live bands. They also have another branch on the beach at Av. Costa Blanca.

DIRECTORY

Consulates UK, Rbla Méndez Núñez 28–32, 965 216 022, www.gov.uk/world/organisations/british-consulate-alicante.

Police C/Isabel La Católica, 965 514 888.

Around Alicante

For a distinct change from Alicante's sun and sand, head inland to the lush palm forest at the lovely town of **Elche**. Further south, explore the region's formidable history in elegant **Orihuela**, which features three medieval churches and a well-preserved old quarter.

Elche

ELCHE (ELX), 20km inland and south from Alicante, is famed for its exotic **palm forest**, El Palmeral, and for the ancient **stone bust** known as *La Dama de Elche*, discovered here in 1897 (and now in the Museo Arqueológico in Madrid). These two assets, plus the School Museum of Pusol, a centre for traditional culture and education, made Elche the first town in Spain to have three cultural properties registered in the different categories of the UNESCO World Heritage List.

The palm trees, originally planted by the Moors, are still the town's chief industry, and not only for tourism: the female trees produce dates, and the fronds from the males are in demand for use in Palm Sunday processions and as charms against lightning.

The **parque municipal** of Elche town is one of the most charming in the region, with palm-shaded gravel paths, a bandstand and water fountains, as well as sports grounds and a municipal pool, plus the amiable restaurant *Dátil de Oro* (see page 775).

Elche is also the home of a remarkable summer **fiesta**, which culminates in a centuries-old mystery play – *Misteri*, held in the eighteenth-century **Basílica Menor de Santa María** over August 14–15. Additional celebrations include one of the best examples of the *Moros y Cristianos* mock battles (see page 768).

Jardín Huerto del Cura

Porta de la Morera 49 • Charge • www.huertodelcura.com

Elche's palm forests, unique in Europe, are all around the outskirts of the city; the finest trees are those in the **Huerto del Cura**, a beautifully landscaped private garden, where you can stroll among the sun-warmed groves.

Museu del Palmeral

Porta de la Morera 12 • Charge, free on Sun • https://www.visitelche.com/cultura/museos/museo-del-palmeral

Set in a traditional farmhouse near the Huerto del Cura, the **Museu del Palmeral** explores the origins, history and evolution of the beautiful palm groves via exhibits, videos and touch screens. A visit also includes a walk through the lush, adjacent palm grove and orchard.

Rio Safari Park

Charge • https://riosafari.com

Ten kilometres out of town, on the way to Santa Pola, lies the **Rio Safari wildlife park**, a home to tigers, monkeys, antelopes, camels and giraffes, as well as sea lions and parrots. It's a conservationist centre, too. There's also an extensive selection of non-creature-related activities, such as trampolines, go-karts and a pool with a water slide – all surrounded by the ever-present palm trees.

ARRIVAL AND INFORMATION   ELCHE

By train and bus Trains and buses run more or less hourly between Alicante and Elche.
Turismo Pza. Parque 3 (April–Oct: Mon–Fri 9am–7pm,

Sat 10am–7pm, Sun 10am–2pm; Nov–March: Mon–Fri 9am–6pm, Sat 10am–6pm, Sun 10am–2pm; 966 658 196, www.visitelche.com).

ACCOMMODATION

Hotel Huerto del Cura Porta de la Morera 14, www. porthotels.es/hotel-huerto-del-cura.html. One of Elche's most elegant hotels, just south of the Huerto del Cura, with wood-beamed rooms leading onto stunning gardens and a graceful ambiance throughout. A gourmet restaurant, wine bar terrace and spa add to the "oasis" feeling. €€€
Jardín Milenio Prolongacion de los Curtidores, www.

porthotels.es/port-jardin-milenio.html. Located within the UNESCO World Heritage Site of the Palmeral, this well-appointed hotel is based around an attractive courtyard with a mosaic water feature. There are big beds and terracotta-colour rooms, plus a restaurant, sauna and pool on site. €€€

EATING AND DRINKING

Keep an eye out for *arroz con costra*, a local speciality (literally "rice with crust"), made with rice, eggs, *embutidos* (cured sausage), chicken and rabbit.
Mestizaje C/Mare de Déu dels Desamparats, 13, www. instagram.com/mestizajeelche. Award-winning chef and TV personality Tomás López cooks up a storm at this stylish spot, serving Mediterranean dishes with a creative twist.

They also serve vegan and vegetarian dishes. €€
Taberna Fuego Lento C/Alpuixarra 10, www.instagram. com/tabernafuegolento. A friendly little restaurant serving dishes that run the gamut from salads and tapas to succulent grilled meats, the house speciality. There's always a board full of daily specials, featuring whatever is freshest at the market. €€

Orihuela

Just over 50km southwest of Alicante lies **ORIHUELA**, capital of the Vega Baja district, where Los Reyes Católicos held court in 1488. The town's aristocratic past is reflected in the restored old quarter; despite its proximity to the coast, Orihuela retains its provincial charm and embraces its Muslim and Baroque origins. One of Orihuela's hidden treasures, the Baroque **Monasterio de la Visitación Salesas** on Pza. de las Salesas Oriheula, has several paintings by the nineteenth-century artist Vincente López displayed in its cloisters and a gorgeous gold altar. The building is usually open only to churchgoers during hours of worship and only very occasionally to the public; enquire at the *turismo*.

Catedral de Orihuela
C/Ramón y Cajal • Charge • www.diocesisoa.org/catedral-de-orihuela
Right in the centre of the old town is the Catalan-Gothic medieval **Catedral**, no bigger than the average parish church, with spiralling, twisted pillars and vaulting. A painting by Velázquez, *The Temptation of St Thomas*, hangs in a museum in the nave. Don't overlook the Mudéjar (Iberian Muslim)-influenced, fourteenth-century *Puerta de las Cadenas*.

Museo Diocesano de Arte Sacro
C/Ramón y Cajal • Charge • https://museodeartesacro.es
The **Palacio Episcopal**, with its impressive Baroque exterior, is home to the **Museo Diocesano de Arte Sacro**, which explores the city's formidable religious past via an unexpectedly rich collection of art and sacred treasures from throughout the town and the region, including works by the early Renaissance painter Pablo de San Leocadio.

12

Iglesia de Santiago

Pza. de Santiago 2 • Free • 965 301 360

The **Iglesia de Santiago** is another of Orihuela's Catalan-Gothic churches, a style you won't find any farther south. The oldest part of the church is the front portal, the Puerta de Santiago, a spectacular example of late fifteenth-century Gothic-Hispano-Flemish architecture. Inside, the furniture is Baroque, and there's a *retablo* by Francisco Salzillo.

Iglesia de Santas Justa y Rufina

Pza. Salesas • Free • 965 300 622

In the town centre, just past the *ayuntamiento*, rises another of Orihuela's medieval churches, the **Iglesia de Santas Justa y Rufina** – its tower is the oldest construction in the parish and has excellent gargoyle sculptures.

Museo de Semana Santa

Pza. de la Merced 1 • Charge • http://semanasantaorihuela.com

Housed in the Iglesia de Nuestra Señora de la Merced, the **Museo de Semana Santa** explores the history of the Semana Santa celebrations, with exhibits on the elaborate costumes and rituals, plus audiovisual presentations and photographs that trace the long timeline of Semana Santa.

Museo de la Muralla

C/Río • Free • 965 304 698

Within the grounds of the Universidad Miguel Hernández, the **Museo de la Muralla** is centred on the extensive underground remains of Orihuela's impressive city walls, plus a well-preserved *baños Árabes* (Arab baths), which includes a room where the water was heated. There's also a Gothic palace and a Baroque building dating from the eighteenth century, plus displays of ancient ceramics.

Museo Fundación Pedrera

C/Doctor Sarget 5 • Free • 966 745 408

The impressive **Museo Fundación Pedrera** is set in the eighteenth-century Palacio de Sorzano de Tejada. It contains a rich permanent collection that includes works by many of the Spanish greats, including Sorolla, Picasso, Murillo, Zurbarán, Goya and Dalí.

Colegio de Santo Domingo

C/Adolfo Claravana 51 • Charge • www.cdsantodomingo.com

The Baroque **Colegio de Santo Domingo**, at the entrance to town near the palm forest, was originally a Dominican monastery. It was converted into a university in 1569 by Pope Pius V, then closed down by Fernando VII in 1824. It is still a school today, so is closed to visitors during term time. The two cloisters are well worth seeing, along with the fine eighteenth-century Valencian tiles in the refectory. For a view of the town and surrounding plains, walk up to the seminary on top of the hill – from Pza. Caturla in the centre of town, take the road leading up on the right; not far from the top, there are a couple of steeper shortcuts to the right.

ARRIVAL AND INFORMATION   ORIHUELA

By train and bus Orihuela is connected by regular trains and buses to Alicante, Murcia and Torrevieja, which arrive and depart from the combined station at the south end of Avda. de Teodomiro.

Turismo C/ Marqués de Arneva 1, (Mon 8am–2pm, Tues–Fri 8am–2pm & 4–7pm, Sat 10am–2pm & 4–7pm, Sun 10am–2pm; 965 304 645, www.orihuelaturistica.es).

ACCOMMODATION AND EATING

Hostal Rey Teodomiro Avda. Teodomiro 10, 965 300 349. Convenient for the bus station, and just five blocks from the train station, this decent *hostal* has clean, bright, unpretentious rooms. €

Hotel Palacio de Tudemir C/Alfonso XIII 1, www. sercotelhoteles.com/es/hotel-sercotel-palacio-de-tudemir. This handsome boutique hotel is suitably palatial, with cosy wood-beamed rooms, a spa and a fine restaurant, inspired by the works of the poet Miguel Hernández. €€

Restaurante Casa Corro Avda. Doctor Garcia Rogel 23, www.instagram.com/casacorro. Tuck into traditional cuisine such as the local speciality of *arroz con costra* at this restaurant with 100 years of history, 1km out of town. They also have a good value set lunch on weekdays. €€

Murcia

MURCIA, according to the nineteenth-century writer Augustus Hare, would "from the stagnation of its long existence, be the only place Adam would recognize if he returned to Earth". Things have certainly changed – today, Murcia is the capital and commercial hub of the region of the same name and boasts a lively cultural scene. Founded by the Moors in the ninth century on the banks of the Río Segura (no more than a trickle now), the city soon became an important trading centre and, four centuries later, the regional capital. It was extensively rebuilt in the eighteenth century, and the buildings in the old quarter are still mostly of this era. Today, a substantial student population ensures that there's a thriving bar and club scene, plus plenty of tapas bars and restaurants to suit all budgets.

The Catedral

Pza. Cardenal Belluga • Charge • https://catedralmurcia.org

The **Catedral** towers over the mansions and plazas of the centre. Begun in the fourteenth century and finally completed in the eighteenth, it's a strange mix of styles, dubbed "Mediterranean Gothic". The outside is more interesting architecturally, particularly the west side with its Baroque facade. The bell tower, the second-tallest campanile in Spain, features some Renaissance architecture and visitors can climb it for great views of the city. Inside, the most remarkable aspect is the florid Plateresque decoration of the chapels – particularly the **Capilla de los Vélez** (1491–1505). Originally designed as a funeral area, but never completed, it's one of the finest examples of medieval art in Murcia and one of the most interesting pieces of Hispanic Gothic; an urn in the niche of the main altar contains the heart of Alfonso the Wise. The **museum** has some fine sculptures and, above all, a giant processional monstrance – 600kg of gold and silver twirling like a musical box on its revolving stand.

The Ayuntamiento

Pza. Cardenal Belluga • Generally closed to the public – enquire at the *turismo*

Looming across the Pza. Cardenal Belluga is the city's Town Hall. Architect Rafael Moneo's extension to the **ayuntamiento** closes the square with a strikingly contemporary building that faces the Catedral facade with a rhythmic twentieth-century version of the Baroque *retablo*.

Museo Salzillo

Pza. de San Agustín 3 • Charge • www.museosalzillo.es

The **Museo Salzillo** has an extraordinary collection of the figures carried in Murcia's renowned Semana Santa procession. They were carved in the eighteenth century by Francisco Salzillo and display all the cloying sentimentality and delight in the "rustic" that was characteristic of that age.

Museo Arqueológico

Avda. Alfonso X 7 • Free • www.museosregiondemurcia.es/web/museosdemurcia/museo-arqueologico-de-murcia

MURCIA

0 — 150 metres

12

■ ACCOMMODATION
Hotel Casa Emilio — 3
Hotel Murcia Rincón de Pepe — 2
Hotel Zenit Murcia — 1

■ DRINKING & NIGHTLIFE
Alter Ego — 3
El Bosque Animado — 4
Guru Dance Club — 2
Luminata Disco — 6
La Muralla — 1
La Ronería y La Gintonería — 5

■ EATING
Las Mulas — 2
Restaurante Hispano — 3
Restaurante Rincón de Pepe — 4
Los Ventanales — 1

AVENIDA DE LA FAMA

Hospital ▲

Estadio de la Condomina

Plaza de Toros

RONDA DE GARAY

Palacio de Justicia

Jardín de la Constitución

Museo de Bellas Artes

OBISPO FRUTOS

Muralla de Santa Eulalia

Universidad

La Merced

Iglesia-Convento de Santa Ana / Domingo

Santo Domingo

Real Casino de Murcia

Catedral

Palacio Episcopal

Jardín de la Fama

Santa Clara

Teatro Romea

Museo Arqueológico

Ayuntamiento

Museo Hidráulico

El Corte Inglés

GRAN VÍA

ESCULTOR SALZILLO

Catalina

Palacio Almudí

San Esteban

Jardín de San Esteban

Muralla Árabe

Mercados Las Verónicas

Iglesia Pasos de Santiago

San Nicolás

Iglesia del Pilar

Jardines del Malecón

Jardín de la Pólvora

Museo Salzillo

Bus Station

Post Office ▲
Hospital ▲

PLAZA CIRCULAR

Albacete & Madrid ▲

Cartagena, Train Station & ■

Cartagena, Airport & Almería ▶

Albacete & Madrid ▲

The **Museo Arqueológico**, housed in the Casa de Cultura, features an extensive collection of ceramics and potsherds (broken fragments of pottery), as well as other archeological finds from around the region, including well-preserved religious and sacred art.

Real Casino de Murcia

C/Trapería 18 • Charge • https://realcasinomurcia.com

Murcia's **casino** is a quirky delight and well worth a visit. The building dates from 1847 and combines an Arabic-style patio and vestibule, an English-style library reading room, a Pompeiian patio with Ionic columns, a billiard room and a French ballroom. The neo-Baroque ladies' powder room (open to all) has a ceiling which depicts angelic ladies among the clouds, powdering their noses and tidying their hair.

Museo de Bellas Artes

C/Obispo Frutos 12 • Free • www.museosregiondemurcia.es/museo-de-bellas-artes-de-murcia

The **Museo de Bellas Artes (MUBAM)**, founded in 1910 and designed by the Murcian architect Pedro Cerdán Martínez, features a representative collection of Renaissance and Golden Age art, contemporary sculpture and even an esoterically carved door said to have belonged to a Portuguese witch.

ARRIVAL AND INFORMATION

MURCIA

By plane The city's airport is 50km away in San Javier on the Mar Menor (www.aena.es/es/internacional-region-de-murcia.html). City buses run to and from the airport six times a day (check timetables at www.interbusmurcia.es); taxi fares into the city cost a fixed rate of €29.

By train The train station is at the southern edge of town on Pza. de La Industria, about a 20min walk into the centre. Destinations Águilas (1 daily; 1hr 45min); Albacete (6 daily; 2hr); Alicante (5 daily; 1hr 30min); Barcelona (5 daily; 6hr–8hr 30min); Cartagena (12 daily; 45min); Lorca (17 daily; 1hr); Madrid (7 daily; 4hr); Málaga (1 daily; 8hr);

Orihuela (5 daily; 20min); Valencia (5 daily; 3hr 20min).

By bus The bus station (968 292 211, https://estaciondeautobusesdemurcia.com) is just west of the centre, within walking distance.

Destinations Águilas (3–5 daily; 4hr); Alicante (20 daily; 1hr 45min); Barcelona (7 daily; 10hr); Cartagena (5 daily; 1hr 45min); Lorca (10 daily; 1hr); Orihuela (7 daily; 45min).

Turismo Pza. Cardenal Belluga, near the Catedral (Mon–Sat 10am–7pm, Sun 10am–2pm; 968 358 749, www.turismodemurcia.es).

ACCOMMODATION

SEE MAP PAGE 778

Hotel Casa Emilio Alameda de Colón 9, 968 220 631. Good budget option, located just south of the river and opposite a big leafy park. Rooms are basic but comfy and have lovely views of the park below. It also sits within walking distance of the train station. €

Hotel Murcia Rincón de Pepe C/Apósteles 34, www.melia.com. One of the finer hotels in Murcia, paved with pink

Portuguese marble and featuring suitably plush rooms plus a well-regarded restaurant and atmospheric bar, La Muralla. €€

Hotel Zenit Murcia Pza. San Pedro 5–6, https://murcia.zenithoteles.com. Comfortable, business-friendly three-star hotel that sits in the thick of things, a few paces from lively Pza. de las Flores. A cool-toned lobby, tidy rooms and all the amenities. €€

EATING

SEE MAP PAGE 778

Murcia is known as *la huerta de Europa* (the orchard of Europe), and although this might be a slight exaggeration, you'll find local produce on most restaurant menus: vegetable soups, grills and paellas are the main specialities. It's also an important rice-growing region, and the local variety, Calasparra, which ripens very slowly, is used to make paella. When talk turns to **tapas**, Murcia doesn't often come up; it should. Come evening, do as the locals and *ir de tapeo* (go out for tapas) in and around Pza. de las Flores, Pza. Santa Catalina and along Gran Vía Alfonso X. For well-

priced traditional Spanish food, it's also worth checking out the *mesones* in the Pza. de Julián Romea (beside the theatre) and on and around Pza. San Juan.

Las Mulas C/Ruiperez 5, 968 220 561, www.instagram.com/lasmulasmurcia. A local tapas experience, with everything from *croquetas* to *montaditos as well as daily specials*. Try the scrambled eggs with potatoes and ham. €

★ **Restaurante Hispano** C/Radio Murcia 2, http://restaurantehispano.es. Owned and run by four brothers, this classy restaurant serves traditional cuisine with a modern

12

twist. Think Mazarrón tuna sashimi-style, *arroz a banda* and baked aubergines; the attached *Barra Picoteo* is perfect for tapas. €€

Restaurante Rincón de Pepe C/Apóstoles 34, www.restauranterincondepepe.com. Located in the hotel of the same name, this elegant restaurant has been one of the best places for a Murcian gastronomic experience for almost a century. Expect inspired combinations of local produce and be sure to leave room for dessert. €€€

Los Ventanales C/Jaime 7, 968 931 240. Popular, wood-panelled tapas bar, cooking up filled *tortillas*, baked potatoes and cheese and meat platters. €€

DRINKING AND NIGHTLIFE   SEE MAP PAGE 778

As a university town, Murcia has a disarmingly vibrant and diverse **nightlife** during termtime, and a scene that hasn't yet succumbed to across-town uniformity. One of the liveliest areas for **bars** is around the university, near the Museo de Bellas Artes, in particular C/Dr Fleming, C/ Saavedra Fajardo and the side streets off them.

La Roneria y La Gintoneria C/Cánovas del Castillo 17, www.la-roneria-y-la-gintoneria.com. This laidback bar has two zones – a Caribbean-themed one dedicated to rum and a stylish area all about gin (seven hundred varieties to sample).

BARS

El Bosque Animado Pza. Cristo del Rescate, www.instagram.com/elbosqueanimado_murcia. This central, aptly named "Animated Forest" has outdoor tables for evening cocktails (try the great *mojitos*) on the breezy plaza and, inside, artificial trees twinkling with lights.

★ **La Muralla** Hotel Rincón de Pepe C/Apóstoles 34, www.instagram.com/lamurallarincondepepe. This underground, low-lit bar is one of Murcia's most memorable places to drink – sip cocktails while surrounded by the original Moorish city walls. They also host regular jazz sessions.

CLUBS

Alter Ego Callejón Burruezo 3, https://grupotemporaneo.com. Stop here for coffee during the day, then head down into the swish cocktail bar and club at night to party to indie pop and eighties tunes.

Guru Dance Club Avda. Ciclista Mariano Rojas, www.gurudanceclub.com. Sprawling modern venue in an industrial park location devoted to electronic dance music, with guest DJs.

Luminata Disco C/ Teniente General Gutierrez Mellado 9, https://grupotemporaneo.com. Bright, flashy disco with lots of lasers, neon-coloured lights and resident DJs.

DIRECTORY

Car rental Europcar, in the Hotel Agalia, at Avda. Arquitecto Miguel Ángel Beloqui, (www.europcar.es); Enterprise Rent-A-Car, Avda. Teniente Montesinos 9 (www.enterprise.es).

Hospital Hospital General Universitario "Reina Sofía", Avda. Intendente Jorge Palacios 1 (968 359 000).

Market Mercado Las Verónicas, C/Plano de San Francisco (Mon–Sat 8am–2pm, www.mercadodeveronicas.es), has stacks of wonderful local produce. Closed Aug.

Police Policía Local de Murcia, Avda. San Juan de la Cruz (968 358 750).

Torrevieja and the Murcian Costa Cálida

The stretch of coast around the south of **Torrevieja** has been developed at a rapid rate, and is now home to a wide mix of Europeans alongside the locals. Beachgoers will find a more sunbathe-able setting at **Las Playas de Orihuela**, and both Playa La Zenía and Playa Cabo Roig are good, clean options with car parks and cafés.

Torrevieja

The town of Torrevieja itself has a nice marina with an active boating and sports scene, as well as some pleasant town squares and seaside restaurants.

ARRIVAL AND INFORMATION   TORREVIEJA

By bus Buses run regularly to and from Alicante, Elche, Cartagena and Murcia.

Turismo Paseo Vista Alegre (Mon–Fri 9am–7pm, Sat 10am–2pm; 965 703 433, https://torrevieja.com).

ACCOMMODATION AND EATING

Hotel Masa International Avda. Alfredo Nobel 150, www.hotelmasa.com. This three-star hotel is located just outside of town, on the pretty Cala de la Higuera bay. Rooms are homely and comfy, and there's also a pool and restaurant. €€€

Tasca Nueva Bahía C/Diego Hernández 32, www. tascanuevabahiatorrevieja.com. This cosy award-winning tapas bar has delectable dishes laid out along the bar.

Try their two specialities – *pastel de chalota* (shallot tart) and *solomillo* (steak) with caramelized apples and Pedro Ximénez wine. €€

Santiago de la Ribera

The Murcian Costa Cálida starts at **Mar Menor** (Lesser Sea), a broad lagoon whose shallow waters (ideal for kids) warm up early in the year, making this a good out-of-season destination. With its high-rise hotels, the "sleeve" (*La Manga*) looks like a diminutive Benidorm; the resort of **SANTIAGO DE LA RIBERA** on the land side of the lagoon is a more appealing place to spend a day or two by the coast, and is popular with Murcians. There's a good sandy beach, an attractive promenade, lookout spots to the atmospheric *Isla Mayor O del Barón* and an important sailing club – the calm sea is perfect for novices.

ARRIVAL AND INFORMATION SANTIAGO DE LA RIBERA

By train The nearest train station is Balsicas (connected with Murcia, San Pedro and Santiago by hourly buses). Trains run direct between Barcelona, Valencia and Madrid.

By bus Buses run regularly to and from Cartagena.

Turismo C/Padre Juan, 300m back from the seafront (July to mid-Sept: Mon–Fri 10am–2pm & 5.30–8.30pm, Sat & Sun 10.30am–1.30pm; mid-Sept to Oct and Easter–July: Mon–Fri 9.30am–2.30pm & 5–7pm, Sat & Sun 10am–1.30pm; Nov–Easter: Mon–Fri 9.30am–2pm & 4–6.30pm; 661 572 285, https://turismo.sanjavier.es/santiago-de-la-ribera).

ACCOMMODATION AND EATING

Cocedero Lonja Mar Menor C/O'Shea 15, 968 573 410. This lively restaurant near the beach is the perfect spot for a seafood feast: you can even select what you'd like them to cook from the displays of incredibly fresh fish laid out on ice. They specialize in seafood rice dishes and paellas, as well as

fish and lobster stews. €€

Hotel El Marino C/Muñoz 2, www.elmarino.es. This family-owned, nautical-themed hotel has homely, summery rooms with good sea views. €€

Cartagena

Whether you're approaching **CARTAGENA** from one of the numerous resorts along Mar Menor, inland from Murcia, or from Almería to the south, it's not a traditionally pretty sight, even if the rusting mineworks that scar the landscape have their own austere appeal. It's only when you reach the old part of town by the port, with its narrow medieval streets packed with bars and restaurants, that the city's real character emerges.

Cartagena was Hannibal's capital city on the Iberian Peninsula, named after his Carthage in North Africa, and a strategic port and administrative centre for the Romans. Many of the old city's sights have been restored and made into visitor attractions, including the theatre and the wonderful **Parque Archeológico del Cerro del Molinete**.

The Mar de Músicas festival in July showcases some of the best in world music; and in September, the town hosts the annual Fiestas de Carthagineses y Romanos, a mock battle of the Second Punic War between the Romans and the Carthaginians, which took place over 2000 years ago. Towards the end of the year, in November, the city hosts both a nationally famous jazz festival and an International Festival of Cinema. The **fiestas** of Semana Santa are some of the most elaborate in Spain, with processions leaving from the church of Santa María de Gracia in the early hours of Good Friday morning.

The best way to get a feel of the city's rich past is to stroll the streets: you'll see a large number of *modernista* buildings. Most of these are the work of former Cartagenian and disciple of Gaudí, Victor Beltri (1865–1935). In particular, have a look at **Casa Maestre** in Pza. San Francisco; **Casa Cervantes**, C/Mayor 15; and the old **Hotel Zapata**, Pza. de España.

12

Castillo de la Concepción

Charge • https://puertodeculturas.cartagena.es

Reached by a signposted path or a **panoramic lift**, the impressive **Castillo de la Concepción** has interesting displays exploring Cartagena's history, and you can also wander around the old walls, where lookout points afford panoramic views of the town and surrounding landscape.

Museo Naval

Paseo Alfonso XII • Charge • www.fundacionmuseonaval.com/

The vast military **Arsenal** that dominates the old part of the city dates from the eighteenth century. Located on the seafront, the well-curated **Museo Naval** provides an in-depth look at Cartagena's naval history, from exhibits on nautical maps and navigational charts to model ships, uniforms, artillery, and a section dedicated to Cartagena-born Isaac Peral, the inventor of the submarine.

Museo del Teatro Romano de Cartagena

Pza. del Ayuntamiento 9 • Charge • https://teatroromano.cartagena.es

The **Museo del Teatro Romano de Cartagena** features relics from Cartagena's past, starting with a tour through a "corridor of history", including the "Neighbourhood of Fisherman" era through to its time as a Byzantine port. You move past exhibits of theatre architecture and exposed sections of the old Islamic medina before stepping out into one of the higher levels of the carefully restored 7000-capacity pink-stone theatre – a huge surprise, given the modest entrance to the museum.

Museo Archeológico Municipal

C/Ramón y Cajal 45 • Charge • https://museoarqueologico.cartagena.es

The **Museo Archeológico Municipal** is built on a Roman burial ground and offers a good introduction to the ancient history of the city. The excellent collection of Roman artefacts includes an impressive display of glass, plus Romanesque art and sculptures.

Muralla Púnica

C/San Diego • Charge • https://puertodeculturas.cartagena.es/

The **Muralla Púnica** visitor and interpretation centre, built on and around one of the city's old Punic walls, explores the city's Carthaginian and Roman history via exhibits and audiovisuals in a roughly 45-minute visit. It also provides helpful information on other sights around the city, including the **Casa de la Fortuna** and the **Military Museum**.

ARRIVAL AND INFORMATION CARTAGENA

By train and bus The main train station (www.renfe.com) is at the end of Avda. America. Services to Los Nietos on the Mar Menor depart from a smaller station (the former FEVE terminal) on C/Carlos Haya. The main bus station is on C/ Trovero Marín, next to the Plaza Puertas de San José.

Turismo Pza. del Ayuntamiento, in the Palacio Consistorial (May–Sept: Mon–Sat 10am–1.30pm & 5–7pm, Sun 10.30am–1.30pm; Oct–April: Mon–Sat 10am–1.30pm & 4–6pm, Sun 10.30am–1.30pm; 968 128 955, https:// turismo.cartagena.es). There are also information points at the Museo-Refugio de la Guerra Civil (C/Gisbert 10) and at the Puertas de San José (Pza. A. Bastarreche).

ACCOMMODATION

Hotel Cartagena Puerto Real 2, Pza. Héroes de Cavite, 968 120 908. Smart, central place with elegant rooms right on the plaza, many with wrought-iron balconies, and a restaurant serving creative regional fare. €€

Hotel Los Habaneros C/San Diego 60, www.hotel habaneroscartagena.com. Comfortable, well-maintained rooms and a very central location near both the bus and train stations. €€

EATING AND DRINKING

La Catedral Pza. Condesa Peralta 7, 868 066 558. One of the most atmospheric dining spots in town, right next to the old *Teatro Romano*, this restaurant is a piece of history itself, built on the site of an old cathedral. Dine on dishes such as sirloin steak smothered in mustard or cod cooked with pine nuts and honey, while surrounded by pieces of ancient wall, glass-floor-covered excavations, artisan lamps and colourful mosaics. There's also a cosy bar downstairs – perfect for wine, cocktails and tapas. €€

El Mejillonera C/Mayor 4, 968 521 179. This lively spot near the Pza. del Ayuntamiento does tasty *mejillones* and Gallego-style *pulpo*. €

Mazarrón

South of Cartagena, much of the scenic coastline down to the border with Andalucia is undeveloped, with a succession of fine coves lying beneath a backdrop of arid, serrated hills. The region's main resorts, **El Puerto de Mazarrón** and **Águilas**, mainly attract Spanish families, but have been undergoing development. The better beaches are often out of town so you'll need your own vehicle; though if you don't have one, note that the south-facing Playa Poniente beach at Águilas is well-maintained and has a fantastic view up to the castle.

El Puerto de Mazarrón

There has been a large amount of development in **EL PUERTO DE MAZARRÓN** in the last few years – so much so that the port area is more of an attraction than Mazarrón town itself. The port has a sweeping, sandy beach just north of the yacht-filled marina, and there are more great **beaches** within easy reach of town. Buses head 6km southwest along the coast to Bolnuevo, where there's a superb stretch of sand. West of Bolnuevo, the route becomes a dirt track, with access to several coves popular with nudists, until you reach the headland of Punta Calnegre, 15km from El Puerto de Mazarrón, where there are more good stretches of sand. Alternatively, if you head northeast from El Puerto de Mazarrón the best beaches are around Cabo Tiñoso, 13km away. When you're tired of sunbathing, visit the nature reserve at **La Rambla de Moreras**, 2km north of Bolnuevo, which has a lagoon that attracts a variety of migratory birds.

INFORMATION
EL PUERTO DE MAZARRÓN

Turismo C/Toneleros 1 (Mon–Fri 8am–9pm, Sat & Sun 9am–2pm & 5–8pm; 968 594 426, www.mazarron.es/es/ turismo).

ACCOMMODATION AND EATING

La Barraca C/Torre 13, 968 594 402, www.instagram. com/labarracamazarron. Enjoy fresh seafood, from lobster and shrimp to sea bream, as well as paellas and *arroz con bogavante* at this long-established restaurant near the port. €€

Hotel Bahía Playa de la Reya, https://30degreeshotels. com/hotel-bahia-2. It may look fairly generic and concrete from the outside, but it's near the beach and offers comfortable, if dated, rooms, a plant-filled lobby and a sun terrace. €€

Playa de Mazarrón Carretera Bolnuevo, www.playa mazarron.com. This well-maintained, massive campsite, with good facilities, is open year-round. Camping €, cottages/bungalows €€

Águilas

ÁGUILAS, 47km from Mazarrón and almost on the border with Andalucia, is hemmed in by the parched hills of the Sierra del Contar. Along with the cultivation of tomatoes – one of the few things that can grow in this arid region – fishing is the mainstay of the economy here, and a fish auction is held at around 5pm every day in the port's modern fish market. **Carnaval** is especially wild in Águilas, and for three days and nights in February the entire population lets its hair down with processions, floats and general fancy-dress mayhem.

Águilas is also popular for its plentiful **beaches**, and the area has a superb year-round climate. The town itself has managed to escape the worst excesses of tourism, and retains much of its rural charm and port-town character. The most important tourist sights are the **Castillo de San Juan** (www.aguilas.es; charge) and the exquisite mosaic staircase at **Rincon Del Hornillo**; ask at the *turismo* (Pza. de Antonio Cortijos; 968 493 285, www.aguilas.es/).

Cuatro calas and Águilas' beaches

You'll find sandy **beaches**, and over thirty small *calas* (coves) in the vicinity – those to the north are rockier and more often backed by low cliffs, while the best are the wonderful, fairly undeveloped **CUATRO CALAS** south of town. You'll need your own wheels to reach these beaches, which get better the farther you get away from Águilas, but all are signposted. The first two, **Calarreona** and **La Higuérica**, have fine sands and are backed by dunes and the odd villa, but 6km south of Águilas, where the coast is completely wild, the ravishing back-to-back sandy coves of **Cala Carolina** and **Cala Cocedores** are simply superb.

If you don't have your own transport, you're better heading for the chain of beaches north of Águilas served by regular buses (generally July to end of Aug only). **Playa Hornillo** is a nice beach with a couple of bars (and you could actually reach it by walking from the train station), while **Playa Amarillo** is decent but in a built-up area. The bus also passes *playas* Arroz, La Cola and finally Calabardina (7km from town). If you feel energetic, you could head across **Cabo Cope** to another chain of beaches beginning at Ruinas Torre Cope.

ACCOMMODATION AND EATING   **ÁGUILAS**

Hotel Restaurante El Paso C/Cartagena 13, https://hotel elpasoaguilas.es. This pleasant small hotel has simple but well-maintained rooms, a central interior courtyard and a bar-restaurant for guests. Prices go down dramatically out of summer season. €€

Restaurante la Veleta C/Blas Rosique Blaya 6, 968 411 798. Dine on fresh seafood, from mussels to octopus to plump shrimp, as well as grilled meats and aromatic rice dishes at this inviting restaurant with terrace bar. €€

Lorca and around

One of the more easily accessible historic villages of inland Murcia is **LORCA**, a former frontier town whose historic centre, on the hill between C/López Gisbert and the castle, still has a distinct aura of the past. For a time, it was part of the Córdoba caliphate, but it was retaken by the Christians in 1243, after which Muslim raids were a feature of life until the fall of Granada, the last Muslim stronghold. Most of the town's notable buildings – churches and ancestral homes – date from the sixteenth century onwards.

Today, Lorca is famed for its **Semana Santa** celebrations, which outdo those of both Murcia and Cartagena, the next best in the region. The high point is the afternoon and evening of Good Friday.

Palacio de Guevara

C/Lope Gisbert • Free, charge for guided tours • www.lorcatallerdeltiempo.es

The **Casa de los Guevara** is an excellent example of civic eighteenth-century Baroque architecture and features all the historical hallmarks of a luxurious mansion, including well-appointed rooms with paintings and period furniture, and a lovely patio and cloister – it's easy to see why the building is nicknamed the "House of Columns". The building underwent extensive renovation after damage by a 2011 earthquake.

Calle Corredera

On the corner of Pza. San Vicente and **Calle Corredera**, the main shopping artery, is the **Columna Milenaria**, a Roman column dating from around 10 BC which marked the distance between Lorca and Cartagena on the *via Heraclea*, the Roman road from the Pyrenees to Cádiz. The Gothic **Porche de San Antonio**, the only gate remaining from the old city walls, and the best preserved in Murica, lies at the far end of C/Corredera.

Plaza de España

Colegiata de San Patricio • Free, charge for guided visit • www.lorcaturismo.es

The **Plaza de España** is the focal point of Lorca life, and holds the imposing **Colegiata de San Patricio**, which reopened in March 2017, after it was damaged by a devastating earthquake in 2011. The restoration project took six years to complete at a cost of 4.8 million euros. During the work, a huge sixteenth-century mural was uncovered, which has now been restored to its former glory and is on display for visitors to see. Originally built between the sixteenth and eighteenth centuries, the Colegiata features an enormous proto-Baroque facade and a refined Renaissance interior. The most important of the works inside is dedicated to the Virgen del Alcázar.

Nearby is the **ayuntamiento**, with its seventeenth- to eighteenth-century facade. An equally impressive front is presented by the sixteenth-century **Posito**, down a nearby side street – originally an old grain storehouse, it's now the municipal archive.

Castillo "La Fortaleza del Sol"

Charge • www.lorcatallerdeltiempo.es

Lorca's brooding thirteenth- to fourteenth-century **Castillo**, overlooking the town, has been turned into a medieval-themed tourist attraction: expect actors prancing around in medieval costume, and reenacted battle scenes. There are also some well-presented exhibits about the castle's undoubtedly formidable history.

Note that although there is a miniature train, which goes up to the castle, it's perfectly possible to walk (or drive) up through the *barrio antiguo* above the Colegiata de San Patricio.

Museo de Bordados del Paso Azul

C/Nogalte • Charge • www.mubbla.org

Timing your visit to coincide with Lorca's famous Semana Santa festivities makes for an unforgettable experience, but if you can't be here for the real thing, it's still worth visiting the **Museo del Paso Azul** to get some insight into the elaborate costumes, history and incredible devotion that the festival is known for.

Centro Regional de Artesanía

C/Lope Gisbert • Free • www.lorcatallerdeltiempo.es

The spacious **Centro de Artesanía**, part of the Palacio de Guevara, displays and sells traditional crafts, and has an area where you can watch local artists at work.

ARRIVAL AND INFORMATION

LORCA

By train and bus Hourly trains and buses connect Lorca with Murcia, although the train is cheaper and a little quicker.

Turismo Centro de Visitantes, Antiguo Convento, C/Puerta de San Ginés (Mon–Sun 10am; 902 441 914). You can also visit the municipal tourism office on Pza. España (Daily 10am–2pm; www.lorcaturismo.es).

ACCOMMODATION AND EATING

Jardines de Lorca Alameda Rafael Méndez, www.hoteljardinesdelorca.com. This hotel and spa sits in a restful residential zone, near the leafy park after which it's named. Prices dip to nearly half in low season. €€

La Parrilla de San Vicente Pza. de San Vicente 4, 968 471 287. For hearty Lorcan cuisine, including excellent grilled meats, head to this friendly, central restaurant with terrace. €€

The Balearic Islands

CALA D'HORT

13 The Balearic Islands

East of the Spanish mainland, the four chief Balearic Islands – Ibiza, Formentera, Mallorca and Menorca – maintain a character distinct from the rest of Spain and from each other. Ibiza is wholly unique: its capital, Ibiza Town, is loaded with historic interest and is a draw for thousands of clubbers and LGBTQ+ visitors, while the north of the island has a distinctly bohemian character. Tiny Formentera has even better beaches than its neighbour and makes up in rustic charm what it lacks in cultural interest. Mallorca, the largest Balearic island, has long since overcome its booze-fuelled package holiday image and these days is better known for its stunning mountain scenery, fantastic hiking and cycling trails, lovely old towns and the vibrant, cosmopolitan city of Palma. Conveniently, most of Mallorca's gaudy clichés are crammed into the mega-resorts of the Bay of Palma and the east coast, and are easy to avoid. And finally, to the east, there's Menorca – more subdued in its clientele, and here, at least, the modern resorts are kept at a safe distance from the two main towns, the capital Maó, which boasts the deepest harbour in the Med, and the charming, pocket-sized port of Ciutadella. With a mild Mediterranean climate and year-round sunshine, all four islands are particularly lovely in the winter months when they are at their quietest and most picturesque.

Access to the islands is easy from Britain and mainland Spain, with plenty of bargain-priced flights in summer, though in winter only Mallorca is really well connected. In addition, ferries and catamarans link Barcelona, Valencia and Denia with the islands, and there are plenty of inter-island ferries, too, though these can be pricey and fully booked in summer. For fuller details on **routes**, see the "Arrival and Departure" sections for individual ports and cities.

The main fly in the ointment is cost: as prime "holiday islands", the Balearics charge considerably above mainland prices for rooms, and eating out can be expensive. Travelling around by **bus**, **moped**, **scooter** and **bicycle** are all perfectly feasible, but note that car-rental companies do not allow their vehicles to be taken from one island to another.

Catalan is spoken throughout the Balearics, and each of the three main islands has a different dialect, though locals all speak Castilian (Spanish). For the visitor, confusion

AIRLINES AND FERRY COMPANIES

Most inter-island **flights** are operated by Iberia (www.iberia.com), Air Europa (www.aireuropa.com) and UepFly (www.uepfly.com/).

Ferries and **catamarans** between the islands and to the Spanish mainland are operated by Trasmed (www.trasmed.com), Baleària (https://balearia.com), Grimaldi Lines (www.grimaldi-lines.com), and GNV (www.gnv.it). Trasmapi (www.trasmapi.com), Baleària (https://balearia.com), Several operators, including Trasmapi, Baleària, Formentera Lines (www.formenteralines.com), Formentera Express (www.formenteraexpress.com) and Aquabus (www.aquabusferryboats.com) run ferries from Ibiza Town to Formentera.

DEIÀ, MALLORCA

Highlights

❶ World clubbing capital Lose yourself to the music of the globe's most sought-after DJs at one of Ibiza's legendary club nights. See page 795

❷ Ibiza sunsets Ibiza's thrills and spills do not come cheap, but, happily, the best spectacle of all is free. See page 799

❸ Formentera's beaches Sweeping white-sand beaches and pellucid waters. See page 801

❹ Palma's old town Charming Renaissance mansions are clustered in this delightful part of Mallorca's capital city. See page 804

❺ Hiking in the Tramuntana mountains An excellent network of well-signposted trails leads you through some of the loveliest scenery in Spain. See page 810

❻ Deià, Mallorca One of Mallorca's prettiest villages, perched high above the ocean. See page 812

❼ Downtown Ciutadella A delightful little Menorcan town of maze-like lanes and fine old mansions. See page 824

HIGHLIGHTS ARE MARKED ON THE MAP ON PAGE 790

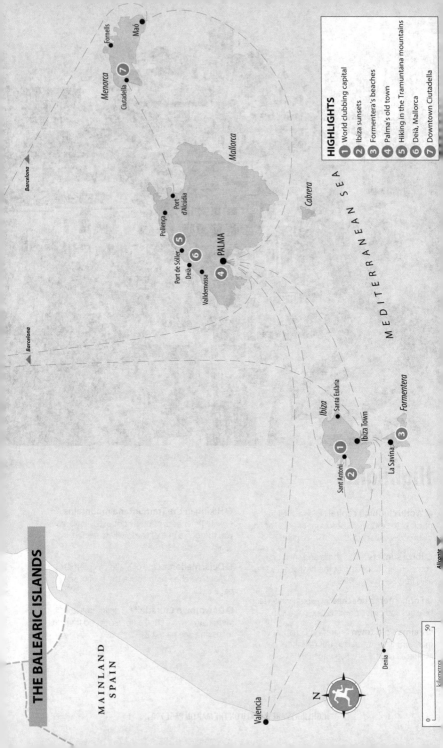

THE BALEARIC ISLANDS

MAINLAND SPAIN

MEDITERRANEAN SEA

Barcelona

Barcelona

Valencia

Denia

Alicante

Ibiza
Sant Antoni
Santa Eulària
Ibiza Town
La Savina
Formentera

PALMA
Mallorca
Pollença
Port d'Alcúdia
Port de Sóller
Deià
Valldemossa
Cabrera

Menorca
Ciutadella
Fornells
Maó

N

0   50
kilometres

HIGHLIGHTS

1 World clubbing capital
2 Ibiza sunsets
3 Formentera's beaches
4 Palma's old town
5 Hiking in the Tramuntana mountains
6 Deià, Mallorca
7 Downtown Ciutadella

13

BALEARIC CUISINE

The influx of the sea-and-sun-seeking masses has brought an **international flavour** – or lack thereof – to many Balearic cafés and restaurants. There are, perhaps, notably few dishes which are unique to the islands, but that's hardly surprising given their history of foreign invasion. Typical dishes, which are often of Catalan descent, consist of hearty stews, soups and spiced meats.

Fish and shellfish are the mainstay of most menus. *Caldereta de llagosta* (a lobster stew cooked with tomatoes) is a common speciality, especially in Menorca, as is salted cod, grilled squid, and prawns cooked in antisocial – but delicious – amounts of garlic.

As in mainland Spain, the most enjoyable way to experiment with local cuisine is by sampling smaller portions in the form of tapas, or *pintxos* (typical of the Basque country). *Pa amb oli* (bread rubbed with olive oil) is an obvious cheap snack and is typically eaten for lunch or breakfast. The sweeter-toothed, should definitely try another source of Balearic culinary pride, a spiral pastry dusted with icing sugar called an *ensaïmada*.

Menorcans were inspired into gin-making by the British, and Xoriguer gin made in Maó has a potent kick – it's often drunk as a *pomada* (gin with lemonade). Mallorcan wine – particularly red from Binissalem – is experiencing something of a resurgence and is worth seeking out.

arises from the difference between the islands' road signs and street names – which are almost exclusively in Catalan – and many of the maps on sale, which are in Castilian. In particular, note that Menorca now calls its capital Maó rather than Mahón, while both the island and town of Ibiza are usually referred to as Eivissa. In this chapter we give the Catalan name for towns, beaches and streets, except for Ibiza and Ibiza Town which are not widely known by their Catalan names outside Spain.

Ibiza

IBIZA, or **Eivissa** in Catalan, is an island of excess – beautiful, and blessed with scores of stunning cove beaches and dense pine forests. Nevertheless, it's the islanders (*eivissencs*) and their visitors who make it special. Ibiza has long attracted hedonistic characters and wealthy bohemians, and the locals remain determinedly blasé about the scantily clad fashionistas and celebrities who flock to the island today.

For years, Ibiza was the European hippy escape, but nowadays it's the extraordinary clubbing scene that most people come here to experience. The island can lay a strong claim to being the globe's **clubbing capital**, with virtually all of the world's top house DJs and many more minor players performing here during the summer season. However, visit between October and May, and you'll find a much more peaceful island – a handful of clubs and a few bars remain open through the winter.

Ibiza Town, the capital, is the obvious place to base yourself: only a short bus ride from two great beaches – **Ses Salines** and **Es Cavallet** – and crammed with bars, restaurants and boutiques. The town of **Sant Antoni** is, for the most part, a sprawling concrete mass of seedy bars and unappealing restaurants, and is best avoided beyond a few choice bars and clubs. The more pleasant, family-oriented town of **Santa Eulària** is a good base for exploring the north of the island. Around the entire shoreline, you'll find dozens of exquisite **cove beaches** (*calas*), many all but deserted even in high season, though you'll need your own transport to reach the best spots. **Inland**, the scenery is hilly and thickly wooded, dotted with a series of tiny hamlets.

Brief history
The **Carthaginians**, who founded Ibiza Town in about 654 BC, transformed the island into a major trading port, with salt as the main export. The **Romans** arrived

IBIZA

13

NIGHTLIFE	
Club Chinois	4
Las Dalias	1
DC10	6
Hï Ibiza	5
Pacha	3
Pikes Hotel	2
Ushuaïa	5

in 123 BC and the island continued to prosper. After the fall of the Roman Empire, Ibiza was conquered by the Moors in the ninth century, and their five-hundred-year reign is still evident in the island's architecture and traditional dress. But thereafter a gradual decline set in, and it wasn't until Beatniks discovered the island in the 1950s that Ibiza began to reinvent itself as one of the chicest locations in the Mediterranean.

Today, almost four million tourists flock to the much-revered "white isle" every year. However, Ibiza's tourism-driven prosperity has seen more and more coastline consumed by **rampant development**. The balance between keeping the tourists coming and maintaining the island's natural allure is keenly felt by the islanders but, for now at least, it's not hard to find a pristine cove or a quiet forested trail if you make the effort.

Ibiza Town

IBIZA TOWN (Ciutat d'Eivissa) is easily the most attractive settlement on the island. Colossal medieval walls guard the maze of cobbled streets of the UNESCO-listed old town quarter of **Dalt Vila**. The walls reach a dramatic climax at the main archway entrance, the imposing **Portal de ses Taules**. Just beyond is the elegant **Pl. de Vila**, which is lined with restaurants and cafés and makes a delightful setting for some tapas or a meal. It's well worth the walk up the steep, winding streets to the Catedral, if only to enjoy the wonderful views out over the harbour.

During summer nights, the whitewashed streets of the port area are packed with people darting between chic boutiques, street market stalls and hip bars. In winter, things are much more peaceful, and the focus of activity shifts to the area around the graceful boulevard – recently pedestrianized and much improved – Passeig de Vara de Rey.

The Catedral

Pl. de la Catedral • Free • www.obispadodeibiza.es

Today's thirteenth-century **Catedral** stands at the highest point in Dalt Vila. It's pleasingly austere, with sombre, sturdy Gothic lines supported by giant buttresses, though inside, the whitewashed decor contains somewhat trite Baroque embellishments.

IBIZA TOWN

MEDITERRANEAN SEA

Port d'Eivissa

● EATING	
La Bodega	5
Comidas Bar San Juan	2
Es Tap Nou	3
Restaurante Jardin	
La Brasa	4
El Zaguan	1

■ DRINKING AND NIGHTLIFE	
Bar 1805	2
Rock Bar	1
Tirapallà	3

■ ACCOMMODATION	
Hostal Marblau	3
Hotel Mirador Dalt Vila	2
Ibiza Boutique Guest House	1

13

Museu Arqueològic d'Eivissa i Formentera

Pl. de la Seu • Charge • https://maef.eu

Opposite the Catedral, the informative **Museu Arqueològic d'Eivissa i Formentera** has some interesting Phoenician and Carthaginian exhibits, including images of the fertility goddess Tanit. Ibiza's Moorish period is dealt with in the Centro de Interpretación Madina Yabisa (charge), which is inside La Cúria, on C/Major 2, a converted courthouse that has some flashy video displays and fine ceramics.

Outside the walls

The port areas of **Sa Penya** and **La Marina** snuggle between the harbour and the ramparts, a maze of raked passages and narrow lanes crimped by balconied, whitewashed houses. This highly atmospheric quarter is packed with boutiques, bars and restaurants. Farther to the west, the **new town** is generally of less interest, but the boulevard-like Passeig de Vara de Rey and the leafy, pedestrianized Pl. des Parc just to the south both host some fine cafés and restaurants.

ARRIVAL AND DEPARTURE   IBIZA TOWN

IBIZA AIRPORT

By plane Ibiza's international airport (www.aena.es/en/ibiza.html) is 7.5km southwest of Ibiza Town.

By bus Buses (check times at https://eivissa.tib.org) run between Ibiza Town and the airport (Route 10: times change regularly, so check online but are roughly every 15–20min in summer and every 30min in winter; €3.60) and also to/from Sant Antoni (Route 9: summer only, approximately every 30min–1hr in summer; €4) and Santa Eulària (Route 24: summer only, hourly; €4).

By taxi A taxi to Ibiza Town will cost around €19–22.

IBIZA TOWN

By bus The town's bus station is at C/Canàries 35, about 1.5km from the port, with which it is linked by regular buses. Full timetables and ticket costs are available at https://eivissa.tib.org/en/autobus. There's a good bus service between Ibiza Town, Sant Antoni, Santa Eulària, Portinatx, the airport and a few of the larger beaches. Note that services are less frequent from Nov to April.

Destinations Airport (20min); Figueretes (5min); Platja

d'en Bossa (10min); Sant Antoni (30min); Sant Carles (45min); Santa Eulària (25min); Sant Joan (35min); Sant Josep (20min); Sant Miquel (30min); Ses Salines (20min). Timetables vary considerably depending on the season, so check up-to-date times on the website (above).

By ferry There are two ferry terminals: one on Avda. Santa Eulària (for Valencia, Dénia on the Spanish mainland, as well as for Formentera, Trasmapi (www.trasmapi.com), Baleària (https://balearia.com), Formentera Lines (www.formenteralines.com) and Aquabus (www.aquabusferryboats.com), and the other at Dique de Botafoc (Barcelona and Mallorca served by Trasmed, www.trasmed.com, and Baleària, https://balearia.com,). Services run all year round but are less frequent in winter.

Destinations Barcelona (1–2 daily; 5–10hr); Denia (daily; 3hr 30min); Es Canar (3–6 daily; 1hr 25min); Formentera (every 30min; 35min); Palma (3–4 daily; 3–5hr); Platja d'en Bossa (every 30min–1hr; 20min); Santa Eulària (3–6 daily; 1hr); Talamanca (every 25–30min; 5min); Valencia (1–2 daily; 5–6hr 30min).

INFORMATION

Turisme Pl. de la Catedral (July–Sept Mon–Sat 10am–2pm & 6–9pm, Sun 10am–2pm; April–June Mon–Sat 10am–2pm & 5–8pm, Sun 10am–2pm; Oct–March Mon–Fri 9am–3pm, Sat & Sun 10am–2pm; https://turisme.eivissa.es). Helpful English-speaking staff, and good maps

and leaflets. The excellent website www.ibiza-spotlight.com is also highly informative and covers everything from clubs and parties to restaurants, beaches, walking, kayaking, cycling and yoga. Their extremely handy events and party calendars are Ibiza essentials.

ACCOMMODATION   SEE MAP PAGE 793

Hostal Marblau C/Faustí Tur I Palau, www.marblauibiza.com. Simple but comfortable rooms in a peaceful location with fantastic views out to sea, only a short walk from Dalt Vila and Passeig Vara de Rey. €€€

Hotel Mirador Dalt Vila Plaza de España 4, www.hotelmiradoribiza.com. Family mansion house converted

into a luxury, five-star hotel located within the walls of Dalt Vila. Includes a small swimming pool, a terrace bar, an excellent restaurant and one of the most important art collections in Ibiza. €€€€

★ **Ibiza Boutique Guest House** Passeig Vara de Rey 7–3°, https://hibiza.com. Housed in an attractive former mansion, the creatively decorated rooms echo the building's grandiose charm. You'll need to climb several flights of stairs but there's a winch for your bags. Rooms all have washbasins; most bathrooms are shared. Prices increase dramatically in high season. €€€

EATING
SEE MAP PAGE 793

★ **La Bodega** C/Bisbe Torres Mayans 2, 971 192 740. In a wonderful setting overlooking the walls of Dalt Vila, this old warehouse has been stylishly converted blending historic architecture with eclectic, bohemian decor. It's a fun, buzzy place to kick off an evening with tapas and cocktails. €€

★ **Comidas Bar San Juan** C/G. de Montgri 8, 971 311 603. Cosy, atmospheric bistro restaurant with dimly lit rooms and excellent-value Spanish and Ibizan cuisine (paella, calamari, *gambas*) in the Dalt Vila. They don't accept reservations to arrive early and expect to share tables. €€

Es Tap Nou C/de Madrid 18, 971 399 841. Lively juice and salad bar attached to a fruit and veg shop a 5min walk from Vara de Rey. The mouthwatering juices range from fresh orange to pineapple, papaya and mango. Also serves salads, *tostadas* and *bocatas* and takeaways. €

Restaurante Jardin La Brasa C/Pere Sala 3, https://labrasaibiza.com. Classy restaurant with a delightful garden terrace shaded by plants and palm trees. The innovative menu concentrates on Mediterranean fish and grilled meat. It's a good place to splash out, particularly on the grilled lobster. €€€

El Zaguan C/Bartolomé Roselló 15, http://elzaguan. es. The decor is not glamorous but locals flock here for excellent, authentic tapas, *pintxos* and *raciones*, such as octopus *a feira*, *patatas bravas* and beef chops, at good value prices. Reservations not possible. €€

DRINKING AND NIGHTLIFE
SEE MAP PAGE 793

Ibiza's **bar and club scene** is nothing short of incendiary. Drink prices at the island's clubs are astronomical but Ibiza Town offers no shortage of reasonably priced bars to get the night started. Stylish bars line the eastern end of C/

CLUBBING IN IBIZA

Some of the globe's most spectacular **clubs** are spread across the southern half of Ibiza. Clubs cost around €30–100 to get in and are open between midnight and 6am – try to blag a guest pass from one of the bars on the harbourfront. The Discobus (May–Sept midnight–6.30am; €4-5; https://discobusibiza.com) ferries partygoers from Ibiza Town to the island's major clubs, leaving from the main port. The highly recommended website www.ibiza-spotlight.com has a party calendar and full details of club nights, events and tickets.

NIGHTLIFE, SEE MAP PAGE 792

Las Dalias San Carles de Peralta, Ibiza Town–Sant Carles road, km12, https://lasdalias.es. This bar-cum-venue with a garden terrace has a legendary place in Ibiza's hippy scene past and present. There's a Saturday hippy market and a summer night market, as well as live music and *Akasha* club nights.

DC10 Carretera de Las Salinas, Sant Josep de sa Talaia, https://dc10ibiza.com. Famed for its underground vibe and after-hours parties, *DC10* is out by the airport – its former open-air areas have been roofed to mask the noise of planes taking off. A long-term favourite for serious hedonists into electro music.

Club Chinois Passeig Joan Carlos 1, 17, Marina Botafoch, www.clubchinoisibiza.com. The dazzling gold and velvet interior, designed to evoke Shanghai in the 1920s, is deliciously louche, and the sound system is among the best on the island. Popular nights include TRIP, BOHO Experience and La Troya.

★ **Hï Ibiza** Platja d'en Bossa, www.hiibiza.com. Regularly voted the best club in the world (including by DJ Mag), this has two main rooms, three outdoor areas, stunning light shows and a new set every night featuring the full spectrum of electronic music.

Pacha Avda. 8 d'Agost 27, Ibiza Town, https://pacha. com. The *grande dame* of the scene and a world-renowned clubbing brand. Multiple rooms playing dance, funk and soul as well as a beautiful garden terrace along with visits from the world's top DJs, including Pete Tong, Peggy Gou and Solomun.

★ **Pikes Hotel** Camí sa Vorera s/n, Sant Antoni de Portmany, www.pikesibiza.com. Legendary hotel/party venue run by the Ibiza Rocks crew famous for its (in)famous guests (George Michael, Grace Jones, Freddie Mercury, among others), the poolside bar (of *Club Tropicana* fame), an eclectic array of artwork and super-fun party nights. Free to get in with guest list; see website.

Ushuaïa Platja d'en Bossa 10, 971 396 710, http://ushuaiabeachhotel.com. A firm fixture on the Ibiza club scene, famous for big names, daytime clubbing, a gorgeous pool area and extraordinary stage productions.

13

Garijo, while the café/bars of Pl. del Parque are best for a quiet beer. Check www.ibiza-spotlight.com for up-to-date opening times and party nights.

BARS

Bar 1805 C/Santa Lucía 7, Sa Penya, http://bar1805ibiza. com. French canteen famed for its absinthe cocktails, including the signature "Green Beast", served up by Ibiza visionary and cocktail maestro Charles Vexenat to a backdrop of electro-swing, rock and jazz.

Rock Bar C/Cipriano Garijo 14, Ibiza Port, www.instagram. com/therockbaribiz. This British-run island institution is a second home for characterful expats and pre-clubbers. Staff are friendly and you'll meet fellow fun-seekers.

Tirapallà C/Alfons XII 10, www.instagram.com/tirapalla ibiza. Soak up the stunning views of the Dalt Vila from this laidback rooftop bar, as you enjoy the top-notch cocktails from expert mixologists.

DIRECTORY

Boat trips Float Your Boat, Passeig de la Mar, San Antonio Abad. Boat trips to less accessible beaches and coves around Ibiza, from €39 per person (www.floatyourboatibiza.com).

Car rental Avis (www.avis.com) and Hertz (www.hertz. es) both have offices at the airport) Class Rent-a-Car, Avda. Cala Llonga 131 (971 307 892, http://classrentacar.es) is also recommended and has offices around the island. The website http://doyouspain.com is an online aggregator of the cheapest car hire companies on the island.

Consulates UK, Avda. d'Isidor Macabich 45, www.gov.

uk, (by appointment only using the online contact form at www.contact.service.csd.fcdo.gov.uk),

Hospital Hospital Can Misses, C/Corona 32–36, Can Misses, 2km west of the port (971 397 000).

Moped rental Cooltra, Avda, Pere Matutes Noguera, 109, Platja d'en Bossa, plus other outlets around the island (672 662 990, https://cooltra.com).

Post office Avda. d'Isidor Macabich 67 (971 399 76, www. correos.es, Mon–Fri 8.30am–2pm, Sat 8.30am–1pm).

Taxi Eivissa Taxi (971 333 333).

The beaches around Ibiza Town

You'll find sea and sand close to Ibiza Town at **Figueretes**, **Platja d'en Bossa** and **Talamanca** beaches, but the first two of these are built-up continuations of the capital (Figueretes is just a 15-minute walk from Ibiza Town) and only at Talamanca is there any peace and quiet. Regular buses and boat taxis run to all three from Ibiza port.

Ses Salines and Es Cavallet

To the **south of Ibiza Town**, stretching from the airport to the sea, are thousands of acres of **salt flats**. For two thousand years, Ibiza's prosperity was dependent on these salt fields (*salines*), a trade that was vital to the Carthaginians. Even today, some salt production continues. Buses from the Ibiza Town bus station leave regularly for the gorgeous beach of **SES SALINES**, whose fine white sand arcs around a bay, the crystal-clear waters fringed by pines and dunes. The beach also has a handful of superb beach bars. From Ses Salines, it's a brief walk through the dunes to **ES CAVALLET**, a popular nudist beach also favoured by LGBTQ+ visitors.

| ACCOMMODATION | THE BEACHES AROUND IBIZA TOWN |

Hostal Boutique La Curandera Salinas Carretera Sa Canal km5, Ses Salines, 971 307 640, http://boutique hostalsalinas.com. Small, family-run sustainable boutique hotel close to Salinas beach. Rooms are tastefully decorated, some with a large terrace overlooking the nature reserve. They offer a range of massages and holistic treatments, a sacred space and a healing cuisine. €€€€

Hostal Giramundo C/Ramón Muntaner 55, Figueretes, https://hostalgiramundoibiza.com. A brightly coloured, backpacker haven very close to Figueretes beach and a 15min walk from the centre. Bonuses include lockers, a

DVD room and a popular in-house bar. Room prices drop significantly in winter months. Dorms €, doubles €€€

OD Ocean Drive Port Deportivo, Playa de Talamanca-Marina Botafoch, on the north side of Ibiza's harbour, www.od-hotels.com/hotel-ocean-drive-ibiza. This luxury boutique hotel is one of Ibiza's most stylish. Its pristine, tasteful rooms are located across the bay from Dalt Vila. Perks include getting your name on the guest lists at the island's most sought-after club nights. Prices drop dramatically outside July and August. €€€€

EATING AND DRINKING

El Chiringuito Playa Es Cavallet, www.elchiringuitoibiza.

com. A classy beachside café-restaurant which serves

everything from breakfast, coffees and cocktails to full meals. The lengthy menu features everything from gourmet beef burgers to *spaghetti frutti di mare* to traditional local favourite: seabream baked in rock salt, which you can enjoy on the terrace facing the waves. €€€

★ **Fish Shack** Sa Punta, Talamanca. Humble shack on the beach serving superb fish. With no telephone number or website, reservations are not possible and there's no menu – only the freshest fish available from the market that morning is served. If available, try the swordfish fillet or the prawns. Everything is cooked on the grill with olive oil and garlic and served with salad. €€

The east coast

Head northeast from Ibiza Town and it's 15km to **SANTA EULÀRIA DES RIU**, a pleasant town with a plush marina but few obvious sights, though it does boast an attractive church – a fortified whitewashed sixteenth-century construction perched on a hilltop to the west of the town centre. **SANT CARLES**, 7km to the north, is an agreeable one-horse village.

East of Sant Carles the road passes through burnt-red fields of olive, almond and carob trees to several almost untouched beaches. **Cala Llenya**, a broad sandy cove with sparkling waters, is the nearest, and is popular with families. Tiny **Cala Mastella**, 2km farther north, is a supremely peaceful spot, with a diminutive sandy beach and crystal-clear sheltered water. Just north of Cala Mastella is **Cala Boix**, another stunning sandy cove, a little larger and more exposed.

Continuing north from Cala Boix, the coastal road follows an exhilarating, serpentine route above the shore, through thick pine forests and past the lovely nudist beach of **Aguas Blancas**.

ACCOMMODATION   THE EAST COAST

Aguas de Ibiza C/Salvador Camacho s/n, Santa Eulària, www.aguasdeibiza.com. Stylish five-star hotel, restaurant and spa that manages to be both luxurious and relaxed. The rooftop bar and terrace (open to non-guests) offer fantastic views across the beautiful bay of Santa Eulària. €€€€

La Bohemia del Río C/del Sol 9, Santa Eulària, www.labohemiadelrio.com. In a quiet but central location in Santa Eulària is this lovely *hostal*, with a bougainvillea-clad terrace, small swimming pool and a dozen charming bedrooms. Adults only. €€€

EATING AND DRINKING

Anita's Bar Sant Carles, C/Venda de Peralta 21, 971 335 090. A milestone in Ibiza's bohemian past, this vine-shaded patio remains a popular meeting point and has an inexpensive menu of burgers, pizza, tapas and a good range of drinks, including its own famous *hierbas* liqueur. The art on the walls allegedly dates from the times when 1960s artists donated their works in exchange for sustenance. €

★ **Babylon Beach** C/Bartomeu Tur Clapés 20, Santa Eulària, www.instagram.com/babylonbeach. Perhaps the nicest beach bar in northeast Ibiza. Tables and rustic loungers overlook crystal-clear waters, the menu focuses on local, organic produce and the bread is home-made. As well as great burgers, they also offer delicious veggie and vegan options. There's also a beach-shack bar, kayaks, a pontoon into the sea and a play area for kids. €€

Project Social C/San Lorenzo 22, Santa Eulària, www.projectsocial.co/. Popular burger and street-food restaurant with a hipster edge that's missing elsewhere in family-oriented Santa Eulària. Try their "Tourist" burger (beef patty, stilton, crispy bacon) or the "Pig & Ting" (pulled pork, coleslaw), washed down with a craft beer or a cocktail. €€

The north

Twenty kilometres from Ibiza Town, **SANT JOAN** is a pretty hilltop village home to a typically minimalist, whitewashed Ibizan church, a sprinkling of café-bars and a lively Sunday morning market. North of the village are some wonderful beaches, especially remote **Cala d'en Serra**, a tiny, exquisite sandy cove, with turquoise waters perfect for snorkelling. **Benirràs**, 9km northwest of Sant Joan, is another beautiful bay, backed by high, wooded cliffs. This is one of Ibiza's prime hippy-centric beaches – dozens gather here to burn herbs and pound drums to the setting sun on Sundays.

13

The next village to the west is **SANT MIQUEL**, where there's an imposing fortified church and a number of simple tapas bars – try *Es Pi Ver* for an inexpensive meal. The once astonishingly beautiful inlet at **PORT DE SANT MIQUEL**, 3km north of the village, has been badly mauled by developers, but outside high season it's not too packed here. Walk 10mins over the headland to the left as you're facing the shore, and you'll reach a quieter bay, **Es Caló d'es Moltons**, which has its own *chiringuito*, *Utopia*, specializing in grilled seafood and cocktails.

ACCOMMODATION — THE NORTH

★ **Agroturismo Atzaró** Sant Joan km15, https://atzaro. com. Serene countryside retreat dotted with orange trees, complete with a heavenly spa, various bars and a top-notch restaurant. Rooms are exquisitely decorated and the grounds breathtakingly beautiful. €€€€
Can Planells Venda de Rubio 2, near Sant Miquel, www.canplanells.com. Located away from the coast, this sumptuous *agroturismo* has spacious and chic but rustic rooms that are nestled into a rural villa that has its own

extensive grounds and a tempting pool. €€€
Hotel Gard du Nord C/de sa Calla 11, www.thegiri destinations.com/ibiza/gare-du-nord. Small boutique hotel with nine individually decorated, light, bright rooms, all en suite and with balcony. Guests have access to the spa and a charming bar and garden restaurant serving Spanish-fusion specialities at their adjoining hotel property, the *Giri Residence*. €€€

EATING AND DRINKING

The Giri Café Pl. España 5, Sant Joan, https://giricafe.com. A relatively small entrance just off the main road running through Sant Joan hides this large, elegant restaurant with shady terrace and garden tables. The separate breakfast, lunch and dinner menus are plentiful, with a focus on seasonal, local and sustainable produce. €€€
La Luna Nell'Orto C/de Missa 16, Sant Miquel, www. lalunanellorto.com. Exceptional Italian food served in a romantic garden attached to a traditional, rustic *casa payesa*, complete with candles, flowers, fig trees and

occasional live music. Famous for its home-made pasta, such as the squid-ink tagliatelle with seafood, and other Mediterranean dishes, such as the slow-cooked lamb. €€€
★ **La Paloma** C/Can Pou 4, Sant Llorenc, https://paloma ibiza.com. Extremely pretty and popular garden restaurant serving a wide range of Mediterranean and Israeli dishes during the day (such as minced lamb stuffed focaccia and fresh salads) and a more expensive Italian menu at night. The wine list features primarily organic wines and much of the produce is sourced from the surrounding garden. €€€

The west and south coast

For years unchallenged at the top of Europe's costa hooligania league table, the package resort of **SANT ANTONI DE PORTMANY** on the island's west coast is trying hard to shake off its tarnished image, with a revamped marina. Nevertheless, the high-rise concrete skyline and gritty British pubs of the "West End" aren't at all enticing. Hordes of young British clubbers flock to San An for its plethora of bars within easy staggering distance – the Sunset Strip on the western side of town is the most appealing place for a drink.

Beaches near Sant Antoni

South of Sant Antoni, it's just a few kilometres to some exquisite coves. Sheltered **Cala Bassa** gets packed with holidaying families in high season, but it does have a campsite, while the more exposed beach of **Cala Comte** is less crowded, and is a beautiful spot to while away an afternoon. The most beguiling beach in the Balearics, **Cala d'Hort**, is in the extreme southwest of the island, and it has an unspoiled, quiet sand-and-pebble shoreline plus three good, moderately priced seafood restaurants. From the shore there are mesmeric vistas of **Es Vedrà**, an incisor-shaped 378-metre-high islet revered by islanders and island hippies alike, and the subject of various myths and legends – including a claim to be Homer's island of the sirens.

Taking the scenic southern road to Ibiza Town you pass via **SANT JOSEP**, a pretty village with a selection of café-restaurants. A handful of beautiful *calas*, such as **Carbó** and **Molí**, are a 15min drive from Sant Josep, the pick of the bunch being **Cala Vedella**, for its calm waters, sunsets and a great restaurant.

INFORMATION, ARRIVAL AND DEPARTURE

Tourist office Passeig de Ses Fonts 1, Sant Antoni (971 343 363, https://visit.santantoni.net).

By bus The modern bus station (971 340 091, https://ibizabus.com) on C/Londres in Sant Antoni is located a couple of blocks behind the "egg" roundabout, on the corner where the main road parallel to the beach meets the road that runs alongside the marina.

Destinations Buses leave Sant Antoni for Ibiza Town every 30–120min 7am–11.30pm, and there are frequent departures to the *calas* Vedella, Comte and Tarida (May–Oct). See https://ibizabus.com for full schedules.

THE WEST AND SOUTH COAST

By ferry Most ferry services to the island arrive and depart from Ibiza Town but Baleària (www.balearia.com) offer a mainland service which calls at Sant Antoni. The port is easily accessible at the end of the marina on the north side of the bay.

Destinations Barcelona (1–2 daily in summer; 8hr 30min); Dénia (2 daily in summer; 2hr 30min–4hr).

Boat trips Cruceros Portmany (www.crucerosportmany. com) do regular trips to Cala Bassa, Comte and Formentera as well as excursions around Es Vedrà.

ACCOMMODATION

Cala Bassa Carretera Cala Bassa, 971 344 599, www.campingcalabassa.com. Just 250m from the beach, this well-established campsite has mobile homes and wooden bungalows, ready erected tents as well as camping pitches. Camping €, bungalows €€

Hostal La Torre Cap Negret 25, Sant Antoni, www.latorre

ibiza.com. Well-located hotel with clean, comfy rooms, fantastic sea views and possibly the best sunsets in Ibiza. Central Sant Antoni is 3km away, Cala Gració a short walk. DJs play from sunset to midnight every night at the bar-restaurant in summer. €€€

EATING

★ **Bon Sol** On the beachfront at Cala Vedella, Sant Josep, 971 808 213. Beachside restaurant offering superb Italian food, gorgeous views over Vedella bay and one of the best sunset vantage points in Ibiza. They offer a wide range of home-made pasta dishes, pizzas and more, and you can finish up with their own ice-cream. €€€

Can Limo Carretera Sant Josep km12.5, Sant Josep, www.canlimoibiza.com. Creative and original Peruvian/Asian fusion restaurant. With a regularly changing but constantly appealing menu of tasty tapas and small dishes to share, it's worth several repeat visits. €€€

Rita's Cantina Paseo Marítimo, Sant Antoni, https://ritas

ibiza.com. Stylish, high-ceilinged, airy and atmospheric bar-restaurant that stands apart from its gaudy, white-plastic neighbours on the Sant Antoni strip. Dutch-run and popular with locals and holiday-makers alike, *Rita's Cantina* is famous for its breakfasts and Indonesian food, such as the *nasi goreng*. €€

Sunset Ashram Cala Comte, www.sunsetashram.com. Looking out over the beach, this is a beautiful spot to dine at as the sun sinks into the Med. International dishes include a range of salads, curries, steaks and fresh fish. It also has a cocktail bar and nightly DJ sets. €€€

DRINKING AND NIGHTLIFE

Blue Marlin Playa Es Jondal, https://bluemarlinibiza.com. A suave beach club in an idyllic spot, attracting top DJs. A great spot for a cocktail, it also has a restaurant, though meals will set you back over €80 a head.

Café Mambo C/Vara de Rey 40, Sant Antoni, https://cafemamboibiza.com. A classic haunt on the Sunset Strip with a deserved reputation for ambient tunes and strong cocktails. Famed for its big-name DJs, party nights and amazing sunsets.

Ibiza Rocks Hotel C/Cervantes 27, Sant Antoni, www.ibizarocks.com. The hotel is no looker but it's the focal point of the Ibiza Rocks brand, hosting the weekly Ibiza Rocks gigs on Tuesdays (past acts have featured Bastille, Clean Bandit and The Kooks) and regular parties in the central swimming pool area on Tues, Thurs & Sun.

TOP 5 IBIZA SUNSETS

Ibiza's southwest coast is home not only to some of the best beaches, but is also the prime location for watching the island's famous fiery red, orange, purple and gold sunsets. Here are our favourite vantage points:

Benirrás beach see page 797
Cala d'Hort, Sant Josep see page 798
Es Vedrà see page 798
Hostal La Torre see page 799
Restaurante Bon Sol, Cala Vedella see page 799

13

★ **Racó Verd** Pl. de la Iglesia, Sant Josep, www.racoverd ibiza.com. There is nightly live music at this bar-restaurant whose outdoor terrace boasts a thousand-year-old olive tree. Music (from 10pm) varies nightly from rock to world music and flamenco. The café-bar serves Mexican food such as tacos and quesadillas as well as wraps, salads and a variety of fruit juices (and cocktails).

Formentera

Just eleven nautical miles south of Ibiza Town, **FORMENTERA** (population around 12,000) is the smallest of the four main Balearic Islands, measuring just 20km from east to west. Formentera's history more or less parallels that of Ibiza, though between 1348 and 1697 it was left uninhabited for fear of pirate raids. Like Ibiza, it was a key part of the 1960s hippy trail (Pink Floyd made an album here), and the island retains a bohemian character.

Formentera is very arid, and mainly covered in rosemary, which grows wild everywhere; it also crawls with thousands of brilliant-green **Ibiza wall lizards** (*Podarcis pityusensis*), which flourish in parched scrubland. The economy is tourism-based, taking advantage of some of Spain's longest, whitest and least-crowded beaches. Development has been limited, and visitors come here seeking escape rather than sophistication. Nude sunbathing is the norm just about everywhere, except in Es Pujols.

La Savina

There's nothing much to keep visitors in **LA SAVINA**, Formentera's only port. Along from the ferry port, there's a smart marina which fills with a fleet of gleaming yachts in

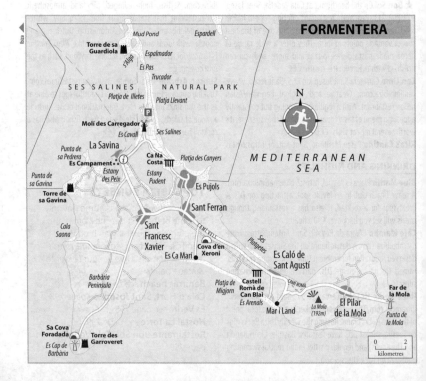

the summer. Beyond that, though, it's a rather functional place with little more than car-rental kiosks and unappealing wholesale stores.

Platja de Illetes and Espalmador

Northwest of La Savina are the absolutely spectacular sands of **Platja de Illetes**, whose clear waters are ideal for watersports and diving. Across a narrow channel lies the uninhabited island of **Espalmador**, a pristine nature reserve, where there's another great beach and the water is turquoise enough to trump any Caribbean brochure. Excursion boats are no longer allowed to serve Espalmador, so the only option is to rent a paddle board, boat or kayak. Don't be tempted to wade across (forbidden, as large signs attest), as currents are deceptive and dangerous.

Sant Francesc Xavier

The island capital, **SANT FRANCESC XAVIER**, is 4km inland from La Savina and serves as Formentera's commercial and shopping centre, with a handful of restaurants, cafés, street stalls and a supermarket, plus the island's main post office, at Pl. de sa Constitució 1. The only real sight here is the mighty fortified **church**, now stripped of its defensive cannon, which sits in the large central square.

Sant Ferran and Platja de Migjorn

There is little to see in the sleepy village of **SANT FERRAN** except a small nineteenth-century church. From here it is a short journey south to one of Formentera's best beaches. Taking up most of Formentera's southern coastline, **Platja de Migjorn** is a sweeping bay with 5km of pale sands and crystalline waters.

Es Pujols

From Sant Ferran, a side road leads to **ES PUJOLS**, Formentera's main resort development – though it's tiny, and tame by mainland standards. Here you'll find two fine sandy beaches and clear, shallow waters, plenty of good seafood restaurants and some late-night bars.

The east

As you head eastwards from Sant Ferran, dusty pathways and tracks – well worth exploration – dart off from the main island road to quieter spots along Platja de Migjorn. After about 6km, the road passes through **Es Caló de Sant Agustí**, a tiny inlet with a café, restaurant and hotel. The road continues eastwards through pine forests as it skirts the northern flanks of **La Mola**, at 192m the island's highest point. After the drowsy little town of **EL PILAR DE LA MOLA**, the road straightens for 2km to the **Far de La Mola** (lighthouse), which stands on cliffs high above the blue ocean. It was here that Jules Verne was inspired to write his *Off on a Comet* as he gazed into the clear night sky.

ARRIVAL AND INFORMATION   **FORMENTERA**

Ferries Several operators, including Trasmapi (www. trasmapi.com), Formentera Lines (www.formenteralines. com), Formentera Express (www.formenteraexpress.com) and Aquabus (www.aquabusferryboats.com) run ferries from Ibiza Town to La Savina. The journey takes about 30 minutes. There are also sailings from Denia, Valencia with Baleária (www.balearia.com).

Turisme Estación Marítima de Formentera, La Savina (May to mid-Oct Mon–Fri 9am–7pm, Sat & Sun 9am–3pm; mid-Oct to April Mon–Fri 10am–2pm & 5–7pm; 971 321 201, www.formentera.es), can help with accommodation and cycle routes, and provide maps.

13

GETTING AROUND

By bus There's a good bus service from the port of arrival, La Savina, to the main settlements; timetable on https://bus formentera.com. There are two tourist routes (L3, each colour-coded): both the blue (€15 return) and yellow route (€10) go to Illetes, but the blue route also takes in the Platja Migjorn.
Destinations La Savina to: Es Pujols (every 20–30min; 10min); Faro de La Mola (6 daily; 50min); San Ferran (every 45min;15min); Sant Francesc Xavier (every 45min; 10min). Single tickets cost from €2.25 to €3.20, depending on the distance travelled.

By bike, scooter and car Getting about by bicycle (including electric bikes) is very popular, since apart from the hill of La Mola, the island is extremely flat; there are several rental places by the ferry dock and in Es Pujols (€15–30 per day). Scooters and cars are also available but be warned that some of the tracks down to the beaches are very uneven and the terrain is covered with sand.

ACCOMMODATION

It's essential to make an **advance reservation** between June and September, as the bulk of the island's limited supply of beds is snapped up early. Off-season prices can be less than half of those in July and August. Camping is not permitted anywhere on the island.

Es Marès Hotel & Spa C/Santa María 15, Sant Francesc, https://hotelesmares.com. Everything from the bright, white walls to the natural, nautical materials used in the furnishings and decor make this hotel a perfect reflection of the island paradise outside. As well as the spa, there's a small pool and garden terrace and a restaurant serving contemporary Mediterranean cuisine. €€€€

Gecko Beach Club Platja de Migjorn, Ca Mari, https://geckobeachclub.com. If you want to enjoy Formentera's simple charms from a sophisticated base, this stylish hotel is one of the island's best. A picture-postcard location on the beach, with gleaming floors, a garden-like pool area, an excellent restaurant, yoga classes and massage sessions. €€€€

Hostal Can Rafalet C/ Sant Agustí 1, Es Caló, https://hostal-rafalet.com. This hotel overlooks a tiny fishing harbour, and its spacious rooms afford magnificent sea views. With welcoming staff and a good bar and restaurant (open to the public), it's the perfect place to unwind. €€€

Hostal Illes Pitiüses Avda. de Juan Castelló Guasch 48, Sant Ferran, www.formenterapassport.com/alojamientos/hostal-illes-pitiuses. A long-established family-run hotel on the main cross-island road. Rooms are comfortable and pleasantly old-fashioned; all have satellite TV, private bathrooms and a/c, but breakfast isn't included. €€

Hostal La Savina Avda. Mediterránea 22–40, La Savina, www.hostal-lasavina.com. This hip *hostal* is right on the beach – rooms, with their own fridges, are bright and fresh, some with balconies facing the sea, and there's a good restaurant and cocktail bar downstairs. €€€

Hotel Voramar Avda. Miramar 33, Es Pujols, www.voramarformentera.com. Friendly, good-value mid-market hotel a short walk from the beach and close to all bars and restaurants in Es Pujols, with a pleasant garden pool and family-friendly atmosphere. €€€

EATING AND DRINKING

★ **Blue Bar** C/San Ferran-La Mola, Platja de Migjorn km8, https://bluebarformentera.com. Chilled-out beachside bar-restaurant with a menu of tasty Mediterranean dishes, as well as pastas and salads. With the ambient tunes and endless sea views, it's the perfect place to enjoy a cocktail under the stars. DJs and/or live music on Saturday evenings. €€

Fonda Platé C/Sant Jaume 1, San Francesc Xavier, 971 322 313. A welcoming, traditional café that has been going for more than a century, with a large interior, a charming vine-shaded patio and a buzzy, local feel. They serve up tapas, sandwiches and light meals. €€

★ **Macondo** C/Major 67, Sant Ferran, https://macondo formentera.com. This highly recommended pizzeria serves giant pizzas and delicious home-made pasta dishes. Gets lively at night when there's live music. €€

DIRECTORY

Car rental Autos Ca Marí, 971 328 855, https://auto scamariformentera.com. Offices in La Savina, Platja de Migjorn and Es Caló.

Emergencies For the police and fire brigade, call 092 and for general emergencies dial 112.

Hospital L'Hospital de Formentera, Vénda des Brolls s/n, Sant Francesc, 971 321 212.

Taxi Radio-Taxi 971 322 342.

Mallorca

Few Mediterranean holiday spots have been as often and as unfairly maligned as **MALLORCA**. Until recently, the island was commonly perceived as little more than

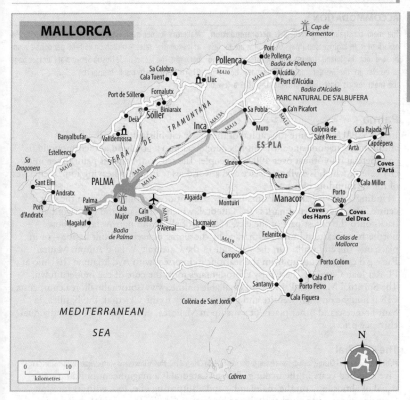

sun, sex, booze and high-rise, an image spawned by the helter-skelter development of the 1960s. In fact, the spread of development, even after fifty years, is essentially confined to the **Badia de Palma** (Bay of Palma), a thirty-kilometre strip flanking the island capital, and a handful of mega-resorts notching the east coast. These resorts are self-contained, remote and so completely at odds with the beguiling beauty of the rest of the island that it's easy to ignore them altogether.

Palma itself, the Balearics' one real city, is a bustling, historic place whose grand mansions and magnificent Gothic Catedral defy the expectations of many visitors. And so does the northwest coast, where visitors delight in the rearing peaks of the rugged **Serra de Tramuntana**, beautiful cove beaches, monasteries at Valldemossa and Lluc, and a string of delightful old towns and villages – such as Deià, Sóller and Pollença. There's a startling variety and physical beauty to the land, which has drawn tourists to visit and well-heeled expatriates to settle here since the nineteenth century, including artists and writers of many descriptions, from Robert Graves to Roger McGough.

GETTING AROUND   MALLORCA

Public transport Palma lies at the hub of an extensive public transport system – the latest timetables are on www.tib.org for island-wide transport or www.emtpalma. cat for local Palma transport. Bus services link the capital to all Mallorca's principal settlements and there are even a couple of train lines – one, a beautiful ride up through the mountains to Sóller (see page 811), is an attraction

in itself. And with your own transport, Palma is within two hours' drive of anywhere on the island. Hiring a bike is also a popular way to seek out the island's quieter spots.

Taxis can work out a reasonable deal, too, if you're travelling in a group – the fare across the island to Port de Pollença from Palma is about €100 for four people, for instance.

13

ACCOMMODATION

The main constraint for travellers is **accommodation**, or lack of it. In high season (May–Oct) rooms are far less booked out in inland towns and villages. Everything is quieter in the winter months but many hotels in the main resorts close. Bear in mind also that a few of Mallorca's former **monasteries** rent out renovated cells at inexpensive rates – reckon on €50–60 per double room per night. The Monestir de Nostra Senyora at Lluc (see page 814) is reachable by public transport.

Palma

In 1983, **PALMA** became the capital of the newly established Balearic Islands autonomous region, since when it has developed into a go-ahead and cosmopolitan commercial hub of just over 400,000 people. The self-confidence is plain to see in the city centre, which is a vibrant place and a world away from the heaving tourist enclaves of the surrounding bay.

Finding your way around Palma is fairly straightforward once you're in the city centre. The obvious landmark is the **Catedral**, which dominates the waterfront and backs onto the oldest part of the city, a cluster of alleys and narrow lanes whose northern and eastern limits are marked by the zigzag of avenues built beside – or in place of – the city walls. On the west side of the Catedral, Avda. d'Antoni Maura/ Passeig d'es Born cuts up from the seafront to intersect with Avda. Jaume III/Unio at Pl. Rei Joan Carles I. These busy thoroughfares form the core of the modern town. The Spiritual Mallorca Palma card (available online: www.spiritualmallorca.com) costs €18 if bought on their website and gives you entry to the Catedral, the Basílica de Sant Francesc and other places of worship in Mallorca, or see page 804 for individual entrance prices.

The Catedral

Pl. de la Almoina s/n • Charge, includes admission to the Museu de la Catedral and Museu Diocesano • https://catedraldemallorca.org/

Five hundred years in the making, Palma's **Catedral** is a magnificent building – the equal of almost any on the mainland – and a surprising one, too, with its interior featuring *modernista* touches designed by Antoni Gaudí. The original church was built following the Christian Reconquest of the city, and the site taken, in fulfilment of a vow by Jaume I, was that of the Moorish Great Mosque. Essentially Gothic, with massive exterior buttresses to take the weight off the pillars within, the church derives its effect through its sheer height, impressive from any angle but startling when glimpsed from the waterside esplanade. On the way into the church, you pass through three rooms of assorted ecclesiastical bric-a-brac, which comprise the **Museu de la Catedral**.

Palau de l'Almudaina

Pl. de la Almoina s/n • Charge, free entry for EU citizens showing their passport on Wed & Sun from 3–7pm • https://www. patrimonionacional.es/visita/palacio-real-de-la-almudaina

Opposite the Catedral entrance stands the **Palau de l'Almudaina**, originally the palace of the Moorish walis (governors) and later of the Mallorcan kings. The interior has been painstakingly restored, but its rabbit warren of rooms are relatively modest, the main decorative highlight being a handful of admirable Flemish tapestries, each devoted to classical themes.

Palau March Museu

C/Palau Reial 18 • Charge • www.fundacionbmarch.es

Along C/Palau Reial stands the opulent late 1930s townhouse of the Mallorcan magnate and speculator Joan March (1880–1962), opened to the public as the **Palau March Museu**. The highlight here is the splendid Italianate courtyard, which is used to display a potpourri of modern art drawn from the March collection. There are two Henry Moore sculptures, a Rodin torso and a fetchingly eccentric *Orgue del Mar* (Organ of the Sea) by Xavier Corbero.

Museu de Mallorca
C/Portella 5 • Free • 971 177 838

Within the medina-like maze of old town streets at the back of the Catedral is the Museu de Mallorca. Occupying one of the many fifteenth- and sixteenth-century patrician mansions that dot this section of town, the museum holds an extensive collection of Mallorcan archeological finds as well as some exceptionally fine medieval religious paintings, including further examples of the work of the Mallorcan Primitives.

Basílica de Sant Francesc
Pl. Sant Francesc 7 • Charge • 971 712 695

Occupying, oddly enough, the site of the old Moorish soap factory, the **Basílica de Sant Francesc** is the finest among the city's bevy of medieval churches. It's a substantial building, founded towards the end of the thirteenth century, and the main facade displays a stunning severity of style, with a great sheet of dressed sandstone stretching up to an arcaded balcony and pierced by a gigantic rose window. Entered via a fine trapezoidal Gothic cloister, the cavernous interior is a little disappointing, but you can't miss the monumental **high altar**, a gaudy affair illustrative of High Baroque.

Baluard Museu d'Art Modern i Contemporani
Pl. Porta de S.Catalina 10 • Charge • www.esbaluard.org

On the west side of the city centre, the **Passeig Mallorca** is bisected by the deep, walled watercourse that once served as a moat and is now an especially handsome feature of the city. One of the old bastions overlooking the watercourse now houses the **Baluard Museu d'Art Modern i Contemporani** (Modern & Contemporary Art Museum), where pride of place goes to a rare and unusual sample of Picasso ceramics, most memorably a striking white, ochre and black vase-like piece entitled *Big Bird Corrida*. Take time, too, to explore the town walls immediately around the museum, remodelled into stylish walkways and viewpoints with great vistas across town.

ARRIVAL AND DEPARTURE   **PALMA**

BY PLANE
By plane Mallorca's whopping international airport is 11km east of Palma. It has car-rental outlets, 24hr ATMs and currency exchange facilities among the package tour operator helpdesks. The airport is linked to the city and the Bay of Palma resorts by the busy MA19 highway. Bus #A1 leaves for Palma every 15min from the main entrance of the terminal building, just behind the taxi rank (5.30am–2.20am; €5), and goes to Pl. Espanya, on the north side of the city centre. A taxi from the airport to the city centre will set you back around €30-35.

By bus Buses from outside Palma arrive and depart from the city's transport Intermodal hub at Pl. Espanya. Go down the escalators and follow the signs.

Destinations Alcúdia (Mon–Sat 18 daily, Sun 5 daily; 1hr); Andratx (hourly; 1hr); Deià (Mon–Fri 7 daily, Sat & Sun 4–6 daily; 45min); Lluc (2 daily; 1hr 15min); Pollença (Mon–Fri 14 daily, Sat & Sun 9 daily; 1hr); Port d'Alcúdia (Mon–Sat 18 daily, Sun 5 daily; 1hr 15min); Port de Pollença (Mon–Fri 14 daily, Sat & Sun 9 daily; 1hr 15min); Port de Sóller (via the tunnel: Mon–Fri approx hourly, Sat & Sun every 2hr, 35min;

via Valldemossa: 4–7 daily, 1hr 30min); Sóller (via the tunnel: Mon–Fri 14 daily, Sat & Sun 6–8 daily, 35min; via Valldemossa: 4–6 daily, 1hr 25min); Valldemossa (Mon–Fri 12 daily, Sat & Sun 6–7 daily; 30min).

By car Parking is problematic especially in the old town, though there are usually places around the seafront Parc de la Mar.

By ferry The Palma ferry terminal is about 4km west of the city centre. Buses #4 and 20 link the port with Plaça d'Espanya in the city centre. The taxi fare for the same journey is about €15-20.

Destinations Trasmed (www.trasmed.com), Baleària (www.balearia.com) and GNV (Grandi Navi Veloci, www.gnv.it) connect Palma with the following destinations in mainland Spain and the other Balearic islands.

Barcelona (2–3 daily; 7–9hr); Denia (1–2 daily; 6hr) Ibiza (3–4 daily; 2–4hr) Maó (1 weekly; 6hr); Valencia (2 daily; 7–8hr). See their websites for full timetables.

By train Palma has two train lines. The scenic trip on the Tren de Sóller is the most popular (see page 811) but a

13

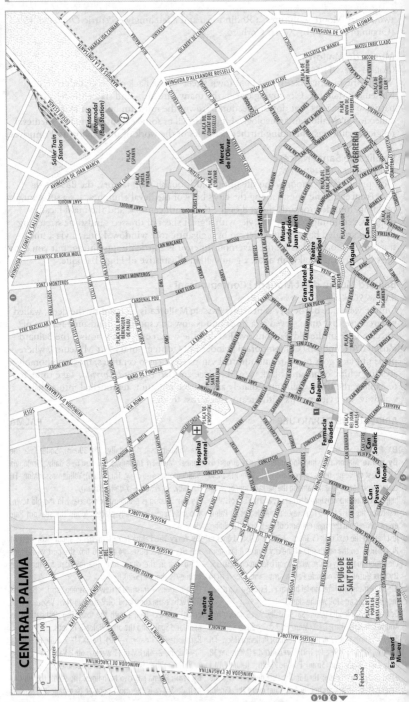

CENTRAL PALMA

0 ——— 100
metres

Soller Train Station

Estació Intermodal (Bus Station)

PLAÇA ESPANYA

AVINGUDA DE JOAN MARCH

AVINGUDA D'ALEXANDRE ROSSELLÓ

AVINGUDA DE GABRIEL ALOMAR

MATEU ENRIC LLADÓ

Mercat de l'Olivar

PLAÇA DE L'OLIVAR

SA GERRERIA

SANT MIQUEL

Sant Miquel

Museu Fundación Juan March

Teatre Principal

L'Àguila

Can Rei

Gran Hotel & Caixa Forum

LA RAMBLA

PLAÇA DEL BISBE BERENGUER DE PALOU

Can Balaguer

Farmacia Buades

Hospital General

PLAÇA DE L'HOSPITAL

Can Solleric

Can Pavesí

Can Moner

AVINGUDA JAUME III

CONCEPCIÓ

EL PUIG DE SANT PERE

PASSEIG MALLORCA

AVINGUDA DE PORTUGAL

Teatre Municipal

PLAÇA DEL FONT

AVINGUDA D'ALEMANYA

VIA ROMA

PASSEIG MALLORCA

Es Baluard Museu

La Feixina

AVINGUDA DE L'ARGENTINA

13

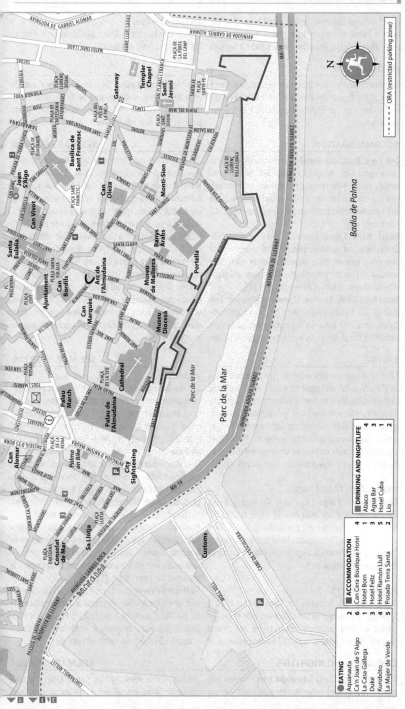

- - - - - ORA (restricted parking zone)

Badia de Palma

Parc de la Mar

● **EATING**
Aquanauta	2
Ca'n Joan de S'Aigo	6
La Casa Gallega	3
Duke	7
Kurobico	4
La Mujer de Verde	5

■ **ACCOMMODATION**
Can Cera Boutique Hotel	4
Hotel Born	1
Hotel Feliz	3
Hotel Ramón Llull	6
Posada Terra Santa	5

■ **DRINKING AND NIGHTLIFE**
Abaco	4
Agua Bar	3
Hotel Cuba	1
Lío	2

13

more functional line serves several inland towns from the modern Palma Intermodal train station (www.trensfm. com), off Pl. Espanya, where you can also find left luggage and bike hire facilities.

Destinations Inca (every 30min; 30min), Manacor (hourly; 1hr 15min), Sa Pobla (hourly; 1hr).

INFORMATION

Turisme In the city centre, the *turisme* nearest the old town is just off the Passeig d'es Born at Pl. de la Reina 2 (Mon–Fri 8.30am–8pm, Sat 8.30am–3pm; 971 173 990, www. mallorca.es).

Municipal tourist office The main office is on the north edge of Pl. Espanya next to the main bus/train station (daily 9am–8pm; 902 102 365, www.visitpalma.com). Both provide island-wide information.

ACCOMMODATION
SEE MAP PAGE 806

Can Cera Boutique Hotel C/Sant Francesc 8, www. cancerahotel.com. Beautifully converted seventeenth-century palace in the centre of the old town with fourteen rooms, a restaurant serving Mallorcan food and tapas, a spa and a private rooftop terrace for the exclusive use of guests. Adults only. €€€€

Hotel Born C/Sant Jaume 3, www.hotelborn.com. Comfortable and justifiably popular hotel in an excellent downtown location. It's a sixteenth-century refurbished mansion and has marvellous high-ceiling rooms and grand communal areas as well as a courtyard café. €€€

Hotel Feliz C/Avda. Joan Miró 74, www.hotelfeliz.com. Each room at this friendly, modern hotel has been individually styled, some with balconies overlooking the sea. Upsides include the two plunge pools, one on the private roof terrace;

the downside is the 20min walk into Palma, although a regular bus service is only a short walk away. €€€

Hotel Ramón Llull C/Ramón Llull 12, https://en.ramon llullhouse.com. Converted historic old town building offering one double room and four private apartments ranging from a studio to a two-bedroom apartment with private patio. Well-located and decorated in a traditional style but with modern fittings and furnishings. An excellent-value option. €€€

★ **Posada Terra Santa** C/Posada Terra Santa 5, www. posadaterrasanta.com. This boutique hotel combines modern flare with the old-world charm of a sixteenth-century manor house on a narrow side street. Rooms come with large flat-screen TVs and beds have Egyptian cotton sheets, while the bar-restaurant is adjacent to an internal courtyard. €€€€

EATING
SEE MAP PAGE 806

Santa Catalina, to the west of the city centre and the Passeig de Mallorca, is Palma's hipster district and where you'll find the highest density of interesting eating options, particularly if you're keen for something non-Spanish. You'll find good-quality Indian, Middle Eastern and East Asian food here, as well as above-average options for vegetarians. The old town and the side streets north of Pl. Llotja are home to more traditional, Spanish-style restaurants, bars and tavernas.

CAFÉS AND TAPAS BARS

Ca'n Joan de S'Aigo C/Can Sanç 10, https://canjoan desaigo.com. In a tiny alley near Pl. Santa Eulàlia, this long-established coffee house has wonderful, freshly baked *ensaimadas* (sweet spiral pastry buns) and is also famous for being the oldest ice-cream parlour in Palma. Charmingly formal, period-piece decor. €

RESTAURANTS

Aquanauta Avda. Argentina 27a, Santa Catalina, 871 804 930. Fun and lively Mexican-Californian café-restaurant serving excellent, authentic tacos, ceviche and tropical cocktails. Veggie options available, booking essential at

weekends. €€

La Casa Gallega Avinguda del Comte de Sallent 19, https:// casagallegamallorca.com. Their excellent seafood tapas are worth braving the crowds and occasional brusque service. The grilled or Galician-style octopus is particularly recommended as is the lunchtime set menu (Mon–Sat only). €€

★ **Duke** C/ Soler 36, Santa Catalina, www.dukepalma.com. The Asian/Middle Eastern-influenced menu is so varied and tempting, it's difficult to choose from the ceviches, stir-fries and curries. With a strong focus on fresh, healthy and seasonal produce, plus lots of vegetarian/vegan options, this superb restaurant gets very busy so be sure to book ahead. €€

Kurobōto C/Cotoner 33, Santa Catalina, https://kurobota palma.com. This stylish restaurant serves an unusual menu featuring Japanese and Italian fusion cuisine, prepared with locally sourced, seasonal ingredients, and every dish is presented like a work of art. €€€

La Mujer de Verde C/Sant Feliu 7, https://lamujerdeverde. com. One of the few fully vegetarian and vegan restaurants on the island, centrally situated off the Passeig d'es Born, with an informal atmosphere and satisfying food at low prices. Good-value three-course set lunch menu. €€

DRINKING AND NIGHTLIFE
SEE MAP PAGE 806

There's a cluster of lively **late-night bars** – mostly with music as the backdrop rather than the main event – among the narrow side streets backing onto Pl. Llotja. The **club scene** in Palma is small but worth investigating after around midnight; entry charges are between €10 and €30, depending on the night and what's happening.

BARS

Abaco C/Sant Joan 1, https://bar-abaco.es. Easily Palma's most unusual bar, with fruits cascading down its stairway, caged birds hidden amid patio foliage and a daily flower bill you could live on for a month. The bizarre surroundings are so mesmerizing that the atmosphere is rather sedate.

Agua Bar C/Jaume Ferrer 6, www.aguabar.com. Friendly New Yorker-run bar with a good range of beer, an impressive collection of rock 'n' roll and a relaxed vibe. Various theme nights, including an open-mic night on Sundays, attract a crowd.

Hotel Cuba C/Sant Magi 1, www.hotelhostalcuba.com. This hotel has an elegant gastrobar (food served all day) with DJ sessions, plus the *Sky Bar* on their amazing roof terrace and a basement club with DJs (free entry).

CLUBS

Lío Passeig Marítim, Avda. Gabriel Roca 31, www.liogroup. com/mallorca. A glossy and glamorous mixture of dining club, cabaret show and nightclub, this is one of the newest kids on the block in Palma. Part of the Pachá Group, you are guaranteed a spectacular night out.

DIRECTORY

Bike rental Palma has an excellent network of cycle lanes and is ideal for cycling round. Nano, at C/ Apuntadors 6, www.nanobicycles.com, rents city bikes, e-bikes and mountain bikes from €10 a day.

Car rental Avis (www.avis.es) has offices in the city and at Palma airport.

Hospital Hospital Universitari Son Espases, C/ de Valldemossa 79, 871 205 000, www.hospitalsonespases.es.

Pharmacy Farmacia Guijarro, Pl. de la Reina 11, Mon–Sat 9am–9pm, 971 715 371, www.instagram.com/farmaciaplazadelareina.

Post office C/Constitució 6, www.correos.es, Mon–Fri 8.30am–8.30pm, Sat 9.30am–1pm.

Around Palma

Anywhere in the west or centre of the island is readily accessible as a **day-trip** from Palma. If you're after a quick **swim** the most convenient option is to stick to the resorts strung along the neighbouring **Badia de Palma** (Bay of Palma). Locals tend to go east on the #15 bus (every 10min; 30min) from Pl. Espanya to **S'Arenal**, where there's an enormously long, albeit often very crowded, sandy beach. Much more appealing, and slightly further out of town is **Illetes** beach, accessible on the #3 bus (every 10min; 22min) from Pl. del Mercat (Audiència) just off Pl. Major.

Castell de Bellver

C/ de Camilo José Cela s/n, Cala Major • Charge • https://castelldebellver.palma.es

An appealing option, though there are no buses to it, is the **Castell de Bellver**, a strikingly well-preserved fortress of canny circular design built for Jaume II at the beginning of the fourteenth century. The castle perches on a wooded hilltop some 3km west of the city centre and offers superb views of Palma and its harbour.

Fundació Pilar i Joan Miró

C/ de Saridakis 29, Palma • Charge • https://miromallorca.com

This wonderful gallery and museum, just outside the city centre and accessible on the #3 bus (every 10min; 12min) from Pl. del Mercat (Audiència) just off Pl. Major, showcases the work of Surrealist artist and sculptor Joan Miró, who lived in Palma and worked in the workshops on display here from 1956 until his death in 1983. In 1979, Miró and his wife, Pilar, donated the workshops, which offer a unique glimpse into the artist's creative process, to the city of Palma, it being their wish that they would serve to inspire future generations of artists.

Andratx, Sant Elm and Sa Dragonera

Inland from the Bay of Palma, you could spend an hour or two exploring **ANDRATX**, a small, reasonably developed town huddled among the hills to the west of the city – there are buses roughly every hour from Palma. From here, it's another

13

forty minutes through a pretty, orchard-covered landscape to low-key **SANT ELM**, with its small beach.

There is not much to the place, but you can take the 15-minute ferry crossing (every 30min–1hr; April–Sept daily 9.45am–2.15pm, return 11.30am–4.50pm; Mar & Oct Tue-Sun 9.45am–12.15pm, return 11.30am–3pm; no service Nov-Feb; €18; https://crucerosmargarita.com) across from Sant Elm's minuscule harbour to the austere offshore islet of **Sa Dragonera**, an uninhabited chunk of rock some 4km long and 700m wide, with an imposing ridge of sea cliffs dominating its northwestern shore; the main pull here – apart from hiking on this traffic-free islet – is the birdlife.

Northern Mallorca

Mallorca is at its scenic best in the gnarled ridge of the **Serra de Tramuntana**, the imposing mountain range that stretches the length of the island's western shore, its soaring peaks and plunging sea cliffs intermittently intercepted by valleys of olive and citrus groves and dotted with some of the island's most attractive towns and villages. An enjoyable way to admire this spectacular scenery at a leisurely pace is to drive or cycle along the coastal road MA10, which runs from Andratx to Pollença – though be aware that some of the twists and turns are quite precarious. If you're reliant on public transport, the easiest way to explore the north is to travel up from Palma to Sóller and use this town as a base, making selected forays along the coastal road. Sóller is within easy striking distance of the mountain village of **Deià** and the monastery of **Valldemossa** to the southwest, or it's a short haul northeast to the monastery of **Lluc**, the quaint town of **Pollença** and the resort of **Port de Pollença**.

As far as **beaches** are concerned, most of the region's coastal villages have a tiny, shingly strip, and only around the bays of Pollença and Alcúdia are there more substantial offerings. The resorts edging these bays have the greatest number of hotel and hostal rooms, but elsewhere **accommodation** requires some forethought.

Sóller

If you're arriving by train at **SÓLLER**, the obvious option is to take the **tram** straight through to the port. If you don't stop, however, you'll miss one of the most laidback and enjoyable towns on Mallorca, though it's the general flavour of the place that appeals rather than any specific sight: the town's narrow, sloping lanes are cramped by eighteenth- and nineteenth-century stone houses, whose fancy grilles and big wooden doors once housed the region's well-heeled fruit merchants.

Plaça Constitució

All streets lead to the main square, **Pl. Constitució**, an informal, pint-sized affair of crowded cafés just down the hill from the train station. The square is dominated by

---

HIKING IN NORTHERN MALLORCA

The **Serra de Tramuntana** provides the best walking on Mallorca, with scores of hiking trails latticing the mountains, the most famous being the GR221 Dry Stone Route, (https://caminsdepedra.conselldemallorca.es/es/ruta-piedra-seca-gr-221), which runs for 135km from Port d'Andratx to Pollença. Generally speaking, paths are well marked, though apt to be clogged with thorn bushes. There are trails to suit all levels of fitness, from the easiest of strolls to the most gruelling of long-distance treks, but in all cases you should come properly equipped – certainly with an appropriate hiking **map** (available in Palma and at the Sóller *turisme*), and, for the more difficult routes, a **compass**. Spring and autumn are the best times to embark on the longer trails; in midsummer, the heat can be enervating and water is scarce. Bear in mind also that the mountains are prone to mists, though they usually lift at some point in the day.

13

the hulking mass of the church of **Sant Bartomeu**, a crude but still somehow rather engaging neo-Gothic remodelling of the medieval original, its main saving grace being the enormous rose window cut high in the main facade.

ARRIVAL AND DEPARTURE   SÓLLER

By bus Buses to and from Port de Sóller to Palma, Deià, Valldemossa and north Mallorca call en route at the Sóller bus station at C/Cetre – about a 5min walk west of the centre. See https://tib.org for full details and timetables in English.

Destinations Deià (6–8 daily; 25min); Palma (via Valldemossa: 6–8 daily, 1hr 25min; via the tunnel: Mon–Fri 14 daily, Sat & Sun 6–8 daily, 35min); Port de Sóller (daily every 30min; 10min); Valldemossa (6–8 daily; 55min); Route 354 (2 daily April–Oct Mon–Sat) runs from Port de Sóller to Sóller (10min), Lluc (1hr 20min), Pollença (1hr 45min), Port Pollença (2hr), Alcudia (2hr 15min) and Port Alcudia (2hr 25min).

By train Easily the best way to cross the Serra de Tramuntana is to take the train (971 752 028, https://

trendesoller.com) from Palma to Sóller (via Bunyola), a 28km journey that takes about an hour on antique rolling stock that seems to have come straight out of an Agatha Christie novel. The rail line, constructed on the profits of the nineteenth-century orange and lemon trade, dips and twists through the mountains and across fertile valleys, offering magnificent views.

Destinations Palma (4–6 daily; 1hr; €28 return, combined with tram ticket to Port de Sóller €35).

By tram Trams leave from outside the station down to the seashore at Port de Sóller, just 5km away (7am–8.20pm, 1–2 hourly; 15min; €7 each way, or €32 combined with return train fare to Palma).

INFORMATION

Turisme Located inside an old tram carriage on Pl. de Espanya; it has a good supply of leaflets as well as a list of

accommodation (Mon–Fri 10am–4.30pm; Sat 9.15am–1pm; 971 638 008).

ACCOMMODATION

★ **Ca's Curial** C/La Villalonga 23, http://cascurial.com. Family-run hotel just a short walk from the centre of Sóller yet in an impossibly romantic location surrounded by orange and lemon groves, lush garden foliage and the Tramuntana mountains. Adults only. €€€€

Hotel El Guía C/Castanyer 2, www.hotelelguia.com.

First opened in 1880, this renovated smart-looking hotel, just metres from the train station, is a family-run Sóller institution, with a pool, sauna and an excellent and reasonably priced restaurant. Expect – and revel in – plenty of old-world charm. €€

EATING AND DRINKING

La Lluna C/de sa Lluna, www.luna36.es. Stands apart from many of its Sóller counterparts in terms of decor, service and the quality of the dishes, which are mainly Mediterranean in style with occasional Asian touches. Try the braised lamb neck with mustard sauce and vegetables or the fish and

scallop ceviche with Sóller lemons, mango and onions. €€

Sá Fàbrica de Gelats Pl. del Mercat, www.gelatsoller.com. Heavenly ice-cream parlour with a choice of forty flavours. It's famed for its hugely refreshing orange ice cream. Take away or enjoy in the garden terrace. €

Port de Sóller

PORT DE SÓLLER is one of the most popular and family-orientated resorts on the west coast, and its horseshoe-shaped bay must be the most photographed spot on the island after the package resorts around Palma. The best **swimming** is along the pedestrianized area of **Platja d'en Repic**, where the water is clear and the beach clean and well maintained. Also good fun is the fifty-minute walk up to the **lighthouse**, which guards the cliffs above the entrance to Port de Sóller's harbour. It's a steep climb but the views out over the wild and rocky coast are spectacular, especially at sunset, and there's even a restaurant at the cape. Directions couldn't be easier: from the centre of the resort, walk round the southern side of the bay past the Platja d'en Repic beach and keep going. At the opposite end of the bay, fifty-minute boat trips run out to Sa Calobra (see page 812).

ARRIVAL AND INFORMATION   PORT DE SÓLLER

By tram Trams from Sóller clank to a halt beside the   waterfront, bang in the centre of town next to the *turisme*.

13

By bus Buses arrive and depart from just off C/Sa Figuera, the second roundabout out of town, or from the Can Miró car park on the Port de Sóller road. See https://tib.org for full details and timetables in English.

Destinations Deià (6–8 daily; 30min); Palma (via Valldemossa: 6–8 daily, 1hr 30min; via the tunnel: Mon–Fri approx hourly, Sat & Sun every 2hr 35min); Sóller (daily every 30min; 5–10min); Valldemossa (6–8 daily; 55min).

Route 354 (2 daily April–Oct Mon–Sat) runs from Port de Sóller to Sóller (5–10mins), Lluc (1hr 20min), Pollença (1hr 45min), Port Pollença (2hr), Alcudia (2hr 15min) and Port Alcudia (2hr 25min).

Turisme C/Marina 7, on the waterfront next to the tram stop (March–Oct Mon–Fri 9am–2.30pm; 659 498 747, https://soller.es). Full details of buses, trams, boat trips and cultural activities throughout Sóller.

GETTING AROUND

Boat trips Several companies based on the waterfront by the *turisme* offer boat and kayak hire, boat charters (with or without captain) and full-day excursions to nearby coves and bays, some only accessible by water, including Sa Calobra, Cala Tuent, Cala Deià and Sa Foradada. Barcos Azules (www.barcoscalobra.com) is the only company to offer a taxi boat service to Sa Calobra (single €22, return

€33), which also stops at Cala Tuent.

Moto hire Bullimoto on C/Antoni Montis 6 (www.bullimoto.com) hire out vintage and modern-style classic Vespas from €46 a day in high season. They also offer private guided tours by Vespa, and can deliver bikes directly to your accommodation (or anywhere on the island).

ACCOMMODATION

Hotel Espléndido Passeig Es Través 5, www.esplendidohotel.com. Standing proud on the waterfront is this modern and stylish hotel whose vintage and vanguard decor, a reflection of the owners' personal taste, sets it apart from its more humdrum neighbours. Includes three pools (one indoor), a spa, a bistro-restaurant and a cocktail bar. €€€€

★ **Hotel Es Port** C/Antonio Montis 10, www.hotelesport.com. Outside peak season, there's a good chance of a reasonably priced room at the attractive *Hotel Es Port*, which occupies a huge old mansion with lovely gardens set back from the main part of the port. There are both indoor and outdoor pools, plus a spa. €€€€

EATING AND DRINKING

★ **Kingfisher** Sant Ramon de Penyafort 25, https://kingfishersoller.com. Deservedly popular for its wonderful views over the harbour, the attentive service and above all the excellent Mediterranean-style food, mainly fish, as well as the specialist gin cocktails. Grilled octopus is a favourite, as are the tuna ceviche and the fish soup. Vegetarian dishes

also available. Reservations essential. €€€

Petit Café Frozen Yoghurt Passeig Es Través 23, 697 434 468. Simple beach bar serving delicious frozen natural yoghurt with fruit and syrup toppings. Also serves freshly made baguettes, salads and organic coffee. Eat in at a couple of shady tables or take away. €

Deià

It's a dramatic, ten-kilometre journey southwest from Sóller along the MA10 to the beautiful village of **DEIÀ**, where the mighty Puig des Teix mountain ramps down to the coast. At times, this thoroughfare is too congested to be much fun, but the tiny heart of the village, tumbling over a high and narrow ridge on the seaward side of the road, still preserves a surprising tranquillity. Here, labyrinthine alleys of old peasant houses curl up to a pretty country church, in the precincts of which stands the grave of **Robert Graves** (1895–1985), the village's most famous resident and author of works including *I, Claudius* and *Goodbye To All That*. The grave is marked simply "Robert Graves: Poeta, E.P.D." (En Paz Descanse: "Rest In Peace"), and the views from the graveyard out over the coast are truly memorable.

La Casa de Robert Graves

Carretera Deià a Sóller • Charge • www.lacasaderobertgraves.org • Buses #203 and 204 from Sóller and Palma

Robert Graves put Deià on the international map, and his old home, **Ca N'Alluny**, a substantial stone building beside the main road about 500m east of the village, was opened to the public in 2006. Graves first lived here in the 1930s and returned after World War II to remain in the village until his death. For the most part, the house has been returned to its 1940s appearance, and its rooms are decorated with Graves' own furnishings and fittings. You can see the study where Graves produced much of his finest work, as well as an exhibition of manuscripts and photos of Graves posing with a few of his well-known visitors.

Cala Deià

Cala Deià, the nearest thing the village has to a beach, comprises some 200m of shingle at the back of a handsome rocky cove of jagged cliffs, boulders and white-crested surf. It takes about thirty minutes to walk from the village to the *cala*, a pleasant stroll down a wooded ravine – or a five-minute drive. Once a quiet place for a swim, the cove can get rather overrun with tourists in high season, largely due to the popularity of one of its two restaurants, *Ca's Patro March* (see page 813).

ARRIVAL AND INFORMATION   DEIÀ

By bus Buses loop through Deià, dropping passengers on the main street.
Destinations Palma (Mon–Fri 7 daily, Sat & Sun 4–6 daily; 45min); Port de Sóller (4–7 daily; 30min); Sóller (4–7 daily;

25min); Valldemossa (4–7 daily; 15min).
Information There's no *turisme* but a useful website with information about the village is https://deia.info.

ACCOMMODATION

★ **Es Moli** Carretera Valldemossa–Deiá, https://esmoli. com. One of the most agreeable hotels on Mallorca, *Es Moli* is a supremely comfortable establishment in an immaculately maintained building with superb gardens overlooking the main road at the west end of the village. It even has its own private cove, served by a free minibus shuttle. €€€€

Hostal Miramar C/de Can Oliver, http://pension miramardeia.com. A slightly old-fashioned-looking *pensión* in lush surroundings, reached by a short, steep walk up above the main road. Rooms are unimaginative but perfectly adequate, and there are smashing views over the village from the terrace. €€

EATING AND DRINKING

Ca's Patro March Cala Deià, 971 369 137, www.instagram. com/caspatromarch; bookings by phone or at https://cas patromarch.myrestoo.net. With an idyllic setting over the crystalline waters of Cala Deià, this seafood restaurant was popular even before the 2016 TV adaption of John le Carré's novel, *The Night Manager*, was filmed here. Now it's a squeeze to get in and booking is essential, but it's still a lovely spot. Cash only. €€€
★ **Sa Foradada** Carretera Valldemossa km6, https:// restaurantesaforadada.com. Built into the cliff face

overlooking the famous Sa Foradada hole in the rock, access is only possible by sea or a 45min walk from the Na Foradada lookout (3.5km along the MA10 from Deià). The spectacular views and traditionally wood-fire cooked paella (min. two people) are more than worth the effort. €€
Trattoria Italiana Viña Vieja 1, https://latrattoriadeia. com. This sophisticated Italian restaurant has a superb terrace with mountain views. It's a good spot for a drink or steak, salmon with dill and various pasta dishes. €€

Valldemossa

Some 10km **southwest of Deià** along the MA10 lies the ancient and intriguing hill town of **VALLDEMOSSA**, a sloping jumble of rusticated houses and monastic buildings set in a lovely valley and with a mountain backdrop. The origins of Valldemossa date to the early fourteenth century, when the asthmatic King Sancho built a royal palace here in the hills, where the air was easier to breathe. Later, in 1399, the palace was given to Carthusian monks from Tarragona, who converted and extended the original buildings into a **monastery**, which now forms part of the **Real Cartuja de Valldemossa** complex and is the island's most visited building after Palma Catedral.

Real Cartuja de Valldemossa

Plaça Cartoixa • Charge • https://cartoixadevalldemossa.com

Remodelled on several occasions, most of the present complex, the **Real Cartuja de Valldemossa**, as it's formally named, is of seventeenth- and eighteenth-century construction, its square and heavy church leading to the shadowy corridors of the cloisters beyond. The monastery owes its present fame almost entirely to the novelist and republican polemicist **George Sand**, who, with her companion, the composer **Frédéric**

13

Chopin, lived here for four months during 1838–39 in a commodious set of vacant cells – their stay is commemorated in Sand's self-important work, *A Winter in Majorca*.

ARRIVAL AND DEPARTURE   VALLDEMOSSA

By bus Valldemossa is easily reached by bus from Deià, Sóller and Palma. Buses stop beside the bypass at the west end of town; from here, it's just a couple of minutes' walk to the monastery.
Destinations Deià (4–7 daily; 15min); Palma (Mon–Fri 12

daily, Sat & Sun 6–7 daily; 30min); Port de Sóller (4–7 daily; 55min).
Turisme Avda. de Palma 7, next to the central car park (April–Sept Mon–Fri 9am–7pm, Sat & Sun 10am–7pm; 971 612 019).

ACCOMMODATION AND EATING

★ **Es Petit Hotel** C/Uetam 1, www.espetithotel-valldemossa.com. Spacious and tastefully decorated rooms in an attractive refurbished old house. All the rooms have a/c and satellite TV, and some have great views over the valley. The price includes an excellent buffet breakfast. €€€

Es Roquissar Pl. de la Cartuja 5, 971 616 208. Superbly located in the pretty square opposite the Cartuja, this place should be a tourist trap, but the excellent quality Mediterranean dishes with an Asian/Peruvian influence, served at charming terrace tables in the square, make it anything but. €€€

Lluc

Without doubt, the most interesting approach to the northernmost tip of the island is the 35km stretch of the MA10 northeast from Sóller to **LLUC**. The road slips through the highest and harshest section of the **Serra de Tramuntana**. Tucked away in a remote mountain valley, Lluc was Mallorca's most important place of pilgrimage from the middle of the thirteenth century, supposedly after a shepherd boy named Lluc (Luke) stumbled across a tiny, brightly painted statue of the Madonna here in the wood.

Monestir de Nostra Senyora

Free • Charge for the car park, refunded with entry to the museum • https://santuaridelluc.com

Lluc is dominated by the austere, high-sided dormitories of the **Monestir de Nostra Senyora**. At the centre of the monastery is the main shrine and architectural highlight, the **Basílica de la Mare de Déu de Lluc**, a dark and gaudily decorated church, whose heaviness is partly relieved by a dome over the central crossing. On either side of the nave, stone steps extend the aisles round the back of the Baroque high altar to a little chapel. You can also stroll along the **Camí dels Misteris del Rosari** (Way of the Mysteries of the Rosary), a pilgrims' footpath that winds its way up the rocky hillside behind the monastery. Don't miss the attractive botanical gardens (to the left of the monastery as you face it), where you can also find an extremely alluring open-air pool.

Museu de Lluc

Charge • 971 871 525

Allow time for a visit to the monastery museum, the **Museu de Lluc**, which includes a fascinating display of archeological finds and gifts offered to the Virgin. The entry fee also allows you to see a small and underwhelming sound and light display about the monastery, adjacent to the ticket office.

ARRIVAL AND DEPARTURE   LLUC

By bus Buses stop at a large car park just a minute's walk from the monastery's main entrance.
Destinations Alcudia (2 daily; 1hr); Palma (2 daily; 1hr 15min); Pollença (May–Oct Mon–Sat 2 daily; 30min); Port

de Alcúdia (May–Oct Mon–Sat 2 daily; 1hr 10min); Port de Sóller (May–Oct Mon–Sat 2 daily; 1hr 15min); Sóller (May–Oct Mon–Sat 2 daily; 1hr 5min).

ACCOMMODATION

Santuari de Lluc Lluc, www.lluc.net. Spending the night at the monastery provides the perfect opportunity to experience the peace and quiet that has been sought here

for centuries. Double rooms are basic but comfortable and there are also apartments available for two to six people. €€€

EATING AND DRINKING

Sa Fonda Santuari de Lluc, Lluc, 971 517 022, www.lluc. net/es/restaurante. Inside the monastery, on the left as you enter, this is grander than you might expect from a former monks' refectory and the pick of Lluc's dining experiences. Lamb is the speciality. €€

Pollença

Heading northeast from Lluc, the MA10 twists through the mountains to travel the 20km on to **POLLENÇA**, a pretty and ancient little town that nestles among a trio of hillocks where the Serra de Tramuntana fades into the coastal flatlands. Following standard Mallorcan practice, the town was established a few kilometres from the seashore to protect it against sudden pirate attack, with its harbour, Port de Pollença (see page 816), left as an unprotected outpost. For once, the stratagem worked. Unlike most of Mallorca's old towns, Pollença avoided destruction, and the austere stone houses that cramp the twisting lanes of the centre mostly date from the eighteenth century. In the middle, **Pl. Major**, the main square, accommodates a cluster of laidback cafés and the dour facade of the church of **Nostra Senyora dels Àngels**, a sheer cliff face of sun-bleached stone pierced by a rose window.

Via Crucis

Pollença's pride and joy is its **Via Crucis** (Way of the Cross), a long, steep and beautiful stone stairway, graced by ancient cypress trees, which ascends **El Calvari** (Calvary Hill) directly north of the principal square. At the top, a much-revered statue of the **Mare de Déu del Peu de la Creu** (Mother of God at the Foot of the Cross) is lodged in a courtyard of the simple **Oratori** (Chapel), whose whitewashed walls sport some of the worst religious paintings imaginable. On Good Friday, a figure of Jesus is slowly carried by torchlight down from the Oratori to the church of Nostra Senyora dels Àngels, in the **Davallament** (Lowering), one of the most moving religious celebrations on the island.

Ermita de Nostra Senyora del Puig

There are magnificent views from the **Ermita de Nostra Senyora del Puig**, a rambling, mostly eighteenth-century monastery that occupies a serene and beautiful spot on top of the Puig de María, a 320-metre-high hump facing the south end of town. The Benedictines now own the place, but the monks are gone and today a custodian supplements the order's income by renting out cells to tourists – the views are spectacular, but the conditions pretty spartan. To get to the monastery, take the signposted turning left off the main Pollença–Inca road just south of town, then head up this steep, 1.5-kilometre lane until it fizzles out, to be replaced by a cobbled footpath that winds up to the monastery entrance. It's possible to drive to the top of the lane, but unless you've got nerves of steel, you're better off leaving your vehicle by the turning near the foot of the hill. Allow just over an hour each way if you're walking from the centre of town.

ARRIVAL AND INFORMATION   POLLENÇA

By bus Buses to Pollença from Palma, Inca and Port de Pollença stop at the bus stop a few blocks south of Pl. Major on C/Cecili Metel. But, inconveniently, buses from Lluc and Sóller drop off passengers about 1km north of the centre on the main MA10 road (Carretera Lluc).
Destinations Alcúdia (Mon–Sat 2 daily; 30min); Palma (Mon–Fri 14 daily, Sat & Sun 9 daily; 1hr); Sóller (May–Oct Mon–Sat 2 daily; 1hr 35min); Lluc (Mon–Sat 2 daily; 30min); Port de Pollença (every 20min; 15min).
Turisme Plaça Major 17 (Apr–Oct Mon–Fri 9am–4pm, Sun 10am–1pm; Nov–April Mon–Fri 8am–3pm; 971 535 077, www.pollensa.com).

ACCOMMODATION

Hotel Juma Pl. Major 9, 971 535 002, www.pollensahotels. com. The most central place to stay is the *Hotel Juma*, with comfortable, a/c modern bedrooms, some of which overlook the main square. Popular with cyclists, this medium-sized hotel is above a café, and has helpful staff. They also operate the slightly more upmarket *L-Hostal*, which offers stylish, rustic rooms in an old stable. €€€

13

13

EATING AND DRINKING

Bar Nou C/Antoni Maura 13, https://barnourestaurante. com. A rustic, wood-panelled restaurant with gingham tablecloths and a menu of classic Spanish favourites, from tapas like *patatas bravas* and *croquetas* to more substantial dishes like paella (they also do a good vegetarian version) and lamb chops. €€

Q11 C/Antoni Maura 11, Pl. Major, www.q11restaurant.

com. Prime location with shaded tables overlooking the church on the main square, but the superb food and the regularly changing, forward-looking menu is the reason to come here. The Mallorcan lamb with mustard crust is a favourite and there are excellent vegetarian options too. €€€

Port de Pollença

Over at **PORT DE POLLENÇA** things are a little more touristy than at Pollença, though still pleasantly low-key. With the mountains as a backdrop, the resort arches through the flatlands behind the Badia de Pollença, a deeply indented bay whose sheltered waters are ideal for swimming. The **beach** is the focus of attention, a narrow, elongated sliver of sand that's easily long enough to accommodate the crowds. There's also a delightful three-kilometre (each way) **hike** across the neck of the Península de Formentor to the remote shingle beach of **Cala Boquer**.

ARRIVAL AND INFORMATION   PORT DE POLLENÇA

By bus Buses to/from all destinations leave/arrive at the bus stops on C/Roger de Flor.
Destinations Palma (Mon–Fri 14 daily, Sat & Sun 9 daily; 1hr 15min); Pollença (every 15min to 1hr; 15min); Port de Sóller (April–Oct Mon–Sat 2 daily; 2hr); Sóller (May–Oct

Mon–Sat 2 daily; 2hr).
Turisme Passeig Saralegui 1 (May–Oct Mon–Fri 9am–8pm, Sat 9am–4pm; Nov–April Mon–Fri 8am–3pm; 971 865 467, www.pollensa.com).

TOURS AND ACTIVITIES

Boat trips Lanchas la Gaviota (www.lanchaslagaviota. com) runs passenger ferries between the marina and Platja de Formentor (May–Oct 4–6 daily; 30min; €17 return), one of Mallorca's most attractive beaches, as well as boat trips around the bay and over to Cap de Formentor; check website for schedules.

Bike rental The flatlands edging the Badia de Pollença make for easy, scenic cycling, and mountain bikes can be rented from around €17 a day (up to €50 day for the top-of-the-line bikes) from Rent March at C/Joan XXIII 89 (971 864 784, https://rentmarch.com).

ACCOMMODATION

Hoposa Hotel Bahía Paseo Voramar 29, www.hoposa. es/puerto-pollensa-hotels. A few minutes' walk north of the marina, this peaceful hotel has a great location right on the seashore. It's a good choice, with small but pleasant rooms and an excellent restaurant. Expect to pay extra for a sea view. €€€
Pension Bellavista C/Monges 14, www.pension

bellavista.com. This simple *pensión* is metres from the seafront. Rooms are small and some face a noisy side street, others open onto an attractive communal terrace at the back. Communal areas are attractively decorated with works by local artists, but the best feature is the patio garden where vegetarian breakfasts are served under the trees. €€

EATING AND DRINKING

★ **Bella Verde** C/Monge 14, www.restaurantebellaverde. com. You don't have to be a vegetarian to appreciate the food at this leafy hideaway. With tables set up under shady trees in a patio garden, you can enjoy vegetarian curries, pumpkin lasagne or tomato tart with asparagus and rosemary potatoes. Lovely cakes and fresh juices, too. €€
Himalaya Nepalese Indian Restaurant Paseo Anglada

Camarasa 13, https://indianrestauranthimalaya.com. Easy to miss among the identical white plastic establishments along the *paseo*, this Indian restaurant serves above average, authentic curries such as king prawn masala and chicken jalfrezi, including a good range of vegetarian options. Also does takeaways. €€

Península de Formentor

Travelling northeast out of Port de Pollença, the road soon weaves up into the craggy hills of the twenty-kilometre-long **Península de Formentor**, the final spur of the Serra

13

de Tramuntana. At first, the road (which suffers a surfeit of tourists from mid-morning to mid-afternoon) travels inland, out of sight of the true grandeur of the scenery, but after about 4km the **Mirador de Mal Pas** rectifies matters with a string of lookout points perched on the edge of plunging, north-facing sea cliffs. From here, it's another couple of kilometres to the woods backing onto the **Platja de Formentor**, a pine-clad beach of golden sand in a pretty cove. From summer 2025, car access will be restricted, and shuttle buses will ferry visitors to the beach.

Alcúdia
It's just 10km round the bay from Port de Pollença to the pint-sized town of **ALCÚDIA**, whose main claim to fame is its impeccably restored medieval walls and incredibly popular open-air market (Tues & Sun) that has everything from souvenir trinkets to fruit and veg. Situated on a neck of land separating two large, sheltered bays, the site's strategic value was first recognized by the Phoenicians and later by the Romans, who built their island capital, Pollentia, here in the first century AD.

Roman City of Pollentia
Avda. Princep d'Espanya s/n • Charge, includes entry to the Museu Monogràfic and Roman Theatre but tickets must be bought at Pollentia • www.alcudia.net/Pollentia

It only takes an hour or so to walk around the antique lanes of Alcúdia's compact centre, and to explore the town walls and their fortified gates. This pleasant stroll can be extended by a visit to the meagre remains of Roman **Pollentia**, whose broken pillars and mashed foundations lie just outside the town walls. The entrance ticket includes admission to the small but excellent **Museu Monogràfic** nearby, just inside the walls, as well as the Roman Theatre.

ARRIVAL AND DEPARTURE   ALCÚDIA

By bus Buses to Alcúdia stop beside – and immediately to the south of – the town walls on Avda. dels Princeps d'Espanya.
Destinations Lluc (2 daily; 1hr); Palma (Mon–Sat 18 daily, Sun 5 daily; 1hr); Pollença (Mon–Sat 2 daily; 30min); Port de Pollença (every 15min; 20min); Sóller (2 daily; 2hr 10min); airport (12 daily; 1hr 5min).
Turisme Passeig Pere Ventayol s/n (daily 8.30am–2.30pm; 971 549 022, https://alcudiamallorca.com/).

EATING

Ca'n Costa C/Sant Vincenc 14, https://cancostaalcudia. com. Hugely popular restaurant serving traditional Mallorcan cuisine, such as *fritos* (seafood or lamb stir fry), *tumbet* (vegetable stack) and *arroz brut* (rice and meat stew). They also do a fixed lunch menu as well as dishes for vegetarians and coeliacs. €€

Port d'Alcúdia
PORT D'ALCÚDIA, 3km south of Alcúdia, is easily the biggest and busiest of the resorts on the Badia d'Alcúdia, its raft of restaurants and café-bars attracting crowds from a seemingly interminable string of high-rise hotels and apartment buildings. The tower blocks are, however, relatively well distributed and the streets neat and tidy. Predictably, the daytime focus is the **beach**, a superb arc of pine-studded golden sand, which stretches south for 10km from the combined marina and fishing harbour.

ARRIVAL AND DEPARTURE   PORT DE ALCÚDIA

By bus Port d'Alcúdia acts as northern Mallorca's summertime transport hub, with frequent bus services to and from all the neighbouring towns and resorts, plus Palma.
Destinations Alcúdia (every 15min; 10min); Lluc (May–Oct Mon–Sat 2 daily; 1hr 10min); Palma (Mon–Sat 18 daily, Sun 5 daily; 1hr 15min); Port de Pollença (every 15–30min; 30min); Sóller (2 daily; 1hr 20min); airport (12 daily; 1hr 20min).

By ferry Ferries run by Menorca Lines (www.menorcalines. com), Baleària (www.balearia.com) and Trasmed (www. trasmed.com) depart from the modern ferry building on the eastern side of the bay to make the crossing to Ciutadella in Menorca (March–Sept 4–5 daily; Oct–Feb 1 daily; 1hr 15min–2hr 30min).
Turisme On the seafront on Passeig Marítim (April–Oct

13

daily 8am–3pm; 971 547 257, https://alcudiamallorca. com). It can supply all sorts of information, most usefully

free maps marked with all the resort's hotels and apartments.

Parc Natural de S'Albufera

Carretera MA12 km26.3 • Charge • www.caib.es/sites/espaisnaturalsprotegits/es/parque_natural_de_salbufera_de_mallorca-21714 • Buses from Port d'Alcúdia to Ca'n Picafort (Mon–Sat 2–3 daily; 30min) stop beside the entrance

Head south around the bay from Port d'Alcúdia and it's about 6km to the **Parc Natural de S'Albufera**, a slice of protected wetland, which is all that remains of the marshes that once extended round most of the bay. The signposted entrance to the park is on the MA12, but access is only on foot or cycle – so if you're driving, you'll need to use the small car park near the entrance. About 1km from the entrance, you come to the park's **reception centre**, from where footpaths radiate out into the reedy, watery tract beyond. It's a superb habitat, with ten well-appointed hides allowing excellent **birdwatching**. Over two hundred species have been spotted: resident wetland-loving birds, autumn and/or springtime migrants, and wintering species and birds of prey in their scores.

Menorca

The second largest of the Balearic Islands, boomerang-shaped **MENORCA** is the least plagued by unsavoury development. An essentially rural island, it features rolling fields, wooded ravines and humpy hills filling out the interior in between its two main – but still notably small – towns of **Maó** and **Ciutadella**. Much of this landscape looks pretty much as it did at the beginning of the twentieth century, and only around the edges of the island, and then only in parts, have its rocky coves been colonized by sprawling villa complexes. Neither is the development likely to spread: determined to protect their island from the worst excesses of the tourist industry, the Menorcans have clearly demarcated development areas and are also pushing ahead with a variety of environmental schemes – the island was declared a UNESCO Biosphere Reserve in 1993, and over forty percent of it now enjoys official protection.

GETTING AROUND   MENORCA

By bus Bus routes are distinctly limited, adhering mostly to the main central road between Maó and Ciutadella, occasionally branching off to the larger coastal resorts.

By car You'll need your own vehicle to reach any of the emptier beaches, which are sometimes down a track fit only for 4WD.

ACCOMMODATION

Accommodation is at a premium, with limited options outside Maó and Ciutadella – and you can count on all the beds in all

the resorts being block-booked by the tour operators from the beginning to the end of the season (May–Oct).

MENORCA'S PREHISTORY

Menorca is dotted with **prehistoric monuments**, weatherworn stone remains that are evidence of a sophisticated culture. Little is known of the island's prehistory, but the monuments are thought to be linked to those of Sardinia and are classified as examples of the **Talayotic culture**, which is usually considered to have ended with the arrival of the Romans in 123 BC. **Talayots** are the rock mounds found all over the island – popular belief has it that they functioned as watchtowers, but it's a theory few experts accept. The megalithic **taulas** –huge stones topped with another to form a T, around 4m high and unique to Menorca – are even more puzzling. They have no obvious function, and they are almost always found alongside a *talayot*. Some of the best-preserved *talayot* and *taula* remains are on the edge of Maó at the **Talatí de Dalt** site. The third prehistoric structure of note is the **naveta** (dating from 1400 to 800 BC), stone slab constructions shaped like an inverted bread tin.

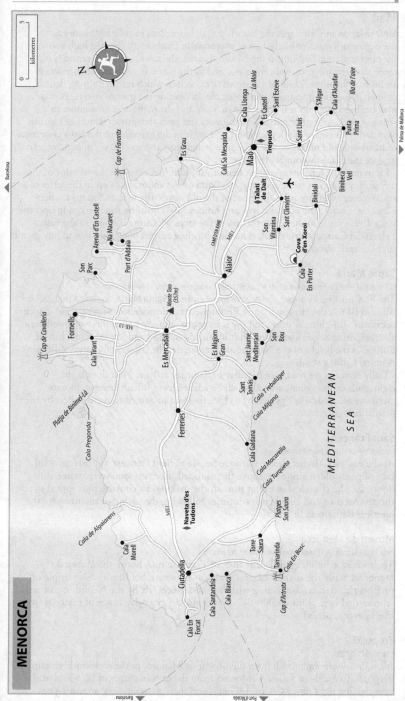

MENORCA

Barcelona

Palma de Mallorca

Barcelona

Port d'Alcúdia

MEDITERRANEAN SEA

La Mola
Cala Llonga
Es Castell
Sant Esteve
S'Algar
Cala d'Alcaufar
Illa de l'aire
Punta Prima
Sant Lluís
Trepucó
Es Grau
Cala Sa Mesquida
Maó
Cap de Favàritx
Bimbeca Vell
Binidalí
Talatí de Dalt
Sant Climent
Binissafúller
Son Vitamina
Cova d'en Xoroi
Cala En Porter
Arenal d'En Castell
Na Macaret
Port d'Addaia
CAMÍ D'EN KANE
ME-1
Alaior
Son Parc
Monte Toro
(357m)
Cap de Cavalleria
Fornells
ME-13
Es Mercadal
Es Migjorn Gran
Sant Jaume Mediterrani
Son Bou
Cala Tirant
Sant Tomàs
Cala Trebalúger
Cala Mitjana
Platja de Binimel·là
Ferreries
Cala Pregonda
Cala Galdana
Cala Macarella
Cala Turqueta
Platges Son Saura
ME-1
Naveta d'es Tudons
Cala de Algaiarens
Torre Saura
Tamarinda
Cala En Bosc
Cala Morell
Ciutadella
Cala Santandría
Cala Blanca
Cap d'Artrutx
Cala En Forcat

0 — 5 kilometres

13

Maó

MAÓ (Mahón in Castilian), the island capital, has a place in culinary history as the eighteenth-century birthplace of **mayonnaise** (*mahonesa*). Perched high above the largest natural harbour in the Mediterranean, the town's compact centre is no more than ten minutes' walk from one end to the other. Its architecture consists of an unusual hybrid of classical Georgian townhouses, which reflect a strong British connection, and tall Spanish apartment blocks shading the narrow streets. Port it may be, but there's no real gritty side to Maó, and the harbour is now home to a string of slick – if rather sedate – restaurants and cafés that attract droves of tourists. Wandering the maze of alleyways and peering into the gateways of the city's collection of handsome old mansions are its charm, rather than any specific sight, and you can explore the place thoroughly in a day.

From near the ferry terminal, set beneath the cliff that supports the remains of the city wall, a generous stone stairway, the **Costa de Ses Voltes**, leads up to the series of small squares that comprise the heart of the old town. The first, **Pl. Espanya**, offers views right across the port and bay, and houses Maó's bustling fish market, in operation since 1927, while to the left at the top of the steps, **Pl. Carme** is home to the vast Església del Carme whose cloisters house a bustling market – a good place to buy picnic supplies and souvenirs.

Santa María

Pl. Constitució • Free but donation requested • https://visitmenorca.com/menorca/iglesia-de-santa-maria

The Pl. Constitució boasts the town's main church, **Santa María**, founded in 1287 by Alfonso III to celebrate the island's Reconquest and remodelled on several subsequent occasions. The church's pride and joy is its **organ**, a monumental piece of woodwork, all trumpeting angels and pipes, built in Austria in 1810 and lugged across half of Europe at the height of the Napoleonic Wars under the concerned charge of Britain's Admiral Collingwood.

Daily concerts are held here Monday to Saturday at 1pm. Next door is the eighteenth-century **ajuntament**, which benefitted from British largesse, too, its attractive arcaded facade graced by a clock that was presented to the islanders by the first British governor.

Sant Francesc

Pla des Monestir • Free but donation requested

At the end of C/Isabel II, the Baroque facade of **Sant Francesc** appears as a cliff face of pale golden stone set above the rounded, Romanesque-style arches of its doorway. The church was a long time in the making, its construction spread over the seventeenth and eighteenth centuries following the razing of the town by the piratical Barbarossa in 1535.

Museu de Menorca

Avda. Doctor Guàrdia s/n • Charge • www.museudemenorca.com

The monastic buildings adjacent to Sant Francesc now house the **Museu de Menorca**, easily the island's biggest and best museum, holding a wide sample of prehistoric artefacts, beginning with bits and pieces left by the Neolithic pastoralists who settled here around 4000 BC; there's also an extensive range of material from the Talayotic period.

Trepucó

Charge • 971 157 800

It's a 35-minute walk south from the Museu de Menorca to the prehistoric remains of Trepucó. To get there, follow C/Moreres from the eastern corner of Pl. S'Esplanada, take the first right down C/Cós de Gràcia and then go straight on, streaming onto

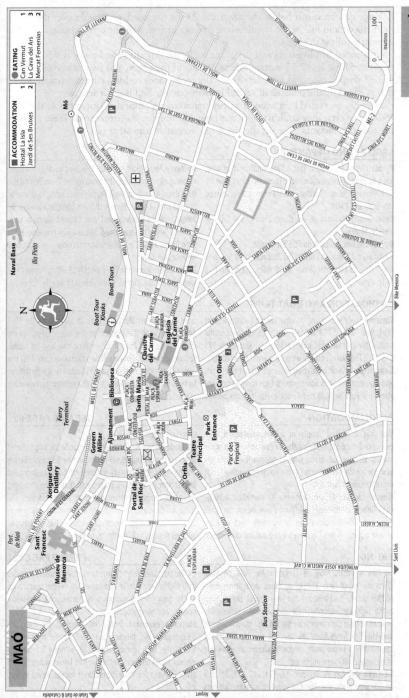

MAÓ

ACCOMMODATION
Hostal La Isla — 1
Jardí de Ses Bruixes — 2

EATING
Can Vermut — 1
La Cava del Ars — 3
Mercat Femenías — 2

13

C/Verge de Gràcia just before the ring road. At the ring road, go straight over the roundabout and follow the twisting lane in front of you, past the cemetery, and thereafter follow the signs.

Surrounded by olive trees and dry-stone walls, the tiny site's focal point is a 4.2-metre-high and 2.75-metre-wide **taula**, one of the largest and best preserved of these T-shaped monoliths on the island. The *taula* stands inside a circular compound that is edged by the remains of several broadly circular buildings. These were thoroughly excavated by a team of archeologists from Cambridge University in the late 1920s, but even they couldn't work out how the complex was structured. There are two cone-shaped **talayots** close by, the larger one accessible, the other not.

ARRIVAL AND DEPARTURE   MAÓ

By air Menorca's airport, just 3.5km southwest of Maó, has a handful of car-rental outlets. There are buses (line 10, €2.80) every hour or 30 minutes to Maó bus station; the taxi fare is about €15-18.

Destinations Mallorca (6–10 daily; 25min) and Ibiza (4 weekly; 50min).

By bus The bus station is on Pl. S'Esplanada.

Destinations Ciutadella (Mon–Fri 20 daily, Sat & Sun 6–8 daily; 1hr); Es Mercadal (Mon–Fri 20 daily, Sat & Sun 6–8 daily; 25min).

By ferry Ferries sail right up the inlet to Maó harbour, mooring directly beneath the town centre. From behind the ferry dock, it's a 5min walk up the wide stone stairway to the old part of town. Ferries to/from Barcelona are run by Balearia (www.balearia.com) and to/from Valencia with Trasmed (www.trasmed.com). Balearia also run services to/from Palma as well as some winter services (see individual websites for details).

Destinations Barcelona (3–7 weekly; 8–9hr); Palma (1–2 weekly; 5hr–5hr 30min); and Valencia (1 weekly; 15hr).

INFORMATION AND BOAT TRIPS

Turisme There is a tourist information desk at the airport (daily 9am–2pm; 971 356 944), plus an office down on the harbourfront, at Moll de Llevant 2 (Mon–Fri 9am–1pm; 971 355 952). The island's official website is www.menorca.es.

Boat trips Several boat companies offer boat hire, taxis and charters as well as accompanied trips ranging from 1hr along the Port de Maó to full-day excursions around the

calas of southeast Menorca. They all leave from the Moll de Llevant near the bottom of the main steps, where ticket offices and further information can also be found. Yellow Catamarans (www.yellowcatamarans.com; €15) run regular hour-long trips out past Es Castell to the fortress of La Mola in glass-bottom boats, with a running commentary in several languages.

ACCOMMODATION   SEE MAP PAGE 821

Maó has a limited supply of **accommodation**, and excessive demand tends to inflate prices at the height of the season. Despite this, along with Ciutadella it remains the best Menorcan bet for good-value lodgings, with a small concentration of *hostales*.

Hostal La Isla C/Santa Caterina 4, www.hostal-laisla. com. Rooms at this amenable *hostal* may be on the small side, but they are clean and comfortable, and all have private bathroom and TV. There's a popular bar downstairs;

breakfast included. €€

★ **Jardí de Ses Bruixes** C/San Fernando 26, https://hotel sesbruixes.com. Exquisitely restored manor house combining original nineteenth-century features, Art Nouveau decor and Mediterranean flourishes, no more so than in the charming courtyard, complete with orange trees and chandeliers. The courtyard doubles up as a café serving breakfast and brunch, and a restaurant offering local specialities such as grilled squid with ink noodles and citric fruits. €€€€

EATING   SEE MAP PAGE 821

★ **Can Vermut** Moll de Llevant 176, Port de Maó, www.canvermut.com. The food, music and atmosphere of this simple harbourfront bar-café reflect the owners' authenticity and integrity. Ingredients are local, sustainable or sourced from their vegetable garden, the meat is organic and the fish fresh from the sea. Try the black octopus carpaccio or a home-made *croquette* accompanied by one of their speciality vermouths. €€

La Cava del Ars Pl Príncipe 12, 971 351 079, https:// arscafe.wordpress.com. This café-music bar-restaurant puts

on live jazz, theatre and comedy as well as hosting regular club nights with DJs. It also serves up decent tapas, such as the pork fillet in whisky, with some good vegetarian options, and great mojitos. €€

Mercat Femenias Inside the Mercat des Peix, Pl. d'Espanya. Lively, bustling food hall on the right of the fish market with several varied stalls offering fish-focused *pintxos*, tapas and *raciones*, as well as larger plates. They'll also cook your fish market purchases for you to eat in situ. €€

DIRECTORY

Hospital Hospital Mateu Orfila, Ronda de Malburguer 1, **Post office** C/Ciutadella 76, www.correos.es.
971 487 000, https://ibsalut.es.

Around Maó

The southeast corner of the island is pretty flat and rural, which makes it a good place
for cyclists, especially as the main roads are shadowed by separate dedicated bike lanes.
There's not much to detain you in this region save the odd low-key resort and what
must be one of the world's most spectacularly sited nightspots.

Cova d'en Xoroi

Carrer de Sa Cova 2, Cala en Porter, Alaior • Check website for details of discos and club nights • www.covadenxoroi.com • A taxi from Maó
costs around €30

The **Cova d'en Xoroi** caves are built into a high cliff face, with terraces and large open
windows hewn out of the rock giving spectacular views over the Med. A winding staircase
leads down from the entrance at the top, punctuated by terraces and seating areas as it
links various colourfully lit caves that tunnel back into the rocks. During the day, you can
wander round the caves and sit on the terraces to marvel at the view, but at night it really
comes into its own as a **nightclub** showcasing some big-name DJs and club nights.

Across the island

The road from Maó to Ciutadella, the **Me-1**, forms the backbone of Menorca, and
what little industry the island enjoys – a few shoe factories and cheese plants – is strung
along it. Here also is the island's highest peak, **Monte Toro**, from the top of which there
are wondrous views.

Talatí de Dalt

4km out of Maó on the Me-1 • Charge, free Oct–April • www.menorcatalayotica.info

Down a country lane, clearly signposted off the Me-1, **Talatí de Dalt** is another
illuminating Talayotic remnant. Much larger than Trepucó, the site is enclosed by a
Cyclopean wall and features an imposing *taula*, which is adjacent to the heaped stones
of the main *talayot*. All around are the scant remains of prehistoric dwellings. The rustic
setting is charming – olive and carob trees abound and a tribe of semi-wild boar root
around the undergrowth.

Es Mercadal and Monte Toro

The old market town of **ES MERCADAL** squats among the hills at the very centre of the
island about 20km west of Maó. It's an amiable little place of whitewashed houses and
trim allotments, whose antique centre straddles a quaint watercourse.

Monte Toro

From Es Mercadal, you can set off on the ascent of **Monte Toro**, a steep 3.2-kilometre
climb along a serpentine road. At 357m, the summit is the island's highest point and
offers wonderful vistas. It has been a place of pilgrimage since medieval times, and the
Augustinians plonked a monastery on the summit in the seventeenth century. Bits
of this original construction survive in the convent there today, though much of the
convent area is closed to visitors.

Naveta d'es Tudons

Just off Me-1, 6km from Ciutadella • Charge, free Oct–April

From Es Mercadal, the Me-1 swings past the village of **FERRERIES** before sliding across
the agricultural flatlands of the western part of the island. There are prehistoric remains

13

to either side of the road, but easily the most interesting is the **Naveta d'es Tudons**, Menorca's best example of a *naveta*. Seven metres high and fourteen long, the structure is made of massive stone blocks slotted together in a sophisticated dry-stone technique. The narrow entrance leads into a small antechamber, which was once sealed off by a stone slab; beyond lies the main chamber where the bones of the dead were stashed away after the flesh had been removed.

Ciutadella

Like Maó, **CIUTADELLA** sits high above its harbour, though navigation is far more difficult here, up a narrow channel too slender for anything but the smallest of cargo ships. Despite this nautical inconvenience, Ciutadella was the island's capital for most of its history; the narrow, cobbled streets of its compact, fortified centre brim with fine old palaces, hidden away behind high walls, and a set of Baroque and Gothic churches very much in the Spanish tradition.

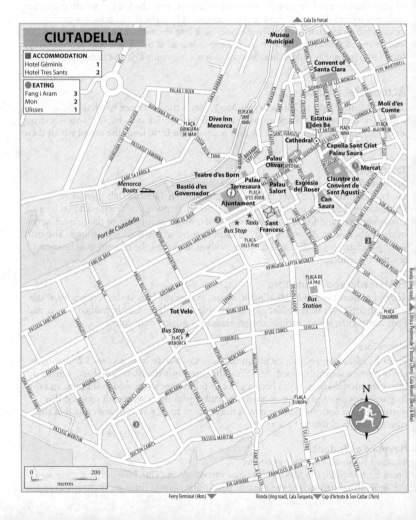

The main plazas, accommodation and points of interest are all within a few strides of each other, on and around the main square, **Pl. d'es Born**, in the middle of which a soaring obelisk commemorates the town's futile defence against the marauding Turks in 1558. To the northwest, the square is bordered by the steep harbour walls, and in the northeast lies the vast nineteenth-century Palau Torresaura. Like many of the city's grand aristocratic mansions, it is still privately owned and off limits to visitors.

Allow at least a couple of days, more if you seek out one of the charming cove beaches within easy striking distance of town – **Cala Turqueta and Calas Macarella and Macarelleta** are the picks of the bunch.

The Catedral

C/Cal Bispe s/n • Charge, includes entry to the Convent and Cloister of Sant Agustí • 971 380 343

From beside Palau Torresaura, C/Major d'es Born leads through to the **Catedral**, built by Alfonso III at the end of the thirteenth century on the site of the town's chief mosque. Built so soon after the Reconquest, its construction is fortress-like, with windows set high above the ground – though the effect is somewhat disturbed by the flashy columns of the Neoclassical west doorway, the principal entrance.

Convent and Cloister of Sant Agustí

C/Seminari 7 • Charge, includes entry to the Catedral • 971 481 297

The dignified **Convent and Cloister of Sant Agustí** (El Socors) dates from the seventeenth century, and is unique in Menorca for its twin towers and Renaissance style. Inside, you can see a collection of Talayotic and early classical archeological finds, notably a superbly crafted miniature bull and a similarly exquisite little mermaid, both Greek bronzes dating from the fifth century BC.

The Mercat

Pl. Llibertat • Fish market Tues–Sat 7am–2pm • Meat market Mon–Fri 7.30am–1.30pm & 5–8pm, Sat 7.30am–1.30pm

The green-and-white-tiled **mercat** (market), known to locals as the *mercat des peix* (fish market), is another delightful corner of the old town, where fresh fruit, vegetable and fish stalls mingle with lively and inexpensive cafés selling the freshest of *ensaimadas*. The benches and café patios are great for people-watching and while the market square lacks the atmospheric chaos, bustle and colour of a typical Spanish town, the produce on sale is second to none.

North of the centre

C/Seminari proceeds north from the Convent of Sant Agustí to intersect with the narrow, pedestrianized main street running through the old town – here **C/J.M. Quadrado**, though it goes under various names along its route. To the east of this intersection is a parade of whitewashed, vaulted arches, **Ses Voltes**, distinctly Moorish in inspiration and a suitable setting for several attractive shops and busy cafés. C/J.M. Quadrado then leads into **Pl. Nova**, a minuscule square edged by some of the most popular pavement cafés in town. Continuing east along C/Maó, you leave the cramped alleys of the old town at Pl. Alfons III.

ARRIVAL AND DEPARTURE   **CIUTADELLA**

By bus Buses to/from Maó (route 1) and some local routes pull in and depart from Pl. de la Pau. Other routes use the bus stop on Pl. dels Pins but this changes frequently so best to check at the *turisme*. The main bus station is the Perimetral, just outside the town centre. Timetables are found at www.tmsa.es.

Destinations Es Mercadal (Mon–Fri 20 daily, Sat & Sun 6–8 daily; 25min); Maó (Mon–Fri 20 daily, Sat & Sun 6–8 daily;

1hr).

By ferry Car ferries dock at the port about 2.5km south of the centre. Buses meet the boats to ferry passengers to the town centre (10min).

Destinations Barcelona (1 daily; 5hr 30min–9hr 30min); Port de Alcúdia (March–Sept 4–5 daily; Oct–Feb 1 daily; 2–2hr 30min).

13

INFORMATION AND TOURS

Turisme The tourist office in the *ajuntament* on Pl. d'es Born (May–Oct Mon–Sat 9am–8.30pm, Nov–April Mon–Fri 9am–2pm; 971 383 724, www.menorca.es) has buckets of information on Menorca as a whole and Ciutadella in particular. Bike hire is available at Velos Joan, C/Vila Juaneda 23 (https://velosjoan.com).

Boat trips Full-day excursions along the southwest coast stopping off at the beaches of Son Saura and Turqueta are offered by Menorca Blava (www.menorcablava.com) and other similar companies located on the Passeig des Moll, from where the boats also depart.

ACCOMMODATION

SEE MAP PAGE 824

Hotel Géminis C/Josepa Rossinyol 4, https://hotelgeminis menorca.com. This well-tended, peaceful two-star hotel on a quiet residential street has thirty simple but comfortable rooms and a small outdoor pool. €€€
Hotel Tres Sants C/Sant Cristòfol 2, https://hoteltres

santsciudadela.com-hotel.com. A boutique-style hotel sensitively converted from an old manor house in the heart of the old town. The roof terrace has great views over the town and harbour, and there's a small pool and Turkish bath in the basement. €€€€

EATING

SEE MAP PAGE 824

For an early **breakfast**, make your way to the **market** on Pl. Llibertat, where a couple of simple cafés serve coffee and fresh pastries. Later in the day, around **lunchtime**, aim for C/J.M. Quadrado, Pl. Nova or Pl. Alfons III, which together hold a good selection of inexpensive café-bars, offering tapas and light meals. In the summer evenings, head to the bars around the harbour for a taste of Ciutadella nightlife.
Fang i Aram C/Gabriel Martí i Bella 11, www.instagram.com/fangiaram. Vegetarian and vegan restaurant serving delicious locally sourced, organic food, including salads, veggie burgers and pasta as well as raw and gluten-free dishes. Highlights include the baked, stuffed aubergine, vegetable lasagne and homemade desserts. €€
★ **Mon** Pg. Sant Nicalau 4, www.monrestaurantfonda.com. This elegant restaurant, the creation of Felip Llufriu,

former chef at Michelin-starred *Roca Moo* in Barcelona, offers a deceptively simple menu, but every dish is packed with flavour. It changes according to what's in season, but might include traditional cod with spinach, sultanas and pine nuts, roast suckling pig with *sobrassada* (cured sausage with paprika), or prawn carpaccio with basil sorbet. €€€
★ **Ulisses** Pl. de la Llibertat 22, https://ulissesbar.com. Very popular café and tapas bar specializing in products sourced directly from the market, which it overlooks. Dishes range from small tapas to large plates such as tiger mussels, grilled squid or the Mercat hamburger with *sobrassada* (cured sausage) and honey. It also has an extensive wine list, thanks to its sister wine shop next door. Highly recommended. €€

Southeast of Ciutadella: Cala Turqueta

Beginning at the traffic island on C/Alfons V, the cross-country **Camí de Sant Joan de Missa** runs southeast from Ciutadella to the remote coves of the south coast. The one to head for is **Cala Turqueta**, an idyllic cove flanked by wooded limestone cliffs. About 3km from town, you reach the clearly marked farmhouse of **Son Vivó**, where the road branches into two with the more easterly (signposted) road leading to the **Ermita de Sant Joan de Missa**, a brightly whitewashed church with a dinky little bell tower. There's a fork here, too, but the signs are easy to follow, and you keep straight with the road slicing across the countryside before swerving round the **Marjal Vella** farmhouse. Shortly afterwards, about 4.3km from the church, you turn at the sign, going through the gateway to reach the car park for Cala Turqueta. The beach is ideal for swimming.

THE TILED "PROVINCE ALCOVES" IN THE PLAZA DE ESPANA

Contexts

History

The first Europeans of whom we have knowledge lived in southern Spain. A recent series of spectacular discoveries at Orce, 115km northeast of Granada, rocked the archeological world, as the date for the arrival of early humans in Europe was pushed back from around 700,000 years ago to perhaps a million years before this, making Orce – the findings were scientifically confirmed in 2013 – the earliest known site of human occupation in Europe by a long way. Other finds of early human remains around 800,000 years old in the Sierra de Atapuerca are further confirmation of early activity on the peninsula. Evidence of occupation by Stone Age societies stretching back some 400,000 years was already known about from discoveries at Venta Micena, close to Orce, where early inhabitants hunted elephant and rhino and left behind tools and camp fires. Some of the earliest human fossils found on the Iberian Peninsula were unearthed inside the Gibraltar caves, with evidence of Neanderthals dating from around 100,000 BC.

In the Paleolithic period, the first **homo sapiens** arrived on the Iberian Peninsula from southern France, settling around the Bay of Biscay as well as in the south. They were cave dwellers and hunter-gatherers, and, at **Altamira** in the Cordillera Cantábrica near Santander, and the Pileta and Nerja caves near Málaga, left behind remarkable **cave paintings** and deftly stylized cave murals depicting the animals they hunted. The finest examples (created about 12,000 BC) are at Altamira – these are mostly closed for general visits, though you can see similar paintings at Puente Viesgo nearby. During the later Neolithic phase, a sophisticated material culture developed in southern Spain, attested to by the finds of *esparto* sandals and baskets as well as jewellery in the **Cueva de los Murciélagos** in Granada. This period also saw the construction of **megalithic tombs** (dolmens) along the perimeter of the Iberian Peninsula, including the superbly preserved examples at Romanya de la Selva, in Catalunya, and **Antequera**, near Málaga.

Subsequent prehistory is more complex and confused, and the focus shifts from the cave cultures of the north, south to Almería, which was settled around 5000–4000 BC by the "Iberians", **Neolithic** colonists from North Africa. They had already assimilated into their culture many of the developments in Egypt and the Near East. Settling in villages, they introduced pastoral and agricultural ways of life and exploited the plentiful supply of copper. Around 1500 BC, with the onset of the **Bronze Age**, they began to spread outwards into fortified villages on the central *meseta*, the high plateau of modern Castile. At the turn of the millennium, they were joined by numerous waves of **Celtic** and **Germanic** peoples. Here, Spain's divisive physical make-up – with its network of mountain ranges – determined its social nature. The incoming tribes formed distinct and isolated groups, conquering and sometimes absorbing each other but only on a very limited and local scale. Hence the Celtic "urnfield people"

1.5 million years ago	25,000 BC	12,000 BC	2500 BC
Early humans active at Orce in the province of Granada after arriving from Africa.	Cave dwellers occupy caves in Málaga province.	Cave paintings made at Altamira in Cantabria and dolmens constructed in Catalunya and Málaga.	Chalcolithic (Copper Age) sites flourish in Almería.

established themselves in Catalunya, the **Vascones** in the Basque Country and, near them along the Atlantic coast, the **Astures**. Pockets of earlier cultures survived, too, particularly in Galicia with its *citanias* of beehive huts.

First colonies

The Spanish coast, meanwhile, attracted colonists from different regions of the Mediterranean. The **Phoenicians** founded the port of Gadir (Cádiz) around 1100 BC and traded intensively in the metals of the Guadalquivir valley. Their wealth and success gave rise to a Spanish "Atlantis" myth, based on the lost kingdom of Tartessus, mentioned in the Bible and probably sited near Huelva. Market rivalry later brought the **Greeks**, who established their trading colonies along the eastern coast – the modern Costa Brava. There's a fine surviving site at Empúries, near Barcelona.

More significant, however, was the arrival of the **Carthaginians** in the third century BC. Expelled from Sicily by the Romans, they saw in Spain a new base for their empire, from which to regain strength and strike back at their rivals. Although making little impact inland, they occupied most of Andalucía and expanded along the Mediterranean seaboard to establish a new capital at Cartagena ("New Carthage"). Under Hannibal they prepared to invade Italy, and in 219 BC attacked Saguntum, a strategic outpost of the Roman world. It was a disastrous move, precipitating the **Second Punic War**; by 210 BC, only Cádiz remained in their control and they were forced to accept terms. A new and very different age had begun.

Romans and Visigoths

The **Roman colonization** of the peninsula was far more intense than anything previously experienced and met with great resistance from the Celtiberian tribes of the north and centre. The conquest took two centuries to complete, and indeed the Basques, although defeated, were never fully Romanized. Nonetheless, Spain became the most important centre of the Roman Empire after Italy itself, producing no fewer than three emperors, along with the writers Seneca, Lucan, Martial and Quintilian. Again, geography dictated an uneven spread of influence, at its strongest in Andalucía, southern Portugal and on the Catalan coast around Tarragona. In the first two centuries AD, the Spanish mines and the granaries of Andalucía brought unprecedented wealth and Roman Spain enjoyed a brief **"golden age"**. The finest monuments were built in the great provincial capitals – Córdoba, Mérida (with impressive remains) and Tarragona – but across the country more practical construction was undertaken: roads, bridges and aqueducts. Many of the latter were used into recent centuries – the most remarkable being those of Segovia and Tarragona – and many bridges, such as that crossing the Guadalquivir in Córdoba, remain in use even today.

Towards the third century, however, the Roman political framework began to show signs of decadence and corruption. Although it didn't totally collapse until the Muslim invasions of the early eighth century, it became increasingly vulnerable to **barbarian incursions** from northern Europe. The Franks and the Suevi (Swabians) swept across the Pyrenees between 264 and 276, leaving devastation in their wake. They were followed two centuries later by further waves of Suevi, Alans and Vandals. Internal

c.1100 BC	c.1000 BC	c.9th–4th century BC	600–300 BC
Phoenicians found Cádiz.	Semi-mythical kingdom of Tartessus flourishes in the southwest of the peninsula.	Celts settle in the north and west of the peninsula. Greeks establish trading posts along east coast.	Greeks establish trading colonies along the Mediterranean coast.

strife was heightened by the arrival of the **Visigoths** from Gaul, allies of Rome and already Romanized to a large degree. The triumph of Visigothic strength in the fifth century resulted in a period of spurious unity, based upon an exclusive military rule from their capital at Toledo. But order was often fragmentary and nominal, with the bulk of the subject people kept in a state of disconsolate servility and the military elite divided by constant plots and factions – exacerbated by the Visigothic system of elected monarchy and adherence to the heretical Arian doctrine. In 589, **King Recared** converted to Catholicism but religious strife was only multiplied: forced conversions, especially within the Jewish enclaves, maintained a constant simmering of discontent.

Moorish Spain

In contrast to the drawn-out Roman campaigns, **Moorish conquest** of the peninsula was effected with extraordinary speed. This was a characteristic phenomenon of the spread of Islam – Muhammad left Mecca in 622 and by 705 his followers had established control over all of North Africa. Spain, with its political instability, wealth and fertile climate, was an inevitable extension of their aims. In 711, Tariq, governor of Tangier, led a force of seven thousand Berbers across the straits and routed the Visigothic army of King Roderic; two years later, the Visigoths made a last desperate stand at Mérida, and within a decade the Moors had conquered all but the wild mountains of Asturias. The land under their authority was dubbed "al-Andalus", a fluid term that expanded and shrank with the intermittent gains and losses of the Reconquest. According to region, the Moors were to remain in control for the next three to eight centuries.

It was not simply a military conquest. The Moors (a collective term for numerous waves of North African Arabs and Berbers) were often content to grant a limited autonomy in exchange for payment of tribute; their administrative system was tolerant and absorbed both Jews and Christians, who became known as "Mozarabs". And al-Andalus was a distinctly Spanish state of Islam. Though at first politically subject to the Eastern Caliphate (or empire) of Baghdad, it was soon virtually independent. In the tenth century, at the peak of its power and expansion, Abd-ar-Rahman III asserted total independence, proclaiming himself caliph of a new **Western Islamic empire**. Its capital was Córdoba – the largest, most prosperous and most civilized city in Europe. This was the great age of Muslim Spain: its scholarship, philosophy, architecture and craftsmanship were without rival and there was an unparalleled growth in urban life, in trade and agriculture, aided by magnificent irrigation projects. These and other engineering feats were not, on the whole, instigated by the Moors, who instead took Roman models and adapted and improved them. In **architecture** and the **decorative arts**, however, their contribution was original and unique – as may be seen in the fabulous monuments of Seville, Córdoba and Granada.

The Córdoban Caliphate for a while created a remarkable degree of unity. But its rulers were to become decadent and out of touch, prompting the brilliant but dictatorial **al-Mansur** to usurp control. Under this extraordinary ruler, Moorish power actually reached new heights, pushing the Christian kingdom of Asturias-León back into the Cordillera Cantábrica and sacking its most holy shrine, Santiago de Compostela. However, after al-Mansur's death the caliphate quickly lost its authority,

c.5th century BC	c.214 BC	210 BC	27 BC
Carthage colonizes southern Spain. Celtiberian culture develops, with Greek influence.	Second Punic War with Rome.	Roman colonization begins.	Octavian-Augustus becomes the first Roman emperor.

> **ALMOHAD ARCHITECTURE**
>
> In the eleventh century, Andalucía fragmented into rival kingdoms or *taifas*, allowing successive waves of Moorish invaders to move into the power vacuum. One of these, the ultra-fundamentalist **Almohads**, left behind a number of remarkable buildings of which the foremost is the magnificent **Giralda** tower in Seville, the surviving minaret of the Friday mosque demolished to construct the Gothic Catedral. At 100m high with elaborate *sebka* brickwork panels adorning its exterior walls, it was started in 1184 under architect Ahmed ibn Baso and completed twelve years later.

and in 1031 it disintegrated into a series of small independent kingdoms, or *taifas*, the strongest of which was Seville.

Internal divisions among the *taifas* weakened their resistance to the Christian kingdoms that were rallying in the north, and twice North Africa had to be turned to for reinforcement. This resulted in two distinct new waves of Moorish invasion – first by the fanatically Islamic **Almoravids** (1086) and later by the **Almohads** (1147), who restored effective Muslim authority until their defeat at the battle of Las Navas de Tolosa in 1212.

The Christian Reconquest

The **Reconquest** of land and influence from the Moors was a slow and intermittent process. It began with a symbolic victory by a small force of Christians at Covadonga in Asturias (722) and was not completed until 1492 with the conquest of Granada by Fernando and Isabel.

The victory at Covadonga resulted in the formation of the tiny Christian kingdom of **Asturias**. Initially just 50 by 65km in area, it had by 914 reclaimed León and most of Galicia and northern Portugal. At this point, progress was temporarily halted by the devastating campaigns of al-Mansur. However, with the fall of the Córdoban Caliphate and the divine aid of Spain's Moor-slaying patron, St James the Apostle, or Santiago (see page 512), the Reconquest moved into a new and powerful phase.

The frontier castles built against Arab attack gave their name to Castile, founded in the tenth century as a county of León-Asturias. Under **Ferdinand I** (1037–65), it achieved the status of a kingdom and became the main thrust of the Reconquest. Other kingdoms were being defined in the north at the same time: the Basques founded **Navarra** (Navarre), while dynastic marriage merged **Catalunya** with **Aragón**. In 1085, this period of confident Christian expansion reached its zenith with the capture of the great Moorish city of Toledo. The following year, however, the Almoravids arrived on invitation from Seville, and military activity was effectively frozen – except, that is, for the exploits of the legendary El Cid (see page 393), a Castilian nobleman who won considerable lands around Valencia in 1095.

The next concerted phase of the Reconquest began as a response to the threat imposed by the Almohads. The kings of León, Castile, Aragón and Navarra united in a general crusade that resulted in the great victory at Las Navas de Tolosa (1212). Thereafter, Muslim power was effectively paralysed, and the Christian armies moved

c.409–415	c.5th–7th century	711	722
Vandals invade Spain.	Visigoths arrive and take control of most of Spain.	Moors under Tariq invade and defeat Visigothic King Roderic near Jerez. Peninsula conquered in seven years.	Pelayo defeats Moors at Covadonga in Asturias in northern Spain marking the start of the Reconquest.

on to take most of al-Andalus. Ferdinand III ("El Santo", The Saint) led Castilian soldiers into Córdoba in 1236 and Seville in 1248. Meanwhile, the kingdom of Portugal had expanded to near its present size, while Jaime I of Aragón was to conquer Valencia, Alicante, Murcia and the Balearic Islands. By the end of the thirteenth century, only the kingdom of Granada remained under Muslim authority, and for the following two centuries was forced to pay tribute to Castile.

Two factors should be stressed regarding the Reconquest. First, its **unifying religious nature** – the spirit of crusade, intensified by the religious zeal of the Almoravids and Almohads, and by the wider European climate (which in 1095 gave rise to the First Crusade). This powerful religious motivation is well illustrated by the subsequent canonization of Ferdinand III, and found solid expression in the part played by the military orders of Christian knights, the most important of which were the Knights Templar and the Order of Santiago. At the same time, the Reconquest was a movement of **recolonization**. The fact that the country had been in arms for so long meant that the nobility had a major social role, a trend perpetuated by the redistribution of captured land in huge packages, or *latifundia*. Heirs to this tradition still remain as landlords of the great estates, conspicuously in Andalucía. Men from the ranks were also awarded land, forming a lower stratum of nobility, the *hidalgos*. It was their particular social code that provided the material for Cervantes in *Don Quixote*.

Any spirit of mutual cooperation that had temporarily united the Christian kingdoms disintegrated during the fourteenth century, and independent lines of development were once again pursued. Attempts to merge Portugal with Castile foundered at the battle of Aljubarrota (1385), and Portuguese attention turned away from Spain towards the Atlantic. Aragón experienced a similar pull towards the markets of the Mediterranean, although pre-eminence in this area was soon passed to the Genoese. It was Castile that emerged the strongest over this period: self-sufficiency in agriculture and a flourishing wool trade with the Netherlands enabled the state to build upon the prominent military role it played under Fernando III. Politically, Castilian history was a tale of dynastic conflict until the accession of the Catholic Monarchs.

Los Reyes Católicos

Los Reyes Católicos – the **Catholic Monarchs** – was the joint title given to **Fernando of Aragón and Isabel of Castile**, whose marriage in 1469 united the two largest kingdoms in Spain. Unity was in practice more symbolic than real: Castile had underlined its rights in the marriage vows and Aragón retained its old administrative structure. So, in the beginning at least, the growth of any national unity or Spanish – as opposed to local – sentiment was very much dependent on the head of state. Nevertheless, from now on it becomes realistic to consider Spain as a single political entity.

At the heart of Fernando and Isabel's popular appeal lay a **religious bigotry** that they shared with most of their Christian subjects. The **Inquisition** was instituted in Castile in 1480 and in Aragón seven years later. Aiming to establish the purity of the Catholic faith by rooting out heresy, it was directed mainly at Jews – resented for their enterprise in commerce and influence in high places, as well as for their faith. Expression had already been given to these feelings in a pogrom in 1391, reinforced by an edict issued in 1492 that forced up to 400,000 Jews to flee the country. A similar spirit was

756	c.9th century	967	1031
Abd-ar-Rahman I proclaims Emirate of Córdoba. Great mosque of Córdoba (Mezquita) begun.	Kingdoms of Catalunya and Navarra founded.	Al-Mansur usurps Caliphal powers of Córdoba Caliphate and forces Christians back into Asturias.	Caliphate disintegrates into *taifas* (petty kingdoms).

COLUMBUS AND THE CATHOLIC MONARCHS

After many frustrating years trying to find backers for his plan **to reach the Indies by sailing west**, Columbus's luck turned in 1491 when he spent a period at the Franciscan monastery of La Rabida in the province of Huelva. The abbot of La Rabida, Juan Pérez, a former confessor to Queen Isabel, was moved to write to her on Columbus's behalf. It was a timely moment as Granada had just fallen, the treasury was empty, and the promise of gold and glory for a resurgent Spain now attracted Isabel and her husband King Fernando. On August 3, 1492, Columbus set out from Palos, a port in Huelva, with three small vessels and 120 men. On October 12, he made landfall on Watling Island (aka San Salvador) in the Bahamas. After leaving a colony of men on Hispaniola (modern Haiti) he returned to Palos on March 15, 1493, to enormous acclaim. The Spanish conquest of the Americas had begun.

embodied in the Reconquest of the **Kingdom of Granada**, also in 1492. As the last stronghold of Muslim authority, the religious rights of its citizens were guaranteed under the treaty of surrender. Within a decade, though, those Muslims under Christian rule had been given the choice between conversion or expulsion.

The year 1492 was symbolic in another way: it was the year that Columbus (Cristóbal Colón) "discovered" America, and of the papal bull entrusting Spain with the conversion of the Native Americans, entrenching its sense of a mission to bring the world to the "True Faith". The next decade saw the systematic conquest, colonization and exploitation of the **New World** stretching from Labrador to Brazil, and new-found wealth poured into the royal coffers. Important as this was for Fernando and Isabel, and their prestige, their priorities remained in Europe, and strategic marriage alliances were made with Portugal, England and the Holy Roman Empire. It was not until the accession of the Habsburg dynasty that Spain could look to the activities of Cortés, Magellan and Pizarro and claim to be the world's leading power.

Habsburg Spain

Carlos I, a **Habsburg**, came to the throne in 1516 as a beneficiary of the marriage alliances of the Catholic Monarchs. Five years later, he was elected emperor of the Holy Roman Empire as Carlos V (**Charles V**), inheriting not only Castile and Aragón, but Flanders, the Netherlands, Artois, the Franche-Comté and all the American colonies to boot. With such responsibilities it was inevitable that attention would be diverted from Spain, whose chief function became to sustain the Holy Roman Empire with gold and silver from the Americas. It was only with the accession of **Felipe II** in 1556 that Spanish politics became more centralized. Felipe lived in the centre of Castile, near Madrid, creating a monument to the values of medieval Spain in his palace, El Escorial.

Two main themes run through his reign: the preservation of his own inheritance, and the revival of the crusade in the name of the Catholic Church. In pursuit of the former, Felipe successfully claimed the Portuguese throne (through the marriage of his mother), gaining access to the additional wealth of its empire. Plots were also woven in support of Mary Queen of Scots' claim to the English throne, launching the ill-fated **Armada** in 1588, its sinking a triumph for English naval strength and Protestantism.

1037	1085	1086	1147
Fernando I unites kingdoms of Castile and León Asturias.	Christians capture Toledo.	Almoravids invade Spain from North Africa.	Invasion by Almohads from Morocco; Seville becomes new Moorish capital in Spain.

This was a period of unusual religious intensity: the **Inquisition** was enforced with renewed vigour, and a rising of Moriscos (subject Moors) in the Alpujarras was fiercely suppressed. Felipe III later ordered the expulsion of half the total number of Moriscos in Spain – allowing only two families to remain in each village in order to maintain irrigation techniques. The **exodus** of both Muslims and Jews created a large gulf in the labour force and in the higher echelons of commercial life – and in trying to uphold the Catholic cause, an enormous strain was put upon resources without any clear-cut victory.

By the middle of the seventeenth century, Spain was losing international credibility. Domestically, the disparity between the wealth surrounding Crown and court and the impoverishment of the masses was a source of perpetual tension. Discontent fuelled regional revolts in Catalunya and Portugal in 1640, and the latter had finally to be reacknowledged as an independent state in 1668.

Bourbons and the Peninsular War

The **Bourbon dynasty** succeeded to the Spanish throne in the person of **Felipe V** (1700); with him began the **War of the Spanish Succession** against the rival claim of Archduke Charles of Austria, assisted by British forces. In the Treaty of Utrecht, which ended the war (1713), Spain was stripped of all territory in Belgium, Luxembourg, Italy and Sardinia, but Felipe V was recognized as king. Gibraltar was seized by the British in the course of the war. For the rest of the century, Spain fell under the French sphere of influence, which was politically defined by an alliance with the French Bourbons in 1762.

Contact with France made involvement in the **Napoleonic Wars** inevitable and led eventually to the defeat of the Spanish fleet at Trafalgar in 1805. Popular outrage was such that the powerful prime minister, Godoy, was overthrown and King Carlos IV forced to abdicate (1808). Napoleon seized the opportunity to install his brother, Joseph, on the throne.

Fierce local resistance was eventually backed by the muscle of the British army commanded by Sir John Moore, then the Duke of Wellington, and the **Peninsular War** resulted in the French being driven out. Meanwhile, however, the **American colonies** had been successfully asserting their independence from a preoccupied centre and with them went Spain's last real claim of significance on the world stage. The entire nineteenth century was dominated by the struggle between an often reactionary monarchy and the aspirations of liberal constitutional reformers.

Seeds of civil war

Between 1810 and 1813 an ad hoc Cortes (parliament) had set up a **liberal constitution** with ministers responsible to a democratically elected chamber. The first act of Ferdinand VII on being returned to the throne was to abolish this, and until his death in 1833 he continued to stamp out the least hint of liberalism. On his death, the right of succession was contested between his brother, Don Carlos, backed by the Church, conservatives and Basques, and his infant daughter, Isabel, who had the support of the liberals and the army. So began the **First Carlist War**, a civil war that

1162	1212	1213
Alfonso II unites kingdoms of Aragón and Catalunya.	Almohad advance halted at Las Navas de Tolosa in Andalucía.	Jaime I "El Conquistador" becomes king of Aragón and leads Christian Reconquest of Balearics (1229), Valencia (1238) and Alicante (1266).

lasted six years. Isabel II was eventually declared of age in 1843, her reign a long record of scandal, political crisis and constitutional compromise. Liberal army generals under the leadership of General Prim effected a coup in 1868 and the queen was forced to abdicate, but attempts to maintain a republican government foundered. The Cortes was again dissolved and the throne returned to Isabel's son, Alfonso XII. A new constitution was declared in 1876, limiting the power of the Crown through the institution of bicameral government, but again progress was halted by the lack of any tradition on which to base the constitutional theory.

The years preceding World War I merely heightened the discontent, finding expression in the growing **political movements** of the working class. The Socialist Workers' Party was founded in Madrid after the restoration of Alfonso XII, and spawned its own trade union, the UGT (1888), successful in areas of high industrial concentration such as the Basque Country and Asturias. Its anarchist counterpart, the CNT, was founded in 1911, gaining substantial support among the peasantry of Andalucía.

The loss of **Cuba** in 1898 emphasized the growing isolation of Spain in international affairs and added to economic problems with the return of soldiers seeking employment where there was none. A call-up for army reserves to fight in **Morocco** in 1909 provoked a general strike and the "Tragic Week" of rioting in Barcelona. Between 1914 and 1918, Spain was outwardly neutral but inwardly turbulent; inflated prices made the postwar recession harder to bear.

The general disillusionment with parliamentary government, together with the fears of employers and businessmen for their own security, gave **General Primo de Rivera** sufficient support for a military coup in 1923 in which the king, Alfonso XIII, was pushed into the background. Dictatorship did result in an increase in material prosperity, but the death of the dictator in 1930 revealed the apparent stability as a facade. New political factions were taking shape: the Liberal Republican Right was founded by Alcalá Zamora, while the Socialist Party was given definition under the leadership of Largo Caballero. The victory of antimonarchist parties in the 1931 municipal elections forced the abdication of the king, who went into exile, and the **Second Republic** was declared.

The Second Republic

Catalunya declared itself a republic independent of the central government and was ceded control of internal affairs by a statute in 1932. **Separatist movements** were powerful, too, in the Basque provinces and Galicia, each with their own demands for autonomy. Meanwhile, the government, set up on a tidal wave of hope, was utterly divided internally and too scared of right-wing reaction to carry out the massive tax and agrarian reforms that the left demanded, and that might have provided the resources for thoroughgoing regeneration of the economy.

The result was the increasing polarization of Spanish politics. **Anarchism**, in particular, was gaining strength among the frustrated middle classes as well as among the workers and peasantry. The **Communist Party** and left-wing **Socialists**, driven into alliance by their mutual distrust of the "moderate" socialists in government, were also forming a growing bloc. On the right, the **Falangists**, basically a youth party

1217	**1469**	**1492**
Fernando III "El Santo" crowned king of Castile, and retakes Córdoba (1236), Murcia (1241) and Seville (1248).	Castile and Aragón united by the marriage of Isabel and Fernando, Los Reyes Católicos (the Catholic Monarchs).	Fall of Granada, the last Moorish kingdom. "Discovery" of America by Cristóbal Colón (Columbus).

founded in 1923 by **José Antonio Primo de Rivera** (son of the dictator), made uneasy bedfellows with conservative traditionalists and dissident elements in the army upset by modernizing reforms.

In an atmosphere of growing confusion, the left-wing Popular Front alliance narrowly won the general election of **February 1936**. Normal life, though, became increasingly impossible: the economy was crippled by strikes, peasants took agrarian reform into their own hands, and the government failed to exert its authority over anyone. Finally, on July 17, 1936, the military garrison in Morocco rebelled under the leadership of **General Francisco Franco**, to be followed by risings at military garrisons throughout the country. It was the culmination of years of scheming in the army, but in the event was far from the overnight success its leaders expected. The south quickly fell into Nationalist hands, but Madrid and the industrialized north and east remained loyal to the Republican government.

Civil War

The ensuing **Civil War** was undoubtedly one of the most bitter and bloody that Europe has seen. Violent reprisals were taken on their enemies by both sides – the Republicans shooting priests and local landowners wholesale, the Nationalists carrying out mass slaughter of the population of almost every town they took. Contradictions were legion in the way the Spanish populations found themselves divided from each other. Perhaps the greatest irony was that Franco's troops, on their "holy" mission to ensure a Catholic Spain, comprised a core of Moroccan troops from Spain's North African colony.

It was, too, the first modern war – Franco's German allies demonstrated their ability to wipe out entire civilian populations with their bombing raids on Gernika and Durango, and radio proved an important weapon, as Nationalist propagandists offered the starving Republicans "the white bread of Franco".

Despite sporadic help from Russia and thousands of volunteers in the **International Brigade**, the Republic could never compete with the professional armies and massive assistance from Fascist Italy and Nazi Germany enjoyed by the Nationalists. In addition, the left was torn by internal divisions that at times led almost to civil war within its own ranks. Nevertheless, the Republicans held out in slowly dwindling territories for nearly three years, with **Catalunya** falling in January 1939 and armed resistance in **Madrid** – which never formally surrendered – petering out over the following months. As hundreds of thousands of refugees flooded into France, General Franco, who had long before proclaimed himself head of state, took up the reins of power.

Franco's Spain

The early reprisals taken by the victors were on a massive and terrifying scale. Executions were commonplace, and upwards of two million people were put in concentration camps until "order" had been established by authoritarian means. Only one party, the **Falange**, was permitted, and censorship was rigidly enforced. By the end of World War II, during which Spain was too weak to be anything but neutral, **Franco** was Europe's only Fascist head of state, one responsible for sanctioning more

1516	1519	1532	1556
Carlos V succeeds to the throne and becomes the Holy Roman Emperor (1520), inaugurating the Golden Age.	Cortés lands in Mexico.	Pizarro "discovers" Peru.	Accession of Felipe II (d.1598).

deaths than any other in Spanish history. Spain was economically and politically isolated and, bereft of markets, suffered – almost half the population were still tilling the soil for little or no return. When President Eisenhower visited Madrid in 1953 with the offer of huge loans, it came as water to the desert, and the price, the establishment of American nuclear bases, was one Franco was more than willing to pay. However belated, economic development was incredibly rapid, with Spain enjoying a growth rate second only to that of Japan for much of the 1960s, a boom fuelled by the tourist industry and the remittances of Spanish workers abroad.

Increased **prosperity**, however, only underlined the political bankruptcy of Franco's regime and its inability to cope with popular demands. Higher incomes, the need for better education, and a creeping invasion of Western culture made the anachronism of Franco ever clearer. His only reaction was to attempt to withdraw what few signs of increased liberalism had crept through, and his last years mirrored the repression of the postwar period. Trade unions remained outlawed, and the rampant inflation of the early 1970s saw striking workers across Spain hauled out of occupied mines and factories and imprisoned, or even shot in the streets. Attempts to report these events by the liberal press resulted in suspensions, fines and censorship. **Basque nationalists**, whose assassination of Admiral Carrero Blanco in 1973 had effectively destroyed Franco's last hope of a like-minded successor, were singled out for particularly harsh treatment. Hundreds of so-called terrorists were tortured, and the Burgos trials of 1970, together with the executions of August 1975, provoked worldwide protest.

Franco finally died in November 1975, nominating **King Juan Carlos** as his successor. Groomed for the job and very much "in" with the army – of which he remained official commander-in-chief – the king's initial moves were cautious in the extreme, appointing a government dominated by loyal Francoists who had little sympathy for the growing opposition demands for "democracy without adjectives". In the summer of 1976, demonstrations in Madrid ended in violence, with the police upholding the old authoritarian ways.

The return of democracy

The violent events leading up to and following his mentor's death persuaded Juan Carlos that some real break with the past and a move towards **democratization** was now urgent and inevitable. Using the almost dictatorial powers he had inherited, he ousted Franco's reactionary prime minister, Carlos Arias Navarro, and replaced him with **Adolfo Suárez**, an ambitious lawyer and former apparatchik in Franco's ruling Movimiento party. Taking his cue from the king, in 1976 Suárez pushed a **Law of Political Reform** through the Cortes, reforming the legislature into two chambers elected by universal suffrage – a move massively endorsed by the Spanish people in a referendum. Suárez also passed legislation allowing the setting up of free trade unions, as well as legitimizing the Socialist Party (PSOE) and, controversially, the Communists. Several cabinet ministers resigned in protest, and an outraged military began planning their coup d'état.

When elections were held in June 1977, Suárez's own hastily formed centre-right party, the **Unión del Centro Democrático** (**UCD**), was rewarded with a 34 percent share of the vote, the Socialists coming in second with 28 percent, and the Communists and

1588	1605	1609
British forces defeat the Spanish Armada. Marks Spain's demise as a sea power.	Miguel de Cervantes writes *Don Quijote* (*Quixote*), considered the first modern novel.	Expulsion of Moriscos, last remaining Spanish Muslims.

THE LAW OF HISTORICAL MEMORY

In Spain as well as abroad the **legacy of Franco** remains controversial. In the years following the restoration of democracy there was no national debate about the dictator's thirty-five-year rule and unlike other countries, such as Germany and Argentina, Spain has never fully come to terms with its former dictatorship. Instead, politicians on both sides of the divide tacitly agreed not to mention the legacy of the Franco regime and no war crimes trials were held. But many others were angry at a pact which meant that crimes committed in the Franco years not only went unpunished, but were not even recognized as having taken place. In 2007 the Spanish PSOE government – led by José Luís Rodrigo Zapatero, whose own grandfather was executed by Franco's forces – decided to address this issue and passed into law **La Ley de Memoria Histórica** (The Law of Historical Memory). This rules that sentences handed down by kangaroo courts during the regime – that led to the imprisonment or execution of thousands of Franco's opponents – were "illegitimate". It also decrees that local governments must locate, exhume from mass graves and identify the victims of the Franco regime. Historians claim that the remains of tens of thousands of Franco's opponents are buried in unmarked graves throughout the country.

The law also stipulates that all statues, plaques and symbols relating to the regime must be removed from public buildings (however, church property was excluded). It deals, too, with the dictatorship's monumental legacy – the vast basilica of the **Valle de los Caídos** near Madrid where the remains of Franco and the founder of the Fascist Falange party, José Antonio Prima de Rivera, are interred. The law prohibits all political events at the site, thus preventing the traditional "Mass for the Caudillo" formerly celebrated each November 20 (the anniversary of Franco's death), and its celebration of the Fascist cause.

Francoist **Alianza Popular** marginalized at 9 percent and 8 percent respectively. Despite the overwhelming victories in Catalunya and the Basque Country of parties appealing to regional sentiment, this was a vote for democratic stability rather than for ideology, something reflected in the course of the parliament, with Suárez governing through "consensus politics", negotiating settlements on all important issues with the major parties.

The first parliament of the "New Spain" now embarked on the formidable task of drawing up a **constitution**, while the Suárez government applied for membership of what was then the EEC. One of the fundamental components of the new constitution was the concept of **autonomy** – the granting of substantial self-rule to the seventeen *autonomías* (autonomous regions) into which Spain was to be divided. In Franco's time, even speaking regional languages such as Catalan or Basque was banned, and the backlash against this policy ensured that nothing less than some form of independence would be acceptable for regions such as the Basque Country and Catalunya. On December 6, 1978, the new constitution was overwhelmingly endorsed in a national referendum and, remarkably, only three years after the death of Franco, Spain became a full democracy.

Elections in March 1979 virtually duplicated the 1977 result, but when the UCD, a fractious coalition of moderates and extremists, started to crack, **Suárez resigned** in January 1981. This provided the trigger for a **military coup**, launched by a

1700	1808	1812	1833–39
War of Spanish Succession brings Felipe V (1683–1746), a Bourbon, to the throne. British seize Gibraltar.	France occupies Spain. Venezuela declares independence, others follow.	Liberal constitution declared in Cádiz.	First Carlist War. Dissolution of the monasteries.

contingent of Guardia Civil loyal to Franco's memory and commanded by the tragi-comic Colonel Antonio Tejero. They stormed into the Cortes with Tejero brandishing a revolver, and submachine-gunned the ceiling as *diputados* (MPs) dived for cover. The crisis was real: tanks were brought out onto the streets of Valencia, and only three of the army's ten regional commanders remained unreservedly loyal to the government. But as it became clear that the king would not support the plotters, most of the rest then affirmed their support. Juan Carlos had taken the decision of his life and emerged with immensely enhanced prestige in the eyes of most Spaniards.

The González era

On October 28, 1982, the Socialist PSOE, led by charismatic **Felipe González**, was elected with the biggest landslide victory in Spanish electoral history to rule a country that had been firmly in the hands of the right for 43 years. The Socialists captured the imagination and the votes of nearly ten million Spaniards with the simplest of appeals: "for change".

Once in power, however, the Socialist Party chose the path of pragmatism, and a relentless drift to the right followed. Four successive election victories kept the party in power for fourteen years, and by the mid-1990s the PSOE government's policies had become indistinguishable from the conservative administrations of Britain or Germany.

González himself, meanwhile, had also undergone transformation – from a radical young labour lawyer into a careworn elder statesman. Control of inflation had become a more urgent target than reducing unemployment, while loss-making heavy industries were ruthlessly overhauled and others privatized. Like most of Spain's left, González had vehemently objected to Spain's membership of NATO but when a referendum was held on the issue in 1986 – which turned out marginally in favour of staying in – his was one of the main voices in favour of continued membership. **European Union** membership came in the same year, and the pride that most Spanish people felt at this tangible proof of their acceptance by the rest of Europe bought the Socialists more valuable time.

After long years of being hopelessly divided, in the late 1980s the **Spanish right** realigned itself when former prime minister Adolfo Suárez's UCD Christian Democrats merged with the Alianza Popular to form the new right-of-centre **Partido Popular** (PP), which came a respectable runner-up in the 1989 elections; a new far-left coalition, **Izquierda Unida** (United Left), composed of the Communists and smaller leftist parties, came third, albeit with the same number of seats (18) in the Congress of Deputies as the Catalan Nationalists, barely a tenth of the PSOE's representation.

The nation's progressive disillusionment with Felipe González's government in the early 1990s saw the rise to prominence of **José María Aznar** as leader of the PP. A former tax inspector, Aznar was dogged in his criticism of government incompetence in dealing with its own sleaze and the growing economic crisis. This debilitated the PSOE's position still further in the build-up to the **1993 elections**. However, the PSOE confounded the opinion polls to hang on to power by the skin of its teeth, albeit as a minority government.

But González's victory was a poisoned chalice, for his past now began to catch up with him. Illegal financing of the PSOE and corruption and commission-taking on

1898	1923	1931	1936
Loss of Cuba, Spain's last American colony,	Primo de Rivera dictatorship Resigns (1930) due to ill health and popular agitation urges a republic.	King Alfonso XIII is forced out and the Second Republic is declared.	Spanish Civil War begins.

government projects by party officials and ministers were only some of numerous scandals now exposed. By far the most serious was the **GAL affair** (Grupo Antiterrorista de Liberación), when it was discovered that a semi-autonomous anti-terrorist unit had been carrying out a dirty war against the ETA terrorists in the 1980s, which included kidnapping and wholesale assassinations of suspected ETA members. The press – and a later judicial investigation – exposed police participation in these crimes and a clear chain of command reaching up to the highest echelons of the PSOE government. Some Guardia Civil police officers were sent to prison for offences connected with the GAL affair, as were (briefly) two ministers for covering up the plot, before being released on appeal. But despite the efforts of prosecutors, González managed to avoid being hauled before the courts.

The swing to the right

The ailing PSOE administration, immersed in endless scandals, limped on towards what looked likely to be a crushing defeat in the **1996 elections**. The surprise result, however, was another **hung parliament**, making everyone a loser. Aznar, the narrow victor, was denied the "absolute majority" he had believed to be his throughout the campaign, and was forced into a deal with the nationalist parties in order to secure a workable parliamentary majority. Meanwhile, the PSOE's avoidance of the expected overwhelming defeat was proclaimed as a vindication by González, who hastily dismissed ideas of retirement. However, unable to make any significant impact on changing public opinion, and with the PSOE still in turmoil, early in 1998 **González resigned** the leadership of the party he had dominated for 23 years.

Elected on a centre-right platform, Aznar, during his first term in office following his narrow 1996 victory, progressively moved his party to the centre, shifting aside remaining hardliners in the hope of gaining the electorate's confidence and a working majority not dependent on alliances with the northern nationalists.

Following the resignation of Felipe González in 1998, a desperate PSOE formed an alliance with the ex-Communist Izquierda Unida, but this failed to convince voters and the outcome of the March 2000 **general election** was a stunning **triumph for Aznar** and the PP: for the first time since the death of Franco, the right was in power with an overall majority.

The result was disaster for the left, and the PSOE then elected **José Luis Rodríguez Zapatero**, a relatively unknown young politician, as leader. A moderate, Zapatero admitted the PSOE's past mistakes, stating emphatically that any government led by him would be radically different. This seemed to go down well with the electorate, and the opinion polls started to move in the PSOE's favour.

The return of the PSOE

In 2001, José María Aznar announced that he would lead the PP up to the next general election but would then resign, and that it must seek a new leader. As leader designate (to take over following the election), the party chose Aznar's nominee, the less prickly, cigar-puffing **Mariano Rajoy**, minister for the interior and deputy prime minister. Early in 2004 all the indicators suggested that the following March general election would

1937	1939	1953
Basque town of Gernika is destroyed by German bombers. Over 1500 civilians are killed.	Civil War ends and Franco dictatorship begins.	US makes economic deal with Franco in return for military bases.

deliver a comfortable victory for the ruling PP and its new leader, Rajoy. Then, on March 11, and three days before polling day, a series of **bombs** exploded on rush-hour commuter trains travelling into Madrid, killing 191 people and injuring almost two thousand others. The nation was thrown into shock at the most savage attack seen in Spain since the Civil War. Despite the discovery by police within hours of a van linked to the bombings containing detonators and a Koranic audiotape, the PP leadership decided that no mention was to be made of any possible link with Islamic militant groups or the Iraq war (which ninety percent of Spaniards had opposed) – the blaming of ETA would conveniently vindicate Aznar's hardline stance against Basque terrorism and separatism.

The scheme failed. Many voters saw through the government's "blame ETA" smokescreen and correctly believed the attack to be the work of **Islamic terrorists** as a retaliation for Spain's participation in the Iraq war. The result was **an unexpected victory** for Zapatero and the PSOE, whose first act was to announce the **immediate withdrawal of Spanish troops from Iraq**, an election promise. This aligned Zapatero firmly with the German and French governments in Europe to whom Aznar had been hostile, but incurred the displeasure of US president George W. Bush, who shunned Zapatero for the rest of his presidency.

Zapatero's initial record was competent if unspectacular. He enjoyed the benefit of a favourable economic climate with consistently high growth figures and an economy producing more jobs than any other euro-zone member. But in the latter part of 2007, the impact of the world **economic downturn** became desperately felt in Spain, as one of the major drivers of the Spanish economy, the huge construction industry, went into meltdown. The **general election of March 2008** took place against a backdrop of economic uncertainty, and although the result was another **PSOE victory** the reality was that they had scraped home seven seats short of an overall parliamentary majority.

The PSOE government's second term was dominated by fallout from the post-2008 world financial and economic crisis. Unemployment rose to above twenty percent, while austerity programmes saw civil service and teachers' salaries cut, benefits and pensions frozen and welfare programmes cancelled. Appearing weary and indecisive, Zapatero announced that he would not lead the party into the next general election, and the party chose a "safe" veteran minister, Alfredo Pérez Rubalcaba, to succeed him. The subsequent 2011 election delivered the predicted **landslide victory** for the PP and the PSOE suffered its most crushing defeat since the return of democracy. In his victory speech the PP leader, and former prime minister, **Mariano Rajoy**, gravely announced that "difficult times are coming" as the financial crisis continued to wreak havoc across world markets.

Difficult times

On taking power the Rajoy government first blamed the Socialists for the economic mess in which they had left the country, and then set about imposing even harsher **austerity measures** than the outgoing administration, dictated by the EU in Brussels and the German government in Berlin. The promise was that cutting government debt would eventually lead to prosperity, but the reality for vast numbers of Spaniards has been unemployment, which soared to 27 percent in 2014, the EU's highest.

1975	1981	1986	2002
Death of Franco. Spain becomes a constitutional monarchy with Juan Carlos I as king.	Attempted military coup fails; members of parliament are held hostage in the Cortes (Spanish Parliament).	Spain joins the European Union.	Spain swaps peseta for euro.

Other headaches for Rajoy's ministers included a **banking crisis** and **endemic corruption** which has left the country with unfinished airports, tramways and metro systems – all constructed during the boom years at eye-watering cost – that are unlikely ever to see a plane, tram or train. Embarrassingly for Rajoy, one of the biggest corruption scandals involved the PP's party treasurer who not only stashed away tens of millions of party funds in Swiss bank accounts, but claimed that the party's senior politicians (including Rajoy) had all received regular and illegal cash payments in brown envelopes (that is, tax free).

The perennial stone in the shoe of Madrid administrations, the autonomous region of **Catalunya**, also caused unwelcome waves by announcing its intention to hold a **referendum on independence** in November 2014. In response, Madrid flatly stated that this would be unconstitutional and therefore illegal "and will not take place". When the Tribunal Constitucional (Constitutional Court) backed the government view and declared the referendum illegal the Catalan government rebranded the poll as a "participation exercise" carrying only a symbolic function. It thus went ahead and when the votes were counted there was an eighty percent majority in favour of independence. However, the turnout was low and the poll was widely boycotted by those opposed to independence. The Constitutional Court later decided that the poll had nevertheless been illegal and the Catalan president Artur Mas and other ministers who had organized the ballot were suspended from office and given heavy fines.

But the new president of Catalunya, Carles Puigdemont, was no less determined than his predecessor that a vote on independence needed to be held. In June 2017 the Govern (Catalunya's government) announced that a new referendum would be held in October of the same year. In a rerun of the 2014 vote the Constitutional Court again declared the referendum illegal under the terms of the constitution. Realizing that this would leave them open to suspensions and heavy fines, some ministers objected, whereupon Puigdemont sacked them and then replaced them with others who supported going ahead. Spain's Supreme Court sentenced nine separatist leaders to prison. This sparked mass protests, of which some were violent. In 2021, the nine leaders were pardoned in the hope that this would help with the ongoing discussions. Later that year, Puigdemont was stripped of the immunity he had held since 2019. In 2021, a European arrest warrant was granted by Spain and Puigdemont was detained in Sardinia, but later released.

A new political landscape

In the spring of 2014 further convulsions were taking place in the PSOE opposition party, after a series of opinion polls ranked the party in second place to a highly unpopular PP government. Blame for their poor showing fell on leader Alfredo Pérez Rubalcaba and, following a disastrous performance by the party in the European elections, he offered his resignation. At a special congress the party chose **Pedro Sánchez**, a telegenic university economics lecturer, as its new leader. Sanchez adopted an uncompromising abrasive style in dealing with the PP government, which did not go down well with many of the party's *barones* ("barons"), such as Felipe Gónzalez and José Luís Rodríguez Zapatero who favoured a more consensual approach. Leading the party into the December 2015 general election he lost to the PP who, despite

2004	2010	2014
Madrid train bombings kill 191 and injure more than 1800, influencing the outcome of the general election held three days later.	Spain's men's football team wins the FIFA World Cup in South Africa for the first time.	Following royal scandals, King Juan Carlos I abdicates; his son is crowned Felipe VI with consort Queen Letizia.

winning the most seats, fell well short of a majority. The PSOE performance was hampered by the arrival of a new radical party, **Podemos** (We Can), which captured a large number of votes from younger Spaniards, tired of the traditional two-party "charade". Podemos's leader, the 38-year-old bearded and pony-tailed **Pablo Iglesias**, attracted large crowds to his hustings, declaring that he was determined to undermine the corrupt regime – including all the major parties – that has governed Spain since the death of Franco.

The governing PP had been stricken by almost constant media stories of corruption at both national and local levels, which had led to a loss of its core supporters. Many of these had been attracted by a new centre-right party, **Ciudadanos** (Citizens), led by a charismatic 37-year-old lawyer, Albert Rivera. A Catalan opposed to the secession of Catalunya from Spain, he has received death threats from Catalan nationalists.

In an attempt to resolve the stalemate following the 2015 election the PP government announced a new election for June 2016. Now a four-party race, the result was once again inconclusive, with the PP again finishing as the largest party but 40 seats short of an overall majority. The result was even worse for the PSOE, whose 85-seat haul was the lowest in its 140-year history. Despite having had to face a new challenge from Podemos, Sanchez was blamed by the *barones* and the PSOE hierarchy for the terrible result and a civil war in the party led to Sanchez resigning from his position as leader and as a member of the Congress. He declared that he would go out on the road to convince the PSOE membership that his policies were the only ones that could win power again. A new election for the leadership was held in May 2017, with Sanchez again as a candidate facing the *barones'* preferred choice of Susana Díez, president of the region of Andalucía. Against most expectations, the rank and file supported him and Sanchez won a remarkable victory.

The 2016 election result produced the most fragmented parliament since the return of democracy in 1977. The negotiations between the four major parties failed to produce a stable coalition and Rajoy and the PP were recently in power as a minority government, dependent upon smaller parties and abstentions to get them through key votes.

The long-term picture is worrying. Spain is only now starting to recover from the property crash and the worst recession in decades: while the jobs market is improving, unemployment is still at around eighteen percent – far lower than the appalling figures of a decade ago, yet more than double the pre-crisis rate of eight and a half percent, and the second highest in Europe behind Greece. Rather than resolving Spain's political problems, the elections have only added to the political uncertainty and instability. With a government unlikely to last a full parliamentary term – with all the implicit damaging consequences for the Spanish economy – the storm clouds do not appear to be lifting any time soon.

Like the rest of the world, the Covid-19 pandemic brought lots of difficulties to Spain. At the time of writing there had been over five million cases of the virus in the country, and close to 88,000 deaths. The country is close to 80% vaccinated.

2020	2021	2023	2024
Covid-19 pandemic breaks out.	The Spanish Canary Island of La Palma is victim to a volcanic eruption. The areas of Los Llanos de Aridane, Tazacorte and El Paso are evacuated.	Spain's women's football team wins the FIFA Women's World Cup.	The men's football team wins the European Championships for Spain for the fourth time.

Wildlife

Despite its reputation as the land of the package holiday, you can't beat
Spain for sheer diversity of landscape and wildlife. When the Pyrenees were
squeezed from the earth's crust they created an almost impenetrable barrier
stretching from the Bay of Biscay to the Mediterranean Sea. Those animals
and plants already present in Spain were cut off from the rest of Europe, and
have been evolving independently ever since. In the same way, the breach
of the land bridge at what is now the Strait of Gibraltar, and the subsequent
reflooding of the Mediterranean basin, stranded typical African species on
the peninsula. The outcome was an assortment of wildlife originating from
two continents, resulting in modern-day Iberia's unique flora and fauna.

Spain is the second most **mountainous** country in Europe after Switzerland. The central
plateau – the *meseta* – averages 600–700m in elevation, slopes gently westwards and
is surrounded and traversed by imposing sierras and cordilleras. To the north, the
plateau is divided from the coast by the extensive ranges of the Cordillera Cantábrica,
and in the south the towering Sierra Nevada and several lesser ranges run along the
Mediterranean shore. Where these southern sierras continue across the Mediterranean
basin, the unsubmerged peaks today form the Balearic Islands. The Pyrenean chain
marks the border with France, and even along Spain's eastern shores the narrow coastal
plain soon rises into the foothills of the sierras of Montseny, Espuña and Los Filabres,
among others. The ancient sierras de Guadarrama and Gredos cross the *meseta* just
north of Madrid, and the Sierra Morena and the Montes de Toledo rise out of the
dusty southern plains. With such an uneven topography, it is not surprising to find an
alpine element in the flora and fauna, with the most strictly montane species showing
adaptations to high levels of ultraviolet light and prolonged winter snow cover.

   Climatic variations have produced a corresponding diversity in Spanish wildlife.
The wet, humid north is populated by species typical of northern Europe, while the
southern foothills of the Sierra Nevada have more in common vegetation-wise with the
Atlas Mountains of Morocco. The continental weather pattern of much of the **interior**
has given rise to a community of drought-resistant shrubs, together with annual herbs
that flower and set seed in the brief spring and autumn rains, or more long-lived plants
that possess underground bulbs or tubers to withstand the prolonged summer drought
and winter cold.

Habitat

Like most of Europe, the Iberian Peninsula was once heavily forested. Today, though,
following centuries of deforestation, only about ten percent of the original **woodland**
remains, mostly in the north. Historically, much of the *meseta* was covered with
evergreen oaks and associated shrubs such as laurustinus and strawberry tree (*madroño*
–the tree is the symbol of Madrid), but the clearance of land for arable and pastoral
purposes has taken its toll, as have the ravages of war. Today, tracts of Mediterranean
woodland persist only in the sierras and some parts of Extremadura. When it was
realized that much of the plateau was unsuitable for permanent agricultural use,
the land was abandoned, and it is now covered with low-growing, aromatic scrub
vegetation, known as *matorral* (maquis). An endangered habitat, the maquis is a haven
for many rare and distinctive plant and animal species, some found nowhere else in
Europe. The southeastern corner of the *meseta* is the only part of Spain that probably

never supported woodland; here the arid steppe **grasslands** (*calvero*) remain basically untouched by man. In northern Spain, where vast areas are still forested, the typical tree species are more familiar: oak, beech, ash and lime on the lower slopes, grading into pine and fir at higher levels – and the appearance is distinctly northern European.

Much of the *meseta* is predominantly flat, arid and brown. Indeed, in Almería, Europe's only true **desert** is to be found, such is the lack of rainfall. But the presence of subterranean water supplies gives rise to occasional **oases** teeming with wildlife. The numerous tree-lined **watercourses** of the peninsula also attract birds and animals from the surrounding dusty plains. The great Ebro and Duero rivers of the north, and the Tajo and Guadiana in the south, have been dammed at intervals, creating **reservoirs** that attract wildfowl in winter.

The Spanish **coastline** has a little of everything: dune systems, shingle banks, rocky cliffs, salt marshes and sweeping sandy beaches. In Galicia, submerged river valleys, or *rías*, are reminiscent of the Norwegian fjords, and the offshore islands are home to noisy sea-bird colonies; the north Atlantic coast is characterized by limestone promontories and tiny, sandy coves; the Mediterranean coast, despite its reputation for wall-to-wall hotels, still boasts many undeveloped lagoons and marshes; and southwest of Seville lies perhaps the greatest of all Spain's coastal wetlands: the Coto Doñana.

While the rest of Europe strives for agricultural supremacy, in Spain much of the land is still **farmed** by traditional methods, and the **landscape** has changed little since the initial disappearance of the forests. The olive groves of the south, the extensive livestock-rearing lands of the north and even the cereal-growing and wine-producing regions of the plains, exist in relative harmony with the indigenous wildlife of the country. It is only since Spain joined the European Union that artificial pesticides and fertilizers and huge machines have made much impact. Even so, compared to its neighbours, Spain is still essentially a wild country. Apart from a few industrial areas in the northeast and around Madrid and large-scale urbanization along parts of the coast, the landscape reflects the absence of modern technology, and the low population density means that less demand is made on the wilderness areas that remain.

Flora

With such a broad range of habitats, Spain's **flora** is nothing less than superb. Excluding the Canary Islands, about eight thousand species occur on Spanish soil, approximately ten percent of which are found nowhere else in the world. The plethora of high **mountains** allows an alpine flora to persist in Spain well beyond its normal north European distribution, and because of the relative geographical isolation of the mountain ranges, plants have evolved which are specific to each. In fact, there are about 180 plants that occur only in the Pyrenees, and over forty species endemic to the Sierra Nevada.

This effect is clearly illustrated by the **buttercup** family. In the Pyrenees, endemic species include the pheasant's-eye *Adonis pyrenaica* and the meadow rue *Thalictrum macrocarpum*; the Sierra Nevada has *Delphinium nevadense* and the monkshood *Aconitum nevadense*, and of the columbines *Aquilegia nevadensis* occurs here alone. *A. discolor* is endemic to the Picos de Europa, *A. cazorlensis* is found only in the Sierra de Cazorla, and *A. pyrenaica* is unique to the Pyrenees. Other handsome montane members of this family include alpine pasqueflowers, hepatica, hellebores, clematis and a host of more obvious buttercups.

The dry Mediterranean grasslands of Spain are excellent hunting grounds for **orchids**. In spring, in the meadows of the Cordillera Cantábrica, early purple, elder-flowered, woodcock, pink butterfly, green-winged, lizard and tongue orchids are ten a penny, and a little searching will turn up sombre bee, sawfly and Provence orchids. Farther into the Mediterranean zone, exotic species to look for include Bertoloni's bee, bumblebee and mirror orchids. Lax-flowered orchids are common on the Costa Brava and high limestone areas will reveal black vanilla orchids, frog orchids and summer lady's tresses a bit later in the year.

PALMAGEDDON FOR THE EMBLEM OF THE SOUTH

A quintessential emblem of Mediterranean lands, the **palm tree** was loved as much by the Romans and Moors as the inhabitants of the Mediterranean world today. Sadly, as you travel across Spain, particularly its southernmost regions, you will not fail to notice countless palm trees with collapsed crowns, caused by the invasion over the last decade of the **red palm weevil** (*Rhynchophorus ferrugineus*). Native to tropical Asia, where natural predators keep down its numbers, the beetle arrived in Europe via imports of infected trees and is now a plague almost out of control. Each adult female weevil lays hundreds of eggs in holes in a tree then larvae then munch their way from top to bottom. When the insects damage the palm's crown, the tree is then unable to produce new fronds and dies within months. Up to four centimetres long, the bugs are so industrious that their burrowing can often be heard if you place your ear against the trunk of a tree. Once the larvae have hatched they are prodigious flyers and can travel up to seven kilometres in a matter of days to infect new trees.

There is no effective way of preventing infestation and to treat every tree is proving to be unsustainable in times of scarce public resources. Mighty trees the length and breadth of Spain – many up to a century old – have fallen victim to this tiny pest and it is proving almost impossible to halt its devastation. It would be tragic indeed if Spain and the Mediterranean world had to say goodbye to this Moorish symbol of welcome.

The Mediterranean **maquis** is a delight to the eye and nose in early summer, as the cistus bushes and heaths come into flower, with wild rosemary, thyme, clary and French lavender adding to the profusion of colour. The *dehesa* grasslands of southwest Spain are carpeted with the flowers of *Dipcadi serotinum* (resembling brown bluebells), pink gladioli and twenty or so different trefoils in May. In the shade of the ancient evergreen oaks grow birthworts, with their pitcher-shaped flowers, bladder senna and a species of lupin known locally as "devil's chickpea".

Even a trip across the **northern meseta**, although reputedly through endless cereal fields, is by no means a dull experience. Arable weeds such as cornflowers, poppies, corncockle, chicory and shrubby pimpernel add a touch of colour and are sometimes more abundant than the crops themselves. Where the coastal **sand dunes** have escaped the ravages of the tourist industry you can find sea daffodils, sea holly, sea bindweed, sea squill and the large violet flowers of *Romulea clusiana*.

Mammals

The great mammalian fauna that roamed Europe in the Middle Ages today survives only as a relict population in the wildest areas of Spain. Forced to seek refuge from hunters and encroaching civilization, it is perhaps surprising that the only species to have succumbed to extinction is the little-known European beaver. Unfortunately, with elusiveness the key to their survival, the mammal species that remain can be almost impossible to see. Endangered, but common in the mountains of the north, the **wolf** (*lobo*) avoids contact with humans as much as possible. Persecuted for centuries in response to the exaggerated menace portrayed in folk tales, they are still today regarded as a major threat to livestock in some quarters, despite their dwindling numbers. Although afforded official protection, many farmers would not think twice about shooting on sight. Similarly, the omnivorous **brown bear** (*oso pardo*) shows none of the inquisitive boldness exhibited by its American cousins, and with numbers as low as a hundred in Spain, anybody catching a glimpse of one should consider themselves exceptionally fortunate.

In the **northern mountains** – the Pyrenees and the Cordillera Cantábrica – you should get at least a glimpse of chamois, roe and red deer, and possibly **wild boar** (*jabalí*), which can be seen at dusk during the winter conducting nightly raids on village potato patches. The **Spanish ibex** (*cabra montés*), the scimitar-horned wild goat, had represented the main quarry of locals since prehistoric times. However, while it was able to sustain low levels of predation, its agility was no match for modern hunters and it almost disappeared in the early years of the twentieth century. Thanks to effective conservation measures, its numbers are slowly beginning to recover and it is becoming an increasingly common sight in the sierras de Cazorla, Grazalema (both Andalucía) and Gredos (Castilla y León). Europe's answer to prairie dogs, **marmots** (*marmotas*) can occasionally be seen in the Pyrenees, where they graze in alpine meadows, while the surrounding pine forests support large numbers of their arboreal relatives – the **red squirrel**. Less well known, and considerably more difficult to see, is the bizarre **Pyrenean desman**, a large, shrew-like creature closely related to the mole, which inhabits mountain streams.

The typical mammals of **southern Spain** have more in common with Africa than Europe, the separation of the two continents leaving several species stranded to evolve in isolation. Specialities of African origin include the sleek, cat-like **spotted genet** and the adaptable, intelligent **Egyptian mongoose**, both of which are active mainly at night but can be glimpsed during the day. The undoubted jewel of the south, though, is the **Iberian lynx** (*lincé ibérico*), paler, more heavily spotted and less heavily built than the northern-European species, in adaptation to the subtropical climate. Highly endangered, and now almost completely confined to parts of the Sierra Morena near Andújar and Parque Nacional Coto Doñana (although a small and previously unknown population has been discovered in Castilla-La Mancha), its haunting cries on spring nights are sadly becoming more and more infrequent. An emergency breeding programme set up in 2005 in Coto Doñana increased the population there to fifty or so individuals, which has remained roughly the same in the years reported since then. A similar programme in the Parque Natural Sierra de Andujár has had greater success and has more than doubled the 2002 population of 60 to over 150 individuals reported in 2009. In April 2013 it was reported that an Andalucía-wide census had found a total wild population of 310 individuals and a 2017 census revised that number upwards to over 500 including populations discovered in Extremadura and Castilla-La Mancha. The survey also discovered that 34 cubs had been born in the wild in the same year. It is hoped that both programmes – in addition to captive breeding programmes in Portugal and Spain – will continue to aid the lynx's regeneration and remove it from the critically endangered species list.

In the air, no fewer than 27 species of **bat** occupy caves and woodlands throughout Spain. Highly visible and often attracted to artificial light sources by clouds of insects, they are among the easiest of wild mammals to see, although identification to species level is best left to experts. Most interesting are the four types of horseshoe bat and Europe's largest bat, the rare **greater noctule**, which, with a wingspan of 45cm, even feeds on small birds.

The most spectacular **aquatic mammals** are the twenty or so species of whale and dolphin, whose presence has encouraged the appearance of numerous boating companies to run trips out to see them. **Pilot whales** and **sperm whales** are common in the Straits of Gibraltar, and **dolphins** will often choose to accompany boat trips in all areas. Isolated and protected coves on the Mediterranean shores shelter some of the last breeding colonies of the **Mediterranean monk seal**, a severely threatened species perhaps doomed to extinction. **Fresh water** also supports a number of mammal species, perhaps the best known being the playful **European otter**, which is still fairly numerous in the north.

Birds

If any country in Europe qualifies as a paradise for **birdwatching**, then it must surely be Spain. Most twitchers head straight for the world-famous Parque Nacional Coto Doñana, where over half of all European bird species have been recorded, but other parts of the country are just as rewarding, even if you have to work a little harder to get a matching list.

Birds of prey are particularly visible, and as many as 25 species of raptor breed here, but it is during the spring and autumn migrations that you will see the most dramatic numbers. Clouds of honey buzzards, black kites and Egyptian vultures funnel across the Straits of Gibraltar, aided by warm currents, followed by less numerous but equally dramatic-looking species such as short-toed and booted eagles. Resident species include the widespread griffon vulture, the surprisingly common red kite and the Bonelli's eagle. Twitchers, though, are likely to have their sights set on four attention-grabbing species: the Eurasian black vulture, fighting against extinction in Extremadura; the bone-breaking bearded vulture (lammergeyer) of the Pyrenees; the diminutive but distinctive black-winged kite of the southern plains; and the endangered, endemic Spanish imperial eagle. The last-named is most easily seen in Coto Doñana, where guides take great delight in pointing out this emblematic hunter.

There is no less variety in other types of bird. Woodpeckers are most abundant in the extensive forests of the **northern mountain ranges**. While white-backed woodpeckers are confined to the Pyrenees, other such rarities as black and middle-spotted woodpeckers may also be seen in the Cordillera Cantábrica, and the well-camouflaged wryneck breeds in the north and winters in the south of the country. Other typical breeding birds of these northern mountains are the turkey-like capercaillie, pied flycatcher, blue rock thrush, alpine accentor, citril and snow finches, and that most sought-after of all montane birds, the unique, butterfly-like wallcreeper.

In the open **grasslands** and cereal fields of the *meseta*, larks are particularly common. Look out for the calandra lark, easily identified by its chunky bill and the trailing white edge to the wing. More rewarding are great and little bustards – majestic at any time of year, but especially when the males fan out their plumage during the springtime courtship display. In a tiny area of the Mediterranean coast, strange nocturnal mooing calls from low-growing scrub betray the presence of the secretive **Andalucian buttonquail**, a tiny, quail-like bird, more closely related to the bustards than the quails. Look out also for the exotically patterned pin-tailed sandgrouse, one of only two European members of a family of **desert-dwelling birds**, as well as stone curlews and red-necked nightjars, the latter seen (and heard) mainly at dusk.

Olive groves are an ornithological treasure-trove playing host to a colourful assemblage of birds – hoopoes, azure-winged magpies, golden orioles, southern grey and woodchat shrikes, bee-eaters, rollers, great spotted cuckoos and black-eared wheatears. On a sunny summer's day, these birds are active and often easy to spot if you are patient.

Fluctuating water levels, particularly in the south, mean that there is no shortage of seasonally flooding **fresh-water** habitats positively teeming with birdlife. In reed beds, you may come across the vividly coloured purple gallinule, the high-stepping Bailon's crake, the thrush-sized great reed warbler or localized colonies of sociable bearded reedlings. In winter, large flocks of migrant waterfowl may gather, but it is the resident species that bring more reward: the exotic red-crested pochard, the rare ferruginous duck, the delicate marbled teal and the threatened white-headed duck among the highlights.

Coastal wetlands and **river deltas** are a must for any serious birdwatcher, with common summer occupants including black-winged stilts, avocets, greater flamingos and all but one of the European representatives of the heron family: cattle and little egrets, purple, grey, squacco and night herons, bitterns and little bitterns. In the right conditions and at the right time of year, almost all the species can be seen breeding together in vast and noisy heronries – an unforgettable sight. Wintering waders are not outstandingly distinctive, though wherever you go, even on the Atlantic coast, you should look for spoonbills. Grey phalaropes visit the northwest corner, as do whimbrels, godwits, skuas and ruffs, taking a break from their northern breeding grounds. For **sea birds**, the Illas Cíes, off the Galician coast, are unbeatable, providing breeding grounds for shags, the rare Iberian race of guillemot and the world's southernmost colony of lesser black-backed gulls.

Even **towns** have their fair share of notable species. The **white stork** (*cigüeña blanca*) is a summer visitor that has endeared itself to Andalucía and south central Spain, and few conurbations are without the unkempt nest atop a bell tower, electricity pylon or war monument. Finches such as serin and goldfinch are numerous, and the airspace above any town is usually occupied by hundreds of swifts, martins and swallows; you may be able to pick out alpine, pallid and white-rumped swifts and red-rumped swallows if you're in the southern half of the country, as well as crag martins in the north.

The **Balearic Islands** can provide you with a few more unusual cliff-nesting species, such as Eleanora's falcon, while deserted islets are ideal for hole-nesting sea birds, including Cory's shearwaters and storm petrels.

Reptiles and amphibians

Around sixty species of reptiles and amphibians occur in Spain, including some of Europe's largest and most impressive. Four species of salamander inhabit the peninsula. The brightly coloured **fire salamander**, an attractive patchwork of black and yellow, is perhaps the best known. Named for its habit of seeking solace in woodpiles and later emerging when the fire was lit, the salamander spawned the legend that it was somehow born out of the flames. The 30cm-long **sharp-ribbed salamander** of the southwest is Europe's largest, and bizarrely pierces its own skin with its ribs when attacked. The two remaining species, the drab, misnamed **golden-striped salamander** and the **Pyrenean brook salamander**, are confined to the cool, wet, mountainous north.

Closely related to the salamanders are the **newts**, of which there are only four species in Spain. If you take a trip into the high mountain pastures of the Cordillera Cantábrica, where water is present in small, peaty ponds all year round, you should see the brightly coloured **alpine newt**, while the aptly named **marbled newt** can be seen round the edges of many of Spain's inland lakes and reservoirs. Searches through tall waterside vegetation frequently turn up the tiny, lurid-green **tree frog**, striped in the north and west, but stripeless along the Mediterranean coast.

Two species of **tortoise** occur in Spain: **spur-thighed tortoises** can still be found along the southern coast and on the Balearic Islands, the latter the only Spanish locality for the other species – **Hermann's tortoise**. European **pond terrapins** and **stripe-necked terrapins** are more widely distributed, but only in fresh-water habitats. Beware of confusion between these native species and the introduced North American **red-eared terrapin**, the result of the release of unwanted pets following the decline of the Teenage Mutant Ninja Turtle craze. **Marine turtles** are uncommon visitors to the Mediterranean and Atlantic coasts –perhaps the most frequently encountered is the protected **green turtle**, especially in the waters around Gibraltar, but **loggerhead** and **leathery turtles** are occasionally reported.

The most exotic reptilian species to occur in Spain is the **chameleon**, although again this swivel-eyed creature is confined to the extreme southern shores where its camouflage skills render it difficult to find. **Lizards** are numerous, with the most handsome species being the large **ocellated lizard** – green with blue spots along the flank. Some species are very restricted in their range, such as Ibizan and Lilford's wall lizards, which live only in the Balearic Islands. In the south, the most noticeable species are **Moorish geckos**, large-eyed nocturnal creatures usually seen on the walls of buildings both inside and out. Adhesive pads on their feet enable them to cling perilously to vertical surfaces as they search for their insect prey.

Similarly, **snakes** are common, although few are venomous and even fewer are ever likely to bite. When faced with humans, evasive action is the snake's preferred option, and in most cases a snake will be long gone before the intruder even knew it was there. The **grass snake** will even play dead rather than bite, if cornered. **Asps** and **western whip snakes** occur in the Pyrenees, while the most common species in the south is the harmless **horseshoe whip snake**, named for the distinctive horseshoe mark on the back of its head.

The most unusual Spanish reptile is undoubtedly the **amphisbaenian**, sometimes misleadingly called the blind snake. Adapted to a subterranean existence, this rarely encountered and harmless creature can sometimes be found by searching through rotten leaves and mulch in forested environments and gardens of the south.

Teresa Farino

Flamenco

Flamenco – one of the most emblematic musics of Spain and its richest musical heritage – has recently enjoyed huge exposure and today is more popular than ever before. Twenty-five years or so ago it looked like a music on the decline, preserved only in the clubs or *peñas* of its aficionados, or in travestied castanet-clicking form for tourists. However, prejudice vanished as flamenco went through a tremendous period of innovation in the 1980s and 1990s, incorporating elements of pop, rock, jazz and Latin, and today there's a new respect for the old "pure flamenco" artists and a huge joy in the new. Fittingly, in 2010 UNESCO added flamenco to its intangible cultural heritage list, as a world-class art form to be encouraged, protected and supported.

The initial impetus for flamenco's new-found energy came at the end of the 1960s, with the innovations of guitarist **Paco de Lucía** (who died in 2014) and, especially, the late, great singer **Camarón de la Isla**. These were musicians who had grown up learning flamenco but whose own musical tastes embraced international rock, jazz and blues.

They have been followed by groups such as **Ketama**, **Raimundo Amador** (ex Pata Negra), **La Barbería del Sur**, **Navajita Plateá** and **Niña Pastori**, who have all reached massive audiences that neither de Lucía nor de la Isla could have dreamt of decades before. At the end of the 1990s, there were successful comebacks from such established artists as the late **Enrique Morente** and **José Mercé**. Morente – the king of flamenco – experimentally revisited old styles and combined them with new moves, releasing a spectacular new album, *Omega*, in 1996, with **Lagarjita Nick**, one of the most emblematic bands of the Spanish indie rock scene. José Mercé collaborated with **Vicente Amigo** – recognized as the most gifted player of the moment – on *Del Amanecer*. Paco de Lucía had acknowledged Amigo as his successor in the innovation of flamenco guitar.

Among others regarded as the best **contemporary singers** are the male singers El Cabrero, Juan Peña "El Lebrijano", the Sorderos, El Fosforito, José Menese, Duquende and El Potito. The most revered women include Fernanda and Bernarda de Utrera, Carmen Linares, Remedios Amaya, Estrella Morente (daughter of Enrique Morente, and the new "star" of Spanish flamenco), Montse Cortés, La Macanita and Carmen Amaya. Until his death, **Camarón** – or more fully **Camarón de la Isla** – was by far the most popular and commercially successful singer of modern flamenco. Collaborating with the guitarists and brothers Paco de Lucía and Ramón de Algeciras, and latterly, Tomatito, Camarón raised *cante jondo* to a new art. A legend in his own lifetime, he died of cancer in 1992 at the age of just 42, having almost single-handedly revitalized flamenco song, inspiring and opening the way for the current generation of flamenco artists.

Origins

Flamenco evolved in southern Spain from many sources: Morocco, Egypt, India, Pakistan, Greece and other parts of the Near and Far East. Most authorities believe the roots of the music were brought to Spain by gypsies arriving in the fifteenth century. In the following century, it was fused with elements of Arab and Jewish music in the Andalucian mountains, where Jews, Muslims and "pagan" gypsies had taken refuge from the forced conversions and clearances effected by the Catholic kings and the church. Important flamenco centres and families are still found today in quarters and towns of *gitano* and refugee origin, such as Alcalá, Jerez, Cádiz, Utrera and the

Triana *barrio* of Seville. Although flamenco is linked fundamentally to **Andalucía**, emigration from that province has long meant that flamenco thrives not only there but also in Madrid, Extremadura, the Levante and even Barcelona – wherever Andalucian migrants have settled.

Flamenco aficionados enjoy heated debate about the purity of their art and whether it is more validly performed by a *gitano* (gypsy) or a *payo* (non-gypsy). Certainly during dark times, flamenco was preserved by the oral tradition of the closed *gitano* clans. Its power and the despair that it overcomes, seem to have emerged from the lives of a people surviving for centuries at society's margins. These days, though, there are as many acclaimed *payo* as *gitano* flamenco artists, and the arrival on the scene of musicians from Barcelona such as Vicente Amigo – who has no Andalucian blood but grew up in a neighbourhood full of flamenco music – has de-centred the debate.

The concept of dynasty, however, remains fundamental for many. The veteran singer **Fernanda de Utrera**, one of the great voices of "pure flamenco", was born in 1923 into a *gitano* family in Utrera, one of the *cantaora* (flamenco singer) centres. The granddaughter of the legendary singer "Pinini", she and her younger sister Bernarda, also a notable singer, both inherited their flamenco with their genes. This concept of an active inheritance is crucial and has not been lost in contemporary developments: the members of Ketama, for example, the Madrid-based flamenco-rock group, come from two *gitano* clans.

While flamenco's exact origins are debated, it is generally agreed that its "laws" were established in the nineteenth century. Indeed, from the mid-nineteenth into the early twentieth century it enjoyed a golden age, the tail end of which is preserved on some of the earliest 1930s recordings. The musicians found a first home in the **café cantantes**, traditional bars that had their own groups of performers (*cuadros*). One of the most famous was the *Café de Chinitas* in Málaga, immortalized by the poet Federico García Lorca in *A las cinco de la tarde* ("At five in the afternoon"), in which he intimates the relationship between flamenco and bullfighting, both sharing root emotions and flashes of erratic genius, and both being a way to break out of social and economic marginality.

The art of flamenco

Flamenco is played at *tablaos* and fiestas, in bars and at *juergas* (informal, more or less private parties). Because the Andalucian public are so knowledgeable about flamenco, even musicians, singers and dancers found at a local club or village festival are usually very good.

Flamenco songs often express pain. Generally, the voice closely interacts with an improvising guitar, which keeps the *compás* (rhythm), the two inspiring each other, aided by the **jaleo** – the hand-clapping *palmas*, finger-snapping *palillos* and shouts from participants at certain points in the song. Aficionados will shout encouragement, most commonly *¡olé!* when an artist is getting deep into a song, but also a variety of other less obvious phrases. A stunning piece of dancing may, for example, be greeted with *¡Viva la maquina escribir!* (Long live the typewriter!), as the heels of the dancer move so fast they sound like a clicking machine; or the cry may be *¡agua!* (water!), for the scarcity of water in Andalucía has given the word a kind of glory.

The encouragement of the audience is essential for the artists, as it lets them know they are reaching deep into the emotional psyche of their listeners. They may achieve the rare quality of **duende** – total communication with their audience, and the mark of great flamenco of any style or generation. Latterly, the word *duende* has been used to describe "innovation", which, while it is significant, does not always capture its real depth.

Flamenco songs

There is a classical repertoire of more than sixty flamenco songs (*cantes*) and dances (*danzas*) – some solos, some group numbers, some with instrumental accompaniment, others a cappella. These different styles (or *palos*) of flamenco singing are grouped in families according to more or less common melodic themes, establishing three basic types of *cante flamenco*: **cante grande** (comprising songs of the *jondo* type), **cante chico**, and **cante intermedio** between the two. Roughly speaking, the *jondo* and *chico* represent the most and the least difficult *cantes* respectively in terms of their technical and emotional interpretation, although any form, however simple, can be sung with the maximum of complexity and depth. **Cante jondo** (deep song) comprises the oldest and "purest" songs of the flamenco tradition, and is the profound flamenco of the great artists, whose *cantes* are outpourings of the soul, delivered with an intense passion, art forms expressed through elaborate vocal ornamentation. To a large extent, however, such categories are largely arbitrary, and few flamenco musicians talk about flamenco in this way; what matters to them is whether the flamenco is good or bad.

The basic *palos* include **soleares**, **siguiriyas**, **tangos** and **fandangos**, but the variations are endless and often referred to by their place of origin: *malagueñas* (from Málaga), for example, *granaínos* (from Granada), or *fandangos de Huelva*. *Siguiriyas*, which date from the golden age, and whose theme is usually death, have been described as cries of despair in the form of a funeral psalm. In contrast, there are many songs and dances such as *tangos*, *Sevillanas*, *fandangos* and *alegrías* (literally "happinesses"), which capture great joy for fiestas. The **Sevillana** originated in medieval Seville as a spring country dance, with verses improvised and sung to the accompaniment of guitar and castanets (rarely used in other forms of flamenco). In the last few years, dancing *Sevillanas* has become popular in bars and clubs throughout Spain, but their great natural habitats are Seville's Feria de Abril and the annual *romería*, or pilgrimage, to El Rocío. Each year wonderful new *Sevillanas* come onto the market in time for the fiestas.

Another powerful and more seasonal form is the **saeta**, songs in honour of the Virgins that are carried on great floats in the processions of Semana Santa (Holy Week). Traditionally, they are quite spontaneous – as the float is passing, a singer will launch into a *saeta*, a sung prayer for which silence is necessary and for which the procession will therefore come to a halt while it is sung.

Flamenco guitar

The guitar used to be simply an accompanying instrument – originally, the singers themselves played – but in the early decades of the last century it developed as a solo instrument, influenced by classical and Latin American traditions. The greatest of these early guitarists was **Ramón Montoya**, who revolutionized flamenco guitar with his harmonizations and introduced a variety of *arpeggios* – techniques of right-hand playing adapted from classical guitar playing. Along with Niño Ricardo and Sabicas, he established flamenco guitar as a solo medium, an art extended from the 1960s onwards by **Manolo Sanlúcar**, whom most aficionados reckon the most technically accomplished player of his generation. Sanlúcar has kept within a "pure flamenco" orbit, and not strayed into jazz or rock, experimenting instead with orchestral backing and composing for ballet.

The best known of all contemporary flamenco guitarists, however, is the undoubtedly late **Paco de Lucía**, who made the first moves towards "new" or "fusion" flamenco. A *payo*, he won his first flamenco prize at the age of 14, and went on to accompany many of the great singers, including a long partnership with Camarón de la Isla. He started forging new rhythms for flamenco following a trip to Brazil, where he was influenced by *bossa nova*, and in the 1970s established a sextet with electric bass, Latin percussion, flute and saxophone. Before his death in 2014, he worked with jazz-rock guitarists such as John McLaughlin and pianist Chick Corea, while his own regular band, the Paco de Lucía Sextet featuring his brother, the singer Pepe de Lucía, was one of the most original and distinctive sounds on the flamenco scene.

Other modern-day guitarists have equally identifiable sounds and rhythms, and fall broadly into two camps, being known either as accompanists or soloists. The former include **Tomatito** (Camarón's last accompanist), Manolo Franco and Paco Cortés, while among the leading soloists are the brothers Pepe and Juan Habichuela; Rafael Riqueni, who is breaking new ground with classical influences; Enrique de Melchor; Gerardo Núñez; and Vicente Amigo. Jerónimo Maya was acclaimed by the Spanish press as the "Mozart of Flamenco" when he gave his first solo performance, aged 7, in 1984.

Nuevo flamenco

The **reinvention of flamenco** in the 1980s was initially disliked by purists, but soon gained a completely new young public. Paco de Lucía set the new parameters of innovation and commercial success, and following in his footsteps came **Lolé y Manuel** and others, updating the flamenco sound with original songs and huge success. **Jorge Pardo**, Paco de Lucía's sax and flute player, originally a jazz musician, has continued to work at the cutting edge. **Enrique Morente** and **Juan Peña "El Lebrijano"** were two of the first to work with Andalucian orchestras from Morocco, and the Mediterranean sound remains important today, together with influences from southern India.

Paco Peña's 1991 *Missa Flamenca* recording, a setting of the Catholic Mass to flamenco, with the participation of established singers including Rafael Montilla "El Chaparro" from Peña's native Córdoba and a classical academy chorus from London, has stayed a bestseller since its first appearance, remaining a benchmark for such compositions.

The encounter with rock and blues was pioneered at the end of the 1980s by Ketama and Pata Negra. **Ketama** were hailed by the Spanish press as creators of the music of the "New Spain" after their first album, which fused flamenco with rock and salsa, adding a kind of rock-jazz sensibility, a "flamenco cool", as they put it. They then pushed the frontiers of flamenco still farther by recording the two *Songhai* albums in collaboration with Malian kora player Toumani Diabate and British bassist Danny Thompson. The group **Pata Negra**, a band led by two brothers, Raimundo and Rafael Amador, introduced a more direct rock sound with a bluesy electric guitar lead, giving a radical edge to traditional styles like *bulerías*. Their *Blues de la Frontera* album caused an equal sensation. After splitting, Raimundo Amador has continued as a solo artist.

Flamenco continues to attract legions of new aficionados in the twenty-first century and with the addition of the new Bienal de Flamenco in Málaga – a six-month festival spread across the province – and the Bienal de Sevilla which has been running for almost forty years, both demonstrate that flamenco is as popular now as it has ever been.

Jan Fairly, David Loscos and Manuel Domínguez

Books

Listings below represent a highly selective reading list on Spain and Spanish matters. Most titles are in print, although we've included a few older classics, no longer in print (indicated by o/p); most of them are easy to find, in secondhand bookshops or on websites such as http://abebooks. co.uk. An excellent specialist source for books about Spain – new, used and out of print – is Paul Orssich, 2 St Stephens Terrace, London SW8 1DH (http://orssich.com). Books marked ★ are particularly recommended.

TRAVEL AND GENERAL ACCOUNTS

THE BEST INTRODUCTIONS

★ **John Hooper** *The New Spaniards*. This authoritative portrait of post-Franco Spain was originally written by *The Guardian's* former Spanish correspondent in the 1980s. A revised second edition published in 2006 is already dated, but is still one of the best introductions to contemporary Spain.

Adam Hopkins *Spanish Journeys: A Portrait of Spain*. Published in the mid-1990s, this is an enjoyable and highly stimulating exploration of Spanish history and culture, weaving its considerable scholarship in an accessible and unforced travelogue form, and full of illuminating anecdotes.

★ **Michael Jacobs** *Andalusia*. A well-crafted, opinionated and wide-ranging introduction to Andalucía, covering everything from prehistory to the Civil War with perceptive pieces on flamenco, architecture, gypsies and food and drink. A gazetteer at the back details major sights. Jacobs died in 2014, but this remains one of the best introductions to the region.

★ **Mark Kurlansky** *The Basque History of the World*. An entertaining take on this much-maligned, misunderstood and misrepresented people. Kurlansky uses history, stories, anecdotes and recipes to concoct this heady brew.

Lucy McCauley (ed) *Spain: Travelers' Tales*. Probably the best anthology of writing on Spain, which gathers its stories and journalism mostly from the last fifteen years. Featured authors include Gabriel García Márquez, Colm Tóibín and Louis de Bernières, whose "Seeing Red", on Buñol's La Tomatina festival, is worth the purchase price alone.

David Mitchell *Travellers in Spain: An Illustrated Anthology* (also published under the title *Here in Spain*). A well-told story of how four centuries of travellers – and most often travel writers – saw Spain. It's interesting to see Ford, Irving, Brenan, Laurie Lee and the rest set in context.

★ **Giles Tremlett** *Ghosts of Spain*. Tremlett (*The Guardian's* Madrid correspondent) digs into the untold story of Spain's Civil War dead and the collective conspiracy of silence surrounding the war's terrors, and goes on to peel away the layers of the post-Franco era to present an enthralling and often disturbing study of contemporary Spain. An updated edition (2014) has a new chapter, "The Fiesta is Over".

RECENT TRAVELS AND ACCOUNTS

Tom Chesshyre *Slow Trains Around Spain: A 3,000-Mile Adventure on 52 Rides*. Veteran British travel writer Tom Chesshyre takes a meandering route from Catalonia to Seville, taking in the country's varied and storied landscapes from the Civil War trenches of Aragon to the Moorish masterpieces of Granada – via the holiday hotspot of Benidorm. A wry and entertaining account of slow train travel through Spain.

★ **Chris Stewart** *Driving Over Lemons: An Optimist in Andalucía*. A funny, insightful and charming account of life on a remote peasant farm, El Valero, in the Alpujarras where Stewart set up home. The sequel, *A Parrot in the Pepper Tree*, has more stories from the farm interspersed with accounts of the author's earlier adventures as a sheep shearer in Sweden, drummer with rock band Genesis and flamenco guitarist in Seville. The saga's next episode, *The Almond Blossom Appreciation Society*, delivered another cocktail of hilarious, improbable and poignant tales. The "fourth book in the trilogy", *The Last Days of the Bus Club*, was published in 2014 and ladles out another enjoyable helping of El Valero bonhomie.

TWENTIETH-CENTURY WRITERS

★ **Gerald Brenan** *South from Granada*. An enduring classic. Brenan lived in a village in the Alpujarras in the 1920s, and records this period and the visits of Virginia Woolf, Lytton Strachey and Bertrand Russell.

★ **Laurie Lee** *As I Walked Out One Midsummer Morning*, *A Rose for Winter* and *A Moment of War*. One Midsummer *Morning* is the irresistibly romantic account of Lee's walk through Spain – from Vigo to Málaga – and his gradual awareness of the forces moving the country towards civil war. As an autobiographical novel, it's a delight; as a piece of social observation, painfully sharp. In *A Rose for Winter* he describes his return, twenty years later, to Andalucía, while in *A Moment of War* he describes a winter fighting with the International

Brigade in the Civil War – by turns moving, comic and tragic.

★ **George Orwell** *Homage to Catalonia*. Stirring account of Orwell's participation in the early exhilaration of revolution in Barcelona, and his growing disillusionment with the factional fighting among the Republican forces during the Civil War.

OLDER CLASSICS

George Borrow *The Bible in Spain* and *The Zincali* (both o/p). On first publication in 1842, Borrow subtitled *The Bible in Spain* "Journeys, Adventures and Imprisonments of an English-man"; it is one of the most famous books on Spain – slow in places but with some very amusing stories. *The Zincali* is an account of the Spanish *gitanos* (gypsies), whom Borrow got to know pretty well.

★ **Richard Ford** *A Handbook for Travellers in Spain* and *Readers at Home* and *Gatherings from Spain*. This must be the best guide ever written to any country. Massively opinionated, it is extremely witty in its British, nineteenth-century manner, and worth reading for the proverbs alone. *The Gatherings* is a timid, yet entertaining, abridgement of the general pieces, intended for a female audience who weren't expected to have the taste for the original. A biography, *Richard Ford, Hispanophile, Connoisseur and Critic* by Ian Robertson, places the great man in context.

Washington Irving *Tales of the Alhambra*. Half of Irving's book consists of stories, set in the Alhambra; the rest are accounts of his own residence there.

George Sand *A Winter in Majorca*. Sand and Chopin spent their winter at the monastery of Valldemossa. They weren't entirely welcomed, in which lies much of the book's appeal. Local editions, including a translation by late Mallorcan resident Robert Graves, are on sale around the island.

HISTORY

PREHISTORIC AND ROMAN SPAIN

James M. Anderson *Spain: 1001 Sights, An Archeological and Historical Guide*. A good guide and gazetteer to 95 percent of Spain's archeological sites.

María Cruz Fernandez Castro *Iberia in Prehistory*. A major study of the Iberian Peninsula prior to the arrival of the Romans, which surveys recent archeological evidence relating to the remarkable technical, economic and artistic progress of the early Iberians.

John S. Richardson *The Romans in Spain*. A look at how Spain became part of the Roman world. It also examines the influences exchanged between Spain and Rome.

EARLY, MEDIEVAL AND BEYOND

J.M. Cohen *The Four Voyages of Christopher Columbus*. Columbus's astonishing voyages as described by Columbus himself in his log are interwoven with opinions of contemporaries on the great explorer, including his biographer son Hernando. A fascinating collection, superbly translated.

Roger Collins *The Arab Conquest of Spain 710–97*. Controversial study documenting the Moorish invasion and the significant influence that the conquered Visigoths had on early Muslim rule. Collins's earlier *Early Medieval Spain 400–1000* takes a broader overview of the same subject.

★ **J.H. Elliott** *Imperial Spain 1469–1716*. The best introduction to the "Golden Age" – academically respected, and a gripping tale.

★ **Richard Fletcher** *The Quest for El Cid* and *Moorish Spain*. Two of the best studies of their kind – fascinating and highly readable narratives. The latter is a masterly introduction to the story of the Moors in Spain.

L.P. Harvey *Islamic Spain 1250–1500*. Comprehensive account of its period – both the Islamic kingdoms and the Muslims living beyond their protection.

David Howarth *The Voyage of the Armada*. An account from the Spanish perspective of the personalities, from king to sailors, involved in the Armada.

★ **Henry Kamen** *The Spanish Inquisition*. A highly respected examination of the Inquisition and the long shadow it cast across Spanish history. *The Spanish Inquisition: An Historical Revision* returns to the subject in the light of more recent evidence, while Kamen's *Philip of Spain* is the first full biography of Felipe II, the ruler most closely associated with the Inquisition. In *Spain's Road to Empire*, Kamen skilfully dissects the conquest of the Americas and the Philippines.

Elie Kedourie *Spain and the Jews: the Sephardi Experience, 1492 and After*. A collection of essays on the three million Spanish Jews of the Middle Ages and their expulsion by Los Reyes Católicos.

John Lynch *Spain 1598–1700* and *Bourbon Spain: 1700–1808*. Two further volumes in the Blackwells project covering Spain from prehistory to modern times, written by the series' general editor and dealing with Spain's rise to empire and the critical Bourbon period.

Hugh Thomas *Rivers of Gold: The Rise of the Spanish Empire*. Thomas's scholarly but accessible history provides a snapshot of Spain's most glorious period – its meteoric imperial rise in the late fifteenth and early sixteenth centuries, when characters such as Fernando and Isabel, Columbus and Magellan shaped the country's outlook for the next three hundred years. This is part one in the trilogy on the Spanish Empire; the second volume, *The Golden Age*, and the third, *World Without End* are equally compelling.

THE TWENTIETH CENTURY

Phil Ball *Morbo – The Story of Spanish Football*. Excellent account of the history of Spanish football from its nineteenth-century beginnings with British workers at the mines of Río Tinto in Huelva to the golden years of Real Madrid and the dark days of Franco. Ever-present as a backdrop is the ferocious rivalry, or *morbo* – political, historical, regional and linguistic – that has driven the Spanish game since its birth.

★ **Gerald Brenan** *The Spanish Labyrinth*. First published in 1943, Brenan's account of the background to the Civil War is tinged by personal experience, yet still makes for an impressively rounded read.

★ **Raymond Carr** *Modern Spain 1875–1980* and *The Spanish Tragedy: the Civil War in Perspective*. Two of the best books on modern Spanish history – concise and well told.

Ronald Fraser *Blood of Spain*. Subtitled *An Oral History of the Spanish Civil War*, this is an equally impressive – and brilliantly unorthodox – piece of research allowing Spaniards to recount their experiences in their own words.

★ **Ian Gibson** *Federico García Lorca, The Assassination of Federico García Lorca* and *Lorca's Granada*. The biography is a compelling book and *The Assassination* a brilliant reconstruction of the events at the end of the writer's life, with an examination of Fascist corruption and the shaping influences on Lorca, twentieth-century Spain and the Civil War. *Granada* contains a series of walking tours around parts of the town familiar to the poet.

Sid Lowe *Fear and Loathing in La Liga: Barcelona and Real Madrid*. Proving that FC Barcelona and Real Madrid are more than mere football clubs, this book examines the explosive rivalry between the two – the wounds left by the Civil War, the games between them which encapsulate the plucky Catalan nation against the overweening Spanish state, the attempts by both clubs to achieve global domination – by means of interviews with ex-players and coaches.

★ **Paul Preston** *Franco* and *Concise History of the Spanish Civil War*. A penetrating – and monumental – biography of Franco and his regime, which provides a clear picture of how he won the Civil War and survived in power so long. *Civil War* is more accessible than Thomas's work (see below). Preston's published and acclaimed *The Spanish Holocaust* documents the brutal and murderous persecution of Spaniards between 1936 and 1945 when some 200,000 were murdered, mostly by Franco's new regime.

★ **Hugh Thomas** *The Spanish Civil War*. This exhaustive thousand-page study is regarded (both in Spain and abroad) as the definitive history of the Civil War.

Gamel Woolsey *Málaga Burning* (US) and under its original title *Death's Other Kingdom* (UK). A long-ignored minor classic written in the late 1930s and reprinted (and retitled) by a US publisher, in which the American poet and wife of Gerald Brenan vividly describes the horrors of the descent of their part of Andalucía into civil war.

Richard Wright *Pagan Spain*. In his eye-opening account of travels in Spain in the 1950s, the celebrated African-American writer provides an astonishing reminder of how much Spain has changed since the Franco era.

ART, ARCHITECTURE, PHOTOGRAPHY, FILM AND DESIGN

Marianne Barrucand and Achim Bednoz *Moorish Architecture*. A beautifully illustrated guide to the major Moorish monuments.

Bernard Bevan *History of Spanish Architecture* (o/p). Classic study of Iberian and Ibero-American architecture, including extensive coverage of the Mudéjar, Plateresque and Baroque periods.

Robert Goff *The Essential Salvador Dalí*. An enjoyable and accessible introduction to Dalí and Surrealism, which examines the artist's bizarre life and obsessions (particularly his intense attachment to Gala, his wife), as well as his most enigmatic paintings.

Godfrey Goodwin *Islamic Spain*. Portable architectural guide with descriptions of virtually every significant Islamic building in Spain, and a fair amount of background.

Gijs van Hensbergen *Gaudi: the Biography*. At last, a worthy biography of one of the world's most distinctive architects. Van Hensbergen puts substantial flesh on the man while also placing his work firmly in context.

Robert Hughes *Goya*. The celebrated author of *The Shock of the New* and *Barcelona* turns his attention to one of Spain's greatest painters in this fabulous biography, a gripping account of Goya's life and work, placed within the context of turbulent eighteenth- and early nineteenth-century Spain.

★ **Michael Jacobs** *Alhambra*. Sumptuous volume with outstanding photographs and expert commentary. Authoritatively guides you through the Alhambra's history and architecture, and concludes with a fascinating essay on the hold the palace has had on later artists, travellers and writers, from Irving and Ford to de Falla and Lorca.

John Richardson *A Life of Picasso*. The definitive biography of one of the twentieth century's major artistic driving forces, currently in three volumes with the final volume due for publication shortly.

Gabriel Ruiz Cabrero *The Modern in Spain*. This readable book is a clear, comprehensive study of postwar Spanish architecture. The author is an architect and professor in the renowned Faculty of Architecture at Madrid's Politécnica.

Meyer Schapiro *Romanesque Art*. An excellent illustrated survey of Spanish Romanesque art and architecture – and its Visigothic and Mozarabic predecessors.

FICTION AND POETRY

SPANISH CLASSICS
Pedro de Alarcón *The Three-Cornered Hat*. Ironic nineteenth-century tales of the previous century's corruption, bureaucracy and absolutism.

Leopoldo Alas *La Regenta*. Alas' nineteenth-century novel, with its sweeping vision of the disintegrating social fabric of the period, is a kind of Spanish *Madame Bovary* (a book that it was in fact accused of plagiarizing at the time of publication).

Ramón Pérez de Ayala *Belarmino and Apolonio* and *Honeymoon, Bittermoon*. A pair of tragicomic picaresque novels written around the turn of the twentieth century.

Emilia Pardo Bazán *The House of Ulloa*. Bazán was an early feminist intellectual and in this, her best-known book, she charts the decline of the old aristocracy in the time of the Glorious Revolution of 1868.

★ **Miguel de Cervantes** *Don Quixote* and *Exemplary Stories*. In 2005 Spain and the Hispanic world celebrated the four-hundredth anniversary of the publication of Cervantes' work. *Quixote* is the classic of Spanish literature and still an excellent and witty read, with much to inform about Spanish character and psychology. J.M. Cohen's fine Penguin translation or the 2005 translation by Edith Grossman, published by HarperCollins, are worth looking out for. To try Cervantes in a more modest dose, the *Stories* are a good place to start. A decent biography, *Cervantes*, by Jean Canavaggio, which won him the Prix Goncourt, places the great author in his historical milieu.

Benito Pérez Galdós *Fortunata and Jacinta*. Galdós wrote in the last decades of the nineteenth century, and his novels of life in Madrid combine comic scenes and social realism; he is often characterized as a "Spanish Balzac". Other Galdós novels available in translation include *Misericordia*, *Nazarín* and the epic *"I"*.

★ **St Teresa of Ávila** *The Life of Saint Teresa of Ávila*. St Teresa's autobiography is said to be the most widely read Spanish classic after *Don Quixote*. It takes some wading through, but it's fascinating in parts.

MODERN FICTION

★ **Bernardo Atxaga** *Obabakoak*. This challenging novel by a Basque writer won major prizes on its Spanish publication. It is a sequence of tales of life in a Basque village and the narrator's search to give them meaning.

★ **Arturo Barea** *The Forging of a Rebel* (o/p). Superb autobiographical trilogy, taking in the Spanish war in Morocco in the 1920s, and Barea's own part in the Civil War. The books have been published in UK paperback editions under the titles *The Forge*, *The Track* and *The Clash*.

Camilo José Cela *The Family of Pascual Duarte* and *The Beehive*. Nobel Prize-winner Cela was considered integral to the revival of Spanish literature after the Civil War, though his reputation is tainted by his role as a censor in Franco's government. *Pascual Duarte*, his first novel, portrays the brutal story of a peasant murderer from Extremadura, set against the backdrop of the Civil War, while *The Beehive*, his best-known work, set in Madrid at the end of the same war depicts the poverty and misery of this period through the lives of the characters.

Ildefonso Falcones *Cathedral of the Sea*. Historical romp tracing the life of the son of a fugitive serf who makes a new life for himself in the thriving medieval port of Barcelona. The title refers to the Gothic church of Santa María del Mar, which provides the backdrop to much of the action.

★ **Juan Goytisolo** *Marks of Identity*, *Count Julian*, *Juan the Landless*, *Landscapes after the Battle* and *Quarantine*. Born in Barcelona in 1931, Goytisolo became a bitter enemy of the Franco regime, and spent most of his life in self-exile. He is perhaps the most important modern Spanish novelist, confronting, above all in his great trilogy (comprising the first three titles listed above), the whole ambivalent idea of Spain and Spanishness, as well as being one of the first Spanish writers to deal openly with homosexuality. The more recent *Quarantine* is a journey into a Dante-esque netherworld in which the torments of hell are set against reportage of the first Gulf War. He died at his home in Morocco in 2017.

Carmen Laforet *Nada*. Written in 1944 but only recently translated, this is a haunting tale of a Barcelona family locked in the violence and despair of post-Civil War Spain. For all the horror, there is beauty also in the portrayal of a teenage girl's longing for consolation.

★ **Javier Marias** *Tomorrow in the Battle Think on Me*. There are many who rate Marias as Spain's finest contemporary novelist – and the evidence is here in this searching, psychological thriller, with its study of the human capacity for concealment and confession. Two other Marias novels, *A Heart So White* and *All Souls*, are also available in English translation.

Ana María Matute *School of the Sun*. The loss of childhood innocence on a Balearic island, where old enmities are redefined during the Civil War.

★ **Eduardo Mendoza** *City of Marvels* and *The Truth about the Savolta Case*. Mendoza's first and best novel, *City of Marvels*, is set in the expanding Barcelona of 1880–1920, full of underworld characters and comic turns. It's a milieu repeated in *The Truth about the Savolta Case*.

★ **Manuel Vázquez Montalbán** *Murder in the Central Committee*, *Southern Seas*, *An Olympic Death*, *The Angst-Ridden Executive*, *Off Side* and *The Man of My Life*. Montalban was, until his death in 2003, one of Spain's most influential writers. A long-time member of the Communist Party, he lived in Barcelona, like his great creation, the gourmand private detective Pepe Carvalho, who stars in all of his wry and racy crime thrillers. The one to begin with – a classic – is *Murder in the Central Committee*.

Merce Redoreda *In Diamond Square*. A transfixing close-up vision of everyday life in Barcelona during and after the Civil War.

Julián Ríos *Larva*. Subtitled *Midsummer Night's Babel*, *Larva* is a large, complex, postmodern novel by a leading Spanish literary figure, published to huge acclaim in Spain.

Carlos Ruiz Zafón *The Shadow of the Wind*. A wonderfully atmospheric and gripping novel in which a young boy tries to unravel the truth behind the life and death of a forgotten writer. Set in post-Civil War Barcelona. Its follow-up, *The Angel's Game*, has recently been translated.

PLAYS AND POETRY

Pedro Calderón de la Barca *Life is a Dream and other Spanish Classics* and *The Mayor of Zalamea*. Some of the best works of the great dramatist of Spain's "Golden Age".

J.M. Cohen (ed) *The Penguin Book of Spanish Verse*. Spanish poetry from the twelfth century to the modern age, with (parallel text) translations from all the major names.

Lope de Vega Spain's first important playwright (b.1562) wrote hundreds of plays, many of which, including *Lo Cierto por lo Dudoso* and *Fuenteobvejuna*, remain standards of classic Spanish theatre.

★ **Federico García Lorca** *Five Plays: Comedies and Tragicomedies, Poet in New York, The House of Bernarda Alba*. Andalucía's great pre-Civil War playwright and poet. These are some of his finest compositions for the stage while *Poet* is a collection of poems he wrote as a student in post-Wall

Street Crash New York, capturing the sprawling city with its brutality and loneliness.

SPAIN IN FOREIGN FICTION

★ **Ernest Hemingway** *The Sun Also Rises* and *For Whom the Bell Tolls*. Hemingway remains a big part of the American myth of Spain and *The Sun Also Rises* – played out against the background of Pamplona's San Fermín *feria* – contains some lyrically beautiful writing, while the latter is a good deal more laboured.

★ **Norman Lewis** *Voices of the Old Sea*. Lewis lived in Catalunya from 1948 to 1952, just as tourism was starting to arrive. This book is an ingenious blend of novel and social record, charting the breakdown of the old ways in the face of the "new revolution".

★ **Amin Malouf** *Leo the African*. A wonderful historical novel, re-creating the life of Leo Africanus, the fifteenth-century Moorish geographer, in the last years of the kingdom of Granada and his subsequent exile in Morocco and world travels.

SPECIALIST GUIDEBOOKS

THE PILGRIM ROUTE TO SANTIAGO

Millán Bravo Lozano *A Practical Guide for Pilgrims: The Road to Santiago*. Colourful, informative guide. Includes separate map pages so you can leave the heavy guide at home.

John Higginson *Le Puy to Santiago – A Cyclist's Guide*. A cyclist's guide to the pilgrim route, which follows as closely as possible (on tarmac) the walkers' path, visiting all the major sites en route.

Edwin Mullins *The Pilgrimage to Santiago* (o/p). This is a travelogue rather than a guide, but is by far the best book on the Santiago legend and its fascinating medieval pilgrimage industry.

Alison Raju *The Way of St James: Le Puy to the Pyrenees* (vol I) and *Pyrenees-Santiago-Finisterre* (vol II); *Vía de la Plata – The Way of St James*. Walking guide to the pilgrim route divided between the French and Spanish sections and written by an experienced Iberian hiker. Both books include detailed maps, background on sights en route as well as practical information such as where to stay. In *Vía de la Plata*, Raju covers the lesser-known pilgrim route to Santiago, starting out from Seville.

David Wesson *The Camino Francés* (Confraternity of St James). Annually updated basic guide to the *camino*, with directions and accommodation. The Confraternity (http://csj.org.uk) publishes the most accurate guides to the route, and there's also an online bookshop.

TREKKING AND CYCLING

David and Ros Brawn *Sierra de Aracena*. A guide covering this magnificent Andalucian sierra in 27 walks, with an accompanying map (sold separately), and all routes GPS waypointed.

Charles Davis *Costa del Sol Walks, Costa Blanca Walks*. Well-written guides to two excellent walking zones describing 34 (32 in *Costa Blanca*) walks of between 3km and 18km; each walk has its own map. The same author's *Walk! the Axarquía* (Discovery, UK; http://walkingdemon.co.uk) is a reliable guide to this Andalucía region describing 30 walks between 5km and 22km, all GPS waypointed. *34 Alpujarras Walks* details GPS waypointed treks, and *Mallorca's Dry Stone Way* (Discovery, UK) is a guide to the Balearic island's long-distance walking route. In the latter books, each walk has its own map.

Harry Dowdell *Cycle Touring in Spain*. Well-researched cycle-touring guide, which describes eight touring routes of varying difficulty in the north and south of Spain. Plenty of practical information on preparing your bike for the trip, transporting it, plus what to take.

★ **Teresa Farino** *Picos de Europa*. An excellent walking and touring guide in the *Landscapes* series detailing a variety of hikes in this spectacular national park, with special emphasis given to flora and fauna.

★ **Guy Hunter-Watts** *Walking in Andalucía, Coastal Walks in Andalucía*. *Walking* is a first-rate hiking guide to the natural parks of Grazalema, Cazorla, Los Alcornocales, Aracena and La Axarquía, as well as the Alpujarras and the Sierra Nevada, with 36 walks, each with a colour map. *Coastal Walks* details 40 hikes along the coast and its hinterland between Vejer and Almería. A new publisher has improved the maps and presentation and the routes can be downloaded as a GPX file to a GPS device or smartphone.

Jacqueline Oglesby *The Mountains of Central Spain*. Walking and scrambling guide to the magnificent sierras de

Gredos and Guadarrama by resident author. Ready for a new edition, but it is still useful.

June Parker *Walking in Mallorca*. This reliable guide details 80 hikes across the island and is now in its fifth edition.

Gisela Randant Wood *Walking in Extremadura*. Second edition of this hiking guide (with clear maps) to one of Spain's less-travelled regions. Covers 32 routes of varying length and includes three city tours – Merida, Caceres and Trujillo.

Kev Reynolds *Walks and Climbs in the Pyrenees*. User-friendly guide for trekkers and walkers, though half devoted to the French side of the frontier.

Bob Stansfield *Costa Blanca Mountain Walks*. Two-volume set (sold separately) of walks in this little-known but spectacular area near Alicante. The first volume covers the western Costa Blanca, the second covers the eastern sector.

Douglas Streetfield-James et al *Trekking in the Pyrenees*. The best west-to-east guide to most of the GR11

and choice bits of the Camino de Santiago, though the GR10 and its variants is half the book. Easy-to-use sketch maps with time courses and details for overnighting in villages.

Robin Walker *Walks and Climbs in the Picos de Europa* and *Walking in the Cordillera Cantábrica*. The first is a guide to walks and rock climbs in the Picos by an experienced resident mountaineer, the second expands beyond this zone to detail treks in the Cordillera mountain range.

Andy Walmsley *Walking in the Sierra Nevada*. Forty-five walks of varying distance and difficulty, from three-hour strolls in the Alpujarras to the arduous Tres Mils peaks. The latest edition also caters for mountain bikers.

Editorial Alpina The Barcelona-based publisher Editorial Alpina (http://editorialalpina.com) has a reliable range of 1:25,000 to 1:40,000 walking maps and guides covering Andalucía, Catalunya, the Pyrenees, the Picos de Europa, the Costa Blanca, the Balearics and other parts of Spain.

WILDLIFE

Teresa Farino and Mike Lockwood *Travellers' Nature Guides: Spain*. Excellent illustrated wildlife guide by two Spanish-based experts (one of whom contributed this guide's wildlife section); it covers all the peninsula's major habitats.

★ **Svensson, Grant, Mullarney and Zetterstrom** *The Collins Bird Guide*. The best bird field guide yet published covers (and illustrates) the birds of Europe including almost everything you're likely to encounter in Spain.

FOOD AND WINE

Coleman Andrews *Catalan Cuisine*. The best available English-language book dealing with Spain's most adventurous regional cuisine.

Nicholas Butcher *The Spanish Kitchen*. A practical and knowledgeable guide to creating Spanish dishes, with informative detail on tapas, olive oil, *jamón serrano* and herbs.

Penelope Casas *The Foods and Wines of Spain*. Superb classic, covering traditional and regional dishes with equal, authoritative aplomb.

Alan Davidson *The Tio Pepe Guide to the Seafood of Spain and Portugal*. An indispensable (and pocketable) book that details and illustrates every fish and crustacean found in restaurants and bars along the Spanish *costas*.

★ **Julian Jeffs** *Sherry*. The story of sherry – history, production, blending and brands. Rightly a classic, and the best introduction to Andalucía's great wine now in a fully

revised and updated sixth edition (older editions are still available for a song). The same author's *Wines of Spain* is an erudite guide to traditional and up-and-coming wine regions, with details of vineyards, grape varieties and vintages.

Jean Claude Juston *The New Spain – Vegan and Vegetarian Restaurants* (available from http://vegetarianguides.co.uk). Very useful guide to vegetarian restaurants throughout Spain by the owner/chef of a vegetarian restaurant in the Alpujarras.

Jan Read *Guide to the Wines of Spain*. Encyclopedic (yet pocketable) guide to the classic and emerging wines of Spain by a leading authority. Includes maps, vintages and vineyards.

★ **Paul Richardson** *Late Dinner*. A joyous dissection of the food of Spain. A celebration of culture and cuisine, this is the best general introduction to what Spanish food (and life) is really all about.

LEARNING SPANISH

★ **Collins Spanish Dictionary** Recognized as the best single-volume bookshelf dictionary. Regularly revised and updated, so make sure you get the latest edition.

Elisabeth Smith *Teach Yourself Instant Spanish*. Good book-based (CD is available) course that gets you from zero to streetwise Spanish in six weeks in thirty minutes per day.

★ **Get By in Spanish** (BBC Publications, UK). One of the BBC's excellent crash-course introductions, which gets you to survival-level Spanish in a couple of weeks.

Hugo Spanish In Three Months One of the best of the CD- and book-linked home-study courses, which aims to give

you reasonable fluency within three months.

Untza Otaola Alday *Colloquial Spanish*. Excellent book-based beginner's course (supporting CDs are sold separately) with well-structured lessons and exercises.

Rough Guide Spanish Dictionary Good pocket-size dictionary that should help with most travel situations.

Michel Thomas Method *Foundation Course* and *Advanced Spanish*. The revolutionary "100 percent audio" CD-based learning system devised by the late polyglot Thomas has been praised by many learners who have struggled with traditional "grammar grind" methods.

Language

Once you give it a try, Spanish (Castellano or Castilian) is among the easier languages to get a grip on. English is spoken, but wherever you are you'll get a far better reception if you at least try communicating with Spaniards in their own tongue. Being understood, of course, is only half the problem –getting the gist of the reply, often rattled out at a furious pace, may prove far more difficult.

Castilian

The rules of **pronunciation** are straightforward and, once you get to know them, strictly observed. Unless there's an accent, words ending in d, l, r and z are **stressed** on the last syllable, all others on the second last. All **vowels** are pure and short; combinations have predictable results.

A somewhere between the A sound of "back" and that of "father".

E as in "get".

I as in "police".

O as in "hot".

U as in "rule".

C is lisped before E and I; otherwise, hard: *cerca* is pronounced "thairka" (though in Andalucía many natives pronounce the soft "c" as an "s").

G works the same way, a guttural "H" sound (like the ch in "loch") before E or I, a hard G elsewhere – *gigante* becomes "higante".

H is always silent.

J the same sound as a guttural G: *jamón* is pronounced "hamon".

LL sounds like an English Y or LY: *tortilla* is pronounced "torteeya/torteelya".

N is as in English unless it has a tilde (accent) over it, when it becomes NY: *mañana* sounds like "man-yana".

QU is pronounced like an English K.

R is rolled, RR doubly so.

V sounds more like B, *vino* becoming "beano".

X has an S sound before consonants, normal X before vowels. More common in Catalan, Basque or Gallego words, where it's "sh" or "zh".

Z is the same as a soft C, so *cerveza* becomes "thairvaitha" (but again much of the south prefers the "s" sound).

The list of a few essential words and phrases here should be enough to get you started, though if you're travelling for any length of time a dictionary or phrasebook is obviously a worthwhile investment. If you're using a **dictionary**, bear in mind that in Spanish CH, LL and Ñ count as separate letters and are listed after the Cs, Ls and Ns respectively.

In addition to Castilian, many Spaniards speak a second, **regional language** – we've given brief pronunciation rules and condensed glossaries for the three most widely spoken: **Catalan** (*Català*), **Basque** (*Euskara*) and **Galician** (*Galego*).

CASTILIAN WORDS AND PHRASES

BASICS

Yes, No, OK Sí, No, Vale
Please, Thank you Por favor, Gracias
Where, When Dónde, Cuando
What, How much Qué, Cuánto
Here, There Aquí, Allí
This, That Esto, Eso
Now, Later Ahora, Más tarde
Open, Closed Abierto/a, Cerrado/a
With, Without Con, Sin

Good, Bad Buen(o)/a, Mal(o)/a
Big, Small Gran(de), Pequeño/a
Cheap, Expensive Barato, Caro
Hot, Cold Caliente, Frío
More, Less Más, Menos
Today, Tomorrow Hoy, Mañana
Yesterday Ayer

GREETINGS AND RESPONSES

Hello, Goodbye Hola, Adiós

Good morning Buenos días
Good afternoon/ night Buenas tardes/noches
See you later Hasta luego
Sorry Lo siento/disculpéme
Excuse me Perdón/Con permiso
How are you? ¿Como está (usted)?
I (don't) understand (No) Entiendo
Not at all/ You're welcome De nada
Do you speak English? ¿Habla (usted) inglés?
I (don't) speak Spanish (No) Hablo español
My name is … Me llamo …
What's your name? ¿Como se llama usted?
I am English/Australian/Canadian/American/Irish Soy inglés(a)/australiano(a)/canadiense(a)/americano(a)/ irlandés(a)

HOTELS AND TRANSPORT

I want Quiero
I'd like Quisiera
Do you know …? ¿Sabe …?
I don't know No sé
There is (is there) (¿)Hay(?)
Give me … (one like that) Deme …(uno así)
Do you have …? ¿Tiene …?
the time la hora
a room una habitación
… with two beds/double bed … con dos camas/cama matrimonial
… with shower/bath … con ducha/baño
It's for one person (two people) Es para una persona (dos personas)
for one night (one week) para una noche (una semana)
It's fine, how much is it? ¿Está bien, cuánto es?
It's too expensive Es demasiado caro
Don't you have anything cheaper? No tiene algo más barato?
Can one …? camp (near) here? ¿Se puede ….? … acampar aquí (cerca)?
Is there a hostel nearby? ¿Hay un hostal aquí cerca?
How do I get to …? ¿Por donde se va a …?
Left, right Izquierda, derecha,
Straight on Todo recto
Where is …? ¿Dónde está …?
… the bus station … la estación de autobuses
… the train station … la estación de station ferro-carril
… the nearest bank … el banco mas cercano
… the post office … el correos/la oficina de correos
… the toilet el baño/aseo/servicio
Where does the bus to … leave from? ¿De dónde sale el autobús para …?
Is this the train for Mérida? ¿Es este el tren para Mérida?

I'd like a (return) ticket to … Quisiera un billete (de ida y vuelta) para …
What time does it leave (arrive in …)? ¿A qué hora sale (llega a…)?
What is there to eat? ¿Qué hay para comer?
What's that? ¿Qué es eso?
What's this called in Spanish? ¿Como se llama este en español?

NUMBERS AND DAYS

one un/uno/una
two dos
three tres
four cuatro
five cinco
six seis
seven siete
eight ocho
nine nueve
ten diez
eleven once
twelve doce
thirteen trece
fourteen catorce
fifteen quince
sixteen diez y seis
twenty veinte
twenty-one veintiuno
thirty treinta
forty cuarenta
fifty cincuenta
sixty sesenta
seventy setenta
eighty ochenta
ninety noventa
one hundred cien(to)
one hundred and one ciento uno
two hundred doscientos
two hundred and one doscientos uno
five hundred quinientos
one thousand mil
two thousand dos mil
two thousand and one dos mil uno
two thousand and two dos mil dos
two thousand and three dos mil tres
first primero/a
second segundo/a
third tercero/a
fifth quinto/a
tenth décimo/a
Monday lunes
Tuesday martes
Wednesday miércoles
Thursday jueves

Friday viernes
Saturday sábado

Sunday domingo

MENU READER

BASICS

Aceite Oil
Ajo Garlic
Arroz Rice
Azúcar Sugar
Huevos Eggs
Mantequilla Butter
Miel Honey
Pan Bread
Pimienta Pepper
Sal Salt
Vinagre Vinegar

MEALS

Almuerzo/Comida Lunch
Botella Bottle
Carta Menu
Cena Dinner
Comedor Dining room
Cuchara Spoon
Cuchillo Knife
La cuenta The bill
Desayuno Breakfast
Menú del día Fixed-price set meal
Mesa Table
Platos combinados Mixed plate
Tenedor Fork
Vaso Glass

SOUPS (SOPAS) AND STARTERS

Ajo blanco Chilled almond and garlic soup
Caldillo Clear fish soup
Caldo Broth
Caldo verde gallego Thick cabbage-based broth
Ensalada (mixta/verde) (Mixed/green) salad
Gazpacho Chilled tomato, peppers and garlic soup
Pimientos rellenos Stuffed peppers
Sopa de ajo Garlic soup
Sopa de cocido Meat soup
Sopa de gallina Chicken soup
Sopa de mariscos Seafood soup
Sopa de pescado Fish soup
Sopa de pasta (fideos) Noodle soup
Verduras con patatas Boiled potatoes with greens

FISH (PESCADOS)

Anchoas Anchovies (canned)
Anguila/Angulas Eel/Elvers
Atún Tuna

Bacalao Cod (often salt)
Bonito Tuna
Boquerones Fresh anchovies
Chanquetes Whitebait
Dorada Bream
Lenguado Sole
Lubina Sea bass
Merluza Hake
Mero Grouper
Pez espada Swordfish
Rape Monkfish
Raya Ray, skate
Rodaballo Turbot
Rosada Rockfish
Salmonete Mullet
Sardinas Sardines
Trucha Trout
Urta Bream family

SEAFOOD (MARISCOS)

Almejas Clams
Arroz con mariscos Rice with seafood
Calamares (en su tinta) Squid (in ink)
Centollo Spider crab
Cigalas King prawns
Conchas finas Large scallops
Gambas Prawns/shrimps
Langosta Lobster
Langostinos Crayfish
Mejillones Mussels
Nécora Sea crab
Ostras Oysters
Paella Classic Valencian dish with saffron rice, chicken, seafood, etc
Percebes Goose barnacles
Pulpo Octopus
Sepia Cuttlefish
Vieiras Scallops
Zarzuela de mariscos Seafood casserole

COMMON TERMS

al ajillo in garlic
a la brasa grilled over embers
a la Navarra stuffed with ham
a la parrilla/plancha grilled
a la Romana fried in batter
al horno baked
alioli with garlic mayonnaise
asado roasted

cazuela, cocido stew
en salsa in (usually tomato) sauce
frito fried
guisado casserole
rehogado sautéed

MEAT (CARNE) AND POULTRY (AVES)

Callos Tripe
Carillada Pork cheeks
Carne de buey Beef
Cerdo Pork
Cerdo Ibérico Black-pig pork
Choto Baby kid
Chuletas Chops
Cochinillo Suckling pig
Codorniz Quail
Conejo Rabbit
Cordero Lamb
Escalopa Escalope
Fabada asturiana/Fabes a la catalana Hotpot with
  butter beans, black pudding, etc
Hamburguesa Hamburger
Hígado Liver
Jabalí Wild boar
Lacón con grelos Gammon with turnips
Lengua Tongue
Lomo Loin (of pork)
Pato Duck
Pavo Turkey
Perdiz Partridge
Pollo Chicken
Rabo de toro Oxtail
Riñones Kidneys
Solomillo Sirloin steak
Solomillo de cerdo (Ibérico) Pork tenderloin
Ternera Beef/Veal
Venado Venison

VEGETABLES (LEGUMBRES)

Acelga Chard
Alcachofas Artichokes
Arroz a la cubana Rice with fried egg and tomato sauce
Berenjenas Aubergine
Cebollas Onions
Champiñones/Setas Mushrooms
Coliflor Cauliflower
Espárragos Asparagus
Espinacas Spinach
Garbanzos Chickpeas
Habas Broad/fava beans
Judías blancas Haricot beans
Judías verdes, rojas, negras Green, red, black beans
Lechuga Lettuce
Lentejas Lentils

Menestra/Panache de verduras Mixed vegetables
Nabos/Grelos Turnips
Patatas Potatoes
Patatas fritas French fries (chips)
Pepino Cucumber
Pimientos Peppers/capsicums
Pisto manchego Ratatouille
Puerros Leeks
Puré Mashed potato
Repollo Cabbage
Tomate Tomato
Zanahoria Carrot

FRUITS (FRUTAS)

Albaricoques Apricots
Cerezas Cherries
Chirimoyas Custard apples
Ciruelas Plums, prunes
Dátiles Dates
Fresas Strawberries
Granada Pomegranate
Higos Figs
Limón Lemon
Manzanas Apples
Melocotones Peaches
Melón Melon
Naranjas Oranges
Nectarinas Nectarines
Peras Pears
Piña Pineapple
Plátanos Bananas
Sandía Watermelon
Toronja/Pomelo Grapefruit
Uvas Grapes

DESSERTS (POSTRES)

Arroz con leche Rice pudding
Crema Catalana Catalan crème brûlée
Cuajada Cream-based dessert served with honey
Flan Crème caramel
Helado Ice cream
Melocotón en almíbar Peaches in syrup
Membrillo Quince paste
Nata Whipped cream
Natillas Custard
Pan de Calatrava Bread pudding
Peras al vino Pears cooked in wine
Pudín Sweet pudding (varies nationwide)
Tarta de almendras Almond tart
Tarta de manzana Apple tart
Tarta de Santiago Classic Galician almond tart
Tocino de cielo Syrup and egg flan (Andalucía)
Yogur Yoghurt

CHEESE

Cheeses (*quesos*) are on the whole local, though you'll get the hard, salty *queso manchego* everywhere. Mild sheep's or goat's cheese (*queso de oveja/cabra*) from León province or the Sierra de Grazalema (Cádiz) is widely distributed and worth asking for.

STANDARD TAPAS AND RACIONES

Aceitunas Olives
Albóndigas Meatballs
Anchoas Anchovies
Berberechos Cockles
Berenjenas fritas Fried aubergine
Bígaros Periwinkles
Boquerones Anchovies
Cabrillas Large snails with tomato
Calamares Squid
Callos Tripe
Caracolas Whelks
Caracoles Snails
Carne mechada Larded meat
Champiñones Mushrooms, usually fried in garlic
Chocos Deep-fried cuttlefish
Chorizo Spicy sausage
Cocido Stew
Costillas Pork ribs
Croquetas Fish or meat croquettes
Empanada Fish/meat pasty
Ensaladilla rusa Russian salad (diced vegetables in mayonnaise)

Escalibada Aubergine and pepper salad
Espinacas con garbanzos Spinach with chickpeas
Garbanzos Chickpeas
Gambas (al ajillo) Prawns (cooked in garlic)
Habas Broad beans
Habas con jamón Broad beans with ham
Hígado (de pollo) Liver (chicken liver)
Jamón Serrano Cured ham (like Parma ham)
Jamón Ibérico Cured black-pig ham (the best)
Langostinos Big, deep-water prawns
Mejillones Mussels
Morcilla Blood sausage (black pudding)
Navajas Razor clams
Papas arrugadas Boiled then baked new potatoes served with spicy sauce (Canary Islands)
Patatas alioli Potatoes in garlic mayonnaise
Patatas bravas Spicy fried potatoes
Pimientos Peppers
Pincho moruno Kebab
Pintxo Basque tapa (on stick)
Pulpo Octopus
Puntillitas Deep-fried baby squid
Riñones al Jerez Kidneys in sherry
Salchicha Sausage
Salchichón Cured, peppery salami
Sepia Cuttlefish
Tabla Tapa served on a wooden board
Tortilla de camarones Prawn fritters
Tortilla española Potato omelette
Tortilla francesa Plain omelette

Catalan

Catalan (Català) is spoken in Catalunya, part of Aragón, much of Valencia, the Balearic Islands and the Principality of Andorra. On paper, it looks like a cross between French and Spanish, and is generally easy to understand if you know those two, but, spoken, it has a distinct, rounded sound and is far harder to come to grips with – the language has eight vowel sounds (including three diphthongs).

The main differences from Castilian in **pronunciation** are:

A as in "hat" when stressed, as in "alone" when unstressed.

C sounds like an English S: *plaça* is pronounced "plassa".

G before E and I is like the "zh" in "Zhivago"; otherwise, hard.

J as in the French "Jean".

N is as in English, though before F or V it sometimes sounds like an M.

NY replaces the Castilian Ñ.

QU before E or I sounds like K; before A or O as in "quit".

R is rolled at the start of the word; at the end, it's often silent.

TX is like the English CH.

V sounds more like B at the start of a word; otherwise, a soft F sound.

W sounds like a B/V.

X like SH in most words, though in some it sounds like an X.

Z like the English Z.

CATALAN GLOSSARY

one un(a)
two dos (dues)
three tres

four quatre
five cinc
six sis

seven set
eight vuit
nine nou
ten deu
Monday Dilluns
Tuesday Dimarts
Wednesday Dimecres
Thursday Dijous
Friday Divendres
Saturday Dissabte
Sunday Diumenge
good morning/hello bon dia
good evening bona nit
goodbye adéu
please per favor
thank you gràcies
today avui
yesterday ahir

tomorrow demà
day before yesterday abans d'ahir
day after tomorrow demà passat
more més
a lot, very força
a little una mica
left esquerre(a)
right dret(a)
near (a) prop
far lluny
open obert(a)
closed tancat
town square plaça
beach praia
where? ¿on?
when? ¿quan?
how much? ¿quant?

Basque

Basque (Euskara) is spoken in the Basque Country and Navarra. According to the official estimates in 2011 around thirty percent of the population of the Basque Country and eleven percent of Navarra are "actively bilingual", speaking Euskara as their first language but understanding Castilian.

It's worth noting a couple of **key letter changes**: notably, the Castilian CH becomes TX (*txipirones* as opposed to *chipirones*), V becomes B and Y becomes I (Bizkaia as opposed to Vizcaya). Above all, Euskara features a proliferation of Ks: this letter replaces the Castilian C (Gipuzkoa instead of Guipúzcoa) and QU (Lekeitio instead of Lequeitio) and is also used to form the plural and the possessive (eg Bilboko means "of Bilbao").

BASQUE GLOSSARY

one bat
two bi
three hiru
four lau
five bost
six sei
seven zazpi
eight zortzi
nine bederatzi
ten hamar
Monday astelehen
Tuesday astearte
Wednesday asteazken
Thursday ostegun
Friday ostiral
Saturday larunbat
Sunday igande
yes, no bai, ez
hello kaixo
good morning egun on
good night gabon

please mesedez
thank you eskerrik asko
today gaur
yesterday bihar
tomorrow atzo
more gehiago
a lot asko
a little gutxi
left ezker
right eskuin
near hurbil
far urruti
open ireki
closed hertsi
town square enpastantza
beach hondartza
shop denda
where? ¿daude?
when? ¿noiz?
how much? ¿zenbat?

Galician

While superficially similar to Castilian, **Galician** (Galego) is closer to Portuguese – in fact, both Galician and Portuguese evolved from a single ancestral tongue – and is the main or only language of seventy percent of the population of Galicia.

The most obvious **characteristic** of Galician is the large number of Xs, which in Castilian might be Gs, Js or Ss; these are pronounced as a soft "sh" – thus *jamón* in Castilian becomes *xamón*, pronounced "shamon", in Galician. Similarly, LL in Castilian often becomes CH in Galician. You'll also find that the Castilian "la" becomes "a" (as in A Coruña), "el" is "o" (as in O Grove), "en la" is "na", "en el" is "no", "de la" is "da" and "del" is "do".

GALICIAN GLOSSARY

one un	**thank you** grazas
two dous	**today** hoxe
three tres	**yesterday** onte
four catro	**tomorrow** mañá
five cinco	**more** mais
six seis	**a lot** moito
seven sete	**a little** pouco
eight oito	**left** esquerda
nine nove	**right** dereita
ten dez	**near** preto
Monday Luns	**far** lonxe
Tuesday Martes	**open** aberto
Wednesday Mécores	**closed** pechado
Thursday Xoves	**town square** praza
Friday Venres	**beach** praia
Saturday Sábado	**shop** tenda
Sunday Domingo	**where?** ¿onde?
good morning bos días	**when?** ¿cándo?
good afternoon boas tardes	**how much?** ¿cánto?
good night boas noites	

Glossary of Spanish and architectural terms

Alameda Park or grassy promenade.

Alcazaba Moorish castle.

Alcázar Moorish fortified palace.

Apse Semicircular recess at the altar (usually eastern) end of a church.

Ayuntamiento/ajuntament Town hall.

Azulejo Glazed ceramic tile work.

Barrio Suburb or quarter.

Bodega Cellar, wine bar or warehouse.

Calle Street.

Capilla mayor Chapel containing the high altar.

Capilla real Royal chapel.

Cartuja Carthusian monastery.

Castillo Castle.

Chiringuito Beach restaurant serving fish, seafood and paella.

Churrigueresque Extreme form of Baroque art named after José Churriguera (1650–1723) and his extended family, its main exponents.

Colegiata Collegiate (large parish) church.

Convento Monastery or convent.

Coro Central part of church built for the choir.

Coro alto Raised choir, often above west door of a church.

Correos Post office.

Corrida de toros Bullfight.

Cortes Spanish parliament in Madrid.

Cuadrilla A bullfighter's team of assistants.

Custodia Large receptacle for Eucharist wafers.

Dueño/a Proprietor, landlord/lady.

Ermita Hermitage.

Gitano Gypsy or Romany.

Hórreo Granary.

Iglesia Church.

Isabelline (Gothic Hispano-Flemish) Ornamental form of late Gothic developed during the reign of Isabel and Fernando.

Lonja Stock exchange building.

Mercado Market.

Mihrab Prayer niche of Moorish mosque.

Mirador Viewing point.

Modernisme (Modernista) Catalan/Spanish form of Art Nouveau, whose most famous exponent was Antoni Gaudí.

Monasterio Monastery or convent.

Morisco Muslim Spaniard subject to medieval Christian rule – and nominally baptized.

Mozarabe Christian subject to medieval Moorish rule; normally allowed freedom of worship, they built churches in an Arab-influenced manner (Mozarabic).

Mudéjar Muslim Spaniard subject to medieval Christian rule, but retaining Islamic worship; most commonly a term applied to architecture which includes buildings built by Moorish craftsmen for the Christian rulers and later designs influenced by the Moors. The 1890s to 1930s saw a Mudéjar revival, blended with Art Nouveau and Art Deco forms.

Palacio Aristocratic mansion.

Parador State-owned luxury hotel, often (but not always) converted from a minor monument.

Paseo Promenade; also the evening stroll thereon.

Patio Inner courtyard.

Plateresque Elaborate Renaissance style, the sixteenth-century successor of Isabelline forms. Named for its resemblance to silversmiths' work (*platería*).

Plaza Square.

Plaza de toros Bullring.

Posada Old name for an inn.

Puerta Gateway, also mountain pass.

Puerto Port.

Raciones Large plate of tapas, often shared.

Reja Iron screen or grille, often fronting an altar or a window.

Reliquary Receptacle for a saint's relics, usually bones; often highly decorated.

Reredos Wall or screen behind an altar.

Retablo Altarpiece.

Ría River estuary in Galicia.

Río River.

Romería Religious procession to a rural shrine.

Sacristía, sagrario Sacristy of church – room for sacred vessels and vestments.

Sardana Catalan folk dance.

Seo, Seu, Se Ancient/regional names for cathedrals.

Sidreria Bar specializing in cider.

Sierra Mountain range.

Sillería Choir stall.

Solar Aristocratic town mansion.

Taifa Small Moorish kingdom, many of which emerged after the disintegration of the Córdoba caliphate.

Transepts The wings of a cruciform church, placed at right angles to the nave and chancel.

Turismo Tourist office.

Tympanum Area between lintel of a doorway and the arch above it.

Small print and index

A ROUGH GUIDE TO ROUGH GUIDES

Published in 1982, the first Rough Guide – to Greece – was a student scheme that became a publishing phenomenon. Mark Ellingham, a recent graduate in English from Bristol University, had been travelling in Greece the previous summer and couldn't find the right guidebook. With a small group of friends he wrote his own guide, combining a contemporary, journalistic style with a thoroughly practical approach to travellers' needs.

The immediate success of the book spawned a series that rapidly covered dozens of destinations. And, in addition to impecunious backpackers, Rough Guides soon acquired a much broader readership that relished the guides' wit and inquisitiveness as much as their enthusiastic, critical approach and value-for-money ethos. These days, Rough Guides include recommendations from budget to luxury and cover more than 120 destinations around the globe, from Amsterdam to Zanzibar, all regularly updated by our team of roaming writers.

Browse all our latest guides, read inspirational features and book your trip at **roughguides.com**.

Rough Guide credits

Editor: Libby Davies
Cartography: Carte
Picture Manager: Tom Smyth
Layout: Pradeep Thapliyal

Publishing technology manager: Rebeka Davies
Production operations manager: Katie Bennett
Head of Publishing: Sarah Clark

Publishing information

Eighteenth edition 2025

Distribution

UK, Ireland and Europe
Apa Publications (UK) Ltd; sales@roughguides.com
United States and Canada
Ingram Publisher Services; ips@ingramcontent.com
Australia and New Zealand
Booktopia; retailer@booktopia.com.au
Worldwide
Apa Publications (UK) Ltd; sales@roughguides.com

Special Sales, Content Licensing and CoPublishing
Rough Guides can be purchased in bulk quantities
at discounted prices. We can create special editions,
personalised jackets and corporate imprints tailored to
your needs. sales@roughguides.com.
roughguides.com

Printed in Czech Republic

This book was produced using **Typefi** automated
publishing software.

A catalogue record for this book is available from the
British Library

The publishers and authors have done their best to
ensure the accuracy and currency of all the information
in **The Rough Guide to Spain**, however, they can accept
no responsibility for any loss, injury, or inconvenience
sustained by any traveller as a result of information or
advice contained in the guide.

Help us update

We've gone to a lot of effort to ensure that this edition
of **The Rough Guide to Spain** is accurate and up-to-
date. However, things change – places get "discovered",
transport routes are altered, restaurants and hotels raise
prices or lower standards, and businesses cease trading. If
you feel we've got it wrong or left something out, we'd like
to know, and if you can direct us to the web address, so
much the better.
   Please send your comments with the subject line
"Rough Guide Spain Update" to mail@uk.roughguides.
com. We'll acknowledge all contributions and send a copy
of the next edition (or any other Rough Guide if you prefer)
for the very best emails.

Photo credits
(Key: T-top; C-centre; B-bottom; L-left; R-right)

ABOUT THE AUTHORS

Libby Davies is a travel editor at Rough Guides and has updated guidebooks to Spain and London. London-based, she still finds the city just as exciting as when she first moved in 2016. She grew up in Yorkshire and still spends time walking around the gorgeous peaks, dales and reservoirs of the north.

Sally Davies settled in Barcelona in 2001 after stints living in Madrid and Seville. She has written guidebooks to most regions of Spain, along with a book on Spanish cuisine. Her work as a journalist leads her all over the country, seeking out culinary and cultural experiences of every stripe – but Barcelona will always be home.

Mary-Ann Gallagher is a writer, translator and editor based in Barcelona. She's explored every nook and cranny of Spain over the last twenty years, and has written and contributed to more than two dozen guidebooks on the country.

Agnish Ray is a journalist based in Madrid, covering travel, culture, gastronomy and current affairs. He has written about destinations across Spain, from Madrid, San Sebastián and Oviedo to Seville, Valencia and the Balearic Islands, and has interviewed a range of Spanish artists, filmmakers, sportspeople, dancers, designers, authors and chefs. His work has been featured in publications such as *The Guardian*, *The Telegraph*, *The Times*, *Financial Times*, *Wallpaper**, *Conde Nast Traveller*, *Sleeper*, *Kinfolk* and *Vogue*, among others.

Daniel Stables is a travel writer based in Manchester, UK. He writes travel articles for *National Geographic* and the BBC, and his debut narrative travel book, *Fiesta: A Journey Through Festivity* is coming out in early 2026. He also hosts a podcast, "Hungry Ghosts", about food and travel. You can find his work on X @DanStables, Instagram @DanStabs, or on his website, www.danielstables.co.uk.

Index

R

Map symbols

The symbols below are used on maps throughout the book

▬▬■	International boundary	⋯⋯⋯	Funicular	⁖	Ruin	🏠	Mountain refuge
──	Province boundary	╍╍╍	Narrow-gauge railway	⊙	Statue	⚲	Church (regional)
━ ━ ━	Chapter division boundary	●–●–●	Cable car	♜	Castle		Rocks
	Major road	─ ─ ─	Ferry route	⛷	Skiing		Swamp
	Minor road	─ ─	Path	⛌	Lighthouse	≍	Bridge
	Motorway road	✡	Synagogue	⌂	Monastery		Building
	Pedestrian road	P	Parking		Spring/spa	□	Market
▬▬	Railway	@	Internet café/access		Swimming pool/area	⊞	Church
─ ─	Ferry route	✉	Post office		Waterfall	○	Stadium
─ ─	River	ⓘ	Information office	⊤	Gardens		Park
✈	Airport	ℂ	Telephone office		Viewpoint		Beach
★	Bus/taxi	●	Museum		Cave	⊟	Saltpan
Ⓣ	Tram stop	✚	Hospital		Campsite/ground	──	Wall
Ⓜ	Metro station	♦	Place of interest		Mountain range		
⊛	Cercanías RENFE station	🕌	Mosque	▲	Mountain peak		

Listings key

- ■ Accommodation
- ● Eating
- ■ Drinking and nightlife
- ● Shopping

YOUR TAILOR-MADE TRIP
STARTS HERE

Tailor-made trips and unique adventures crafted by local experts

Rough Guides has been inspiring travellers with lively and thought-provoking guidebooks for more than 35 years. Now we're linking you up with selected local experts to craft your dream trip. They will put together your perfect itinerary and book it at local rates.

Don't follow the crowd – find your own path.

HOW ROUGHGUIDES.COM/TRIPS WORKS

STEP 1

Pick your dream destination, tell us what you want and submit an enquiry.

STEP 2

Fill in a short form to tell your local expert about your dream trip and preferences.

STEP 3

Our local expert will craft your tailor-made itinerary. You'll be able to tweak and refine it until you're completely satisfied.

STEP 4

Book online with ease, pack your bags and enjoy the trip! Our local expert will be on hand 24/7 while you're on the road.

BENEFITS OF PLANNING AND BOOKING AT
ROUGHGUIDES.COM/TRIPS

PLAN YOUR ADVENTURE WITH LOCAL EXPERTS

Rough Guides' English-speaking local experts are hand-picked, based on their experience in the travel industry and their impeccable standards of customer service.

SAVE TIME AND GET ACCESS TO LOCAL KNOWLEDGE

When a local expert plans your trip, you save time and money when you book, even during high season. You won't be charged for using a credit card either.

MAKE TRAVEL A BREEZE: BOOK WITH PEACE OF MIND

Enjoy stress-free travel when you use Rough Guides' secure online booking platform. All bookings come with a money-back guarantee.

WHAT DO OTHER TRAVELLERS THINK ABOUT ROUGH GUIDES TRIPS?

Trip to Spain

This Spain tour company did a fantastic job to make our dream trip perfect. We gave them our travel budget, told them where we would like to go, and they did all of the planning. Our drivers and tour guides were always on time and very knowledgable. The hotel accommodations were better than we would have found on our own. Only one time did we end up in a location that we had not intended to be in. We called the 24 hour phone number, and they immediately fixed the situation.

Don A, USA

Trip to Morocco

Our trip was fantastic! Transportation, accommodations, guides – all were well chosen! The hotels were well situated, well appointed and had helpful, friendly staff. All of the guides we had were very knowledgeable, patient, and flexible with our varied interests in the different sites. We particularly enjoyed the side trip to Tangier! Well done! The itinerary you arranged for us allowed maximum coverage of the country with time in each city for seeing the important places.

Sharon, USA

PLAN AND BOOK YOUR TRIP AT
ROUGHGUIDES.COM/TRIPS